LET'S GO

FRANCE
2003

ANNALISE NELSON EDITOR
PAUL EISENSTEIN ASSOCIATE EDITOR
SARAH LEVINE-GRONNINGSATER ASSOCIATE EDITOR

RESEARCHER-WRITERS
EMILY BUCK
EDWARD B. COLBY
LAURE "VOOP" DE VULPILLIÈRES
ROBERT MADISON
GENEVIEVE SHEEHAN
JULIA STEELE

HARRIETT GREEN MANAGING EDITOR
NICK DONIN MAP EDITOR
MELISSA RUDOLPH TYPESETTER

ST. MARTIN'S PRESS  NEW YORK

HELPING LET'S GO If you want to share your discoveries, suggestions, or corrections, please drop us a line. We read every piece of correspondence, whether a postcard, a 10-page email, or a coconut. Please note that mail received after May 2003 may be too late for the 2004 book, but will be kept for future editions. **Address mail to:**

Let's Go: France
67 Mount Auburn Street
Cambridge, MA 02138
USA

Visit Let's Go at **http://www.letsgo.com,** or send email to:

feedback@letsgo.com
Subject: "Let's Go: France"

In addition to the invaluable travel advice our readers share with us, many are kind enough to offer their services as researchers or editors. Unfortunately, our charter enables us to employ only currently enrolled Harvard students.

HOW TO USE THIS BOOK

ORGANIZATION. This book is divided into 18 regions, which generally correspond to French governmental divisions and local identities. Our coverage begins in Paris and the Ile-de-France, moving up to the northwest coast and sweeping counter-clockwise around the country. At the beginning of each chapter, a high-light box gives you a run-down of each town and city in the region to help you decide what's really worth your time.

PRICE RANGES AND RANKINGS. Our researchers list establishments in order of value from best to worst. Our absolute favorites are denoted by the *Let's Go* thumbs-up (🖾). Since the best value does not always mean the cheapest price, we have incorporated a system of price ranges in the guide. The table below lists how prices fall within each bracket.

FRANCE	❶	❷	❸	❹	❺
ACCOMMODATIONS	€1-15	€16-25	€26-35	€36-55	€56-100
FOOD	€1-6	€7-9	€10-15	€16-24	€26-50

WHEN TO USE IT

TWO MONTHS BEFORE. The first chapter, **Discover France**, contains highlights of the region, including Suggested Itineraries (see p. 4) that can help you plan your trip. For itineraries further off the beaten path, check out the **Alternatives to Tourism** chapter, with listings for schools, volunteer activities and teaching opportunities in France. The **Essentials** (see p. 31) chapter has practical information on arranging transportation, planning a budget, making reservations, and renewing a passport.

ONE MONTH BEFORE. Take care of insurance, and write down a list of emergency numbers and hotlines. Make a list of packing essentials (see **Packing**, p. 48) and shop for anything you are missing. Read through the coverage and make sure you understand the logistics of your itinerary (catching trains, ferries, and buses). Make any reservations if necessary.

2 WEEKS BEFORE. Leave an itinerary and a photocopy of important documents with someone at home. Take some time to peruse the **Life and Times** (see p. 7), which has info on history, the arts, recent political events, and cuisine.

ON THE ROAD. The **Appendix** contains a French glossary, a temperature chart, and a measurement converter. As you wait to catch your train, take a cultural crash course with one of our in-depth articles on French regionalism (p. 30) and urban development in Paris (p. 143), update your French vocab with our mini guide to slang phrases (p. 17), and check out our exclusive interviews with locals—from a monk on Mont St-Michel (p. 210) to France's premier chef (p. 662). Now, grab your travel journal and hit the road!

A NOTE TO OUR READERS The information for this book was gathered by *Let's Go* researchers from May through August of 2002. Each listing is based on one researcher's opinion, formed during his or her visit at a particular time. Those traveling at other times may have different experiences since prices, dates, hours, and conditions are always subject to change. You are urged to check the facts presented in this book beforehand to avoid inconvenience and surprises.

CONTENTS

RESEARCHER-WRITERS

Emily Buck   *Loire Valley, Poitou-Charentes, Berry-Limousin, Périgord*

Plucky and indomitable, this distinguished Phi Beta Kappa scholar and musical talent accepted nothing but the truth in the former home of the French nobility. Her sweet smile and friendly demeanor didn't stop her from voraciously seeking out bargains and new scenes or giving frank opinions on everything she encountered. Even the undercover police in Saumur didn't make her flinch.

Edward B. Colby   *Provence, Lyon and the Auvergne, Burgundy*

Ned earned his nickname, "the Neditor," as a freelance journalist and college newspaper editor. A modern European history major, he combined his studies with his journalistic energy for the grand cause of travel writing. His experience as a *Let's Go: USA 2001* R-W helped him conquer a challenging route of virulent Vichy water and unforgiving stick shifts. In his wake, Ned left charmed *provençal* girls and a speechless four-star chef.

Laure "Voop" de Vulpillières   *Champagne, Alsace-Lorraine, Flanders, Languedoc*

Returning to her native France as a tourist, Voop put her sociology and women's studies degrees to good use, chatting unabashedly with locals to find the best scenes for both gays and straights. Sending back exhaustive copy, she expanded our understanding of French fashion, youth culture, and regional identity. She showed us an untouristed France we never knew existed.

Robert Madison   *Cote d'Azur, Corsica, the Alps*

A literature scholar, French film expert, and seasoned budget traveler, Rob found his calling in France. Thorough and persistent, this amateur food critic gave his approval to only the best *pains aux raisins*. Our food coverage expanded almost as much as his knowledge of Corsican politics. He managed to have a little fun on the way, engaging Monaco's underground Twister world, befriending canines in Corsica, and defying the mountain gods (from a heated gondola).

Genevieve Sheehan   *Brittany and Normandy*

The rugged Northern coast was ill-prepared for this force of nature, who reviewed dozens of new accommodations and restaurants. Always good-spirited, Genevieve put her Celtic background and International Relations knowledge to good use dancing the jig at a Breton festival. All this while reaching back in time with vets on the D-day beaches and quizzing a monk-webmaster about the secrets of Mont-St-Michel.

Julia Steele   *Languedoc-Roussillon, Aquitaine, Pays Basque*

Hired for her knowledge of four languages and her travel experience on four continents, Julia developed additional talents in the field: vividly depicting the fine cuisine of Perpignan and Biarritz, describing the hospitality of Cauterets, and chasing away the amorous locals of Cahors. In expert French, she illuminated the transportation complexities of Aquitaine and helped expand coverage of the overshadowed southwestern beaches.

Sarah Robinson   *Editor, Paris*

Sarah Eno   *Researcher-Writer, Paris*

Dehn Gilmore   *Researcher-Writer, Paris*

Nathaniel Mendelsohn   *Researcher-Writer, Paris*

CONTRIBUTING WRITERS

Matthew Lazen spent two years in Brittany and Alsace on a Chateaubriand Fellowship for dissertation research on regional cultures in post-modern France. Currently a History & Literature lecturer at Harvard University, he is revising his dissertation for publication and organizing a conference on post-War French regionalism at Harvard University.

Charlotte Houghteling is the editor of *Let's Go: Middle East 2003*, *Egypt 2003*, and *Israel 2003*. She wrote her senior thesis on the development of department stores during the Second Empire and will complete her M.Phil. at Cambridge on the consumer society of Revolutionary Paris.

Sara Houghteling was a Researcher-Writer for *Let's Go: France 1999*. She taught at the American School in Paris for a year. She is now a graduate student in creative writing at the University of Michigan, and is currently in Paris researching Nazi art theft during World War II.

Couper Samuelson, a History & Literature and French Studies graduate, channeled a fierce obsession with French cinema to write his thesis on *policier* films. A quarter French, he spends his summers in Paris, in the cool, darkened cinemas of the 5th and 6th *arrondissements*.

ACKNOWLEDGMENTS

LET'S GO

Team France thanks: Our lovely and talented researchers for their dedication. Harriett for advice and ice cream, Nick for amazing maps, and Scrobins for fab crunching. Tom Conley and Matthew Lazen for scholarly help. Team SPAM for girlz gone wild, Moroccan hustlers and ball-pits. Suzanne for being a FinAss. Mrs. Nelson for the brownies. Metaphorically, The Wrap.

Annalise thanks: Everyman for Darnel and amazing good humor, Sarah for swan poses and crossing the great divide, Cody for the pinot egrigio, Andy for sharing Andorra and the squalor of 2a Hingham, Irin for music and NYC, Lucy for 4pm dance breaks, Karoun for kebabs, Suzanne for outdoor concerts, Mangela for hula hooping, Moudy for compliments. Word to the foomigators, and an utter weakness for Keif. To Ma and Pa, all my love.

Paul thanks: Annalise for vision and naf-naf, Sarah for caustic wit and lingerie, Moudy, Alex, and Eli for advice and distractions, Karoun for my classical expertise, Irin for falling into my arms, Lucy for Beirut babes, Andy for being an island in a sea of estrogen. Evan, Adam, Seth, Laurel, Becca, and everyone else back home. Mamma, Pappa, Anna, Carin, and Ostrich, I'll call soon, I swear.

Sarah thanks: Anna for her "story" and mussels. Everyman for Hugo Boss and Tolstoy. Cody for "hi." SPAM for taking a chance on a SAF-pod girl. Liz for Cape Cod. Jen/Ben G. for Cape Codders. Scrobs for Paris. Stefan for "coffee." Irene for Newport. Taylor for the McFlurries. Noah for the morning song. Doulo for more than I ever deserved. Eno for frozen bananas and the love. The Seneca. My family, the original LG enterprise.

Nick thanks: Mom and Pops for their phone calls and level heads, Ali, Chris, Noah, and Fatsendio for keeping me tipsy. And Jackie, for always being my "bro" and my brother.

Editor
Annalise Nelson
Associate Editors
Paul Eisenstein, Sarah Levine-Gronningsater
Managing Editor
Harriett Green
Map Editor
Nick Donin

Publishing Director
Matthew Gibson
Editor-in-Chief
Brian R. Walsh
Production Manager
C. Winslow Clayton
Cartography Manager
Julie Stephens
Design Manager
Amy Cain
Editorial Managers
Christopher Blazejewski,
Abigail Burger, D. Cody Dydek,
Harriett Green, Angela Mi Young Hur,
Marla Kaplan, Celeste Ng
Financial Manager
Noah Askin
Marketing & Publicity Managers
Michelle Bowman, Adam M. Grant
New Media Managers
Jesse Tov, Kevin Yip
Online Manager
Amélie Cherlin
Personnel Managers
Alex Leichtman, Owen Robinson
Production Associates
Caleb Epps, David Muehlke
Network Administrators
Steven Aponte, Eduardo Montoya
Design Associate
Juice Fong
Financial Assistant
Suzanne Siu
Office Coordinators
Alex Ewing, Adam Kline,
Efrat Kussell

Director of Advertising Sales
Erik Patton
Senior Advertising Associates
Patrick Donovan, Barbara Eghan,
Fernanda Winthrop
Advertising Artwork Editor
Leif Holtzman
Cover Photo Research
Laura Wyss
President
Bradley J. Olson
General Manager
Robert B. Rombauer
Assistant General Manager
Anne E. Chisholm

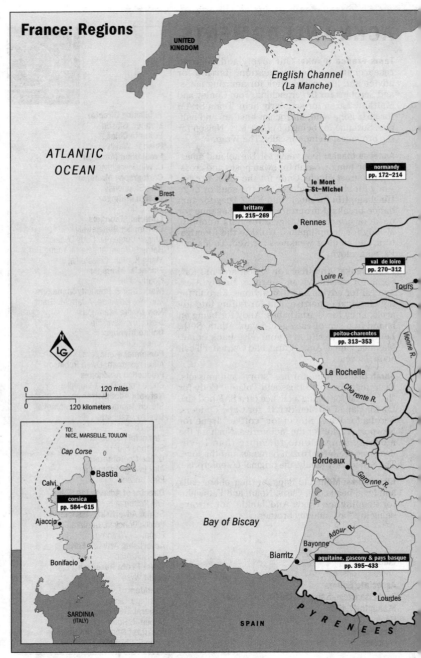

France: Regions

UNITED KINGDOM

English Channel (La Manche)

ATLANTIC OCEAN

Brest

normandy pp. 172–214

le Mont St-Michel

brittany pp. 215–269

Rennes

val de loire pp. 270–312

Loire R.

Tours

poitou-charentes pp. 313–353

Vienne R.

La Rochelle

Charente R.

0   120 miles
0   120 kilometers

Bordeaux

Garonne R.

Bay of Biscay

Adour R.

Bayonne

Biarritz

aquitaine, gascony & pays basque pp. 395–433

Lourdes

PYRENEES

SPAIN

TO: NICE, MARSEILLE, TOULON

Cap Corse

Bastia

Calvi

corsica pp. 584–615

Ajaccio

Bonifacio

SARDINIA (ITALY)

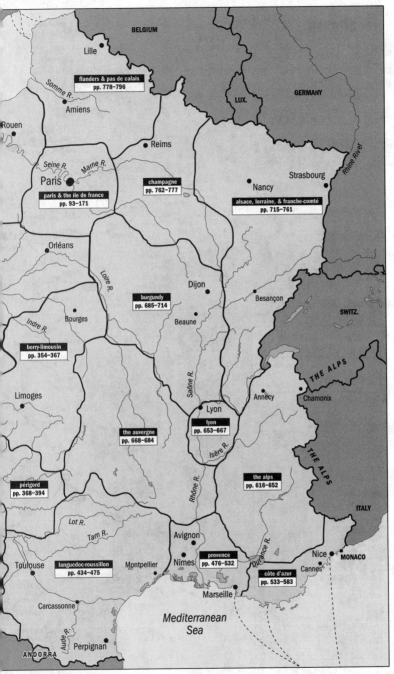

BELGIUM

Lille

Somme R.

flanders & pas de calais
pp. 778–796

LUX.

GERMANY

Amiens

Rouen

Reims

Seine R.

Marne R.

Strasbourg

Rhine River

Paris

Nancy

paris & the ile de france
pp. 93–171

champagne
pp. 762–777

alsace, lorraine, & franche-comté
pp. 715–761

Orléans

Loire R.

Dijon

Besançon

SWITZ.

burgundy
pp. 685–714

Bourges

Indre R.

Beaune

berry-limousin
pp. 354–367

Limoges

Saône R.

THE ALPS

Annecy

Chamonix

Lyon

lyon
pp. 653–667

the auvergne
pp. 668–684

Isère R.

THE ALPS

périgord
pp. 368–394

the alps
pp. 616–652

ITALY

Lot R.

Rhône R.

Tarm R.

Avignon

Durance R.

Nice

MONACO

Toulouse

languedoc-roussillon
pp. 434–475

Montpellier

Nîmes

provence
pp. 476–532

Cannes

côte d'azur
pp. 533–583

Carcassonne

Marseille

Aude R.

Mediterranean
Sea

ANDORRA

Perpignan

Highways

GREAT BRITAIN

English Channel
(La Manche)

ATLANTIC OCEAN

CHANNEL ISLANDS

Southampton
Portsmouth
Exeter
Étretat
Cherbourg
Le Havre
Deauville
A13
Guernsey
Jersey
Bayeux
Coutances
Caen
N138
Granville
N175
Paimpol
St-Malo
Avranches
Brest
Morlaix
St Brieuc
N12
Dinan
N175
Alençon
N12
Quimper
Carhaix-Plouguer
N164
Rennes
A81
A11
Le Mans
N165
Lorient
Concarneau
Vannes
Angers
N147
Tour
Quiberon
N137
A11
N152
St-Nazaire
Saumur
N147
Belle-Ile
Nantes
N149
Hills of Vendée
Poitiers
Ile d'Yeu
N137
Niort
A10
Les Sables d'Olonne
La Rochelle
Rochefort
N141
Saintes
N137
Royan
Cognac
Angoulême
le Verdon-sur-Mer
A10
N10
Périgueux
N89
Bordeaux
Bergerac
N21
Arcachon
A63
A62
Agen
Bay of Biscay
N10
Mont-de-Marsan
Auch
Bayonne
Biarritz
St-Jean-de-Luz
A63
Anglet
A64
Pau
N21
Bilbao
San Sebastian
St-Jean-Pied-de-Port
Lourdes
Cauterets
SPAIN
PYRENEES

0 — 120 miles
0 — 120 kilometers

A10 Highways Roads (Autoroutes)
N76 National Roads (Routes Nationales)
- - - - Ferry

TO: NICE, MARSEILLE, TOULON
Cap Corse
Bastia
Calvi
CORSICA
Corte
Ajaccio
Aléria
Propriano
Sarténe
Porto-Vecchio
Bonifacio
SARDINIA (ITALY)

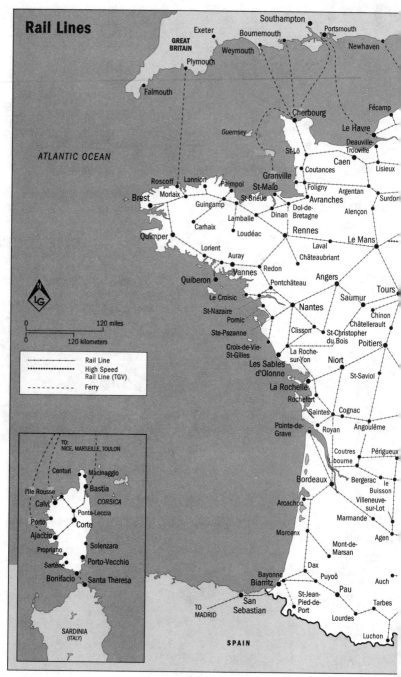

Rail Lines

GREAT BRITAIN

Southampton
Portsmouth
Exeter
Bournemouth
Weymouth
Newhaven

Plymouth

Falmouth

Fécamp

Cherbourg
Le Havre

ATLANTIC OCEAN

Guernsey

Deauville-Trouville

St-Lô
Caen
Lisieux

Coutances
Granville
Foligny
Argentan
Surdon

Roscoff
Lannion
Paimpol
St-Malo
Avranches
Alençon

Brest
Morlaix
St-Brieuc
Dol-de-Bretagne

Guingamp
Dinan

Lamballe
Rennes
Le Mans

Carhaix
Loudéac
Laval

Quimper
Châteaubriant

Lorient
Auray
Redon
Angers
Tours

Vannes
Saumur

Quiberon
Pontchâteau
Chinon

Le Croisic
Nantes
Châtellerault

St-Nazaire
Clisson
St-Christopher du Bois
Poitiers

Pornic
La Roche-sur-Yon
Niort

Ste-Pazanne

Croix-de-Vie-St-Gilles

Les Sables d'Olonne
St-Saviol

La Rochelle

Rochefort

Saintes
Cognac

Pointe-de-Grave
Royan
Angoulême

Coutres
Périgueux

Libourne

Bordeaux
Bergerac
le Buisson

Arcachon
Villeneuve-sur-Lot

Marmande

Morcenx
Agen

Mont-de-Marsan

Dax
Auch

Bayonne
Puyoô
Pau

Biarritz

St-Jean-Pied-de-Port
Tarbes

San Sebastian

Lourdes
Luchon

SPAIN

N

0 ____ 120 miles
0 ____ 120 kilometers

─────── Rail Line
••••••••• High Speed Rail Line (TGV)
- - - - - Ferry

TO:
NICE, MARSEILLE, TOULON

Centuri
Macinaggio

l'Ile Rousse
Bastia

Calvi
CORSICA

Porto
Ponte-Leccia

Ajaccio
Corte

Propriano
Solenzara

Sartène
Porto-Vecchio

Bonifacio
Santa Theresa

TO MADRID

SARDINIA (ITALY)

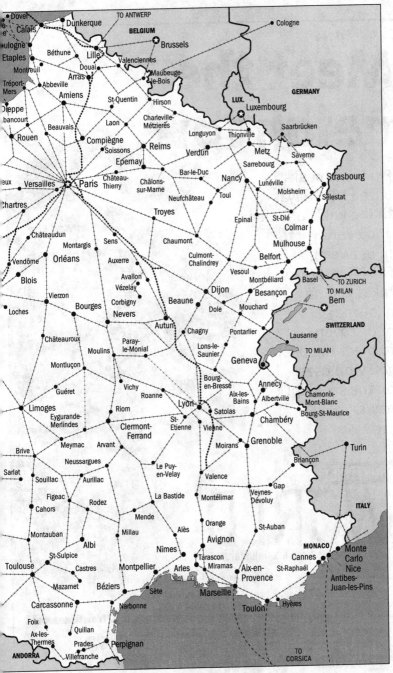

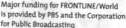

DISCOVER FRANCE

But the true travelers...are never separated from their fate,
And, without knowing quite why, always say: Let's Go.
—Charles Baudelaire, *Les Fleurs du Mal*

Whatever Baudelaire might say, travelers know exactly why they're going to France. With the world's grandest art museums, an infinite number of châteaux, and all the glorious vestiges of aristocratic life, France arguably remains *the* cultural capital of the world. The French reign supreme in the smaller details of life, creating the most impossibly intricate pastries, the most prestigious wines, the most elegant cuts of clothing, and raises them all to the level of an aesthetic experience. And if that isn't quite enough, there is simply nothing comparable to France's natural beauty: the breathtakingly misty isles off Brittany, the lush rows of vines in sleepy towns in Alsace, the dazzling turquoise beaches of the Riviera, the fields of lavender and poppies in Provence.

But perhaps Baudelaire does have a point, for France has a draw far more elusive than anything you will see in a glossy brochure. France has the original *je ne sais quoi*—that certain "I don't know what"—and you will discover it when and where you least expect it. You might find it in a fierce, high-stakes game of *pétanque* with old cronies in a *provençal* village. You might find it haggling for the perfect piece of *batik* in a North African market in Marseille. Or it might come to you in a single impression: as you bite into a warm chocolate croissant at dawn after a night of clubbing in Lille, as you eavesdrop on the low conversation of an elegant Parisian couple beside you in a bistro, as you witness the slight, bent frames of World War II veterans paying tribute to the gray beaches of Normandy.

But our suggestions are nothing more than a starting point. It's up to you to weave your own fate in France.

FACTS AND FIGURES

OFFICIAL NAME: République Française

POPULATION: 59,551,227

CAPITAL: Paris

GDP per capita: US$24,400

PRESIDENT: Jacques Chirac

MAJOR RELIGIONS: 90% Catholic, 3% Muslim, 2% Protestant, 1% Jewish

WINE PRODUCED PER YEAR: Equivalent to 1,927 Olympic-sized pools.

BAGUETTES CONSUMED PER YEAR: Laid end-to-end, they would span the Earth's circumference 1.14 times.

ESTIMATED NUMBER OF ROMANTIC ENCOUNTERS PER DAY: 4,959,476 in Paris alone. *Ah, l'amour!*

WHEN TO GO

In July, Paris starts to shrink; in August, it positively shrivels. The city in August is devoid of Parisians, animated only by tourists and the pickpockets who love them. At the same time, the French themselves hop over to the Norman coast, swell the beaches of the western Atlantic coast from La Rochelle down to Biarritz, and move along the shores of rocky Corsica. From June to September, the Côte d'Azur becomes one long tangle of halter-topped, khaki-shorted anglophones; a constant, exhausting party. Early summer and autumn are the best times to visit Paris, while winter there can be abominable, presided over by a terrible *grisaille*—chill "grayness." The north and west of France are prone to wet but mild winters and springs, while summers are warm but undependable. The center and east of the country have a more continental climate, with harsh winters and long, dry summers; these are also generally the least crowded and most unspoiled regions. During the winter, the Alps provide some of the best skiing in the world, while the Pyrénées offer a calmer, if less climatically dependable, alternative.

As a general rule, the further south you travel in the summer, the more crucial hotel reservations become. Reserve a month in advance for the Côte d'Azur, Corsica, Provence, Languedoc, and the Pays Basque.

WHERE ALL THE LIGHTS ARE BRIGHT

While **Paris** (pp. 93-171) is one of the world's great cities, you'll find plenty to do in France's major regional centers. **Lyon** (p. 653), France's second city, has had a reputation for staid *bourgeoisie*, but today it provides non-stop action and France's best cuisine. In **Marseille**'s (p. 476) 2600-year history, this multicultural working city has never failed to make itself heard. **Nice** (p. 534) is a party town packed with museums, and only a pebble's throw from the rest of the sandy Côte d'Azur. With a hybrid Franco-German culture, **Strasbourg** (p. 729) is the obvious home for the European Parliament. In Brittany, **Rennes** (p. 216) mixes a medieval *vieille ville* and major museums with frenzied party kids. In the southwest, sophisticated **Montpellier** (p. 470) is the gay capital of France, while rosy **Toulouse** (p. 434) holds Languedoc together with student-filled nightlife and modern art.

ONCE UPON A TIME...

French châteaux range from imposing feudal ruins to the well-preserved country homes of 19th-century industrialists. The greatest variety and concentration is found in the **Loire Valley** (pp. 270-312), where the defensive hilltop fortresses of **Chinon** (p. 296) and **Saumur** (p. 298) contrast with the Renaissance grace of **Chenonceau** (p. 294) and **Chambord** (p. 283). The Loire has no monopoly on châteaux, though. Near Paris you can find a tribute to the great Louis XIV's even greater ego at **Versailles** (p. 165). In Provence, you'll be hard-pressed to decide whether the Palais des Papes in **Avignon** (p. 495) is a castle or a palace, while nearby the craggy ruins of **Les Baux** (p. 514) will take you back to the age of chivalry. Perhaps the most impressive château is the fortress of **Carcassonne** (p. 447), a medieval citadel which still stands guard over the Languedoc. If you prefer smaller, less-touristed castles, head to the **Route Jacques Cœur** near **Bourges** (p. 359).

Paris's **Notre Dame** (p. 127) is the most famous Church building in France, but a more exquisite Gothic jewel is the nearby **Sainte-Chapelle** (p. 129). The Gothic style first reached maturity at **Chartres** (p. 168), while other medieval masterpieces await at **Strasbourg** (p. 729) and **Reims** (p. 763). A more modern sensibility animates Le Corbusier's post-war masterpiece at **Ronchamp** (p. 750).

AU NATUREL

Everyone's heard about the **Alps,** where some of the best hiking and skiing in the world can be found around **Val d'Isère** (p. 646) and **Chamonix** (p. 637). But the Alps are just one of France's four major mountain ranges. To the north, you'll find the rolling **Jura** mountains (p. 756) in Franche-Comté, while **Le Mont-Dore** (p. 674), in the **Massif Central,** provides spectacular hiking near extinct volcanoes. To the southwest, you can climb into Spain from the western **Pyrénées** (p. 427). If snow-capped peaks aren't your thing, lowland pleasures can be found exploring the fla-mingo-filled plains of the **Camargue** (p. 517) or canoeing the rapids of the **Grand Canyon du Verdon** (p. 572). For advanced hikers, it's possible to trek the length of rugged **Corsica's** interior (p. 584), but those less advanced can find great day and overnight hikes everywhere on the island, especially on the **Cap Corse** (p. 610).

LA VIE EN *ROSÉ*

Let's Go: France was shocked and dismayed to read that France ranks second in international wine consumption, being trumped by her neighbor Italy. Luckily, we can still say France produces some of the finest wines and inebriants in the world. Start with an *apéritif* of a champagne cocktail from one of **Reims's** spectacular *caves* (p. 763). To try a little bit of everything, check out the red wines in **Bordeaux** (p. 395) and **Burgundy** (p. 685), or the whites of Alsace's **Route du Vin** (p. 737) and the **Loire Valley** (p. 270). Top it all off with an after-dinner drink—either **Cognac** in the eponymous town (p. 326), or Calvados, made throughout **Normandy** (p. 172).

HERE COMES THE SUN

The Côte d'Azur attracts two types of people—the stars who create its glamor, and the masses who come looking for it. You'll party among the tanned youth of Europe in **Nice** (p. 534) and **Juan-les-Pins** (p. 563). Surfers should head straight for the big rollers of the Atlantic coast in **Anglet** (p. 415). If sun and sand are your only desires, try **Ile Rousse** (p. 600) in Corsica or the dune beaches near **Arcachon** (p. 405). Some of France's most beautiful beaches await in foggy Brittany, at **Belle-Ile** (p. 260) and **St-Malo** (p. 226). Find solitude on the pristine untouched *plages* of **Ile de Ré** and **Ile d'Aix** (p. 340).

▨ LET'S GO PICKS

BEST PLACE TO KISS: Dusk on **Pont Neuf** (p. 111), on the Ile de la Cité in Paris.

BEST MUSES: The gorgeous orchards and harbor of **Collioure** (p. 455) inspired Matisse, Dalí and Picasso. Van Gogh left his heart and his ear in **Arles** (p. 508), where he painted cafés and starry nights. Follow in the footsteps of Cézanne in **Aix-en-Provence** (p. 490).

LONGEST SHOTS: The **bar-o-mètre** in Nice's Tapas la Movida (p. 545); the still-loaded **German artillery** in Longues-sur-Mer (p. 200); your chances at the famous **Monte-Carlo Casino** (p. 555).

BEST INDOOR RAINSHOWERS: Inside the funky **Maison Satie** in Honfleur (p. 185). Each room is a surprise!

MOST WHIMSICAL PALACE: Le Palais **Idéal** in Hauterives (p. 625), assembled stone by stone by the local postman.

BEST ISLANDS: White homes with blue shutters cover idyllic **Ile d'Yeu** (p. 349). Sheep and stone crosses are the main inhabitants of **Ile d'Ouessant** (p. 250). Neither island is larger than a Peugeot.

BEST REASONS FOR WORLD PEACE: Normandy's World War II **D-Day beaches** (p. 197); tiny **Oradour-sur-glane** (p. 367), untouched since Nazis massacred its entire population; the bones of 130,000 unknown soldiers at the Ossuaire outside **Verdun** (p. 726).

MOST CREATIVELY LEWD MUSEUM: The **Musée de Tire-Bouchon** in Ménerbes (p. 506) features perhaps the dirtiest corkscrews you'll ever see. Really, now.

SCARIEST GARGOYLES: Viollet-le-Duc's *chimera* on the **Cathédrale de Notre-Dame** in Paris (p. 127); Front Nationale leader and defeated presidential candidate **Jean-Marie Le Pen** (p. 13).

DISCOVER

SUGGESTED ITINERARIES

The following itineraries are designed to give you the highlights of France's distinct regions, from its cosmopolitan hubs to its sleepy villages. While these itineraries are intended for those who haven't traveled around France very much, even initiated Francophiles can use them as a template for additional daytrips and excursions. There are many Frances, however, and these are not the only ones; in fact, we've left out more than half the country. For more ideas, see "Other Trips" below or the regional chapter introductions.

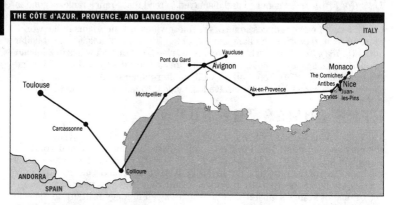

THE CÔTE d'AZUR, PROVENCE, AND LANGUEDOC

COTE D'AZUR, PROVENCE AND LANGUEDOC (3 WEEKS)

Visit the Côte d'Azur for beaches and glamor, inland Provence for scented fields and sun-drenched villages, and Languedoc for orchards and crumbling monuments. **Nice** is the unofficial capital of the Côte d'Azur, a nonstop anglophone beach party with more beaches, nightlife, and budget housing than you can shake a glowstick at (2 days; p. 534). Don't neglect the nearby clifftop villages of the **Corniches** (2 days; p. 548). If you have any money left, you'll want to daytrip east to the micro-state of **Monaco,** which is absolutely the richest place on the Riviera (1 day; p. 552). Twin towns **Antibes** and **Juan-les-Pins** have enough beauty and nightlife for ten towns; don't miss them (1 day; p. 560). **Cannes,** home to the famous and exclusive film festival, is star-packed all year round, and has some of the cheapest housing on the coast (1 day; p. 564). **Aix-en-Provence** is a slow *provençal* city full of fountains, twisty streets, and Cézanne paintings (2 days; p. 490). **Avignon,** city of Popes, hosts a yearly drama festival (2 days; p. 495). It's also the closest city to the lovely **Vaucluse,** a group of sleepy, ruin-dotted, quintessentially *provençal* little towns, and the Roman aqueduct, **Pont du Gard** (2 days; p. 503 and p. 526). **Montpellier** is a city with intellectual and cultural sophistication and unbeatable gay nightlife (3 days; p. 470). Tiny **Collioure,** sandwiched between the Pyrénées and the Mediterranean, is a paradise of vineyards and orchards (1 day; p. 455). Brave the hordes of tourists to climb the ancient ramparts of **Carcassonne** (1 day; p. 447) and top it all off in **Toulouse,** the pink-bricked capital of the southwest (3 days; p. 434).

LOIRE VALLEY, BRITTANY AND NORMANDY (2 WEEKS)

The northeast has it all; from vibrant student cities to isolated rugged coasts, from the monastic austerity of Mont St-Michel to the monarchic decadence of the Loire châteaux. **Blois** houses one of France's most famous châteaux and serves as a base for the magnificent many-chimneyed **Chambord** (2 days; p. 278). The bustling, student-filled **Tours** serves as a daytrip hub for the medieval town of **Chinon** and the graceful lines of the river-spanning Renaissance chateau of **Chenonceau**

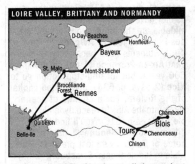

LOIRE VALLEY, BRITTANY AND NORMANDY

ALSACE, BURGUNDY AND THE ALPS

(2 days; p. 287). Check out all the student hotspots in the bustling Breton university town of **Rennes** (3 days; p. 216). The nearby **Brocéliande forest,** the ancient haunt of Merlin and Guinevere, is one of Brittany's most legend-steeped sites. Just off the Western coast of Brittany, the wind-swept cliffs of **Belle Ile** (reached by ferry from mainland **Quiberon**) set the scene for a perfect day-long bike ride (2 days; p. 260). Soak your tired muscles at the sandy beaches of the seaside resort town **St-Malo** (1 day; p. 226). **Mont St-Michel** simply can't be missed for the breathtaking view of sunlight on the monastery's stark walls (1 day; p. 209). Visit **Bayeux,** home to the 1000-year-old tapestry that recounts William the Conqueror's invasion of England, then head to the nearby **D-Day beaches,** which memorialize the events of 1944 with striking honesty (2 days; p. 194). **Honfleur**'s multicolored houses provide a bohemian backdrop to the funky museum of composer Erik Satie (1 day; p. 185).

ALSACE, BURGUNDY AND THE ALPS (2 WEEKS) Spanning from the gentle Vosges mountains to the peak of Mont Blanc, France's eastern border is the perfect destination for history buffs, nature enthusiasts and wine connoisseurs alike. While **Reims**'s architectural claim to fame is its immense medieval cathedral, no traveller will want to miss a light-headed tour of the city's palatial *maisons de champagne* (2 days; p. 763). The capitol of Lorraine, **Nancy** boasts gardens, airy *places*, and fab nightlife (2 days; p. 717). **Strasbourg** is a cosmopolitan center of Alsatian culture, and serves as the the hub for the tiny villages amidst the vineyards of the *Route du*

Vin (3 days; p. 729). **Colmar** stands at the heart of the Route with pastel half-timbered houses and an exquisite museum (1 day; p. 742). Fill up on *boeuf bourgignon* and scrutinize the wines of the Cote d'Or in **Dijon,** and glimpse glazed-tile roofs in nearby **Beaune** (3 days; p. 692). **Lyon** serves up world-class cuisine in a capital city second only to Paris (2 days; p. 653). Nestled in the Alps and perched on a pristine lake, **Annecy** belongs in a fairy tale (1 day; p. 631), while **Chamonix** is the gateway to the majestic Mont Blanc (2 days; p. 637).

LA CRÈME DE LA CRÈME (1 MONTH) To see everything worth seeing in France in only a few weeks is impossible, but you can still try! You'll need at least 4-5 days to see the sights and shops of **Paris** (p. 93)—be sure to make time for a daytrip to **Versailles** (p. 165). Next, slip down to the Loire Valley. **Chambord** (1 day; p. 283), which is perhaps as grand as Versailles, has as many chimneys as there are days in a year. The château of **Amboise** (1 day; p. 286) was home to four French kings, while **Saumur** (1 day; p. 298) is famous for its castle, riding school, and sparkling wines. Then travel up to the island abbey of **Mont-St-Michel** (1 day; p. 209). A little farther along the coast is popular **St-Malo** (1 day;

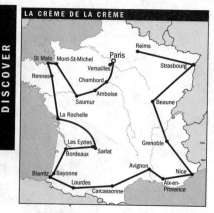

LA CRÈME DE LA CRÈME

sonne (1 day; p. 447), guarding the town as they have done for centuries. No less formidable are the fortifications of the Palais-des-Papes in festive **Avignon** (1 day; p. 495). Students have been partying in elegant **Aix-en-Provence** (1 day; p. 490) for 600 years, but for non-stop action go to **Nice** (2 days; p. 534), undisputed capital of the Riviera. For a change of scenery, climb into the Alps to reach dynamic **Grenoble** (2 days; p. 616). You'll find highs of a different sort in **Beaune** (1 day; p. 692), home of Burgundy's most precious wines, while to the northeast, **Strasbourg** (2 days; p. 729) offers Alsatian wines and a hybrid Franco-German culture. Finally, finish off in style with a tasting at one of the champagne *caves* in **Reims** (1 day; p. 763).

p. 226), with ramparts, beaches, and fantastic seafood. Next, head down to **Rennes** (2 days; p. 216) for medieval sights and modern nightlife, before soaking up the sun in beach-blessed, historical **La Rochelle** (1 day; p. 334). For a change of pace, contemplate times past in medieval **Sarlat** (1 day; p. 375), and the 17,000-year-old cave paintings of **Les-Eyzies-de-Tayac** (1 day; p. 374). Test your taste buds in the vineyards of **Bordeaux** (2 days; p. 395) before zipping southward to *basque* on the beach in **Biarritz** or **Bayonne** (2 days; p. 407). From there, follow the pilgrims to miraculous **Lourdes** (1 day; p. 423). Keep heading east to reach the stunning walls of **Carcas-**

OTHER TRIPS France's best hiking and windsurfing are in the rugged, rocky, sun-blasted island of **Corsica** (p. 584), which is ringed with beautiful beaches and crumbling Genoese watchtowers. **Burgundy** (p. 685) is known for its great wines and sleepy villages, as are the towns surrounding **Bordeaux** (p. 395) in the southwest. Finally, don't forget the exquisite **Dordogne,** a river-cut valley of walnut trees, lazy flowing water, and enough *pâté* for several coronaries (p. 382).

LIFE AND TIMES

Fifty years after Galileo's death, France's Louis XIV proved the astronomer a heretic; the earth revolved around the Sun King, and France was the navel of the cosmos. Four revolutions later, patriotic Frenchmen and -women still argue that France is the cultural center of the world. The greatest *artistes*, the most elaborate fashions, the most pungent cheeses; the clichés may be well worn, but to a great extent, they're all true. Yet the more you explore France, the more the clichés fail to capture the complexities of French culture. The *liberté, égalité, fraternité* ideology of the Revolution inevitably faces off with current debates over immigration, minorities, and national identity. France's centralized bureaucracy must acknowledge the nation's cultural and geographic diversity from the Celtic traditions on the shores of the north to the Basque language in the mountains of the south. To paraphrase Alexis de Tocqueville, France to outsiders might be an object of admiration, hatred, pity or terror, but never indifference.

LAND

France's 543,965 sq. km fit into a hexagonal shape: to the southwest, the **Pyrénées mountains** form a frontier with Spain, to the east the snowcapped peaks of the **Alps** and **Jura** separate France from Italy and Switzerland, and just above the Jura, the **Rhine River** marks the divide between France and Germany. France's only artificial border is with Belgium, in the northeast corner of the country. The **English Channel** (*La Manche*) keeps Normandy's chalky cliffs at a 35km distance from England at its narrowest point. The **Atlantic Ocean** laps upon beaches of fine sand in the west and the **Mediterranean** greets the pebbly beaches of the south. The interior of France is primarily characterized by low-lying plains and river valleys, while the rugged *massif central* plateau in the southeast boasts a landscape of extinct volcanoes, deep gorges and stalagmites. **Corsica,** France's Mediterranean island territory, is 170km off the French coast. Its 8681 sq. km are mostly mountainous, with high cliffs and craggy rocks on its west coast and a lagoon-spotted east coast.

FLORA, FAUNA & THE ENVIRONMENT

France was once almost entirely covered in forest. Today, trees cover 25% of the terrain and provide a home to France's larger mammals, such as red deer, roe deer and wild boar. Other common animals include hares, rabbits and foxes. The Alpine chamois and marmot, Pyrenean lynx and brown bear, and Atlantic seals are all endangered species. In April 2002, President Chirac announced at the G-8 Environmental Summit that France would take an active role in leading European initiatives to protect ancient forests. These efforts earned accolades from Greenpeace—an organization that has not always had the fondest relations with France. In 1985, the French secret service blew up Greenpeace's ship, the *Rainbow Warrior,* which was stationed in the South Pacific in protest to France's nuclear testing in the French Polynesian islands. International controversy surrounding these tests continued into the 1990s, and the last test was concluded in 1996. In 1998, France signed the **United Nations Comprehensive Test Ban Treaty.**

For more information on French national parks, check out www.parcsnationaux-fr.com; for more on French environmental concerns, see the French Institute for the Environment's website: www.ifen.fr.

HISTORY

FROM GAULS TO GOTHS. In 1868, the skull of a 27,000-year-old advanced hominid was unearthed at Cro-Magnon, in **Périgord.** 10,000 years later, his descendants left their mark on history in the graffiti-filled caves of the **Dordogne Valley,** and by 4500 BC Neolithic peoples were carving huge stone monuments at **Carnac.** These mysterious creations were admired by the Celtic **Gauls,** who arrived from the east around 600 BC. Gauls traded and co-existed peacefully with the Greek colonists who settled during the 7th century BC at Massilia (modern day **Marseille**). In a clever substitution of vowels, Rome made **Provence** a province in 125 BC and quickly conquered the rest of the South. Fierce resistance from France's northern Gauls kept the Romans out of their territory until **Julius Caesar's** victory at Alesia in 52 BC. By the time Rome itself fell in AD 476, Gaul had suffered Germanic invasions for centuries. While many of the Gothic tribes plundered and passed on, the **Franks** eventually dominated Gaul. The Frankish **Clovis** founded the Merovingian dynasty and was baptized a Christian in 507. His empire was succeeded by the grander Carolingian dynasty of **Charlemagne.** While his **Holy Roman Empire** did not actually live up to its literal name, Charlemagne did succeed in adding what are now Germany, Austria and Switzerland to his domains. The territorial squabbles following his death in were resolved with the **Treaty of Verdun,** which divided the empire among his three grandsons.

FRANCE AND ENGLAND DUKE IT OUT. The territorial conflict between the French and the English that began with the fall of the Carolingian empire and ended 500 years later with bittersweet victory of Joan of Arc reads, at best, like a soap opera. In the wake of the Carolingians, the noble-elected **Hugh Capet** quickly consolidated power. His distant descendant **Louis VII** made the fatal error of not signing a pre-nuptial agreement, and when his ex-queen **Eleanor of Aquitaine** married into the English Plantagenêt dynasty in the 12th century, a broad swath of land stretching from the Channel to the Pyrénées became English territory. In a comedic turn of events, King **Philippe-August** won much of northern France from England's bumbling King John that same century. The plot thickened in the 14th century, when England's **Edward III** tried to claim the throne after the fall of the Capetian dynasty. The French **Philippe de Valois** responded to this indignation by encroaching upon English-owned Aquitaine. Edward III landed his troops in Normandy, triggering the **Hundred Years War** in 1328. All seemed lost when the English crowned their own **Henry VI** king of France 90 years later, but salvation soon followed for France with a 17-year-old peasant girl. Leading the French army, **Joan of Arc** won a string of victories before her capture by Burgundians, who were allied with the English. While she burned at the stake in **Rouen** (p. 172) in 1430, the tide of war had already turned, and only Calais was left in English hands by 1453.

STRANGE BEDFELLOWS: RELIGIOUS DEVOTION AND WAR. As always, fervor and violence made an uneasy liaison in the Middle Ages and Renaissance. Medieval townspeople raised cathedrals to the honor of God, and monasteries and convents swelled with novitiates. The power of the monasteries was often as great as that of the aristocracy, and in the 11th century, the abbot of **Cluny** (p. 699) was as influential as any monarch. **Pope Innocent II** proclaimed the first Crusade from **Clermont** (p. 668), hoping to wrest Jerusalem from the Saracens. Thousands, from kings to peasants, flocked to take the cross, swayed by the promise of salvation and the probability of plunder. Though few crusades had any military success, exposure to the advanced civilizations of the east and a revival of international trade helped stir Europe from her intellectual slumber. The balance between the papacy and monarchies was tested and then tipped when **Philip IV** challenged **Pope Boniface VIII**

at the opening of the 14th century. The king arrested the pope to prevent his imminent excommunication; old Boniface died after the arrest, and his French successor, **Pope Clement V,** moved the pope's court from Rome to church-owned **Avignon** (p. 495). Six more popes held mass in France, increasing French power but spawning the **Black Death** (according to the superstitious and the Italians); the papacy finally returned to Rome in 1377. In the 16th century, religious conflict between **Huguenots** (French Protestants) and **Catholics** initiated the **Wars of Religion.** When the fervently Catholic **Catherine de Médici** claimed the throne, she orchestrated a marriage between her daughter and the Huguenot **Henri de Navarre** in 1572. What appeared at first as a peaceful political move was soon revealed as a deadly trap. Their wedding day is known today as the **St-Bartholomew's Day Massacre;** a murdering spree that slaughtered 2000 Huguenots. Henri survived, quickly converted to Catholicism, and ascended the throne as the first **Bourbon** monarch. In 1598 he issued the **Edict of Nantes,** granting tolerance for French Protestants and quelling religious warfare for almost a century.

BOURBON ON THE ROCKS. The French Bourbon monarchy reached the height of its power and extravagance in the 17th century. **Louis XIII's** capable and ruthless minister, **Cardinal Richelieu,** consolidated political power in the hands of the monarchy and created the centralized, bureaucratic administration characteristic of France to this day. When Richelieu and Louis died within months of each other in 1642, they were succeeded by another king-and-cardinal combo, **Louis XIV** and **Cardinal Mazarin.** Since Louis was only five years old at the time, the cardinal again took charge, but by 1661 the 24-year-old monarch had decided he was ready to rule alone. Not known for his modesty, Louis styled himself as the **Sun King** and took the motto *"l'état, c'est moi"* ("I am the state"). He brought the nobility with him to the fabulously opulent palace of Versailles, hoping that there he could keep a close watch over them and avoid any unpleasant uprisings. Yet for all his elaborate displays of power, Louis could not long hide the state's growing financial problems, and resentment toward the monarchy began to brew.

When **Louis XVI** succeeded to the throne in 1774, the country was in desperate financial straits. Peasants blamed the soon-to-be-**Old Regime** for their mounting debts, while aristocrats detested the king for his attempts at reform. In 1789, in an attempt to resolve this no-win situation, Louis XVI called a meeting of the **Estates General,** an assembly of delegates from the three classes of society: aristocrats, clergy, and the bourgeois-dominated **Third Estate.** The Third Estate soon broke away and proclaimed itself the National Assembly, moving to the tennis courts of Versailles and promising to draft a new constitution in their **Oath of the Tennis Court.** As rumors multiplied, the initiative passed to the Parisian mob, known as the *sans-culottes* (those without breeches) who were angered by high bread prices. When they stormed the old fortress of the **Bastille** on July 14th, a destructive orgy stormed across the nation as peasants burned records of their debts. The Assembly soon authored the **Declaration of the Rights of Man,** which embodied the principles of *liberté, égalité,* and *fraternité.* When the petrified king tried to flee the country in 1791, he was arrested and imprisoned; in 1792 his monarchy was officially abolished and replaced by the **First Republic.** Meanwhile, Austria and Prussia mobilized in order to stamp out the democratic disease. In 1793, as the revolutionary armies miraculously defeated the invaders, the radical **Jacobin** faction, led by **Maximilien Robespierre,** took over the Convention and guillotined the King and his cake-savoring Queen, **Marie-Antoinette.** By this point, the revolution had taken a radical turn. Robespierre's Committee of Public Safety began its **Reign of Terror** and ordered the execution of Robespierre's popular rival, **Danton.** Robespierre himself met with the guillotine blade in 1794. With his death, the Terror was over and power was entrusted to a five-man Directory.

THE LITTLE DICTATOR. Meanwhile, war continued as a young Corsican general swept through northern Italy and into Austria. Fearful of his rising popularity, the Directory jumped at **Napoleon Bonaparte**'s idea of invading Egypt to threaten Britain's colonies in India. Although successful on land, the destruction of his fleet at the Battle of the Nile left his disease-ridden army marooned in Cairo. Napoleon responded by hurrying back to France to salvage his political career. Riding a wave of public support, he deposed the Directory, ultimately crowning himself **Emperor** in 1804. His **Napoleonic Code** re-established slavery and limited the legal rights of women. After crushing the Austrians, Prussians and Russians, he left only Britain undefeated, safe in her island refuge after **Horatio Nelson**'s 1807 victory at Trafalgar. In 1812, after occupying a deserted Moscow, Napoleon was forced to withdraw at the onset of winter. The freezing cold decimated the French ranks; of the 700,000 men he had led out to Russia, barely 200,000 returned. Napoleon lost the support of a war-weary nation. In return for abdicating in 1814, he was given the Mediterranean island of **Elba,** and the monarchy was reinstated under **Louis XVIII,** brother of his headless predecessor. The story has a final twist: Napoleon left Elba and landed near Cannes on March 26th, 1815. He marched north as the king fled to England. The adventure of the ensuing **Hundred Days' War** ended on the field of **Waterloo** in Flanders, where the **Duke of Wellington** triumphed as much by luck as by skill. Napoleon was banished to **St-Helena** in the south Atlantic, where he died in 1821. Thousands still pay their respects to Napoleon's Corsican hometown of **Ajaccio** (p. 586).

REVOLUTION AGAIN…AND AGAIN…AND AGAIN. The **Bourbon Restoration** was quick to step into the power vacuum left by Napoleon. France's reinstated monarchy soon returned to its despotic ways of the Old Regime. But when **Charles X** restricted the press and limited the electorate to the landed classes, the people spoke up. Following the **July Revolution of 1830,** Charles, remembering the fate of his brother, abdicated quickly, and a **constitutional monarchy** was created under the head of the new Orléan regime, "bourgeois king" **Louis-Philippe.** While the middle classes prospered, the industrialization of France created a class of urban poor receptive to the new ideas of socialism. They provided the muscle behind the **February Revolution of 1848,** which culminated in the declaration of the **Second Republic** and the adoption of universal male suffrage. Playing on the myth of his name, the emperor's nephew **Louis Napoleon** was elected president. He seized power in an 1851 coup, and declared himself Emperor Napoleon III in 1852. During his reign, the Second Empire, France was economically revived: her factories hummed and **Baron Haussmann** rebuilt Paris, creating the grand boulevards.

The confident French did not notice the storm clouds gathering across the Rhine, where **Bismarck** had almost completed the unification of Germany. Tricking the French into declaring war, Bismarck's troops overran the country. The emperor was captured, and as German armies advanced, the **Third Republic** was declared by Parisian deputies. The city kept the Germans at bay for four months, finally capitulating just as its citizens were reduced to eating rats. Germany pulled out after receiving the Alsace-Lorraine territory and an exorbitant occupation indemnity. After this humiliation, the Parisian mob revolted and declared the **Commune,** a brief-lived governmental coup which was quickly and bloodily crushed as over 10,000 *communards* died under the rifles of French troops. The Third Republic was further undermined by the **Dreyfus Affair,** a product of the humiliated army's search for a scapegoat. Dreyfus, a Jewish captain in the French army, was convicted in 1894 on trumped-up charges of treason, and exiled. Dreyfusard momentum became unstoppable after Emile Zola condemned the army, the government, and society for its anti-semitic prejudice in his dramatic diatribe *J'accuse;* Dreyfus was finally pardoned in 1904.

COSTLY VICTORIES: THE TWO GREAT WARS. Germany's 1871 unification changed the balance of power in Europe. After centuries of conflict, the **Entente Cordiale** brought the British and the French into cooperation in 1904. With the addition of Czarist Russia, Britain and France formed the **Triple Entente** and faced the **Triple Alliance** of Germany, Italy, and the Austro-Hungarian Empire. When **World War I** erupted in 1914, German armies rapidly advanced on France in a seeming replay of the previous conflict, but a stalemate soon developed as the opposing armies dug trenches along the length of the country. The withdrawal of newly revolutionary Russia in 1917 was balanced by the entry of the US, and victory for the West came in 1918. It is still possible to visit the battle-scarred fields where Europe lost an entire generation (see **Memorials near Verdun**, p. 728). Devastated by four years of fighting on her territory, and with 1.3 million men dead, France pushed for crippling reparations from Germany; these and accompanying humiliations were often invoked by Hitler in his rise to power.

During the great depression of the 1930s, internal tensions between the right and the left, Fascists and Socialists, bourgeois and workers left France ill-equipped to deal with the dangers of **Hitler's** rapid rise to power and his impending mobilization on the opposite shores of the Rhine. **World War II** began with the German invasion of Poland in 1939, and France declared war on Germany in response. In May 1940, the German flank swept through Belgium, bypassing the **Maginot line**, a string of fortresses along the German border which had formed France's main defensive position. Allied defenses collapsed, and France capitulated in June. The country was partitioned, with the north under German occupation, and a puppet state in the south ruled from **Vichy** (p. 681) by WWI hero **Maréchal Pétain**. Those French forces that escaped the Germans were commanded by the French government-in-exile, under **General Charles de Gaulle**. It was at his insistence that French troops led the **liberation of Paris** on August 25th, 1944. Today, several stunning monuments pay tribute to the losses of World War II. The beaches of Normandy still see British and American veterans every June 6th, who come to honor the anniversary of **D-Day** (see p. 197). The unrestored ruins of the ghost town **Oradour-sur-glane** (p. 367) remain a mute testimony to the horror of war and a memorial to the inhabitants massacred by Nazi troops in 1944. **Le Struthof-Natzwiller** concentration camp (p. 739) in Alsace and the **Resistance** headquarters in Lyon (p. 653) are equally compelling reminders of the war.

FOURTH REPUBLIC AND POST-COLONIAL FRANCE. The **Fourth Republic** was proclaimed in 1944 under the leadership of de Gaulle. In the next two years, his vision of a restructured society led to female suffrage and nationalized energy companies. He quit in 1946, unable to adapt to the deadlock of democratic politics. The Fourth Republic lacked a strong replacement for de Gaulle, and the next 14 years saw 25 governments. The end of the war also signaled great change in France's residual 19th-century **colonial empire**. France's defeat in 1954 at the Vietnamese liberation of **Dien Bien Phu** inspired the colonized peoples of France's other protectorates and colonies. Morocco and Tunisia gained **independence** in 1956, followed by Mali, Senegal, and the Ivory Coast in 1960. But in Algeria, France drew the line when Algerian nationalists moved for independence. With a population of over one million French colonists, or **pied-noirs** (literally "black feet" in French), France was reluctant to give up the colony it regarded as an extension of its own culture. De Gaulle was voted into power in 1958 to deal with the impending crisis, but even he could not stop the **Algerian Revolution** from erupting in 1962. Later that year, with a new **constitution** in hand, France declared itself the **Fifth Republic.** Yet the constitution did nothing to keep the Algerian conflict from worsening. At a peaceful demonstration in Paris against curfew restrictions in 1961, police opened fire on the largely North African crowd, killing hundreds and dumping their bodies into the Seine. Amid the violence in Paris and the war in Algeria, a 1962 referendum reluctantly granted Algeria independence. One hundred years of French colonial rule in Algeria abruptly came to an end, and the French colonial empire crumbled in its wake.

The 1960s saw another kind of revolution occur within France itself. In **May 1968**, what started as a student protest against racism, sexism and problems in the university system rapidly grew into a full-scale revolt as 10 million state workers went on strike in support of social reform. The government responded by deploying tank and commando units into the city. The National Assembly was soon dissolved and things looked to be heading for revolution yet again, averted only when fresh elections returned the Gaullists to power. However, the aging General had lost his magic touch, and he resigned following a referendum defeat in 1969.

THE 80S AND 90S. After de Gaulle's exit, many feared the Fifth Republic's collapse. It has endured, but with change. De Gaulle's Prime Minister, **Georges Pompidou**, won the presidency, during which he held a *laissez-faire* position toward business and a less assertive foreign policy than de Gaulle. In 1974, Pompidou died suddenly, and his successor was conservative **Valéry Giscard d'Estaing.** D'Estaing's term saw the construction of the **Centre Pompidou**, a center for the arts incorporating galleries and performance spaces. D'Estaing carried on de Gaulle's legacy by concentrating on economic development and strengthening French presence in international affairs. In 1981, Socialist **François Mitterrand** took over the presidency and the Socialists gained a majority in the *Assemblée Nationale*. Within weeks, they had raised the minimum wage and added a fifth week to the French worker's annual vacation. The political collapse of the Left during Mitterrand's presidency forced him to compromise with the Right. Mitterrand began his term with widespread nationalization, but the international climate could not support a socialist economy. The Socialists had serious losses in the 1986 parliamentary elections, and Mitterrand had to appoint the conservative **Jacques Chirac** as Prime Minister.

At the same time, the **far right** began to flourish under the leadership of **Jean-Marie Le Pen.** He formed the **Front National (FN)** on an anti-immigration platform. The dissolution of France's colonial empire and healthy post-war economy led to the development of a new working class from North Africa and other former colonies. Le Pen was able to capitalize on racism toward these immigrants, phrasing it, euphemistically, as "cultural difference." In the 1986 parliamentary elections, the FN picked up 10% of the vote by blaming France's woes (unemployment in particular) on immigrants and foreigners. Meanwhile, in an unprecedented power-sharing relationship known as "cohabitation," Mitterrand withdrew to control foreign affairs, allowing Chirac to assume domestic power. Chirac privatized many industries, but a large-scale transport strike and widespread terrorism hurt the right, allowing Mitterrand to win a second term in 1988. During his second term, he planned a decentralization of financial and political power from Paris to local governments outside the Ile-de-France. In 1995, Mitterrand chose not to run again because of his failing health, and Jacques Chirac was elected president. With **unemployment** at 12.2% at the time of the election, Chirac faced a difficult year. In 1996, the nation mourned the loss of François Mitterrand, who died in early January, and later that year, Chirac was denounced around the globe for conducting underground **nuclear weapons tests** in the South Pacific. The ascendancy of the right was short-lived; in 1997, Chirac dissolved the parliament, and elections reinstated a Socialist government. Chirac was forced to accept his one-time presidential rival **Lionel Jospin,** head of the Socialist majority, as Prime Minister in 1998.

One of the most important challenges in the 80s and 90s has been the question of European integration. Despite France's support of the creation of the **European Economic Community (EEC)** in 1957, the idea of a unified Europe has met with considerable resistance. Since the inception of the 1991 **Maastricht Treaty**, which significantly strengthened economic integration by expanding the 13-nation EEC to the **European Union (EU),** the French have manifested fear of a loss of French national character and autonomy. Hoping that a united Europe would strengthen cooperation between France and Germany, Mitterrand led the campaign for a "Oui" vote in France's 1992 referendum on the treaty. This position lost him prestige; the referendum scraped past with a 51% approval rating. The **Schengen agreement** of 1995 created a six-nation zone without border controls. 1999 saw the extension of this zone to the entire EU (barring the UK, Ireland, and Denmark), and 2002 witnessed the birth of the **Euro** as the single European legal tender.

PAINLESS HISTORY READS

Barbara Tuchman. *A Distant Mirror.* Details the bloodiest events of the 14th century (plagues, crusades, wars) from the viewpoint of a French nobleman.

Natalie Zemon Davis. *The Return of Martin Guerre.* Infinitely readable account of a 16th-century impostor who wins the affections of a tiny Pyrenean town.

Robert Darnton. *The Great Cat Massacre.* A fun, quirky cultural history about the world views of ordinary people during the Enlightenment.

Alexis de Tocqueville. *The Old Regime and the French Revolution.* Still the classic explanation, written by a leading 19th-century historian and cultural critic.

T.J. Clark. *The Painting of Modern Life: Paris in the Art of Manet.* An often dense but worthwhile study of Impressionism and its cultural influences. Gorgeous glossy photos.

Modris Eksteins. *The Rites of Spring.* Simply the best account of the military and cultural history of World War I. A must-read for anyone going to Verdun (p. 726).

Stephen Ambrose. *D-Day, June 6, 1944.* The most recent account of the Normandy beaches by the popular American historian.

Kristin Ross. *May '68 and its Aftermath.* Traces the political and social goals of the student rebellion. Shows the influence of Algerian anti-imperialist movements and the student and worker movements that lasted into the 1970s.

TODAY

2002 ELECTION UPSET. While the presidential election was initially slated by the media to be a lackluster showdown between the scandal-riddled rightist president **Jacques Chirac** and his dry academic Socialist prime minister **Lionel Jospin,** things got interesting when the far-right nationalist **Jean-Marie Le Pen** edged out Jospin in the April preliminary elections. Throughout France, protesters took to the streets to condemn Le Pen's policies, citing his dismissive comments about the Holocaust as proof of his racism. On May 5, voters shrugged off their previous apathy and entered the booths in droves, electing Chirac by a 82% majority. The parliamentary elections on June 16 marked the end of cohabitation between President and Prime Minister. With a landslide victory for the center-right and the appointment of conservative **Jean-Pierre Raffarin** as Prime Minister, Chirac should face few barriers in fulfilling his pledges for tax cuts and institutional reform. Theoretically, that is.

THE IMMIGRATION DEBATE. The steady popularity of Le Pen and his anti-immigration platform is only the most visible sign of the constant national debate on immigration policy, a debate which has expanded in the last few years to encompass issues of national identity, migrant incorporation, and terrorism. France has passed a record amount of legislative change in its immigration policy, issuing forth no less than seven reforms in the last 25 years. Anti-immigration sentiment increased substantially in 1993 when then Interior Minister Charles Pasqua proposed "zero-immigration" and initiated the **Pasqua Law,** allowing police greater freedom to interrogate immigrants in France. Jospin's 1998 law on immigration allows foreign scientists and scholars more relaxed conditions of entry.

SYNAGOGUE BOMBINGS. In March and April of 2002, France experienced an alarming wave of anti-Semitic violence. Jewish schools, synagogues and cemeteries all became targets of terrorist activities. Synagogues in Marseille, Lyon and Strasbourg were badly damaged by fire and bombs, while the Israeli embassy in Paris met a similar fate. Pro-Palestinian and pro-Israeli groups clashed on several other occasions, including several public fist fights. Thousands of French police were called in to protect Jewish neighborhoods. The violence has reflected not only the escalating conflict in the Middle East, but also the growing tension in France and across Europe over demographic changes.

GAY RIGHTS AND ADOPTION. In 1999, France became the first traditionally Catholic country in the world to legally recognize homosexual unions. The **Pacte Civil de Solidarité,** known by its acronym **PACS,** was designed to extend to homosexual and unmarried heterosexual couples greater welfare, tax and inheritance rights. While PACS is now such a common term that it is used as both a noun *(pacser)* and an adjective *(pacsé),* it is has faced a share number of detractors. For many, PACS is strictly a legal term, for gay marriage is still an unwelcome concept to many conservative French. Gay activists are currently struggling to attain the same rights to adoption and reproductive technologies that married couples enjoy.

CULTURE

FOOD & DRINK

Charles de Gaulle complained that no nation with 400 types of cheese could ever be united; watch a pack of ravenous Frenchwomen tearing through a *fromagerie* and you'll agree. Though *le fast-food* and *le self-service* have invaded France, many still shop daily for their ingredients, and restaurants observe the traditional order of courses. One could hardly expect less from the people who coined *haute cuisine.*

MEALS. The French ease into their food consumption for the day with a breakfast *(le petit déjeuner)* which is usually light, consisting of bread *(le pain)* or sometimes croissants plus an espresso with hot milk *(café au lait)* or a hot chocolate *(le chocolat).* The largest meal of the day is lunch *(le déjeuner)* between noon and 2pm. Dinner *(le dîner)* begins quite late, and restaurants may not serve you if you want to dine at 6pm. A complete French meal includes an *apéritif* (drink), an *entrée* (appetizer), a *plat* (main course), salad, cheese, dessert, fruit, coffee, and a *digestif* (after-dinner drink). *Kir,* white wine with *cassis* (black currant liqueur), and *pastis,* a licorice liqueur diluted with water, are the most common *apéritifs.*

MENUS. Most restaurants offer a *menu à prix fixe* (fixed-price meal) that costs less than ordering *à la carte.* The menu may include an *entrée, plat, fromage* (cheese), and dessert. The *formule* is a cheaper, two-course version. Bread is served with every meal; it is perfectly polite to use a piece to wipe your plate. Etiquette dictates keeping one's hands above the table, not in one's lap, but elbows shouldn't rest on the table. Order sparkling water *(eau pétillante* or *gazeuse)* or flat mineral water *(eau plate);* for a pitcher of tap water, ask for *une carafe d'eau.* Finish the meal with espresso *(un café),* which comes in little cups with blocks of sugar. When *boisson comprise* is written on the menu, you are entitled to a free drink (usually wine) with the meal. Vegetarians will probably have the best luck at *crêperies,* ethnic restaurants, and places catering to a younger crowd.

GROCERIES. For an occasional €15 spree you can have a marvelous meal, but it's easy to assemble inexpensive meals yourself with a ration of cheese, *pâté*, wine, and bread. Start with bread from the *boulangerie* (bakery), and then proceed to the *charcuterie* for *pâté*, *saucisson* (hard salami), and *jambon* (ham), or buy a delicious freshly roasted chicken from the *boucherie* (butcher's). If you want someone else to do the work, boulangeries often sell fresh sandwiches. *Pâtisseries* will sate nearly any sweet tooth with treats ranging from candy to ice cream to pastries.

CAFÉS. Cafés in France, brooding ground of upstart poets and glooming existentialists, figure pleasantly in the daily routine. When choosing a café, remember that you pay for its location. Those on a major boulevard can be much more expensive than smaller establishments a few steps down a sidestreet. Prices in cafés are two-tiered, cheaper at the counter *(comptoir)* than in the seating area *(salle)*; outdoor seating *(la terrasse)* may charge a third level. Coffee, beer, and (in the south) the anise-flavored *pastis* are the staple café drinks, while *citron pressé* (lemonade) and *diabolo menthe* (peppermint soda) are popular non-alcoholic choices. If you order *café*, you'll get espresso; for coffee with milk, ask for a *café crème*. *Bière à la pression*, or draft beer, is 660ml of either pale *(blonde)* or dark *(brune)* lager; for something smaller ask for a *demi* (330ml).

THE ELIXIR OF LIFE

Wine *(le vin)* pervades French culture, and no occasion is complete without a glass or four. The range and variety of wines available are tremendous. Not only does the character and quality of a wine depend on which of the 60 grape varieties it is made from, but the climate and soil type also have a crucial effect. **White wine** *(vin blanc)* can be made from both white grapes *(blanc de blancs)* or red *(blanc de noirs)*; in the latter case care must be taken to prevent the skins from coloring the wine. **Red wine** *(vin rouge)* and *rosé* are always made from red grapes.

Wine-producing regions are scattered throughout France, each with its own specialty. On the Dordogne and Garonne rivers, the famous **Bordeaux** region produces mostly reds, including Pomerol, Médoc and Graves, and sweet white Sauternes. Red Bordeaux is often called "claret" in English. **Burgundy** is especially famous for its reds, from the wines of Chablis and the Côte d'Or in the north, to the Beaujolais and Mâconnais in the south. The northeast offers **Alsatian** whites that tend to be dry and fruity, complementing spicy foods. Delicately-bouqueted whites predominate in the **Loire Valley.** In Provence, the **Côtes de Provence** around Marseille are recognized for their *rosés*, while the **Côtes du Rhône** produce the sweet white *Muscat de Beaumes-de-Venise* and celebrated reds such as the famous *Châteauneuf du Pape*. Although many areas produce sparkling wines *(vins mousseux)*, only those grown and produced in **Champagne** can legally bear its name.

Other grape-based delights include **Cognac** and **Armagnac,** which come from Charente and Gascony respectively. Technically distinguished from brandy by strict government regulations, Cognac is a double-distilled spirit and so has a higher alcohol content than the single-distilled but more flavorful Armagnac. Unlike other wines, Cognac and Armagnac are usually enjoyed as *digestifs*.

A budget traveler in France can be pleasantly surprised by even the least expensive *vins de tables* (table wines), which are what most French drink. When buying wine, look for the product of the region you're in. Don't feel that you have to splurge to drink well; bad wine is virtually unheard of in France, and you can buy a decent red for as little as US$5. Table wines in restaurants can be bought by the liter *(une carafe)*, the half-liter *(une demi-carafe)*, and sometimes the quarter-liter. Many cities have wine bars where you can buy vintage wine by the glass; this is a good way to learn about wine without the prices you'd otherwise have to pay. To indulge for absolutely nothing, visit regions with vineyards, like Burgundy and Bordeaux, where wine producers frequently offer free *dégustations* (tastings).

GASTRONOMIC TOUR DE FRANCE

NORMANDY AND BRITTANY. Brittany's trademark *crêperies* offer savory buckwheat **galettes** wrapped around eggs, mushrooms, seafood, or ham, and dessert crepes filled with chocolate, fruit, or jam. The freshest of *huîtres* (oysters) come from Brittany, and seafood should be a part of any good meal. Norman cuisine has maximized the potential of fermented apples; *cidre, calvados* (apple brandy) and *pommeau* (the regional apératif of choice), are the region's most beloved alcoholic offerings. Normandy's pungent **camembert** cheese is best when it's soft.

POITOU-CHARENTES, LOIRE VALLEY AND BERRY-LIMOUSIN. Poitou-Charentes is known for its **moules à la mouclade** (mussels in a wine, cream, and egg sauce), and **fricassée d'anguilles** (eels in a red wine sauce). *Escargots* (snails), known locally as *cagouilles,* are prepared with a meat stuffing *(à la saintongeaise)* or with a red wine sauce *(aux lumas).* The rich soil of the Loire Valley nurtures asparagus, strawberries, and sunflowers. In the *caves* once used as quarries for the châteaux, tubs of mushrooms neighbor barrels filled with wine. In Berry-Limousin, try **poulet en barbouille,** chicken roasted over a fire, cut in pieces, and then simmered in a creamy sauce made of its own blood mixed with cream, egg yolk, and liver. Limousin is renowned throughout France for its beef and lamb, often garnished with walnuts, honey, *chèvre,* and local mushrooms.

AQUITAINE, GASCONY, PAYS BASQUE, PERIGORD AND LANGUEDOC. Aquitaine's glory is its wine, which complements food flavored with the elusive *truffe noir* (black truffle). The Pays Basque has a distinctly Spanish influence in its cuisine. The *jambon cru* (cured ham) of Bayonne, the *thon* (tuna) of St-Jean-de-Luz, and the ubiquitous **piperade** (omelette filled with green peppers, onions, tomatoes, and thyme) are among the most notable of the region's dishes. Périgord is famous for its *cèpe* mushrooms and truffles which are used in its traditional meat dishes. These also make use of walnuts, honey, and *chèvre.* In the Languedoc, one popular regional dish is **cassoulet,** a hearty stew of white beans, sausage, pork, mutton, and goose.

LYON, THE AUVERGNE AND BURGUNDY. Within the heartland of France, the farm kitchens of the Auvergne simmer with rich food—pork, cabbage, veal, turnips, and potatoes. Tarts and jams are filled with apricots from local orchards. Lyon reigns supreme in the world of *haute cuisine.* A typical delicacy consists of an unmentionable bull's organ prepared in a subtle, creamy sauce. Other delicacies include organs such as brain, stomach, and intestines. Finish off with **tarte tatin,** an apple tart baked upside-down. While Burgundy's diverse wines may stretch the limits of your vocabulary, don't forget to check out other regional delicaies: **gougères** (puffed pastry filled with cabbage or cheese), **hélix pomatia** (snails) in butter and garlic, and the esteemed **bœuf bourguignon.** The **jambon persillé** (a gelatin mold of ham and parsley) may be an acquired taste, but the traditional **coq au vin** (chicken in wine sauce) is fantastic from the start.

PROVENCE AND CORSICA. Along the Mediterranean, Provence has simple and fresh food. Regional specialities include **bouillabaisse** (a hearty fish and seafood stew), **soupe au pistou** (a brew of pine nuts, fresh basil, and garlic), **aïoli** (a creamy garlic dip), and fresh seafood. In Corsica, herbs from the *maquis* (an impenetrable tangle of lavender, laurel, myrtle, rosemary, and thyme growing on Corsica's hillsides) impart a distinct flavor to local specialties. The island's most famous specialties are *sanglier* (wild boar), *brocciu* (ewe's cheese), **gâteau de chataigne** (chestnut cake), and **charcuterie corse,** free-range pork products.

ALPS, ALSACE-LORRAINE AND FLANDERS. Food in the French Alps has a Swiss twist. Regional specialties include **fondue savoyarde** (bread dipped in a blend of cheeses, white wine, and kirsch), **raclette** (strong cheese melted and served with boiled potatoes and onions), and **gratin dauphinois** (sliced potatoes baked in a creamy cheese sauce). In contrast, Germanic influences are rampant in Alsatian cuisine. Traditional dishes are **tarte à l'oignon** (onion pie), **choucroute garnie** (sauerkraut cooked in white wine sauce and topped with sausages and ham), and **coq au Riesling** (chicken in white wine sauce). Cooks in Lorraine make up in heartiness what they lack in delicacy; bacon, butter, and cream are key ingredients in artery-hardening dishes like **quiche lorraine.** In Belgian-influenced Flanders, try beer and *moules* (mussels) swathed in an astounding variety of sauces.

CUSTOMS & ETIQUETTE

In Paris they simply stared when I spoke to them in French; I never did succeed in making those idiots understand their language.
-Mark Twain

BLENDING IN. A good rule of thumb in France: don't evoke their stereotype of the American tourist and they won't evoke yours—that nasty, nasal Frenchman. What may look perfectly innocuous in Miami will mark you out instantly in Menton. The French are known for their conservative stylishness—it's unlikely you'll be able to compete with them. Go for restrained sneakers or closed shoes, solid-color pants or jeans, and plain T-shirts or button-down shirts, rather than Teva sandals, baggy pants, or torn jeans. French people rarely wear shorts, but if you choose to wear them, they shouldn't be too short. For women, skirts or dresses are more appropriate. Be sure to dress respectfully in churches. Blending in is a great excuse to shop for French clothes. If you're traveling in January or August, be sure to take advantage of massive sales *(les soldes)*—prices are often slashed as much as 75%.

ETAGES. The French call the ground floor the *rez-de-chaussée* and start numbering with the first floor above the ground floor *(premier étage)*. The button labeled "R" and not "1" is typically the ground floor. The *sous-sol* is the basement.

HOURS. Most restaurants open at noon for lunch and close in the afternoon before reopening for dinner. Some bistros and cafés remain open during the afternoon. Small businesses, banks and post offices close daily noon-3pm. Many establishments shut down on Sundays, and most museums are closed on Mondays.

LANGUAGE AND POLITESSE. Even if your French is near-perfect, waiters and salespeople who detect the slightest accent will often immediately respond in English. If your language skills are good, continue to speak in French. More often than not, the waiter or salesperson will respect and appreciate your fortitude, and respond in French. The French put a premium on polite pleasantries, particularly in the service industry. Always say *"Bonjour Madame/Monsieur"* when you come into a business, restaurant or hotel, and *"Au Revoir"* when you leave. If you knock into someone on the street, always say *"Pardon."* The proper way to answer the phone is *"Âllo,"* but if you use this on the street, you'll blow your cover. When meeting someone for the first time, a handshake is appropriate. However, friends and acquaintances greet each other with a kiss on each cheek (the exception is men kissing men). If you are unsure of how to appropriately greet someone, let them make the first move. Don't use first names unless the person uses your first name or is obviously younger than you are.

POCKET CHANGE. Cashiers and tellers will constantly ask you *"Avez-vous de la monnaie?"* ("Do you have the change?") as they would rather not break your €20 note for a pack of gum. If you don't have it, smile ever-so-sweetly and say *"Non, désolée."*

PUBLIC RESTROOMS. The streetside public restrooms that have emerged all over France are worth the €0.30 they require. You are guaranteed a clean restroom, as these magic machines are self-cleaning after each use. Toilets in train stations, métro stops, and public gardens are tended to by *gardiens* and generally cost €0.40-0.60. Most cafés reserve restrooms for their clients only, but fast food chains usually won't notice if you use their facilities.

SAFETY AND SECURITY. Personal safety in France is on par with the rest of Western Europe, with a far lower rate of violent crime than the US. It's best not to be complacent, though, especially since tourists are often seen as (and often are) easy victims for robbery. As big cities go, Paris is relatively safe. Certain areas of Paris can be rough at night, including Les Halles and the Bastille area. Travelers should not walk around Pigalle, Barbès-Rochechouart, Montmartre, rue St-Denis in the 2ème, or Belleville alone at night. In general, the northern and eastern *arrondissements* are less safe than the southern and western ones, and the Right Bank less safe than the Left. In Marseille, be especially careful of the northern section of the city, in the Quartier Belsunce. The south of France—especially the Côte d'Azur and Provence—has a reputation for being more dangerous than the north. Exercise caution and common sense—keep bags under your arm and be particularly vigilant in crowded areas. In an emergency, dial ☎ 17 for police.

SERVICE AND TIPPING. There is no assumption in France that "the customer is always right," and complaining to managers about poor service is rarely worth your while. Your best bet is to take your business elsewhere. When engaged in any official process (e.g., opening a bank account, purchasing insurance, etc.), don't fret if you get shuffled from one desk to another or from one phone number to the next. Hold your ground, patiently explain your situation as many times as necessary, and you will prevail. Service is always included in meal prices in restaurants and cafés, and in drink prices at bars and clubs; look for the phrase *service compris* on the menu or just ask. If service is not included, tip 15-20%. Even when service is included, it is polite to leave a *pourboire* at a café, bistro, restaurant, or bar—a few francs to 5%. Do tip your hairdresser well; do not tip taxis more than a few francs.

THE ARTS

ARCHITECTURE

ANCIENT BEGINNINGS. Long before the arrival of the "civilizing" Greeks and Romans, Frenchmen were making their own impressive buildings. The prehistoric murals of **Lascaux** (p. 378) and the huge stones of **Carnac** (p. 262) testify to the presence of ancient peoples in France. No such monuments stand to the ancient Gauls, whose legacy was virtually swept away by Roman conquerors. Rome's leavings are most visible in Provence, in the theater at **Orange** (p. 528) and the arena and temple at **Nimes** (p. 521). Nearby, the golden arches of the **Pont du Gard** aqueduct (p. 526) served up 44 million gallons of water to Nîmes's thirsty citizens every day.

MEDIEVAL CATHEDRALS. The first distinctively "Western" style emerged during the 9th century, when artists under Charlemagne's patronage combined elements of the Classical legacy with elements of the northern Barbarian tradition to create a highly symbolic art form. The Carolingian church of **Germigny-des-Près** (p. 277) houses a 9th-century Byzantine mosaic in its chapel. The same religious sentiment is conveyed by French churches of the 11th and 12th centuries. Dubbed **Romanesque** and characterized by round arches and barrel-vaulting, their beauty is one of simple grandeur. These churches, like the **Basilique St-Sernin** in Toulouse (p. 439) and the **Basilique Ste-Madeleine** at Vézelay (p. 711), were designed to accommodate large crowds of worshippers and pilgrims, while the monastery of **Mont St-Michel** (p. 209) provided a secluded religious haven. The architecture that characterizes the later Middle Ages is known as the **Gothic** style. Gothic architecture utilizes a system of arches that distributes weight outward. Flying buttresses (the stone supports jutting out from the sides of cathedrals) counterbalance the pressure of the ribbed vaulting, relieving the walls of the roof's weight. As a result, the walls of Gothic churches seem to soar effortlessly skyward, and light streams in through enormous stained glass windows. The cathedral at **Laon** (p. 787) in northern France embodies the early Gothic style. The high Gothic style of the later Middle Ages embodied more elaborate ornamentation which can be seen in the cathedrals of **Amiens** (p. 795), **Chartres** (p. 168), and **Reims** (p. 763).

RENAISSANCE AND NEOCLASSICAL. François I, who hired Italian artists to improve his lodge at **Fontainebleau,** also commissioned the remarkable **Château de Chambord** (p. 283) and additions to the **Louvre** (p. 152), combining flamboyant French Gothic motifs with aspects of Italian design. But kings were not the only ones building palaces during the Renaissance. As French aristocrats moved away from Paris to the surrounding countryside, they demanded suitably lavish living quarters, and great châteaux began to spring up in the Loire Valley. In the 17th century, **Nicolas Fouquet,** Louis XIV's finance minister, commissioned **Le Vau, Le Brun,** and **Le Nôtre** to build for him the splendid Baroque **Château de Vaux-le-Vicomte,** which inspired Louis XIV to enhance Versailles. Louis used the same team of architect, artist, and landscaper to expand his mansion at **Versailles** (p. 165). He moved there in 1672, shifting the seat of the French government away from the ancient capital. Here Louis commissioned the world's largest royal residence, an exorbitantly beautiful palace full of crystal, mirrors, and gold, and surrounded by formal gardens. The rise of Neoclassicism is exemplified by **Jacques-Germain Souf-flot**'s grandiose **Eglise Ste-Geneviève** (1757) in Paris, which was deconsecrated during the revolution and rededicated as the **Panthéon** (p. 137). It serves as the resting place of Voltaire and Rousseau. This style ruled from 1804 to 1814.

NINETEENTH-CENTURY HAUSSMANIA. Today's city is the Paris remade under the direction of **Baron Georges-Eugène Haussmann.** From 1852 to 1870, Haussmann transformed Paris from an intimate medieval city to a centralized modern metropolis. Commissioned by Napoleon III to modernize the city, Haussmann tore long, straight boulevards through the tangled clutter and narrow alleys of old Paris, creating a unified network of **grands boulevards.** These avenues were designed not only to increase circulation of goods and people, but also to make Paris a work of art, reflecting the elegance of Second Empire style. Not incidentally, the wide avenues also impeded insurrection, limiting once and for all the effectiveness of street barricades.

Engineering came onto the architectural scene in the latter part of the 19th century, as **Gustave Eiffel** and architect **Louis-Auguste Boileau** designed Le Bon Marché, the world's first department store. Eiffel's later project, the star exhibit of the Universal Exhibition of 1889, was first decried by Parisians as hideous and unstable. The **Tour Eiffel** (p. 140) is now the best-loved landmark in the city. The ornate and organic style of **Art Nouveau** developed in the late 19th century. The movement's characteristic ironwork can best be seen in Paris, where **Hector Guimard**'s vinelike Métro stops sprout from the pavement.

TWENTIETH-CENTURY MODERNISM AND SUBURBAN MISERY. In the interwar period, radical French architects began to incorporate new building materials in their designs. A Swiss citizen who lived and built in Paris, Charles-Edouard Jeanneret, known as **Le Corbusier,** was the architectural pioneer in reinforced concrete. A prominent member of the **International School,** Le Corbusier dominated his field from the 1930s until his death in 1965, and is famous for his mushroom-like chapel at **Ronchamp** in Alsace. The post-war years were not kind to the architecture and urban development of France's northern coast. Badly damaged during World War II, Le Havre, Dunkerque and Calais were hurriedly rebuilt in loathsome chunks of concrete. Paris too capitulated to the cheap lure of cement. Large housing projects or **HLMs** *(habitations à louer modéré)* were originally intended as affordable housing, but have since become synonymous with suburban misery, racism, and the exploitation of the immigrant poor. In the 80s, Paris became the hub of Mitterand's 15-billion Franc endeavor known as the *Grands Projets,* which included the construction of the **Musée d'Orsay,** the **Parc de la Villette,** the **Institut du Monde Arabe,** the **Opéra** at the Bastille, and **I.M. Pei**'s glass pyramid at the **Louvre.** Skyscrapers have been exiled to the business suburb of **La Défense,** home to the **Grande Arche,** a giant, hollowed-out cube of an office building aligned with the Arc de Triomphe, the smaller arch in the Tuileries, and the Louvre. In recent news, the **ZAC project** aims to build a new university, sports complex, public garden and métro in the 13*ème.*

FINE ARTS

MEDIEVAL MASTERPIECES. Much of France's surviving **medieval art** instructed the average 12th-and 13th-century churchgoer on religious themes. As most commoners were illiterate, brilliant stained glass and intricate stone facades, like those at **Chartres, Reims,** and **Sainte-Chapelle** in Paris, served as large reproductions of the Bible. Monastic industry brought the art of illumination to its height, as monks occupied their long days by adding ornate illustrations to manuscripts. Chantilly now houses the breathtaking **Très Riches Heures du Duc de Berry,** a gem-like illuminated prayer book whose realistic portrayal of peasants ushered in the Northern Renaissance. During the Middle Ages, artisans perfected the skill of weaving. The famous 11th century **Bayeux tapestry,** which unravels a 70-meter-long narrative of the Battle of Hastings, can still be seen in its original Norman town (p. 194). The mysterious 15th-century allegorical tapestry series, **The Lady and the Unicorn,** still charms visitors at the **Musée Cluny** in Paris.

THE RENAISSANCE IN FRANCE. Inspired by the painting, sculpture, and architecture of the **Italian Renaissance,** 16th-century France imported its styles from Italy. François I had viewed the new wave of art during his Italian campaigns, and when he inherited France in 1515, he decided the time had come to put France on the artistic map. He gathered a variety of Italian artists to create his château at **Fontainebleau,** and on his invitation, **Leonardo da Vinci** trekked up from Florence bearing the smiling **Mona Lisa** in tow. Da Vinci's final home and a number of his sketches for inventions can still be seen in **Amboise** (p. 286). Rosso and Francesco Primaticcio arrived in France in the 1530s to introduce the French to Italian Mannerist techniques, which were soon adopted by the **Ecole de Fontainebleau.**

BAROQUE AND ROCOCO. Italy remained the arbiter of France's aesthetic taste in the 17th century, when Louis XIV imported the gilded, baubled excesses of the **Baroque** style to his own court at Versailles. The enduring masterpieces of French Baroque, however, remain the more realist paintings of the brothers **Le Nain** and **Georges de La Tour,** who created representations of everyday life. Baroque exuberance was also subdued by the classical subjects and serene landscapes of **Nicolas Poussin,** who was fortunate enough to enjoy the support of the French **Académie Royale.** Under director **Charles Le Brun,** the Academy, founded in 1648, became the sole arbiter of taste in matters artistic, holding annual **salons,** the "official" art exhibitions held in vacant halls of the Louvre. The early 18th century brought on the even more frilly **Rococo** style. Catering to the tastes of the nobility, **Antoine Watteau** painted the *fêtes* and secret *rendez-vous* of the aristocracy, and **François Boucher** painted landscapes and rosy-cheeked shepherdesses. **Elisabeth Vigée-Lebrun** painted Europe's rich and famous; her portrait of Marie Antoinette and her children is on display at Versailles. Far from the glitz of the court, **Jean-Baptiste Chardin** captured the lustre of pewter and heavy softness of dead hares in his stunning still-lifes.

NEOCLASSICAL AND ROMANTIC SCHOOLS. The French Revolution inspired painters to create heroic depictions of scenes from their own time. **Jacques-Louis David's** *Death of Marat* paid gory tribute to the Revolutionary leader. Napoleon I's reign saw the emergence of **Neoclassicism** as the emperor tried to model his empire, and his purple capes, on the Roman version. Following David, and encouraged by the deep pockets of Napoleon, painters created large, dramatic pictures, often of the emperor as Romantic hero and god, all rolled into one *petit* package. But after Napoleon's fall, nineteenth-century France was ready to settle into respectable bourgeois ways, and few artists painted nationalistic *tableaux.* One exception was **Theodore Géricault,** whose *Raft of the Medusa* (1819) can be seen in the Louvre. The paintings of **Eugène Delacroix** were a shock to the salons of the 1820s and 1830s. His *Liberty Leading the People* (1830) and *The Death of Sardanapalus* (1827) display an extraordinary sense of color and a penchant for melodrama. Delacroix went on to do a series of "Moroccan" paintings, and he soon shared this orientalist territory with another painter, **Jean-Auguste-Dominique Ingres.** Ingres's most famous painting is the nearly liquid reclining nude, *La Grande Odalisque* (1814).

REALISM AND IMPRESSIONISM. If the Revolution of 1789 ushered in an art with a political conscience, the Revolution of 1848 introduced an art with a social conscience. **Realists** like **Gustave Courbet** scrutinized and indeed glorified the "humble" aspects of peasant life. His *Burial at Ornans* (1850) caused a scandal when first exhibited because it used the huge canvases associated with history painting to depict a simple village scene. Fellow Realist **Jean Millet** showed the dignity of peasants, the value of their work, and the idyllic simplicity of their lives. Another group of mid-19th-century painters, particularly **Camille Corot** and **Théodore Rousseau,** transformed landscape painting, depicting rural subjects from direct observation while paying close attention to light and atmosphere. **Edouard Manet** facilitated the transition from Courbet's Realism to what we now consider **Impressionism** by flattening the fine shading and sharp perspectives of academic art and turning his focus to texture and color. His portrait of the nude, unabashed prostitute *Olympia* and his recycling of classical poses in *Déjeuner sur l'herbe* scandalized his colleagues but held center stage at the Salon des Refusés in 1863.

By the late 1860s Manet's new aesthetic had set the stage for **Claude Monet, Camille Pissarro,** and **Pierre-Auguste Renoir,** who began to further explore Impressionist techniques. They strove to attain a sense of immediacy; colors were used to capture visual impressions as they appeared to the eye, and light became subject matter. Claude Monet's studies of haystacks and the Rouen cathedral revealed how different moments of light could transform a subject. His *Impression: Soleil Levant* (1872) inspired one mocking critic to dub the ensemble of artists "Impressionists" after their first group exhibition in 1874. The name stuck, and the Impressionist movement went on to inspire **Edgar Degas**'s ballerinas and racehorses, **Gustave Caillebotte**'s rainy streets of Paris, and **Berthe Morisot**'s tranquil studies of women. Monet's garden at **Giverny** (p. 170), which inspired his monumental *Waterlilies* series, remains a popular daytrip from Paris. The influence of Impressionism extended to sculpture, where **Auguste Rodin** captured barely-constrained energy in his life-sized bronzes. His *Burghers of Calais* (1886) honors the town's nobles for preparing to sacrifice their lives during the Hundred Years War.

POST-IMPRESSIONISM. The fragmented inheritors of the Impressionist tradition share the label of **Post-Impressionism. Paul Cézanne** worked in Aix-en-Provence and created still-lifes, portraits, and geometric landscapes (among them his many versions of the prominent *Mont Ste-Victoire*, 1885-87), using planes of orange, gold, and green, and bold, geometric blocks of color. **Georges Seurat** took this fragmentation of shape a step further with **Pointillism,** a style in which thousands of tiny dots of paint merge to form a coherent picture in the viewer's eye. **Paul Gauguin** used large, flat blocks of color with heavily drawn outlines to paint "primitive" scenes from Brittany, Arles, Tahiti, and Martinique. He had gone to **Arles** (p. 508) to join his friend **Vincent Van Gogh,** a Dutch painter who had moved to the south of France in search of new light, color, and imagery. The poverty and mental illness that plagued Van Gogh throughout his short life are reflected in his work. Similarly tortured in his art and life was **Henri de Toulouse-Lautrec,** a man of noble lineage who was disabled by a bone disease and a childhood accident. Toulouse-Lautrec's vibrant posters, many of which are displayed in his hometown of **Albi** (p. 443), capture the brilliant and lascivious nightlife of 19th-century Paris. Struggling with Pointillism during a trip to **Collioure** in the Languedoc (p. 455), **Henri Matisse** abandoned the technique and began squeezing paint from the tube directly onto the canvas. This aggressive style earned the name **Fauvism** (from *fauves*, wild animals) and characterizes Matisse's mature works like *The Dance* (1931-32).

CUBISM AND THE SCHOOL OF PARIS. Former Fauve artist **Georges Braque** and Spanish-born **Pablo Picasso** developed **Cubism,** a technique of composing the canvas with shaded planes. By converting everyday objects—fruits, glasses, vases, newspapers—into these cross-cutting planes, Braque and Picasso sought to analyze pictorial space as an overlapping system of geometric shapes. After developing Cubism in the mid-1910s, Braque's and Picasso's careers diverged. Picasso became arguably the greatest artist of the 20th century, constantly innovating and breaking new artistic ground. His career, spanning many decades and movements, is chronicled at the **Musée Picasso** in Paris (p. 154) and at the beautiful seaside **Musée Picasso** in Antibes (p. 560). In the 1920s and 30s, Picasso was the brightest star in a group of talented artists who came to Paris from all over the world to practice their craft in the exciting, avant-garde atmosphere of inter-war Paris.

DADAISM, SURREALISM, AND THE SCENE TODAY. The sense of loss and disillusionment that pervaded Europe after WWI prompted a group of artists to reject the very bourgeois culture that had begun the war. The anarchy and nonsense of the

Dada movement found its best expression in the works of **Marcel Duchamp,** who scrambled artistic conventions by drawing a moustache on a copy of Mona Lisa and signing a factory-made urinal (*La Fontaine*, 1917) as if it were a piece of high art. **Surrealism's** goal was a union of dream and fantasy with the everyday world in "an absolute reality, a surreality," according to poet and leader of the movement, **André Breton.** The bowler-hatted men of **René Magritte,** the dreamscapes of **Joan Miro,** the textures and patterns of **Max Ernst,** and the melting timepieces of **Salvador Dalí** arose from time spent in Paris. Later 20th-century experiments in photography, installation art, video, and sculpture can be seen in the collections and temporary exhibitions of the **Centre Pompidou** and the **Fondation Cartier pour l'Art Contemporain.**

LITERATURE AND PHILOSOPHY

MEDIEVAL AND RENAISSANCE LITERATURE. Medieval France produced an extraordinary number of literary texts, starting at the beginning of the 12th century with popular **chansons de gestes,** stories written in verse that recount tales of 8th-century crusades and conquests. The aristocracy enjoyed more refined literature extolling knightly honor and courtly love, such as the *Lais* (narrative songs) of **Marie de France** and the romances of **Chrétien de Troyes.** During the 13th century, popular satirical stories called **fabliaux** celebrated bawdy humor with tales of cuckolded husbands, saucy wives, and shrewd peasants. The 14th and 15th centuries produced the feminist writings of **Christine de Pisan,** and the ballads of **François Villon.** Literary texts of the Renaissance challenged medieval notions of courtly love and Christian thought. Marguerite de Navarre's *Héptaméron* (1549) employed pilgrim stories to explore the innovative ideas of Humanism. **John Calvin's** humanist treatises criticized the Catholic Church and opened the road to the ill-fated Protestant Reformation in France. **François Rabelais's** fantastical *Gargantua and Pantagruel* (1562) imaginatively explored the world from giants's point of view, and **Michel de Montaigne's** *Essais* (1595) pushed the boundaries of individual intellectual thought.

RATIONALISM AND THE ENLIGHTENMENT. The **Académie Française** was founded in 1635 to regulate and codify French literature and language. French philosophers reacted to the mushy musings of humanists with **Rationalism,** a school of thought that championed logic and order. In his 1637 *Discourse on Method,* **René Descartes** proved his own existence with the catchy deduction, "I think, therefore I am." **Blaise Pascal** misspent his youth inventing the mechanical calculator and the science of probabilities. He later became a devotee of Jansenism, a Catholic reform movement that railed against the worldliness of the Jesuit-dominated Church. **La Fontaine's** *Fables* and **Charles Perrault's** *Fairy Tales of Mother Goose* (1697) explored right and wrong in more didactic ways. **Molière,** the era's comic relief, satirized the social pretensions of his age, and his actors initiated the great **Comédie Française.** The Enlightenment in France was informed by advances in the sciences and aimed at the promotion of reason and tolerance in an often backward and bigoted world. **Denis Diderot's** *Encylopédie* (1752-1780) took no smaller ambition than to record the entire body of human knowledge. **Voltaire** gained fame with his satire *Candide* (1758), a refutation of the claim that "all is for the best in the best of all possible worlds." Voltaire's witticisms paled before with the curmudgeonly advice of **Jean-Jacques Rousseau's** *Confessions* (1769), which instructed readers to abandon society altogether rather than remaining in a corrupt world.

ROMANTICISM AND REALISM. The 19th century saw an emotional reaction against Enlightenment rationality. The expressive ideals of **Romanticism** first came to prominence in Britain and Germany rather than analytically minded France. **François-René de Chateaubriand** drew inspiration for his novel *Attala* (1801) by his experiences with Native Americans near the mighty Niagara Falls. The stylish

Madame de Staël reflected upon the injustices of being a talented woman in a chauvinist world in *Delphine* (1802). The novel became the pre-eminent literary medium, with such great writers as **Stendhal** (*Le Rouge et le Noir*) and **Balzac** (*La Comédie Humaine*), but it was **Victor Hugo** who dominated the Romantic age with the publication of *The Hunchback of Notre Dame* in 1831. That same year, the young Aurore Dupin left her husband and childhood home of La Châtre, took the *nom de plume* of **George Sand,** and published passionate novels condemning chauvinist social conventions. The heroine of **Gustave Flaubert**'s *Madame Bovary* (1856) spurned provincial life for romantic daydreams in his famous Realist novel. Provoking moral outrage from his critics, Flaubert was prosecuted for immorality and narrowly acquitted in 1857. **Charles Baudelaire** was not so lucky; the same tribunal fined him 50 francs. The poet gained a reputation for obscenity, but his *The Flowers of Evil* (1861) is now considered the most influential piece of 19th-century French poetry.

BELLE EPOQUE TO WWII. Like artistic Impressionism, literary **Symbolism** reacted against stale conventions and used new techniques to capture instants of perception. Led by **Stéphane Mallarmé, Paul Verlaine,** and the precocious **Arthur Rimbaud,** the movement was instrumental in the creation of modern poetry. *Fin de siècle* high society decadence was combined with an inquiry into the nature of time, memory and love in **Marcel Proust**'s seven volumes of *Remembrance of Things Past* (1913-1927). His portrayal of homosexuality was matched by **André Gide**'s novel *l'Immoraliste* and **Colette**'s sensual descriptions of cabarets in *Le pur et l'impur.* Meanwhile, the avant-garde poet **Guillaume Apollinaire** published *Calligrammes* (1918), which created visual poems by using words to form pictures on the page. The anarchy of **Dada** art was verbally represented in the incoherent scrambled poems of **Tristan Tzara.** In 1924, André Breton abandoned the Dada movement to argue for the artistic supremacy of the subconscious in his *Surrealist Manifesto.* **Jean-Paul Sartre** dominated France's intelligentsia in the years following World War II. His theory of **Existentialism** held that life in itself was meaningless; only by committing yourself to a cause could existence take on a purpose. While Sartre worked under censorship in occupied Paris, Algerian-born **Albert Camus** edited the Résistance newspaper *Combat.* He achieved fame with his debut novel *The Outsider* (1942), in which a dispassionate social misfit is condemned to death for murder.

THE BEST EXPATRIATE LITERATURE

Ernest Hemingway. *A Moveable Feast.* The quintessential tale of a young expat in Paris. With cameo appearances by F. Scott Fitzgerald and Gertrude Stein.

George Orwell. *Down and Out in London and Paris.* A writer takes grimy jobs in the dark underbelly of Paris. Beautifully descriptive and funny.

W. Somerset Maugham. *The Moon and Sixpence.* A dull London businessman leaves his family to paint in Paris and Tahiti. Loosely based on the life of Paul Gauguin.

Henry James. *The American.* The New World meets the Old in this classic story of friendship, love and betrayal in turn of the century Paris.

F. Scott Fitzgerald. *Tender is the Night.* No one could capture the 1920s flapper set quite like Fitzgerald—his story of scandal and intrigue on the Riviera is a classic.

Peter Mayle. *A Year in Provence.* A staple of bookclubs everywhere, a lighthearted autobiography, travelogue and culinary guide to life in the rural town of Ménerbes (p. 506).

Julian Barnes. *Flaubert's Parrot.* And elderly English doctor journeys to France to research Flaubert's life and inspiration for his short story *Un Coeur Simple.*

Adam Gopnik. *Paris to the Moon.* A New Yorker journalist settles down in Paris with his family. Small observations on Parisian life, lyrically woven into larger cultural themes.

FEMINISM AND LA PRÉSENCE AFRICAINE. Existentialist and feminist **Simone de Beauvoir** made waves with *The Second Sex* (1949), an essay attacking the myth of femininity. Its famous statement, "One is not born, but becomes a woman" inspired a whole generation of second-wave **feminism** in the 50s, 60s, and 70s. In turn, writers like **Marguerite Duras** *(The Lover)*, **Hélène Cixous** *(The Laugh of the Medusa)*, and **Luce Irigaray** *(This Sex Which is Not One)* explored gender identity, challenged the Freudian concept of 'penis envy' and sparked feminist movements in France and abroad. The founding of the publishing house *Des Femmes* in the 70s ensured that French women writers would continue to express themselves in print. Throughout the 20th century, France's colonial exploitation has been powerfully condemned by writers from the **Antilles, Haiti, Québec,** the **Maghreb** (Algeria, Tunisia, Morocco), and **West Africa** (Senegal, Mali, Ivory Coast, Congo, and Cameroon). With the foundation of the **Négritude** movement in the 1920s by intellectuals **Aimé Césaire** (Martinique) and **Léopold Sédar Senghor** (Senegal), Francophone literature began to flourish. Their work and the subsequent founding of the press **Présence Africaine** inspired generations of Francophone intellectuals on both sides of the Atlantic. North African immigration to France in the 80s and 90s has had a profound impact on French language, culture, and politics. Many second- and third-generation Maghrebian writers in France, such as **Mehdi Charef** *(Le thé au harem d'Archi Ahmed*, 1983), have written about *beur* (slang for an Arab resident of France) culture and the difficulties of cultural assimilation.

FILM

BEGINNINGS. Not long after he and his brother Louis presented the world's first paid screening in a Paris café in 1895, **Auguste Lumière** remarked, "The cinema is a medium without a future." In defiance of this statement, the French strive to reveal the broadest possibilities of film. The trick cinema of magician-turned-filmmaker **Georges Méliès** astounded audiences with "disappearing" objects, and his *Journey to the Moon* (1902) was the first motion picture to realize the story-telling possibilities of the medium. Paris was the Hollywood of the early days of cinema, dominating production and distribution worldwide. While WWI stunted the growth of French film, the interwar period yielded a diverse number of influential films. **Luis Buñuel** and **Salvador Dalí**'s *Un Chien Andalou* (1928) was a Surrealist marvel of jarring associations. **Jean Renoir**, son of the Impres-

IN THE WAKE OF THE NEW WAVE

There's a saying used to describe someone who invents something while simultaneously creating its most perfect application: "It's like the Lumière Brothers creating Citizen Kane." There's a certain assumption here: France may have invented the cinema, but it was America who perfected it. While Hollywood's blockbusters may dominate the global cinema industry today, French cinema has proved time and again that it is possible to get it right on the first try.

The French New Wave of the 1960s pioneered a new generation of filmmakers. Using experimental techniques (hand-held cameras, disjointed soundtracks, jump sequences) and small budgets, young directors like Jean-Luc Godard and François Truffaut created a new cinema. The New Wave in fact turned the lens on American movies by borrowing and critiquing Hollywood genres such as crime flicks. In short, the films of the New Wave put into question the comfortable realistic appearance of film by exposing its raw edges.

But a cinema that deconstructs that praises and subverts old genres and character types—where could French cinema possibly go from there? In effect, everywhere. French cinema today may not fit a generalized title like so many brilliant films of the 1960s did, but it does run a wide spectrum, from comedies and dramas to *cinéma beur*. Cynics may complain that recent French film has gone the way of generic international-marketed films. Luc Besson is an example of an _auteur_ turned Hollywood director, rading in the style of his edgy drug-addict-turned-assassin _Nikita_ (1990) with popular high-budget flicks like _he Fifth Element_ and _Messenger_.

But sellout? That's for you to decide. French critics can be a tough ot, and even films that use French subjects and storylines have earned his epithet in recent year. Case in point: the 1990s witnessed an obsession with classy period epics from France's swashbuckling past. Jean-Paul Rappeneau's _Cyrano de Bergerac_ was a long-nosed swordsman with a rapier wit, while the royal court set the stage for Patrice Leconte's _Ridicule_. Such films earned the wrath of some critics, who argued, for better or worse, that the French film establishment was trading in on the country's historical image. Yet many of these films earned Oscar nominations.

All said, an experimental, idiosyncratic edge to French film persists today. Claire Denis' compelling, difficult _Trouble Every Day_ (about cannibalism) may not earn the adoration of popcorn-fed teens, but her work has earned international acclaim. Meanwhile, Jean-Pierre Jeunet's whimsical _Amélie_ was the summer hit of 2001. A series of minute-long sequences, _Amélie_ depicts a reclusive Montmartre waitress turned do-gooder. For the French, the film stood like a municipal monument, unbowed to any global cinema. _Amélie_ was new, _Amélie_ was different, and _Amélie_ was French.

Amélie doesn't look like a new New Wave, as some have claimed, but it does serve as an appropriate metaphor for the best of French cinema. It obeys no rules, it can be willfully incoherent and then suddenly full of poise. The only generalization one can make is that there is a searching spirit behind all the good French movies, a spirit that transcends its particulars. –_contributed by Couper Samuelson_

sionist painter, directed the powerful anti-war film _La Grande Illusion_ (1937) and depicted the erosion of French bourgeois society in _La Règle du Jeu_ (1939). Censorship during the Occupation led to a move from political films to nostalgia and escapism. **Marcel Carné** and **Jacques Prévert's** epic _Children of Paradise_ (1943-45) found in 1840s Paris the indomitable spirit of the French.

NEW WAVE. In the 1950s, **André Bazin** and a group of young intellectuals used their magazine **Cahiers du Cinéma** to take issue with the slick insubstantial popular films of the day. Encouraged by government subsidies, they swapped pen for the camera in 1959. **François Truffaut's** coming-of-age story _The 400 Blows_ and **Jean-Luc Godard's** gangster flick _A Bout du Souffle (Breathless)_ were joined the same year by **Alain Resnais's** _Hiroshima, Mon Amour_ and announced the **French New Wave (Nouvelle Vague).** Three years earlier, a star was born when **Jean Vadim** sent the incomparable **Brigitte Bardot** shimmying naked across the screen in _And God Created Woman_. Other directors associated with the New Wave are **Louis Malle** (_The Lovers_, 1958), **Eric Rohmer** (_My Night with Maud_, 1969), and **Agnès Varda** (_Cléo from 5 to 7_, 1961). These directors are united by their interest in categories of fiction and documentary, the fragmentation of linear time, the thrill of youth, speed, cars, and noise.

CONTEMPORARY CLASSICS AND CINÉMA BEUR. The world impact of French cinema in the 60s brought wider recognition of French film stars in the 70s and 80s, such as stunning **Catherine Deneuve** (_Belle de jour_), gothic priestess **Isabelle Adjani** (_La Reine Margot_), and omnipresent **Gérard Depardieu** (_Danton, Camille Claudel_). **Edouard Molinaro's** campy _La Cage aux Folles_ (1975) and **Colline Serraud's** _Trois hommes et un couffin_ ("Three Men and a Baby," 1985) have inspired American remakes. **Claude Berri's** _Jean de Florette_ (1986) and Polish **Krzysztof Kieslowski's** _Three Colors_ trilogy, _Bleu_ (1993), _Blanc_ (1994), and _Rouge_ (1994) have become instant classics of the late 20th-century French cinema. Several recent French films explore the issue of gay identity and sexual orientation, including Belgian **Alain Berliner's** transgender tragicomedy _Ma vie en rose_ (1997). Some of the most explosive Parisian films today are the production of _cinéma beur_, the work of second-generation North Africans coming to terms with life in the housing projects of suburban Paris. Rich with graffiti art and rap music, films like **Mehdi Charef's** _Le thé au harem d'Archi Ahmed_ (1986) and **Mathieu Kassovitz's** _La Haine_ (1995) expose the horrors of urban racism.

MUSIC

The early years of music in France date back to the Gregorian chant of 12th-century monks in cathedrals across the country. Other early highlights include the 13th-century ballads of medieval troubadours, the Renaissance masses of **Josquin des Prez** (1440-1521), the lavish Baroque Versailles court operas of **Jean-Baptiste Lully** (1632-87), and the organ fugues of **Jean-Philippe Rameau** (1683-1764). During the terrifying reign of **Robespierre,** the people rallied to the strains of **revolutionary music,** such as **Rouget de Lisle's** *War Song of the Army of the Rhine.* Composed to rally French forces fighting the Prussians, it was adored by volunteers from Marseille; dubbed *La Marseillaise,* it became the national anthem in 1795. Paris became the center of influence for 19th century European music. With the rise of the middle class in the early part of the 19th century came the spectacle of **grand opera,** as well as the simpler **opéra comique.** These styles later merged and culminated in the Romantic **lyric opera,** a mix of soaring arias, exotic flavor, and tragic death best exemplified by **Georges Bizet's** *Carmen* (1875). Paris served as musical center for foreign Romantic composers as well, including **Frédéric Chopin, Franz Liszt** and **Félix Mendelssohn.**

Music at the turn of the 20th century began a new period of intense, often abstract invention. **Claude Débussy** (1862-1918), whose style is called **Impressionist,** used tone color and nontraditional scales in his *Prelude to the Afternoon of a Fawn* (1894). **Erik Satie,** whose funky museum now resides in **Honfleur** (see p. 186), composed in a sarcastic, anti-sentimental spirit, in striking contrast to that of Debussy. **Ravel's** use of Spanish rhythm betrayed his Basque origins in his most famous work, *Boléro* (1928). The music of **Igor Stravinsky,** whose ballet *The Rite of Spring* caused a riot at its 1913 premiere at the Théâtre des Champs-Elysées, was violently dissonant and rhythmic. **Olivier Messaien** suffered from synesthesia, a sensory disorder which confuses sound and vision; different harmonies appeared to him in different colors. Messaien's student, the innovative composer **Pierre Boulez,** now directs the **IRCAM** institute in the Pompidou Center in Paris.

JAZZ, CABARET, AND THE NEXT BIG THINGS. France has been particularly receptive to jazz and recognized its artistic worth sooner than the US. Jazz singer **Josephine Baker** left the US for Paris in 1925, finding the French to be much more accepting than her segregated home. **Cabaret,** which grew in popularity in the 1930s, was made famous by the iconic voice of Edith Piaf in her ballads "La Vie en Rose" and "Non, je ne regrette rien." In this same decade, French musicians copied the swing they heard on early Louis Armstrong sides, but the 1934 Club Hot pair of violinist **Stéphane Grapelli** and stylish Belgian-Romany guitarist **Django Reinhardt** were already innovators. After WWII, a stream of American musicians came to Paris. A jazz festival in 1949 brought the young **Miles Davis** across the pond.

In the late 50s and 60s, a unique French take on American rock emerged: the movement was termed, in a stroke of onomatopoetic genius, **yé-yé.** Teen idol **Johnny Hallyday** took the limelight, and youth-oriented **Salut les Copains** was the moment's rage. Contemporary music is divided between music played on the radio and the various forms of electronica that dominate dance clubs. Radio pop music includes soundtracks from French musicals like *Notre Dame de Paris,* and *Romeo and Juliet,* as well as solo artists like French-Canadian **Céline Dion** and French **Lara Fabien.** France's hip-hop and rap scene includes artists like **Nique Ta Mère, MC Solaar,** and **Lunatic.** World music also dominates the airwaves, coming from North Africa (including raï musicians **Cheb Khaled, Cheb Mami,** and **Faudel**), the Middle East (**Natacha Atlas**), Latin America (**Manu Chao** and **Yuri Buenaventura**), and the West Indies (with the sounds of **reggae** and **zouk**).

SPORTS & RECREATION

There are really only two sports in France. The rest is stamp collecting. The French take **le football** very seriously. Their national team, *Les Bleus*, has emerged from a half-century of mediocrity to perform spectacularly. They captured the 1998 **World Cup,** routing perennial favorite Brazil 3-0 in the newly built Stade de France outside Paris. The victory ignited celebrations from the Champs-Elysées to the Pyrénées. In the 2000 European Championship, the Blues took the trophy in an upset against Italy, and in the 2001 *Coupe des Confederations*, France completed the Triple Crown of football. The charismatic star of the French team, **Zinedine Zidane,** has attained a hero status second only to de Gaulle. The son of an Algerian immigrant, "Zizou" has helped unite a country divided by tension over immigration. Sadly, France failed to make it past the qualifying round of the 2002 *Cup Mondiale*, finishing behind even Uruguay. So shocking was the failure that President Chirac issued a message of condolence. Nonetheless, watching a football match remains an adventurous experience.

If the French take soccer seriously, **cycling** is a national obsession. France annually hosts the only cycling event anyone can name: the grueling 3-week, 3500km **Tour de France.** *Malheureusement,* the hosts haven't had much success the past three years, as the American Lance Armstrong has biked over the rest of the field to capture four straight championships. Ideal for those who prefer a bit less exertion, the game of **petanque,** once dominated by old men, has been gaining popularity among all ages. The basic idea of petanque, which is like bocce or bowls, is to throw a large metal ball as close as possible to a small metal ball. It is hard to miss "pickup" games of petanque on the beaches and dirt roads of Southern France, often for substantial sums of money. **Alpine** and **cross-country skiing,** particularly in the Alps, is also popular. Chamonix, Grenoble, and Albertville all hosted Winter Olympics and continue to dazzle skiers from around the world. Despite the objections of French traditionalists, sports from other continents are gaining a foothold in France, including **rugby, golf,** and even the heresy that is **American football.**

HOLIDAYS & FESTIVALS

The most important national holiday is **Bastille Day,** July 14, which commemorates the anniversary of the storming of the Bastille in 1789. The day is celebrated with a solemn military march up the Champs-Elysées followed by dancing, drinking and fireworks all over the country. When Bastille Day falls on a Tuesday or Thursday, the French often also take off the Monday or Friday, a crafty practice known as *faire le pont* (making the bridge). The dates listed below are for 2003.

DATE	NATIONAL HOLIDAY
January 1	Le Jour de l'an (also called la St-Sylvestre): New Year's
April 21	Le lundi de Pâques: Easter Monday
May 1	La Fête du travail: Labor Day
May 8	Fête de la Victoire 1945: Celebrates the end of World War II in Europe
May 29	L'Ascension: Ascension day
June 9	Le Lundi de Pentecôte: Whit Monday
July 14	La Fête Nationale: Bastille Day
August 15	L'Assomption: Feast of the Assumption
November 1	La Toussaint: All Saints' Day
November 11	L'Armistice 1918: Armistice Day
December 25	Noël: Christmas

In addition to national holidays, there are many regional and city festivals, especially throughout the summer. *Let's Go* provides coverage of these major *fêtes et manifestations* throughout the guide. For more information on specific events, check out the customized search engine on the French Government Tourist Office's website (www.franceguide.com, under "Culture and Art de vivre")

ONE NATION UNDER PARIS?
Regional identities in modern France

Paris, that luminous center of the French solar system, can often blind us to the rest of the country. France is one of the most centralized countries in the West, both politically and culturally, and its notorious defense of its language has only reinforced the image of a unified French culture. The French State was unified through annexation of several ethnically diverse territories: parts of Catalonia and the Basque Country in the South, the ever volatile island of Corsica in the Mediterranean, the rest of Southern France (which goes by the name of Occitania), the Germanic regions of Alsace and part of Lorraine, Celtic Brittany, and the Flemish northern tip of France. Until this last century, these regions were like foreign countries on French soil.

The Revolution replaced the hodge-podge of semi-autonomous provinces with *départements*, administrative sub-divisions operating under one law for all. Opponents of the Revolution saw the provinces as threats. In 1793, Bertrand Barère famously declared "Federalism and superstition speak Lower Breton; emigration and hatred of the Republic speak German [Alsatian]; the counter-revolution speaks Italian [Corsican]; and fanaticism speaks Basque." The project of unifying French language and culture never had much support, until public school became mandatory in the 1880s. In many schools, children who spoke with a local tongue were punished with a *symbole*, usually a dunce cap or scarlet letter. In return, however, schools assigned readings on rural France like the enduring *Le Tour de la France par deux enfants*, a picaresque journey around France by two Alsatian boys (and the inspiration for today's famous nationwide bike race). It was only after World War II that France was fully synchronized by mass media, consumerism, and the decline of the traditional peasantry. In France today, travelers see mostly the same stores, television, post offices, and phone booths, and rarely hear a peep of local parlance, spoken mostly in the home and by the elderly, if spoken at all.

Yet, local identity has not disappeared. Rather, it has made a startling comeback since the 1960s. Most conspicuously, Corsican terrorist attacks (often involving criminal corruption as much as autonomist movements) have made front-page news for years. There are also many quieter manifestations of local identity around France. In 1986, regional governments were elected for the first time since the Revolution, and regional languages have entered some school curricula, though not without controversy. Whereas the French State had once gone so far as to prohibit the use of non-French names on birth certificates, ethnic names such as Yann (the Breton equivalent of the French Jean or the English John) have caught on strong. In the 1980s and 1990s, French television suddenly discovered what other countries had long known, that local news was extremely popular, a rather belated realization considering that the regional newspapers like *Ouest-France* and *Les Dernières Nouvelles d'Alsace* had long outsold the national press. As for movies, France every year produces several paeans to community and rural life, such as the many film adaptations of the mid-twentieth century regional novelist Marcel Pagnol (*Jean de Florette*, *My Mother's Castle*). And of course tourists are treated to a parade of folkloric festivals, dance, and souvenirs.

Anyone looking for elusive "authenticity" should be skeptical, however; local culture isn't what it used to be. At a Breton village festival, for instance, the "drunken peasant" you encounter could be a Belgian professor who abandoned his career for the pastoral life. After the radical transformations that France has undergone, it is no surprise that some of the more apparently authentic images of regional culture are little more than show. This is not to say, however, that all displays of local difference and identity are mere sham. Vestiges of regional culture combine creatively with other cultures these days, as in the regionalist rap or world music of the Celtic maestro Alan Stivell or the Southern bands The Fabulous Troubadours, Massilia Sound System, and Zebda. And of course, as any traveler knows, no two places are exactly alike. Local variations persist, and the French continue to nurture an intimate bond to community and place.

Matthew Lazen is History and Literature lecturer at Harvard University. He is currently revising his dissertation on regional cultures in post-modern France for publication, and organizing a conference on post-War French regionalism at Harvard.

ESSENTIALS

FACTS FOR THE TRAVELER

ENTRANCE REQUIRMENTS
Passport (p. 33). Required for all non-EU citizens, plus UK and Irish citizens.
Visa (p. 34). For all stays, required of citizens of South Africa. Over 90 days, required of Australian, Canadian, New Zealand, and US citizens.
Work Permit (p. 34). Required for Australian, Canadian, New Zealand, South African, and US citizens.

EMBASSIES AND CONSULATES

FRENCH CONSULAR SERVICES ABROAD

Travelers visit these consulates to inquire about obtaining visas or travel to France in general. Services have different opening hours; those listed are for visa concerns. Most consulates receive inquiries in the afternoon by appointment.

Australia: Consulate General, Level 26, St. Martins Tower, 31 Market St., Sydney NSW 2000 (☎02 92 61 57 79; fax 02 92 83 12 10; www.consulfrance-sydney.org). Open M-F 9am-1pm.

Canada: Consulate General, 1 pl. Ville-Marie, suite 2601, 26th floor, **Montréal**, QC H3B 4S3 (☎514-878-4385; fax 514-878-3981; www.consulfrance-montreal.org). Open M-F 8:30am-noon. Consulat général de France à Québec, Maison Kent, 25 rue Saint-Louis, **Québec**, QC G1R 3Y8 (☎418-694-2294; fax 418-694-1678; www.consulfrance-quebec.org). Open M-F 9am-12:30pm. Consulat Général de France à Toronto, 130 Bloor St. West, Suite 400, **Toronto**, ON M5S 1N5 (☎416-925-8041; fax 416-925-3076; www.consulfrance-toronto.org). Open M-F 9am-1 pm.

Ireland: French Embassy, Consulate Section, 36 Ailesbury Rd., Ballsbridge, Dublin 4 (☎01 260 16 66; fax 01 283 01 78; www.ambafrance.ie). Open M-F 9:30am-12:30pm.

New Zealand: New Zealand Embassy and Consulate, 34-42 Manners St., P.O. Box 11-343, **Wellington** (☎04 384 25 55; fax 04 384 25 77). Open M-F 9am-1pm. French Honorary Consulate in Auckland, P.O. Box 1433, **Auckland** (☎09 379 58 50; fax 09 358 70 68; www.ambafrance-nz.org).

South Africa: Consulate General at Johannesburg, 191 Jan Smuts Ave., Rosebank. If you live in Gauteng, KwazuluNatal, Free State, Mpumalanga, Northern Province, North West Province or Lesotho, mail inquiries to P.O. Box 1027, Parklands 2121 (☎011 778 56 00, visas ☎011 778 56 05; fax 011 778 56 01). Open M-F 8:30am-1pm. If you live in the Northern Cape, Eastern Cape or Western Cape, inquire at the Consulate General, **Cape Town**, 2 Dean St. (☎021 423 15 75; fax 021 424 84 70; www.consulfrance.co.za). Open M-F 9am-12:30pm. Send mail to P.O. Box 1702 Cape Town 800.

United Kingdom: Consulate General, P.O. Box 520, 21 Cromwell Rd., London SW7 2EN (☎020 7073 1200; fax 020 7073 1201; www.ambafrance-uk.org). Open M-W 8:45am-3pm, Th-F 8:45am-noon. Visa service: P.O. Box 57, 6a Cromwell Pl., London SW7 2EW (☎020 7073 1250). Open M-F 8:45-11:30 am.

United States: Consulate General, 4101 Reservoir Rd. NW, Washington D.C. 20007-2185 (☎202-944-6195; fax 202-944-6148; www.consulfrance-washington.org). Open M-F 8:45am-12:45pm. Visa service ☎202-944-6200 M-F 2-5pm, answering machine 8:45am-12:45pm; fax 202-944-6212. Consulates also in Atlanta, Boston, Chicago, Houston, Los Angeles, Miami, New Orleans, New York, and San Francisco. See www.info-france-usa.org/intheus/consulates.asp for more info.

FOREIGN CONSULAR SERVICES IN FRANCE

Travelers visit these embassies only when they encounter trouble and need assistance. The most common concern is a loss of passport or worry about potentially dangerous local conditions. In serious trouble, your country's embassy or consulate usually can provide legal advice and may be able to advance money. But don't expect them to get you out of every scrape: you must always follow French law in France. In the case of arrest, your consulate can do little more than suggest a lawyer. Dual citizens of France cannot call on the consular services of their second nationality for assistance. Call before visiting any of these embassies, as hours vary. Visa services tend to be available only in the morning.

Australia: Australian Embassy and Consulate, 4 rue Jean Rey, 75724 Paris Cédex 15 (☎01 40 59 33 00, after-hours emergency 01 40 59 33 01; fax 01 40 50 33 10; www.austgov.fr). Open 9:15am-noon and 2-4pm.

Canada: Canadian Embassy and Consulate, 35 Ave. Montaigne, 75008 Paris (☎01 44 43 29 00; www.amb-canada.fr). Open 9am–5pm. General Delegation of **Quebec,** 66 rue Pergolèse, 75116 Paris (☎01 40 67 85 00; www.mri.gouv.qc.ca/paris/).

Ireland: Embassy of Ireland, 4 rue Rude, 75016 Paris (☎01 44 17 67 00, emergencies 01 44 17 67 67; fax 01 44 17 67 60; www.irlande.tourisme.fr). Open M-F 9:30am-noon. Also in Antibes, Cherbourg, Lyon, and Monaco.

New Zealand: New Zealand Embassy and Consulate, 7*ter* rue Leonardo de Vinci, 75116 Paris (☎01 45 00 24 11; fax 01 45 01 26 37; NZEMBASSY.PARIS@wanadoo.fr). Open July-Aug. M-Th 8:30am-1pm and 2-5:30pm, F 8:30am-2pm; Sept.-June M-F 9am-1pm and 2-5:30pm.

South Africa: South African Embassy, 59 Quai d'Orsay, 75007 Paris. Send mail to 59 Quai d'Orsay 75343 Paris Cédex 07 (☎01 53 59 23 23, emergencies 86 09 67 06 93; fax 01 53 59 23 68; www.afriquesud.net). Open M-F 8:30am-5:15pm; consular services M-F 8:30am-noon.

United Kingdom: British Embassy, Consulate Section, 18bis rue d'Anjou, 75008 Paris (☎01 44 51 31 00; fax 01 44 51 31 27; www.amb-grandebretagne.fr). Open M-F 9:30am-12:30pm and 2:30-5pm.

United States: Consulate General, 2 rue St-Florentin 75001, Paris Cédex 08 (☎01 43 12 22 22; www.amb-usa.fr). Send mail to 2 rue Saint-Florentin 75382. Open M-F 9am-12:30pm and 1pm-6pm, notarial services Tu-F 9am-noon. Don't wait in line; tell the guard that you desire American services. Also in **Bordeaux, Lille, Lyon, Marseille, Nice, Rennes, Strasbourg,** and **Toulouse;** visa services only in Paris.

TOURIST OFFICES

The **French Government Tourist Office (FGTO),** also known as Maison de la France, runs tourist offices in French cities and offers tourist services to travellers abroad. The FGTO runs the website **www.franceguide.com,** which offers very useful info for travelers from many countries. Each country also typically has a helpline. Check the website for more information. *Let's Go* lists the tourist office in every town where one exists.

DOCUMENTS & FORMALITIES

PASSPORTS

REQUIREMENTS. Citizens of Australia, Canada, Ireland, New Zealand, South Africa, the UK, and the US need valid passports to enter France and to re-enter their own country. France does not allow entrance if the holder's passport expires in under three months after the expected date of departure from France; returning home with an expired passport is illegal and results in a fine.

NEW PASSPORTS. Citizens of Australia, Canada, Ireland, New Zealand, the UK, and the US can apply for a passport at the nearest post office, passport office, or court of law. Citizens of South Africa can apply for a passport at the nearest office of Foreign Affairs. New passport or renewal applications must be filed well in advance of the departure date, although most passport offices offer rush services for a steep fee. Citizens living abroad who need a passport or renewal services should contact the nearest consular service of their home country. Passport office hours vary greatly, so call ahead.

Australia: Apply at a post office or passport office in Adelaide, Brisbane, Canberra, Darwin, Hobart, Melbourne, Newcastle, Perth, or Sydney (info ☎ 13 12 32; www.dfat.gov.au/passports), or overseas diplomatic mission. 32-page AUS$136, children AUS$68; 64-page AUS$204, children AUS$102. Adult valid 10 years, children 5 years.

Canada: Canadian Passport Office, Department of Foreign Affairs and International Trade, Ottawa, C.D. Howe Building, 249 Sparks Street Level C, East Tower (☎ 819-994-3500 or 800-567-6868; www.dfait-maeci.gc.ca/passport). Applications available at passport offices, Canadian missions, and post offices. Passports CDN$85; valid for 5 years (non-renewable).

Ireland: Department of Foreign Affairs, Passport Office, Setanta Center, Molesworth St., Dublin 2 (☎ 01 671 1633; fax 671 1092; www.irlgov.ie/iveagh). For residents of Clare, Cork, Kerry, Limerick, Tipperay, and Waterford, send inquiries to Passport Office, Irish Life Building, 1A South Mall, Cork (☎ 021 27 25 25). Pick up your application at a Garda station or post office, or request it in the mail at the above locations. Passports €57; valid for 10 years. Under 18 or over 65 €12; valid for 3 years.

New Zealand: Passport Office, Department of Internal Affairs, P.O. Box 10-526, Wellington, New Zealand (☎ 0800 22 50 50 or 4 474 8010; fax 4 474 8010; passports@dia.govt.nz; www.passports.govt.nz). Standard processing time is 10 working days. Passports NZ$71; valid for 10 years. Children NZ$36; valid for 5 years. 3 day "urgent service" NZ$146; children NZ$111.

South Africa: Department of Home Affairs, Civitas Building, 242 Struben Street, Pretoria (☎ 012 314 8911; home-affairs.pwv.gov.za). Issues passports, but all applications must be submitted or forwarded to the nearest South African consulate. Processing time is 6 weeks or more. Passports around ZAR120; valid for 10 years. Under 16 around ZAR90; valid for 5 years.

United Kingdom: Request an application from a passport office, main post office, travel agent, or online at www.ukpa.gov.uk/forms/f_app_pack.htm, then apply by mail or at a passport office (☎ 0870 521 0410; www.open.gov.uk). Passports UK£30, valid for 10 years; under 15 UK£16, valid for 5 years. Processing time 2 weeks; faster service by personal visit to a High Street Partner (extra UK£4) or a Passport Office (same-day £45, one-week £30).

United States: Apply at any federal or state courthouse, authorized post office, or US Passport Agency (☎ 202-647-0518; www.travel.state.gov/passport_services.html). Processing time 5-6 weeks. New passports US$60, valid 10 years; under 16 US$40, valid 5 years. 3-day expedited service extra US$35. Passport renewal by mail or in person (US$40).

ONE EUROPE. European unity has come a long way since 1958, when the European Economic Community (EEC) was created to promote solidarity and cooperation between its six founding states. Since then, the EEC has become the European Union (EU), with political, legal, and economic institutions spanning 15 member states: Austria, Belgium, Denmark, Finland, France, Germany, Greece, Ireland, Italy, Luxembourg, the Netherlands, Portugal, Spain, Sweden, and the United Kingdom.

How does this affect the average non-EU tourist? In 1999 the EU established **freedom of movement** across the entire EU, excluding Ireland and the UK, but including Iceland and Norway. Border controls between participating countries have been abolished and visa policies harmonized. You're still required to carry a passport (or government-issued ID card for EU citizens) when crossing an internal border, but it will not be checked for travel from one participating country to another. The UK and the Republic of Ireland have also formed a **common travel area,** abolishing passport controls between their borders. The only times you'll see a border guard within the EU are traveling between the British Isles and the Continent.

For more important consequences of the EU for travelers, see **Customs in the EU** (p. 36).

PASSPORT MAINTENANCE. Make sure to photocopy the page of your passport with your photo, passport number, and other identifying information, as well as your visas, traveler's check serial numbers, plane tickets, travel insurance policies, and any other important documents. Carry one set of copies in a safe place, apart from the originals, and leave another set at home. Consulates also recommend that you carry an expired passport or an official copy of your birth certificate in a part of your baggage separate from other documents.

If you lose your passport, immediately notify the local police and the nearest embassy or consulate of your home government. Because of September 11, many countries no longer reissue passports abroad, including the United States and the the United Kingdom. Most countries, including the US and UK, will issue temporary passports abroad for urgent travel, which expire in a short time and are valid only for limited travel. In emergencies, almost all countries issue immediate temporary traveling papers that will permit you to re-enter your home country. At the time of publishing, Australia, Canada, Ireland, New Zealand, and South Africa still reissue passports abroad, but that may change. To expedite obtaining a replacement or temporary passport, you will need to know all info contained in the lost passport and show ID and proof of citizenship. In some cases, a replacement may take weeks to process, and may involve an elaborate investigation into the circumstances of its loss. Any visas stamped in your old passport will be irretrievably lost. Your passport is a public document belonging to your nation's government. You may have to surrender it to a foreign government official; if not returned in a reasonable amount of time, inform the nearest mission of your home country.

VISAS, INVITATIONS, & WORK PERMITS

In certain cases of travel or short residence, the government of France requires the traveler to obtain a visa. French visas are valid for travel in any of the states of the EU common travel area (see **"One Europe"** above), but if your primary destination is a country other than France, you should apply to that country's consulate for a visa. All visitors to France are required to register with the police in the town in which they plan to reside; you are automatically registered when you rent a hotel or hostel room or sign a lease. Before departure, check at the nearest French Embassy or Consulate (listed under **Embassies & Consulates,** on p. 31) for up-to-date info on entrance requirements. US citizens can also consult the website at www.pueblo.gsa.gov/cic_text/travel/foreign/foreignentryreqs.html.

VISITS OF UNDER 90 DAYS. Citizens of South Africa need a **short-stay visa** *(court séjour)*. To obtain this visa, your passport must be valid for three months past the date you intend to leave France. You must submit two passport-sized photos, a return ticket, proof of medical insurance, and documentary evidence of your socio-professional situation and means of support in France. You will also need to provide either a certificate of accommodation stamped by a police station or town hall (2 copies) if you plan to stay with friends, a letter from your employer if you plan to work, or evidence of a hotel reservation or organized tour. Apply at your nearest French consulate; short-stay visas for South African nationals take up to 2 weeks to process. (Transit visa (1 or 2 entries of 1 or 2 days each) ZAR87; single/multiple entry visa up to 30 days ZAR217; single/multiple entry visa for 31-90 days ZAR260.)

VISITS OF OVER 90 DAYS. All non-EU citizens need a **long-stay visa** *(long séjour)* for stays of over 90 days. You must present the same info as for the *court séjour* (see above). The visa can take two months to process and costs €95.16. US citizens can take advantage of the **Center for International Business and Travel** (CIBT, ☎800-925-2428), which secures visas for travel to almost all countries for a variable service charge. All foreigners (including EU citizens) who plan to stay over 90 days must apply for a temporary residence permit *(carte de séjour temporaire)* at the prefecture in their town of residence within 60 days of their arrival in France.

STUDY AND WORK PERMITS. Only EU citizens have the right to work and study in France without a visa. Others must apply for a special student visa or work permit. For more information, see **Alternatives to Tourism** chapter (p. 84).

IDENTIFICATION

French law requires that all people carry an official form of identification, either a passport or an EU government-issued identity card. The police have the right to demand identification at any time; refusal or lack of identification merits a large fine. Minority travelers, particularly black and Arab travelers, should be especially mindful. It is advisable to carry two or more forms of photo identification. Many establishments, like banks, demand several forms of ID to cash traveler's checks. A passport combined with a driver's license or birth certificate is almost always adequate. Never carry all your IDs together, in case of theft. You may want to bring a supply of passport-size photos to affix to the railpasses or other IDs you acquire in France; you can also find photo booths at almost every *métro* station.

Below are some useful forms of identification. For more info, contact the **International Student Travel Confederation (ISTC),** Herengracht 479, 1017 BS Amsterdam, Netherlands (☎20 421 2800; fax 20 421 2810; www.istc.org).

TEACHER, STUDENT & YOUTH IDENTIFICATION. The **International Student Identity Card (ISIC),** the most widely accepted form of student ID, provides discounts on sights, accommodations, food, and transport; access to 24hr. emergency helpline (in North America call ☎877-370-ISIC; elsewhere US collect 715-345-0505); and, for US cardholders, insurance benefits (see **Insurance,** p. 47). ISIC holders receive discounts of 10-50% on Paris sights like the Eiffel Tower, Musée d'Orsay, Pantheon, and Museum of Modern Art. The ISIC is more likely than an institution-specific card (such as a university ID) to be recognized and honored abroad. Applicants must be be at least 12 years of age and be degree-seeking students of a secondary or post-secondary school. Because fake ISICs are common, some services (particularly airlines) require additional proof of student identity, such as a school ID or a letter from your registrar attesting to your student status and stamped with your school seal.

The **International Teacher Identity Card (ITIC)** offers teachers the same insurance coverage as ISIC, as well as limited discounts. The **International Youth Travel Card (IYTC;** formerly the **GO 25** Card) offers many of the same benefits as the ISICF for travelers who are 25 years old or under but are not students.

Each of these identity cards costs US$22. ISIC and ITIC cards are valid for roughly one and a half academic years, IYTC cards for one year. Many student travel agencies (see p. 60) issue the cards, including STA Travel in Australia and New Zealand; Travel CUTS in Canada; usit in the Republic of Ireland and Northern Ireland; SASTS in South Africa; Campus Travel and STA Travel in the UK; and Council Travel and STA Travel in the US.

CUSTOMS

CUSTOMS IN THE EU. Travelers in the EU member countries (Austria, Belgium, Denmark, Finland, France, Germany, Greece, Ireland, Italy, Luxembourg, the Netherlands, Portugal, Spain, Sweden, and the UK) can take advantage of the freedom of movement of goods. There are no customs controls at internal EU borders and travelers may transport legal substances for their personal (non-commercial) use—up to 800 cigarettes, 10L of spirits, 90L of wine (60L of sparkling wine), and 110L of beer. Duty-free was abolished in 1999 for travel between EU member states, but travelers between the EU and the rest of the world still get a duty-free allowance when passing through customs.

RECLAIMING VALUE-ADDED TAX. Most purchases in France include a 20.6% value-added tax (**TVA** is the French acronym, VAT the English). Non-EU residents in France for less than six months can reclaim the tax for purchases made over €175 in one store. Only certain stores participate in this **vente en détaxe** refund porgram. You must show a non-EU passport or proof of non-EU residence at the time of purchase and ask the vendor for a *bordereau de détaxe* form in triplicate; make sure that the vendor fills out his part. Present the purchase receipt and the completed form to a French customs official within 3 mon. of the purchase. Have the purchased goods at hand. At an airport, look for the window labeled *douane de détaxe*. On a train, find an official or get off at a station close to the border. Budget at least two hours for this exquisitely painful encounter with French bureaucracy. Some shops will exempt you from paying the tax at the time of purchase, though you must still complete the above process. Food products, tobacco, medicine, firearms, unmounted precious stones, (sorry!) cars, and "cultural goods" do not qualify for a refund. For more information, contact the Europe Tax-Free Shopping office in France, 4 pl. de l'Opéra, Paris 75002 (☎01 42 66 24 14).

GOING HOME. Upon returning home, you must declare all articles acquired abroad and pay duty on those exceeding the allowance established by your country. There is normally a separate, smaller allowance for goods and gifts purchased at **duty-free** shops abroad; if you exceed this you must pay duty and possibly sales tax as well. ("Duty-free" means that you did not pay a tax in the country of purchase; see **Customs in the EU,** p. 36, for more info.)

To speed up your return, make a list of any valuables brought from your home country, along with their serial numbers, and register them with customs before traveling. Keep all receipts for goods acquired abroad. For more info, contact:

Australia: Australian Customs, Syndey Central Building, 477 Pitt Street, Sydney NSW 2000 (☎1300 363 263, from elsewhere 61 2 6275 6666; www.customs.gov.au).

Canada: Canadian Customs, 2265 St. Laurent Blvd. 1st fl., Ottawa, ON K1G 4K3 (☎800-461-9999 24hr., from elsewhere 204-983-3500; www.revcan.ca).

Ireland: Customs Information Office, Irish Life Mall, Lower Abbey St., Dublin 1 (☎01 878 8811; www.revenue.ie).

New Zealand: New Zealand Customhouse, 17-21 Whitmore St., Box 2218, Wellington (☎04 473 6099; fax 04 473 7370; www.customs.govt.nz).

South Africa: Customs and Excise, P.O. Box 13802, Tramshed, Pretoria 0001 (☎012 334-6400; fax 012 328 6478; www.sars.gov.za).

United Kingdom: Her Majesty's Customs and Excise, Passenger Enquiry Team, Wayfarer House, Great South West Road, Feltham, Middlesex TW14 8NP (☎0845 010 9000 in UK, elsewhere ☎208 929 0152; www.hmce.gov.uk).

United States: US Customs Service, 1300 Pennsylvania Ave., NW, Washington, D.C. 20229 (☎202-927-1000; www.customs.gov).

MONEY

If you stay in hostels and prepare your own food, you'll spend €17-22 per person per day. **Accommodations** start at about €20 per night for a double; a basic sit-down meal with wine costs €10. Personal checks from home will be met with blank refusal, and traveler's checks are not widely accepted outside tourist-oriented businesses; many establishments only accept euro-denominated traveler's checks.

CURRENCY AND EXCHANGE

The **franc français** has now been superseded completely by the **euro** (symbol €). The euro is divided into 100 cents.

The currency chart below is based on published exchange rates from August 2002 between European Union euros (EUR€) and Australian dollars (AUS$), Canadian dollars (CDN$), Irish pounds (IR£), New Zealand dollars (NZ$), South African Rand (ZAR), British pounds (UK£), and US dollars (US$). Check the currency converter on financial websites such as www.bloomburg.com and www.xe.com, or a large newspaper, for the latest exchange rate.

EUROS (€)		
AUS$1 = €0.56		€1 = AUS$1.78
CDN$1 = €0.65		€1 = CDN$1.53
NZ$1 = €0.48		€1 = NZ$2.10
ZAR1 = €0.10		€1 = ZAR10.33
UK£1 =€1.58		€1 = UK£0.63
US$1 = €1.02		€1 = US$0.98

It is generally cheaper to convert money in France. Bring enough foreign currency to last for the first 24-72 hours of a trip, since banks tend to find many excuses to be closed. **International Currency Express** (☎888-278-6628) will deliver over 120 foreign currencies or traveler's checks overnight (US$15) or second-day (US$12) at competitive exchange rates. Check newspapers for the standard rate of exchange to make sure you are not charged outrageous commissions. Look elsewhere if there is more than a 5% margin between buy and sell prices. Banks generally have the best rates. Since you lose money on each transaction, convert in large sums (unless the currency is depreciating rapidly). Carry some of your bills and traveler's checks in small denominations (US$50 or less) in case you have to exchange money at disadvantageous rates; carry some in large denominations because charges are often levied per check cashed. Store your money in a variety of forms—cash, traveler's checks, and an ATM or credit card.

TRAVELER'S CHECKS

Traveler's checks are one of the safest and least troublesome means of carrying funds. They are readily accepted in France, though a number of places only take checks in euros and a passport is often required to cash them. Check issuers provide refunds if the checks are lost or stolen, as well as additional services like toll-free refund hotlines abroad, emergency message services, and stolen credit card assistance. **American Express** and **Visa** are the most widely recognized brands. Many banks and agencies sell them for a small commission. Order checks, particularly large ones, from banks well in advance. American Express offices often sell traveler's checks in major currencies over the counter. When purchasing checks, inquire about toll-free refund hotlines and the location of refund centers.

To ensure a **refund** for lost or stolen checks, keep your check receipts separate from your checks in a safe place or with a traveling companion. Record check numbers when you cash them and leave a list of check numbers with someone at home. Never countersign your checks until you are ready to cash them.

American Express: Checks available with commission at select banks and all AmEx offices. US residents can also purchase checks by phone (☎888-887-8986) or online (www.aexp.com). AAA (see p. 74) offers commission-free checks to its members. Checks available in US, Australian, British, Canadian, Japanese, and Euro currencies. *Cheques for Two* can be signed by either of 2 people traveling together. For purchase locations or more info contact AmEx's service centers (US and Canada ☎800-221-7282; UK 0800 521 313; Australia 800 25 19 02; New Zealand 0800 441 068; elsewhere US collect 801-964-6665).

Visa: Checks available (generally with commission) at banks worldwide. For the location of the nearest office, call Visa's service centers (US ☎800-227-6811; UK 0800 89 50 78; elsewhere UK collect 44 020 7937 8091). Checks available in US, British, Canadian, Japanese, and Euro currencies.

Thomas Cook: In the US and Canada call ☎800-287-7362; UK 0800 62 21 01; elsewhere UK collect 1733 31 89 50. Checks available in 100 currencies at 2% commission. Thomas Cook offices cash checks commission-free.

Citicorp: In the US and Canada call ☎800-645-6556; elsewhere call US collect +1 813-623-1709. Traveler's checks are available in US dollars, British pounds, and German marks at 1-3% commission. Call 24hr.

CREDIT, ATM, AND DEBIT CARDS

Credit cards are generally accepted in France for purchases over €15. Where they are accepted, credit cards often offer superior exchange rates—up to 5% better than the retail rate used by banks and other establishments. Credit cards may also offer services such as insurance or emergency help, and are sometimes required to reserve hotel rooms or rental cars. **MasterCard (EuroCard)** and **Visa (Carte Bleue)** are the most welcomed; American Express cards work at some ATMs and at AmEx offices and major airports. Credit cards are accepted in most businesses in France, though normally only for purchases of over €15. Major credit cards can be used to extract cash advances in euros from associated banks and cash machines throughout France. Such machines require a **Personal Identification Number (PIN**; see p. 39).

French-issued credit cards are fitted with a micro-chip (known as *cartes à puce)* rather than a magnetic strip *(cartes à piste magnétique);* in untouristed areas, cashiers may attempt to scan the card with a microchip reader. In such circumstances you should explain: *"Ceci n'est pas une carte à puce, mais une carte à piste magnétique."* Self-service and cash machines should have no problem scanning magnetic cards.

24hr. **ATMs** (also called **cash machines**) are widespread in France; they can normally be found at post offices and banks. Depending on the system that your home bank uses, you can usually withdraw money from your personal bank account through an ATM machine. ATMs get the same wholesale exchange rate as credit cards. There is normally a limit on the amount of money you can withdraw per day (generally €125-450). Your home bank may charge a fee for using ATM facilities abroad, typically US $1-5 per withdrawal. The two major international money networks are **Cirrus** (US ☎ 800-424-7787) and **PLUS** (US ☎ 800-843-7587). To locate ATMs around the world, call the above numbers, or consult www.visa.com/globalgateway/gg_selectcountry.html or www.mastercard.com/cardholderservices/atm.

ATM CARD ALERT. To withdraw money from a machine in France with a cash or credit card, you must have a four-digit **Personal Identification Number (PIN).** These are not usually automatically assigned to credit cards, so ask your card issuer to assign you one before you leave. If your PIN is longer than four digits, ask your bank whether the first four digits will work. There are no letters on the keypads of most French cash machines; use the following chart to convert your PIN: 1=QZ; 2=ABC; 3=DEF; 4=GHI; 5=JKL; 6=MNO; 7=PRS; 8=TUV; and 9=WXY. If you punch the wrong code into a French machine three times, it will swallow your card. If you **lose your card** in France, call the following numbers, all of which have English-speaking operators: **AmEx** (☎ 01 47 77 72 00), **Mastercard** (☎ 08 00 90 13 87), and **Visa** (☎ 08 00 90 11 79).

Visa TravelMoney allows you to access money from any ATM that accepts Visa cards. You deposit an amount before you travel (plus a small administrative fee), and can withdraw up to that sum while traveling. The cards, which give you the same favorable exchange rate for withdrawals as a regular Visa, are especially useful for travel through many countries. Obtain a card at a Thomas Cook or Citicorp office (toll-free US ☎ 877-394-2247) or possibly at your local bank. For customer assistance in France, call ☎ 08 00 90 12 35.

American Express cardholders can withdraw cash from their checking or current accounts without charge at any major AmEx office (and some other offices), up to US$1000 every 21 days or US$1000 every seven days with a Green Card. AmEx offers Express Cash at their ATMs in France. Express Cash withdrawals are automatically debited from the cardmember's checking account or line of credit. For more info on Express Cash, call: in the US ☎ 800 CASH-NOW (227-4669); UK 01273 696 933; Canada 800-716-6661; Australia 800 230 100; New Zealand 0800 109 109. The AmEx national number in France is ☎ 01 47 77 70 00.

Visa (US ☎ 800-336-8472) and **MasterCard** (US ☎ 800-307-7309) are issued in cooperation with banks and other organizations. **American Express** (US ☎ 800-843-2273; yearly fee $55) allows cardholders to cash personal checks at AmEx offices abroad, access an emergency 24hr. medical and legal assistance hotline (North America ☎ 800-554-2639, elsewhere US collect 715-343-7977), and enjoy various benefits (plane, hotel, and car rental reservations; baggage loss and flight insurance; mailgram and international cable services). The **Discover Card** (US ☎ 800-347-2683, elsewhere US collect 801-902-3100) offers cashback bonuses on most purchases, but may not be accepted in France.

Debit cards withdraw money directly from the holder's checking account. A debit card can be used wherever its associated credit card company (usually Mastercard or Visa) is accepted. Debit cards often double as ATM cards. Debit cards can be obtained from your local bank.

GETTING MONEY FROM HOME

WIRING MONEY. It is possible to arrange a **bank money transfer** from your home bank to a French bank. This is the cheapest and slowest way to transfer cash. Some banks may release your funds only in local currency, potentially at a poor exchange rate. Money transfer services like Western Union are faster and more convenient but pricier. Western Union has branches in many French post offices. Western Union has many locations worldwide. (US ☎ 800-325-6000, Canada 800-235-0000, UK 0800 83 38 33, Australia 800 501 500, New Zealand 800 27 0000, South Africa 0860 100031, France 08 25 00 98 98; www.westernunion.com.) Money transfer services are also available at **American Express** and **Thomas Cook** offices.

US STATE DEPARTMENT (US CITIZENS ONLY). In dire emergencies, the US State Department will forward money within hours to the nearest consular office at a US$15 fee. Contact the Overseas Citizens Service division of the US State Department (☎ 202-647-5225; nights, Sundays, and holidays 202-647-4000).

COSTS

PRICE RANGES Price ranges, marked by the numbered icons below, are now a part of food and accommodation descriptions. They are based on the lowest cost for one person, excluding special deals or prices. In the case of campgrounds, we include the cost of parking a car. The table below is a guide to how prices and icons match up.

SYMBOL	❶	❷	❸	❹	❺
ACCOMM.	€1-15	€16-25	€26-35	€36-55	€56-100
FOOD	€1-6	€7-9	€10-15	€16-24	€25-50

The cost of your trip will vary considerably, depending on where you go, how you travel, and where you stay. The most significant expenses will be your round-trip **airfare** to France (see **Getting to France: By Plane,** p. 58) and a **railpass** (see p. 69) or **bus pass** (p. 73). Calculate a reasonable per-day **budget** to meet your needs. Don't forget to factor in emergency reserve funds (at least US$200) when deciding how much money to bring.

STAYING ON A BUDGET. A bare-bones day in France (camping or sleeping in hostels/guesthouses, buying food at supermarkets) costs about €20 (US$20); a slightly more comfortable day (sleeping at budget hotels, eating one meal a day at a restaurant, going out at night) runs about €45 (US$45).

TIPS FOR SAVING MONEY. There are a couple of easy ways to save money: search out opportunities for free entertainment; split accommodation and food costs with trustworthy fellow travelers; buy food in supermarkets rather than fine restaurants. Bring a sleepsack (see p. 48) to avoid sheet charges in European hostels. Do your **laundry** in the sink (unless explicitly prohibited).

TIPPING & BARGAINING

By law, service must be included at all **restaurants, bars,** and **cafés** in France. It is not unheard of to leave extra change at a café or bar, maybe half a euro per drink, even 5-10% for exceptionally good service. Otherwise, tipping is only expected for **taxis** and **hairdressers,** where 10-15% is the norm. People like concierges may also expect to be tipped for services beyond the call of duty, never less than €1.50.

Though you should inquire about discounts and less pricey options, do not try to bargain at established places—i.e., hotels, hostels, restaurants, cafes, museums, nightclubs. Although not encouraged, bargaining is acceptable at outdoor markets, though you shouldn't expect to get any deals.

TAXES

The **value-added tax (VAT)** is a general tax on doing business in France; it applies to a wide range of goods (entertainment, food, accommodations) and services. The tax can be up to 20.6% of the price of the good. Some of the VAT can be recovered (see **Reclaiming Value-Added Tax,** p. 36). There is also tax on staying at a hotel, hostel, or other accommodation *(taxe de séjour)*, which is typically included in the price of a stay and the price quoted in *Let's Go: France.*

SAFETY AND SECURITY

EMERGENCY AND CRISIS TELEPHONE NUMBERS

MEDICAL EMERGENCY: Dial ☎ **15.**

POLICE EMERGENCY: Dial ☎ **17.**

FIRE EMERGENCY: Dial ☎ **18.**

NATIONAL ENGLISH-LANGUAGE CRISIS LINE: Dial ☎ **01 47 23 80 80,** in Paris (3-11pm).

DIRECTORY ASSISTANCE: Dial ☎ **12.**

SNCF RESERVATIONS AND INFORMATION: Dial ☎ **08 36 35 35 35.**

Tourists are the biggest targets for crime in France. When confronted by a suspicious individual, do not respond or make eye contact. Walk quickly away, and keep a solid grip on your belongings. Contact the police if a hustler is insistent or aggressive. When driving, lock your doors and keep bags away from windows; scooter-borne thieves often snatch purses and bags from cars stopped at lights. In **Paris,** be especially careful on public transportation at rush hour and traveling to and from the airport. Pick-pocketing is common on the Paris Métro, especially on line #1 and the RER B line to de Gaulle Airport, and at department stores, particularly on the escalators. Be vigilant with your baggage at **airports** and **train stations.** Take a **licensed taxi.** Outside Paris, tourist-related crime is most prevalent on the **Côte d'Azur,** in **Marseille,** and in **Montpellier.**

PERSONAL SAFETY

EXPLORING. To avoid unwanted attention, blend in. What may look perfectly innocuous in Miami will mark you out instantly in Menton. The French are known for their conservative stylishness. Go for restrained sneakers or closed shoes, solid-color pants or jeans, and plain T-shirts or button-down shirts. Avoid sport sandals, baggy pants, or torn jeans. French people rarely wear shorts, and only

ESSENTIALS

ESSENTIALS

long ones. For women, skirts or dresses are more appropriate. Carrying a large bag with you everywhere will reveal your true identity as a tourist.

Women and men should dress especially conservatively when visiting churches. Women should wear long pants or a long skirt and cover their shoulders; men should remove their hats and cover their upper bodies.

Familiarize yourself with your surroundings before setting out; if you must check a map on the street, duck into a café, shop, or doorway. Carry yourself with confidence. If you are traveling alone, be sure that someone at home knows your itinerary and **never admit that you're traveling alone.** When night falls, walk along busy, well-lit streets.

SELF DEFENSE. Impact, Prepare, and Model Mugging can refer you to local self-defense courses in the US (☎800-345-5425; www.impactsafety.org). Workshops (2-3hr.) start at US$50; full courses run US$350-500.

DRIVING. Despite being blessed with excellent roads, the French have deservedly earned a reputation for aggressive and dangerous driving. They regularly flout the speed limit, often while drunk. Corsica's narrow and twisting roads are among the most lethal in Europe, often because cars try to pass in dangerous situations. Watch out for mopeds, especially in the south; they sometimes speed out from alleys or sidewalks. By law, all passengers must wear a seatbelt. Children under 40 lbs must ride in a specially-designed carseat, available at a small fee from most car rental agencies. Study a map of your route before hitting the road. For long drives, bring spare parts and invest in a cellular phone and a roadside assistance program (see p. 74). If your car breaks down without either of these, wait for the police to drive by. In cities, and especially on the Côte d'Azur, park your car in a well-lit area and secure it with a steering wheel locking device. Sleeping in your car is dangerous and often illegal. *Let's Go* also does not recommend hitchhiking under any circumstances—see **Getting Around,** p. 68, for more about its perils.

TERRORISM. Terrorism has not been as serious of a problem in France as in other European countries. In the post-September 11 world, however, the old mantras about terrorism no longer apply. As a Western nation, France is a potential target. Since colonialism, France has always been an enemy of unstable Algeria. France contains cells of al Qaeda and other terrorist groups; several September 11 hijackers lived in neighboring Germany. Several cities have recently experienced unrest, though because of immigrant conditions rather than terrorism. Several Jewish synogogues have been firebombed, though by domestic anti-Semites rather than al Qaeda. The French government has heightened security at public places. Certain train stations no longer permit luggage storage, for example.

If you are concerned about terrorism, avoid areas with lots of people—popular restaurants and shops, public transportation, famous sights. That said, it will be very hard to enjoy your vacation without being around other people. See the box on **travel advisories** below for more info.

FINANCIAL SECURITY

PROTECTING YOUR VALUABLES. A few steps minimize the financial risks of traveling. **Bring as little with you as possible.** Buy combination **padlocks** to secure your belongings in hostel lockers or in your pack. Label the inside and outside of every piece of luggage. Don't put your wallet in your back pocket. Buy a sturdy handbag with a secure clasp and carry it crosswise on the side, away from the street with the clasp against you. Keep your bag in sight at all times. **Carry as little cash as possible** and never count your money in public. Keep your traveler's checks and ATM/

TRAVEL ADVISORIES. The following government offices provide travel information and advisories by telephone, by fax, or via the web:

Australian Department of Foreign Affairs and Trade: ☎1300 55 5135; faxback service 02 6261 1299; www.dfat.gov.au.

Canadian Department of Foreign Affairs and International Trade (DFAIT): In Canada and the US call ☎800-267-6788, elsewhere call +1 613-944-6788; www.dfait-maeci.gc.ca. Call for their free booklet, *Bon Voyage...But.*

New Zealand Ministry of Foreign Affairs: ☎04 494 8500; fax 494 8506; www.mft.govt.nz/trav.html.

United Kingdom Foreign and Commonwealth Office: ☎020 7008 0232; fax 7008 0155; www.fco.gov.uk.

US Department of State: ☎202-647-5225, faxback service 647-3000; http://travel.state.gov. For *A Safe Trip Abroad,* call ☎512-1800.

credit cards in a **money belt** or a less accessible **neck pouch**. Keep a small cash reserve (about US$50), your traveler's check numbers, and important photocopies separate from your primary stash, sewn into or stored in the depths of your pack.

CON ARTISTS & PICKPOCKETS. Con artists often come in the form of groups of children. Often, one child will distract you, jostling you or spitting on your shoulder, while another snatches your bag. **Pickpockets** operate in city crowds and on public transportation. Be alert in public telephone booths. Speak your calling number quietly and make sure no one can look over your shoulder if you punch it in.

ACCOMMODATIONS & TRANSPORTATION. Never leave your belongings unattended; crime occurs in the best hotel or nicest parking lot. Bring your own **padlock** for hostel lockers and don't store valuables there.

Be alert on **buses** and **trains**. Thieves often pounce as soon as travelers fall asleep. When traveling with others, sleep in shifts. Never sleep alone in an empty train compartment. Bed down on the top bunk; lock your luggage pack to the rack above you and keep valuables on your person.

DRUGS, DRINKS, AND SMOKES

Possession of **illegal drugs** (including marijuana) in France can result in a substantial jail sentence or fine. Drug-dealers often sell drugs to tourists and then turn them in to authorities for a reward. In France, police may arbitrarily stop and search anyone on the street. **Prescription drugs,** particularly insulin, syringes, or narcotics, should be left in their original, labeled containers and accompanied by their prescriptions and a doctor's statement. In case of arrest, your home country's consulate can suggest attorneys and inform your family and friends, but can't get you out of jail. For more info, write to the Bureau of Consular Affairs, Public Affairs #6831, Department of State, Washington, D.C. 20520 (US ☎202-647-5300).

The French love alcohol, but they drink carefully. Virtually no one drinks "to get drunk." Drinking on the street is similarly uncouth. Restaurants may serve alcohol to anyone 14 or over.

Smoking is banned in public places, but the French light up almost anywhere. Some restaurants have non-smoking sections, but they are often not respected.

HEALTH

Avoid common traveling ailments by drinking lots of fluids, wearing sturdy, broken-in shoes and clean socks, and keeping your feet dry with talcum powder.

ESSENTIALS

BEFORE YOU GO

Bring a **first-aid kit** for minor problems. Take along moleskin or other blister protection. Women report having difficulty finding applicator **tampons** in France, though other kinds are available at pharmacies and groceries.

In your **passport,** write the names of any people you want contacted in case of a medical emergency and list any **allergies** or medical conditions. Allergy sufferers should obtain a full supply of their medication before leaving. Finding the foreign equivalent of a prescription is not always easy or safe. Carry up-to-date, legible prescriptions or a statement from your doctor giving the medication's trade name, manufacturer, chemical name, and dosage.

IMMUNIZATIONS & PRECAUTIONS

Travelers over two years old should keep the following vaccines up to date: *MMR* (measles, mumps, and rubella); *DTaP* or *Td* (diptheria, tetanus, and pertussis); *OPV* (polio); *HbCV* (haemophilus influenza B); and *HBV* (hepatitis B). For recommendations on immunizations and prophylaxis, consult the CDC (see below) in the US or the equivalent in your home country, as well as a doctor.

USEFUL ORGANIZATIONS & PUBLICATIONS

The US **Centers for Disease Control and Prevention** (CDC; ☎877-FYI-TRIP; fax 888-232-3299; www.cdc.gov/travel) maintains an international travelers' hotline and an informative website. The CDC's comprehensive booklet *Health Information for International Travel,* an annual rundown of disease, immunization, and general health advice, is free online or US$25 via the Public Health Foundation (☎877-252-1200). Consult the appropriate government agency of your home country for consular info sheets on health issues and entry requirements (use the listings in the box on **Travel Advisories,** p. 43). For quick info on health and other travel warnings, call the **Overseas Citizens Services** (☎202-647-5225, after-hours 202-647-4000, hotline 1-888-407-4747), or contact a passport agency, embassy, or consulate abroad. US citizens can send a self-addressed, stamped envelope to the Overseas Citizens Services, Bureau of Consular Affairs, #4811, US Department of State, Washington, D.C. 20520, for info. For material on medical evacuation services and travel insurance firms, see the US government's website at http://travel.state.gov/medical.html or the **British Foreign and Commonwealth Office** (www.fco.gov.uk).

For detailed info on travel health, including a country-by-country overview of diseases, try the **International Travel Health Guide,** by Stuart Rose, MD (US$19.95; www.travmed.com). For general health info, contact the **American Red Cross** (☎800-564-1234; www.redcross.org).

MEDICAL ASSISTANCE ON THE ROAD

Medical care in France is as good (and as expensive) as anywhere in the world. All but the smallest towns have a hospital, generally with English-speaking staff, which are listed under the Practical Information in each city listing. Every town has a **24hr. pharmacy** *(pharmacie de garde).* Different pharmacies assume the duty at different times. The police can direct you to the right one; pharmacies also post this info on their doors on Sundays.

EU citizens get "reciprocal health benefits" (including immediate urgent care) if they fill out an **E-111** form, available at most post offices, before departure. EU citizens studying in France qualify for long-term care. Other travelers should get adequate medical insurance before leaving; regular **insurance** policies may require you to purchase additional coverage for travel abroad. Medicare does not cover travel abroad. For more info, see **Insurance, p. 47.**

If you need a doctor **(un médecin),** call the local hospital for a list of nearby practitioners or inquire at a pharmacy. If you are receiving reciprocal health care, make sure you call an **honoraires opposables** doctor (linked to the state health care system). Legally, they may not charge more than €17 for a consultation. Doctors registered as **honoraires libres** can charge whatever they like, and their fees will not be reimbursed under reciprocal health care agreements.

If you are concerned about **medical support,** try one of the following services. The *MedPass* from **Global Emergency Medical Services (GEMS),** 2001 Westside Dr., #120, Alpharetta, GA 30004, USA (☎800-860-1111; www.globalems.com), provides 24hr. international medical assistance, support, and medical evacuation resources. The **International Association for Medical Assistance to Travelers (IAMAT)** has free membership and lists English-speaking doctors worldwide. (US ☎716-754-4883, Canada 519-836-0102, New Zealand 03 352 2053; www.sentex.net/~iamat.)

Travelers with medical conditions (diabetes, allergies to antibiotics, epilepsy, heart conditions) may want to obtain a stainless-steel **Medic Alert** ID tag (first yr. US$35, thereafter US$20 per yr.), which identifies the condition and gives a 24hr. collect-call number. Contact the Medic Alert Foundation, 2323 Colorado Ave, Turlock, CA 95382, USA (☎888-633-4298; www.medicalert.org). Diabetics can contact the **American Diabetes Association,** 1701 N. Beauregard St., Alexandria, VA 22311 (☎800-342-2383; www.diabetes.org).

ONCE IN FRANCE

ENVIRONMENTAL HAZARDS

Hikers should be especially attentive to their health. The summer heat can cause rapid dehydration and sunburn, especially in the South. In the Alps, the Pyrénées, or Corsica, storms strike unpredictably, killing several hikers each year.

Heat exhaustion and dehydration: The symptoms of heat exhaustion include fatigue, headaches, and nausea. To avoid it, eat salty foods; drink clear fluids; stay away from alcohol and caffeine; wear a hat and a lightweight long-sleeved shirt in the sun; and acclimatize to hot regions before serious physical activity. Continuous heat stress may lead to **heatstroke,** characterized by rising body temperature, severe headache, and the cessation of sweating. Heatstroke is rare but potentially fatal; cool off victims with a wet towel and take them to a doctor immediately.

Hypothermia and frostbite: A rapid drop in body temperature is the clearest warning sign of **hypothermia.** Victims may also shiver, feel exhausted, exhibit poor coordination or slurred speech, hallucinate, or suffer amnesia. If these symptoms appear, seek medical help immediately. **Do not let hypothermia victims fall asleep**—it may prove fatal. To avoid hypothermia, keep dry, wear layers, and stay out of the wind. In wet weather, wool and synthetics (such as pile) retain heat. Most other fabrics, including cotton, will make you colder. **Frostbite** strikes when the temperature is below freezing. If a region of skin turns white, waxy, and cold, do not rub the area. Instead, drink warm beverages, get dry, and slowly warm the area with dry fabric or steady body contact, then find a doctor.

High altitude: If traveling at high altitude, give your body a couple of days to adjust to the thinner air before exerting yourself. At high altitudes alcohol is more potent and the risk of sunburn is greater (even in cold weather).

PREVENTING DISEASE

INSECT-BORNE DISEASES

Many diseases are transmitted by mosquitoes, fleas, ticks, and lice. **Mosquitoes** are most active from dusk to dawn and in wet or forested areas. Use insect repellents, such as DEET, spray your gear with permethrin (licensed in the US for use on clothing), wear long pants, closed shoes, and long sleeves, and wear a mosquito net. Tuck long pants into socks. Calamine lotion or topical cortisones (like Cortaid) may stop insect bites from itching, as can a bath with a half-cup of baking soda or oatmeal. **Ticks** can be particularly dangerous in rural and forested regions. Periodically run a fine-toothed comb on your neck and scalp to brush off ticks. **Do not** try to remove the little nuisances by burning them or coating them with nail polish remover or petroleum jelly. Instead, grasp the head of the tick with tweezers, as close as possible to your skin, and apply slow, steady traction. Removing a tick within 24 hours greatly reduces the risk of infection.

Tick-borne encephalitis: A viral infection of the central nervous system transmitted by tick bite or by consumption of unpasteurized dairy products. The risk of contracting the disease is generally low but higher in the summer and in dark, forested areas.

Lyme disease: A bacterial infection carried by ticks and identified by a circular bull's-eye rash of 2 in. or greater diameter. Advanced symptoms include fever, headache, fatigue, and aches and pains. Antibiotics are effective if administered early. Left untreated, Lyme disease can cause problems in joints, the heart, and the nervous system.

Other insect-borne diseases: Filariasis is a roundworm infestation transmitted by mosquitoes. Infection causes enlargement of extremities and has no vaccine. **Leishmaniasis,** a parasite transmitted by sand flies, strikes in Central and South America, Europe, Africa, and the Middle East, and on the Indian subcontinent. Common symptoms are fever, weakness, and swelling of the spleen. There is a treatment, but no vaccine.

FOOD- AND WATER-BORNE DISEASES

Cook everything properly and thoroughly and drink clean water. Clean water is not usually a problem in France, though most French people drink mineral water as a matter of taste and style.

Traveler's diarrhea in France is usually only the body's temporary reaction to bacteria in unfamiliar food ingredients; it tends to last 3-7 days and causes nausea, bloating, and urgency. To keep your strength up, eat quick energy, non-sugary foods with protein and carbohydrates. Over-the-counter remedies (such as Immodium) provide symptomatic relief, but may complicate serious infections unless used in conjunction with rehydration salts. A simple recipe for rehydration salts: mix one cup of clean water with half a teaspoon of sugar or honey and a pinch of salt. If diarrhea lasts longer than 5 days or you develop a fever, see a doctor. Treatment is different for children; consult a doctor.

INFECTIOUS DISEASES

Rabies is transmitted through the saliva of infected animals and is fatal if untreated. If you are bitten, wash the wound thoroughly and seek immediate medical care. Once you begin to show symptoms (thirst and muscle spasms), the disease is in its terminal stage. A rabies vaccine is available but is only semi-effective.

Hepatitis B is a viral infection of the liver transmitted by bodily fluid contact, needle sharing, and unprotected sex. Its incubation period varies widely; a person may not show symptoms until many years after infection. Vaccination is recommended for health-care workers, sexually active travelers, and anyone planning to seek medical treatment abroad. Vaccination consists of 3 shots taken over several months, and must begin at least 6 months before departure.

Hepatitis C is like Hepatitis B, but primarily strikes intravenous drug users, those exposed occupationally to blood, hemodialysis patients, and recipients of blood transfusions. It can, however, be tranmitted through sexual contact and the sharing of items like razors and toothbrushes.

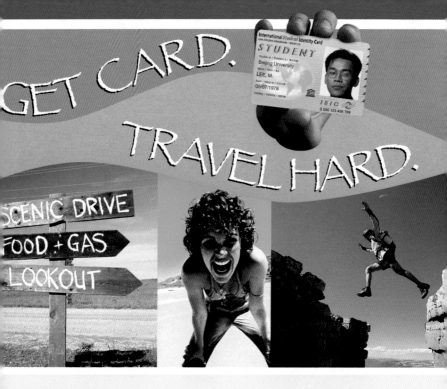

There's only one way to max out your travel experience and make the most of your time on the road: The International Student Identity Card.

 Packed with travel discounts, benefits and services, this card will keep your travel days and your wallet full. Get it before you hit it!

Visit **ISICUS.com** to get the full story on the benefits of carrying the ISIC.

90 minutes, wash & dry (one sock missing).
5 minutes to book online (Detroit to Mom's

Save money & time on student and faculty
travel at **StudentUniverse.com**

AIDS, HIV, STDS

Acquired Immune Deficiency Syndrome (AIDS; SIDA in French) is a major problem in France; Paris has the largest HIV-positive community in Europe. France has only recently lifted immigration bans on HIV-positive individuals. There are as many heterosexuals infected as homosexuals in France. HIV is most *easily* transmitted through direct blood-to-blood contact; *never* share intravenous drug or tattooing needles. HIV is most *commonly* transmitted through sexual intercourse; using latex condoms greatly reduces your risk. (See **Women's Health,** p. 47.)

For detailed info on **AIDS** in France, call the **US Centers for Disease Control's** 24hr. hotline at ☎ 800-342-2437 or contact the **Joint United Nations Programme on HIV/AIDS (UNAIDS),** 20 av. Appia 20, CH-1211 Geneva 27, Switzerland (☎ 41 22 791 36 66; fax 41 22 791 41 87). France's AIDS hotline is ☎ 01 44 93 16 16. The Council on International Educational Exchange's pamphlet, *Travel Safe: AIDS and International Travel,* is posted on their website (www.ciee.org/Isp/safety/travelsafe.htm), along with links to other online and phone resources.

Sexually transmitted diseases (STDs) such as gonorrhea, chlamydia, genital warts, syphilis, and herpes are easier to catch than HIV and just as deadly. They include **Hepatitis B** and **C** (see **Infectious Diseases,** above). Oral or even tactile sexual contact can transmit these diseases. Warning signs include swelling, sores, bumps or blisters on sex organs, the rectum, or mouth; burning and pain during urination or bowel movements; itching around sex organs; swelling or redness of the throat; and flu-like symptoms. If these symptoms develop, see a doctor immediately.

Contraception is readily available in most pharmacies and supermarkets. To obtain **condoms** in France, visit a pharmacy and tell the clerk, *"Je voudrais une boîte de préservatifs"* (zhuh-voo-DRAY oon BWAHT duh PREY-zehr-va-TEEF).

WOMEN'S HEALTH

Women traveling in parts of France are susceptible to **vaginal yeast infections,** a treatable but uncomfortable illness that flares up in hot and humid climates. Wearing loosely fitting trousers or a skirt and cotton underwear helps prevent it. Yeast infections can be treated with over-the-counter remedies like Monistat (generic name "miconazole") or Gyne-Lotrimin (generic name "clotrimazole"). Bring supplies from home if you are prone to infection, as these may be difficult to find.

Recent changes have relaxed restrictions on surgical and pharmaceutical **abortions,** permitting them up to 12 weeks into pregnancy. Minors now need the permission of a legal adult rather than their parent or guardian. EU citizens have a reciprocal health care agreement whereby abortions are covered if deemed medically necessary. Non-EU citizens should check with their home insurance provider to ascertain whether abortions are covered. Contact the French branch of the International Planned Parenthood Federation, the **Mouvement Français pour le Planning Familial (MFPF),** which can supply the names of French hospitals and OB/GYN clinics performing abortions. (☎ 01 48 07 29 10. €550 if not covered by insurance.) More info about family planning centers can also be obtained through the **International Planned Parenthood Federation,** European Regional Office, Regent's College Inner Circle, Regent's Park, London NW1 4NS (☎ 020 7487 7900).

INSURANCE

Travel insurance covers medical/health problems, property loss, trip cancellation/interruption, and emergency evacuation. Check whether your regular insurance policies extend to travel-related accidents; even if they do, consider purchasing travel insurance if the cost of potential trip cancellation/interruption or emergency medical evacuation is greater than you can immediately absorb.

US residents' **medical insurance** (particularly university policies) often covers costs incurred abroad. **US Medicare does not cover foreign travel.** Canadians are protected by their home province's health insurance plan for up to 90 days after leaving the country; check with the provincial Ministry of Health or Health Plan Headquarters for details. **Homeowners' insurance** often covers theft during travel and loss of travel documents (passport, plane ticket, railpass) up to US$500.

SIC and **ITIC** (see p. 35) provide several insurance benefits: US$100 per day of in-hospital sickness up to 60 days, US$3000 of accident-related medical reimbursement, and US$25,000 for emergency medical transport. Cardholders have access to a toll-free 24hr. helpline (run by insurance provider **TravelGuard**) for medical, legal, and financial emergencies overseas (US and Canada ☎ 877-370-4742, elsewhere US collect 715-345-0505). **American Express** (US ☎ 800-528-4800) grants most cardholders automatic car rental insurance (collision and theft, but not liability) and accident coverage of US$100,000 on flight purchases made with the card.

INSURANCE PROVIDERS. Council and **STA** (see p. 47) offer a range of supplementary plans to your basic coverage. Other private insurance providers in the US and Canada are: **Access America** (☎ 800-284-8300); **Berkely Group/Carefree Travel Insurance** (☎ 800-323-3149); **Globalcare Travel Insurance** (☎ 800-821-2488); and **Travel Assistance International** (☎ 800-821-2828). **Columbus Direct** (☎ 020 73 75 0011) is a **UK** provider. In **Australia**, try **AFTA** (☎ 02 93 75 4955).

PACKING

Pack lightly. If you plan to hike a lot, see **Camping & the Outdoors,** p. 53.

LUGGAGE. If you plan to walk a lot, buy a sturdy **frame backpack** (see p. 53). Toting a **suitcase** or **trunk** works if you explore from a base of one or two cities, but not if you frequently switch residences. Bring a **daypack** (a small backpack or courier bag) in addition to your main piece of luggage.

CLOTHING. The weather in France is highly variable. Take along a **warm jacket** or wool sweater, a **rain jacket** (Gore-Texhhh is both waterproof and breathable), sturdy shoes or **hiking boots,** and **thick socks. Flip-flops** or waterproof sandals make grubby hostel showers more bearable. Consider packing nicer clothes and shoes, especially for when you visit religious and cultural sights.

SLEEPSACK. Some hostels require that you either provide your own linen or rent sheets from them. Save cash by making your own sleepsack: fold a full-size sheet in half the long way, then sew it closed along the long side and one of the short sides.

CONVERTERS & ADAPTERS. In France, electricity is 220 volts AC, enough to fry any 110V North American appliance. **Americans** and **Canadians** should buy an **adapter** (which changes the shape of the plug) and a **converter** (which changes the voltage) for US$20. Using only an adapter is a common mistake. **New Zealanders** and **South Africans** (who use 220V at home) as well as **Australians** (who use 240/250V) will need only an adapter.

TOILETRIES. Toothbrushes, towels, cold-water soap, talcum powder, deodorant, razors, and tampons are difficult to find; bring enough from home. The same is true of **contact lenses,** which also tend to be expensive. Take along your glasses and a copy of your prescription in case you need emergency replacements. If you use heat disinfection, switch temporarily to a chemical disinfection system (check to make sure it's safe with your brand of lenses) or buy a converter.

FIRST-AID KIT. A good first-aid kit pack includes bandages, pain reliever, antibiotic cream, a thermometer, a Swiss Army knife, tweezers, moleskin, decongestant, motion-sickness remedy, diarrhea or upset-stomach medication (Pepto Bismol or Imodium), an antihistamine, sunscreen, insect repellent, burn ointment, and a syringe for emergencies (get an explanatory letter from your doctor).

FILM. Film and developing in France is fairly expensive (about US$7 for a 36-roll). Less serious photographers may want to use a **disposable camera**. Despite disclaimers, airport security X-rays *can* fog film; buy a lead-lined pouch at a camera store or ask security to hand-inspect it. Always pack film in your carry-on luggage, as higher-intensity X-rays are used on checked luggage.

OTHER USEFUL ITEMS. For safety purposes, you should bring a **money belt** and small **padlock**. Basic **outdoors equipment** (plastic water bottle, compass, waterproof matches, pocketknife, sunglasses, sunscreen, hat) may also prove useful. Torn garments can be **quickly repaired** on the road with a needle and thread or with electrical tape. If you want to wash laundry by hand, bring detergent, a small rubber ball to stop up the sink, and string for a makeshift clothes line. **Other things** you might forget: umbrella; sealable **plastic bags**; **alarm clock;** safety pins; rubber bands; flashlight; earplugs; garbage bags; and a small **calculator.**

IMPORTANT DOCUMENTS. Don't forget your passport, traveler's checks, ATM and/or credit cards, and adequate ID (see p. 35). Check if you need the following: a hosteling membership card (see p. 49); driver's license (see p. 35); travel insurance forms; and/or rail or bus pass (see p. 69).

ACCOMMODATIONS

HOSTELS

Hostels generally offer dormitory accommodations in large single-sex or coed rooms with 4-10 (up to 60) beds, though some offer private rooms at reasonable prices. Hostels sometimes provide kitchens and utensils, bike rental, storage, laundry facilities, and occassionaly internet access. Some hostels close during certain daytime "lock-out" hours, have a curfew, don't accept reservations, and/or enforce a maximum stay. In France, a bed in a hostel costs around €7.50-16.

If you plan on staying at a lot of hostels, it is worth joining **Hostelling International (HI).** In France, Hostelling International's affiliate, the **Fédération Unie des Auberges de Jeunesse (FUAJ),** operates 178 hostels. Officially, all HI hostels require that you purchase a **membership card** to stay there. Alternatively, you can buy a €3 stamp with each night's stay at an HI hostel; once you have six stamps, you are entitled to full membership. Hostels that enforce this restriction are listed as **"Members only"** in *Let's Go*. Some hostels accept reservations via the **International Booking Network** (Australia ☎ 02 9261 1111, Canada 800-663-5777, England and Wales 1629 58 14 18, Northern Ireland 1232 32 47 33, Republic of Ireland 01 830 1766, NZ 03 379 9808, Scotland 8701 55 32 55, US 800-909-4776; www.hostelbooking.com). HI's umbrella organization's web page (www.iyhf.org) lists the web addresses and phone numbers of all national associations. Other hosteling resources include www.hostels.com/fr.html, www.hostelplanet.com, and www.eurotrip.com/hostels.

Australian Youth Hostels Association (AYHA), Level 3, 10 Mallett St., Camperdown NSW 2050 (☎02 9565 1699; fax 9565 1325; www.yha.org.au). AUS$52, under 18 AUS$16.

Hostelling International-Canada (HI-C), 400-205 Catherine St., Ottawa, ON K2P 1C3 (☎800-663-5777 or 613-237-7884; fax 237-7868; www.hostellingintl.ca). CDN$35, under 18 free.

ESSENTIALS

An Óige (Irish Youth Hostel Association), 61 Mountjoy St., Dublin 7 (☎830 4555; fax 830 5808; www.irelandyha.org). IR£10, under 18 IR£4.

Youth Hostels Association of New Zealand (YHANZ), P.O. Box 436, 193 Cashel St., 3rd Floor Union House, Christchurch 1 (☎03 379 9970; fax 365 4476; www.yha.org.nz). NZ$40, under 17 free.

Hostels Association of South Africa, 3rd fl., 73 St. George's St. Mall, P.O. Box 4402, Cape Town 8000 (☎021 424 2511; fax 424 4119; www.hisa.org.za). ZAR45.

Scottish Youth Hostels Association (SYHA), 7 Glebe Crescent, Stirling FK8 2JA (☎01786 89 14 00; fax 89 13 33; www.syha.org.uk). UK£6.

Youth Hostels Association (England and Wales) Ltd., Trevelyan House, 8 St. Stephen's Hill, St. Albans, Hertfordshire AL1 2DY, UK (☎0870 870 8808; fax 01727 84 41 26; www.yha.org.uk). UK£12.50, under 18 UK£6.25, families UK£25.

Hostelling International Northern Ireland (HINI), 22-32 Donegall Rd., Belfast BT12 5JN, Northern Ireland (☎02890 31 54 35; fax 43 96 99; www.hini.org.uk). UK£10, under 18 UK£6.

Hostelling International-American Youth Hostels (HI-AYH), 733 15th St., NW, #840, Washington, D.C. 20005 (☎202-783-6161; fax 783-6171; www.hiayh.org). US$25, under 18 free.

HOTELS

Two or more people traveling together can save money by staying in cheap hotels rather than hostels. The French government assigns hotels between zero and four stars, solely based on quality. *Let's Go* chooses and ranks hotels according to such characteristics as charm, friendliness, convenience, and value for money; *Let's Go* lists mainly zero or one stars, with the occasional two or three. Hotels in each town are listed in order of our preference; particularly outstanding ones are awarded the **Let's Go thumb (🖢)**. Prices are generally per room, although *demi-pension* (half-board; includes room and breakfast) and *pension* (room and all meals) are quoted per person. Amenities—TV, A/C, etc.—are typically but not necessarily mentioned in the listings. Hotels without 24hr. reception generally give out keys to allow entry after the reception closes.

Expect to pay at least €18 for a single room and €25 for a double. If you want a room with twin beds, ask for *une chambre avec deux lits* (oon chAMBR-avEK duh LEE); otherwise you may find yourself in *une chambre avec un grand lit* (oon chAMBR avEK anh grANH LEE; a room with a double bed). A **taxe de séjour** (residency tax) of €0.75-1.50 per person per night is generally included in the quoted price. Hotel breakfast normally runs €3.50-6.25, usually consisting of coffee or hot chocolate as well as bread and/or croissants. Local cafés may give you a better deal. French hotels must display a list of the prices of rooms, breakfast, and any residency tax on the back of each room's door. It is illegal to charge more than shown. Rooms in cheap hotels normally have no *en suite* facilities—even the sink is in the hall. Occasionally you must pay extra for a hot shower (€2.30-3.80). Some very cheap hotels have no washing facilities at all. Otherwise, rooms can come *avec WC* or *avec cabinet* (with sink and toilet), *avec douche* (with shower), and *avec salle de bain* (with full bathroom). Many bathrooms also have a *bidet*, a low toilet-like apparatus used to clean your genitalia and your arse. "Turkish toilets"—porcelain-rimmed holes in the floor—still exist in parts of France; put your feet where indicated, don't fall over, and make sure the light timer doesn't run out.

Hotels listed in *Let's Go* are generally small, family-run establishments close to sights of interest. *Let's Go* doesn't list the budget chains like *Hôtels Formule 1*, *Etap Hôtel*, and *Hôtels Première Classe*, which can usually be found on the out-

skirts of town. These typically charge €27-31 for one to three person rooms, have rooms with sink, TV, hall showers, toilets, and telephones, and allow you to rent with a credit card when the reception is closed.

When visiting a popular tourist area, especially during a festival, write or fax ahead for reservations. Most hotel owners require either a deposit or credit card number as a guarantee of your reservation. If you don't show up or stay less time than you reserved, they have the right to charge you for their loss of earnings.

OTHER OPTIONS

GÎTES D'ETAPE AND MOUNTAIN REFUGES. Gîtes d'étape are rural accommodations for cyclists, hikers, and other outdoorspeople. These farmhouses, cottages, and campgrounds are located in less populated areas, normally beside major biking and hiking trails. Though they vary widely in price (averaging €10) and quality, *gîtes* generally have beds, kitchen facilities, and a resident caretaker. During the high season, *gîtes* in resort towns fill up quickly; reserve in advance. Don't confuse *gîtes d'étapes* with *gîtes ruraux*, country houses rented by the week.

Hikers and skiers on extended treks frequently make use of the *refuge*, a rustic shelter overseen by a do-it-all caretaker. *Refuge* accommodations range in price €6.50-12.50. Hot, homecooked meals typically cost up to €12. *Refuges* are not always guarded year-round, but their doors generally remain open all year for hikers and skiers on the road.

CHAMBRES D'HÔTE (BED AND BREAKFASTS). Some French house-owners supplement their income by letting rooms to travelers. These **chambres d'hôte,** or bed-and-breakfasts, range from acceptable rooms in modern townhouses to palatial chambers in Baroque châteaux. Most cost €30-45 per night. For a comprehensive listing of *chambres d'hôte* in France, buy **Selected Bed & Breakfasts in France 2001** in a bookstore or from Thomas Cook Publishing, P.O. Box 227, Units 19-21, Thomas Cook Business Park, Peterborough PE3 8XX, UK (☎ 44 1733 416477; www.thomascook.com/books). **Fleurs de Soleil** (www.fleurs-soleil.tm.fr) and **B&B** (www.bedbreak.com) list *chambres d'hôte* throughout France. For more info on B&Bs around the world and in France, contact **InnFinder,** 6200 Gisholt Dr., #105 Madison, WI 53713 (www.inncrawler.com) or **InnSite** (www.innsite.com).

UNIVERSITY HOUSING. Many universities open their clean dorm rooms to travelers when classes are out, and occassionally in term-time, at low rates. The *Let's Go* listings for each town mention available university accommodations.

HOME EXCHANGE AND RENTALS. In a **home exchange** program, you get to live for free in a French residence (a house, apartment, villa, even a castle) while a French family lives in yours. Some exchange services are listed below. It is also possible to **rent homes**, which can be a cheap bet for large groups.

HomeExchange, P.O. Box 30085, Santa Barbara, CA 93130, USA (☎ 310-798-3864; fax 310-798-3865; www.HomeExchange.com). US$30 for a 1yr. listing.

Intervac International Home Exchange, 230 bd. Voltaire, 75011 Paris (☎ 01 43 70 21 22; fax 01 43 70 73 35; info@intervac.fr; www.intervac.org/france).

The Invented City: International Home Exchange, 41 Sutter St., Suite 1090, San Francisco, CA 94404, USA (☎ 415-252-1141; www.invented-city.com). US$40 per year for unlimited access to a database of thousands of homes.

FURTHER READING. *The Complete Guide to Bed and Breakfasts, Inns and Guesthouses in the US, Canada, and Worldwide,* by Pamela Lanier (Ten Speed Press, US$17).

CAMPING AND THE OUTDOORS

The French are avid campers, but not in the sense you might be used to. After three thousand years of settled history, there is little wilderness in France. It is illegal to camp in public spaces or light your own fires. Forget those romantic dreams of roughing it and prepare to share organized *campings* (campsites) with hundreds of fellow campers. Sites generally cost around €3. Most campsites have toilets, showers, and electrical outlets, though often at extra expense (€1.50-6.00). Cars may incur an additional €3.00-7.50 charge.

PUBLICATIONS AND WEB RESOURCES

For info about camping, hiking, and biking, write or call the publishers listed below. Campers heading to Europe should consider buying an **International Camping Carnet.** Like the hostel membership card, it's required at a few campgrounds and provides discounts at others. It is available in North America from the **Family Campers and RVers Association** and in the UK from **The Caravan Club** (see below). The **Great Outdoor Recreation Pages** (www.gorp.com) is an excellent resource for travelers in the outdoors.

Automobile Association, Contact Centre, Car Ellison House, William Armstrong Drive, Newcastle-upon-Tyne NE4 7YA, UK. (General info ☎0870 600 0371; fax 0191 235 5111; www.theaa.co.uk). Publishes Big Road Atlases for Europe, France, Spain, Germany, and Italy.

The Caravan Club, East Grinstead House, East Grinstead, West Sussex, RH19 1UA, UK (☎01342 326 944; fax 410 258; www.caravanclub.co.uk). For UK£27.50, members get equipment discounts, a 700page directory and handbook, and monthly magazine.

The Mountaineers Books, 1001 SW Klickitat Way, #201, Seattle, WA 98134, USA (☎800-553-4453 or 206-223-6303; fax 223-6306; www.mountaineersbooks.org). Over 400 titles on hiking, biking, mountaineering, natural history, and conservation.

Hikers will want to bring or acquire guidebooks for their travels. The **Institut Géographique National (IGN)** publishes the acclaimed **Blue Series** of maps for hikers, as well as many road maps. The Blue Series is sold throughout France; for more info contact their map superstore in Paris, **Éspace IGN,** 107 rue La Boétie, 75008 Paris (☎01 43 98 80 00; espace-ign@ign.fr; www.ign.fr/GP/adresse). You can buy IGN maps in **Australia** from **Hema maps,** P.O. Box 4365, Eight Mile Plains QLD 4113 Australia (☎07 334 00 00), in **Canada** from **Ulysse,** 4176 St. Denis, Montreal, Québec H2W 2M5 (☎514-843-9447; www.ulysse.ca), in the **UK** from Travellers World Bookshop, Newmarket Court, Derby DE24 8NW (☎01332 57 37 37; www.mapworld.co.uk), and in the **US** from Map Link Inc., 30 S. La Patera Lane, Unit #5, Santa Barbara, CA 93117 (☎805-692-6777; fax 962-6787; www.maplink.com).

CAMPING AND HIKING EQUIPMENT

Sleeping Bag: Sleeping bags are identified by the season they are designed for ("summer" means 30-40°F at night; "four-season" or "winter" means below 0°F). They are made either of **down** (warm and light, but disgusting when wet) or **synthetic** material (durable and less soggy when wet). Prices range US$80-210 for a summer synthetic, US$250-300 for a quality down winter bag. Sleeping bags can be accompanied by foam pads (US$10-20), air mattresses (US$15-50), and Therm-A-Rest self-inflating pads (US$45-80). A **stuff sack** stores your sleeping bag and keeps it dry.

Tent: Low-profile dome tents are your best bet; they are free-standing and set up quickly. Good 2-person tents start at US$90, 4-person US$300. Seal the seams of your tent with **waterproofer**, and bring a **battery-operated lantern**, a **plastic ground-cloth**, and a **nylon tarp**.

Backpack: Flexible **internal-frame packs** mold to your back and maintain a low center of gravity. Less flexible **external-frame packs** are more comfortable for long hikes over even terrain; they keep weight higher and distribute it more evenly. Your pack should have a strong, padded hip-belt to transfer weight to your legs. Serious backpackers need at least 4000 in^3 (16,000cc) of pack space. Sturdy backpacks cost US$125-420. Before buying a pack, fill it up, walk around, and evaluate the weight distribution. Buy a **waterproof backpack cover** or store all of your belongings in plastic bags.

Boots: Bring hiking boots with good **ankle support** that fit snugly and comfortably over 2 pairs of socks (wool and thin liner). Break in your boots before hiking.

Other Necessities: Synthetic layers (like polypropylene) and a **pile jacket** maintain warmth even when wet. A **space blanket** (US$5-15) retains your body heat and doubles as a groundcloth. Bring shatter- and leak-proof plastic **water bottles** and **water-purification tablets** in case you cannot boil water. Since most French campgrounds forbid making fires, you'll need a **camp stove** (the classic Coleman starts at US$40) and a propane **fuel bottle**. Also don't forget a **first-aid kit, pocketknife, insect repellent, calamine lotion**, and **waterproof matches** or a **lighter**.

CAMPERS AND RVS

Renting an RV is more expensive than tenting or hosteling, but cheaper than staying in hotels and renting a car. Plus you get to have your own bedroom, bathroom, and kitchen. Rates vary widely by region, season (July and August are most expensive), and type of RV. Rental prices for a standard RV are around US $1200.

Auto Europe (US ☎800-223-5555, UK toll-free 0800 169 6414; www.autoeurope.com) rents RVs in Paris, Lyon, and Marseilles.

ORGANIZED ADVENTURE TRIPS

Organized adventure tours are structured ways of exploring the wild through organized activities like hiking, biking, skiing, canoeing, kayaking, rafting, climbing, photo safaris, and archaeological digs. Tourism bureaus and stores that specialize in camping and outdoor equipment will have info about these tours (see above).

Specialty Travel Index, 305 San Anselmo Ave., #313, San Anselmo, CA 94960, USA (☎800-442-4922 or 415-459-4900; fax 415-459-9474; info@specialtytravel.com; www.specialtytravel.com). Tours worldwide.

WILDERNESS SAFETY

Stay warm, stay dry, and stay hydrated. Follow this mantra and you will avoid most life-threatening wilderness situations. Prepare for the unexpected by packing raingear, a hat and mittens, a first-aid kit, a reflector, a whistle, high energy food, and extra water. Dress in wool or warm synthetic layers. The weather can change suddenly: check **weather forecasts** and pay attention to the sky; www.intellicast.com/LocalWeather/World/Europe and www.meteo.fr provide up-to-date meteorological info. Let a friend, hostel owner, park ranger, or local hiking organization know when and where you are hiking. Do not attempt a hike beyond your ability. See **Health,** p. 43, for info about outdoor ailments and medical concerns.

ENVIRONMENTALLY RESPONSIBLE TOURISM. Responsible tourism means leaving nothing behind when you leave the outdoors. Use a campstove rather than a fire or make a small fire of dead branches and brush. Place your campsite at least 150 ft. (50m) from bodies of water. Find a toilet or bury human waste (but not paper) at least four inches (10cm) deep and above the high-water line, 150 ft. or more from any sources of water or campsites. Pack your trash in a plastic bag and carry it until you reach a trash receptacle. For more info, contact one of these organizations.

Earthwatch, 3 Clock Tower Pl. #100, Box 75, Maynard, MA 01754, USA (☎800-776-0188 or 978-461-0081; info@earthwatch.org; www.earthwatch.org).

International Ecotourism Society, 28 Pine St., Burlington, VT 05402, USA (☎802-651-9818; fax 802-651-9819; ecomail@ecotourism.org; www.ecotourism.org).

National Audubon Society, Nature Odysseys, 700 Broadway, New York, NY 10003, USA (☎212-979-3000; fax 979-3188; webmaster@audubon.org; www.audubon.org).

Tourism Concern, Stapleton House, 277-281 Holloway Rd., London N7 8HN, UK (☎020 7753 3330; fax 7753 3331; info@tourismconcern.org.uk; www.tourismconcern.org.uk).

KEEPING IN TOUCH

MAIL

SENDING MAIL FROM FRANCE

Surface mail is by far the cheapest and slowest way to send mail. It takes one to three months to cross the Atlantic and two to four to cross the Pacific. **Airmail** is the fastest way to send mail home. **Aerogrammes,** printed sheets that fold into envelopes, more private versions of post cards, travel by air and are faster than regular airmail. Purchase an aerogramme at a post office and write *par avion* on the front. It is usually impossible or expensive to send enclosures with aerogrammes.

SENDING MAIL TO FRANCE

Mark envelopes *air mail* or *par avion* or your letter or postcard will never arrive. In addition to the standard postage system, **Federal Express** (US and Canada ☎800-247-4747, Australia 13 26 10, New Zealand 0800 73 33 39, UK 0800 12 38 00; www.fedex.com) handles express mail services from many countries to France; they can get a letter from New York to France in 2 days for US $75 and from London to Paris in 2 days for US$42.

RECEIVING MAIL IN FRANCE

Mail can be sent Poste Restante (French for General Delivery) to a city or town to be picked up by the addressee at a later date. Address letters in this format:

PICARD, Jean-Luc
Poste Restante: Recette Principale
[5-digit postal code] TOWN
FRANCE.
HOLD.

Let's Go lists post offices and postal codes and notes when a town's Poste Restante code differs from its postal code. To pick up Poste Restante mail, bring a passport and €0.45. Mail can be held for a maximum of 15 days. Post offices will not accept courier service deliveries (e.g. Federal Express) or anything requiring a signature for *Poste Restante*.

BY TELEPHONE

CALLING HOME FROM FRANCE

A calling card is the cheapest way to call home. Cards are either billed or prepaid. **Billed** cards can be obtained for a small fee and charge the recipient of your call or bill you upon your return home. These tend to be more expensive but need not be constantly renewed. **Prepaid** calls subtract calling charges from a predetermined amount. These are cheaper, but less convenient. Do not use cards to call within France—the company will bill you for the call to the overseas access number and then for the call from the access number to France. You can frequently call collect without buying a company's calling card by dialing their access number and following instructions (see **International Direct Dial,** below). To obtain a calling card or the access number, contact your national telecommunications service.

COMPANY	TO OBTAIN A CARD, DIAL:	COLLECT NUMBER:
AT&T (US)	888-288-4685	0 800 99 00 11
British Telecom Direct	800 34 51 44	0 800 99 02 44
Canada Direct	800-668-6878	0 800 99 00 16
Ireland Direct	800 40 00 00	0 800 99 03 53
MCI (US)	800-444-3333	0 800 99 00 19
New Zealand Direct	0800 00 00 00	0 800 99 00 64
Sprint (US)	800 877-4646	0 800 99 00 97
Telkom South Africa	10 219	0 800 99 00 27
Telestra Australia	13 22 00	0 800 99 00 61

Let's Go has recently partnered with ekit.com to provide a calling card that offers a number of services, including email and voice messanging. Before purchasing any calling card, always be sure to compare rates with other cards, and to make sure it serves your needs (a local phonecard is generally better for local calls, for instance). For more information, visit www.letsgo.ekit.com.

You can place direct international calls on pay phones without a phone card, but you will need to drop coins as fast as you talk. Placing a collect call through an international operator is even more expensive; consider it only in an emergency.

CALLING WITHIN FRANCE

The simplest way to call within France is to use a coin-operated phone. Unfortunately, finding one is nearly impossible. A better option is a **prepaid phone card,** or *Télécarte* (available at newspaper kiosks and tobacco stores). Most often, you pay beforehand for a certain amount of phone time and swipe the card at the phone to place calls. Another kind of prepaid telephone card comes with a Personal Identification Number (PIN) and a toll-free access number and can be used to make international as well as domestic calls. *Télécartes* are available in 50-unit (€7.50) and 120-unit (€15) denominations; one minute of a local call uses about one unit. When you use the card, a small digital screen on the phone issues a series of simple commands; press the small button marked with a British flag to get them in English. If no button exists, proceed with caution, since French pay-

PLACING INTERNATIONAL CALLS. To call France from home or to call home from France, dial:

1. The **international dialing prefix.** To call out of France, dial ☎00; **Australia,** 0011; **Canada** or the **US,** 011; the **Republic of Ireland, New Zealand,** or the **UK, 00; South Africa,** 09.
2. The **country code** of the country you want to call. For **Australia,** dial ☎61; **Canada** or the **US,** 1; the **Republic of Ireland,** 353; **New Zealand,** 64; **South Africa,** 27; the **UK,** 44; **France,** 33.
3. The **city/area code.** *Let's Go* lists the city/area codes for each French city and town; find it after the ☎ symbol next to the city/town name. Omit the first zero of this number when calling from abroad (e.g. dial 20, not 020, to reach London from Canada).
4. The **local number.**

phones are notoriously unforgiving. *Décrochez* means pick up; *patientez* means wait. Do not dial until you see *numérotez* or *composez*. *Raccrochez* means "hang up," usually because you did something wrong. To make another call, press the green button instead of hanging up. French phone boxes normally display a complicated wall chart showing phone rates, which tend to be high in the morning, intermediate in the evening, and low on Sundays and late at night. Calls with a 120-unit card are 50% cheaper after 7pm Monday to Friday, from noon to midnight Saturday, and all day Sunday. Expect to pay about €0.45 per minute to the UK, Ireland, and North America and about €1.50 per minute to Australia, New Zealand, and South Africa. Use only public **France Télécom** payphones; private ones often charge more.

Calling collect, *faire un appel en PCV*, is an expensive alternative to the calling card, and only very good friends will accept the call. Though convenient, in-room hotel calls often incur arbitrary and pricey surcharges (as much as US$10).

CELL PHONES

A cell phone from outside Europe can be used in France if it has been registered at home for international service and if its band has been switched to 900/1800. Switching bands will automatically register your phone with one of the three French cell phone servers: Bouygue, Itineris, or France Télécom.

I'LL TRADE MY '52 MANTLE FOR YOUR '88 GERARD LONGUET

If you're in France for any length of time, you'll eventually give up the futile search for coin-operated telephones and invest in a *télécarte*. To you, the card is merely a useful item, but to some it might as well be a Babe Ruth rookie card or a unique coin. The ads and artwork on the cards turn some designs into valuable commodities; an entire *télécarte* collection business has developed around the credit-card sized *chef d'oeuvres*. Common and uncommon cards are sold in stores for several euros; rare specimens lie protected in acrylic cases. The condition of a card affects its value, as does the artist who drew its images. A 1987-88 *carte* by Gerard Longuet is one of the gems in the *télécarte* collector's crown. Only 40 exist; an unblemished one will net you €6,000. For the real prize, seek out the November 1988 card "Les Boxeurs," with artwork by Gilles Chagny. There are 100 out there, but only one is signed by the artist. Maybe it's down at your feet right now as you make your call—if it is, you've just stumbled across a cool €15,000.

EMAIL

Most major **post offices** and some branches now offer Internet access at special "cyberposte" terminals; you can buy a rechargeable card that gives you 50 minutes of access at the post office for €8. Note that *Let's Go* **does not list** "cyberposte" locations. Most large towns in France have at least one cybercafé, which can be found in the Practical Information section of the town listing. Rates and speed of connection vary widely; on rare occasions, you can find free terminals in technologically-oriented museums or exhibitions. **Cybercafé Guide** (www.cyberiacafe.net/cyberia/guide/ccafe.htm#working_france) can find a cybercafé near you.

Beware: many hotel switchboards use the **PBX** system, which fries modems without a **converter** (US$50). The cost of a modem call is steep, unless your phone card defrays the cost (check with the phone card company).

MEDIA IN FRANCE

LES JOURNAUX. *Le Monde* is France's newspaper of record. Most French papers are politically oriented. *Le Figaro* is slightly right-of-center and popular. *Le Parisien* targets readers in the capital. *Le Libération* ("Libé") is big among left-wingers, *L'Humanité* among the Communist fringe. Many French read newsmagazines, including the liberal *Nouvel Observateur*; the conservative and airy *L'Express*; the vacuous *Paris-Match*; and the witty, complex *le Canard Enchaîné*. The *New York Times*, the *Times of London*, and the *International Herald Tribune* can be purchased in major cities.

LA RADIO. Most corporate and public radio stations are national. Popular national stations are *Fun Radio*, *NRJ*, and *Skyrock* for teens; *Nostalgie* for older listeners; and *Europe 1* with news. Public stations include *France Inter*, a general-interest station, and *France Info*, a news channel. Most music played is anglophone: a French law requires that radios play 40% francophone music, but stations typically fill the quota between 1 and 6 am. Check local radio frequencies at www.mobiquid.com/fr/frequence.v22.asp.

TELEVISION. France has six major national TV channels. Three are public: **France 2** with news, educational, and entertainment shows; **France 3** with regional programs and occasional news; **La Cinquième** with cartoons, game shows, and documentaries until 7 pm, when it becomes **Arte**, a cultural channel. Three channels are private. **Canal+** exhibits foreign and French films; **TF1,** the most popular station in France, produces news, sports, and general-interest programs; **M6,** a more vacuous version of the American MTV, is geared towards teenagers and young adults. France has 25 cable channels, as well as numerous local stations.

GETTING TO FRANCE

BY PLANE

Putting in a little effort searching for flights pays off. If you are able to tolerate certain restrictions, cheap courier fares are ideal. Purchasing from consolidators or flying standby save money; taking advantage of last-minute specials, airfare wars, and charter flights saves even more. Students, seniors, and youths should never pay full price for a ticket.

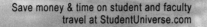
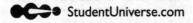

AIRFARES

Airfares to France peak between June and September and at Easter and Christmas. The cheapest fares involve a Saturday night stay. Traveling with an "open return" ticket is pricier than fixing a return date. Most fixed budget tickets don't allow date or route changes. Round-trip flights are much cheaper than "open-jaw" trips (arriving and departing from different cities). Flights between capitals or regional hubs have the cheapest fares. Paris is the most affordable point of entry from outside Europe, though other cities offer good fares to travelers from Ireland and the UK. Globe-hoppers should consider a **Round-the-World (RTW)** ticket, which includes at least 3 stops, is priced by total mileage, and remains valid for a year after purchase. Prices range US$3500-5000. Try **Northwest Airlines/KLM** (US ☎800-447-4747; www.nwa.com) or **Star Alliance,** a consortium of 13 airlines including United Airlines (US ☎800- 241-6522; www.star-alliance.com). Round-trip fares to Paris from the US range from US$250-500 (off-season) to US$300-800 (summer); from Australia, between AUS$1600 and AUS$2500; from New Zealand, NZ$5000-9000; from the Britain, UK£60-80; from Dublin to Paris, as little as IR£120. When flying internationally, pick up tickets well in advance of the departure date and reconfirm by phone within 72 hours of departure. Most airlines require that passengers arrive at the airport at least two hours before departure. Travelers flying out of EU countries are entitled to full compensation if their flight is overbooked and they have a confirmed ticket and checked in on time. Most non-courier international flights permit one carry-on item (max 5kg) and two pieces of checked baggage (up to 60kg total); flights within Europe generally allow travelers to check baggage up 20-30kg, regardless of the number of pieces.

BUDGET & STUDENT TRAVEL AGENCIES

Though travel agencies can make your life easier, they may not always find the lowest possible fare since they get paid on commission. Travelers holding **ISIC** and **IYTC cards** (see p. 35) can get discounts on student travel agency services.

usit world (www.usitworld.com). Over 50 **usit campus** branches in the UK, including 52 Grosvenor Gardens, **London** SW1W 0AG (☎08702 401010); **Manchester** (☎01612 731880); and **Edinburgh** (☎0131 668 3303). Nearly 20 **usit NOW** offices in Ireland, including 19-21 Aston Quay, O'Connell Bridge, **Dublin** (☎016 021600), and **Belfast** (☎02890 327111). Offices also in Athens, Auckland, Brussels, Frankfurt, Johannesburg, Lisbon, Luxembourg, Madrid, Paris, Sofia, and Warsaw.

Council Travel (www.counciltravel.com; 800-226-8624). Countless US offices, including branches in Atlanta, Boston, Chicago, L.A., New York, San Francisco, Seattle, and Washington, D.C. Also an office at 28A Poland St., Oxford Circus, **London**, W1V 3DB (☎02074 377767). In May 2002, Council declared bankruptcy and was subsumed by STA. However, their offices are still open and transacting business.

CTS Travel, 44 Goodge St., **London** W1T 2AD, UK(☎0207 636 0031; fax 637 5328; ctsinfo@ctstravel.co.uk).

STA Travel, 7890 S. Hardy Dr., Suite 110, Tempe, AZ 85284, USA (24hr. reservations and info ☎800-781-4040; www.sta-travel.com). A student and youth travel organization with over 150 offices worldwide, including US offices in Boston, Chicago, L.A., New York, San Francisco, Seattle, and Washington, D.C. Ticket booking, travel insurance, railpasses, and more. In the UK, walk-in office 11 Goodge St., **London** W1T 2PF (0207-436-7779). In New Zealand, Shop 2B, 182 Queen St., **Auckland** (☎09 309 0458). In Australia, 366 Lygon St., **Carlton** Vic 3053 (☎03 9349 4344).

Travel CUTS (Canadian Universities Travel Services Limited), 187 College St., **Toronto,** ON M5T 1P7 (☎416-979-2406; fax 979-8167; www.travelcuts.com). 60 offices across Canada. Also in the UK, 295-A Regent St., **London** W1R 7YA (☎02072 551944).

ESSENTIALS

Wasteels, Skoubogade 6, 1158 Copenhagen K. (☎3314 4633 fax 7630 0865; www.wasteels.dk/uk). A huge chain with 165 locations across Europe. Sells BIJ tickets discounted 30-45% off regular fare.

Contiki Holidays (888-CONTIKI; www.contiki.com) offers a variety of European vacation packages designed for 18- to 35-year-olds. For an average cost of $60 per day, tours include accommodations, transportation, guided sightseeing and some meals.

✈ FLIGHT PLANNING ON THE INTERNET.

Many airline sites offer special last-minute deals on the Web. Other sites do the legwork and compile the deals for you—try www.bestfares.com, www.flights.com, www.hotdeals.com, www.lowestfare.com, www.onetravel.com, and www.travelzoo.com.

▧ StudentUniverse (www.studentuniverse.com), STA (www.sta-travel.com), Council (www.counciltravel.com) and **Orbitz.com** provide quotes on student tickets. **Expedia** (www.expedia.com) and **Travelocity** (www.travelocity.com) offer full travel services. **Priceline** (www.priceline.com) has you specify your desired price and obligates you to buy any ticket that meets or beats it, including ones with late hours and odd routes. **Skyauction** (www.skyauction.com) allows you to bid on both last-minute and advance-purchase tickets.

An indispensable Internet resource is the *Air Traveler's Handbook* (www.cs.cmu.edu/afs/cs/user/mkant/Public/Travel/airfare.html), a comprehensive listing of links to everything you need to know before you board a plane.

COMMERCIAL AIRLINES

TRAVELING FROM NORTH AMERICA

Basic round-trip fares to Western Europe range roughly US$200-750; to Frankfurt, US$300-750; London, US$200-600; Paris, US$250-700. Standard commercial carriers like American (☎800-433-7300; www.aa.com) and United (☎800-241-6522; www.ual.com) offer the most convenient flights, but rarely the cheapest. You might find a better deal on one of the following airlines.

Icelandair, ☎800-223-5500; www.icelandair.com. Stopovers in Iceland for no extra cost on most transatlantic flights. New York to Frankfurt May-Sept. US$500-730; Oct.-May US$390-$450. For last-minute offers, subscribe to their email *Lucky Fares.*

Finnair, ☎800-950-5000; www.us.finnair.com. Cheap round-trips from San Francisco, New York, and Toronto to Helsinki; connections throughout Europe.

Martinair, ☎800-627-8462; www.martinair.com. Fly from California or Florida to Amsterdam mid-June to mid-Aug. US$880; mid-Aug. to mid-June US$730.

Air France, ☎802-802-802; www.airfrance.com. France's national airline, connecting France to the world with 162 flights per week to the US alone.

United Airlines, ☎800-538-2929; www.ual.com. Mammoth US carrier offers last-minute special e-fares deals available only online.

Cathay Pacific, in France ☎01 41 43 75 75; in Australia ☎13 17 47. Reasonable RTW fares and flights to Paris, connecting to Australia via Hong Kong.

TRAVELING FROM THE UK & IRELAND

The **Air Travel Advisory Bureau** in London (☎020 7636 5000; www.atab.co.uk) refers you to travel agencies and consolidators with discounted airfares from the UK.

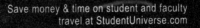

Aer Lingus, Ireland ☎0818 365000; www.aerlingus.ie. Return tickets from Dublin, Cork, Galway, Kerry, and Shannon to Amsterdam, Brussels, Dusseldorf, Frankfurt, Helsinki, Madrd, Milan, Munich, Paris, Rennes, Rome, Stockholm, and Zurich (IR£102-244).

British Midland Airways, UK ☎08706 070555; www.flybmi.com. London to Paris UK£71.

buzz, UK ☎0870 2407070; www.buzzaway.com. A subsidiary of KLM. London to Paris UK£50-80. Tickets can not be changed or refunded.

easyJet, UK ☎0870 600000; www.easyjet.com. London to Amsterdam, Athens, Barcelona, Geneva, Madrid, Nice, Palma, and Zurich (UK£47-136). Online tickets.

KLM, UK ☎08705 074074; www.klmuk.com. Cheap return tickets from London and elsewhere to Amsterdam, Brussels, Frankfurt, Düsseldorf, Milan, Paris, and Rome.

Ryanair, Ireland ☎0818 303 030, in UK 0870 156 95 69; www.ryanair.ie. From Dublin, London, and Glasgow to destinations in France, Ireland, Italy, Scandinavia, and elsewhere. Deals from as low as UK£9 on limited weekend specials.

Virgin Express, UK ☎02077 440004; France ☎0800 528528; www.virgin-express.com. Connects London to Nice via Brussels from UK£39 one-way.

TRAVELING FROM AUSTRALIA & NEW ZEALAND

Air New Zealand, New Zealand ☎0800 737000; www.airnz.co.nz. Auckland to London and Frankfurt.

Qantas Air, Australia ☎13 13 13, New Zealand ☎0800 808767; www.qantas.com.au. Flights from Australia and New Zealand to London around AUS$2400.

Singapore Air, Australia ☎13 10 11, New Zealand ☎0800 808909; www.singaporeair.com. From Auckland, Sydney, Melbourne, and Perth to Western Europe.

Thai Airways, Australia ☎1300 65 19 60, New Zealand ☎093 770268; www.thaiair.com. Auckland, Sydney, and Melbourne to Amsterdam, Frankfurt, and London.

TRAVELING FROM SOUTH AFRICA

Air France, ☎01 17 70 16 01; www.airfrance.com/za. Johannesburg to Paris; connections throughout Europe.

British Airways, ☎0860 011747; www.british-airways.com/regional/sa. Cape Town and Johannesburg to the UK and the rest of Europe from SAR3400.

Lufthansa, ☎0861 842538; www.lufthansa.co.za. From Cape Town, Durban, and Johannesburg to Germany and elsewhere.

Virgin Atlantic, ☎0113 403400; www.virgin-atlantic.co.za. Flies to London from Cape Town and Johannesburg.

AIR COURIER FLIGHTS

If you travel light, consider courier flights. As a courier, you take only carry-on and allow the airline to use your luggage space to transport cargo. Most courier flights are round-trip only, with short fixed length stays (usually one week) and many restrictions. Most flights leave from New York, Los Angeles, San Francisco, or Miami in the US; and from Montreal, Toronto, or Vancouver in Canada. Round-trip courier fares from the US to France vary greatly, but can be as low as US$200. Generally, couriers must be over 21. In summer, the most popular destinations usually require an advance reservation of about two weeks.

FROM NORTH AMERICA

Round-trip courier fares from the US to Western Europe run about US$200-500. The organizations below provide members with lists of opportunities and courier brokers for an annual fee. Quoted prices are round-trip.

Air Courier Association, 350 Indiana St., #300 Golden, CO 80401 (☎800-282-1202; www.aircourier.org). Ten departure cities throughout the US and Canada to London, Madrid, Paris, Rome, and throughout western Europe (high-season US$150-360). One-year membership US$49.

International Association of Air Travel Couriers (IAATC), P.O. Box 980, Keystone Heights, FL 32656 (☎352-475-1584; fax 475-5326; www.courier.org). From 9 North American cities to Western European cities, including London, Madrid, Paris, and Rome. One-year membership US$45.

Global Courier Travel, P.O. Box 3051, Nederland, CO 80466 (www.globalcourier-travel.com). Searchable online database. 6 departure points in the US and Canada to Amsterdam, Athens, Brussels, Copenhagen, Frankfurt, London, Madrid, Milan, Paris, and Rome. Lifetime membership US$40, 2 people US$55.

NOW Voyager, 315 W 49th St., New York, NY 10019 (☎212-459-1616; fax 262-7407). To Amsterdam, Brussels, Copenhagen, Dublin, London, Madrid, Milan, Paris, and Rome (US$499-699). Usually 1wk. max. stay. 1yr. membership US$50. Non-courier discount fares also available.

FROM THE UK, IRELAND, AUSTRALIA, & NEW ZEALAND

The minimum age for couriers from the **UK** is usually 18. **Brave New World Enterprises,** P.O. Box 22212, London SE5 8WB (info@courierflights.com; www.courier-flights.com) publishes a directory of all the companies offering courier flights in the UK (UK£10, in electronic form UK£8). **Global Courier Travel** (see above) also offers flights from London and Dublin to continental Europe. **British Airways Travel Shop** (☎08702 400747; info@batravelshops.com; www.batravelshops.com) arranges some flights from London to destinations in continental Europe (specials may be as low as UK£60). **Global Courier Travel** (see above) has listings from Sydney and Auckland to London and occasionally Frankfurt.

STANDBY FLIGHTS

Companies dealing in standby flights sell vouchers rather than tickets with the promise to get you to or near your destination within a certain window of time (typically one to five days). Call in before your window of time to hear your flight options, including the probability that you will be able to board each flight. Then decide which flights you want to try to make, show up at the appropriate airport at the appropriate time, present your voucher, and board if space is available. You may receive a monetary refund if every available flight within your date range is full but you will receive only credit (if that) if you do not attempt to board an available flight. Carefully read agreements with standby companies, as there can be unfavorable fine print. To check on a company's service record in the US, call the Better Business Bureau (☎212-533-6200). One established standby company in the US is **Whole Earth Travel,** 325 W. 38th St., New York, NY 10018, USA (☎800-326-2009, Los Angeles ☎888-247-4482; fax 212-864-5489; www.4standby.com), which offers one-way flights to Europe from the US (US$169-249) and intracontinental connecting flights within the US for Europe (US$79-139).

TICKET CONSOLIDATORS

Ticket consolidators, or **"bucket shops,"** buy unsold tickets in bulk from commercial airlines and sell them at discounted rates. The best place to look is in the Sunday travel section of any major newspaper (such as the *New York Times*), where many bucket shops place tiny ads. Call quickly, as availability is limited. Not all bucket shops are reliable; insist on a receipt that gives full details of restrictions, refunds, and tickets, and pay by credit card (in spite of the 2-5% fee) so you can stop payment if you never receive your tickets. For more info, see www.travel-library.com/air-travel/consolidators.html.

TRAVELING FROM THE US & CANADA

Travel Avenue (☎ 800-333-3335; www.travelavenue.com) searches for best available published fares and then uses several consolidators to attempt to beat that fare. **NOW Voyager,** 74 Varick St., Ste. 307, New York, NY 10013 (☎ 212-431-1616; fax 219-1793; www.nowvoyagertravel.com) arranges discounted flights, mostly from New York, to Barcelona, London, Madrid, Milan, Paris, and Rome. Other worthwhile consolidators are **Interworld** (☎ 305-443-4929; fax 443-0351); **Pennsylvania Travel** (☎ 800-331-0947); **Rebel** (☎ 800-227-3235; travel@rebeltours.com; www.rebeltours.com); **Cheap Tickets** (☎ 800-377-1000; www.cheaptickets.com); and **Travac** (☎ 800-872-8800; fax 212-714-9063; www.travac.com); **Internet Travel Network** (www.itn.com); **Travel Information Services** (www.tiss.com); **TravelHUB** (www.travelhub.com); and **The Travel Site** (www.thetravelsite.com). *Let's Go* does not in any way endorse these agencies.

TRAVELING FROM THE UK, AUSTRALIA, & NEW ZEALAND

In London, the **Air Travel Advisory Bureau** (☎ 0207-636-5000; www.atab.co.uk) provides names of reliable consolidators and discount flight specialists. From Australia and New Zealand, look for consolidator ads in the travel section of the *Sydney Morning Herald* and other papers.

CHARTER FLIGHTS

Tour operators contract charters with an airline to fly sizeable numbers of passengers during peak season. Charter flights fly less frequently than major airlines and are often fully booked. Flights may be cancelled or change their schedule as late as 48 hours before the trip without a full refund. Check-in, boarding, and baggage claim are often slow. Charter flights are, however, usually cheaper.

Discount clubs and **fare brokers** offer savings to members on last-minute charter and tour deals. Study contracts closely, as they may involve an overnight layover. **Travelers Advantage,** Trumbull, CT, USA (☎ 203-365-2000; www.travelersadvantage.com; US$60 annual fee includes discounts and cheap flight directories) specializes in European travel and tour packages.

BY CHUNNEL FROM THE UK

Traversing 27 mi. under the sea, the Chunnel is undoubtedly the fastest, most convenient, and least scenic route from England to France.

BY TRAIN. Eurostar, Eurostar House, Waterloo Station, London SE1 8SE (UK ☎ 0990 186 186; US ☎ 800-387-6782; elsewhere call UK 020 7928 5163; www.eurostar.com) runs frequent trains between London and the continent. Ten to twenty-eight trains per day run to Paris (3hr., €75-159), Brussels (3hr., 50min., €75-159), and Eurodisney. Routes include stops at Ashford in England, and Calais and Lille in France.

BY BUS. Both **Eurolines** and **Eurobus** provide bus-ferry combinations (see p. 67).

BY CAR. Eurotunnel, P.O. Box 2000, Folkestone, Kent CT18 8XY (www.eurotunnel.co.uk) shuttles cars and passengers between Kent and Nord-Pas-de-Calais. Return fares for vehicle and all passengers UK£219-317 with car, UK£259-636 with campervan. Same-day return UK£110-150, five-day return UK£139-195. Book online or via phone.

BY BUS

For British travelers, buses are the cheapest way to get to France, with return fares starting around UK£50 including ferry/chunnel transport. Often cheaper than railpasses, **international bus passes** typically allow unlimited hop-on, hop-off travel between major European cities. Note that **Eurobus,** a onetime UK-based bus service, is no longer in operation.

> **Eurolines,** 4 Cardiff Rd., Luton LU1 1PP, UK (☎08705 808080; fax 01582 400694); 52 Grosvenor Gardens, **London** SW1W OAU (☎01582 404 511; welcome@euro-lines.uk.com; www.eurolines.com). Roundtrip London to Paris fares from UK£49.

> **Busabout,** 258 Vauxhall Bridge Rd., London SW1V 1BS, UK (☎020 7950 1661; fax 020 7950 1662; www.busabout.com). Five interconnecting bus circuits covering 60 cities and towns in Europe. Consecutive day passes and Flexi Passes available. Consecutive Day passes are valid for 15 days (US$249), 21 days (US$359), 1 mon. (US$479), 2 mon. (US$739), 3 mon. (US$909), or for the season (US$1089). Student discounts.

BY BOAT

The fares below are **one-way** for **adult foot passengers** unless otherwise noted. Though standard return fares are usually just twice the one-way fare, **fixed period returns** (usually within five days) are almost invariably cheaper. Ferries run **year-round** unless otherwise noted. Bringing a **bike** is usually free, although you may have to pay up to UK£10 in high season. For a **camper/trailer** supplement, you will have to add UK£20-140 to the "with car" fare. A directory of ferries in this region can be found at www.seaview.co.uk/ferries.html.

> **P&O Stena Line,** UK ☎08706 000611, from Europe 1304 864003; www.posl.com. **Dover** to **Calais** (1¼hr., 30 per day every 45min.; UK£24).

> **Hoverspeed,** UK ☎0870 524024, France 080012 111211; www.hoverspeed.co.uk. **Dover** to **Calais** (35-55min., every hr., UK£24) and **Ostend, Belgium** (2hr., 5-7 per day, UK£28); **Newhaven** to **Dieppe, France** (2¼-4¼hr., 1-3 per day, UK£28).

> **SeaFrance,** UK ☎08705 711711; France 08 03 04 40 45; www.seafrance.co.uk. **Dover** to **Calais** (1½hr., 15 per day, UK£15).

> **DFDS Seaways,** UK ☎08705 33 30 00; www.dfdsseaways.co.uk. **Harwich** to **Hamburg** (20hr.) and **Esbjerg, Denmark** (19hr.). **Newcastle** to **Amsterdam** (14hr.); **Kristiansand, Norway** (19hr.); and **Gothenburg, Sweden** (22hr.).

> **Brittany Ferries,** UK ☎08703 665 333, France 08 25 82 88 28; www.brittany-ferries.com. **Plymouth** to **Roscoff, France** (6hr., June-Aug. 1-3 per day, off-season 1 per wk.; UK£20-58 or €21-46) and **Santander, Spain** (24-30hr., 1-2 per week, return UK£80-145). **Portsmouth** to **St-Malo** (8¾hr., 1-2 per day, €23-49) and **Caen, France** (6hr, 1-3 per day, €21-44). **Poole** to **Cherbourg** (4¼hr., 1-2 per day, €21-44). **Cork** to **Roscoff, France** (13½hr., Apr.-Sept. 1 per week, €52-99).

> **P&O North Sea Ferries,** UK ☎08701 296002; www.ponsf.com. Daily ferries from **Hull** to **Rotterdam, Netherlands** (13½hr.) and **Zeebrugge, Belgium** (14hr.). Both UK£38-48, students UK£24-31, cars UK£63-78.

> **Fjord Line,** Norway ☎55 54 88 00, UK ☎0191 296 1313; www.fjordline.no. **Newcastle, England** to **Stavanger** (19hr.) and **Bergen, Norway** (26hr.; UK£50-110, students £25-110). Also between **Bergen** and **Egersund,** Norway, and **Hanstholm,** Denmark.

> **Irish Ferries,** France ☎01 44 88 54 50, Ireland ☎1890 313131, UK ☎087 051717 17; www.irishferries.ie. **Rosslare** to **Cherbourg** and **Roscoff** (17-18hr.; Apr.-Sept. 1-9 per wk.; €60-120, students €48); **Pembroke, UK** (3¾hr.; €25-39, students €19); **Holyhead, UK** to **Dublin** (2-3hr.; return £20-31, students £15).

ESSENTIALS

Stena Line, UK ☎1233 64 68 26; www.stenaline.co.uk. **Harwich** to **Hook of Holland** (5hr., UK£26); **Fishguard** to **Rosslare** (1-3½hr.; UK£18-21, students £14-17); **Holyhead** to **Dublin** (4hr.; UK£23-27, students £19-23); **Dún Laoghaire** (1-3½hr.; £23-27, students £19-23); **Stranraer** to **Belfast** (1¾-3¼hr.; UK£14-36, students £10).

GETTING AROUND FRANCE

France's rail system is comprehensive; its network of high-speed services and local trains connects all but the most minor towns. Buses can be very useful where they fill in gaps in train service, but are inferior in speed and not definitively superior in price to trains in areas served by both trains and buses. Though France is blessed with an extremely efficient and well-maintained network of roads, steep *autoroute* tolls and gasoline costs alone (not to mention car rental fees) can make driving more expensive than train-riding for one or two people. Then again, cars offer greater freedom to explore the countryside and greater flexibility in travel.

To buy a one-way ticket for a train, bus, or plane in France, ask for **un billet aller-simple;** for a roundtrip ticket, request **un billet aller-retour.** Roundtrip fares are often cheaper than two one-ways.

HOW TO USE TRANSPORTATION LISTINGS: CENTER-OUT

Let's Go employs the 'center-out' principle for transportation listings: for each town, we describe only how to reach towns of similar or greater importance. If you're in a big city, information on reaching neighboring small towns will be in the small towns themselves rather than in the big city.

BY PLANE

Only high-rollers get around France by plane. With most major cities linked by high-speed rail lines, taking a train can be just as fast as flying once you account for the time it takes to travel to oft-remote airports, check in, taxi around runways, wait for luggage, and then travel from the airport to the city in your destination. The one exception is travel to **Corsica;** frequent air services from Nice, Marseille, and Paris to Ajaccio and Bastia compare competitively to the 10hr. ferry crossing. Expect to pay about US$100 round-trip from **Nice** to Corsica or US$150 from **Paris;** see **Corsica: Getting There,** p. 584, for details.

BY BOAT

FERRIES. Aside from accessing the many islands along the French seaboard, the only time you will take a ferry in France is to reach Corsica. Though far slower than flying (the trip lasts 7-12 hr.) and not much cheaper, ferries provide an opportunity to relax and meet people. Overnight ferry travel will also help you save time for sightseeing. Expect to pay about €92.50 roundtrip per person and €30.50-91.50 per car. An additional option, high-speed hydrofoil service from Nice to Calvi and Bastia, takes about 3 hours. For details, see **Corsica: Getting There,** p. 584.

RIVERBOATS. France has over 5300 miles of navigable rivers and canals. Experts and tourists alike can boat through France from the English channel to the Mediterranean. For details on regulations, have the the French Government Tourist Office send you a copy of their English-language pamphlet *Boating on the Waterways.* For a list of companies renting out boats and organizing waterborne vacations, contact the **Fédération des Industries Nautiques,** Port de Javel Haut, 75015 Paris (☎01 44 37 04 00; fax 01 45 77 21 88). or check out the *Maison de la France* website (www.francetourism.com/activities/boatrent.htm).

BY TRAIN

SNCF HOTLINE ☎08 36 35 35 35 for timetable info and reservations.

The French national railway company, **SNCF**, operates one of the most efficient transportation systems in the world; their **TGVs** (*trains à grande vitesse*, or high-speed trains) are among the fastest in the world. If not in a hurry, take the slower but cheaper **Rapide** service. Ironically, local trains, called **Express** or sometimes **TER** (*Train Express Régionale*), are slowest of all. On long trips, trains sometime split at crossroads; make sure you're in the right carriage. Trains are not always safe; for safety tips, see p. 41.

RESERVATIONS. A ticket or railpass does not guarantee you a seat; during busy periods, it's advisable to buy a **reservation** for a small fee (US$3-10). Most TGVs sell a limited number of **standby** tickets, which guarantee travel on the train but not necessarily a seat. Reservations (with optional seat or couchette) can be made by a travel agent or in person at the train station. On especially fast or comfortable sections of the *TGV*, if you do not have Eurailpass or Europass, you will need to purchase a **supplement** (US$10-50). *TGV* reservations can be made up to a few minutes before departure, but other services should be arranged before noon the day of a post-5pm departure and before 8pm the day before a pre-5pm departure.

! COMPOSTEZ! Before boarding a train, you must validate your ticket by having it *composté* (stamped with the date and time) by one of the orange machines near the platforms. You must re-validate your ticket at any connection in your trip.

OVERNIGHT TRAINS. Night trains don't waste valuable daylight hours and defray the costs of staying at a hotel. Unfortunately, they also uncomfortable and potentially boring. You can sleep upright in your seat, purchase a reclining seat, or buy a slighlty more luxurious open-bunk **couchette** (about US$20 per person). These co-ed compartments are, to put it mildly, cozy, sleeping up to six men and women in triple-stacked bunks. **Sleepers** (beds) in private sleeping cars offer more privacy and comfort for a bigger price tag (US$40-150). For those with limited-day railpasses, note that an overnight train that departs after 7pm uses only one travel day.

SHOULD YOU BUY A RAILPASS? Ideally, a railpass would allow you to spontaneously jump on any train, head anywhere, and alter your plans at whim. In practice, things are not so simple. You still wait in line to pay for supplements and seat and couchette reservations. Worse, railpasses aren't necessarily cost-effective. There are many forms of discounts on regular rail travel in France (see **Discount Rail Tickets,** p. 72), especially for those under 25. Those planning on train-hopping from city to city on trains will profit from a railpass. To evaluate your options more precisely, get the prices of relevant point-to-point tickets from the SNCF website, add them, and compare with railpass prices.

MULTINATIONAL RAILPASSES

EURAILPASS. Eurailpass is valid in most of Western Europe: Austria, Belgium, Denmark, Finland, France, Germany, Greece, Hungary, Italy, Luxembourg, the Netherlands, Norway, Portugal, the Republic of Ireland, Spain, Sweden, and Switzerland. It is not valid in the UK. **Continuous Eurailpasses** are valid for a predetermined number of consecutive days; they work best if you spend a lot of time on

ESSENTIALS

trains every few days. **Flexipasses,** valid for any 10 or 15 days within a two-month period, are more cost-effective for those traveling long distances but less frequently. **Saverpasses** and **Saver Flexipasses** provide 1st-class travel for travelers in groups of two to five. **Youthpasses** and **Youth Flexipasses** give similar perks for those under 26. Starting in January 2003, Eurail will offer the **Selectpass,** which allows you to travel in your choice of 3, 4, or 5 adjoining countries for any 5, 6, 8, or 10 days in a two-month period. This pass replaces the **Europass.** For more information, visit www.eurail.com.

EURAILPASSES	15 DAYS	21 DAYS	1 MONTH	2 MONTHS	3 MONTHS
1st class Eurailpass	US$588	US$762	US$946	US$1338	US$1654
Eurail Saverpass	US$498	US$648	US$804	US$1138	US$1408
Eurail Youthpass	US$414	US$534	US$664	US$938	US$1160

EURAIL FLEXIPASSES	10 DAYS IN 2 MONTHS	15 DAYS IN 2 MONTHS
1st class Eurail Flexipass	US$694	US$914
Eurail Saver Flexipass	US$592	US$778
Eurail Youth Flexipass	US$488	US$642

SELECTPASSES		5 DAYS	6 DAYS	8 DAYS	10 DAYS	15 DAYS
Selectpass:	3-country	US$356	US$394	US$470	US$542	N/A
	4-country	US$398	US$436	US$512	US$584	N/A
	5-country	US$438	US$476	US$552	US$624	US$794
Saver:	3-country	US$304	US$336	US$400	US$460	N/A
	4-country	US$340	US$372	US$436	US$496	N/A
	5-country	US$374	US$406	US$470	US$560	US$674
Youth:	3-country	US$249	US$276	US$329	US$379	N/A
	4-country	US$279	US$306	US$359	US$409	N/A
	5-country	US$307	US$334	US$387	US$437	US$556

Passholders receive a timetable for major routes and a map with instructions on receiving reduced ferry, bus, car rental, hotel, and Eurostar (see p. 66) fares.

SHOPPING AROUND FOR A EURAIL PASS. Eurailpasses are designed by the EU itself, and can be bought only by non-Europeans and almost exclusively from non-European distributors. These passes are sold at uniform prices set by the EU. Some travel agents tack on a US$10 handling fee while others offer bonuses with purchase; shop around. Pass prices usually increase each year; purchase a pass before January 1 if you plan to travel within 3 months into the year (passed must be validated within 3 months of purchase).

Purchase your Eurailpass before leaving, since only a few places in major European cities sell them (at marked-up prices). You can get a replacement for a lost pass only if you have purchased insurance on it (US$14). Eurailpasses are available through travel agents, student travel agencies like STA and Council (see p. 60), and **Rail Europe,** 500 Mamaroneck Ave., Harrison, NY 10528 (US ☎888-382-7245, Canada 800-361-7245, UK ☎0990 84 88 48; fax US 800-432-1329, Canada 905-602-4198; www.raileurope.com) or **DER Travel Services,** with several posts across the US (US ☎888-337-7350; fax 800-282-7474; www.der.com).

OTHER MULTINATIONAL PASSES. Regional passes are good values for travels limited to one area. The Benelux Tourrail Pass for Belgium, the Netherlands, and Luxembourg (5 days in 1 month 2nd-class US$155, under 26 US$104; 50% discount for companion traveler) may be especially useful for travelers to France.

InterRail Passes provide discounts on unlimited rail travel for travelers who have lived at least six months in Europe. There are eight zones in the InterRail Pass system—France is in Zone E (along with Belgium, the Netherlands, and Luxembourg). The **Under 26 InterRail Card** gives either 21 consecutive days or one month of unlimited travel within one, two, three or all eight zones (UK£119-249, costlier for more zones). A card can also be purchased for 12 days of travel in one zone (UK£119). The **Over 26 InterRail Card** provides the same services, but at UK£169-355, as does the new **Child Pass** (ages 4-11) for UK£85-178. Passholders receive **discounts** on rail travel, Eurostar journeys, and most ferries to Ireland, Scandinavia, and the rest of Europe. The pass generally does not cover **supplements** for high-speed trains. For info and ticket sales in Europe contact **Student Travel Centre,** 24 Rupert St., 1st fl., London W1V 7FN (☎020 74 37 81 01; fax 77 34 38 36; www.student-travel-centre.com). The pass is also sold by travel agents, ticketbooths at major train stations, and online (www.railpassdirect.co.uk).

DOMESTIC RAILPASSES

A national pass is valid on all rail lines of the national rail company. Many national passes don't offer free or discounted travel on private railways and ferries.

NATIONAL RAILPASSES. Analagous to the Eurailpass, national railpasses are valid either for a set number of consecutive days or days within a given time period. National railpasses must normally be purchased before leaving home. For more info, check out http://raileurope.com/us/rail/passes/single_country_index.htm.

EURO DOMINO. Like the Interrail Pass, the Euro Domino pass is available to anyone who has lived in Europe for at least six months. Euro Domino can give access to any one of 29 European countries plus Morocco. Reservations must be purchased separately, but **supplements** are covered by the pass. The pass must be bought within your country of residence; the price is different in each country. Inquire with your national rail company for more info.

> **Euro-Domino France pass:** 3 days €180, 4 days €212, 5 days €244, 6 days €275, 7 days €307, 8 days €339.

> **Euro-Domino France Youth pass:** Must be under 26. 3 days €132, 4 days €158, 5 days €183, 6 days €209, 7 days €234, 8 days €260.

REGIONAL PASSES. This type of pass covers a specific area within a country or a round-trip from any border to a particular destination and back; these can supplement areas where your main pass isn't valid.

> **France Railpass:** 4 days unlimited rail travel in any 30-day period. US$210 for 1 adult, $171 each for 2 or more traveling together. Additional days (up to 6) $30.

> **France Rail'n'Drive pass:** 3 days unlimited rail travel and 2 days Avis car rental with unlimited mileage excluding insurance. US$245 for 1 adult, US$175 each for 2 traveling together. Additional rail days (up to 7) $31; additional car days $37.

> **France Youthpass:** For travelers under 26. 4 days of unlimited travel within 1 month US$148. Additional days (up to 6) $18.

RAIL-AND-DRIVE PASSES. Many countries (as well as Eurail) offer rail-and-drive passes, which combine car rental with rail travel. Prices range €245-509 per person, with discounts for children under 11 (see **By Car,** p. 74).

DISCOUNTED TICKETS

For travelers under 26, **BIJ** tickets (*Billets Internationaux de Jeunesse;* operated by **Wasteels**) are a great alternative to railpasses. Available for international trips within Europe as well as most ferry services, they knock 20-40% off 1st- and 2nd-class fares. Tickets are good for 2 months after purchase and allow stopovers along the normal direct route of the train journey. Issued for a specific international route between two points, they must be used in the direction and order of the designated route and must be bought in Europe. The equivalent for those over 26, **BIGT** tickets provide a 20-30% discount on 1st- and 2nd-class international tickets. Both types of tickets are available from European travel agents, Wasteels offices, and sometimes at the ticket counter. For more info, contact Voyages Wasteels Paris, 5 Saint Michel, 113 bd. Saint Michel, 75005 Paris (☎ 08 25 88 70 03) or Voyages Wasteels Marseille, 67 rue La Canabiere, 13001 Marseille (☎ 08 25 88 70 46) or www.wasteels.com.

SNCF offers a wide range of discounted roundtrip tickets called **tarifs Découvertes**. SNCF calendars designate days as **période bleue, période blanche**, and **période rouge**, depending on passenger traffic; trips in the blue period get many discounts, while trips in red get none. The **Découverte à deux, Découverte Séjour**, and **Découverte 12-25** are discounted 5% any journey via TGV beginning during a blue period. The *Découverte à deux* is for two adults traveling together on both legs of a roundtrip journey; the *Découverte Séjour* is for travelers making a roundtrip journey of at least 200km and staying over a Saturday night; *Découverte 12-25* is for travelers aged 12-25. The *Carte Senior* and *Carte Enfants+* offer similar discounts. Travelers under the age of 25 can also take advantage of the **Carte 12-25**. This is available for €41.20 at SNCF stations (with proof of age and a passport-sized photo) and is valid for a year from the date of purchase. The Carte gives 50% off trips that start during a blue period and 25% off those that start in a white period. It also provides savings on Avis rental cars. SNCF often offers other discounts for youth travelers.

BY BUS

In France, long-distance buses are a 2nd-class means of transportation, with comparatively rare and infrequent service. Within a given region, however, buses provide vital (often speedy) service to outlying towns and villages. Bus stations are usually adjacent to the train station, and many bus services are operated by SNCF and accept railpasses. Other services are operated by regional companies, which vary in price and punctuality. *Let's Go* lists the local bus companies and relevant destinations for each town. Bus schedules usually indicate whether a bus runs during the *période scolaire* (school year), *période de vacances* (summer vacation), or both. Few buses run on *jours feriés* (Sundays and holidays).

BY CAR

Unless in a large group, traveling by car is not cost-effective, accounting for highway tolls, gasoline costs, and rental charges. Occassionally, though, a combination of train and bus works well; RailEurope and other railpass vendors offer rail-and-drive packages. Fly-and-drive packages are also often available from travel agents.

DRIVING PERMITS & CAR INSURANCE

INTERNATIONAL DRIVING PERMIT (IDP). Anybody with a valid EU-issued driving license is unconditionally entitled to drive on French roads. Others may be legally permitted to drive in France on the strength of their national licenses for a few months, but not all police are aware of that. It's advisable to obtain an **International Driving Permit (IDP),** which is essentially your regular license translated into 10 languages, including French. You must be 18 years old to obtain the IDP. The IDP, valid for one year, must be issued in your home country before you depart. The IDP is an addition, not a replacement, for your home license and is not valid without it. To apply, contact the national or local branch of your home country's Automobile Association.

Australia: Contact your local Royal Automobile Club (RAC) or the National Royal Motorist Association (☎08 9421 4444; www.rac.com.au/travel). Permits AUS$15.

Canada: Contact any Canadian Automobile Association (CAA) branch office or write to CAA, 1145 Hunt Club Rd., #200, K1V 0Y3 (☎613-247-0117; www.caa.ca/CAAInternet/travelservices/internationaldocumentation/idptravel.htm). CDN$10.

Ireland: Contact the nearest Automobile Association (AA) office or write to: Irish Automobile Association, 23 Suffolk St., Rockhill, Blackrock, Co. Dublin (☎016 179 841). Permits IR£4.

New Zealand: Contact your local Automobile Association (AA) or their main office at Auckland Central, 99 Albert St., Auckland City (☎09 377 4660; www.nzaa.co.nz.). Permits NZ$10.

South Africa: Contact the Travel Services Department of the Automobile Association of South Africa at P.O. Box 596, 2000 Johannesburg (☎011 799 1000; www.aasa.co.za). Permits ZAR28.50.

UK: Contact the Automobile Association, International Documents, Fanum House, Erskine, Renfrewshire PA8 6BW (☎0870 600 0371; www.theaa.co.uk/motoringandtravel/idp/index.asp). Permits UK£4.

US: Visit any American Automobile Association (AAA) office (call ☎800-564-6222 for the office nearest you) or write to AAA Florida, Travel Related Services, 1000 AAA Drive (mail stop #100), Heathrow, FL 32746 (☎407-444-7000). You do not have to be a member of AAA to purchase an IDP. Permits US$10.

RENTING A CAR

You can **rent** a car from an international firm (e.g. Avis, Budget, or Hertz) with European offices, from a European-based company with local representatives (e.g. Europcar), or from a tour operator (e.g. Auto Europe, Europe By Car, or Kemwel Holiday Autos), which will arrange a rental for you from a European company, often at a good deal.

The minimum age for renting is usually 21, though some agencies won't rent to anyone under 23. Renters under 25 often must pay a surcharge. Otherwise, most agencies require only a valid drivers' license and one year of driving experience.

You can generally make reservations before you leave by calling major international offices in your home country. Reserve long before leaving for France and pay in advance. Occasionally the price and availability information from home offices do not coincide with that from local offices in France. Check with both sources to get the best price and accurate information. Local desk numbers are included in town listings; for home-country numbers, call your toll-free directory.

Many websites search out deals from multiple companies. Check out **Travel Now** (www.travel.com/mall/2) and the **Internet Travel Network** (www.itn.net/cgi/get?itn/cb/traveldotcom/index. Rental agencies in France include:

Auto Europe: US ☎888-223-5555, UK 08001 696414, Australia 800 22 35 55 55; www.autoeurope.com.

Avis: US ☎800-230-4898, Canada 800-272-5871, UK 08706 060100, Australia toll-free 136 333, New Zealand 0800 655 111; www.avis.com.

Budget: US ☎800-404-8033, Canada 212-581-3040, international 800-472-3325; www.budgetrentacar.com.

Europe by Car: US ☎800-223-1516; www.europebycar.com.

Europcar: US ☎800-227-3876, Canada 877-940-6900, France 03 35 23 52; www.europcar.com. Unusually, rents to ages 21-24 at many sites.

Hertz: US ☎800-654-3001, Canada 800-263-0600, UK 08708 448844; Australia 38 38 38; www.hertz.com.

COSTS & INSURANCE. Expect to pay at least US$200 per week, plus 20.6% tax, as the base rate for a small car rental. Automatic gearboxes cost extra and are often unavailable on cheaper cars. 4WD and air conditioning each generally cost US$7 extra per day. Many rental packages offer unlimited kilometers; others allow 250 km per day with a surcharge of approximately US$0.35 per kilometer after that. Some airlines offer fly-and-drive packages, which may give you up to a week of free or discounted rental. National chains often allow one-way rentals—dropping a rental off in a different city than it was obtained, but usually with a minimum hire period and a drop-off charge of several hundred dollars.

EU residents driving their own cars do not need any extra insurance coverage in France. Gold credit cards (or standard American Express cards) often cover basic insurance, though cars rented on **American Express, Visa/Mastercard Gold,** or **Platinum** credit cards might *not* carry automatic insurance. Home car insurance often covers liability overseas, but only with proof provided by a **green card** or **International Insurance Certificate**, obtained at travel agents or border crossings. Accidents abroad, if reported, will show up on your domestic records and in your premium thereafter. If these options fail, be prepared to shell out US$5-10 per day for insurance on a rental car. Insurance plans almost always come with an **excess** (or deductible) of around US$500 for conventional vehicles; excess ranges up to around US$2500 for younger drivers and for 4WD. This means you pay for all damages up to that sum, unless they are the fault of another vehicle. The excess you will be quoted applies to collisions with other vehicles; collisions with non-vehicles, such as trees, will cost even more. The excess can often be reduced or waived entirely if you pay an additional charge, around US$9 per day. Accidents while driving a conventional vehicle on an **unpaved road** in a rental car are almost never covered by insurance; inquire at the rental agency.

LEASING A CAR

An option only for non-EU residents, **leasing** can be cheaper than rental for periods longer than a few weeks and is often the only option for travelers aged 18-21. The cheapest leases are agreements to buy the car and then sell it back to the manufacturer at a prearranged price. The base price of a lease (US$1200 for 60 days) may not appear to differ much from a regular car rental, but it includes comprehensive insurance, unlimited mileage, and avoids taxes. Contact **Auto Europe** or **Europe by Car** (see above) at least 30 days before your departure.

BUYING A CAR

Buying a used vehicle in France and then reselling it before leaving can be less expensive than renting and leasing on long trips. If you decide to keep your car, check with consulates about import-export laws concerning used vehicles, registration, and safety and emission standards. Camper-vans and motor homes provide the advantages of a car with the benefits of a hotel on the road.

ON THE ROAD

The French drive on the right-hand side of the road. On *autoroutes*, the speed limit is 130km/h (81 mph); on smaller highways, 110km/h (68mph); in cities, 50-60km/h (about 35 mph). Since *autoroute* toll tickets are stamped with the time you left the booth, ticket-takers at the end of your trip can calculate your speed and penalize you. **Fines** range €137-762, though they are reduced by 30% if paid within 24 hours of the ticketing. France has a **mandatory seatbelt law** and prohibits children under 10 from riding in the front car seat.

By French law, cars entering a road from the right have the right of way over cars already on the road, even on major thoroughfares; be prepared for cars to turn into the road ahead without warning. Inverted-triangle road signs with exclamation marks and text *"vous n'avez pas la priorité"* or *"cédez le passage"* mean that the rule does not apply—normally the case on major roundabouts. In another reverse of practices in most countries, a driver who flashes his highbeams wants to send the message: "I AM going first," rather than "Go right ahead." Check out **Itinéraire** (www.iti.fr) if you plan to drive in France; enter your start and end points, your desired speed and budget, and you will receive directions as well as estimates of driving time and toll and gas costs. **Gas stations** in most towns won't accept cash after 7pm, but they will take the French *Carte Bleue* (analagous to VISA); in a pinch, get a passerby to charge it on his card and reimburse him in cash. Gas generally costs around €0.85-1.15 per liter. Diesel *(gazole)* fuel tends to be cheaper than unleaded *(essence sans plomb)*.

> **!** **DRIVING PRECAUTIONS.** When traveling in the summer, bring substantial amounts of water (a suggested 5L of **water** per person per day) for consumption and for the radiator. Register with the police before taking long treks to unpopulated areas. Check with the local automobile club for details. For long distance travel, bring good maps and make sure tires are in good repair. Always carry: a **compass, car manual, spare tire** and **jack, jumper cables, extra oil, flares, a torch (flashlight),** and **heavy blankets.** Make sure you know how to **change a tire.** If you experience a blowout in deserted areas, **stay with your car;** if you wander off, trackers are less likely to find you.

DANGERS

In general, French roads are some of the best in Europe and the world. There are a few exceptions: the roads in the Alps and on Corsica tend to be narrow, twisty, and prone to unpredictable weather conditions. Moreover, the French tend to drive fast, impolitely, and aggressively. Good roads near Paris and in southern France become stressful and dangerous during the crowded high season.

BY BICYCLE

Some airlines count bikes as a second piece of luggage, but others charge US$60-110 each way to transport them. Bikes must be packed in a cardboard box (available at the airport for US$10) with the pedals and front wheel detached. Trains almost always have room for a bike, at variable costs. Most ferries charge a nominal fee or nothing at all. Bike rental is probably a better idea; Let's Go lists rental places for most towns. Some hostels rent bicycles cheaply.

Riding with a frame pack strapped on your bike or back is not safe; use a **basket** or **panier**. Buy a suitable **bike helmet** (US$25-50). The most secure locks are U-shaped **Citadel** or **Kryptonite** locks (from US$30).

For those nervous about striking out on their own, **Blue Marble Travel** (Canada ☎519-624-2494, US 215-923-3788, France 01 42 36 02 34; www.bluemarble.org) organizes bike tours of France and many other countries for adults aged 20 to 50. Full-time graduate and professional students may get discounts; "stand-by" rates may be obtained in Europe through the Paris office. **CBT Tours**, 2506 N. Clark St., #150, Chicago, IL 60614 (US ☎800-736-2453; www.cbttours.com), offers full-package 7-12 day biking, mountain biking, and hiking tours June to late Aug. (around US$200 per day).

For further info, **Mountaineers Books**, 1001 S.W. Klickitat Way #201, Seattle, WA 98134 (☎206-223-6303; www.mountaineers.org), sells *Europe By Bike*, by Karen and Terry Whitehill (US$15), and country-specific biking guides.

BY MOPED AND MOTORCYCLE

Motorbikes (mopeds) eliminate the negatives of costly car travel and short-ranged bicycling. However, they are uncomfortable for long distances, dangerous in the rain, and unpredictable on rough roads and gravel. Always wear a helmet and never ride with a backpack. Expect to pay about €15.25-23 per day. Motorcycles are more expensive and require a license, but are better for long distances. **Bosenberg Motorcycle Excursions**, Mainzer Str. 54, 55545 Bad Kreuznach, Germany (☎49 671 673 12; www.bosenberg.com), arranges tours in the Alps, Austria, France, Italy, and Switzerland and rents motorcycles Apr.-Oct. For **further info**, consult *Europe by Motorcycle*, by Gregory Frazier (Arrowstar Publishing, US$20).

BY FOOT

France's best scenery can only be reached on foot. *Let's Go* outlines daytrips and short hikes in every region; tourist offices, locals, and fellow travelers are also good resources. France is criss-crossed by over 30,000km of signposted footpaths, known as **sentiers de grandes randonnées** or just **GR**. The **Fédération française de randonnée pédestre (FFRP)**, 14 rue Riquet, 75019 Paris (☎01 44 89 93 93; fax 01 40 35 85 67; www.ffrp.asso.fr) publishes the valuable *Topoguide* series, which describes, maps, and lists accommodations for each GR route in French. The GR routes are heir to a lot of history. The GR65 route, running from Le Puy-en-Velay in the Massif Central to St-Jean-Pied-de-Port on the way to Santiago de Compostella in Spain, was trodden for centuries before hiking became popular. Thousands of people still undertake **pilgrimages** on foot. Pilgrims stay free at monasteries and special hostels on the way, with a letter from a priest certifying that they are *bonafide* pilgrims. For more info, check out **France on Foot** (www.franceonfoot.com) and **Hiking in France** (www.hejoly.demon.nl/countries/france.html).

BY THUMB

No one should hitchhike *("faire l'autostop")* without seriously considering the risks. Hitching entrusts your life to a stranger, putting you at risk of theft, assault, sexual harassment, unsafe driving, and endless reminiscences about the Crimean War. If you're a woman traveling alone, don't hitch, period. A man and a woman are a safer combination; two men will have trouble getting lifts; three people will go nowhere. France is considered the most difficult country in Europe to get a lift.

> ❗ **THUMBS DOWN?** *Let's Go* urges you to consider the dangers before you choose to hitch-hike. We do not recommend hitching, nor is any of the information presented here intended to do so.

Where you stand is very important. Experienced hitchers choose spots outside built-up areas, where drivers have time to assess potential passengers in the distance and stop safely. Hitching (or even standing) on *autoroutes* is illegal; thumbing is legal only at rest stops, tollbooths, and highway entrance ramps.

Success also depends on your appearance, which means looking clean and not wearing sunglasses. Veteran hitchers travel light and stack their belongings in a compact but visible cluster. Most Europeans signal with an open hand, rather than a thumb. Many write their destination on a sign in large, bold letters with a smiley-face or "S.V.P." under it (*s'il vous plaît*).

Safety should always be your paramount concern. Smart hitchikers never sit in the back of a two-door car or any automobile they can't exit quickly and always hold tight to their backpacks. Hitchhiking at night can be particularly dangerous; experienced hitchers stand in well-lit places and expect drivers to be leery of nocturnal thumbers. If they ever feel threatened, hitchers insist on being let out, regardless of the location. Acting as if you're going to open the car door or vomit on the upholstery will usually get a driver to stop. A thorough website on hitchhiking is **H's Guide to Everywhere** (www.suite101.com/welcome.cfm/hitch_hiking).

A relatively safe alternative to hitching is the ride service, which pairs drivers with riders at variable fees. **Eurostop International** (**Allostop** in France; www.ecri-tel.fr/allostop/) is one of the largest European ride services. Riders and drivers can post their names on the Internet through the **Taxistop** (www.taxistop.be). Not all of these organizations screen drivers and riders.

SPECIFIC CONCERNS

WOMEN TRAVELERS

NATIONAL RAPE HOTLINE	**SOS Viol:** ☎0800 05 95 95 offers counseling and assistance in French. Open M-F 10am-6pm.

Women exploring alone inevitably face additional safety concerns. Stay in hostels with single rooms that lock from the inside or in religious organizations with exclusively female rooms. Choose centrally located accommodations, avoid solitary late-night treks or metro rides, and think twice about using communal hostel showers.

Carry extra money for a phone call, bus, or taxi. **Hitchhiking** is never safe for lone women or even for two women traveling together. On overnight or long train rides, pick either a women-only compartment or one that happens to be occupied by women or couples. Approach older women or couples for directions if necessary.

The less like a tourist you appear, the better. That may mean dressing conservatively, especially in rural areas. Wearing a conspicuous **wedding band** can forestall unwanted overtures.

The best answer to verbal harassment is one perfected by French women: a withering, icy stare. Acknowledging *dragueurs* (as the French call these men), even with "NO!," only invites a reply. The extremely persistent may need to be dissuaded by a loud *"laissez-moi tranquille!"* (leh-SEH mwa tranhk-EEL; leave me alone!) or *"au secours!"* (oh-S'KOOR; help!). Consider carrying a whistle on your keychain for extra effect and don't hesitate to seek out a police officer. **In an emergency, dial ☎ 17 for police assistance.** *Let's Go* also lists local police authorities in the Practical Information section of cities. A self-defense course will give you additional tips on how to deal with dangerous situations (see **Self Defense,** p. 42).

TRAVELING ALONE

Traveling alone brings an increased risk of harassment and street theft. Lone travelers should appear confident, hide the fact that they are alone, be especially careful in deserted or crowded areas, and maintain regular contact with someone at home who knows their itinerary.

For more tips, try *Traveling Solo* by Eleanor Berman (Globe Pequot Press; US$17) or subscribe to **Connecting: Solo Travel Network,** 689 Park Road, Unit 6, Gibsons, BC V0N 1V7, Canada (☎604-886-9099; www.cstn.org; membership US$35). **Travel Companion Exchange,** P.O. Box 833, Amityville, NY 11701, USA (☎631-454-0880; www.whytravelalone.com; US$48), links solo travelers with companions of similar travel habits and interests.

OLDER TRAVELERS

Almost all museums and sights in France offer discounts for senior citizens; many cities also offer special rates for public transportation. Many restaurants offer special senior discounts, but don't list them. Major sights are typically well equipped to deal with any special needs. The same is not true of budget accommodations, which usually have extremely steep stairs in place of elevators.

The books *No Problem! Worldwise Tips for Mature Adventurers,* by Janice Kenyon (Orca Book Publishers; US$16), and *Unbelievably Good Deals and Great Adventures That You Absolutely Can't Get Unless You're Over 50,* by Joan Rattner Heilman (NTC/Contemporary Publishing; US$13), are excellent resources for senior travelers.

ElderTreks, 597 Markham St., Toronto, ON M6G 2L7 (☎800-741-7956; www.eldertreks.com). Adventure travel programs for 50+ travelers in France.

Elderhostel, 11 Ave. de Lafayette, Boston, MA 02111 (☎877-426-8056; www.elderhostel.org). Organizes 1-4 wk. educational adventures on varied subjects for those 55+.

The Mature Traveler, P.O. Box 15791, Sacramento, CA 95852 (☎800-460-6676). Deals, discounts, and travel packages for the 50+ traveler. Subscription $30.

Walking the World, P.O. Box 1186, Fort Collins, CO 80522 (☎800-340-9255; www.walkingtheworld.com), organizes trips for 50+ travelers to France.

ESSENTIALS

BGLT TRAVELERS

France is changing its traditional attitude towards gay communities; help-lines, bars, and meeting places have sprung up in all its major cities and in a number of smaller cities. The **Marais**, in Paris, has a notably gay-friendly atmosphere, as do parts of Bordeaux and the French Riviera. **Montpellier** is regarded as the center of gay life in southern France. However, the French countryside and many towns (especially in the southwest, northeast, and northwest) retain their traditional perspectives. To avoid uncomfortable situations, use discretion when interacting with your significant other in public and don't assume that a stretchy shirt or a little flamboyance is a blip on your gay-dar. In general, you won't see many butch lesbians in France—gay women often fit the traditional feminine norms and have been known to regard butches as *camioneuses* ("truck drivers"). In Paris, the **Centre Gai et Lesbien**, 3 rue Keller, has resources on health, legal, counseling and soc social issues. (☎ 01 43 57 21 47; fax 01 43 57 27 93; www.cglparis.org. Open M-Sa 4-8pm.) The monthly gay magazine **Têtu** is sold in newstands around France, and contains information on gay bars and clubs throughout France.

▼ **FURTHER READING: BISEXUAL, GAY, & LESBIAN.**
Spartacus International Gay Guide 2001-2002. Bruno Gmunder Verlag. US$33.
Damron's Accommodations and *The Women's Traveller.* Damron Travel Guides. US$14-19. For more info, call ☎ 800-462-6654 or visit www.damron.com.
Ferrari Guides' Gay Travel A to Z, Ferrari Guides' Men's Travel in Your Pocket, and *Ferrari Guides' Inn Places.* Ferrari Publications (www.ferrariguides.com). US$16-20.
The Gay Vacation Guide: The Best Trips and How to Plan Them, Mark Chesnut. Citadel Press. US$15.
Gayellow Pages USA/Canada, Frances Green (www.gayellowpages.com). Gayellow pages. US$16. Smaller regional editions available.

TRAVELERS WITH DISABILITIES

Rail is probably the most convenient form of travel for disabled travelers in France. SNCF offers wheelchair compartments on all TGV services. Ask for the *Guide du voyageur a mobilité réduit* at train stations for more details. Guide dog owners from Britain and Ireland will have trouble getting their pooches past quarantine on their return; contact the PETS helpline at ☎ 087 0241 1710 or www.defra.gov.uk for details. Others should inquire as to the specific quarantine policies and regulations of their own country and France. In Paris and other major cities, public transport has seats earmarked for disabled or infirm passengers. Taxis are obliged to take wheelchair-bound passengers and help them enter and exit the taxi. Hertz, Avis, and National car rental agencies have hand-controlled vehicles at some locations, which must be reserved at least 48 hours in advance.

Unfortunately, budget hotels and restaurants are generally ill-equipped for handicapped visitors. Very few handicapped-accessible bathrooms can be found in the one- to two-star range (and below). The brochure *Paris-Ile-de-France for Everyone* (available in French and English for €9 at most Parisian tourist offices) lists accessible sites, hotels, and restaurants, as well as useful tips.

Many museums and sights are wheelchair-accessible. Some provide guided tours in **sign language**. The following organizations provide useful info.

Mobility International USA (MIUSA), P.O. Box 10767, Eugene, OR 97440, USA (☎541-343-1284; info@miusa.org; www.miusa.org). Sells *A World of Options: A Guide to International Educational Exchange, Community Service, and Travel for Persons with Disabilities* (US$35).

Society for the Advancement of Travel for the Handicapped (SATH), 347 Fifth Ave., #610, New York, NY 10016, USA (☎212-447-7284; www.sath.org). An advocacy group that publishes free online travel info and the travel magazine *OPEN WORLD* (US$18, free for members). Annual membership US$45, students and seniors US$30.

Directions Unlimited, 123 Green Ln., Bedford Hills, NY 10507, USA (☎800-533-5343; www.travel-cruises.com). Specializes in arranging individual and group vacations, tours, and cruises for the physically disabled.

FURTHER READING. *Access in Paris,* by Gordon Couch (Quiller Press, US$12); *Resource Directory for the Disabled,* by Richard Neil Shrout (Facts on File; US$14); *Wheelchair Through Europe,* by Annie Mackin (Graphic Language Press; US$13); *Global Access* (www.geocities.com/Paris/1502/disabilityl-inks.html) has links for disabled travelers in France.

MINORITY TRAVELERS

Like much of Europe, France has experienced a wave of immigration from former colonies in the past few decades. North Africans compose the greatest part of the immigrants, at over a million, followed by West Africans and Vietnamese. Many of the immigrants are uneducated and face discrimination, causing poverty and crime in the predominately immigrant inner cities. In turn, there has been a surge in support for the far-right National Front party and its cry of *"la France pour les français."* In fact, extreme right presidential candidate Jean-Marie Le Pen (see p. 13), campaigning on an anti-immigration platform, shockingly beat his more moderate competitors in the 2002 primary before being soundly defeated by incumbent Jacques Chirac. Anyone who might be taken for **North African** may encounter verbal abuse and is more likely than other travelers to be stopped and questioned by the police. Racism is especially prevalent in the Southeast. The following organizations can give advice about your travel and help in the event of a racist encounter.

S.O.S. Racisme, 28 rue des Petites ecuries, 75010 Paris (☎01 53 24 67 67; www.sos-racisme.org). Provides legal services and helps negotiate with police.

MRAP (Mouvement contre le racisme et pour l'amitié entre les peuples), 43 bd. Magenta, 75010 Paris (☎01 53 38 99 99; fax 01 40 40 90 98; www.mrap.asso.fr/mrap.htm). Handles immigration issues; monitors racist publications and propaganda.

TRAVELERS WITH CHILDREN

If you are considering staying at a B&B, **call ahead** and make sure it's child-friendly. If you rent a car, make sure the rental company supplies a car seat for younger children. French law mandates that children sit in the rear. **Be sure that your child carries some sort of ID** in case there is an emergency or (s)he gets lost.

Museums, tourist attractions, accommodations, and restaurants often offer discounts for children, usually included in the *Let's Go* listings. Children under 2 generally fly for 10% of the adult airfare on international flights. International fares are usually discounted 25% for children aged 2-11. Parents of **fussy eaters** should check out menus before sitting down. Cheaper restaurants often have children's menus.

For more information, consult one of the following books:

Take Your Kids to Europe, Cynthia W. Harriman. Cardogan Books (US$18).

Have Kid, Will Travel: 101 Survival Strategies for Vacationing With Babies and Young Children, Claire and Lucille Tristram. Andrews McMeel Publishing (US$9).

Adventuring with Children: An Inspirational Guide to World Travel and the Outdoors, Nan Jeffrey. Avalon House Publishing (US$15).

DIETARY CONCERNS

Those with special dietary requirements may feel left behind in France. **Vegetarians** will find dining out difficult (see **Food & Drink,** p. 14) and **vegans** will find it near impossible. Contact the **North American Vegetarian Society**, P.O. Box 72, Dolgeville, NY 13329 (☎518-568-7970; www.navs-online.org) for *Transformative Adventures, Vacations, and Retreats* (US$15). The **International Vegetarian Union** (www.ivu.org) is another valuable resource.

Kosher food exists in France, which has one of Western Europe's largest Jewish populations, but finding it may prove difficult, particularly in rural regions. Kosher travelers should contact synagogues in larger cities for info on restaurants. Your home synagogue or college Hillel should have lists of Jewish institutions throughout the world. **The Jewish Travel Guide,** edited by Michael Zaidner, lists synagogues, kosher restaurants, and Jewish institutions in over 100 countries and is available in Europe from Vallentine Mitchell Publishers, Crown House, 47 Chase Side, Southgate, London N14 5BP, UK (☎02089 202100; fax 84 478548), in the US at 5824 NE Hassalo St., Portland, OR, 97213 (☎800-944-6190; fax 503-280-8832).

FURTHER READING. *The Vegetarian Traveller: Where to Stay if You're Vegetarian, Vegan, or Environmentally Sensitive*, by Jed and Susan Civic (US$16); *Europe on 10 Salads a Day*, by Greg and Mary Jane Edwards (Mustang Publishing; US$10); *The Jewish Travel Guide*, by Betsy Sheldon (Hunter; US$17).

OTHER RESOURCES

USEFUL PUBLICATIONS

We like these books and think you might as well.

Fragile Glory: A Portrait of France and the French, Richard Bernstein. Plume, 1991 (US$14.95). A witty look at France by the former New York Times Paris bureau chief.

Portraits of France, Robert Daley. Little, Brown & Co., 1991 (US$23). An engaging, informed collection of essays on France and the French, organized by region.

Culture Shock: A Guide To Customs and Etiquette, Sally Adamson Taylor. Graphic Arts Center Publishing Company, 1991 (US$13.95). Tips and warnings.

Merde! The Real French You Were Never Taught at School, Michael Heath Genevieve. Fireside, 1998 ($9). Lots of gutter slang and a collection of very dirty things to say.

French or Foe? Getting the Most Out of Visiting, Living and Working in France, Polly Platt. Distribooks Intl., 1998 (US$16.95). A popular guide to getting by in France.

A Traveller's Wine Guide to France, Christopher Fielden. Traveller's Wine Guides, 1999 (US$19.95). Exactly what it says it is, by a well-known oenophile.

THE WORLD WIDE WEB

Below are general, all-purpose sites.

Maison de la France (www.francetourism.com), the French government's site for tourists. Tips on everything from accommodation to smoking laws. English version.

Youth Tourism (www.franceguide.com). For youths planning long stays in France. Mostly in English.

France Diplomatie (www.france.diplomatie.fr/) is the site of the Department of Foreign Affairs. Info on **visas** and current affairs. Mostly in English.

Secretariat for Tourism (www.tourisme.gouv.fr) has a number of government documents about French tourism; links to all French tourist authorities. In French.

Tourism in France (www.tourisme.fr) has info in French and mildly amusing English.

Nomade (www.nomade.fr) is a popular French search engine.

TF1 (www.tf1.fr) is the home page of France's most popular TV station.

Météo-France (www.meteo.fr) has 2-day weather forecasts and maps. In French.

THE ART OF BUDGET TRAVEL

How to See the World: www.artoftravel.com. A compendium of great travel tips.

Rec. Travel Library: www.travel-library.com. Fantastic general info and travelogues.

Lycos: http://cityguide.lycos.com. Introductions to cities and regions throughout France.

Backpacker's Ultimate Guide: www.bugeurope.com.

Backpack Europe: www.backpackeurope.com. Helpful tips, a bulletin board, and links.

INFORMATION ON FRANCE

CIA World Factbook: www.odci.gov/cia/publications/factbook/index.html. Vital stats.

Foreign Language for Travelers: www.travlang.com. Online translating dictionary.

Geographia: www.geographia.com. Highlights, culture, and people of France.

Atevo Travel: www.atevo.com/guides/destinations. Travel tips. Suggested itineraries.

World Travel Guide: www.travel-guides.com/navigate/world.asp. Helpful practical info.

AND OUR PERSONAL FAVORITE...

WWW.LETSGO.COM Our newly designed website now has lots of extra information about our guides, the countries we cover, and travel in general. Trial versions of all nine City Guides are available for download on Palm OS™ PDAs. Our website also contains our newsletter, links for photos and streaming video, online ordering of our titles, info about our books, and a travel forum buzzing with stories and tips.

ALTERNATIVES TO TOURISM

Without doubt, a budget itinerary is the best way for travelers with limited funds and time to see the highlights of France's incomparable cultural heritage and natural beauty. But let's face it, touring a Loire Valley château or buying a hat in the shape of Mont St-Michel is not going to give you the most realistic view of daily life in France, let alone a firm grasp of the current political, social and cultural challenges the country faces. If you are interested in getting a more in-depth perspective on life in France and in forming lasting relationships with local residents, consider working, volunteering, or studying in France. There is no formula to finding the perfect job or study program in France—your best tools are persistence, thorough research, and luck. Of course, being fluent in French and fabulously connected couldn't hurt either, particularly in light of France's highly competitive job market. This chapter provides information on France's education and employment systems and outlines several programs and work options to serve as starting points for your own research.

VISA INFORMATION
Students belonging to the EU have the right to work and study in France without obtaining a visa, but they are required to have a residency permit. Students and paid workers from non-EU countries must apply for both a visa and a residency permit. In order to get a student visa (US$47), you must have a passport and offer of admission from a French university. The process for obtaining a working visa is more complicated. Your employer must get authorization from the French Ministry of Labor in order to allow you to apply for a long-stay visa (US$93) through the French Consulate in the United States. After entering France, you must apply at the local prefecture of police for a residency permit *(Carte de Séjour)*. International students looking for part-time work (up to 20 hours per week) can apply for a provisional work authorization upon completing their first academic year in a French university.

STUDYING ABROAD

Study abroad programs in France range from basic language and culture courses to college-level classes, often for credit. In order to choose a program that best fits your needs, you will want to find out what kind of students participate in the program and what sort of accommodations are provided. In programs that have large groups of students who speak the same language, there is a trade-off. You may feel more comfortable in the community, but you will not have the same opportunity to practice French or to interact with other international students. For accommodations, dorm life provides a better opportunity to mingle with fellow students, but there is less of a chance to experience the local scene. If you live with a family, there is a potential to build lifelong friendships with natives and to experience day-to-day life in more depth, but conditions can vary greatly from family to family. A good resource for finding programs that cater to your particular interests is www.studyabroad.com, which has links to various semester abroad programs based on a variety of criteria, including desired location and focus of study.

For those who are fluent in French, direct enrollment in a French university can be more rewarding than a class filled with native English speakers. It can also be up to four times cheaper, although academic credit at home is not a guarantee. As a student at a French university, you will receive a student card *(carte d'étudiant)* upon presentation of a residency permit and a receipt for your university fees. In addition to basic student benefits, additional benefits are administered by the **Centre Régional des Oeuvres Universitaires et Scolaires (CROUS)**. Founded in 1955 to improve the living and working conditions of students, CROUS welcomes foreign students. The brochure *Le CROUS et Moi* lists addresses and info on student life. Pick up their free guidebook *Je Vais en France*, in French or English, from any French embassy.

AMERICAN PROGRAMS

American Institute for Foreign Study, College Division, River Plaza, 9 W. Broad St., Stamford, CT 06902, USA (☎800-727-2437, ext. 5163; www.aifsabroad.com). Organizes programs for high school and college study in universities in France.

Central College Abroad, Office of International Education, 812 University, Pella, IA 50219, USA (☎800-831-3629 or 641-628-5284; www.central.edu/abroad). Offers internships, as well as summer-, semester-, and year-long programs in France. US$25 application fee.

School for International Training, College Semester Abroad, Admissions, Kipling Rd., P.O. Box 676, Brattleboro, VT 05302, USA (☎800-336-1616 or 802-257-7751; www.sit.edu). Semester- and year-long programs in France run US$10,600-13,700. Also runs the **Experiment in International Living** (☎800-345-2929; fax 802-258-3428; www.usexperiment.org), 3- to 5-week summer programs that offer high school students cross-cultural homestays, community service, ecological adventure, and language training in France and cost US$1,900-5,000.

Study Abroad, 1450 Edgmont Ave., Suite #140, Chester, PA 19013, USA (☎610-499-9200; www.studyabroad.com), maintains a compilation of countless international exchanges and study programs, including about 175 in France.

Council on International Educational Exchange (CIEE), 633 3rd Ave., 20th fl., New York, NY 10017-6706 (☎800-407-8839; www.ciee.org/study) sponsors work, volunteer, academic, and internship programs in France.

International Association for the Exchange of Students for Technical Experience (IAESTE), 10400 Little Patuxent Pkwy., Suite 250, Columbia, MD 21044-3519, USA (☎410-997-2200; www.aipt.org). 8- to 12-week programs in France for college students who have completed 2 years of technical study. US$25 application fee.

FRENCH UNIVERSITIES

Paris conjures practically every archetypal image of student life imaginable: flirting over a volume of Sartre in a candlelit café, leisurely reading in the Luxembourg garden, tracking down elusive late-night parties. However, there are distinct advantages to studying in France's other major student city centers. The lower cost of living and proximity to beaches, mountains, and a variety of cultural destinations make Montpellier, Grenoble, Toulouse, Aix-en-Provence, Marseille, Strasbourg and Rennes very attractive student centers. French universities are segmented into three degree levels. Programs at the first level (except the **Grandes Ecoles,** below) are two or three years long, generally focus on science, medicine, and the liberal arts, and must admit anyone holding a *baccalauréat* (French graduation certificate) or recognized equivalent. A certificate or diploma of secondary-school completion in most countries is enough, although French competency or other testing may be required (for Americans, two years of college French are expected). The more selective and more demanding **Grandes Ecoles** cover specializations from physics to photography to veterinary medicine. These have notoriously difficult entrance examinations which require a year of preparatory schooling.

French universities are far cheaper than their American equivalents; however, it can be hard to receive academic credit at home for a non-approved program. Expect to pay at least €500 per month in living expenses. EU citizens studying in France can take advantage of the 3- to 12-month **SOCRATES** program, which offers grants to support inter-European educational exchanges. Most UK and Irish universities will have details of the grants available and the application procedure. EU law dictates that educational qualifications be recognized across the Union (with the exception of some professional subjects). These organizations can supply further info on academic programs in France. For information on programs of study, requirements, and grants or scholarships, visit www.egide.asso.fr.

Agence EduFrance, 173 bd. St-Germain, 75006 Paris (☎01 53 63 35 00; www.edufrance.fr), is a one-stop resource for North Americans thinking about studying for a degree in France. Info on courses, costs, grant opportunities, and other major student cities in France.

American University of Paris, 31 av. Bosquet, 75343 Paris Cedex 07 (☎01 40 62 06 00; www.aup.fr), offers US-accredited degrees and summer programs taught in English at its Paris campus. Intensive French language courses offered. Tuition US$9,000 per quarter, not including living expenses.

Université Paris-Sorbonne, 1 rue Victor Cousin, 75005 Paris Cédex 05 (☎01 40 46 25 42; www.paris4.sorbonne.fr), the grand-daddy of French universities, was founded in 1253 and is still going strong. Inscription into degree courses costs about €400 per year. Also offers 3-9 month-long programs for American students.

LANGUAGE SCHOOLS

Many French universities offer language courses during the summer, while independent organizations run throughout the year. The American University of Paris also runs a summer program (see above). For more info on language courses in France, contact your national **Institut Français**, official representatives of French culture attached to French embassies around the world (contact your nearest French embassy or consulate for details). Other well-known schools include:

Alliance Française, Ecole Internationale de Langue et de Civilisation Française, 101 bd. Raspail, 75270 Paris Cédex 06 (☎01 42 84 90 00; www.alliancefr.org). Instruction at all levels, with courses in legal and business French. Courses are 1-4 months in length, costing €267 for 16 2hr. sessions and €534 for 16 4hr. sessions.

Cours de Civilisation Française de la Sorbonne, 47 rue des Ecoles, 75005 Paris (☎01 40 46 22 11; www.fle.fr/sorbonne). Courses in the French language at all levels, along with a comprehensive lecture program of French cultural studies taught by Sorbonne professors. Must be at least 18 and at *baccalauréat* level. Semester- and year-long courses during the academic year and 4-, 6-, 8-, and 11-week summer programs.

Eurocentres, 101 N. Union St., Suite 300, Alexandria, VA 22314, USA (☎703-684-1494; www.eurocentres.com) or in Europe, Head Office, Seestr. 247, CH-8038 Zurich, Switzerland (☎14 85 50 40; fax 04 81 61 24). Language programs for beginning to advanced students with homestays in France. Schools located in **Paris, Amboise, Tours La Rochelle, Lausanne,** and **Neuchatel.**

Language Immersion Institute, 75 S Manheim Blvd., SUNY-New Paltz, New Paltz, NY 12561-2499, USA (☎845-257-3500; www.newpaltz.edu/lii). 2-week summer language courses and some overseas courses in French. Program fees are around US$1,000 for a 2-week course.

Institut de Langue Française, 3 av. Bertie-Albrecht, 75008 Paris (☎01 45 63 24 00; fax 01 45 63 07 09; www.inst-langue-fr.com). M: Charles de Gaulle-Etoile. Language, civilization, and literature courses. Offers 4-week up to year-long programs, 6-20hr. per week, starting at €185.

Institut Parisien de Langue et de Civilisation Française, 87 bd. de Grenelle, 75015 Paris (☎01 40 56 09 53; fax 01 43 06 46 30; www.institut-parisien.com). M: La Motte-Picquet-Grenelle. French language, fashion, culinary arts, and cinema courses. Intensive language courses for 10 (€95-117 per week), 15 (€143-177 per week), or 25 (€238-294 per week) hours per week.

CULINARY AND ART SCHOOLS

One final—and pricier—study abroad option for students and amateurs of all ages is to enroll in a French culinary institute or art school. While the very best of France's trade schools are oriented toward pre-professionals, many programs allow budding chefs and closet Van Goghs to participate in semester- or year-long programs, or in some cases individual class sessions. For smaller, more intimate courses based in farms and homes, amateur cooks should check out www.CookingSchools.com, which lists small private schools and gastronomy tours throughout France.

Grande Ecole des Arts Culinaires et de l'Hôtellerie de Lyon (Lyon Culinary Arts and Hotel Management School), Château de Vivier–BP25, 69131 Lyon-Ecully Cedex (☎04 72 18 02 20; fax 04 78 43 33 51; www.each-lyon.com; info@each-lyon.com). Premier school affiliated with Paul Bocuse, located in France's capital city of *haute cuisine*. 8- and 16-week summer courses in French and English for amateurs (€4200-7000). Offers individual day courses ranging €62-76 (reserve in advance to dchabert@each-lyon.com).

Cordon Bleu Paris Culinary Arts Institute, 8 rue Léon Delhomme, 75015 Paris (☎01 53 68 22 50; fax 01 48 56 03 77; www.cordonbleu.edu; infoparis@cordonbleu.edu). M: Porte de la Chapelle. The *crème de la crème* of French cooking schools. A full-year diploma course will run you about €29,500 in debt, but Gourmet Sessions are also available, ranging from half-days to 4 weeks.

Pont Aven School of Art, 66 Commonwealth Ave., Concord, MA, USA (☎978-369-9740; fax 369-6954; www.pontavensa.org; artists@pontavensa.org) or in France, 5 pl. Paul Gaugin, 29930 Pont Aven (☎02 98 09 10 45; fax 02 98 06 17 38; psa.france@wana-doo.fr). English-speaking school in Brittany offers studio courses in painting and sculpture, art history, and French language. 4- and 6-week sessions €3200-6200, including room and board.

Lacoste School of Art, P.O. Box 3146, Savannah, GA 31401, USA (☎912-525-5803; www.scad.edu/lacoste; lacoste@scad.edu). Based in the tiny medieval town of Lacoste in Provence, this school is administered by the Savannah College of Art and Design. Summer and fall courses in architecture, painting, and historical preservation. Tuition €3850-5925; room and board €2350.

Painting School of Montmiral, rue de la Porte Neuve, 81140 Castelnau de Montmiral (☎/fax 05 63 33 13 11; www.painting-school; fpratt@painting-school.com). Teaches 2-week classes for student, amateur, teacher, and professional levels. In English or French. €1180, including accommodations and half-board.

WORKING

Anyone hoping to come to France and slip easily into a job will face the tough reality that employers are still understandably more sympathetic toward French job-seekers than unqualified or very qualified foreigners. On the bright side, many employers look favorably on English-language skills; if you're bilingual, your chances of obtaining employment can be greater. Before stating your job hunt, make sure you understand France's **visa requirements** for working abroad. See the box on p. 84 for more information. For US college students, recent graduates, and young adults, the simplest way to get legal permission to work abroad is through **Council Exchanges Work Abroad Programs.** Fees range from US$300 to 475. Council Exchanges can help you obtain a three- to six-month work permit/visa and also provides assistance finding jobs and housing.

LONG-TERM WORK

If you're planning on spending a substantial amount of time (more than three months) working in France, search for a job well in advance. International placement agencies are often the easiest way to find employment abroad, especially for teaching English. **Internships,** usually for college students, are a good way to segue into working abroad, although they are often unpaid or poorly paid; many say the experience, however, is well worth it. For an international internship and job database, try www.jobsabroad.com. Be wary of advertisements or companies that claim the ability to get you a job abroad for a fee—often times the same listings are available online or in newspapers, or even out of date. It's best, if going through an organization, to use one that's somewhat reputable. Some good ones include:

Council Exchanges, 52 Poland St., London W1F 7AB, UK (☎44 020 7478 2000, US 888-268-6245; www.councilexchanges.org). Council Exchanges offers the simplest way to get legal permission to work abroad, charging a US$300-475 fee for arranging a three- to six-month work permit/visa. They also provide extensive information on different job and housing opportunities in France.

French-American Chamber of Commerce (FACC), International Career Development Programs, 1350 Avenue of the Americas, 6th fl., New York, NY 10019 (☎212-765-4598; fax 765-4650) has *Work In France* programs, internships, teaching, and public works.

TEACHING ENGLISH
Many private and public schools in France require teachers to have a **Teaching English as a Foreign Language (TEFL)** certificate. This does not necessarily exclude you from finding a teaching job, but certified teachers often find higher paying jobs. In almost all cases, you must have at least a bachelor's degree to be a full-fledged teacher, although often times college undergraduates can get summer positions teaching or tutoring. The Fulbright Teaching Assistantship and French Teaching Assistantship program through the French Ministry of Education are the best options for students and recent grads with little experience teaching. Another alternative is to make contacts directly with schools or just to try your luck once you get there. If you are going to try the latter, the best time of the year is several weeks before the start of the school year. The following organizations are extremely helpful in placing teachers in France.

Fulbright English Teaching Assistantship, U.S. Student Programs Division, Institute of International Education, 809 United Nations Plaza, New York, NY 10017-3580, USA (☎212-984-5330; www.iie.org). Competitive program sends college graduates to teach in France.

French Ministry of Education Teaching Assistantship in France, Cultural Service of the French Embassy, 972 Fifth Ave., New York, NY 10021, USA (☎212-439-1400; fax 439-1455; www.frenchculture.org/education). Program for US citizens sends 1500 college students and recent grads to teach English part-time in France.

International Schools Services (ISS), 15 Roszel Rd., Box 5910, Princeton, NJ 08543-5910, USA (☎609-452-0990; fax 609-452-2690; www.iss.edu). Hires teachers for more than 200 overseas schools including ones in France; candidates should have experience teaching or with international affairs; 2-year commitment expected.

AU PAIR WORK
Au-pairs are typically women aged 18-27 who work as live-in nannies, caring for children and doing light housework in foreign countries in exchange for room, board, and a small spending allowance or stipend. Most former au pairs speak favorably of their experience, which allowed them to get to know a region without the high expenses of traveling. Drawbacks, however, often include long hours of constantly being on-duty, and the mediocre pay (wages are often range from US$75-120 per week). Much of the au pair experience really does depend on the family you're placed with. The agencies below are a good starting point for looking for employment as an au pair.

L'Accueil Familial des Jeunes Etrangers, 23 rue du Cherche-Midi, 75006 Paris (☎01 42 22 50 34; fax 01 45 44 60 48; accueil@afje-paris.org). Arranges summer and 18-month au pair jobs (placement fee €108). Also arranges similar jobs for non-students which require 30hr. of work per week in exchange for room, board, employment benefits, and a métro pass.

Au Pair Homestay, World Learning, Inc., 1015 15th St. NW, Suite 750, Washington, DC 20005, USA (☎800-287-2477; fax 202-408-5397).

Au Pair in Europe, P.O. Box 68056, Blakely Postal Outlet, Hamilton, Ontario, Canada L8M 3M7 (☎905-545-6305; fax 905-544-4121; www.princeent.com).

Childcare International, Ltd., Trafalgar House, Grenville Pl., London NW7 3SA (☎20890 63116; fax 8906-3461; www.childint.co.uk).

InterExchange, 161 Sixth Ave., New York, NY 10013, USA (☎212-924-0446; fax 924-0575; www.interexchange.org).

FINDING WORK ONCE THERE

Those looking for work can check help-wanted columns in French newspaper, especially *Le Monde*, *Le Figaro*, and the English-language *International Hera Tribune*, as well as *France-USA Contacts (FUSAC)*, a free weekly circular fill, with classified ads, available at Yankee hangouts. Many of these jobs are "unofficia and therefore illegal (the penalty is deportation), but many people find them conv nient because they often don't ask for presentation of a work permit. However, t best tips on jobs for foreigners come from other travelers. Be aware of your rights an employee, and always get written confirmation of your agreements, includi official job offers. Youth hostels frequently provide room and board to travelers exchange for work. Those seeking more permanent employment should have **résumé** in both English and French. Type up your résumé for a prospecti employer, but write the cover letter by hand. Handwriting is considered an imp tant indicator of your character to French employers. Also, expect to be asked int view questions that might be considered inappropriate in another culture, such your stance on ethical or political issues. The French workplace tends to be mo conservative than Anglo offices, so your and your employer's morals must (as far your employer knows) correspond.

American Church, 65 quai d'Orsay, 75007 Paris (☎01 40 62 05 00; fax 01 40 62 11; www.americanchurchparis.org). Posts a bulletin board full of job and housi opportunities targeting Americans and anglophones. Open M-Sa 9am-10pm.

The Information Center, 65 quai d'Orsay, 75007 Paris (☎01 45 56 09 50). Located the garden level at the American Church. A clearing house of information and referr providing immediate service to the English speaking people of Paris. The Center ma tains a comprehensive database of resources available to those in need of informati regarding legal matters, medical resources, housing, language courses, and mo Open Tu-Th 1:15-4pm.

Agence Nationale Pour l'Emploi (ANPE), 4 impasse d'Antin, Paris (☎01 43 59 62 www.anpe.fr). Has specific info on employment opportunities. Interested parties sho bring a work permit and *carte de séjour*. Open M-W and F 9am-5pm, Th 9am-noon.

Centre d'Information et de Documentation Jeunesse (CIDJ), 101 quai Branly, 757 Paris (☎01 44 49 12 00; fax 01 40 65 02 61; www.cidj.asso.fr). An invaluable sta run youth center provides info on education, résumés, employment, and caree English spoken. Jobs are posted on the bulletin boards outside. Open M, W, F 10a 6pm; Tu and Th 10am-7pm; Sa 9:30am-1pm.

European Employment Services (EURES) (☎08 00 90 97 00) facilitates employm between EU countries. For EU citizens only.

Chamber of Commerce in France, 156 bd. Haussmann, 75008 Paris (☎01 56 43 67; fax 01 56 43 45 60; www.amchamfrance.org). An association of American b nesses in France. Keeps résumés on file for 2 months and places them at the dispo of French and American companies. Open M-Th 9:30am-1pm and 2-5pm.

SHORT-TERM WORK

Traveling for long periods of time can get expensive; many travelers try their ha at odd jobs for a few weeks to make some extra cash. Bartending, serving, a working in the tourist industry are options commonly available to travele Another popular option is to work several hours a day at a hostel in exchange free or discounted room and/or board. Most often, these short-term jobs are fou by word of mouth, or simply by talking to the owner of a hostel or restaurant. L to the high turnover in the tourism industry, many places are always eager help, even if only temporary. Youth centers *(centres de jeunesse)* often have listings; check out our practical information sections in larger cities.

Farm work is another option; the autumn *vendanges* (grape harvest) provides plentiful opportunities for backbreaking work in return for a small allowance and cheap wine. Check out **WWOOF** (Willing Workers on Organic Farms; WWOOF International, P.O. Box 2675, Lewes BN7 1RB, UK; www.phdcc.com/wwoof), which maintains an international list of farms seeking temporary workers in exchange for room and board.

VOLUNTEERING

Volunteering in France runs the wide range from work camps to historical preservation to working with homeless individuals. At its best, volunteering in France can be a fulfilling way to see French culture and society while making an active contribution to its improvement and preservation. But finding a program that is both well-run and cost effective for you may require some research. Many volunteer services charge participation fees which can be surprisingly hefty (although they frequently cover airfare and living expenses). Try talking to people who have previously participated and find out exactly what you're getting into, as living and working conditions can vary greatly. Different programs are geared toward different ages and levels of experience, so be sure to make sure that you are not taking on too much or too little. The more informed you are and the more realistic expectations you have, the more enjoyable the program will be.

Archaeological Institute of America, 656 Beacon St., Boston, MA 02215, USA (☎617-353-9361; www.archaeological.org). The *Archaeological Fieldwork Opportunities Bulletin,* available on the organization's website, lists field sites throughout Europe.

Club du Vieux Manoir, Abbaye Royale du Moncel, 60700 Pontpoint (☎03 44 72 33 98; cvmclubduvieuxmanoir.free.fr). Offers year-long and summer programs restoring castles and churches throughout France. €13.72 membership/insurance fee, €13.72 per day, including food and tent.

Concordia International Volunteer Programs, Heversham House, 20-22 Boundary Rd., Hove, BN34ET, England (☎+44(0)1273 422218, www.concordia-iye.org.uk). Free volunteer activities (food and lodging provided) in France for ages 18-30, including archaeological restoration, environment, arts/culture.

Elderhostel, Inc., 11 av. de Lafayette, Boston, MA 92111-1746, USA (☎877-426-8056; fax 877-426-2166; www.elderhostel.org). Sends volunteers age 55 and over around the world to work in construction, research, teaching, and many other projects. Costs average $100 per day plus airfare.

REMPART, 1 rue des Guillemites, 75004 Paris (☎01 42 71 96 55, www.rempart.com), enlists volunteers to care for endangered monuments. Membership fee €35; most projects charge €6-8 per day.

Service Civil International Voluntary Service (SCI-IVS), SCI USA, 3213 W. Wheeler St., Seattle, WA 98199, USA (☎/fax 206-350-6585; www.sci-ivs.org). Arranges placement in work camps in France for those 18+. Registration fee US$65-125.

United Nations Educational, Scientific, and Cultural Organization (UNESCO), (www.unesco.org). Offers unpaid internships of 3-6 months for university graduates. For more information check the web site above or write, to the attention of your country's delegation, to UNESCO PER-Staff Training Section, 1 rue Miollis, 75732 Paris.

Volunteers for Peace, 1034 Tiffany Rd., Belmont., VT 05730, USA (☎802-259-2759; www.vfp.org). Arranges placement in work camps in France. Membership required for registration. Annual *International Workcamp Directory* US$20. Programs average US$200-500 for 2-3 weeks.

ALTERNATIVES
TO TOURISM

FOR FURTHER READING ON ALTERNATIVES TO TOURISM

French or Foe? Getting the Most Out of Visiting, Living and Working in France, by Polly Platt. Distribooks Intl, 1998 (US$17).

How to Get a Job in Europe, by Sanborn and Matherly. Surrey Books, 1999 ($US22).

How to Live Your Dream of Volunteering Oversees, by Collins, DeZerega, and Heckscher. Penguin Books, 2002 (US$17).

International Directory of Voluntary Work, by Whetter and Pybus. Peterson's Guides and Vacation Work, 2000 (US$16).

International Jobs, by Kocher and Segal. Perseus Books, 1999 (US$18).

Living, Studying, and Working in France, by Reilly and Kalisky. Henry Holt and Company, 1999 (US$16).

Overseas Summer Jobs 2002, by Collier and Woodworth. Peterson's Guides and Vacation Work, 2002 (US$18).

Work Abroad: The Complete Guide to Finding a Job Overseas, by Hubbs, Griffith, and Nolting. Transitions Abroad Publishing, 2000 (US$16).

PARIS

City of light, site of majestic panoramas and showy store windows; unsightly city, invisible city—Paris somehow manages to do it all. From alleys that shelter the world's best bistros to broad avenues flaunting the highest of *haute couture*, from the old stone of Notre Dame's gargoyles to the futuristic motions of the Parc de la Villette, from the relics of the first millennium to the celebration of the third, Paris presents itself as both a harbor of tradition and a place of impulse. You can't conquer Paris in one week or in thirty years, but you can get acquainted in a day, and in a week, you may find you're old friends.

SUGGESTIONS

Paris is first and foremost an international city, and second the capital of France. Wandering around the grand **Champs-Elysées** (p. 142), the student-filled **Latin Quarter** (p. 136), the formerly aristocratic and now supremely fun **Marais** (p. 132), and bohemian **Montmartre** (p. 149) will give you a good feel for the city. No one can visit Paris without seeing the **Louvre** (p. 152), the **Eiffel Tower** (p. 140), and **Notre Dame** (p. 127), but don't neglect Paris's Latin past in the **Musée de Cluny** (p. 154), Gothic architecture's finest jewel, **Ste-Chapelle** (p. 129), and the mecca of Impressionism, the **Musée d'Orsay** (p. 153). Near Paris, Louis XIV's palace **Versailles** (p. 165), is the best-known château, while **Chartres** (p. 168) is the best-known cathedral.

ORIENTATION

Flowing from east to west, the **Seine River** crosses the heart of Paris. Two islands, the **Ile de la Cité** and the **Ile St-Louis**, sit at the geographical center of the city. To the north, the **Rive Droite** (Right Bank) has historically been the center of Paris, with the oldest streets and most expensive restaurants. To the south, the **Rive Gauche** (Left Bank) was once associated with the lifestyle of impoverished students but now hosts a lively café and bar scene. By the time of Louis XIV, the city had 20 *quartiers*. Modern Paris is divided into 20 *arrondissements* (districts) that spiral clockwise around the Louvre, each labeled with a number (e.g. the 3rd, 12th). The French equivalent of the English "th," as in 8th, is *"ème."* Thus, the 5*ème* is the *cinquième* (SANK-yem). The exception is the 1st, for which the French abbreviation is 1*er*, spelled out as *premier* (PREM-yay). For more on individual *arrondissements*, see **Sights,** p. 127.

■ GETTING INTO PARIS

TO AND FROM THE AIRPORTS

ROISSY-CHARLES DE GAULLE. Transatlantic flights. 24hr. English-speaking info center. (☎ 01 48 62 22 80; www.parisairports.com.)

RER: From Roissy-CDG to Paris, take the free shuttle bus (*Navette*) from Terminal 1 (every 10min.). From there, the RER B (one of the Parisian commuter rail lines) runs to central Paris. To transfer to the métro, get off at Gare du Nord, Châtelet-Les-Halles, or St-Michel. **To Roissy-CDG from Paris,** take the RER B to "Roissy," which is the end of the line. Then change to the free shuttle bus if you need to get to Terminal 1 (30-35min.; RER every 15min. 5am-12:30am; €7.60, children €5.30).

Shuttle Buses: Roissybus (☎01 49 25 61 87) runs between 9 rue Scribe, near M: Opéra, and terminals 1, 2, and 9. Tickets can be purchased on the bus (45min.; to airport every 15min. 5:45am-11pm, from airport every 15min. 6am-11pm; €8.05). **Air France Buses** (recorded info in English ☎08 92 35 08 20) run daily to two sections of the city. Buy tickets on board. **Line 2** runs to and from the Arc de Triomphe (M: Charles de Gaulle-Etoile) at 1 av. Carnot, and to and from pl. de la Porte de Maillot/Palais des Congrès (M: Porte de Maillot) on bd. Gouvion St-Cyr (both lines: 35min.; every 15min. 5:45am-11pm; one-way €10, children €5, round-trip €17; %15 group discount). **Line 4** runs to and from rue du Commandant Mouchette opposite the Méridien Hotel (M: Montparnasse-Bienvenüe) and to and from Gare de Lyon (M: Gare de Lyon) at 20b bd. Diderot (both lines: to airport every 30min. 7am-9:30pm; one-way €11.50, children €5.75, round-trip €19.55; %15 group discounts). The shuttle stops at or between terminals 2A and 2F and at terminal 1 on the departures level.

ORLY. 18km south of the city. Charters and many continental flights. (Info in English ☎01 49 75 15 15, 6am-11:45pm.)

RER: From Orly Sud gate G or gate I, platform 1, or Orly Ouest level G, gate F, take the **Orly-Rail** shuttle bus (every 15min. 6am-11pm; €5.15, children €3.55) to the **Pont de Rungis/Aéroport d'Orly** train stop, where you can board the **RER C2** for a number of destinations in Paris (info ☎08 36 68 41 14 in English; 35min., every 15min. 6am-11pm, €5.15.) The **Jetbus** (every 15min. 6am-10pm, €4.58), provides a quick connection between Orly Sud, gate H, platform 2, or Orly Ouest level O, gate C and M: Villejuif-Louis Aragon on line 7 of the métro.

Bus: The RATP **Orlybus** (☎01 40 02 32 94) runs between métro and RER stop Denfert-Rochereau, 14ème, and Orly Sud (30min., every 10-15min. 6am-11:30pm from Orly to Denfert-Rochereau, 5:35am-11pm from Denfert-Rochereau to Orly; €5.60). You can also board the Orlybus at Dareau-St-Jacques, Glacière-Tolbiac, and Porte de Gentilly. **Air France Buses** run between Orly and **Gare Montparnasse**, near the Hôtel Méridien, 6ème (M: Montparnasse-Bienvenüe), and the Invalides Air France agency, pl. des Invalides (30min.; every 15min. 6am-11pm; one-way €7.50, round-trip €12.75). Air France shuttles stop at Orly Ouest and then Orly Sud, at the departures levels.

Orlyval: RATP also runs **Orlyval** (☎08 36 68 41 14), a combination of métro, RER, and VAL rail shuttle, and probably the fastest option. The VAL shuttle goes from Antony (a stop on the RER line B) to Orly Ouest and Sud. You can either get a ticket just for the VAL (Orly to Antony, €7), or a combination VAL-RER ticket that includes the VAL ticket and the RER ticket (€8.65 and up). Be careful when taking the RER B from Paris to Orly, because it splits into 2 lines right before the Antony stop; make sure you're on the train labeled "St-Rémy-Les-Chevreuse." Buy tickets at any RATP booth or from the Orlyval agencies. (35min. from Châtelet, 40min. from Charles de Gaulle-Etoile, 50min. from La Défense; every 10min. M-Sa 6am-10:30pm, Su and holidays 7am-11pm.) **From Orly,** trains arrive at Orly Ouest 2min. after stopping at Orly Sud (32min. to Châtelet; 45min. to La Défense; every 10min. M-Sa 6am-10:30pm, Su 7am-11pm.)

TRAINS

Each of Paris's six train stations is a veritable community of its own, but all you really need is the ticket counters (*guichets*), platforms (*quais*), and tracks (*voies*). Each terminal is divided into the *banlieue* (suburban trains) and the *grandes lignes* (major trains). Some cities can be reached by both regular trains and **trains à grande vitesse** (TGV; high speed trains), which are more expensive, much faster, and require reservations for a small fee. For **train info** or to make reservations, contact **SNCF.** (☎08 36 35 35 35; www.sncf.fr; €0.34 per min.) Yellow **ticket machines** (*billetteries*) at every train station sell tickets to anyone with a Mastercard or Visa who knows his or her PIN.

BUSES

International buses arrive in Paris at **Gare Routière Internationale du Paris-Gallieni** (M: Gallieni), just outside Paris at 28 av. du Général de Gaulle, Bagnolet 93170. **Eurolines** (☎ 08 36 69 52 52; www.eurolines.fr) sells tickets to most destinations in France and neighboring countries. Pick up schedules for departures from the station or the office at 55 rue St-Jacques, *5ème* (M: Maubert-Mutualité).

⊏ GETTING AROUND PARIS

RATP helpline (☎ 08 92 68 41 14 in English daily 6am-9pm; www.ratp.fr; €0.34 per min.).

FARES AND PASSES

Individual tickets for the RATP cost €1.30 each and €9.30 for a book of 10 (*un carnet*). Each métro ride takes one ticket; the bus takes at least one, sometimes more, depending on the number of connections and the time of day. For directions on using the tickets, see **Métro,** below. If you're staying in Paris for several days or weeks, a **Carte Orange** can be very economical. Bring a photo ID (photo machines are found in most stations; €3.81) to the ticket counter and ask for the weekly *carte orange hebdomaire* (€13.75) or the monthly *carte orange mensuelle* (€46.05). Prices quoted here are for passes in Zones 1 and 2 (the métro and RER in Paris and suburbs), which work on all métro, bus, and RER modes of transport in these zones. If you intend to travel to the suburbs, you'll need to buy RER passes for more zones (up to 5). If you're only in town for a day or two, a cheap option is the **Carte Mobilis** (available in métro station; €5), which provides one day of unlimited métro, bus, and RER transportation within Zones 1 and 2. Always write the number of your *carte* on your coupon. **Paris Visite tickets** are valid for unlimited

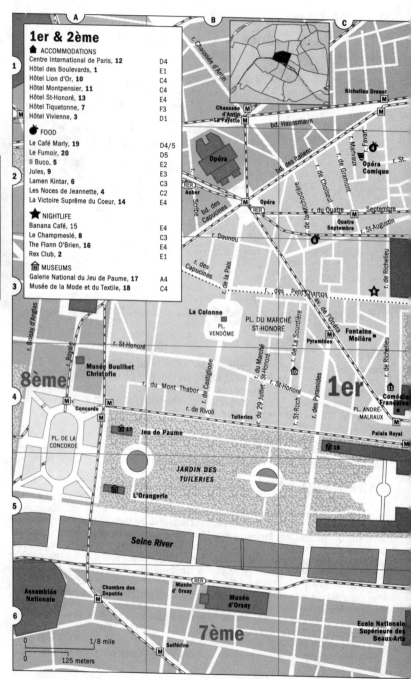

1er & 2ème

🏠 ACCOMMODATIONS

Centre International de Paris, **12**	D4
Hôtel des Boulevards, **1**	E1
Hôtel Lion d'Or, **10**	C4
Hôtel Montpensier, **11**	C4
Hôtel St-Honoré, **13**	E4
Hôtel Tiquetonne, **7**	F3
Hôtel Vivienne, **3**	D1

🍴 FOOD

Le Café Marly, **19**	D4/5
Le Fumoir, **20**	D5
Il Buco, **5**	E2
Jules, **9**	E3
Lamen Kintar, **6**	C3
Les Noces de Jeannette, **4**	C2
La Victoire Suprême du Coeur, **14**	E4

⭐ NIGHTLIFE

Banana Café, **15**	E4
Le Champmeslé, **8**	C3
The Flann O'Brien, **16**	E4
Rex Club, **2**	E1

🏛 MUSEUMS

Galerie National du Jeu de Paume, **17**	A4
Musée de la Mode et du Textile, **18**	C4

PARIS

PARIS

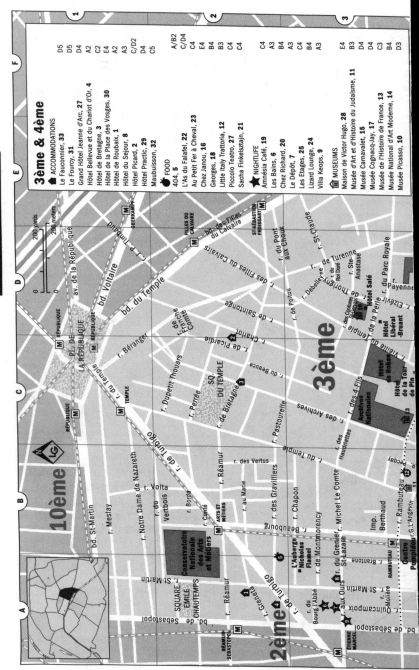

3ème & 4ème

♦ ACCOMMODATIONS

Le Fauconnier, 33	D5
Le Fourcy, 31	D5
Grand Hôtel Jeanne d'Arc, 27	D4
Hôtel Bellevue et du Chariot d'Or, 4	A2
Hôtel de Bretagne, 3	C2
Hôtel de la Place des Vosges, 30	E4
Hôtel de Roubaix, 1	A2
Hôtel du Séjour, 8	A3
Hôtel Picard, 2	C/D2
Hôtel Practic, 29	D4
Maubuisson, 32	C5

☀ FOOD

404, 5	A/B2
L'As du Falafel, 22	C/D4
Au Petit Fer à Cheval, 23	C4
Chez Janou, 16	E4
Georges, 18	B4
Little Italy Trattoria, 12	B3
Piccolo Teatro, 27	C4
Sacha Finkelsztajn, 21	C4

❏ NIGHTLIFE

Amnésia Café, 19	C4
Les Bains, 6	A3
Chez Richard, 20	B4
Le Dépôt, 7	A3
Les Etages, 25	C4
Lizard Lounge, 24	B4
Villa Keops, 9	A3

🏛 MUSEUMS

Maison de Victor Hugo, 28	E4
Musée d'Art et d'Histoire du Judaïsme, 11	B3
Musée Carnavalet, 15	D4
Musée Cognacq-Jay, 17	D4
Musée de l'Histoire de France, 13	C3
Musée National d'Art Moderne, 14	B4
Musée Picasso, 10	D3

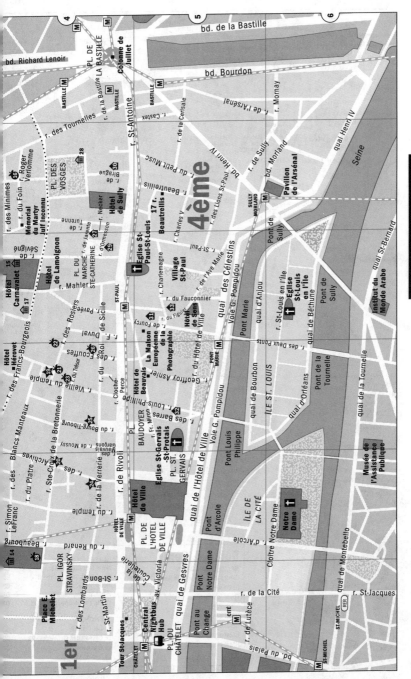

PARIS

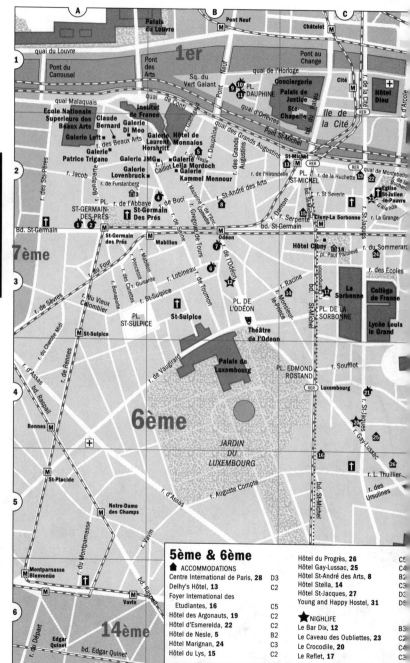

5ème & 6ème

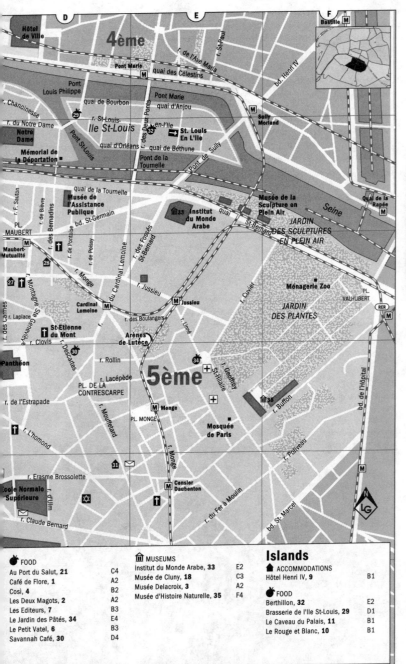

PARIS

🍴 **FOOD**

Au Port du Salut, **21**	C4
Café de Flore, **1**	A2
Cosi, **4**	B2
Les Deux Magots, **2**	A2
Les Editeurs, **7**	B3
Le Jardin des Pâtés, **34**	E4
Le Petit Vatel, **6**	B3
Savannah Café, **30**	D4

🏛 **MUSEUMS**

Institut du Monde Arabe, **33**	E2
Musée de Cluny, **18**	C3
Musée Delacroix, **3**	A2
Musée d'Histoire Naturelle, **35**	F4

Islands

🔺 **ACCOMMODATIONS**

Hôtel Henri IV, **9**	B1

🍴 **FOOD**

Berthillon, **32**	E2
Brasserie de l'Ile St-Louis, **29**	D1
Le Caveau du Palais, **11**	B1
Le Rouge et Blanc, **10**	B1

PARIS

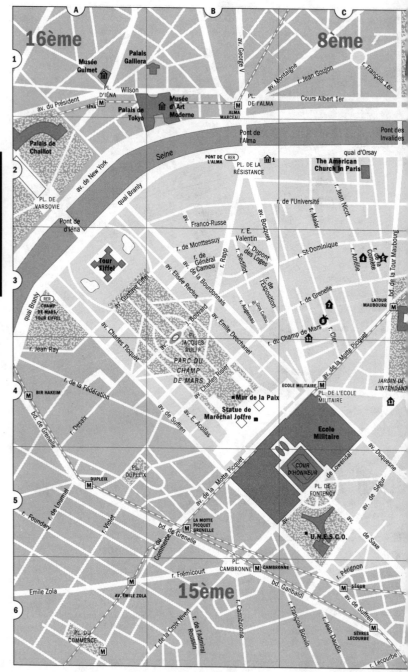

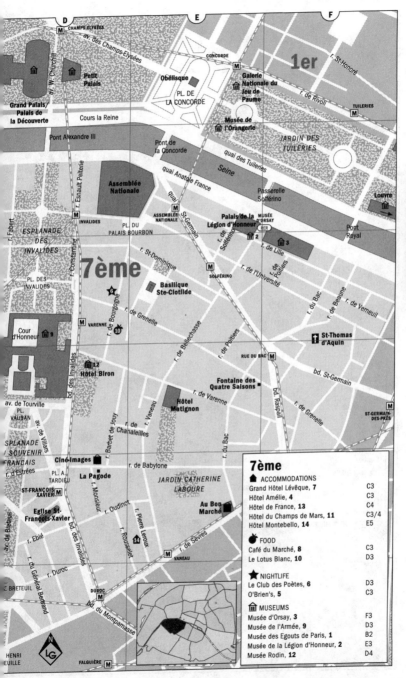

7ème

♠ ACCOMMODATIONS

Grand Hôtel Lévêque, **7**	C3
Hôtel Amélie, **4**	C3
Hôtel de France, **13**	C4
Hôtel du Champs de Mars, **11**	C3/4
Hôtel Montebello, **14**	E5

🍅 FOOD

Café du Marché, **8**	C3
Le Lotus Blanc, **10**	D3

★ NIGHTLIFE

Le Club des Poètes, **6**	D3
O'Brien's, **5**	C3

🏛 MUSEUMS

Musée d'Orsay, **3**	F3
Musée de l'Armée, **9**	D3
Musée des Egouts de Paris, **1**	B2
Musée de la Légion d'Honneur, **2**	E3
Musée Rodin, **12**	D4

8ème

♣ ACCOMMODATIONS
Hôtel Europe-Liège, **10**	F1
Hôtel Madeleine Haussmann, **7**	E4
UCJF/YWCA, **5**	E1

🍴 FOOD
Bagel & Co., **4**	C3
Bangkok Café, **9**	F1
Fauchon, **8**	E4

★ NIGHTLIFE
buddha-bar, **6**	E4
House of Live, **3**	B3
Latina Café, **1**	B3
Le Queen, **2**	B3

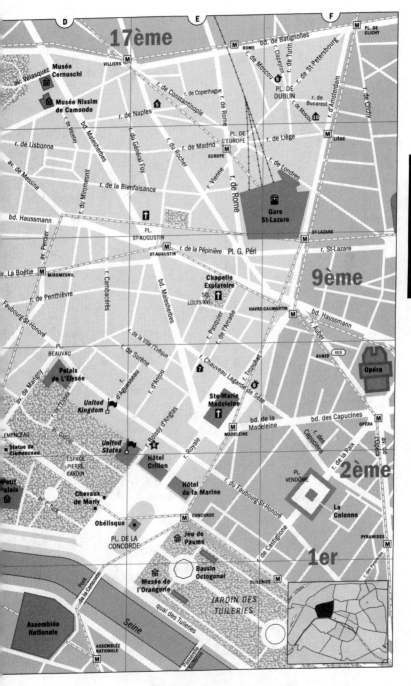

PARIS

PARIS

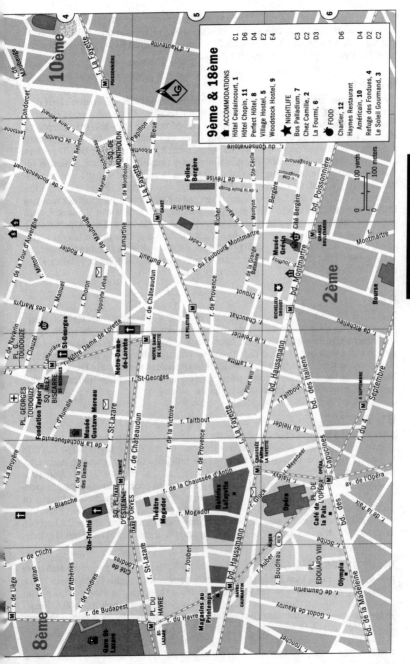

9ème & 18ème

▲ ACCOMMODATIONS	
Hôtel Caulaincourt, 1	C1
Hôtel Chopin, 11	D6
Perfect Hôtel, 8	D4
Village Hostel, 5	E2
Woodstock Hostel, 9	E4

★ NIGHTLIFE	
Bus Palladium, 7	C3
Chez Camille, 2	C2
La Fourmi, 6	D3

● FOOD	
Chartier, 12	D6
Haynes Restaurant	
Américain, 10	D4
Refuge des Fondues, 4	D2
Le Soleil Gourmand, 3	C2

PARIS

travel on bus, métro, and RER, and provide discounts on sightseeing trips, bike rentals, and stores (available at the airport or métro/RER stations; 1-day €8.35, 2-day €13.70, 3-day €18.25, 5-day €26.25). This discounted ticket will not always save you money, depending upon how much you travel.

MÉTRO

Métro stations are marked with an "M" or with fancy "*Métropolitain*" lettering designed by Art Nouveau legend Hector Guimard. The first trains start running around 5:30am, and the last ones leave the end-of-the-line stations (the "*portes de Paris*") for the center of the city at about 12:15am. Connections to other lines are indicated by orange *correspondance* signs, exits by blue *sortie* signs. Transfers are free if made within a station; it is not always possible to reverse direction on the same line without exiting the station. To pass through the turnstiles, insert the ticket into the small slot in the metal divider just to your right as you approach the turnstile. It disappears for a moment, then pops out about a foot farther along; a little green or white circle will light up, reminding you to retrieve the ticket. **Hold onto your ticket** until you pass the point marked **Limite de Validité des Billets** on the way to the exit. Do not count on being able to buy a métro ticket late at night; some ticket windows close as early as 10pm. Stay away from the most dangerous stations at night (Barbès-Rochechouart, Pigalle, Anvers, Châtelet-Les-Halles, Gare du Nord, Gare de l'Est). If concerned, take a taxi.

RER

The RER *(Réseau Express Régional)* is the RATP's suburban train system, which passes through central Paris. Within the city, the RER travels much faster than the métro. There are five RER lines, marked A-E, with different branches designated by a number, such as the C5 line to Versailles-Rive Gauche. The principal stops within the city, which link the RER to the métro system, are Gare du Nord, Nation, Charles-de-Gaulle-Etoile, Gare de Lyon, and Châtelet-Les-Halles. The RER runs from about 5:15am to midnight, like the métro.

BUS

Although slower and often more costly than the métro, buses can act as cheap sight-seeing tours and helpful introductions to the city's layout. The RATP's *Grand Plan de Paris* includes a map of the bus lines for day, evening, and night-time (free at métro stations). The free bus map *Autobus Paris-Plan du Réseau* is available at the tourist office and at métro information booths. Bus tickets are identical to those used on the métro, and can be purchased either in métro stations or on the bus from the driver. *Cartes oranges* and other transport passes (Paris Visite, Mobilis), are equally valid in buses and subways (see **Métro,** above). When you wish to leave the bus, press the red button and the *arrêt demandé* sign will magically light up.

NIGHT BUSES. Most buses run daily 6:30am-8:30pm; those marked **Autobus de nuit** continue until 1am. Those named **Noctambus** run all night. Night buses (from €2.30, depending on how far you go) run from the Châtelet stop to the *portes* (end-of-the-line stations) of the city (daily every hr. on the half hr. 1:30-5:30am). Buses also run from the suburbs to Châtelet (every hr. on the hr. 1-6am). Noctambuses I through M, R, and S run along the Left Bank to the southern suburbs. Buses A through H, P, T, and V run on the Right Bank heading north. Look for bus stops marked with a bug-eyed moon sign. Ask at a major métro station for more info.

TOUR BUSES. Balabus (call RATP at ☎08 36 68 41 14 for info in English) visits virtually every major sight in Paris in 1¼hr. (Bastille, St-Michel, Louvre, Musée d'Orsay, Concorde, Champs-Elysées, Charles-de-Gaulle-Etoile). The fare is the same as that for any bus that covers more than two zones (3 tickets). The loop starts either at the Grande Arche de La Défense or Gare de Lyon.

TAXIS

Taxis are expensive. They normally take three passengers; a fourth costs around €2.45. Prominent taxi companies include: **Alpha Taxis** ☎01 45 85 85 85; **Taxis 7000** ☎01 42 70 00 42; **Taxis Bleus** ☎0 800 25 16 10 10; **Taxis G7** ☎01 47 39 47 39.

BIKE RENTAL

Paris-Vélo, 2 rue de Fer-à-Moulin, 5ème (☎01 43 37 59 22). M: Censier-Daubenton. €13.75 per day, includes accident insurance. Deposit €305. Open M-Sa 10am-12:30pm and 2-7pm.

Paris à vélo, c'est sympa!, 37 bd. Bourdon, 4ème (☎01 48 87 60 01). M: Bastille. Deposit €200 (or credit card). €16 per day; €9.50 per half-day (9am-2pm or 2-7pm). Open daily 9am-1pm and 2-6pm.

🔢 USEFUL SERVICES

For consulates and embassies, see **Essentials,** p. 31.

TOURIST OFFICES

Bureau d'Accueil Central, 127 av. des Champs-Elysées, 8ème (☎08 36 68 31 12; www.paris-touristoffice.com). M: Georges V. Open June-Aug. daily 9am-8pm; Sept.-May M-Sa 9am-8pm, Su 11am-6pm.

Bureau Gare de Lyon, 12ème (☎01 43 43 33 24). M: Gare de Lyon. Open M-Sa 8am-8pm.

Bureau Tour Eiffel, Champs de Mars, 7ème (☎08 92 68 31 12). M: Champs de Mars. Open May-Sept. daily 11am-6pm.

GUIDED TOURS

Bateaux-Mouches (☎01 42 25 96 10; info ☎01 40 76 99 99). M: Alma-Marceau. 70min. English tours. Tours every 30min. 10:15am-10:40pm (none 1-2pm) from the Right Bank pier near Pont d'Alma. €7, ages 4-12 and over 65 €4, under 4 free.

Mike's Bullfrog Bike Tours (☎01 56 58 10 54; www.mikesbiketours.com). Tours May daily 11am; June-July 11am and 3:30pm; Aug.-Nov. 11am. No reservations necessary, but call ahead to confirm meeting times. Night tours May and Aug.-Nov. Su, Tu, and Th 7:30pm; June-July Su-Th 7:30pm. Reservations required. Tours meet by the south leg (Pilier Sud) of the Eiffel Tower. Day tour €19, night tour €23.

USEFUL PUBLICATIONS AND LISTINGS

The weeklies **Pariscope** (€0.40; www.pariscope.fr) and **Officiel des Spectacles** (€0.35), both published on Wednesdays, have the most comprehensive listings of movies, plays, exhibits, festivals, clubs, and bars. *Pariscope* also includes an English-language section called **Time Out Paris.** The tourist office's free monthly **Where: Paris** highlights exhibits, concerts, walking tours, and events. The Mairie de Paris, 29 rue de Rivoli, 4ème (☎01 42 76 42 42; M: Hôtel-de-Ville), publishes the free monthly **Paris le Journal,** with articles about what's hot in the city. On Wednesday, the newspaper *Le Figaro* includes **Figaroscope,** a supplement about Paris happenings. **Free Voice,** a monthly English-language newspaper published by the American Church, and the bi-weekly **France-USA Contacts (FUSAC),** list jobs, housing, and info for English speakers and are available for free from English-speaking bookstores, restaurants, and travel agencies.

CURRENCY EXCHANGE

Many banks will exchange money during bank hours (9am-noon and 2-4:30pm). Beware of *bureaux de change* at airports, train stations, and touristy areas, which usually have bad exchange rates. Consider **American Express,** 11 rue Scribe, 9*ème*. (☎01 47 14 50 00. M: Opéra or Auber. Open M-Sa 9am-6:30pm, exchange counter open Su 10am-5pm.). Don't forget **Thomas Cook,** 73 av. des Champs-Elysées, 8*ème*. (☎01 45 62 89 55. M: Georges V. Open M-Sa 9am-7pm, Su 1-7pm.)

LOCAL SERVICES

Dry Cleaning: Pressing Villiers, 93 rue de Rocher, 8*ème* (☎01 45 22 75 48). M: Villiers. Open M-F 8am-7:30pm, Sa 8am-12:30pm. MC/V. **Arc en Ciel,** 62 rue Arbre Sec, 1er (☎01 42 41 39 39). M: Louvre. Open M-F 8am-1:15pm and 2:30-7pm, Sa 8:30am-1:15pm.

Gay/Lesbian Resources: ACT-UP Paris, 45 rue de Sedene, 11*ème* (☎01 48 06 13 89). M: Bréguet-Sabin. **Centre Gai et Lesbien,** 3 rue Keller, 11*ème* (☎01 43 57 21 47). M: Ledru-Rollin or Bastille.

Disability Resources: L'Association des Paralysés de France, Délégation de Paris, 17, bd. Auguste Blanqui, 13*ème* (☎01 40 78 69 00; www.apf.asso.fr). M: Place d'Italie. Open M-F 9am-12:30pm and 2-5:30pm.

HEALTH AND CRISES

Emergency Numbers: Ambulance (SAMU) ☎ **15. Police** ☎ **17. Fire** ☎ **18. Poison** ☎01 40 05 48 48. In French, but some English assistance available. **Rape: SOS Viol** (☎0 800 05 95 95; open M-F 10am-7pm) or the anonymous, confidential English crisis hotline S.O.S Help! (☎01 47 23 80 80). Open daily 3-11pm.

Hospitals: Hôpital Américain de Paris, 84 bd. Saussaye, Neuilly (☎01 46 41 25 25). M: Port Maillot, then bus #82 to the end of the line. Private. **Hôpital Franco-Britannique de Paris,** 3 rue Barbès, in the Parisian suburb of Levallois-Perret (☎01 46 39 22 22). M: Anatole-France. Some English spoken, but don't count on it. **Hôpital Bichat,** 46 rue Henri Buchard, 18*ème* (☎01 40 25 80 80). M: Port St-Ouen. Emergency services.

24hr. Pharmacies: Every arrondissement has a **pharmacie de garde** which will open in emergencies. The locations change, but the name of the nearest one is posted on every pharmacy's door. **British & American Pharmacy,** 1 rue Auber, 9*ème* (☎01 42 65 88 29). M: Auber or Opéra. Open M-Su 8am-8:30pm.

Birth Control: Mouvement Français pour le Planning Familial (MFPF), 10 rue Vivienne, 2*ème* (☎01 42 60 93 20). M: Bourse. Phone calls M-F 9:30am-5:30pm. A clinic is held at 94 bd. Massanna, 13*ème* (☎01 45 84 28 25), M: Porte Ivry, on the 1st fl. of the Tour Mantoue on Fridays (10am-4pm); door code 38145; call ahead.

Emotional Health: SOS Crisis Help Line Friendship: ☎01 47 23 80 80 (English). Open daily 3-11pm. **International Counseling Service (ICS)** ☎01 45 50 26 49. Access to psychologists, psychiatrists, social workers, and clergy. Open M-F 8am-8pm, Sa 8am-4pm.

COMMUNICATIONS

Internet Access: Internet cafés are widespread throughout the city. Our favorite is ▨ **Easy Everything**, 37 bd. Sébastopol, 1er (☎01 40 41 09 10). M: Châtelet-Les-Halles. Purchase a User ID for any amount above €3 and recharge the ID in increments of €1.50. Minutes/euro depends on the time of day and how busy the store is. Open daily 24hr.

Federal Express: ☎08 00 12 38 00. Call M-F before 5pm for pick-up. Drop off at 2 rue du 29 Juillet, between Concorde and rue du Rivoli, 1er or at 63 bd. Haussmann, 8ème. Open M-Sa 9am-7pm; drop off by 4:45pm.

Poste du Louvre: 52 rue du Louvre, 1er (info ☎01 40 28 20 40). M: Louvre. Open 24hr.

▐ ACCOMMODATIONS

ILE DE LA CITÉ

▨ **Hôtel Henri IV,** 25 pl. Dauphine (☎01 43 54 44 53). M: Pont Neuf. One of Paris's best located and least expensive hotels, in a 400-year-old building where Henri IV once kept his printing presses. Big windows and charming views of the tree-lined pl. Dauphine. Spacious rooms with sturdy, mismatched furnishings. Showers €2.29. Reserve one month in advance, June-Aug. earlier. Singles €21-29; doubles €25-34, with shower and toilet €53; triples €40, with shower €47.50; quads €47.50. ❷

FIRST ARRONDISSEMENT

▨ **Hôtel Montpensier,** 12 rue de Richelieu (☎01 42 96 28 50; fax 01 42 86 02 70). M: Palais-Royal. Walk around the left side of the Palais-Royal to rue de Richelieu. Clean rooms, lofty ceilings, bright decor. Its good taste distinguishes it from most hotels in this region and price range. Friendly English-speaking staff. Elevator. TV in rooms with shower or bath. Internet access €1 per 4min. Breakfast €6.10. Shower €4. June-Aug. reserve 2 months in advance. Singles and doubles with toilet €53, with toilet and shower €74, with bath €87. Extra bed €12. AmEx/MC/V. ❹

▨ **Centre International de Paris (BVJ): Paris Louvre,** 20 rue Jean-Jacques Rousseau (☎01 53 00 90 90; fax 01 53 00 90 91). M: Louvre or Palais-Royal. From M: Louvre, take rue du Louvre away from the river, turn left on rue St-Honoré, and right on rue J.-J. Rousseau. 200-bed hostel draws an international crowd. Courtyard hung with brass lanterns and strewn with *brasserie* chairs. Bright, dorm-style rooms. English spoken. Internet €0.15 per min. Breakfast and showers included. Lockers €2. Reception 24hr. For Sa-Su reserve up to 1 week in advance by phone. Rooms held only 10-30min. after your expected check-in time; call if you'll be late. €24 per person. ❷

Hôtel Lion d'Or, 5 rue de la Sourdière (☎01 42 60 79 04; fax 01 42 60 09 14). M: Tuileries or Pyramides. From métro, walk down rue du 29 Juillet away from the park and turn right on rue St-Honoré, then left on rue de la Sourdière. Clean and carpeted, in a quiet area. Phone and TV in most rooms. Friendly, English-speaking staff. Breakfast €5.30. June-Aug. reserve 1 month in advance. Price 5% lower for stays of more than 4 nights. Singles with shower, toilet, and double bed €58-74, with bath €68-80; doubles €74-85/€80-95; triples €84-95/€90-105. Extra bed €10. AmEx/MC/V. ❺

Hôtel St-Honoré, 85 rue St-Honoré (☎01 42 36 20 38 or 01 42 21 46 96; fax 01 42 21 44 08; paris@hotelsainthonoré.com). M: Louvre, Châtelet, or Les Halles. From M: Louvre, cross rue de Rivoli onto rue du Louvre and turn right on rue St-Honoré. Friendly, English-speaking staff and young clientele. Recently renovated with breakfast area and sizable modern rooms. Internet €6 per hr. All rooms have shower, toilet, and TV. Breakfast €4.50. Reserve 3 weeks ahead by fax, phone, or email. Singles €49; doubles €68, with bathtub €75; triples and quads €83. AmEx/MC/V. ❹

PARIS

SECOND ARRONDISSEMENT

■ **Hôtel Tiquetonne,** 6 rue Tiquetonne (☎01 42 36 94 58; fax 01 42 36 02 94). M: Etienne-Marcel. Walk against traffic on rue de Turbigo; turn left on rue Tiquetonne. It's near Marché Montorgueil, some tasty eateries on rue Tiquetonne, the rowdy English bars near Etienne-Marcel, and rue St-Denis's sex shops—what more could you ask for? This affordable 7-story hotel is a study in faux finishes, from fake-marble corridors to "I-can't-believe-it's-not-wood" doors. Elevator. Breakfast €5. Hall showers €5. Reserve 2 weeks in advance. Closed Aug. and 1 week for Christmas. Singles with shower €23.46-35.46; doubles with shower and toilet €40.92. AmEx/MC/V. ❷

■ **Hôtel Vivienne,** 40 rue Vivienne (☎01 42 33 13 26; fax 01 40 41 98 19; paris@hotel-vivienne.com). M: Grands Boulevards. Follow the traffic on bd. Montmartre, pass the Théâtre des Variétés, and turn left on rue Vivienne. Elegant, with hardwood floor reception area and spacious rooms with armoires. Some rooms with balconies. Elevator. Breakfast €6. Singles with shower €48, with shower and toilet €78; doubles €63/€78; extra person add 30%, under 10 no extra charge. MC/V. ❹

Hôtel des Boulevards, 10 rue de la Ville Neuve (☎01 42 36 02 29; fax 01 42 36 15 39). M: Bonne Nouvelle. Walk against traffic on av. Poissonnière and make a right on rue de la Ville Neuve. Funky, but slightly run-down neighborhood. Quiet, simple rooms with TV, phones, wardrobes, and new carpets. The higher the room, the brighter. Breakfast included. Reserve 2 weeks ahead. Singles and doubles €39, with shower €49, with bath €53-55; extra bed €10. 10% discount with *Let's Go.* AmEx/MC/V. ❹

THIRD ARRONDISSEMENT

■ **Hôtel du Séjour,** 36 rue du Grenier St-Lazare (☎/fax 01 48 87 40 36). M: Etienne-Marcel or Rambuteau. From M: Etienne-Marcel, follow the traffic on rue Etienne-Marcel, which becomes rue du Grenier St-Lazare. One block from Les Halles and the Centre Pompidou. Bright rooms and a warm atmosphere. Reserve at least one week in advance. Showers €4. Reception 7am-10:30pm. Singles €30; doubles €42.55, with shower and toilet €54; extra person €23. ❸

Hôtel de Roubaix, 6 rue Greneta (☎01 42 72 89 91; fax 01 42 72 58 79). M: Réaumur-Sébastopol or Arts et Métiers. From the métro, walk opposite traffic on bd. de Sébastopol and turn left on rue Greneta. Advice-dispensing staff, clean rooms with flowered wallpaper, soundproofed windows, and new baths. All rooms have shower, toilet, telephone, locker, and TV. Breakfast included. Reserve one week in advance. Singles €52-58.15; doubles €64-68; triples €78-81; quads €87; quints €92. MC/V. ❹

Hôtel Picard, 26 rue de Picardie (☎01 48 87 53 82; fax 01 48 87 02 56). M: Temple. From the métro, walk against traffic down rue du Temple, take the first left on rue du Petit Thouars, and turn right at the end of the street. Next door to cyber café WebBar. Not much English spoken. In a good location. TV in rooms with showers. Elevator. Breakfast €4.50. Hall showers €3. Apr.-Sept. reserve two weeks ahead. Singles €33, with shower €41, with shower and toilet €51; doubles €40-43/€52/€63; triples €59-82. 5% discount with *Let's Go.* MC/V. ❸

Hôtel Bellevue et du Chariot d'Or, 39 rue de Turbigo (☎01 48 87 45 60; fax 01 48 87 95 04). M: Etienne-Marcel. From the métro, walk against traffic on rue de Turbigo. A Belle Epoque lobby, with bar and breakfast room. Clean and modern rooms with phone, TV, toilets, and bath. Breakfast €5.25. Reserve 2 weeks in advance. Singles €51; doubles €57; triples €74; quads €91. AmEx/MC/V. ❹

Hôtel de Bretagne, 87 rue des Archives (☎01 48 87 83 14). M: Temple. Take rue du Temple against traffic and turn left onto rue de Bretagne; the hotel is on the right, at the corner with rue des Archives. Friendly reception and well-kept rooms. Breakfast €4.58. Reserve 1 week in advance. Singles €29, with shower and toilet €55; doubles €35-38/€61; triples €84; quads €92. ❸

FOURTH ARRONDISSEMENT

■ **Hôtel des Jeunes (MIJE)** (☎01 42 74 23 45; fax 01 40 27 81 64; www.mije.com). Books beds in Le Fourcy, Le Fauconnier, and Maubuisson (see below), 3 small hostels on cobblestone streets in beautiful old Marais residences. The following applies to all. No smoking. English spoken. Internet €0.15 per min. Public phones and free lockers with €1 deposit. Breakfast, shower, and sheets included. Reception 7am-1am. Check-in noon; call if late. Lockout noon-3pm. Curfew 1am. Groups reserve 1 year in advance, individuals 2-3 weeks ahead. 7-day max. stay. **Ages 18-30 only.** Dorms €21.80 per person; singles €37.40; doubles €27.30; triples €24.10; quads €22.60. ❷

> **Le Fourcy,** 6 rue de Fourcy. M: St-Paul or Pont Marie. From M: St-Paul, walk opposite the traffic for a few meters down rue François-Miron and turn left on rue de Fourcy. Hostel surrounds a large courtyard ideal for meeting travelers and picnicking, but disturbing for light sleepers. La Table d'Hôtes restaurant offers a main course with drink (€7.80), coffee, and 3-course "hosteler special" (€9.40). Elevator.

> **Le Fauconnier,** 11 rue du Fauconnier. M: St-Paul or Pont Marie. From M: St-Paul, take rue du Prevôt, turn left on rue Charlemagne, and turn right on rue du Fauconnier. Ivy-covered building steps away from the Seine and Ile St-Louis.

> **Maubuisson,** 12 rue des Barres. M: Hôtel-de-Ville or Pont Marie. From M: Pont Marie, walk opposite traffic on rue de l'Hôtel-de-Ville and turn right on rue des Barres. A half-timbered former girls' convent on a silent street by the St-Gervais monastery. Elevator.

■ **Grand Hôtel Jeanne d'Arc,** 3 rue de Jarente (☎01 48 87 62 11; fax 01 48 87 37 31; www.hoteljeannedarc.com). M: St-Paul or Bastille. From métro walk opposite traffic on rue de Rivoli and turn left on rue de Sévigné, then right on rue de Jarente. On a quiet side-street. Rooms have shower, toilet, and TV. Elevator. 2 wheelchair-accessible rooms. Breakfast €5.80. Reserve 2 months in advance. Singles €53-64; doubles €67-92; triples €107; quads €122; extra bed €12. MC/V. ❹

Hôtel de la Place des Vosges, 12 rue de Birague (☎01 42 72 60 46; fax 01 42 72 02 64; hotel.place.des.vosges@gofornet.com). M: Bastille. Take rue St-Antoine; rue de Birague is the 3rd right. Only steps away from pl. des Vosges. Beautiful interior with exposed beams and stone walls. TV and full baths in all rooms. Elevator. Breakfast €6. Reserve by fax 2 months ahead with 1 night's deposit. Singles €76; doubles €101, with twin beds €106; triples €120; quads €140. AmEx/MC/V. ❺

Hôtel Practic, 9 rue d'Ormesson (☎01 48 87 80 47; fax 01 48 87 40 04). M: St-Paul. Walk opposite the traffic on rue de Rivoli, turn left on rue de Sévigné and right on rue d'Ormesson. A clean hotel in the heart of the Marais. Rooms are modest but bright, and all have TV and hair dryers. Breakfast €6. Reserve by fax 1 month in advance. Singles with toilet €49, with shower €75, with both €91; doubles €58/€80/€98; triples with both €112. Extra bed €12. MC/V. ❹

FIFTH ARRONDISSEMENT

■ **Young and Happy (Y&H) Hostel,** 80 rue Mouffetard (☎01 45 35 09 53; fax 01 47 07 22 24; smile@youngandhappy.fr). M: Monge. From the métro, cross rue Gracieuse and take rue Ortolan to rue Mouffetard. A funky, lively hostel. The laid-back staff, clean rooms, and commission-free currency exchange are ideal for young travelers looking to crash for a few weeks, though the bathrooms can get a bit dirty. Kitchen and Internet access. Breakfast included. Sheets €2.50. Towels €1. Laundry. Lockout 11am-4pm. Curfew 2am. Doubles €50; triples €66; quads €88; Jan.-Mar. prices €2 lower. ❷

■ **Hôtel St-Jacques,** 35 rue des Ecoles (☎01 44 07 45 45; fax 01 43 25 65 50). M: Maubert-Mutualité; RER: Cluny-La Sorbonne. Turn left on rue des Carmes, then left on rue des Ecoles. Spacious, faux-elegant rooms at reasonable rates, with balconies, bathrooms, and TV. English spoken. Elevator. Internet. Breakfast €6.50. Singles €44, with toilet and shower €68; doubles €76.50/€102. AmEx/MC/V. ❹

PARIS

Hôtel Marignan, 13 rue du Sommerard (☎01 43 54 63 81; fax 01 43 25 16 69; www.hotel-marignan.com). M: Maubert-Mutualité. From the métro, turn left on rue des Carmes, then right on rue du Sommerard. Amenable rooms great for larger groups. Friendly multilingual owner welcomes backpackers and families with a hotel's privacy and a hostel's warm atmosphere. TV in every room. Shower open until 9pm. Laundry. Kitchen. Internet. Breakfast €3. Reserve 2 months in advance. Singles €42-45; doubles €60, with shower and toilet €86-92; triples €100-110; quads €120-130. Mid-Sept. to Mar. 15% discount. AmEx/MC/V accepted for stays longer than 5 nights. ❹

Hôtel d'Esmeralda, 4 rue St-Julien-le-Pauvre (☎01 43 54 19 20; fax 01 40 51 00 68). M: St-Michel. Walk along the Seine on quai St-Michel toward Notre Dame, then turn right at Parc Viviani. Clean but creaky rooms with an ancient, professorial feel. Near a small park, with views of the Seine and the pealing of Notre Dame's bells. Breakfast €6. Singles €30, with shower and toilet €60; doubles €60-85; triples €95; quads €105. ❸

Hôtel des Argonauts, 12 rue de la Huchette (☎01 43 54 09 82; fax 01 44 07 18 84). M: St-Michel. With your back to the Seine, take the first left off bd. St-Michel onto rue de la Huchette. Ideally located in a bustling, Old Paris pedestrian quarter (a stone's throw from the Seine). Clean rooms flaunt a cheerful blue and yellow Mediterranean motif. Breakfast €4. June-Aug. reserve 3-4 weeks in advance. Singles with shower €44; doubles with bath and toilet €63-71. AmEx/MC/V. ❹

Centre International de Paris (BVJ): Paris Quartier Latin, 44 rue des Bernardins (☎01 43 29 34 80; fax 01 53 00 90 91). M: Maubert-Mutualité. Walk with traffic on bd. St-Germain and turn right on rue des Bernardins. Boisterous, generic hostel. English spoken. Internet €1 per 10min. Microwave, TV, and message service. Showers in rooms. Breakfast included. Lockers €2. Reception 24hr. 5- and 6-person dorms €25; singles €30; doubles and triples €27 per person. ❸

Hôtel du Progrès, 50 rue Gay-Lussac (☎01 43 54 53 18). M: Luxembourg. From the métro, walk away from Jardin du Luxembourg on rue Guy-Lussac. One of the last places in the area to offer really cheap rooms with no frills. The fairly clean rooms can be noisy from street traffic, but have beautiful views of the Panthéon. Elevator. Reservation with deposit; call 2-3 weeks in advance. Breakfast included. Singles €27-41, with shower and toilet €54; doubles €42-46/€57. ❸

Hôtel Gay-Lussac, 29 rue Gay-Lussac (☎01 43 54 23 96; fax 01 40 51 79 49). M: Luxembourg. Friendly owner and clean, stately old rooms, some with fireplaces. Lots of neighborhood traffic, but the peaceful shade of the Luxembourg gardens is just a few blocks away. Elevator. Reserve by fax 2-4 weeks in advance. Singles €31, with toilet €48, with shower and toilet €60; doubles €52, with shower and toilet €64; triples €54/€57/€73; quads €95. Dec.-Feb. occasional discounts. ❸

SIXTH ARRONDISSEMENT

▨ **Hôtel de Nesle,** 7 rue du Nesle (☎01 43 54 62 41; www.hotelnesle.com). M: Odéon. Walk up rue Mazarine, take a right onto rue Dauphine, then a left on rue du Nesle. Fantastical and absolutely sparkling, the Nesle (pronounced "Nell") stands out in a sea of nondescript budget hotels. Unique, recently renovated rooms. Garden with duck pond. Laundry nearby. Singles €50-70; doubles €70-100; extra bed €12. AmEx/MC/V. ❹

▨ **Hôtel St-André des Arts,** 66 rue St-André-des-Arts (☎01 43 26 96 16; fax 01 43 29 73 34; hsaintand@minitel.net). M: Odéon. From the métro, walk one block down rue de l'Ancienne Comédie and take the first right on rue St-André-des-Arts. A hotel in the heart of St-Germain with the feel of a country inn. New bathrooms (with showers, sinks and toilets), free breakfast, and friendly owner. Reservations recommended. Singles €51.65-61.65; doubles €76.30-80.30; triples €92.95; quads €103.60. MC/V. ❹

Delhy's Hôtel, 22 rue de l'Hirondelle (☎01 43 26 58 25; fax 01 43 26 51 06). M: St-Michel. Just steps from pl. St-Michel and the Seine. Wood paneling, flower boxes, modern facilities, and quiet location. Satellite TV and phone in all rooms. Breakfast included. Hall showers €3.81. Toilets in the hallways. Reserve 15-20 days ahead with deposit. Singles €40-58, with shower €66-73; doubles €58-64/€71-79; triples €79-93/€93-115; extra bed €15. Each night must be paid in advance. MC/V. ❹

Hôtel du Lys, 23 rue Serpente (☎01 43 26 97 57; fax 01 44 07 34 90). M: Odéon or St-Michel. From either subway stop, take rue Danton; rue Serpente is a side street. Worthwhile splurge. Floral wall-prints, rusticated beams, and porcelain tiles with old French coats of arms in the hallway give this sparkling hotel a sublime French country feel. All rooms have bath or shower, TV, phone, and hair dryer. Breakfast included. June-Aug. reserve one month ahead. Singles €93; doubles €105; triples €120. MC/V. ❺

Foyer International des Etudiantes, 93 bd. St-Michel (☎01 43 54 49 63). RER: Luxembourg. Across from the Jardin du Luxembourg. Marbled reception area, library, laundry facilities, and TV lounge. Kitchenettes, showers, and toilets in hallways. Rooms are elegant (if faintly musty). Breakfast included. **Oct.-June women only;** rooms are rented by the month—call or write for info. July-Sept. hotel is coed. Reserve in writing as early as Jan. for June-Aug., with €30.50 deposit. 2-bed dorms €39; singles €27. ❷

Hôtel Stella, 41 rue Monsieur-le-Prince (☎01 40 51 00 25 or 06 07 03 19 71; fax 01 43 54 97 28; www.site.voila.fr/hotel_stella). M: Odéon. From the métro, walk against traffic on bd. St-Germain and make a left on rue Monsieur-le-Prince. This hotel takes the exposed-beam look to a whole new level, sporting some woodwork reportedly several centuries old. Spacious triples have pianos. All rooms have shower and toilet. Reserve ahead with deposit. Singles €40; doubles €50; triples €70; quads €80. ❹

SEVENTH ARRONDISSEMENT

🖾 **Hôtel du Champs de Mars,** 7 rue du Champ de Mars (☎01 45 51 52 30; fax 01 45 51 64 36; www.hotel-du-champs-de-mars.com). M: Ecole Militaire. Just off av. Bosquet. Pricey, but above its competitors in quality and elegance. Rooms have phone and satellite TV. Breakfast €6.50. Reserve 1 month ahead. Small elevator. Singles and doubles with shower €66-72; triples with bath €92. MC/V. ❺

🖾 **Hôtel Montebello,** 18 rue Pierre Leroux (☎01 47 34 41 18; fax 01 47 34 46 71). A bit far from the 7ème's sights, but amazing prices for this upscale neighborhood. Behind the miserable facade are clean, cheery rooms with full baths. Breakfast €3.50. Reserve at least 2 weeks ahead. 1 person €37; 2 people €42-45. ❹

Hôtel de France, 102 bd. de la Tour Maubourg (☎01 47 05 40 49; fax 01 45 56 96 78; www.hoteldefrance.com). M: Ecole Militaire. Across from the Hôtel des Invalides. Clean rooms with amazing views. Phone, cable, minibar, and full bath in all rooms. Two wheelchair accessible rooms (€76.25). Connecting rooms for 4-5 people. Reserve 1 month ahead. Breakfast €7. Singles €64; doubles €81. AmEx/MC/V. ❺

Hôtel Amélie, 5 rue Amélie (☎01 45 51 74 75; fax 01 45 56 93 55; www.123france.com). M: La Tour-Maubourg. Walk in the direction of traffic on bd. de la Tour Maubourg, make a left onto rue de Grenelle, then a right onto rue Amélie. On a picturesque back street, tiny Amélie is charmingly decorated and has a friendly owner. Minibar and full bath in all rooms. Breakfast €6.10. Reserve 2 weeks in advance. Singles €61-72; doubles €71-82. AmEx/MC/V. ❺

Grand Hôtel Lévêque, 29 rue Cler (☎01 47 05 49 15; fax 01 45 50 49 36; www.hotel-leveque.com). M: Ecole Militaire. Take av. de la Motte-Picquet to cobbled and colorful rue Cler. Cheery and clean. Elevator. English spoken. Satellite TV, phone, ceiling fan, and computer plug in all rooms. Breakfast €7. Safe €3. Luggage storage. Reserve 6 months ahead. Singles €50-53; doubles with shower and toilet €76-84, with twin beds, shower, and toilet €76-91; triples with shower and toilet €106-114. Hall showers are on the 5th floor. AmEx/MC/V. ❹

EIGHTH ARRONDISSEMENT

■ **Hôtel Europe-Liège,** 8 rue de Moscou (☎01 42 94 01 51; fax 01 43 87 42 18). M: Liège. From the métro, walk down rue d'Amsterdam and turn left on rue de Moscou. Very pleasant, quiet, and reasonably priced hotel (for the 8ème) with newly painted rooms and a friendly staff. Many restaurants nearby. All rooms have TV, hair dryer, phone, shower, or bath. 2 wheelchair accessible rooms on the ground floor. Breakfast €6. Reserve 15 days in advance. Singles €65; doubles €80. AmEx/MC/V. ❺

Union Chrétienne de Jeunes Filles (UCJF/YWCA), 22 rue Naples (☎01 53 04 37 47; fax 01 53 04 37 54). M: Europe. From the métro, take rue de Constantinople and turn left onto rue de Naples. Also at 168 rue Blomet, 15ème (☎01 56 56 63 00; fax 01 56 56 63 12); M: Convention. Men should contact the YMCA Foyer **Union Chrétienne de Jeunes Gens,** 14 rue de Trévise, 9ème (☎01 47 70 90 94). The UCJF has spacious and quiet (if a bit worn) rooms with sinks and large desks. Large common room with fireplace, TV, books, theater space, and dining room. Guests permitted until 10pm; men not allowed in bedrooms. Kitchen. Laundry. Breakfast and dinner included; monthly rates include *demi-pension.* Reception M-F 8am-12:25am, Sa 8:30am-12:25pm, Su 9am-12:25pm and 1:30pm-12:30am. Curfew 12:30am. June-Aug. 3-day min. stay; Sept.-May longer stays for women ages 18-26. Singles €26, per week €155.50, per month €497; doubles €46/€250/€793; triples €23/€375/€1189. Mandatory YWCA membership fee (€4.60) and processing fee (1 week €7.60, 1 month €15.25). ❷

Hôtel Madeleine Haussmann, 10 rue Pasquier (☎01 42 65 90 11; fax 01 42 68 07 93; www.3hotels.com). M: Madeleine. From the métro, walk up bd. Malesherbes and turn right on rue Pasquier. Centrally located and comfortable. Bathroom, hair dryer, TV, safe box, and minibar in every cheery room. One small wheelchair accessible room on the ground floor. Breakfast €7. Reserve 1 month ahead. Singles €100-120; doubles €120-130; triples €140; quads €180. ❺

NINTH ARRONDISSEMENT

■ **Hôtel Chopin,** 46 passage Jouffroy (☎01 47 70 58 10; fax 01 42 47 00 70). M: Grands Boulevards. Walk west on bd. Montmartre until no. 10 and make a right into passage Jouffroy. Inside a spectacular old *passage* lined with shops. Very clean, new rooms decorated in a tasteful style. A cut above most budget hotels. Elevator. Breakfast €7. Singles with shower €55, with shower and toilet €62-70; doubles with shower and toilet €69-80; triples with shower and toilet €91. AmEx/MC/V. ❺

Perfect Hôtel, 39 rue Rodier (☎01 42 81 18 86 or 01 42 81 26 19; fax 01 42 85 01 38; perfecthotel@hotmail.com). Across from the Woodstock Hostel, see directions below. While "perfect" is an overstatement, the hotel comes close. Some rooms have balconies, and the upper floors have a beautiful view. Phones, communal refrigerator and kitchen access, free coffee, beer vending machine (€1.50), and a helpful, English-speaking staff. Elevator. Breakfast free with *Let's Go.* Singles €30, with shower and toilet €48; doubles €36/€48; triples €45/€60. MC/V. ❸

Woodstock Hostel, 48 rue Rodier (☎01 48 78 87 76; fax 01 48 78 01 63; www.woodstock.fr). M: Anvers. From the métro, walk against traffic on pl. Anvers, turn right on av. Trudaine and left on rue Rodier. From M: Gare du Nord, turn right on rue Dunkerque (with the station at your back); at pl. de Roubaix, veer left on rue de Maubeuge, then right on rue Condorcet, and left on rue Rodier. (15min.) Incense, reggae music, tie-dye paraphernalia, and a Beatles-themed VW Bug hanging from the ceiling. The nicest rooms are off the courtyard. Safe deposit box, Internet (€1 per 10min.), and fax. English spoken. Breakfast included. Kitchen. Sheets €2.50, towels €1. Showers, on every floor, are free and clean. Reserve ahead by phone. 2-week max. stay. 4- to 8-person dorms €19; doubles €22 per person. ❷

TENTH ARRONDISSEMENT

■ **Cambrai Hôtel**, 129bis bd. de Magenta (☎01 48 78 32 13; fax 01 48 78 43 55; www.hotel-cambrai.com). M: Gare du Nord. Follow traffic on rue de Dunkerque to pl. de Roubaix and turn right on bd. de Magenta. The hotel is on the left. Clean, 50s-style rooms with high ceilings and TV. Wheelchair accessible family suite (€84). Breakfast €5.34. Showers €3. Singles €30, with toilet €35, with shower €41, with bath €46; doubles €41/€46/€52-58; triples €76. MC/V. ❸

Hôtel Montana La Fayette, 164 rue La Fayette (☎01 40 35 80 80; fax 01 40 35 08 73). M: Gare du Nord. Walk up rue La Fayette towards Gare de l'Est. The hotel is on the right. Conveniently close to the Gare du Nord, yet still blessedly quiet. Enjoy the clean rooms with largish bathrooms. Breakfast €5. Most rooms have shower, toilet, and TV. Singles €39; doubles €52, with twin beds €55. MC/V. ❹

ELEVENTH ARRONDISSEMENT

■ **Modern Hôtel**, 121 rue de Chemin-Vert (☎01 47 00 54 05; fax 01 47 00 08 31; www.modern-hotel.fr). M: Père Lachaise. Chemin-Vert is an exit. Newly renovated, with modern furnishings, pastel color scheme, and spotless marble bathrooms. All rooms have hair dryer, modem connection, and safe-deposit box. No elevator. Breakfast €5. Singles €60; doubles €70; quads €95; extra bed €15. MC/V. ❺

Hôtel Beaumarchais, 3 rue Oberkampf (☎01 53 36 86 86; fax 01 43 38 32 86; www.hotelbeaumarchais.com). M: Oberkampf. Exit on rue de Malte and turn right on rue Oberkampf. Newly renovated, with colorful, modern furniture, clean baths, and TV, this hotel is worth the extra money. Small elevator. A/C. Breakfast €6.10. Reserve 2 weeks in advance. Singles €69-85; doubles €99; luxurious suites €140. AmEx/MC/V. ❺

Plessis Hôtel, 25 rue du Grand Prieuré (☎01 47 00 13 38; fax 01 43 57 97 87; hotel.plessis@club_internet.fr). M: Oberkampf. From the métro, walk north on rue du Grand Prieuré. 5 floors of clean, bright rooms. Rooms with showers have hair dryers, fans, TV, and balconies. Lounge with TV and vending machines. Breakfast €5.80. Open Sept.-July. Singles €35.50, with shower and toilet €60, with bath €63; doubles €35.50-63, with twin beds and shower €63. AmEx/MC/V. ❹

Auberge de Jeunesse "Jules Ferry" (HI), 8 bd. Jules Ferry (☎01 43 57 55 60; fax 01 43 14 82 09; auberge@easynet.fr). M: République. Walk east on rue du Faubourg du Temple and turn right on the far side of bd. Jules Ferry. Wonderful location in front of a park and next to pl. de la République. 100 bunk beds. Clean rooms with sinks, mirrors, and tiled floors. Doubles with big beds. Party atmosphere. Internet €0.15 per min. Breakfast, showers, and sheets included. Lockers €1.55. Laundry. Reception in dining room 24hr. Lockout 10am-2pm. No reservations; arrive by 8am. 1-week max. stay. 4- to 6-bed dorms €18.50; doubles €37. MC/V. ❷

TWELFTH ARRONDISSEMENT

■ **Hôtel de l'Aveyron**, 5 rue d'Austerlitz (☎01 43 07 86 86; fax 01 43 07 85 20). M: Gare de Lyon. Walk away from the train station on rue de Bercy and take a right on rue d'Austerlitz. On a quiet street, with clean, unpretentious rooms. Downstairs lounge with TV. Helpful English-speaking staff. Breakfast €4. Reserve 1 month in advance. Singles and doubles €30, with shower €42; triples €39/€49. MC/V. ❸

■ **Centre International du Séjour de Paris: CISP "Ravel,"** 6 av. Maurice Ravel (☎01 44 75 60 00; fax 01 43 44 45 30; cisp@csi.com). M: Porte de Vincennes. Walk east on cours de Vincennes, take the first right on bd. Soult, turn left on rue Jules Lemaître, and right on av. Maurice Ravel. Large, clean rooms, art exhibits, auditorium, and outdoor public pool. Internet €1.50 per 10min. Breakfast, sheets, and towels included. Cafeteria open daily 7:30-9:30am, noon-1:30pm, and 7-8:30pm. Restaurant open noon-

1:30pm. Reception 6:30am-1:30am; arrange to have the night guard let you in after 1:30am. 1-month max. stay. Reserve at least a few days ahead by phone. 8-bed dorm with hall shower and toilet €15.40; 2-to 4-bed dorm €19.21 per person ; singles with shower and toilet €30; doubles with shower and toilet €24. AmEx/MC/V. ❶

THIRTEENTH ARRONDISSEMENT

Maison des Clubs UNESCO, 43 rue de Glacière (☎01 43 36 00 63; fax 01 45 35 05 96; clubs.unesco.paris@wanadoo.fr). M: Glacière. Exiting the métro, look for rue de Glacière and walk north. Enter through the garden on the right. Reasonably close to the 5ème. Small but clean rooms with large windows. Knowledgeable, friendly staff. Breakfast included. Hallway shower and toilet. Groups call months in advance, individuals and couples 10 days ahead. Singles €28; doubles €46; triples €60; quads €80. Cheaper, single-sex rooms with multiple beds available. MC/V. ❸

FOURTEENTH ARRONDISSEMENT

▧ **Hôtel de Blois,** 5 rue des Plantes (☎01 45 40 99 48; fax 01 45 40 45 62). M: Mouton-Duvernet. From the métro, turn left on rue Mouton Duvernet then left on rue des Plantes. One of the better deals in Paris. Glossy wallpaper, ornate ceiling carvings, and velvet chairs—like staying with your very own (extremely nice) French grandmother. TV, phones, hair dryers, and big, clean baths. Laundromat across the street, pool next door. Breakfast €5. Hall showers. Reserve 10 days ahead. Singles €39, with shower €43, with shower and toilet €45, with bath and toilet €51; doubles €41/€45/€47/€56; triples €61; extra bed €12. AmEx/MC/V. ❹

▧ **Ouest Hôtel,** 27 rue de Gergovie (☎01 45 42 64 99; fax 01 45 42 46 65). M: Pernety. Walk against traffic on rue Raymond Losserand and turn right on rue de Gergovie. A clean hotel with modest furnishings, outstanding rates, and friendly staff. A small library and a charming dining room perfect for munching on *panini* and chatting it up with fellow travelers. Breakfast €5. Hall shower €5. Singles €22-28; doubles €28, with shower €37, with twin bed and shower €39. MC/V. ❷

FIAP Jean-Monnet, 30 rue Cabanis (☎01 43 13 17 00, reservations 01 43 13 17 17; fax 01 45 81 63 91; www.fiap.asso.fr). M: Glacière. From the métro, walk straight down bd. Auguste-Blanqui, turn left on rue de la Santé and then right on rue Cabanis. With a high-end, pre-fab feel, this international student center offers spotless rooms with toilet and shower. Game room, TV rooms, laundry, sunlit piano bar, restaurant, outdoor terrace, and disco. Breakfast included. Curfew 2am. Reserve 2-4 weeks in advance. Be sure to specify if you want a dorm bed, or you will be booked for a single. Wheelchair accessible. Rooms cleaned daily. Check-in 2:30pm, check-out 9am. 3-month max. stay. 5- and 6-bed rooms €22; singles €48.50; doubles €62.60; triples and quads €27.40 per person. €15 check or credit card deposit per person per night. MC/V. ❹

FIFTEENTH ARRONDISSEMENT

▧ **Hôtel Printemps,** 31 rue du Commerce (☎01 45 79 83 36; fax 01 45 79 84 88; hotel.printemps.15e@wanadoo.fr). M: La Motte-Picquet-Grenelle. In a pleasant neighborhood, surrounded by shops (including Monoprix) and budget restaurants, this hotel is clean, and cheap. Breakfast €4. Hall showers €3. Reserve 3-4 weeks ahead. Singles and doubles with sink €30, with shower €36, with shower and toilet €38. MC/V. ❸

▧ **Three Ducks Hostel,** 6 pl. Etienne Pernet (☎01 48 42 04 05; fax 01 48 42 99 99; www.3ducks.fr). M: Félix Faure. Walk against traffic on the left side of the church; the hostel is on the left. With palm trees in the courtyard and beach-style shower shacks, this hostel is aimed at Anglo fun-seekers. In-house bar—probably the best late-night option in the 15ème. 15min. from the Eiffel Tower. Kitchen, lockers, and small 2- to 8-

bed dorm rooms. Shower and breakfast included. Sheets €2.30; towels €0.80. Reception daily 8am-2am. Lockout daily 11am-5pm. Curfew 2am. 1-week max. stay. Reserve with credit card a week ahead. Mar.-Oct. dorms €21; doubles €48; triples €67.50. Nov.-Feb. dorms €19; doubles €45. MC/V. ❷

La Maison Hostel, 67bis rue Dutot (☎01 42 73 10 10). M: Volontaires. Cross rue de Vaugirard on rue des Volontaires, take the second right, and go 2 blocks. Doubles and clean 3- or 4-bed dorms in a quiet neighborhood. All rooms have shower and toilet. Internet. Breakfast included. Kitchen. Sheets €2.50, towels €1; free with doubles. Reception 8am-2am. Lockout 11am-5pm. Curfew 2am. Reserve 1 month ahead. June-Oct. 2- and 3-bed dorms €21; doubles €24; Nov.-May dorms €19; doubles €22.50. ❷

SIXTEENTH ARRONDISSEMENT

▨ **Hôtel Boileau,** 81 rue Boileau (☎01 42 88 83 74; fax 01 45 27 62 98; www.cofrase.com/boileau). M: Exelmans. From the métro, walk down bd. Exelmans toward the Seine and turn right on rue Boileau. Marble busts, Oriental rugs, vintage cashboxes, a sunny breakfast room, and a sunny staff. Cable TV, Internet access, and clean rooms. Breakfast €6. Singles €69; doubles €77-86; triples €109. AmEx/MC/V. ❺

Villa d'Auteuil, 28 rue Poussin (☎01 42 88 30 37; fax 01 45 20 74 70). M: Michel-Ange Auteuil. Walk up rue Girodet and turn left on rue Poussin. At the edge of the Bois de Boulogne, on a peaceful street is the Parisian Fawlty Towers, with eccentric staff members and (of course) a parrot. Rooms have wood-frame beds, shower, toilet, phone, and TV. High rooms have you working off those croissants—there's no elevator. Breakfast €5. Singles €48-52; doubles €56-60; triples €68. MC/V. ❹

SEVENTEENTH TO TWENTIETH ARRONDISSEMENTS

▨ **Hôtel Caulaincourt,** 2 sq. Caulaincourt, 18ème (☎01 46 06 46 06; fax 01 46 06 46 16; bienvenue@caulaincourt.com). M: Lamarck-Caulaincourt. Walk up the stairs to rue Caulaincourt; it's between #63 and #65. Half hotel, half hostel, this friendly place is in a nice, quiet area of Montmartre. Formerly artists' studios, its large, simple rooms get great light and wonderful views of Montmartre and the Paris skyline, as well as TV and phone. Breakfast €5. Reserve up to one month ahead. Singles €30, with shower €38, with shower and toilet €46, with bath and toilet €52; doubles €40-43/€47-50/€55-58/€60-63; triples with shower €56-59, with shower and toilet €64-67. MC/V. ❸

▨ **Eden Hôtel,** 7 rue Jean-Baptiste Dumay, 20ème (☎01 46 36 64 22; fax 01 46 36 01 11). M: Pyrénées. Turn right from the métro; off rue de Belleville. A hotel with good value for its two stars. Clean rooms with TV and toilets. Elevator. Breakfast €4.50. Bath or shower €4. Reserve 1 week in advance. Singles €35, with shower €48; doubles with shower €50-53, with bath €53. Extra bed €10. MC/V. ❸

Rhin et Danube, 3 pl. Rhin et Danube, 19ème (☎01 42 45 10 13; fax 01 42 06 88 82). M: Danube; or bus #75 from M: Châtelet. Just steps from the métro. Spacious, unexceptional suites. Many look onto a quaint place. All rooms have kitchen, fridge, dishes, coffee maker, hair dryer, shower, toilet, and satellite TV. Singles €46; doubles €61; triples €73; quads €83. MC/V. ❹

Hôtel Champerre Héliopolis, 13 rue d'Héliopolis, 17ème (☎01 47 64 92 56; fax 01 47 64 50 44). M: Porte de Champerret. Turn left off av. de Villiers. 22 brilliant and sparkling blue-and-white rooms, some with wooden balconies that overlook a palm-lined terrace. Beautiful, central location (for the 17ème) close to the métro, with pleasant eateries nearby. Welcoming and helpful staff. All rooms have shower, TV, telephone, hair dryer. One wheelchair-accessible room. Breakfast €7. Reserve 15 days ahead. Singles €65; doubles €77, with bath €84; triples with bath €91. AmEx/DC/MC/V. ❺

Village Hostel, 20 rue d'Orsel, 18ème (☎01 42 64 22 02; fax 01 42 64 22 04; www.villagehostel.fr). M: Anvers. Go uphill on rue Steinkerque and turn right on rue d'Orsel. In the midst of the heavy Sacré-Coeur tourist traffic, but clean and cheap. Doubles and 3- to 5-bed dorms, some in sight of Sacré-Coeur, some off a large patio, and some facing the noisy street. Lounge has kitchen, beer dispenser, TV, stereo, telephones, and Internet. Toilet and shower in all rooms. Breakfast included. Sheets €2.50; towel €1. Curfew 2am. Lockout 11am-4pm. Reserve by fax or email. Accepts same-day telephone reservations—call at 8am. 7-day max. stay. Dorms €21.50; doubles €50; triples €69. ❷

◻ FOOD

ILE DE LA CITÉ

▨ **Le Caveau du Palais,** 19 pl. Dauphine (☎01 43 26 04 28). M: Cité. Le Caveau is a chic, intimate restaurant serving traditional, hearty French food from an old-style brick oven. The proprietor specializes in Basque food, which includes lots of steak (€15-24) and fish (€19.50-24.40). A local favorite. Reservations encouraged. MC/V. ❸

Le Rouge et Blanc, 26 pl. Dauphine (☎01 43 29 52 34). M: Cité. This simple, *provençal* bar and bistro is the creation of Rigis Tillet, a young man who is proud of his southern roots and treats his customers like old friends. *Menus* €17 and €22; *plats* €14-20. Open M-Sa 11am-3pm and 7-10:30pm. Closed when it rains. MC/V. ❹

ILE ST-LOUIS

Brasserie de l'Ile St-Louis, 55 quai de Bourbon (☎01 43 54 02 59). M: Pont Marie. Cross the Pont Marie and turn right on rue St-Louis-en-l'Île; walk to the end of the island. This *brasserie* is known for Alsatian specialties such as *choucroute garnie* (sausages and pork on a bed of sauerkraut; €16), but also for omelettes and other café fare (€7-10). Open M-Tu and F-Su noon-1am, Th 5pm-1am. AmEx/MC/V. ❸

FIRST AND SECOND ARRONDISSEMENTS

▨ **Jules,** 62 rue Jean-Jacques Rousseau, 1er (☎ 01 40 28 99 04). M: Les Halles. Take the rue Rambuteau exit from the métro, walk toward the church St-Eustache, then go left on rue Coquillère and a right on rue Jean-Jacques Rousseau. Named after chef and owner Eric Teyant's son, this restaurant feels like home, with a mantelpiece and blinds on the windows. Subtle blend of modern and traditional French cooking from an award-winning chef; selections change by season. 4-course *menu* €20.58-28.50 includes terrific cheese course. Open M-F noon-2:30pm and 7-10:30pm. AmEx/MC/V. ❺

▨ **La Victoire Suprême du Coeur,** 41 rue des Bourdonnais, 1er (☎01 40 41 93 95). M: Châtelet. From the métro, take the rue des Halles exit. Follow traffic on rue des Halles and turn left on rue des Bourdonnais. La Victoire's owners have both body and soul in mind when creating dishes like *gratinée aux champignons* (mushrooms and green beans in cheese sauce). It's all vegetarian, and all very tasty. Meals marked with a "V" can be made vegan upon request. 3-course *formule* €16. *Entrées* €4.20-9. Open M-F 11:45am-2:45pm and 7-10pm, Sa noon-4pm and 7-10pm. MC/V. ❹

▨ **Le Fumoir,** 6 rue de l'Amiral Coligny, 1er (☎01 42 92 05 05). M: Louvre. On rue du Louvre, cross rue de Rivoli and rue du Louvre will become rue de l'Amiral Coligny. Conveniently close to the Louvre. Decidedly untouristy types drink their chosen beverage in deep leather sofas. Part bar, part tea house. Serves the best brunch in Paris (€19). Coffee €2.40. Open daily 11am-2am. AmEx/MC/V. ❹

■ **Les Noces de Jeannette,** 14 rue Favart, and 9 rue d'Amboise, 2ème (☎01 42 96 36 89). M: Richelieu-Drouot. Exit onto bd. des Italiens, turn left, and go left onto rue Favart. Elegant, with a wonderfully diverse clientele. *Menu du Bistro* (€27.50) includes large salad *entrées*, roasted fish, duck, and grilled meat *plats*. Free *kir* with meal. Reservations recommended. Open daily noon-1:30pm and 7-9:30pm. ❺

Le Café Marly, 93 rue de Rivoli, 1er (☎01 49 26 06 60). M: Palais-Royal. One of Paris's classiest cafés; located in the Richelieu wing of the Louvre. Terraces face the famed I.M. Pei pyramids and the Louvre's Cour Napoléon. Breakfast €12.50, served until 11am. Main dishes €16-30. Open daily 8am-2am. MC/V. ❺

Il Buco, 18 rue Léopold Bellan, 2ème (☎01 45 08 50 10). M: Sentier. Though away from the hustle and bustle of rue Montorgueil, this Italian restaurant is energized by the hip, well-dressed Parisians who frequent its closely-packed tables. The menu changes daily but always stays affordable. Large *entrées* €9-10.50, *plats* €10-13. Reservations recommended. Open M-F noon-2:30pm and 8-11pm; Sa dinner only. MC/V. ❸

Lamen Kintar, 24 rue St-Augustin, 2ème (☎01 47 42 13 14). M: Quatre Septembre. From the métro, walk with traffic down rue Monsigny and turn right onto rue St-Augustin. A low-priced Japanese restaurant. Noodle bowls €7.80; lunch *menu* (€13.73-20.59) includes *entrée*, sushi, sashimi, and soup. Open M-Sa 11:30am-10pm. MC/V. ❹

THIRD AND FOURTH ARRONDISSEMENTS

■ **Chez Janou,** 2 rue Roger Verlomme, 3ème (☎01 42 72 28 41). M: Chemin-Vert. From the métro, take rue St-Gilles and turn left on rue des Tournelles. It's on the corner of rue Roger Verlomme. Hip and friendly restaurant lauded for its reasonably priced gourmet food. The *ratatouille* entrée (€7) and the goat cheese and spinach salad (€7.50) are both delicious. Savory main courses like *thon à la provençale* (€9.50-14). Open M-F noon-3pm and 7:45pm-midnight, Sa-Su noon-5pm and 7:45pm-midnight. ❸

■ **Au Petit Fer à Cheval,** 30 rue Vieille-du-Temple, 4ème (☎01 42 72 47 47). M: Hôtel-de-Ville or St-Paul. From St-Paul, go with the traffic on rue de Rivoli and turn right; the restaurant is on the right. An oasis of *chèvre, kir,* and *Gauloises,* and a loyal local crowd. *Filet mignon de veau* (€15); excellent house salads (€3.50-10). Desserts €4-7. Open daily 10am-2am; food served noon-1:15am. MC/V. ❸

■ **L'As du Falafel,** 34 rue des Rosiers, 4ème (☎01 48 87 63 60). M: St-Paul. This kosher falafel stand and restaurant has some of the best falafel in Paris (€4). Thimble-sized (but damn good) lemonade €2.50. Open Su-F 11:30am-11:30pm. MC/V. ❶

Piccolo Teatro, 6 rue des Ecouffes, 4ème (☎01 42 72 17 79). M: St-Paul. Walk with the traffic down rue de Rivoli and take a right on rue des Ecouffes. A romantic vegetarian hideout. Weekday lunch *menus* €8.20, €9.90, or €13.30. *Entrées* €3.60-7.10; *plats* €7.70-12.50. Open Tu-Sa noon-3pm and 7-11:30pm. AmEx/MC/V. ❷

404, 69 rue des Gravilliers, 3ème (☎ 01 42 74 57 81). M: Arts et Métiers. Walk down rue Beaubourg and take a right on rue des Gravilliers. Metal hanging lights and rich red curtains lie behind the plain stone facade of this classy but comfortable North African restaurant. Mouth-watering couscous (€13-23) and *tagines* (€13-19). Lunch *menu* €17. Open daily noon-2:30pm and 8pm-midnight. AmEx/MC/V. ❹

Georges, on the 6th fl. of the Centre Pompidou, 4ème (☎01 44 78 47 99). M: Rambuteau. Ultra-sleek, Zen-cool, in-the-spotlight café; don't miss the terrace. Wine €8; champagne €10; gazpacho €8; fresh fruit salad €9.50. Open W-M noon-2am. ❸

Little Italy Trattoria, 13 rue Rambuteau, 4ème (☎01 42 74 32 46). M: Rambuteau. Walk along rue Rambuteau in the direction of traffic; it's on the right. A delicious-looking *salumeria* with indoor and outdoor tables. Amazing *antipasti* selection for two €21.50, delicate fresh pastas €8-13. Pitcher of wine €7-7.50. Open M-Sa 8:30am-11:30pm, food served M noon-4pm, Tu-Sa noon-4pm and 7:30-11:30pm. MC/V. ❸

PARIS

Sacha Finkelsztajn, 27 rue des Rosiers, 4ème (☎01 42 72 78 91). M: St-Paul. This Yiddish deli makes sandwiches for around €5. Go with an open mind, leave the cookin' up to the friendly owners, and come away with delicious combos like smoked salmon and green olive paste. Open M and W-Th 10am-2pm and 3-7pm, F-Su 10am-7pm. ❶

FIFTH AND SIXTH ARRONDISSEMENTS

▨ **Savannah Café,** 27 rue Descartes, 5ème (☎01 43 29 45 77). M: Cardinal Lemoine. Follow Cardinal Lemoine uphill, turn right on rue Clovis, and walk 1 block. Decorated with eclectic knick-knacks, this cheerful yellow restaurant prides itself on its Lebanese food and other "selections from around the world." Dishes include eggplant caviar, tabouli, and traditional French cuisine. *Entrées* €6-11.50. *Menu gastronomique* €21.65. Open M-Sa 7-11pm. MC/V. ❹ Around the corner is Savannah's little sister, the **Comptoir Méditerranée,** 42 rue du Cardinal Lemoine (☎01 43 25 29 08), with takeout and lower prices. Select from 20 hot and cold dishes to make your own plate (4 items €5.34, 6 items €7.32). Open M-Sa 11am-10pm. ❶

▨ **Au Port Salut,** 163bis rue St-Jacques, 5ème (☎01 46 33 63 21). M: Luxembourg. Exit onto bd. St-Michel, turn right onto rue Soufflot, then right on rue des Fossés St-Jacques at pl. de l'Estrapade; it's on the corner of rue St-Jacques. Behind its iron portcullis, this old stone building (once a cabaret of the same name) houses 3 floors of traditional French gastronomic joy: geraniums decorate the quiet, non-smoking dining room upstairs; the *rez-de-chaussée* has a bar with a piano and a usually boisterous crowd. 3-course *menus* (€11.80 and €20.90) include *confit de canard* and *escargots*. Open Tu-Sa noon-2:30pm and 7-11:30pm. MC/V. ❸

Le Petit Vatel, 5 rue Lobineau, 6ème (☎01 43 54 28 49). M: Mabillon. From the métro, follow traffic on bd. St-Germain, turn right on rue de Seine, and then take the second right onto rue Lobineau. This charming little home-run bistro with sunny yellow walls and pictures of Carmen Miranda serves Mediterranean French specialties like *catalan pamboli* (bread with puréed tomatoes, ham, and cheese), all for €10. Lunch *menu* (€11) usually has a vegetarian option. Open Tu-Sa noon-2pm and 8-10:30pm. ❸

Les Editeurs, 4 carrefour d'Odéon, 6ème (☎01 43 26 67 76). The newest and classiest café on the block, Les Editeurs pays homage to St-Germain's literary pedigree with books—on everything from Marilyn Monroe to Brassaï—overflowing its plush red and gold dining rooms, and outlets for struggling, laptop-toting young writers. Jazz music and a piano upstairs. *Croque Monsieur* €9.50. *Café* €2.50, draft beer €4.50, cocktails €9. Ice creams like *mandarine des montagnes* or pistachio €7.50. Happy hour daily 6-8pm with cocktails €6-8. Open daily 8am-2am. AmEx/MC/V. ❷

Café de Flore, 172 bd. St-Germain, 6ème (☎01 45 48 55 26). M: St-Germain-des-Prés. Walk against traffic on bd. St-Germain. Sartre wrote *Being and Nothingness* here; Apollinaire, Picasso, Breton, and Thurber sipped brew. Espresso €4, *salade Flore* €12.20, pastries €6.10-10.40. Open daily 7:30am-1:30am. AmEx/MC/V. ❹

Les Deux Magots, 6 pl. St-Germain-des-Prés, 6ème (☎01 45 48 55 25). M: St-Germain-des-Prés. Blocks from the Eglise St-Germain-des-Prés. The cloistered area behind the famous high hedges has been home to the ghosts of literati (like Mallarmé and Hemingway) since 1885, but now is favored by Left Bank residents and tourists. Coffee €3.80, pastries €6.70, sandwiches €6.10-7.60. Open daily 7:30am-1:30am. AmEx/V. ❷

Le Jardin des Pâtés, 4 rue Lacépède, 5ème (☎01 43 31 50 71). M: Jussieu. From the métro, walk up rue Linné and turn right on rue Lacépède. In a space best described as "yuppie zen," this restaurant serves organic food best described as "delicious." Mostly pasta and vegetables, but there is still meat on the menu, including the *pâtés de seigle* (ham, white wine, and sharp comté cheese; €8.84). Many vegetarian options. Appetizers €3-5, main dishes €6.40-12. Open daily noon-2:30pm and 7-11pm. MC/V. ❷

Così, 54 rue de Seine, 6ème (☎01 46 33 35 36). M: Mabillon. From the métro, walk down bd. St-Germain and make a left onto rue de Seine. Named for the Mozart opera, this hip sandwicherie sells enormous, tasty, inexpensive sandwiches on fresh, brick-oven bread. Sandwiches €5.20-7.60. Desserts €2.80-3.40. Open daily noon-11pm. ❶

SEVENTH AND EIGHTH ARRONDISSEMENTS

▨ **Café du Marché,** 38 rue Cler, 7ème (☎01 47 05 51 27). M: Ecole Militaire. Walk up rue de la Motte Piquet and turn left onto rue Cler. Watch the chic residents of the 7ème doing their errands from this beautiful terrace on an adorable street. Good, American-style food like a Caesar salad (€8) along with customary French dishes (duck confit €9.50). Open M-Sa 7am-1am, food served until 11pm; Su 7am-3pm. MC/V. ❷

▨ **Bangkok Café,** 28 rue de Moscou, 8ème (☎01 43 87 62 56). M: Rome. From the métro, take a right onto rue Moscou. A talented Thai chef and her French husband serve inventive seafood salads and soups (€8-10) and a choice of meats cooked in coconut milk, curry, or satay sauce (€12-18). Plenty of vegetarian options. Open M-F noon-2:30pm and 7-11:30pm, Sa 7-11:30pm. AmEx/MC/V. ❸

Le Lotus Blanc, 45 rue de Bourgogne, 7ème (☎01 45 55 18 89). M: Varenne. On bd. des Invalides, walk towards the Invalides; turn left onto rue de Varenne and left again onto rue de Bourgogne. Chef Pham-Nam Nghia has been making Vietnamese food for 25 years. Lunch *menu* €9-29. Veggie *menu* €6.50-10.50. Reservations encouraged. Open M-Sa noon-2:30pm and 7-10:30pm. Aug. closed two weeks. AmEx/MC/V. ❸

Bagel & Co., 31 rue de Ponthieu, 8ème (☎01 42 89 44 20). M: Franklin D. Roosevelt. Walk toward the Arc de Triomphe on the Champs-Elysées, then go right on av. FDR and left on rue de Ponthieu. One of the only cheap options in the 8ème, this bright, modern, New York-inspired deli offers a large array of creative bagel and specialty sandwiches (€3-5), like the *Los Angeles* (bagel with smoked turkey, cheddar, and avocado). Intimate upstairs eating area and cafeteria-bar. Homemade dessert €2-3. Lots of vegetarian and kosher options. Open M-F 7:30am-9pm, Sa 10am-8pm. AmEx/MC/V. ❶

NINTH AND TENTH ARRONDISSEMENTS

▨ **Haynes Restaurant Américain,** 3 rue Clauzel, 9ème (☎01 48 78 40 63). M: St-Georges. Head uphill on rue Notre-Dame-de-Lorette and turn right on rue H. Monnier, then right on rue Clauzel. The first African-American owned restaurant in Paris (1949), a center for expatriates, and a former hangout for hep cats like Louis Armstrong, James Baldwin, and Richard Wright, Haynes is famous for its "original American Soul Food" and down-home hospitality. Very generous portions, most under €16. Ma Sutton's fried chicken with honey €14. Sister Lena's BBQ spare ribs €14. Vocal jazz concerts F nights; funk and groove Sa nights. Open Tu-Sa 7pm-12:30am. AmEx/MC/ V. ❸

▨ **Au Bon Café,** 2 bd. St-Martin, 10ème (☎01 42 00 21 45). M: République. Just to the right of pl. de la République if you exit the station facing the statue. This delightful eatery is a haven from the frenzy of the pl. de la République and a nice alternative to the *place's* pizza chain stores. Superb salads with scallops, grapefruit, pear, avocado and tomato. Salads €9-10; quiches €6-8. AmEx/MC/V. ❷

Chartier, 7 rue du Faubourg-Montmartre, 9ème (☎01 47 70 86 29). M: Grands Boulevards. This Parisian fixture has been serving well-priced French cuisine since 1896. Far from stuffy, with high ceilings and a large, open space. As tradition dictates, the waitstaff still add up the bill on the tablecloth. Main dishes €7-9.50. Side dishes of vegetables €2.20. Open daily 11:30am-3pm and 7-10pm. MC/V. ❷

Cantine d'Antoine et Lili, 95 quai de Valmy, 10ème (☎01 40 37 34 86). M: Gare de l'Est. From the métro, go down rue Faubourg St-Martin and turn left on rue Récollets; Cantine is on the corner of quai de Valmy. This canal-side café-bistro is one quarter of the Antoine and Lili operation, which also includes a neighboring plant store, furniture outlet, and clothing boutique. The counter staff and the vibrant decor are welcoming, and the light, café-style food is tasty. Pasta salads €5; salads €6; quiches €6. Open W-Sa 11am-1am, Su-Tu 11am-8pm. AmEx/MC/V. ❶

ELEVENTH AND TWELFTH ARRONDISSEMENTS

▨ **Chez Paul,** 13 rue de Charonne, 11ème (☎01 47 00 34 57). M: Bastille. Go east on rue du Faubourg St-Antoine and turn left on rue de Charonne. Worn exterior hides a kicking vintage bistro. From succulent salmon to peppercorn steak (€12.50), Paul dishes up a menu to make your palate sing. Reservations required. Open daily noon-2:30pm and 7pm-2am; food served until 12:30am. Aug. 1-Aug.15 closed for lunch. AmEx/MC/V. ❸

▨ **Café de l'Industrie,** 16 rue St-Sabin, 11ème (☎01 47 00 13 53). M: Breguet-Sabin. This huge, hip café pays tribute to France's colonialist past with photos of natives, palm trees, and weapons on the walls. The gramophone plays, the populace gets restless, and l'Industrie is full by the end of the night. Coffee €2; *vin chaud* €4; salads €7-7.50. After 10pm prices €0.60 higher. Open Su-F 10am-2am; lunch served noon-1pm. ❷

L'Ebauchoir, 45 rue de Citeaux, 12ème (☎01 43 42 49 31). M: Faidherbe-Chaligny. Walk down rue du Faubourg St-Antoine, turn left on rue de Citeaux. L'Ebauchoir has a dressed-up diner feel, but the mix of funky and Frenchie works. The lunch *menu* (€12) includes drink; all-day *menu* €15; *plats* from €11. Open M-Th noon-2:30pm and 8-10:30pm, F-Sa noon-2:30pm and 8-11pm. MC/V. ❸

THIRTEENTH AND FOURTEENTH ARRONDISSEMENTS

▨ **Café du Commerce,** 39 rue des Cinq Diamants, 13ème (☎01 53 62 91 04). M: Place d'Italie. Take bd. Auguste Blanqui and turn left onto rue des Cinq Diamants. This is very much a local establishment, serving traditional food with a funky twist. Dinner *menus* €15.50, lunch *menu* €10.50. Both feature options like *boudin antillais* (spiced blood-wurst) or steak with avocado and strawberries. Dinner reservations recommended. Open daily noon-3pm with service until 2:30pm and 7pm-2am with service until 1am. Sa-Su brunch until 4pm. AmEx/MC/V. ❸

▨ **Phinéas,** 99 rue de l'Ouest, 14ème (☎01 45 41 33 50). M: Pernety. Follow the traffic on rue Pernety and turn left on rue de l'Ouest. The restaurant is on your left. Wild ferns, hand-painted stained-glass windows, and one oversized crown decorate the pink walls of this restaurant's two dining rooms. In the open kitchen the chef makes *tartes salées* (€6.50-8) and *tartes sucrées* (€6-6.50). The restaurant doubles as a comic-book shrine. Vegetarian options available. Open Tu-Sa 9am-noon for take-out and noon-11:30pm for dine-in. Su brunch 11am-3pm. AmEx/MC/V. ❸

La Coupole, 102 bd. du Montparnasse, 14ème (☎01 43 20 14 20). M: Vavin. Half-café, half-restaurant, La Coupole's Art Deco chambers have hosted Lenin, Stravinsky, Hemingway, and Einstein. Though fairly touristy and overpriced it's still worth the nostalgic splurge: coffee (€2), hot chocolate (€3), or a *croque monsieur* (€5). The food proper, though unabashedly expensive, is considered to be among the best in Paris. Dancing (salsa, disco, R&B) Tu, Th, Sa 10pm-5am. Cover €15. Open M-F 8:30am-1am, Sa-Su 8:30am-1:30am. AmEx/MC/V. ❺

Aquarius Café, 40 rue de Gergovie, 14ème (☎01 45 41 36 88). M: Pernety. Walk against traffic on rue Raymond Losserand and turn right on rue de Gergovie. A vegetarian oasis and celebrated local favorite. The "mini mixed grill" dish includes tofu sausages, wheat pancakes, brown rice, and vegetables in a mushroom sauce (€9.91). They even have organic wines. Open M-Sa noon-2:15pm and 7-10:30pm. Also at 54 rue Ste-Croix de la Bretonnerie, 4ème (☎01 48 87 48 71). AmEx/MC/V. ❸

FIFTEENTH AND SIXTEENTH ARRONDISSEMENTS

▨ **Thai Phetburi,** 31 bd. de Grenelle, 15ème (☎01 41 58 14 88). M: Bir-Hakeim. From the métro, walk away from the river on bd. de Grenelle; the restaurant will be on your left. Award-winning food, friendly service, low prices, and a relaxing atmosphere. The *tom yam koung* (shrimp soup flavored with lemongrass; €6.80) and the *keng khiao wan kai* (chicken in spicy green curry sauce; €7.80) are both superb. AmEx/MC/V. ❷

▨ **La Rotunde de la Muette,** 12 Chaussée de la Muette, 16ème (☎01 45 24 45 45). M: La Muette. From the métro, head 2min. down Chaussée de la Muette toward the Jardin de Ranelagh. Located in a beautiful *fin-de-siècle* building overlooking the tree-lined Chaussée de la Muette. Indoors, the stylish red and yellow lamps, hip music, and plush burgundy seats are a sleek diversion from the patio's classic feel. Sandwiches €5-9.60, salads €4-9.15. Open daily noon-11pm. AmEx/MC/V. ❷

Le Tire Bouchon, 62 rue des Entrepreneurs, 5ème (☎01 40 59 09 27). M: Charles Michels. A charming couple serves classic French cuisine with a creative touch to a mix of Parisians and Americans. Try the *terrine de pennes* (€8), the *fricassée d'agneau* with delicious tomato chutney (€13), and for dessert a shortbread pastry with tea-flavored ice cream (€6). Open Tu-F noon-2:30pm and 7:30-11pm, M and Sa 7:30-11pm. MC/V. ❸

Byblos Café, 6 rue Guichard, 16ème (☎01 42 30 99 99). M: La Muette. Walk down rue Passy one block and turn left on rue Guichard. This airy, modern, Lebanese restaurant serves cold *mezzes* (think Middle Eastern *tapas*), tabouli, moutabal, moussaka, and a variety of hummus dishes €5.80-8. Warm *mezzes* include hot Lebanese sausages and falafel (€6.10). *Menu* €15. Takeout 15-20% lower. Vegetarian options available. Open daily 11am-3pm and 5-11pm. AmEx/MC/V. ❷

SEVENTEENTH AND EIGHTEENTH ARRONDISSEMENTS

▨ **Le Patio Provençal,** 116 rue des Dames, 17ème (☎01 42 93 73 73). M: Villiers. Follow rue de Lévis away from the intersection and go right on rue des Dames. High quality rustic farmhouse-style restaurant serves staples of southern France, such as *filet de canard* (€12). Glass of wine €3-4. Super-busy, making service a bit slow and reservations a must. Open M-F noon-2:30pm and 7-11pm. MC/V. ❸

▨ **Le Soleil Gourmand,** 10 rue Ravignan, 18ème (☎01 42 51 00 50). M: Abbesses. Facing the church in Place des Abbesses, head right down rue des Abbesses and go right (uphill) on rue Ravignan. Two sisters run this local favorite with funky artistic flare. Inventive and light *provençal* food. Try the specialty *bricks* (fried stuffed filo dough; €11), 5-cheese *tartes* with salad (€10), and house-baked cakes (€4.50-7). Vegetarian options. Dinner reservations required. Open daily 12:30-2:30pm and 8:30-11pm. ❸

Refuge des Fondues, 17 rue des Trois Frères, 18ème (☎01 42 55 22 65). M: Abbesses. Walk down rue Yvonne le Tac and turn left on rue des Trois Frères. Only two main dishes: *fondue bourguignonne* (meat fondue) and *fondue savoyarde* (cheese fondue). The wine is served in baby bottles with rubber nipples; leave your Freudian hang-ups at home. *Menu* €15. Open daily 5pm-2am. Closed for parts of July and Aug. ❸

L'Endroit, 67 pl. du Dr. Félix Lobligeois, 17ème (☎01 42 29 50 00). M: Rome. Follow rue Boursault to rue Legendre, and turn right. As cool during the day as it is at night, L'Endroit is the place to go in the 17ème. 4-course Su brunch (noon-3:30pm; €16) heads a long *menu* with items like melon and *jambon* (€10.80), salads (€10.70), and toasted sandwiches (€9.30). Open daily noon-2am. MC/V. ❸

NINETEENTH AND TWENTIETH ARRONDISSEMENTS

▨ **Café Flèche d'Or,** 102 rue de Bagnolet, 20ème (☎01 43 72 04 23). M: Alexandre Dumas. Follow rue de Bagnolet until it crosses rue des Pyrénées; the café is on the right. Near Porte de la Réunion at Père Lachaise. This bar/performance space/café is housed in a defunct train station. North African, French, Caribbean, and South American cuisine with jazz, ska, folk, salsa, and samba (cover €5-6). Psychology cafés the first Su morning of every month, political debates other Su mornings. Greek, Middle Eastern, Vietnamese, and Mexican-themed dinner *menus* €17-20. Su brunch *menu* €11. Open daily 10am-2am; dinner daily 8pm-1am. MC/V. ❹

Lao-Thai, 34 rue de Belleville, 19*ème* (☎01 43 58 41 84). M: Belleville. Thai and Laotian specialties on an all-you-can-eat buffet with 12 different dishes, rice, and dessert. Perfect for the poor and hungry traveler (though the ambience is somewhat lacking). At €2.30, a martini is only €0.45 more than a Coke. Lunch M-F €7.55, Sa-Su €8.70. Dinner Su-Th €11.60, F-Sa €13. Open Tu-Su noon-2:30pm and 7-11:15pm. MC/V. ❸

SALONS DE THÉ

Parisian *salons de thé* (tea rooms) fall into three categories: those stately salons straight out of the last century piled high with macaroons, Seattle-inspired joints for pseudo-intellectuals, and cafés that simply want to signal they also serve tea.

▨ **Angelina's,** 226 rue de Rivoli, 1*er* (☎01 42 60 82 00). M: Concorde or Tuileries. Where *grandmère* takes little Delphine after playing in the Tuileries. Audrey Hepburn's favorite; apparently the tourists agree. *Chocolat africain* (hot chocolate; €6) and *Mont Blanc* (meringue with chestnut nougat; €6.15) are the sinful house specialties. Afternoon tea €5.20. Open daily 9am-7pm. AmEx/MC/V.

▨ **Mariage Frères,** 30 rue du Bourg-Tibourg, 4*ème* (☎01 42 72 28 11). M: Hôtel-de-Ville. Started by 2 brothers who found British tea shoddy, this salon prepares 500 varieties of tea (€6.10-12.20), from Russian to Vietnamese. A classic and classy French institution. Tea *menu* (€24) includes sandwich, pastry, and tea. Excellent brunch (brioche, eggs, tea, cakes) €23. Afternoon tea 3-6:30pm; Su brunch 12:30-6:30pm. Open daily 10:30am-7:30pm; lunch M-Sa noon-3pm. AmEx/MC/V. Also at 13 rue des Grands Augustins, 6*ème* (☎01 40 51 82 50), M: St-Michel; and at 260 rue du Faubourg St-Honoré, 8*ème* (☎01 46 22 18 54).

▨ **Ladurée,** 16 rue Royale, 8*ème* (☎01 42 60 21 79). M: Concorde. Ever wondered what it would be like to dine inside a Fabergé egg? The traditional rococo decor of this classic tea salon attracts the shoppers that frequent the pricey boutiques in the area. Famous for the macaroons stacked in the window (€4). Pastry counter. Specialty tea *Ladurée mélange* €5.45. Open daily 8:30am-7pm; lunch until 3pm. AmEx/MC/V. Also at 75, av. des Champs-Elysées, 8*ème* (☎01 40 75 08 75). M: FDR.

MARKETS

Marché rue Montorgueil, 2*ème*. M: Etienne-Marcel. From métro, walk along rue Etienne Marcel away from the river. Rue Montorgueil is the 2nd street on your right. A center of food commerce and gastronomy since the 13th century, the marble Mount Pride Market sells wine, cheese, meat, and produce. Open Tu-Su 8am-7:30pm.

Marché Port Royal, 5*ème*. M: Censier-Daubenton. Make a right on bd. du Port-Royal in front of the Hôpital du Val-de-Grâce. Colorful, fun, and busy. Sells fresh produce, meat, fish, and cheese, as well as shoes, cheap chic clothing, and housewares. Open Tu, Th, and Sa 7am-2:30pm.

Marché Mouffetard, 5*ème*. M: Monge. Walk through pl. Monge and follow rue Ortolan to rue Mouffetard. Cheese, meat, fish, produce, and housewares sold here. The bakeries are reputedly among the best in Paris. Open Tu-Su 8am-1:30pm.

SPECIALTY SHOPS

Food shops, particularly *boulangeries* and *pâtisseries*, are on virtually every street in Paris, or at least it seems like it. Not surprisingly, most of them are excellent. The following listings are the best specialty food shops in Paris.

■ **Fauchon**, 26 pl. de la Madeleine, 8ème (☎01 47 42 60 11). M: Madeleine. Paris's favorite gourmet food shop (with gourmet prices), this *traiteur/pâtisserie/épicerie/charcuterie* has it all. Go home with a prettily packaged tin of *madeleines*, or browse their wine cellar, one of the finest in Paris. Open M-Sa 10am-7pm.

■ **Ice cream: Berthillon**, 31 rue St-Louis-en-l'Île, 4ème (☎43 54 31 61), on Ile-St-Louis. M: Cité or Pont Marie. Forget the Louvre and the Eiffel Tower. This place is reason enough to visit Paris. The best and most famous ice cream and sorbet in the city. Choose from dozens of *parfums* (flavors), ranging from passion fruit and gingerbread to the standard chocolate. Open Sept.-July 14: take-out W-Su 10am-8pm; eat-in W-F 1-8pm, Sa-Su 2-8pm. Closed 2 weeks in Feb. and Apr.

■ **Wine: Nicolas**, locations throughout Paris. This wine-loving country's version of Starbucks, at least in terms of number of locations. Super-friendly English-speaking staff is happy to help you pick the perfect Burgundy. They will even pack it up in travel boxes with handles. Most branches open M-F 10am-8pm. AmEx/MC/V.

■ **Bakery: Poujauran**, 20 rue Jean-Nicot, 7ème (☎01 47 05 80 88). M: La Tour-Maubourg. Sells a wide range of *petit pains* (miniature breads; €0.65) alongside their bigger brothers (and sisters). Open Tu-Sa 8:30am-8:30pm.

■ **Chocolates: La Maison du Chocolat**, 8 bd. de la Madeleine, 9ème (☎01 47 42 86 52). M: Madeleine. The whole range, from milk to a mysterious distilled chocolate essence drink. Box of 2 chocolates €3.15. Also at 19 rue de Sèvres, 6ème (☎01 45 44 20 40). Open M-Sa 10am-7pm. MC/V.

◎ SIGHTS

ILE DE LA CITÉ

Until the 5th century, when it became the first spot to be named "Paris," Ile de la Cité was called Lutetia by the Gallic tribe that inhabited it. In the 6th century, Clovis crowned himself king of the Franks, and until the 14th century, Ile de la Cité was the seat of the monarchy. Today, all distance points in France are measured from *kilomètre zéro*, a circular sundial in front of Notre Dame.

NOTRE DAME

The Cathedral of Notre Dame does not budge an inch for all the idiocies of the world.
   —e.e. cummings

Notre Dame was once the site of a Roman temple to Jupiter, and this holy spot housed three churches before Maurice de Sully began the construction of the cathedral in 1163. Sully, the bishop of Paris, aimed to create an edifice filled with air and light, in a style that would later be dubbed **Gothic.** He died before his plan was completed, and it was up to later centuries to rework the cathedral into the composite masterpiece, finished in 1361, that stands today. Notre Dame has seen royal weddings, Joan of Arc's trial, and Napoleon's coronation. Revolutionary secularists renamed the cathedral *Le Temple de la Raison* (The Temple of Reason), hiding Gothic arches behind plaster facades of virtuous Neoclassical design. Although reconsecrated after the Revolution, the building fell into disrepair and was used to shelter livestock. Victor Hugo's 1831 novel *Notre-Dame de Paris*

(The Hunchback of Notre Dame) revived interest in the cathedral and inspired Napoleon III and Haussmann to invest time and money in its restoration, including modifications by Eugène Viollet-le-Duc like a new spire, gargoyles, and a statue of himself admiring his own work. In 1870 and again in 1940 thousands of Parisians attended masses here to pray for deliverance from invading Germany. On August 26, 1944, Charles de Gaulle braved Nazi sniper fire to come and give thanks for the imminent liberation of Paris.

EXTERIOR. Notre Dame has been and still is in the throes of a massive cleaning project, but at least now its newly glittering **West Facade** has been set free from scaffolding. The oldest work is found above the **Porte de Ste-Anne** (right), mostly dating from 1165-1175. Revolutionaries wreaked havoc on the facade during the 1790s. Not content with decapitating Louis XVI, they attacked the statues of the Kings of Judah above the doors, which they incorrectly thought were his ancestors. The heads are now exhibited in the Musée de Cluny (see p. 154).

■**TOWERS.** The two towers—home to the cathedral's most famous fictional resident, Quasimodo the Hunchback—were a mysterious, imposing shadow on the Paris skyline for years. The claustrophobia-inducing staircase emerges onto a spectacular perch, where rows of gargoyles survey the city, particularly the Latin Quarter and the Marais. In the south tower, a tiny door opens onto the 13 ton bell that even Quasimodo couldn't ring: it requires the force of eight people to move.

INTERIOR. From the inside, the cathedral seems to be constructed of soaring, weightless walls. This effect is achieved by the spidery **flying buttresses** that support the vaults of the ceiling from outside, creating room for delicate stained glass walls. The transept's **rose windows,** nearly 85% 13th-century glass, are the most spectacular feature of the interior. The cathedral's **treasury,** south of the choir, contains an assortment of gilded artifacts. The famous Crown of Thorns, which is supposed to have been worn by Christ, was moved to Notre Dame at the end of the 18th century. The relic is presented only on Fridays during Lent (5-6pm). Far below the cathedral towers, the **Crypte Archéologique,** pl. du Parvis du Notre Dame, houses artifacts unearthed in the construction of a parking garage. *(M: Cité. ☎01 42 34 56 10, crypt 01 43 29 83 51. Cathedral open daily 8am-6:45pm. Towers open daily 10am-5pm. €5.50, 18-25 €3.50. Tours begin at the booth to the right as you enter. In English W-Th noon, Sa 2:30pm; in French M-F noon, Sa 2:30pm. Free. Roman Catholic Mass M-F 8, 9am, noon, 6:15pm; Sa 8, 8:45, 10, 11:30am, 12:45, 6:30pm. Vespers sung 5:30pm in the choir. Treasury open M-Sa 9:30-12:30pm and 1:30-5:30pm, Su 1:30-5:30pm; last entry 5pm. €2.50, students and ages 12-17 €2, 6-12 €1, under 6 free. High Mass with Gregorian chant Su 10am. Free organ recital daily 4:30pm. Crypt open daily 10am-5:30pm; last entry 30min. before closing. €3.30, over 60 €2.20, under 27 €1.60, under 13 free.)*

PALAIS DE LA CITÉ

The Palais de la Cité is known for the infamous **Conciergerie,** a Revolutionary prison, **Ste-Chapelle,** and the **Palais de Justice,** which was built after the great fire of 1776 and is now home to the district courts of Paris. *(M: Cité. 4 bd. du Palais.)*

PALAIS DE JUSTICE. A wide set of stone steps at the main entrance of the Palais de Justice leads to three doorways marked *Liberté, Egalité,* or *Fraternité.* All trials are open to the public so you can choose a door and make your way through the green gates that stand beyond "Equality." Climb the stairs to the second floor and go immediately left (look for signs for "Cour d'Appel") and guards will let you into a viewing gallery. *(M: Cité. 4 bd. du Palais, enter at Ste-Chapelle. ☎01 44 32 51 51. Courtrooms open M-F 9am-noon and 1:30-6pm. Free.)*

■ **STE-CHAPELLE.** Ste-Chapelle remains the foremost example of flamboyant Gothic architecture and a tribute to the craft of medieval stained glass. Construction of the chapel began in 1241 to house the most precious of King Louis IX's possessions: the Crown of Thorns from Christ's Passion. Although the crown itself—minus a few thorns that St-Louis gave away in exchange for political favors—has been moved to Notre Dame, Ste-Chapelle is still a wonder to explore. No mastery of the lower Chapel's dim gilt can prepare the visitor for the **Upper Chapel,** where light pours through walls of stained glass and frescoes of saints and martyrs shine. *(M: Cité. 4 bd. du Palais. ☎ 01 53 73 58 51 or 01 53 73 78 50. Open Apr.-Sept. daily 9:30am-5:30pm. Last admission 30min. before closing. €5.50, seniors and ages 18-25 €3.50, under 18 free. Twin ticket with Conciergerie €8, seniors and ages 18-25 €5, under 18 free.)*

CONCIERGERIE. This dark monument to the Revolution stands over the Seine. Originally an administrative building, then a royal prison, it was taken over by the Revolutionary Tribunal after 1793. You can see rows of cells complete with preserved props and plastic people. Plaques explain how the rich and famous could buy themselves private rooms with tables for writing while the poor slept on straw in pestilential cells. Among the 2700 people awaiting execution between 1792 and 1794 were Robespierre and Marie Antoinette. *(M: Cité. 1 quai de l'Horloge, entrance on bd. du Palais. ☎ 01 53 73 78 50. Open Apr.-Sept. daily 9:30am-6:30pm; Oct.-Mar. 10am-5pm. Last ticket 30min. before closing. €5.50, students €3.50. Includes tour in French daily 11am and 3pm. For English tours, call in advance.)*

OTHER ISLAND SIGHTS

MÉMORIAL DE LA DÉPORTATION. This is a haunting memorial to the 200,000 French victims of Nazi concentration camps. The focal point is a tunnel lined with 200,000 quartz pebbles, reflecting the Jewish custom of memorializing the dead by placing stones on their graves. On the sides are empty cells and wall carvings of concentration camp names and humanitarian quotations. Near the exit the injunction, *"Pardonne. N'Oublie Pas"* ("Forgive. Do Not Forget.") is the simplest and most arresting. *(M: Cité. At the very tip of the island on pl. de l'Ile de France, a 5min. walk from the back of the cathedral, and down a narrow flight of steps. Open Apr.-Sept. daily 10am-noon and 1-7pm; Oct.-Mar. 10am-noon and 1-5pm. Free.)*

PONT NEUF. Leave Ile de la Cité by the oldest bridge in Paris, Pont Neuf (New Bridge), located just behind pl. Dauphine. Before the construction of the Champs-Elysées, it was Paris's most popular thoroughfare, attracting peddlers, performance artists, and thieves. More recently, Christo, the Bulgarian performance artist, wrapped the entire bridge in 44,000 square meters of nylon.

ILE ST-LOUIS

Originally two small islands—the Ile aux Vâches (Cow Island) and the Ile de Notre Dame—the Ile St-Louis was considered suitable for duels, cows, and little else throughout the Middle Ages. The two islands merged in the 17th century, and Ile St-Louis became residential; its inhabitants included Voltaire, Mme. de Châtelet, Daumier, Ingres, Baudelaire, Balzac, Courbet, George Sand, Delacroix and Cézanne through the years in its *hôtels particuliers*. Ile St-Louis retains a certain distance from the rest of Paris. Older residents say "Je vais à Paris" ("I'm going to Paris") when leaving by one of the four bridges linking Île St-Louis and the mainland.

QUAI DE BOURBON. Sculptor **Camille Claudel** lived and worked at **no. 19** from 1899 until 1913, when her brother, the poet Paul Claudel, had her incarcerated in an asylum. The protegé and lover of sculptor Auguste Rodin, Claudel's most striking work is displayed in the Musée Rodin (see p. 153). At the intersection of the

IN RECENT NEWS

BEACH BUMMING

As the saying goes, if you can't stand the heat, then get the hell out of town. Among those who heed this mantra are the citizens of Paris, who, come August, flee their beloved city for the shores of Normandy and the Côte d'Azur. But in the summer of 2002, the city figured out how to bring the beach to Paris. Bertrand Delanoe, the city's mayor, decided to transform 2km of Seine riverfront into "Paris Plage." The result was five patches of "beach"—one of sand, two of grass, and two of pebbles—that stretched from **quai Tuileries** to **quai Henri IV.** Equipped with lounge chairs, parasols, palm trees, and even a volleyball court, the beach drew hordes of sun-hungry citizens. The city has also temporarily closed the road next to the plage to cars so that visitors can enjoy the sand and sunshine by inline skating and riding their bicycles along the edge of the beach.

True, the plage, for which the city shelled out €1.5 million, has fallen short of paradise. Pollution by Parisians past, who failed to foresee the city's beach potential, makes the Seine unfit for swimming. More tragically, perhaps, the city discourages one of Europe's age-old customs: nude sunbathing.

Despite these setbacks, the plage was a resounding success. With any luck, this year it will again be drawing crowds eager to, if not beat the summer heat, then at least get a tan for their trouble. Just not a seamless one.

quai and rue des Deux Ponts sits the café **Au Franc-Pinot,** whose wrought-iron facade is almost as old as the island itself. Closed in 1716 when authorities discovered a basement stash of anti-government tracts, the café-cabaret reemerged as a center for treason during the Revolution. Cécile Renault, daughter of the proprietor, mounted an unsuccessful attempt on Robespierre's life in 1794 and was guillotined the following year. Today the Pinot houses a mediocre jazz club. (Immediately to the left after crossing the Pont St-Louis, the quai wraps around the northwest edge of the island.)

EGLISE ST-LOUIS-EN-L'ILE. Louis Le Vau's 17th-century Rococo interior is lit by a surprising number of windows. The third chapel has a splendid gilded wood relief, The Death of the Virgin. (19bis rue St-Louis-en-l'Ile. ☎01 46 34 11 60. Open Tu-Su 9am-noon and 3-7pm. Check with FNAC or call the church for details on concerts.)

FIRST ARRONDISSEMENT

Paris's royal past is conspicuous in much of the 1er. Its prized possession, the Louvre, is the former home of French royalty. Today, the bedchambers and dining rooms of innumerable rulers house the world's finest art, and the Sun King's prized gardens are filled with sunbathers, cafés, and carnival rides. Royalty still dominates here, though: Chanel, the Ritz, and upscale shops hold court in the **pl. Vendôme.** Souvenir shops crowd **rue du Louvre** and **Les Halles.** To the west, smoky jazz clubs pulse on **rue des Lombards** while restaurants on **rue Jean-Jacques Rousseau** serve up divine cuisine. **Safety:** Although above ground the 1er is one of the safest areas in Paris, the métro stops Châtelet and Les Halles are best avoided at night.

EAST OF THE LOUVRE

JARDIN DES TUILERIES. Sweeping down from the Louvre to the pl. de la Concorde, the Jardin des Tuileries celebrates the victory of geometry over nature. Missing the public promenades of her native Italy, Catherine de Médici had the gardens built in 1564. In 1649, André Le Nôtre (gardener for Louis XIV and designer of the gardens at Versailles) imposed straight lines and sculpted trees. The elevated terrace by the Seine offers remarkable views of the **Arc de Triomphe du Carrousel** and the glass pyramid of the Louvre's Cour Napoléon. Sculptures by Rodin and others stand amid the gardens's cafés and courts. In the summer, the rue de Rivoli terrace becomes an amusement park with children's rides, food stands, and a huge ferris wheel. The **Galerie National du Jeu de Paume** and the **Musée de l'Orangerie** flank the pathway at the Concorde end of the Tuileries. *(M: Tuileries. ☎01 40 20 90 43. Open daily Apr.-Sept. 7am-9pm; Oct.-Mar. 7:30am-7:30pm. Tours in English from the Arc de Triomphe du Carrousel; free; call for details. Amusement park open late June to mid-Aug. and Dec.-early Jan. Rides €2-15.)*

PLACE VENDÔME. Stately pl. Vendôme, three blocks north of the Tuileries, was begun in 1687 by Louis XIV. Designed by Jules Hardouin-Mansart, the square was built to house embassies, but bankers created lavish private homes behind the elegant facades. Today, the smell of money is still in the air: bankers, perfumers, and jewelers, including Cartier (at no. 7), line the square.

PALAIS-ROYAL

One block north of the Louvre along rue St-Honoré lies the once regal and racy Palais-Royal, constructed in the 17th century as Cardinal Richelieu's Palais Cardinal. After the Cardinal's death in 1642, Queen Anne d'Autriche moved in, bringing with her a young Louis XIV. In the central courtyard, the controversial **colonnes de Buren**, a set of black and white striped pillars, were installed by artist Daniel Buren in 1986. *(Open June-Aug. daily 7am-11pm; Sept. 7am-9:30pm; Oct.-Mar. 7am-8:30pm; Apr.-May 7am-10:15pm.)*

LES HALLES AND SURROUNDINGS

EGLISE DE ST-EUSTACHE. There is a reason why Richelieu, Molière, and Mme. de Pompadour were all baptized in the Eglise de St-Eustache, why Louis XIV received communion in its sanctuary, and why Mozart chose to have his mother's funeral here. This church is a magnificent blend of history, beauty, and harmony, honoring Eustache (Eustatius), a Roman general who adopted Christianity upon seeing the sign of a cross between the antlers of a deer. As punishment for converting, the Romans locked him into a brass bull that was placed over a fire. The chapels contain paintings by Rubens, as well as the British artist Raymond Mason's bizarre relief *Departure of the Fruits and Vegetables from the Heart of Paris*, commemorating the closing of the market at Les Halles. *(M: Les Halles. Above rue Rambuteau. ☎01 42 36 31 05. Open M-F 9:30am-7:30pm and Su 9:15am-7:30pm. High Mass Su 11am and 6pm. Free organ recital Su 5:30-6pm. Summer organ concerts €12.20-22.90.)*

LES HALLES. The métro station Les Halles exits directly into the underground mall. To see the gardens, ride the escalators up toward daylight. A sprawling market since 1135, Les Halles received a much-needed face-lift in the 1850s with the construction of large iron-and-glass pavilions to shelter the vendors's stalls. In 1970, when authorities moved the old market to a suburb, planners destroyed the pavilions to build a subterranean transfer-point between the métro and the new commuter rail and a subterranean shopping mall, the **Forum des Halles,** with over 200 boutiques and three movie theaters. Watch out for pickpockets.

SECOND ARRONDISSEMENT

The 2*ème* has a long history of trade and commerce, from 19th-century passageways full of goodies to the ancient Bourse where stocks and bonds were traded. The oldest and most enduring trade of the area, prostitution, has thrived on rue St-Denis since the Middle Ages. Many cheap little restaurants and hotels populate this mostly working class area, making it an excellent place to stay. Abundant fabric shops and cheap women's clothing stores line **rue du Sentier,** while upscale boutiques keep to the streets in the 2*ème's* western half. The Opéra Comique, now the **Théâtre Musicale,** lies between bd. des Italiens and rue de Richelieu. **Safety:** Rue St-Denis is Paris's seedy center of prostitution and pornography. Use caution, especially at night.

TO THE WEST

GALLERIES AND PASSAGES. Behold the world's first shopping malls. In the early 19th century, speculators built **passageways** designed to attract window shoppers using sheets of glass held in place by lightweight iron rods. This startling new design allowed the daylight in, and gas lighting and electric heating attracted customers (of every sort) at all hours of the day and night.

For a tour, begin at the most beautiful remaining passage, the **Grand Cerf,** 10 rue Dussoubs to 145 rue St-Denis. Worth visiting for its stained-glass portal windows and exquisite ironwork, the Grand Cerf has the highest glass and iron arches in Paris. Returning to rue Etienne Marcel, walk 10min. until you reach rue Montmartre on your right. Follow rue Montmartre onto bd. Montmartre. Between bd. Montmartre and rue St-Marc is the oldest of the galleries, **Passage des Panoramas,** 10 rue St-Marc and 11 bd. Montmartre. Built in 1799, it contains a 19th-century glass-and-tile roof and a collection of ethnic restaurants. A chocolate shop (François Marquis), a printer (at no. 8), and an engraver (at no. 47) have all managed to stay open since the 1830s. Across bd. Montmartre, mirroring the Passage des Panoramas, **Passages Jouffry** and **Verdeau** are filled with charming toy shops, bookstores, and gift shops. From bd. Montmartre, make a left onto rue Vivienne. On your left just before you reach the Palais-Royal are the most fashionable *galeries* of the 1820s. Inlaid marble mosaics swirl along the floor, and stucco friezes grace the entrance of **Galerie Vivienne,** 4 rue des Petits Champs to 6 rue Vivienne. Built in 1823 as the *grande dame* of the passageways, Vivienne today boasts the boutique of bad boy Jean-Paul Gaultier.

BIBLIOTHÈQUE NATIONALE: SITE RICHELIEU. With a 12 million volume collection including Gutenberg Bibles and first editions from the 15th century, the Bibliothèque Nationale, of which Richelieu is a branch, is possibly the largest library in Continental Europe. Since 1642, every book published in France has been legally required to enter the national archives. At one point, books considered a little too titillating for public consumption descended into a room named "Hell". In the late 1980s, the French government built the mammoth **Bibliothèque de France** in the 13*ème*, where the collections from the 2*ème's* Richelieu branch were relocated between 1996 and 1998.

Richelieu still holds collections of stamps, money, photography, medals, and maps, as well as original manuscripts written on everything from papyrus to parchment. Scholars must pass through a strict screening process to gain access to the main reading room; bring a letter from your university, research advisor, or editor stating the nature of your research and two photo IDs. For the general public, the **Galerie Mazarin** and **Galerie Mansart** host excellent temporary exhibits of books, prints, and lithographs. Upstairs, the **Cabinet des Médailles** displays coins, medallions, and confiscated *objets d'art* from the Revolution. *(M: Bourse. 58 rue de Richelieu. Info* ☎ *01 53 79 59 59, galleries 01 47 03 81 10, cabinet 01 47 03 83 30; www.bnf.fr. Just north of the Galeries Vivienne and Colbert, across rue Vivienne. Library open M-Sa 9am-5:30pm. Tours in English and French of the former reading room first Tu of the month 2:30pm; €6.83.* ☎ *01 53 79 86 87. Galleries open Sa 10am-7pm and Su noon-7pm when there are exhibits. €5, students €4. Cabinet des Médailles open M-F 1-6pm, Sa 1-5pm. Free.)*

THIRD ARRONDISSEMENT

Drained by monks in the 13th century, the Marais ("swamp"), comprised of the 3*ème* and 4*ème*, was landfilled to provide building space for the Right Bank. With Henri IV's construction of the **pl. des Vosges** (see **Sights,** p. 135) at the beginning of the 17th century, the area became the city's center of fashionable living. Leading architects and sculptors of the period designed elegant *hôtels particuliers* with large courtyards. Under Louis XV, the center of Parisian life moved to the *fau-*

bourgs (then considered suburbs) **St-Honoré** and **St-Germain,** and construction in the Marais ceased. But a thirty-year period of gentrification has attracted trendy boutiques, cafés, and museums. Once-palatial mansions have become exquisite museums, and the tiny twisting streets have been adopted by fashionable boutiques and galleries and some terrific accommodations at reasonable rates.

RUE VIEILLE-DU-TEMPLE. This street is lined with stately residences including the 18th-century **Hôtel de la Tour du Pin** (no. 75) and the more famous **Hôtel de Rohan** (no. 87). Built for Armand-Gaston de Rohan, Bishop of Strasbourg and alleged love-child of Louis XIV, the *hôtel* has housed many of his descendants. Frequent temporary exhibits allow access to the interior *Cabinet des Singes* and its original decorations. The Hôtel also boasts an impressive courtyard and rose garden. Equally engaging are the numerous art galleries that have taken root on the street. At the corner of rue des Francs-Bourgeois and rue Vieille-du-Temple, the flamboyant Gothic **Hôtel Hérouët** and its turrets were built in 1528 for Louis XII's treasurer, Hérouët. *(M: Hôtel-de-Ville or St-Paul. Info on guided tours ☎ 01 40 27 63 94.)*

ARCHIVES NATIONALES. In the 18th-century Hôtel de Soubise, the **Musée de l'Histoire de France** exhibits the most famous documents of the National Archives, including the Treaty of Westphalia, the Edict of Nantes, the Declaration of the Rights of Man, Marie-Antoinette's last letter, Louis XVI's diary, letters between Benjamin Franklin and George Washington, and Napoleon's will. Louis XVI's entry for July 14, 1789, the day the Bastille was stormed, reads simply *"Rien"* ("Nothing")— out at Versailles, the hunting had been bad that day. Documents are displayed only in temporary exhibits. *(60 rue des Francs-Bourgeois. Upcoming events ☎ 01 40 27 60 96. M: Rambuteau. Open M-F 10am-12:30pm and 2-5:30pm, Sa-Su 2-5:30pm.)*

MÉMORIAL DU MARTYR JUIF INCONNU. The Memorial to the Unknown Jewish Martyr is the child of a 1956 committee that included de Gaulle, Churchill, and Ben-Gurion; it commemorates European Jews who died at the hands of the Nazis and their French collaborators. Usually located in the *4ème*, the memorial is under renovation in 2003; the address below is temporary. *(M: St-Paul. 37 rue de Turenne. ☎ 01 42 77 44 72; fax 01 48 87 12 50. Exposition open M-Th 10am-1pm and 2-5:30pm, F 10am-1pm and 2-5pm. Archives open M-W 11am-5:30pm, Th 11am-8pm.)*

FOURTH ARRONDISSEMENT

The *4ème* is an especially fun section of the Marais. It's accessible. It's soft-core hip. It's just-barely-affordable, sort-of-designer. It's falafels and knishes. It's gay men out for brunch. It's antiques and sparkly club wear. Let the festivities begin.

TO THE NORTH: BEAUBOURG

RUE DES ROSIERS. At the heart of the Jewish community of the Marais, the rue des Rosiers is packed with kosher shops, butchers, bakeries, and falafel counters. Until the 13th century, Paris's Jewish community was concentrated in front of Notre Dame. When Philippe-Auguste expelled Jews from the city limits, many families moved just outside the city walls to the Marais. The street's Jewish population grew with the influx of Russian Jews in the 19th century and North African Sephardim fleeing Algeria in the 1960s. This mix of Mediterranean and Eastern European Jewish cultures gives the area a unique flavor, with kugel and falafel served side by side. During WWII, many who had fled to France to escape the pogroms of Eastern Europe were murdered by the Nazis. Assisted by French police, Nazi soldiers stormed the Marais and hauled Jewish families to the Vélodrome d'Hiver, an indoor cycling stadium, before transporting them to concentration camps. The Jewish community has been reborn in the Marais, with two synagogues at 25 rue des Rosiers and 10 rue Pavée, designed by art nouveau architect Hector Guimard. The gay community also thrives here, though the beautiful androgynous types for which the Marais is famous are more visible on rue Vieille-du-Temple and rue Ste-Croix de la Bretonnerie. (*M: St-Paul. Four blocks east of Beaubourg, parallel to rue des Francs-Bourgeois.*)

RUE VIEILLE-DU-TEMPLE AND RUE STE-CROIX DE LA BRETONNERIE. As in a scene from the movie *Grease*, hair-slicked men in muscle-tees and tight-pants women in heels fill the shops and outdoor café-bars of this *super-hyper-chic* neighborhood. This is the heart of Paris's vibrant gay community, but a prominent straight hangout as well. (*M: St-Paul or Hôtel-de-Ville. One block north of rue de Rivoli runs the parallel rue du Roi de Sicile, which becomes rue de la Verrerie; rue Vieille-du-Temple intersects it and then meets rue Ste-Croix de la Bretonerie one block farther north.*)

HÔTEL DE VILLE AND SURROUNDINGS

HÔTEL DE VILLE. Paris' grandiose city hall dominates a large square with fountains and Belle Epoque lampposts. The present edifice is a 19th-century creation built to replace the original medieval structure, a meeting hall for the cartel that controlled traffic on the Seine. The building witnessed municipal executions on pl. Hôtel-de-Ville; in 1610, Henri IV's assassin Ravaillac was quartered here—not as a house guest, but by four horses bolting in opposite directions. On May 24, 1871, the *communards* doused the building with petrol and set it on fire. The blaze, which lasted eight days, spared only the frame. The Third Republic built a virtually identical structure on the ruins. The pl. Hôtel-de-Ville made a vital contribution to the French language. Poised on a marshy embankment (*grève*) of the Seine, the medieval square served as a meeting ground for angry workers, giving France the useful phrase *en grève* (on strike). Strikers and riot police still gather here. Less frequently, the square hosts concerts, TV broadcasts, and light shows against the Hôtel-de-Ville; during the 1998 World Cup and the Euro 2000, fans watched the French victory on huge screens erected in the square. (*M: Hôtel-de-Ville. 29 rue de Rivoli. ☎ 01 42 76 43 43. Open M-F 9am-6:30pm, until 6pm if there is no exhibit.*)

TOUR ST-JACQUES. The Tour St-Jacques stands alone in the center of its own park. This flamboyant Gothic tower is the only remnant of the 16th-century Eglise St-Jacques-la-Boucherie. The 52m tower's meteorological station and the statue of Pascal at its base commemorate Pascal's experiments on the weight of air, performed here in 1648. The tower is **closed for renovations in 2003** and is scheduled to reopen in 2004. (*M: Hôtel-de-Ville. Two blocks west of the Hôtel-de-Ville. 39-41 rue de Rivoli.*)

SOUTH OF RUE ST-ANTOINE AND RUE DE RIVOLI

HÔTEL DE BEAUVAIS. The Hôtel de Beauvais, which will be **under renovation until June 2003,** was built in 1655 for Pierre de Beauvais and his wife Catherine Bellier. Bellier, Anne d'Autriche's chambermaid, had an adolescent tryst with the Queen's son, 15-year-old Louis XIV. Later, from the balcony of the *hôtel*, Anne d'Autriche and Cardinal Mazarin watched the entry of Louis XIV and his bride, Marie-Thérèse, into Paris. A century later, as a guest of the Bavarian ambassador, Mozart played his first piano recital here. (*M: Hôtel-de-Ville. 68 rue François-Miron.*)

HÔTEL DE SENS. The Hôtel de Sens is one of the city's few surviving examples of medieval residential architecture. Built in 1474 for Tristan de Salazar, the Archbishop of Sens, its military features reflect the violence of those times. The turrets were designed to guard the streets outside; the square tower served as a dungeon. An enormous Gothic arch entrance is carved with chutes for pouring boiling water on invaders. The former residence of Queen Margot, Henri IV's first wife, the Hôtel de Sens has witnessed some of Paris's most daring romantic escapades. In 1606, the

55-year-old queen drove up to her beautiful courtyard to find her two lovers-of-the-month arguing. One opened the lady's carriage door, and the other shot him dead. Unfazed, the queen ordered the perpetrator's execution. The *hôtel* now houses the **Bibliothèque Forney.** *(M: Pont Marie. 1 rue du Figuier. Courtyard open to the public. Library open Tu-F 1:30-8:30pm, Sa 10am-8:30pm. Closed July 1-16.)*

EGLISE ST-PAUL-ST-LOUIS. The Eglise St-Paul-St-Louis dominates rue St-Antoine and dates from 1627 when Louis XIII placed its first stone. Its large dome—a trademark of Jesuit architecture—is visible from afar, but hidden by ornamentation on the facade. Paintings inside the dome depict four French kings: Clovis, Charlemagne, Robert the Pious, and St-Louis. Before being destroyed during the Revolution, the embalmed hearts of Louis XIII and Louis XIV were kept in vermeil boxes guarded by gilded silver angels. The church's Baroque interior is graced with three 17th-century paintings of the life of St-Louis, as well as Eugène Delacroix's dramatic *Christ in the Garden of Olives* (1826). The holy-water vessels were gifts from Victor Hugo. *(M: St-Paul. 99 rue St-Antoine. ☎01 49 24 11 43. Open M-Sa 9am-8pm, Su 9am-8:30pm. Free tours 2nd Su of every month 3pm. Mass Sa 6pm; Su 9:30, 11:15am, 7pm.)*

PLACE DES VOSGES AND SURROUNDINGS

■ **PLACE DES VOSGES.** At the end of rue des Francs-Bourgeois sits the magnificent pl. des Vosges, Paris's oldest public square. The *place* is one of Paris's most charming spots for a picnic or an afternoon siesta. The central park, lined with immaculately manicured trees centered around a splendid fountain, is surrounded by 17th-century Renaissance townhouses. Kings built several mansions on this site, including the Palais de Tournelles, which Catherine de Médicis ordered destroyed after her husband Henri II died there in a jousting tournament in 1563. Henri IV subsequently ordered it re-built.

Each of the 36 buildings lining the square has arcades on the street level, two stories of pink brick, and a slate-covered roof. The largest townhouse, forming the square's main entrance, was the king's pavilion. Originally intended for merchants, the pl. Royale attracted elites like Mme. de Sevigné and Cardinal Richelieu. Molière, Racine, and Voltaire filled the grand parlors with their *bon mots*, and Mozart played a concert here at the age of seven. Even when the city's nobility moved across the river to the Faubourg St-Germain, pl. Royale remained among the most elegant spots in Paris. During the Revolution, however, the 1639 Louis XIII statue in the center of the park was destroyed (the statue there now is a copy), and the park was renamed pl. des Vosges after the first department in France to pay its taxes. **Victor Hugo** lived at no. 6, which is now a museum of his life and work. *(M: Chemin Vert or St-Paul.)*

HÔTEL DE SULLY. Built in 1624, the Hôtel de Sully was acquired by the Duc de Sully, minister to Henri IV. Often cuckolded by his young wife, Sully would tease when giving her money, *"Voici tant pour la maison, tant pour vous, et tant pour vos amants."* ("Here's some for the house, some for you, and some for your lovers.") The small inner courtyard offers the fatigued tourist several stone benches and an elegant formal garden. The *Hôtel* occasionally hosts small exhibits. *(M: St-Paul. 62 rue St-Antoine. Open M-Th 9am-12:45pm and 2-6pm, F 9am-12:45pm and 2-5pm.)*

FIFTH ARRONDISSEMENT

The 6*ème* and the western half of the 5*ème* make up the Latin Quarter, which takes its name from the language used in the 5*ème*'s prestigious *lycées* and universities prior to 1798 (including the Sorbonne). The 5*ème* has been right in the intellectual thick of things ever since then. Its student population played a large role in the uprisings of May 1968. Today, areas like **bd. St-Michel** (the boundary between the 5ème and 6ème) are notable victims of commercialization, but the smaller byways of the student quarter still hold fast to their progressive, edgy, and multiethnic tone, with dusty bookstores, art-house cinemas, and Lebanese foodcounters aplenty. Pl. de la Contrescarpe and rue Mouffetard, which has one of the liveliest street markets in all of Paris, are quintessential Latin Quarter.

TO THE WEST: THE LATIN QUARTER

PLACE ST-MICHEL. The busiest spot in the Latin Quarter, pl. St-Michel is heir to much political history: the Paris Commune began here in 1871, as did the student uprising of 1968. The majestic 1860 fountain (one of the 5ème's great meeting places) features bronze dragons, an angelic St-Michel slaying the dragon, and a WWII memorial commemorating the citizens who fell here defending their *quartier* in August 1944. For those with more of a bent for books than battles, the *place* is still eager to please. Several branches of Gibert Jeune dot the beginning of bd. St-Michel; there are scores of antiquarian booksellers and university presses in the area (see **Shopping,** p. 162). For the gastronomically inclined, the surrounding streets offer a panoply of delights; ice cream shops and crêpe stands line **rue St-Séverin,** while Greek *gyro* counters compete for customers on the bustling corridors and bazaarlike alleyways of **rue de la Huchette.**

The *quartier* also has some awe-inspiring sights. The nearby **Eglise St-Julien-le-Pauvre** (a right off bd. St-Michel and another right onto rue St-Julien le Pauvre), which dates back to 1170, is one of the oldest churches in Paris. Across bd. St-Jacques is another architectural behemoth, the huge, bizarre, and wonderful **Eglise St-Séverin.** Inside, spiraling columns and modern stained glass ornament this Gothic complex. At the intersection of bd. St-Germain and bd. St-Michel, the **Musée de Cluny**'s extraordinary collection of medieval art, tapestries, and illuminated manuscripts has something to suit just about everyone (see **Museums,** p. 154). A major tourist thoroughfare, **bd. St-Michel** (or "*boul' Mich'*") doesn't give an authentic impression of local life—for that, visitors need only travel a bit farther afield, as many of the traditional bistros of the quarter hold their ground on nearby streets, like **rue Soufflot** and **rue des Fossés St-Jacques.**

LA SORBONNE. Started in 1253 by Robert de Sorbon as a dormitory for 16 poor theology students, the Sorbonne is one of Europe's oldest universities. Soon after its founding, it became the administrative base for the University of Paris and the site of France's first printing house. As it grew in power and size, the Sorbonne often contradicted the authority of the French throne, even siding with England during the Hundred Years' War. But today, the university is safely in the folds of governmental administration, officially known as *Paris IV,* the fourth of the University of Paris's 13 campuses. Its main building, **Ste-Ursule de la Sorbonne,** which is closed to the public, was commissioned in 1642 by Cardinal Richelieu. Security has been tightened following the events of September 11, but visitors can still stroll through the **Chapelle de la Sorbonne** (entrance off of the pl. de la Sorbonne), an impressive space which displays temporary exhibitions on the arts and letters. Nearby **pl. de la Sorbonne,** off bd. St-Michel, contains an assortment of cafés, bookstores, and—during term-time—students. *(M: Cluny-La Sorbonne or RER: Luxembourg. 45-7 rue des Ecoles. Walk away from the Seine on bd. St-Michel and turn left on rue des Ecoles to see the main building. Entrance to main courtyard off pl. de la Sorbonne. Open M-F 9am-6pm.)*

COLLÈGE DE FRANCE. Created by François I in 1530 to contest the university's authority, the Collège de France stands behind the Sorbonne with the humanist motto "Doce Omnia" ("Teaches Everything") in mosaics on the interior courtyard. The outstanding courses at the Collège, given by such luminaries as Henri Bergson, Pierre Boulez, Paul Valéry, and Milan Kundera, are free and open to all. *(M: Maubert-*

Mutualité. 11 pl. Marcelin-Berthelot. ☎ 01 44 27 12 11; www.college-de-france.fr. From the métro, walk against traffic on bd. St-Germain, turn left on rue Thenard; the entrance to the Collège is at the end of the road, across rue des Ecoles and up the steps. Courses run Sept.-May. Lecture schedules posted in the kiosk in Sept. Closed Aug.)

THE PANTHÉON. The Panthéon is one of the most beautiful buildings in the world. Visible all the way from the Luxembourg gardens to St-Germain to the Ecole Normale Supérieure, it is an extravagant landmark in a city known for its extravagance. Unreal airiness and geometric grandeur are its architectural claims to fame. But the architecture itself can't take all the credit; the crypt beneath the structure is the final resting place of some of France's most distinguished citizens—scientists Marie and Pierre Curie, politician Jean Jaurès, Louis Braille, and writers Voltaire, Rousseau, Zola, and Hugo. At Hugo's burial in 1885, two million mourners and Chopin's *Marche Funèbre* followed the coffin to its resting place.

The stone inscription across the front of the Panthéon dedicates it: "To great men from a grateful fatherland," but the Panthéon was originally one man's tribute to his wife. In 507, King Clovis converted to Christianity and had a basilica designed to accommodate his tomb and that of his wife, Clotilde. In 512, the basilica became the resting place of **Ste-Geneviève,** who supposedly protected Paris from the attacking Huns with her prayers. Her tomb immediately became a pilgrimage site; her legend grew so much that a set of worshippers dedicated themselves to the preservation of her relics and remains, calling themselves Génovéfains.

Louis XV was also feeling grateful after surviving a grave illness in 1744, a miracle he ascribed to the powers of Ste-Geneviève. He vowed to build a prestigious monument to the saint and entrusted the design of the new basilica to the architect Jacques-Germain Soufflot. Louis laid the first stone himself in 1764; after Soufflot's death, the Neoclassical basilica was completed by architect Jean-Baptiste Rondelet. The Revolution converted the church into a mausoleum of heroes on April 4, 1791, but the act was really a hurried attempt to find a place for proletariat poet Mirabeau's body. The poet was interred, only to have his ashes expelled the next year when his correspondence with King Louis XVI was revealed. In 1806, Napoleon reserved the crypt for those who had given "great service to the State."

The Panthéon's other main attraction is **Foucault's Pendulum.** The plane of oscillation of the pendulum stays fixed as the Earth rotates around it. The pendulum confirmed the Earth's rotation to nonbelievers, such as Louis Napoleon III and a large crowd in 1851. *(M: Cardinal Lemoine. Pl. du Panthéon. ☎ 01 44 32 18 00. From the métro, walk down rue Cardinal Lemoine and turn right on rue Clovis; walk around to the front of the building to enter. Open June-Aug. daily 10am-6:30pm; Sept.-May 10am-6:15pm; last admission 5:45pm. Admission €7, students €4.50, under 18 free. Free entrance 1st Su of every month from Oct.-Mar. Guided tours in French leave from inside the main door daily at 2:30 and 4pm.)*

TO THE EAST: PLACE DE LA CONTRESCARPE

South on rue Descartes, past the prestigious Lycée Henri IV, **pl. de la Contrescarpe** is the geographical center of the 5*ème*. Lovely outdoor restaurants and cafés cluster around a circular fountain. From Contrescarpe, it's only a 5min. walk to St-Germain, the Panthéon, or the Jardin des Plantes.

RUE MOUFFETARD. South of pl. de la Contrescarpe, **rue Mouffetard** plays host to one of the liveliest street markets in Paris (see p. 126), and, along with **rue Monge,** binds much of the Latin Quarter's tourist and student social life. But the storied rue Mouff wasn't always a snaking alley of gourmet shops and touristy jazz clubs. It was the main thoroughfare of a wealthy villa from the 2nd century until the 13th century. Poet Paul Verlaine died at 39 rue Descartes in 1844. Hemingway lived down the Mouff at 74 rue du Cardinal Lemoine. Perfect for a picturesque afternoon stroll or people-watching is the winding stretch up rue Mouffetard past pl. de la Contres-carpe, and onto **rue Descartes** and **rue de la Montagne Ste-Geneviève**. *(M: Cardinal Lemoine, Place Monge, or Censier Daubenton.)*

JARDIN DES PLANTES. In the eastern corner of the 5ème, the Jardin des Plantes has 45,000 square meters of carefully tended flowers and lush greenery. Opened in 1640 by Louis XIII's doctor, the gardens originally grew medicinal plants to promote His Majesty's health. Today, the Jardin's exquisite greenery attract Parisian families and sprawling sunbathers in the summer. The **Ecole de Botanique** is a landscaped botanical garden tended by students, horticulturists, and amateur botanists; the **Roserie** is a luscious, fragrant display of roses from all over the world (in full bloom in mid-June); the two big, botanical boxes of the **Grandes Serres** (big greenhouses) span two climates. The gardens also include the tremendous **Musée d'Histoire Naturelle** and the **Ménagerie Zoo**. Although no match for the Parc Zoologique in the Bois de Vincennes, the zoo will gladden anyone's day with its 240 mammals, 500 birds, and 130 reptiles. *(M: Gare d'Austerlitz, Jussieu, or Censier-Daubenton. ☎01 40 79 37 94. Jardin des Plantes, Ecole de Botanique, Jardin Alpin, and Roserie open June-Aug. daily 7:30am-8pm; Sept.-May 7:30am-5:30pm. Free. Grandes Serres, 57 rue Cuvier. Open W-M 1-5pm; Apr.-Oct. also Sa-Su 1-6pm. €2, students €1.50. Menagerie Zoo, 3 quai St-Bernard and 57 rue Cuvier. Open daily 10am-5:30pm in the winter, Apr.-Sept. until 6pm. Last entry 30min. before closing. €6, students €3.50.)*

MOSQUÉE DE PARIS. The Institut Musulman houses the beautiful Persian gardens, elaborate minaret, and shady porticoes of the Mosquée de Paris, constructed in 1920 by French architects to honor the role played by the countries of North Africa in WWI. The cedar doors open onto an oasis of blue and white, where Muslims from around the world come to meet around the fountains and pray in the carpeted prayer rooms (visible from the courtyard but closed to the public). Frenzied tourists can also relax in the steam baths at the exquisite *hammam*, or Turkish bath. *(M: Jussieu. Behind the Jardin des Plantes at pl. du Puits de l'Ermite. ☎01 48 35 78 17. From the métro, walk down rue Linne, turn right on rue Lacépède, and left on rue de Quatrefages; entrance to the left. Open daily 10am-noon and 2-5:30pm; June-Aug. closes 6:30pm. Tour €3, students €2. Hammam Open for men Tu 2-9pm and Su 10am-9pm; for women M, W-Th, Sa 10am-9pm and F 2-9pm; €15. 10min. massage €10, bikini wax €11. MC/V.)*

ALONG THE SEINE

SHAKESPEARE & CO. BOOKSTORE. The absolute center of young Anglophone Paris. While not the original Sylvia Beach incarnation (at no 8 rue Dupuytren), this rag-tag bookstore has become a cultish landmark all to itself. Frequented by Allen Ginsberg, Lawrence Ferlinghetti, and run by the purported grandson of Walt Whitman, Shakespeare hosts poetry readings, Sunday evening tea parties, and other funky events. For more, see **Shopping**, p. 162. *(M: St-Michel. 37 rue de la Bucherie. Open daily noon-midnight.)*

INSTITUT DU MONDE ARABE. The Institut du Monde Arabe (IMA) resides in one of the city's most striking buildings. Facing the Seine, the IMA was built to resemble a boat, such as those on which many Algerian, Moroccan, and Tunisian immigrants flee to France. Inside, the IMA houses permanent and rotating exhibitions on Maghrébin, Near Eastern, and Middle Eastern Arab cultures as well as a library, research facilities, lecture series, film festivals, and a rooftop terrace; you don't have to eat in the Institut's restaurant to see the gorgeous views of the Seine, Montmartre, and Île de la Cité. *(M: Jussieu. 1 rue des Fossés St-Bernard. ☎01 40 51 38 38. Walk down rue Jussieu away from the Jardin des Plantes and make your first right onto rue des Fossés St-Bernard. Museum open Tu-Su 10am-6pm. €3, under 12 free. Library open Tu-Sa 1-8pm; free.)*

SIXTH ARRONDISSEMENT

The 6ème is the home to two of Paris's still-vibrant cultural staples: literary cafés and innovative art galleries. The art exhibits of the Left Bank's prestigious gallery district display some of the area's most exciting contemporary work. Head west from St-Michel if you want a more classically Parisian flavor. Crossing bd. St-Michel and running east-west, bd. St-Germain lends its name to the neighborhood **St-Germain-des-Prés**, whose cafés amused Rimbaud, Hemingway, Sartre, and just about anyone who was anyone in Paris during the first half of the 20th century. St-Germain still draws a trendy and intellectual crowd, but the 6ème is not impervious to the passing of time. The Picassos and Picabias have moved to the outskirts, replaced by the *haute bourgeois* and their designer boutiques.

JARDIN DU LUXEMBOURG AND ODÉON

JARDIN DU LUXEMBOURG. Parisians flock to these formal gardens to sunbathe, write, read, and gaze at the rose gardens, central pool, and each other. A residential area in Roman Paris, the site of a medieval monastery, and later the home of naughty 17th-century French royalty, the gardens were liberated during the Revolution and are now free to all. *(M: Odéon or RER: Luxembourg. Open daily dawn to dusk. Main entrance are on bd. St-Michel. Tours in French Apr.-Oct. 1st W of every month 9:30am.)*

PALAIS DU LUXEMBOURG. The Palais du Luxembourg, located within the park and now serving as the home of the French Senate, was built in 1615 at Marie de Médici's request. The palace went on to house a number of France's most elite nobility; in later years, it incarcerated those same nobles. One of the palace-jails' most famous residents was Beauharnais, the future Empress Josephine. During the Nazi occupation, the palace was the headquarters of the *Luftwaffe*.

EGLISE ST-SULPICE. The balconied, Neoclassical facade of the huge Eglise St-Sulpice dominates the enormous square of the same name. Designed by Servadoni in 1733, the church remains unfinished. St-Sulpice's claims to fame are a set of fierce, gestural Delacroix frescoes in the first chapel on the right, a *Virgin and Child* by Jean-Baptiste Pigalle in a rear chapel, and an enormous organ. *(M: St-Sulpice or Mabillon. ☎01 46 33 21 78. From the Mabillon métro, walk down rue du Four and make a left on rue Mabillon which intersects rue St-Sulpice at the church. Open daily 7:30am-7:30pm. Guided tour in French daily 3pm.)*

ST-GERMAIN-DES-PRÉS

Known as *le village de Saint-Germain-des-Prés*, the crowded area around **bd. St-Germain** between St-Sulpice and the Seine is packed with cafés, restaurants, galleries, cinemas, and expensive boutiques.

BOULEVARDE ST-GERMAIN. Known by most as the ex-literati hangout of Existentialists (who frequented the Flore) and Surrealists like André Breton (who frequented the Deux Magots), the bd. St-Germain is stuck somewhere in between a nostalgia for its intellectual café culture past and an unabashed delight with the cutting edge of materialism. The boulevard is home to scores of new and old cafés. The long-standing—if now virtually meaningless—rivalry between **Café de Flore** and **Les Deux Magots,** (see **Food & Drink**, p. 120) remains the *noblesse oblige* version of Family Feud. The Boulevard and its many side-streets around rue de Rennes have become a serious shopping neighborhood in recent years (see **Shopping**, p. 162), filled with designer boutiques from Louis Vuitton to Emporio Armani. *(M: St-Germain-des-Prés.)*

EGLISE DE ST-GERMAIN-DES-PRÉS. The Eglise St-Germain-des-Prés is the oldest standing church in Paris, and it shows; its only ornate decorations are the pink and white hollyhocks growing to the side. King Childebert I commissioned a church on this site to hold relics he had looted from the Holy Land. Completed in 558, it was consecrated by St-Germain, Bishop of Paris, on the day of King Childebert's death—the king had to be buried inside a church's walls. The rest of the church's history reads like an architectural Book of Job. It was sacked by the Normans and rebuilt three times. During the Revolution, 15 tons of gunpowder that had been stored in the abbey exploded, devastating much of the church. Baron Haussmann destroyed the last remains of the deteriorating abbey walls and gates when he extended rue de Rennes to the front of the church to create pl. St-Germain-des-Prés.

Completely redone in the 19th century, the magnificent interior is painted in shades of maroon, deep green, and gold with enough regal grandeur to counteract the building's modest exterior; especially striking are the royal blue and gold-starred ceiling, frescoes depicting the life of Jesus, and decorative mosaics along the archways. In the second chapel, a stone marks the interred heart of 17th-century philosopher René Descartes, as well as an altar dedicated to the victims of the September 1793 massacre, in which 186 Parisians were slaughtered in the courtyard. The information window at the church's entrance has a schedule of the Eglise's frequent concerts; see **Entertainment,** p. 156. *(M: St-Germain-des-Prés. 3 pl. St-Germain-des-Prés. ☎ 01 55 42 81 33. From the métro, walk into pl. St-Germain-des-Prés to enter the church from the front. Open daily 8am-8pm. Info office open Tu-Sa 10:30am-noon and 2:30-6:45pm, M 2:30-6:45pm.)*

ODÉON. Cour du Commerce St-André is one of the most picturesque walking areas in the 6*ème*, with cobblestone streets, centuries-old cafés (including **Le Procope**), and outdoor seating. Beyond the arch stands the **Relais Odéon,** a Belle Epoque bistro whose stylishly painted exterior, decked with floral mosaics and a hanging sign, is a fine example of art nouveau. Just to the south of bd. St-Germain-des-Prés, the **Carrefour d'Odéon,** a favorite Parisian hangout, is a delightful, tree-lined square filled with bistros, cafés, and more outdoor seating. The **Comptoir du Relais** still holds court here, while newcomer cafés strut their flashy selves across the street.

PONT DES ARTS. The wooden footbridge across from the Institut, appropriately called the Pont des Arts, is celebrated by poets and artists for its delicate ironwork, beautiful views of the Seine, and spiritual locus at the heart of France's prestigious Academy of Arts and Letters.

SEVENTH ARRONDISSEMENT

The construction of the controversial Eiffel Tower here in 1889 cemented the 7*ème's* identity as elegant and quintessentially Parisian. Home to the National Assembly, countless foreign embassies, the Invalides, the Musée d'Orsay (see **Museums,** p. 153), and (yes, still) the Eiffel Tower, this section of the Left Bank is a medley of France's diplomatic, architectural, and military achievements. Whether in the Musée Rodin's rose gardens or the public markets of the rue Cler, the 7*ème* offers some of the most touristy and most intimate sights in Paris.

TO THE WEST

■ **THE EIFFEL TOWER.** Gustave Eiffel, its designer, wrote: "France is the only country in the world with a 300m flagpole." Designed in 1889 as the tallest structure in the world, the Eiffel Tower was conceived as a monument to engineering that would surpass the Egyptian pyramids in size and notoriety. Before construction had begun, shockwaves of dismay reverberated through the city. Critics dubbed it a "metal asparagus" and a Parisian tower of Babel. Writer Guy de Maupassant ate lunch every day at its ground-floor restaurant—the only place in Paris, he claimed, from which he couldn't see the offensive thing.

Nevertheless, when it was inaugurated in March 1889 as the centerpiece of the Universal Exposition, the tower earned the love of Paris; nearly 2 million people ascended during the event. *(M: Bir-Hakeim or Trocadéro.* ☎ *01 44 11 23 23; www.tour-eiffel.fr. Open mid-June to Aug. daily 9am-midnight; Sept.-Dec. 9:30am-11pm (stairs 9:30am-6pm); Jan. to mid-June 9:30am-11pm (stairs 9:30am-6:30pm). Elevator to 1st fl. €3.70, under 12 € 2.10; 2nd fl. €6.90/€3.80; 3rd fl. €9.90/€5.30. Stairs to 1st and 2nd fl. €3, under 3 free. Last access to top 30min. before closing.)*

NEAR THE TOWER

CHAMPS DE MARS. The Champs de Mars (Field of Mars) is a tree-lined expanse stretching from the Ecole Militaire to the Eiffel Tower. The field is close to the *7ème*'s military monuments and museums, but it celebrates the god of war for other reasons. The name comes from the days of Napoleon's Empire, when the field was used as a drill ground for the adjacent Ecole Militaire. During the Revolution, it witnessed civilian massacres and political demonstrations. Today, the god of war would be ashamed by the daisy-strewn lawns filled with tourists and hordes of children, not to mention the new glass monument to international peace.

TO THE EAST

INVALIDES. The gold-leaf dome of the Hôtel des Invalides shines at the center of the *7ème*. The green, tree-lined **Esplanade des Invalides** runs from the *hôtel* to the **Pont Alexandre III,** a bridge with gilded lampposts from which you can catch a great view of the Invalides and the Seine. The **Musée de l'Armée, Musée des Plans-Reliefs,** and **Musée de l'Ordre de la Libération** are housed in the Invalides museum complex (see **Museums,** p. 151), as is **Napoleon's tomb,** in the **Eglise St-Louis.** Enter from either pl. des Invalides or pl. Vauban and av. de Tourville. To the left of the Tourville entrance, the **Jardin de l'Intendant** is a shady break from guns and emperors. *(M: Invalides. 127 rue de Grenelle (main entrance) or 2 av. de Tourville.)*

■ **LA PAGODE.** A Japanese pagoda built in 1895 by the Bon Marché department store magnate M. Morin as a gift to his wife, La Pagode is a testament to the 19th-century Orientalist craze in France. When Mme. Morin left her husband just prior to WWI, the building became the scene of Sino-Japanese soirées. In 1931, La Pagode opened its doors to the public, becoming a cinema and swank café where silent screen stars like Gloria Swanson were known to raise a glass. The theater closed during the Nazi occupation, despite its friendliness towards German patrons. It reopened under a private owner in November 2000. See **Entertainment,** p. 156. *(M: St-François-Xavier. 57bis rue de Babylone.* ☎ *01 45 55 48 48. Café open daily between show times; coffee €2.50. MC/V.)*

EIGHTH ARRONDISSEMENT

The showy elegance of the *8ème* has a tendency to make tourists feel schlumpy, especially alongside the Parisians who walk determinedly down the neighborhood's *grands boulevards*. Full of expansive mansions, expensive shops and restaurants, and grandiose monuments, the *8ème* is decidedly Paris's most glamorous *arrondissement*. Obscenely upscale *haute couture* boutiques (Hermès, Louis Vuitton, and Chanel) line the Champs-Elysées, the Madeleine, and the eternally fashionable rue du Faubourg St-Honoré. For the most part, budget travelers should visit the *8ème* for a peek at the high life and then dine elsewhere.

ALONG THE CHAMPS-ELYSÉES

■ **ARC DE TRIOMPHE.** It is hard to believe that the Arc de Triomphe, looming gloriously above the Champs-Elysées at pl. Charles de Gaulle-Etoile, was first designed as a huge, bejeweled elephant. The world's largest triumphal arch crowns a flattened hill between the Louvre and Pont de Neuilly—an ideal vantage point that in

1758 excited the imagination of the architect Ribart, whose ambition it was to erect an animal of monumental proportions. Fortunately for France, construction of this symbol of her military prowess was not started until 1805, when Napoleon envisioned a monument somewhat more appropriate for welcoming troops home. Construction stalled during Napoleon's exile, but Louis XVIII ordered it completed in 1823 to commemorate the war in Spain, though still allowing the names of Napoleon's generals and battles to be engraved inside.

Since Napoleon, the arch has been a magnet for various triumphal armies. The victorious Prussians marched through in 1871, inspiring mortified Parisians to later purify the ground with fire. On July 14, 1919, the Arc provided the backdrop for an Allied celebration parade headed by Maréchal Foch. During WWII, Frenchmen were reduced to tears as the Nazis goose-stepped through their beloved arch. After the torturous years of German occupation, a sympathetic Allied army made sure a French general would be the first to drive under the famous edifice.

The **Tomb of the Unknown Soldier** has been under the Arc since November 11, 1920. Its marker bears the inscription, "Here lies a French soldier who died for his country, 1914-1918," but represents the 1.5 million men who died during WWI. Inside the Arc, 205 winding steps lead up to the *entresol* between the Arc's two supports; the museum is 29 farther up. There is an elevator for the less ambitious. 46 steps beyond the museum, the observation deck, at the top of the Arc, provides a brilliant view of the Champs-Elysées, the tree-lined av. Foch, and the "Axe Historique"—from the Arc de Triomphe du Carrousel and the Louvre Pyramid at one end to the Grande Arche de la Défense at the other. *(M: Charles de Gaulle-Etoile. ☎01 44 09 89 84. Open Apr.-Sept. daily 10am-11pm; Oct.-Mar. 10am-10:30pm. Last entry 30min. before closing. €7, ages 18-25 €4.50, under 17 free. Expect lines even on weekdays. Buy your ticket in the pedestrian underpasses before going up to the ground level. AmEx/MC/V for charges over €14.)*

■ **AVENUE DES CHAMPS-ELYSÉES.** The av. des Champs-Elysées is the most famous of the 12 symmetrical avenues radiating from the huge rotary of pl. Charles de Gaulle-Etoile. The Champs remained unkempt until the early 19th century, when the city built sidewalks and installed gas lighting. From that point on, the avenue flourished, and where elegant houses, restaurants, and less subdued bars and panoramas sprung up, the *beau monde* was guaranteed to see and be seen. The infamous Bal Mabille opened in 1840 at no. 51. At no. 25, visitors have the rare chance to see a true *hôtel particulier* from the Second Empire, where the famous courtesan, adventuress, and spy Marquise de Paiva entertained the luminaries of the era. In recent years, the Champs has become thoroughly commercialized. But Jacques Chirac made an effort to resurrect the avenue, widening the sidewalks, planting more trees, and building underground parking lots. The tree-lined streets merge with park space just past av. Franklin D. Roosevelt, one of the six avenues that radiate from the Rond Point des Champs-Elysées. Av. Montaigne, lined with Paris's finest houses of *haute couture*, runs southwest. For help conquering the Champs-Elysées (and the rest of Paris), visit the enormous **tourist office** at no. 127 (see **Useful Services,** p. 109).

GRAND AND PETIT PALAIS. At the foot of the Champs-Elysées, the Grand and Petit Palais face one another on av. Winston Churchill. Built for the 1900 World's Fair, they were called a combination of "banking and dreaming," exemplifying the ornate art nouveau architecture. While the Petit Palais (**closed for renovations** until winter 2004-05) houses an eclectic mix of artwork, its big brother has been turned into a space for temporary exhibitions on architecture, painting, sculpture, and French history. The Grand Palais also houses the **Palais de la Découverte,** a science museum/playground for children (see **Museums,** p. 154). The Palais is most beautiful at night, when its statues are backlit and the glass dome glows greenly from within.

HAUSSMANIA
How Paris cleaned up its act

Like a clock that has lost an hour, eleven straight boulevards radiate outwards from the pl. Charles de Gaulle. A view through the arc at the foot of the Louvre aligns with the Obelisk in the pl. de la Concorde, the Arc de Triomphe, and the modern arch at La Défense. Café-lined streets seem as organic to Paris as its wide tree-lined boulevards and the murky snaking of the Seine. Yet none of this is an accident. And, despite our modern notions that Paris is a city to which pleasure—be it amorous, gastronomic, artistic, or commercial—comes naturally, the city's charm is as calculated as the strategic applying of paint to a courtesan's lips, and the city wasn't always so beautiful.

Social commentator Maxime Du Camp observed in the mid-19th century: "Paris, as we find it in the period following the Revolution of 1848, was uninhabitable. Its population...was suffocating in the narrow, tangled, putrid alleyways in which it was forcibly confined." Sewers were not used in Paris until 1848, and waste and trash rotted in the Seine. Streets followed a maddening 12th-century design; in some *quartiers*, winding thoroughfares were no wider than 3.5m. Toadstool-like rocks lined the streets allowing pedestrians to jump to safety as carriages sped by. In the hands of the prefect of the Seine, Baron Georges-Eugène Haussmann, bureaucrat and social architect under Emperor Louis Napoleon, nephew of the Corsican emperor, the medieval layout of the city was demolished and replaced with a new urban vision.

Haussmann replaced the tangle of medieval streets with his sewers, trains, and grand boulevards. The prefect's vision bisected Paris along two central, perpendicular axes: the rue de Rivoli and the bd. de Sébastopol (which extended across the Seine to the bd. St-Michel). Haussmann, proclaiming the necessity of unifying Paris and promoting trade among the different *arrondissements*, saw the old streets as antiquated impediments to modern commercial and political progress. His wide boulevards swept through whole neighborhoods of cramped row houses and little passageways; incidentally, he displaced 350,000 of Paris's poorest residents.

The widespread rage at Haussmann's plans reinforced the emperor's desire to use the city's layout to reinforce his authority. The old, narrow streets has been ideal for civilian insurrection in preceding revolutions; rebels built barricades across street entrances and blocked off whole areas of the city from the government's military. Haussmann believed that creating *grands boulevards* and carefully mapping the city could bring to an end the use of barricades and prevent future uprisings. However, he was gravely mistaken. During the 1871 revolt of the Paris Commune, which saw the deposition of Louis Napoleon and the rise of the Third Republic, the *grands boulevards* proved ideal for the construction of higher and stronger barricades.

Despite the underlying political agenda of Haussmannization, many of the prefect's changes were for the better. Haussmann transformed the open-air dump and grave (for the offal of local butchers and the bodies of prisoners) at Montfauçon with the whimsical waterfalls, cliffs, and grottoes of the Park Buttes-Chaumont. Paris became eminently navigable, and to this day a glance down one of Paris's many grands boulevards will offer the *flâneur* an unexpected lesson in the layout of Paris. Stroll down the bd. Haussmann, the street bearing its architect's name. En route to the ornate Opéra Garnier, one glimpses the Church of the Madeleine and the Gare St-Lazare; Haussmann's layout silently links these monuments to religion, art, and industry.

It is hard to imagine Paris as a sewer-less, alley-ridden metropolis; but it is perhaps all the more beautiful today if we do so.

Charlotte Houghteling *is the editor of* Let's Go: Middle East 2003, Egypt 2003 *and* Israel 2003. *She wrote her senior thesis on the development of department stores during the Second Empire and will complete her M.Phil. at Cambridge on the consumer society of Revolutionary Paris.* ***Sara Houghteling*** *was a Researcher-Writer for* Let's Go: France 1999. *She taught at the American School in Paris for a year. She is now a graduate student in creative writing at the University of Michigan, and is currently in Paris researching Nazi art theft during World War II.*

PLACE DE LA CONCORDE AND SURROUNDINGS

PLACE DE LA CONCORDE. Paris's largest and most infamous public square forms the eastern terminus of the Champs-Elysées. With your back to av. Gabriel, the Tuileries Gardens are to your left; across the river lie the gold-domed Invalides and the columns of the Assemblée Nationale. Behind you stands the Madeleine. Constructed between 1757 and 1777 to provide a home for a monument to Louis XV, it later became pl. de la Révolution, the site of the guillotine that severed 1343 necks from their blue-blooded bodies. On Sunday, January 21, 1793, Louis XVI was beheaded by guillotine on a site near where the Brest statue now stands. The celebrated heads of Marie-Antoinette, Lavoisier, Danton, Robespierre, and others rolled into baskets here and were held up to cheering crowds. After the Reign of Terror, the square was optimistically renamed **pl. de la Concorde** (place of Harmony), though the noise pollution of the cars zooming through this intersection today hardly makes for a harmonious visit.

In the center of the *place* is the **Obélisque de Luxor.** Erected in 1836, Paris's oldest monument dates back to the 13th century BC. At night the obelisk, fountains, and cast-iron lamps are illuminated, creating a romantic glow, somewhat dimmed by the hordes of cars rushing by. Flanking the Champs-Elysées at pl. de la Concorde stand replicas of Guillaume Coustou's **Chevaux de Marly,** also known as *Africans Mastering the Numidian Horses*. The originals are now in the Louvre.

THE MADELEINE. Mirrored by the Assemblée Nationale across the Seine, the Madeleine was begun in 1764 by Louis XV and modeled after a Greek temple. Construction was halted during the Revolution, but was completed in 1842. The structure stands alone amongst a medley of Parisian churches, distinguished by four ceiling domes that light the interior, 52 exterior Corinthian columns, and a curious altarpiece. A sculpture of the ascension of Mary Magdalene, the church's namesake, adorns the altar. A colorful flower market thrives alongside the church. (*M: Madeleine. Pl. de la Madeleine. ☎01 44 51 69 00. Open daily 7:30am-7pm. Regular organ and chamber concerts; contact the church for a schedule and **Virgin** or **FNAC** for tickets.*)

TO THE NORTH

CHAPELLE EXPIATOIRE. Pl. Louis XVI includes the Chapelle Expiatoire, its monuments to Marie Antoinette and Louis XVI. Although Louis XVIII had his brother and sister-in-law's remains removed to St-Denis in 1815, the Revolution's Most Wanted still lie here. Marat's assassin Charlotte Corday and Louis XVI's cousin Philippe-Egalité are buried on either side of the staircase. (*M: Madeleine. 29 rue Pasquier, just below bd. Haussmann. ☎01 44 32 18 00. Open Th-Sa 1-5pm. €2.50, under 18 free.*)

PARC MONCEAU. The Parc Monceau, an expansive urban oasis guarded by gold-tipped, wrought-iron gates, borders the elegant bd. de Courcelles. An array of architectural follies—a pyramid, a covered bridge, an East Asian pagoda, Dutch windmills, Roman ruins, and roller rink—make this formal garden and kid's romping ground a Kodak commercial waiting to happen. (*M: Monceau or Courcelles. Open Apr.-Oct. daily 7am-10pm, Nov.-Mar. 7am-8pm. Gates close 15min. earlier.*)

CATHÉDRALE ALEXANDRE-NEVSKI. Built in 1860, the onion-domed Eglise Russe, also known as Cathédrale Alexandre-Nevski, is a Russian Orthodox church. The spectacular and recently restored domes were intricately painted by artists from St-Petersburg in gold, deep reds, blues and greens. The cathedral is the modern center of Russian culture in Paris. (*M: Ternes. 12 rue Daru. ☎01 42 27 37 34. Open Tu, F, Su 3-5pm. Services in French and Russian, Su at 10am, Sa at 6-8 pm.*)

NINTH ARRONDISSEMENT

The 9ème is a veritable diagram of Paris's cultural extremes. The lower half offers the highest of highs: the extravagant Opéra Garnier, the high-falutin' panoramic cinemas, and the glitzy shopping malls **Galeries Lafayette** and **Au Printemps.** Near the northern border, you'll find the lowest of lows: the infamous porn shops, X-rated cinemas, prostitution, and drugs. The 9ème has tons of hotels, but many to the north are used for the local flesh trade. Nicer but not-so-cheap hotels are available near the respectable bd. des Italiens and bd. Montmartre. **Safety:** The pl. Pigalle and M: Barbès-Rochechoart are notorious for prostitution and drugs, which become very visible at an astonishingly early hour.

THE OPÉRA AND SURROUNDINGS

The area around the southernmost border of the 9ème is known as l'Opéra after the area's distinguishing landmark, the **Opéra Garnier.** To the north of the Opéra is the most trafficked area in the 9ème, the enormous shopping malls **Galeries Lafayette** and **Au Printemps** (see **Shopping,** p. 163), which offer some of the best shopping in Paris—especially in July, when the summer sale season begins.

■ **OPÉRA GARNIER.** The stunning facade of the Opéra Garnier—with its stately flamboyance, newly restored multi-colored marble facade, and sculpted golden goddesses that glitter in the sun—is one of the most breathtaking sights in all of Paris. Designed by Charles Garnier under Napoleon III, the Opéra is perhaps most famous as home to the legend of the Phantom of the Opera. But it is also one of the city's most extravagant architectural wonders, the brilliant facade shimmering like alabaster and gold. *(M: Opéra. General info and reservations ☎ 08 36 69 78 68, tour info 01 40 01 22 63; www.opera-de-paris.fr. Concert hall and museum open Sept. to mid-July daily 10am-5pm, last entry 4:30pm; mid-July to Aug. 10am-6pm, last entry 5:30pm. Admission €4.58; ages 10-16, students, and over 60 €3. English tours June-Aug. daily noon and 2pm; €10; students, ages 10-16, and over 60 €8; under 10 €4. See also **Entertainment,** p. 156.)*

NORTH OF THE OPÉRA

EGLISE NOTRE-DAME-DE-LORETTE. The Eglise Notre-Dame-de-Lorette was built in 1836 to "the glory of the Virgin Mary." This Neoclassical church is filled with statues of saints and frescoes of scenes from the life of Mary. **Rue Notre-Dame-de-Lorette,** however, is a different animal. Somewhat less saintly than its namesake, this street was the debauched hangout of Emile Zola's Nana and a thoroughfare of serious ill-repute in the late 1960s. *(M: Notre-Dame-de-Lorette. Leave the métro and the church will be in front of you on pl. Kossuth.)*

PIGALLE. Farther north, at the border of the 18ème, is the infamous area named Pigalle, the extravagant un-chastity belt of Paris. Stretching along the trash-covered bd. de Clichy from pl. Pigalle to pl. Blanche is a salacious, voracious, and generally pretty naughty neighborhood. The home of famous cabarets-cum-nightclubs (Folies Bergère, Moulin Rouge, Folies Pigalle) and well-endowed newcomers with names like "Le Coq Hardy" and "Dirty Dick," this neon neighborhood is raunchy enough to make even Jacques Chirac blush. The areas to the north of bd. Clichy and south of pl. Blanche are comparatively calmer, but visitors should **exercise caution at all times.** *(M: Pigalle.)*

TENTH ARRONDISSEMENT

The pl. de la République was once a hotbed of Revolutionary fervor, but Haussmann put an end to that with a some clever urban planning. The area is today one of striking juxtapositions—regal statues scrawled with graffiti and peaceful

PARIS

squares next to hectic boulevards full of seedy wares. Though the 10*ème* is not known for drawing tourists, it should not be ignored. Good, cheap ethnic restaurants abound, and the area near the canal is pleasant. **Safety:** Most of the tenth is unsafe at night, especially around pl. de la République and rue du Château d'Eau. Bd. St-Martin and rue de Faubourg St-Denis are unsafe at all hours.

ELEVENTH ARRONDISSEMENT

The 1989 opening of the Opéra Bastille on the bicentennial of the Revolution breathed new life into the 11*ème*. In the early 1990s, the neighborhood near the Opéra, called simply the **Bastille,** was touted as the next Montmartre, the next Montparnasse, and the next Latin Quarter. With numerous bars along **rue de Lappe,** impressive dining options on **rue de la Roquette,** and a good number of off-beat cafés and Art Nouveau galleries, the Bastille has met expectations. Five mĕtro lines converge at M: République and three at M: Bastille, fueling the 11*ème*'s reputation as a center of action. Often vacant budget accommodations line **rues Oberkampf** and **Ménilmontant. Safety:** Watch out for pickpockets on pl. de la République.

THE BASTILLE PRISON. Originally commissioned by Charles V to safeguard the eastern entrance to Paris and later made into a state prison by Louis XIII, the Bastille was hardly the hell-hole the Revolutionaries who tore it down imagined. Titled inmates were allowed to furnish their suites and bring their own servants.

Having sacked the Invalides for weapons, Revolutionaries stormed the Bastille for munitions. Surrounded by armed rabble, too short on food to entertain a siege, and unsure of the loyalty of the Swiss mercenaries who defended the prison, the Bastille's governor surrendered. Defarge & Co. demolished it the next day. Today, the **July Column,** at one corner of the pl. de la Bastille, commemorates the site where the prison once stood. Since the late 19th century, July 14 has been the official state holiday of the French Republic and is usually a time of glorious firework displays and equally glorious alcohol consumption. *(M: Bastille.)*

TWELFTH ARRONDISSEMENT

The 12*ème* was a center of revolutionary fervor during in 1830 and 1848. In the mid-1900s, the neighborhood calmed down, only to raise up its hackles much later in response to the building of the controversial **Opéra Bastille.** Today, its northwestern fringes are decidedly funky (the **Viaduc des Arts** and **rue du Faubourg St-Antoine** are lined with galleries and stores), but its core is working class, with a large immigrant population. The streets around the Bois de Vincennes offer some of the city's most pleasant places to stay, but are removed from the city center.

OPÉRA BASTILLE. Like its namesake, the Opéra Bastille has stirred up a lot of opposition. One of Mitterrand's *Grands Projets*, the Opéra, designed by a Canadian, opened in 1989 to protests over its unattractive design. On the tour (expensive but extremely impressive) you'll see a different side of the largest theater in the world. The immense auditorium seats 2703 people, but 95% of the building is taken up by exact replicas of the stage for rehearsals and workshops. *(M: Bastille. 130 rue de Lyon. ☎01 40 01 19 70; www.opera-de-paris.fr. 1hr. tour daily 1 or 5pm; call ahead. Tours in French, but groups can arrange for English. €10; over 60 €8, students and under 26 €5.)*

VIADUC DES ARTS AND PROMENADE PLANTÉE. The *ateliers* in the **Viaduc des Arts** house artisans who make everything from *haute couture* fabric to handpainted porcelain. Restorers of all types fill the arches of the old railway viaduct, and they can make your oil painting, 12th-century book, or childhood dollhouse look as good as new. Interspersed among the stores are gallery spaces that are rented by new artists each month. High above the avenue, on the "roof" of the viaduct, runs the lovely, rose-filled **Promenade Plantée**, Paris's skinniest park. *(M: Bastille. 9-129 av. Daumesnil. Entrances at Ledru Rollin, Hector Malot, and bd. Diderot. Open M-F 8am, Sa-Su 9am; closing hours vary, around 5:30pm in winter and 9:30pm in summer.)*

THIRTEENTH ARRONDISSEMENT

Until the 20th century, the 13ème (which, together with the 14ème, comprises the area called **Montparnasse**), was one of Paris's poorest neighborhoods. But the area has of late shown signs of a rebirth. A new project called ZAC (Zone d'Aménagement Concerté) is set to make the quai banks of the 13ème into the largest cultural center in Paris. Next to come are a new university, numerous blocks of office space, a cinema complex and film education center. The 13ème is also home to several immigrant communities and the large new Bibliothèque de France. **Safety:** Nightlife around the northern end of av. du Maine has a decidedly sleazy feel.

CHINATOWN. Paris's Chinatown (see sidebar, **Insider's City**) lies in the area bounded by rue de Tolbiac, bd. Masséna, av. de Choisy, and av. d'Ivry. It is home to large Chinese, Vietnamese, and Cambodian communities, and a host of Asian restaurants, shops, and markets like Tang Frères. Av. de Choisy and av. d'Ivry give a taste of the neighborhood, whose shop windows are filled with beautiful embroidered dresses, elegant chopstick sets, ceramic Buddha statuettes, fresh vegetables, and Asian *à la vapeur* specialties.

FOURTEENTH ARRONDISSEMENT

The first of many generations of immigrants to settle in the 14ème were 19th-century Bretons, and Breton *crêperies* and cultural associations still line **rue du Montparnasse**. But the 14ème got its true start in the 1920s, when Picasso, Hemingway, and Gertrude Stein occasionally stepped over the border from the Latin Quarter to wile away afternoons in its cafés. The area just south of the Latin Quarter still attracts young artists and students with its affordable café culture.

▓ THE CATACOMBS. A series of tunnels 20m below ground and 1.7km in length, the Catacombs were originally excavated to provide stone for building the city. By the 1770s, much of the Left Bank was in danger of caving in and digging promptly stopped. The former quarry was then used as a mass grave, relieving Paris's foul and overcrowded cemeteries. During WWII, the Resistance set up headquarters among the departed. They formed an underground city, with street names on walls lined with femurs and craniums. The catacombs are not recommended for the

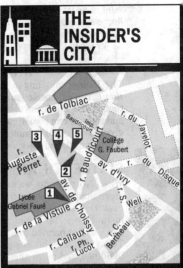

faint of heart; there are 85 steep steps to climb up. *(M: Denfert-Rochereau. 1 pl. Denfert-Rochereau. ☎01 43 22 47 63. From the métro, take exit pl. Denfert-Rochereau, cross av. du Général Leclerc; the entrance is the dark green structure straight ahead. Open Tu 11am-4pm, W-Sa 9am-4pm. €5, seniors €3.30, ages 14-26 €2.50, under 14 free. Tour lasts 45min.)*

FIFTEENTH ARRONDISSEMENT

The 15*ème*, middling in incomes and politics, is the most populous *arrondissement*. The expansive **Parc André Citroën** attracts families on weekends. Aside from that, the 15*ème* doesn't have many sights. Hotels scramble for guests in the summer, and tourists can sometimes bargain for rates. Locals have their favorites among the grocers on rue du Commerce, the cafés at the corner of rue de la Convention and rue de Vaugirard, and the specialty shops along av. Emile Zola.

SIXTEENTH ARRONDISSEMENT

When Notre Dame was under construction, this now elegant suburb was little more than a couple of tiny villages in the woods, and so it remained for several centuries, as kings and nobles chased deer and boar through its forests. Haussmann (see p. 143) transformed the area. The wealthy villages of Auteuil, Passy, and Chaillot banded together and joined the city, forming what is now the 16*ème*. Today, the area houses some of the most interesting Art Nouveau and Art Deco buildings, and more museums than any other *arrondissement*. Wealthy and residential, the 16*ème* is a short walk from the Eiffel Tower but a 20min. métro ride away from the center of Paris.

TROCADÉRO AND SURROUNDINGS

The pl. d'Iéna positions you next to the rotunda of the **Conseil Economique** and in front of a sweep of popular museums, including the round facade of the **Musée Guimet**, the **Musée de la Mode et du Costume** (see **Museums**, p. 155), and the **Palais de Tokyo,** just down the street. Henri Bouchard's impressive facade for the **Eglise St-Pierre de Chaillot** (1937) lies between rue de Chaillot and av. Pierre I de Serbie, 5min. away. *(M: Iéna. Open M-Sa 9:30am-12:30pm and 3-7pm, Su 9:30am-12:30pm.)*

PLACE DU TROCADÉRO. In the 1820s, the Duc d'Angoulême built a memorial to his victory in Spain at Trocadéro. Jacques Carlu's modern design for the 1937 World Exposition (which beat out Le Corbusier's plan) for the **Palais de Chaillot** features two white stone wings cradling an austere, Art Deco courtyard that extends from the place over spectacular cannon-shaped fountains. Surveyed by Henri Bouchard's 7.5m bronze **Apollo** and eight other figures, the terrace attracts tourists, vendors, skateboarders, and in-line skaters and offers brilliant panoramic views of the Eiffel Tower and Champs de Mars, particularly at night. Be aware of possible pickpockets and of traffic as you gaze upward.

SEVENTEENTH ARRONDISSEMENT

Hugging the northwestern edge of the city and sandwiched between more luxurious and famous *arrondissements*, the 17*ème* suffers from a bit of multiple personality disorder. In between the aristocratic 8*ème* and 16*ème* *arrondissements* and the more tawdry 18*ème* and Pigalle, the 17*ème* is a working-class residential district. Some of its hotels cater to prostitutes, others to businesspeople. **Safety:** Safety is an issue on the border with the 18*ème*, especially near pl. de Clichy.

EIGHTEENTH ARRONDISSEMENT: MONTMARTRE

Montmartre is one of the few Parisian neighborhoods Baron Haussmann left intact when he redesigned the city and its environs. A rural area outside the city limits until the 20th century, the hill used to be covered with vineyards, wheat fields, windmills, and gypsum mines. Its picturesque beauty and low rent attracted bohemians like Toulouse-Lautrec and Erik Satie as well as performers and impresarios like Aristide Bruant during the area's Belle Epoque heyday. Filled with bohemian cabarets like "Le Chat Noir," satirical journals, and proto-Dada artist groups like *Les Incohérents* and *Les Hydropathes*, the *butte* became the Parisian center of free love, fun, and *fumisme*. Just before WWI smashed its spotlights and destroyed its crops, the area welcomed Picasso, Modigliani, and Apollinaire into its artistic circle.

Nowadays, Montmartre is a mix of upscale bohemia (above rue des Abbesses) and sleaze (bd. de Clichy). The legions of tourists are hard to miss near Sacré-Coeur, the front of which provides a dramatic panorama of the city. The northwestern part of the *butte* retains some village charm, with streets speckled with shops and cafés. At dusk, gas lamps light the stairways leading to the basilica. Hotel rates rise as you climb the hill to the Basilique Sacré-Coeur, and food near the church and pl. du Tertre is pricey. **Safety:** At night, avoid M: Anvers, M: Pigalle, and M: Barbès-Rochechouart, which let out into the slummy Goutte d'Or area; use M: Abbesses instead. Downhill at seedy pl. Pigalle, hotels tend to rent by the hour.

MOUNTING MONTMARTRE

One does not merely visit Montmartre; one climbs it. The standard approach is from the south, via M: Anvers or M: Abbesses, although other directions provide interesting, less-crowded paths up. For a less difficult ascent, use the glass-covered **funicular** from the base of rue Tardieu. From M: Anvers, walk up rue Steinkerque and take a left on rue Tardieu. *(Funicular runs every 2min. 6am-12:30am. €1.30 or métro ticket. 2hr. walking tours in French May-Oct. Su 2:30pm. Meet at funicular station. €6.)*

■ **BASILIQUE DU SACRÉ-COEUR.** The Basilica of the Sacred Heart is like an exotic headdress floating above Paris. In 1873, the Assemblée Nationale selected the birthplace of the *Commune* as the location for Sacré-Coeur, "in witness of repentance and as a symbol of hope," although politician Eugène Spuller called it "a monument to civil war." The Catholic establishment hoped that the Sacré-Coeur would "expiate the sins" of France after the bloody civil war in which thousands of *communards* (leftists who declared a new populist government, known as the Commune of Paris) were massacred by government troops. After a massive fund-raising effort, the basilica was completed in 1914 and consecrated in 1919. Its hybrid style of onion domes, arches, and white color set it apart from the smoky grunge of most Parisian buildings. Most striking inside the basilica are the **mosaics,** especially the depiction of Christ on the ceiling and the mural of the Passion at the back of the altar. The narrow climb up the dome offers the highest vantage point in Paris and a view that stretches as far as 50km on clear days. Farther down, the **crypt** contains a relic of what many believe to be a piece of the sacred heart of Christ. While the views up the grassy slopes to the Basilica are among the most beautiful in Paris, the streets beneath the winding pedestrian pathways leading up to the Basilica are hideously over-touristed; to circumvent the onslaught, walk up rue des Trois Frères instead. *(M: Anvers, Abbesses, or Château-Rouge. 35 rue du Chevalier de la Barre. ☎ 01 53 41 89 00. Open daily 7am-11pm. Free. Dome and crypt open daily 9am-6pm. €5.)*

DOWNHILL

RUES ABBESSES AND LEPIC. These days great restaurants, trendy cafés, and *boulangeries* crowd this corner of Montmartre around rue des Abbesses and rue Lepic. Tall iron gates hide the beautiful gardens of 18th-century townhouses. Walking down rue Lepic will carry you past the **Moulin Radet,** one of the last remaining windmills on Montmartre. Farther down is the site of the **Moulin de la Galette,** depicted by Renoir during one of the frequent dances held there, and one of van Gogh's former homes at no. 54 rue Lepic.

CIMETIÈRE MONTMARTRE. Parallel to rue Lepic, rue Caulaincourt leads downhill to the secluded Cimetière Montmartre, where writers Dumas and Stendhal, painter Degas, physicists Ampère and Foucault, composer Berlioz, filmmaker Truffaut, and dancer Nijinksy are buried. In 1871, the cemetery held the mass graves from the siege of the Commune. *(M: Place de Clichy or Blanche. 20 av. Rachel.* ☎ *01 43 87 64 24. Follow rue Caulaincourt parallel to rue Lepic downhill to the cemetery. Open M-F 8am-6pm, Dec.-Feb. until 5:30pm; opens Sa 8:30am and Su 9am.)*

BAL DU MOULIN ROUGE. Along the bd. de Clichy and bd. de Rochechouart, you'll find many of the cabarets and nightclubs that were the definitive hangouts of the Belle Epoque, including the infamous cabaret Bal du Moulin Rouge, immortalized by the paintings of Toulouse-Lautrec, the music of Offenbach, and, most recently, a certain Hollywood blockbuster. At the turn of the century, Paris's bourgeoisie came to the Moulin Rouge to play at being bohemian. After WWI, Parisian bohemians relocated to the Left Bank and the area around pl. Pigalle became a world-renowned seedy red-light district (see p. 145). Today, the crowd consists of tourists out for an evening of sequins, tassels, and skin. The revues are still risqué, but the price of admission is prohibitively expensive—a show and dinner cost €125. *(M: Blanche. 82 bd. de Clichy.* ☎ *01 53 09 82 82. Directly across from the métro. Shows 7, 9, 11pm.)*

NINETEENTH ARRONDISSEMENT

Like Paris's other peripheral *arrondissements*, the 19*ème* is a predominantly working-class quarter, a 30min. métro ride from Paris's central sights. Cheap high-rises dot the hillsides, but a few charming streets preserve the old-Paris feel. Parisians pay handsomely for houses with views of one of Paris's two finest parks, the Parc des Buttes-Chaumont and the Parc de la Villette. The 19*ème* is also home to a large Asian community, and has wonderful, inexpensive eateries. **Safety:** Be careful at night, particularly in the emptier northwestern corner of the *arrondissement* as well as along rue David d'Angiers, bd. Indochine, av. Corentin Cariou, rue de Belleville, and by the "Portes."

PARC DE LA VILLETTE. Cut in the middle by the **Canal de l'Ourcq** and the **Canal St-Denis,** the **Parc de la Villette** separates the Cité des Sciences from the Cité de la Musique. Rejecting the 19th-century notion of the park as natural oasis, Bernard Tschumi designed a 20th-century urban park which feels like a step into the future. Constructed in 1867 as the La Villette beef building, the steel-and-glass **Grande Halle** (☎ 01 40 03 75 03) now hosts frequent plays, concerts, temporary exhibitions, and films. Unifying the park is a set of red cubical structures that form a grid of squares, known as **Folies.** The **Promenade des Jardins** links several thematic gardens, such as the **Mirror Garden,** which uses an array of mirrors to create optical illusions, the **Garden of Childhood Fears,** which winds through a wooded grove resonant with spooky sounds, and the roller coaster **Dragon Garden.** The promenade ends at Jardin des Dunes and the Jardins des Vents, a playground for kids ages 12 and under accompanied by parents. *(Promenade open 24hr. Free.)*

PARC DES BUTTES-CHAUMONT. To the south, Parc des Buttes-Chaumont is a mix of man-made topography and transplanted vegetation. Nostalgic for London's Hyde Park, where he spent much of his time in exile, Napoleon III built Parc des Buttes-Chaumont. Before the construction of the Buttes-Chaumont, the *quartier* was home to a *gibbet* (an iron cage filled with the rotting corpses of criminals), a dumping-ground for dead horses, and a gypsum quarry (the source of "plaster of Paris"). Making a park out of this mess took four years and 1000 workers; all of the soil was replaced and the quarried remains built up with new rock to create enormous fake cliffs and an artificial lake. *(M: Buttes-Chaumont and Botzaris both exit onto the park. Open daily 7am-10:45pm.)*

TWENTIETH ARRONDISSEMENT

As Haussmannization expelled many of Paris's workers from the central city, thousands migrated east to the *20ème*. By the late Second Republic, it was known as a "red" *arrondissement*, characterized as both proletarian and radical. Some of the heaviest fighting during the suppression of the Commune took place in these streets. Those workers who survived the retributive massacres following the government's takeover kept themselves to the *20ème*. Today, the *arrondissement* retains its isolated feel, with busy residential areas and markets that cater to locals. The area is also the home to sizeable Greek, North African, Russian, and Asian communities.

■ **CIMITIÈRE PÈRE LACHAISE.** With its winding paths and elaborate sarcophagi, Cimetière du Père Lachaise has become the final resting place of French and foreign giants. Balzac, Colette, David, Delacroix, La Fontaine, Haussmann, Molière, and Proust are buried here, as are Chopin, Jim Morrison, Gertrude Stein, and Oscar Wilde. With so many tourists around, they're hardly resting in peace.

The cemetery is a 19th-century neighborhood-of-the-dead laid out in streets. Many of the tombs in this landscaped grove remind visitors of the dead's worldly accomplishments: the tomb of French Romantic painter **Géricault** wears a reproduction of his *Raft of the Medusa;* on **Chopin's** tomb sits the muse Calliope. **Oscar Wilde**'s grave is marked by a larger-than-life striking Egyptian figure. **Haussmann,** the man of the boulevards, wanted to destroy the cemetery as part of his urban-renewal project, but relented and now occupies a mausoleum in Père Lachaise. Plaques here commemorate dancer **Isadora Duncan,** author **Richard Wright,** opera diva **Maria Callas,** and artist **Max Ernst.** The most visited grave is that of **Jim Morrison,** the former lead singer of The Doors. His graffiti-covered bust was removed from the tomb, allowing his fans to fill the rest of the memorial with their messages. In summer, dozens of young people bring flowers, joints, beer, poetry, and Doors paraphernalia to his tomb. At least one guard polices the spot at all times.

Perhaps the most moving sites in Père Lachaise are those that mark the deaths of collective groups. The **Mur des Fédérés** (Wall of the Federals) has become a site of pilgrimage for left-wing sympathizers. In May 1871, a group of *communards* murdered the Archbishop of Paris, who had been taken hostage at the beginning of the Commune. They dragged his mutilated corpse to their stronghold in Père Lachaise and tossed it in a ditch. Four days later, the victorious Versaillais found the body. In retaliation, they lined up 147 Fédérés against the eastern wall of the cemetery, shot them, and buried them on the spot. Near the wall, a number of moving monuments commemorate the Résistance fighters of WWII as well as Nazi concentration camp victims. *(M: Père Lachaise. 16 rue du Repos. ☎01 55 25 82 10. Open Mar.-Oct. M-F 8am-6pm, Sa 8:30am-6pm, Su and holidays 9am-6pm; Nov.-Feb. M-F 8am-5:30pm, Sa 8:30am-5:30pm, Su and holidays 9am-5:30pm. Last entry 15min. before closing. Free. Free maps available at guard booths by main entrances, but they're usually out; it is worth the €1.50 to buy a detailed map from a nearby tabac before entering. 2hr. guided tour in English June-Sept. Sa 3pm; in French Sa 2:30pm, occasionally Tu 2:30pm and Su 3pm. €5.70, students €3.90. Tours meet at the bd. de Ménilmontant entrance. Call ☎01 40 71 75 60 for info.)*

▥ MUSEUMS

The **Carte Musées et Monuments** offers admission to 70 museums in the Paris area. It will save you money if you visit three or more museums per day, and it will enable you move to the front of most museums's lines. It's sold at major museums and in almost all métro stations. 1-day pass €15, 3 consecutive days €30, 5 consecutive days €45. For more info, call Association InterMusées, 4 rue Brantôme, 3ème (☎01 44 61 96 60; www.intermusees.com).

■ **MUSÉE DU LOUVRE.** Construction of the Louvre began in 1190, and it still isn't finished. Under King Philippe-Auguste, the structure was a fortress attached to the city walls, designed to defend Paris while he was away on a crusade. In the 14th century, Charles V built a second city wall beyond what is now the Jardin des Tuileries (see **Sights**, p. 130), thus rendering the Louvre useless. Not one to let a good castle go to waste, Charles converted the fortress into a residential château. In 1528, François Ier returned to the Louvre in an attempt to flatter the Parisian bourgeoisie. He razed Charles's palace and commissioned Pierre Lescot to build a new royal palace in the open style of the Renaissance. The old foundations are displayed in an exhibit entitled **Medieval Louvre,** on the ground floor of the Sully wing. Henry II's widow, Catherine de Médici, had the Tuileries Palace built looking onto an Italian-style garden. Henri IV completed the Tuileries and embarked on what he called the **Grand Design**—a project to link the Louvre and the Tuileries with the two large wings you see today in a "royal city." He only built a fraction of the project before his death in 1610. Louis XIV moved back to Paris and into the Louvre in 1650, hiring a trio of architects—Le Vau, Le Brun, and Perrault—to transform it into the grandest palace in Europe, but he later abandoned it in favor of Versailles.

In 1725, after years of relative abandonment, the Academy of Painting inaugurated annual salons in the halls to show the work of its members. In 1793, the exhibit was made permanent, creating the Musée du Louvre. Napoleon filled the Louvre with plundered art, most of which had to be returned. He happily continued Henri IV's Grand Design, extending the Louvre's two wings to the Tuileries palace and remodeling the facades of the older buildings. Mitterrand's *Grands Projets* campaign transformed the Louvre into an accessible, well-organized museum. Architect I.M. Pei came up with the idea of moving the museum's entrance to the center of the Cour Napoléon, on an underground level surmounted by his stunning and controversial **glass pyramid.**

Renaissance works include Leonardo da Vinci's *Mona Lisa (La Joconde)* and canvases by Raphael and Titian, while among the French paintings are David's *Oath of the Horatii*, Ingres's sensual *Odalisque*, Géricault's gruesome *Raft of the Medusa*, and Delacroix's patriotic *Liberty Leading the People*. Sculptures include Michelangelo's *Slaves*, as well as an incredible collection of antiquities; be sure to see the *Venus de Milo* and the *Winged Victory of Samothrace*. The underground complex beneath the Pyramid also houses temporary exhibits. Visitors can either enter through the pyramid or directly from the métro into the new Carrousel du Louvre mall—follow the signs; if you have a *Carte Musée et Monuments*, you can enter directly from the Richelieu entrance, in the passage connecting the Cour Napoléon to the rue de Rivoli. Otherwise, you can buy full-price tickets from machines underneath the pyramid; reduced-rate tickets must be bought from ticket offices. The Louvre is less crowded on weekday afternoons and on Monday and Wednesday evenings, when it stays open until 9:45pm. The museum is enormous; you'll only be able to cover a fraction of it in any one visit. Pick up an updated **map** at the info desk below the pyramid. (M: Palais-Royal/Musée du Louvre. 1er. ☎01 40 20 51 51. Open M and W 9am-9:30pm, Th-Su 9am-6pm. Last entry 45min. before closing. M and W-Sa 9am-3pm €7.50; Su-M and W-Sa 3pm-close €5.30, under 18 and first Su of the month free. Temporary exhibits in the Cour Napoléon open 9am. English tours M and W-Sa 11am, 2, 3:45pm; €3.)

OTHER MAJOR MUSEUMS

■ **CENTRE POMPIDOU.** Often called the Beaubourg, the **Centre National d'Art et de Culture Georges Pompidou** fulfills former French President Pompidou's desire for Paris to have a cultural center embracing music, cinema, books, and the graphic arts. The Centre has inspired architectural controversy ever since its inauguration in 1977. Richard Rogers and Renzo Piano's building-turned-inside-out bares its circulatory system to all. Piping and ventilation ducts in various colors run up, down, and sideways along the outside (blue for air, green for water, yellow for electricity, red for heating). It attracts more visitors per year than any other museum or monument in France—eight million annually compared to the Louvre's three million. The **Musée National d'Art Moderne,** the Pompidou's main attraction, houses a rich selection of 20th-century art, from the Fauvists and Cubists to Pop and Conceptual Art. *(M: Rambuteau or Hôtel-de-Ville; RER: Châtelet-Les-Halles. Pl. Georges-Pompidou, 4ème.* ☎ *01 44 78 12 33, wheelchair info 01 44 78 49 54. Centre open W-M 11am-10pm; museum open W-M 11am-9pm, last tickets 8pm. Permanent collection €5.50, students and over 60 €3.50, under 13 free, 1st Su of month free. Permanent collection, current exposition, and the Atelier Brancusi €8.50, students and seniors €6.50. Audio guides €4.50.)*

■ **MUSÉE D'ORSAY.** If only the old cronies who turned the Impressionists away from the Louvre could see the Musée d'Orsay today! Hundreds come daily to see these famous rejects. Paintings, sculpture, decorative arts, architecture, photography, and cinema are presented in this former railway station, with works spanning the period from 1848 until WWI. An escalator at the far end of the building ascends directly to the Impressionist level. If it's your first visit, start from the right-hand side of the first floor as you enter, and follow the signs—it's organized very well.

The best plan of attack for the museum is (counterintuitively) to visit the ground floor, the top floor, and then the mezzanine. This is clearly indicated both by signs and maps. The central atrium is dedicated to **sculpture** and highlights the likes of Jean-Baptiste Carpeaux. Galleries around the atrium display 19th-century works of the **Neoclassical, Romantic, Barbizon,** and **Realist** schools; important canvases include Manet's *Olympia,* Ingres's *La Source,* Delacroix's *La Chasse aux lions,* and Courbet's *Un Enterrement à Ornans.* The top floor is dedicated to the **Impressionists,** with important works by virtually all of the school of light's movers and shakers; famous works include Monet's *Gare St-Lazare* and Manet's *Déjeuner sur l'herbe.* The **Post-Impressionist** collection includes van Gogh's *Portrait of the Artist* (1889) and still lifes and landscapes by Cézanne. The small mezzanine, meanwhile, is dedicated to **Rodin,** and is dominated by his huge *La Porte de l'Enfer.* The museum is least crowded on Sunday mornings and Thursday evenings. *(M: Solférino; RER: Musée d'Orsay. 62 rue de Lille, 7ème.* ☎ *01 40 49 48 14. Open mid-June to mid-Sept. Tu-W and F-Su 9am-6pm, Th 9am-9:45pm; mid-Sept. to mid-June Tu-W and F-Su 10am-6pm, Th 10am-9:45pm. Last tickets 45min. before closing. €7, ages 18-25 and Su €5, under 18 free. Tours in English Tu-Sa 11:30am and 2:30pm; 90min.; €5.50. MC/V.)*

■ **MUSÉE RODIN.** The elegant 18th-century **Hôtel Biron,** where Auguste Rodin lived and worked at the end of his life, is now his museum. He was among the country's most controversial artists, classified by some as Impressionism's sculptor and by others as the father of modern sculpture. This is one of Paris's best museums, housing many of Rodin's better known sculptures *(La Main de Dieu* and *Le Baiser).* Many sculptures rest on beautiful antiques that are labeled for their own merits, and the walls are adorned with paintings and photographs by artists like Renoir, Van Gogh, Meunier, and Steichen. The museum also has several works by **Camille Claudel,** Rodin's muse, collaborator, and lover. The *hôtel's* expansive garden displays Rodin's work amongst rose trees and fountains, including the collection's star: *Le Penseur (The Thinker).* On the other side of the garden stands one version of Rodin's largest sculpture, *La Porte de l'Enfer (The Gates of Hell,* 1880-1917), the final version of which sits in the Musée d'Orsay. *(M: Varenne. 77 rue de Varenne, 7ème.* ☎ *01 44 18 61 10. Open Apr.-Sept. Tu-Su 9:30am-5:45pm; Oct.-Mar. 9:30am-4:45pm. Last entry 30min. before closing. €5; seniors, ages 18-25, and all on Su €3. Park open Apr.-Sept. Tu-Su 9:30am-6:45pm; Oct.-Mar. 9:30am-5pm. €1. Audio tour €4. MC/V.)*

PARIS

MUSÉE DE CLUNY. The **Musée National du Moyen Age** is one of the world's finest collections of medieval art, jewelry, sculpture, and tapestries. In the 15th century, this *hôtel* was the home of the monastic Order of Cluny, led by the powerful Amboise family. In 1843, the state converted the *hôtel* into the medieval museum; excavations after WWII unearthed Roman baths below. The museum's collection includes art from Paris's most important medieval structures: Ste-Chapelle, Notre Dame, and St-Denis. The museum's unequivocal star is the stunning series of allegorical tapestries, ■*The Lady and the Unicorn*. (M: Cluny-Sorbonne. 6 pl. Paul Painlevé, 5ème. ☎ 01 53 73 78 00. Open W-M 9:15am-5:45pm, last entry 5:15pm. €6.70; students, under 25, over 60, and all on Su €5.20; under 18 free. Weekly concerts; prices and schedules vary; call ☎ 01 53 73 78 16.)

CITÉ DES SCIENCES ET DE L'INDUSTRIE. Dedicated to bringing science to young people, the ■**Explora science museum** is the star of La Villette, a park-museum complex dedicated, in Mitterrand's words, to "intelligent leisure." The architecture of the buildings is impressive by itself, but the exhibits can only be described as absolutely fabulous, and kids will love them. The museum features a **planetarium**, a **3-D cinema**, a modest **aquarium**, and the **Médiathèque**. (M: Porte de la Villette. ☎ 01 40 05 70 00 in French. Museum open Tu-Sa 10am-6pm, Su 10am-7pm. €7.50, students €5.50, under 7 free. Planetarium €2.50, under 7 free. Médiathèque open Tu noon-7:45pm, W-Su noon-6:45 pm. Free. Cité des Enfants programs Tu-Su every 2hr.; 1½hr.; €5.)

CITÉ DE LA MUSIQUE. At the opposite end of La Villette from the Cité des Sciences is the Cité de la Musique. Designed by Franck Hammoutène and completed in 1990, the complex of buildings is visually stunning, full of curves and glass ceilings. The highlight is the **Musée de la Musique,** a collection of paintings, sculptures, and 900 musical instruments. Visitors can don a pair of headphones that tune in to musical excerpts and explanations of each instrument. The building's two performance spaces—the **Salle des Concerts** and the **Amphithéâtre**—host an eclectic range of shows and concerts year-round. The Cité also has a **music information center** and the **Médiathèque Pédagogique.** (M: Porte de Pantin. 19ème. ☎ 01 44 84 44 84, Médiathèque 01 44 84 46 77. Musée open Tu-Sa noon-6pm, Su 10am-6pm. €6.10, students €4.60, children 6-18 €2.30, under 6 free; €2.30 more for temporary exhibits. Tours in French; €10, reduced €7.60, under 18 €4.60. Médiathèque open Tu-Su noon-6pm. Free.)

THE BEST OF THE REST

PALAIS DE LA DÉCOUVERTE. Kids tear around the Palais's interactive science exhibits, pressing buttons to start comets on celestial trajectories, spinning on seats to investigate angular motion, and seeing all kinds of creepy-crawlies. The **planetarium** has 4 shows per day. (M: FDR or Champs-Elysées-Clemenceau. In the Grand Palais, av. Franklin D. Roosevelt, 8ème. ☎ 01 56 43 20 20, planetarium 01 40 74 81 73. Open Tu-Sa 10am-6pm, Su 10am-7pm. €5.60, students, seniors, and under 18 €3.65, under 5 free. Planetarium €3.05. Family entrance for two adults and two children over 5 €12.20. AmEx/MC/V.)

PETIT PALAIS. Also called the Palais des Beaux-Arts de la Ville de Paris. Built for the 1900 Universal Exposition, the Palais houses 17th- to 20th-century Flemish, French, and Dutch painting and sculpture, but will be **closed for renovations** until winter 2005. (M: Champs-Elysées-Clemenceau. 3 av. du Général Eisenhower, 8ème. ☎ 01 44 13 17 30 or 01 44 13 17 17. Follow av. W. Churchill toward the river; the museum is on your right. Open Th-M 10am-8pm, W 10am-10pm; last entry 45min. before closing. Admission varies by exhibit; around €8, ages 13-26 €5.50, under 13 free; call ahead for info.)

MUSÉE PICASSO. When Picasso died in 1973, his family paid the French inheritance tax in artwork. The French government put this collection on display in 1985 in the 17th-century **Hôtel Salé.** The museum leads the viewer through Pablo Picasso's early work in Spain to his Cubist and Surrealist years and his Neoclassical work in France. *(M: Chemin-Vert. 5 rue de Thorigny, 3ème. ☎ 01 42 71 63 15. Open Apr.-Sept. W-M 9:30am-6pm; Oct.-Mar. 9:30am-5:30pm; last entrance 30min. before closing. €5, ages 18-25 and Su €4, under 18 free.)*

MUSÉE D'ART MODERNE DE LA VILLE DE PARIS. In the magnificent Palais de Tokyo, this museum contains one of the world's foremost collections of 20th-century art. Two works stand out: Matisse's *La Danse Inachevée* and Dufy's epic of electricity, *La Fée Électricité. (M: Iéna. 11 av. du Président Wilson, 16ème. ☎ 01 53 67 40 00. From Iéna, follow av. du Président Wilson with the Seine on your right. Open Tu-F 10am-5:30pm, Sa-Su 10am-6:45pm. Permanent exhibits free, special exhibits €5, students €2.20-3.)*

■ **MUSÉE JACQUEMART-ANDRÉ.** The former home of Nélie Jacquemart and her husband contains a collection of Renaissance artwork worthy of the most prestigious museums in Paris. The collection includes a *Madonna and Child* by Botticelli and *St-George and the Dragon* by Ucello. Visitors can also eat a light lunch in the tearoom under a fresco by Tiepolo or admire the museum's impressive facade while resting in the courtyard. *(M: Miromesnil. 158 bd. Haussmann, 8ème. ☎ 01 45 62 11 59. Open daily 10am-6pm; last entry 5:30pm. €8, students, ages 7-17 €6; under 7 free. Headsets with presentations in English are free with admission).*

■ **MUSÉE CARNAVALET.** Housed in Mme. de Sévigné's 16th-century hôtel particulier, this amazing museum traces Paris's history, with exhibits on the city from prehistory and the Roman conquest to 18th-century splendor and Revolution, 19th-century Haussmannization, and Mitterrand's *Grands Projets. (M: Chemin-Vert. 23 rue de Sévigné, 3ème. ☎ 01 44 59 58 58. Take rue St-Gilles as it turns into rue de Parc Royal, and turn left onto rue de Sévigné. Open Tu-Su 10am-5:40pm; last entry 5:15pm. Free.)*

MUSÉE D'HISTOIRE NATURELLE. Three museums in one. The new-fangled **Grande Galerie de l'Evolution** tells the story of evolution via a Genesis-like parade of naturalistic stuffed animals. Next door, the **Musée de Minéralogie** contains some lovely jewels. The ■**Gallery of Comparative Anatomy and Paleontology,** at the other end of the garden, whose exterior looks like a Victorian house of horrors, is filled with a ghastly collection of fibias, rib-cages, and vertebrae formed into historic and pre-historic animals. *(M: Gare d'Austerlitz. 57 rue Cuvier, in the Jardin des Plantes, 5ème. ☎ 01 40 79 30 00. Grande Galerie de l'Evolution: open M-W 10am-6pm, Th 10am-10pm. €7, students €5. Musée de Minéralogie: open W-M 10am-6pm, Sa-Su 10am-6pm. €5, students €3. Galeries d'Anatomie open Apr.-Oct. W-M 10am-5pm, Sa-Su 10am-6pm. €5, students €3.)*

■ **MUSÉE DE LA MODE ET DU COSTUME.** With 30,000 outfits, 70,000 accessories, and a relatively small space in which to work, the museum must rotate exhibitions showcasing fashions of the past three centuries. With exhibits that have a wide appeal, this is *the* place to go to see the history of Paris high fashion and society. *(M: Iéna. In the Palais Galleria, 10 av. Pierre I-de-Serbie, 16ème. ☎ 01 47 20 85 23. From the métro, walk down either av. du Président Wilson or av. Pierre 1er de Serbie with the Eiffel Tower to your right. The museum entrance is in the center of the Palais and is reached from the pl. de Rochambeau side. Open Tu-Su 10am-6pm; last entry 5:30pm. €7, students and seniors €5.50. Audio tour in French; free. MC/V for charges over €7.)*

GALERIE NATIONALE DU JEU DE PAUME. Connoisseurs and tourists alike come to appreciate the changing contemporary art exhibitions. Scheduled upcoming exhibitions for 2003 include Magritte. *(M: Concorde. Tuileries garden, 1er. ☎ 01 47 03 12 50, recorded info 01 42 60 69 69. From the métro, walk up the steps on rue Rivoli to the upper level of the Tuileries gardens. Open Tu noon-9:30pm, W-F noon-7pm, Sa-Su 10am-7pm. €6, students under 26, seniors, and ages 13-18 €4.50. Tours in French W and Sa 3pm, Su 11am.)*

MUSÉE MARMOTTAN MONET. Owing to generous donations by the family of Monet, the Empire-style house has been transformed into a lucrative shrine to Impressionism. The top floor is dedicated to paintings by Berthe Morisot, the First Lady of Impressionism, but the basement is the reason most visitors come: walls covered with late Monets, mostly the famed water lilies. *(M: La Muette. 2 rue Louis-Boilly, 16ème.* ☎*01 44 96 50 33. Follow Chaussée de la Muette as it becomes av. Ranelagh, through the Jardin du Ranelagh. Open Tu-Su 10am-6pm. €6.50, students €4, under 8 free.)*

MUSÉE D'ART ET D'HISTOIRE DU JUDAISME. Recently renovated and housed in the grand **Hôtel de St-Aignan,** once a tenement populated by Jews fleeing Eastern Europe, this museum displays a history of Jews in Europe, France, and North Africa. The collection includes an ornate 15th-century Italian ark, letters written to wrongly accused French general Dreyfus, a small collection of Chagall and Modigliani paintings, Lissitzky lithographs, and modern art collections looted from Jewish homes by the Nazis. *(M: Hôtel de Ville. 71 rue du Temple, 3ème.* ☎*01 53 01 86 53. Open M-F 11am-6pm, Su 10am-6pm; last entry 5:15pm. €6.10, students and 18-26 €3.80, under 18 free; includes an excellent English audioguide. Wheelchair accessible.)*

🎭 ENTERTAINMENT

FREE CONCERTS

Paris Selection, available at tourist offices, has listings of concerts. Free concerts are often held in churches and parks, especially during summer festivals; they are extremely popular, so arrive early. The **American Church in Paris,** 65, quai d'Orsay, 7ème, sponsors free concerts. (☎01 40 62 05 00; M: Invalides or Alma Marceau. Concerts Sept.-May Su 6pm.) **Eglise St-Germain-des-Prés** (see **Sights,** p. 139) also has free concerts; check the information booth just inside the door for times. **Eglise St-Merri,** 78 rue St-Martin, 4ème (M: Hôtel-de-Ville), also hosts free concerts (Sept.-July Sa at 9pm, Su at 4pm); contact Accueil Musical St-Merri, 76, rue de la Verrerie, 4ème (☎01 42 71 40 75; M: Châtelet). Concerts take place Wednesday through Sunday in the **Jardin du Luxembourg's** band shell, 6ème (☎01 42 34 20 23); show up early for a seat or prepare to stand. Concerts in the **Musée d'Orsay,** 1, rue Bellechasse, 7ème (☎01 40 49 49 66; M: Solférino), are occasionally free.

OPERA

Opéra de la Bastille, pl. de la Bastille, 12ème (☎08 92 69 78 68; www.opera-de-paris.fr). M: Bastille. Opera and ballet with a modern spin. Because of acoustical problems, it's not the place to splurge for front row seats. Subtitles in French. Call, write, or stop by for a free brochure of the season's events. Tickets can be purchased by Internet, mail, fax, phone (M-Sa 9am-7pm), or in person (M-Sa 11am-6pm). Tickets €57-105. Rush tickets for students under 25 and anyone over 65 15min. before show. For wheelchair access, call 2 weeks ahead (☎01 40 01 18 08). MC/V.

Opéra Garnier, pl. de l'Opéra, 9ème (☎08 92 69 78 68; www.opera-de-paris.fr). M: Opéra. Hosts operas, symphonies, chamber music, and the Ballet de l'Opéra de Paris. Tickets available 2 weeks before shows. Box office open M-Sa 11am-6pm. Tickets usually €19-64. Last-minute discount tickets available 1hr. before showtime. For wheelchair access, call 2 weeks ahead (☎01 40 01 18 08). AmEx/MC/V.

Opéra Comique, 5 rue Favart, 2ème (☎01 42 44 45 46). M: Richelieu-Drouot. Operas on a lighter scale—from Rossini to Offenbach. Box office open M-Sa 11am-7pm. Tickets €10-100. Student rush tickets available 15min. before showtime.

CABARET

Au Lapin Agile, 22 rue des Saules, 18ème (☎01 46 06 85 87). M: Lamarck-Coulaincourt. Turn right on rue Lamarck, then right up rue des Saules. Picasso, Verlaine, Renoir, and Apollinaire hung out here during the heyday of Montmartre; now a mainly tourist audience crowds in for comical poems and songs. Shows Tu-Su 9pm-2am. Admission and first drink €24, Su-F students €17. Subsequent drinks €6-7.

THEATER

La Comédie Française, 2 rue de Richelieu, 1er (☎01 44 58 15 15; www.comediefrancaise.fr). M: Palais-Royal. Founded by Molière, now the granddaddy of all French theaters. Expect wildly gesticulated slapstick farce; you don't need to speak French to understand the jokes. Performances take place in the 896-seat Salle Richelieu. This season: canonized plays by French greats Molière, Racine, and Corneille. Box office open daily 11am-6pm. Tickets €4.50-30, under 27 €4.50-7.50. Student rush tickets (€9) available 1hr. before showtime. The *comédiens français* also mount the same sort of plays in the 330-seat **Théâtre du Vieux Colombier,** 21 rue des Vieux Colombiers, 6ème (☎01 44 39 87 00 or 01 44 39 87 01). M: St-Sulpice or Sèvres-Babylone. Tickets €25, over 60 €17.50. Student rush tickets (€9-13) 45min. before showtime.

Odéon Théâtre de l'Europe, 1 pl. Odéon, 6ème (☎01 44 41 36 36; www.theatreodeon.fr). M: Odéon. Programs in this elegant Neoclassical building range from classics to avant-garde, but the Odéon specializes in foreign plays in their original language. 1042 seats. Also **Petit Odéon,** an affiliate with 82 seats, which in the past has presented the poetry of Lou Reed and *Medea* by Euripedes. Box office open daily 11am-7pm. Tickets €5-28 for most shows. Under 27 rush tickets (€7.50) available 90min. before showtime. Cheaper rates available Th and Su; call ahead. Petit Odéon €10. Call ahead for wheelchair access. MC/V; no credit card purchases over the phone.

JAZZ

■ **Au Duc des Lombards,** 42 rue des Lombards, 1er (☎01 42 33 22 88; www.jazzvalley.com/duc). M: Châtelet. From rue des Halles, walk down rue de la Ferronerie and turn right on rue St-Denis and right again on rue des Lombards. Murals of Ellington and Coltrane cover the exterior of this premier jazz joint. Still the best in French jazz, with occasional American soloists, and some world music. Cover €12-23, music students €7.40-18.60. Beer €5-8, cocktails €9. Music 9:30pm-1:30am. Open M-Sa 8pm-2am. MC/V.

■ **Le Petit Opportun,** 15 rue des Lavandières-Ste-Opportune, 1er (☎01 42 36 01 36). M: Châtelet. From the métro, walk down rue des Halles and make a right onto rue des Lavandières-Ste-Opportune. Some of the best modern jazz around, including American musicians. Show up early for a spot in the front room. Cover €13-16. Drinks €5-9. Open Aug.-June Tu-Sa 9pm-5am; music begins between 9:30 and 10:30pm.

Le Caveau de la Huchette, 5 rue de la Huchette, 5ème (☎01 43 26 65 05). M: St-Michel. From bd. St-Michel, make a right onto rue de la Huchette. Come prepared to listen, watch, and dance the jitterbug, swing, and jive in this popular, if somewhat touristy, club. Bebop dance lessons at 9:30pm; call ☎01 42 71 09 09. Varied age group. Cover Su-Th €10.50, F-Sa €13. Students €9 during the week. Dance School €8. Drinks €5.50-8.50. Open daily 9:30pm-2:30am, F until 3:30am, Sa until 4am. AmEx/MC/V.

CINEMA

There are scores of cinemas throughout Paris, particularly in the *Quartier Latin* and on the Champs-Elysées. Many theaters in Paris specialize in programs featuring classic European film, current independent film, Asian and American

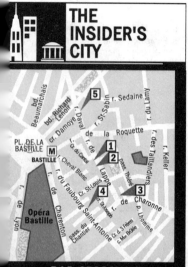

THE INSIDER'S CITY

BAR STORMING

The 11ème may have been the site of the Revolution's send-off party, but the only places being stormed in the Bastille nowadays are its nightspots. The 11ème has been called the next Montmartre, the next Montparnasse, and the next Latin Quarter. But the next bar is your only concern; here are a few to get you started:

1 **Bar des Familles.** Small and low-key (though still not the place to take your parents). (☎01 43 14 64 77. Open daily 6pm-2am.)

2 **Bar Bat.** This one draws a young and lively crowd, good for kicking the revelry up a notch. (☎01 43 14 26 06. Open daily 5pm-2am.)

3 **Le Bar Sans Nom.** The jazz will go right along with your buzz. (☎01 48 05 59 36. Open M-Sa 7pm-2am.)

4 **Sanz Sans.** Popular and upbeat, with a screen that projects scenes from the bar. (☎01 44 75 78 78. Open daily 9:30pm-1am.)

5 **Wax.** A Parisian miracle: a club that is both free and fun. Set up in a concrete bunker. House music only. (☎01 48 05 88 33. Open M-Su 6pm-2am; closed Su in summer.)

classics, and Hollywood blockbusters. The two big theater chains—**Gaumont** and **UGC**—offer *cartes privilèges* discounts for five visits or more. Paris's cinemas offer student, senior, and family discounts. On Mondays and Wednesdays, prices drop by about €1.50 for everyone. Check *Pariscope* or *l'Officiel des Spectacles* (available at any newsstand, €0.40) for weekly film schedules, prices, and reviews.

Musée du Louvre, 1er (info ☎01 40 20 53 17, schedules and reservations 01 40 20 52 99; www.louvre.fr). M: Louvre. Mainly art and silent films. Open Sept.-June. Free.

Les Trois Luxembourg, 67 rue Monsieur-le-Prince, 6ème (☎01 46 33 97 77). M: Cluny. Turn left on bd. St-Michel, right on rue Racine, and left on rue M-le-Prince. Independent, classic, and foreign films, all in original language. €6.40, students and seniors €5.

La Pagode, 57b rue de Babylone, 7ème (☎01 45 55 48 48). M: St-François-Xavier. A Japanese pagoda built in 1895 and reopened as a cinema in 2000. Foreign and independent films, and the occasional American film. Stop in at the café in between shows. Tickets €7, over 60, under 21, students, M and W €5.50. MC/V.

Cinémathèque Française, pl. du Trocadéro, 16ème (☎01 45 53 21 86, schedule ☎01 47 04 24 24; www.cinemathequefrancaise.com). M: Trocadéro. At the Musée du Cinéma in the Palais de Chaillot; enter through the Jardins du Trocadéro. **Branch** at 18 rue du Faubourg-du-Temple, 11ème. M: République. A must for film buffs. Two to three classics, near-classics, or soon-to-be classics per day. Foreign films usually in original language. €4.70, students €3. Open W-Su 5-9:45pm.

⬛ NIGHTLIFE

Those on the prowl for dancing may be frustrated by Paris's rather closed-off club scene, but *Let's Go* has tried to list clubs that admit non-models. If you'd rather just drink and watch the world go by, bars and cafés that are open late will not disappoint. As far as gay nightlife goes, the Marais is the place to see and be seen.

PLACE DE LA RÉPUBLIQUE: 3ÈME, 4ÈME, 11ÈME

⬛ **L'Apparement Café,** 18 rue des Coutures St-Gervais, 3ème. M: St-Paul. Beautiful wood-and-red lounge complete with games and a calm, young crowd. Late-night meals €10-13, served until closing.

⬛ **Chez Richard,** 37 rue Vieille-du-Temple, 4ème (☎01 42 74 31 65). M: Hôtel-de-Ville. Inside a courtyard off rue

Vieille-du-Temple, with an atmosphere reminiscent of Casablanca. Jumping on weekends but chill during the week. Beer €3.70-4.50, cocktails €8.40-9.21. Open daily 6pm-2am. AmEx/MC/V.

■ **Lizard Lounge,** 18 rue du Bourg-Tibourg, 4ème (☎01 42 72 81 34). M: Hôtel-de-Ville. A hot, split-level space for Anglo/Franco late 20-somethings. Cellar has DJ every night. Happy hour 6-10pm (cocktails €4.60). Pint of lager €5.20. Open daily noon-2am. Food served noon-3pm and 7-10:30pm, weekend brunch noon-4pm. MC/V.

Café Charbon, 109 rue Oberkampf, 11ème (☎01 43 57 55 13). M: Parmentier or Ménilmontant. A spacious bar that proudly wears traces of its *fin-de-siècle* dance hall days but still manages to pack in a crowd of young locals and artists. Beer €2.80. Happy Hour 5-7pm. Open daily 9am-2am. MC/V.

Villa Keops, 58 bd. Sébastopol, 3ème (☎01 40 27 99 92). M: Etienne-Marcel. Walk east on rue Etienne Marcel; the bar is on the corner with bd. Sébastopol. Stylish, candlelit couch bar decorated with beautiful people. *The* place to show your face (before doing the same at Les Bains; see **Dance Clubs,** below). Open M-Th noon-2am, F-Sa noon-4am, Su 4pm-3am. AmEx/MC/V.

Les Etages, 35 rue Vieille-du-Temple, 3ème (☎01 42 78 72 00). M: St-Paul. Set in an 18th-century hotel. Its 3 floors are filled with chill kids basking in dim lighting. Sangria €4.50. Brunch buffet €14.50, Su 11am-4pm. Open daily 3:30pm-2am. MC/V.

Amnésia Café, 42 rue Vieille-du-Temple, 3ème (☎01 42 72 16 94). M: Hôtel-de-Ville. A largely gay crowd comes to lounge on plush sofas in Amnésia's classy wood-paneled interior. This is one of the top see-and-be-seen spots in the Marais, especially on Sa nights. Espresso €2; *kir* €4. Open daily noon-2am. MC/V.

DANCE CLUBS

Les Bains, 7 rue du Bourg l'Abbé, 3ème (☎01 48 87 01 80). M: Etienne-Marcel or Réaumur-Sébastopol. From Etienne-Marcel, take rue Etienne Marcel east, turn left onto bd. Sébastopol, and take the next right. Ultra-selective, super-crowded, and expensive. Madonna and Mick Jagger have been spotted here recently. Funky house and garage grunge, W is hip-hop. Cover and 1st drink Su-Th €16; F-Sa €19. Clubbing daily 11pm-6am; open for dinner until 9pm; reservations a must. AmEx/MC/V.

Le Dépôt, 10 rue aux Ours, 3ème (☎01 44 54 96 96; www.ledepot.com). M: Etienne-Marcel. Take rue Etienne Marcel east; it becomes rue aux Ours. A veritable pleasure complex for gay men. Dance, mingle, or take your boy toy to one of the rooms in the downstairs labyrinth. Women welcome upstairs after 11pm, and W is lesbian night. Su Gay Tea Dance is especially popular. Disco M, House/Techno W, Latin Th, visiting DJ F, House Sa (called *"Putas"* at Work"). Cover includes first drink: M-Th €7.50, F €10, Sa €12, Su €10; W free for ladies. Open daily 2pm-8am. V.

LEFT BANK: 5ÈME, 6ÈME, 7ÈME, 13ÈME

■ **Le Reflet,** 6 rue Champollion, 5ème (☎01 43 29 97 27). M: Cluny-La Sorbonne. Walk away from the river on bd. St-Michel, then make a left on rue des Ecoles. Take the first right. Small and low-key; and crowded with students and younger Frenchies. Beer €1.90-2.70 at the bar, *kir* €2. Open M-Sa 10am-2am, Su noon-2am. MC/V.

■ **Le Caveau des Oubliettes,** 52 rue Galande, 5ème (☎01 46 34 23 09). M: St-Michel. Walk away from pl. St Michel on quai de Montebello and turn right on rue Petit Pont, then turn left onto rue Galande. Three entertainments in one: the bar upstairs has a real-live guillotine; downstairs, there's an outstanding jazz club; and beneath the club, the narrow tunnels of a former prison where criminals were locked up and forgotten. Attracts a (mostly local) set of mellow folk. Jazz concerts every night; free *soirée boeuf*

PARIS

(jam session) Su-Th from 10:30pm-1:30am; F-Sa concerts €7.50. Beer €3.70-4.10. Rum cocktail €3.80. Happy Hour 5-9pm. Open daily 5pm-2am.

■ **Le Bar Dix (Bar 10)**, 10 rue de l'Odéon, 6ème (☎01 43 26 66 83). M: Odéon. From the métro, walk against traffic on bd. St-Germain and make a left on rue de l'Odéon. A classic student hangout. Catch up with old friends, American collegiates, young intellectuals and laid-back yuppies. Sangria (€3) makes their great jukebox, which plays everything from Edith Piaf to Aretha Franklin to The Police, even better. Open daily 5:30pm-2am.

Le Crocodile, 6 rue Royer-Collard, 6ème (☎01 43 54 32 37). M: Cluny-La Sorbonne. Walk up bd. St-Michel about 7 blocks and make a left onto rue Royer Collard (10min.). A lively crowd of cool 20-somethings packs into this unassuming bar that lurks behind boarded-up windows on a quiet side street. Ring to be let in. With 238 tasty cocktails (€8) to choose from, this local bar is not for the beer-swigging crowd. Pick a number from the menu (or at random if you're feeling adventurous), write it down, and hand it across the bar. Open M-Sa 10:30pm-4am.

Le Club des Poètes, 30 rue de Bourgogne, 7ème (☎01 47 05 06 03). M: Varenne. Walk up bd. des Invalides with the Invalides behind you and to your left; go right on rue de Grenelle and left onto rue de Bourgogne. For 40 years, Jean-Pierre Rosnay has been making "poetry contagious and inevitable." A restaurant by day, at 10pm, a troupe of readers, including Rosnay's family, transform the place into a poetry salon. If you arrive after 10pm, wait to enter until you hear clapping or a break in the performance. The food is not cheap, but come for a drink to be part of the fun. Drinks €9.15, for students €6.86. Open M-Sa noon-2:30pm and 8pm-1am; food served until 10pm. AmEx/MC/V.

O'Brien's, 77 rue St-Dominique, 7ème (☎01 45 51 75 87). M: Latour-Maubourg. Follow traffic along bd. de La Tour Maubourg. A lively Irish pub. Locals gather around the big screen TV for soccer matches. Happy hour M-F from opening time until 8pm, pints €5. Otherwise, beer €4-7, cocktails €7. Open M-Th 6pm-2am, F-Su 4pm-2am. MC/V.

DANCE CLUBS

■ **Batofar**, facing 11 quai François-Mauriac, 13ème (☎01 56 29 10 33). M: Quai de la Gare. Facing the river, walk right along the quai—Batofar has the red lights. This barge/bar/club has made it big with the electronic music crowd but maintains a friendly vibe. During June, a trailer parked outside provides free music for the many who get down right on the quai. Open Tu-Th 9pm-3am, F-Sa until 4am; hours change for film and DJ events. Cover €6.50-9.50; usually includes first drink. MC/V.

RIGHT BANK: 1ER, 2ÈME, 8ÈME

■ **Banana Café**, 13-15 rue de la Ferronnerie, 2ème (☎01 42 33 35 31). M: Châtelet. From the métro, take rue Pierre Lescot to rue de la Ferronerie. This *très branché* (way cool) evening arena is the most popular gay bar in the 1er. Legendary theme nights. The "Go-Go Boys" W-Sa midnight-dawn. Happy hour 4-10pm: two for one drinks. Beer €5.18 weekdays, €6.71 weekends. Open daily 4pm-dawn. AmEx/MC/V.

■ **Le Champmeslé**, 4 rue Chabanais, 1er (☎01 42 96 85 20). M: Pyramides or Quatre Septembre. From the métro, walk down av. de l'Opéra, make a right on rue des Petits Champs, and another right onto rue Chabanais. Make another right onto rue Cabanais. This lesbian bar is Paris's oldest and most famous. Mixed crowd in the front, women-only in back. Beer €4. Cabaret show Th 10pm. Free drink during the month of your birthday. Monthly photo exhibits. Open M-Th 2pm-2am, F and Sa 2pm-5am. MC/V.

■ **House of Live**, 124 rue La Boétie, 8ème (☎01 42 25 18 06). M: Franklin D. Roosevelt. Walk toward the Arc on the Champs-Elysées, and rue La Boétie will be the second street on your right. Formerly the Chesterfield Café. Friendly and happening American bar with first-class live music. Americans and Frenchies mix with the attractive wait staff. Snack bar has good ole Yankee fare. Cocktails €8.10, beer €6, coffee €2-4. No cover Su-Th. Open daily 10am-5am. AmEx/MC/V.

buddha-bar, 8 rue Boissy d'Anglas, 8ème (☎01 53 05 90 00). M: Madeleine or Concorde. Step off your private jet, slip on your stilettos, and come here to be seen. Stereotypically snobbish, but once you make it past the door, you won't find a hotter place in the 8ème. The ground floor is where the *really* important people sit; upstairs is more relaxed. Mixed drinks and martinis €11, the mysterious Pure Delight (€12.20) is indeed that. Open M-F noon-3pm, daily 6pm-2am.

The Flann O'Brien, 6 rue Bailleul, 1er (☎01 42 60 13 58). M: Louvre-Rivoli. From the métro, walk away from the Seine on rue du Louvre and make the first right after crossing rue de Rivoli. Arguably the best Irish bar in Paris. Often packed, especially on live music nights (F, Sa, Su). Go for the Guinness and stay for the reportedly good "crack" downstairs (Irish for good fun). Demi €3.40, full pint €6. Open daily 4pm-2am.

DANCE CLUBS

▨ **Latina Café,** 114 av. des Champs-Elysées, 8ème (☎01 42 89 98 89). M: George V. Draws one of the largest nightclub crowds on the glitzy Champs-Elysées with an energetic world music mix. Drinks €9-11. €16 cover includes first two drinks. Live concerts Th. Café open daily 7:30pm-2am, club open daily 11:30am-6:30am.

Le Queen, 102 av. des Champs-Elysées, 8ème (☎01 53 89 08 90). M: George V. Where drag queens, superstars, models, moguls, and go-go boys get down to the mainstream rhythms of a 10,000 gigawatt sound system. Her majesty is one of the cheapest and most fashionable gay clubs in town. Mostly male crowd. M disco; Th-Sa house; Su 80s. Cover Su-Th €9, F-Sa €18. All drinks €9. Open daily midnight to dawn. AmEx/MC/V.

Rex Club, 5 bd. Poissonnière, 2ème (☎01 42 36 10 96). M: Bonne-Nouvelle. A nonselective club which presents the most selective of DJ line-ups. Young break-dancers and veteran clubbers fill this casual, subterranean venue to hear cutting-edge techno, jungle, and house fusion. Large dance floor and lots of seats as well. Shots €4-5, beer €5-7. Cover €8-12.50. Open Th-Sa 11:30pm-6am.

PLACE PIGALLE: 9ÈME, 18ÈME

The sleazy southernmost end of the *butte* around the red-light district near **Place Pigalle** and **bd. Rochechouart,** contains streets lined with aggressive peepshow hawkers and prowling drug dealers. Avoid making eye contact with strangers and stay near well-lit, heavily trafficked areas. Tourists traveling alone, especially women, should avoid M: Pigalle, M: Anvers, and M: Barbès-Rochechouart at night.

▨ **Chez Camille,** 8 rue Ravignan, 18ème (☎01 46 06 05 78). M: Abbesses. From the métro, walk down rue de la Veuville and make a left on rue Drevet and another left on rue Gabrielle which becomes rue Ravignan. Small, trendy, bright yellow bar on the safe upper slopes of Montmartre with pictures of Serge Gainsbourg, funky charm, and a pretty terrace looking down the *butte* to the Invalides dome (especially dramatic at night when the floodlights go on). Coffee €1, tea €2. Beer €1.70-2.50, wine from €2.50, cocktails €3-8. Open Tu-Sa 9am-2am, Su 9am-8pm.

La Fourmi, 74 rue des Martyrs, 18ème (☎01 42 64 70 35). M: Pigalle. Walk east on bd. Rochechouart and make a left on rue des Martyrs. A popular stop-off before clubbing, this bar has an artsy atmosphere, with a large zinc bar and industrial-chic decor. Draws a hyper-hip, energetic young crowd. Beer €2.30-3.20, wine €2.50, cocktails €7-10. Open M-Th 8:30am-2am, F-Sa 8:30am-4am, Su 10:30am-2am. MC/V.

DANCE CLUBS

Bus Palladium, 6 rue Fontaine, 9ème (☎01 53 21 07 33). M: Pigalle, Blanche, or St-Georges. From Pigalle, walk down rue Jean-Baptiste Pigalle and turn right on rue Fontaine. A young, trendy, and beautiful crowd hit this rock 'n' roll club, which still sports vintage posters and faded gilded decor. Getting past the bouncers can be tough. Cover €16. Tu free for ladies; Th rock. Drinks €13. Open Tu-Sa 11pm-6am. AmEx/V.

▢ SHOPPING

Like its food, nightlife, and conversation, Paris's fashion is an art. From the wild wear near rue Etienne-Marcel to the boutiques of the Marais to the upscale shops of St-Germain-des-Prés, everything Paris touches turns to gold (or, on the runways, trendy black). The great *soldes* (sales) of the year begin after New Year's and at the very end of June, with the best prices at the beginning of February and the end of July. If at any time of year you see the word *braderie* (clearance sale) in a store window, march in without hesitation.

BY ARRONDISSEMENT

ETIENNE-MARCEL AND LES HALLES (1ER AND 2ÈME). Fabrics here are a little cheaper, and the style is younger. The stores on rue Etienne-Marcel and rue Tiquetonne are best for clubwear and outrageously sexy outfits. *(M: Etienne-Marcel.)*

▨ **Zadig & Voltaire,** 15 rue du Jour, 1er (☎01 42 21 88 70). M: Etienne-Marcel. Also at 1, rue des Vieux Colombiers, 6ème (☎01 43 29 18 29; M: St-Sulpice); and 12 rue Ste-Croix-de-la-Bretonnerie (☎01 42 72 15 20; M: St-Paul). Funky but sleek men's and women's designs by DKNY, T. Gillier, and Helmut Lang. Their own label does soft, feminine designs; sweater sets and jerseys. A big selection of handbags. Opening hours vary by branch. Main branch open Tu-Sa 10:30am-7:30pm, M 1-7:30pm. AmEx/MC/V.

▨ **Le Shop,** 3 rue d'Argout, 2ème (☎01 40 28 95 94). M: Etienne-Marcel. Two levels, 1200 sq. meters, and 24 corners of Asian-inspired club wear. Prices range from reasonable (€15.25) to ludicrous (€465). Open M 1-7pm, Tu-Sa 11am-7pm. AmEx/MC/V.

MARAIS (4ÈME AND THE LOWER 3ÈME). The Marais has a line-up of affordable, trendy boutiques, mostly mid-priced clothing chains, independent designer shops, and vintage stores that line **rue Vieille-du-Temple, rue de Sévigné, rue Roi de Sicile,** and **rue des Rosiers.** Lifestyle shops line **rue de Bourg-Tibourg** and **rue des Francs-Bourgeois.** The best selection of affordable-chic menswear in Paris can be found along **rue Ste-Croix-de-la-Bretonnerie.** *(M: St-Paul or Hôtel de Ville.)*

▨ **Karine Dupont Boutique,** 22 rue de Poitou, 3ème (☎01 40 27 84 94). M: St-Sébastien Froissart. Karine Dupont makes ingenious bags in every shape and color imaginable out of unassuming, waterproof tent material. For under €100, you can be the proud owner of a conical or diagonally-cut sports bag. Open M-Sa noon-7:30pm. MC/V.

Plein Sud, 21 rue des Francs-Bourgeois, 4ème (☎01 42 72 10 60). M: St-Paul. A sweep of delicate, shimmering tops and dead-sexy dresses. Adds a spark to any woman's wardrobe. Again, a splurge—but you'll wear these clothes for years to come. Open M-Sa 11am-7pm, and Su 2-7pm. AmEx/MC/V.

Culotte, 7 rue Malher, 4ème (☎01 42 71 58 89). M: St-Paul. Japanese designs ranging from ripped printed tees to 40s-style dresses and skirts. Funky vintage jewelry, especially of the mod and 80s variety. Open Tu-Sa 11am-7pm, Su 1-7pm. AmEx/MC/V.

Loft Design By Paris, 12 rue de Sévigné, 4ème (☎01 48 87 13 07). Open M-F 11am-7pm, Sa 10am-7pm, Su 11:30am-7pm. Also at 12 rue du Faubourg-St-Honoré, 8ème

(☎01 42 65 59 65). Mostly men's clothing, including well-tailored shirts and casual sweaters and pants. Elegant and minimalist. Open M-Sa 10am-7pm. AmEx/MC/V.

Alternatives, 18 rue de Roi de Sicile, 4ème (☎01 42 78 31 50). M: St-Paul. This upscale second-hand shop sells quality clothes, including many designers at reasonable (if not exactly cheap) prices. Open Tu-Sa 11am-1pm and 2:30-7pm. MC/V.

ST-GERMAIN-DES-PRÉS (6ÈME AND EASTERN BORDER OF 7ÈME). St-Germain-des-Prés, particularly the triangle bordered by **bd. St-Germain, rue St-Sulpice,** and **rue des Sts-Pères,** is saturated with high-budget names like **Paul and Joe** (men's, no. 40; ☎01 45 44 97 70; open daily 11am-7:30pm) and **Sinéquanone** (women's, no. 16; ☎01 56 24 27 74; open M-Sa 10am-7:30pm). Closer to the Jardin du Luxembourg, **rue de Fleurus** hosts **A.P.C.** as well as interesting designs at no. 7 (M: St-Placide). In the 7ème, visit **rue de Pré-aux-Clercs** to check out the avant-garde jewelry at **Stella Cadente,** 22 rue de Grenelle. In general, the 7ème is expensive, but there are some impressive little boutiques around the Bon Marché department store on rue de Sèvres, and rue du Cherche-Midi. (M: Vaneau, Duroc, Sèvres-Babylone, Rue du Bac.)

▨ **Petit Bateau,** 26 rue Vavin, 6ème, and other locations throughout the city (☎01 55 42 02 53). M: Vavin or Notre-Dame-des-Champs. T-shirts, tanks, undies, and pajamas in the softest of cottons. A children's store, but the stylish Parisian mothers are not there for their children—the size for age 16 is about the same as an American 6, and the maximum size is age 18. Tees and tanks €6.50, long sleeved tees €12. Other locations throughout the city. Open M-Sa 10am-7pm; M in Aug. 2-7pm. AmEx/MC/V.

▨ **Tara Jarmon,** 18 rue du Four, 6ème (☎01 46 33 26 60) and 51 rue de Passy (01 45 24 65 20). Also at 73 av. des Champs-Elysées, 8ème (☎01 45 63 45 41). Classic, upscale feminine styles in lovely fabrics and bright colors.

Vanessa Bruno, 25 rue St-Sulpice, 6ème (☎01 43 54 41 04). M: St-Sulpice. Chic, trendy, simple, exotic, conservative, wild...all describe Vanessa Bruno's beautiful, well-cut creations for women. Army-inspired velvet coats, flapper-style lace tanks, below-the-hip skirts, and shiny leather flower-adorned belts are just a few of her trademark pieces. Blazers €150, skirts €160, belts €90. Open M-Sa 10:30am-7:30pm. AmEx/MC/V.

DEPARTMENT STORES

▨ **Au Printemps,** 64 bd. Haussmann, 9ème (☎01 42 82 50 00). M: Chaussée d'Antin-Lafayette or Havre-Caumartin. Also at 30 pl. d'Italie, 13ème (☎01 40 78 17 17), M: Place d'Italie; and 21-25 cours de Vincennes, 20ème (☎01 43 71 12 41), M: Porte de Vincennes. One of the two biggies in the Parisian department store scene. Most hotels have 10% discount coupons for the store. Haussmann open M-W and F-Sa 9:30am-7pm, Th 9:30am-10pm. Other locations open M-Sa 10am-8pm. AmEx/MC/V.

Galeries Lafayette, 40 bd. Haussmann, 9ème (☎01 42 82 34 56). M: Chaussée d'Antin. Also at 22 rue du Départ, 14ème (☎01 45 38 52 87), M: Montparnasse. Chaotic and crowded, with mini-boutiques of Kookaï, agnès b., French Connection, and Cacharel. Lafayette Gourmet, on the first floor, has everything from a sushi counter to a mini-boulangerie. Haussmann open M-W, F, Sa 9:30am-7:30pm, Th 9:30-9pm; Montparnasse open M-Sa 9:45am-7:30pm. AmEx/MC/V.

Samaritaine, 67 rue de Rivoli, on the quai du Louvre, 1er (☎01 40 41 20 20). M: Pont Neuf, Châtelet-Les Halles, or Louvre-Rivoli. 4 large historic Art Deco buildings connected by tunnels and bridges. Not as chic as Galeries Lafayette or Bon Marché, daring to sell merchandise at reasonable prices. Most hotels give out 10% discount coupons for the store. Open M-W and F-Sa 9:30am-7pm, Th 9:30am-10pm. AmEx/MC/V.

Au Bon Marché, 22 rue de Sèvres, 7ème (☎01 44 39 80 00). M: Sèvres-Babylone. Paris's oldest department store, Bon Marché has it all, from scarves to smoking acces-

THE INSIDER'S CITY

MARCHÉ ST-OUEN

Rare records, Victorian-era corsets, 1950s Paris paraphernalia—this flea market has everything you never knew you wanted. Here are some of the gems of St-Ouen's official market.

1 **Marché Malassis: Trésors de Perse, stall #41.** Start high class: ivory-inlaid chairs and Persian carpets.

2 **Marché Malassis: Stalls #51 and #100.** These two gallery-esque stalls sell paintings from Provence.

3 **Marché Dauphine: Les Nuits de Satin, #284-85.** Maybe this was Victoria's secret: vintage lingerie in every shape, style, and size.

4 **Marché Vernaison: Stall #6.** A huge collection of antique beads for poring over, for only €16 per cup.

5 **Chez Louisette, 130, av. Michelet.** Stop for lunch at this boisterous and kitschy bar, complete with Christmas lights and an Edith Piaf cover singer. (☎01 40 12 10 14. Open Sa-M 8am-4pm, Tu-F 8am-5pm.)

6 **Marché Biron: Les Verres de Nos Grandmères, #2.** Shelf upon shelf of antique glassware—make sure to tread carefully!

sories, designer clothes to home furnishings. Across the street is *La Grande Epicerie de Paris,* Bon Marché's celebrated gourmet food annex. Open M-W and F 9:30am-7pm, Th 10am-9pm, Sa 9:30am-8pm. AmEx/MC/V.

OUTLET STORES

Stock is French for outlet store, but it really translates into big name clothes for less. Outlet clothes often have small imperfections or are out of date by a season. Many are on rue d'Alésia in the 14*ème* (M: Alésia), including **Cacharel Stock,** no. 114 (☎01 45 42 53 04; open M-Sa 10am-7pm; AmEx/MC/V); **Stock Chevignon,** no. 122 (☎01 45 43 40 25; open M-Sa 10am-7pm; AmEx/MC/V); **S.R. Store** (Sonia Rykiel) at nos. 110-112 and no. 64 (☎01 43 95 06 13; open Tu 11am-7pm, W-Sa 10am-7pm; MC/V); and **Stock Patrick Gerard,** no. 113 (☎01 40 44 07 40). A large **Stock Kookaï** bustles at 82 rue Réamur, 2*ème* (☎01 45 08 93 69; open M 11:30am-7:30pm, Tu-Sa 10:30am-7pm); **Apara Stock** sits at 16 rue Etienne Marcel (☎01 40 26 70 04); **Haut-de-Gomme Stock,** selling lines like Armani, Khanh, and Dolce & Gabbana, is at 9 rue Scribe, 9*ème* (☎01 40 07 10 20; M: Opéra; open M-Sa 10am-7pm) and 190 rue de Rivoli, 1*er* (☎01 42 96 97 47; M: Louvre-Rivoli; open daily 11am-7pm).

BOOKS

Paris overflows with high-quality bookstores. The 5*ème* and 6*ème* are particularly bookish: interesting shops line every large street in the Latin Quarter, not to mention the endless stalls *(bouquinistes)* along the quais of the Seine. Some specialty bookshops serve as community centers, too. English bookshops like **Shakespeare & Co.** (below) and **The Village Voice,** 6 rue Princesse, 6*ème*, have bulletin boards for posting events and housing notices. (Village Voice ☎01 46 33 36 47. M: Mabillon. Open M 2-8pm, Tu-Sa 10am-8pm, Su 2-7pm; Aug. closed Su.) **Les Mots à la Bouche,** 6 rue Ste-Croix de la Bretonnerie, 4*ème*, carries literature, essays, and art relating to homosexuality, and has info for gays and lesbians. (☎01 42 78 88 30; www.motsbouche.com. M: Hôtel-de-Ville. Open M-Sa 11am-11pm and Su 2-8pm.) **L'Harmattan,** 21b rue des Ecoles, 5*ème*, can direct you to Caribbean, Maghrébin, and West African resources. (☎01 46 34 13 71. M: Cluny la Sorbonne. Open M-Sa 10am-12:30pm and 1:30-7pm. MC/V.)

The large, English-language **W.H. Smith,** 248 rue de Rivoli, 1*er*, has many scholarly works and magazines. Sunday *New York Times* available Monday after 2pm. (☎01 44 77 88 99. M: Concorde. Open M-Sa 9am-7:30pm, Su 1-7:30pm. AmEx/MC/V.) **Brentano's,** 37 av.

de l'Opéra, 2ème, is an American and French bookstore with an extensive selection of English literature. (☎01 42 61 52 50. M: Opéra. Open M-Sa 10am-7:30pm. AmEx/MC/V.) **Shakespeare & Co.**, 37 rue de la Bûcherie, 5ème, across the Seine from Notre-Dame, is run by *bon vivant* George Whitman. Walt's grandson sells a quirky and wide selection of new and used books, including bargains (€2.50) in bins outside the shop. (M: St-Michel. Open daily noon-midnight.)

MARCHÉ AUX PUCES DE ST-OUEN

Located in St-Ouen, a town just north of the 18ème. M: Porte-de-Clignancourt. Open Sa-M 7am-7:30pm; most vendors only open M 9am-6pm; many of the official stalls close early, but renegade vendors may open at 5am and close at 9pm.

This is the granddaddy of all flea markets. The Puces de St-Ouen began in the Middle Ages, when merchants resold the cast-off clothing of aristocrats (crawling with its namesake insects) to peasant-folk. Today it's an overwhelming smorgasbord of stuff. It opens early and shuts down late, and serious hunters should allow themselves the better part of a day in order to cover significant ground, although the market tends to be least crowded before noon.

RENEGADE MARKET. The 10min. walk along av. de la Porte de Clignancourt, under the highway, and left on rue Jean Henri Fabre, is jammed with tiny unofficial stalls. Vendors sell flimsy clothes, T-shirts, African masks, and teenage jewelry. It's a tourist trap and pickpockets know it, so be vigilant.

■ OFFICIAL MARKET. If the renegade bazaar turns you off, continue down rue Fabre to the official market, on rue des Rosiers and rue Jules Vallès. Here you can browse leisurely in a much less crowded setting. The whole enterprise is officially divided into a number of sub-markets, each specializing in a certain type of item, but they generally all have the same eclectic and engaging collection of unusual antiques (see sidebar, **The Insider's City**).

NEAR PARIS

VERSAILLES

By sheer force of ego, the Sun King converted a simple hunting lodge into the world's most famous palace. The sprawling château and bombastic gardens stand as a testament to the despotic playboy-king, Louis XIV, who lived, entertained, and governed here on the grandest of scales. A century later, young King Louis XVI and his bride Marie-Antoinette would discover that the dream of ridiculous luxury at the expense of near-universal poverty could not last forever.

A child during the aristocratic insurgency called the Fronde, Louis XIV is said to have entered his father's bedchamber one night only to find (and frighten away) an assassin. Fearing conspiracy, upon his coronation, Louis chose to move the center of royal power out of Paris and away from potential aristocratic insubordination. In 1661, the Sun King renovated his small hunting lodge in Versailles. Naturally, the nobility followed him there, but on Louis's terms.

No one knows just how much it cost to build Versailles; Louis XIV burned the accounts to keep the price a mystery. At the same time, life there was less luxurious than one might imagine: courtiers wore rented swords and urinated behind statues in the parlors; wine froze in the drafty dining rooms; dressmakers invented the color *puce* (literally, "flea") to camouflage the insects crawling on the noblewomen.

Louis XIV died in 1715 and was succeeded by his great-grandson Louis XV in 1722. His most memorable act was to commission the Opéra, in the North Wing, for the marriage of Marie-Antoinette and the future Louis XVI. The newlyweds inherited the throne and Versailles when Louis XV died of smallpox in 1774. The Dauphin and Marie-Antoinette changed little of the exterior, but redecorated inside to make an imaginary playland for Marie, called the Hamlet. On October 5, 1789, 15,000 Parisian fishwives and National Guardsmen marched out to the palace and hauled the royal family back to Paris, where they were guillotined in 1793.

In the 19th century, King Louis-Philippe established a museum to preserve the château, against the wishes of many French, who wanted Versailles demolished like the Bastille. In 1871, the château took the limelight again, when Wilhelm of Prussia became Kaiser Wilhelm I of Germany in the Hall of Mirrors. That same year, as headquarters of the Thiers regime, Versailles sent an army against the Parisian Commune. The *Versaillais* pierced the city walls and crushed the *communards*. On June 28, 1919 at the end of WWI, France forced Germany to sign the ruinous Treaty of Versailles in the Hall of Mirrors.

⓰ PRACTICAL INFORMATION

Tours: ☎01 30 83 76 79; www.chateauversailles.com. Open Tu-Su May-Sept. 9am-6:30pm; Oct.-Apr. 9am-5:30pm. Last admission 30min. before closing. Admission to palace and **self-guided tour, entrance A:** €7.50, over 60 and after 3:30pm €5.30, under 18 free. Supplement for **audio tour, entrance C:** 1hr.; €4, under 7 free. Supplement for **guided tour, entrance D:** 1hr. tour of Chambres du Roi €4, under 18 €2.70; 1½hr. tour of the apartments of Louis XV and the opéra €6, ages 7-17 €4.20. **Full-day tour** "A Day at Versailles" (two 1½hr. segments, in the morning and afternoon) €17.84. Sign-language tours available; make reservations with the Bureau d'Action Culturelle (☎01 30 83 77 88).

Trains: The **RER** runs from M: Invalides or any stop on RER Line C5 to the Versailles Rive Gauche station (30-40min., every 15min.; round-trip €4.90). From the Invalides or other RER Line C stop, take trains with labels beginning with "V." From the RER Versailles train station, turn right down av. de Général de Gaulle, walk 200m, and turn left at the first big intersection on av. de Paris; the entrance is ahead.

Tourist Office: Office de Tourisme de Versailles, 2bis av. de Paris (☎01 39 24 88 88; fax 01 39 24 88 89; tourisme@ot-versailles.fr; www.versailles-tourisme.fr). From the RER Versailles train station, follow directions to the château; the office will be on your left on av. de Paris before you reach the château.

ⓞ SIGHTS

Arrive early in the morning to avoid the crowds, which are worse on Sundays from May to September, and in late June. Pick up a map at one of the entrances or the info desk in the center of the courtyard. Figuring out how to get into the château is the hardest part; there are half a dozen entrances, many of which offer different sights. Most visitors enter at **Entrance A,** on the right-hand side in the north wing, or **Entrance C,** in the archway to the left (either ticket allows free entrance to the other; native speakers of Russian, Chinese, Japanese, Spanish, or Italian start at C). **Entrance B** is for groups; **Entrance D** is where tours with a living, breathing guide begin, and **Entrance H** is for those in wheelchairs. **General admission** allows entrance to the following rooms: the *grands appartements;* the War and Peace Drawing Rooms; the *Galerie des Glaces* (Hall of Mirrors); and Marie-Antoinette's public apartment. Head for Entrance C to purchase an **audioguide.** From Entrance D, at the left-hand corner as you approach the palace, you can choose between four excellent **tours** of different parts of the château (the best is the 1½hr. tour of the Louis XV apartments and opéra). Arrive before 11am to avoid long tour lines.

SELF-GUIDED TOUR. Begin at **Entrance A.** Start in the **Musée de l'Histoire de France,** created in 1837 by Louis-Philippe. Along its walls are portraits of those who shaped the course of French history. The 21 rooms (arranged in chronological order) seek to construct a historical context for the château.

Up the staircase to the right is the dual-level **royal chapel,** designed by architect Hardouin-Mansart. Back toward the staircase and to the left is a series of gilded **drawing rooms** in the **State Apartments** that are dedicated to Hercules, Mars, and the ever-present Apollo (the Sun King identified with the sun god). The ornate **Salon d'Apollo** was Louis XIV's throne room. Framed by the **War and Peace Drawing Rooms** is the **Hall of Mirrors,** which was originally a terrace until Mansart added a series of mirrored panels and windows to double the light in the room and reflect the gardens outside. In their time, these mirrors were at the boundaries of 17th-century technology. Le Brun's ceiling paintings (1679-1686) tell the story of Louis XIV, culminating with *The King Governs Alone.*

The **Queen's Bedchamber,** where royal births were public events, is now furnished as it was on October 6, 1789, when Marie-Antoinette left the palace for the last time. A version of the David painting of Napoleon's self-coronation dominates the **Salle du Sacré** (also known as the Coronation Room). The **Hall of Battles** installed by Louis-Philippe is a monument to 14 centuries of the French military.

THE GARDENS

*Open daily sunrise-sundown. €3, ages under 18 and after 6pm free. **Fountains** turned on for special displays (like the **Grandes Eaux Musicales** (Apr.-Oct. Sa-Su 11am-noon and 3:30-5:30pm; €5.50). **Discovering Groves Tour,** call ☎ 01 30 83 77 88; 1½hr.; €5. The most convenient place for **bike rentals** is across from the base of the canal; 2 other locations: one to the north of the Parterre Nord by the Grille de la Reine, and another by the Trianons at Porte St-Antoine (☎ 01 39 66 97 66). Open Feb.-Nov Sa-Su 10am-closing and M-F 1pm-closing. €5 per hr. Rent **boats** for 4 at the boathouse to the right side of the base of the canal (☎ 01 39 66 97 66). Open Tu-F noon-5:30pm, Sa-Su 11am-6pm. €11 per hr., €8 per 30min.; €7.63 deposit. **Horse-drawn carriages** run Tu-Su, departing from just right of the main terrace (☎ 01 30 97 04 40).*

Numerous artists—Le Brun, Mansart, Coysevox—executed statues and fountains, but master gardener André Le Nôtre provided the overall plan for Versailles's gardens. Louis XIV wrote the first guide to the gardens himself, entitled the *Manner of Presenting the Gardens at Versailles.* Tours should begin, as the Sun King commanded, on the terrace.

To the left of the terrace, the **Parterre Sud** graces the area in front of Mansart's **Orangerie,** once home to 2000 orange trees. In the center of the terrace lies the **Parterre d'Eau;** the **Bassin de Latone** fountain below features Latona, mother of Diana and Apollo, shielding her children as Jupiter turns villains into frogs. Past the fountain is one of the garden's gems: the flower-lined sanctuary of the **Jardin du Roi,** accessible only from the easternmost side facing the **Bassin du Miroir.** Near the south gate of the grove is the magnificent **Bassin de Bacchus,** one of four seasonal fountains depicting the god of wine. Working your way north toward the center of the garden, you can see where the king used to take light meals amid the exquisite **Bosquet de la Colonnade**'s 32 violet-and-blue marble columns, sculptures, and basins, just east of the Jardin du Roi. The north gate to the Colonnade exits onto the 330m-long **Tapis Vert** (Green Carpet), the central mall linking the château to the garden's conspicuously central fountain, the **Bassin d'Apollon,** whose charioted Apollo rises, youthful and god-like, out of the water to enlighten the world.

On the north side of the garden is Marsy's incredible **Bosquet de l'Encelade.** When the fountains are turned on, a 25m high jet bursts from Titan's enormous mouth, which is plated with shimmering gold and half buried under a pile of rocks. Flora reclines on a bed of flowers in the **Bassin de Flore,** while a gilded Ceres luxuriates in sheaves of wheat in the **Bassin de Cérès.** The **Parterre Nord,** full of flowers, lawns, and trees, overlooks some of the garden's most spectacular fountains. The **Allée d'Eau,** a fountain-lined walkway, provides the best view of the **Bassin des Nymphes de Diane.** The path slopes toward the sculpted **Bassin du Dragon,** where a dying beast slain by Apollo spurts water 27m high into the air. Ninety-nine jets of water attached to urns and seahorns surround Neptune in the **Bassin de Neptune,** the gardens's largest fountain. Beyond the classical gardens stretch wilder woods, meadows, and farmland perfect for a picnic away from the manicured perfection of Versailles. Stroll along the **Grand Canal,** a rectangular pond beyond the Bassin d'Apollon measuring 1535m long.

THE TRIANONS AND MARIE-ANTOINETTE'S HAMLET

Shuttle trams from the palace to the Trianons and the Hameau leave from behind the palace facing the canals. Round-trip €5, ages 3-12 €3. The walk takes 25min. Both Trianons open Nov.-Mar. Tu-Sa noon-5:30pm; Apr.-Oct. noon-6pm; last entrance 30min. before closing. Admission to the Trianons €5, under 18 free.

The Trianons and Hameau provide a racier counterpoint to the château: here kings trysted with lovers, and Marie-Antoinette lived like the peasant she wasn't.

PETIT TRIANON. On the right down the wooded path from the château is the **Petit Trianon,** built between 1762 and 1768 for Louis XV and his mistress Madame de Pompadour. Marie Antoinette took control of the Petit Trianon in 1774, and it soon earned the nickname "Little Vienna." In 1867, the Empress Eugénie, who worshipped Marie Antoinette, turned it into a museum.

Exit the Petit Trianon, turn left, and follow the marked path to the libidinous **Temple of Love,** a domed rotunda with 12 white marble columns and swans. Marie Antoinette held many intimate nighttime parties in the small space, during which thousands of torches would be illuminated in the surrounding ditch. The Queen was perhaps at her happiest and most ludicrous when at the **Hameau,** her own pseudo-peasant "hamlet" down the path from the Temple of Love. Inspired by Rousseau's theories on the goodness of nature and the hameau at **Chantilly,** the queen aspired fashionably for a more simple life. She commissioned Richard Mique to build a compound of 12 buildings (including a mill, dairy, and gardener's house, all surrounding a quaint artificial lake) in which she could play at country life, though the result is something of a cross between English Romanticism and Euro-Disney. At the center is the **Queen's Cottage;** any illusions of country-style slumming disappear after crossing the doors. The rooms contained ornate furniture, marble fireplaces, and walk-in closets for linens, silverware, and footmen.

GRAND TRIANON. The single-story, stone-and-pink-marble Grand Trianon was intended as a château-away-from-château for Louis XIV. Here the king could be reached only by boat along the **Grand Canal.** The palace consists of two wings joined together by a central porch. **Formal gardens** are located behind the colonnaded porch. The mini-château was stripped of its furniture during the Revolution but was later restored and inhabited by Napoleon and his second wife.

CHARTRES

Were it not for a piece of fabric, the cathedral of Chartres and the town that surrounds it might be only a sleepy hamlet. Because of this sacred relic—the cloth that the Virgin Mary supposedly wore when she gave birth to Jesus—Chartres became a major medieval pilgrimage center. The spectacular cathedral that towers above the surrounding rooftops is not the only reason to take the train ride here: the *vieille ville* (old town) is also a masterpiece of medieval architecture.

🔒 PRACTICAL INFORMATION

Trains: Frequent trains run to Chartres from **Gare Montparnasse, Grandes Lignes.** (☎08 36 35 35 35; June-Aug. 1 per hr. 7am-10pm.; call ahead for winter schedule; 50-75 min.; round-trip €22.70, under 26 and groups of 2-4 €17.20, over 60 €11.50.) To reach the cathedral from the station, walk straight along rue Jehan de Beauce to pl. de Châtelet, then right onto rue Ste-Même, and left onto rue Jean Moulin.

Tourist Office: (☎02 37 18 26 26; fax 02 37 21 51 91; chartres.tourism@wanadoo.fr). On pl. de la Cathédrale, in front of the cathedral's main entrance. Reservations service (€9.15 surcharge, €7.63 of which goes toward your hotel bill). Helpful free map guide with a walking tour and a list of restaurants, hotels and sights. (Open Apr.-Sept. M-Sa 9am-7pm, Su and holidays 9:30am-5:30pm; Oct.-Mar. M-Sa 10am-6pm, Su and holidays 10am-1pm and 2:30-4:30pm.) *Le petit train Chart'train* runs 35min. narrated tours (in French) of the old city. (☎02 37 21 87 60. Tours Apr.-Oct.; leave from in front of the tourist office; check board outside for daily departure times. €5, under 12 €3.)

👁 SIGHTS

☎02 37 21 75 02. **Open** *Easter through Oct. daily 8am-8pm, Nov. through Easter daily 8:30am-7pm. No casual visits during mass.* **Masses** *M-F 11:45am and 6:15pm; Sa 11:45am and 6pm; Su 9:15 (Latin), 11am, and 6pm (in the crypt).* **North Tower** *open May-Aug. M-Sa 9am-6pm, Su 1-6:30pm; Sept.-Oct. and Mar.-Apr. M-Sa 9:30-11:30am and 2-6:30pm, Su 2-5pm; Nov.-Feb. M-Sa 10-11:30am and 2-4pm, Su 2-4pm.* **Tower admission** *€3.96, ages 18-25 €2.44, under 18 and some Sundays free. English audioguides available at the gift shop (€3-5, depending on tour) and require a piece identification as a deposit.* **English tours** *of the cathedral by Malcolm Miller; call ☎02 37 28 15 58 for tour availability during winter months. €8, students €5.* **French tours of the crypt** ☎*02 37 21 56 33. 30min. tours Apr.-Oct. M-Sa 11am, 2:15, 3:30, 4:30pm; Nov.-Mar. 11am and 4:15pm; June 22-Sept. 21 additional 5:15pm tour; Su 11am no tours. €2.30, students €1.60, under 7 free.*

The Cathédrale de Chartres is the best-preserved medieval church in Europe, escaping major damage during the Revolution and WWII. A patchwork masterpiece of Romanesque and Gothic design, the cathedral was constructed by generations of unknown masons, architects, and artisans who labored for centuries.

SANCTA CAMISIA. The year after he became emperor in AD 875, Charlemagne's grandson, Charles the Bald, donated to Chartres the Sancta Camisia, the cloth believed to have been worn by the Virgin Mary when she gave birth to Christ. Unfortunately, it cannot be seen until the Treasury reopens. A church already existed on the site, but the emperor's bequest required a new cathedral to accommodate the growing number of pilgrims. The sick were nursed in the crypt below the sanctuary. In 911, the powers of the relic supposedly saved the city; just as he started to besiege Chartres, the Viking leader Rollon converted to Christianity.

STAINED GLASS. At a time when most people were illiterate, the cathedral served as an educational beacon. Most of the stained glass dates from the 13th century and was preserved through World War I and II by heroic town authorities, who dismantled and stored the windows in the Dordogne. The famous Blue Virgin, Tree of Jesse, and Passion and Resurrection of Christ windows are among the surviving 13th-century stained glass. Bring binoculars.

LABYRINTH. A winding labyrinth is carved into the floor in the rear of the nave. Designed in the 13th century, the labyrinth was laid out for pilgrims as a substitute for a journey to the Holy Land. By following this symbolic journey on their hands and knees, the devout would act out a voyage to heavenly Jerusalem.

TOUR JEHAN-DE-BEAUCE. The adventurous can climb the cathedral's north tower for a stellar view of the cathedral roof, the flying buttresses, and the city below. The tower, a wonderful example of flamboyant Gothic style, provides a striking counterpart to its more sedate partner, the Romanesque **octagonal steeple** (the tallest in its style still standing), built just before the 1194 fire.

CRYPT. Parts of Chartres's crypt, such as a well down which Vikings tossed the bodies of their victims, date back to the 9th century. You can enter the 110m long subterranean crypt only as part of a tour that leaves from La Crypte, the store opposite the cathedral's south entrance. *(Tour in French. English info sheets available.)*

ELSEWHERE IN THE CATHEDRAL. Inside the church, the Renaissance choir screen, begun by Jehan de Beauce in 1514, depicts the Virgin Mary's life. The lovely, candlelit shrine to *Notre Dame de Pilier* is near the Santa Camista. Both are worth a visit. The only English-language **tours** of the cathedral are given by veteran tour-guide **Malcolm Miller,** an authority on Gothic architecture. His presentations on the cathedral's history and symbolism are intelligent, witty, and enjoyable for all ages. If you can, take both his morning and afternoon tour—no two are alike.

GIVERNY

Drawn to the verdant hills, haystacks, and lily pads on the Epte river, painter Claude Monet and his eight children settled in Giverny in 1883. By 1887, John Singer Sargent, Paul Cézanne, and Mary Cassatt had placed their easels beside Monet's and turned the village into an artists's colony. Today, the town remains much as it did back then (the cobblestone street that was the setting for Monet's *Wedding March* is instantly recognizable), save for the tourists, who come in droves.

🔋 PRACTICAL INFORMATION

Trains: The **SNCF** runs trains sporadically from Paris **Gare St-Lazare** to **Vernon,** the nearest station to Giverny. Take the métro (M: St-Lazare), and take the rue d'Amsterdam exit, then walk straight into the right-hand entrance of the Gare. From there, go to the Grandes Lignes reservation room. €21 round-trip, couples €31.60. Take the bus (☎02 32 71 06 39) from Vernon to Giverny (10min.; Tu-Su 4 per day 15min. after the train arrives in Vernon; return only 3 per day, schedule for return inside the info office in the train station; €2, round-trip €4). Coordinate train and bus schedules before your trip to avoid 3hr. delays.

👁 SIGHTS

FONDATION CLAUDE MONET. Today, Monet's serenely beautiful house and gardens are maintained by the Fondation Claude Monet. From April to July, the gardens overflow with wild roses, hollyhocks, poppies, and the scent of honeysuckle. The water lilies, the Japanese bridge, and the weeping willows of the Orientalist Water Gardens look like—well, like *Monets*. The only way to avoid the rush is to go early in the morning and, if possible, early in the season. In Monet's thatched-roof home, big windows, solid furniture, and pale blue walls complement his collection of 18th- and 19th-century Japanese prints. *(84 rue Claude Monet. ☎02 32 51 28 21. Open Apr.-Oct. Tu-Su 10am-6pm. €5.50, students and ages 12-18 €4, ages 7-12 €3. Gardens €4.)*

MUSÉE D'ART AMÉRICAIN. Near the foundation, the incongruously modern but respectfully hidden Musée d'Art Américain houses a small number of works by American expatriates, such as Theodore Butler and John Leslie Breck, who came to Giverny to learn the Impressionist style. *(99 rue Claude Monet. ☎02 32 51 94 65. Open Apr.-Oct. Tu-Su 10am-6pm. €5.34; students, seniors, teachers €3.05; under 12 €2.29.)*

DISNEYLAND PARIS

It's a small, small world and Disney is hell-bent on making it even smaller. When Euro-Disney opened on April 12, 1992, Mickey Mouse, Cinderella, and Snow White were met by the jeers of French intellectuals and the popular press, who called the Disney theme park a "cultural Chernobyl." Resistance seems to have subsided since Walt & Co. renamed it Disneyland Paris and started serving wine. Despite its dimensions, this Disney park is the most technologically advanced yet, and the special effects on some rides are incredible.

🛂 PRACTICAL INFORMATION

Everything in Disneyland Paris is in English and French. The detailed *Park Guide Book* (free at Disney City Hall to the left of the entrance) has a map and information on everything from restaurants and attractions to bathrooms and first aid. The *Guests Special Services Guide* has info on wheelchair accessibility. For more info on Disneyland Paris, call ☎ 01 60 30 60 81 (from the US) or 01 60 30 63 53 from all other countries, or visit their web site at www.disneylandparis.com.

Trains: Take **RER A4** from either M: Gare de Lyon or Châtelet-Les Halles (dir: Marne-la-Vallée) to the terminus (M: Marne-la-Vallée-Chessy). Before boarding the train, check on the boards hanging above the platform to if there's a light next to the Marne-la-Vallée stop; otherwise the train doesn't stop there (45min., every 30min., round-trip €11). The last train to Paris leaves Disney at 12:22am, but the métro closes at midnight, so catch an earlier train. **TGV** service from de Gaulle Airport reaches the park in a mere 15min., a good option for travelers with Eurail passes. **Eurostar** trains now run directly between Waterloo Station in London and Disneyland. (☎ 08 36 35 35 39. Departs 9:15am, return 7:30pm. Prices from €135-375. Reserve far in advance.)

Car: Take the A4 highway from Paris to Exit 14, marked "Parc Disneyland Paris," about 30min. from the city. Parking €8 per day; 11,000 spaces in all.

Bus: Buses make the rounds between the terminals of **Orly** and **de Gaulle airports** and the bus station near the **Marne-la-Vallée RER.** (40min.; every 45-60min. 8:30am-7:30pm, F and Su 8:30am-9:30pm at CDG; round-trip €14, ages 3-11 €11.50.)

Tickets: Instead of selling tickets, Disneyland Paris issues **passeports,** valid for 1 day and available at the ground floor of the Disneyland Hotel. *Passeports* are also sold at the Paris tourist office on the Champs-Elysées (see p. 109), FNAC, Virgin Megastores, the Galeries Lafayette, or at any of the major stations on RER line A (Châtelet-Les Halles, Gare de Lyon, Charles de Gaulle-Etoile). Early Apr. to early Jan. passeports €38, ages 3-11 €29; early Jan. to early Apr. €29/€25; 2- and 3-day *passeports* available.

Hours: Apr.-Sept. 9am-11pm; Oct.-Apr. M-F 10am-9pm, Sa-Su 10am-10pm. Hours subject to change, especially during winter; call ahead for details.

NORMANDY (NORMANDIE)

In AD 911, Rollo, the leader of a band of Vikings who had settled around Rouen, accepted the title of Duke of Normandy from King Louis the Simple. After being baptized, Rollo assumed the name of Robert and over the next few centuries, Norman power grew beyond even Robert's wildest dreams. The most famous Norman achievement was the successful 1066 invasion of England, celebrated in a magnificent tapestry that still hangs in Bayeux. The tables later turned, however, and Normandy was occupied in 1346 by English King Edward III. By 1450, Normandy was reincorporated into France. The English did not attempt another invasion until June 6, 1944, when they returned with American and Canadian allies to wrest Normandy from German occupation.

In the intervening centuries, Normandy exchanged its warlike reputation for a quiet agricultural role. Far removed from the border wars which raged between France and its neighbors, Normandy's towns and villages remained virtually unchanged from the Middle Ages—an architectural heritage mostly destroyed during the heavy fighting following the D-Day landings. Gustave Flaubert, Normandy's most famous author, set his tale of provincial malcontent, *Madame Bovary*, in his homeland. Later in the 19th century, a landscape painter from Honfleur, Eugène Boudin, persuaded a young Claude Monet to take up serious painting. Monet and his friends became regular visitors to the stormy coast and calm Seine estuary in the 1860s.

ROUEN

However Gustave Flaubert criticized his hometown through the eyes of his famous malcontent housewife in *Madame Bovary*, Rouen (pop. 108,000) is no petty provincial hamlet. From the 10th to 12th centuries, this Norman capital

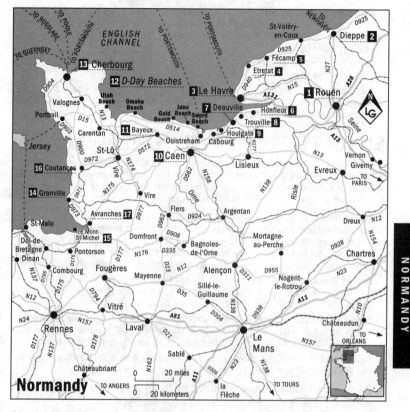

Normandy

bloomed with Gothic architecture and half-timbered houses. Fifteenth-century Rouen witnessed the trial of Joan of Arc, who burned at the stake in 1431 after her life sentence was generously commuted by Burgundian clerics. The pathos of Joan's story and the Gothic splendor of Rouen's churches have provided constant inspiration for artists and writers; in the 19th century, Victor Hugo dubbed it the "city of a hundred spires," and Monet's fascination with the play of the light on the cathedral's facade has made it a fixture in museums around the world. If post-World War II reconstruction didn't exactly beautify Rouen, it hasn't marred the architectural and historical appeal at its heart. A hip, young population has inherited the *vieille ville;* Madame B. would be jealous.

⌐ TRANSPORTATION

Trains: rue Jeanne d'Arc, on pl. Bernard Tissot. Info office open M-Sa 7:45am-7pm. To: **Caen** (2hr., 7 per day, €18.20); **Dieppe** (1hr., 13 per day, €8.70); **Le Havre** (1hr., 15 per day, €11.40); **Lille** (3hr., 5 per day, €25.30); **Paris** (1½hr., every hr., €16.50).

Buses: SATAR and CNA, both at rue Jeanne d'Arc, in front of the Théâtre des Arts (☎08 25 07 60 27). Info office open M-F 8am-6:30pm. Most buses depart from quai du Havre or quai de la Bourse. To **Le Havre** (2½hr., 8 per day, €12.35), as well as various small towns in the **Seine Valley.**

Public Transportation: Métrobus, office with SATAR and CNA (☎02 35 52 52 52). Info office open M-Sa 7am-7pm. Most buses run 6am-8pm, some night lines until midnight. Subway runs 5am-11pm. For both, 1hr. ticket €1.20, *carnet* of 10 €10. Day pass €3.50, 2-day €5.

Taxis: 67 rue Jean Lecanuet (☎02 35 88 50 50). Stands at the train and bus stations, as well as the Palais de Justice on rue Jeanne d'Arc. 24hr.

Bike Rental: Rouen Cycles, 45 rue St-Eloi (☎02 35 71 34 30), a few streets behind the Métrobus station. €18.30 per day. Deposit of the bike's value required. Open Tu-Sa 9am-noon and 2-7pm. AmEx/MC/V.

■✚ 🛈 ORIENTATION AND PRACTICAL INFORMATION

To get to the city center from the station, exit straight out and follow **rue Jeanne d'Arc** several blocks. A left onto the cobblestoned rue du Gros Horloge leads to **place de la Cathédrale** and the tourist office; a right leads to **place du Vieux-Marché.** Continuing almost to the Seine, the Gare Routière is on the right.

Tourist Office: 25 pl. de la Cathédrale (☎02 32 08 32 40; fax 02 32 08 32 44). Free map (available in a variety of languages). Commission-free **currency exchange.** For info regarding excursions from Rouen, ask for the brochure *Day Trips around Rouen;* for a hip look at student favorites, pick up the student guide *Le Viking.* Open May-Sept. M-Sa 9am-7pm, Su 9:30am-12:30pm and 2-6pm; Oct.-Mar. M-Sa 9am-6pm, Su 10am-1pm.

English Bookstore: ABC Bookshop, 11 rue des Faulx, behind Eglise St-Ouen (☎02 35 71 08 67). Windows display ads for au pairs and tutors for hire. Open Tu-Sa 10am-6pm, July Tu-Sa 10am-3pm. Usually closed late July to mid-Aug.

Work Opportunities: Centre Rouen Information Jeunesse (CRIJ), 84 rue Beauvoisine (☎02 32 10 49 49), helps find work—mainly for "animateurs" (guides/hosts) but also at hotels—and has info on activities. Free Internet access. Open M-F 10am-6pm.

Laundromat: 87 rue Beauvoisine. Open daily 8am-8pm. Also at rue Cauchoise near pl. du Vieux Marché. Open daily 7am-9pm.

Police: 9 rue Brisout de Barneville (☎02 32 81 25 00), off rue Barbey d'Aureyville.

Hospital: 1 rue de Germont (☎02 32 88 89 90), near pl. St-Vivien.

24hr. Pharmacy: Grande Pharmacie du Centre, pl. de la Cathédrale (☎02 32 08 04 30 or 02 32 88 89 95 for info), beside tourist office. A number of pharmacies in Rouen provide service on nights (8pm-9am) and holidays. Call for more info.

Internet Access: Free at **Centre Rouen Information Jeunesse (CRIJ). Place Net,** 37 rue de la République (☎02 32 76 02 22), near the Eglise St-Maclou. €4 per hr. Open M-Sa 11am-midnight, Su 2-10pm. Also **le Cœur Net,** 54 rue Cauchoise (☎02 35 15 45 42), near pl. du Vieux Marché. €4 per hr. Open M-Sa 10am-midnight, Su 2-8pm.

Post Office: 45bis rue Jeanne d'Arc (☎02 35 15 66 73). **Currency exchange.** Open M-F 8am-7pm, Sa 8:30am-1:30pm. **Branch** at 122 rue Jeanne d'Arc, just left from the train station. Open M-F 8:30am-6:30pm, Sa 9am-noon. **Postal code:** 76000.

🏠 ACCOMMODATIONS AND CAMPING

Cheap lodgings lie on the side streets between the train station and the Hôtel de Ville; unfortunately, Rouen no longer has a hostel.

Hôtel Normandya, 32 rue du Cordier (☎02 35 71 46 15), near the train station, off rue du Donjon. Owned by an exuberantly friendly, *Let's Go*-loving couple. Nicely decorated with excellent views of the city; a few dark, windowless rooms. Reception 8am-8pm. Singles and doubles €19-23. No credit cards. ❷

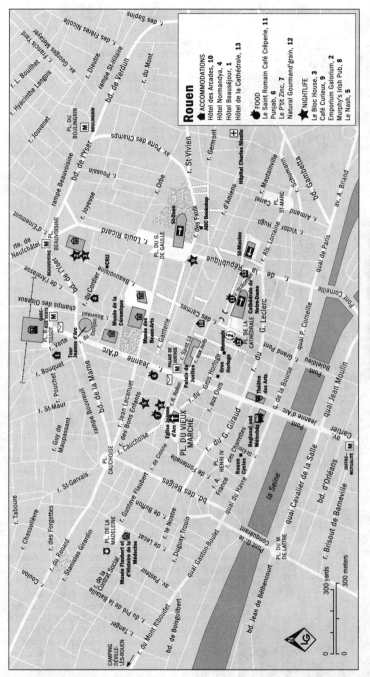

Rouen

ACCOMMODATIONS
Hôtel des Arcades, **10**
Hôtel Normandya, **4**
Hôtel Beauséjour, **1**
Hôtel de la Cathédrale, **13**

FOOD
Le Saint Romain Café Créperie, **11**
Punjab, **6**
Le P'tit Zinc, **7**
Natural Gourmand'grain, **12**

NIGHTLIFE
Le Bloc House, **3**
Café Curieux, **9**
Emporium Galorium, **2**
Murphy's Irish Pub, **8**
Le Nash, **5**

**IN
RECENT
NEWS**

IFS, ANDS, AND BUTTS

Over ten years ago, France adopted the **Evin** law, intended to jump-start a movement toward a tobacco-free society. Under the law, smoking is prohibited in public areas. Tobacco companies are forbidden to advertise their products and are required to place labels on boxes warning of the hazards of tar, nicotine, and other cigarette components. At the time, anti-smoking associations cheered; now they despair over the lack of real change that has been effected in the past decade. Smokers are out in force not only in bars and cafés, but in schools and hospitals as well. Half the compartments on trains are still commonly given to those who wish to smoke. Furthermore, follow-up measures to the law, such as stiffer penalties, have not come to fruition.

However, since the Evin Law came into effect in 1992, there have been some positive changes. Some experts point to the general recognition of tobacco as a drug; others to increased awareness of the health problems associated with tobacco use. The anti-smoking campaign is still active in its attempt to diminish the use of tobacco products in France. May 31 is known as Tobacco Free Day (*la Journée Nationale sans Tabac*), a day of parades and demonstrations in cities like Rouen. Continued anti-smoking activism may eventually lead to a decline in tobacco use in public places. For now, however, both national and regional initiatives have yet to get to the heart—or the butt—of the problem.

Hôtel Beauséjour, 9 rue Pouchet (☎02 35 71 93 47; fax 02 35 98 01 24; www.lerapporteur.fr/beausejour), very near the train station off pl. B. Tissot. 2-star hotel at extremely reasonable prices. Cheery rooms with comfortable beds overlook the small street or the charming garden courtyard; access to hotel bar and sitting room. Breakfast €4.50. Reception 6am-11pm. Singles €23, with shower €26, with bath €31; doubles with shower €34, with bath €39. MC/V. ❷

Hôtel des Arcades, 52 rue de Carmes (☎02 35 70 10 30; fax 02 35 70 08 91). Bright, clean, color-coordinated rooms in a central location, with an extremely helpful proprietor. Breakfast €5.50. Reception M-F 7am-8pm, Sa-Su 7:30am-8pm. Singles and doubles €25, with toilet €30, with shower €34-40. AmEx/MC/V. ❷

Hôtel de la Cathédrale, 12 rue St-Romain (☎02 35 71 57 95; fax 02 35 70 15 54; www.hotel-de-la-cathedrale.fr), off pl. de la République, behind Cathédrale de Notre Dame and in front of Eglise St-Maclou. Attractive, spacious rooms, some with extra features like chandeliers. Features a bar, an elevator, Internet access, parking services, and tea room (open 11am-8pm). Buffet breakfast €7.50. Singles with shower €45, with bath €53; doubles €53/€61. MC/V. ❹

Camping Municipal de Déville, rue Jules Ferry in Déville-les-Rouen (☎02 35 74 07 59), 4km from Rouen. Take the *métro* from the train station (dir: Technopole or Georges Braque) to "Théâtre des Arts," transfer to Métrobus line TEOR (T2; dir: Mairie), and get off at "Mairie de Deville-les-Rouen." Continue down the street one block and turn left on Rue Jules Ferry; campground is on the right. A few shady grass patches with a gravel parking lot for caravans. Showers free. Open June-Sept. for tents; year-round for caravans. Reception open M-F 9-11am and 4:30-6:30pm; Sa-Su 9:30-11am and 3-5pm. Gates close at 10pm. €3.90 per person, €1.50 per tent, €1.40 per car, €2.75 per caravan. Electricity €1.95. Daily tax €0.15 per person. ❶

▌ FOOD

Outdoor cafés and *brasseries* crowd around **pl. du Vieux-Marché.** A **market** is held on the *place* itself. (Tu-Su 6am-1:30pm) There are also plenty of eateries near the **Gros Horloge** and the **Cathédrale de Notre Dame.** A **Monoprix supermarket** is at 73-83 rue du Gros Horloge (open M-Sa 8:30am-9pm), and a **Marché U** on pl. du Vieux-Marché (open M-Sa 8:30am-8pm). Just a few feet from the Cathédrale de Notre-Dame, the tiny welcoming **Saint Romain Café Crêperie ❶**, 52 rue St-Romain, offers sweet crepes and savory buckwheat galettes that will satisfy both your hunger and your wallet. (☎02 35 88 90 36. Lunch €3-4. Dinner with salad €7.

Open Tu-Sa noon-2pm, Th-Sa 7pm-10pm. MC/V.) Vegetarianism and other organic obsessions are indulged at the cheerful **Natural Gourmand'grain ❷**, 3 rue du Petit Salut, off pl. de la Cathédrale beside tourist office. (☎02 35 98 15 74. *Plat* and salad €7.95. Restaurant open Tu-Sa noon-2pm; store open 10am-7pm. MC/V.) **Restaurant Punjab ❸**, 3 rue des Bons Enfants, just off rue Jeanne D'Arc, provides the taste of the subcontinent in a central location. Lunch menus (€8-10) and dinner menus (€16-20). Dinner (from €10) includes many vegetarian selections as well as a full bar and wine list. (☎02 35 88 63 48. Open M-Su 11:30am-3pm and 7-11:30pm. MC/V.) **Le P'tit Zinc ❸**, pl. du Vieux-Marché, is a cozy bistro with a prime view of the Eglise Ste-Jeanne D'Arc. (☎02 35 15 96 22. Dinners €10-15. Open M-F 10am-3pm and 7-10pm, Sa 10am-3pm.)

🔂 SIGHTS

Sights in Rouen fall into three basic categories: museums, churches, and museums and churches related to Joan of Arc. The real show-stoppers are the cathedral, the Musée des Beaux-Arts, and Flaubert's former house. Sorry, Joan.

CATHÉDRALE DE NOTRE-DAME. The cathedral is among the most important in France, incorporating nearly every intermediate style of Gothic architecture. It also gained artistic fame as the subject of Monet's famous studies of light. Of the stained glass windows that survived bombings during World War II, the beheading of St-Jean the Baptist and the legend of St-Julien in the **Chapelle St-Jean de la Nef** are the best. To the left of Notre-Dame stands the 12th-century **Tour St-Romanus,** to the right the 17th-century **Tour de Beurre (Tower of Butter),** which was funded by cholesterol-loving parishioners who chose to pay a dispensation rather than go without butter during Lent. The cathedral, whose central spire is the tallest in France (151m), is illuminated nightly in summer. *(Pl. de la Cathédrale. Open M-Sa 8am-7pm, Su 8am-6pm. Tours in French June-Sept. daily 3pm; Oct.-May Sa-Su 3pm.)*

MUSÉE DES BEAUX-ARTS. This renowned museum houses a modest but worthwhile collection, with a wallop of Dutch and Italian masters and a less impressive 19th- and 20th-century array. Occasional gems, such as Caravaggio's *Flagellation of Christ* and Monet's representation of the sun-drenched cathedral, provide a nice reprieve from the roomfuls of gloomy religious painting. *(Sq. Verdel, down rue Jeanne d'Arc from the train station. ☎02 35 71 28 40. Open W-M 10am-6pm; some exhibits closed 1-2pm. €3, ages 18-25 and groups €2, under 18 free.)*

MUSÉE FLAUBERT ET D'HISTOIRE DE LA MÉDECINE. Gustave Flaubert grew up on these premises, since converted into a fascinating museum. The building houses a few of Flaubert's possessions (including the iconic parrot that inspired his short story *Un Coeur Simple*), as well as an old midwifery mannequin and a collection of gruesome medical instruments used by his physician father. *(51 rue de Lecat, next door to the Hôtel-Dieu hospital. Follow rue de Crosne from pl. du Vieux Marché. ☎02 35 15 59 95. Open Tu 10am-6pm, W-Sa 10am-noon and 2-6pm. Free English brochure. €2.20, ages 18-25 €1.50, students and under 18 free.)*

EGLISE STE-JEANNE D'ARC. This massive structure was designed in 1979 to resemble an overturned Viking longboat. The interior "church in the round" is small compared to the huge external structure; a wall of luminous stained glass, recovered from the Eglise St-Vincent, which was destroyed during WWII, relieves the drabness of poured cement. Outside, a 6.5m cross marks the spot where Joan was supposedly burned, although the exact location is much contested. *(Pl. de Vieux Marché. Open M-Th and Sa 10am-12:30pm and 2-6pm, F and Su 2-6pm.)*

TOUR JEANNE D'ARC. This is the last remaining tower of the château which confined Joan of Arc before she was burned at the stake in 1431, in the pl. du Vieux-Marché. Visitors can ascend the spiral staircase to the small rooms on each level of the tower, which feature 10ft. thick walls and models of Rouen in the days of Joan of Arc. *(To the left of the station on rue du Donjon. Due to renovations, the entrance is on rue Bouvreuil. Open Apr.-Sept. W-M 10am-12:30pm and 2-6pm, Su 2-6:30pm; Oct.-Mar. W-M 10am-12:30pm and 2-5pm, Su 2-5:30pm. €1.50, students and under 18 free.)*

EGLISE ST-MACLOU. St-Maclou's uniformly Gothic facade, with a delicate freestanding flamboyant grille, may outgrace the cathedral's; inside, the elaborately carved friezes of the organ are the most stunning feature. Look for *les enfants pisseurs*, two urinating cherubs in the left corner of the facade. *(Open to tourists M-Sa 10am-noon and 2-5:30pm, Su 3-5:30pm. Concerts July and Aug. Tickets available 30min. before concert at the church. For more info, pick up a brochure at the church or call ☎ 02 35 70 84 90. €8, students €5.)* Beyond the church to the left, a poorly marked passage at 186 rue de Martainville leads to the **Aître St-Maclou.** This cloister served as the church's slaughterhouse and cemetery during the Middle Ages, including the years of the deadly plagues; hence the grisly 15th-century frieze that decorates the beams of the inner courtyard. The *Rouennais* entombed a live black cat inside the walls to exorcise spirits; the shriveled feline is still suspended behind a glass panel for all to see. *(Pl. Barthélémy, behind the cathedral. Open M-Sa 10am-noon and 2-5:30pm, Su 3-5:30pm. Aître closed indefinitely for renovation starting in 2002).*

OTHER SIGHTS. Built into a bridge across rue du Gros Horloge, the ornately gilded **Gros Horloge** ("Big Clock") is charmingly inaccurate; look up when passing under at the friezes of the Lamb of God. The belfry is still under renovations; when it's completed, visitors will be able to ascend for a view of the 14th-century clockwork and the rooftops of Rouen. Under the war-marked Palais de Justice stands the 11th-century **Monument Juif** (Jewish Monument), uncovered in the 1970s. Hebrew inscriptions on the walls confirmed that the structure had been a Jewish one, perhaps dating as far back as 1100 AD, though whether it was a synagogue, Talmudic school, or private house is unknown. *(Call tourist office two days in advance for a tour in French.)*

◢ NIGHTLIFE

Rouen's bars tend to be fairly quiet; for a jumpin' drinking scene, check out **Murphy's Irish Pub,** 12 pl. du Vieux-Marché, where a bustling crowd spills onto the sidewalk (☎ 02 35 71 17 33. Open M-Su 4pm-midnight. MC/V). The best of the mellow establishments is the zebra-pillowed **Le Nash,** 97 rue Ecuyère, just off rue des Bons Enfants, where beer is €3 and the porch encourages open-air interaction. (☎ 02 35 98 25 24. Open M-F 10am-2pm, Sa 6pm-2am, Su 7pm-2am.) Smoky **Emporium Galorium,** 151 rue Beauvoisine, plays live bands and concerts on a regular basis. (☎ 02 35 71 76 95. Beers and mixed drinks from €4. Open M-Sa 7pm-2am.) The gay and lesbian **Le Bloc House,** 138 rue Beauvoisine, provides an upbeat clubbing atmosphere where live DJs spin house Sa night. (☎ 02 35 07 71 97. Open M-Sa 7pm-2am. MC/V.) **Café Curieux,** 3 rue des Fossés Louis VIII off rue de la République opposite Eglise St-Ouen, blasts a clubber's delight of house, reggae and hiphop. (☎ 02 35 71 20 83. €1 cover. Open F-Sa 10pm-late.)

NEAR ROUEN

THE SEINE VALLEY

The lazy Seine unwinds toward the sea, trailing behind it natural and historic gems: castles, abbeys, and national parks spread among rolling farmland and craggy cliffs. You can theme-trek along the river on an Impressionist route, an Emma Bovary route, a route of major castles and mansions, or the best-known itinerary, the Route des Abbayes. The first you'll encounter out of Rouen is the still-functioning **Abbaye St-Martin de Boscherville,** but the star of the bunch is the **Abbaye de Jumièges,** founded by St-Philibert in 654. A fixture in local history and legend since Merovingian times, the abbey became a stone quarry during the Revolution, but was bought and restored by the state in 1947. Now it's a splendid ruin, set in lush grounds that incorporate a 17th-century French garden. (☎ 02 35 37 24 02. Open Apr. 15-Sept. 15 daily 9:30am-7pm Sept. 16-Apr. 14 9:30am-1pm and 2:30-5:30pm. Tours available in French every hr. €4, students €2.50, under age 18 free.) The **Parc Naturel Régional de Brotonne** sprawls across the Seine midway to Le Havre; before you hit the concrete jungle, get in some green time on this network of trails (inquire at the Rouen tourist office). The town of **Caudebec-en-Caux,** easily accessible by bus from Rouen or Le Havre, makes an excellent base to explore the park. A bit farther on toward the sea, the town of **Villequiers,** the site of the tragic drowning of Victor Hugo's daughter Léopoldine and her husband Charles Vacquerie, now houses the **Musée Victor Hugo,** rue Ernest Binet. (☎ 02 35 56 78 31. Open M, W-Sa 10am-12:30pm and 2-6pm, Su 2-6pm. Tours available upon request. €3.) The museum holds memorabilia from the Hugo and Vacquerie families, as well as drawings and first editions by Hugo himself. Cap off your tour of the valley with a peak at the enormous **Pont de Normandie,** the stark, futuristic bridge that joins the northern and southern banks of the Seine just above Le Havre.

It's easiest to get around the valley by car, but **CNA buses** (☎ 08 25 07 60 27) hit most of the major sites. Line #30A runs from Rouen's bus station to several of the abbeys, including Jumièges (45min., 4 per day, €5.50). Change buses at Caudebec-en-Caux to reach Villequiers and the Musée Victor Hugo. Biking is feasible as well, though distances are great. The Rouen tourist office can provide you with info on excursions and a map detailing all the major sights along the valley; its publication *Day Trips around Rouen* may prove helpful as well.

DIEPPE

Somewhere between the mixed bag of the Channel Ports and the concrete block of Le Havre is Dieppe (pop. 36,000), a longtime vacation spot for British and Parisian vacationers. They come for the beach, for Dieppe has little to offer beyond the seaside strip of pebbles that runs along one edge of the town. Though an impressive château and some WWII monuments will help you pass the time until your ferry leaves, nothing here merits a detour.

■ ▮ **ORIENTATION AND PRACTICAL INFORMATION. Hoverspeed** ferries leave for **Newhaven,** England. (☎ 08 00 12 11 12 11. 2hr.; 2-3 per day; €38-43, car €206-235.) Ferry ticket holders can take a free shuttle between the ferry terminal and the train station, bd. Clemenceau (☎ 02 35 06 69 33). **Trains** go to **Rouen** (1¼hr., 10 per day, €8.40), where you can change for other major destinations. (☎ 02 35 06 69 33. Ticket office open M-F 5:35am-7:30pm, Sa 6:15am-7:30pm, Su 7:15am-8:50pm.) **CNA buses,** next to the train station, go to **Rouen** (2hr., 4 per day, €11.50). Buy tickets on board. (☎ 02 35 84 21 97. Info office open M-Sa 8am-12:15pm and 2-6:30pm.) **Stradbus,** 56 quai Duquesne (☎ 02 32 14 03 03), runs **local buses** (tickets €1, *carnet* of 10 €6.80). For a 24hr. **taxi** call ☎ 02 35 84 20 05.

A courtesy bus runs from the ferry terminal to the **tourist office,** Pont Ango. Otherwise, follow the fishy smell to the waterfront in the town center, taking quai Berigny straight out from the train station until you reach the Pont Ango on your right. The solicitous staff books rooms (€3.50) and provides maps and info about the town. (☎ 02 32 14 40 60; fax 02 32 14 40 61. Open July-Aug. M-Sa 9am-1pm and

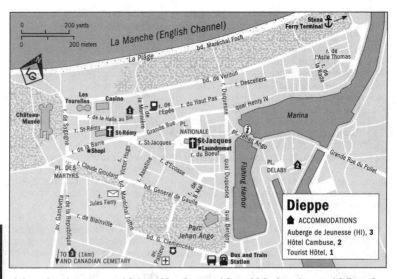

Dieppe

⚓ ACCOMMODATIONS
Auberge de Jeunesse (HI), **3**
Hôtel Cambuse, **2**
Tourist Hôtel, **1**

2-8pm, Su 10am-1pm and 3-6pm; May-June and Sept. M-Sa 9am-1pm and 2-7pm, Su 10am-1pm and 3-6pm; Oct.-Apr. M-Sa 9am-noon and 2-6pm.) Check out the biweekly *Les Informations Dieppoises*, which lists local happenings and hotspots (€1 at *tabacs*). There's a **laundromat** on rue du Mortier d'Or facing the Eglise St-Jacques. (Open daily 7am-9pm.) The **police** are on bd. Clemenceau, next to the station (☎02 32 14 49 00), and the **hospital** is on av. Pasteur. (☎02 35 14 76 76.) **La CyberCab**, 48 rue de l'Epée, has **Internet** access. (☎02 35 84 64 36. €4 per hr. Open Tu-Sa noon-7pm, Su 2-6pm.) The **post office**, 2 bd. Maréchal Joffre, has **currency exchange** and offers Internet access through the cyberposte service. (☎02 35 06 99 20. Open M-F 8-6pm, Sa 8am-12:30pm.) **Postal code:** 76200.

🖪🖸 ACCOMMODATIONS AND FOOD. Inexpensive hotels are scattered throughout town, although truly cheap rates are hard to come by. There are more expensive two-stars all along the beach. Reserve well in advance for August.

The **Auberge de Jeunesse (HI) ❶**, 48 rue Louis Fromager, has spacious, modern, single-sex rooms with bunk beds. To get there, take bus #2 (dir: Val Druel) from the Chambre de Commerce (200m down quai Duquesne from the station) or from the tourist office, to "Château Michel." Walk back down the hill 200m and take the first left. To walk there from the station, turn left onto bd. Clemenceau, which becomes rue de Blainville. At the end of the street, turn right on rue de la République and make a sharp left on rue Gambetta. Climb the hill and keep going. Turn right at the roundabout onto D925, and left again 200m up the hill (rue Louis Fromager). The hostel is on your right. (30min.) Women should not walk here alone at night. (☎02 35 84 85 73. Breakfast €3. Sheets €2.60. Reception 8-10am and 5-10pm. Bunks €8. **Members only.**) The **Tourist Hôtel ❷**, 16 rue de la Halle au Blé, is just behind the beach. From quai Duquesne, turn left onto rue du Haut Pas, which becomes rue de l'Epée and eventually rue de la Halle au Blé. The rooms, which overlook a small courtyard, are basic but comfortable, and the owner is welcoming. (☎02 35 06 10 10; fax 02 35 84 15 87. Breakfast €5. Reception 7am-2am. Singles with shower from €21.50; doubles with toilet €26, with shower from €31.) **Hôtel Cambuse ❸**, 42 rue Belle Teste, is across the Pont Ango, near the tourist office.

From pl. Delaby on the other side of the bridge, take a left onto rue Belle Teste. Rooms are spotless and well-maintained. (☎02 35 84 19 46. Breakfast €5. Reception 7am-10pm. Singles and doubles €28-38.50. MC/V.)

Inexpensive *brasseries*, bakeries, and *crêperies* are on Grande Rue, quai Henri IV, and around Eglise St-Jacques. The sidestreets hold small restaurants that proudly serve up local fish specialties: *harengs marinés* (marinated herring), *soupe du poisson* (fish soup), and *marmite dieppoise* (a fish and shellfish chowder). **Shopi** has a supermarket at 59 rue de la Barre. (☎02 35 84 04 09. Open M-Sa 8:30am-8pm, Su 9:30am-noon.) If canned tuna gets you down, check out the **marché de poissons** in front of the tourist office when the weather is good enough for fishing boats to go out. (Open M-Sa 8am-noon.) There's a **market** surrounding the Eglise St-Jacques (Tu and Th mornings), and a larger one takes over the town center all day Saturday.

◑ ▣ SIGHTS AND ENTERTAINMENT. Most of Dieppe's summer visitors come to roast on the long stone beach, bordered by cliffs to the west and the port to the east. Atop these cliffs rises an imposing 15th-century **château,** now a civic museum that summarizes itself with two words: "maritime" and "ivory." The castle itself gives a commanding view of Dieppe after a steep climb from the town below. (☎02 35 84 19 76. Open June-Sept. daily 10am-noon and 2-6pm; Oct.-May W-M 10am-noon and 2-5pm. €2.40, children €1.10, groups €1.85.) In town, the eerily beautiful, Gothic **Eglise St-Jacques** has been undergoing repairs, but still displays some lovely modern stained glass and detailed friezes. A somber testament to more recent events is the chilling **Canadian Cemetery** in nearby **Hautot-sur-Mer.** Thousands of Canadians died in the famous Allied raid on Dieppe (August 19, 1942); today each identified gravestone bears an inscription in English. To get there, turn right from the hostel, walk for 20 min., and turn right at the cross and sign. Or take bus #2 (dir: Val Druel), which leaves every 20min. from the tourist office and the Chambre de Commerce, 200m down quai Duquesne from the station. In the eastern part of town, atop the cliffs, the **Chapelle de Notre-Dame-de-Bon-Secours** commands a stunning view of the harbor. It's a long way, but you'll get terrific pictures of the city and cliffs. Take bus #1 (dir: 4 Poteaux) or #8 (dir: Puys). In this tourist town, the best bet for a night out is to follow the vacationing crowds to the bars clustered on **Grande Rue** and **rue du Haut Pas.**

LE HAVRE

Everybody comes through Le Havre (pop. 200,000), but few stay. Founded in 1517 by François 1er, the town can boast of being the largest transatlantic port in France, but little else. In the 1930s, Jean-Paul Sartre served as a teaching assistant in Le Havre, which he renamed Bouville (Mudtown) in his first novel, *Nausea.* Le Havre's answer to the devastating damage of WWII was to call in architect Auguste Perret, who spewed reinforced concrete everywhere, compounding the unsightliness of the already utilitarian harbor. The town is trying desperately to improve its image with a good museum and a few tree-lined boulevards, but it is still best as a stopover. Get in, get out, and nobody gets hurt.

▣ TRANSPORTATION

Trains: cours de la République (☎08 36 35 35). Info office open M-Sa 9:30am-6:15pm. To: **Fécamp** via Etretat (1hr., 9 per day, €6.70); **Paris** (2hr., 8 per day, €23.70); **Rouen** (50min., 13 per day, €11.40). The **bus station,** connected to the train station (exit from the platforms your left), is on bd. de Strasbourg (☎02 35 26 67 23). Info office open M-Sa 7am-7pm. **CNA** runs to **Rouen** (3hr.; M-Sa 7 per day, 2 on Su; €13.35).

Buses: Bus Verts (☎08 01 21 42 14) goes to **Caen** (1½hr., 5 per day, €19) and **Honfleur** (30min., 4 per day, €5.60); ask about student fares. See p. 190 for Caen-Le Havre express info. **Autocars Gris** (☎02 35 28 19 88) runs to **Fécamp** via Etretat (45-100min.; 10 per day; €7.20, 50% reduction on same-day return).

Ferries: P&O European Ferries, av. Lucien Corbeaux (☎08 03 01 30 13 or 08 25 013 013; www.poportsmouth.com), leave from Terminal de la Citadelle (☎02 35 19 78 78) for **Portsmouth** (see **Getting to France: By Boat,** p. 67, for details). Ticket and info office open M-F 8:30am-7pm, Sa 9am-5pm. Terminal closes at 11pm.

Taxis: Radio-Taxis wait at the train station (☎02 35 25 81 81). 24hr.

✴ ⁊ ORIENTATION AND PRACTICAL INFORMATION

To get to the tourist office from the station, follow **bd. de Strasbourg** across town as it changes to **av. Foch** and eventually hits the beach; turn left onto **bd. Clemenceau,** and the tourist office will be on your left. From the ferry terminal, walk left down quai de Southampton and then right up bd. Clemenceau; the office will be on your right. Beware of walking anywhere alone at night, especially around the train station and harbor.

Tourist Office: 186 bd. Clemenceau (☎02 32 74 04 04; fax 02 35 42 38 39; www.lehavretourism.com). Info on outdoor activities, a list of hotels and restaurants, a small guide to regional nightlife ("Bazart"), and a free map. Open May-Sept. M-Sa 9am-7pm, Su 10am-12:30pm and 2:30-6pm; Oct.-Apr. M-Sa 9am-6:30pm, Su 10am-1pm.

Hospital: 55bis rue Gustave Flaubert (☎02 32 73 32 32).

Police: 16 rue de la Victoire (☎02 32 74 37 00).

Internet Access: Cybermetro, cours de la République (☎02 35 25 40 43), a café across from the train station. €2.30 per 15min., €3.05 per 30min., €4.60 per hr. Open daily 11am-10pm. Or try the **library,** 17 rue Jules Lecesne (☎02 32 74 07 40). By appointment only, but you can use a computer when people (often) don't show up. Open July-Aug. Tu-W and F-Sa 10am-5pm, Th noon-5pm; Sept.-June Tu and F 10am-7pm, W and Sa 10am-6pm, Th noon-6pm.

Post Office: 62 rue Jules Siegfried (☎02 32 92 59 00). **Internet** kiosk. Open M-F 8am-7pm, Sa 8am-noon. **Postal code:** 76600.

⌐⌐ ACCOMMODATIONS AND FOOD. Cheap one-star hotels, offering mostly singles, line the seedy cours de la République across from the train station. Pricier and marginally prettier two-star establishments line bd. de Strasbourg. **Hôtel Le Monaco ❷,** 16 rue de Paris, near the ferry terminal, has spacious rooms in a classy, countryside decor above a popular *brasserie,* serving 3-course *menus* for €10. (☎02 35 42 21 01. Reception 6:30am-11pm. Breakfast €4.60. Singles €22.90, with shower €28.30-33.55; doubles €26.70, with bath or shower €33.10. AmEx/MC/V.)

Le Havre has no shortage of cheap eateries, but don't set your sights too high. Restaurants crowd **rue Victor Hugo** near the Hôtel de Ville, while the streets between **rue de Paris** and **quai Lamblardie** frame a range of neighborhood restaurants frequented by locals. Stock up for the ferry at **Monoprix,** 38-40 av. René Coty, in the *Espace Coty* shopping center. (Open M-Sa 8:30am-9pm.) **Super U,** bd. François 1er, is almost a full turn around the block behind the tourist office (open M-Sa 7am-8pm), and a **Marché Plus** near the Volcan on rue de Paris (open M-Sa 7am-9pm, Su 8:30am-12:30pm). For unusually fresh food, try the morning **market** at pl. Thiers by the Hôtel de Ville (M, W, F) or the all-day market on cours République (Tu, Th, Sa). A list of all markets is available from the tourist office.

⊙ ⏏ SIGHTS AND ENTERTAINMENT. The **Musée des Beaux Arts André Malraux,** 2 bd. Clemenceau, features a small but delightful collection of pre-Impressionist works in an airy modern space. The museum houses Monet, Manet, Gaugin, and a host of local artists; Boudin has painted every cow in Normandy, and most of those paintings seem to be on the second floor. (☎ 02 35 19 62 62. Open M and W-F 11am-6pm, Sa-Su 11am-7pm. €3.80, students €2.20, under 18 free.) The quiet shade of the weeping willows in the **Jardin Sarraute,** off av. Foch, provides a refreshing counterpoint to the town's griminess, as do the ivy-covered walkways and sparkling fountains on **pl. de l'Hôtel de Ville.**

The skyscraper visible from practically everywhere in town is actually the **Eglise St-Joseph,** yet another chapter in Perret's sermon on the wonders of concrete. That's not actually a giant felled mushroom in the middle of the city; it is Le Havre's center of performing arts. Nicknamed **Le Volcan,** the Maison de la Culture du Havre, in pl. Gambetta, looks like the unholy union of a nuclear power plant and an overturned toilet bowl, and houses a state-of-the-art theater for renowned orchestras and plays, as well as a cinema that screens new releases and classics. (☎ 02 35 19 10 10. Closed July 20-Aug.)

For evening entertainment in Le Havre, the fresh-off-the-ferry crowds head to a number of night spots. **Havana Café,** 173 rue Victor Hugo (the end farthest from the beach), exudes a Cuban vibe with €5 cocktails and Thursday night karaoke. (☎ 02 35 42 35 77. Open Tu-Sa.) If in search of a DJ, try **Le Plazza,** 159 bd. de Strasbourg, near the train station. (☎ 02 35 43 04 28. Cocktails €6. Open Tu-Sa 6pm-2am.)

THE HIGH NORMANDY COAST

ETRETAT

Heading northeast along the coast from Le Havre, you'll arrive at the small, touristy town of Etretat (pop. 1640), whose natural beauty overpowers its chintzy feel. A favorite destination of British and French vacationers, Etretat occupies perhaps the most spectacular spot on the Channel coast, its pebble beach sandwiched between soaring chalk cliffs. The arching western cliff, known as the **Falaise d'Aval,** was likened to an elephant dipping its trunk into the sea by Guy de Maupassant. Climb the steps on the west end of the promenade (to the left facing the sea) to ramble along the clifftop, which has spectacular views. Perched atop the eastern cliff (Falaise d'Amont) is the tiny **Chapelle Notre Dame de la Garde,** constructed by the Jesuits in 1854; note the spitting dolphins at the gutters on the roof. The hike to the top of the cliff is worth it for the view alone. Behind it sits the miniscule **Musée Nungesser et Coli** and a modern wishbone of a monument dedicated to the first aviators to attempt a trans-Atlantic flight, whose plane was lost off the coast of Etretat in 1927. (☎ 02 35 27 07 47. Open June 15-Sept. 15 W-M 10:30am-noon and 2-5pm; Sept. 16-June 14 Sa-Su only. €0.90, children €0.60.) The town itself is just a handful of crooked streets wending between the main avenue, Georges V, and the beach, strewn with eateries and small shops. Stowed among them are the former house and gardens of crime novelist Maurice Leblanc, who created Arsène Lupin, the original "gentleman burglar." Solve a murder mystery at **Le Clos Lupin,** 15 rue de Maupassant—with the help of headphones, you can foil Lupin in the rooms of the antique home. (☎ 02 35 10 59 53. Open Apr.-Sept. M-Su 10am-7pm; Oct.-Mar. F-Su 11am-7pm. €5.60. Available in French or in English.)

The **tourist office,** just behind the bus stop, can outfit you with a free map, **bike** rental information, and a **tour.** (☎ 02 35 27 05 21; fax 02 35 28 87 20. Open June 15-Sept. 15 daily 10am-7pm; Sept. 16-Nov. and Apr.-June 14 10am-noon and 2-6pm; Dec.-Mar. Sa-Su only.) **Les Autos Cars Gris** (☎ 02 35 27 04 25) runs buses from **Fécamp** (35min., 9 per day, €4.50) and **Le Havre** (1hr., 10 per day, €6) to the center of Etretat.

There are plenty of hotels in town, but no truly budget ones; the closer to the beachfront, the higher the rates. Reservations are crucial in summertime. **Hôtel l'Angleterre ❹**, 35 av. Georges V, and the posh **Hôtel de la Poste ❸**, 6 av. Georges V, may not be cheap, but they're the best you can do in Etretat. Both feature immaculate, luxurious rooms with shower, toilet, and TV. (☎ 02 35 27 01 34; fax 02 35 27 76 28. Shared reception 8am-8pm at the Hôtel de la Poste down the street. Buffet breakfast €7. Angleterre singles and doubles €37; triples and quads €58. Poste singles €29; doubles €40. Lower prices Sept.-Easter. MC/V.) Campers can bed down at the **town campsite ❶**, straight down rue Guy de Maupassant from the tourist office (10 min. walk, or the some buses stop opposite). It's dirt cheap, probably because it's the only place in town far from the beach. (☎ 02 35 27 07 67. Reception 9am-noon and 3-7pm. Gates 7:30am-10pm. Open Easter-Sept. 15. €2.20 per person, €2.20 per car with tent, €2.50 per car with caravan. Electricity €3.50. Showers free.)

FÉCAMP

Tucked among craggy cliffs, Fécamp (pop. 22,000) is one of the jewels of the High Normandy coast, well worth a daytrip from Dieppe or Rouen. Fécamp first found fame as a pilgrimage site in the 6th century, when some drops of *précieux-sang* (Christ's blood) allegedly washed ashore in a fig-tree trunk. Few pilgrims still come to adore the holy plasma, which is held in the **Eglise Abbatiale de la Trinité**, rue des Forts. According to legend, the bishops were arguing over the church's dedication when an angel appeared to command patronage to the Holy Trinity; the footprint he left behind can still be seen to the right of the altar. At the eastern end of the nave sits a gold box containing the *précieux-sang*.

Most visitors to Fécamp are after a different precious liquid entirely—*Benedictine*. Between the 16th and 18th centuries, Fécamp's Benedictine monks created a mysterious concoction of 27 local plants and Asian spices for use as a healing agent. Local wine merchant Alexandre Le Grand rediscovered the recipe, which had been lost during the Revolution, and built a palace in 1888 to distill the spirit, named after the monks who invented it. Today the magnificent **Palais Bénédictine**, 110 rue Alexandre Le Grand, remains the town's greatest draw; follow up a visit to the excellent collection of medieval and Renaissance artifacts and contemporary art with a swill of the fiery liqueur. (☎ 02 35 10 26 10. Open July-Sept. daily 2 9:30am-7pm; Sept. 3-30 10am-1pm and 2-6:30pm; Oct.-Dec. and Feb. 3-28 10am-12:15pm and 2-6pm; Mar.-June 10am-1pm and 2-6:30pm. Last admission 1hr. before closing. €5, under age 18 €1.75, family €11.)

If you plan on spending the night, try the **Hôtel Vent d'Ouest ❹**, 3 av. Gambetta, across the street from the bus stop and just up the steps from the train station. While a bit pricey, lodgings in Fécamp don't come any cheaper, and each of the bright clean rooms has its own shower, toilet, TV, and phone. (☎ 02 35 28 04 04; fax 02 35 28 75 96. Breakfast €4.60. Reception 8am-10pm. June-Sept. singles €31.90, each additional person €6.10; Oct.-May singles €25.80, each additional person €4.60. MC/V.) Travelers can also bed down at the truly picturesque campground, **Camping Municipal de Reneville ❶**, chemin de Nesmond, which overlooks the ocean and affords a spectacular cliff view from its grassy heights. From the train station or bus stop, turn right onto ave. Gambetta, which becomes quai Berigny; turn left onto rue du Président Coty, right onto rue Caron, left onto rue d'Yport, and right onto ch. de Nesmond. (☎ 02 35 28 20 97. Office 8am-noon and 2-6pm. Gates 7am-10pm. €6.10 per tent, €7.95 per caravan, €2.08 per extra person. Electricity €2. Tax €0.15. Showers free.) For supplies, there's a **Marché-Plus** supermarket at 83 quai Berigny. (Open M-Sa 7am-9pm, Su 9am-1pm)

The town center (the location of the main Fécamp bus stop) is behind Eglise St-Etienne, across the street from the train station and up the steps. To reach the **tourist office,** 113 rue Alexandre Le Grand, turn right onto av. Gambetta, which becomes quai Berigny. Turn left onto rue du Domaine, and then right onto rue le Grand; it's across the street from the Palais Bénédictine. They dispense maps and book rooms for €1.60. (☎02 35 28 51 01; fax 02 35 27 07 77. Open July-Aug. M-F 10am-6pm; May-June and Sept. M-F 9am-12:15pm and 1:45-6pm, Sa 10am-noon and 2:30-6:30pm, Su 10am-noon and 2-6pm; Oct.-Mar. M-F 9am-12:15pm and 1:45-6:30pm, Sa 10am-noon and 2:30-6:30pm.) Fécamp is accessible by **train** from **Bréauté-Beuzeville** with connections to **Le Havre** (45min., 5 per day, €7); **Paris** (2½hr., 6 per day, €24); and **Rouen** (1¼hr., 6 per day, €11). Get there by **bus** on **Les Autos Cars Gris,** 55 chemin de Nid Verdier, pl. St-Etienne. (☎02 35 27 04 25. Open open M-Tu and Th-F 8:30am-11:45am and 1:30pm-5:45pm, W 8:30am-11:45am and 1:30pm-5pm, Sa 8:30am-12:30pm.) The stop is across from the church on av. Gambetta. Buses run from **Le Havre** ("rapidbus" 45min., 7 per day; regular bus 1¼hr., 17 per day; €8. Buy tickets on board). There is a **taxi** stand on pl. St-Etienne at the top of av. Gambetta (☎02 35 28 17 50).

THE CÔTE FLEURIE

In contrast to Normandy's working port cities, the smaller villages along the northeastern coast of Lower Normandy, known as the Côte Fleurie, are decidedly playful. Doubling as resort towns and thalassotherapy centers (seaside health spas), these coastal towns have served as weekend destinations for Paris's elite since the mid-19th century. Today, they cater to a more international crowd, which means that they won't turn up their noses at your French, but they might take exception to your attire. The Côte's reputation as the "Norman Riviera" stems mostly from its fixation on wealth and style, and the budget lifestyle is little accommodated. Caen's hotels or hostels can make good budget bases, and Bus Verts provides regular connections between coastal towns and to Caen and Bayeux. Consider their *Carte Liberté* bus passes if you'll be doing a lot of touring (see **Transportation,** p. 190).

HONFLEUR

Among the picturesque, carefully-preserved towns in northwestern France, Honfleur (pop. 6000) stands out as a true gem of culture and architecture. The town emerged from WWII miraculously unharmed, and its narrow, multicolored houses surrounding the old port look the same as they have for centuries. The beautiful wilds around the town have attracted a close-knit community of artists, whose works can be seen in the many local galleries. While the waterfront *Vieux Bassin* bustles with tourists, Honfleur's idyllic tranquility is found just a few streets away.

🚩 **PRACTICAL INFORMATION.** The **bus station** is located at the end of quai Lepaulmier, near the Bassin de l'Est. **Bus Verts** (☎08 10 21 42 14) connects Honfleur to Caen (1½hr., 15 per day, €13.50) and Le Havre (30min., 12 per day, €6.40) by lines #20 and #50. Ask about student discounts. To get to the **tourist office,** 33 pl. Arthur Boudin, turn right out of the bus station and follow rue des Vases along the Avant Port until you see a glass library on your left, at rue de la Ville. The office is in the stone section of the library. The *guide pratique* has a good town map that lays out 4 walking tours (2½-7km) in the streets of the town and the surrounding forests, and also lists all of the town's business establishments, restaurants, and hotels. (☎02 31 89 23 30; fax 02 31 89 31 82. Open July-Aug. M-Sa 9:30am-7pm, Su 10am-5pm; Oct.-Easter M-Sa 9:30am-noon and 2-6pm; Easter-June and Sept. M-Sa 9:30am-12:30pm and 2-6:30pm, Su 10am-5pm.)

♫ ⬚ ACCOMMODATIONS AND FOOD. The budget-conscious should make Honfleur a daytrip—hotels here have more stars than most constellations. That said, **Les Cascades ❹,** 17 pl. Thiers, on cours des Fossés, offers comparatively inexpensive rooms in an ideal location right next to the port. Huge begonia-filled boxes adorn the windows of comfortable rooms, some with skylights and half-timbered walls. You may be asked to take dinner *(demi-pension)* at the hotel restaurant in summer. (☎ 02 31 89 05 83; fax 02 31 89 32 13. Breakfast €5.35. Open Feb.-Nov. Doubles with bath €30.50-45.75; triples €38.15-53.40; quads €54.90. AmEx/DC/MC/V.) The seaside **Le Phare ❶** campsite, 300m from the town center at the end of rue Haute, is conveniently located near the beach and just minutes from the town center. It gets crowded in summer, so arrive early to get a shady spot. (☎ 02 31 89 10 26. Reception July-Aug. 8am-10pm; low season hours vary. Car curfew 10pm-7am. Open Apr.-Sept. and July-Aug. €4.30 per person, children under 7 €3, day visitor €4.30; Apr.-June and Sept. €4.10, children under 7 €2.90, day visitor €4.10; Apr.-Sept. €5.35 per tent and car. Electricity €4-5.80. Shower €1.20.)

Restaurants and *brasseries* line the *Vieux Bassin;* splurge on a meal at one of the many eateries vying for sidewalk space to get a taste of local seafood (most fixed menus range €13-25). Less expensive to-go food is available from a number of storefronts on the quai Ste-Catherine and on quieter streets off the main pedestrian thoroughfare. One hundred flavors of homemade ice cream make **Pom'Cannelle,** 60 quai Ste-Catherine, worth the price. (☎ 02 31 89 55 25. 1 scoop €1.50, 2 scoops €3. Open daily 11am-11pm.) For groceries, drop by the **Champion** supermarket, pl. Sorel. (Open July-Aug. M-F 8:30am-1pm and 2:30-7:30pm, Sa 8:30am-7:30pm, Su 9am-1pm; Sept.-June hours slightly shorter.) A **market** goes up in pl. Ste-Catherine, in front of the church (Sa morning), while pl. St-Léonard has an organic **Marché Bio** (W morning). Be sure to pick up some *pain Breton.*

◙ SIGHTS. Honfleur is for the curious; the city's tight corners and tucked-away streets hide lesser-known architectural marvels and any number of delights. The *Pass Musées* gives access to all four of Honfleur's museums and bell tower. (€8.50, students and children €5.50, under 10 free.) Worth the trip to Honfleur alone is the **▓Maisons Satie,** 67 bd. Charles V, the 1866 birthplace and museum of composer, musician, artist, and author Erik Satie. Breathtaking, fanciful, and a little psychedelic, this maze of rooms feels like a stroll through the mind of an artist. Expect starry ceilings, indoor rainshowers, and the whimsical *laboratoire des émotions.* (☎ 02 31 89 11 11. Open May-Sept. W-M 10am-7pm; Oct.-Dec. and Feb. 16-Apr. 11am-6pm. €5, students and seniors €3, under 10 free.)

The wonderful **Musée d'Ethnographie et d'Art Populaire,** quai St-Etienne, consists of two 15th-century houses, decorated as they would have been during Honfleur's glory days; a walk through a prison and a soldier's quarters gives a glimpse into the lives of the town's past inhabitants. The almost-adjacent **Musée de la Marine,** quai St-Etienne, in the former Eglise St-Etienne, is a tiny but informative museum that recounts Honfleur's affair with the sea engagingly enough for even the most earthy landlubber. (☎ 02 31 89 14 12. Both open July-Aug. daily 10am-1pm and 2-6:30pm; Apr.-June and Sept. Tu-Su 10am-noon and 2-6pm; Feb. 15-Mar. and Oct.-Nov. 15 Tu-F 2-5:30pm, Sa-Su 10am-noon and 2-5:30pm. Closed Nov. 16-Feb. 14. €2.30, students and children €1.50; with Musée d'Ethnographie €3.80, students €2.30.)

Part of the ramparts that once surrounded the village, the **Porte de Caen** at the end of quai Ste-Catherine is the only remaining gate through which the king would ride into the fortified town. A block away from the Bassin's waters is the 15th-century **Eglise Ste-Catherine.** The largest wooden church in France, it was built hurriedly and cheaply by pious sailors after the first one burned down in 1450. The result is a splendidly carved church that resembles a cross between an ornamented market hall and a half-timbered house. (Open July-Aug. daily 8am-8pm, Sept.-June 8:30am-noon and 2-6pm.) The **belltower** across the street is open for climbing. (Open Mar. 15-Sept. daily 10am-noon and 2-6pm; Oct.-Nov. 11 M-F 2:30-5pm and Sa-Su 10am-noon. Included with Musée Eugène Boudin, see below.)

Paintings of Honfleur by Eugène Boudin and his circle became popular in the 19th century and are considered by many critics to be the precursors of Impressionism. A vast collection by a variety of artists, as well as mini-displays on each coastal town of the region and an exhibit of 18th-century Norman tradition, are displayed at the **Musée Eugène Boudin,** pl. Erik Satie, off rue de l'Homme de Bois. (☎ 02 31 89 54 00. Open Mar. 15-Sept. W-M 10am-noon and 2-6pm; Oct.-Mar. 14 M and W-F 2:30-5pm, Sa-Su 10am-noon and 2:30-5pm. €5, students and children €3.50, under 10 free.) The shaded **public gardens** on the bd. Charles V, just beside the port, make the perfect spot for a picnic. Flower beds, swingsets, a wading pool, and a waterfall should help wile away the hottest hours of the day. A spectacular photo opportunity of the looming Pont de Normandie awaits at the peak of **Mont-Joli.** Fill your water bottle and follow rue du Puits from pl. Ste-Catherine to a steep asphalt ramp sloping up to the right (1.5 km). In mid-September, Honfleur invites comedians for the newest of its festivals, the **Estuaire en Rire.**

DEAUVILLE AND TROUVILLE

Deauville and Trouville are traditionally treated as a pair, with their twin casinos, beaches, and boardwalks, but each manages to retain a distinct identity on its own bank of the river Touques. Since its founding in 1861, **Deauville** (pop. 4518) has consistently drawn Parisian elite to its sandy shores and ritzy boutiques. Fortunately for the budget traveler, the fun of Deauville lies in people-watching and window-shopping. Across the river, **Trouville**'s streets (pop. 5500) are smaller, its crowds less absurdly wealthy, its shops less expensive and its selection of restaurants more varied; its overall feel is more "family holiday" than "resort haven."

▐ TRANSPORTATION. These siamese twins are joined at the station. **Trains** (SNCF ☎ 08 36 35 35 35) go to **Caen** (1hr., 5 per day, €11.75); **Paris** (2hr., 5-6 per day, €24.40); **Rouen** (2½-3hr., 3 per day, €16.35). **Bus Verts** (☎ 08 01 21 42 14) goes to: **Cabourg** (20min., €4.80); **Caen** (70min., €8.80); **Honfleur** (20min., €3.20); **Houlgate** (30 min., €4); **Le Havre** via Honfleur (1hr., €9.60). **Agence Fournier,** pl. du Maréchal Foch in Trouville, runs **shuttles** between Deauville and Trouville (☎ 02 31 88 16 73; €1.60). The **Bac de Deauville/Trouville,** pl. du Marechal Foch in Trouville, ferries passengers across the canal from Deauville to Trouville's Monoprix when the tide is high enough. (Mar. 15-Sept. daily 8:30am-6:45pm, €.90.) For a **taxi,** call ☎ 02 31 88 35 33 or 08 00 51 41 41.

▐▐ ORIENTATION AND PRACTICAL INFORMATION. To get to **Trouville** from the train station, turn right and cross the bridge (Pont des Belges) onto the main bd. Fernand Moureaux; turn left and the **tourist office** is one minute away in the direction of the town center, at 32 quai Fernand Moureaux. The staff distributes vacationing guides, which include listings of Trouville's lodgings and dining establishments; also available are two walking tours (map €.50) and a town map. (☎ 02 31 14 60 70; fax 02 31 14 60 71; www.trouvillesurmer.org. Open July-Aug. M-Sa 9:30am-7pm, Su 10am-4pm; Apr.-June and Sept.-Oct. M-Sa 9:30am-noon and 2-6:30pm, Su 10am-1pm; Nov.-Mar. M-Sa 9:30am-noon and 2-6pm, Su 10am-1pm.)

To get to **Deauville** from the train station, turn left as you exit; at the second roundabout take the second right (rue Désiré le Hoc) and follow it two blocks to pl. Morny. Cut straight through the *place* and continue another block; the **tourist office,** pl. de la Mairie, will be in front of you. (10min.) Info on town and prestigious film and music festivals, pretentious star sightings, and frequent horse races and polo games. (☎02 31 14 40 00; fax 02 31 88 78 88; www.deauville.org. Open July-Sept. 9 M-Sa 9am-7pm, Su 10am-1pm and 3-6pm; Sept. 10-Apr. M-Sa 9am-12:30pm and 2-6:30pm, Su 10am-1pm and 2-5pm; May-June M-Tu and Th 9am-12:30pm and 2-6:30pm, W 10am-12:30pm and 2-6:30pm, F-Sa 9am-6:30pm, Su 10am-1pm and 2-5pm.) Rent **bikes** at **La Deauvillaise,** 11 quai de la Marine. (☎02 31 88 56 33. €4.50 per hr., €12 for 5hr., €40 per week. Open July-Aug. daily 9am-6:30pm; Sept.-June Tu-Su 9am-12:30pm and 2-6:30pm.)

⌂◫ ACCOMMODATIONS AND FOOD. You'll have to stay in Trouville if you want to sleep without pawning your pack. **Au Ch'ti-mi ❸,** 28 rue Victor Hugo, has airy, well-decorated rooms, each with a shower in the corner. Up a tiny stairs and over a little bar, the location is equally convenient to the beach and the boulevard. (☎02 31 88 49 22. Breakfast €4.60. Reception at bar. Doubles with shower €30.50; triple with shower and toilet €46.) **Camping Le Chant des Oiseaux ❶,** 11 rte. d'Honfleur, is a well-maintained site 2km from town on cliffs overlooking the sea. To walk from bd. Fernand Moureaux, follow rue Victor Hugo through many name changes until it becomes rue du General Leclerc, past the Musée Montebello. When the road forks, go right, up the steep incline and past the giant crucifix. When this route merges with the main road, continue for 5min. and it will be on the left. (☎02 31 88 06 42; fax 02 31 98 16 09. Open Apr.-Nov. 1. Reception July-Aug. 8am-10pm; in low season, someone is almost always in the office or nearby. €4.30 per person, ages 2-7 €2.70; €5 per tent; €2.70 per car. July-Aug. shower €0.50.)

Since many of the restaurants along the beach face west, toward the setting sun, beachcombers and locals flock to Trouville's terraces to dine in the last light of the day. A multitude of reasonably priced seafood restaurants, pizzerias, and *crêperies* line the pedestrian **rue des Bains** and **bd. Fernand Moureaux.** One of the best meals in town may be the traditional **Tivoli Bistro ❹,** 27 rue Charles Mozin in Trouville. *Menus* €14-24. (☎02 31 98 43 44. Open F-Tu 12:15-2pm and 7:15-10pm, W 12:15-2pm. MC/V.) In Deauville, find respite from haughty boutique prices at **Manny Crêpes ❶,** 57 rue D. LeHoc, where delicious sandwiches are €3 and desert crêpes and flan are a mere €2. (☎02 31 14 96 44. Open 9am-11pm. MC/V.) For basic supplies, head to **Monoprix** supermarket on the corner of bd. Fernand Moureaux and rue Victor Hugo in Trouville. (Open July-Aug. M-Sa 9am-8pm, Su 9:30am-1pm; Sept.-June daily 9am-12:30pm and 2-7:30pm.) A **market** fills Trouville's pl. Maréchal Foch (W and Su morning), and local fishermen sell their fresh catch daily at the *poissonerie* along the waterfront of bd. Moureaux.

◳◪ SIGHTS AND ENTERTAINMENT. The original and best attraction at both towns is the **beach.** Their boardwalk promenades are the pride of each town. In Trouville, a stroll along the wooden planks affords a view of the spectacular houses that inspired realist novelist Gustave Flaubert; and in Deauville, a path lined with names of movie stars. The **Natur'Aquarium de Trouville,** on the boardwalk, feels more like a disturbed collector's house, but will delight the prepubescent set. The glass cases hold the stuffed and the breathing, everything from finches to tarantulas, guinea pigs to geckos, dried larvae to preserved organs. (☎02 31 88 46 04. Open July-Aug. daily 10am-7:30pm; Sept.-Oct. 10am-noon and 2-7pm; Nov.-Easter 2-6:30pm; Easter-June 10am-noon and 2-7pm. €6.50, students and seniors €5.50, ages 6-14 €4.50, ages 3-6 €3.50.)

The **Casino Barrière de Trouville,** pl. du Maréchal Foch (☎02 31 87 75 00), has an adjoining nightclub and cinema, and offers a more laid-back atmosphere than the **Casino de Deauville** (☎02 31 14 31 14). **Café Trouville,** a series of café-side concerts held in July and August (4-5 per week), can be enjoyed from the terrace of the café du jour or for free on the sidewalk. The 3rd weekend in June sees both the **Festival**

Folklorique in Trouville, with music and dance groups from all over the world, and the town's **Carnaval.** The wine bar/café **La Maison,** 66 rue des Bains in Trouville, offers a sophisticated and laid-back setting. Grass mats and wrought-iron furniture give a dreamy, Spanish flavor to the terrace. (☎ 02 31 81 43 10. Open July-Aug. daily 11am-1am; Sept.-May Th-M 11am-1am.)

Deauville aptly demonstrates France's continuous love-affair with the horse. The town has two hippodromes: **Clairefontaine,** dedicated to racing, and **La Touques,** where the polo games are held. Deauville also hosts several festivals, including **Swing'In Deauville** (3rd week of July) and the **American Film Festival.** (Sept.)

NEAR TROUVILLE AND DEAUVILLE

HOULGATE

Quieter and more affordable than its eastern neighbors, Houlgate (pop. 2000) was one of the first resorts to appear on the Norman coast. Its several expensive villas and 1.5km of seashell-strewn beaches make for a pleasant daytrip from Honfleur, and campers will love its wealth of well-equipped campsites. East of Houlgate, the sea swells crash into the **Vache Noir** (Black Cow) cliffs, so named because of the dark hue of the fossil deposits against the cliffs's exposed limestone. The cliffs and beach below offer a remarkable walk that alternates between lush verdure and moonscape (best taken at low tide).

SNCF trains frequently run to Trouville/Deauville (35min., 15 per day, €6.80). **Bus Verts** #20 runs to Caen (1hr., 12 per day, €5.60) via Cabourg (11min., €1.60), as well as to Le Havre (80min., 2 per day, €11.20); ask about student discounts. A tide table and walking tours are available at Houlgate's **tourist office,** on bd. des Belges, down the hill from the Bus Verts stop. (☎ 02 31 24 34 79; fax 02 31 24 42 27; www.houlgate.com. Open daily 10am-12:30pm and 2-6:30pm.) The **post office,** at the corner of bd. des Belges and bd. de St-Philbert, **exchanges currency.** (☎ 02 31 28 10 05. Open M-F 9am-noon and 2-5pm, Sa 9am-noon.) **Postal code:** 14510.

Three kilometers east of Houlgate, between the town and the neighboring Villers-sur-Mer, are wonderful **campgrounds** on the rte. de la Corniche (D163). From the tourist office, head toward the beach and turn right on rue des Bains; continue straight ahead as it becomes rue Baumier, takes you up dozens of stairs, through the woods, then to the paved rue de la Corniche. In 30 minutes, the campsites will be on your left, one after the other. Alternately, for easier access from Honfleur and other places (and a way to get there by car), take Bus Verts #20 to Auberville (stop: "Mairie") and walk the 1km, continuing along the road and turning right at the first intersection, the monument to soldiers; turn at the first left at the small roundabout, continue onward and the campsites will be on your left. ◪**Camping les Falaises ❶,** rte. de la Corniche (D163), is a 450-spot campground with a restaurant and bar, market, heated pool, life-size chessboard, and—most importantly—huge sites with ocean views. (☎ 02 31 24 81 09; fax 02 31 28 04 11; camping.lesfalaises@voila.fr. Open Apr.-Oct. €4 per person, child under 7 €2.50; car and tent €4.70. Electricity €3.50-4.10. July-Aug. minimum total fee €15.60 per night.) ◪**Les Ammonites ❶,** rte. de la Corniche (D163), is a few steps closer to the bus stop and a few minutes farther from Houlgate. The jovial proprietor maintains a welcoming campsite that boasts a restaurant, bar, market, game room, heated pool, giant chessboard, and tennis courts. Overlooking the ocean, the plots are picturesque, with flowers, neat paths, and manicured lawns. Has many mobile home and bungalow sites ranging from €275 to €535 per week depending on month, and ample room for caravans. (☎ 02 31 87 06 06; fax 02 31 87 18 00; www.camping-les-ammonites.com. Open Apr.-Oct. €7 per person; car and tent €8. Electricity €3.)

NORMANDY

CAEN

Caen (population 120,000) suffered more during World War II than almost any other city in Normandy; by the end of the fighting, two-thirds of its citizens were homeless and three-quarters of its buildings reduced to dust. The city is notable for the skill and care with which it was rebuilt; today, the finely restored abbeys commissioned by William the Conqueror have returned to their stunning pre-war form. Closer than Bayeux to a good third of the D-Day beaches, and equally convenient to the resort towns of the Côte Fleurie, Caen combines its central location with the assets of a chic student population and several good museums.

▮ TRANSPORTATION

Trains: pl. de la Gare. Info office open M-Sa 8am-6pm, Su 9:15am-6:45pm. To: **Cherbourg** (1½hr.; 10 per day, 5 on Su; €15.70); **Paris** (2½hr., 12 per day, €44.60); **Rennes** (3hr., 3 per day, €25.70); **Rouen** (2hr., 5 per day, €18.20); **Tours** (3½hr., 2 per day, €26.70).

Buses: Bus Verts, to the left of the train station and at pl. Courtonne in the center of town (☎08 10 21 42 14), covers the region. Office open M-F 7:30am-7pm, Sa 8:30am-7pm, Su 9am-2:30pm. See p. 197 for coverage of the D-Day beaches. To **Bayeux** (1hr.; M-Sa 2-3 per day; €5.60, students €4.55) and **Le Havre** (2-3hr.; M-Sa 6 per day, Su 5 per day; €16, students €13). Also **Caen-Le Havre** express (1½hr., 2 per day, €19) stops in **Honfleur** (1hr. from Caen, 2 per day, €13.50). Full-day **Carte Liberté** €17.50, 3 days €27, 7 days €43; accepted on local bus Twisto.

Public Transportation: Twisto, 15 rue de Geôle (☎02 31 15 55 55), at "Château," pl. St-Pierre. Kiosks at "Théâtre" (at square where bd. Maréchal Leclerc terminates), "St-Pierre" (top of bd. Maréchal Leclerc), "SNCF" (pl. de la Gare). Tickets €1, carnet of 10 €8.50, day pass €2.70. Open M-F 7:15am-6:45pm, Sa 10am-4:45pm; hours vary seasonally).

Ferries: Brittany Ferries go to **Portsmouth, England** from Ouistreham, 13km north of Caen. See **Getting There: By Boat,** p. 67. Bus Verts #1 links Ouistreham to Caen's center and train station (40min., 8 per day, €3.20).

Taxis: Abbeilles Taxis Caen, 19 pl. de la Gare (☎02 31 52 17 89). 24hr. **Late-night taxi kiosk** at bd. Maréchal Leclerc near rue St-Jean (10pm-3am).

▮ ▮ ORIENTATION AND PRACTICAL INFORMATION

Caen's train station and youth hostel are on the south side of the Orne River, far enough from the center of town that you may want to take the bus. The city is in the midst of constructing a new tramway, causing traffic patterns and bus stop locations to change constantly. All of the buses leaving from the front of the train station stop in the vicinity of the Eglise St-Pierre and the city center. Ask about changes in bus routes at the Twisto kiosk near the tourist office. From the station, **avenue du 6 Juin** and **rue St-Jean** run parallel to each other toward the city center and the lively commercial districts between **rue St-Pierre** and **rue de l'Oratoir.**

Tourist Office: pl. St-Pierre (☎02 31 27 14 14; fax 02 31 27 14 18; www.ville-caen.fr), on rue St-Jean by the Eglise St-Pierre. **Hotel booking** €1.50. Free map and multilingual visitor's guide. *Le Mois à Caen* lists concerts and events. Daytime city **tours** July-Sept. (1hr.; €4, students and children over 5 €3.10). Theatrical performances at night in French mid-July to Aug. (2hr.; €10.75, students and children over 5 €7.75; reservations required.) Office open July-Aug. M-Sa 9:30am-7pm, Su 10am-1pm and 2-5pm; Sept.-June M-Sa 9:30am-1pm and 2-6pm, Su 10am-1pm.

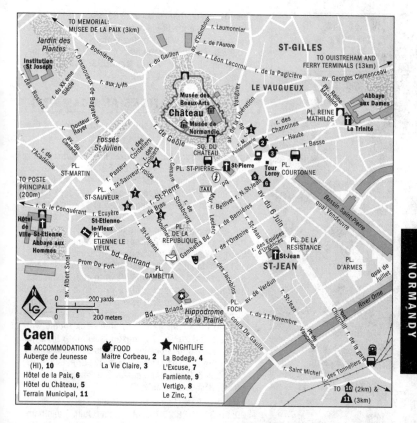

Caen

🏠 ACCOMMODATIONS
Auberge de Jeunesse (HI), **10**
Hôtel de la Paix, **6**
Hôtel du Château, **5**
Terrain Municipal, **11**

🍎 FOOD
Maitre Corbeau, **2**
La Vie Claire, **3**

⭐ NIGHTLIFE
La Bodega, **4**
L'Excuse, **7**
Farniente, **9**
Vertigo, **8**
Le Zinc, **1**

Money: Currency exchange at the post office, and in most of the banks in the area. Credit Agricole has a streetfront booth on bd. Maréchal Leclerc, at intersection with rue St-Jean. Open M 10am-12:30pm and 2-6pm, Tu-F 9am-12:30pm and 2-6pm, Sa 9am-12:30pm and 2-5pm.

Youth Center: Centre Information Jeunesse, 16 rue Neuve-St-Jean (☎02 31 27 80 80; fax 02 31 27 80 89; crij.bn@wanadoo.fr), off av. du 6 Juin next to the Hôtel de la Paix. Brochures on events, jobs, and lodging. Many work opportunities listed, particularly secretarial, marketing, human resources, or with children's groups or camps. The EU Information booth offers free Internet access.

Laundromat: rue de Geôle (☎06 60 55 75 60). Open daily 7am-9pm. Also at 16 rue Ecuyère (☎06 80 96 08 26). Open daily 7am-8pm.

Hospital: Centre Hospitalier Universitaire, av. Côte de Nacre (☎02 31 06 31 06).

Police: rue Thiboud de la Fresnaye (☎02 31 29 22 22). Kiosk near the tourist office on rue Maréchal Leclerc.

Internet Access: Free access at CIJ (see Youth Center, above). 30 computers at **Espace Micro,** 1 rue Basse (☎02 31 53 68 68). €1 for 15min., €4 for 1hr. plus (30min. free). Open M 1pm-11pm, Tu-Sa 11am-11pm, Su 3pm-7pm.

IN RECENT NEWS

BUS FUSS

When Caen first rose to prominence under William the Conqueror a thousand years ago, its streets were obviously not clogged with honking traffic as they are today. While the *Caennais* have no desire to return to medieval times, Caen has recently taken action to reduce the traffic that fills its historic streets with a new initiative: le *Tramway*. This €190 million, 15.7km project, which opened in September 2002, promises to change the face of the city. To combat high-volume traffic and to reduce atmospheric pollution, Caen intends for this metropolitan tram system to connect the city center, the many nearby schools, and outlying suburbs.

As Caen digs up its streets to lay more Tramway lines, other initiatives are also being undertaken: cycling is being encouraged with bike lanes and the creation of "bike parks" (parking lots for cyclists), and pedestrian routes are being restored along busy shopping thoroughfares. This makes for an interesting and varied urban landscape, populated by all modes of transport and peppered with the modern sleek shapes of the jointed trams zooming around the *centre ville*.

With a seating for 37 per car and comfort capacity" of a cramped 145, Tramway might be how you zoom past the Eglise St-Pierre on your visit to Caen. As a pedestrian, though, watch out: the primary golden rule is that Tramway always has the right of way as it darts into the lives of the Caen population.

Post Office: pl. Gambetta (☎02 31 39 35 78). From pl. St-Pierre, take rue St-Pierre and turn left on rue St-Laurent; post office will be at the bottom of the street on your left. **Currency exchange.** Open M-F 7:30am-7pm, Sa 8am-12:30pm. **Poste Restante:** "14016 Gambetta." **Postal code:** 14000.

ACCOMMODATIONS AND CAMPING

There are many hotels in the center of Caen, but few go for under €23.

Auberge de Jeunesse (HI), Foyer Robert Reme, 68bis rue Eustache-Restout (☎02 31 52 19 96; fax 02 31 84 29 49). From the station, turn right and then left onto rue de Falaise. Walk up a block and look for the bus stop on your right. Take bus #5 or 17 (dir: Fleury or Grâce de Dieu) to "Lycée Fresnel." On foot, take a right out of the station and cross the street. Follow it until the road (now rue de Falaise) curves to the left and up the hill. Walk uphill until you see bd. Leroy on the left, and then turn right onto bd. Maréchal Lyautey and continue about 10min. Turn left onto rue Eustasche-Restout and continue 10min. through a residential area. The road turns right after a large school; the hostel will be on your right, far away (3km) from where you want to be. Clean 4-person, single-sex rooms with showers and stoves. The hostel is within a foyer for young workers; the loitering residents can occasionally be a little *too* social. Breakfast €2. Sheets €2.30. Reception 5-10pm. 24hr. guard. Check-in 5-9pm. Beds €9.45. **HI members only. ❶**

Hôtel de la Paix, 14 rue Neuve-St-Jean (☎02 31 86 18 99; fax 02 31 38 20 74), off av. du 6 Juin. Clean bathrooms, firm beds, and TVs right in the center of town. Breakfast €5.50. Reception 24hr. Singles €26, with toilet or shower €29, with bath €32; doubles €29/€35/€37; triples with shower €40/€49; quads with bath €52; extra bed €5. MC/V. ❸

Hôtel du Château, 5 av. du 6 Juin (☎02 31 86 15 37; fax 02 31 86 58 08). Exceptionally large, bright rooms with TVs and tasteful furniture on what will soon be a pedestrian street near the château. Breakfast €6. Reception 24hr. Singles and doubles €35, with sink €45. Extra bed €10. Prices lower Oct.-Easter. MC/V. ❹

Terrain Municipal, rte. de Louvigny (☎02 31 73 60 92). Take bus #13 (dir: Louvigny) to "Camping" (every 30min. M-Sa, every 2hr. Su). Pretty campground at a bend in the river at the edge of town, shaded by weeping willows. Reception 8am-1pm and 5-9pm. Gates closed 11pm-7am. Open June-Sept. €2.75 per person, children under 7 €1.60, €1.60 per tent, €1.60 per car. Electricity €2.75. ❶

🧡 FOOD

Brasseries vie with Chinese eateries and African restaurants in the **Quartier Vaugueux** near the château as well as between the Eglise St-Pierre and the Eglise St-Jean. Large **markets** are held Fridays at pl. St-Sauveur and on Sundays in front of the Eglise St-Pierre, on pl. Courtonne, and at quai Vendeuvre. Smaller markets abound on Grace de Dieu and rue de Bayeux (Tu); bd. Leroy (W and Sa); and La Guernière and Le Chemin Vert (F); all open 8am-1pm. There's a **Monoprix** supermarket at 45 bd. du Maréchal Leclerc (open M-Sa 9am-8:30pm), and a small **7-11** market at 1167 rue de Caen near the hostel. (Open Tu-Sa 9:15am-1pm and 3-11pm.) Locals flock to 🟦**Maître Corbeau ❸,** 8 rue Buquet, to feast on *Fondue Normande* (with camembert and calvados; €11.45) amidst giant sunflowers and stuffed cows. It's so popular, in fact, that you'll probably have to reserve 2-3 days in advance just to get a table. (☎02 31 93 93 00. Open M and Sa 7-10:30pm, Tu-F noon-1:30pm and 7-10:30pm. Closed last week in Aug. and 1st week in Sept.) La Vie Claire ❷, 3 rue Basse, serves an ever-changing, always-scrumptious 3-course vegetarian *menu* ranging €8.50-12.50. (☎02 31 93 66 72. Open Tu-Sa noon-2pm. Organic bakery and take-away store open 9am-7pm.)

🔘 SIGHTS

Though pricey, some of Caen's sights are discounted with the purchase of a full-price ticket to other sights or museums in the area; the tourist office has details.

🟦**MEMORIAL DE CAEN.** This must-see memorial serves as a powerful reminder of the precious and precarious nature of peace and is without a doubt the best of Normandy's many WWII museums. It traces the "failure of peace" through spiraling galleries beginning with the end of WWI and incorporates a unique collection of WWII footage, high-tech audio-visual aids, models, and displays. The three films are striking, particularly "D-Day, the Battle of Normandy," and the detailed exhibitions give human faces to soldiers and civilians alike. A new wing continues in time beyond the war to explore the Cold War. Count on spending at least three hours here to see it all. *(Take bus #17 to "Mémorial." ☎02 31 06 06 44; www.memorial-caen.fr. Open July 13-Aug. 26 daily 9am-8pm; Feb. 3-July 12 and Aug. 27-Oct. 9am-7pm; Jan. 15-Feb. 2 and Nov.-Dec. 9am-6pm. Closed first two weeks in Jan. Last entry 1¼hr. before closing. €16, students, seniors, and ages 10-18 €14, may be less Oct.-Mar.)*

ABBEYS AND CHURCHES. Caen got its start as the seat of William the Conqueror's duchy; the city's legacy of first-class Romanesque architecture is due chiefly to William's guilty conscience. Despite the pope's explicit interdiction, William married his distant cousin Mathilda. To get themselves back on the gold-paved road to Heaven, the duke and his wife built several ecclesiastical structures, most notably Caen's twin abbeys. In 1066, William began the **Abbaye-aux-Hommes,** off rue Guillaume le Conquérant, which now functions as Caen's Hôtel de Ville. (☎02 31 30 42 81.) The adjacent **Eglise St-Etienne** contains William's tomb and an enormous organ you can climb into. In one of the chapels off the choir is a small collection of photographs taken in Caen during and after the bombings. Many of the city's displaced citizens took shelter in the abbey; stunning photographs show upper-class women struggling for normalcy as they glance at the mirror by candlelight between the church's columns. *(Open daily 9:15am-noon and 2-6pm. 1¼hr. tours of church in French at 9:30am, 2:30, 4pm; of Hôtel de Ville at 11am. €2, students €1, under 18 free.)* Across the street from the abbey's gardens are the tower and remaining arches of the **Eglise St-Etienne-le-Vieux,** a raw, unrestored reminder of the destruction of the bombings. The smaller Eglise de la Trinité of the **Abbaye-aux-Dames,** off rue des Chanoines, has two 16th-century towers and modern windows illuminating Mathilda's trapezoidal tomb. To visit the crypt, go through the low doorway in the left side of the south transept, on the right when you enter the church. *(Open M-Sa 8am-5:30pm, Su 9:30am-12:30pm. Free 1hr. tours in French at 2:30 and 4pm.)*

CHÂTEAU. Centered between the two abbeys to its east and west sprawl the ruins of William's enormous **château,** overlooking Caen below. Its construction began in 1060, but a community may have existed here since the first century AD. *(Open May-Sept. daily 6am-1am; Oct.-Apr. 6am-7:30pm. Free. Tours may be available.)* The château's outer walls hide the sparkling but confusingly laid-out **Musée des Beaux-Arts,** which contains a fine selection of 16th- and 17th-century Italian, French, Dutch, and Flemish works, Impressionist paintings of Normandy, and eclectic 20th-century art. *(☎02 31 30 47 70. Open W-M 9:30am-6pm. €4, students €2.50, art history students and under age 18 free, W free. Joint ticket with Musée de Normandie €6, students €4.)* The small **Jardin des Simples** within the château holds a collection of plants used in the Middle Ages. *(Same hours as château.)*

OTHER SIGHTS. Just beyond the château is the **Musée de Normandie,** which traces the origins of Norman craftsmanship and farming. *(☎02 31 30 47 60. Open W-M 9:30am-12:30pm and 2-6pm. €2, students €1, under 18 free.)* For a break from the bustle of Caen's center, take a walk around the château walls on rue de Geôle, turning left on rue Bosnières, to reach the sheltered, romantic **Jardin des Plantes** on pl. Blot. *(Open June-Aug. daily 8am-sunset; Sept.-May 8am-5:30pm.)*

♫ ENTERTAINMENT

Caen parties every night, especially during the school year. **Rue de Bras, rue des Croisiers, quai Vendeuvre,** and **rue St-Pierre** are packed with well-attended bars and clubs. Crowds of laid-back university students can be found at **Vertigo,** 14 rue Ecuyère, gathering around outdoor tables to wait for the night to heat up. *(☎02 31 85 43 12. House cocktails €3. Open July-Sept. M-W noon-1am, Th-Sa noon-2am; Oct.-June M-Sa noon-1am.)* **Farniente,** 13 rue Paul Doumer, draws the young and the chic who warm up for the clubs by grinding to Latin music and throwing back tequila. *(☎02 31 86 30 00. Open M-W 6pm-1am, Th-Sa 6pm-2am.)* Glance at the funky modern artwork of **L'Excuse,** 20 rue Vauquelin, on your way to the dance floor, where they work it to everything from house to Arab-inspired techno. *(☎02 31 38 80 89. Beer and liquor €5.50. Occasional €4 cover. Open June-Aug. Th-Sa 11pm-4am, Sept.-May Th-Sa 10pm-4am. Doors close 2am.)* Large, loud **La Bodega,** 11 rue des Croisiers, is yet another pub to keep the young Caennais happy—with its bustling feel and happy hour 5-8pm. *(☎02 31 85 22 33. Sangria and beer €1.70. Open most days 5pm-2am.)* Steamy **Le Zinc,** 12 rue du Vaugueux, supplies a mixed gay and straight crowd with heart-pounding techno. *(☎02 31 93 20 30. Beer €2.50, liquor €5.60. Open Tu-Th 6pm-2am and F-Sa 6pm-4am.)*

BAYEUX

Bayeux (pop. 15,000) was unharmed by Nazi occupation and Allied liberation; as a result, the town retains its original river-hugging architecture and resplendent cathedral. Bayeux is most visited for its celebrated 900-year-old tapestry, which narrates William the Conqueror's victory over England in 1066. Bayeux is a beautiful base for exploration of the D-Day beaches, but it should by no means be treated simply as a stopover. Some visitors skip the tapestry to see the beaches, but this masterpiece narrates an equally significant invasion.

🛈 PRACTICAL INFORMATION

Trains: pl. de la Gare (☎02 31 92 80 50). Ticket counters open M-F 6am-8pm, Sa-Su 8am-8pm. To: **Caen** (20min., 15 per day, €4.90); **Cherbourg** (1hr., 12 per day, €12.50); **Paris** (2½hr., 12 per day, €26.75).

Buses: Bus Verts, pl. de la Gare (☎02 31 92 02 92). Open M-F 9:15am-noon and 1:30-6pm. Buses head west to small towns and east to **Caen** (1hr., M-Sa 2-3 per day, €5.60). See p. 197 for coverage of the D-Day beaches. Buy tickets from the driver or at the office. **Bybus,** pl. de la Gare (☎02 31 92 02 92). In-town bus circuit runs about 9am-6pm. €0.85 or €0.65 9-11:30am and 2-4pm.

Taxis: Les Taxis du Bessin (☎02 31 92 92 40).

Bike Rental: Available at the hostel, €10 per day, with a €20 deposit.

Tourist Office: Pont St-Jean (☎02 31 51 28 28; fax 02 31 51 28 29; www.bayeux-tourism.com). To find it from the station, turn left onto the highway (bd. Sadi-Carnot), then bear right at the roundabout, still on bd. Sadi-Carnot, following the signs to the *centre ville*. Once there, continue up rue Larcher and turn right on rue St-Martin, Bayeux's commercial avenue. The office will be on your left, at the edge of the pedestrian zone. The staff offers a comprehensive regional brochure, gaspingly expensive **Internet access** (€4.50 per 15min., €9 per 50min., €16 for 100min.), and books rooms anywhere in Calvados for €1.50. Open June 15-Sept. 15 M-Sa 9am-7pm, Su 9am-1pm and 2-6pm; Sept. 16-June 14 M-Sa 9am-12:30pm and 2-6pm.

Laundromat: 10 rue Maréchal Foch. Open daily 7am-9pm.

Police: 49 av. Conseil (☎02 31 92 94 00).

Hospital: 13 rue de Nesmond (☎02 31 51 51 51), next to the tapestry center.

Post Office: rue Larcher (☎02 31 51 24 90). **Currency exchange. Internet access** through Cyberposte. Open M-F 8am-6:30pm, Sa 8am-noon. **Postal code:** 14400.

🛏 ACCOMMODATIONS AND CAMPING

There are several inexpensive lodgings in Bayeux, but demand often outstrips supply, especially in summer. You'll need to plan with military precision to get a room around June 6, the anniversary of D-Day.

■**The Family Home/Auberge de Jeunesse (HI),** 39 rue Général de Dais (☎02 31 92 15 22; fax 02 31 92 55 72), is right in the center of town. From the tourist office, turn right onto rue St-Martin (the name changes) and turn left onto rue Général de Dais. The hostel will be on your left. (5min.) Or, from rue Larcher, turn left on rue L. Leforestier, then right onto rue Général de Dais; the hostel will be on the right. Amazing accommodations in 1- to 7-person rooms branching off a main courtyard. Communal laundry, kitchen, TV, and dining room make meeting other guests a cinch. Huge breakfast included; most diners take advantage of the fantastic dinner fare at night (€10), which may be the best meal you'll eat all week. Reception hours inconsistent, but someone is always around during the day. So popular in the summer that you may be displaced after one night. Beds €16, without HI membership €18; single room €28. Help clean the kitchen and they promise lunch and a free bed for the night. ❷

Centre d'Accueil Municipal, 21 chemin des Marettes (☎02 31 92 08 19; fax 02 31 92 12 40). From the station, follow bd. Sadi-Carnot and bear left at the rotary onto bd. Maréchal Leclerc, which becomes bd. Fabien Ware. (10-15min.) Perseverance is key to getting the door answered. This *centre d'accueil* has the look of a 60s-era hotel, with sterile, spartan singles inside. Don't expect a hostel atmosphere here; the center is huge and quite impersonal. Breakfast €2.50. Sheets included. Reception 8am-8pm; call if arriving late. Beds €11.90. ❶

Le Maupassant, 19 rue St-Martin (☎02 31 92 28 53). Small but central, clean rooms above a street and *brasserie* heavy with pedestrian traffic. Breakfast €5.35. Reception 8am-10pm. Singles with or without shower €26; doubles with shower or toilet €33.55; quads with bath €61. ❸

Camping Municipal, bd. d'Eindhoven (☎02 31 92 08 43), is within easy reach of the town center and the N13. Follow rue Genas Duhomme to the right off rue St-Martin and continue straight on av. de la Vallée des Prés. The campground is on your right, across from a Champion Supermarket. (10min.) Immaculate sites and shiny facilities next to the municipal swimming pool. Laundry, great showers. Gates close 10pm-7am. Office open July-Aug. 7am-9pm; May-June and Sept. 8-10am and 5-7pm. Open May-Sept. €2.85 per person, children under 7 €1.55, €3.52 per tent and car. Electricity €2.90. Showers included. 10% reduction on stays of 5 or more days. ❶

🍴 FOOD

Markets are on pl. St-Patrice on Saturdays, and rue St-Jean on Wednesdays, both about 7am-1pm. The area around the tourist office has small grocery stores and there is a **Champion** supermarket on bd. d'Eindhoven, near the campground. Most of the towns eateries populate the rue St-Martin, rue St-Jean and their sidestreets. One of the heartiest and most engaging restaurants in the city is **La Table du Terroir** ❹, 42 rue St-Jean, down the street from the tourist office. The jovial chef-owner and his family serve local meat dishes and delicious desserts at communal wooden tables. (☎02 31 92 05 53. *Menus* €16, €20, and €26. Open Tu-Sa noon-2:30pm and 7-10pm, Su noon-2:30pm; Oct.-May F-Sa 7-10pm.)

👁 SIGHTS

■ **TAPISSERIE DE BAYEUX.** The exquisite tapestry illustrates in vibrant detail the events leading up to the Battle of Hastings. In the famed year 1066, William the Bastard earned himself a more sociable nickname by crossing the Channel with a large cavalry to defeat his cousin Harold who, according to the Norman version of the tale, had stolen the English throne from William. William's victory, following a grueling 14-hour battle in which Harold was dramatically killed by an archer, would be the last successful invasion of England. A mere 50cm wide but 70m long, the tapestry, now over 900 years old, hangs in all its glory at the **Centre Guillaume le Conquérant,** rue de Nesmond. Take note of the horses, the soldiers flailing in quicksand at Mont-St-Michel (frames 16-17), Halley's comet (32-33), and poor Harold, with the fatal arrow in his eye (57). A lengthy, elaborate exhibit details the tapestry's contents and depicts 11th-century life; the film before the tapestry gives a comprehensive step-by-step overview of the events depicted, making the audio guide necessary only for the more minute details. Everything is translated into English. (☎02 31 51 25 50. *Open May-Aug. daily 9am-7pm; Mar. 15-Apr. and Sept.-Oct. 15 9am-6:30pm; Oct. 16-Mar. 14 9:30am-12:30pm and 2-6pm. €6.40, seniors €5, ages 10-26 €2.60, under 10 free; includes Musée Baron Gérard and Hôtel du Doyen, a religious art museum and center for lace production. Audio guide €1.*)

CATHÉDRAL NOTRE-DAME. Nearby is the original home of the tapestry, the **Cathédrale Notre-Dame.** Above the transept are Gothic arches with dizzyingly intricate carvings, while the 11th-century crypt reveals chipping 15th-century frescoes. To the left of the entrance is the *salle capitulaire,* which contains the only *chemin de Jerusalem* in France, a tile labyrinth on the floor that retraces the twists and turns of Jesus's *via crucis;* the route that he followed on the way to

Calvary. *(Open July-Aug. M-Sa 8am-7pm, Su 9am-7pm; Sept.-June M-Sa 8:30am-noon and 2:30-7pm, Su 9am-12:15pm and 2:30-7pm. Informal tours of the cathedral July-Aug. Tu-F approximately 10am-noon and 3-7pm. Tours of the salle capitulaire July-Aug. M-F 1, 3, and 5pm.)*

MUSÉE BARON GERARD. Next to the cathedral, the **Musée Baron Gérard,** on pl. de la Liberté, houses a large collection of porcelain, along with tapestries, 16th- and 17th-century paintings, and the delicate lace characteristic of Bayeux. Just before you enter the museum, glance at the enormous tree, planted in 1793 to commemorate the French Revolution, that fills the *place.* *(☎02 31 51 60 50. Open June-Sept. 15 daily 9am-7pm; Sept. 16-May 10am-12:30pm and 2-6pm. Prices same as to the tapestry, but admission to tapestry gets you in free to Musée Baron Gérard.)*

LOCAL D-DAY SIGHTS. The events of the D-Day landing and the subsequent 76-day battle are recounted in the overwhelming **Musée de la Bataille de Normandie,** bd. Fabian Ware. American, English, French, and German newspapers of the time are presented along with photos, weapons, and innumerable uniform-clad mannequins. It is impossible to cover the entire exhibit, though—there's just too much small type. *(☎02 31 51 46 90. www.maire-bayeux.fr. Open May-Sept. 16 daily 9:30am-6:30pm; Sept. 17-Apr. 10am-12:30pm and 2-6pm. 30min. film in English approx. every 2hr. Closed last two weeks in Jan. €5.70, seniors and military €4.40, students €2.50, under age 10 free.)* In contrast, the strikingly simple **British Cemetery** across the street provides an understated but more moving wartime record.

THE D-DAY BEACHES

By 1944, the German forces stationed along the northern coasts of France had been waiting for an Allied invasion for the four years since they had taken over the Republic. The area around Calais, at the English Channel's narrowest point, had been heavily fortified. Normandy was slightly less prepared for a full-scale invasion, but German General Erwin Rommel's command still made it a treacherous landing zone. Preparations for the attack began in 1943, when the Allied leaders concluded that the only way to defeat Hitler was to recapture what he had dubbed "Fortress Europe." The attack, a gamble from the outset, would come mostly from the sea. Allied counterintelligence disseminated false attack plans, inflated dummy tanks near Norway, and flooded the radio waves with retired military men. Meanwhile, the British, Canadian, and American masterminds of "Operation Overlord" planned a landing on the Normandy coast between the Cotentin Peninsula and the Orne. In the pre-dawn hours of **June 6, 1944,** 16,000 British and US paratroopers tumbled from the sky; a few hours later, 135,000 troops and 20,000 vehicles landed in fog from a rough sea onto the beaches code-named Utah and Omaha (American), Gold and Sword (British), and Juno (Canadian). The D-Day landings caused devastating losses on both sides, but were a crucial precursor to great successes for the Allies. The Battle of Normandy raged on for two and a half months until August 21. On August 24, free French forces entered and liberated Paris. Less than a year later, Allied forces rolled into Berlin, and Germany surrendered.

The **Voie de la Liberté** (Liberty Highway) follows the US army's advance from Utah Beach to Bastogne in Belgium. For a complete description of the sites and museums which commemorate the battle, pick up *The D-Day Landings and the Battle of Normandy,* a brochure available from most tourist offices in the area. Today, the battle's traces are visible in remnants of German bunkers and the few unfilled bomb craters dotting the coast. Monuments, cemeteries, and museums commemorating the battle and its victims are strewn across Normandy from Cherbourg to Le Havre. The anniversary of D-Day, June 6, is a powerfully moving experience as veterans return to pay their respects at memorial services.

NORMANDY

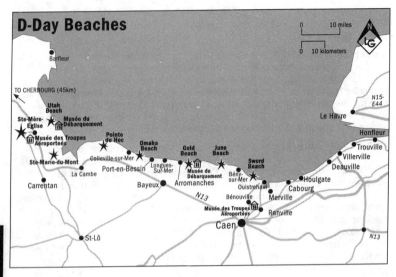

D-Day Beaches

TO CHERBOURG (45km)

Barfleur

Utah Beach
Ste-Mère-Eglise
Musée du Débarquement
Musée des Troupes Aéroportés
Pointe du Hoc
Omaha Beach
Gold Beach
Juno Beach
Ste-Marie-du-Mont
Colleville-sur-Mer
Longues-Sur-Mer
Sword Beach
La Cambe
Port-en-Bessin
Musée du Débarquement
Bény-sur-Mer
Carrentan
Bayeux
Arromanches
Ouistreham
Bénouville
Merville
Musée des Troupes Aéroportés
Ranville
Caen
St-Lô
N13
N13
Le Havre
Honfleur
Trouville
Villerville
Deauville
Houlgate
Cabourg
N15-E44

0 ——— 10 miles
0 ——— 10 kilometers

■ **TRANSPORTATION.** Although the most convenient way to see the beaches is undoubtedly by car, most of the beaches and museums can be reached from Caen and Bayeux with the help of **Bus Verts** (☎08 10 21 42 14). Ask about the special **"D-Day" line** that runs from Arromanches to the Pointe du Hoc, stopping at the US Cemetery and Omaha Beach along the way. The bus leaves from Caen for Arromanches at 9:30am and returns at 6pm (unit ticket €12); from Bayeux take **#75** in time for a 2pm departure from Arromanches (buy the *Carte Liberté*, €17.50 for one day or €27 for 3 days). To get to Benouville and Ouistreham, take **Bus Verts #1** from Caen; **#20** links Caen to the British cemetery at Ranville. Line **#70** (M-Sa 5 per day, 3 on Su) runs from Bayeux to Pointe du Hoc, the American Cemetery, and Port-en-Bessin. Line **#75** goes to Arromanches and Ouistreham (3 per day). You may want to buy a day-pass if you plan to make many stops. Ste-Mère-Eglise is accessible by **STN** bus (☎02 33 77 44 88) from Carentan (15min.; 1 per day at 12:50pm, return at 6:35pm; €2.90). Call the Carentan tourist office (☎02 33 42 74 01) for more info. To get to Carentan, you can take the train from Bayeux (30min., 10 per day, €6.70). Utah Beach and the Musée du Débarquement are only accessible by car, foot, or thumb from Ste-Mère-Eglise, though *Let's Go*, as always, does not recommend hitchhiking.

Before renting a car or heading off by bus, consider a **tour.** All three companies listed here include admission to the museum in Arromanches. **Normandy Sightseeing Tours,** formerly **Bus Fly,** rue des Cuisiniers in Bayeux, runs tours with impeccable English-speaking guides, also available in German, Spanish, Italian, Japanese, and Chinese. (☎02 31 22 00 08 or 02 31 51 70 52; fax 02 31 92 35 10; www.normandywebguide.com; françois.gauthron@wanadoo.fr. 4hr. tour €35, students €30; 8hr. tour €70. Pick-up 8:30am and 1:30pm from your hotel or hostel. Reservations required.) **Victory Tours** leads tours in English that leave from behind the tourist office in Bayeux. (☎02 31 51 98 14; fax 02 31 51 07 01; www.victory-tours.com or www.lignerolles.homestead.com. 4hr. tour at 12:30pm, €31. 8hr. tour at 9:15am, €54. Reservations required.) **Normandy Tours,** 26 pl. de la Gare, based in Bayeux's Hôtel de la Gare, runs flexible tours with less commentary in both English and French. (☎02 31 92 10 70; fax 02 31 51 95 99. 4hr. tour €31, 8:30am and 1pm.) Tipping tour guides is gracious, but not mandatory.

NORMANDY

⌂ ACCOMMODATIONS. Camping Reine Mathilde, in Etreham, near Port-en-Bessin, is 5km from the sea and Omaha Beach, 10km from Bayeux, and always packed. (☎ 02 31 21 76 55; fax 02 31 22 18 33; camping.reine-mathilde@wanadoo.fr. Open Apr.-Sept. Reception daily 8:30am-12:30pm and 2:30-7:30pm. €4.50 per person, children under age 7 €2, €4.20 per tent and car, electricity €3.55.) Bayeux's tourist office can help you find accommodations in *chambres d'hôte* or in one of the many campgrounds along the coast.

BEACHES NEAR BAYEUX

Local tourist offices distribute a list of D-Day museums and sights that offer discounted admission with a full-price ticket to another museum or sight.

▨ UTAH BEACH. The Americans spearheaded the western flank of the invasion at **Utah Beach,** near Ste-Marie du Mont. Utah was one of the more successful operations of the day; all objectives were completed on schedule, and with fewer casualties than expected. This feat of military planning is honored by the **American Commemorative Monument** and the **Musée du Débarquement.** Films and models in the latter show how 836,000 soldiers, 220,000 vehicles, and 725,000 tons of equipment came ashore. (☎ 02 33 71 53 35. Open June-Sept. daily 9:30am-7pm; Apr.-May and Oct. 10am-12:30pm and 2-6pm; Nov.-Mar. Sa-Su 10am-12:30pm and 2-5:30pm. €4.50, ages 6-16 €2.) Nearby **Ste-Mère-Eglise** was one of the most important targets of the invasion. The town was on the road to Carentan, which held a German depot, and Cherbourg, the port the Allies hoped to recapture. Many paratroopers had been misdropped, and in the pre-dawn hours these soldiers fell directly into the town. Visible as targets for German artillery and encumbered by heavy equipment, 16% were killed before they hit the ground. Even so, a badly outnumbered group of paratroopers broke through heavy German defenses after six hours of fighting. The parachute-shaped **Musée des Troupes Aéroporteés,** 14 rue Eisenhower, houses one of the planes that dropped them. (☎ 02 33 41 41 35. Open Apr.-Sept. daily 9am-6:45pm; Feb.-Mar. and Oct.-Nov. 9:30am-noon and 2-6pm; closed Dec.-Jan. and Nov. 5, 2002-Mar. 22, 2003 for construction. €5, ages 6-14 €2.)

POINTE DU HOC. The most difficult landing was that of the First US Infantry Division at **Pointe du Hoc.** Not only was this the most strongly fortified of all the coastline strongholds, but it stood above 30m cliffs that had to be scaled with ropes and hooks. Of the 225 specially trained US Rangers who climbed the bluff, neutralized a key German position, and single-handedly defended it for two days, only 90 survived. German losses were even heavier: only 40 prisoners were left among the 2000 stationed there. The Pointe is considered to be a military cemetery because so many casualties still remain there, crushed beneath collapsed 5m thick concrete bunkers. Dozens of unfilled bomb craters dive into the earth surrounding the rubble in one of the few areas that still reflects the day's destruction; it is possible to enter some surviving bunkers.

▨ OMAHA BEACH. Next to Colleville-sur-Mer and just east of the Pointe du Hoc, **Omaha Beach** is perhaps the most famous of all the beaches—often referred to as "bloody Omaha." Nothing went right here on D-Day: scouts failed to detect a German presence, and aerial and naval bombardment of the fortifications were entirely ineffective due to foggy conditions. The beach was protected by three veteran battalions (instead of the single motley division that the Americans had expected), was covered with mine-topped jack-and-pole devices called "Rommel's asparagus," and ended in concrete walls, anti-tank ditches, minefields, and barbed wire. The first waves of troops to hit the shores suffered casualties of nearly 100%, and of 32 amphibious tanks initially launched, only one made it ashore. 6,000 men

ROBERT HALLIDAY, D-DAY VETERAN

Mr. Halliday served as a parachutist in the 12th Yorks Battalion, 6th British Airborne Division, nicknamed the "Red Berets." His division, which captured the Pegasus Bridge at Benouville, was one of the first to arrive in Normandy on the early morning of June 6, 1944.

Q: How often do you come back to the battle site?

A: We [the Red Berets] come over every year. Most of us are from England. We gradually get fewer and fewer, because the men are now in their eighties. It gets sadder every year.

Q: What was your experience at Normandy?

A: The American aircraft we jumped out of was hit, and as soon as we left, the plane crashed. The outcome of the crew we don't know; that sort of thing happened all the time.

Q: How do the tributes to the D-Day vets here personally affect you?

A: The nicest thing was someone who spoke to me the year before last. He was French. He had our insignias on his jacket, and also he showed me an original photograph of the beaches that he had given his son.

Q: Do you think films and museums teach real lessons about WWII?

A: Hollywood films today really fabricate stories about D-Day, with these big handsome guys doing impossible things. It was blokes like us, who had next to nothing, on a few shillings a week, all volunteers. I myself was 17 when I joined the army.

of the initial wave of 35,000 died within the first hour of fighting, and an additional 8,000 were killed the same day. After a heavy rain, pieces of 57-year-old German barbed wire can still be found peeking out of the sand near the grass at the back of the beach.

AMERICAN CEMETERY. Overlooking Omaha beach, 9,387 American graves stretch across a 172-acre coastal reserve. The **American Cemetery,** in Colleville-sur-mer, contains rows of immaculate white crosses and stars of David, among them the graves of a father and his son and 38 pairs of brothers. A simple marble chapel and a 7m bronze statue, *The Spirit of American Youth Rising from the Waves,* face the soldiers's graves, while the Garden of the Missing, behind the memorial, lists the names of the 1557 individuals whose remains were never recovered. The cemetery contains only a fraction of all those killed here, as many soldiers were buried in the US instead. (☎ 02 31 51 62 00; fax 02 31 51 62 09; www.abmc.gov. *Open Apr. 16-Sept. daily 8am-6pm; Oct.-Apr. 15 9am-5pm. The American staff at the office can help locate specific graves.)* Not far from Omaha Beach, in La Cambe, is the **German Military Cemetery**. This memorial area contains the graves of 21,300 German casualties of World War II, often overlooked by the victorious Allied side, and a Peace Garden of maple trees. (☎ 02 31 22 70 76; fax 02 31 22 05 27; www.volksbund.de. *Open Apr-Oct. daily 8am-7pm; Nov.-Mar. 8am-5:30pm.)*

BATTERIES DE LONGUES. Six kilometers west of Arromanches in tiny **Longues-sur-Mer,** the **Batteries de Longues** are an ominous reminder of the German presence. Visitors can climb through these four bunkers, constructed in 1944, which still hold their original artillery; one contains the only cannon in the region still loaded with its original ammunition. The D-Day naval bombardment destroyed the town a kilometer inland, but left the bunkers intact for the most part. On June 7, surrender by the German and Polish troops stationed here to British troops was almost instantaneous, leaving no casualties. (☎ 02 31 06 06 45; fax 02 31 06 01 66. *Tours in French and English daily through the Caen Memorial 10am-5:30pm; Apr.-May none M-Tu. €4, €3.50 with ticket stub from almost any other area museum. Open June-Aug. 10am-7pm, Sept.-May 10am-6pm.)*

GOLD BEACH. At **Arromanches,** a small town at the center of **Gold Beach,** the British used retired ships and 600,000 tons of concrete towed across the Channel to build **Port Winston,** the floating harbor that was to supply the Allied forces until Cherbourg was liberated months later. The hulking ruins of a port built in six days and designed to last 18 months remain 57 years later in a broken semicircle just off the coast. The **Musée du Débarquement** on the beach uses models to show how the port was built, towed, and assembled under fire. Two short, effective films and frequent tours make this one of the better museums in the area, though nowhere near the stylistic masterpiece of the Caen memorial. (☎ 02 31 22 34 31; www.normandy1944.com. Open May-Aug. daily 9am-7pm; Sept. 9am-6pm; Oct. and Mar. 9:30am-12:30pm and 1:30-5:30pm; Apr. 9am-12:30pm and 1:30-6pm; Nov.-Dec. and Feb. 10am-12:30pm and 1:30-5pm. Opens at 10am on Sunday, except June-Aug (9am). Closed Dec. 30-Jan. 28. €6, students and children over 6 €4.) The **Arromanches 360° Cinéma** shows a well-made 18-minute film, Le Prix de la Liberté (The Price of Freedom), on its circular screen. The movie combines battle footage with peaceful images of pre-war Normandy. To reach the cinema from the museum, turn left on rue de la Batterie and follow the steps to the top of the cliff. (☎ 02 31 22 30 30. Open June-Aug. daily 9:40am-6:40pm; May 15-31 and Sept. 1-14 10:10am-6:10pm; Sept. 15-Oct. 10:10am-5:40pm; Mar.-May 14 and Nov. 10:10am-5:10pm; Dec. and Feb. 10:10am-4:40pm. Closed Jan. Movies at 10 and 40min. past the hour. €3.65, children 10-18 €3.20.)

BEACHES NEAR CAEN

These eastern beaches were landing sites for the Canadian and British armies; German defenders fired on them from expensive stone vacation houses along the beach. The beaches have changed considerably since 1944. The bunkers of Juno, Sword, and Gold Beaches have been replaced by resorts, and the somber taboos against recreation which characterize the American sites are not maintained here.

JUNO BEACH. East of Arromanches, **Juno Beach** was the Canadian battlefront. The last Canadian amphibious attack, in Sicily in 1942, had resulted in 75% casualties and ultimate failure. Bent on revenge at Juno, they pushed their attacks through without air or naval support and despite terrible losses. The **Canadian Cemetery** is located at **Bény-sur-Mer-Reviers** (take Bus Verts #4 from Caen). The British anchored the easternmost flank of the invasion with their landing at **Sword Beach.** This enormously successful mission was accomplished with the help of the quirky "Hobart's Funnies," tanks outlandishly fitted with bridge-building, mine-sweeping, and ditch-digging apparatus.

BENOUVILLE. It was here that British paratroopers of the 6th Airborne Division captured Pegasus Bridge within 10 minutes of landing and held it until their Scottish reinforcements arrived. The **Musée des Troupes Aéroportées,** also known as the **Memorial Pegasus,** at the Pegasus Bridge between Benouville and Ranville, tells the story of the Parachute Brigades's operations on the Dives River. To reach it, take Bus Verts #1 from Caen and get off "Mairie" in Benouville; continue down the road, take a right at the roundabout, cross the bridge, and the entrance is on your left. (☎ 02 31 44 62 54; fax 02 31 78 19 42; www.normandy1944.com. Open May-Sept. daily 9:30am-6:30pm; Oct.-Nov. and Feb.-Apr. 10am-1pm and 2-5pm. €5, students and children €3.50.) One of the largest of the 16 British cemeteries is 1.5km away in **Ranville.** The only French troops involved in the D-Day landings came ashore at **Ouistreham,** at the mouth of the Orne River. They and Normandy's resilient citizens are memorialized in the **N°4 Commando Museum,** pl. Alfred Thomas. (☎ 02 31 96 63 10. Open mid-Mar. to Oct. daily 10:30am-6pm. €4, students and children 10 and over €2.50.) and in **le Grand Bunker: Musée du Mur de l'Atlantique** (€6, children 6-12 €4). The museums and the Ouistreham **tourist office** lie in a row: take Bus Verts #1 from Caen and get off at "Centre" in Ouistreham; walk right down rue Général Leclerc, turn left on av. de la Mer and follow it to the beach. The tourist office will be directly in front of you, N°4 Commando Museum will be on your left, and the Grand Bunker will be down the street to your right.

CHERBOURG

Strategically located at the tip of the Cotentin peninsula, Cherbourg (pop. 44,000) was the Allies' "Gateway to France," their major supply port following the D-Day offensive of 1944. Today, the town's numerous ferry lines shuttle tourists from France to England and Ireland. Don't go out of your way to visit Cherbourg; the city is short on both sights and charm. But if you find yourself there on your way in and out of France, don't despair. There's just enough to keep you busy until the next train or ferry leaves.

◪ PRACTICAL INFORMATION. Ferries leave from the *gare maritime*, northeast of the town center, along bd. Maritime (open daily 5:30am-11:30pm). Irish Ferries goes to Rosslare about every other day. P&O European Ferries go to Portsmouth, and Brittany Ferries to Poole (see **Getting There: By Boat,** p. 67). It is essential to both reserve ahead and check the most up-to-date ferry schedules; many travelers find themselves stranded in Cherbourg if they don't plan ahead. To reach the **train station,** go left at the roundabout onto av. Aristide Briand and follow it as it becomes av. Carnot. Turn right at the end of the canal onto av. Millet; the station will be ahead on the left. (25min.) **Trains** run to Bayeux via Lison (1hr., 8 per day in the afternoon, €12.80); Caen (1½hr., 10 per day, €15.70); Paris (3hr., 7 per day, €34.20); Rennes via Lison (3½hr., 3 per day, €27.10); Rouen (4½hr., 4 per day, €29.10). Station open daily 5:30am-7:30pm. To walk from the train station to the *gare maritime* for a ferry, turn right onto av. Millet, and then left onto av. Carnot, which becomes av. Aristide Briand. Go right at the roundabout onto bd. Felix Amiot; continue and the ferries will be on the left. **STN** (☎ 02 33 88 51 00) sends **buses** around the region (€1 per ride); the bus station is across the street from the train station. (Open M-F 8am-noon and 2-6pm.) You can rent **bikes** from the hostel in the summertime, or from **Station Voile,** rue Diablotin. (☎ 02 33 78 19 29. Open June 15-Sept. 15 daily 10am-6pm. €7 per half-day, €12 per day. Deposit of €305 or credit card number required. MC/V.) Catch a **taxi** at the train station and at the top of Quai Alexandre III by the tourist office and the bridge (☎ 02 33 53 36 38).

To get to the **tourist office** and the center of town, turn right from the terminal onto bd. Felix Amiot. At the roundabout, go straight and continue around the bend to the left. Make a right at the first bridge to cross the canal; you will see the tourist office ahead on your left. (20min.) The **tourist office,** 2 quai Alexandre III, leads hikes and tours in summer, and books rooms for free. (☎ 02 33 93 52 02; fax 02 33 53 66 97; www.ot-cherbourg-cotentin.fr. Open 9am-12:30pm and 2-6pm.) An **annex** at the *gare maritime* is open for ferry arrivals and departures. (☎ 02 33 44 39 92. Open daily approx. 7am-noon and 2-8pm; Sept.-May closes at 6pm.) There's **currency exchange** at the ferry terminal or at banks around **place Gréville. Internet access** is available upstairs at the **Forum espace culture,** pl. Centrale, a large bookstore off rue au Blé. (☎ 02 33 78 19 30. Open M 2-7pm, Tu-Sa 10am-7pm. €1.50 per 10 min., €3.25 per 30min.) The **post office** is on rue de l'Ancien Quai, at place Divette. There's a **branch** on av. Carnot near the ferry terminal. (☎ 02 33 08 87 00. Open M-F 8am-7pm, Sa 8am-noon.) **Postal code:** 50100.

◪◪ ACCOMMODATIONS AND FOOD. Cherbourg's few budget accommodations are often available, since most people leave town as soon as they step off the ferry, but check the possibilities a few days in advance. The tourist office has lists of *chambres d'hôte* (around €23) and nearby campsites. The cheapest option is the **Auberge de Jeunesse (HI) ❶,** 57 rue de l'Abbaye. From the tourist office, go left onto quai de Caligny and then left again on rue de Port, which becomes rue Tour Carrée and then rue de la Paix. Bear left onto rue de l'Union, which feeds into rue de l'Abbaye; the hostel is on the left. (10min.) From the station, take bus #3 or 5 to "Arsenal" (last bus around 7:30pm); the hostel is across the street from the bus stop. The hostel has 100 beds in spotless 2- to 5-person rooms, each with a sink, shower, and lockers (bring your own lock), a kitchen, and bar. (☎02 33 78 15 15; fax 02 33 78 15 16; cherbourg@fuaj.org. Bike rental available, approx €8 per half-day, €12.50 per day. Sheets €2.70. Reception 8am-noon and 6-11pm. Lockout from 10am-6pm; can enter after 1pm if you've already checked in. No curfew. Bunks and breakfast €14.90 1st night, €12.20 2nd night; non-HI members €17.80/€15.10.) Opposite the station, **Hôtel de la Gare ❸**, 10 pl. Jean Jaurès, lets large, colorful, lovingly tended rooms that seem miles away from the asphalt. (☎02 33 43 06 81; fax 02 33 43 12 20. Bacon and egg breakfast €5.50. Reception 24hr. Singles and doubles with shower €28-31, with toilet €34-42; triples and quads €46-57. All rooms with TV. MC/V.)

A huge **market** is held on pl. du Théâtre on Tuesday morning and on Thursday until 3pm. Stock up at the **Carrefour** supermarket, quai de l'Entrepôt, next to the station (open M-Sa 8:30am-9pm) or at the **Proxi**, rue de l'Union, near the hostel. (Open daily 8:30am-1pm and 3-7:30pm.) **Rue de la Paix** is lined with inexpensive ethnic restaurants and small bars. **Crêperie Ty-Billic ❷**, 73 rue au Blé, is a tourist-free haven. Get two *galettes*, two crepes, and one cider for €9. (☎02 33 01 11 90. Open daily noon-2:30pm and 7-11:15pm.)

◨ ◪ SIGHTS AND ENTERTAINMENT. Cherbourg's latest attraction, **La Cité de la Mer,** is by far its best. Located at the Gare Maritime Transatlantique, across the bridge from the tourist office and most of Cherbourg's tourist locales, the vast complex is dedicated to the underwater exploits of man and animals. An impressive array of interactive exhibits on topics from scuba to sonar to sharks are both accessible to children and interesting to adults. The high point of the visit is a full audio-guided walking tour (in French or English) of *Le Redoubtable*, a nuclear submarine (children under 6 not allowed). Convenient to the ferry terminal and equipped with a post office branch, restaurant, and bar, La Cité de la Mer promises the best way to pass a rainy afternoon in this transit town. (☎02 33 20 26 26. Open June-Sept. 15 9:30am-7pm; Sept. 16-May 10am-6pm. May-Sept. €13, under 17 €9.50, under 7 free; Oct.-Apr. €11.50, under 17 €8.50, under 7 free.)

Founded by Mathilde, granddaughter of William the Conqueror and mother of England's King Henry the First, the 12th-century semi-ruined **Abbaye du Vœu** and its gardens are at the western edge of town, past the hostel. (Free entrance to gardens. Occasional guided tours of abbey at 2:30pm.) With intricate lacework and dark, angular windows in the transept, the **Basilique de la Trinité**, pl. Napoléon, off Quai de Caligny, has meshed centuries of architectural styles. Sixteenth-century carvings above the nave include a grotesque skeleton on the left, who gives the reminder that "death comes for us all."

The streets around pl. Central are filled with bars and late-night eateries that are happy to help you drink away your layover. Multilingual crowds congregate nightly at **Art's Café**, 69 rue au Blé. (☎02 33 53 55 11. Live DJ F-Sa. Beer €1.85. Open M-Sa 11am-1am.) Or try mellow **Le Solier**, 52 rue Grande Rue, with cushy stools, Celtic music, and cheap cider. (☎02 33 94 76 63. Open June-Sept. M-Sa 6pm-2am; Oct.-May M-Sa 6pm-1am.) The second week of October, Cherbourg hosts the **Festival des Cinemas d'Irlande et de Grande Bretagne,** a festival of Irish and British films.

GRANVILLE

In 1439, the expatriate Lord Jean d'Argouges sold his great-grandmother's dowry to the English. This dowry—the rocky peninsula of Granville—quickly became an entire fortified city, from which the English spent 30 years trying to take Mont-St-

Michel. Now thoroughly pardoned by France, Granville (pop. 13,700) crams a lot of variety into a small area. The center is a bustling and attractive shopping district, and on the sea is a popular resort with rugged cliffs and ribbons of white sand. Granville's distance from Paris keeps it less crowded and less expensive than you might expect, and proximity to Mont-St-Michel and the Channel Islands, a great beach, and exceptional museums give the town a definite appeal.

⚏ 🎫 ORIENTATION AND PRACTICAL INFORMATION. Granville's ancient streets can be difficult to navigate, even with a map. Particularly tricky are the narrow sloped routes that crisscross the *haute ville*, the old English walled city—access to the *haute ville* comes only at a few points, such as the stairs at the side of the casino and at the rue des Juifs. Getting to town from the train station is the one easy trip: just follow av. Maréchal Leclerc straight into the heart of Granville. The **train station,** pl. Pierre Semard, off av. Maréchal Leclerc, has service to: Bayeux (2hr., 4 per day, €14.20); Cherbourg (3hr., 3 per day, €17.90) via Lison; Paris (3hr., 4 per day, €31.30). Info open M-Sa 9:10am-noon and 2-6:30pm, Su 10:10am-noon and 1:45-7:30pm. **SNCF buses** go to Coutances (30min., 3 per day, €6.30), and **STN,** on cours Jonville, to Avranches (1hr., 3 per day, €5.30). STN also runs a mostly extraneous **local bus** circuit. (☎ 02 33 50 77 89. Office open M-F 8:30am-noon and 1:30-6:30pm, Sa 9:15am-noon and 2:15-4:15pm.) **Emeraude Lines** (☎ 02 33 50 16 36), at the *gare maritime*, sails to the Chausey Islands (1hr.; 1-2 per day; €16.76, ages 3-14 €10.26); Guernsey (2hr.; 3 per week; €56, ages 16-23 €38, ages 4-15 €34); Jersey (1¼hr.; 3 per week; €46, ages 16-23 €34, 4-15 €26). Ask about family rates. **Vedette "Jolie France"** (☎ 02 33 50 31 81; fax 02 33 50 39 90; open daily 8:30am-12:30pm and 1:30-7pm) also sails to the Chausey Islands (50min.; 1-3 boats per day; €16.30, children ages 3-14 €10.30; reserve 2 days ahead July-Aug.). Rent **bikes** at **Sport Evasion,** av. Maréchal Leclerc (☎ 02 33 68 10 00), for €7.62 per day with a security deposit. Call in advance. Access the **Internet** at the post office through Cyberposte, or at the back of the bar **Les Bals des Oiseaux,** rue St-Sauveur. (☎ 02 33 51 35 51. Open Tu-Sa 10:30am-2am. Open M evening. €1 per 15 min., €3.50 per hr.)

To get to the center of town, leave the station and follow av. Maréchal Leclerc downhill as it becomes rue Couraye. (10min.) The **tourist office,** 4 cours Jonville, is around the corner on your right as soon as you reach the main place. They offer **tours** of the city. In the summer, ask for a copy of the *Calendrier des manifestations* for a list of events in town. (☎ 02 33 91 30 03; fax 02 33 91 30 19; www.ville-granville.fr. Tours in French July-Aug. Tu and F at 2pm, €2. Office open July-Aug. M-Sa 9am-1pm and 2-6:30pm, Su 10am-1pm; Apr.-June M-Su 9am-12:30pm and 2pm-6:30pm; Sept.-Mar. M-Su 9:30am-noon and 2-6pm.) Down the street, the **post office,** 8 cours Jonville, has **currency exchange.** (☎ 02 33 91 12 30. Open M-F 8am-12:30pm and 2:30-6:30pm, Sa 8:30am-noon.) **Postal code:** 50400.

🏠🍴 ACCOMMODATIONS AND FOOD. In summer you're unlikely to find either solitude or a surplus of hotel rooms in Granville. To get to the **Auberge de Jeunesse (HI) ❶,** bd. des Amiraux Granvillais, from the train station, turn right onto av. Maréchal Leclerc and follow it downhill. Just before the town center, turn left onto rue St-Sauveur; head right when the road forks and look for "Centre Nautisme" signs straight ahead—the hostel is part of the Station Voile complex. Part of a huge sailing center, it runs week-long camps during July and August. Comfortable and newly redone dorms. Be sure to reserve well in advance in the summer. (☎ 02 33 91 22 62; fax 02 33 50 51 99. Prices listed for HI members, followed by non-HI members: Breakfast €2.35/€3.59. Meals €8.85/€11.15. Sheets €3.60/€4.55. Office open for check-out 8:30-10am and 3-6pm for check-in. Code for late entry. Singles €17.70/€20.08; one bed in double €14.60/€16.68; quads €9.85/€11.43.)

To reach ▧**Hôtel Michelet ❷**, 5 rue Jules Michelet, from the tourist office, head straight across pl. de Gaulle onto rue P. Poirier. When that ends, take a right onto rue Georges Clemenceau (becomes av. de la Libération), then a sharp left up the hill onto rue Jules Michelet. Comfortable, modern rooms, some with balconies, in a calm location near the beach. (☎ 02 33 50 06 55; fax 02 33 50 12 25. Breakfast €4.80. Reception 7:30am-10pm. Doubles €21.50, with toilet €29, with shower, toilet, and TV €37.50, with bath, toilet, and TV €46.50. MC/V.) Run by accommodating owners conveniently close to the train station, **Hôtel Terminus ❷**, 5 pl. de la Gare, feels like a Victorian dollhouse. All rooms have toilet and TV. (☎ 02 33 50 02 05. Breakfast €4. Singles €20, with shower €25; doubles €25, with shower €30, with bath €33; triples €30-40; quads €38-45.)

There are **markets** on cours Jonville all day Saturday and pl. du 11 Novembre 1918 on Wednesday mornings. For more groceries, head to **Marché Plus,** 107 rue de Couraye. (Open M-Sa 7am-9pm, Su 9am-1pm.) Restaurants in town are plentiful, but tend to be a bit pricey. Bypass these and head to one of the small *crêperies* of the *haute ville* near the Eglise de Notre-Dame. Try **La Gourmandise ❷**, 37 rue St-Jean, where savory dishes run around €7 and desserts about €3. (☎ 02 33 50 65 16. Open daily for lunch and dinner. AmEx/MC/V). Near the hostel, **Monte Pego ❷**, 13 rue St-Sauveur, serves delicious pastas, pizzas, and salads for €6.70-9. (☎ 02 33 90 74 44. Open July-Aug. daily noon-2:30pm and 7-10:30pm; Sept.-June closed Su-M. MC/V.) Near the beach, you'll find kebab vendors and ice cream stands. The town also has an enormous number of *boulangeries* and *pâtisseries*.

🖸 🖪 **SIGHTS AND ENTERTAINMENT.** Granville's old English walled city, known as the *haute ville*, occupies the top of a point that stretches from the casino to the **Eglise de Notre-Dame** (where classical concerts are held on summer weekends). Stretching northward from the old city is Granville's most popular **beach,** but you'll also find quiet stretches of sand past the port on the opposite side of the point. Anchored at the edge of the *haute ville*, at the pl. de l'Isthme, is its most modern addition: the **Musée Richard Anacréon,** the area's only 20th-century art museum. The museum focuses on the first half of the century, and on Fauvism in particular. Temporary exhibitions supplement the permanent collection during the summer. (☎ 02 33 51 02 94. Open July-Sept. W-M 11am-6pm, Oct.-June W-Su 2-6pm. €1.50, students and children €1.) The area just outside affords a marvelous view of the city and the ocean below.

You can take a coastal path from the beach promenade to the stairs that deposit you at the clifftop **Musée Christian Dior,** in the childhood home of Granville's most famous son. The museum offers a showcase of the extravagant creations of the house of Dior, with themed exhibits that change each year; some dresses are as flowery as the villa's immaculate gardens, designed from 1905 to 1930 by Dior and his mother. (☎ 02 33 61 48 21. Open mid-May to Sept. 10am-12:30pm and 2-6:30pm. Gardens 9am-8pm. €5, students and over 60 years €4, under 12 free.)

From May to September, boats leave daily for the **Chausey Islands,** a sparsely inhabited archipelago of 52 to 365 islets, depending on the tide (for ferry info see **Orientation and Practical Information,** p. 204).

Nightlife is limited and pleasantly low-key; bar-hopping in your flip-flops will not earn you disapproving stares. **Les Bals des Oiseaux,** rue St-Sauveur, serves a laid-back, hemp-strung clientele, offers Internet use at reasonable rates, and hosts occasional reggae and ska concerts. (☎ 02 33 51 35 51. Open Tu-Sa 10:30am-2am and M evening.) The **Bar les Amiraux,** bd. des Amiraux, across from the hostel, pulls in relaxed, mid-summer crowds fresh off the beach in search of €2 brews. (☎ 02 33 50 12 83. Open June-Sept. M-Sa noon-2am, Su 2pm-1am; Oct.-May Su-Th until 1am, F-Sa until 2am.) Granville hosts *Carnaval* every year on the Sunday before Mardi Gras and the **Fête des Marins** at the end of July.

COUTANCES

Miraculously unscathed by World War II, the 13th-century cathedral of Coutances (pop. 11,000) is second in beauty perhaps only to Chartres. Flanked by the churches of St-Pierre and St-Nicholas, the cathedral forms the centerpiece of the town's three-spired skyline, which is visible from miles into the surrounding countryside. The beautiful abbeys and châteaux, within walking distance of town, provide a true respite from the heavily touristed D-Day beaches and Mont-St-Michel.

■■ ▐ ORIENTATION AND PRACTICAL INFORMATION. The **train station** (☎02 33 07 50 77; open M 9:30am-noon, Tu and Th 9:15-11:45am and 2:30-5:45pm, W 8:30am-noon, F 9:15-11:50am and 2:05-3:30pm), has service to Avranches (1hr., 3 per day, €7); Caen (1½hr., 8 per day, €12.90); Cherbourg (1½hr., 6 per day, €14.75); Paris (3½hr., 8 per day, €32); Rennes (2hr., 3 per day, €16.85). Adjacent is the **STN bus office** (☎02 33 45 00 50), from which buses run to Granville (30min., 3 per day, €6.30).

To reach the cathedral from the train station, walk straight ahead to the roundabout and turn right onto bd. Legentil de la Galaisière and turn at the first left onto rue de la Mission. Take the second right onto rue Maréchal Foch, then turn at the first left. From the front of the cathedral, take rue Tancrède to the right, down to rue St-Nicolas, the main commercial area of the town center. The **tourist office**, pl. Georges Leclerc, is one block from the front of the cathedral, behind the Hôtel de Ville. (☎02 33 19 08 10; fax 02 33 19 08 19; tourisme-coutances@wanadoo.fr. Open July-Aug. M-Sa 10am-12:30pm and 1:30-7pm, Su 2-6pm; Sept. 16-June M-Sa 10am-12:30pm and 2-6pm; Oct.-Apr. closes Su at 5pm.) There's **currency exchange** at **Crédit Agricole**, pl. de la Poste, a block to the right as you leave the cathedral. (Open Tu-Sa 9am-noon and 1:30-6pm.) The **post office** is on pl. de la Poste. (☎02 33 76 64 10. Open M-F 8:30am-12:30pm and 1:30-6:30pm, Sa 8:30am-noon.) **Postal code:** 50200.

▐▐ ACCOMMODATIONS AND FOOD. Coutances is best seen as a daytrip from Granville, but there are a couple of decent budget options. Spacious, comfortable and surprisingly colorful rooms open off the hospital-sterile hallways of **Hôtel de Normandie ❷**, pl. du Général de Gaulle, near the cathedral. All rooms have a view of one steeple or another. (☎02 33 45 01 40; fax 02 33 46 74 54. Breakfast €5. Singles €24, with shower and TV €30.50, with bath, TV, and toilet €35; doubles €30.50, with shower and TV €38, with bath, TV, and toilet €44. MC/V.) The **Hôtel des Trois Pilliers ❷**, 11 rue des Halles, also near the cathedral, offers pleasant, modern rooms. The bar downstairs overflows with local teens. (☎02 33 45 01 31. Breakfast €4.50. Singles or doubles €21, with shower €23. Extra bed €6. MC/V.)

On Thursday mornings, **markets** fill pl. de Gaulle. (9am-1pm) The **Champion** supermarket, rue de la Verjustière, is at the bottom of the hill behind Eglise St-Nicolas (open M-F 9am-12:45pm and 2:30-7:30pm, Sa 9am-1pm and 2-7:30pm), but you can find smaller stores around the cathedral. There is a small supermarket near the campsite, across from the stadium. (Open M-Sa 9am-noon and 2-7pm.) Restaurants around the cathedral tend to be reasonably priced. **Le Râtelier ❷**, 3 bis rue Georges Clemenceau, is a homey *crêperie* with funky decor that draws a large local clientele, serving up savory and sweet crepes from €2-7. (☎02 33 45 56 52. Open Tu-Sa for lunch and dinner. MC/V.)

◪ SIGHTS. The carved, patterned spires of Coutances's grand **cathedral** are the foreground for its even more impressive lantern-tower, a three-tiered structure that catapults upward from the choir, filling it with light. Visitors can ascend to its galleries during tours, which are organized by the tourist office. (Open daily 9am-7pm. Tours at the end of May, June, and Sept. in French at 2:30pm; July-Aug. 3 per day in French 10:30am, 2:30, 4pm; in English Tu at 2pm. Tours €5.35, ages 10-18 and students €4. Under 10 not permitted.)

The **Jardin des Plantes,** near the tourist office, is among the oldest in France and has creative flowerbeds, including one arrangement in the shape of a ship, and illuminated gardens on summer nights. (Open July-Aug. daily 9am-11:30pm; Apr.-June and Sept. 9am-8pm; Oct.-Mar. 9am-5pm.) At the entrance is the **Quesnel-Morinière museum,** which houses temporary exhibits along with regional paintings and artifacts, including one of the best collections of ceramics in Normandy. Gape at the *Christ de la Mission,* a crucifix three times larger than life. (☎02 33 45 11 92. Open July-Aug. W-M 10am-noon and 2-6pm, closed Su morning; Sept.-June 10am-noon and 2-5pm. €2.30, students and children under 18 free.)

There are many treasures within 4 to 5km of town. If you are up for walking (there is no bike rental in Coutances), ask the tourist office for the brochure *Monuments et Lieux de Visite* (in English too), which covers a number of châteaux, manors, museums, and abbeys. The **Château de Gratot,** an easy 40- to 50-minute walk from Coutances, offers a look at the renovations old châteaux undergo. (☎02 33 45 18 49. Open daily 10am-7pm. €3, ages 10-18 €2.) On the week of Ascension Thursday (May 24-31, 2003), Coutances hosts **Jazz sous les Pommiers,** a week of more than 30 concerts in the streets and bars (☎02 33 76 78 61).

AVRANCHES

From its hilltop corner of the bay of Mont-St-Michel, Avranches (pop. 9000) watches proudly over the fortified island, satisfied that its residents have safeguarded the monastery's real treasures (its manuscripts) since the French Revolution. The town's link to the Mont goes back to its beginnings, when Bishop Aubert was visited here by the Archangel Michael. Apart from the exquisite manuscripts and a smattering of religious relics, Avranches offers an unexpected wealth of churches and beautiful vistas of the Mont from afar.

ORIENTATION AND PRACTICAL INFORMATION. Trains and buses to and from Avranches are sporadic; be prepared for a long wait and plan a carefully-timed exit. The Caen-Rennes train line passes through Avranches's **train station** (☎02 33 58 00 77) at the bottom of the hill. Destinations include Caen (2 per day, €17.30); Granville (15min., 2 per day, €6.40); Paris (5hr., 2 per day, €35.50); Pontorson (25min., 1 or 2 per day, €5.40). Station open M-Th and Sa 8:45am-noon and 1:45-6:45pm; F 8:45am-noon, 2-7:45pm, and 8:30-9:15pm; Su and holidays 1:45-7:30pm and 8:30-10:05pm. **STN,** 2 rue du Général de Gaulle (☎02 33 58 03 07), around the back of the tourist office, sends buses to Granville (70min.; M-F 3 per day, Sa-Su 2-3 per day; €5.50) and Mont-St-Michel (40min.; July-Aug. 1 per day, Apr., June, and Sept. W only; €4.25). Office open M-F 10:15am-noon and 4-6pm. **Rent bikes** from **Decathalon,** 2½km from town, for €11 per day, leaving a check as a deposit. (☎02 33 89 28 50. Open July-Aug. M-Sa 9:30am-8pm; Sept.-June M-Sa 9:30am-7:30pm.)

To get to the center of town from the station, cross the highway via the footbridge to the right of the station and lean into the grueling hike uphill. At the top of the hill, head straight across rue du Général de Gaulle at the intersection. The **tourist office,** 2 rue du Général de Gaulle, will be 250m ahead on the left. (10min.) The office reserves rooms for €1.50 and gives out free town maps. There is a skimpier **annex** outside the Jardin des Plantes from July to August. (☎02 33 58 00 22; fax 02 33 68 13 29; www.ville-avranches.fr; annex ☎02 33 58 59 11. Open daily 10am-12:30pm and 2-6pm. Main office open July-Aug. M-Sa 9am-12:30pm and 2-7:15pm, Su 9am-12:30pm and 2-7:15pm; Sept.-June M-F 9am-noon and 2-6pm, Sa 9:30am-noon and 2-6pm, Su 10am-noon and 2-5pm.) **Le Point Information Jeunesse,** 24 pl. du

NORMANDY

Marché, between the market halls and to the left, offers **Internet access** when they're not running training workshops. (☎02 33 79 39 41. €1.52 per hr., plus a €1.52 membership fee. Open M-Tu 1:30-5:30pm, W 9:30am-12:30pm and 1:30-6:30pm, Th 1:30-6:30pm, F 9:30am-12:30pm and 1:30-5:30pm, Sa 9:30am-12:30pm. Call ahead.) The **post office** on rue St-Gervais has **currency exchange.** (☎02 33 89 20 10. Open M-F 8am-12:15pm and 1:30-6:15pm, Sa 8am-12:15pm.) **Postal code:** 50300.

▐ ◖ ACCOMMODATIONS AND FOOD. The popular **Hôtel de Normandie ❷**, bd. L. Jozeau-Marigné, sits at the end of the steep path you'll hit after crossing the footbridge to the right of the station. The ivy-covered building, run by three generations of the same family, has large and lovely rooms with fluffy eiderdowns, immaculate bathrooms, and views of the patchwork countryside. (☎02 33 58 01 33. Breakfast €4.60. Singles €22.90, with bath €27.45; doubles €27.45, with bath €36.60. MC/V.) **Hôtel La Renaissance ❷**, 17 rue des Fosses, located just off the main square behind the Hôtel de Ville, offers rooms over a bar that are large, plain, and comfortable. (☎02 33 58 03 71. Breakfast €5. Rooms for 1-2 people €23, for 1-3 people €28, for 1-4 €33. AmEx/MC/V.) The tourist office lists *chambres d'hôte*, which are often the cheapest option (€15.25).

A **market** is held on pl. du Marché (a.k.a. place des Halles), off rue des Chapeliers (Sa morning). You'll pass a **Champion** supermarket on the right side of rue du Général de Gaulle before you reach the tourist office. (Open M-Sa 9am-7:30pm, Su 9:30-11:45am.) Numerous cheap *brasseries* and restaurants surround the tourist office. **◪Pizzeria l'Anticario ❷**, at pl. St-Gervais, serves up a creative lunchtime *formule* for €7.50, but dinner is the better time to make an appearance at this three-tiered candle-lit restaurant. The only thing better than the atmosphere is the food—huge delicious portions of pizza with every topping imaginable. (☎02 33 58 32 10. Open Tu-Sa noon-2pm and 7pm-midnight, Su 7pm-midnight.) The scent of exotic spices lures diners from the street to the creatively-named **George's Indian Restaurant ❸**, 22 rue St-Gervais, which offers reasonably priced Indian and Pakistani fare. (☎02 33 48 19 07. Lunch *formules* €9 and €12, dinner entrees about €10. Open W-Su 12-2pm and 7-10pm. MC/V.)

◪ ◨ SIGHTS AND FESTIVALS. The town's treasures are the 10th- to 15th-century **manuscripts** copied and illuminated by the monks of Mont-St-Michel and now kept in the **Hôtel de Ville's library,** in the square next to the tourist office. In a single silent room, 30 of the 200 surviving manuscripts are displayed each summer. Line after line of sharply executed script detail the finer points of theology, philosophy, astronomy, and music. Those who studied the books sometimes added their own notes in equally perfect script, making each a repository of centuries of thought. (☎02 33 89 29 40. Open June-Sept. daily 10am-6pm. €3.05, students €1.55, under 10 free. Combined ticket with the museum and treasury €4.60, students €2.30, under 12 free.) The **Musée Municipal,** rue d'Office, houses reproductions of local craftsmen's workshops and a rural Norman home. Downstairs is a replica of a medieval scriptorium (the room in which the manuscripts were created), where you can attempt the monks's trade. (☎02 33 58 25 15. Open Easter-Sept. daily 9:30am-noon and 2-6pm. €2.30, students €1.25, under 10 free.)

The granite 19th-century **Eglise St-Gervais,** pl. St-Gervais, has a stratospheric 74m bell-tower and a treasury containing one of the holiest heads this side of the Seine. After Avranches's Bishop Aubert twice refused the archangel Michael's command to build a church on the Mont, the exasperated angel scolded Aubert with a rap on the forehead emphatic enough to leave the future saint with a perfectly circular hole in his skull. The sacred cranium is in a monumental gold-plated reliquary, to the right as you enter the church. (Open June-Sept. daily 10am-noon and 2-6pm. Closed Su morning in June and Sept. €1.55, students €0.75, under 10 free.)

The **Jardin des Plantes,** pl. Carnot, is built around the remains of an 1803 Ursuline monastery destroyed in WWII. Rose gardens and lush grass ring the Romanesque arches. The garden provides a spectacular view of the distant Mont-St-Michel, directly in line with the winding river that appears to lead to its gates—a can't-miss sight on summer evenings when the island is illuminated. (Open daily 8:30am-11:30pm.) Down rue de la Constitution is the **Patton Memorial,** officially American soil. The huge obelisk commemorates Operation COBRA's successful break through the German front between St-Lô and Périers in July of 1944.

In the beginning of July, Avranches hosts **Musiques en Baie,** a concert series that covers the spectrum from Baroque to jazz. (3-concert pass €22.90, students €13.75. The tourist office has details.) The third weekend of June is the popular **Eclats de Rire,** during which comedians and actors take to the streets, devoting themselves entirely to the art of laughter.

MONT-ST-MICHEL

The fortified island of Mont-St-Michel (pop. 42) rises from the sea like a vision from another world. It is one of a kind, a dazzling 8th-century labyrinth of stone arches, spires, and stairways that climb to an abbey overlooking both Brittany and Normandy, the disputed jewel of each. Pilgrims have flocked to the island for centuries, braving the area's fickle tides and quicksand to set foot in the eighth wonder of the occidental world. Modern, secular visitors arrive in RVs and double-decker tour buses, invulnerable to these natural trials, but invariably victimized by the holy isle's hawkers. With three million visitors annually, there are few chances to see the Mont as its peaceful Benedictine inhabitants must have known it; to avoid the crowds, arrive early or stay late. An exploration of the abbey at midnight provides an unforgettable view of the heavens in perfectly pitch-black skies.

☞ TRANSPORTATION

Trains: In Pontorson (☎02 33 60 00 35). Open M-Th and Sa 9:15am-noon and 2:45-7:10pm, F 9:15am-noon and 2:45-7:20pm, Su 1:10-7:15pm. To: **Dinan** (1hr., 2-3 per day, €7.10); **Granville** (1hr.; 3 per day, Sa-Su 2 per day; €7.30) via Folligny; **Paris St-Lazare** (3½hr., 3 per day, €37 plus TGV supplement) via Caen; and **St-Malo** (90min., 2-3 per day, €6.60) via Dol—don't miss the brief stop or you'll end up in Rennes.

Buses: Courriers Bretons, 104 rue Couesnon (☎02 99 12 70 70) in Pontorson. Buses leave Mont-St-Michel from its entrance at Porte de l'Avancée, and leave Pontorson from just outside the train station and the Courriers Bretons office. Buy tickets on board. Mont and Pontorson buses run about 12 per day, 6 on Su, last bus back from the Mont 8pm; €1.70. The same company also runs to **Rennes** (1½hr.; June-Sept. M-Sa 5 per day, Su 3 per day; Sept.-June 6 per day, 1 on Su; €11) and **St-Malo** (1½hr.; July-Aug. 3-4 per day, Sept.-June 1-2 per day; €9). Office open M-F 10am-noon and 4-7pm.

Bike Rental: Couesnon Motoculture, 1bis rue du Couesnon (☎02 33 60 11 40), in Pontorson. €7 per half-day, €12 per day, €23 for 2 days, €32 for 3 days. Passport deposit. Open Tu-Sa 8:30am-noon and 2-7pm. V/MC.

▄✴ 🛈 ORIENTATION AND PRACTICAL INFORMATION

Mont-Saint-Michel is at the northeastern tip of Brittany, or the southwestern tip of Normandy. **Pontorson,** 9km due south down D976, has the closest train station, supermarket, and affordable hotels. Just inside the Porte de l'Avancée, the only entrance to the Mont, lies the tourist office; **Grande Rue,** the town's major thoroughfare, is to the right. All hotels, restaurants, and sights are on this steep, spiraling street. There's no public transportation off the Mont late at night—you'll need

FRÈRE TOBIE, BROTHER OF JERUSALEM

Frère Tobie, age 25, is a native Breton and monk at Mont St-Michel. He is a serious-looking young man, thin, with closely cropped red hair, and he wears a monk's full-length dark blue robe and simple sandals. Attached to his belt, along with his prayer beads, is a mobile phone.

Q: What is it like to live on Mont St-Michel?

A: It's an exceptional monument. Life on the Mont is entirely different than elsewhere, because this is not just a monastery but also a tourist site, a place of pilgrimage, and an ancient monument. Life varies each day, but for us essentially this is a place of sanctuary, even though almost three million people visit each year. Living in the midst of the sea, we have to pay attention to the tides, because they dictate when we can venture off the island. At night and in the early morning the Mont is completely deserted. When you look out on the bay, with 500km of sand, it is a great desert.

Q: What is the monastic community like here?

A: We have two communities, who live in parallel and have liturgies together. We have four monks and seven nuns. We hope to become more numerous over time, with more brothers and sisters from other communities. The community is here indefinitely; our superior can send us elsewhere, because we have pledged obedience.

Q: What is a normal day for you?

A: Our day begins at 6am. At 6:30 we

a car. Biking from Pontorson takes about one hour on relatively flat terrain, though not always on bike-friendly roads; try the path next to the Couesnon River instead.

Tourist Office at Mont-St-Michel: Just behind the wall to your left after you enter the island (☎02 33 60 14 30; fax 02 33 60 06 75; OT.Mont.Saint.Michel@wanadoo.fr). Busy but helpful multilingual staff can set you up with info on sites and nearby lodging. A free *Horaire des Marées* (tidetable) will inform you whether your view from the Mont will be of ocean or sandy marsh. Hours vary in the off-season, so you may want to call first. Open July-Aug. daily 9am-7pm; Apr.-June and Sept.-Oct. 9am-12:30pm and 2-6pm; Nov.-Mar. 9am-noon and 2-5:30pm.

Tourist office in Pontorson: pl. de l'Eglise (☎02 33 60 20 65; fax 02 33 60 85 67; MONT.ST.MICHEL.PONTORSON@wanadoo.fr) has maps and info on walking tours, as well as lots of Mont-St-Michel information. **Internet access** €4.50 per hour. Open July-Aug. M-F 9am-12:30pm and 2-6:30pm, Sa 10am-12:30pm and 3-6:30pm, Su 10am-12:30pm; Sept.-June M-F 9am-noon and 2-6pm, Sa 10am-noon and 3-6pm.

Laundromat: on the rue St-Michel next to the Champion supermarket (see below), north of Pontorson on the road to the Mont. From the train station, take an immediate right on rue Dr. Bailleul, following the road as it becomes bd. Général de Gaulle; at the roundabout, take the road to your right (the D.976) to Mont-Saint-Michel, and the laundromat will be just ahead on the right. Open daily 7am-9pm.

Police: entrance just to the left of the Porte de l'Avancée before you enter (☎02 33 60 14 42). Open daily 11am-1pm and 5:30-7:30pm.

Hospital: Emergency services are in Avranches. There is a small **clinic** on the Mont, across from the post office.

Internet Access: At the Pontorson tourist office (see above).

Post Office: Grande Rue (☎02 33 89 65 00), about 100m to the right of Porte de l'Avancée. **Currency exchange** at tolerable rates. Open June-Aug. M-F 9am-5:30pm, Sa 9am-4pm; Mar.-May and Sept.-Oct. M-F 9am-noon and 2-5pm, Sa 9am-noon; Nov.-Feb. 9am-noon and 1:30-4:30pm. **Postal code:** 50116.

◪ ACCOMMODATIONS

If you are on a tight budget, forget about actually staying on the Mont unless St-Michel himself is bankrolling your visit; hotels on location start at €50 per night. More affordable indoor lodging is available in Pontorson, and some travelers choose to visit Mont-St-Michel as a daytrip from St-Malo. There are also a number of campsites and *chambres d'hôte* near Beauvoir. Plan ahead to reserve a room you can afford, since prices climb faster than the spring tide.

Centre Duguesclin (HI), rue Général Patton, Pontorson (☎/fax 02 33 60 18 65; aj@ville-pontorson.fr). From the station, turn right onto the main road, then left after a block onto rue Couesnon. Take the third right onto rue St-Michel. When you see the tourist office on your left, cut diagonally across the square, following signs toward the church. Bear left in front of the church onto rue Hédou. Follow that to the end, then turn right on rue Gén. Patton. The hostel is on your left. (10min.) Clean dorm-style 3-, 4-, and 6-person rooms in a 1910 stone house; with communal lounge, kitchen, and dining area. Breakfast €3.20. Sheets €2.70. Reception July-Aug. 8am-9pm; Sept.-June 8am-noon and 5-9pm. Lockout Sept.-June noon-5pm. Call at least 1 week ahead, 1 month in the summer, as many groups stay here. Dorms €8, €8.40 without HI membership. ❶

Hôtel le Grillon, 37 rue du Couesnon, on the right after rue St-Michel, Pontorson (☎02 33 60 17 80). Pleasant owners offer 5 quiet, like-new rooms (all with showers), behind a perky *crêperie*. Breakfast €5. Reception F-W 7am-11pm. Reserve 1-2 weeks ahead July-Aug. Doubles €29, with toilet €32. Extra bed €5. MC/V. ❸

Hôtel de Guesclin, Grande Rue, Mont-St-Michel (☎02 33 60 14 10, fax 02 33 60 45 81) about halfway up the Grande Rue on the right-hand side. One of the best bets for staying on the Mont itself, the ten rooms offer comfort at comparatively reasonable cost. Half board available at the downstairs restaurant. Breakfast €7. Open Apr.-Nov. Double with shower, toilet, TV, and telephone €55-75. MC/V. ❺

Hôtel de France et Vauban, 50 bd. Clemenceau, Pontorson (☎02 33 60 03 84, fax 02 33 60 35 48, www.hotel-france-vauban.fr), across the street from the station on the left, with reception in the Restaurant l'Orson Bridge Café. Agreeable, sparkling bedrooms (all with shower or bath) provide a quiet, unremarkable night's rest. Breakfast €6. Doubles €32, with toilet €38-41; triples €39/€42; quads with toilet €59. Mention *Let's Go* for a 10% discount. MC/V. ❸

Hôtel de L'Arrivée, 17 rue de Docteur Tizon, Pontorson (☎/fax 02 03 60 01 57) over a bar right across the street from the station, on the other side of the Courriers Bretons office. This no-frills accommodation is a good choice for its low prices and proximity to bus and train. Breakfast €4.60. Reception 8am-10pm. Shower €2.50. Singles and doubles €15.40-18.90, with shower €25; triples €28, with shower €37.50; quads €34, with shower €40.40. Extra bed €5. Prices drop slightly in the winter. MC/V.

have a half-hour of silent prayer, and then *laudes*, the first services of the day. After breakfast we have *lectio divino*, a reading from the Bible. We listen to an hour of this every day, because the word of God is the basis of our life. At noon we have daily mass—in the abbey in summer, and the crypt in winter. We eat lunch in silence. In the afternoon we work. At 6:30pm, we have the adoration of the sacrament for an hour and vespers, in which the public can participate. Later we eat dinner, also in silence, and then *complies*, our final service.

Q: What kind of work do you do during the day?

A: Our vocation is being monks in the town, among people. Here at Mont St-Michel, we divide up our daily tasks: we have one brother who cooks, one brother who cleans and gardens, our superior who coordinates the masses. I am the webmaster, so I develop Internet sites.

Q: Why did you pick the monastic life?

A: The monastic life is chosen in response to a call from God. This is our answer. This call from God isn't an apparition, but a verification of spirituality. In the community, we have all possible routes: there is one brother who converted after spending 20 years as a communist, because he had such a strong personal experience. There are also those from Christian families, who joined very young, just after finishing high school.

Q: How do you feel about all the tourists who come to the Mont?

A: For us, it's not difficult, because we need to interact with people. When people arrive at the top of the Mont, they are panting and out of breath. Tired like this, they are perhaps more able to receive the message of Mont St-Michel, the calm of the environment. We have a mission here, and it allows this place to touch the hearts of those who come.

NORMANDY

🏕 CAMPING

Camping Haliotis at Pontorson, chemin des Soupirs (☎/fax 02 33 68 11 59; camping-monto@ville-pontorson.fr). Follow hostel directions to rue Hédou, then take a left on rue Général Patton and the first right onto chemin des Soupirs. The campsite will be 300m ahead on the left. Hedges and cornfields hide this well-kept, 3-star site from the road and the nearby Couesnon river. Clean, extensive central bathrooms and showers, newly-built heated pool. Reception July-Aug 7:30am-10pm; Apr.-June and Sept. 8-10am and 6-7pm. July-Aug. €2.70 per person, €1.50 per child; €3.70 per tent and car. Electricity €2.10. Apr.-June and Sept. €2 per person, €1.25 per child, €2.90 per tent and car. Electricity €2. Handicapped-accessible. ❶

Camping du Mont-St-Michel is a mere 1.8km from the Mont at the junction of D275 and N776 (☎ 02 33 60 22 10; fax 02 33 60 20 02). More like a small town with 350 spots and many dependent businesses. They also **rent bikes** (€4.80 per hr., €16 per day). Open mid-Feb. to Oct. €6.50 per site, €3 per person. Electricity included. ❶

Camping St-Michel, rte. du Mont-St-Michel (☎ 02 33 70 96 90), is by the bay in Courtils. This 3-star campground is a bit far from the Mont (9km). It was named the most garden-like campsite in the *département*—flowers surround the heated swimming pool, common room, grocery store, breakfast room, and snack bar. They **rent bikes** (€5 per half-day, €8 per day). Open mid-Mar. to mid-Oct. July-Aug. $4 per person, €1.60 per child under 7, €3.50 per car and tent; prices slightly lower in off-season. ❶

🍴 FOOD

If you dare invest in more than a postcard and sandwich on the Mont, look for local specialties such as *agneau du pré salé* (lamb raised on the surrounding salt marshes) and *omelette poulard,* (a fluffy soufflé-like dish; about €10-14). **Chapeau Rouge ❸,** Grande Rue, serves these delicacies at lower prices than most (lamb €8.50) in a homey wood-furnished dining room. (☎ 02 33 60 14 29. 3-course *menus* €11-19. Open daily 11:30am-2:30pm and 7-9pm. Sometimes closed at night.) To eat in a room with a view, walk along the ramparts and take your pick; all restaurants sport terraces or glass walls. You could be lured to a sticky end at **La Sirène ❷,** Grande Rue, past the post office—bind yourself to avoid the temptation of choco-late-banana crepe (€4.80), stuffed to bursting and topped with a *mont* of chocolate sauce. (☎ 02 33 60 08 60. *Menu* €9.15. Open daily 11am-9pm.) For a splurge, get your eggs from **La Mère Poulard ❹,** Grande Rue, Mont-St-Michel, just on your left as you walk through the gates. While the prices seem exorbitant (*menus* €19-50), the experience of watching cooks in traditional garb crafting your omelettes in copper pots over a wood fire justifies the expense for one evening. (☎ 02 33 89 68 68. Open 11:30am-10pm.) If you plan to picnic, arrive prepared as there are no grocery stores within the walls, just vendors hawking sweet treats and sand-wiches. Pontorson has a morning **market** on rue Couesnon and at pl. de la Mairie. (Open W.) Or stop by the **Champion supermarket,** rue St-Michel, just outside Pontor-son. (☎ 02 33 60 37 38. Open July-Aug. M-Sa 9am-7:30pm; reduced hours in the off-season.)

🔭 SIGHTS

Grande Rue is quite a spectacle in itself—jam-packed with restaurants and shops selling Mont-motif souvenirs of every size, shape, and description. For more detailed information on Mont architecture, you may want to pick up one of the many guidebooks (€5-40), although brochures and tours are on offer for free within the abbey walls. While you're free to explore the bay, don't wander off too far on the sand without company—the broad expanses are riddled with quicksand, and the bay's tides, changing every six hours or so, are the highest in France. During the bi-monthly spring tides, the *mascaret* (initial wave) rushes in at 2m per second, flooding the beaches along the causeway. To see this spectacle, you must be within the abbey two hours ahead of time. New surprises await in every nook and cranny on the Mont, and it's near-impossible to get lost.

HISTORY. Legend holds that the Baie de St-Michel was created by a tidal wave that flooded the surrounding forest and left three islands: Tombelaine, Mont Dol, and Mont Tomba (meaning "mound" or "tomb"). So appealing was the last island that heaven wanted a piece of it. In 708, the Archangel Michael appeared to St. Aubert, Bishop of Avranches, instructing him to build a place of worship on the barren island. However, construction of the hill-top church did not begin until Benedictine monks from Fontenelle were sent to the Mont in 966 at the request of Richard I, the third duke of Normandy. Four crypts were built, one at each cardinal point, to support the base of a church on Tomba's 80m high point. These became the monastery's first chapels, beginning with Notre-Dame-sous-Terre later in the 10th century. The Mont became an increasingly important destination for pilgrims, comparable in importance to Rome and Jerusalem.

In the 14th and 15th centuries, it was fortified against a 30-year English attack with ramparts designed by Abbot Jolivet; and the Benedictines continued their life-long work, the copying and illumination of the *manuscrits du Mont-St-Michel*, the remains of which are now on display in nearby Avranches (see p. 207). In 1789, the Revolutionary government turned the island into a prison, first jailing 600 monks, followed by Robespierre and 14,000 others who ranged from royalists to ordinary criminals. The prison was closed in 1863, and shortly thereafter, in 1874, Mont-St-Michel was classified as a national monument. In 1897, the church was topped with a neo-Gothic spire identical to the one atop Ste-Chapelle in Paris, and a copper and gold leaf statue of St-Michel. Around that time a new dike made the island a peninsula, facilitating tourist access. Today the abbey is again home to a small community of monks—not Benedictines, but instead the *moines* (monks) and *moniales* (nuns) of the Brothers and Sisters of Jerusalem.

ABBEY AND CRYPTS. The twisting road and ramparts end at the abbey entrance, but the steps continue to the **west terrace** and entrance to the **abbey church,** the departure point for five 1hr. free English tours daily during the summer. (French tours leave every half-hour. Mass is held daily at 12:15pm; entry to the abbey church for the service only is free noon-12:15pm.) The **church,** the most ornate portion of the abbey, spans an impressive 80m in length, thanks to ingenious planning of the original architects over 1000 years ago. The interior's hodgepodge of architectural styles is the result of reconstruction following the collapse of half of the nave in 1103, the Romanesque choir in 1421, and 13 separate fires over the past 1000 years. The adjacent **cloister,** lined with small columns and focused around an empty space, is the center of **La Merveille** ("the Marvel"), the 13th-century Gothic monastery. Beneath the church and the cloister are the Mont's frigid **crypts,** which can only be seen on 2hr. tours. The descent passes through the **refectory,** where the monks took their meals in silence as St. Benedict's rules were read. The **Chapelle St-Etienne,** below, was the chapel of the dead. Prisoners held on the Mont's **treadmill** during the Revolution would walk on the wheel for hours, as their labor powered an elaborate pulley system that carried supplies up the side of the Mont. Many actually volunteered for the grueling task, since it meant they got more food to keep them strong. The **Crypte des gros piliers** is directly under the choir and was built at the same time; its pillars, 6m in circumference, were described by Victor Hugo as a forest of palm trees. The narrow abbey gardens, clinging to the side of the rock, surround the compound's exit. (☎02 33 89 80 00. Open July 13-Aug. daily

9am-7pm; May-July 12 and Sept. 9am-5:30pm; Oct.-Apr. 9:30am-4:30pm, until 5pm during school holidays. Closed Jan. 1, May 1, Nov. 1 and 11, and Dec. 25. €7, ages 18-25 €4.50; Oct.-Mar. first Su of the month free. A 2hr. conference tour with a guide (only in French) leaves once a day at 2pm (July-Aug. 4 times per day) and costs €4, ages 12-25 €3. Audio tour €4, or €5 for two sets of headphones.)

SPECTACLES. Nightly illumination transforms the Mont into a glowing jewel best seen either from the causeway entrance or from across the bay in Avranches. *(Illumination June-Sept. from 9 or 10pm.)* Dusk is also the time to revisit the crypts of the Abbey. **D'un autre songe** is a memorable nighttime display that immerses the sanctuary's corridors in a flood of light and music. *(☎ 02 33 89 80 00. July-Aug. M-Sa and Sept. F-Sa 9pm-midnight, last entry at 11pm. €9, ages 12-25 €6.50, under 12 free.)* On Sunday, May 5, 2002, the Mont will celebrate the **St-Michel de Printemps** folk festival, when costumed men and women parade through the streets and re-enact local traditions. The **St-Michel d'Automne** festival, held on the Sunday before Michaelmas (late September), is similar but more religious.

BRITTANY
(BRETAGNE)

Brittany tugs away from mainland France, maintaining its Celtic traditions despite Paris's centuries-old effort to Frenchify the province. In recent years the government has softened its stance, allowing schools to teach in Breton; it is still, however, illegal to advocate independence. Present-day Breton culture has its roots in the 5th-7th centuries, when Britons fled Anglo-Saxon invaders for this beautiful, wild peninsula. Reminders of earlier inhabitants are plentiful; Neolithic people, who settled here before the Gauls, erected the thousands of megaliths visible today. The Romans, who conquered the area in 56 BC, decorated some of these monuments and incorporated them into their own rituals. In the centuries that followed, Brittany fought for and retained its independence from Frankish, Norman, French, and English invaders, uniting with France only after the last Duchess ceded it to her husband, François I, in AD 1532.

Brittany is lined with spectacular beaches and misty, almost apocalyptic headlands. If you dislike crowds, beware of visiting in summer. In the off-season, some coastal resorts such as St-Malo, Quiberon, and Concarneau close down, but the churches, beaches, and cliffs are as eerie and romantic as ever. The traditional costume of Breton women—a black dress and an elaborate white lace *coiffe* (head-dress)—appears in folk festivals and some markets, and lilting *Brezhoneg* is spoken energetically at pubs and ports in the western part of the province.

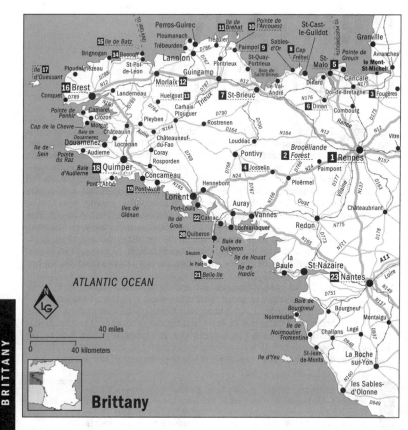

ATLANTIC OCEAN

0   40 miles

0   40 kilometers

Brittany

RENNES

Rennes (pop. 210,000) tempers its Parisian sophistication with college town revelry and the relaxed Breton spirit. During the day, its *vieille ville* of half-timbered houses seems frozen in time; come 4pm, locals flock to the cafés and bars, the narrow streets fill with traffic, and students rush to take advantage of the city's sizzling nightlife. Rennes is a popular stopover for medieval folklore enthusiasts traveling to the mythical forests of King Arthur's clan, as well as for those heading north to Mont-St-Michel (p. 209) and St-Malo (p. 226), and west to the coastal beaches. Everything can be squeezed into a couple of jam-packed days, but save some energy for the super-charged club scene.

⌐ TRANSPORTATION

Trains: pl. de la Gare (☎02 99 29 11 92). Info and ticket office open M-Sa 8:45am-7:45pm, Su and holidays 11am-7:45pm. To: **Brest** (2-2½hr., at least 1 per hr., all TGV, €26.90); **Caen** (3hr., 8 per day, €25.70); **Nantes** (1¼-2hr., 7 per day, €17.40); **Paris Montparnasse** (2hr., 1 per hr., €44.80); **St-Malo** (1hr., 15 per day, €10.70); **Tours** (2½-3hr., every 2-3hr., €27.60) via **Le Mans.**

Buses: 16 pl. de la Gare (☎02 99 30 87 80), to the right of the train station's north entrance. **Cars 35** (☎02 99 26 11 11) services **Dinan** (1¼hr.; M-Sa 6-7 per day, Su 3 per day; €8.30); **Fougères** (1hr.; M-F 10 per day, Sa 3 per day, Su 2 per day; €8.20); **Paimpont**, site of the Brocéliande Forest (1¼hr.; M-F 3-4 per day, Sa 2 per day; €2.70); **Josselin** (1¼hr.; M-Th and Sa 4 per day, F 6 per day, Su 2 per day in the evening; €10.70); **St-Malo** (3hr.; 1 per day, W 2 per day, Su no service; €9.60). **Nantes** (2hr.; M 3 per day, Tu-Th and Sa 2 per day, F 4 per day; €15) is covered by **Cariane Atlantique** (☎02 40 20 46 99, 08 25 08 71 56 in Nantes). **Anjou Bus** (☎02 41 69 10 00) goes to **Angers** (2½-3hr.; 3-4 per day; €15.90, express €19.80). **Mont-St-Michel** (2½hr., 1-2 per day, €11) is served by **Les Courriers Bretons** (☎02 99 19 70 70).

Public Transportation: Star, 12 rue du Pré Botté (☎ 02 99 79 37 37). Office open M-Sa 7am-7pm. **Buses** run daily 5am-8pm; lines in areas with hopping nightlife run as late as midnight. Purchase tickets on bus or from bus office or newsstands. A **métro** line runs through the heart of Rennes on the same ticket. Dir: Kennedy runs from the train station to the pl. de la République; dir: Poterie runs the other way (€1, *carnet* of 10 €8.40, 1-day pass €3).

Taxis: 4 rue Georges Dottin (☎02 99 30 79 79), at the train station. 24hr.

Bike Rental: Guedard, 13 bd. Beaumont (☎02 99 30 43 78), near station. €12 per day. Open M 2-7pm, Tu-Th 9am-12:30pm and 2-7pm, F 10am-7pm, Sa 9am-6:30pm.

■ 🛈 ORIENTATION AND PRACTICAL INFORMATION

The **Vilaine river** bisects the city, with the train station to the south and most of its historic sights in the north. **Av. Jean Janvier,** in front of the north exit of the station, runs through the center of town. Across the river on this street, the old city begins about 5 blocks to the left. You'll find most clubs, bars and other nightlife around **pl. Ste-Anne, pl. des Lices,** and **pl. St-Michel** just north of the *vieille ville,* but there are some hotspots on the southern bank. To the east and west lie Rennes' modern, sometimes architecturally abysmal sectors, and its suburbs.

BRITTANY

Tourist Office: 11 rue St-Yves (☎02 99 67 11 11; fax 02 99 67 11 10). From the station, take av. Jean Janvier to quai Chateaubriand. Turn left and walk along the river and through the pl de la République. Turn right on rue George Dottin, then right again on rue St-Yves. The office is on the right, just past the church on the corner. Free maps, directions, and lists of hotels, restaurants, and shops. Hotel reservations (€1). Call in advance to reserve tours of the Parliament, the *vieille ville*, the Jardin du Thabor, or themed visits of historical houses (July-Aug. daily; Sept.-June 1-3 times per week; €6.10, students €3.05). Open Apr.-Sept. M-Sa 9am-7pm, Su and holidays 11am-6pm; Oct.-Mar. M-Sa 9am-6pm, Su and holidays 11am-6pm.

Hiking and Biking Information: France Randonnée, 4 rue Ronsard (☎02 99 26 13 56). Info on **GR trails.** Open M-F 10am-6pm, Sa 10am-1pm.

American Consulate, 30 quai Duguay-Trouin (☎02 23 44 09 60; fax 02 99 35 00 92). Does not issue visas.

Youth Center: Centre Information Jeunesse Bretagne (CIJB), Champ du Mars, 6 cours des Alliés (☎02 99 31 47 48; fax 02 99 30 39 51; cijb@cijb.asso.fr) has info on summer jobs. Free **Internet** (Sept.-May M and Th 1-9pm, W and F 1-6pm, Sa 2-6pm; June-Aug. Tu-F 1-6pm). Open Tu and Th 10am-9pm, W and F 10am-6pm, Sa 2-6pm.

Laundromat: 25 rue de Penhoet. Open daily 8am-10pm. Also at 45 rue St-Malo. Both open daily 9am-noon and 2-7pm.

Police: 22 bd. de la Tour d'Auvergne (☎02 99 65 00 22).

Hospital: Rennes has a number of hospitals. The most central is on Pontchailloux, past rue St-Malo. In an **emergency,** dial 16.

Internet Access: Free at the Youth Center **(CIJB),** above. The tourist office has a full list. **Cyberspirit,** 22 rue de la Visitation (☎02 99 84 53 30). €0.75 per 15min., €2.30 per 30min., €4.50 per hr. Half-price daily 2-3pm, 6-7pm, and after 9pm. Open July-Aug. Tu-Sa 2-10pm; Sept.-June M 2-9pm, Tu noon-9pm, W-F noon-10pm, Sa 2-10pm. **Cybernet Online,** 22 rue St-Georges (☎02 99 36 37 41). €0.80 per 5min., €6 per hr. Open M 2-8pm, Tu-Sa 10am-8pm. Closed Aug. 1-20.

Post Office: 27 bd. du Colombier (☎02 99 01 22 11), 1 block left of the train station exit. **Postal Code:** 35032. **Branch** office, pl. de la République (☎02 99 78 43 35). From the station, walk up av. Jean Janvier and turn left onto the quai three blocks over. **Currency exchange** with 2.5% commission. **Western Union** at branch. Both open M-F 8am-7pm, Sa 8am-noon. **Postal code:** 35000.

▐ ACCOMMODATIONS AND CAMPING

You must reserve for the first week of July, during the *Tombées de la Nuit* festival, but many hotels recommend reservations year-round. A number of moderately priced hotels lie to the east of av. Jean Janvier between quai Richemont and the train station. Most of the budget hotels, unfortunately, are not central.

▨ **Au Rocher de Cancale,** 10 rue St-Michel (☎02 99 79 20 83). From the north entrance of the train station, walk along av. Jean Janvier and turn left on bd. de la Liberté. After 5 blocks, turn right on rue de Nemours/rue Tronjolly. Follow the street north through many name changes to pl. du Champ-Jacquet; head across the *place* and left on rue Leperdit. Pl. St-Michel will be in front of you; the hotel is up the street to the right. Alternately, take the *métro* (dir: Kennedy) to pl. Ste-Anne; rue St-Michel is in the southwest corner of the square. An ancient half-timbered building protects charming, stylish, modern rooms, all with tiled shower and toilet, right in the heart of the old quarter. Traditional restaurant downstairs (*menus* €13-23). Breakfast €5.50. Reservations recommended. Doubles €34; triples €43. MC/V. ❸

Auberge de Jeunesse (HI), 10-12 canal St-Martin (☎02 99 33 22 33; fax 02 99 59 06 21; rennes@fuaj.org). From the station, take av. Jean Janvier straight to the canal, where it becomes rue Gambetta. Go 5 blocks, then take a left onto rue des Fossés. Take rue de la Visitation to pl. Ste-Anne. Follow rue de St-Malo on the right down the hill and through its intersection with rue Dinan and rue St-Martin. Cross the canal and immediately turn right into a gravel parking lot. The hostel is ahead on the left. (30min.) Or take the *métro* (dir: Poterie) to pl. Ste-Anne and change to #18 (dir: St-Grégoire) to the "Auberge de Jeunesse." Simple, plain beds on clean, color-coded floors. Kitchen, common room, cafeteria, and **Internet.** Discount bus fares to Mont-St-Michel and St-Malo. Breakfast included. Showers in rooms. Lockers in most rooms. Bottom sheet and blanket provided, but top sheet €2.70. Laundry. Handicapped-accessible. Reception 7am-11pm. Singles €21.20; doubles, triples, and quads €12.20 per person. MC/V. ❶

Hôtel d'Angleterre, 19 rue Maréchal Joffre. (☎02 99 79 38 61; fax 02 99 79 43 85). See directions for Hôtel Maréchal Joffre, below. Single-star establishment with views of the street or a courtyard. Breakfast €4.90. Reception 7am-10:30pm, Su 7am-noon and 6-10:30pm. Singles €22; doubles €34-44. MC/V. ❷

Hôtel Maréchal Joffre, 6 rue Maréchal Joffre (☎02 99 79 37 74; fax 02 99 78 38 51). From the north entrance of the train station, follow av. Jean Janvier and turn left on bd. de la Liberté. After 3 blocks, take a right on rue Maréchal Joffre; the hotel is 2 blocks up the street on the left. (15min.) Alternately, take the métro (dir: Kennedy) to pl. de la République, walk towards the river and turn right onto rue Jean Jaurès; the hotel is on the right. Small, cheerful rooms in a very central location, with a little chipped paint and a few dingy carpets. No lock on front door. Breakfast €5. Reception 24hr. Closed last week of July and 1st week of Aug. Singles €20, with shower and toilet €31; doubles €22/€35.50; triples with shower, toilet, and TV €41. MC/V. ❷

BRITTANY

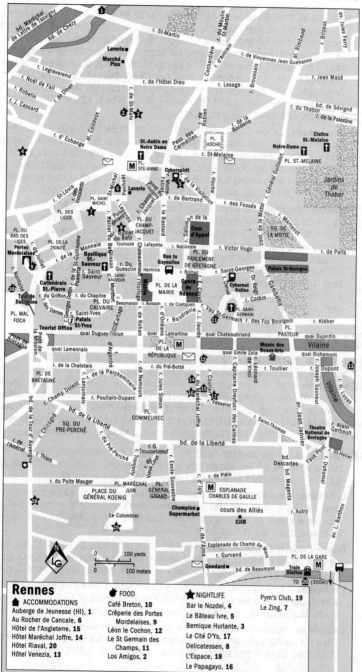

Rennes

♠ ACCOMMODATIONS

Auberge de Jeunesse (HI), **1**
Au Rocher de Cancale, **6**
Hôtel de l'Angleterre, **15**
Hôtel Maréchal Joffre, **14**
Hôtel Riaval, **20**
Hôtel Venezia, **13**

🍴 FOOD

Café Breton, **10**
Crêperie des Portes
  Mordelaises, **9**
Léon le Cochon, **12**
Le St Germain des
  Champs, **11**
Los Amigos, **2**

★ NIGHTLIFE

Bar le Nozdei, **4**
Le Bâteau Ivre, **5**
Bernique Hurlante, **3**
Le Cité D'Ys, **17**
Delicatessen, **8**
L'Espace, **18**
Le Papagayo, **16**

Pym's Club, **19**
Le Zing, **7**

Hôtel Riaval, 9 rue Riaval (☎02 99 50 65 58; fax 02 99 41 85 30). Leave the train station through the southern "Cour d'Appel" exit; walk across the open plaza and down the metal stairs. Turn left onto rue de Quineleu, and proceed until the first intersection. Cross the street, and rue de Quineleu will become rue Riaval. Follow the sign to the hotel, 100m ahead on the left. (5min.) Though hardly central, the rooms are clean and in a quiet residential neighborhood. Breakfast €4.50. Showers €2.50. Reception M-F 7am-10pm, Sa-Su 8am-1pm and 8-10pm. Reserve ahead. Singles and doubles €23, with shower, toilet, and TV €33.50; doubles with twin beds €29/€35-39.50; triples and quads €39.50-44. AmEx/MC/V. ❷

Hôtel Venezia, 27 rue Dupont des Loges (☎02 99 30 36 56; fax 02 99 30 78 78). From the station's north entrance, walk up av. Jean Janvier for about 10min. Turn right onto rue Dupont des Loges (one street before quai Richemont), and cross the bridge; the hotel is on the left. On an island surrounded by the Vilaine River; spectacular views of the canal. Unremarkable but comfortable rooms. Breakfast €5. Reservations recommended. Singles €22.50, with shower, toilet, and TV €29; doubles €28/37. MC/V. ❷

Camping: Municipal des Gayeulles, in Parc des Gayeulles (☎02 99 36 91 22; fax 02 23 20 06 34; www.ville-rennes.fr/camping). Take bus #3 (dir: Gayeulles/St-Laurent) from pl. de la Mairie to "Piscine/Gayeulles" (last bus 8:30pm). Follow the path around the swimming pool dome until you see a paved road. Turn left and follow signs to the campground, deep within the lush Parc des Gayeulles. Reception June 15-Sept. 15 7:30am-1pm and 2-8pm; Sept. 16-June 14 9am-12:30pm and 4:30-8pm. June 15-Sept. 15 gates close 11pm; off-season 10pm. Laundry €2.30. €3.05 per person, €1.50 per child under 10. €1.50 per car. Electricity €2.60. Nov.-Mar. prices 10% lower. MC/V. ❶

◖ FOOD

Rue St-Malo, rue St-Georges, and **pl. St-Michel** have traditional *crêperies*, cafés, kebab stands, Chinese restaurants, and even a Pizza Hut. Every Saturday, a huge ■market livens pl. des Lices with flowers, fresh fruit, vegetables, baked goods, cheeses, and other delights. (Open 6am-1pm.) Local **supermarkets** include **Galeries Lafayette** on quai Duguay-Trouin, **Champion** on the rue d'Isly near the train station, and **Marché Plus** in the apartment complex on the left side of rue de St-Malo on the way from rue de l'Hôtel Dieu to the youth hostel. (All open M-Sa 9am-8pm.)

■ **Café Breton,** 14 rue Nantaise (☎02 99 30 74 95). An ever-changing menu of Breton cuisine in an upscale atmosphere reminiscent of a country kitchen. *Plats* €7-9; desserts €3.50-4. Open M and Sa noon-4pm, Tu-F noon-3pm and 7-11pm. ❷

Le St Germain des Champs (Restaurant Végétarien-Biologique), 12 rue du Vau St-Germain (☎02 99 79 25 52). The organic restaurant's chef-owners welcome guests to their popular open kitchen and bamboo-accented dining room. *Menus* €9-17. Open M-Sa noon-2:30pm and Th-Sa 7-10pm. Closed Aug. MC/V. ❸

Léon le Cochon, 1 rue Maréchal Joffre (☎02 99 79 37 54; fax 02 99 79 07 35). Enticing local dishes and dried chili pepper decorations fuse modern and traditional at this elegant restaurant. Open daily noon-2pm and 7-11pm. July-Aug. Su closed. MC/V. ❸

Los Amigos, 13 rue de St-Malo (☎02 99 36 86 86), across from #40. Savor an evening drink at the fur-lined bar and follow it with heaping platters of local oysters or duck hearts. Six *plats du jour* each €11-14. Open M-Sa 8pm-midnight. ❸

Crêperie des Portes Mordelaises, 6 rue des Portes Mordelaises (☎02 99 30 57 40). Below the old city walls, this *crêperie* is one of the best in the city. *Galettes* and crepes €3.50-6.40. Open M-Sa 11:30am-2pm and 6:30-11pm, Su 6:30-11pm. ❶

⊙ 🔂 SIGHTS AND EXCURSIONS

SIGHTS. Rennes' *vieille ville* bears a strong architectural resemblance to the prototypical Western European medieval village. Striking half-timbered buildings, now filled with bars and pubs, can be found throughout the old city, on **rue St-Georges,** in **pl. Ste-Anne,** and **pl. St-Michel.** For a good tour of the old buildings, upon exiting the tourist office turn left on rue St-Yves and right on rue Georges Dottin, checking out the buildings on rue du Chapitre. Continuing on rue Georges Dottin, take a look at the old buildings on **rue de la Psalette** which becomes **rue St-Guillaume.** At the end of rue St-Guillaume, turn left onto rue de la Monnaie, which becomes rue de la Cathédrale, to visit the Cathédrale St-Pierre (on the left).

The imposing **Cathédrale St-Pierre** was founded in 1787 on a site previously occupied by a pagan temple, a Roman church, and a Gothic cathedral. The 5th chapel houses the cathedral's treasures: a delicately-carved, glass-encased 16th-century altarpiece tracing the life of the Virgin Mary. (Open daily 9:30am-noon and 3-6pm. Closed to visitors during high mass Su 10:30-11:30am, July-Aug. also M and Su afternoon.) Across the street from the cathedral, tucked in an alleyway bearing the same name, the **Portes Mordelaises,** once the entrance to the city, is a last vestige of the medieval city walls, accompanied by the crumbling **Tour de Duchesne.** The best view is from pl. du Maréchal, reached by taking rue de la Monnaie from the Portes.

The **Musée des Beaux-Arts,** 20 quai Emile Zola, has 17th-century French, Flemish, Pont-Aven, and modern/surrealist collections. (☎ 02 99 28 55 85. Open W-M 10am-noon and 2-6pm. €4, students €2, children under 18 free.)

Rennes' **Jardin du Thabor** is among the most beautiful gardens in France. Its lush grounds contain sculptures, fountains, a carrousel, a massive bird cage, and the "caves of hell." The rose garden alone holds an amazing 1700 types of the *fleur d'amour.* Concerts are often held here; a small gallery on the north side exhibits local artwork on a rotating basis. (Open daily June-Sept. 7:15am-9:30pm.)

EXCURSIONS. The **Parc des Gayeulles** is a 15min. bus ride from the center of Rennes (see **Accommodations** for directions to the campground and bus info). Gayeulles' forests are interspersed with an indoor pool, several lakes (with paddleboats in the summer), sports fields, tennis courts, mini-golf, and a campground. Many walking paths and bikepaths cut through the park. (Check the maps posted in the park to be sure you're cycling legally.) The park is also home to a working farm and animal reserve. The farm, an instructional facility where local youngsters are taught about gardening, milking cows, and feeding horses, is open to guests of the campground who are accompanied by a parent. (☎ 02 99 36 71 73. Open July-Aug. M-F 9am-5:30pm; Sept.-June Tu and Th-F 4:30-6pm. Free.)

🔂 NIGHTLIFE

With enough bars for a city twice its size and a collection of clubs that draws students from Paris and beyond, Rennes is the partying mecca of northwestern France. After the sun sets (as late as 10:30pm in the summer) the city's population seems to double, and the kids don't disappear until the sun rises. Much of the action centers around **pl. Ste-Anne, pl. St-Michel,** and the radiating streets, but don't limit yourself—there are hot nightspots all over the city, including a few great bars and discothèques to the south of the Vilaine. In 2001, new laws changed the closing times for *bars de nuit* from 3am to 2am, and for discos from 5am to 4am. But don't fret: the laws don't seem to have cramped the average reveler's style.

BRITTANY

Swing by **Bar le Nozdel,** 39 rue de Dinan, where you can sip cider (€2) and admire the prominent disco ball hanging amidst centuries-old timbered walls. (☎02 99 30 61 64. Open M-Sa 11am-1am.) **Le Bateau Ivre,** 28 rue de la Visitation, whose funky ceiling is covered with small plastic grazing sheep (☎02 99 38 76 93) and the intimate book-lined **Bernique Hurlante,** 40 rue de St-Malo (☎02 99 38 70 09), are also great options for starting out the evening right.

BARS

■ **Le Zing,** 5 pl. des Lices (☎02 99 79 64 60). Zing's 2 floors and 8 rooms are packed with the young and the beautiful, who look all the more mysterious in the seductively dim amber lighting. Beer €2.20 before midnight, €3 after; cocktails €7.50. Open from 2pm; filled from around midnight until the crowd heads for the discos at 2am.

Le Papagayo, 10 rue Maréchal Joffre (☎02 99 79 65 13). An unassuming tapas bar by day, this place is transformed to a party after dark—especially on tequila nights (tequila €1.50), when salsa music blares. Open M-Sa 8am-1am.

La Cité D'Ys, 31 rue Vasselot (☎02 99 78 24 84), is so Breton that regulars refuse to speak French. 2 floors, decorated with Celtic knots and crosses and a spiraling staircase, with a fabulous variety of traditional music. Coreff €2.40. Open M-Sa 11am-1am.

CLUBS

■ **Delicatessen,** 7 allée Rallier du Baty (☎02 99 78 23 41), tucked around the corner from pl. St-Michel in a former prison, has swapped jailhouse bars for dance cages to become one of Rennes' hottest clubs. Open Tu-Sa midnight-5am. Beer €5, after 2am €8. Cover Th-Sa after 1:30am €10, F-Sa after 1:30am €13.

L'Espace, 45 bd. La Tour d'Auvergne (☎02 99 30 21 95). From 2am on, L'Espace plays host to dancers of all sexual orientations, who gyrate on its stage and dance floor as house music blasts through the cavernous hall. (F and Sa 40-50% gay, W and Th mostly mixed). Upstairs is **L'Endroit,** which attracts a more relaxed, mixed crowd, which reclines on wicker furniture and grooves to techno. Both open Th 11pm-4am, F-Sa 11pm-5am, Su-W midnight-4am. Cover F and Su €9, Sa €10.

Pym's Club, 27 pl. du Colombier (☎02 99 67 30 00). Look for the signs for Colombier, not Colombes, from pl. Maréchal Juin. The club is just below a cinema. The most posh of Rennes' discothèques; 3 rooms filled with scarlet benches and couches, with only the most chic clientele. **Planète** draws the largest, youngest crowd with techno; **Le Salon**'s mellow music caters to an older set; **Club**'s hits from the 80s and 90s attract a mix of the two. Cover F-Sa €13, students before 1am €8, students after 1am €10; Su-Th free until 1:30am, after 1:30am €8. Open daily 11pm-5am; music stops 4am.

♫ THEATRE AND FESTIVALS

For a more sedate evening search out theater, dance, and classical music performances in *Contact Hebdo Le Guide-Loisirs,* available at the tourist office or hostel. For information on **Orchestre de Bretagne** concerts, call ☎02 99 27 52 83.

The best-known of Rennes' summer festivals, **Les Tombées de la Nuit,** is a week-long riot of music, theater, mime, and dance (complete with a 14hr. traditional Breton dancefest) in early July. (For info, contact the tourist office or www.ville-rennes.fr/tdn). The **Festival Transmusicales** fills the city from mid-May to late June, exhibiting local artists and international bands. (www.transmusicales.com.)

DAYTRIPS FROM RENNES

BROCÉLIANDE FOREST

Just an hour from Rennes, **Brocéliande** is enshrouded by legend. Its connections with King Arthur and his knights are countless; a 75km road through the forest passes Merlin's Tomb, the Fountain of Youth, the Valley of No Return, and the field where Lancelot confessed his forbidden love for Guenevère and stole the kiss that ended an age. Many of the forest's supposedly Arthurian structures are probably the remnants of stone-age megaliths (*à la* Stonehenge) dating from 3000 to 2000 BC; they're so worn that there's almost nothing there anymore. They're also fenced in and heavily touristed by myth-seekers. Though the Tomb of Merlin is covered in bouquets and notes from people seeking his aid, the real magic emanates from the misty forest, where some trees have lived 6000 years and the terrain ranges from mysterious woods to mystical moors.

To get a real sense of the forest, you might want to camp or stay in a nearby *gîte*. If you don't have a car, rent a mountain bike at **Le Bar Brecilien,** 1 rue Général Charles de Gaulle, behind the tourist office. (☎02 99 07 81 13. €3 per hr., €9 per half-day, €14 per day. Open July-Aug. daily 8am-8pm; Sept.-June closed Su-M.)

TIV buses leave from Rennes (1hr.; M-F 3-4 per day, Sa 2 per day; €2.70) and stop in the village of **Paimpont,** in the middle of the forest. From the Paimpont bus stop, turn around and walk back 200m in the direction from which the bus came. Before the road crosses the water, there is a sign for the "Syndicat d'initiative" on the left. Turn left and proceed toward the old abbey ahead, now a Presbyterian church and town hall. The **tourist office** is next to the abbey. It has info on bike and car routes and local accommodations, as well as maps of the forest. (☎02 99 07 84 23. Basic map free; hiking routes €4; complete road map €7.95. 4hr. tours in French M-Tu, Th-F, Su 2pm, W, Sa 10am-12:30pm and 2-6:30pm; €4.50-7 per person; reserve a spot by phone. July-Aug. guided car tours to major forest sites. Open Feb.-Dec. M-F 10am-noon and 2-5pm, Sa-Su 10am-noon and 2-6pm.)

FOUGÈRES

Atop a hill overlooking the pristine Nançon Valley, picturesque Fougères has been a center for feudal lords and ladies, home to craftsmen, and a haven for artists and authors. Today, it is a modern town with a perfectly preserved historic center and a breathtaking château. To reach the château from pl. Aristide Briand, turn left onto rue Porte Roger (near the tourist office) and head to the right of the fountain (up one block) onto rue de la Pinterie, the main artery of the medieval city. Proceed downhill until a view of the château opens up ahead. You can proceed directly to the castle, or make a detour into the garden immediately to the left.

As you exit the garden, bear right at the fork to stay on rue de la Pinterie. Just ahead you will see the tri-towered, moat-traversing entrance to Fougères' awe-inspiring **château,** sitting on a promontory flanked by rock walls and the Nançon river. Its construction began around AD 1000 as part of a plan to reinforce the entire Breton duchy. The château fell into disrepair centuries later, but a number of architectural ingenuities are still standing. You can venture up into the towers, including the behemoth **Tour Mélusine,** built by the Lusignans of Poitou to honor their half-human half-snake ancestor. It stands 30m high, with 3m thick walls and a dungeon to boot—peak through the trap door to check it out. (☎02 99 99 79 59. Open June 15-Sept. 15 daily 9am-7pm; Sept. 16-Oct. and Apr.-June 14 daily 9am-noon and 2-6pm; Nov.-Dec. and Feb.-Mar. daily 10am-noon and 2-5pm. French tours July-Aug., on the hr., 10-11am and 2-5pm. English tours leave 5min. later. €4.50, students €3.50, ages 10-16 €2, under 10 free. Off-season prices lower.

THE LOCAL STORY

AS FÊTE WOULD HAVE IT

M. Jean-Louis Courchinoux is president of the Josselin Festival Médiéval. A landscaper and architect by trade, he swaps his polo shirt and khakis once a year on July 14 for the swords-and-tights garb of his city's past.

Q: How did your festival get its start?

A: The Festival Médiéval was created to commemorate the château, which was built 1000 years ago. The entire town participates in the festival, decorating the streets and dressing is costumes from *le Moyen Age*.

Q: So what kind of events go on?

A: Local groups coordinate many of the activities, but we also bring in 15 professional troupes. There is everything from falconry to men on stilts to medieval harpists—you could not possibly see it all in one day.

Q: Do you get to dress up, too?

A: Of course, but I never wear the same costume twice. The first year of our festival it was all about disguise; now it's more like a carnival. Often, people clothe themselves *en gue*, in peasant clothing. It's funny, a lot of the far-left liberals dress themselves as nobles. Even M. Rohan, who lives in the château his family owned for hundreds of years, has a costume for the festival. Very handsome, and very expensive, of course.

Q: It's interesting that you've chosen Bastille Day, which is such a democratic celebration, as the date for this decidedly medieval festival.

A: July 14 naturally has a festive feeling in the air. It's a chance to celebrate the whole of France, as well as our own traditions.

Clocktower €2.) Look for signs to the **Jardin Public,** which has a breathtaking panoramic view of the château and surrounding countryside.

Fougères is 50km from Rennes. The only way to get here is by bus. **TIV buses** (☎02 99 99 02 37) run from Rennes (1hr.; M-F 10 per day, Sa 4 per day, Su 2 per day; €8.20). Get off at "Fougères Jean Jaurès" for the historic center of the city. It's easiest to leave on the return trip from the **bus terminal** (☎02 99 99 08 77), pl. de la République. From "Fougères Jean Jaurès," walk downhill on bd. Jean Jaurès for about seven minutes until you reach the fountain in the center of the traffic circle. The terminal is on the left side of the fountain. (Office open M-Sa 9:30am-noon and 2-7pm.) **Les Courriers Bretons** (☎02 99 19 70 70; www.lescouriersbretons.fr) run from St-Malo (2¼hr., 2 per day, €12.50) via Pontorson (1hr., 2 per day, €7). To get to the **tourist office,** pl. Aristide Briand, walk uphill on bd. Jean-Jaurès; at the traffic circle, continue straight uphill on rue de Paris. Follow it to the end and pl. Aristide Briand will be on your right. Walk to the end of the *place* and turn left at the Marché Plus; the tourist office, 2 rue Nationale, is ahead to the left of the Théâtre. (☎02 99 94 12 20; fax 02 99 94 77 30. Open July-Aug. M-Sa 9am-7pm, Su 10am-noon and 2-4pm; Sept.-June M-Sa 9:30am-12:30pm and 2-6pm, Su 1:30-5:30pm.)

NEAR RENNES

JOSSELIN

Wreathed in flowers, the charming village of Josselin (pop. 2650) seems to have changed little since its medieval beginnings. While kids here are up on the latest looks, the general pace of life still seems to match the speed of the canal that meanders past the château that made the town famous.

🖪🎫 TRANSPORTATION AND PRACTICAL INFORMATION. CTM buses (☎02 97 01 22 10) run to Rennes (1¼hr.; M-Th and Sa 4 per day, F 6 per day, Su 2 per day; €10.70). Buses from Rennes to Josselin leave in the afternoon, while buses from Josselin to Rennes run mostly in the morning. Buses stop at pl. de la Résistance.

To get to the **tourist office,** pl. de la Congrégation, take your first right upon exiting the bus onto rue Olivier de Clisson and head downhill to pl. Notre-Dame. Turn left on rue des Vierges; the office is at its intersection with rue de Château, on the left side of rue de Château before the château's entrance. The office has free maps, info on activities and accommodations, as well as local and regional bike routes with English explanations (€2-4). Walkers and bikers alike will enjoy the beautiful paths along the canal. (☎ 02 97 22 36 43; fax 02 97 22 20 44. Open July-Aug. daily 10am-6:30pm; Apr.-June and Sept.-Oct. M-Sa 10am-noon and 2-6pm, Su 2-6pm; Nov.-Mar. M-F 10am-noon and 2-6pm, Sa 10am-noon.) For those who want to venture into the canal, **canoe and kayak rental** is available right beside the *gîte*. (See below. ☎ 02 97 22 24 68 or 06 64 33 80 84. €5-7 per hr., €10-11 per half-day, €14-16 per day. Open June 15-Sept. 9am-noon and 1:30-6pm; off-season closed W and Sa). The **police** are at the top of town on the corner of rue de Pont Mareuc and rue de Carouges. (☎ 02 97 22 20 26.) The **hospital** is on rue St-Jacques. (☎ 02 97 73 13 13.) The **post office**, rue Olivier de Clisson, has **currency exchange.** (☎ 02 97 22 20 00. Open M-F 9am-noon and 2-5pm, Sa 9am-noon.) **Postal code:** 56120.

📍🏠 **ACCOMMODATIONS AND FOOD.** The *gîte d'étape* **L'Ecluse 35 de Josselin** ❶ shelters guests in salmon pink and blue rooms inside a brightly lit, impeccably clean restored farmhouse right on the canal. From the bottom of the château, proceed to the left along the canal and through the parking lot until you reach a small cluster of houses that face one of the canal's lochs—then ask for the *gîte*. They have a kitchen, dining room, one single, two doubles, and 12 dorm-style beds. (☎ 02 97 75 67 18 or 02 97 22 24 17. Shower €1.52. €7.50 per person, Nov.-Feb. €8.) A 25min. walk from Josselin, **Camping du Bas de la Lande** ❶ is situated on the canal; the site has beautiful views and fishing, as well as the human joys of laundry, ping pong, and mini golf. No buses run here; from the château, walk to the right along rue de Canal (on the actual road, not the path immediately beside the canal) as it becomes rue Glatinier. Take a left at the first roundabout and then a right after the bridge. The campsite is on the left, across from the mini golf course. They also rent mobile-home chalets, by the week during July and August and by the weekend the rest of the year. (☎ 02 97 22 22 20; fax 02 97 73 93 85; campingbasdelalande@wanadoo.fr. Reception July-Aug. 9:30am-noon and 3-9pm; Apr.-June and Sept.-Oct. 9:30am-noon and 2:30-8pm. Open Apr.-Oct. and July-Aug. €3 per person, €2 per car, €3 per tent; Apr.-June and Sept.-Oct. €2.50 per person, €1.60 per car, €2.10 per tent.)

🔵🎭 **SIGHTS AND ENTERTAINMENT.** A millennium has passed since its construction, but Josselin's stately **château** still presides over the Canal de Nantes à Brest under the stewardship of the Rohan family. England's King Henry II razed the original wooden structure in 1168 to punish the feudal Bretons for opposing his attempted takeover of the duchy. New buildings were built, and a 15th-century longhouse, distinctive for its intricate granite lacework, remains standing. The building was not complete without the prominent display of the Rohan motto, "A Plus" (without better), on its facade and interior fireplaces. In spring and summer the gardens, with their 300-year old cedar trees, are beautiful. Since the castle is a private home, its interior can be viewed only on a tour, available in impeccable English (45min.; July-Aug. 11am and 2:30pm, June and Sept. 2:30pm). The château's stables are now the **Musée de Poupées**, 3 rue des Trente, a 19th- and 20th-century doll collection. (Château and museum ☎ 02 97 22 36 45. Open July-Aug. daily 10am-6pm; June and Sept. daily 2-6pm; Apr.-May and Oct. Sa-Su 2-6pm. Château €6, children €4.10; museum €5.35, children €3.80; combined €10.70, children €7.50.)

The **Basilique Notre Dame,** a Romanesque structure dating back to the 9th century, is in a *place* bearing the same name, on the route from the bus station to the château. There is toothpick-sized remnant of the statue of the Virgin (in a reliquary to the left of the choir) that reportedly inspired the church's construction.

Bastille Day (July 14) brings the **Festival Médiéval** to Josselin (see sidebar, **The Local Story**), sending the town back to the Middle Ages with period-clad dancers, troubadours, jugglers, plays, and medieval delicacies. Festivities include jousting tournaments, a banquet, fireworks, and a medieval market. (Open 10am-7:30pm.) Starting in 2003 Josselin will host medieval festivities every month. (Call tourist office for more info.)

ST-MALO

With its modern-meets-medieval combination of fabulous beaches and ancient city walls, St-Malo (pop. 52,000) draws a varied crowd of tourists to bake on the soft brown sand of its beaches and ramble on its ramparts. Eighty percent of the city was destroyed in World War II, but St-Malo has been rebuilt so thoughtfully that it's difficult to distinguish the old from the new. Within its towering stone walls, a maze of cobblestone streets winds among 15th- to 17th-century-style buildings, where artisans' workshops have been replaced by the Body Shop, Lacoste, and more than a few merchants vying to sell you a little piece of Brittany.

▐▀ TRANSPORTATION

Trains: pl. de la Grande Hermine (☎02 99 40 70 20). Info open daily 9:30am-7pm. Trains run, all via **Dol,** to: **Caen** (3½hr., 8 per day, €22.80); **Dinan** (1hr., 5 per day, €7.30); **Paris** (5hr., 3 per day, €49.60); **Pontorson** (45min., 5 per day, €6.50); **Rennes** (1hr., 8-12 per day, €10.70).

Buses: At espl. St-Vincent. Offices beside tourist office and pick-up across the street. **Tourisme Verney** (☎02 99 82 26 26) runs to: **Cancale** (30min., 3 per day, €3.40); **Dinard** (30min., 11 per day, €3.30); **Rennes** (1½hr.; M-F 4 per day, Sa 2 per day, Su 1 per day; €9.40). Purchase tickets on the bus. Office open July-Aug. M-Sa 8:30am-12:30pm and 1:30-7pm; Sept.-June M-F 8:30am-noon and 2-6:30pm, Sa 8:30am-noon. **Courriers Bretons** (☎02 99 19 70 80; www.lescourriersbretons.fr) goes to: **Cancale** (45min., 4 per day, €3.70) and **Mont-St-Michel** (1½hr.; M-Sa 4 per day, Su 3 per day; €9). Buses also stop at the hostel.

Tours in summer to **Fréhel** (5hr., €15); **Dinan** (5hr., €15); **Ile de Bréhat** (full day, €26); and **Mont-St-Michel** (half-day W and Th 1:45-6:15pm; full-day Tu and Sa 9:30am-6:15pm; €20.50, ages 4-11 €11). 10% discount for students, children under 18, adults over 60; child fares for age 4-11. Office open July-Aug. M-F 8:30am-6:30pm; Sept.-June 8:30am-12:15pm and 2-6:15pm.

Ferries: Gare Maritime de la Bourse. **Brittany Ferries** (☎02 99 40 64 41; www.brittany-ferries.fr) serves **Portsmouth** (9hr.; 1 per day in summer, less frequently in the winter; €45). See **Getting There: By Boat,** p. 67, for details. **Condor Ferries** (☎02 99 20 03 00; www.condorferries.co.uk) travels to **Jersey** (70min.) and **Guernsey** (1¾hr.; 4 per day; round-trip €46, ages 4-15 €24, car €20). **Emeraude Lines** (☎02 33 18 01 80; fax 02 99 18 15 00; www.emeraudelines.com) runs to **Jersey** (70min.; 3 per day; round-trip €45), **Guernsey** via Jersey (2 hr., round-trip €55), and **Sark** via Jersey (2¼hr., round trip €45) and has all-inclusive vacation packages. Reduced fares for ages 23 and under. Bikes €8-10 round-trip; call for car prices (around €55).

Public Transportation: St-Malo Bus (☎02 99 56 06 06), in the bus office pavilion. Buses run July-Aug. daily 8am-midnight; Sept.-June 8am-7pm. The tourist office and the hostel have free copies of the master map and schedule. Tickets €1.10 (valid 1hr.), *carnet* of 10 €7.80, 24hr. pass €3.20.

Taxis: ☎02 99 81 30 30 or 06 60 21 59 95. Stands at St-Vincent and the train station.

Bike Rental: Les Velos Bleus, 47 quai du Duguay-Trouin (☎02 99 40 31 63; fax 02 99 56 35 72; www.velos-bleus.fr), has bikes and mountain bikes. €8-10 per half-day, €11-13 per day, €46-75 per week. €100-150 or passport deposit. Open June-Aug. daily 9am-noon and 2-6pm.

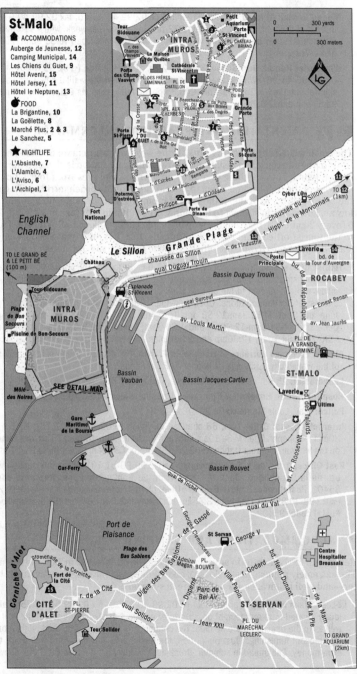

Moped Rental: M'Road, 2 pl. de l'Hermine (☎02 99 40 13 15; fax 02 99 40 97 24), in front of the train station. Scooters €32 per day, €148 per week, with €915 deposit; mopeds €15 per day, €78 per week, with €610 deposit. Open Tu-Sa 9am-12:15pm and 2-7pm.

Windsurfer Rental: Surf School St-Malo, 2 av. de la Hoguette (☎02 99 40 07 47; fax 02 99 56 44 96). Walk along Grande Plage, away from the walled city, until you see sign (about 1km). €25.15 per hr., €40.35 per half-day. Lessons €30 per hr. Open daily 9am-noon and 2-6pm.

✦ 7 ORIENTATION AND PRACTICAL INFORMATION

The small walled city *(intra-muros)* is the westernmost point of St-Malo and the heart of the shopping and restaurant district. The train station is closer to the town center, which holds nothing of interest to tourists. The area from four blocks to the west of the train station down to the old city is prime beach territory. To get to the *intra-muros,* as you exit the train station, cross bd. de la République and follow av. Louis-Martin straight to the tourist office (10min.), or take bus #1, 2, 3, 4, or 6 (every 20min., €1.10) from the stop on bd. de la République to St-Vincent. To get to the tourist office from the ferry terminals, turn left onto quai St-Louis as you leave the *gare maritime;* the office is beside the port and the bus station.

Tourist Office: espl. St-Vincent (☎02 99 56 64 48; fax 02 99 56 67 00; www.saint-malo-tourisme.com), near the entrance to the old city. Cross bd. de la République and follow espl. St-Vincent to the office. (10min.) Free map (or a very detailed one for €1) and list of accommodations. Open July-Aug. M-Sa 8:30am-8pm and Su 10am-7pm; June and Sept. M-Sa 9am-12:30 and 1:30-7pm, Su 10am-12:30pm and 2:30-6pm; Oct.-Easter M-Sa 9am-12:30pm and 1:30-6pm; Easter-June M-Sa 9am-12:30pm and 1:30-7pm, Su 10am-12:30pm and 2:30-6pm.

Money: Exchange currency at **Banque de France,** rue d'Asfeld at the southeast corner of the walled city. Exchange desk open M-F 9am-noon.

Laundromat: 25 bd. de la Tour d'Auvergne. Open daily 7am-9pm.

Hospital: Centre Hospitalier Broussais, 1 rue de la Marne (☎02 99 21 21 21).

Police: 5 av. Louis Martin (☎02 23 18 18 18).

Internet Access: Cyber L@n, 68 chauseé du Sillon (☎02 99 56 07 78). €2.50 per 30min., €4 per hr. Open M-Sa 10am-1am and Su 10am-3pm. **Ultima,** 75 bd. des Talards, on the left from the train station (☎02 23 18 18 23). €3 per hr. Open Tu-Sa 9am-1am.

Post Office: 1 bd. de la Tour d'Auvergne (☎02 99 20 51 70), at the intersection with bd. de la République. Open M-F 8am-7pm, Sa 8am-noon. **Poste Restante code:** 35401. **Postal code:** 35400. **Branch office,** pl. des Frères Lamennais in the *vieille ville* (☎02 99 40 89 90). Open M-F 8:45am-12:15pm and 1:30-5:45pm, Sa 8:45am-noon. **Postal code:** 35402.

⌂ ACCOMMODATIONS AND CAMPING

Reserve up to six months in advance to stay in the *vieille ville* in July and August. The extremely popular hostel doesn't take phone reservations; book by fax or letter—and well in advance—to stay there in summer.

■ **Les Chiens du Guet,** 4 pl. du Guet (☎02 99 40 87 29; fax 02 99 56 08 75). Fabulously located *intra-muros* right on a *porte* gives direct access to the top of the wall as well as to the beach and promenade. The charming owner has coordinated bright rooms with elegant furnishings. Just 5min. from the restaurants and bars, and well worth the extra money. Call ahead in summer. Breakfast €5. July-Aug. doubles €31, with shower

€38, with shower and toilet €45; triples €34, with shower and toilet €55; quads €66. Off-season prices €5-6 lower. Closed Nov. 12-Jan. MC/V. ❸

Auberge de Jeunesse/Centre Patrick Varangot/Centre de Rencontres Internationales (HI), 37 av. du Révérend Père Umbricht (☎02 99 40 29 80; fax 02 99 40 29 02; info@centrevarangot.com). From the train station, take bus #5 (dir: Paramé or Davier) or bus #1 (dir: Rothéneuf) to "Auberge de Jeunesse" (last bus 7:30pm). You can also take bus #1 from St-Vincent and the tourist office. From July to Aug. 25, #1 runs about once per hr. 8am-11:30pm. By foot, follow bd. de la République to the right from the front of the station. After 2 blocks, turn right onto av. Ernest Renan. When it ends, turn left onto av. de Moka. Turn right on av. Pasteur, which becomes av. du Rév. Père Umbricht, and keep right at the sign saying "Auberge de Jeunesse." (30min.) The professional staff runs an enormous establishment, more hotel than hostel. Clean 2- to 6-person rooms with new furniture, sinks and bathrooms. Athletic facilities. 3 blocks from the beach. Kitchen with individual refrigerators (€1.60). Laundry. Sheets €2.70. After 10:45pm, guard in the neighboring Foyer des Jeunes Travailleurs can let you in. M-F meals €6.40. Handicapped-accessible. Reception 24hr. 4- to 6-person rooms with sink €12.20; 2- to 3-person rooms with shower €12.60; 2- to 5-person rooms with bunk beds, toilet, and shower €13.70; 2- to 3-person rooms with toilet and shower €14.90. Oct.-Apr. prices are about €0.50 lower. ❶

Hôtel le Neptune, 21 rue de l'Industrie (☎02 99 56 82 15). On an empty street 5min. from both station and *intra-muros* and just one block removed from the beach. From the station, turn right onto bd. de la République and bear left when it ends, passing the post office on your right. Keep straight; rue de l'Industrie will be on the left. Unremarkable hotel, situated convenient to the old and new parts of the city, featuring relatively recent renovations. Breakfast €5. Reception 8am-midnight. Singles and doubles with shower €25, with shower and toilet €28; quads €32/€35; quint €40. MC/V. ❷

Hôtel Avenir, 31 bd. de la Tour d'Auvergne (☎02 99 56 13 33). From the station, turn right onto bd. de la République and then right onto bd. de la Tour d'Auvergne (just before the post office); the hotel is on your left. Provides simple, small, yet spotless rooms over a modest bar. Breakfast €4. Singles €20, with shower €24.50; doubles €21.50/€26; quad/quint (3 beds) €43. No credit cards. ❷

Hôtel Jersey, 53 chaussée du Sillon (☎02 99 56 10 41; fax 02 99 40 52 70; www.antineahotel.com). From the station, follow directions to Hôtel Neptune but instead of turning left on rue de l'Industrie keep straight until you hit the beach and turn right; the hotel will be on your left. The plush, well-appointed rooms (all with shower and toilet, TV and phone) are a bargain by beachfront standards; prices vary based on rooms' proximity to the ocean. Breakfast €7. Open mid-Feb. to Dec. Singles €38.10-76.20; doubles €41.15-79.25. June-Sept. prices higher. ❹

Camping Municipal La Cité d'Alet, at the western tip of St-Servan (☎02 99 81 60 91). Buses #1 and #6 run to "Alet" about twice per day (otherwise, take a bus to "St-Servan" and head northwest to Alet). From the bus stop, head uphill and bear left at the ruined 4th- to 10th-century Cathédrale St-Pierre onto allée Gaston Buy; the campground is 50m away. 350 spots in quiet, scenic location. Reception July-Aug. 8am-9pm; Sept.-June 11am-noon and 2-7:30pm. Gates closed 11pm-7am. 2 people and tent €10, 2 people and caravan with electricity €14. €5 per person, ages 2-7 €2.30. ❶

⬛ FOOD

Numerous indistinguishable **restaurants** cluster along the main roads of *intra-muros*, particularly along rue Jacques Cartier; there are less generic and less populated spots along the side streets. **Outdoor markets** (8am-12:30pm) are on pl. Bouvet in St-Servan, at the Marché aux Légumes *intra-muros* (Tu and F) and on pl.

du Prieuré in Paramé (W and Sa). There is an underground **Marché Plus,** 9 rue St-Vincent, near the entrance to the city walls at Porte St-Vincent. (Open M-Sa 7am-9pm and Su 9am-1pm.) A **Champion supermarket** is on av. Pasteur near the hostel. (Open M-F 8:30am-1pm and 3-7:30pm, Sa 8:30am-7:30pm, and Su 9:30am-noon. July-Aug. longer hours.) Try the homey setting of **La Goëlette ❶,** 3 rue de la Pie qui boit (☎02 99 40 59 00, fax 02 99 20 14 48. Salads €6, specialty galettes €6 and crepes €4. Open daily 11am-2pm and 7-10pm. MC/V) or the classy country interior of **La Brigantine ❷,** 13 rue de Dinan (☎02 99 56 82 82, fax 02 23 15 14 40. Open Th-M 11am-2pm and 6:30-10pm. Galettes €7 and crepes €4. MC/V). Sweet-toothed travelers will love the exotic flavors of homemade gelato at **Le Sanchez,** pl. du Pilori. (☎02 99 56 67 17. Scoop €1.60, two €2.50. Open daily about 11am-11pm.)

◎ SIGHTS

St-Malo's miles of **beaches** attract sunbathing beauties, volleyball and sand soccer enthusiasts, and brave cold-blooded swimmers. Just outside the city walls, you'll find the area's warmest water in the large, square **Piscine de Bon-Secours,** a pool filled by the sea at high tide and by local youth at all other times. To the east of the city, **Grand Plage** is the most popular beach; further up the coast is the slightly calmer, couple-filled **Plage Rochebonne.**

The best view of St-Malo is from its **ramparts,** the high wide walls which kept invaders from entering the *intra-muros* but now attract visitors to the city in droves. All entrances to the city have stairways leading up to the old walls. From the northern side of the city, you can see a series of small islands drifting out into the sea. The three largest, Fort National, Le Grand Bé, and Le Petit Bé, can be reached at low tide over a sandy, pebbly, squelching path strewn with stranded mollusks. **Fort National** (look for the French flag) was built in 1689 by the military's master architect, Vauban, to protect St-Malo from the English. It's not really worth paying for a tour of the empty, stony fortresses, save for the fabulous view of the bay and the city from the top. (☎02 99 69 03 17 or 02 99 85 34 44. Open June-Sept. daily; Easter-May Sa-Su only. Hours depend on the tides; call the tourist office for a schedule. Tours in French every 20min; written explanations in English. €3, children 6-15 €1.50.) The other two islands, west of the Fort and near the Piscine de Bon-Secours, are worth a visit for their strange rocky seclusion. **Le Grand Bé** holds the grave of native son **Chateaubriand** (1768-1848), who asked to be buried amid the wind and waves that inspired his books. "Bé" means "tomb" in Breton; on that note, don't set out for **Le Petit Bé** if the sea is within 10m of the walkway.

The **Grand Aquarium** (not to be confused with the smaller aquarium *intra-muros*) displays an impressive marine bestiary hailing from Atlantic to Amazonian climes, as well as a frightening robotic creature that welcomes you to the site. The new Nautibus gives visitors an up-close look at underwater treasures, and the giant wraparound CineMerScope will get you as close to the sharks as you'll want to be. Take bus #5 (dir: Moinerie or Grassinais) from the station, the tourist office, or the hostel; in summer, ask about the special A line (€1.10) straight there from the tourist office. (☎02 99 21 19 00; fax 02 99 21 19 01; www.mysteresdelamer.com. Open July-Aug. daily 9:30am-8pm; Apr.-June and Sept. 10am-7pm; Oct.-Mar. 10am-6pm. Last entry 1hr. before closing. €12, ages 4-17 €9.)

St-Malo native Jacques Cartier, who discovered Canada, is buried in the 12th-century **Cathédrale St-Vincent,** which has been carefully restored following heavy damage in WWII. Look for the funky 20th-century altar and bright modern stained glass contrasting the ancient edifice. (Open June-Aug. M-Sa 9:45am-6pm, Su 9:30am-6pm; Sept.-May closed from noon-2pm.) During July and August, the cathedral presents a series of classical and choral music concerts through the **Festival de Musique Sacrée.** (☎02 99 56 05 38, reservations 06 08 31 99 93.)

♪ ENTERTAINMENT

L'Absinthe, 1 rue de l'Orme, is a great place to meet locals, world-class sailors, and beach bums, who stand elbow-to-elbow in the large front room downing anything and everything from beer to mojitos. As the night goes on, the clientele spreads out to three surrounding rooms of tatami-style tables, red velvet couches, and movie-theater seats. (☎02 99 40 85 40. Frozen margaritas €1.50 and €3.90. Open daily 2pm-2am, 4pm-2am if it's sunny. Closed M off-season.) **L'Alambic,** 8 rue du Boyer, which looks like a brewery with its brass lamps, stone walls, and timbered ceilings, draws a crowd even on quiet evenings. (☎02 99 40 86 41. Open Apr.-Sept. daily 10am-2am; Oct.-Mar. 10am-1am.) **L'Aviso,** 12 rue Point du Jour, sells 300 types of beer (starting at €2.60), 12 whiskeys, and more kinds of juice than you're interested in drinking. (☎02 99 40 99 08. Open May-Sept. daily 6pm-3am, Oct.-Apr. 6pm-2am.) Intimate, cave-like **L'Archipel,** 18 rue Sainte Barbe, seats a chic crowd of regulars around just a few tables and the massive, curling wood-paneled bar. (☎02 99 56 75 10. Beer €2. Open July-Aug. daily 4pm-2am; Sept.-June noon-2am.)

St-Malo draws even bigger crowds during its many festivals. **Etonnants Voyageurs,** the pre-eminent international literary festival in France, brings travel and adventure writers to the city in mid-May. The **Festival des Folklores du Monde** brings in international folk musicians and dancers the first week of July. The **Route du Rock** draws 20 bands to the city during the 2nd weekend of August. The **Quai des Bulles,** held the last weekend in October, lets you meet the creators of your favorite comic strips. The **Route du Rhum,** named for its participants' beverage of choice, is a sailing race that begins in St-Malo in November and ends in the French Antilles.

DINAN

Tranquil Dinan (pop. 10,000) may be the best-preserved medieval town in Brittany, and shows all the signs of a town that has reaped the benefits of its tourist-friendly status. Its *vieille ville* teeters intact 66m above the river Rance, and its 15th-century streets house artisans and postcard hawkers in roughly equal numbers. In spite of the tourist hordes, Dinan maintains a quiet dignity, and its scenery will take you back centuries.

⬅ TRANSPORTATION

Trains: pl. du 11 Novembre 1918 (☎02 96 39 22 39). Office open M-Th 6am-7pm, F-Sa 7:10am-7pm, Su 9am-8pm. To: **Morlaix** (1½hr., 2-3 per day, €18.70) via St-Brieuc; **Paris** (3hr., 8 per day, €49.60); **Rennes** (1hr., 8 per day, €11.20); **St-Brieuc** (1hr., 2-3 per day, €8.60); **St-Malo** (1hr., 7 per day, €7.30) via Dol.

Buses: CAT/TV buses (☎02 96 39 21 05) leave from train station and pl. Duclos. Office open M-F 8am-noon and 2-6pm. To **St-Malo** (45min.; M-Sa 5 per day, Su 3 per day; €5.30). July-Aug. leads **tours** of Mont-St-Michel (1-2 per week, €18). **TAE buses/Cars 35** (☎02 99 26 16 00), leave from the station. To **Dinard** (30min., 7 per day, €1.80) and **Rennes** (70min., 7 per day, €8.20).

Taxis: ☎02 98 39 06 00.

Bike Rental: Cycles Scardin, 30 rue Carnot (☎02 96 39 21 94). Bikes €12.20-14 per day, €73.20-84 per week. €150 deposit. Open Tu-Sa 9am-noon and 2-7pm. MC/V.

Canoe and Kayak Rental: Port de Dinan, **Club de Canoë** (☎02 96 39 01 50), 12 rue du Quai Talard, across from rue du Quai. Canoes €15.25 per half-day, €22.90 per day. Kayaks €12.20 per half-day, €18.30 per day. Passport deposit. Open July-Aug. daily 10am-noon and 2-5:30pm.

BRITTANY

☀❓ ORIENTATION AND PRACTICAL INFORMATION

To get from the station to the **tourist office,** rue du Château, bear left across pl. du 11 Novembre 1918 onto rue Carnot, then right onto rue Thiers, which brings you to pl. Duclos. Turn left to go inside the old city walls, and immediately bear right onto rue du Marchix, which becomes rue de la Ferronnerie. Pass the parking lots on pl. du Champ and pl. Duguesclin to your left; the tourist office is ahead on the right.

Tourist Office: rue du Château (☎02 96 87 69 76; fax 02 96 87 69 77; www.dinan-tourisme.com). Provides free walking tour map of city and offers historical guide with circuits in the city and region for €2; also sells a "Keys to the City" pass, which gives access to Dinan's major sights (€6). Will make hotel reservations for €1.50. Tours Apr.-Sept. daily €5, children €2.50. Open June 15-Sept. 15 M-Sa 9am-7pm, Su 10am-12:30pm and 2:30-6pm; Sept. 16-June 14 M-Sa 9am-12:30pm and 2-6:15pm.

Laundromat: 19 rue de Brest, off rue Thiers on rue des Rouairies, which becomes rue de Brest. Open M 2-7pm, Tu and Th 8:30-noon and 2-7pm, W and F-Sa 8:30am-7pm.

Police: 16 pl. du Guesclin (☎02 96 39 03 02), near the château.

Hospital: rue Chateaubriand (☎02 96 85 72 85), in Léhon.

Internet Access: Arospace Cybercafé, 9 rue de la Chaux (☎02 96 87 04 87), off rue de l'Horloge. €3.05 for the first 30min., €1.55 for each additional 15min. Open Tu-Sa 10am-7pm.

Post office, pl. Duclos (☎02 96 85 83 50), has **currency exchange.** Open M-F 8am-6:30pm, Sa 8am-noon. **Postal code:** 22100.

⌂ ACCOMMODATIONS AND CAMPING

The best place to **camp** is at the hostel in a shaded field behind the main building (€4). The tourist office lists other, more urban sites.

Auberge de Jeunesse Moulin du Méen (HI), (☎02 96 39 10 83; fax 02 96 39 10 62; dinan@fuaj.org), slightly outside town in Vallée de la Fontaine-des-Eaux. Turn left from train station, turn left across tracks, then turn right and follow tracks and signs downhill for 1km. Turn right and continue through wooded lanes (be careful of traffic as there is no sidewalk) for 0.5km until you reach the hostel on the right. (30min.) Beautiful old stone house by a brook. Small, clean 2- to 8-bed rooms. Summer photo workshops and equestrian activities. Breakfast €3.20. Dinner €8. Kitchen access. Lockers. Sheets €2.70. Laundry. Reception 8am-noon and 5-8pm. Curfew 11pm. Beds €8.50. ❶

Hôtel du Théâtre, 2 rue Ste-Claire (☎02 96 39 06 91), above quiet bar of same name, has bright rooms, some with large windows, in the heart of the *vieille ville.* Cheaper top-floor rooms are a bit cramped. Breakfast €4-5.50. Singles with sink €14.50; doubles €20.50-22, with shower and toilet €27; triples with shower and toilet €36. ❶

Hôtel de la Gare, pl. de la Gare (☎02 96 39 04 57; fax 02 96 39 02 29), right across from the station and a 10min. walk from the historic quarter. Friendly owners provide simple but bright and clean rooms over a corner bar. Breakfast €4.60. Shower €1.60. Singles €22; doubles €24, with shower and TV €27; triples with shower, TV, and toilet €37; quads with shower, TV, and toilet €40. MC/V. ❷

🍴 FOOD

Simple bars and *brasseries* line the streets linking rue de la Ferronnerie with pl. des Merciers, especially on narrow **rue de la Cordonnerie. Monoprix supermarket** is on rue du Marchix. (Open M-Sa 9am-7:30pm.) There is also a **Marché Plus,** 28 pl.

Duclos, near the post office. (☎02 96 87 50 51. Open M-Sa 7am-9pm, Su 9am-1pm.) Buy a picnic of fruit and crepes at the outdoor **market** on pl. du Champ and pl. du Guesclin in the *vieille ville*. (Open Th 8am-noon.) Small restaurants cluster in the cobbled streets just outside the ramparts and along the port. For a break from the indistinct tourist-heavy cafés of the old town, head away from the walls for a meal. **Crêperie des Artisans ❶**, 6 rue Petit Fort, lies just beyond the Jerzual gate, on the charming street that leads down to the river. A rustic atmosphere to enjoy crepes and galettes. (☎02 96 39 44 10. Crepes €4-7. Open daily July-Aug., Apr.-Oct. Tu-Su.)

👁 SIGHTS

Dinan's city walls and the churches and houses within make the town a sight unto itself. The tourist office provides two separate walking tours to guide your visit of the ramparts and the *intra muros*.

On the ramparts, the 13th-century **Porte du Guichet** is the entrance to the **Château de Dinan**. Its former keep in the Tour de la Duchesse Anne houses a small museum of local art and history. At the top of the 34m tower and its 150 steps, you'll be greeted with a great view of the town and a congratulatory sign for making it to the top. On the same ticket is the 15th-century **Tour de Coëtquen,** adjacent to the keep. Along with the occasional temporary exhibit, its dank, drafty basement possesses a fine collection of funerary ornaments—seven eerie stone slabs portray 14th-century noblemen clutching shields, wives, and weapons. (Open June-Sept. daily 10am-6:30pm; Oct.-Nov. 15 and Mar. 16-May W-M 10am-noon and 2-6pm; Nov. 16-Dec. and Feb. 7-Mar. 15 W-M 1:30-5:30pm. €3.90, ages 12-18 €1.50.) The **Jardin du Val Cocherel,** on the ramparts far from the château, begins hilly, twisting, and dense, but gives way to huge bird cages, a rose garden, a checkerboard for life-sized chessmen, a small zoo, and a children's library. (Garden open daily 8am-7:30pm. Library open daily 10am-noon and 1:30-6:30pm.)

The **Basilique St-Sauveur** was built by a local man grateful to have been spared in the Crusades. The Romanesque facade, including the lion and bull above the doorway and the four statues in the side arches, date back to AD 1120. Within is the heart of the unfortunate Bertrand du Guesclin, perhaps the only Frenchman to ever have 5 tombs for various body parts.

The **Maison d'Artiste de la Grande Vigne,** 103 rue du Quai, past the port, is the former home of painter Yvonne Jean-Haffen (1895-1993). Reaching it entails a long but pleasant walk from the town through Jerzual gate, down the steep rue du Petit Fort, and left along the rue du Quai. The whole house is a work of art—exhibitions of Jean-Haffen's work are displayed, her murals adorn the walls, and the garden outside is an artist's dream. (☎02 96 87 90 80 or 02 96 39 22 43. Open June-Sept. daily 10am-7pm. €2.50, students and ages 12-18 €1.60.)

The **Eglise St-Malo,** on Grande Rue, contains a remarkable 19th-century organ with blue and gold pipes and a massive Baroque altar. The 30m 15th-century **Tour de l'Horloge,** on rue de l'Horloge, commands a brilliant view of Dinan's jumbled streets and the countryside. On the way up, you'll pass through the stone rooms that once held the town archives, now a museum of Arthurian legend and lore. (☎02 96 87 02 26. Open June-Sept. daily 10am-6:30pm. €2.50, ages 12-17 €1.60.) Every two years (next in 2004), Dinan hosts the two-day **Fête des Remparts** during the second half of July, when the whole town dons medieval garb for jousting tournaments, markets, and merrymaking. (☎02 96 87 94 94; fax 02 96 87 99 99; http://perso.wanadoo.fr/fete-remparts.dinan. 11am-9pm each day. €15 per day for access to all activities, those under 12 and in medieval garb free.)

BRITTANY

ST-BRIEUC

As most locals will tell you, St-Brieuc (pop. 48,000) is much more of a commercial center than a tourist trap; its small *vieille ville* and city center are surrounded by an industrial port and economically diverse suburbs. The university students enliven the city, and create a lively bar scene. However, the main reason most visit St-Brieuc is its position between the Côte d'Emeraude and the Côte de Granite Rose. It's a perfect launch pad for daytrips, particularly the stunning Cap Fréhel.

▐ TRANSPORTATION

Trains: bd. Charner (☎02 96 01 61 64). Info open M-Sa 8am-7pm, Su 9:30am-7pm. To: **Dinan** (1hr., 2-3 per day, €8.60); **Morlaix** (1hr., 8-11 per day, €13.10); **Rennes** (1hr., 15 per day, €14.40); **Vannes** (2hr., 6 per day, €15.90).

Buses: CAT is at both the train station and the **bus station** at rue du Combat des Trente (☎02 96 68 31 20), next to the main intra-city bus terminal at Champs de Mars. To: **Fréhel** (1½hr.; July-Sept. M-Sa 6 per day, Su 3 per day; Oct.-June 3 per afternoon; €7.20, students €5.80) and **Paimpol** (1½hr.; M-Sa 5 per day; €7.20, students €5.80). **TUB,** 8 rue Jouallan (☎02 96 68 14 87), runs throughout the city (every 15min. 6:30am-8pm); **NOCTUB** takes the duties of line #3 every 30min. from 8-11:15pm. Tickets €0.95, *carnet* of 10 €8.10.

Bike Rental: at the **hostel** (see below).

▗▌ ORIENTATION AND PRACTICAL INFORMATION

To get to the center of town from the station, walk straight ahead onto rue de la Gare. When you reach rue du 71*ème* Régiment d'Infanterie, the main bus terminals will be to the right at pl. du Champ de Mars. Continue straight on rue de la Gare (through name changes), following it to the left as it becomes rue de Rohan, and turn right onto rue St-Gouéno; the **tourist office** is on the left.

Tourist Office: 7 rue St-Gouéno (☎02 96 33 32 50; fax 02 96 61 42 16; www.baie-saintbrieuc.com). Guided tours of the cathedral and old quarters (80min.; July 3-Aug. 25 M-F 10:30am and 3pm; meet outside of the cathedral; €2.60). Pick up the free *Le Griffon* at a newsstand for info on regional events. Open July-Aug. M-Sa 9am-12:30pm and 2-7pm, Su 10am-1pm; Sept.-June M-Sa 9am-12:30pm and 2-6pm.

Currency Exchange: banks line pl. Champ de Mars.

Laundromat: Behind the cathedral in pl. du Martray (☎06 08 05 29 84). Has a terrifying automatic locking system. Open Apr.-Sept. daily 7am-9pm, Oct.-Mar. 7am-8pm.

Police: 17 rue Joullan (☎02 96 33 36 66).

Hospital: rue Marcel Proust (☎02 96 01 71 23).

Internet Access: MediaCap, 4 rue Joullan (☎02 96 68 90 31), off rue St-Guillaume. €0.75 for 15min. or €3 per hr. Open M-F 9:30am-7pm and Sa 2-7pm. The tourist office can suggest other places.

Post Office: pl. de la Résistance (☎02 96 61 10 60). Open M-F 8am-noon and 2-6pm, Sa 8am-noon. **Postal code:** 22000.

▐▐ ACCOMMODATIONS AND FOOD

Decent budget accommodations are extremely hard to come by in town. Most inexpensive hotels are cheap for a reason. To escape from the dingy city feel, try the **youth hostel ❶**, 3km outside town, in a 15th-century house surrounded by fields and hiking trails. From the train station, cross the street and take bus #2 (dir: Centre Commercial les Villages) and get off at the last stop, "Vau Méno"; continue in the direction of the bus and then turn right onto rue de la Ville Guyomard, where you'll find the hostel on the left. You can also go to the bus terminal at pl. du Champs de Mars and take bus #3 (dir: Centre Commercial les Villages), which stops at the hostel about half of the time and at les Villages the other half. If the bus doesn't stop at Vau Méno, get off at "Brocéliande" and turn right up rue de Brocéliande. After 300m that dead-ends; turn left onto rue du Vau Méno and then right onto rue de la Ville Guyomard, where you'll find the hostel on the left. Tennis, bike rental, sea kayaking, and horseback riding are all available. Call ahead, as they are often full. (☎02 96 78 70 70. Breakfast included. Hearty meals €8.40. Sheets €3.05. Bikes €11.45 per day with passport deposit. No lockout or curfew. Reception 8am-noon, 2-4pm, and 8-10pm, but someone is always around. Bunks €12.20. All prices increase by about €3 for non-HI members. MC/V.) **Hotel de l'Arrivée ❶**, 35 rue de la Gare, has small, clean rooms (all with shower, toilet, TV, and phone) on a busy street near the train station and 500m from the bus terminal, only a 10min. walk from the cathedral and tourist office. (☎02 96 94 05 30. Breakfast €4.85. Reception 7am-3pm and 5-9:30pm. Singles €30.50-33.60, doubles €35.10-38.20. Extra bed €8. MC/V.)

Bars and outdoor cafés cluster in the area behind the tourist office and along the small rue Fardel behind the Cathédrale St-Etienne; rue des Trois Frères le Goff is lined with inexpensive Moroccan, Italian, Chinese, Mexican, and Indian restaurants. If you are in the mood for crepes with a Breton flavor, head to **Le Cabestan ❶**, 6 rue Fardel. (☎02 96 61 30 03. Crepes €4-6. Open daily for lunch and dinner. MC/V.) Meals of more substance can be found at nearby **Le Chaudron ❸**, 19 rue Fardel, which offers tasty *fondues* for €13, and *grillades* for €14. (☎02 96 33 01 72. Open daily for lunch and dinner, except W lunch. MC/V.) There's a **Monoprix supermarket** on pl. de la Résistance. (Open M-Sa 8:30am-7:15pm.) The enormous **Géant** supermarket is at the Centre Commercial Les Villages near the hostel. (Open M-Sa 8am-9pm.) The public **market** sells cloth, leather, and beaded goods around the cathedral, and food in front of the post office. (W and Sa 8am-1pm.)

👁 🎵 SIGHTS AND ENTERTAINMENT

St-Brieuc doesn't offer much in the way of sights, with the exception of **Cathédrale St-Etienne**, pl. de Gaulle, a multi-century work of art. The first wooden monastery was built here in 848; construction of the stone edifice was more or less complete by the 14th century, but additions continued for the next 500 years. Of particular interest are the 12th-century column capital on the left of the south transept, and a 1950s-era set of stations of the cross that mixes modern art with the flatness of icon painting. Guided visits offered by tourist office (see above) give a good sense of the history of the cathedral and the region. For a better sense of old St-Brieuc, ask the tourist office for the **Circuit de découverte du centre historique**, a self-guided walking tour past the city's monuments and older neighborhoods.

St-Brieuc's bars accommodate a large range of ages and types; on any given night, the same place may be filled with a chic student crowd or a familiar group of middle-aged shopkeepers. **Chez Rollais**, 25 rue du Général Leclerc off rue St-Barbe, first opened its carved oak door in 1912; locals still sip Loire wines under the frescoed ceiling of this beautiful old wine bar. (☎02 96 61 23 03. Wine €1.90-3.10 a glass. Open Tu-Sa 9am-11pm.) St-Brieuc's most popular lounge is **Le Piano Bleu**, 4 rue Fardel. The front room sees frequent concerts; the back has cushy couches and padded benches. During the summer, young businessmen lounge alongside students halfway into the narrow street at outdoor tables. (☎02 96 33

BRITTANY

41 62. Cocktails €5.35, liquor €4.60. Open daily 5pm-3am.) **Kafé de la Plage,** 2 pl. de General de Gaulle, indeed has a beachy tropical feel despite its inland setting; its specialty is the ultimate island drink, rum. (☎ 02 96 33 19 06. Open daily 8am-1am, F and Sa until 2am, Su 4pm-1am. MC/V.) **Le Chapeau Rouge,** 13 rue Fardel, welcomes a loyal clientele (whose photos decorate the walls) into a single, intimate wood-paneled room in one of the oldest buildings in St-Brieuc. Signs out front proclaim its gay-friendly status. In the summer months, the outdoor tables have a great view of the other bars' patios down the hill. (☎ 02 96 33 83 13. Open M-F 7pm-3am, Sa 8pm-3am, Su 9pm-3am.) Escape into the Celtic sanctum of **O'Kenny Irish Pub,** 10 rue Mireille Chrisostome, dominated by an oval island bar that serves up pints of Guinness (€5) into the wee hours. (☎ 02 96 61 37 36. Open daily 4pm-1am. MC/V.)

St-Brieuc's innovative festivals include **ArtRock,** a combined music and street art festival held on the last weekend in May or first weekend in June. Every Thursday and Friday in July and August, **L'Eté en Fête** brings at least three street concerts or presentations to pl. du Martray, near the tourist office.

NEAR ST-BRIEUC

CAP FRÉHEL

*To get to the Cap, you'll need to catch a **CAT bus** from St-Brieuc (1½hr.; July-Sept. M-Sa 6 per day, Su 3 per day; Oct.-June 3 per afternoon; €7.20, students €5.80). The last stop is in the town of Fréhel, which is 6km from the hostel and the Cap, so be ready for a hike. In low season, buses are scheduled so that you only have an hour to visit the Cap; spending the night makes sense.*

When landscape artists go to sleep at night, they dream of Cap Fréhel. The flora here is reason enough to come: green expanses dotted by royal purple spiny petals and wild orchids. Add rust-hued cliffs, which drop 70m to inlets beaten by a raging sea, and you'll begin to understand why this peninsula is so popular with hikers, postcard photographers, and those in search of self. The Cap does not offer much solitude in the summer, as hundreds flock here to hike the well-marked **GR34 trail** that follows the peninsula's edge. Wander off the trail, and you're bound to find a less crowded set of winding paths. However, be sure not to get too adventurous— the terrain can be challenging and there are several fatalities every year.

The small Fréhel **tourist office,** down the street from the bus stop in Fréhel *bourg* and across from the post office, can give advice on local terrain. (☎ 02 96 41 53 81; fax 02 96 41 59 46. Open M 2-5pm; Tu, Th, F 8:45am-12:30pm and 3-5pm; W 8:45am-12:30pm.) At the northernmost point of the Cap there's a great view from the **lighthouse,** set in the middle of an ornithological reserve (access to the point free, €1.55 per car). An easy walk southwest leads to a breathtaking, secluded little beach. You can also take a scenic walk (90min.) to the **Fort de la Latte,** a 13th-century castle complete with drawbridges. (☎ 02 96 41 40 31. Open June-Sept. Tours daily 10am-12:30pm and 2:30-6:30pm. €3.35, under 12 €1.70.)

If you're adventurous enough to make the trek, plan on spending the night at the **Auberge de Jeunesse Cap Fréhel (HI) ❶,** Ville Hadrieux, Kerivet, near the town of Plévenon. The hostel's two-tiered eight-person rooms are clean and perfectly acceptable, but some prefer to sleep in the three tents beyond the bonfire pit outside, where they can be closer to the sandbox, the goats, the horses, and, of course, the Chinese pigs. It's very popular with groups, so be sure to call ahead. The hostel also **rents bikes** (€7.35 per half-day) and has maps of the GR34. (☎ 02 96 41 48 98; Sept. 16-Apr. ☎ 02 96 78 70 70. Breakfast €2.90. Dinner €7.65. Sheets €2.60. Lock-out noon-5:30pm. Open May-Sept. €7 inside or out.)

PAIMPOL

Anchored on the border of the Côte de Granite Rose and the Côte de Goëlo, Paimpol (pop. 8200; pronounced "PAM-pol") is a pretty little fishing village. Paimpol has kept its traditional ties to the rod and reel, but the port now harbors a string of snazzy bars, restaurants, and yachts. Although Paimpol itself has few sights, the town provides easy access to the surrounding islands, cliffs, beaches, hiking trails, and the picturesque ruins of the Abbaye de Beauport.

▉ TRANSPORTATION

Trains: av. du Général de Gaulle. Office open M-Sa 6:40-7:10am and 8am-7pm, Su and holidays 9am-7pm. To: **Pontrieux** (18min., 4 per day, €2.70). At Guingamp (☎02 96 20 81 22), there are connections to **Morlaix** (1¼hr., 4 per day, €12) and **St-Brieuc** (1hr., 4-5 per day, €10).

Buses: CAT (☎02 96 22 67 72) runs from the train station to **Pointe de l'Arcouest** (15min.; M-Sa 7 per day, Su 5 per day; €1.75) and **St-Brieuc** (1¼hr.; 8 per day; €7.20, students €5.80). The same well-organized bus system runs throughout the Côtes d'Armor and also serves the campground. Buy tickets on the bus.

Bike Rental: Cycles du Vieux Clocher, pl. de Verdun (☎02 96 20 83 58). €6 per half-day, €11 per day. Open M-Sa 8:30am-12:30pm and 2-7:30pm, Su 8am-noon.

▉ ▉ ORIENTATION AND PRACTICAL INFORMATION

To reach the port and the tourist office on **pl. de la République,** turn right onto av. du Général de Gaulle and follow it to the roundabout. Bear left; the tourist office will be on the left opposite the Marché Plus, and the port will be to the right.

Tourist Office: pl. de la République (☎02 96 20 83 16; fax 02 96 55 11 12; tourisme.paimpol@wanadoo.fr). They have a map of the hiking trails that lead from Paimpol to the Pointe de l'Arcouest. Pick up *La Presse d'Armor,* a local publication with a schedule of events (€1), at a newsstand. Open July-Aug. M-Sa 10am-7pm, Su 10am-1pm; Sept.-June Tu-Sa 10am-12:30pm and 2:30-6pm.

Currency Exchange: Société Générale, 6 pl. de la République (☎02 96 20 81 34).

Hospital: chemin de Malabry (☎02 96 55 60 00), off the right side of the port.

Police: rue Raymond Pellier (☎02 96 20 80 17), the 3rd road on the roundabout at the non-portside end of pl. de la République.

Laundromat: Au Lavoir Pampolais, 23 rue du 18 juin (☎02 96 20 96 41), near the station. Rents sheets. Open daily 8am-8pm. Also near the port on rue de Labenne. Open daily 7:30am-9pm; July-Aug. until 9:30pm.

Internet Access: Cybercommune, Centre Dunant, (☎02 96 20 74 74), near the church. €0.09 per min., €5.40 per hr. Open M-F 3-8pm, Tu-W also 9am-12:30pm, Sa 2-6pm.

Post Office: av. du Général de Gaulle (☎02 96 20 82 40). **Currency exchange.** Open M and W-F 8am-noon and 1:30-5:30pm, Tu 8am-12:30pm and 1:30-5:30pm, Sa 8am-12:30pm. **Postal code:** 22500.

▉ ACCOMMODATIONS

A good choice for accommodations in Paimpol is **Hôtel Berthelot ❸,** 1 rue du Port (☎02 96 20 88 66). From the tourist office, walk straight ahead toward the port and turn left after several blocks onto rue du Port. You'll see a bright blue "H" on the right at the hotel's entrance. On a quiet side street, it has friendly reception and large, comfy rooms with big windows. (Breakfast €4.50. Singles and doubles €26, with toilet €28, with bath €36, with TV €38. MC/V.) **Le Terre-Neuvas ❸,** quai Dug-uay-Trouin, is located on the water over the restaurant of the same name (see below). Small, welcoming rooms with a vaguely nautical theme, some with views of the harbor. (☎02 96 55 14 14; fax 02 96 20 47 66. Breakfast €5. Call ahead in summer. Doubles with shower and toilet €31, with harbor view €37; triples with shower and toilet €39, with harbor view €45. MC/V.)

The **Auberge de Jeunesse (HI) ❶,** Château de Kéraoul, 20min. uphill on the western edge of town, is closed indefinitely for renovations. Check first with the tourist office to find out if it has reopened. To get there from the train station, turn left onto av. du Général de Gaulle, right onto rue du Marne at the first light, and left at the next light onto rue Bécot. When the road forks, veer right onto rue de Pen Ar Run. Turn left at the end of the street; the hostel will be on your right behind a school. (☎02 96 20 83 60. 2- to 6-person rooms. Camping allowed.) The very popular sea-side **Camping Municipal de Cruckin ❶,** off the plage de Cruckin, is right by the Abbaye de Beauport. From the train station, turn right onto av. du Général de Gaulle and take the third option at the roundabout, rue du Général Leclerc. Follow the street as it twists through four name changes. Take rue de Cruckin from rue du Commandant le Conniat. The entrance is 150m down the hill, on the right. (25min.) Or take the CAT bus (dir: St-Brieuc) from the train station to "Kerity" (5min., 8 per day, €1.75). (☎02 96 20 78 47. Reception June 11-Aug. daily 8am-10pm; Apr.-May 15 and Sept. M-Sa 8am-noon and 4-8pm, Su 9-11am and 7-8pm; May 16-June 10 M-Sa 8am-noon and 4:30-8:30pm, Su 9-11am and 7:30-8:30pm. June-Aug. 10pm-6am gates close to cars, but there's a night watchman. Apr.-May gates close 10pm-7am without watchman. Open Apr.-Sept. Handicap-accessible. 1 person and tent €7; 2-3 people and tent €11.40. Extra person €1.35. Electricity €2.30-2.80.)

⬛ FOOD

Picnickers can find supplies either at Paimpol's Tuesday morning **market,** held in squares throughout the town, or at the **Marché Plus,** rue St-Vincent, across from the tourist office. (Open M-Sa 7am-9pm and Su 10am-noon.) Seafood fans will be happy at portside **Le Terre-Neuvas ❷,** quai Duguay-Trouin, where there is elegant food at backpacker prices. The specialties of the house are *moules frites* (€7.50, €12.50 with *entrée* and dessert). In July and August, five *grandes assiettes gourmandes* are served with grilled and seasoned bread, the catch of the day, salad, vegetables, and a side dish for €9-12. (☎02 96 55 14 14; fax 02 96 20 47 66. Open July-Aug. daily noon-2pm and 7-10pm; Sept.-June closed M.)

⬛ SIGHTS

Hidden from the road by vegetation, the ruins of the ▨**Abbaye de Beauport,** chemin de l'Abbaye, look dreamily out to sea. First built in 1202, the abbey, east of Paimpol, has been revamped as an 800th birthday present. The now-roofless church has flowers sprouting from its flying buttresses, and the book-guided self-tour (in French, English, or German) gives a complete account of the many other portions of the abbey, from the intact cellars to the picturesque garden. To get there, follow directions to the campground, but continue past rue de Cruckin to the next major left turn; the abbey is at the end of the lane. (☎02 96 55 18 58; www.abbaye-beauport.com. Open June 15-Sept. 15 daily 10am-7pm; Sept. 16-June 14 daily 10am-noon and 2-5pm. English tours July-Aug. daily 11am; 3-4 tours in French per day. €5, students and seniors €4.50, ages 11-18 €3.50, ages 5-10 €2.50.)

The **Musée de la Mer,** rue de Labenne, on the opposite side of the roundabout from the tourist office, is the town's tribute to its Icelandic fishing industry. Nautical experts will likely take the plunge to view local fishermen's memorabilia, but others may find the museum as fun as a dip in the North Atlantic. (☎02 96 22 02 19 or 02 96 20 83 16. Open June 15-Sept. 10:30am-12:30pm and 2:30-6pm, Apr.-June 15 2:30pm-6pm. €4.05, students €2.)

🎵 ENTERTAINMENT

The port is boxed in by bars and restaurants on all sides except on the water, where it's overrun by private yachts. As the sun sets, the crowds head across the port to bars along quai de Kernoa. **La Falaise**, 2 quai de Kernoa, blasts house music from the top of the port. (☎02 96 20 89 79. Open daily 10am-1am, F-Sa until 2am.) For a more Breton atmosphere, walk a few doors down to the **Tavarn An Tri Martolod** (Tavern of the Three Sailors), 11 quai de Kernoa. (☎02 96 20 75 15. Open July-Aug. Su-Th 11am-1am, F-Sa 11am-2am; Sept.-June W-M 11am-1am.) Nearby side-streets have even more interesting options. Just around the corner from Hôtel Berthelot, **Le Corto Maltese**, 11 rue du Quai, draws locals and tourists of all ages. (☎02 96 22 05 76. Open July-Aug. M-F 10am-1am, Sa-Su 10am-2am; Sept.-June Tu-Su 10am-1am.) For a cozier atmosphere, try **Le Cargo**, 15 rue des 8 Patriotes, with its plaid-draped windowsills and chunky wooden tables. (☎02 96 20 72 46. Open Su-Th 12:30pm-1am, F-Sa 12:30pm-2am.) More than likely, you'll end up at one of Paimpol's few late-night bars. **Le Pub**, 3 rue Islandais, lurks behind a heavy oak door, but even that doesn't contain the revelry into the early hours. (☎02 96 20 82 31. Open June-Sept. daily 7pm-3am; Oct.-May Th-Sa 7pm-3am and Su 10pm-3am.) Set back from the street in an alley, **La Ruelle**, 26 rue des 8 Patriotes, doesn't get going until other bars close, but stays open until 3am, sending the sounds of ska and reggae out through open doors into the street. (☎02 96 20 56 96. Beer €2. Open July-Sept. daily 6:30pm-3am; Oct.-June Th-Sa 6:30pm-3am, Su 10:30pm-3am.)

The **Festival du Chant de Marin** draws sailor-musicians from around the world to the port of Paimpol in August. For three days the city dedicates itself to dancing, boating, and general merriment. Call the tourist office for more info.

🚶 DAYTRIP: POINTE DE L'ARCOUEST AND ILE DE BRÉHAT

To reach the Pointe, take a **CAT bus** (☎02 96 68 31 20) from Paimpol (12min.; M-Sa 8 per day, Su 7; last bus from the Pointe 5:20pm; €1.75). Drivers can follow the clearly marked GR34 from the Paimpol port. **Les Vedettes de Bréhat** (☎02 96 55 79 50; www.vedettesdebrehat.com) sends boats from the Pointe to the island (10min.; 10-15 per day; round-trip €6.50, ages 4-11 €5.50; passenger and bike €14.50; 45min. tours €11, ages 4-11 €8).

Six kilometers north of Paimpol, the peninsula ends in the tumble of pink granite that is the **Pointe de l'Arcouest.** The archipelagos and blue-green waters flowing around this point provide some of France's best sea kayaking. Two kilometers across the water lies a mesh of rocky beaches, flower-covered mansions, and fields of elbow-high grasses. Only 3.5km in length, cinched to a little bridge in the middle, the idyllic **Ile de Bréhat** (pop. 450) is divided into the rugged northern half, with a lighthouse, and the southern half, where the *bourg* and the port lie. What most refer to as the Ile de Bréhat is actually the largest landmass in an archipelago of 96 islets, some of them so minute that they essentially amount to single rocks. If you can, take the first boat of the day, then head north to avoid the crowds. For a few extra euros, you can stay on the boat for a 45min. tour of the island from the sea, allowing you to take in its cliff-strewn beauty before setting a foot on shore. Empty, isolated beaches dot the coastline; be sure to bring a mat since most of Bréhat's beaches are rocky. The view from the white **Chapelle St-Michel,** on the west side of the island, is unparalleled—except by that from the **Phare du Paon,** a lighthouse at the island's northern tip (a 40-50min. walk from the center of town).

The *bourg* is a 15min. walk from the port, which is at the southernmost point of the island and has restaurants, a **post office,** and an **8 à Huit** supermarket. (Open M-Sa 8:30am-8pm and Su 9am-1pm.) To get to the **tourist office,** follow the main road toward the *bourg*, passing the 8 à Huit, until you reach the large square. Turn right and it will be in front of you, before the church. Maps of Bréhat (€0.30 and €0.50). Info about camping on the island. (☎02 96 20 04 15. Open Tu-F 10am-6pm, M and Sa 10am-12:30pm and 2-6:30pm.) **Bike** rental is available just past the port at **Loca-cycle.** (☎06 89 69 35 33. €8 per half-day, €11 per day.)

MORLAIX

A half-dozen stone stairways and two rivers descend sharply from the hills on either side of Morlaix (pop. 17,000) and pour cars, water, and people into the squares and port of the narrow town center, giving it a fast-paced, crowded, big-city feel. Founded in Gallo-Roman times, when Armorican Celts built a fort here called "Mons Relaxus" (Mount of Rest), the town was continually invaded during the Middle Ages by the Duchy of Brittany, the French crown, and the British, all of whom sought to control Morlaix's enviably located port. British invaders made the mistake of celebrating their victory to drunken excess and were unhappily surprised when Morlaix's avenging citizens returned. From this event came Morlaix's name and motto: *"S'ils te mordent, mords-les!"* ("If they bite you, bite them back!"). Luckily, their ancestors are significantly less blood-thirsty, but still take pride in their Celtic roots and medieval past.

▛ TRANSPORTATION

Train Station: rue Armand Rousseau (☎08 36 35 35 35). Info open M 4:30am-10:30pm, Tu-Sa 5am-10:20pm, Su 8am-midnight. To: **Brest** (45min., 8-10 per day, €8.30); **Paimpol** (1¼hr., 5 per day, €12); **Quimper** via **Landerneau** (2hr., 5-7 per day, €15); **Roscoff** (30min., 2 per day, €7); **St-Brieuc** (45min., 6-10 per day, €11.40).

Buses: SNCF also leaves from the train station for **Roscoff** (30-45min., 4 per day, €4.60). **CAT** (☎02 98 72 01 41) runs to: **Huelgoat** (1hr., 2-3 per day, €1.50); **Quimper** (2hr., 3-5 per week, €10); **Roscoff** (30-45min.; M-Sa 3-4 per day, 1 on Su; €7.20). You can catch some buses at the Morlaisiennes stop, in front of the Monoprix on rue d'Aiguillon, or at the station.

Public Transportation: TIM, pl. Cornic (☎02 98 88 82 82). Tickets €.90, *carnet* of 10 €8.40. Buses run 7:30am-7pm.

Taxis: Radio Taxis (☎02 98 15 12 73) are usually at pl. des Otages and the station.

✦ ▯ ORIENTATION AND PRACTICAL INFORMATION

All roads run downhill from the station to the port and up into the surrounding hills. There are three ways to get down to the town center. The most direct (and fat-burning) route is **rue Courte,** also known as the Cent Marches, a set of exactly 109 steps interspersed with a series of ramps. From the station, walk straight ahead on **rue Gambetta** for 100m and turn left onto the stairs, which lead directly to the central **pl. Emile Souvestre.** The switchbacking **rue Gambetta** and the steep **rue Longue** (the next road to the left after rue Courte) get you to the same place without stairs. If you climb up any of the three, especially with heavy luggage, you may be using muscles you didn't know existed. To get from the station to the **tourist office,** follow the directions above to pl. Emile Souvestre. Turn left and you will shortly be in **pl. des Otages.** The tourist office is the free-standing brown building across the *place*, directly in front of the viaduct.

Tourist Office: pl. des Otages (☎02 98 62 14 94; fax 02 98 63 84 87). Helpful, peppy staff gives out maps and a complete city guide. Tours of the city in French July-Aug. Th at 2:30pm. Open July-Aug. M-Sa 10am-noon and 2-7pm, Su 10:30am-12:30pm; Sept.-June Tu-Sa 10am-noon and 2-6pm.

Laundromat: 4 rue de Lavoirs or pl. Charles de Gaulle. Both open daily 8am-8:30pm.

Police: 17 pl. Charles de Gaulle (☎02 98 88 17 17).

Hospital: Hôpital Général, 15 rue Kersaint Gilly (☎02 98 62 61 60).

Internet Access: Le Millenium Café, 9 rue Gambetta (☎02 98 63 99 78), just off pl. Emile Souvestre at the bottom of rue Courte. €1.50 per 15min., €3.80 per hr. Open Tu-F 8am-8pm, Sa 1-8pm. Also at the **post office** with Cyberposte. Surf the web for free at the **public library,** "Les Ailes du Temps," 5 rue Gambetta (☎02 98 15 20 60), with the purchase of a 2 month membership (€4). Open W 10am-noon and 1:30-6pm, F 1:30-6pm, Sa 10am-5pm.

Post Office: 15 rue de Brest, off pl. Emile Souvestre (☎02 98 88 93 22). **Currency exchange.** Open M-F 8:30am-6:30pm, Sa 8:30am-noon. **Postal code:** 29600.

▟ ACCOMMODATIONS

Morlaix is small enough that few areas are undesirable or inconvenient. Ask the tourist office about local *gîtes d'étape* (around €8) or *chambres d'hôte* (€15-30).

Hôtel Le Roy d'Ys, 8 pl. des Jacobins (☎02 98 63 30 55). In a historic building located almost in the center of Morlaix, near many restaurants and sights. Follow directions to pl. Emile Souvestre and head straight on rue Carnot, which is slightly to the right; follow to the end and turn right on rue au Fils. When you reach pl. des Jacobins, the hotel is on the left. The hotel boasts fantastic original wooden spiral stairs; the front rooms overlooking the *place* are fitted with stained glass while the back rooms are more tranquil. All rooms are spacious and brightly decorated. Doubles with shower and/or toilet €30.55. MC/V. ❸

Hôtel de la Gare, 25 pl. St-Martin (☎02 98 88 03 29; fax 02 98 63 97 80), on rue Gambetta just south of the train station, across the street from the top of rue Courte. In a quiet location with quick access to the center of town via the Cent Marches, the hotel has large, clean rooms (all with showers) with spare but pretty furniture and futon-like mattresses. Doubles €31, with toilet €37. ❸

Auberge de Jeunesse (HI), 3 rte. de Paris (☎02 98 88 13 63; fax 02 98 88 81 82). The hostel may not be open in the off-season (any time other than July-Aug.) so call first to check. Far from the train station but not from sights, nightlife, and a lovely canal. From the station, follow the directions in **Orientation,** above, to pl. Emile Souvestre, and bear slightly to the right onto rue Carnot. Take a right onto rue d'Aiguillon (the sign for the hostel will be one among many), which becomes rue de Paris as it bears left 200m ahead. Proceed another 200m and take a left at the roundabout onto rte. de Paris. The road immediately curves to the right and goes up the hill. You'll find the hostel 250m ahead, just after the road curves to the right again. (25min.) The hostel has bright, simple 2- to 9-bed rooms, a kitchen, and a huge dining room. Breakfast €3.20. Dinner €8. Sheets €3.20. Reception M-F 8-10am and 5-8pm, Sa-Su 6-10pm. Lockout 10am-6pm. Curfew off-season 11pm; ask for a key if you'll be late. Dorms €8. ❶

Camping à la Ferme (☎/fax 02 98 79 11 50), in Croas-Men. Worth the 7km walk. From the center of town, follow signs first to Plouigneau and then to Garlan, and then look for the sign. The campsite will be past Garlan on your left. The owners, 3rd-generation farmers of this land, want you to love their farm. To this end, they offer breakfast in the 1840s farmhouse, a petting farm, tractor rides for kids, and sell fresh yogurt and cider. Reception 8am-10pm; gates open 24hr. Open Apr.-Oct. €4 per site, €2.50 per person, children under 7 €2. Electricity €2.50. Pets €1. ❶

FROM THE ROAD

DANCING AT MORLAIX

Traveling around Brittany I've made one key realization about French towns in the summertime: they really like festivals. My most memorable evening was in Morlaix on the longest day of the year, which is celebrated with a music festival. As I wandered from square to square listening to bands, I discovered a much more interesting spectacle: dancing. In a large area in front of the *hôtel de ville*, with the illuminated viaduct behind, a large group of people had joined hands and were spinning around in time to the music.

I watched their clockwise rotation, enthralled. As the band played on, with guitar, accordion, and horn, I noted the basic steps—left, right, 1, 2, 3. The circle was enlarging, so I did the natural thing and joined in. Linked by my pinkies to people on either side of me, I managed to find the beat and skip around. Just as I got the hang of it, the music changed and so did the steps: 2 in, 2 out, and kick. I stayed in the circle, song after song, joining locals whose feet knew the dances instinctively but were more than happy to welcome a stranger. I sat out a do-si-do, only to join back in for a Celtic conga line that spiraled back on itself endlessly. As darkness gathered, the numbers in the square swelled. By midnight we had three circles, one within the other; hundreds all participating in the revelry. As the last song played, the rain that had been threatening all day came down, but we finished the dance, modern people joined in age-old merriment together.
—*Genevieve Sheehan*

🍴 FOOD

There are many places to eat in **quartier St-Mathieu** and on **rue Ange de Guernisac**. For *crêperies* and inexpensive restaurants, head to **rue au Fil**. Saturday brings an all-day **market** that stretches from pl. des Otages to pl. Allende, spilling over into neighboring streets where local craftsmen sell their wares. A Marché Plus **supermarket** is on rue de Paris. (Open M-Sa 7am-9pm, Su 9am-noon.)

👁 🎵 SIGHTS AND ENTERTAINMENT

The **Circuit des Venelles,** a walking tour through medieval Morlaix, is the best way to see the city. The steep, sometimes stairwayed alleys *(venelles)* were the city's main thoroughfares in ancient times. They lead you past Morlaix's churches, wooden architecture, and views, along with all the sights listed here. The tourist office has a map of the circuit and theatrical tours of the *venelles* in summer.

The **viaduct,** 58m high and 285m long, is Morlaix's most visible sight. Though the airy walkway is now closed to the public, you can get a good view of steep, near-vertical Morlaix from its gates. **La Maison de la Duchesse Anne,** across pl. Allende on rue du Mur, commemorates the Queen's 1505 visit to the city. The house is a prime example of a Morlaisienne *maison à pondalez,* or lantern house. (☎ 02 98 88 23 26. Open July-Aug. daily 10am-6:30pm; Apr.-May Tu-Sa 10am-noon and 2-5:30pm; June and Sept. 10am-noon and 1-6pm. €1.60, ages 10-18 €0.80, under 10 free.) The collection at the **Musée des Jacobins,** in the 13th-century Jacobin church on pl. des Jacobins, mixes traditional Bretonalia like carved *lits-clos* (cabinet-like beds) with temporary art exhibits and a collection of paintings all themed around Brittany. The museum contains one of the few existing statues of Ankou, the Breton figure of death, who appears as a wooden skeleton lurking on the top floor, as well as two sarcophagi and a hodge-podge of Breton objects. (☎ 02 98 88 68 88. Open July-Aug. daily 10am-12:30pm and 2-6:30pm; Easter-June and Sept.-Oct. W-M 10am-noon and 2-6pm, Sa 2-6pm; Nov.-Easter W-M 10am-noon and 2-5pm, Su 2-6pm. €4, students €2, under 12 free. Families €6.10. Joint ticket with Maison €5.30, students €3.10.)

The **Ty Coz Pub,** 10 venelle au Beurre, overlooking the pl. Allende, looks straight out of an Arthurian legend; there's Breton music, Breton beer, and tables that are really thick cylindrical sections of trees. (☎ 02 98 88 07 65. Coreff beer €2. Open M-Sa 11am-

1am. Closed Th mornings.) The bar-*brasserie* **Café de L'Aurore**, 17 rue Traverse, on the other side of the square, attracts folks of all ages, who crowd the sidewalk until late at night. It also has an **Internet** kiosk with *télécarte* access. (☎02 98 88 03 05. €0.15 per min. Open M-Sa 7:30am-1am.)

NEAR MORLAIX

FORÈT D'HUELGOAT

Although **Argoat** (ar-gwah), the Old Breton term for inland Brittany, literally translates as "wooded country," centuries of clearing have made Brittany one of the least forested regions in France. Only a few scattered plots remain of the great oak and beech forest where menhir-carvers once lived. Brocéliande (see p. 223), Merlin's legendary stronghold, is one; Huelgoat (wel-gwaht), meaning "tall woods" in Breton, is another. The boulder-strewn, rugged forest enjoys significant governmental protection as part of the **Parc Régional d'Armorique,** which stretches 70 hectares eastward from the coast. On the eastern edge of a sparkling lake, the tiny **village** of the same name (pop. 1700) serves as a pit stop for hikers; the area is too hilly and rough for comfortable biking. The park service has excellent topographic maps (available at the tourist office for €1.50) that include hiking tours. There are scrupulously marked trails from one *gîte* to the next. (About €8 per night.)

The forest's marvels include the **Mare au Sangliers** (Pond of Boars), a tree-lined pool at the base of an intricate rock structure, and the **Roche Tremblante,** a 137-ton rock monster balanced precariously on the hillside. Guides (July-Aug. only) somehow set the entire thing a-trembling with a tap in just the right place. Most impressive is the **Grotte du Diable** (Devil's Grotto), a cave formed by building-sized boulders that hang over the raging Argent river into which you can climb down from the trail.

In town, you'll find the **tourist office** beside the **Moulin du Chaos,** a mill next to a tumble of boulders along the Argent river. From the bus stop, facing the 8 à Huit, turn right and walk out of the main square, follow the road to the left, and the office will be on your right just under the bridge. The office has a list of *chambres d'hôte* (€25-40) within 15km of town. They also have regional maps (€1.50, guides €3.85) and information on the grottoes. (☎02 98 99 72 32. Open July-Aug. M-Sa 10am-12:30pm and 2-5:30pm, some Su mornings; Sept.-June until 4pm.)

Huelgoat is best visited as a daytrip, but if you decide to stay, check out the in-town **Camping Municipal du Lac,** rue du Général de Gaulle. From the bus stop, facing the 8 à Huit supermarket, turn left and go to the end of the square. Take the first right onto rue du Docteur Jaco, then left onto rue du Général de Gaulle (the road closest to the lake); the campsite is past the lake on the right. (10min.) It has 75 orderly sites near the lake and a pool in summer. (☎02 98 99 78 80. Reception M-Sa 9am-11am and 4:15-7:30pm, Su 9-10:30am and 5:45-7:30pm, but you can get a spot at any hour. Open June 15-Sept. 15. €2.75 per person, children under 7 €1.70, €3.20 per tent. Showers €1.10. Electricity €1.85.) Huelgoat's **market** is on pl. A. Briand and along rue du Lac (open 1st and 3rd Th of the month, 8am-1pm); alternate Thursdays host a smaller version. Across from the bus stop on pl. A. Briand is a small **8 à Huit** supermarket. (Open M-Sa 8am-12:30pm and 2:30-7:15pm, Su 9am-noon.) Past the tourist office just outside of town is a larger **Intermarché.**

CAT buses (☎02 98 93 06 98) go to **Morlaix** (1hr.; M-Sa 2-3 per day, Su 1 per day, with no return; €1.50) and **Quimper** (70min., 3-5 per week, €6.80), stopping by the church on pl. A. Briand. The **post office** is on rue de Cieux. (☎02 98 99 73 90. Open M-F 9am-noon and 2-5pm, Sa 9am-noon.) **Postal code:** 29690.

ROSCOFF

Although the ferries streaming into Roscoff (pop. 3700) are its longtime livelihood, the town has for the most part evaded "harbor blight." The turreted houses of the port area and the attractive beaches on either side of the town are noteworthy, but Roscoff's prime location, amazing campsite, and famous thalassotherapy centers (spas with heated seawater) are its true prizes. Roscoff is also the prime embarkment point to the nearby gem Ile de Batz.

■■ ■ **ORIENTATION AND PRACTICAL INFORMATION.** Roscoff's port is the center of the action. Turn right after exiting the bus station and make an immediate right onto rue Ropartz (unmarked). Follow the scent of the sea and the signs to the *centre ville* (you'll be bearing left more than right). **Brittany Ferries** (☎ 02 98 29 28 00; www.brittany-ferries.fr) sends boats to **Plymouth, England** and west to **Cork, Ireland,** while **Irish Ferries** (☎ 02 98 61 17 17; fax 02 98 61 17 46; shamrock@wanadoo.fr) serves **Rosslare, Ireland** (see **Getting There,** p. 67, for details of service). Both offer Eurail discounts of up to 50%. **SNCF trains** and **buses** (☎ 02 98 69 70 20) go from the station to Morlaix (30-45min., 7-11 per day, €7) with connections to Brest and Paris, and the train station offers free long-term parking. **CAT buses** (☎ 02 98 90 68 40) go to Morlaix (30-45min.; M-Sa 3-4 per day, 1 on Su; €4.60) and Quimper (2hr., 2 per day, €15.25).

The **tourist office,** 46 rue Gambetta, set back slightly from the center of the port, has transportation schedules, walking tours, maps, info on *chambres d'hôte,* and a shiny visitor's guide. (☎ 02 98 61 12 13; fax 02 98 69 75 75. Open July-Aug. M-Sa 9am-12:30pm and 1:30-7pm, Su 10am-12:30pm; Sept.-June M-Sa 9am-noon and 2-6pm.) A **laundromat** is at 23 rue Jules Ferry. (Open daily 9am-8pm.) Though you shouldn't need a **bike** in Roscoff itself, you can rent one at **Cycles Desbordes,** 13 rue Brizeux. (☎ 02 98 69 72 44. Bikes €6.50-9.50 per day.) The **post office,** on 17 rue Gambetta, offers **currency exchange.** (☎ 02 98 69 71 28. Open July-Aug. M-F 9am-12:30pm and 1:30-5:30pm, Sa 9am-12:15pm; Sept.-June M-F 9am-noon and 2-5:30pm, Sa 9am-12:15pm.) **Postal code:** 29680.

■ ■ **ACCOMMODATIONS, CAMPING, AND FOOD.** Budget hotels are in short supply in Roscoff, so true backpackers might prefer the youth hostel on Ile de Batz (see below), which is only 15min. away by ferry. There are, however, two excellent options on the mainland. The **Hôtel d'Angleterre ❸,** 28 rue Albert de Mun, is in an old mansion that has retained its original Breton furniture and stained-glass windows in the restaurant downstairs. An adjacent sunroom looks onto the enormous, beautiful backyard garden. (☎ 02 98 69 70 42; fax 02 98 69 75 16. Breakfast €5.80. Singles and doubles €30, with toilet €37.20, with bath €47.70; 3- to 4-person rooms €39/€46/€56. Apr.-May and Sept.-Oct. prices €3-5 lower. Open Apr.-Oct. 15. AmEx/MC/V.) ■**Camping de Kérestat Peoc'h ❶,** rue de Pontigou, is on the estate of a 15th-century manor 25min. from town on foot. From the train station, turn left onto rue Brizeux, and head left when it ends on rue Albert de Mun and rue Laennec, which becomes rue du Pontigou. Continue down this road, straight through the car-ferry roundabout (bearing slightly right); the campsite is at the end of the first lane on the right. With a 19th-century mini-labyrinth, a tower built under Louis XIV, remnants of Gallo-Roman walls, and flower-tufted wilds stretching to the sea, this campground is almost reason enough to visit Roscoff. The estate and its tennis courts are open to campers. (☎/fax 02 98 69 71 92. Open June 28-Sept. 2. Reception 10am-noon and 5-8pm. €4 per person, €7 per tent, €2 per car, under 10 €2, caravans €15. Hot water included. Electricity €3.)

Restaurants serving seafood *menus* (€12.20-15.25) line the port, and there is a **market** every Wednesday morning on quai Auxerre and a Casino **supermarket,** between the town and Camping de Kérestat (see above) before the roundabout on the right-hand side. For fresh local catch, try **Le Surcouf ❸**, 14 rue Admiral Réveillère, which dishes up fishes from €12 (delectable pan-fried sole is €17), with a €21.50 *menu*. (☎02 98 69 71 89. Open Th-M. MC/V.)

◙ SIGHTS. This spa town was not made for the budget-conscious—sitting by the port is probably the cheapest activity around, but there are a few worthwhile free sights. The 16th-century **Eglise Notre-Dame de Kroaz-Batz,** which is reminiscent of an overgrown sand castle with its turreted spires, two-tiered belfry, and massive, golden Baroque choir, merits a look. (Open daily 9am-noon and 2-7pm.) On the far right of the port is the **Pointe St-Barbe,** a tall rock outcropping wrapped in spiraling stone steps and crowned with a white chapel, which provides a wonderful panoramic view of the coast, the port, and the Ile de Batz. To get a better sense of the environs of Roscoff, which are well worth the minimal effort involved in a visit, take one of the 1½-3hr., or 6-12km, walking tours explained in the free *Circuits Pedestre* brochure, available at the tourist office.

ILE DE BATZ

Just 15min. off the coast from Roscoff, this tiny, wind-battered island has an unmistakable appeal. Thanks to unusual meteorological phenomena, Batz experiences quite temperate weather. Even when clouds build over Roscoff, the skies over Batz stay deep blue and cloud-free. Expect to find serenity, rather than civilization, here, especially in the afternoon when the crowds are thin.

▣ ▨ ORIENTATION AND PRACTICAL INFORMATION. Ferry companies **Armein** (☎02 98 61 77 75) and **CFTM** (☎02 98 61 78 87) connect Roscoff and Batz in 10-15min. Boats leave from the port during high tide or from the long walkway extending into the harbor at low tide. (June 26-Sept. 10 every 30min.; Sept. 11-June 25 8-9 per day. Round-trip €6, ages 4-12 €3.50.) There are free trail maps at the **tourist office** on the island, which is in the town hall; turn left out of the port and follow the signs. (Open Sept.-June daily 9am-noon and 2-5pm. Annex at port open July-Aug. M-Sa 9am-1pm and 2-5pm.) There are a number of bike rental places in convenient locations, including **Vélos et Nature,** just left of the port, which also gives maps and guided tours. (☎02 98 61 75 75. Bikes €3 per hr., €6 per half-day, €10 per day.) The **laundromat** is in a private home 50m to the right of the 8 à Huit supermarket. (Open daily 8am-9pm.) The **post office** is up the hill in the center of town; look for the signs. (☎02 98 99 73 90. Open M-F 9:30am-noon and 1:30-4:30pm, Sa 9:30am-noon.) **Postal code:** 29253.

▛ ▗ ACCOMMODATIONS AND FOOD. To reach the **Auberge de Jeunesse Marine ❶** from the port, take the road that goes sharply uphill immediately to the left of the hotel. Signs clearly mark the path to the hostel, uphill and to the right. (5min.) Perched on a hill, the five-building hostel has amazing views of Roscoff and access to a private beach down the hill. In July and August, the hostel doubles as a sailing school—call ahead to enroll in a course. (☎02 98 61 77 69; fax 02 98 61 78 85. Breakfast €3.20. Dinner €3.50. Sheets €3.20. Reception hours vary, but there is usually someone around. Open Apr.-Oct. Beds €7.60, bunk cots in big tent €6, camping €5.15.)

The *chambres d'hôte* **Ti Va Zadou ❸,** which overlook the port, are more expensive but a good value. From the ferry, head left toward town. The stone house with light blue shutters is at the top of a hill, on the right fork just before the church. The four guest rooms are carefully color-coordinated and decorated with lovely old dark wood furniture. (☎02 98 61 76 91. Breakfast included. All rooms with bath. Open Mar.-Nov. 15. Reserve at least a month in advance July-Aug. Singles

€35; doubles €50; 2-room family suite €65-75.) The **Hôtel Roch Ar Mor ❸**, facing the port, lets ten spacious singles and doubles, some with magnificent views, as well as larger family rooms for up to six people. The dock-side location makes up for the scarcity of showers; there's exactly one. (☎ 02 98 61 78 28; fax 02 98 61 78 12. Breakfast €5.50. Reception 8am-8pm. Rooms €34.50. Extra bed €10.)

The grassy, wind-scoured **Terrain d'Hébergement de Plein Air ❶**, on the beach near the lighthouse, is the only legal campground on the island. Head toward the town center, keeping it to your right and the water to your left, then follow the signs to the campsite or to the *phare*, or lighthouse. (45min.) As there are no official sites, finding a spot is sort of a free-for-all, but there's plenty of room. There are three little beaches but only two toilets, two sinks, and one shower. (☎ 02 98 61 75 70. €1 per person, €0.50 per child; €1 per tent.)

At the highest point in town is an **8 à Huit** supermarket. (☎ 02 98 61 78 79. Open July-Aug. M-Sa 9am-1pm and 2:30-8pm, Su 9am-12:30pm; Sept.-June Tu-Sa 9am-12:30pm and 2:30-7:30pm, Su 10am-12:30pm.)

◖▮ ◪ **SIGHTS AND HIKES.** The best way to see the Ile de Batz is to take the *sentier côtier*, 14km of trails that follow the coastline. The tourist office has maps, but the trails are well-marked, and on an island this size, it's hard to get lost. The trails are technically private property, but that doesn't stop most from using them. They run past the *côte sauvage* on the west side of the island, along small white sandy beaches, over massive rocks, and beside inland lakes. The hike is easy and well worth the four hours it takes. You can find the trails from any point on the island by heading toward water or by following signs from the port.

West of the town center is a **lighthouse** with great views of the island, Roscoff, and the occasional Channel ferry. There are 190 steps to the top, where you'll likely have to brave a howling wind. (Open July-Sept. 15 daily 1-5:30pm; June and Sept. 16-30 Th-Tu 2-5pm. €1.50, over age 6 €1.) At the southeast tip of the island, a tranquil **botanical garden** is the brainchild of Georges Delaselle, a Parisian transplant who decided in 1897 that Batz needed a little exotic plant life. (☎ 02 98 61 75 65. Open July-Aug. daily 1-6pm; Apr.-June and Sept. W-M 2-6pm; Oct. Sa-Su 2-6pm. Guided visits Su at 3pm. €4, students and seniors €3.50, children €2.)

Slightly inland, to the west of the garden, stand the ruins of the 12th-century **Chapelle Ste-Anne,** first the site of a Viking structure in AD 878. During the **Fête de Ste-Anne,** on the last Saturday in July, everyone on the island comes out to light a massive bonfire on the dunes as part of the largest celebration of the year. The festivities are followed by a more solemn mass in the chapel the next morning, perhaps to atone for the previous night's festivities.

BREST

Brest was transformed into a somber wasteland in 1944 by Allied bombers driving out the occupying German flotilla. Now home to the French Atlantic Fleet, Brest (pop. 156,000) has slowly replaced its toppled historic buildings with concrete ones. But despite its reputation as one of the dreariest places in Brittany, the city is slowly being rejuvenated with an active downtown and a summer concert series. Brest now combines the pleasures of a major port and a university town, and boasts one of the largest aquariums around.

▮ **TRANSPORTATION**

Trains: pl. du 19ème Régiment d'Infanterie (☎ 02 98 31 51 72). Info open M-F 8:30am-7:30pm, Sa 8:30am-7pm, Su 9:30am-7pm. To: **Morlaix** (€8.30); **Nantes** (€33.30); **Paris** (€59.30); **Quimper** (30min., 5 per day, €12.80); **Rennes** (1½hr., 15 per day, €25.30).

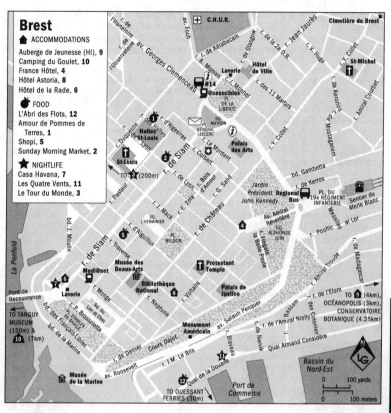

Brest

⌂ **ACCOMMODATIONS**
Auberge de Jeunesse (HI), **9**
Camping du Goulet, **10**
France Hôtel, **4**
Hôtel Astoria, **8**
Hôtel de la Rade, **6**

🍎 **FOOD**
L'Abri des Flots, **12**
Amour de Pommes de
Terres, **1**
Shopi, **5**
Sunday Morning Market, **2**

★ **NIGHTLIFE**
Casa Havana, **7**
Les Quatre Vents, **11**
Le Tour du Monde, **3**

BRITTANY

Buses: next to train station (☎02 98 44 46 73). Open July-Aug. M-F 7am-12:30pm and 1-7pm, Sa 7:15-11am and 1-6:30pm, Su 8:45-10:15am, 1-2pm, and 5:15-7:45pm; Sept.-June M-F 7am-12:30pm and 1-7pm, Sa 8am-1:15pm and 2:30-6:30pm, Su 6-7pm. To: **Crozon** and **Camaret** (1½hr.; M-Sa 2 per day, Su 1 per day; €9.30); **Quimper** (1¼hr.; 4 per day, 1 on Su; €12.80); **Roscoff** (30-45min., 7-11 per day, €8.50).

Ferries: For ferry lines serving Brest, see **Ile d'Ouessant** (p. 250).

Local Transportation: Bibus, 33 av. Georges Clemenceau (☎02 98 80 30 30). Service from about 6am-8pm followed by erratic service by a special letter-designated route until about 10pm, F-Sa until midnight. Buses run infrequently, particularly in the summer months, so plan ahead. Ask at the tourist office or the Bibus *"point d'accueil"* at the Hôtel de Ville (M-F 8:15am-12:15pm and 1:15-6:45pm, Sa 9am-noon and 1:30-6pm) for a bus map and a book-sized schedule. Buy tickets on the bus: €1, *carnet* of 10 €8, full-day €3, students for 1 week €8.

Taxis: Allô Taxis, 234 rue Jean Jaurès (☎02 98 42 11 11).

✚ 🛈 ORIENTATION AND PRACTICAL INFORMATION

To the right of the train station, av. Georges Clemenceau leads to the tourist office and the central **pl. de la Liberté,** the main terminal for the city's internal bus system. **Rue Jean Jaurès,** to the north of the *place,* is prime shopping territory, but exercise caution at night. **Rue de Siam,** to the south of the *place*, is the city's most vibrant street. Bookshops, clothing stores, markets, and bars spill out onto the thoroughfare overlooking the water. The city's only remaining **old quarter** is across the space-age Pont de Recouvrance (Bridge of Recovery) at the end of rue de Siam.

Tourist Office: 8 av. Georges Clemenceau, on pl. de la Liberté near the Hôtel de Ville (☎02 98 44 24 96; fax 02 98 44 53 73). Makes hotel and ferry reservations. Free map; info on food, sights, and tours; *Jeunes à Brest* for young people. Open July-Aug. M-Sa 9:30am-7pm, Su 2-4pm; Sept.-June M-Sa 10am-12:30pm and 2-6pm.

Laundromat: Point Blue, 7 rue de Siam. Open daily 8am-9:30pm. **Le Père Denis,** rue J. Monnet, at the top of pl. de la Liberté. Open daily 7am-8:30pm.

Police: 15 rue Colbert (☎02 98 43 77 77).

Hospital: av. Foch (☎02 98 22 33 33).

Youth Center: Bureau Information Jeunesse Brest, 4 rue Morvan, off pl. de la Liberté (☎02 98 43 01 08; bij@wanadoo.fr). Info on jobs and free **Internet.** Open M and F 1:30-6pm, Tu and Th 1:30-6pm and 8-10pm, W and Sa 9:30am-noon and 1:30-6pm.

Internet Access: @cces.cibles, 31 av. Clemenceau (☎02 98 46 76 10). Cyberdeath-seeking pre-pubescent males. €3 per hr. Open M-Sa 11am-1pm, Su 2-11pm. Also **Medi@net,** 31 rue Monge (☎02 98 46 48 79). €3 per hr. Open M-Sa noon-1am.

Post Office: rue de Siam (☎02 98 33 73 07), on pl. Général Leclerc. **Currency exchange.** Open M-F 8am-7pm, Sa 8am-noon. **Poste Restante:** 29279. **Postal code:** 29200.

ACCOMMODATIONS AND CAMPING

Brest is a haven for the budget traveler, with oodles of inexpensive hotels and an incredibly friendly hostel. Call two to three weeks ahead in July and August.

▨ **Auberge de Jeunesse (HI),** 5 rue de Kerbriant (☎02 98 41 90 41; fax 02 98 41 82 66), about 4km from the train station, near Océanopolis, next to the artificial beach in Le Moulin Blanc. Leave the train station, walk past the bus station, cross the street, and head left down the street to the bus stop. Take bus #7 to its terminus "Port de Plaisance" (M-Sa 6:45am-7:30pm, Su 2-5:45pm; €1). With your back to the bus stop, go left toward the beach, take an immediate left, and follow signs to the hostel; look for a sign in Breton reading *"ostaleri ar yaouankiz."* Looks like an IKEA ad set in the tropics. Rémy, the caretaker, can answer any and all questions. Ping-pong, foosball, and TV room. Kitchen. Breakfast included. Dinner €7.60. Reception M-F 7-9am and 5-8pm, Sa-Su 7-10am and 6-8pm. Lockout 10am-5pm. July-Aug. curfew midnight; Sept.-June 11pm; ask for a key if you'll be late. Beds €11.30. ❶

▨ **Hôtel Astoria,** 9 rue Traverse (☎02 98 80 19 10; fax 02 98 80 52 41; www.hotel-astoria-brest.com), off rue de Siam. From the station, walk straight ahead, cross av. Georges Clemenceau onto av. Amiral Réveillère, which bears slightly to the left at the first intersection onto rue Voltaire. Take your 4th right onto rue Traverse. The hotel will be on your right. (8min.) Central, quiet, and spotless. Modern, airy rooms (with TV) and helpful staff. Call ahead, especially July-Aug. Discounts on ferries and Océanopolis. Breakfast €5.50. Shower €4. Reception M-Sa 7am-11pm, Su 8am-noon and 6-11pm. Singles and doubles €23, with shower €38-43, with bath €44; triples €46. AmEx/MC/V. ❷

France Hôtel, 1 rue Amiral Réveillère (☎02 98 46 18 88; fax 02 98 44 44 33). Out of the train station, head straight ahead 1 block down rue Amiral Réveillère; the hotel will be down a block on the right. Courteous reception and plain, comfortable rooms (all with TV) that are larger than most. Large windows look onto Jardin Kennedy or quiet back area. Bar and restaurant downstairs. Breakfast €4.60. Singles with toilet €26.70, with toilet and shower €32, with toilet and bath €42; doubles €30.50/37.35/47.80; quads €62.50. MC/V. ❸

Hôtel de la Rade, 6 rue de Siam (☎ 02 98 44 47 76; fax 02 98 80 10 51). The hotel's giant windows open onto the lively bar and restaurant scene of the rue de Siam near the water and the château. 44 immaculate and identical, cheery rooms; quieter ones lie port-side. Breakfast buffet €5.35. All rooms have toilets and showers or baths. Singles €38.20; doubles €42.70; triples €47.30. MC/V. ❹

Camping du Goulet (☎ /fax 02 98 45 86 84), 7km from downtown in Ste-Anne du Portzic; take bus #14 (dir: Plouzané) to "Le Cosquer." (15min.) At night take bus B route "A" (dir: Plouzané). Follow signs 100m down the side road to this large, often crowded site. Clean facilities, manicured hedges, and hot showers. Laundry. Reception M-F 10am-noon and 2:30-7pm, Sa 9am-noon, longer hours July-Aug. €3.40 per person, children under 7 €2; €3.90 per tent; €1.20 per car. Electricity €1.70-2.50. ❶

🔲 FOOD

Markets are held every day in various locations; the traditional and organic market on rue du Moulin à Poudre is notable. (Open Tu 4-8pm and Sa mornings.) Every Sunday morning, the area around St-Louis is closed down for an enormous market that sells everything from *moules* to melons at decent prices. There is a slightly pricey **indoor market** at Les Halles St-Louis, a block from rue de Siam. (Open daily 7am-1pm and 4-7:30pm.) Bakeries, *pâtisseries*, and vegetable stores can be found on and around rue de Siam, as can a **Shopi supermarket.** (Open M-Sa 8am-8pm.) **Amour de Pommes de Terre ❷,** 23 rue des Halles, just behind the indoor market, is a spuds-only establishment: every main course is a potato, topped with tasty and inventive treats. (☎ 02 98 43 48 51. *Menus* €9.50-18. Open daily for lunch and dinner.) **L'Abri des Flots,** 8 quai de la Douane, at the Port de Commerce, will satisfy all with its jovial ambiance, huge portions, and relatively low prices. They serve *galettes* and crepes (€1.60-5.50) but are known for their seafood couscous. (☎ 02 98 44 07 31. Seafood meals priced €10-18. Open noon-2pm and 7pm-midnight.)

👁 🎵 SIGHTS AND ENTERTAINMENT

Brest's **château** was the only major building to survive the bombings of World War II. In over 1700 strife-laden years, through Roman, Breton, English, French, and German occupations, no attacker has ever taken the château by force; it now holds the distinction of being the world's oldest active military institution. You can only enter the château through the **Musée de la Marine,** which occupies most of the sprawling fortress. Its dungeons are multiple massive towers that are filled with exhibits ranging from early copper scuba gear to torpedoes to a display chronicling the invention of the comic book pirate. (☎ 02 98 22 12 39. Open Apr.-Sept. daily 10am-6:30pm; Oct.-Mar. W-M 10am-noon and 2-6pm. €4.60, students €3, ages 6-18 €2.30, under 6 free.) The rose-tinted **Monument Américain,** on rue de Denver, overlooks the Port du Commerce, a reminder of the Americans' landing in 1917. Locals joke that you need a passport to visit this American-built monument to the US, guarded by American officers on American-owned soil.

Océanopolis, port de Plaisance, welcomes you into its temperate pavilion, which emphasizes Brittany's marine life (much of it in tidal tanks) and the Iroise Sea (which surrounds the Ile d'Ouessant). There's a polar pavilion with a 3-D theater that opens onto the penguin playland, and a tropical pavilion, complete with coral reef. Océanopolis is huge and can have massive lines; don't expect to spend less than a day here. To get there, take bus #7 (dir: Port de Plaisance) from the Liberty terminal (every 30min. M-Sa until 7:30pm; €1) to "Océanopolis." (Aquarium ☎ 02 98 34 40 40; fax 02 98 34 40 69. Open Apr.-Aug. daily 9am-6pm; Sept.-Mar. Tu-Sa 10am-5pm, Su 10am-6pm. €13.50, ages 4-17 €10, under 4 free.) Five minutes away is the beautiful **Conservatoire Botanique de Brest** park, with a trail stretching lengthwise through 3km of exotic plantlife, bamboo groves, and trickling brooks that seem miles away from the city.

Nightlife centers around the Port de Commerce, the pont de Recouvrance end of rue de Siam, and the streets near pl. de la Liberté. You may want to avoid the neighborhoods on the other side of pl. de la Liberté after dark. The popular **Jeudis du Port** concerts dominate the Port with the sounds of Breton music, rock, and jazz on Thursdays. (Open July-Aug. 7:30pm-midnight.) Locals pack **Les Quatres Vents,** quai de la Douane, rocking the boat-bar from 10pm to 1am. (☎02 98 44 42 84. Open M-Sa 10am-1am, Su 2pm-1am.) The sea-themed **Le Tour du Monde,** port du Moulin Blanc, near the aquarium, is owned by a famous navigator and draws crowds with cheap beer, mussels, and port views. (☎02 98 41 93 65. Open daily 11am-1am.) The young, fresh crowd in **Casa Havana,** 2 rue de Siam, munches tapas and mingles amidst tropical plants and Latin music. (☎02 98 80 42 87. Cocktails €4; beer €2.50. Open daily noon-2:30pm and 7:30-11:30pm; bar open 10am-1am.)

ILE D'OUESSANT

As the westernmost point in France, windswept Ouessant (pop. 951; *Enez Eussa* in Breton) is an isolated haven for hikers and naturalists, an hour's boat ride from the nearest point of mainland Brittany. Ouessant's mysterious jagged rock formations rise up from rugged grounds covered in wildflowers and grazing sheep.

⬛ TRANSPORTATION. Two **ferry** companies offer service to Ouessant. Buy tickets at the port or at the Brest tourist office, and reserve in advance in summer. **Penn Ar Bed** sails year-round between Ouessant and Brest, via Le Conquet (2¼hr.) It also serves the islands of Molène and Sein. (☎02 98 80 80 80; www.penn-ar-bed.fr. 1-2 per day; July-Aug. 4-6 per day. Brest-Ouessant round-trip €29, students €25.45, children €17.40; Le Conquet-Ouessant €25, students €21.25, children €15. Reservations required.) **Finist'mer** runs "fast ferries" from Ouessant to Camaret (1hr.) and Ouessant to Le Conquet. (30min.) (☎02 98 89 16 61; www.finist-mer.fr. Camaret July-Aug. 9:30am; Apr.-June and Sept. 8:45am; return departure 5:30-6:15pm. Le Conquet July-Aug. 4-6 times per day; Apr.-June and Sept. 2-3 times per day. €24-28, students and over 60 €20-24, ages 4-16 €13.40-16.40.) To get to **Le Conquet,** take the **Cars de St-Mathieu bus** (☎02 98 89 12 02) from **Brest** (40min., €4.30), though it's difficult to coordinate the bus schedule with Finist'mer departures. Both ferry companies charge €6 one-way for bikes.

Boats dock at **Port du Stiff,** 3.5km from Lampaul, the main town on the Ile d'Ouessant. **Riou** (☎02 98 48 81 57) and **Jean Avril** buses (☎02 98 48 85 65) await the boats' arrival at the port and take you into town in a few air-conditioned minutes (both €2). On foot it's a 45min. stroll. Four companies **rent bikes** at the port and in Lampaul (€10 per day, €11 for a beach bike, €14 for a mountain bike; €7/8/10 per half day, €37/39/50 per week).

⬛⬛ ORIENTATION AND PRACTICAL INFORMATION. Lampaul's **tourist office,** near the church in the center of town, sells a pedestrian guide (€2.30) to the island with four routes that cover every inch of the coastline in 1½-3hr. hikes. The island's bike paths are marked on a separate map since cycling is forbidden on the foot paths. (☎02 98 48 85 83; fax 02 98 48 87 09; www.ot-ouessant.fr. Office open July-Aug. M-Sa 9:30am-6pm and Su 9:30am-12:30pm; Apr.-June and Sept. M-Sa 10am-noon and 2:30-6pm, Su 10am-noon; Oct.-Mar. M-Sa 10am-noon and 2:30-5pm.) **Police** only operate on the island in July and August (☎02 98 48 81 61). The **post office** (☎02 98 48 81 77) is to the left of the church and 30m downhill. (Open June 15-Sept. 15 M-F 9:15am-12:30pm and 2-5:15pm, Sa 9-12:15am; Sept. 16-June 14 M-F 9:30am-noon and 2-5pm, Sa 9am-noon.) **Postal code:** 29242.

■■ ACCOMMODATIONS AND FOOD. It's a good idea to make hotel reservations in advance, as tourism is slowly but incessantly encroaching on the island. The cheerful and spotless ⬛**Auberge de Jeunesse d'Ouessant ❶** is just a five-minute walk from the tourist office and the center of Lampaul. Take the stairs to the right of the SPAR supermarket across from the church and turn right onto the first road the stairs bring you to (not at the top of the stairs); then turn right at the crossroads. The hostel is on your right, across from a garage. 48 beds in sunny, clean 2- to 6-person rooms, a communal kitchen, and a dining area with views of the water. (☎02 98 48 84 53 or 06 81 23 72 95; fax 02 98 48 87 42. Breakfast included. Sheets €3.52. Dorms €13, students and under 25 €11.28. *Demi-pension* (dinner included) for €22.42/€20, full *pension* (all meals included) for €32/€28.81.) **Roc'h Ar Mor ❹** is a lovely hotel with spacious blue and yellow bedrooms and bathrooms, in a prime seaside location just beyond the center of Lampaul, with an appealing seafood restaurant downstairs. Room prices vary depending on view; all have bath, shower, toilet, telephone, and TV. (☎02 98 48 80 19; fax 02 98 48 87 51; http://perso.wanadoo.fr/rocharmor. Breakfast €7.60, €5.80 for children. Singles and doubles €48-75; triples €58-70; quads €70; discounts Oct.-Dec. Extra bed €8. Handicapped accessible. MC/V.) **Le Fromveur ❸** has simpler rooms with plain pastel decor in the dead center of Lampaul, over a popular restaurant that serves up local catches and has *menus* €11-26. (☎02 98 48 81 30. Breakfast €4.50. Singles €26, with TV, toilet, and shower €38. MC/V.) **The Centre d'Etude du Milieu Ouessantin ❶,** an environmental studies and ornithological center, doubles as a hostel. From Lampaul's tourist office, bear right onto the road just past the supermarket and follow the signs for the Musée des Phares. Continue on the same road to the center, which is at Keridreux on the left, the last major building before you reach the lighthouse. (30min.) The beds and facilities aren't as spiffy as those at the Auberge, but it's just down the road from the lighthouse and the spectacular coast. In July and August, you can also reserve a spot on one of their nature hikes by calling ahead. (☎02 98 48 82 65; fax 02 98 48 87 39. Reception M-F 8:30am-noon and 1:30-5:30pm. Sheets €3.50. Reserve early, especially for July. 4- to 5-person dorms €11, students €9, under 15 €8.50. Price €0.50 lower for 2nd-6th nights.) **Camping Municipal ❶,** 2km from the port on the main road, is on the left about 300m before the church in Lampaul. (☎02 98 48 84 65. Laundry €2.30. Showers €1.60. Reception July-Aug. 7am-10pm; call ahead in the off-season. Open Apr.-Sept. €2.60 per person, under 7 €1.25; €2.60 per tent, bed in communal tent €3.10.)

A **SPAR supermarket** is next door to the tourist office (open M-Sa 8:30am-7:30pm, Su 9:30am-12:30pm), and an **8 à Huit supermarket** lies just downhill (open Tu 8:30am-12:30pm, W-Sa 8:30am-7:30pm, Su 9:30am-12:30pm); together they have the island's only cash machines. There is also a small market, **Le Marché des Iles,** 50m from the campground. (☎02 98 48 88 08. Open M-Sa 8:30am-7:30pm and Su 8:30am-12:30pm.) For food more filling than a picnic lunch, head to **Ty Korn ❸** (☎02 98 48 87 33) in Lampaul. They offer a variety of marine delights, with *menus* at €16 and €24; for a challenge, set yourself to the sumptuous €70 feast (order 24 hr. ahead).

◪ SIGHTS. Walking Ouessant will allow you to appreciate the rugged simplicity of its landscape, but the island's well-paved roads, which are almost devoid of cars, are ideal for biking. Some bike trails exist, but for safety reasons, it is strictly forbidden to bike along the coast. A good hiking companion is the complete and accurate tourist booklet of coastline paths (€2.30), which contains details of all of the ruins and rocks along each route, although a free basic map is also available. If you only have time to choose one path, take the 14km northwest trail to the **Pointe de Pern,** whose breathtaking rock formations rising from the ocean are the westernmost point in Europe.

The northwest path takes you past Ouessant's two museums, which, unlike the coast, are easily accessible by bike. The **Musée des Phares et Balises,** in du Créac'h, once Europe's most powerful lighthouse, is devoted to the history of lighthouses and maritime signaling. The exhibit includes two short films on lighthouses in Brittany and their caretakers (in French), and displays dozens of intricate lights that have now been retired from use. (☎02 98 48 80 70. Open May-Sept. daily 10:30am-6:30pm; Oct.-Mar. Tu-Su 2-4pm; Apr. Tu-Su 2-6:30pm. €3.85, ages 8-14 €2.30, under 8 free. Joint ticket with Ecomusée €6, ages 8-14 €3.85.) The **Ecomusée and Maison du Niou,** 1km northwest of Lampaul, has a display of traditional local women's clothing and a replica of a traditional *ouessantine* home. (☎02 98 48 86 37. Hours same as Musée des Phares. €3.05, children 8-14 €1.85.)

QUIMPER

Quimper (kem-PAIR, pop. 63,000), ancient capital of the Cornouaille kingdom, is reminiscent of Paris, with its central waterway lined by stately homes and its theater and cathedral occupying opposite banks of the river Odet. However, Quimper (or "Kemper" in Breton) is also among the most aggressively Breton cities in the region. Many street signs appear in both languages, most masses are conducted in Breton, and one high school even teaches exclusively in the old tongue. Breton *faïencerie* (stoneware) is hand-painted in Quimper just as it was 300 years ago, and each year between the third and fourth Sundays of July, the city celebrates its links to tradition in the *Festival de Cornouaille.*

☞ TRANSPORTATION

Trains: av. de la Gare (☎08 36 35 35 35). Info open M-Sa 8:15am-7pm. To: **Auray** (1hr., €14.40); **Brest** (1½hr., 4 per day, €12.80); **Nantes** (2¾hr., 4 per day, €25.90); **Paris** Montparnasse (4¾hr., 8 TGVs per day, €59.70); **Rennes** (2¼hr.; 10 per day, 4 TGV; €26.90); **Vannes** (€16.10).

Buses: next to the train station (☎02 98 90 88 89). To: **Brest** (1¼hr.; M-Sa 4 per day, 2 on Su; €12.80); **Pointe du Raz** (1½hr., 2-4 per day, €7.65); **Pont-Aven** (1¼hr.; M-Sa 3 per day, 2 on Su; €5.80); **Roscoff** (2hr., July-Aug. 1 per day, €22.)

Local Transportation: QUB (Quartabus), 2 quai Odet (☎02 98 95 26 27). **Buses** run 6am-7:30pm. Tickets €0.95; day pass €2.90; *carnet* of 6 €5.18; *carnet* of 10 €7.93. Bus #1 serves the hostel and campground. The office has schedules and a map of the bus lines. Open M-F 8am-12:15pm and 1:30-6:30pm, Sa 9am-noon and 2-6pm.

Taxis: ☎02 98 90 21 21. In front of the station.

Car Rental: Hertz (☎02 98 53 12 34, reservations 08 03 86 18 61), across the street from the train station. Open M-F 8am-noon and 2-7pm, Sa 8am-noon and 2-6pm.

Bike Rental: MBK s.a. Lennez, 13 rue Aristide Briand (☎02 98 90 14 81), off av. de la Gare. Bikes €7.65 per half-day, €12.20 per day. Passport or check deposit. Open Tu-Sa 9am-noon and 2-6:30pm. **Torch'VTT,** 58 rue de la Providence (☎02 98 53 84 41), has bikes. €14 per day. €450 deposit. Open Tu-Sa 9:30am-12:30pm and 2:30-7pm.

■✦❷ ORIENTATION AND PRACTICAL INFORMATION

Quimper is in the heart of the Cornouaille region; rich farmland separates it from the sea and port towns about 20km. to its south and west. The center of town is to the west of the train station, which is on the edge of town; from the train station, go right onto av. de la Gare and follow the river Odet, keeping the river and its

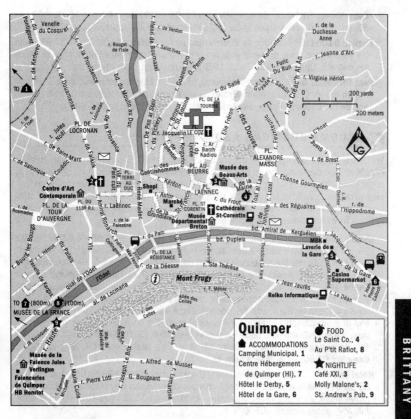

Quimper

ACCOMMODATIONS
Camping Municipal, **1**
Centre Hébergement
de Quimper (HI), **7**
Hôtel le Derby, **5**
Hôtel de la Gare, **6**

FOOD
Le Saint Co., **4**
Au P'tit Rafiot, **8**

NIGHTLIFE
Café XXI, **3**
Molly Malone's, **2**
St. Andrew's Pub, **9**

numerous footbridges to your right. It will become bd. Dupleix and lead to pl. de la Résistance. The tourist office will be on your left, the *vieille ville* across the river to your right. (10min.)

Tourist Office: 7 rue de la Déesse (☎02 98 53 04 05; fax 02 98 53 31 33; www.bretagne-4villes.com), off pl. de la Résistance. Free, detailed map. **Tours** of city in English (1½hr.; July-Aug. 1 per week; call to reserve). Office open July-Aug. M-Sa 9am-7pm, Su 10am-12:45pm and 3-5:45pm; Apr.-June and Sept. 9am-12:30pm and 1:30-6:30pm; Oct.-Mar. 9am-12:30pm and 1:30-6pm.

Laundromats: Point Laverie, 47 rue de Pont l'Abbé, about 5min. from the hostel. Open daily 8am-10pm. **Laverie de la Gare,** 2 av. de la Gare. Open daily 8am-8pm.

Police: 1 rue de Pont l'Abbé (☎02 98 55 09 24).

Hospital: Centre Hospitalier Laënnec, 14 bis av. Yves-Thépot (☎02 98 52 60 60).

Youth Center: Bureau Information Jeunesse, pl. Louis Armand, next to the train station. Open M and F 1:30-5:30pm, Tu-Th 10am-noon and 1:30-5:30pm, Sa 10am-4pm.

Internet Access: Reiko Informatique, 1 bis rue Jean Jaurès (☎02 98 90 71 82), at the top of rue Aristide Briand, is close to the station. €3.80 per hr., billed by the minute. Open M-Sa 9am-noon and 2-7pm. So is **CyberCopy,** 3 bd. A. de Kerguelen (☎02 98 64 33 99). €2.30 per 15min., €3.05 per 30min., €4.50 per hr. Open M-Sa 9am-7pm.

CyberVideo, 51 bd. A. de Kerguelen (☎02 98 95 31 56). €2 per 15min., €3 per 30min., €4.50 per hr. Open M-Sa 10:30am-noon and 2-8:30pm, F-Sa until 9pm.

English bookstore: Librairie de Mousterlin, 19 rue de Frout (☎02 98 64 37 94), with the yellow shop front, stocks a wide range of mainly fiction paperbacks, most of which are only €5. Open June-Aug. Tu-Su 10:30am-7pm, Sept.-May 11am-7pm.

Post Office: 37 bd. A. de Kerguelen (☎02 98 64 28 28). **Currency exchange.** Open M-F 8am-6:30pm, Sa 8am-noon. **Branches** on chemin des Justices, 2min. from hostel, and on rue Châpeau Rouge. **Poste Restante:** 29109. **Postal code:** 29000.

⌐ ACCOMMODATIONS AND CAMPING

While the hostel and campsite are far away from the city center, several affordable hotels are located near the train station. Travelers should be particularly careful at night (and even on smaller streets during the day); Quimper is a big city with big-city problems. Ask at the tourist office about private homes offering bed and breakfast (doubles around €23). In July and August, it's a good idea to make reservations in writing as early as possible.

Centre Hébergement de Quimper (HI), 6 av. des Oiseaux (☎02 98 64 97 97; fax 02 98 55 38 37). Take bus #1 from pl. de la Résistance (dir: Kermoysan) to "Chaptal" (last bus 7:30pm). The hostel will be 50m up the street on your left. On foot, cross the river from pl. de la Résistance and go left on quai de l'Odet. Turn right onto rue de pont l'Abbé and continue past 2 major intersections until the large roundabout; continue straight for 50m, and the hostel will be on your left. Dormitory-style rooms hold bunks for 8-14. Clean facilities, with TV, foosball, and a communal kitchen. The hostel is at the end of a questionable street on the edge of town; the building is secure from the outside, but individual rooms don't have locks. Breakfast €3.20. Sleepsack €2.70, sheets €3. Reception 8-11am and 5-9pm; call if arriving later. Bunks €8; singles €9.80. **Camping €4.80. HI members only. ❶**

Hôtel Le Derby, 13 av. de la Gare, facing the train station (☎02 98 52 06 91; fax 02 98 53 39 04). These rooms over a bright bar are cheerful and very tastefully decorated, if rather small; all with shower and toilet. Breakfast €5.35. Singles €25; doubles €35; July-Aug. prices increase €3. ❷

Hôtel de la Gare, 17 av de la Gare, facing the train station (☎02 98 90 00 81; fax 02 98 53 21 81). Modern, freshly redone rooms are set back from the noise and the traffic of the street and face an inner courtyard/parking lot. Nearly all rooms have bath, TV, and kitchenette. Breakfast €5. Singles €31; doubles €49; triples €54. MC/V. ❸

Camping Municipal, av. des Oiseaux (☎/fax 02 98 55 61 09), next to the hostel. A forested area with plenty of shady trees, if not quite removed from all the reminders of city life. Reception M 1-7pm; Tu, Th, Sa 8-11am and 3-8pm; W and Su 9am-noon; F 9-11am and 3-8pm. €2.90 per person, children under 7 €1.50; €1.10 per car; €0.65 per tent. Electricity €2.55. ❶

⌐ FOOD

The lively **covered market (Les Halles),** off rue Kéréon on rue St-François, always has shops open to provide good bargains on produce, seafood, meats, and cheeses (as well as fabulous crepes), but the earlier you get there the better. (Open M-Sa 7am-8pm, Su 9am-1pm.) An **open market** is held twice a week. (W in Les Halles, Sa outside Les Halles and in pl. des Ursulines. Both open June-Aug. 9am-6pm; Sept.-May 9am-1pm.) A **Casino supermarket** is on av. de la Gare. (Open M-Sa 8:30am-7:30pm, Su 9:30am-1pm and 5-7:30pm.) There is a **Shopi** downstairs at 20 rue Astor.

(Open M-Sa 8:30am-7:30pm, Su 9:30am-12:30pm.) On a quiet street just around the corner from the cathedral, the classy, modern bistro **Le Saint Co. ❸**, 20 rue Frout, offers a tasteful (and tasty) variety of steak *plats*, as well as creative and filling salads and mussels. (☎02 98 95 11 47. Steak €12-14; salads €3-7; mussels €7-8. *Menu* €16-20. Open July-Aug. daily 11:30am-midnight; Sept.-June noon-2pm and 7:30pm-midnight. MC/V.) For your pick of the aquarium, head a little farther afield to **Au P'tit Raflot ❹**, 7 rue de Pont-l'Abbé, which serves enormous helpings of such marina favorites as *bouillabaisse* and *cassoulet marin* for €19.40. (☎02 98 53 77 27. Open M and Sa 7:30-10pm, Tu-F noon-1:30pm and 7:30-10pm.)

🔆 🎵 SIGHTS AND ENTERTAINMENT

The unmistakable, magnificent dual spires of the **Cathédrale St-Corentin,** built between the 13th and 15th centuries, mark the entrance to the old quarter from quai St-Corentin. Quimper's patron is one of dozens of Breton saints not officially recognized by the Church. (Open M-Sa 8:30am-noon and 1:30-6:30pm, Su 8:30am-noon, except during mass, and 2-6:30pm.) **Mont Frugy,** next to the tourist office, offers an amazing view of the cathedral spires and some relief from the bustle of the city center. It's an easy hike, with numerous wooded walking trails.

The ▧**Musée Départemental Breton,** 1 rue du Roi Gradlon, through the cathedral garden, cleverly presents local history, archaeology, and ethnography exhibits. Highlights include an elaborate display of traditional Breton clothing and innovative temporary exhibitions. (☎02 98 95 21 60. Open June-Sept. daily 9am-6pm; Oct.-May Tu-Sa 9am-noon and 2-5pm, Su 2-5pm. €3.80, students €2.50, under 11 and on Su free. July-Aug. tours in French, at least 1 per day; call for details and reservations; €1.50.) The **Musée des Beaux-Arts,** 40 pl. St-Corentin, holds a collection of large-scale interpretations of Breton folktales and the joys and trials of everyday life. A fascinating exhibit about the poet and artist Max Jacob, a Quimper native killed in the Holocaust, contains portraits by several of his friends, including Picasso. (☎02 98 95 45 20. Open July-Aug. daily 10am-7pm; Sept.-June W-M 10am-noon and 2-6pm. Tours daily July-Aug.; call for info. €3.85, ages 18-26 and over 60 €2.30, under 18 free.) The **Musée de la Faïence,** 14 rue J-B Bousquet, has a surprisingly beautiful permanent exhibit on Quimper's characteristic earthenware, as well as temporary exhibits. (☎02 98 90 12 72. Open Apr.-Oct. 27 M-Sa 10am-6pm.) For a more hands-on experience, head to **Faïenceries de Quimper H. B. Henriot,** rue Haute. Henriot's studio allows visitors to tour the facilities and watch potters at work. (☎02 98 90 09 36. Open M-F 9-11:15am and 1:30-4:45pm; June closed F. Tours every 15-30min. Call in advance for English tours. €4, 18-25 €3.20, children 7-17 €2.30, under 7 free.)

The 21st century meets the 11th in glittering **Café XXI,** 38 pl. St-Corentin, across from the cathedral and next to the Musée des Beaux Arts. This popular daytime people-watching venue doubles as a glam nightspot, serving its "XXI" specialty (white rum, curaçao, and fresh citrus juice; €3.20) to its sophisticated clientele. (☎02 98 95 92 34. Open daily 8:30am-11pm.) Or try the spectacular ▧**Molly Malone's,** pl St-Mathieu, on rue Falkirk. The magnificent decoration of this pub makes approaching the bar feel like walking past a street of traditional cottages, down to the details of battered wood and illumined windows. (☎02 98 53 40 42. Guinness €3, pint €5.20. Open daily 11am-1am. MC/V.) **St. Andrew's Pub,** 11 pl. Styvel, is just across the river from rue de Pont l'Abbé. A breezy terrace next to the Odet is the perfect setting for a relaxed drink served by the pub's friendly managers. (☎02 98 53 34 49. Drinks €2-3. Open daily 11am-1am.)

Those who miss the *Festival de Cornouaille* can still catch Breton cultural celebrations. Every Thursday from late June to early September, the cathedral gardens, next to the Odet, fill with **Breton dancers** in costume, accompanied by lively

A BAD TIME TO BE AN ERMINE The black-and-white Breton flag bears a striking resemblance to the Stars and Stripes, which it long predates. Where the American flag has stars, the Breton flag has a mysterious figure: a trio of small diamonds at the top and an elongated one at bottom. These represent a caped ermine, symbol of the king of Brittany. Legend tells that the first king came across an ermine while hunting and, taken by its beauty, pursued it to the edge of a bog. There the unfortunate animal turned around and declared that it would rather die than soil its coat. Struck by the animal's gallantry—though not struck enough to save its life—the king insisted on placing its hide before him at every meal.

biniou (bagpipes) and *bombarde* (similar to an oboe) players (9pm, €3.05). Quimper holds its **Semaines Musicales** during the first three weeks in August. Orchestras and choirs perform nightly in the Théâtre Municipal and cathedral, and during the last half of August, brass bands fill the streets for the **Festival Extérieurs Cuivres;** call the tourist office for more information.

NEAR QUIMPER

PONT-AVEN

Between Quimper and Quimperlé lies Pont-Aven (pop. 3000), a jewel immortalized on countless canvases, its air of the surreal unspoiled even by the tourists who descend upon the town in search of inspiration. The first to paint the town was Paul Gauguin (1848-1903), who, fed up with mainstream Impressionism, came here in 1886. Inspired by Gauguin, the Pont-Aven School, comprising 20 artists, developed into a movement emphasizing pure color, absence of perspective, and simplified figures. The town now claims some of the finest art galleries and museums in France, along with acres of woodland that inspired their contents.

The tourist office provides maps detailing a number of short hikes in the surroundings, many of them passing through places where these artists congregated. In the town center, you can follow the **Promenade Xavier Graal,** a series of bridges hovering over the swift river Aven on their way to the **Chaos de Pont-Aven,** a set of flat rocks around which the river swirls. A path through the tranquil **Bois d'Amour** (Lover's Wood) meanders along the Aven beneath the rich, dappled load of gnarled old trunks. The most enticing part of the walk in the woods is closest to town and runs next to the river. If you choose to do the entire circuit (about 40min.), you may want to start from the Chapelle de Trémalo, since it's all downhill from there! Above the woods, amidst thriving farmland, is the **Chapelle de Trémalo.** This simple 16th-century church has ancient granite walls and a wooden barrel-vaulted ceiling edged with lively, cherubic faces and one irreverent rear end. The chapel also houses the 17th-century wooden painted crucifix that inspired Gauguin's "Yellow Christ." The **Musée de L'Ecole de Pont-Aven,** pl. de l'Hôtel de Ville, up the street to the left when facing the tourist office, showcases the works of Gauguin, Serusier, and many of the school's other artists. Those familiar with the northwestern tip of Brittany may experience a pleasant sense of *déjà vu*—canvases depicting the cliffs of Ile d'Ouessant and other regional attractions are prominently displayed on the museum's walls. (☎02 98 06 14 43. Open July-Aug. daily 10am-7pm; Apr.-Oct. 10am-12:30pm and 2-6:30pm; Feb.-Dec. 10am-12:30pm and 2-6pm. €4, off-season €3, students and ages 13-20 €2.30, under 12 free.) The year 2003 marks the centenary of Gaugin's death; in commemoration, the museum is presenting a special temporary exhibit, "Gaugin and the Pont-Aven School," with five Gaugins and 40 other works. (June 28-Sept. 29, 2003.)

Pont-Aven's few hotels cater to the same crowd that comes to town for the express purpose of leaving with less money and more paintings than they started with. So you might do best to make Pont-Aven a daytrip from Quimper or Concarneau. If you're willing to splurge a little to stay in a restored farm house, Mme. Larour's ⊠gîte d'étape ❹, rue Kermentec, past the pedestrian trail on the road to Tremalo, a mere 600m walk from the town or the chapel, is the perfect place. Surrounded by enough flowers to inspire any artist, the *gîte* has a kitchen, common areas, and large, exquisitely furnished, sky-lit bedrooms. (☎ 02 98 06 07 60. Breakfast included. Doubles €41. Children €12.) The tourist office may also be able to help you find less expensive *chambres d'hôte* (€25-31), depending on the season. If Pont-Aven's exhibitions on Gaugin heighten your taste for exotic climes, sate your hunger at **Restaurant Tahiti ❷**, 21 rue de la Belle Angele, route de Bannalec. The cook, a Tahitian native, offers Pacific specialties (around €9) amidst tropical decor. (☎ 02 98 06 15 93. Open Tu-Su for lunch and dinner.)

Pont-Aven is connected by **Transports Caoudal buses** (☎ 02 98 56 96 72) to **Quimper** (1¼hr.; 3 per day; €5.80, €9 round-trip) and nearby towns. The **tourist office,** pl. de l'Hôtel de Ville, is a block from the bus stop on pl. Gauguin. Turn away from the river and walk toward the square and the museum beyond; the office is on the right side of the street. The staff sells a walking-tour guide (€0.30) and organizes **tours**, in French, of the town and museum (town €4, museum €5, both €6). The office can also provide information on the "Fleurs d'ajonc" **folk festival** on the first Sunday of August. (☎ 02 98 06 04 70; fax 02 98 06 17 25. Tours June-Sept. 11am and 4:30pm. Call to inquire about tours in English. Open July-Aug. M-Sa 9:30am-7:30pm, Su 10am-1pm and 3-6:30pm; Apr.-June and Sept. M-Sa 9:30am-12:30pm and 2-7pm, Su 10am-1pm; Oct.-Mar. M-Sa 10am-12:30pm and 2-6pm.)

QUIBERON

Connected to the mainland by just a narrow strip of land, this peninsula is almost overwhelmed in summer with tourists who come to sun themselves on the smooth stretch of the Grande Plage on the southern tip, or to surf, kayak, and sail on the smaller, but spectacular, beaches on the eastern side of the peninsula. Stunning Belle-Ile is only a 45min. ferry ride away, but the countryside of Quiberon (pop. 4500) offers many opportunities for excursions. Save time for a hike or bike ride along the peninsula's wave-battered, seaward-facing coast, the Côte Sauvage.

▣❼ TRANSPORTATION AND PRACTICAL INFORMATION. Most of the year, the train to Quiberon stops at Auray (☎ 02 97 24 44 50). A special train connects Auray and Quiberon (1 hr., July-Aug. 6-12 per day, €2.50). Trains run through Auray on their way to Brest, Paris, and Quimper (call ☎ 08 36 35 35 35 for schedules). **TIM buses** (☎ 02 97 47 29 64) run from Auray (1hr., M-Sa 7-9 per day, €6), Carnac (30min., M-Sa 7-9 per day, €3.35), and Vannes (2hr., M-Sa 7-9 per day, €8). **Quiberon Voyages,** 21 pl. Hoche (☎ 02 97 50 15 30), runs trips all over the province, including an afternoon excursion to **Carnac** and **Vannes** (€20) and a full-day trip to **Concarneau, Pont-Aven,** and **Quimper** (€34). **SMN,** in Port Maria, serves **Belle-Ile** from the **gare maritime,** quai de Houat. (☎ 08 20 05 60 00, for foreigners 02 97 35 02 00; fax 02 97 31 56 81. 5-13 per day; round-trip €20.60-22.80, under 25 €12.55-13.85, seniors €14-15.40. Bikes €10.50, cars €84.40-197.50.) Cruise the beachfront or explore the Côte Sauvage on **bikes,** tandems, or scooters from **Cyclomar,** 47 pl. Hoche (☎ 02 97 50 26 00), which also has an **annex** at the train station. (Bikes €7.35 per half-day, €10 per day, €44 per week. Scooter €24.40 per half-day, €35.85 per day plus insurance. Moped €14.35 per half-day, €22.90 per day. 10% off with *Let's Go* guide, ISIC card, or note from the youth hostel. Credit card, personal ID, or passport deposit. Open July-Sept. daily 7:30am-11pm; Oct.-June 8:30am-12:30pm and 1:30-7:30pm. Annex open July-Aug. daily 8:30am-8pm.)

IN RECENT NEWS

CAFÉ CULTURE—AN ENDANGERED SPECIES?

Searching for a restaurant but faced by a string of take-out joints? It's no surprise. The reason is not a question of cuisine but of accounting. France has had to change its tax codes in several ways to align with the practices of the European Union. While most of these boring bureaucratic changes will hardly affect travelers, some alterations have serious effects on restaurant business and culture. Under the new rules, owners of sit-down restaurants pay significantly higher taxes than their take-out counterparts. Consequently, many less expensive restaurants are going under or changing their wares.

The results are the most obvious in summer havens like Quiberon: the small *brasseries* that pepper the beachside boardwalks are being replaced by kebab stands. Those that remain are altering the way that they conduct business. The encroachment of fast food is more than just the spread of outside influence; it's also the result of hard business practices.

Restauranteurs are steeling themselves for the toll that taxes can take on their businesses. With the tough choice of raising prices or cutting profits, it is becoming more difficult to run the small sidewalk cafés for which France is famous.

On your journey through France, you won't starve or be forced to subsist on take-out. However, when you stumble across that perfect gem of a *brasserie*, enjoy it with the knowledge that it's an increasingly rare find.

To find the **tourist office,** 14 rue de Verdun, turn left from the train station and walk down rue de la Gare. When you see the church ahead on your left, bear right down rue de Verdun. (5min.) The staff distributes a detailed guide to six pedestrian tours of the peninsula. (☎ 02 97 50 07 84; fax 02 97 30 58 22; www.quiberon.com. Open July-Sept. M-Sa 9am-1pm and 2-7pm, Su 10am-1pm and 3-7pm, Aug. 1-15 M-Sa until 8pm; Nov. and Feb.-June M-Sa 9am-12:30pm and 2-6pm; Dec.-Jan. M-Sa 9am-12:30pm and 2-5pm.) The **Centre Hospitalier du Pratel** (☎ 02 97 29 20 20) in Auray is the nearest hospital, but has 24hr. service only during July and August. (Sept.-June open until 8pm.) The **Centre Hospitalier Bretagne Atlantique** in Vannes (bd. Maurice Guillaudot, ☎ 02 97 01 41 41) has year-round emergency service. The **post office,** pl. de la Duchesse Anne, has **currency exchange.** (☎ 02 97 50 11 92. Open July-Aug. M-F 9am-12:30pm and 2-5:30pm, Sa 9am-noon; Sept.-June M-F 9am-noon and 2-5pm, Sa 9am-noon.) **Postal code:** 56170.

⌐ ACCOMMODATIONS AND CAMPING. Quiberon is generally expensive, but the small, comfy, personal **Auberge de Jeunesse (HI) ❶,** 45 rte. du Roch-Priol, will silence any complaints. From the station turn left and take rue de la Gare toward the beach and the church. Turn left onto rue de Port-Haliguen, then right onto bd. Anatole France, and left on rte. du Roch-Priol. The hostel will be on your left. (12min.) Guillaume, the manager, lets eight-person rooms with a woodsy feel that'll take you back to summer camp. With the outdoor eating area, communal kitchen, and tents in the garden, you'll be making friends in no time. (☎ 02 97 50 15 54. Breakfast €2.90. Sheets €0.45. Reception 8:30-10am and 6-8:30pm. Open May-Sept. Bunks €8. Camping €5 per person, tents €1.) The central **Hôtel de l'Océan ❸,** 7 quai de l'Océan, offers bright, florally decorated rooms, some facing the harbor. An enormous sunny salon with views of the quai makes for a lovely place to people-watch. (☎ 02 97 50 07 58; fax 02 97 50 27 81. Breakfast €5.50. Singles and doubles €28-36, with shower €39-43, with bath €44-52. Extra bed €12.20. MC/V.)

The campsite closest to the city is **Camping Municipal du Goviro ❶.** Windswept and consequently a little dusty, it nonetheless provides the best access to the quiet, intimate beach across the street. Make reservations, as it's almost always full in high season. (☎ 02 97 50 13 54. Reception July-Aug. M-Sa 8:30am-7:30pm, Su 9am-7pm; June and Sept.-Oct. 5 M-Sa 9am-12:30pm and 2-6pm, Su 9am-noon. Reservation deposit €34.15-35. Open Mar. 16-Oct. 14. €2.40 per tent; €1.60 per car; €3.95 per person, children under 10 €0.95. Electricity €3. 10% price reduction with *Carte Jeune*.) Just a bit farther from the beach, behind Goviro, is the slick and spacious and well-landscaped **Camping Bois d'Amour ❶**. (☎02 97 50 13 52 or 04 42 20 47 25. Reception July-Aug. 8:30am-8pm; Apr.-May and Sept. 9:30am-12:30pm and 2-6:30pm. €4-7.50 per person, children under 10 €3-5; tent or caravan with car €7-14. Electricity €4. Prices vary based on time of year.)

❏ FOOD. Quiberon's many port-side eateries are prime territory for two particular gastronomic delights: as many kinds of seafood and shellfish as you can fit on your plate and the lollipop-topped, caramel-like *niniche* candy. For a little taste of the sea, try **La Criée ❸**, 11 quai de l'Océan. The fish are displayed on ice as you walk through the door. The *plateau gargantua*, an awesome array of oysters, crab, and other ocean-dwellers (€46), is perfect for a large group. Otherwise, try the €14 three-course *menu*. (☎02 97 30 53 09. Open July-Aug. daily noon-2pm and 7-10:30pm; Sept.-Dec. and Feb.-June Tu-Sa noon-2pm and 7-9:30pm, Su noon-2pm. MC/V.) Down the quai toward the Grande Plage is **L'Elfenn ❸**, 1 rue de Kervozes, a slightly less expensive alternative with great views of the port. (☎02 97 30 40 43. *Menus* €12.50-15.25; fish €7-12; mussels €6-8. MC/V.)

For groceries, try **Marché Plus**, on rue de Verdun (open M-Sa 7-9pm, Su 9am-noon), or the **Casino supermarket**, close to the hostel on rue de Port Haliguen (open M-F 9am-8pm, Sa 9am-noon). There are produce **markets** in pl. du Varquez (Sa mornings) and at Port Haliguen (June 15 to September 15 W morning).

◪ BEACHES. The craggy Côte Sauvage is aptly named; this "savage" coastline stretches a wild and windy 10km along the western edge of the Quiberon peninsula. Though it seems as if the amazing views from the easy road cannot be surpassed, you must drop your car and take to the foot paths to fully enjoy these boulder-strewn beaches and eroded bedrock archways. But heed the signs marked *Baignades Interdites* (Swimming Forbidden); many have drowned in these tempting but treacherous waters. The flag system is as follows: green means safe supervised bathing; orange means dangerous but supervised bathing; red means bathing prohibited. There are SOS posts dotting the coastline with flotation devices attached. The weather here can be as brutal and fleeting as the crashing waves; storms assault the coast and then retreat just as quickly.

Grande Plage is the most popular beach, while the small, rocky **plage du Goviro** appeals to those who prefer solitude. To reach it from the port, follow bd. Chanard east along the water as it becomes bd. de la Mer and then bd. du Goviro. The east side of the peninsula is dotted with sandy beaches, perfect for sunbathing after a quick dip in the cool waters.

⧉ ENTERTAINMENT AND FESTIVALS. The beaches don't empty until it's too dark to see the volleyball. At 11:30pm, the still energized crowd heads to the **Hacienda Café**, 4 rue du Phare, off pl. Hoche. It's packed with young teenage *Quiberonnais*, who drink flaming cocktails and dance until 3am. Brush that sand off carefully—black lights illuminate fluorescent murals that cover every surface, including the bar. (☎02 97 30 51 76. *Rhum vanille* or beer €2.50. Open July-Aug. daily 6pm-3am; Oct.-Apr. F-Su only 10pm-3am.) To escape the teenybopper crowd, try the nightclub **Le Surtoit**, 29 rue Port Maria, where the music and the clientele are both older but present in smaller quantities. Watch out at the bar—vodka is €8. (Open daily 10pm-4am, Sa until 5am.) **Le Nelson,** pl. Hoche, the local *rhumerie* (rum joint), may have walls covered with naval paraphernalia, but the boisterous crowd is more surfer than sailor, inundated with giddy teenage girls rather than hardened fishermens' wives. (☎02 97 50 31 37. A zillion types of rum €4.50-8; fabulous punch €4. Open daily 4pm-3am; Oct.-Easter closed Su.) During the second week in August, the **festival** "La Flibuste" takes the town by storm with dance, music, plays, and even pirates.

BELLE-ILE

The coast of Belle-Ile (pop. 4800), just 45min. away from Quiberon, is even more breathtaking than that of its neighboring *presqu'île*. At least five boats depart daily from Quiberon's Port-Maria for Belle-Ile, an island also known as "Le Bien-Nommé" (The Well-named). Throughout French history, Belle-Ile's high cliffs, crashing seas, and heathered fields have attracted residents of all sorts, from menhir-carvers to monks, from pirates to German POWs. At 20km in length, Belle-Ile is large enough to make bike rental or a few shuttle rides necessary; consider spending the night if you want to explore the island to your satisfaction.

□ TRANSPORTATION. Boats dock on the northern coast at **Le Palais**, the island's largest town. The ferry ride takes 45min., and you can take your bike along (round-trip €21; see **Quiberon: Transportation,** p. 252). The other main towns—**Bangor, Locmaria,** and **Sauzon**—lie in the center, on the east coast, and on the northwest tip respectively. A shuttle system linking the four ports makes travel between them much easier, though there are fewer routes and buses in June and September than July and August. **Buses** run from Le Palais to: Bangor (33min., 7 per day); Locmaria (30min., 5 per day); Sauzon (15-25min., 10 per day). Tickets are available on the bus or at **Point Taoi Mor,** quai Bonelle in Le Palais. (☎ 02 97 31 32 32. Single ticket €2.50, 2-day pass €10; children 4-12 years old €1.60.) **Cars Verts,** Gare Maritime at Quiberon, runs one-day bus tours of the island, beginning in Le Palais and exploring all major towns and coastal hot spots before returning to Le Palais in the evening. (☎ 02 97 50 11 60. €10.70, children 4-12 years €6; does not include ferry to the island.) There is a clearly marked, well-kept trail running along much of the coast. Alternate bike routes are well-marked on smaller, more scenic, and occasionally unpaved roads. The most spectacular area, the island's own Côte Sauvage, is also accessible by boat (see **Quiberon Beaches,** p. 259, for safety info).

▨ PRACTICAL INFORMATION: LE PALAIS. The **tourist office** is on the left end of the dock. The energetic staff distributes a thorough guide to the island (€1), a comprehensive French brochure with hiking and biking plans, and a map (€7) essential for exploring the island on foot or bike. They also have info on sailing, sea kayaking, and numerous other island activities. (☎ 02 97 31 81 93; fax 02 97 31 56 17; www.belle-ile.com. Open July-Aug. M-Sa 9am-7:30pm, Su 10am-12:30pm; Apr.-June and Sept.-Nov. M-Sa 9am-1pm and 2-6pm, Su 10am-12:30pm.) Rent **bikes** and mountain bikes at **Cyclotour,** quai de Bonnelle, near the tourist office. (☎ 02 97 31 80 68. Bikes €8 per half-day, €10 per day. Passport deposit. Open July-Aug. daily 8:30am-7pm; Sept.-June M-Sa 9am-12:30pm and 2-7pm.) Those 14 and over can rent **motorscooters** at **Au Bonheur des Dames,** quai Jacques Le Blanc. (☎ 02 97 31 80 52. €25-35 per half-day, €35-45 per day. Open daily 9am-7pm.) The **police** are at Les Glacis (☎ 02 97 31 80 22); the **hospital** (☎ 02 97 31 48 48) is in Le Palais. There is a **pharmacy** on rue de l'Eglise. (☎ 02 97 31 81 30; fax 02 97 31 49 06.) The **post office,** on quai Nicolas Foucquet across from quai Gambetta, has **currency exchange.** (☎ 02 97 31 80 40. Open M-F 9am-12:30pm and 2-5pm, Sa 9am-noon.) **Postal code:** 56360.

◪ ACCOMMODATIONS AND CAMPING. The tourist office in Le Palais can help you find cheap rooms and has info about the island's *chambres d'hôte,* rudimentary *gîtes d'étape,* and numerous campsites. Both the Palais campground and the hostel are near the citadel, a 10min. hike, partly uphill, from Le Palais' port. Upon disembarking from the ferry, look for rue J. Simon (directly in front of you, perpendicular to the quai) and walk about a block to pl. de la République, where you'll see quai J. Le Blanc and the water ahead to your right. Follow quai Le Blanc to the first footbridge (it leads to the citadel). Cross the bridge, go up the steep hill directly ahead, and follow the road as it turns to the left. Keep going through the parking lot and take a right at the end; **Camping Les Glacis ❶** will be on your right. You can also take the shuttle bus (€1) from the port to the "Les Glacis" stop, which is not on the schedule. Perched on a hillside, the campground offers several sites with beautiful views of the port and the citadel. (☎02 97 31 41 76; fax 02 97 31 57 16. Reception July-Aug. 8am-8pm; Apr.-June and Sept. 9am-noon and 5:30-7pm. Reservation required July-Aug., recommended at all times. Open Apr.-Sept. €3 per person, children under 10 €2; €3-4 per tent; €2 per car; €1 per bike. Electricity €2.50.) The large **HI hostel ❶** is another 7min. walk up the same road on the right, just past the *gendarmerie* and down the driveway to the right—follow the signs. The shuttle system also has an "Auberge de Jeunesse" stop. Suited to large groups, this hostel has fantastic facilities. The manager leads week-long hiking tours of the island that involve day hikes that return to the hostel in the evening. To camp on the lawn, you must rent a tent. **HI members only.** (☎02 97 31 81 33; fax 02 97 31 58 38; belle-ile@fuaj.org. Breakfast €3.20. Dinner €8. Unlocked luggage storage. Sheets €2.70. Reception 8:30am-noon and 6-8pm; July-Aug. 6-10pm. Open Mar.-Sept. and Nov.-Dec. Doubles €8.50 per person. Camping €6.70 per person.) **La Frégate ❷**, quai de l'Acadie, in front of the dock, has small, cheap, and sunny, if somewhat musty, rooms, each individually named and decorated. Downstairs, a bright sitting room has fabulous views of the port. (☎02 97 31 54 16. Breakfast €6. Reception Apr.-Nov. 15 8am until just after the last boat from Quiberon. Singles and doubles €22-29, doubles with bath €39; triples with bath €45. MC/V.)

⬛ FOOD. A small **market** is held every morning in Le Palais at pl. de la République; on Tuesday and Friday it takes over the *place*. (Open 8am-1pm.) There is a **Super U supermarket** on rue de l'Eglise. (Open Sept.-June M-Sa 8am-12:30pm and 3:30-7pm, Su 8am-noon; July-Aug. M-Sa 8am-1pm and 3-8pm, Su 8am-12:30pm.)

⬛⬛ SIGHTS AND FESTIVALS. The massive **Citadelle Vauban,** built in 1549 by Henri II to protect monks from pirates, grew to an impressive network of snaking passageways between 30ft. walls. Today, they protect a grass-roofed museum with displays on famous visitors such as Sarah Bernhardt, Monet, and 400 German POWs housed here during WWI. (☎02 97 31 84 17. Open July-Aug. daily 9am-7pm; Apr.-June and Sept.-Oct. 9:30am-6pm; Jan. 11-Mar. 9:30am-noon and 2-5pm. €6.10, ages 7-16 €3.05, under 7 free.)

Belle-Ile's natural treasures lie scattered along the coastline. The **plage de Donnant**, on the western coast, with its expansive dunes and mysterious stone facade, is the widest and most popular beach. Equally gorgeous are the pristine **plage Port-Maria,** on the eastern shore, and the powder-white **plage Grands Sables,** southeast of Le Palais. To see the more rugged side of the island's coastline, head 6km northwest from Le Palais to postcard-like **Sauzon.** The narrow port fills with sailboats rocking gently on the turquoise water. Gentle breezes (the remnants of gusts of wind softened by the nearby hills) bring salt-tinged air into the crisp white houses with multicolored shutters that line the port and face the mossy rock cliffs on the other side. Massive rock formations rise over the thunderous **Grotte de l'Apothicairerie,** southwest of **Pointe des Poulains** on the northern tip of the island, and at the **Aiguilles de Port Coton,** where needle-like rock formations shoot up through electric-green water. From late July to mid-August, the **Festival Lyrique** brings Mozart concerts and several operas to the island. (☎06 16 34 25 06; www.belle-ile.net.)

CARNAC

I would express the irrefutable, indisputable, irresistible...Here is my opinion: the stones of Carnac are big stones.
—Gustave Flaubert

Carnac (pop. 4500) is home to one of the world's most impressive series of ancient megalithic monuments, collectively the oldest prehistoric site in Europe. Carnac's rock formations come in various shapes and sizes. Many still go by their ancient Breton names. Here's a little glossary to get you started: **menhir:** from the ancient Celtic, a large upright stone (men = stone, hir = long); **dolmen:** a table-like structure which served as a funeral chamber; **dolmen corridors:** allowed the living to visit with the dead; **cairn** or **tumulus:** a pile of stones on top of one or many dolmens. If miles of monster rocks aren't your thing, try small granular ones—the smooth stretch of beach is a great place to frolic and unwind.

▣⬚ TRANSPORTATION AND PRACTICAL INFORMATION. To get to Carnac, take the **TIM bus** (☎02 97 21 28 29 in Vannes) from Auray (30min., 9 per day, €3.60); Quiberon (30min., 7 per day, €3.40); Vannes (1¼hr., 9 per day, €6.10). Or take the **train** to Plouharnel (July-Aug. only; July 1-5 6 per day, July 6-Sept. 1 12 per day; €2.50) and then catch a local bus (5min.; M-Sa 9 per day; €1). There are two **bus stops** corresponding to Carnac's two tourist offices: "Carnac-Ville" is close to the town center and its sights; "Carnac-Plage," in front of the main tourist office, is close to the beach. Carnac runs **Tatoovu**, a local shuttle, from major sites to Carnac-Ville and Carnac-Plage. (Buses run June-Sept. daily 9:15am-1pm and M-Sa 2:30-8pm. Tickets €1, *carnet* of 11 €10.50. Buy tickets on bus. Tourist has schedules.) The main **tourist office** is at 74 av. des Druides. (☎02 97 52 13 52; fax 02 97 52 86 10. Open July-Aug. M-Sa 9am-7pm, Su 3-7pm; June M-Sa 9am-12:30pm and 2-6:30 pm; May 9am-noon and 2-6pm.) To walk back to the town center, leave the tourist office and turn left onto av. des Druides. It will curve to your right and become av. de la Poste, which will lead to the tourist office **annex** at pl. de l'Eglise, just behind the church. (Open Apr.-Sept.) **Bikes** are useful in this area; go to **Cycles Lorcy**, 6 rue de Courdiec. (☎02 97 52 09 73. €4.50-5.50 per half-day, €5.50-€9.25 per day, €28-37 per week. Deposit €120 or passport. Open July-Aug. Tu-Sa 8:30am-noon and 2-7pm, Su 8:30am-12:15pm; Sept.-June Tu-Sa only.) The **police station** is at 40 rue St-Cornély. (☎02 97 52 06 24.) The **post office**, av. de la Poste, just outside the town center, has **currency exchange.** (☎02 97 52 03 90. Open July-Aug. M-F 9am-6pm, Sa 9am-noon; Sept.-June M-F 9am-noon and 2-5pm, Sa 9am-noon.) **Postal code:** 56430.

▣⬚ ACCOMMODATIONS AND FOOD. Carnac is best as a daytrip, since hotel prices rise in summer. B&Bs and *chambres d'hôte* are the cheapest housing options—doubles run €16-24; the tourist office has a list. The most reasonably-priced, coziest place is ▣**Hôtel Chez Nous ❸**, 5 pl. de la Chapelle. From the Carnac town center bus stop, facing the road, turn left and head down rue St-Cornély toward pl. de l'Eglise. A block before the church turn left onto rue de Courdiec, then right onto rue Kervarail. The hotel will be on your left, though you may have to cross the street to the right to find the exceptionally friendly owner. The bedrooms are beautifully decorated and perfectly clean; wood furniture and floral motifs complement the bower downstairs. (☎02 97 52 07 28; fax 02 97 52 74 28. Breakfast €5.75. Singles and doubles with shower €33-38; doubles with bath €43; triples €50-53. July-Aug prices rise about €3. MC/V.) **Camping Kerabus ❶**, allée des Alouettes, off rte. d'Auray, is 10min. from the Alignements de Kermario. Hedges separate each campsite, and paths lead to the menhirs. (☎/fax 02 97 52 24 90.

Bring toilet paper. July-Aug. reserve well in advance Open Apr.-Sept. 15. Gates close 10:30pm. Sept.-June €8.25 per person; July-Aug. €9.75. Car €2.60/2.75 extra per person, children under 7 €1.40/1.60, car and tent €5.30/5.80 extra per person. Electricity €2/2.15.)

There's a **Marché U supermarket**, 68 av. des Druides, next to the beach and tourist office, and a **Casino** on av. des Salines, close to the city. (Both open M-Sa 8:30am-8pm, Su 8:30am-noon.) There's also a **Proxi** on rue St-Cornély, between the church and the Carnac *centre ville* bus stop. (Open Tu-Sa 8am-1pm and 3-7:30pm, Su 8:30am-1pm.) At the **market** behind the church at pl. du Marché vendors sell clothing in addition to meat, fish, fruits, and veggies. (Open W and Su 8am-1pm.)

🔲 **SIGHTS.** The stone alignments at Carnac are the most prominent example of the neolithic monuments scattered throughout the area. Built from 4500 to 2500 BC, Carnac's 3000 menhirs stretch along the horizon for 4km, steadily increasing in height as they extend westward. Their origin is explained in a Celtic myth in which St. Cornély allegedly turned a Roman legion to stone as he fled religious persecution, but recent scholarship suggests they served as archeo-astronomic indicators of important sunrises and sunsets. The closest menhirs to town are the **Alignements du Ménec,** the largest of its kind in the world. More than 1000 menhirs, some over 3m tall, stretch more than 2km in a line along the horizon. The **Alignement de Kermario** stands adjacent to the **Géant du Manio** (a big rock) and the **Quadrilatère** (rocks in a square). Due to concerns that receding vegetation and erosion could destabilize their foundations, these menhirs have been fenced in. Sheep still roam unfazed among the wonders, but tourists must keep to the observation boardwalk and surrounding hills. Call the **Centre d'Accueil** to reserve a spot on one of the guided tours. (☎02 97 52 29 81 or 02 97 52 89 99; www.culture.gouv.fr/culture/arcnat/megalithes. Open July-Aug. daily 9am-10pm; Mar.-June and Sept.-Oct. daily 9am-6pm; Nov.-Feb. daily 10am-5:30pm. Hours likely to change; call in advance. Tours in French, occasionally English. €4, under 25 €3, under 12 free.)

In the center of town, behind the church, is the **Musée de Préhistoire,** 10 pl. de la Chapelle. The museum's interesting but sterile exhibits of tools, burial chamber contents, jewelry, and artifacts ranging from 450,000 BC to the early Middle Ages are a good prelude to the actual megaliths. (☎02 97 52 22 04. Open June-Sept. M-F 10am-6:30pm, Sa-Su 10am-noon and 2-6pm; Oct.-May W-M 10am-noon and 2-5pm. €4.65; Oct.-Mar. €3.80; students €2.30; children under 12 free. Combined admission with tour of alignments or Table des Marchands in Locmariaquer available.)

The **Archéoscope,** just across the street from the Alignements du Ménec, provides a flashy, dramatic introduction to the region's dozens of megalithic sites through the use of lasers, films, and life-sized moving menhirs. From the museum, go back toward the church, take a right on rue St-Cornély, and then a right onto rue de Courdiec. Walk directly up the street (about 1km), then turn left onto route des Alignements and the Archéoscope will be ahead on your left. (☎02 97 52 07 49. Open July-Aug. daily 9am-6pm; mid-Feb. to mid-Nov. 10am-noon and 1:30-5pm. Showings in French every 30min.; July-Aug. in English 10:30am, 2:30, 6pm; also twice daily in German. Call for off-season showings. €7, students and ages 13-18 €5, ages 6-12 €4, under 6 free.)

If you take the train to Plouharnel and have a few spare minutes, check out the **Dolmen de Rondossec,** a cairn with 3 graves, dating from 4000 BC, accessible to visitors. Walk from the train station towards Plouharnel and take the first right onto rue Hoche. What looks like a pile of stones as you approach is actually the roof of the cairn, which you can explore from the tiny path to the left.

BRITTANY

NANTES

The gory history of Nantes (pop. 550,000) would liven any dull textbook reading. It was here in 1440 that the infamous pirate Bluebeard (the Maréchal de Retz) was brought to trial for grisly murders and burned at the stake. Between the 16th and 18th centuries, Nantes established itself as a nexus of the slave trade, a brutal business that made it France's largest port. Putting the efficiency of the guillotine to shame, bloodthirsty and impatient *Nantois* revolutionaries resorted to mass drownings in the Loire. Modern Nantes pays very little heed to its gruesome past; instead, it successfully blends high-tech industry with its lively pedestrian districts. Just down the street from the modern, gargantuan train station and towering buildings, cafés and 15th- and 16th-century wood-paneled houses line winding cobblestone streets. Locals gather for the street musicians who perform on summer nights in the central squares.

▐ TRANSPORTATION

Flights: The airport is 10km south of Nantes (☎02 40 84 80 00). **Air Inter** (☎02 51 88 31 08) flies daily to **Lyon, Marseille, Nice,** and **Paris. Air France** (info ☎02 40 47 12 33; reservations ☎08 02 80 28 02) sends at least 6 flights per week to **London.** A **Tan Air shuttle** (☎02 40 29 39 39) runs to the airport from pl. du Commerce and the station (25min., M-F 13 shuttles per day, Sa 8 per day, Su 3 per day). Tickets €5.80, *carnet* of 4 €15.25.

Trains: There are two entrances to the train station: North, at 27 bd. de Stalingrad and South, across the tracks on rue de Loumel. Info and tickets at northern entrance. To: **Angers** (40min., about 20 per day 5am-11pm, €13.10); **Bordeaux** (4hr., 6-8 per day, €34.60); **La Rochelle** (2hr., 8-11 per day, €17.20); **Paris** (2-4hr., 20 per day, €46.30); **Rennes** (2hr., 10 per day Su 10am and 9pm only, €17.20); and **Saumur** (70min., 7 per day, €15.70).

Buses: Cariane Atlantique sends buses to **Rennes** (2hr.; Sept.-June only 2 per day; €14.95) and **Vannes** (1½hr., 1 per day, €18.15). Info office is at 5 allée Duquesne. (Open M-F 9:15am-noon and 2:15-6:15pm.) Buses leave from the train station's south entrance and from the parking lot on allée Baco.

Public Transportation: TAN, 3 allée Brancas, opposite pl. du Commerce (☎08 01 44 44 44). Runs buses and two tram lines until 8pm. Ticket €1.20, day pass €3.30. Open M-F 7:15am-7pm.

Taxis: Allô Radio-Taxis Nantes Atlantique at the train station (☎02 40 69 22 22). 24hr. €7.60-12.20 to the hostel in Beaulieu.

Car Rental: Europcar is conveniently located in the parking garage, to the left of the north exit from the train station (☎02 40 29 05 10). Open M-F 7:45am-10:15pm. **Budget** is on the right of the south exit from the train station (☎02 40 35 75 75). Open M-F 7:30am-10pm, Sa 8am-12:30pm and 2:30-6pm.

Bike Rental: The tourist office rents bikes (☎02 51 84 94 51) with pick-up locations in several parking garages. €1.50 per hr., €7.50 per day. Open daily 9am-7pm.

Canoe Rental: Contre Courant, on the Ile de Versailles (☎02 40 14 31 24). Take Tram line #2 (dir: Orvault Grand Val) to "St. Mihiel." Cross the bridge to the island. €5 per hr., €15 per day. Open M-F 10am-12:30pm and 2-7pm, Sa-Su 10am-8pm.

▐ ✦ ORIENTATION AND PRACTICAL INFORMATION

Nantes' tangle of neighborhoods, hills, and pedestrian streets spreads along the north bank of the Loire. Shadowed by a modest skyscraper, the Tour Bretagne, the

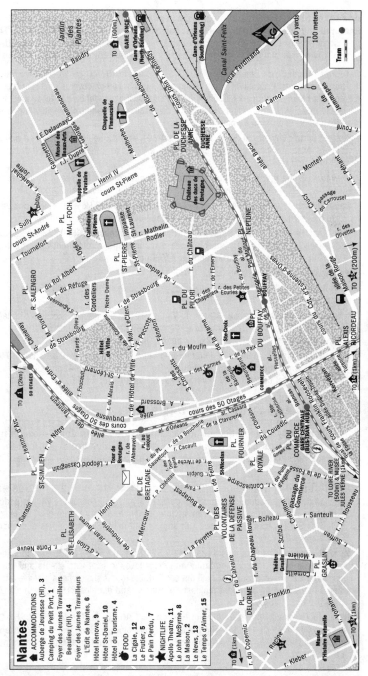

Nantes

▲ ACCOMMODATIONS
Auberge de Jeunesse (HI), **3**
Camping du Petit Port, **1**
Foyer des Jeunes Travailleurs
Beaulieu (HI), **14**
Foyer des Jeunes Travailleurs
L'Edit de Nantes, **6**
Hôtel Renova, **9**
Hôtel St-Daniel, **10**
Hôtel du Tourisme, **4**

● FOOD
La Cigale, **12**
Le Frutier, **5**
Le Pain Perdu, **7**

★ NIGHTLIFE
Apollo Theatre, **11**
Le John McByrne, **8**
La Maison, **2**
Le News, **13**
Le Temps d'Aimer, **15**

Tram

110 yards
100 meters

BRITTANY

city's axes run east-west along **cours John Kennedy,** which becomes **cours Franklin D. Roosevelt** and later quai de la Fosse, and north-south along **cours des 50 Otages.** The pedestrian district between the château and the place du Commerce is the liveliest part of town, and place du Commerce serves as the hub for local transportation.

Tourist Office: pl. du Commerce (☎02 40 20 60 00; fax 02 40 89 11 99; www.reception.com/Nantes). Excellent maps. Tours of the city in French cover a variety of topics, from its history to its parks. Tours €6 for adults, €3 for students; call for a schedule. Office open M-Sa 10am-7pm. **Branch** at the château entrance. Open July-Aug. daily 10am-6pm; Sept.-June Su only 10am-6pm.

Budget travel: Voyage au Fil (☎02 51 72 94 60), at CRIJ (see below). Ground and air tickets. Matches travelers with drivers. Same hours as CRIJ except closed 12:30-1:30pm. AmEx/MC/V.

Currency Exchange: Good rates at **Change Graslin,** on rue Rousseau in pl. Graslin (☎02 40 69 24 64), right next to *La Cigale.* Open M-F 9am-noon and 2-5:15pm.

Laundromat: 3 rue de Bouffay. Open M-Sa 9am-7pm. Also at 7 Hôtel de Ville (open daily 7am-8:30pm), and 11 rue Chaussée de la Madeleine (open M-Sa 10am-8pm).

Youth Information: Centre Régional d'Information Jeunesse (CRIJ), 28 rue du Calvaire (☎02 51 72 94 50). Info on youth discounts and employment opportunities. Open Tu, W, F 10am-6:30pm; Th and Sa 2-6:30pm.

Police: pl. Waldeck-Rousseau (☎02 40 37 21 21).

Hospital: Centre Hospitalier Régional, pl. Alexis Ricordeau (☎02 40 08 33 33). Emergency for women: ☎02 40 73 57 32.

Internet Access: Cyberkebab, 30 rue de Verdun, serves up Internet access with falafel and kebabs. €3 per hr., discounts for students. Open daily 9am-2am. **Cybercity,** 14 rue de Strasbourg (☎02 40 89 57 92). €3 per hr. Open daily 11am-midnight.

Post Office: 4 rue du Président Edouard Herriot, at pl. de Bretagne (☎02 40 12 62 74), near Tour Bretagne. **Currency exchange.** Open M-F 8:30am-6:45pm, Sa 8:30am-12:30pm. **Postal code:** 44000. **Poste restante:** Nantes RP, 44000.

┏ ACCOMMODATIONS AND CAMPING

Nantes has plenty of good budget hotels and lots of student dorm space in the summer. Avoid the hotels across from the station, which are overpriced for a seedy neighborhood. Most budget places are within a 10min. walk or bus ride of pl. du Commerce.

Hôtel St-Daniel, 4 rue du Bouffay (☎02 40 47 41 25; fax 02 51 72 03 99; hotel.st.daniel@wanadoo.fr), just off pl. du Bouffay, in the heart of the vibrant pedestrian district. A great value, with small clean rooms and cozy comforters. Breakfast included. Singles €24.40; doubles with shower and toilet €27.45; triples and quads €36. AmEx/MC/V. ❷

Hôtel Renova, 11 rue Beauregard (☎02 41 4 57 03; fax 02 51 82 06 39), off cours des 50 Otages. Amiable, accommodating proprietor loves to chat with clients and make stays as pleasant as possible. Small but comfortable rooms should be in a house rather than a hotel. Central location. Breakfast €3. Singles and doubles €19-21, with shower €25-34. AmEx/MC/V. ❷

Hôtel du Tourisme, 5 allée Duquesne (☎02 40 47 90 26; fax 02 40 35 57 25). 20 clean, bright rooms, all with TV and phone. Free bike storage. Breakfast €4.50. Reserve ahead. Singles and doubles with shower €26, with shower and toilet €30-35; extra bed €8. MC/V. ❷

Auberge de Jeunesse (HI). 2, place de la Manu (☎02 40 29 29 20; fax 02 51 12 48 42). From the north exit of the train station, turn right and walk down Boulevard de Stalingrad; the hostel is on the left side of the road. (5 min.) This hostel is located in a former factory. 83 beds in bare, 2- to 5- bed rooms. €14.55 the 1st night, €11.55 afterwards. Lockout 11am-3pm, 11am-5pm on the weekends. No curfew. ❶

Foyer des Jeunes Travailleurs L'Edit de Nantes, 1 rue du Gigant (☎02 40 73 41 46; fax 02 40 69 11 55). From the north exit of the train station, take tram line 1 (dir: François Mitterand) to the pl. du Commerce, where you can catch bus #24 (dir: Bellevue) or #56 (dir: Hermeland) to "Edit de Nantes," across the street from the hostel. 60 beds in unspectacular double rooms with shower and toilet; lively *foyer* with friendly residents and pleasant cafeteria. Lunch or dinner €6.85. Reception M-F 9am-9pm. Min. 2-night stay. Call ahead. Beds €9.15. ❶

Foyer des Jeunes Travailleurs Beaulieu (HI), 9 bd. Vincent Gâche (☎40 12 24 00; fax 02 51 82 00 05). From the north exit of the train station, take tram line 1 (dir: François Mitterand) to the pl. du Commerce, and switch to line 2 (dir: Trocadie) to "Vincent Gâche". Bd. Vincent Gâche is ahead on the left. By foot, exit via *accès nord* and turn left onto cours John F. Kennedy. Turn left onto av. Carnot and continue straight for about 10-15min. until you cross the river. Vincent Gâche will be one block up on the left, past the Holiday Inn. (20min.) 200 beds in 1- to 4-person rooms with baths. Modern set-up makes up for industrial neighborhood. Breakfast €2.20. Meals €6.10. Sheets €3. Reception 8am-9pm. Beds €9.50, non-members €20. ❶

Camping du Petit Port, 21 bd. du Petit Port (☎02 40 74 47 94; fax 02 40 74 23 06; camping-petit-port@nge-nantes.fr). From the pl. du Commerce, take tram line 2 (dir: Orvault Grand Val) to "Petit Port Facultés." (10 min.) Superb 4-star site with activities to keep children busy. Laundry and pool access. Reception 9am-9pm. Reserve in writing or arrive early in summer. €4 per person, €2.80 per tent, €7.60 per tent and car. Electricity €2.80. Sept.-May. prices. ❶

🍴 FOOD

Local specialties include *fruits de mer au beurre blanc* (seafood with butter sauce) and *canard nantais* (duck prepared with grapes), as well as Muscadet and Gros Plant white wines. *Le Petit Beurre* cookies are a local invention, as are *muscadines* (chocolates filled with grapes and Muscadet wine). Explore the streets behind **pl. du Bouffay,** where the *crêperies* are especially good.

THE BIG SPLURGE

LA CIGALE

It's not every day that you get to eat in a national historic monument, and dining at La Cigale ❸ is no ordinary experience. Stepping into this *brasserie,* you will be transported from modern-day Nantes into the gilded elegance of turn-of-the-century Art Nouveau. Mosaics in brilliant blues and greens decorate the walls, while enormous chandeliers hang from the ceiling. In the summer, outdoor tables offer the perfect spot for people watching, while in the winter you can gaze into the mirrors reaching from the floor to the soaring ceiling. Gold detail tops of the decor, making the entire room sparkle. The atmosphere rivals the best cafés of Paris, *sans* the crowds of gawking tourists.

La Cigale's specialty is a very fresh lobster soup (€6.50), which is best accompanied by one of their generous-portioned salads. Three-course menus, which start around €15, may not win any awards for creativity, but all the old standards of *brasserie* fare are prepared with extra care. Travelers on a tighter budget can get a lighter snack while taking in the view—coffee (€2) and mountainous ice cream sundaes (€5-8) are served at all hours. For a romantic evening, dine at La Cigale before catching a show at the Theater Graslin, across the *place.* An elegant evening gown is optional, but reservations are recommended, especially on weekends and before shows at the theater. (*4 pl. Graslin, opposite the Théâtre Graslin.* ☎*02 51 84 94 94. Open daily 7:30am-12:30am. Reserve for dinner. MC/V.*)

The biggest **market** in Nantes is the **Marché de Talensac,** along rue de Bel-Air near pl. St-Similien behind the post office. (Open Tu-Sa 9am-1pm.) On **pl. du Bouffay,** a smaller market has the same hours, while another stretches down pl. de la Petite Hollande opposite pl. du Commerce. (Open Sa 8am-1pm.) The best selection of fresh fruit in town can be found at **Le Frutier,** 17 rue des Carmes. (☎02 40 12 08 09. Open M-Sa 8am-8pm.) **Monoprix,** 2 rue de Calvaire, is off cours des 50 Otages, down from the Galeries Lafayette. (Open M-Sa 9am-9pm. MC/V.)

■ **La Cigale,** 4 pl. Graslin (☎02 51 84 94 94), facing the Théâtre Graslin, is one of the most beautiful *brasseries* in France. (See sidebar, **The Big Splurge.**) ❸

Le Pain Perdu, 12 rue Beauregard (☎02 40 47 74 21), shouldn't be missed by fish lovers. The menu of traditional French seafood dishes is spiced up with sushi offerings. *Menus* €11-23. Open daily noon-2:30pm and 7:30-11pm. ❸

🔲 SIGHTS

Ask the tourist office about the **Nantes City Card,** a pass to the château, the Musée des Beaux-Arts, the Musée d'Histoire Naturelle, and the Musée Jules Verne. The pass includes free access to trams and buses and a tour guided by the tourist office. Most of Nantes' museums have free entrance one Sunday a month, on a rotating basis; check with the tourist office for a schedule. Walk around the city to experience Nantes' elaborate 19th-century facades are fashioned with wrought-iron balconies. Make sure to see **Passage Pommeraye,** an unusual shopping arcade off pl. du Commerce.

CHÂTEAU DES DUCS DE BRETAGNE. Currently under renovation, this château has seen as much history as any in the Loire. Its imposing walls once held Gilles de Retz, the original Bluebeard, who was convicted of sorcery in 1440 for sacrificing hundreds of children in gruesome rituals. In 1598, Henri IV composed the Edict of Nantes here in an effort to soothe religious tensions. All of the château's museums are closed until 2004, but the château grounds are open and the interim **Musée du Château des Ducs de Bretagne** hosts a number of temporary exhibits. (☎02 40 41 56 56. Courtyard open July-Aug. daily 10am-7pm; Sept.-June 10am-6pm. Free. Call the tourist office for a schedule of guided tours that take you inside the castle. Museum open July-Aug. daily 10am-6pm; Sept.-June closed Tu. €3, students €1.50, under 18 free. Free after 4:30pm.)

CATHÉDRALE ST-PIERRE. Gothic vaults soar 38m in this remarkably bright cathedral, which holds the body of King François II in the south transept. Built in stages from 1434 to 1891, the edifice has survived Revolutionary pillagers, WWII bombs, and a 1972 fire. A restoration has masterfully undone the ravages of time—except for the stained glass, which was almost entirely shattered during WWII. One glass remains, the largest in France, 25m above François's tomb. (Open daily 10am-7pm.)

MUSÉE DES BEAUX-ARTS. This museum prompted Henry James to reflect on provincial museums: "The pictures may be bad, but...from bad pictures, in certain moods of the mind, there is a degree of entertainment to be derived." James' assessment notwithstanding, the collection includes works by Delacroix, Ingres, Monet and Kandinsky. (10 rue Clemenceau. ☎02 40 41 65 65. Take bus #11 (dir: Jules Verne) or #12 (dir: Colonière) to "Trébuchet." Open M and W-Su 10am-6pm; F until 8pm. €3.10, students €1.60; first Su of the month and F 6-9pm free.)

MUSÉE JULES VERNE. Journey to the center of the Verne world through novels, letters, and photographs at this innovative museum, which holds original editions of the author's most famous works, including *Around the World in Eighty Days* and *Twenty Thousand Leagues Under the Sea.* Paintings and posters depict the bustling 19th century Nantes that inspired Jules Verne. (3 rue de l'Hermitage. ☎02 40 69 72 52. Open M and W-Sa 10am-noon and 2-5pm, Su 2-5pm. €1.50, students €0.75.)

THE JARDIN DES PLANTES. Behind the Musée des Beaux Arts, grassy hills, duck ponds, and greenhouses with exotic flowers mark this green oasis. *(Tours every hr. Open M-Sa 8am-7:45pm, Su 2-5pm)* For more greenery, take tram line #2 (dir: Orvault Grand Val) to "St. Mihiel" and cross the bridge to the Ile de Versailles, a tiny island converted into a peaceful and shady Japanese garden. *(Open Mar.-Sept. daily 8am-8pm; Oct.-Feb. daily 8am-5:30pm).*

🎭 🎵 ENTERTAINMENT AND FESTIVALS

A lot of nightlife is listed in the weekly *Nantes Poche* (free at the tourist office, €0.50 at any *tabac*). **The Katorza,** 3 rue Corneille (☎ 08 36 68 06 66), projects nightly films from around the world in their original languages. The **Apollo Theatre,** on rue Racine, shows movies nightly for €2 with an occasional English selection. Nearby **rue Scribe** is full of late-night bars and cafés. A favorite of the young and funky, **quartier St-Croix,** near pl. Bouffay, has about three bars per block and just as many cafés. More clubs and discotheques await the adventurous traveler further out from the *vieille ville.*

La Maison, 4 rue Lebrun, off rue Maréchal Joffre, on the other side of town, offers a silly carefree time with its cantina lighting and ice cream bars. Its beach party atmosphere primarily attracts young people. (☎ 02 40 37 04 12. Open daily 3pm-2am.)

Le John McByrne, 21 rue des Petites Ecuries (☎ 02 40 89 64 46), is a good pub to pull up a chair and enjoy a brew. Live Irish music on Friday nights. Open daily noon-2am.

Le Canotier, 21 quai de Versailles (☎ 02 40 12 06 29), hosts local musicians 3-4 times per week, with blues, jazz, and French accordion music on weekends and a nightly piano bar. Open Tu-Su 2pm-2am.

Le News, 4 pl. Emile Zola off bd. Pasteur (☎ 02 40 58 01 04), spins house and garage in one room and new jack, funk, and dance in another. To get there, take tram line #1 (dir.: François Mitterand) to "Egalité." Walk north two blocks on the rue de l'Egalité and you will reach pl. Emile Zola. The last tram return at 12:45am. Open until 4am.

Le Temps d'Aimer, 14 rue Alexandre Fourny (☎ 02 40 89 48 60), is Nantes' favorite gay disco. From pl. de la République on Ile Beaulieu, follow rue Victor Hugo until rue Fourny on the left. Open daily 9pm-1am.

Eastern Orthodox chanters, blues rockers from Mali, and masqueraders from Trinidad and Tobago perform at the international **Festival d'Eté** in early July. Up-and-coming Asian, African, and South American filmmakers show up for the **Festival des Trois Continents** in late November and early December. (☎ 02 40 69 74 14.) Locals boast that their **Carnaval** is one of the biggest in France, with parades and an all-night party on Mardi Gras. (Info ☎ 02 40 35 75 52.)

BRITTANY

LOIRE VALLEY
(VAL DE LOIRE)

In the heart of France, the Loire Valley beckons travelers with sweeping landscapes dotted with famous castles. The Loire river has attracted settlers from prehistory to the Middle Ages, when the kings of France made this region their home. The Loire also raised some of the brightest stars of French thought, including Rabelais, Descartes, and Balzac; the French spoken on its banks is considered the purest in the country. Today, the Loire Valley's rolling hills are perfect for an afternoon bike ride, while its fertile soil grows some of the nation's best wines.

France owes much to the history of the Loire's châteaux, which goes back to the 9th century, when a splintered France was crumbling under Viking invasions. Local communities, under the leadership of feudal lords, erected fortresses to protect important landholdings from the new invaders. Later the region was a focal point of the incessant Anglo-French wars, beginning when Henry Plantagenêt (the Duke of Anjou) inherited the English crown. During the Hundred Years' War, the region was one of the few to effectively resist the English. In Chinon in 1429, Joan of Arc persuaded the Dauphin to give her an army in order to liberate Orléans. With the introduction of effective artillery in the 16th century, the age of the defensive fortress was over and battles moved into the plains. Most of the surviving castles were converted into comfortable palaces, adapting the new Italian style to fit local tastes. These elegant Renaissance homes, reflected in pools and framed by spectacular gardens, were heaped with masterworks of fine art, fostering an opulence hardly imagined before or since.

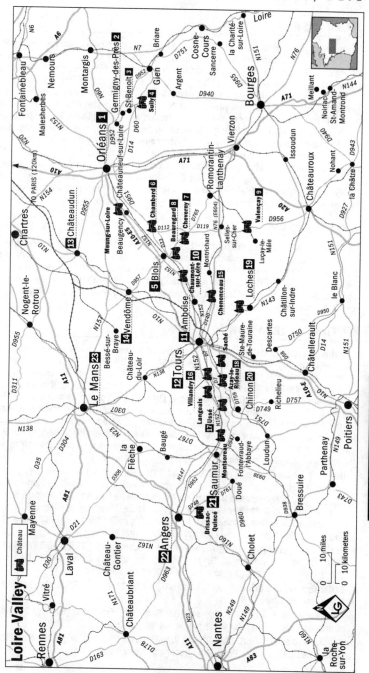

LOIRE VALLEY

▐▀ TRANSPORTATION

An ambitious itinerary in the Loire Valley doesn't pay; two châteaux a day is a good limit. Trains don't reach many châteaux, and they often have inconvenient schedules. Those that do are scheduled inconveniently. Tours, connected to 12 châteaux, is the region's best rail hub, while the smaller city of Blois is also a convenient base from which to explore the châteaux. A group of four renting a car can generally undercut tour bus prices, but biking might be the best way to see the most of the region. Distances between châteaux and hostels tend to be short, and many small flat roads cut through fields of brilliant poppies and sunflowers. Many stations distribute the useful booklet **Châteaux pour Train et Vélo,** with train schedules, distances, and information on bike and car rental. The Michelin map of the region and tourist biking guides will steer you away from truck-laden highways and onto delightful country roads. Nature buffs should ask at tourist offices for the excellent free bilingual booklet **Loisirs and Randonnées of the Val de Loire,** which has info on hiking, biking, canoeing, horse-riding, rock climbing and parachuting.

ORLÉANS

Orléans's location, an hour from Paris, is both a blessing and a curse. Considered by many a suburb of the capital, Orléans (pop. 117,000) clings tightly to its history, especially that which involves Joan of Arc. There are at least 45 public statues of the savior of 1429. This sense of a defined past, combined with a lively shopping district and a *vieille ville* filled with intimate cafes and restaurants, makes it a perfect transition from Paris into the Loire.

▐▀ TRANSPORTATION

Trains: 2 separate stations. Most trains make both stops, but a few routes only stop at Les-Aubrais. **Gare d'Orléans,** on pl. Albert 1er (☎08 36 35 35 35), is in the center of town and better for tourists. Info office open M-Sa 9am-7:30pm. Ticket booths open daily 5:30am-9pm. To: **Blois** (30min., 12 per day 7am-9pm, €8.30); **Nantes** (2hr., M-F 3 per day 6:45am-7:20pm, €30); **Paris** (1¼hr., about 3 per hr. 4am-10pm, €14.60); **Tours** (1hr., 12 per day, €14.10). There is a huge shopping mall complete with supermarket attached to the train station, so you can grab food, buy sneakers, or acquire new clothing while you wait for the train. **Gare Les-Aubrais,** rue Pierre Semard (☎02 38 79 91 00), is a 30min. walk north from the town center. A train **shuttles** new arrivals from quai 2 to Gare d'Orléans for €1.20.

Buses: 2 rue Marcel Proust (☎02 38 53 94 75), connected to the Gare d'Orléans by an overpass. Info desk open M-Tu and Th 10am-1pm and 4-7pm, W and F 10am-1pm and 3-7pm, Sa 10am-1pm. **Les Rapides du Val de Loire** (☎02 38 61 90 00) runs to **Sully** via **Germingy** and **St. Benoît-sur-Loire** (1hr.; M-Sa 3 per day 6:40am-5:30pm, Su 5:30pm; €7.30). **TransBeauce** (☎02 37 18 59 00, in Chartres) runs to **Chartres** (2hr.; 3 per day 12:45pm-6:50pm, 1 on Su; €10.40, under age 20 €5.20).

Public Transportation: SEMTAO, 2 rue de la Hallebarde (☎02 38 71 98 38), off pl. du Martroi, under shopping mall. Tickets €1.20 (good for 1hr.), *carnet* of 10 €10.50, day pass €3.05. Free city bus map available here and at tourist office.

Taxis: Taxi Radio d'Orléans, rue St-Yves (☎02 38 53 11 11). €5.35-6.10 to hostel from train station. 24hr.

Car Rental: Ecoto, 19 av. Paris (☎02 38 77 92 92). From €40 per day. Open daily 9am-noon and 2-6pm. **Car Go,** 1 rue de Bourgogne (☎02 38 53 65 60).

Scooter and Bike Rental: CAD, 95 fbg. Bannier (☎02 38 81 23 00). Scooters €20 per day. Bikes €15 per day. Open M-Su 9am-noon and 2-7pm.

Orléans

▲ ACCOMMODATIONS
Auberge de
Jeunesse (HI), **9**
Hôtel l'Abeille, **3**
Hôtel Blois, **2**
Hôtel de Paris, **1**

● FOOD
Les Alpages, **6**
Mijana, **7**

★ NIGHTLIFE
Cinema des Carmes, **5**
Entr-acte, **4**
Havana, **8**

■ Centre de
Conférences

✦ 🛈 ORIENTATION AND PRACTICAL INFORMATION

Most places of interest in Orléans are on the north bank of the Loire, a 5min. walk south of the train station. Leave the station and go left under the tunnel to pl. Jeanne d'Arc; the tourist office will be across the street to your right. To get to the city center from the station, turn right onto **rue de la République,** which leads to **place du Martroi.** Here, rue de la République becomes **rue Royale** and runs to the river, intersecting **rue de Bourgogne** and **rue Jeanne d'Arc,** two pedestrian-dominated streets home to most of the city's sights, restaurants, and bars.

Tourist Office: 6 pl. Albert 1er (☎02 38 24 05 05; fax 02 38 54 49 84). Maps (€0.30) and excellent walking tour guide of the *vieille ville.* For €2, you can buy a tour book containing info and maps of all of the museums and tourist sites in town. The tourist office also runs French tours (€4) with a variety of themes, from the gardens of Orléans to its historic cathedral (July-Aug. daily 2:30pm; call office for a schedule). Open Apr.-Sept. M 10am-1pm and 2-7pm, Tu-Sa 9am-1pm and 2-7pm; Apr. Su 10am-noon; Oct.-Mar. M 10am-1pm and 2-6:30pm, Tu-Sa 9am-1pm and 2-6:30pm, Su 10am-noon.

Budget Travel: Havas Voyages, 34 rue de la République (☎02 38 42 11 80). Open M-F 9:30am-12:30pm and 2-6:30pm, Sa 9am-noon and 2-6pm.

JNE SALADE, SANS OGM

n the Loire Valley, where farmers have long prided themselves on producing some of the best fruits and vegetables in France, traditions are meeting modern science with the development of genetically modified products (**OGM**, or *organisme géné-tiquement modifié*). Scientists in France and around the world are altering the DNA of plants to introduce genes that confer resistance to pests and add extra nutritional value.

These scientific experiments have met with controversy in France. The opposition to OGM ranges from the occasional vehement activist who burns or cuts down a field of crops to the government officials who have refused to allow the sale of OGM that were approved by the EU. According to the Ministry of Agriculture, OGM present potential health risks to the health of consumers, who may develop allergies to the new foods. Consumers's interest in the debate over OGM is manifested in the new market for food that is described as "biologique," grown in conditions that maximize the productivity of the land without using methods that carry risk to the consumer's health or the environment.

Despite the concerns, however, the Ministry of Agriculture maintains that development of OGM, provided that their potential risks are thoroughly researched before releasing them into the market, are essential in order for France to maintain a dynamic agricultural industry and avoid dependence on other countries.

Money: Banks are on rue de la République and pl. du Martroi. ATMs are everywhere. For the best **currency exchange,** head to the post office (see below).

English Bookstore: Librairie Loddé, 41 rue Jeanne d'Arc (☎02 38 65 43 43), off rue Royale. Good selection. Open Tu-F 9:15am-12:30pm and 1:30-7pm, Sa 9am-12:30pm and 1:30-7pm. MC/V.

Youth Information: Centre Régional d'Information Jeunesse (CRIJ), 5 bd. de Verdun (☎02 38 78 91 78; fax 02 38 78 91 71). Very friendly and helpful staff. Open M and Th 10am-6pm, Tu and F 10am-1pm and 2-6pm, W 10am-6pm, Sa 2-6pm.

Laundromat: Laverie, 26 rue du Poirier (☎02 38 88 23 84). Open daily 7am-11pm.

Emergency: 24hr. (☎17).

Police: 63 rue du fbg. St-Jean (☎ 02 38 24 30 00).

Crisis Lines: Battered women (☎08 00 05 95 95); Battered men (☎01 40 24 05 05).

Hospital: Centre Hospitalier Régional, 1 rue Porte Madeleine (☎02 38 51 44 44). For medical emergencies, call ☎02 38 54 44 44. 24hr.

Internet Access: Médiathèque, pl. Gambetta (☎02 38 65 45 45). 4 free computers. Wait of up to 30min. Open Tu-W 10am-6pm, Th and F-Sa 1pm-8pm. **Odysseüs Cyber Cafe,** 32 rue du Colombier (☎02 38 77 98 48). €1.50 for the 1st 15min., €4.50 per hr. Open M-W 9am-9pm, Th-F 9am-1am, Sa 11am-1am.

Post Office: pl. du Général de Gaulle (☎02 38 77 35 35). **Currency exchange.** Open M-F 8am-7pm, Sa 8am-noon.

Postal code: 45000.

◤ ACCOMMODATIONS AND CAMPING

Inexpensive hotels are hard to find in Orléans; the few that exist are spread throughout the city. They fill up by early evening in July and August, and many have an annual closure in August. Call ahead.

Auberge de Jeunesse (HI), 1 bd. de la Motte Sanguin (☎02 38 53 60 06; asse.crju@libertysurf.fr). A 15min. walk from the train station. By bus: from pl. d'Arc, bus "RS" (dir: "Rosette") or "SY" (dir: "Concyr/La Bolière") will get you to "Pont Bourgogne" (€1.15, until 8pm). From the train station, take #4 and tell the driver you want to get off by the *auberge*. Once you exit the bus, follow the boulevard straight down; the hostel is in the middle of the road on your right. 51 beds in spacious, clean 2 to 4 person rooms. Kitchen facilities and bike storage. Breakfast €3.40. Sheets €3.20. Reception M-F 8am-7pm, Sa-Su 9-11am and 5-7pm. Dorms €7.80; singles €13.80. ❶

Hotel L'Abeille, 64 rue Alsace-Lorraine (☎02 38 53 54 87; hotel-de-labeille@wanadoo.fr). A 5min. walk from the train station, this 2 star hotel welcomes its guests with charming rooms in the *vieille ville* style. Enjoy breakfast in bed for €6.90. Singles and doubles with toilet €38-46, with shower €49-54; triples €49. ❹

Hôtel de Paris, 29 rue du fbg. Bannier (☎02 38 53 39 58). 13 light, simple, renovated rooms in a pleasant area off pl. Gambetta. The friendly owner speaks English. *Brasserie* on the ground floor. Breakfast €4. Singles and doubles with toilet €23, with shower €26-31; triples €28-37. Extra bed €6.50. AmEx/MC/V. ❷

Hôtel Blois, 1 av. de Paris (☎/fax 02 38 62 61 61). Conveniently located across the street from the train station. Clean yet unexciting rooms overlook a busy intersection. The front door locks around 10pm—be sure to get the code from the owner. Breakfast €4.30. Singles and doubles €20, with shower and toilet €31. AmEx/MC/V. ❷

🍴 FOOD

In late summer and autumn, locals feast on *gibier* (game) freshly procured in the nearby forests. Specialty sausages include the *andouillettes de Jargeau*, while *saumon de Loire* (salmon) is grilled fresh from the river. Orléans's most important culinary contribution is its tangy wine vinegars, which you can taste on salads and in marinades at many local *brasseries*. The local cheeses are *frinault cendré*, a savory relative of camembert, and a mild *chèvre*. Wash it all down with Gris Meunier or Auvergnat wines or nearby Olivet's pear and cherry brandies.

Les Halles Châtelet, pl. du Châtelet, is an indoor market attached to Galeries Lafayette. (Open Tu-Sa 7am-7pm, Su 7am-1pm.) Though there are many supermarkets, you'll gravitate to the massive **Carrefour** that occupies the back of the mall at pl. d'Arc (open M-Sa 8:30am-9pm). Just three blocks from the hostel is a **Marché-plus supermarket,** on the corner of rue de la Manufacture and bd. Alexandre Martin. (Open M-Sa 7am-9pm, Su 9am-1pm.)

At night, the area around **Les Halles Châtelet** and **rue de Bourgogne** is the best bet for food, having an endless array of *brasseries* and bars. There are several inexpensive Chinese, Indian, and Middle Eastern restaurants between rue de la Fauconneries and rue de l'Université, including **Mijana ❷**. This restaurant serves traditional Lebanese cuisine, including kebabs and Lebanese wines (☎02 38 62 02 02. Entrees €5-7. *Plats* from €9. *Menus* from €13. Open M 7-11pm, Tu-Sa noon-2pm and 7-11pm. MC/V). **Les Alpages ❷,** 182 rue de Bourgogne, serves traditional French cuisine with seasonings and prices that will keep you coming back for more. (☎02 38 54 12 34. Open M-Sa 7:30am-10pm. Salads €7.50. *Plats* €9-11. Desserts €5.20. *Menus* €7.50. Fondue for 2 €12-14.)

👁 SIGHTS

Most of Orléans's historical and architectural highlights are near **place Ste-Croix**. In 1429, having liberated Orléans from a seven-month siege, Joan of Arc triumphantly marched down nearby **rue de Bourgogne,** the city's oldest street; the scene is vividly captured in *Jeanne d'Arc*, at the Musée des Beaux-Arts. There are 11th- to 15th-century churches throughout the city. The **Eglise St-Paterne,** pl. Gambetta, is a particularly massive showcase of modern stained glass. *(Pass Orléans gives half-price admission to almost all sites in town for €11. Passes on sale at tourist office starting June 1.)*

CATHÉDRALE STE-CROIX. With towering Gothic buttresses, an intricate facade, and slender, dramatic interior arches, the cathedral makes the visit to Orléans worthwhile. On May 8, 1429, Joan of Arc came here to join the first procession of thanks for the deliverance of the town from the English. A series of vivid 19th-century stained glass windows in the nave depict her life's story, down to the flames that consumed her. *(Pl. Ste-Croix. Open July-Aug daily 9:15am-noon and 2:15-7pm; Apr.-Sept. 9:15am-6:45pm; Oct.-Mar. 9:15am-noon and 2:15-5pm. Free. Tours of the upper sections of the cathedral are organized by the tourist office.)*

HÔTEL GROSLOT D'ORLÉANS. Built in 1550 by bailiff Jacques Groslot, this Renaissance mansion was the king's local residence for two centuries. In 1560, François II died here amid scandal after calling the Estates Général. Charles IX, Henri III, and Henri IV also stayed here. The sumptuously decorated rooms evoke the atmosphere of centuries past. Behind the *hôtel*, a garden invites locals and tourists seeking a quiet spot to rest. Now an annex to the town hall, the *hôtel* and garden are open to the public. *(Pl. de l'Etape. ☎02 38 79 22 30. Open daily 9am-6pm.)*

MUSÉE DES SCIENCES NATURELLES. This thoughtfully designed museum makes natural history fun, from the collections of bugs displayed in front of artwork that evokes their natural environment to the tropical and Mediterranean greenhouses on the top floor. Don't miss the human skulls in the "Cabinet des Curiosités." *(6 rue Marcel Proust. ☎02 38 54 61 05. Open daily 2-6pm. €3.05, students and under 16. €1.55.)*

MUSÉE DES BEAUX-ARTS. This fine collection of Italian, Flemish, and French works displays painting, sculpture, and *objets d'art* from the 15th to the 20th centuries. Good modern art and archaeological exhibitions come through regularly. *(1 rue Fernand Rabier, to the right as you exit the cathedral. ☎02 38 79 21 55; fax 02 38 79 20 08. Open M 1:30-6pm, Tu-Sa 10am-noon and 1:30-6pm. €3, students €1.50, under 16 free.)*

PARC LOUIS PASTEUR. The park has large grassy areas for picnicking or lazing around and a great jungle gym for kids. *(Rue Jules Le Maitre, 10min. from the tourist office in the direction of the youth hostel, on a side street that runs perpendicular to the main bd. Alexandre Martin. Turn left onto rue Eugène Vignat to get to Jules Le Maître. Open Apr.-Sept. daily 7:30am-8pm; Feb.-Mar. and Oct. 7:30am-6:30pm; Nov.-Jan. 8am-5:30pm.)*

OTHER SIGHTS. The **Maison de Jeanne d'Arc** is a reconstruction of the original house where the medieval *mademoiselle* stayed, consisting of fragments of other 15th-century houses. Explanations in English accompany dioramas narrating the main events of her life. The museum also displays reconstructions of clothes and armor from the late middle ages. *(3 pl. de Gaulle. ☎02 38 52 99 89. Open May-Oct. Tu-Su 10am-noon and 1:30-6pm; Nov.-Apr. 1:30-6pm. €2, students €1, under 16 free.)* The one-room **Musée Historique et Archéologique de l'Orléanais** displays the treasure of Neuvy-en-Sullias, a remarkable set of Gallo-Roman statues discovered in 1861, along with relics from the Middle Ages to the Neoclassical period. *(Sq. Abbé Desnoyers. ☎02 38 79 21 55. Open July-Aug. daily M 1:30-6pm, Tu-Sa 10am-12:15pm and 1:30-6pm; May-June and Sept M-Sa 1:30-6pm. €3, €1.50 for students, under 16 free. Admission to the Musée Historique is included with admission to the Musée des Beaux Arts.)*

🎵 ENTERTAINMENT AND FESTIVALS

Most locals head to Paris for action, but the bars along **rue de Bourgogne** and near **Les Halles-Châtelet** keep the home front happy. **Paxton's Head,** 264 rue de Bourgogne, is a laid-back British pub that features live jazz on Saturday nights. *(☎02 38 81 23 29. Open daily 3pm-3am.)* For a lively night out, head to **Havana Café,** 28 pl. du Châtelet. *(☎02 38 52 16 00. Open daily 10pm-3am.)* At **Entr-acte,** 81 bd. Alexandra Martin, you can make your own music with Thursday night karaoke. *(☎02 38 62 71 37. Open daily until 11pm.)* **Bowling,** 2 rue Moreau, proves that the appeal of smoke, cheap beer, bowling and billiards is universal. *(☎02 38 66 31 55. Open M-Th 2pm-1am, F and Su 2pm-2am, Sa 2pm-3am.)* For the adventurous, **Cabaret Restaurant**

l'Insolite, 14 rue du Coq St. Marceau, serves dinner with a cabaret show. (☎ 02 38 51 14 15. *Menus* from €10.70. Dinner 8:30pm, show begins at 10:30pm. Open F-Sa.)

Select-Studios, 45 rue Jeanne d'Arc, shows a few first-run English language movies and French films. (☎ 08 36 68 69 25. €4.60-7.30, matinee €3.80.) There's also **Cinema des Carmes,** just up the block at 7 rue des Carmes. During the month of June, Orléans hosts a **Jazz festival** (tickets €6.10-22.90). On weekends in November and December, the **Semaines Musicales Internationales d'Orléans (SMIO)** brings in the Orchestre National de France.

NEAR ORLÉANS

GERMIGNY, ST-BENOÎT, AND SULLY

A day's drive eastward along the Loire takes in these three small towns, each dating from a different era of the Middle Ages. About 30km southeast of Orléans lies the squat Carolingian church of **Germigny-des-Près,** heavily restored but nonetheless the oldest in France. The private chapel preserves a restored 9th-century Byzantine-style mosaic. The monks offer a 45 minute tour of the church for groups. (☎ 02 38 58 27 97. Open Apr.-Sept. daily 8:30am-7pm; Oct.-Mar. 8:30am-6pm. Free. Call ahead to arrange a tour. €46 per group.)

The prize of **St-Benoît-sur-Loire,** 35km southeast of Orléans, is an exquisite 11th-to 12th-century Romanesque basilica. Originally part of the Abbaye de Fleury, the church was destroyed during the French Revolution. Its charms now include its Romanesque mosaic floor, intricate carvings, and 75 arched pillars supporting a barrel vault. Twice daily, the church rings with sung services. The monks offer a tour of the monastery in French in exchange for donations. (☎ 02 38 35 72 43; fax 02 38 35 77 71. Masses M-Sa noon, Su 11am; vespers daily 6:15pm. Church open daily 6:30am-10pm. Call ahead for English tours.)

The 14th-century fortress of **Sully-sur-Loire** lies 42km from Orléans, dominating the countryside from the southern bank of the Loire. The château is a commanding and regal presence on the wooded grounds that guard the intersection of four major roads. At one time three drawbridges were needed to protect the main residence. The white-turreted castle housed a somnolent Charles VII, a frustrated Joan of Arc, a fleeing Louis XIV, and an exiled Voltaire. Written guides in English explain the details of the artwork and architecture of the château (€1.70). Intricate tapestries tell the story of Psyche, who fell in love with Cupid, and horse and carriage rides are available around the grounds. Throughout the year, there are special themed tours, including one with guides in medieval costume for children and one focused on the restoration of the castle. Contact the château for schedules. (☎ 02 38 36 36 86. Open Apr.-Sept. 30 daily 10am-6pm; Feb.-Mar. and Oct.-Dec. daily 10am-noon and 2-5pm; closed Dec. 25-Feb. 1. English tours July 29-Aug. 12 M at 1:30pm. French tours Feb.-Mar. and Oct.-Dec. Sa-Su at 2:30 and 4pm; Apr.-Sept. daily 2:30 and 4pm. €4.90, students and children €3.40, €1.70 extra for tours.) Sully's sprawling, grassy grounds and wooded pathways are perfect for picnics and walks. (Park open daily 9am-nightfall.) In June, the grounds become a stage for a music festival that draws classical musicians from all around the world. (Call tourist office for details.) **Camping Sully-sur-Loire ❶,** chemin de la Salle Verte, surveys the château from the riverbank. (☎ 02 38 36 23 93. Reception M-Sa 7am-noon and 2-7pm. Open Apr.-Oct. €1.25 per site; €2 per person, under age 8 €1; €2.30 per car. Electricity €1.35-2.60.) The **tourist office** is in the center of town on pl. de Gaulle. (☎ 02 38 36 23 70; fax 02 38 36 32 21. Open May-Aug. M 9am-12:30pm and 2-7pm, Tu-F 9am-12:30pm and 2-7pm, Sa 9am-7pm, Su 10:30am-1pm; Sept.-June M-Sa 9:30am-noon and 12:30-6:30pm.)

LOIRE VALLEY

The same **bus** from **Orléans** serves the three towns (Germigny 45min., €5.70; St-Benoît 50min., €6.70; Sully 1hr., €7.30), and comes around five times a day (M-Sa 6:40am-6:25pm). Although bus travel between the towns is difficult, the walk from St-Benoît to Germigny takes only 45 minutes. The trek from Sully to St-Benoît takes 75 minutes. The adventurous may choose to make the challenging 45km **bike ride** to Sully from Orléans, with a scenic route that winds along the south bank of the Loire and passes tiny villages and sunflower fields along the way. **To drive,** take eastbound 152, which becomes the D955, in the direction of Châteauneuf-sur-Loire; signs point you to the D60, which will take you to the towns.

BLOIS

Blois (pop. 50,000) is one of the Loire's must-see cities. Its château, once home of the great French monarchs Louis XII and François, sits at the heart of the town. Amidst the bustle of tourists who come from around the world to the château, the town's blue slate roofs, red-brick chimneys, and narrow cobblestone lanes evoke the simple beauty of a Vermeer village. Blois is the best base for a visit to Chambord and Cheverny, arguably the most famous châteaux in the Loire Valley; each is just an hour's bike trip or a 20min. bus ride away.

⊏ TRANSPORTATION

Trains: pl. de la Gare. Info office (☎08 92 35 35 35) open daily 9am-noon and 2-6:30pm. To: **Angers** via Tours (3hr., 10 per day, €18.20); **Orléans** (30min., 14 per day 6am-11pm, €8.30); **Paris** via Orléans (1¾hr., 8 per day 6am-9pm, €20); **Tours** (1hr., 10 per day 7am-11pm, €8).

Buses: Point Bus, 2 pl. Victor Hugo (☎02 54 78 15 66). Info on buses to châteaux. Open M 1:30-6pm, Tu-F 8:30am-noon and 1:30-5:30pm, Sa 9am-noon. **Transports Loir-et-Cher** (TLC; ☎02 54 58 55 44) sends a bus to nearby **Chambord** and **Cheverny,** as well as **Vendôme** (1¼hr., 4 per day 6:30am-6:10pm, €5.30). Buses leave from the station and pl. Victor Hugo. Tickets can be bought on the bus, and schedules are available at the train station or by calling TLC.

Taxis: Taxis Radio, pl. de la Gare (☎02 54 78 07 65). €8.40 to hostel near Blois; €10.70 with baggage. 24hr.

Bike Rental: Cycles Leblond, 44 levée des Tuileries and 17 rue de Sanitas (☎02 54 74 30 13; fax 02 54 74 06 07). About 1km down the river from the city center, near the "Verdun" bus stop on line #4. The owner rents bikes and has advice on the best routes to nearby châteaux. €4.60-12.20 per day. Passport deposit. Open daily 9am-9pm.

Canoe Rental: la chaussée St-Victor (☎02 54 78 67 48). Open daily 9am-6pm. €20.15 per half-day, €46.50 per day.

✴ ⁊ ORIENTATION AND PRACTICAL INFORMATION

The train station is 10min. north of the château and the town center. Leaving the station, turn left and go straight down av. Jean Laigret; the tourist office will be on the left, near the bottom of the hill before sq. Augustin-Thierry. The streets between the château and **rue Denis Papin** form a bustling cafe-lined pedestrian quarter. When in doubt, descend, as all roads lead down to the city center.

TOURIST AND FINANCIAL SERVICES

Tourist Office: 3 av. Jean Laigret (☎02 54 90 41 41; fax 02 54 90 41 49; www.loire-deschateaux.com), in Anne de Bretagne's Renaissance pavilion. Next year, the office will move to **pl. de ka Voüte de Château.** The office offers a map of the city (€0.50)

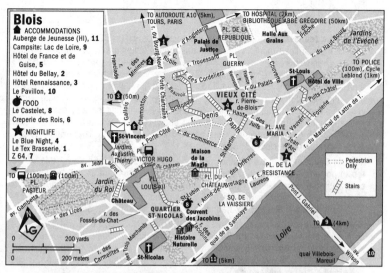

Blois

♠ **ACCOMMODATIONS**
Auberge de Jeunesse (HI), **11**
Campsite: Lac de Loire, **9**
Hôtel de France et de
  Guise, **5**
Hôtel du Bellay, **2**
Hôtel Rennaissance, **3**
Le Pavillon, **10**

🍎 **FOOD**
Le Castelet, **8**
Creperie des Rois, **6**

★ **NIGHTLIFE**
Le Blue Night, **4**
Le Tex Brasserie, **1**
Z 64, **7**

and popular bike maps (€2.50). Complete info on châteaux, including tickets for bus circuits. **Currency exchange** with a 3% commission. **Accommodations service** €2.30. Open Apr. 1-Sept. 30 Tu-Sa 9am-7pm, Su-M and holidays 10am-7pm; Jan.-Mar. and Oct.-Dec. M 10am-12:30pm and 2-6pm, Tu-Sa 9am-12:30pm and 2-6pm, Su 9:30am-12:30pm. MC/V. Around the corner, **Maison du Loir-et-Cher**, 5 rue de la Voûte du Château (☎02 54 57 00 41; fax 02 54 57 00 47), provides info and brochures on events, festivals, lodging, and camping. Open M-F 9am-7pm, Sa-Su 10am-1pm and 1:30-7pm.

Money: In summer, stores displaying *No Francs, No Problem* sign accept currencies from dollars to yen at no commission—but check rates. **Banque de France,** 4 av. Jean Laigret (☎02 54 55 44 00), is on the right as you walk down the hill to the tourist office. **Currency exchange** available M-F 9am-12:15pm.

LOCAL SERVICES

English Bookstore: Librairie Labbé, 9 rue Porte Chartraine. Open Tu-F 10am-7:15pm, Sa 9am-7:15pm, Su 2-7:15pm.

Laundromat: Laverie, 11 rue St. Lubin, pl. Louis XII (☎02 54 74 89 82). Open daily 7am-9pm.

Youth Center: Bureau Information Jeunesse de Loir-et-Cher, 7 av. Wilson (☎02 54 78 54 87). Brochures, job info, and cheap train tickets. Open M-F 9am-12:30pm.

EMERGENCY AND COMMUNICATIONS

Police: 42 quai St-Jean (☎02 54 55 17 99).

Hospital: Centre Hospitalier de Blois, mail Pierre Charlot (☎02 54 55 66 33).

Internet Access: Bibliothèque Abbé Grégoire, pl. Jean Jaurès (☎02 54 56 27 40).€0.30 per 5min. Open M-Tu and F 1-6:30pm, W 10am-6:30pm, Sa 10am-6pm. **Le Tex Brasserie,** 9 rue de Bourg-Neuf (☎02 54 78 46 93). €6 per hr. Open M-Th 11am-10:30pm, F 11am-midnight, Sa 11am-2am.

Post Office: 2 rue Gallois (☎02 54 57 17 17). **Currency exchange.** Open M-F 8am-7pm, Sa 8am-12:30pm.

Postal code: 41000.

▐ ACCOMMODATIONS AND CAMPING

Auberge de Jeunesse (HI), 18 rue de l'Hôtel Pasquier (☎/fax 02 54 78 27 21), 5km west of Blois in Les Grouets. From the tourist office, follow rue Porte Côté, bear right, following rue Denis Papin down to the river, and take bus #4 (dir: "Les Grouets") to "Auberge de Jeunesse." (2 buses per hr. 7am-7pm.) The bus also leaves from the SNCF train station each night at 7:20pm. The hostel is atop a small hilly driveway. Two 24-bed, single-sex dorms in a rural setting. The auberge attracts guests of all types, from children on school trips to backpackers to older travelers visiting the châteaux. Excellent kitchen facilities and hot press-and-repeat showers in bathroom complex outside. Breakfast €3. Reception 6:45-10am and 6-10:30pm. Lockout 10am-6pm. Curfew 10:30pm. Open Mar.-Nov. 15. Bunks €7. ❶

Hôtel du Bellay, 12 rue des Minimes (☎02 54 78 23 62; fax 02 54 78 52 04), at the top of porte Chartraine, 2min. above the city center. Family-run establishment offers cozy, carpeted rooms overlooking a quiet back street. The cheapest rooms come with a choice of toilet or shower. Breakfast €4. Closed Jan. 5-25. Singles and doubles €22-30; triples €38.90; quads €45. Call ahead. Reception 9am-noon, 5-9pm. MC/V. ❷

Hôtel Renaissance, 1 rue de la Garenne (☎02 54 78 02 63; fax 02 54 74 30 95; hotel.renaissance@wanadoo.fr). Carpeted, color-coordinated rooms in an unexciting 2-star hotel that is conveniently close to the train station. Breakfast €4.15. Singles with shower €23-31, with bath €28-37; doubles €26-40; triples and quads €37-61. Prices rise about €7.60 in July-Aug. ❷

Le Pavillon, 2 av. Wilson (☎02 54 74 23 27; fax 02 54 74 03 36), overlooking the Loire. 20min. walk from the train station, or take the local bus, line 3A, from the station. Bright, pretty rooms right on the Loire. Breakfast €5. Singles and doubles €20-36; quads €48. Extra bed €9.15. MC/V. ❷

Hôtel du France et de Guise, 3 Rue Gallois (☎02 54 78 00 53; fax 02 54 78 29 45). This hotel occupies an ideal location, right next to the château. Beautifully decorated rooms give it the feel of a luxury hotel, though the prices are affordable. Breakfast €3.35. Singles €38-43, doubles €42-54, triples €54-70. All rooms come with toilet, TV, telephone, and shower or bath. MC/V. ❹

Campsite: Lac de Loire (☎02 54 78 82 05; fax 02 54 78 62 03). From the station or city center, take bus #S7 to "Lac de Loire" (20min., 3 per day, €1). 2-star site. Open mid-June to Aug. 30. Tent and 1 person €4.30, €2.30 per extra person, €1.50 per child. Hot showers free. Electricity €3. MC/V. ❶

▐ FOOD

Locals have been perfecting *le chocolat blésois* ever since Catherine de Medici brought her own pastry-makers from Italy. Sumptuous *pavés du roi* (chocolate-almond cookies) and *malices du loup* (orange peels in chocolate) peer invitingly from *pâtisseries* along **rue Denis Papin.** There are *crêperies* on almost every block, but for the widest selection, from dinner crepes with cheese or ham (€6-8) to decadent ice cream and crepe sundaes (€6), try **La Crêperie des Rois ❷,** 3 rue Denis Papin (☎02 54 90 01 90. Open M-F noon-2pm and 7-10pm, Sa noon-2pm and 7-11pm). For those who cling to the dinner-before-dessert convention, homey restaurants are along **rue St-Lubin** and around **place Poids du Roi.** For inexpensive Chinese and Greek restaurants try the streets around the **place de la Résistance. Le Castelet ❸,** 40 rue St-Lubin, offers regional delicacies for vegetarians (*menu* €14), children (€7.5), and everybody else (*formules* from €12). (☎02 54 74 66 09; fax 02 54 56 18 77. Entrees from €5, salads €3-6. Open July-Aug. M-Tu and Th-Sa noon-2pm and 7-10pm, W and Su 7-10pm; Sept.-June M-Tu and Th-Sa noon-2pm and 7-

10pm. MC/V.) Bakeries and fruit stands are in the central pedestrian area. An **Inter-marché supermarket** is at 16 av. Gambetta (open M-Th 9am-12:30pm and 3-7:15pm, F-Sa 9am-7:15pm), and at **Utile** at 6 rue Drussy (open M-Sa 9am-9pm, Su 9:30am-noon and 5-9pm). **Place Louis XII** holds an open-air **market** with great deals on fresh fruits, vegetables, cheese, and breads (Sa 8am-12:30pm), and pl. du Château a **gourmet market** (July-Aug. Th 11am-6:30pm).

🜚 SIGHTS

CHÂTEAU DE BLOIS. Brilliantly decorated with gold trimming, carved pillars, and stained glass, this château is unique in the Loire. Home to the French monarchs Louis XII and François Ier, Blois's château was as influential in the late 15th and early 16th centuries as Versailles was in later years. François Ier (1494-1547), whose motto *Nutrisco et extingo* (I feed on fire and I extinguish it) explains the abundance of carved and painted fire-breathing salamanders, made his court a center for art and science. He also enforced unprecedented codes of respect for court women. Though not as grandiose as other châteaux of the Loire, Blois was meticulously restored by 19th-century architect Félix Duban. Located in the château are three excellent museums: the recently renovated **Musée de Beaux-Arts,** with a remarkable 16th-century portrait gallery in the former apartments of Louis XII; the **Musée d'Archéologie,** displaying locally-excavated glass and ceramics; and the **Musée Lapidaire,** preserving sculpted pieces from nearby 17th-century châteaux. (☎ 02 54 78 06 62. *Open July-Aug. daily 9am-7:30pm; Apr.-June and Sept. 9am-6pm; Jan.-Mar. and Oct.-Dec. daily 9am-12:30pm and 2-5:30pm. €6, students under 25 and children under 17 €4. Tours in French May-Sept. approximately every hr; tours begin in the courtyard and continue into the rooms of the château, focusing mainly on the history of the château and its inhabitants; free with admission to the chateau; call ahead to request in English. Tours of the city by carriage depart from the entrance to the château (25min.) €5. Son-et-lumière show May-Sept. 15 daily 10:15pm; €9.50 for adults, €6.50 for students; English show on W. Combined tickets for the château and son-et-lumière, or for the château and Maison de la Magie: €11.50, students €8, and children €5. Ticket for all three attractions: adults €15, students or children €11. MC/V.)*

CATHOLIC GUISE ARE EASY
In its long spell as a royal residence, Blois saw its fair share of scandals and intrigue. The most famous is the murder of the fanatically Catholic duc de Guise, who was committed to stamping out the Protestant heresy in France. When Henry III recognized a Protestant (Henri de Navarre) as the legitimate heir to the throne, de Guise was outraged and raised an army in revolt. As de Guise advanced on Paris, the unpopular king fled Paris and the duke found himself in control of the capital. Emboldened, he called for a meeting of the Estates General at Blois, which he stacked with his own supporters to depose the king and elect himself. Henri had other plans for the duke. On the morning of December 23, 1588, de Guise was invited to discuss some points in private with the king. On his way to the royal chamber, the king's bodyguards fell on the seven-foot duke with knives. When the drama was over, Henri stepped out from behind a tapestry and exclaimed coolly, "He looks even bigger dead than alive." The next day, the duke's brother was dispatched in a similar manner. Unfortunately for Henri, he didn't have long to enjoy his newly-won freedom; he himself was murdered by a monk eight months later. You can go to the scene of the duke's murder on your visit to the castle (see château above); the stabbing occurred in the King's Chamber, room no. 12.

VIEILLE VILLE. Blois holds its own in a land of monuments and cathedrals, but you're likely to most enjoy its hilly streets and ancient staircases, outlined on the tourist office's walking guide. **Rue St-Lubin** and **rue des Trois Marchands** are lined with inviting bars and bakeries en route to the 12th-century Abbaye St-Laumer, now the **Eglise St-Nicolas.** *(Open daily 9am-6:30pm.)* East of **rue Denis Papin** are the most beautiful streets of all, lined with timber-framed houses narrowing into intimate alleys and courtyards. The 12th- to 17th-century **Cathédrale St-Louis,** whose 11th-century crypt is open for viewing upon demand, is a fascinating mix of architectural styles thanks to centuries of additions. *(Open daily 7:30am-6pm; crypt open June-Aug.)* At sunset, cross the Loire and turn right onto **quai Villebois Mareuil** for a view of the château rising above the homes of the commonfolk.

OTHER SIGHTS. The **Musée de la Résistance, de la Déportation et de la Libération** is a powerful memorial to the French victims of the Holocaust and the citizens of Blois who fought in the Résistance. The four small rooms of the museum are packed with photos, newspaper clippings, and narratives gathered and presented by veterans of the Résistance. *(1 pl. de la Grève. ☎02 54 56 07 02. Open Tu-Sa 2-6pm. €3, students and children €1).* The one-room **Musée d'Histoire Naturelle** features minerals, flora, and fauna from the Loire region, plus tropical specimens. *(Past the château off rue Anne de Bretagne. ☎02 54 90 21 00; fax 02 54 90 20 01. Open Tu-Su 2-6pm. €2.30, students and children €0.75.)* The **Musée Diocésain des Arts Religieux,** one floor lower, displays religious objects dating back to the 15th century. *(☎02 54 78 17 14. Open Tu-Sa 2-6pm. Free.)* The **Maison de la Magie,** next to the château, entertains children with its mostly simple tricks. One amateur trickster was so impressed by the museum's godfather, Blois native Jean-Eugène Robert-Houdin, that he adopted the name Houdini. *(1 pl. du Château. ☎02 54 55 26 26. Open July-Aug. daily 10am-12:30pm and 2-6:30pm; Apr.-June and Sept. Tu-Su 10am-noon and 2-6pm. Live shows once per morning, 1-2 times per afternoon. Also open during Christmas holidays, call for hours. €7.50, ages 12-17 €6, ages 6-11 €4.50.)*

🎵 ENTERTAINMENT

Blois seems tame, but only till the lights go down. Neon signs invite you to descend into the modern, swanky **Z 64,** 6 rue Maréchal de Tassigny, near the center of town, which is a combination discothèque, lounge bar, and karaoke joint. (☎02 54 74 27 76. Cocktails €3.80-7.60. Open Tu-Su 8:30pm-4am, but the crowds don't start showing up until midnight.) Near the *place* is **Le Blue Night,** 15 rue Haute, serving over 80 international beers for €3-8 in a bar that looks like a medieval chapel. (☎02 54 74 82 12. Open daily 6pm-4am.) **L'Elite Club,** 19 rue des Ponts Chartrains, rocks the night with disco music. (☎02 54 78 17 73. Open Th-Sa 11pm-5am.) For the cheapest night out in town, head to **Le Tex Brasserie,** 9 rue du Bourg Neuf, where beers go for €1-3. This busy spot also functions as a cyber-café, so you can check your email while you down your Heineken. (☎02 54 78 46 93. Open M-Th until 10:30pm, F until midnight, Sa until 2am.)

From Sept-May, the city hosts world class jazz and classical musicians, dancers, and actors in the Halle Aux Grains, 1 pl. de la République. Schedules available by phone (☎02 54 90 44 00, Tu-F 1-7pm and Sa 2-7pm. Tickets cost €18-22, €16-19 for students.) In July and August, for **Le Soleil a Rendez-Vous avec la Lune,** the city holds free concerts in the street nearly every night, including jazz, classical, and traditional French music. (Schedules available at the tourist office.)

CHÂTEAUX NEAR BLOIS

Blois would be the perfect base from which to explore surrounding châteaux, were it not for transportation difficulties; all those listed below are inaccessible by train. On the bright side, **TLC buses** runs a châteaux circuit to Chambord and Cheverny, giving you two hours at each. Buses leave outside the Blois train station.

If you'd prefer to travel on your own, the châteaux are within easy biking range over beautiful terrain. From Blois, it's 10km to **Cheverny** and only 6km to **Beauregard**. The châteaux and towns are well-marked along the roads. Cyclists are advised to stay off the major—and narrow—French highways. The **tourist office** branch at the Châteaux de Blois has small maps of routes which will lead you safely and efficiently to the châteaux of your choice. Pay attention to route numbers on road maps—roads are marked by their destination. The **Regional Tourism Committee** (☎ 02 54 78 62 52) offers one-week cycling packages which include bike rental, meals, accommodations, and admission to châteaux.

CHAMBORD

*Take the TLC **bus** from the SNCF station in Blois (45min., departs at 9:10am and 1:20pm, €3.20) or enjoy the hour-long **bike** ride. To bike or **drive**, cross the Loire in central Blois and ride 1km down av. Wilson. At the roundabout, take route D956 south for 2-3km followed by a left onto D33. **Château:** ☎ 02 54 50 40 00. Open July-Aug. daily 9am-6:45pm; Sept.-Oct. 9am-6:15pm; Nov.-Mar. 9am-5:15pm; Apr.-June 9am-6:15pm. Last entry 30min. before closing. €7, ages 18-25 €4.50, under 18 free.*

Built by François Ier between 1519 and 1545 for his hunting trips and orgiastic fêtes, Chambord is the largest and most extravagant of the Loire châteaux, on a level with Versailles. With 440 rooms, 365 chimneys, and 83 staircases, the castle is a realization of the ambitious king's most egomaniacal fantasies. The Greek cross floor design used for the keep was formerly reserved for sacred buildings, but François liked the idea of co-opting it for his mansion. To complete his blasphemy, in the center of the castle, where the altar would stand in a church, he built a spectacular double-helix staircase whose design is attributed to Leonardo da Vinci. Not to leave his purpose underemphasized, François stamped Chambord with 70 of his trademark stone salamanders, commissioned 14 four-meter tall tapestries depicting hunting conquests, and left his initials splayed across the stone chimneys on the rooftop terrace. Nevertheless, François stayed at Chambord only 42 days.

While rooms in the château are adequately labeled in English, you can get more detailed explanations of the chateau's architecture by renting a CD headset for €3.80. In summer, visitors are given lanterns to visit the castle at their own pace on incomparable **night tours** that feature whispering voices, mysterious eyes peeking through the castle walls, dancing shadows, and colorful frescoes projected onto the outer walls of the castle. Though exciting, the night tour only takes you through the empty front foyers of the castle, so be sure to take the day tour to see castle rooms and their furniture, tapestries, and personal items. (Night tours July-Aug. M-Sa 10:30pm-1am, last entry midnight. €12, ages 12-25 €7, under 12 free).

There is no currency exchange in the small town, but an **ATM** stands next to the snack shops and restaurants outside the tourist office. While the stretch of forlorn lawn in front of the château is less than inspiring, the lush forest that surrounds it begs to be explored. **Boat** and **bike rentals** are available from a little shelter in front of the château. (☎ 06 07 17 88 13. 2-person boats €10.75 per hr, electric boats €6.10, children €5.30 for 55min.; bikes €5.20 per hr., €12.25 per day, €9.15 each additional day. If you call ahead, you can have your bike brought to the SNCF gare in Blois at 8am, to be returned there between 7-8pm. Open June-Sept. daily 10:30am-7:30pm; Oct. and Mar.-Apr. 11am-6pm. Closed Nov.-Feb.) Campers can trek to **Camping Huisseau-sur-Cosson ❶**, 6 rue de Châtillon, about 5km southwest of Chambord on D33. (☎ 02 54 20 35 26. Open May-Sept. 9am-8pm. €2 per tent; €3.50 per person, children under 7 €2. Shower included. Electricity

€2.50.) Or try **Camping des Châteaux,** between Chambord and Cheverny in **Bracieux.** (☎ 02 54 46 41 84; fax 02 54 46 09 15. Open Mar. 30-Oct. 15 daily 8:30am-noon and 3-7:30pm. Tent €4.40, €3.50 per adult, €1.50 per child. Showers included; electricity €1.50.)

CHEVERNY

*To **bike** or **drive** to the château, take D956 or D765 south for 45min. Four-star **Camping Les Saules** is 2km away on the road to Contres. (☎02 54 79 90 01; fax 02 54 79 28 34. Open Apr.-Sept. 8:30am-8:30pm. €3.80-5.20 per person depending on the season, ages 3-11 €2.60, €4.90-6.10 per tent.) **Château:** ☎02 54 79 96 29. Open July-Aug. daily 9:15am-6:45pm; Apr.-June and Sept. 1-15 9:15am-6:15pm; Oct. and Mar. 9:30am-noon and 2:15-5:30pm; Nov.-Feb. 9:30am-noon and 2:15-5pm. €5.80, students €3.80, ages 7-14 €2.60. MC/V. The same **bus** that leaves from the SNCF station to Chambord also goes to Cheverny, after a 2hr. stop at the first château.*

Since its completion in 1634, Cheverny has been privately owned by the Hurault family, whose members served as financiers and officers to several kings of France. The wealth of the family is reflected in the impeccably maintained grounds and luxurious decor of the château, which was inhabited as recently as 1985. While perhaps lacking the royal intrigues of others, Cheverny retains magnificent furnishings. With murals, armor, and elegant tapestries covering every inch of its wall space with tales of Greek gods, ancient war stories, and Latin axioms about love and bravery, Cheverny is at the height of decadence. Fans of Hergé's **Tintin** books may recognize Cheverny's Renaissance facade as the inspiration for the design of Captain Haddock's mansion. Cheverny housed the **Mona Lisa** in its Orangerie while German artillery shelled Paris during WW II. Animal lovers may want to skip the kennels, which still hold 70 mixed English-Poitevin hounds who stalk stags in hunting expeditions. (Oct.-Mar. every Tu and Sa.) The **soupe des chiens** is not a dubious regional dish but a bizarre opportunity to see these hounds gulp down bins of ground meat in less than 60 seconds. (W-F and Su-M 5pm.) Next to the kennels, thousands of antlers poke out of the ceiling of the morbid **trophy room,** around a striking stained glass window depicting a hunt.

BEAUREGARD

*Transport **Butte** runs **buses** from the SNCF station in Blois (15 min.; departs 6:50am, 11:20 am, and 5:50pm; €1.45). It's 30min. by **bike** from Blois. Off D956, en route to Cheverny. Ask when you rent your bike for more detailed directions. A **taxi** from Blois costs €12.20. **Château:** ☎02 54 70 36 74 or 02 54 70 40 05; fax 02 54 70 36 74. Open July-Aug. daily 9:30am-6:30pm; Apr.-June and Sept. daily 9:30am-noon and 2-6:30pm; Oct.-Jan. M-Tu and Th-Su 9:30am-noon and 2-5pm; Feb. 8-Mar. daily 9:30am-noon and 2-5pm. €6, students and children over 7 €4.50, under 7 free. Gardens only €4.50.*

Before François Ier unleashed his fancy on Chambord, he designed Beauregard as a hunting lodge for his uncle René. Located 6km south of Blois, Beauregard is cozier than its flashy cousin. Paul Ardier, treasurer to Louis XIII, commissioned Jean Mosnier to paint what was to become the world's largest portrait gallery. This collection of over 300 paintings is a *Who's Who* of European powers, from Philippe de Valois (1378) through Louis XIII (1638) and includes all of the Valois monarchs, as well as Elizabeth I, Thomas Moore, and Columbus. The floor's 5616 hand-painted Delft tiles, undergoing a 20-year restoration project, portray Louis XIII's army solemnly marching to war. Outside the château, the ruins of a 14th-century chapel invite a walk into the woods. Tours are available in French and English; times vary depending on the season and the availability of tour guides. Call ahead to check tour times. English guide sheets are always available.

VALENÇAY

Trains run from rue de la Gare to Salbris, which connects to Orléans (2hr.; M-Sa 7 per day, 2 on Su; €14.80) and Paris (3hr.; M-Sa 7 per day, 2 on Su; €24.25). Buses run from the train station in Blois to Valençay (90min., 3 per day 7:40am-5:15 pm, €7.90). To get to the château from the bus stop at pl. de la Halle, continue straight down rue de l'Auditoire and take your second right into pl. Talleyrand. Château: ☎ 02 54 00 10 66. Open July-Aug. daily 9:30am-7:30pm; Apr.-June and Sept.-Oct. 9:30am-6pm; call ahead for schedule Nov.-Mar. €8.50, students 18-25 €5.80. Free shows in French feature actors in traditional dress (daily July-Aug. 11am-5:30pm). The tourist office is on av. de la Résistance. (☎ 02 54 00 04 42, open M-Sa 9:30am-7pm and Su 10am-7pm.)

Midway between the châteaux of the Loire to the west and the castles of the Route Jacques Cœur to the east, the majestic château of Valençay has Renaissance and Neoclassical architecture to match any of them. Dominating the quiet town and ripe vineyards that surround it, the luxurious château was built in 1540 on the site of an earlier 12th-century fortress. Its rich owner Jacques d'Etampes intended it to compete with the likes of Chambord and Chenonceau.

Unlike many château of the Loire, which are a mélange of styles, Valençay is almost entirely in the Imperial style that developed under the reign of Napoleon I. This decor reflects the influence of the château's 19th-century owner, the cunning Charles-Maurice Talleyrand-Périgord. Even though Talleyrand began his career under Louis XVI, he survived the Revolution and was made Minister of Foreign Affairs by Napoleon. It was the Emperor who bought the château for Talleyrand, desiring that he entertain important guests here to build the empire's popularity. After Napoleon deposed King Ferdinand VII of Spain in 1808, he sent the Spanish royal family to Talleyrand at Valençay. Here the princes and at least 50 ladies-in-waiting remained until 1814, when Ferdinand was reinstated as monarch. The exquisite interior contains a number of remarkable items, including the table used for the Congress of Vienna and a sumptuous dining room in which some of the most celebrated culinary creations in all of Europe slipped down the throats of Talleyrand's guests four nights a week.

Admission to the château comes with a free audio guide in English and includes visits to the wine cellars, the underground kitchens, and an animal park complete with peacocks, ponies, goats, hens, and horses. Don't mistake the wallabies for kangaroos. Kids will delight in the oversized maze just outside the château.

CHAUMONT

Chaumont is easily accessible by a flat 1hr. bike ride or 20min. car ride from Blois (16km along N152 in the direction of Tours, follow the sign that directs you across the bridge to Chaumont). Buses also run from Blois. The tourist office, 24 rue Maréchal Leclerc, right across the bridge from N152, rents bikes for €10 per day, €8 for children, €5 for a half-day and €2 per hr. (☎ 02 54 20 91 73. Open daily 9am-12:30pm and 1:30-7pm.)

Chaumont, which occupies a strategic position atop a high hill overlooking the Loire, was originally built in the 10th century by the Comte de Blois to protect his territories from his rival, the Comte d'Anjou. In 1465, most of the original fortress was burnt by Louis XI to punish its owner, Pierre d'Amboise, for rebelling against the throne. The present castle, which was rebuilt in the following decade, reflects the stylistic transition between the late middle ages and the Renaissance. It also reflects renovations made by subsequent owners, including Marie-Charlotte Say, the daughter of a wealthy sugar trader, who acquired the château at age seventeen. While Chaumont is not the most lavish or elegant of the Loire châteaux, it is the most creatively decorated, with giant fake flowers hanging from staircases and sprawling across tables.

The grounds and gardens of Chaumont are spectacular enough to merit a visit of their own. The coutryard of the château offers an expansive view of the Loire valley. Every summer the château hosts an international **garden festival.** Part botanical garden, part modern sculpture museum, the festival features work by landscape artists from around the world. (☎02 54 51 26 26. Admission to gardens €8, students €6.50, children €3.20. Festival runs daily 9:30am-dusk.)

AMBOISE

One of the oldest cities in the Loire Valley, Amboise was home to the first *tourangeaux* (people from Tours) in 100 BC. Over one thousand years later, Charles VIII, Louis XI, Louis XII, and the bacchanalian François Ier ruled France from its hillside château, enjoying the extraordinary panorama of the river valley below. Neither as ornate as Chambord nor as charming as Chenonceau, the château has a medieval, fortress-like character which is appealing in its own right. Amboise's most famous former resident may be Leonardo da Vinci, who spent his last years in the town. Not to be missed are the life-size versions of da Vinci's unrealized projects in his home-turned-museum.

■ ⁊ ORIENTATION AND PRACTICAL INFORMATION. Trains run from bd. Gambetta to: Blois (20min., 15 per day, €5.34); Orléans (1hr., 14 per day, €11.59); Paris (2¼hr., 5 per day, €22.40); Tours (20min., 14 per day, €4.27). (☎02 47 23 18 23. Ticket office open M-Sa 6am-9:30pm, Su 7:30am-9:30pm.) **Fil Vert buses** leave the tourist office for Chenonceau (30min., 3 per day, roundtrip €6.10) and Tours (35min., 3 per day 6:45am-9am, €2.10). To rent **bikes,** head out to **V.T.T. Cycles Richard,** 2 rue de Nazelles, on the north bank by the first bridge as you walk away from the station. (☎02 47 57 01 79. €13.72 per day. Passport or €122 deposit. Open Tu-Sa 9am-noon and 2:30-7pm.) To reach the **tourist office,** follow rue Jules-Ferry from the station and cross both bridges past the residential Ile d'Or. The office is 30m to the right of the bridge, on quai du Général de Gaulle. (15min.) The staff has info about bus tours to nearby châteaux. (☎02 47 57 09 28; fax 02 47 57 14 35. Open July-Aug. M-Sa 9am-8pm, Su 10am-6pm; Sept.-June M-Sa 9am-1pm and 2-6:30pm, Su 10am-1pm and 2-6pm.) The **police** are at 1 bd. A. France (☎02 47 57 26 19), and the **hospital** is on rue des Ursulines (☎02 47 23 33 33). The **post office** sits at 20 quai du Général de Gaulle, three blocks down the street to the left as you face the tourist office and it offers **currency exchange.** (Open M-F 8:30am-noon and 1:30-6:15pm, Sa 8:30am-noon.) **Postal code:** 37400.

⌂⌂ACCOMMODATIONS AND FOOD. There are plenty of hotels in Amboise, but most of them are quite expensive; expect to pay at least €40 a night for a single or double. The **Hôtel Belle-Vue ❹,** 12 Quai Charles Guinot, is at the end of the two bridges that lead from the train station to the château. The Hôtel lives up to its name, offering some of the nicest rooms in town, overlooking the Loire. (☎02 47 30 40 40. Breakfast €6. Singles €43 with shower and toilet; doubles €48-57, triples €57-66.) Your best bet for inexpensive accommodations is the **Centre International de Séjour Charles Péguy (HI) ❶,** Ile d'Or. Follow rue Jules-Ferry from the station and head downhill to the right after the first bridge onto Ile d'Or. (10min.) The industrial feel is offset by a quiet setting. Guests, most of whom are students or young travelers, are housed in 3- to 4-bed dorm rooms; ask for one with a view of the Loire and the château. (☎02 47 30 60 90; fax 02 47 30 60 91. Breakfast €2.30. Sheets €2.90. Reception M-F 3-7pm. Dorms €8.40.) **Ile d'Or camping ❶** has clean, well-maintained facilities, including a swimming pool, and a spectacular view of the Loire and the château. (☎02 47 57 23 37. Open Apr. 6-Sept. 23. Reception 8am-10pm; Sept.-June 8:30am-noon and 2:30-7pm. €2.30 per person, €3.05 per site, children under 12 years €1.52. Electricity €1.83.)

The rue Victor Hugo and rue Nationale, both at the base of the château, are lined with *brasseries* and bakeries. For a cheap picnic with a great view of the Loire, climb the hill to **ATAC supermarket,** at pl. de la Croix Bernard, at the intersection of rue Grégoire de Tours. (Open M-F 8:30am-12:30pm and 2:30-7:30pm, Sa 8:30am-7:30pm, Su 9:30am-12:30pm.) There's also a **Netto** on av. de Tours. (☎ 02 47 57 00 98. Open M-Th 9am-12:30pm and 2:30-7:30pm, F-Sa 9am-7:30pm, Su 9am-noon.)

■ **SIGHTS.** The battlements of the 15th-century **château** that six French kings called home once stretched out along the hill, at times holding as many as 4000 people. In 1560, a failed Protestant conspiracy against the influential, arch-Catholic de Guise family in 1560 led to grisly murder; Huguenots were thrown into the Loire in sacks and others killed on the château balcony, now described by smiling tour guides as the "Balcony of the Hanging People." During the French Revolution, most of the château was destroyed, but the remaining parts have been restored and opened to the public. The **Logis de Roi,** the main part of the château, remains decorated to fit the 15th- and 16th-century royalty who once inhabited it. Intricately carved Gothic chairs stand over 6ft. high in order to prevent surprise attacks from behind. In contrast, the 2nd floor is decorated with 19th-century furniture that recalls the period when it was inhabited by nobles of the house of Orléans, including the mother of King Louis Philippe. The jewel of the grounds is the **Chapelle St-Hubert,** outside the château, the final resting place of Leonardo da Vinci. In summer, people flock to the "Court of King François" **son-et-lumière,** while Renaissance entertainment is held at the nearby park. (☎ 02 47 57 00 98. Château open July-Aug. daily 9am-7pm; Sept.-Oct. 9am-6pm; Nov.-Jan. 9am-noon and 2-5pm; Mar. 9am-noon and 2-5:30pm; Apr.-June 9am-6:30pm. Nearby park open same hours as château. €6.55, students €5.50, ages 7-14 €3.50. *Son-et-lumière* July W and Sa 10pm; Aug. 10:30pm €12.20, children €6.10.)

Just beneath the château, the **Caveau de Dégustation,** rue Victor Hugo, offers free tastings of the region's wines, cheeses, and pâté. (☎ 02 47 57 23 69. Open Mar. 2-Sept. M-Sa 11am-7pm.) From the château, follow the cliffs along rue Victor Hugo beside centuries-old **maisons troglodytiques,** houses hollowed out of the cliffs and still inhabited today. Four hundred meters away is **Clos Lucé,** the manor where Leonardo da Vinci spent his last years. Inside are his bedroom, library, drawing room, and chapel, but the main attraction is a collection of 40 unrealized inventions, built with materials contemporaneous to da Vinci's lifetime. Long before their respective "inventions," Leo had envisioned everything from the helicopter to the machine gun. (☎ 02 47 57 62 88; fax 02 47 30 54 28. Open July-Aug. daily 9am-8pm; Mar. 23-June 9am-7pm; Sept.-Oct. 9am-7pm; Nov.-Dec. 9am-6pm; Jan. 10am-5pm; Feb.-Mar. 22 9am-6pm. €6.55, students €5.50, ages 6-15 €3.50. MC/V.)

TOURS

After Roman Cæsardom was wiped off the map by a barbarian invasion in the 3rd century, three separate towns made use of the site until the Hundred Years' War (1337-1453) compelled them to unite into one city—Tours. In the 15th and 16th centuries, Tours (pop. 250,000) was the heart of the French kingdom, and although the government has long since migrated north, the city is still the urban mouthpiece of the Loire region. The birthplace of Balzac looks firmly toward the future, and the modern day city caters to the 30,000 students who call Tours home. Clothing stores, coffee shops, bakeries, and shoe racks line the wide boulevards filled with young people; warm spring and summer evenings see joggers, musicians, and bar-hoppers along the strollable paths lining the Loire River. The prettiest view is at sunset, when the bridges are illuminated above the rushing waters. Tours is conveniently located near about half of the Loire châteaux, and budget travelers should use it as a base.

LOIRE VALLEY

▐ TRANSPORTATION

Trains: 3 rue Edouard Vaillant, pl. du Maréchal Leclerc. Info open M-Th 5:45am-9:45pm, F 5:50am-10:30pm, Sa 5:50am-9:30pm, and Su 7:15am-11:30am. Many destinations require a change at **St-Pierre-des-Corps,** 5min. outside Tours; check schedule. To: **Bordeaux** (2½hr., 6 per day, €35.50); **Paris** (2¼hr., 7 per day, €24.20; TGV via St-Pierre 1hr., 6 per day, €32.79-42.69); **Poitiers** (45min., 7 per day, €12.60).

Local Transportation: Fil Bleu (☎02 47 66 70 70). Tickets €1.05, *carnet* of 10 €9. Day pass €4.12. Buses run throughout the city 7am-8:30pm; map available from the tourist office or Fil Bleu office near the train station.

Taxis: Artaxi (☎02 47 20 30 40). 24hr.

Car Rental: The tourist office has a list of companies in town. **Avis** (☎02 47 20 53 27; fax 02 47 66 70 70) is in the station. AmEx/DC/MC/V. Similarly priced agencies include **Europcar,** 76 rue B. Palissy (☎02 47 64 47 76) and **Hertz,** 57 rue Marcel Tribut (☎02 47 75 50 00). The cheapest cars can be found at **Ada,** 49 bd. Thiers.

Bike Rental: Amster Cycles, 5 rue du Rempart (☎02 47 61 22 23; fax 02 47 61 28 48). €14 per day. Passport or credit card deposit. Open M-Sa 9am-12:30pm and 1:30-7pm, Su 9am-12:30pm and 6-7pm. AmEx/MC/V.

▐▐ ORIENTATION AND PRACTICAL INFORMATION

Place Jean-Jaurès, vertex of four big boulevards, is the main street. The busy, shop-lined **rue Nationale,** once part of the main road between Paris and Spain, runs north to the Loire, while **av. de Gramont** runs south to the Cher river. **Bd. Béranger** and **bd. Heurteloup** run west and east, respectively, from pl. Jean Jaurès. The mostly pedestrian *vieille ville,* the lively **pl. Plumereau,** and the tourist draws are northwest of pl. Jean Jaurès, toward the Loire. To reach the **tourist office** from the station, cross the park across from the station and turn right at bd. Heurteloup. The office is a glass building on the left, past the futuristic Centre des Congrès.

Tourist Office: 78-82 rue Bernard Palissy (☎02 47 70 37 37; fax 02 47 61 14 22; www.ligeris.com). Free maps and info booklets; finds rooms. Arranges **châteaux tours.** 2hr. historical walking tour departs daily at 10am July 15-Aug. 15. (€5, children 6-12 years €3.81). Call in advance to arrange English tours. The best tours are the 1½hr. walking **night tours** (July-Aug. every F 9:30pm from the tourist office). €7.62, children €6.10. Office open mid-Apr. to mid-Oct. M-Sa 8:30am-7pm, Su 10am-12:30pm and 2:30-5pm; mid-Oct. to mid-Apr. M-Sa 9am-12:30pm and 1:30-6pm, Su 10am-1pm.

Money: Best rates at **Banque de France,** 2 rue Chanoineau (☎02 47 60 24 00), off bd. Heurteloup. Exchange desk open Tu-Sa 8:45am-noon.

English Bookstore: La Boîte à Livres de l'Etranger, 2 rue du Commerce (☎02 47 05 67 29). Open M-Sa 9:30-7pm. MC/V.

Police: 70-72 rue de Marceau (☎02 47 60 70 69).

Hospital: Hôpital Bretonneau, 2 bd. Tonnelle (☎02 47 47 47 47).

Laundromat: Cyber-Laverie, 16bis pl. de la Victoire. **Internet** access available while you wait for laundry. Open daily 9am-7pm. **Lavo 2000,** 17 rue Bretonneau (☎02 47 73 14 69). Open daily 7am-8:30pm.

Internet access: Cyber Gate, 11 rue de Président Merville (☎02 47 05 95 94). €1 per 15min., €5 for 1hr. of access, a sandwich, and a beverage. Open M 1-10pm, Tu-Sa 11am-10pm, Su 2-10pm. **Net@ccess,** 21 rue de Marceau, has an American keyboard. Printing available. Open M 2pm-midnight, Tu-Sa 11am-midnight, Su 2-7pm. €0.06 per min., €4 per hr.

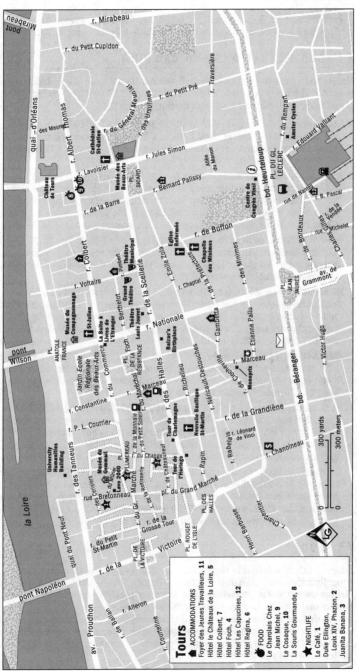

LOIRE VALLEY

Tours

▲ ACCOMMODATIONS
Foyer des Jeunes Travailleurs, 11
Hôtel le Châteaux de la Loire, 5
Hôtel Colbert, 7
Hôtel Foch, 4
Hôtel Les Capucines, 12
Hôtel Regina, 6

● FOOD
Le Charolais Chez
  Jean Michel, 9
Le Cosaque, 10
La Souris Gourmande, 8

★ NIGHTLIFE
Le Café, 1
Duke Ellington,
  Louix XIV, Phazion, 2
Juanita Banana, 3

Post Office: 1 bd. Béranger (☎02 47 60 34 20). **Currency exchange.** Open M-F 8am-7pm, Sa 8am-noon. Branch office on 92 rue Colbert. **Postal code:** 37000.

ACCOMMODATIONS AND CAMPING

Many good, cheap hotels can be found within a 10min. walk of the station. In peak season, call a week or two in advance. **CROUS** (☎02 47 60 42 42) can provide info about discount meals and long-term housing for students.

- ■ **Hôtel Regina,** 2 rue Pimbert (☎02 47 05 25 36; fax 02 47 66 08 72). Hosts make you feel like family. The hostess might throw in a free knitting lesson. Near beautiful river strolls and good restaurants. Spotless hallway showers. Breakfast €4.12. Singles €20-26; doubles €26-30. MC/V. ❷

- ■ **Foyer des Jeunes Travailleurs,** 16 rue Bernard Palissy (☎02 47 60 51 51). This centrally located accommodation fels a bit like a college dorm, albeit a very clean one. Many of the long-term residents are students at the university in Tours, but there are also tourists from around the world, especially in the summer. Meals €7. One-time €3.05 membership. Singles with shower €15.25; doubles with bath €24.39. ❷

- **Hôtel le Châteaux de la Loire,** 12 rue Gambetta (☎02 47 05 10 05, fax 02 47 20 20 14). This hotel earns its 2-star rating with elegant furnishings at a reasonable price. All rooms come with a shower (or bath) and toilet. Singles €36.50-45; doubles €43-48; up to quints available. Breakfast €6.10. ❹

- **Hôtel Foch,** 20 rue du Maréchal Foch (☎02 47 05 70 59; fax 02 47 20 95 10, hotel-foch.tours@wanadoo.fr), just off pl. Plumereau. 14 large rooms. Unbeatable location, and a friendly proprietor eager to help you plan your day. Most rooms have shower; no hallway showers are available. Breakfast €4.57. Singles €19-34; doubles €23-46; triples €37-58; quads €50-58. MC/V. ❷

- **Hôtel Colbert,** 78 rue Colbert (☎02 47 66 61 55, fax 02 47 66 01 55). Large rooms with views of the restaurant-lined rue Colbert or the lovely garden behind the hotel. All rooms come with shower or bath, toilet, and TV. Singles €35-45; doubles €40-50; extra beds €12.20 each. Breakfast €5.35. ❸

- **Hôtel Les Capucines,** 6 rue Blaise Pascal (☎02 47 05 20 41; fax 02 47 05 20 41), just 1min. from train station. Turn left out of train station, and cross rue Nantes. Rue Blaise Pascal is next left. Less-than-sparkling hallways lead to newly renovated rooms with bathrooms, showers, and TVs. Breakfast €3.81. Singles €19-29; doubles €29-35; triples and quads with bath €40. MC/V. ❷

- **Camping:** Tourist office lists campsites within 30km. The closest is **Camping St-Avertin,** 63 rue de Rochepinard in St-Avertin (☎02 47 27 27 60), accessible by bus #5 from Tours. Ask for stop nearest campsite, and follow signs. (5min.) Tennis, volleyball, pool. Open Apr.-Oct. 15. €3 per person, €2.80 per child under 7, €5 per site, €1.30 per car. Electricity €2.50. Reception 8am-noon and 3-8pm. ❶

FOOD

Tours is full of affordable restaurants serving everything from traditional *tourangelle* cuisine to Parisian bistro fare to Indian, Greek, and Chinese specialties. The **rue Colbert** and **pl. Plumereau** have dozens of pleasant outdoor options serving *menus* under €12. The area between the train station and bd. Berganger is full of bistros that sprawl into the street and offer everything from drinks and *assiettes* to full *menus*. Look out for melt-in-your-mouth macaroons, and anything *aux pruneaux* (with prunes). Connoisseurs esteem such local wines as the light, fruity whites of **Vouvray** and **Montlouis.**

Budding chefs, or anyone seeking farm fresh fruits at bargain prices, can browse the **indoor market**, pl. des Halles, which spreads outdoors Wednesdays and Saturdays. (Open M-Sa 6am-7:30pm, Su 6am-1pm.) The first Friday of the month brings the **Marché Gourmand** to pl. de la Résistance, an epicurean's daydream. (Open 4-10pm.) **Supermarkets** are all over town. **ATAC**, 7 pl. Maréchal Leclerc, faces the train station. (Open M-Sa 8:30am-8pm, Su 9:30am-12:30pm.) The **Monoprix** supermarket is in the Galeries Lafayette on the corner of rue Etienne Pallu and rue Nationale, just north of pl. Jean Jaurès. (Open M-Sa 9am-7:30pm.)

▨ **La Souris Gourmande,** 100 rue Colbert (☎ 02 47 47 04 80). More cheese than a 1970s disco night with your parents. Dive into a melting pot of fondue, crepes, omelettes and more at this excellently-priced restaurant. Staff is happy to suggest regional wines that compliment the fondue options. Open Tu-Sa noon-2pm and 7-10:30pm. ❷

    Le Charolais Chez Jean Michel, 123 rue Colbert (☎ 02 47 20 80 20; fax 02 47 66 66 25). Regional French cuisine, exceptional regional wines, big portions, and good prices. €10.50 and €13. 3-course lunch *menus*. Dinner *menus* €19-25. Open M 7:30-10:30pm, Tu-Sa noon-2pm and 7:30-10:30pm. MC/V. ❷

    Le Cosaque, 41 rue Lavoisier (☎ 02 47 61 75 13). This Eastern European restaurant features live musicians performing everything from Tzigane gypsy music to Viennese waltzes to jazz. Russian, Polish, Romanian, and Hungarian cuisine served in generous portions (*menus* from €13 include *entrée, plat, and dessert*). And, of course, there is plenty of vodka (over 50 varieties) to keep the most dedicated drinker happy. ❸

◶ SIGHTS

A €7.62 **Carte Multivisite,** *available at the tourist office, includes admission to seven museums and the 2:30pm city tour.*

Those in search of peace and quiet can leave the city behind at the beautiful **Lac de la Bergeonnerie** (also called Lac de Tours), a 10min. ride away (bus #1), on the banks of the Cher.

CATHÉDRALE ST-GATIEN. Several centuries's worth of architectural caprice have gone into the wildly intricate facade. Solid Roman columns were embellished with delicate Gothic micro-carvings in the Middle Ages, and graceful turrets were added to church spires during the Renaissance. The cathedral is celebrated for its balanced arrangement of windows and for one of the most dazzling displays of stained glass in the Loire. *(Rue Jules Simon. ☎ 02 47 70 21 00. Cathedral open daily 9am-7pm. Cloister open Easter-Sept. 9:30am-12:30pm and 2-6pm; Oct.-Mar. W-Su 9:30am-12:30pm and 2-5pm. Mass on Su 10am and 6:30pm.)*

MUSÉE DU GEMMAIL. These mosaics of **gemmes** (brightly colored shards of glass), assembled by artisans, include original works and interpretations of classic paintings, including the Mona Lisa, Monet's water lily series, and Degas's ballet dancers. The play of light on the multi layered glass is enhanced by illuminating the works from behind. *(7 rue du Murier. Off rue Bretonneau, near pl. Plumereau. ☎ 02 47 61 01 19; fax 02 47 05 04 79. Open Apr.-Nov. 15 Tu-Su 10am-noon and 2-6:30pm; Nov. 16-Mar W-Su Sa-Su 10am-noon and 2-6:30pm. €4.57, students €3.05, under 10 €1.52.)*

MUSÉE DES BEAUX-ARTS. The upper floors of the museum house primarily 17th- and 18th-century French paintings, but a few works by Degas, Monet, Delacroix, and Rodin add variety. The *primitif* collection downstairs includes two paintings by Andrea Mategna, astoundingly well-preserved since the 1430s. The Lebanese cedar outside was planted during Napoleon's reign. *(18 pl. François Sicard, next to the cathedral. ☎ 02 47 05 68 73; fax: 02 47 05 38 91. Open W-M 9am-12:45pm and 2-6pm. €4, students €2. Gardens open in summer daily 7am-8:30pm; off-season 7am-6pm.)*

MUSÉE DE COMPAGNONNAGE. The museum houses the works of **compagnons**, or "companions," members of artisans' guilds dating back to the Middle Ages. While the exhibits on the history of *compagnonnage* may be difficult for those who do not speak French to follow, anyone can appreciate the intricate handiwork displayed in their. Amid the curios is an impressively detailed cathedral model and miniature spiral staircases carved in wood. (*8 rue Nationale. ☎02 47 61 07 93; fax 02 47 21 68 90. Open June 16-Sept. 15 daily 9am-12:30pm and 2-6pm; Sept. 16-June 15 W-M 9am-noon and 2-6pm. €3.81, students and seniors €2.29, under 12 free.*)

THE TWIN TOURS OF TOURS. The **Tour de l'Horloge** and the **Tour de Charlemagne**, flanking rue des Halles, are fragments of the 5th-century Basilique St-Martin, a gargantuan Romanesque church that fell to fire in 994 and then collapsed in 1797, a few years after Revolutionary looters removed its iron reinforcements. St-Martin himself, the city's first bishop, was carried here following his death in Candes-St-Martin and now slumbers undisturbed in the **Nouvelle Basilique St-Martin**, a *fin-de-siècle* church in the popular Neo-Byzantine style. (*Rue Descartes. ☎02 47 05 63 87. Open daily 8am-noon and 2-6:45pm. Closed Jan.-Dec. Mass daily 11am.*)

🎵 ENTERTAINMENT AND FESTIVALS

Pl. Plumereau (or just plain **pl. Plum**) is the *place* to be, with cheerful students sipping drinks and chattering at cafés and bars. Three clubs on the square are stacked one above the other. A bust of the Sun King keeps the crowd in line upstairs at **Louis XIV;** even higher is the chill, jazzy **Duke Ellington,** while the basement rocks with the rhythms of the **Phazion** discothèque. (All 3 open daily until 2am; only Louis XIV open June-Aug.) Find more jazz a few blocks off the *place* in **Le Petit Faucheux,** 23 rue des Cerisiers. (☎02 47 38 29 34. Live combos play weekly, call ahead for a schedule. Cover varies, but is generally €14, students €10.) For a little dancing, head to **Juanita Banana,** 13 rue du Change, which keeps the customers coming with its spicy food and salsa music. (Open until midnight, 2am on weekends.) Low-key **Le Café** is on 39 rue Bretonneau. (☎02 47 61 37 83. Open daily noon-2am.)

In late June Tours hosts the **Fêtes Musicales en Touraine,** a 10-day celebration of voices and instruments playing selections from Saint-Saëns to Gershwin. (☎02 47 21 65 08. €12.20-42.70 per night.) The end of September sees the annual **Jazz en Touraine** jazz festival, while the end of October offers the **acteurs-acteurs** festival of film and theater. Call the tourist office for more info. There's theater year-round at the **Théâtre Louis Jouvet,** 12 rue Leonardo da Vinci (☎02 47 64 50 50), and the **Théâtre Municipal,** 34 rue de la Scellerie (☎ 02 47 60 20 00).

📍 DAYTRIP FROM TOURS

CHÂTEAUDUN AND VENDÔME.

Trains and SNCF buses run from Tours through Vendôme (1hr.; 11 per day, 3 on Su; €9.60) to Châteaudun (1¾hr; €13.90, €6.40 from Vendôme). Trains return to Tours 6:40am-7:30pm from both towns. The Vendôme station is on bd. de Tremault (☎02 54 23 50 04); Châteaudun's is at pl. Armand Lhullery (☎02 37 45 00 54).

Northeast of Tours is the small **Loir Valley,** the rocky older brother of the Loire. The hilly countryside, dotted with troglodyte cave dwellings and strained by crisscrossing brooks, makes for easy ambling. The little town of Châteaudun (pop. 15,000) and its Gothic château preside over the valley from a bluff 60m above the river. Joan of Arc's companion Jean Dunois, the Bastard of Orléans, rebuilt the castle in the 1450s, adding Gothic touches to the 12th-century structure. Fifteen pillars in the Ste-Chapelle raise 15 perfectly preserved statues from Dunois's additions. Fifty years later, Dunois's grandson began the Longueville wing, whose flamboyant Gothic facade is lined with nasty looking gargoyles. Beside the château is the 12th-century **Eglise de la Madeleine,** pl. Cap de la Madeleine, perched 20m above the southern edge of the town center. The church was never completed and suffered severe fire damage during WWII. Its sparse white interior is now eerily empty. (Open daily 10am-noon and 2-5pm.) Down the road are the chilling and attractive **Grottes du Foulon,** 35 rue des Fouleries. A one-hour French tour takes you through the caves all the way beneath the center of town, call in advance to arrange English tours. (☎02 37 45 19 60. Open M-Su 2-6pm.) The **tourist office,** 1 rue de Luynes, has brochures with helpful walking tours taking you past some of the towns prettiest houses and oldest alleyways, dating back to the 16th century. (☎02 37 45 22 46; fax 02 37 66 00 16; www.eureetloir-tourism.com. Open M-Sa 9am-noon and 2-6pm.)

Vendôme (pop. 18,000), the village of Balzac's childhood, would be unremarkable (by the Loire's blooming, bubbling standards) were it not for the **Abbaye de la Trinité,** rue de l'Abbaye, built at the site where Geoffrey Martel had a vision of three burning spears piercing the ground. The **Eglise Abbatiale** is everything but a cathedral, lacking only a bishop to claim the title. Its prickly 1506 facade is the definition of High Gothic and inside remains an elaborate shrine to the Holy Tear, empty since its lachrymose contents were appropriated by Rome in the 19th century. The 12th-century belltower has been pealing a pleasant tune ever since the Hundred Years' War. The cloister today holds the **Musée Municipal de Vendôme,** which features a number of mural paintings from Loire churches along with religious and archaeological artifacts. The **tourist office,** Hôtel du Bellay in parc Ronsard, can give you plenty of info about the entire valley. (☎02 54 77 05 07; fax 02 54 73 20 81; www.tourisme.fr. Open M-Sa 10am-12:30pm and 2-6pm.)

CHÂTEAUX NEAR TOURS

Dozens of beautiful, historic châteaux lie within 60km of Tours; *Let's Go* covers the most popular sites, but it is often surprisingly worthwhile to visit one of the equally appealing, lesser-known châteaux. Driving is by far the most convenient, though generally most expensive, way to travel. Highways are well-marked with arrow-shaped signs leading to most châteaux. Biking along the Loire between châteaux is enchanting, although **bus tours** are more efficient. You can travel in air-conditioned luxury on one of the many minibuses which leave Tours every day; expect to shell out €16-40, which normally includes admission fees to the châteaux. **Valleybus** (www.touring-france.com.) offers English-language day excursions. The price includes one or two châteaux and museums, lunch, and transportation. Daytrips vary in price, beginning at €25. For other tour companies, contact **Saint-Eloi Excursions** (☎02 47 37 08 04), **Touraine Evasion** (☎06 07 39 13 31), **Acco-Dispo Excursions** (☎02 47 57 67 13), or **Sillonne Val** (☎02 47 59 13 14). **Service Touristique de la Touraine** (☎02 47 05 46 09) sits right in Tours's train station, but is the most expensive. All tours have English-speaking guides. Most châteaux have free tours (with printed translations or English guides), as well as performances and special events during the summer. *Son-et-lumière* (sound and light shows) are a fun break from daylight visits. Wine cellars often offer free *dégustations.* **Vouvray's** 30 cellars, 9km east of Tours on the N152, specialize in sweet white wine. (☎02 47 52 75 03. Open daily 9am-noon and 2-7pm.) By bus, take #61 from pl. Jean Jaurès to "les Patis" (20min., M-Sa 14 per day, €2.75). In **Montlouis,** across the river to the south, 10 *caves* pour forth wonderful dry whites. You can take the train from Tours (20min., M-Sa 3 per day, €2.29).

CHENONCEAU

*Trains run to Chenonceau from Tours (45min., 8 per day 9am-11pm, €5.50); the station is 2km from the château. Fil Vert **buses** leave for Chenonceau from Amboise (30min., 3 per day, round-trip €6.10) and Tours (25min., 2 per day, €2). **Château:** ☎ 02 47 23 90 07. Open Mar. 15-Sept. 15 daily 9am-7pm. Call for off-season hours. €7.60, students €6.10. July-Aug. son-et-lumière at 10pm. Entry to Château des Dames wax museum €3.05.*

Perhaps the most exquisite château in France, Chenonceau arches gracefully over the Cher river, flanked by shaded woods and gardens. The site of many outrageous parties in the Renaissance, the château owes its beauty to centuries of female designers. Royal tax-collector Thomas Bohier originally commissioned a château on the ruins of a medieval mill on a tiny island in the Cher river. While he fought in the Italian Wars (1513-21), his wife Catherine oversaw its practical design, which features four rooms radiating from a central chamber and straight Italian-style staircases. In 1547, Henri II gave the château to his mistress, Diane de Poitiers, who added symmetrical gardens and constructed an arched bridge over the Cher so she could hunt in the nearby forest. When Henri II died in 1559, his widow Catherine de Medici forced Diane to exchange her beloved castle for Chaumont. Catherine then designed her own set of gardens and the most spectacular wing of the castle, the two-story gallery atop the bridge built by Diane. In the 18th century, Mme. Dupin brought in Jean-Jacques Rousseau to Chenonceau as her son's tutor, the inspiration for his influential work on children's education, *Emile.*

There's wine at **La Cave Cellar,** on the château grounds (open 11am-7pm; free.) Chenonceau's idyllic setting makes it a tempting stopover. Of the few hotels in the area, the pleasant **Hostel du Roy ❹,** 9 rue Bretonneau, is the best deal. (☎ 02 47 23 90 17; fax 02 47 23 89 81. Breakfast €6. Singles and doubles with shower and toilet €38-42. MC/V.) A tiny **campground ❶** is a few blocks left of the entrance to the château. (☎ 02 47 23 90 13. Open Easter-Sept. €2.10 per adult, €1.40 for children under 10; €1.40 per site, €1.80 with car. Showers included. Electricity €2.)

VILLANDRY

*Trains leave from the station in Tours to Savonnières, which is 4km from the château (10 min.; 4 per day noon-7pm; €3). Many **minibus** tour agencies run a circuit to Villandry and Ussé (see section intro on p. 293 for phone numbers). From Tours, **cyclists** should follow the tiny D16, a narrow marvel that winds along the bank of the Cher past Villandry to Ussé; **drivers** should stick to the D7. **Château:** ☎ 02 47 50 02 09. Gardens open July-Aug. daily 9am-7:30pm; Sept.-June daily 9am-7pm. Château open July-Aug. daily 9am-6:30pm; mid-Feb. to June and Sept. to mid-Nov. 9am-6pm. Château and gardens €7, students €5. Gardens only €5, students €3. The **tourist office,** across D7 from the château, has maps and train schedules. (☎ 02 47 50 12 66, Open M-Sa 9:30am-6:30pm, Su 9:30am-12:30pm and 1-6:30pm.) Fifteen km from Tours, Villandry is one of the closest châteaux, but it is still hard to reach via public transportation.*

Villandry lives up to its claim to be *"le plus beau des jardins du jardin de la France"* ("the most beautiful of gardens of the garden that is France"). They certainly are among the largest gardens, with 125,000 flowers and 85,000 vegetables, all weeded by hand! Built on the banks of the Cher by Jean le Breton, minister to François Ier, the château was purchased in 1906 by Dr. Joachim Carvallo, the present owner's great-grandfather. He renovated the decaying structure and reconstructed the surrounding gardens, which had previously been redone in the popular English style. Today, the formal French gardens are Villandry's main attraction and probably the most beautiful in the Loire Valley. Be sure to stroll underneath the romantic covered arbors and lose yourself in the passageways of the recently opened hedgerow maze. The grounds have three levels. The kitchen garden, designed in the style of an Italian monastery, produces just enough to sell a little at the market. The middle level is the most artistic, forming patterns out of hedges and flowers. The peaceful upper level is lined with lime groves, swan pools, waterfalls, and a view of all the grounds. Inside, don't miss the medieval Moorish ceiling tiled with 3000 gold-leafed wooden pieces.

USSÉ

*Ussé is most easily accessed on a château minibus tour. Service Touristique runs buses from the Tours train station to the château for €18 (☎ 02 47 05 46 09). **Château:** ☎ 02 47 95 54 05. Open Apr.-Sept. daily 9am-6:30pm; Oct.-Nov. 15 and Feb. 15-Mar. 1 daily 10am-noon and 2-5:30pm. Tours only. €9, ages 8-16 €2.90.*

Though no king ever laid his head on the fancy four-poster bed of Ussé's **chambre du Roi,** its fairy-tale spires inspired one 17th-century visitor: Charles Perrault, who penned the tale of **Sleeping Beauty** during his stay here in 1697. It's now billed as the *"château de la belle au bois dormant"* ("the château of the beauty sleeping in the woods"), complete with costumed mannequins that illustrate the story's unfolding—watch out for the Beauty's fancy lace underwear. The rest of the 15th- to 16th-century château can be seen during a 50min. English tour. While waiting, explore Le Nôtre's fabulous gardens, the follow-up to his work at Versailles. You can also check out the Gothic chapel, wine **caves,** and stables. A small door leads from the moat to the prison, a single tiny room deep within the walls; graffiti scratched by former prisoners looks suspiciously well-preserved.

AZAY-LE-RIDEAU

***Trains** run from Tours (30min., 3 per day 5:40am-8:15pm, €4.50) to the town of Azay-le-Rideau, a 2km walk from the château. Turn right from the front of the station and head left on the D57. **Buses** run from the Tours train station to the tourist office (45min.; M-Su 3 per day, 6:40am-5:50pm; pay on bus). **Château:** ☎ 02 47 45 42 04. Open July-Aug. daily 9:30am-7pm; Apr.-June and Sept.-Oct. daily 9:30am-6pm; Nov.-Mar. daily 9:30am-12:30pm and 2-5:30pm, last entrance 45min. before closing. €5, ages 18-25 €3.50, under 18 free. Audio commentary available in English €4. Son-et-lumière July daily 10:30pm; Aug 10pm; €9. Joint ticket for night show and daytime visit €12, 18-25 €7, under age 18 €5. The **tourist office,** pl. de L'Europe, 1km from the train station along av. de la Gare, can give you a small map and help with rooms, although few are cheap. (☎ 02 47 45 44 40; fax 02 47 45 31 46. Open Apr.-Oct. M-Sa 9am-1pm and 2-6pm, Su 10am-1pm and 2-7pm; Nov.-Feb. M-Sa 2-6pm.) You can stay at the **Camping Parc de Sabot ❶,** across from the château at a picturesque sight along the banks of the Indre. (☎ 02 47 45 42 72. Open Easter-Oct. €8 per 2 people with tent, €2.50 each additional person, children €1.22. Electricity €2. Showers available.)*

Azay-le-Rideau gazes peacefully at its reflection atop an island in the Indre. Surrounded by acres of breeze-ruffled trees and grass, the existing château was built on the ruins of an earlier fortress. The town acquired the nickname "Azay-le-Brulé" (Azay the Burned) in 1418 after Charles VII razed the village in revenge against a Burgundian guard who had refused to let him in. The corrupt financier Gilles Berthelot bought the land in 1518, and his wife Philippa set about designing a new castle. Though smaller than François Ier's Chambord, the château which rose from the ashes was intended to rival its contemporary in beauty and setting; the Berthelots succeeded so well that François seized the château before its third wing was completed. On the exterior walls, salamanders without crowns mark the castle as a non-royal residence built under François. Azay's flamboyant style is apparent in the furniture and the ornate Italian second-floor staircase, the latter carved with the faces of 10 Valois kings and queens and lit through open, glassless windows. Azay's *son-et-lumière* is perhaps the most highly rated in the Loire. Guests wander around the castle amidst lights and music and dance in the courtyard.

THE LOCAL STORY

IFESTYLES OF THE RICH AND FAMOUS

Most travelers think of châteaux as attractions, sites where anyone who pays the admission fee can spend a few hours marveling at the extravagance of nobles from centuries past. Even today, a château can be much more than a place to visit; it can be a prime piece of real estate. Châteaux, which have long attracted wealthy French families as a symbol of status and power, are now sold on an international market. Agencies specialize in selling châteaux, often aided by websites like www.france-chateau.fr that allow customers across the world to view pictures of châteaux for sale in the French countryside.

Prices for these classy lodgings range from a few hundred thousand euros to a few million, depending on the size of the building, its condition, and its historical importance. Of course, once you've got the château your expenses have just begun. Many of the châteaux are in need of restoration. A Gothic facade may be romantic, but there is nothing attractive about medieval plumbing. And then there's decorating. Furniture from a local store doesn't quite cut it, and many owners comb through antique stores to find paintings, furniture, even silverware. With these expenses, it's no wonder many families decide to open their châteaux to the public.

If all this sounds like too much hassle, you can always opt for a little taste of the life of nobility. Many châteaux now rent rooms for weekend getaways, weddings, and even business conferences.

LOCHES

Trains and *buses* cover the 40km from Tours's train station to Loches (50 min., 13 per day, €7.50) The tourist office is in a pavilion near the station on brasserie-lined pl. de la Marne. (☎ 02 47 91 82 82. Open June-Aug. daily 9:30am-7pm; Sept.-May daily 9:30am-12:30pm and 2-6pm.) **Château:** ☎ 02 47 59 01 32; fax 02 47 59 17 45. Open Apr.-Sept. daily 9am-7pm; Oct.-Mar. 9:30am-12:30pm and 2-5pm. Donjon or Logis Royal €3.80, students €2; both €4.88, students €2.70. Son-et-lumière F-Sa and occasionally once a week in July at 10:30pm and Aug. at 10pm, call for specific dates. €11, ages 6-12 €6.10.*

It was in the state room of Loches that Joan of Arc, on the heels of her victory over the English at Orléans in 1429, told the indifferent Dauphin that she had cleared the way for him to travel to Reims to be crowned king. Surrounded by a walled medieval town whose ramparts and 15th-century church merit a visit in themselves, the château consists of two distinct structures at opposite ends of a hill. To the north, the 11th-century keep and watchtowers switched from keeping enemies out to keeping them in when Louis XI turned them into a state prison. The posh cell of art lover Ludovico Sforza is perfectly preserved, its frescoes slightly peeling around the latrine and heating system. Additional curiosities include a torture chamber, galleries 20m underground, and a replica of the suspension cages used to hold revolutionary prisoners. While the floors in the three-story tower have fallen out, the walls and stairs remain; you can climb the narrow staircase and take in a view of the village below. The **Logis Royal** pays tribute to the famous ladies who held court here. It was in Loches that Agnès Sorel, lover of Charles VII, became the first woman to hold the official title of Mistress of the King of France, and here she was entombed following her early death at age 28. Anne de Bretagne later added a lacy, stone chapel in the logis. The terrace atop the round tower offers a magnificent view of the medieval city.

CHINON

High above Chinon (pop. 9120) looms the crumbling, majestic château where Richard the Lionheart drew his last breath. This quaint little village was one of the most important cities of France. During the Hundred Years War, the future French king Charles VII sought refuge in Chinon. Later, Chinon became part of the estates of the powerful Duke of Richelieu, who dismantled parts of the château to build his own grandiose residence. Chinon is proud of its heritage, and cares for its many historical sights with frequent renovation projects. Chinon makes an ideal daytrip from Tours.

◪ PRACTICAL INFORMATION. Trains and **SNCF buses** run via St-Pierre-des-Corps to Saumur (1½hr., 2 per day, €10.80) and Tours (45min.; 10 per day M-Sa, 5 on Su; €7.17). A train runs from Saumur to Port Boulet (40min., 5 per day, €3) where you can then take a bus to Chinon (15min., 5 per day, €2.40). From the station (☎02 47 93 11 04), walk along quai Jeanne d'Arc, and turn right at Café de la Paix to get to pl. de l'Hôtel de Ville. Then, turn right onto the little road at the back of the square to get to the **tourist office** at pl. d'Hofheim. (☎02 47 93 17 85; fax 02 47 93 93 05. Walking tours July-Aug. Tu-Th and F-Su 3:30pm; mid-July to Aug. additional tour 9:30am. €4.60, students €2.30. Mini-train tour June-Sept. 6 per day 2:30-6:15pm. €4, students €3. Open May-Sept. daily 10am-7pm; Oct.-Apr. M-Sa 10am-noon and 2-6pm.) If you prefer to explore the region on your own wheels, **bike rentals** are available at the Hôtel Agnès Sorel, 4 quai Pasteur, which can be reached by walking to the end of the quai Jeanne d'Arc. (☎02 47 93 04 37. €8 per half-day, €14 per day.)

The best **currency exchange** rates are at **Crédit Agricole,** 2 pl. de l'Hôtel de Ville. (☎02 47 39 88 88. Open Tu-F 8:45am-12:30pm and 2-5:15pm, Sa 9am-12:30pm and 2-4pm.) The **post office** is at 80 quai Jeanne d'Arc. (Open M-F 8am-noon and 1:30-5:45pm, Sa 8am-noon.) **Postal code:** 37500.

▐◖ ACCOMMODATIONS AND FOOD. The **Auberge de Jeunesse (HI) ❶,** rue Descartes, is five minutes from town along quai Jeanne d'Arc, around the corner from the train station, but it is indefinitely closed for renovations with no set date to reopen. The big rooms at **Hôtel des Menestrels ❷,** 102 quai Jeanne d'Arc, are a good value, despite the noisy street. (☎02 47 93 07 20. Breakfast €5. Reservations recommended. Singles and doubles €20, with shower €25; quads €44-47.) The pleasant but crowded two-star **Camping de l'Ile Auger ❶,** across the river at Ile Auger, off N749, provides a stunning view of the château. (☎02 47 93 08 35. Open mid-Mar. to Oct. 15. €1.72 per person, €1.14 per child, €2.20 per tent. Electricity €1.65.) There is a **Shopi** supermarket at 22 pl. de l'Hôtel de Ville (open M-Sa 9am-1pm and 2:30-7pm) and an **open-air market** every Thursday on pl. Jeanne d'Arc. Find the best cheap meals around **rue Voltaire** and **pl. de l'Hôtel de Ville.**

◪ SIGHTS. Chinon's **château** presides in august rubble on a hilltop overlooking the Vienne river. First erected in the 10th century, the château has crumbled not under attack but by neglect. The stone walls nevertheless convey a sense of history and past glory unexpected for their partially crumbled state and capture the imagination even more than some of the fully renovated châteaux in the region. The three-part château has recently-discovered tunnels which originally connected each fortress during sieges. Additional tunnels, just wide enough for a man to crawl through on his stomach, lead to the main well and the town center. Thanks to a belief that anyone who captured the Tour Marie-Javelle would die a horrible death, the 14th-century belltower has withstood the Hundred Years' War, the Wars of Religion, and the French Revolution without a blemish—and its bell has proudly struck every half-hour since 1399. A wonderful **Joan of Arc Museum** occupies the three-story tower, with audio-visual presentations in English and French about Joan's military travels and numerous artistic tributes to the young warrior, as well as a copy of her 14th-century signature. (Open Apr.-Sept. daily 9am-7pm; Oct.-Mar. 9:30am-12:30pm and 2-5:30pm. €4.60, students ages 7-14 €2.45.)

Wine tastings can be had in the less forbidding tunnels of **Maison Plouzeau,** 94 rue St-Maurice, where M. Plouzeau's sons conduct free tours and pour their superb red wines in a *cave* beneath the château. (☎02 47 93 16 34. Open Easter-Aug. Tu-Sa 11am-1pm and 3-7pm.) The **Musée Animé du Vin et de la Tonnellerie,** 12 rue Voltaire, illustrates wine-making from grape-crushing to barrel building; costumed automata in bad wigs lace the 20min. tour with Rabelais quotes, exhorting you to "drink always and never die." Their free *dégustations* of wine and wine jam are sure to lift your spirits. (☎ 02 47 93 25 63. Tours in French and English. Open Apr.-Sept. daily 10:30am-12:30pm and 2-7pm. €4, children €3.20.)

The exhibits of the **Maison de la Rivière,** 12 quai Pasteur, celebrate the role that both the Loire and the Vienne have played in the lives of this region's people. This small museum has a variety of exhibits on subjects ranging from the aquatic life of the rivers to the traditional craft of making boats. Throughout the year, the museum also offers excursions on the Vienne that focus on the river's wildlife. (☎ 02 47 93 21 34. ☎ 02 47 95 93 15 to reserve a boat ride. Open Apr.-June and Sept.-Nov. Tu-F 10-12:30 and 2-5:30pm, Sa and Su 2-5:30pm; July-Aug. Tu-F 10am-12:30pm and 2-6:30pm, Sa and Su 3-6:30pm. €5 per person, under 12 €1.50).

▶ DAYTRIP FROM CHINON

CHAPELLE SAINTE-RADEGONDE
High up on the hill of Chinon, this chapel in a cave is well worth the hike. Way back in the 6th century, the hermit John the Recluse, a Celt who had fled the Anglo-Saxons in Britain, led the life of a hermit in this cave. Legend has it that he was visited there by Queen Radegonde, who had herself fled her husband, and would later become a nun and, after her death, a saint. This ancient chapel contains a remarkably well preserved fragment of an 11th century wall painting which is believed to represent Henry II Plantagenêt. In addition to the chapel, these caves contain a collection of objects from the daily life of the Chinonais, who have donated everything from old butter churners to scythes used to cut grain. *(To get to the Chapelle from the tourist office, follow the rue Diderot to the Collegiale Saint-Mexme, then follow the sings to the chapelle. It's about a 20 min. walk from the vieille ville. Open July-Aug 10am-7pm, schedule subject to change. Call the tourist office for details.)*

SAUMUR

Saumur (pop. 30,000) is known best for its wine, its musty mushroom caves and its equestrian tradition. Saumur is home to the national cavalry school, whose elite *Cadre Noir* (Black Corps) has trained the country's best riders since the 18th century. As a refreshing break from the usual castle-heavy Loire and with an enchanting old quarter, it's not hard to see why Saumur has won a spot on *le pôle touristique*, the official government list of eight places in France you must see. Munch a mushroom and enjoy, as Balzac did, "the essential strangeness of the place."

▐ TRANSPORTATION

Trains: av. David d'Angers, a 10min. walk from the pl. Bilange. To get to station by bus, take bus A from the pl. Bilange (dir: St-Lambert or Chemin Vert). Ticket office open until 9:30pm. SNCF trains and buses run to: **Angers** (30min., 15 per day, €6.56); **Nantes** (1hr., 9 per day, €15.60); **Paris** (1½hr., 1 per day at 7:50pm, €29.20); **Poitiers** (2½hr., 6 per day, €16.30); **Tours** (45min., 21 per day, €8.80).

Buses: Autocars Val de Loire, pl. St-Nicolas (☎ 02 41 40 25 00), runs buses from here or the train station to **Angers** (1½hr., 6 per day, €5.30) and to **Fontrevaud** (25 min., 5 per day, €2.18).

Local Transportation: Bus Saumur, 19 rue F. Roosevelt (☎ 02 41 51 11 87). Office open M 2-6pm, Tu-F 9am-12:15pm and 2-6pm, Sa 9am-noon. Buses run M-Sa 7am-7:30pm. Maps and schedules are available here or at the tourist office; schedules are unreliable in July and Aug. Tickets €1.16.

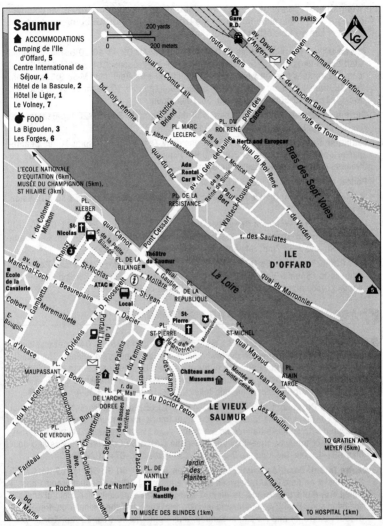

Saumur

ACCOMMODATIONS
Camping de l'Ile d'Offard, **5**
Centre International de Séjour, **4**
Hôtel de la Bascule, **2**
Hôtel le Liger, **1**
Le Volney, **7**

FOOD
La Bigouden, **3**
Les Forges, **6**

Car Rental: Cheapest at **Ada,** 29 av. Général de Gaulle (☎ 02 41 50 46 77). Open M-Sa 8am-noon and 2-6:30pm. **Hertz,** 78/80 av. Général de Gaulle (☎ 02 41 67 20 06), Open M-F 8am-noon and 2-7pm, Sa 8am-noon and 2-5:30pm.

Bike Rental: Camping Municipal, on Ile d'Offard (☎ 02 41 40 30 00; fax 02 41 67 37 81). €7 per half-day, €11 per day, €48 per week. Passport or €152.50 deposit.

ORIENTATION AND PRACTICAL INFORMATION

The tourist office and sights are on the left bank of the Loire, a 10-15min. walk from the train station, which is on the right bank; the hostel sits on an island

LOIRE VALLEY

between the two. Many of the sights are outside of the center of town, so you may want to pick up a bus schedule and map from the tourist office before you set out to discover the diverse attractions of Saumur.

Tourist Office: pl. de la Bilange (☎02 41 40 20 60; fax 02 41 40 20 69). Multilingual staff books beds for €0.75. Free maps and tour suggestions. "14 Sites/14 Privileges" card, guarantees free gift when you visit a pictured site. Open May M-Sa 9:15am-7pm, Su 10:30am-12:30pm; June-Sept. M-Sa 9:15am-7pm, Su 10:30am-5:30pm; Oct.-Apr. M-Sa 9:15am-12:30pm and 2-6pm, Su 10am-noon.

Currency Exchange: Best rate generally at the **Banque de France**, 26 rue Beaurepaire (☎02 41 40 12 00). Open M-F 8:45am-noon.

Laundromat: 12 rue Maréchal Leclerc. Open daily 7am-9:30pm. Also at 16 rue Beaurepaire, open daily 7:30am-9:30pm, until 10pm in the summer. Also at 74 rue du Général de Gaulle; open daily 7am-9pm.

Police: rue Montesquieu (☎02 41 83 73 00).

Medical Assistance: Centre Hospitalier, rue de Fontevraud (☎02 41 53 30 30). **Emergency** ☎ 15.

Internet Access: Welcome Services Copy, 20 rue Portail-Louis (☎02 41 67 75 15). €5.30 for up to 1hr. Open M 2:30-7pm, Tu-F 9am-12:30pm and 2-7pm, Sa 10am-12:30pm and 2:30-7pm; July-Aug closed M.

Post Office: rue Volney (☎02 41 40 22 05). **Currency exchange.** For **Poste Restante,** address to "Saumur Volney 49400." Open M-F 8am-6:30pm, Sa 8am-noon. There is another office across from the train station. **Postal code:** 49400.

🏠 ACCOMMODATIONS AND CAMPING

📖 **Le Volney,** 1 rue Volney (☎02 41 51 25 41; fax 02 41 38 11 04; contact@le-volney.com), on a quiet street in the town center, one block off rue d'Orléans. The friendly proprietor recently renovated each of these rooms with a personal touch, resulting in a fresh, beautiful establishment with a bed-and-breakfast feel. Breakfast €5.50. Singles and doubles with TV, telephone, and toilet €25-27; with shower €35-49. MC/V. ❷

Hôtel de la Bascule, 1 pl. Kléber (☎02 41 50 13 65), near Eglise St-Nicolas on quai Carnot. For those willing to spend a few more francs, these rooms are worth it. Newly renovated with spotless bathrooms. All rooms have TV and showers. Many have excellent views of the river. Breakfast €5. Reception closed Su Oct.-June. Singles and doubles €37-43; one big room for 2-4 people €37. Extra bed €7. MC/V. ❹

Centre International de Séjour, rue de Verdun (☎02 41 40 30 00; fax 02 41 67 37 81). Hostel on Ile d'Offard, between station and tourist office. Adequate rooms host a young crowd of students and travelers. 2-person rooms especially nice. Helpful English-speaking staff. Pool, TV, pinball, and laundry. Breakfast and sheets included. Reception 8:30am-12:30pm and 2-8pm; in summer until 9pm. Closed Dec. 15-Jan. 15. 2- to 8-bed dorms €13.30; 2- to 4-bed dorms with shower €23 for first person, €9.15 for each additional person. Ask at reception for free tickets to Grottien and Meyer *caves.* ❶

Hotel le Liger, 17 av. David d'Angers (☎02 41 67 40 04; fax 02 41 67 40 04), across the street from the train station. This hotel offers bright, if slightly worn, rooms. Singles and doubles with sink and toilet €20, with shower €26, with shower and toilet €33.10; extra bed €7.10. Breakfast €4.50. ❷

Camping de l'Ile d'Offard (☎02 41 40 30 00; fax 02 41 67 37 81), same site as hostel. 4-star site with pool, laundry, tennis, snack shop, minigolf, and TV. Reception 8:30am-12:30pm and 2-8pm. Closed Dec. 15-Jan. 15. June-Aug. €6.50 for one person with car, €4 for each additional person, €2 per child. €3 for electricity. ❶

◘ FOOD

Saumur is renowned for its sparkling **crémant de Loire** wine and its mountains of mushrooms, grown in caves hollowed out along the riverbank. Stock up on fungi at the indoor **market** at the far end of pl. St-Pierre (Su-F until 1pm, Sa until noon), or its outdoor brethren on pl. de la République (Th morning) and pl. St-Pierre (Sa morning). The **ATAC supermarket**, 6 rue Franklin D. Roosevelt, sits inside the shopping center across from the Printemps department store, with a back entrance on rue St-Nicolas. (☎02 41 83 54 54. Open M-F 9am-1pm and 2:15-7:30pm, Sa 9am-12:30pm, Su 9am-12:30pm.) An assortment of cheap restaurants are sprinkled along **rue St-Nicolas.** For creative crepes (€4-10) stuffed with everything from fresh seafood to hamburger to the classic ham and cheese, try **La Biguoden ❶**, 67 rue St-Nicolas. (☎02 41 67 12 59. Open July-Aug. daily noon-2pm; Sept.-June Th-M noon-2pm.). While the town sleeps Sunday away, **pl. St-Pierre** and its offshoots are a great option for light food and drinks. **Les Forges ❸**, 1 pl. St-Pierre, specializes in grilled meats. House specialty *steak tartare* served with a crazy assortment of condiments. The sparkling *saumur rouge* goes for €2.29 per glass. (☎02 41 38 21 79. 3-course *menus* €12.80-22.50. Open M and W-Sa noon-2pm and 7-10pm; winter closed Su. MC/V.)

◎ SIGHTS

The impressive number of museums and festive *caves* will keep you busy all day, but that doesn't mean you can't enjoy the city's quieter gems as well. Already housing three 12th- to 15th-century churches in its main district, Saumur also tucks a very pretty **Jardin des Plantes** between rue Docteur Peton and rue Marceau, on the other side of the château. The picturesque **Pont Cessart** has a fantastic view, and the promenades along the river are nice for sunset strolls.

ECOLE NATIONALE D'EQUITATION. The spectacular Cadre Noir tradition is kept up within this civilian national riding school, whose students compete at an international level and often go on to train equestrians around the country. The palatial 20th-century premises, 15min. from the center of town, boast over 50km of training grounds, 400 fine purebreds, and the world's best veterinarians. Tradition demands unwavering obedience from the horses and irreproachable decorum from the riders, who have, since 1825, donned "black dress decorated with gold, and 'lampion' hats worn ready for battle." Tours discuss facilities and the rigorous demands of equestrianism; morning visits include a half-hour viewing of daily training. *(☎02 41 53 50 60. Take bus B (dir: St. Hilaire) to "Alouette;" continue along the road in the same direction until signs direct you the remaining 3km. Visitors are only allowed to view the grounds on tours, available in French and English. Visits with a peek at equestrian drills Apr.-Sept. Tu-Sa 9:30-11am (last tour at 11). Visits without drills M-F 2:30-4pm (last tour 4pm), Sa morning visits only. €6.50 for adults, €3 for children. The Ecole also offer shows throughout the year, call ahead for schedule and prices.)*

CHÂTEAU. Saumur's 14th-century château is best known for its cameo appearance in the famous medieval manuscript *Les très riches heures du duc de Berry* and lives up to its reputation as "the very image of a fairy tale château." For two centuries, Huguenots studied at the prestigious Protestant academy inside before the château was pillaged, abandoned, and finally converted into a prison by Napoleon. Today, most of the château is dedicated to housing two small museums. The horse-crazy **Musée du Cheval** holds tack from all over the world and traces the evolution of man's second best friend. Guided tours, available in French or English, lead the visitor through the **Musée des Arts Décoratifs,** which has a collection of medieval and Renaissance painting and sculpture, tapestries, and brightly decorated **faïence** (stoneware). The south wing of the château, now closed, is undergoing a major restoration that is expected to be completed in four to five years. (☎ 02 41 40 24 40. Open June-Aug. daily 9:30am-6pm; July and Aug. additional hours W and Sa 8:30-10:30pm; Sept.-May W-M 10am-1pm and 2-5:30pm; Nov.-Mar. closed. English tours (70min.) June-Sept. €6 adults, €4 students; gardens only €2.)

GRATIEN ET MEYER. Saumur's wines have been prized since the 12th century, when Plantagenêt kings took their favorite casks with them to England. The popular Gratien et Meyer offers tastings and tours (€2.29) that describe the wine making process from grape harvest until it hits your tongue. (Rte. de Montsoreau. ☎ 02 41 83 13 32. Take bus D (dir: Dampierres) from pl. Bilange to "Beaulieu." Open Apr.-Nov. daily 9am-noon and 2-6pm, last entry 11am in the morning and 5pm in the afternoon; Nov. 12-Mar. Sa-Su 10am-12:30pm and 3-6pm. In Nov-Mar. groups of 10 or more may also reserve a visit M-F 9am-noon and 2-6pm.)

L'ECOLE DE LA CAVALERIE. Saumur is famous for its equestrian associations, of which this 18th-century mouthful, whose full name is *l'Ecole d'application de l'armée blindée et de la cavalerie*, is the most notable. In 1939, its lightly-armed cadets deemed surrender dishonorable and held back the mighty Wehrmacht for three days. These stables served as the training grounds for Saumur's celebrated equestrian troops until 1984, but now only house their uniforms, weapons, and horse tackle in **Musée de la Cavalerie.** (Pl. Charles de Foucauld. June-Aug. ☎ 02 41 83 92 10, off-season ☎ 02 41 83 93 15. Open May 26-July 22 Tu-Su 10am-noon and 3-6pm. Tours last 1hr., but are by appointment only. €2.29.)

MUSÉE DU CHAMPIGNON. This is what you'd expect—a dark, dank cave full of exotic mushrooms. Tours in English trace the history of the mushroom, with emphasis on its cultivation in France, the world's 3rd largest mushroom producer. The mushroom grill outside serves gourmet *hors d'oeuvres* (€4.57-7.02) from noon to 3pm. (Rte. de Gennes, St-Hilaire-St-Florent. ☎ 02 41 50 70 04. Take bus B (dir: St. Hilaire) to "Pompiers." From there, follow the signs on the 2km (20 min.) walk to the museum. Open Feb.9-Nov. 11 daily 10am-7pm. €6.50, children 5-14 €4.)

MUSÉE DES BLINDES. This museum traces the evolution of warfare in the 20th century with displays of over 150 guns and armored cars from 15 different countries. Keep an eye out for the camouflaged Tiger I, a monstrous German cruiser, and the Leclerc, France's first tank. Once a year, in mid-July, French soldiers drive the unwieldy tanks around like bumper cars. (1043 rte. de Fontevraud. ☎ 02 41 53 06 99. Take bus C (dir: Chemin Vert) to "Fricotelle." Then walk down rue du Tunnel 1km to the museum. Visit lasts 90min. Open May-Sept. daily 9:30am-6:30pm; Oct.-Apr. 10am-5pm. €3.90, children €2.30.)

■ **DAYTRIP FROM SAUMUR**

FONTEVRAUD-L'ABBAYE
The #16 bus makes the 14km trip from the **Saumur** train station. (25min., 3-5 per day, €2.15.) The **tourist office** can give you a free map of the town, which also houses the Gothic **Eglise St-Michel.** (☎ 02 41 51 79 45. Open Easter-Oct. 15 M-Sa-10:30am-12:30pm and 2:30-6:30pm, June Su 10:30am-12:30pm and 2:30-5:30, July-Aug. Su 10:30am-12:30pm and 1:30-5:30pm.) One stop before Fontevraud, in **Montsoreau,** are curious **troglodyte cliff dwellings.** Call the tourist office in Montsoreau (☎ 02 41 51 70 22) for info.

The **Abbaye de Fontevraud,** the largest monastic complex in Europe, has awed nine centuries of visitors. The founder of this now-defunct community, Robert d'Arbrissel, settled in the forest of Fontevraud in 1101. To increase the humility of his monks, he placed a woman at the head of the order. Of its 32 abbesses, 16 were of royal blood; under their rule the abbey became a place of refuge for women of all classes—from reforming prostitutes to princesses escaping unhappy marriages. Following the Revolution the abbey became a prison, and so it remained from 1804 until 1963. The 12th-century abbey church serves as a Plantagenêt necropolis; **Eleanor of Aquitaine,** who lived out her days here after being repudiated by her second husband, **Henry II,** now lies next to him along with their son **Richard the Lionheart.** The British government has repeatedly sought to transfer the royal remains to Westminster, but the French insist that the Plantagenêts were dukes of Anjou first, kings of England second. The walls of the abbey's **chapter house** are painted with scenes that depict Christ's last hours. The most notable decoration is the carving of God holding the world in his hands that sits above one of the carved archways in the Abbey. Throughout the centuries, part of the timeline has been obstructed by intruding nuns—seven abbesses have had themselves added to the wall paintings. Outside, the gardens are organized into patches of legumes, tubers, greens, and medicinals; they bloom behind the abbey kitchen, whose spire-like chimney led 19th-century restorers to take it for a chapel. Be sure not to miss the 12th-century kitchens and the ceiling models's fascinating architecture of a square superimposed inside an octagon, that culminates in a circle at the top. An English booklet and signs help visitors along; don't bother waiting for one of the hour-long English tours. The themed visits put a different spin on life in the abbey and are worth the extra price, but are only available in French. (☎02 41 51 71 41. Abbey open June-3rd Su of Sept. daily 9am-6:30pm; 3rd Su of Sept-May 9:30am-12:30pm and 2-5pm. Tours last 1 hr.; theme tours €1.50.)

🎭 ENTERTAINMENT AND FESTIVALS

The **Théâtre de Saumur** (☎02 41 83 30 85), next to the tourist office, hosts everything from *galas de danse* to jazz and classical concerts in its 19th-century hall. Dance the night away at **Le Blues Rock Magazine,** 7 rue de la Petite Bilange. (☎02 41 50 41 69. Drinks €3-6. Open May-Sept. daily; Oct.-Apr. Tu-Su 11pm-4am. MC/V.) For a few games of pool, head to **Le Général,** 67 av. de Général de Gaulle. (☎02 41 67 31 77. €1 per game, €2 per beer. Open M-Sa 6:30am-11pm.) Late-night lingerers loiter in pl. St-Pierre beside the illuminated cathedral, while livelier crowds and louder music beat around the Irish **pubs** in pl. de la République.

In the first week of July, the three-day **Estivales de Saumur** bring a fun, festive atmosphere to rue St-Nicolas with vendors, outdoor dining, music, and free food. The **International Festival of Military Music** bugles in late June every other year, with the next one occurring in 2003. Alternating years, during the same time slot, there's the **Festival des Géants,** a march of over-sized puppets that pays tribute to Saumur's eternal fascination with carnivals. In late July, the cavalry school and the local tank school join forces in the celebrated **Carrousel.** After two hours of graceful equestrian performances, the spectacle degenerates (or evolves) into a three-hour motorcycle show and dusty tank parade. (Info and reservations ☎02 41 40 20 66. Tickets €18.30.) Saumur annually hosts dozens of (often free) equestrian events. The tourist office has the information.

ANGERS

From behind the imposing walls of their fortress in Angers (pop. 160,000), the medieval dukes of Anjou ruled over the surrounding territory as well as a smallish island across the Channel called Britain. Angers's 13th-century château and cathedral remain well preserved, as does its world-famous apocalyptic tapestry. Today, Jean Lurçat's vibrant 20th-century tapestry, "The Song of the World," reflects the lively atmosphere of modern Angers. Filled with an energetic and youthful population, the town bustles with shops, museums, gardens, and good restaurants.

⌐ TRANSPORTATION

Trains: rue de la Gare. Ticket office open daily 5:45am-9:30pm. To: **Le Mans** (30min., 6-7 per day, €12.30); **Nantes** (1hr., 15 per day, €11.40); **Orléans** (3-4hr., 6 per day, €23.10) change at St-Pierre des Corps; **Paris** (2-4hr., 3 per day); **Poitiers** (2-2½hr., 4-5 per day, €23.20) change at St-Pierre or Tours; **Tours** (1hr., 7 per day, €13.12).

Buses: pl. de la République (☎02 41 88 59 25). To **Rennes** (3hr., 2 per day, €14.80). Open M-Sa 6:15am-7:15pm.

Public Transportation: COTRA buses (☎02 41 33 64 64). Buses leave from pl. Kennedy or pl. Ralliement 6am-8pm. Limited night service 8pm-midnight. Tickets €1.

Taxis: Angers Taxi-Anjou Taxi (☎02 41 87 65 00). **Accueil Taxi Radio-Angers Taxi** (☎02 41 73 98 20). Open daily 5am-11pm; call ahead after-hours.

Car Rental: Several agencies are near the train station: **Hertz,** 18 rue Denis Papin (☎01 39 38 38 38; open M-F 8am-noon and 2-7pm, Sa 8am-noon and 2-6pm) and **Europcar,** 4 rue Paul Bert (☎02 41 24 05 89). Open M 7:30am-noon and 2-6:30pm, Tu-F 8am-noon and 2-6:30pm.

Bike Rental: Available at the **tourist office.** €8 per day, €6.50 for students.

✳ ? ORIENTATION AND PRACTICAL INFORMATION

The heart of the cities lies in the *vieille ville*, around the Cathédrale St-Maurice and pl. du Ralliement. Most of the restaurants and nightlife are concentrated in these pedestrian-only streets, though more hotels are around the train station. To reach the château and tourist office, leave the train station and walk straight onto rue de la Gare. Turn right at the roundabout one block from the train station, at pl. de la Visitation, onto rue Talot. At the traffic light, a left onto bd. du Roi-René will take you to the château at pl. du Président Kennedy. The tourist office is on the right across from the château.

Tourist Office: pl. Kennedy (☎02 41 23 50 00; fax 02 41 23 50 09; accueil@angers-tourisme.com). Staff organizes trips to châteaux, reserves rooms, sells tickets to local events, hands out free maps, and **exchanges currency.** Open June-Sept. M-Sa 9am-7pm, Su 10am-6pm; Oct.-Apr. M 2-6pm, Tu-Sa 9am-6pm, Su 10am-1pm; May M-Sa 9am-6pm, Su 10am-6pm. Offers **walking tours** in English that explore the city's history. (☎02 21 23 50 10. M-Sa 11:30am. €4, €3 students.)

Money: Banque de France, 13 pl. Mendès-France (☎02 41 24 25 00), has good rates of **currency exchange.** Exchange desk open M-F 9am-noon.

Youth Services: Centre d'Information Jeunes, 5 allée du Haras (☎02 41 87 74 47). Job and student info and discount services. Open M-F 1-3:30pm, Sa 10am-noon.

Laundromat: Laverie du Cygne, pl. de la Visitation (☎02 41 86 11 20). **Laverie des Justices,** 10 pl. Justices (☎02 41 47 24 22). Both open daily 8am-noon and 2-8pm.

Police: Gendarmerie, 33 rue Nid de Pie (☎02 41 73 56 10).

Hospital: Centre Hospitalier, 4 rue Larrey (☎02 41 35 36 37).

Internet Access: Cyber Espace, 25 rue de la Roë (☎02 41 24 92 71). €2.30 per 30min., €3.80 per hr. Open M-Th 10am-10pm, F-Sa 10am-midnight.

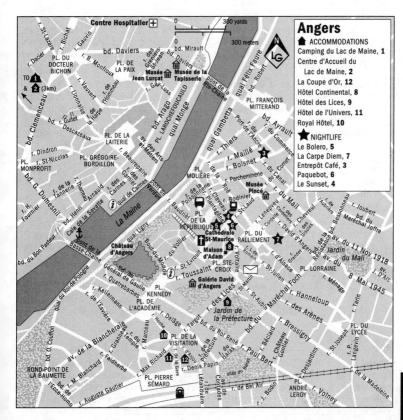

Angers

🏠 ACCOMMODATIONS
Camping du Lac de Maine, 1
Centre d'Accueil du
Lac de Maine, 2
La Coupe d'Or, 12
Hôtel Continental, 8
Hôtel des Lices, 9
Hôtel de l'Univers, 11
Royal Hôtel, 10

⭐ NIGHTLIFE
Le Bolero, 5
La Carpe Diem, 7
Entrepôt Café, 3
Paquebot, 6
Le Sunset, 4

LOIRE VALLEY

Post Office: 1 rue Franklin Roosevelt (☎02 41 20 81 81), just off Corneille near rue Voltaire. **Currency exchange.** Open M-F 8am-7pm, Sa 8:30am-12:30pm. **Postal code:** 49100. **Poste Restante:** "Angers-Ralliement 49052."

🏠 ACCOMMODATIONS AND CAMPING

▨ **Hôtel Continental,** 12 rue Louis de Roman (☎02 41 86 94 94; fax 02 41 86 96 60; le.continental@wanadoo.fr). This hotel, located near the center of Angers, earns its two stars with charming, cutely decorated rooms. Breakfast €6. Singles and doubles with toilet and shower or bath €35-38; €8 for an extra bed. ❸

Hôtel de l'Univers, 2, pl. de la Gare (☎02 41 88 43 59; fax 02 41 86 97 28). The couple who runs this hotel are eager to help their guests plan their stay in Angers. 45 large but plain rooms, decorated in white. Singles and doubles with toilet €24, with shower €31-33, with shower and toilet €43-52. ❷

Centre d'Accueil du Lac de Maine (HI), 49 av. du Lac de Maine (☎02 41 22 32 10; fax 02 41 22 32 11; infos@lacdemaine.fr). Take bus #6 or 16 to "Accueil Lac de Maine," turn around, cross the busy road, and follow signs on the right-hand side to the

Centre d'Accueil. A lakeside setting, extensive sporting facilities, and a mini-golf course justify the 10-15min. ride. Breakfast €3.35, meals €6.85. Call ahead to make sure there's space; school groups often book the Centre in summer. Individuals may not reserve a room more than 3 weeks in advance. Singles and doubles with shower €23.90. **Members only. ❷**

Royal Hôtel, 8bis pl. de la Visitation (☎02 41 88 30 25; fax 02 41 81 05 75). Walk straight down rue de la Gare for one block and the hotel will be ahead on the corner of rue d'Iena. 40 spacious, high-ceilinged rooms with big windows and TVs. Good enough for the budget traveler, though probably not for a king. Breakfast €4.60. Reception M-F 6:45am-midnight, Sa 6am-noon and 2pm-midnight, Su noon-6pm. Singles and doubles with sink €24-26, with shower and toilet €35-41; quad €55. AmEx/MC/V. ❷

Hôtel des Lices, 25 rue des Lices (☎02 41 87 44 10), near the château and center of town. 13 bare but clean rooms above a pleasant bistro in a great location. Don't worry about the name—it refers to jousting, which is what you'll have to do to get a room in summer. Breakfast €4.30. Reception M-F 7am-9pm, Sa-Su 4:30-9pm. Singles and doubles €21, with bath €25-35; triples €39. ❷

La Coupe d'Or, 5 rue de la Gare (☎02 41 88 45 02; fax 02 41 78 31 59), 200m from the train station. Charming owner maintains 18 small, comfortable, but plain rooms with TVs at the top of a narrow winding staircase. Breakfast €4.60. Showers €2.30. Singles and doubles €24-26, with shower and toilet €31; extra bed €8. MC/V. ❷

Camping du Lac de Maine, av. du Lac de Maine (☎02 41 73 05 03; fax 02 41 73 02 20), near the Centre d'Accueil on CD 111, rte. des Pruniers. Take bus #6 to "Camping du Lac de Maine." 4-star campsite on a sandy lakeside. Open Mar. 25-Oct. 10. July-Aug. 2 people, tent, and car €13; off-season €9.60. Electricity €2.90. ❶

🍴 FOOD

Angers caters to its largely student population with cheap, unexceptional food, from crepes to pizza to Chinese, especially on **rue St-Laud** and **rue St-Aubin.** A **covered market** sells inexpensive produce and baked goods in the basement of **Les Halles,** on rue Plantagenêt behind the cathedral, down the street from pl. du Ralliement. (Open Tu-Sa 7am-8pm, Su 7am-1:30pm.) You'll find a grocery store in the basement of **Galeries Lafayette** at the corner of rue d'Alsace and pl. du Ralliement. (Open M-Sa 9:30am-7:30pm.)

🔆 SIGHTS

A €4.50 **ticket** gives admission to 5 museums; the €8 **billet jumelé** also includes château. Both are sold at the tourist office and at museums. Angers is famous for its cherished tapestries, which are hung in many of the city's main sights. The town is situated near several beautiful parks, including the little **Jardin du Mail** to the expansive **Parc du Lac du Maine.**

CHÂTEAU D'ANGERS. St-Louis built this defensive masterpiece from 1228 to 1238 as the symbol of his power. Bristling with 17 towers and protected by a 900m-long, 15m-high wall, it does its job well. The Renaissance Duke René added an inner courtyard in the 15th century as a shelter for inhabitants of the city and a space for courtly artists and market-sellers. During the Wars of Religion, Henry III ordered the château's demolition; fortunately, his subjects only managed to lower the towers by one story. In the 19th century, the château was converted to a prison, undoubtedly a great crime deterrent. Today, its only inmates are beautiful tapestries. The most notable is the **Tapisserie de l'Apoca-**

lypse, the largest of its kind in the world. Commissioned by Duke Louis I, it was inspired by an illuminated manuscript of the Book of Revelation. The six segments of the tapestry mirror the life of St-John in his battle against evil, subtly weaving in references to the war between France (represented by John himself) and Britain, the evil aggressor. Brace yourself for the tapestry's monsters and beasts, including a seven-headed Satan gobbling down babies. *(2 promenade du Bout du Monde, pl. Kennedy. ☎ 02 41 86 81 94. Open May-Sept. 15 daily 9:30am-7pm; Sept. 16-Apr. daily 10am-5:30pm. French tours leave from the chapel 5 times daily, English tours 1-3 times daily. €5.50, students €3.50, under 17 free.)*

GALÉRIE DAVID D'ANGERS. A beautifully restored and glass-topped 13th-century Toussaint Abbey showcases the 19th-century sculptor's work. His animated and lifelike human sculptures include literary characters and famous historical figures. Among the impressive pieces are a scale replica of David's masterwork for the Panthéon in Paris, as well as many of the 30 statues he designed for city squares. *(37bis rue Toussaint. ☎ 02 41 87 21 03. Open mid-June to mid-Sept. daily 9:30am-6:30pm; late Sept.-early June Tu-Su 10am-noon and 2-6pm. €2, under age 16 €1.)*

MUSÉE JEAN LURÇAT. You'll find Angers's second woven masterpiece in this former 12th-century hospice. The 80m long **Chant du Monde** (*Song of the World*), is a symbolic journey through human destiny, representing life's joys and sorrows in 10 enormous panels filled with blazing colors and morbid skulls. Lurçat, inspired by the Apocalypse tapestry, abandoned his career as a painter and turned to weaving, completing this surprisingly modern work in the 1930s. Next to the Chant du Monde is a permanent collection of textile and tapestry, called the **Musée de la Tapisserie Contemporaire,** including pieces by the renowned cloth sculptor Magdalena Abakanowicz. *(4 bd. Arago. ☎ 02 41 24 18 45 for the Musée Jean Lurçat. Open mid-June to mid-Sept. daily 9:30am-6:30pm; late Sept.-early June Tu-Su 10am-noon and 2-6pm. €3.50 for each museum, under 18 free.)*

CATHÉDRALE ST-MAURICE. The 12th-century building is a hodgepodge of historical periods, with a Norman porch, a 13th-century chancel intersecting a 4th-century Gallo-Roman wall, and some of the oldest stained-glass windows in France, dating back to the 12th and 15th centuries. Like everything in Angers, the church is decorated with a rotating exhibit of beautiful tapestries. Linger long enough, and you might get a free tour in English from the lovely local nuns. *(Pl. Monseigneur Chappoulie. ☎ 02 41 87 58 45. Open July-Aug. daily 8:30am-7pm; Sept.-June 8:30am-5:30pm.)*

OTHER SIGHTS. The **Musée Pincé,** housed in a 15th century building, displays an eclectic collection of ancient art from Japan, China, Egypt, and the Roman Empire, from little jade snuff boxes to miniature statues of horses. Though tiny, these works are impressively crafted. *(32bis rue Lenepveu. ☎ 02 41 88 94 27. Open mid-June to Sept. Tu-Su 9:30am-6:30pm; Oct.-early June Tu-Sa 10am-noon and 2-6pm. €2 adults, under 18 free.)* The colorful **Musée d'Histoire Naturelle** displays fun, educational exhibits on the entire animal kingdom for kids and adults who just can't get enough of stuffed animals. Due to its extensive bird collection, the museum is sometimes called the "musée des oiseaux." *(43 rue Jules Guitton. ☎ 02 41 86 05 84; www.ville-angers.fr/museum. Open Tu-Su 2-6pm.)* The heart of the *vieille ville* and a few blocks from the château, pl. du Ralliement is home to numerous stores and cafes and a magnificent **theater,** rebuilt in the 19th century and decorated by local painter Lenepveu. The *vieille ville* gains its name from the ancient, low-roofed, 16th century stone houses here, including the oldest house in Angers, **La Maison d'Adam,** a beautiful timber-framed house just behind the cathedral on pl. Ste-Croix.

LOIRE VALLEY

⟦⟧⟦⟧ ENTERTAINMENT AND FESTIVALS

Although the discos are out in the suburbs, nightlife in Angers can be lively. The cafes along **rue St-Laud** are always packed, and a few bars on student-dominated **rue Bressigny** start getting down before the sun does. Shoot a game and taste the local beer in the laid-back atmosphere of the spacious and bright **Paquebot**, 45 rue St-Laud. (☎02 41 81 06 20. Open daily 11am-2pm.) Just across the street, **Le Sunset**, 44 rue Saint-Laud, is dimmer but no less popular, on account of Le Sun, its smooth tropical punch. (☎02 41 87 85 58. Open daily noon-2am.) **Le Carpe Diem**, 15 rue St-Maurille, schedules philosophical discussions but also encourages patrons to live by its motto. (Bar ☎02 41 87 50 47, schedule of events 02 41 87 50 47. Open M-Sa noon-1am.) Music of all sorts echoes through Angers's cobblestone streets, some from the blues band at **Entrepôt Cafe**, 23 rue Boisnet (☎ 02 41 25 08 21; open daily until 2am) and some from the salsa at **Le Bolero**, 38 rue St-Laud (☎02 41 88 61 19).

In late June and early July, Angers hosts the **Festival d'Anjou.** One of the largest summer theater festivals in France, it attracts renowned French comedy and dramatic troupes to the château; Albert Camus once staged a play here in front of a nationwide TV audience. (Info at 1 rue des Arènes. ☎02 41 88 14 14; www.festivaldanjou.com. €28 per show, students €12.)

LE MANS

From its large, modern apartment buildings to 12th century churches, from ancient Roman walls to the circuit of its world famous 24hr. car race, Le Mans (pop. 150,000) is a city of contrasts. Le Mans may not be the most beautiful city of the Loire Valley, but it is unique. The city boasts possibly the most beautiful *vieille ville* in France, and is worth a night for its unique sights and zippy nightlife.

⟦⟧ TRANSPORTATION

Trains: bd. de la Gare, off pl. du 8 Mai 1945 (☎08 36 35 35 35). Info open M-F 5am-10:30pm, Sa 6am-10:30pm, Su 5am-11pm. To: **Nantes** (1hr., 7 per day, €21.90); **Paris** (1-3hr., 12 per day, €22.30); **Rennes** (1hr., 7 per day, €19.90); **Tours** (1hr., 6 per day, €12.20).

Buses: SNCF (☎02 43 25 30 12) sends buses to **Saumur** (1½hr.; 3 per day M-Sa, 1 on Su at 9pm) from the station.

Public Transportation: SETRAM buses, 65 av. Général de Gaulle (☎02 43 24 76 76), run 5:30am-8 or 9pm (depending on the bus line), after which the city's four **Hi'bus** lines take over until 2am. Pick up a bus map at the SETRAM office or tourist office if you're planning on moving and shaking. The city is fairly big, and well covered by public transportation. Ticket €0.95, *carnet* of 10 €7.47. Info office open M-F 7am-7pm, Sa 8:30am-6:30pm.

Taxis: Radio Taxi (☎02 43 24 92 92). 24hr.

Bike Rental: Top Team, 9 pl. St-Pierre (☎02 43 24 88 32). From €15.25 per day. €305 and ID deposit. Open Tu-Sa 9:30am-noon and 2-7pm. MC/V.

⟦⟧⟦⟧ ORIENTATION AND PRACTICAL INFORMATION

Place de la République is the center of modern Le Mans. The sights and restaurants of the *cité médiévale* are propped up by Roman walls on the bank of the Sarthe. The tourist office is a 15min. walk from the train station, or head up rue Gastelier across from the post office and take bus #5 (dir: Villaret) to "Etoile." Cross pl. Lecouteux and head down rue de l'Etoile; the office is two blocks down to the left.

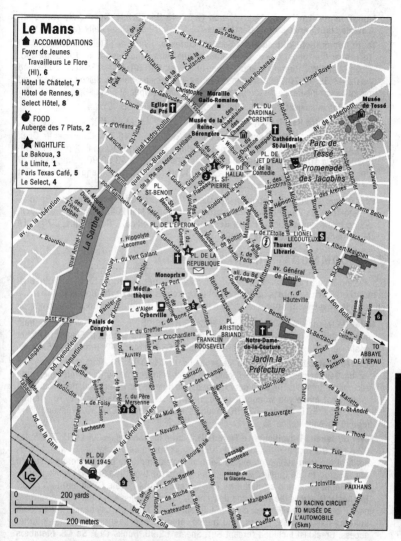

Le Mans

⌂ ACCOMMODATIONS
Foyer de Jeunes
 Travailleurs Le Flore
 (HI), 6
Hôtel le Châtelet, 7
Hôtel de Rennes, 9
Select Hôtel, 8

🍴 FOOD
Auberge des 7 Plats, 2

★ NIGHTLIFE
Le Bakoua, 3
La Limite, 1
Paris Texas Café, 5
Le Select, 4

Tourist Office: rue de l'Etoile (☎02 43 28 17 22; fax 02 43 28 12 14), in the 17th-century Hôtel des Ursulines. The staff distributes maps and info booklets. Historical **walking tours** in French depart from the cathedral fountain (1½-2hr.; July-Aug. M-F 3pm; €5.50, students €3). Open June-Aug. M-F 9am-6pm, Sa 10am-noon and 2-6pm, Su 10am-noon; Sept.-May M-Sa 9am-6pm, Su 10am-noon.

Money: Best currency exchange rates are at **Banque de France,** 2 pl. Lionel Lecouteux (☎02 43 74 74 00). Exchange desks open M-F 8:45am-noon.

English Bookstore: Thuard Librairie, 24 rue de l'Etoile (☎02 43 82 22 22), has best-sellers and some classics in English. Open M-Sa 8:30am-7:30pm. MC/V.

Laundromats: Lav'Ideal, 4 pl. l'Eperon (☎02 43 24 53 99). Open daily 7am-9pm. **Laverie Libre Service,** 4 rue Gastelier (☎02 43 43 99 18) Open daily 7am-9pm.

Youth Information: Ville du Mans Service Jeunesse, 13 rue de l'Etoile (☎02 43 83 00 09), near the tourist office. Offers student discounts and has job and housing info. Open M and W-F 9am-noon and 1-5pm, Tu 1-5pm. **SMEBA,** 34 av. François Mitterrand (☎02 43 39 90 20), is a student travel agency which arranges discount tickets and offers health insurance for foreign students in France. Open M-F 9am-6pm.

Police: Commissariat Central, 6 rue Coeffort (☎02 43 61 68 00).

Hospital: Centre Hospitalier, 194 av. Rubillard (☎02 43 43 43 43).

Internet Access: Médiathèque, 54 rue du Port (☎02 43 47 48 74). €3.20 per hr. Open July-Aug. Sa 10am-noon and 2-5pm; Sept.-June Tu-W and F 10am-6:30pm, Th 1:30-6:30pm, Sa 10am-5pm. **Cyberville,** 8 rue d'Alger (☎02 43 43 90 90), charges €0.20 per min. Open M-F 10am-noon and 1:30-6:30pm, Sa 10am-noon and 1:30-6pm. Get free Internet access at the **hostel** (see below).

Post Office: 13 pl. de la République (☎02 43 21 75 00). **Currency exchange.** Open M-F 9am-7pm, Sa 8am-noon. **Branch office,** 1 pl. du 8 Mai 1945, right by the station. Same hours and services. **Poste Restante** (at main office): "République, 72013 Le Mans Cedex 2." **Postal code:** 72000.

ACCOMMODATIONS AND CAMPING

It's a good idea to call ahead in Le Mans, as spontaneous renovations and closings seem to be favorite sports of local hotel proprietors. Most of the hotels in town are either within a five minute walk of the train station or on the outskirts of town.

Hôtel De Rennes, 43 bd. de la Gare (☎02 43 87 02 95), is right across from the train station, and offers modern, newly renovated rooms in good condition. Singles (no toilet or shower) €34; Doubles with shower and toilet €38; triples €42. Breakfast €5.40. ❸

Hôtel le Châtelet, 15 rue du Père Mersenne (☎02 43 43 92 36). From station, head up av. du Gén. Leclerc and turn left onto rue de la Pélouse; rue du Père Mersenne is the second on the right. The worn-out exterior of this hotel hides 9 beautiful, newly-carpeted rooms that make you wonder if the owners realize what a bargain they're offering. Breakfast €3.81. Singles €22.90; doubles €30.50; triples €44.30. Weekend stays require advance notice. ❷

Foyer de Jeunes Travailleurs Le Flore (HI), 23 rue Maupertius (☎02 43 81 27 55; fax 02 43 81 06 10; florefjt@noos.fr). A 20min. walk from the train station. Or walk 1 block north of the train station on av. du Général Leclerc and take bus #5 from the station (dir: Villaret) to "de Gaulle," walk down a block to the bright red SETRAM kiosk near pl. de la République, and catch the #4 (dir: Gazonfier) or #12 (dir: Californie) to "Erpell." The hostel is across the street and down rue Maupertius. Blissfully clean and quiet *foyer* near the Jardins des Plantes, close to the tourist office and the city center. The modern building has doubles, triples, and quads, plus kitchen, laundry, and free Internet access. Breakfast included (except Su). Sheets €2.90. Bunks €11, Sa €8. **Members only.** Wheelchair accessible. ❶

Select Hôtel, 13 rue du Père Mersenne (☎02 43 24 17 74), just up the street from le Châtelet. 15 rooms in fairly good condition off darkly wallpapered halls. Breakfast €4. Shower €2. Singles and doubles with sink €21, with sink and micro-shower €26; triples €44. MC/V. ❷

Campsites: The tourist office has a list of campsites in the Sarthe region. The closest is the two-star **Camping Le Vieux Moulin,** 9km away in Neuville-sur-Sarthe (☎02 43 25 31 82; fax 02 43 25 38 11). Take the train from Le Mans (8min., 4 per day, €2.44). The riverside site has bikes (€6.10 per day), laundry, a pool, and tennis courts. Open June-Sept. 2 people €10.67, €3.05 per extra person. Electricity €3.05. MC/V. ❶

▶ FOOD

Renowned for its poultry, regional cuisine commonly includes dishes of **pintade** (guinea fowl) and **canard** (duck). The succulent **marmite sarthoise,** a warm casserole of rabbit, chicken, ham, carrots, cabbage, and mushrooms, bubbling in a bath of Jasnière wine, is an omnivore's dream. The best **menus** are in the *brasseries* that line **pl. de la République,** a favorite area for midday meals and late-evening lounging. Pleasant, affordable restaurants settle along Grande Rue and behind pl. de l'Eperon in the *vieille ville*. The **indoor market** sells portable goodies in Les Halles, pl. du Marché, while an **outdoor market** waits in pl. des Jacobins. (Open W and Su 7am-12:30pm.) There is a **Monoprix** supermarket at 30 pl. de la République. (Open M-Sa 9am-8pm.) The eponymous seven *plats* of **Auberge des 7 Plats ❸,** 79 Grande Rue, lend themselves to diverse combinations in the €14 *à la carte menu*. (*Formule* €11. Open Tu-Sa noon-1:30pm and 7-10:30pm. MC/V.)

◉ SIGHTS

*The combined **billet couple** includes visit to two of the following: Musée de Tessé, Musée Vert, or Musée de la Reine-Bérengère. €5.20, students €2.60.*

Roman walls, medieval streets, a Gothic cathedral, and a 20th-century race-car museum make Le Mans a city to savor. Le Mans also holds a remarkable set of beautiful **churches,** sprinkled throughout the city, including the **Maison-Dieu** founded by Henry Plantagenêt. The tourist office brochure *"Les Plantagenêts"* maps out all the churches, accompanied by detailed descriptions.

THE VIEILLE VILLE. Rising up behind thick Roman walls and the river Sarthe, Le Mans's *vieille ville* is considered to be one of the most picturesque in France, though the city becomes a bit of an eyesore outside the central downtown area. The winding streets and alleys, in which **Cyrano de Bergerac** was filmed, are lined with 15th- to 17th-century houses. Before you set out strolling, stop at the tourist office for the English-language brochure *Le Mans: An Art and History Town*, which will allow you to identify the houses as they go by. If your French is up to it, join the **tour** that meets at the cathedral fountain. *(2hr.; daily 3pm; €5.50, students €3.)* The petite **Musée de la Reine-Bérengère,** 9 rue Reine-Bérengère, inside a 1460 residence in the *vieille ville*, displays art and artifacts from Le Mans's past, and often has a good temporary exhibition, too. *(Open May-Sept. daily 10:30am-12:30pm and 2-6pm, Oct.-Apr. T-Su 2-6pm. €2.80, students and children €1.40.)*

CATHÉDRALE ST-JULIEN. One of France's most famous cathedrals, this great fireball of Romanesque and Gothic architecture was originally constructed in the 11th and 12th centuries. The sculpted front of the south porch, dating from this time, is considered one of Europe's finest. After a fire destroyed the town in 1134, the cathedral was repaired using Gothic techniques, hence the pointed arch reinforcements you can see on either side in the nave. The great chancel with twelve chapels was added in the 13th century, doubling the size of the cathedral and necessitating the tangle of flying buttresses which encircle the exterior. The chapel still retains its original 14th-century paint job, including dark violet walls and a blood-red ceiling upon which angels float in painted plasma. *(Pl. des Jacobins. Open daily 9am-noon and 2-6pm.)*

MURAILLE GALLO-ROMAINE. The stocky 4th-century Roman walls which hug the city's southwestern edge are Le Mans's pride and joy, and rightly so. Punctured with arched gates and fortified with massive towers, the 1.3km-long *muraille* is the longest and perhaps best preserved in all of France. Pink mortar gives the entire structure an earthy orange glow.

RACING CIRCUIT AND MUSÉE DE L'AUTOMOBILE. Those who are really into cars can gawk at the 13.5km stretch of racetrack that lies south of the city. Since 1923, the circuit has hosted the annual **24 Heures du Mans,** a gruelling feat of either endurance or misused patience. During the race, drivers receive special massage treatments to help them stay awake. The race is held in the second week of June, but other events take place during the summer. *(Tickets ☎ 02 43 40 24 75 or ☎ 02 43 40 24 77. €2 to enter and walk around track.)* Just outside the track's main entrance is the massive **Musée de l'Automobile,** which traces the evolution of motor vehicles all the way up to the present, including scores of shiny racing cars and cycles of premium vintage. Check out the slick Ford GT40, the only one of its kind. *(From bd. Levasseur off pl. de la République, take bus #6 to "Raineries," the end of the line. (25min.) Continue on foot down rue de Laigne, following signs to the track and museum. (12min.) (☎ 02 43 72 72 24. Open June-Sept. daily 10am-7pm; Oct.-Dec. and Feb.-May 10am-6pm; Jan. Sa-Su 10am-6pm. €6, students and ages 12-18 €5.)*

MUSÉE AND PARC DE TESSÉ. Housed in the former 19th-century bishops's palace, this fabulous collection celebrates over 600 years of art. The modern interior displays 17th- to 19th-century painting and sculpture, temporary exhibits of modern art, and recreations of Egyptian tombs. Check out the mummy lying next to its full-body X-ray. The highlight is a 12th-century enamel portrait of Geoffrey Plantagenêt that originally decorated his tomb in the Cathédrale St-Julien. When you've seen the collection, bask in the sun in the beautiful **Parc de Tessé,** with a fountain, a waterfall, shady trees, and acres of grass. *(2 av. de Paderborn, a 15min. walk from pl. de la République. Take bus #3 (dir: Bellevue) from rue Gastelier by the station or from av. du Gén. de Gaulle, a block down from pl. de la République, to "Musée." Bus #9 (dir: Villaret) also goes there from av. du Gén. de Gaulle. ☎ 02 43 47 38 51. Open July-Aug. Tu-S 10:30am-12:30pm and 2-6:30pm; Sept.-June Tu-Sa 9am-noon and 2-6pm, Su 10am-noon and 2-6pm. €4, students up to 18 €2, half-price Su.)*

📙 ENTERTAINMENT AND FESTIVALS

Le Mans packs most of its nocturnal revelry in narrow side streets off of the **pl. de la République.** The young, funky scene is down **rue du Dr. Leroy,** whose bars resonate with techno or rock. **Paris Texas Café,** 21 rue du Dr. Leroy, is a little club that looks like a saloon out of the American Wild West. (☎ 02 43 23 71 00. Open daily 11am-2am.) A few blocks away, the **Rue des Ponts Neuf** has its own share of bars that are decorated with everything from model cars to artistic film projections onto their walls. **Le Bakoua,** 5 rue de la Vieille Porte, off pl. de l'Eperon, feels like a beach party, complete with calypso music and tropical drinks. (☎ 02 43 23 30 70. Open June-Sept. daily 6pm-2am; Oct.-May 5pm-2am.) Several discothèques are right in town, including **Le Select,** 44 pl. de la République, with wild strobe lights and good beats. (☎ 02 43 28 87 41. Open Th-Su 11pm-5am. Cover €8 with drink.) There's also the gay-friendly **La Limite,** 7 rue St-Honoré, in the *vieille ville.* (☎ 02 43 24 85 54. Cover €19.82, under age 25 €9.15. Open Th-Su until midnight.)

Cannes film festival winners are featured nightly at the *vieille ville*'s ultra-cool **Ciné-Poche,** 97 Grande Rue (☎ 02 43 24 73 85). For the entire month of April, the city attracts contemporary jazz artists of every creed for the **Europa Jazz Festival.** (Info and tickets at 9 rue des Frères Greban; ☎ 02 43 23 78 99.) On the first weekend of July, over 40 theater companies hit the streets for **Les Scénomanies,** a festival presenting over 100 different shows on the streets of old Le Mans. The excitement brings out all sorts of street entertainment, including international music, dance, and acrobatics. If you've missed *Les Scénomanies,* worry not—throughout July and August, **Les Soirs d'Eté** feature free theater, musical comedy, and music performances in the streets. Pick up a **L'Eté au Mans** schedule from the tourist office.

POITOU-CHARENTES

Poitou-Charentes could be France's best-kept secret. The Côte d'Azur may be tops in topless beaches, and the Loire Valley may be the king of châteaux, but no other region of France has so impressive a collection of both. Poitou-Charentes is a brilliant collage of pristine natural sights and coastal towns, tucked away on the western shore of France.

With the acceptance of Christianity in the 4th century AD, the area emerged as an influential political and religious center. The 8th century saw Charles "the Hammer" Martel fend off Moorish attempts to conquer the region. Eleanor of Aquitaine's marriage to England's Henry II in the 12th century marked the start of 300 years of British rule in Poitou-Charentes. In the 17th century, Cardinal Richelieu laid siege to the Protestant stronghold of La Rochelle, relegating it to a century of obscurity until trade with Canada restored it to prosperity.

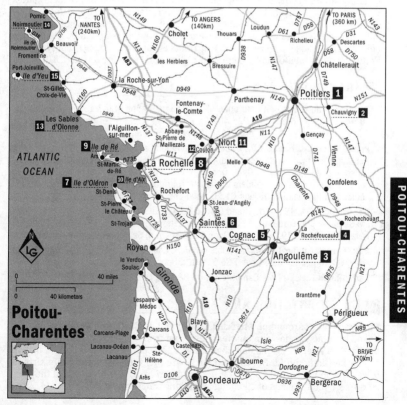

1	**Poitiers:** Steep hills dotted with a few famous, ancient churches and a theme park **(p. 314)**
2	**Chauvigny:** An escape from Poitiers; five towering châteaux, one now a bird's nest **(p. 319)**
3	**Angoulême:** Museum-packed, nightlife-heavy city of interest mostly to comic book fans **(p. 321)**
4	**La Rouchefoucauld:** Daytrip with huge Renaissance château and Gothic cloister **(p. 326)**
5	**Cognac:** Visit for the liquor, but no reason to stay; it's near Saintes and Angoulême **(p. 326)**
6	**Saintes:** A medieval market town with a certain quiet charm **(p. 328)**
7	■ **Ile d'Oléron:** Large island has forests, museums, chapels, enormous citadel **(p. 332)**
8	**La Rochelle:** Beach town full of vacationing French families; near great islands **(p. 334)**
9	**Ile de Ré:** Bike paths, huge untouched beaches, immense marshy bird preserve **(p. 340)**
10	■ **Ile d'Aix:** Smaller and less accessible than Ré; full of backwoods trails, tiny coves **(p. 343)**
11	■ **Niort:** Eastern anchor of the Marais Poitevin, a serene, green wetlands preserve **(p. 345)**
12	**Coulon:** Base for exploring the Marais canals by boat **(p. 346)**
13	**Les Sables d'Olonne:** Crowded family beach town; outdoor activities abound **(p. 347)**
14	**Noirmoutier:** Well-touristed, beachy-pinprick of an island; salt farming, oysters **(p. 349)**
15	■ **Ile d'Yeu:** 10km of sand dunes, mini-forests, rocky cliffs, and secluded inlets **(p. 349)**

POITIERS

The many renowned churches of Poitiers (pop. 120,000) stand as testament to the power of the Church here in the early Middle Ages. It was here that Clovis struck a blow for Christianity by defeating the Visigoths in 507 and Charles Martel repulsed invading Moors in 732. In 1432, when Poitiers was the capital of France, Charles VII founded the Université de Poitiers. However, don't let the beautiful façades deceive you. Despite its spiritual origin, this city has lost the tranquil spirit that still characterizes the rest of Poitou-Charentes. Poitiers is now a bustling, businesslike city, whose most remarkable attribute is not breathtaking scenery but the Futuroscope cinematography theme park 10km outside of town (see p. 319).

▐ TRANSPORTATION

Trains: bd. du Grand Cerf. Info open M-Sa 7:15am-9:45pm, Su 7:15am-10:45pm. To: **Bordeaux** (2hr., 8 per day, €25.40); **La Rochelle** (1¾hr., 8 per day, €17.10); **Paris** (2hr., 6 per day, €41.30); **Tours** (1hr., 5 per day, €12.60).

Public Transportation: S.T.P., 6 rue du Chaudron-d'Or (☎05 49 44 77 00). Open July 15-Aug. 16 M-F 1:30-6:30pm; mid-Aug. to mid-July M-F 9am-noon and 2-7pm. Buses crisscross the city 7am-8:30pm. One night bus (line #2) runs around the centre ville and to the University of Poitiers Campus (4 per day, 10-11pm). Timetables at tourist office and train station. Tickets €1.20, valid 1hr; *carnet* of 5 €4.80.

Car Rental: ADA, 19 bd. du Grand Cerf (☎05 49 50 30 20). From €40 for 24hr. Open M-Sa 8am-6pm. **Europcar,** 48 bd. du Grand Cerf (☎05 49 58 25 34). **Avis,** 135 bd. du Grand Cerf (☎05 49 58 13 00). Open M-F 8am-7pm, Sa 8am-noon and 2-5pm.

Bike Rental: Atelier Cyclaman, 60bis bd. Pont Achard (☎05 49 88 13 25). €13 per day, €8.40 per half-day. Open T-Su 9am-12:30pm and 3-7pm.

Taxis: Radio Taxis, 22 rue Carnot (☎05 49 88 12 34). €9.90 to hostel. 24hr.

■✦▐ ORIENTATION AND PRACTICAL INFORMATION

Poitiers centers around **pl. Maréchal Leclerc** and **pl. Charles de Gaulle**, which are linked by a busy pedestrian quarter. Buses run from opposite the train station to the **Hôtel de Ville**, on the pl. Marechal Leclerc. The *centre ville* is bordered by two rivers, Le Clain and La Boivre, and parks are plentiful around the outskirts of town. The book *"Poitiers et ses environs à pied et à VTT,"* available at the tourist office, contains maps of 20 biking and hiking trails around Poitiers.

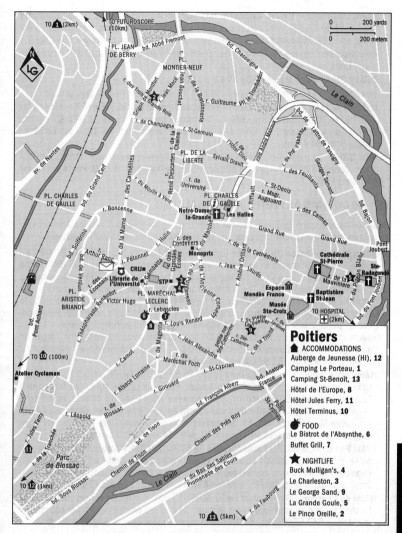

Poitiers

↟ ACCOMMODATIONS
Auberge de Jeunesse (HI), **12**
Camping Le Porteau, **1**
Camping St-Benoît, **13**
Hôtel de l'Europe, **8**
Hôtel Jules Ferry, **11**
Hôtel Terminus, **10**

🍴 FOOD
Le Bistrot de l'Absynthe, **6**
Buffet Grill, **7**

★ NIGHTLIFE
Buck Mulligan's, **4**
Le Charleston, **3**
Le George Sand, **9**
La Grande Goule, **5**
Le Pince Oreille, **2**

POITOU-CHARENTES

Tourist Office: 45 pl. Charles de Gaulle (☎05 49 41 21 24; fax 05 49 88 65 84). Well-labeled maps and lists of hotels and campgrounds. Ask for the brochure *Laissez-vous conter Poitiers*. For info on current events, snag the free *Affiche*. Hotel reservations €2.30. **City tours** (1½hr.) in French run July-Sept. at 11am and 3pm; English tours on demand (€3). Open June 21-Sept. 23 M-Sa 9:30am-7:30pm, Su 10am-6pm; Sept. 24-June M-Sa 10am-6pm. **Comité Régional de Tourisme,** 62 rue Jean Jaurès (☎05 49 50 10 50), has info on hiking, biking, and other modes of transport.

English Books: Librairie de l'Université, 70 rue Gambetta (☎05 49 41 02 05), off pl. M. Leclerc. Open M-Sa 9am-7:30pm. MC/V.

Youth Information: Centre Regionale Information Jeunesse (CRIJ), 64 rue Gambetta (☎05 49 60 68 68), near pl. Leclerc. Help with jobs, lodging, budget travel, and planning activities. **Internet access** for students €0.80 per 30min. Open M-F 10am-6pm.

Laundromat: 2bis rue de le Tranchée. Open daily 7am-8:30pm. Also at 182 Grande Rue. Open daily 8am-9pm.

Police: 38 rue de la Marne (☎05 49 60 60 00).

Hospital: 350 av. Jacques Caire (☎05 49 44 44 44), on the road to Limoges.

Internet Access: Centre Regionale Information Jeunesse (CRIJ). Email for students for €0.80 per 30min. **Cybercafé LRM,** 171 Grande Rue (☎05 49 39 51 87). €7 per hr., €4 per hr. with student ID. Open M-F 10am-noon and 2-8pm, Sa 10:30am-12:30pm and 2-6pm, Su 4-7pm.

Post Office: 16 rue A. Ranc (☎05 49 55 50 00). **Currency exchange** with no commission. Open M-F 8:30am-7pm, Sa 8:30am-noon. **Postal code:** 86000. **Poste Restante:** "Poitiers 86000."

▶ ACCOMMODATIONS AND CAMPING

The hostel and campgrounds are far from the city center, but respectable, cheap hotels in the town center and near the train station make good alternatives.

Auberge de Jeunesse (HI), 1 allée Tagault (☎05 49 30 09 70; fax 05 49 30 09 79). On foot, turn right at station and follow bd. du Pont Achard to av. de la Libération. At the fork in the road, take a right onto rue B. Pascal, then turn right on rue de la Jeunesse, then left onto allée Tagault. The hostel will be ahead on left. (35min.) Or, catch a bus from the stop near the traffic light to the right of the station. Take #3 (dir: Pierre Loti) to "Cap Sud" (M-Sa every 30min., until 7:50pm; €1.20). Perfectly adequate. Family-oriented, clean hostel rents bikes and organizes soccer and volleyball games in a large backyard. Breakfast €2.70. Lunch €8. Dinner €8. Sheets €2.70. Reception 7am-noon and 4pm-midnight. Bunks in 4-bed rooms €8.50. **Tents** and groundpad available for pitching in backyard (€4.80). **Members only. ❶**

Hôtel Jules Ferry, 27 rue Jules Ferry (☎05 49 37 80 14; fax 05 49 53 15 02). From train station, turn right onto bd. Pont Achard, and walk up the street (slightly uphill). Turn left onto rue J. Brunet and left again onto rue Jules Ferry; the hotel is on the right. Slightly worn, dark, carpeted rooms with narrow but spotless showers. Breakfast €4.50. Reception M-Sa 7am-11pm. For Su reservations, call ahead. Door code for late night entry. Singles and doubles with toilet €22, with shower €28; triples €37-46. ❷

Hôtel Terminus, 3 bd. Pont-Achard (☎05 49 62 92 30). Good insulation blocks out the noise from the train station across the street. Rose-colored rooms with large windows, enormous triples/quads on the top floor. All rooms have toilet and shower or bath. Breakfast €6. Singles €41-45, doubles €46-51, triples and quads €51-66. MC/V. ❹

Hôtel de l'Europe, 39 rue Carnot (☎05 49 88 12 00). This hotel is pricey, but offers by far the best and most unique rooms in town. Singles and doubles with toilet and shower in old wing €47-57; singles, doubles, and triples in fancier new wing €72-75. ❹

Camping:

Le Porteau, (☎05 49 41 44 88), on rue de Porteau 2km from town. Take bus #7 from near the station (dir: Centre de Gros; 7:15am-7:20pm, €1.20) to "Porteau." Tiny, rock-hard field encircled by roads. Reception 7am-10pm. Open mid-June to Sept. 2-person site €7.40; extra person €2.50, child €1.60. Electricity €2.30. ❶

Camping St-Benoit, rte. de Passelourdin (☎05 49 88 48 55), 5km from Poitiers. Slightly better (there's grass), but very hard to reach by public transport. From the station, take bus #2, 3, 6, 8, 7, 9, or 11 to "Hôtel de Ville." Walk to the bus stop at the corner of rue. Carnot and pl. Marechal le Clerc and take bus #5 (dir: La Varenne; 9:30am-7:20pm) to "Rue du Clain." Cross the Rocade Sud-Est and follow the rte. de Passelourdin for 1km until you reach the campground. Or take a taxi from train station to campground (€13). Reception 8am-noon and 3-8pm. Open July-Aug. 2-person site €8.40; extra person €2.50, child €1.60. Electricity €2.30. ❶

🟫 FOOD

Poitiers's cuisine specializes in lamb from nearby Montmarillon, *chèvre* (goat cheese), macaroons, and the wines of Haut-Poitou. The problem is finding a *menu* that fits your budget—most hover around €15-30. Many hotel bars post adequate 3-course *menus* for €10.50-15. Inexpensive pizzerias line the pedestrian streets between pl. Leclerc and Notre-Dame-la-Grande. There is a **market** at **Les Halles**, on pl. Charles de Gaulle, which expands beyond your wildest dreams on Saturdays. (Open M-Sa 7am-1pm.) There is a **Monoprix supermarket** at Ile des Cordeliers on rue des Grandes Ecoles. (Open M-Sa 9am-7:30pm.) **Buffet Grill ❸**, 11 rue Lebascles (☎ 05 49 01 74 00), off pl. Leclerc, has two all-you-can-eat buffets, one with salads and *hors d'oeuvres*, the other with desserts. More chocolate mousse than you could ever eat! (Buffets €9.50 each; menus start at €12. Open daily 11:30am-2pm and 7-10:30pm. MC/V.) For a more formal meal that's just as fun, try **Le Bistrot de l'Absynthe ❸**, 6 rue Carnot, which serves French favorites like *escargot* (snails), *cuisses de grenouille* (frog legs), and of course absinthe, straight-up or on top of an ice cream sundae. (☎ 05 46 43 77 52. *Plats* €10.50, *menus* €15.50-20, Absinthe €3.80. Open daily 9am-8pm.)

🟫 SIGHTS

Poitiers's churches, which date back to the conversion of France to Catholicism in the 4th century, are by far the city's most impressive attractions. (All open daily 9am-6pm, June-Aug. until 7pm; free.) Many hold organ concerts in the summer; check the *Guide des Manifestations* or call *Les Nuits en Musique* (☎ 05 49 41 21 24) or *Les Concerts du Marché* (☎ 05 49 41 34 18) for schedules.

NOTRE-DAME-LA-GRANDE. Despite its modest proportions, this is one of France's most important Romanesque churches. The figures of its 12-century statuary stand in a double row. Inside, an original fresco on the choir ceiling depicts Christ in glory, the Virgin and Child, and the Lamb of God in a cruciform. The rest of the interior was restored and is in a different style. In summertime, a not-to-be-missed special ▓**lighting show** projects the original polychrome detail onto the façade, reviving the splendor of the original colors and details. *(On pl. de Gaulle, off Grande Rue. Projections June-Aug. daily 10:30pm; Sept. 1-16 daily 9:30pm.)*

CATHÉDRALE ST-PIERRE. The 1162 construction of the light-stoned St-Pierre was funded by Eleanor of Aquitaine and her husband King Henry II Plantagenêt, who lived in Poitiers in the current Palais de Justice. During two hundred years of construction, the builders remained faithful to the original plan, resulting in a uniform 12th-century cathedral. The church is celebrated for its elaborate Cliquot classical organ (1787-1791), one of only two intact that predate the Revolution, and its central stained-glass window, one of the oldest crucifixion scenes in France. Carefully examine the column capitals and the junctions of the wall and the ceiling, where you'll discover 267 of the church's original carvings, human and bestial in subject. *(On pl. de la Cathédrale, off rue de la Cathédrale.)*

EGLISE STE-RADEGONDÉ. The church's belltower porch was built on the ravaged foundations of a 6th-century chapel erected by Ste-Radegonde, a Thuringian princess who fled to the church when she was forced to marry a Frankish prince. The church now holds the tomb of Radegonde and some of the dragon-slaying legends surrounding her. In AD 587, Christ supposedly appeared to Radegonde on this site and foretold her imminent death, calling her "one of the most precious diamonds in His crown." Helpfully, He left a footprint in the stone floor before vanishing, providing the doomed nun with proof and the abbey with pilgrims and income for centuries. The legend has even spurred the construction of a Radegonde museum next-door. *(Off rue de la Mauvinière, down the street from the cathedral.)*

BAPTISTÈRE ST-JEAN. This 4th-century baptistry is the oldest Christian structure in France. No longer a sacred building, the Baptistère is now a museum of Roman, Merovingian, and Carolingian sarcophagi and capitals. The earliest Christians kept these fragments when they destroyed Poitiers's fine Roman baths, arches, and amphitheater in order to rebuild inferior structures of their own. *(On rue Jean Jaurès, near the cathedral. Open July-Aug. daily 10am-12:30pm and 2:30-6pm; Apr.-June and Sept.-Oct. daily 10:30am-12:30pm and 3-6pm; Nov.-Mar. W-M 2:30-4:30pm. €0.80, under 12 €0.40.)*

MUSÉE STE-CROIX. This multi-purpose museum takes viewers through four millennia with everything from prehistoric artifacts to Roman coins, medieval sepulchres, and a fine-arts collection spanning the Renaissance to the present. Summer events include special exhibits, guest lectures, and concerts; check the bulletin outside for details. *(Open June-Sept. M 1:15-6pm, Tu 10am-8pm, W–F 10am-noon and 1:15-6pm, Sa-Su 10am-noon and 2-6pm; Oct.-May M 1:15-5pm, Tu 10am-5pm, W and F 10am-noon and 1:15-5pm, Sa-Su 2-6pm. €3.50, students free; no charge on Tu and the 1st Su of each month. Guided tours in French on Tu.)*

PARC DE BLOSSAC. This 18th-century park is one of the most beautiful in the region. Inside, a classic *jardin à la française* (French-style garden) is crisscrossed by perfectly rectilinear paths and Dutch linden trees. The park's small but noisy zoological garden is home to goats and a few birds, the most exotic being the numerous varieties of duck swimming in the pond. *(Rue de Blossac, down rue Carnot, near the river Clain. Open Apr.-Sept. daily 7am-10:30pm; Oct.-Mar. 7am-9:30pm. Jardin Anglais open Apr.-Sept. 7am-8pm; Oct.-Mar. daily 8am-sundown.)*

OTHER SIGHTS. Next to the Cathédrale St-Pierre but a millennium younger, the **Espace Mendes France** is a hands-on science museum perfect for youngsters. *(1 pl. de la Cathédrale. ☎ 05 49 50 33 00. Exhibits in French and English. Open July-Aug. M-F 9:30am-6pm; Sa-Su 2-6pm; Sept.-June M-F 2-6pm. Planetarium shows July-Aug. daily 5pm. Admission to exhibits €4, children €2.50; planetarium shows €5.50, children €3.)* In a homey interior, the **Musée Rupert de Chièvres** collects Dutch, Flemish, and Italian paintings, many anonymous, and displays scientific antiquities like the earliest Diderot encyclopedia. *(9 rue Victor Hugo. ☎ 05 45 41 07 53 or 05 49 41 42 21. Open June-Sept. M 1:15-6pm, W and F 10am-noon and 1:15-6pm, Th 10am-9pm, Sa-Su 10am-noon and 2-6pm; Oct.-May M 1:15-5pm, Tu 10am-noon and 1:15-5pm, W-F 10am-noon and 1:15-5pm, Sa-Su 2-6pm. €3.50; students free; all free on Tu and the first Su of each month. Guided tours in French on Tu.)*

🎵 ENTERTAINMENT AND FESTIVALS

Poitiers is more exciting than its size would suggest, particularly during the school year. **Pl. Leclerc** is the liveliest square in town. Locals and students belt out tunes in the pubs and restaurants along its side streets. Pick up the booklet *Café-Concerts, Bars avec Animations* at the tourist office for more information.

   Le Charleston, 10 rue l'Eperon (☎05 49 41 13 36), is home to a karaoke bar with popular French and American tunes. Belt out your own personal rendition of "I Will Survive" before a lively crowd. Open Tu-F 9pm-2am.

   Buck Mulligan's, 5 rue du Chaudron d'Or (☎05 49 30 11 48), around the corner, is an Irish pub in every respect—from hospitality to board games to the *Irish Times*. Happy Hour daily 7-9pm. Open M-Sa 4:30pm-2am, Su 6pm-2am.

   Le Pince Oreille, 11 rue des Trois Rois (☎05 49 60 25 99), hosts a blues or jazz band almost every W, Th, and F night; the mood of the club varies with the band. The armchairs and painted walls create a welcoming and decorative atmosphere. The dimly-lit social bar is full of students almost every night of the week. Stop by on Sundays in the winter to join the "philosophical cabaret" discussion. Cover €5 on music nights. Open M-Th 5pm-2am, F 5pm-3am, Sa 9pm-3am; Dec.-Feb. also on Su for the cabaret.

La Grande Goule, 46 rue du Pigeon Blanc (☎05 49 50 41 36), is the most popular nightclub in Poitiers. The disco brings in teens early on and an older crowd. Open Tu-Sa 11pm-4am. Cover €7.80, students €6.10, free for women before midnight; includes one drink.

Le George Sand, 25 rue St-Pierre le Puellier (☎05 49 55 91 58), is officially gay but draws a mixed crowd with house and 80s music and a great dance scene. Open daily 11pm-4am, W and Sa 11pm-5am.

The **Festival du Cinéma** in March draws film students from international schools all over the world for artsy and mainstream showings. Throughout July and August, rock, opera, jazz, and fireworks thunder through town during the **Places à l'Eté** festival. Concerts, mostly free, begin around 9pm 3-4 nights per week. **La Nuit des Orgues,** only three years old, organizes a series of (mostly free) organ performances in local churches from May to October. Contact the tourist office for tickets and details. In late August and early September, a more formal organ festival, **Voix Orgues,** plays host to organ players from all over the region. Book tickets in advance. (Call ☎05 49 47 13 61 for more info. Tickets €6-15.25.)

▶ DAYTRIPS FROM POITIERS

FUTUROSCOPE

*10km north of Poitiers near Chasseneuil. ☎05 49 49 30 80; fax 05 49 49 59 38; www.futuroscope.com. Take bus #16 or 17 from Poitiers (20min., 18 per day, €1.20). Catch the bus at the Hôtel de Ville or across the street from the train station, in front of the Printania Bar-Hôtel. Schedules are subject to change. For info, contact **STP** (6 rue du Chaudron d'Or; ☎05 49 44 66 88) or the tourist office. Buy tickets from the bus driver. Get off at "Parc De Loisirs" and follow directions to the park entrance. By car, follow A10 (dir: Paris-Châtellerault) to Exit 18. The park is also accessible by **TGV** from Bordeaux (1½hr., 1-2 per day, €30.50) and Paris (80min., 2-3 per day, €30.50). Open daily May-June 9am-6pm; July-Aug. 9am-11pm; Sept.-Mar. 10am-6pm; Sept.-June Sa-Su often open later. Apr.- Aug. daily and Sept.-Oct. weekends €30, children €22, after 6pm €15; low-season €21, children €16. All main attractions included in the price, though the video games on Cyber Avenue require additional tokens.*

The Futuroscope amusement park is essentially a silvery, slick, and stylish collection of high-tech film theaters. Spherical and hemispherical screens, virtual reality, and high-definition 3-D trickery engineer simulation rides and the occasional straight-up film experience. A headset obtained in the Maison de Vienne near the entrance gives the English translation for many films. If you stay late to watch the exciting laser show, you will miss the last bus to Poitiers.

CHAUVIGNY

*SNCF buses leave Poitiers for Chauvigny from outside the station (dir: Châteauroux; 30min., 5 per day, Su at 4:20pm and 8:50pm only; €4.40). Buy tickets in the SNCF train station in Poitiers, on board on your return. The bus will drop you off at pl. de la Poste, in the center of modern-day Chauvigny. The cité médiévale, where you can find all the castle ruins, lies up on the hill. To get there, walk back on rue du Marché in the direction the bus came from. At the end of pl. du Marché, turn right onto rue de Châtellerault. At the end of rue de Châtellerault, turn right onto bd. des Châteaux, which will take you to the cité médiévale. The **tourist office** is on rue St.Pierre, a left off of bd. des Châteaux. (☎05 49 46 39 01. Open July-Aug. daily 10am-7pm; Sept.-June 10:30am-12:30pm and 2-6pm. Tours July-Aug. W-M 2:30pm and 4pm; €4.60. Call ☎05 49 46 35 45 in advance for English tours.)*

IN RECENT NEWS

SMIC: JUST ANOTHER FUNNY FRENCH ACRONYM?

Open *Le Monde*, and you don't need to know French to realize that French politics is full of acronyms, from political parties (RPR, UMP, PS, PC) to labor unions (CGT, CFDT). One nice-sounding acronym, SMIC, is particularly important. SMIC stands for *salarie minimal interprofessional de croissance*—in short, the minimum wage. 2.7 million *SMICards* (14% of the workforce), as they're called, earn this wage. SMIC is big news every June and July, when the government conducts its annual review of minimum wage policy.

SMIC is not a straightforward minimum wage. The government sets five different monthly minimum wages. There are five levels because not all firms changed their workweek.

With the reelection of President Chirac and the success of his RPR party, SMICards have been wondering what will happen to their SMIC. The RPR traditionally opposes raising the minimum wage, in the interests of industry efficiency. Chirac acted quickly, announcing in June that SMIC would be raised 2.4%, equal to the inflation rate, to bring the minimum wage to €1154 a month. In addition, all SMICs would be equalized by 2003. The liberal socialist and communist parties and the worker's unions, who wanted a 6% raise, opposed these decisions. Yet, for the moment, Chirac is in power and the *SMICards* will have to wait another year.

Twenty-three kilometers east of Poitiers, Chauvigny's beauty hides its bloody history; it was conquered four times during the Hundred Years' War, razed during the Wars of Religion, and shelled by the retreating Wehrmacht in 1944. Today the town's tiny medieval citadel and the pretty restaurant-lined walkways around tranquil pl. du Donjon make a worthwhile half-day escape from bustling Poitiers.

Five ruined 11th- to 15th-century chateaux give Chauvigny a striking skyline. Farther down, the 12th-century **Eglise St-Pierre** is known for its choir capitals, engraved with dragons, vultures, and images of Satan.

The ultra-modern **Espace d'Archéologie Industrielle** nestles under a glass ceiling in the ruins of the Gouzon keep, showcasing regional quarrying, porcelain-firing, milling, and steam-engine activity. There's a great view of the city and countryside below from the museum's glass elevator. (☎05 49 46 35 45. Open Apr.-June 15 andSept.-Oct. daily 2-6pm; June 16-Aug. M-F 10am-12:30pm and 2:30-6:30pm, Sa 2:30-6:30pm, Su 11am-6:30pm; the rest of the year Sa-Su 2-6pm. €4.60, students €3, under 14 free.) The crumbling walls of **Les Géants du Ciel** (☎05 49 46 47 48; fax 05 49 44 10 45), once home to Chauvigny's bishops, now host 60 eagles, falcons, vultures, owls, buzzards, storks, parrots, and countless other winged species. The squeamish should avoid the dark room of *chauves* (bats), who fly unrestrained in between visitors. The highlight is a bird show, in which the flock swoops over the city and returns, flying centimeters above your head. (Open daily Apr.-Nov. 4. May-Aug. daily shows at 11:15am, 2:30, 4, and 5:30pm; Apr. and Sept.-Nov. daily shows at 2:30 and 4pm, Sa-Su additional show at 5:30pm. €8.15, students €7; ruins €3.)

For a truly unique glimpse of the countryside, take a ride on the **Vélo-Rails.** These contraptions on rails, powered by pedaling, can take passengers along the viaduct that traverses the Vienne River on a 17km loop around the Chauvigny valley. Reservations must be made at least one day in advance. (10 rue de la Folie. ☎05 49 46 39 01. To get there from pl. de la Poste, walk down rue du Marché, cross the Vienne River and continue straight as the road changes names to rue de Poitiers. When you reach rue de la Verrerie, turn right, and then left onto rue de la Folie. Open July-Aug. daily 10am-9pm; Sept. and May-June daily 2-7pm; Oct. and Mar.-Apr. daily 2-6pm; Nov. daily 1-5pm; Dec.-Feb. by reservation. July-Aug. 2hr. ride €21.40, low-season €18.30.)

From June to August, the **Festival d'Eté** (☎05 49 45 99 10) fills the city with (occasionally free) jazz, dance, and theater performances. Purchase tickets in advance at the tourist office.

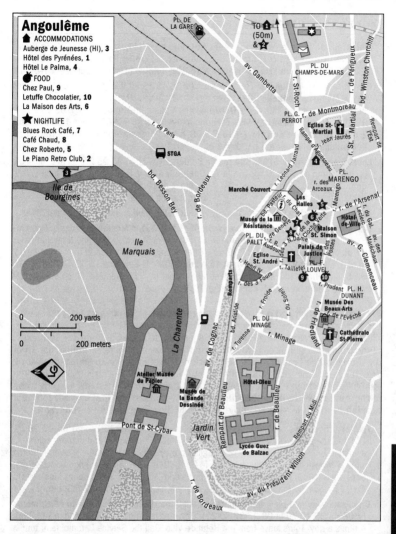

Angoulême

🏠 ACCOMMODATIONS
Auberge de Jeunesse (HI), **3**
Hôtel des Pyrénées, **1**
Hôtel Le Palma, **4**

🍎 FOOD
Chez Paul, **9**
Letuffe Chocolatier, **10**
La Maison des Arts, **6**

★ NIGHTLIFE
Blues Rock Café, **7**
Café Chaud, **8**
Chez Roberto, **5**
Le Piano Retro Club, **2**

ANGOULÊME

A secret well-kept from hordes of tourists, Angoulême (pop. 46,000) sits high on a plateau and affords a magnificent view of the Charente river. The cradle of the French paper industry in the 1600s, the town and its ready supply of writing pads brought Jean Calvin here in 1534. Wood pulp is no less an obsession today, for Angoulême reigns supreme as the capital of French comic strip production, with countless Lucky Luke and Astérix volumes rolling off the town's presses and streets marked with dialogue bubbles and carton graffiti. The winding hilly streets of the *vieille ville* are filled with modern stores, restaurants, and movie theaters.

🗐 TRANSPORTATION

Trains: pl. de la Gare (☎05 45 69 91 65). Info open M-F 9:30am-7pm, Sa 9:30am-6:30pm. To: **Bordeaux** (55min., 8-10 per day, €17.80); **Paris** (2¾hr., 7 per day, €48.60-59); **Poitiers** (1hr., 5 per day, €15.30); **Saintes** (1hr., 4-5 per day, €10.40).

Buses: Autobus Citram, rue Louis Pergaud (☎05 45 25 99 99). To **Cognac** (1hr., 8 per day, €7) and **La Rochelle** (3hr., 3 per day, €16). Buses stop at pl. du Champ de Mars. Buy tickets on board. Info at the **Cartrans** office, pl. du Champ de Mars (☎05 45 95 95 99). Open July to mid-Aug. M-F 2-6:15pm; mid-Aug. to June M-F 9:15am-12:15pm and 2-6:15pm. **CFTA Périgord** (☎05 53 08 43 13), goes from the train station to **Périgueux** (1½hr.; M-Sa 2 per day, 1 on Su; €11.60).

Local Transportation: STGA, 554 rue de Bordeaux (☎05 45 65 25 25), is in a kiosk on pl. du Champ de Mars. Maps available. Open July-Aug. M-F 1-5pm; Aug. 20-June M-F 1-6pm, Sa 9am-12:30pm. Tickets €1.15, *carnet* of 10 €8. Buses run M-Sa 6am-8pm, and are a good way to get to many of the museums on the edge of town.

Taxis: Radio Taxi (☎05 45 95 55 55), in front of the train station. €7 to hostel. 24hr.

Car Rental: Ada, 19 pl. de la Gare (☎05 45 92 65 29), offers the best deals. Open M-Sa 8am-noon and 2-7pm. **National Rent-A-Car** is right across from the train station at 21 pl. de la Gare (☎05 45 37 39 49). Open M-Sa 8am-noon and 2-7pm. Must be 21 to rent. MC/V. A few doors down at 15 pl. de la Gare is **Europcar** (☎05 45 92 02 02), which sometimes has special student rates. Must be 21. Open M-F 8am-noon and 2-7pm, Sa 8am-noon and 2-6pm. AmEx/MC/V.

🛂 🛈 ORIENTATION AND PRACTICAL INFORMATION

The *vieille ville* sits among the ramparts just south of the Charente and southwest of the train station. It is easy to get lost in this maze of streets, so grab a map from the tourist office branch outside the station. To get to the main **tourist office** at pl. des Halles, follow av. Gambetta right and uphill to pl. G. Perrot, and continue straight up the rampe d'Aguesseau and turn right onto bd. Pasteur, keeping close to the railing overlooking the valley, pass the market building on your left, and turn left beyond the market onto rue du Chat; the office will be on your right.

Tourist Office: 7bis rue du Chat, pl. des Halles (☎05 45 95 16 84; fax 05 45 95 91 76). Indispensable city guide with restaurants, hotels, museums, and outdoor activities; available only in French with a few English paragraphs that describe the main tourist sites in the *vieille ville*. Open July-Aug. M-Sa 9:30am-7pm, Su 10am-noon and 2-5pm; Sept.-June M-F 9:30am-6pm, Sa 10am-noon and 2-5pm, Su 10am-noon. **Kiosk** (☎05 45 92 27 57), by the train station. Open daily M-Sa 9am-noon and 2-6:30pm.

City Tours: Day and night tours offered through the Hôtel de Ville's **Service Patrimoine** (☎05 45 38 70 79 or 08 25 88 70 29). Day trips leave daily at 4pm and in July-Sept. 4 times a day. Tours leave from the Hôtel de Ville. Call the Service Patrimoine or tourist office for more info. €5, children €3. English tours available, call in advance.

Budget Travel: Voyages Wasteels, 2 pl. Francis Louvel (☎05 45 92 56 89; fax 05 45 94 01 31). 20-30% savings on train and plane tickets. Open M-F 9am-12:30pm and 2-6:30pm, Sa 10am-12:30pm and 2-5:30pm. **Jet tours,** 5bis rue de Perigeux (☎05 45 92 07 94), can also arrange cheap trips with excellent deals on airfare. Open M-F 9:30am-12:30pm and 2-6:30pm, Sa 6pm closes.

Currency Exchange: Good rates at **Banque de France,** 1 rue de Général Leclerc (☎05 45 97 60 00), on pl. de l'Hôtel de Ville. **Exchange** desk open M-F 8:40am-noon. Post office also has good rates and no commission for US dollars.

Youth Center: Centre Information Jeunesse, L'Espace Franquin, 1ter bd. Bertholet (☎05 45 37 07 30; fax 05 45 38 65 51), around the corner from the Hôtel de Ville. Friendly staff provides info on jobs and events, cheap concert tickets, and general advice. Open July-Aug. M-F 9am-12:30pm and 2-6pm; Sept.-June M-F 9am-6pm, Sa 2-6pm. Email access also available for €2 per hr.

Laundromat: Lavomatique, 3 rue Ludovic Trarieux, near the Hôtel de Ville. Open daily 7am-9pm. Also **Washmatic,** 11 rue St-Roch. Open M-Sa 9am-7pm.

Police: pl. du Champs de Mars (☎05 45 39 38 37), next to the post office.

Hospital: Hôpital de Girac, rte. de Bordeaux (☎05 45 24 40 40). Closer to town is the private **Clinique St-Joseph,** 51 av. Président Wilson (☎05 45 38 67 00).

Internet Access: Café Arobase, 121 rue de Bordeaux (☎05 45 38 65 65), inside the CNBDI (see p. 324). Open Sept.-June Tu-F 10am-6pm, Sa-Su 2-6pm; July-Aug. 10am-7pm, Sa-Su 2-7pm. €3 per hr. for students. If you come to CNBDI when the Café is closed, the receptionist might let you use the museum computers for free. Museum open July-Aug. M-F 10am-7pm, Sa-Su 2-7pm; Sept.-June Tu-F 10am-6pm, Sa-Su 2-6pm. The best deal in town is at the **Centre Information Jeunesse,** see above, €2 per hr.

Post Office: pl. du Champs de Mars (☎05 45 66 66 00; fax 05 45 66 66 17). **Currency exchange.** Open M-F 8am-7pm, Sa 8am-noon. **Branch office,** pl. Francis Louvel, near the Palais de Justice (☎05 45 90 14 30). Open M-F 8am-6:45pm, Sa 8:30am-12:30pm. **Postal code:** 16000.

▐ ACCOMMODATIONS AND CAMPING

Cheap hotels cluster near the intersection of av. Gambetta and the pedestrian district, which slopes downhill from the *vieille ville*. The hostel is on the Ile de Bourgines, an island in the Charente 2km from the town center.

Auberge de Jeunesse (HI), on Ile de Bourgines (☎05 45 92 45 80; fax 05 45 95 90 71). To walk, turn left out of the train station onto av. de Lattre de Tassigny and take the first left onto bd. du 8 Mai 1945. Just before the big bridge, turn left onto bd. Besson Bey and cross the footbridge. Follow the dirt path beside the river to the left; the hostel is just ahead. (30min.) To get there by bus, leave the station, turn right onto av. Gambetta, and right again onto rue Denis Papin, which crosses over the tracks. Continue straight onto Passage Lamaud, a pedestrian shortcut that leads to rue de Paris. (5-10min.) Turn right onto rue de Paris and take bus #7 (dir: Le Treuil; last bus 8pm) to "St-Antoine." Gorgeous location along the Charente. 15 bright 2- to 6-bed rooms with skylights and sinks in a modern building; fiendish press-and-repeat showers get warm when they want to. Breakfast €3.20. Meals €10 with wine and coffee. Lockout 10am-5pm. No curfew. Call ahead in summer. Dorms €8.50. ❶

Hôtel Le Palma, 4 rampe d'Aguesseau (☎05 45 95 22 89; fax 05 45 94 26 66), near the Eglise St-Martial, about 3 blocks up the hill from the train station. Ten large, newly renovated rooms lie along a narrow winding staircase. Quiet atmosphere with excellent location—5min. from both the train station and the center of town. Breakfast €4.50. Reception M-Sa only; call in advance for Su. Singles 21.50, with shower €28; doubles €26, with shower €33-37. AmEx/DC/MC/V. ❷

Hôtel des Pyrénées, 80 rue St-Roch (☎05 45 95 20 45; fax 05 45 92 16 95), off pl. du Champ de Mars. From the train station, follow rue Gambetta until the second large intersection, and take a very sharp left. (10min.) Bright, spacious, well-kept rooms with spotless bathrooms. Breakfast €5. Reception 7am-10:30pm. Singles and doubles €17, with shower and TV €33-39. Extra bed €7. MC/V. ❷

◻ FOOD

The local specialty, *cagouilles à la charentaise* (snails prepared first with garlic and parsley, then with sausage, smoked ham, and spices; €6.50-8.50), can be found in the restaurants of the *vieille ville*. A favorite sweet is the flower-shaped *marguerite* chocolate, named for François I's sister, Marguerite de Valois. Bars, cafés, and bakeries line rue de St-Martial and rue Marengo, but the food becomes funkier and the crowds more interesting as you weave your way into the narrow streets of the quadrant formed by Les Halles, pl. du Palet, Eglise St-André, and the Hôtel de Ville. The recently renovated covered **market** on pl. des Halles sells the town's freshest produce two blocks down rue de Gaulle from the Hôtel de Ville. (Open daily 7am-12:30pm.) There is a **Stoc supermarket**, 19 rue Périgueux, right by the Champ de Mars. (Open M-Sa 8:30am-7:15pm, Su 9am-noon. MC/V.) Be prepared to wait in line. ◼**La Maison Des Arts ❷**, 24 rue de la Cloche Verte, is perfect for diners with a flare for the artistic. The restaurant sells glass and ceramic pottery and paintings by local artists within its 17th century walls. Meals are served in the courtyard in summer under the shade of trees strung with lights; in the winter the tables and plants are moved inside to create a winter garden inside the gallery. Fresh salads and fruit tarts are €6.50 for the set. Feel free to practice their piano after dinner. (☎05 45 93 91 77. Open Tu noon-8pm, W-Sa 10am-11pm. MC/V.) **Chez Paul ❸**, 8 pl. Francis Louvel, has an unassuming exterior, but opens out to a paradise-themed garden with flowers, candles, sculptures and a mini river running through the middle. Excellent regional food served in a summer menu (€16), and lunch express menu (€10.80). The *brasserie* also hosts non-professional acting shows on every F on the mini-theatre upstairs. (☎05 45 90 04 61. Open daily 7am-midnight. MC/V.) **Letuffe Chocolatier**, 10 pl. Francis Louvel, specializes in marguerite chocolates and gives free samples and tours. (☎05 45 95 00 54. €11.43 per 250g. Open M-Sa 9am-noon, 2-7pm. MC/V.)

◻ SIGHTS

CATHÉDRALE ST-PIERRE. The splendid 12th-century cathedral of Angoulême is textbook Romanesque, but for one missing element: the structure was built without internal columns, to permit an uninterrupted view of the interior. The original 6th-century structure also lacked vertical windows; before Byzantine renovations bathed the transept in pale blue light, it was lit only by lanterns. The edifice exerted a considerable influence, not only on other churches in the diocese, but also on more distant buildings like Fontevraud in the Loire and Notre-Dame-la-Grande of Poitiers. A splendid facade depicts the Ascension of Christ and scenes from the Last Judgment. Other notable features include the distinguished capitals below the belfry, the graceful arch-lined walls, and a four-domed nave characteristic of the region. *(Pl. St-Pierre. ☎05 45 95 20 38. Open daily 9am-7pm.)*

MUSÉE DE LA BANDE DESSINÉE. Housed in the **Centre Nationale de la Bande Dessinée et de L'Image (CNBDI)**, this museum is a tribute to Angoulême's leading role in the development of computerized graphics and the *B.D.—la bande dessinée* (comic strips). Here you'll find small exhibits on French cartoons from the 19th and 20th centuries, including favorites like *Tintin*, *Astérix*, and *Popeye*. Entrance to the museum also gives free access to its library and one free hour of Internet access. The extensive bookshop filled with comics from all over the world is by far the best asset of the CNBDI. *(121 rue de Bordeaux. From pl. du Champ de Mars and pl. de l'Hôtel de Ville, take bus #3 or 5 to "Nil-CNBDI." or walk along the remparts, following the signs. (10min.) ☎05 45 38 65 65; cnbdi@cnbdi.fr. Open July-Aug. M-F 10am-7pm, Sa-Su 2-7pm; Sept.-June Tu-F 10am-6pm, Sa-Su 2-6pm. €5, students €3, children €2, under 6 free.)*

MUSÉE DES BEAUX-ARTS. Inhabiting a restored 12th-century bishop's palace, the museum displays a pleasing mélange of media. A labyrinth of 16th to 19th-century paintings, 19th-century *charentais* archaeological digs, North and West African pottery, Oceania, and locally created sculptures surrounds one of the museum's prized possessions, Etienne Barthélémy's 1800 *Grief of Priam's Family*. *(1 rue Friedland, behind the cathedral. ☎ 05 45 95 07 69; fax 05 45 95 98 26. Open M-F noon-6pm, Sa-Su 2-6pm. €3; students and children under 18 free; free noon-2pm.)*

EGLISE ST-ANDRÉ. The 12th-century church, originally Romanesque, was reworked in a Gothic style. It combines paintings from the 16th to the 19th centuries with a massive altarpiece and a superb baroque oak pulpit. The facade was redone in the early 19th century, but the church still retains its original tower and entrance. *(8 rue Taillefer, on the pl. de Palet in the town center. Open daily 9am-7pm.)*

GARDENS AND WATER SPORTS. Angoulême's ramparts and green riverside areas are a refreshing escape from the medieval gloom of its interiors. At the bottom of av. du Président Wilson, the flowers and waterfalls of the **Jardin Vert** soothe tourists. The 4th-century ramparts that surround the town provide a view of the red-roofed houses and green countryside. To canoe or kayak on the Charente, call **SCA Angoulême** at ☎ 05 45 94 68 91. The tourist office has lots of info on sports in the area including canoeing, kayaking, water skiing, and tennis. For water skiing, call **CAM's water skiing.** *(☎ 05 45 92 76 22. €8.50 per session. Open June-Oct daily noon-8pm. Cash or check only.)* The Bourgines Olympic **swimming pool,** next to the hostel, is perfect for splashing under the blue sky. *(Open July-Aug. daily 10am-8pm.)*

OTHER SIGHTS. The **Atelier-Musée du papier** consists of two open-air rooms, illustrating the history of Charente's paper-making industry and the industrial history of the area, in French. *(134 rue de Bordeaux. ☎ 05 45 92 73 43; fax 05 45 92 15 99. Across from the CNBDI. Open Sept.-June Tu-Su 2-6pm; July-Aug. Tu-Sa noon-6:30pm. Free.)* The **Musée de la Résistance et de la Déportation** has taken over the one-time home of 16th-century religious reformer Jean Calvin, and now chronicles Angoulême's experience under Nazi occupation. In particular, it details the development and courage of the French resistance fighters, many of whom were captured and tortured to death by the Nazis. The exhibits are all in French, with limited English texts available. *(34 rue de Genève. ☎ 05 45 38 76 87; fax 05 45 93 12 66. Open July-Aug. M-Sa 9am-noon and 2-6pm; Sept.-June Tu-Sa 2-6pm. €2.50, students €1.50, children and students free.)*

🎵 ENTERTAINMENT AND FESTIVALS

As the sun sets, folks move toward the cafés on rue Massillon and pl. des Halles, and av. Gambetta comes alive with numerous bars and restaurants. Have a hot coffee or a cold drink at **Café Chaud,** 1 rue Ludovic Trarieux. The lively music, wooden spiral staircase, and cushioned wicker seats hold mostly locals. (☎ 05 45 38 26 32. Occasional live music. Open M-Th noon-2am, F-Sa noon-4am, Su 3pm-2am.) **Blues Rock Café,** 19 rue de Genève, caters to a mature crowd and packs the square outside with drinks, smoke, laughter, and, occasionally, live music. Extensive salad menu (€5-8.40), beer €2.20. (☎ 05 45 94 05 98. Open daily 11am-2am.) Live concerts almost nightly make worthwhile the hike out to **Le Piano Rétro Club,** 210 rue St-Roch. (☎ 05 45 92 87 11. Open Tu-Sa 10:30pm-2am.) **Chez Roberto,** 6 rue de Genève, fills with talkative twenty-somethings. This restaurant becomes a bar at night, filling with loud Mexican music and dancing. Occasional concerts and theme nights are sporadically enlivened by striptease acts. (Beer €2. Happy hour 7pm-8pm. Open daily 11am-2am, busiest Th-Sa nights.)

The world-famous **Salon International de la Bande-Dessinée** (☎05 45 97 86 50; www.bdangouleme.com) breezes into town the last weekend in January (Jan. 24-27, 2003). Over 200,000 visitors spend four days admiring comic-strip exhibits throughout town, where Astérix and Obélix can occasionally be sighted. (For tickets, call ☎08 20 07 20 20 or visit the Hotel de Ville. €9.15 for one day, €18.25 for all four days.) The **Festival Musiques Métisses,** 6 rue du point-du-Jour, features French-African and Caribbean music each year during Pentecost. (☎05 45 95 43 42, www.musiques-metisses.com. Tourist office sells tickets. 4 nights €54, students €39.) The popular **Circuit des Remparts,** 2 rue Fontgrave, revs its engine in mid-September, as antique cars hold free races and exhibitions for three days in the town center (☎05 45 94 95 67). International pianists of all genres participate in the two-week **Festival International de Piano, "Piano en Valois,"** in late September and early October. (☎05 45 90 91 57. Concerts free-€39.) In November **Gastronomades,** a celebration of culinary arts, offers cooking lessons, food displays, and free tastings (☎05 45 67 39 30), and **Ludoland** pays homage to video games. (☎05 45 94 75 61; www.ludo-angouleme.com; three-day pass €8.) Finally, like many French cities, Angoulême welcomes all sorts of artistic festivity in the summertime. Call the tourist office after mid-June for info about the **Eté au Ciné,** a series of outdoor films shown evenings during the summer and the **Jeux de Rue,** an open air theater festival with free outdoor performances on every Th during July and August.

For those who love to wine and dine with the gentle sway of the river, **Les Croisières au pays d'Angoulême** are a series of themed cruises that run July to August. Themes include the paper cruise with a stop at the paper museum, the wine cruise, and the chocoholic cruise. Breakfast, lunch and dinner cruises also available. The themes tend to change each summer, but may include fireworks, or a Spanish fiesta. Prices, depending on the cruise, range from €13-37, children €4.50-23. Call the tourist office for info and reservations.

▶ DAYTRIP FROM ANGOULÊME

LA ROCHEFOUCAULD

Get to La Rochefoucauld by train (M-Sa 5 per day, Su 3 per day; €4.60). At the train station, walk around the back and across the parking lot to the traffic circle. Go halfway around the traffic circle and keep walking straight for 4 blocks through the town center. The château will be straight ahead. (8min.) The tourist office is at 1 rue des Tanneurs. (☎05 45 63 07 45. Open M-Sa 9:30am-12:30pm and 2:30-7pm.)

La Rochefoucauld (pop. 3000) has been home to the more than 43 generations of the aristocratic Foucauld family. The present **château,** known as the "pearl of Angoumois," was built by Duke Francis II in 1528 on a feudal-era foundation, with twin towers, a medieval fortress, and an elegant chapel on a plateau overlooking the town. The magnificent central spiral staircase, built in 1520, is a perfect work of renaissance art and was designed by Leonardo Da Vinci. The classical music playing in the inner courtyard adds a touch of humanity to the stone building. (☎05 45 62 07 42. Open M-Sa 10am-7pm, Su and holidays 2-7pm.) The surrounding village, which takes its name from the family ("La Roche à Foucauld" or "The Rock of Foucauld"), houses a well-preserved Gothic cloister, **Le Couvent des Carmes,** in good condition for having been built in 1329, and a church dating from 1266.

COGNAC

Cognac (pop. 20,000) rises along the banks of the Charente, which Henry IV called the "gentlest and most beautiful river in France." According to French law, crops produced in the Cognac region are the only ones in the world fit to become the liquor that bears the Cognac name; distilleries today give tours and samples of the sweet liqueur. Anyone besides the most passionate liqueur enthusiasts will want to daytrip Cognac from Saintes and Angoulême, as there is little else to do in town.

■ ⁊ ORIENTATION AND PRACTICAL INFORMATION. Trains come from **Angoulême** (40min., 5 per day, €7.30) and **Saintes** (20min., 6 per day, €4.30). To get to the **tourist office,** 16 rue du 14 Juillet, follow av. du Maréchal Leclerc out of the train station to the first circle and take a right, following signs to the town center. Turn right on rue Bayard and go straight across pl. Bayard onto rue du 14 Juillet. (15min.) You'll find information, maps, and a free accommodations service. The office arranges tours of the city, including nocturnal trips (July 12-Aug. Th at 9:30pm; €6.50, under 12 €5), and *petit train* tours for €5, English text available. (☎05 45 82 10 71; fax 05 45 82 34 47; office.tourisme.cognac@wanadoo.fr. Office open July-Aug. M-Sa 9am-7pm, Su 10am-4pm; Sept.-June M-Sa 9am-12:30pm and 2-6:15pm; May-June and Sept. M-Sa 9:30am-5:30pm; Oct.-Apr. M-Sa 10am-5pm.) **Hospital** (☎05 45 36 38 50), and **Police** (05 45 36 75 95). Find the **Banque de France,** 39 bd. Denfert-Rochereau, for the best rates. (☎05 45 82 25 10. Open M-F 8:45am-noon.) The **post office,** 2 pl. Bayard, also has **currency exchange.** (☎05 45 36 31 82. Open M-F 8am-6:30pm, Sa 8:30am-noon.) **Postal code:** 16100.

⁊ ACCOMMODATIONS AND CAMPING. Unfortunately, there is no hostel in Cognac. **Le Saint Martin ❷,** 112 av. Paul Firino Martell, about 1km from the center of town, has the cheapest rooms in town. To get here, turn left onto av. Martell from pl. Martell. Singles and doubles, recently redone, are small, accommodating, and kept very clean. Reception 8am-10:30pm. (☎05 45 35 01 29; http://perso.wanadoo.fr/hotel.stmartin. Breakfast €4.20. Singles €21, with shower €24; doubles with shower €25-29.) Three-star **Cognac Camping ❶,** bd. de Châtenay, on rte. de Ste-Sévère, is a 30min. walk from the town. A bus runs twice daily from pl. François 1ᵉʳ (☎05 45 82 01 99; 2 per day, June 16-Sept. 4; €0.60, under 18 €0.30, 6-trip *carnet* €3). Get off at "Camping." (☎05 45 32 13 32. Pool. Laundry. Open May-Oct. July-Aug. 2 people with site, showers, and electricity €12; Sept.-June €10. 3 people with site €10-14. MC/V.)

⁊ FOOD. Tasting Cognac's famous product doesn't necessarily mean drinking it. Restaurants around **pl. François 1ᵉʳ** serve pricey local specialties drenched in the stuff. Right in the town center, **La Boune Goule ❷,** 42 allées de la Corderie, is at the intersection of rue Aristide Briande. Huge, fresh portions of local cuisine served in an almost American diner setting. (☎05 45 82 06 37. Omelettes €5.34, lunch *menu* €11.44. Open daily noon-2:30pm and 7-11:30pm. MC/V.) More basic needs can be satisfied at **Supermarket Eco,** on pl. Bayard, right down the street from the tourist office. (Open M-Sa 9am-12:30pm and 3-7:30pm, Su 9-11:45am.) There is an **indoor market** at pl. d'Armes (Tu-Su 7am-1pm), and a lively **outdoor market** brightens pl. du Marché on the second Saturday of each month.

⁊ COGNAC DISTILLERIES. The joy of visiting Cognac lies in making your way from one brandy producer to the next, touring warehouses, watching films on the history of each house, and collecting nip bottles. If a nip is not enough, Hennessy's "Timeless" Cognac, created especially for the millennium with the best stock of the past century and bottled in pure crystal, costs a mere €3200. If you want the drink, you'll have to take the tour. In the summer, most houses regularly give tours in English; call in advance during the winter.

Hennessy, quai Richard Hennessy (☎05 45 35 72 68; fax 05 45 35 79 49). The indus-try's biggest player has the longest and most interesting presentation, which includes a trip to "paradise," where the oldest cognacs are kept, and a short boat ride along the Charente river. If you have time for only one, this should be it. Their tour is the most expensive, but also the most elegant. Open June-Sept. daily 10am-6pm; Mar.-May and Sept.-Dec. 10am-5pm; Jan.-Feb. call ahead for a reservation. Several excellent English tours per day, call ahead for times. €8, students €5, under 16 free.

Otard and the Château François Ier, 127 bd. Denfert-Rochereau (☎05 45 36 88 86), is housed in the Château de Cognac, the 1494 birthplace of François Ier. Dressed in medieval costumes, the tour guides are proud of the history of their house. The 50min. tour begins with the history of the building, ending with a tour of the damp castle cellar where the cognac is produced and stored. Be sure to notice the fungus growing on the walls—it consumes in vapors the equivalent of 23,000 bottles each year. Open July-Aug. daily 10am-7pm; Apr.-June and Sept.-Oct. daily 10am-noon and 2-6pm; Nov.-Dec. M-Th 11am-noon and 2-5pm, F 11am-noon and 2-4pm. Last tours leave 1hr. before closing. €3.80, 18 and under €2.30, under 12 free.

Martell, pl. Edouard Martell (☎05 45 36 33 33), is the oldest of the major cognac houses, and ships to cities around the world. Today, it is the only tour that will take you into the bottling room itself, where you can see its 11 automatic assembly lines that with clockwork computer precision fill, wrap, and package over 10,000 bottles of Cognac a day. Open June-Sept. M-F 9:30am-5pm, Sa-Su noon-5pm; Oct. and Mar.-May M-Th 9:30am-noon and 2:30-5pm, F 9:30am-noon; Nov.-Feb. call ahead to reserve. English tours given daily, call ahead to arrange. €4, under 16 free.

■ **SIGHTS.** The **Musée Municipal du Cognac,** 48 bd. Denfert-Rochereau, details the history of Cognac and cognac through regional clothing, ceramics, and viticul-ture tools, and displays Marie Curie's cognac bottle bust. (☎05 45 32 07 25. Open June-Sept. W-M 10am-noon and 2-6pm; Oct.-May 2-5:30pm. €3.20, students €1.10, under 18 free.) Despite all the cognac mania, a stroll through the friendly, pedestrian center of town, full of flowers and marketware in the summertime, is always worthwhile. Step into the **Eglise Saint Léger,** off rue Aristide Briand, to admire its two grand 18th-century tableaux, gold-lined altar, and stunning arches. (Open daily 8am-7pm.)

∥ OUTDOOR PURSUITS. Cognac's valley provides great hiking among vine-yards, fields, groves, and forests. The tourist office provides four Sentiers de Randonnées maps (€2.30 each) with paths around Cognac; off-trail surprises include abbeys, historic ruins, and châteaux. (Info about canoeing ☎05 45 82 44 51. Kayak rental €4 per hr., €10 per half-day. Canoe rental €6-14 per hr., €8-24 per half-day.) Parks in Cognac include the **Jardin de l'Hôtel de Ville** around the museum and the large, tree-lined **Parc François Ier** , northwest of the city center between allée Bassée and allée des Charentes. (Jardin open June-Sept. daily 7am-10pm; Apr.-May and Oct. 7am-9pm; Nov.-Mar. 7am-7pm. Parc open 24hr.)

SAINTES

Gracefully bisected by the Charente river and named for the local Gallic Santon tribe, the ancient city of Mediolanum Santonum was founded by Romans in the first century AD. Connected by a major road to Lyon, the city served as the capital of Aquitaine for nearly 100 years; today Saintes's first-century ruins bear testimony to the Roman city's importance. The city's impressive architecture feels out of pro-portion with modern Saintes (pop. 27,000), whose quiet charm is on a smaller level. The city merits a stopover on the way to the larger tourist hubs.

⌐ TRANSPORTATION

Trains: pl. Pierre Senard. Info open M 5:40am-8pm, Tu-F 8am-8pm, Sa 8am-7pm, Su 8am-9:30pm. To: **Bordeaux** (1½hr., 5 per day, €14.80); **Cognac** (20min., 5 per day, €4.40); **La Rochelle** (50min., 5 per day, €10.10); **Niort** (1hr., 5 per day, €9.90); **Paris** (2¼hr., 6 per day, €53.90-61.20); **Poitiers** (2hr., 6 per day, €21.90); **Royan** (30min., 6-7 per day, €5.80).

Buses: Autobus Aunis et Saintonge, 1 cours Reverseaux (☎05 46 97 52 03). To: **Royan** (1hr., 8 per day, €5.30); **Le Château** and **St-Pierre d'Oléron** on the Ile d'Oléron (1½hr., 2 per day, €9.30-10.10). Office open M-F 9am-noon and 2-6pm. **Océcars** (☎05 46 99 23 65), in Rochefort, goes to **La Rochelle** (2½hr., 1-2 per day, €8.70). An operator answers calls M-F 8:30am-noon and 2-7pm.

Public Transportation: Buses cross the city regularly (€0.85). Schedules at tourist office or **Boutique Bus**, in the Galerie du Bois d'Amour (☎05 46 93 50 50).

Car Rental: Budget, 51 av. de la Marne (☎05 46 74 28 11). 21+. Open M-Sa 8am-noon and 2-6:30pm. **Europcar,** 43 av. de la Marne (☎05 46 92 56 10). 21+. Open M-F 8am-6:30pm, Sa 8am-noon and 2-6:30pm.

Taxis: at the train station (☎05 46 74 24 24). €1 per km.

Bike Rental: Groleau, 9 cours Reverseaux (☎05 46 74 19 03). €8 per day. Open Tu-Sa 9am-12:15pm and 2-7pm. MC/V.

✚ 🛈 ORIENTATION AND PRACTICAL INFORMATION

Saintes lies on the Charente River, along the La Rochelle-Bordeaux railway line 25km from Cognac. To get to the **tourist office,** take a sharp left upon leaving the train station and follow av. de la Marne until you hit hopping av. Gambetta. Turn right and follow it to the river; the Arc Germanicus will be on your left. Cross the bridge over the river at pont Palissy and continue straight on leafy green **cours National.** The tourist office is on your right in a villa set back from the street. (20min.) The hub of the mellow pedestrian district is **rue Victor Hugo,** three blocks to the left after the bridge.

Tourist Office: 62 cours National (☎05 46 74 23 82; fax 05 46 92 17 01; saintonge-tour@wanadoo.fr; www.ot-saintes.fr), in Villa Musso. Free maps. Organizes walking tours of the city, abbey, and Roman ruins. Office open July-Aug. M-Sa 9am-1pm and 2-7pm, Su 10am-1pm and 2-6pm; Sept.-June M-Sa 9am-12:30pm and 2-6pm. Tours June-Sept. M-Sa. €6 for one tour, €10 for two, €13 for all three, under 16 free.

Money: Banque de France, 1 cours Lemercier (☎05 46 93 40 33). **Currency exchange** desk open M-F 8:45am-12:15pm and 2-3:30pm.

Laundromat: Laverie de la Saintonge, 18 quai de la République (☎05 46 74 47 18). Open M-Sa 8:30am-7pm, Su 2-6pm. **Laverie et Cie,** 46*ter* cours Reverseaux (☎05 46 74 34 79).

Police: rue de Bastion (☎05 46 90 30 40), or **Gendarmerie,** 17 rue du Chermignac (☎05 46 93 01 19).

Hospital: pl. du 11 Novembre (☎05 46 92 76 76).

Internet Access: France Telecom, 22 rue Alsace-Lorraine, has one terminal available. *Télécarte* necessary. Open M 1:30-6:30pm, Tu-Sa 9:30am-12:30pm and 1:30-6:30pm, or at the **Post Office** with a cyberposte card.

Post Office: 6 cours National (☎05 46 93 84 50). **Currency exchange.** Open M-F 8:30am-7pm, Sa 8:30am-noon. **Postal code:** 17100.

▐ ACCOMMODATIONS AND CAMPING

Hotels fill for the festivals from early to mid-July; otherwise rooms should be easy to find. Most of the cheap beds cluster on the train station side of the Charente.

■ Auberge de Jeunesse (HI), 2 pl. Geoffrey-Martel (☎05 46 92 14 92; fax 05 46 92 97 82; www.hostelbooking.com), next to the Abbaye-aux-Dames. From the station, take a sharp left onto av. de la Marne and then turn right onto av. Gambetta, left onto rue du Pérat, and right onto rue St-Pallais; 25m up at pl. St-Pallais, turn left through the archway into the courtyard of the abbey. Go straight through the courtyard and out through the arch at the back, and the hostel will be on your right. (15min.) A clean, renovated building that feels like part of the abbey itself. Cozy, pine-scented, cabin-like rooms. Breakfast included. Sheets €2.70. Camping €4.20, with breakfast €6. No lockout or curfew. Reception 7am-noon and 5-11pm; Oct.-May until 10pm. Dorms €11. MC/V. ❶

Le Parisien, 29 rue Frédéric-Mestreau (☎05 46 74 28 92), by the train station. The floral arch over the main entrance leads to small, friendly rooms with bright, mismatched bedcovers. Reception 7am-11pm. Breakfast €3-4.50. Call several weeks ahead for July-Aug. June-Aug. singles or doubles €25; Sept.-May €22. Extra bed €7. AmEx/MC/V. ❷

Camping Au Fil de L'Eau, 6 rue de Courbiac (☎05 46 93 08 00; fax 05 46 93 61 88), 1km from the center of town. From the train station, follow directions to hostel until av. Gambetta and turn right onto quai de l'Yser after crossing the bridge. (25-30min.) Signs mark the way. By bus, take #2 (dir: La Recluse) from the train station; get off at "Théâtre" and catch the #3 (dir: Magezy) to "Courbiac" (25min., €0.85). Three-star site by the Charente, next to municipal pool (free for campers) and mini-golf (€3.80). Individual lots are crowded, but enhanced by an on-site market and *brasserie.* Certain buildings are handicapped-accessible. Reception July-Aug. 8am-1pm and 3-9pm; May 15-June and Sept. 1-15 9:30am-noon and 4-8pm. €5 per person, €1.50 per child; €4.50 per site; car included. Electricity €3. MC/V. ❶

▐ FOOD

Menus in Saintes flaunt the region's seafood as well as *escargot* dishes and *mojettes* (white beans cooked in Charenté). Start things off with *pineau,* a sweeter relative of Cognac. Saintes is blessed with plenty of family-run restaurants and bars, especially in the pedestrian district by rue Victor Hugo. Saintes holds **markets** on cours Reverseaux (Tu and F), near Cathédrale St-Pierre (W and Sa), and on av. de la Marne and av. Gambetta (Th and Su), all 8am-12:30pm. On the first Monday of every month **Le Grand Foire** open-air market stretches from the cours National to av. Gambetta. A huge **Leclerc supermarket** and general store are on cours de Gaulle near the hostel. (Open M-Th and Sa 9am-7:15pm, F 9am-8:15pm.) A smaller **Co-op** supermarket can be found on both rue Urbain Loyer, off cours National (open M-Sa 8:30am-12:45pm and 3-7:45pm), and at 162 av. Gambetta, near the train station. (Open Tu-Sa 8:30am-1pm and 3:30-8pm, Su 8:30-11am.) For sit-down fare, try the friendly **Le Gourmandin ❸,** av. de la Marne, near the station. In nice weather, the outdoor seating at Le Gourmandin takes the prize. Sit under an umbrella in a quiet courtyard next to a small manmade waterfall. (☎05 46 93 27 60. Entrees €7.50-€13.50, salads €5.50-10. Open daily noon-2:30pm and 7-10pm. MC/ V.) For a cheap, hot meal, try **Cafétéria du Bois-d'Amour ❶,** 7 rue du Bois-d'Amour, off cours National in the Galérie Marchandise, a pay-by-the-plate cafeteria, offering €1-4.50 *entrées* and €4-€7 *plats.* (☎05 46 97 26 54. Open daily 11:30am-10:30pm; hot food available 11:30am-12:30pm and 6:30-9:45pm. MC/V.) For a fancy treat or quick sandwich, sit yourself down on the velvet chairs of **Chez Alexandre ❶**, 21 rue du Gros Raisin. The *darioles au chocolat* (€4), a cake filled with melting chocolate, is a taste of pure happiness. Don't offer the well-tempered cat a sip of your drink—she's on a diet. (☎ 05 46 28 04 04. Open M-Sa 10pm-7pm. MC/V.)

🔯 SIGHTS

International flags line both sides of the **pont Bernard Palissy,** which looks out onto most of Saintes's sights. Built in AD 18 as the entrance to the city, the Roman **Arc Germanicus** rises on the left bank of the river to honor Emperor Tiberius of Gaul and his nephew Germanicus. First located at the entrance to a bridge that crossed the Charente, the Arc tried to become an aqueduct as the river widened over the centuries. The bridge was extended, but around its 1800th birthday the Arc began to lose stability. The bridge was demolished in 1843, and replaced by the pont Bernard Palissy slightly to the north, but the Arc was spared and moved to the right bank of the river, 15m from its original location.

Behind the Arc, the **Jardin Public** offers refuge on shaded benches next to colorful flower beds. A peaceful mini-zoo in the center houses a few small goats, deer, rabbits, and birds. In July and August, the garden hosts free Sunday afternoon performances, ranging from traditional folk dancing to—grab your Stetson—country line-dancing. Next door, on esplanade André Malraux, the popular **Musée Archéologique** displays the remains of architecture and chariots from the first-century city. A partially finished puzzle of Roman columns, friezes, and cornices, most dating from the demolition of the town's ramparts in the 4th century, lies in another chamber. A comprehensive guide in English and French explains the Roman craftsmanship. (☎ 05 46 74 20 97. Open May-Sept. Tu-Su 10am-noon and 2-6pm; Oct.-Apr. Tu-Sa 10am-noon and 2-5:30pm, Su 2-6pm. Free.)

Rue Arc de Triomphe, which becomes rue St-Pallais, leads to the Romanesque **Abbaye-aux-Dames.** Built in 1047, the abbey led a quiet life for a while—some Gothic touch-ups here, another gallery there—until plagues, fires, and wars prompted centuries of constant construction and reconstruction. During the anti-religious fervor of the Revolution, the abbey was shut down and turned into a prison. Today, it serves as the musical and cultural center of Saintes. Frequent exhibitions by local artists brighten the pale stone walls of the **Salle Capitulaire,** which was once the daily meeting place of Benedictine nuns. The pinecone-shaped belltower of the **Eglise Notre-Dame** dates from the 12th century, when Eleanor of Aquitaine gave the nuns some friendly pointers during renovations. Climb to the top to scan the stunning horizon or check out contemporary tapestries depicting the six days of the Creation. Unlocked doors, winding stairways, and isolated passageways welcome leisurely wanderers. See the *L'Abbaye aux Dames: Eté* pamphlet at the tourist office for summer concerts. (☎ 05 46 97 48 48. Exhibition and ramparts open July-Sept. 15 daily 10am-12:30pm and 2-7pm; Sept. 16-June Th-F and Su-Tu 2-6pm, W and Sa 10am-12:30pm and 2-7pm. Church free. Abbey €3, students and under age 16 free. French tours €6. Concerts €12-45.)

Cross the flower-lined pedestrian bridge as you head for the **Cathédrale St-Pierre** on rue St-Pierre. With its metal helmet, the cathedral hovers over the town, visible from almost anywhere. The 12th-century church was later redone in Gothic style, but the steeple and portal were left unfinished. (☎ 05 46 93 09 92. Open daily 10am-7pm.) Turn away from the center of town and descend the steps of less traveled rue St-Eutrope, which crawls through tree-lined fields to the crypt of the saint who names the road. Known as the saint of recovery, **St-Eutrope** lies in a **crypt** treasured for its healing powers by many, including Joseph de Compostela, who paid a visit on his way to Santiago. (Open daily 9am-7pm.) Follow the path as it curves to the left and turn right onto rue de La Croix Boisnard. The road leads to the **Arènes Gallo-Romaines,** now a crumbled and peaceful amphitheater in a residential neighborhood. Built in AD 40, the structure seated 20,000 spectators who flocked to see gladiators battle wild animals or each other to the death. Don't bother paying the €1 admission: you can see just as well from outside the fence. (Open Apr.-Oct. daily 9am-7pm; Nov.-Mar. Tu-Su 10am-12:30pm and 2-4:30pm.)

🖼 ENTERTAINMENT AND FESTIVALS

Come nightfall, unwind with an evening of conversation and sunset-watching in a Saintes café or pub. Try your game (€1) at **Billiard Saintais,** 126 av. Gambetta, accompanied by €2 beers. (☎06 83 46 02 37. Open W-M 10am-2am. Cash only.) Where rue Gambetta runs into pont Palissy you'll find **Bar Le Palissy,** a gathering place for students who listen to jazz or rock, or sing to classics on Thursday karaoke nights. (☎05 46 74 30 65. Occasional live music. Beer €2. Open Sept.-June only daily 10am-2am. MC/V.) If you've got a car, you can dance up a storm with partying students at the **Le Santon** club, Ste-Vegas, on rte. de Royan. In summer, the adjoining **swimming pool** provides a respite from steamy body heat. (☎05 46 97 00 00. Cover €10.20 for both club and pool. Open daily 10:30pm-3am.)

For ten days in mid-July, the **Festival de Folklore en Charente Maritime** celebrates international folk music, food, and dance. The Arènes Gallo-Romaines host the opening and closing events. (office at 43 rue Gautier; ☎05 46 74 47 50; www.jeux-santons.net. Events free-€30.) At the same time, be sure to join the **Académies Musicales** celebration, in which more than 30 classical music concerts are packed into 10 days at the Abbaye aux Dames. (☎05 46 97 48 48; fax 05 46 92 58 56; www.festival-saintes.org. Tickets €12-43, some are free. Passport for the entire festival €315, students €240.)

ILE D'OLÉRON

Hovering only a couple of miles from the mainland, Oléron is the second-largest French island after Corsica, but not easily accessible from mainland France. Some of France's most renowned oyster beds, first cultivated by the Romans, encircle the island; the 90km coastline also includes 20km of fine beaches.

🖼 TRANSPORTATION. Buses leave for Le Château from 1 cours Reverseaux (☎05 46 97 52 03) in Saintes (1½hr., 3-4 per day, €10.10), and from Rochefort's bus station (☎05 46 99 98 97; 1hr., 6-8 per day, €7), and train station (☎05 46 93 21 41). Ask your driver or check a bus schedule to see whether the bus continues on to other parts of the island; if it does, stay on until the next stop, in the center of town right next to the tourist office. If the bus ride ends at the port in Le Château, turn your back to the water, and follow av. du Port and the signs to the town center. From Le Château, a **shuttle bus** runs to: Grand Village, near the beaches (20min.; M-Sa 5-6 per day, Su 2 per day; €1.60); St-Denis (1hr., 3 per day, €4.90); St-Pierre-d'Oléron (45min.; M-Sa 6-8 per day, Su 4 per day; €2.70).

🖼 ORIENTATION AND PRACTICAL INFORMATION. A 3km bridge links the island to the continent, best traversed by buses that circulate between Saintes, Rochefort-sur-Mer, and Le Château, the main town on the southern end of the island and the best base from which to explore it. For the ultimate escape, rent a bike in Le Château and pedal through the **Marais aux Oiseaux** bird sanctuary in the middle of the island to St-Pierre d'Oléron, the main town in the north, then into the evergreen Forêt des Saumords in the northeast corner. Return by way of the coastal villages. Be forewarned: bike trails are not clearly marked and do not always offer direct paths between towns. Turn right onto bd. Victor Hugo and head up the hill toward the tourist office, pl. de la République, for a chock-full info packet, free maps of the island and the city, and hotel reservations. (☎05 46 47 60 51; fax 05 46 47 73 65; chatolero@ot-chateau-oleron.fr; www.ot-chateau-oleron.fr. Open July-Aug. M-Sa 9:30am-12:30pm and 3-7pm, Su 10am-12:30pm; Sept.-June M-Sa 9:30am-12:30pm and 3-6:30pm.) Rent **bikes** at **Cycles-Peche Locavente,** 5 rue Maréchal Foch, just off pl. de la République. (☎05 46 47 69 30. €5.50-7.85 per half-day, €7-€10.20 per day; deposit €100-150. Open July-Aug. daily 9am-12:15pm and 2-7:15pm; Sept.-June Tu-Sa 9am-12:30pm and 2-7pm, Su 9am-12:30pm. MC/V.) **Crédit Maritime,** near the tourist office on bd. Thiers, charges €2.30 to change foreign traveler's checks. (☎05 46 47 62 23. Open M-Sa 8:30am-12:15pm and 1:30-5pm.) Le Château's **post office** is on bd. Victor Hugo. (☎05 46 47 61 99. Open M-F 9am-noon and 1:30-4:30pm, Sa 9am-noon.) Postal code: 17480.

◘ ACCOMMODATIONS AND FOOD. Reserve several weeks in advance if you want a cheap place to crash. In Le Château, **Le Castel ❸,** 54 rue Alsace-Lorraine, lets cheerful, spotless rooms, which would be spacious were it not for all the furniture. (☎05 46 75 24 69; fax 05 46 75 25 41. Breakfast €5. Reception 9am-noon and 6-10pm. Singles and doubles with bath €26-40. Extra bed €5. MC/V.) In the center of town near the tourist office, **Le Jean-Bart ❷,** pl. de la République, offers four barren, white stucco rooms with a great view. Wake up to the sounds of the morning market and merry-go-round tunes. (☎05 46 47 60 04. Breakfast €5.50. Doubles with shower €25. Extra bed €8. MC/V.)

Most people on a budget take tents, since 34 **campsites** are spread along the coast. Two-star **Les Remparts ❶,** on bd. Philippe Daste, is also in Le Château, right next to the beach. It's the most convenient site for those without a car, but also more crowded. Beach camping available. Laundry. (☎05 46 47 61 93; fax 05 46 47 73 65; www.les-remparts.com. Open Mar.-Oct. June 15-Sept. 15 car and tent €13.87; off-season €11.74. MC/V.) Two and a half kilometers northeast of Le Château, on rte. des Huitres, reigns the four-star **La Brande ❷,** with 199 luxury sites, a pool, tennis courts, mini-golf, laundry, mini-grocery store and a waterslide. (☎05 46 47 62 37; fax 05 46 47 71 70; www.camping-labrande.com; la.brande@wanadoo.fr. Reception 8:30am-10pm. Open Mar. 15-Nov. 15. July-Aug. €32 for 2 people; Sept.-June €15.50. Extra person €6. Electricity €3. MC/V.) Near **Grand-Village** and the beaches lies **Camping Municipal des Pins ❶,** on allée des Pins. With 268 sites, this campground can hold as many people as the nearby town. Campgrounds are a bit crowded, but tall trees help keep an isolated feeling. (☎05 46 47 50 13; fax 05 46 75 17 71. Open Easter-Sept. July-Aug. 2-person site €14, Easter-June and Sept. €12.20; €4 per person. Electricity €3.20. MC/V.)

Each town has a Sunday morning market, and many have weekday morning versions as well. In Le Château, vendors fill the covered building across from the tourist office in pl. de la République (daily 7:30am-12:30pm). **The Coop,** 3 rue Reytre Frères, right behind Hôtel Jean-Bart off pl. République, is a modest grocery just across from the market square. (Open M-Sa 8:30am-12:30pm and 4-7:30pm, Su 9am-1pm.) **Super U Supermarché,** 15 av. d'Antioches, 250m out of Le Château, has a larger selection. (Open M-Sa 8:30am-8pm, Su 9am-12:30pm.) St-Pierre's **Lidl,** on av. de Vel Air (the main route from Le Château), has the cheapest prices. Grand Village also has a large **Super U** in its commercial center. (Both open July-Aug. M-Sa 8:30am-8pm, Su 9am-12:30pm; Sept.-June M-Sa 9am-12:30pm and 3-7:30pm, Su 9am-12:30pm.)

◘◙ ISLAND TOWNS AND SIGHTS. The mighty but crumbling **citadel** in Le Château was built on the ruins of a medieval fortress. In 1621, following a revolt in La Rochelle, skittish Louis XIII had it destroyed to prevent its falling into Protestant hands, only to rebuild it nine years later; the current structure dates to this 1630 reconstruction. Louis XIV and Richelieu were some of its more famous guests; WWI German POWs were some of the more infamous. Allied bombs destroyed much of the citadel in 1945 to keep German squadrons left on Oléron from regrouping. The fortress ruins have since been taken over by grass and pic-nickers. Various exhibits come and go in the more habitable chambers; call ☎ 05 46 75 53 00 for hours and activities, some of which take place in pl. de la République. (Exhibits open daily 10am-7pm. Free.)

St-Pierre d'Oléron, with a bustling pedestrian sector, is the island's geographic and administrative center; it also houses the tomb of French writer and naval officer Pierre Loti. The staff of the St-Pierre **tourist office,** pl. Gambetta, is all-know-ing. (☎ 05 46 47 11 39; fax 05 46 47 10 41; office-tourisme-saint-pierre-ole-ron@wanadoo.fr. Open July-Aug. M-Sa 9am-7pm, Su 10am-1pm; Sept.-June M-Sa 9:15am-12:30pm and 2-6pm.) A lively, brightly colored port graced by a modern chapel makes **La Cotinière** the most picturesque of the island towns. **Le Grand Vil-lage,** 4km southwest of Le Château, is the inappropriately named smallest town, with 910 locals and the island's glitziest, most flamboyantly topless beach, **Les Allassins.** (Tourist office ☎ 05 46 47 58 00; fax 05 46 47 42 17.) Another beach, **Plage du Vert Bois,** near Grand Village and separated from the main road by a thick pine forest, feels almost like an island itself. Near the northwestern tip, **St-Denis** invites tourists to climb the 54m **lighthouse** and peer down at the colorful collage below. (Open daily 10am-noon and 2-6:30pm; Sept.-June 10am-noon and 2-6pm. €2, chil-dren 7-12 €1, under 7 free.) The **tourist office** on bd. d'Antioche has more info (☎ 05 46 47 95 53; fax 05 46 75 91 36; office-tourisme-saint-denis-oleron@wanadoo.fr).

■ **NIGHTLIFE.** Larger towns have some nightlife. In Le Château, **La Cigale,** 25-27 rue Clemenceau, has a lively crowd. (☎ 05 46 47 61 37. Open daily 7am-2am.) St-Denis is home to **Le Panoramic,** 3 bd. d'Antioche, a relaxed jazz and blues bar. (☎ 05 46 75 98 18. Open daily 8am-2am.) In La Cotinière, a city that stays up late in sum-mer, check out **Café de la Marine,** on rue du Port. (☎ 05 46 47 10 38. Open 10am-2am.)

LA ROCHELLE

Though it cannot boast of beautiful beaches or sandy shores, La Rochelle (pop. 120,000) does have one great claim to fame—fish, and lots of it. La Rochelle's posi-tion as one of France's best-sheltered seaports helped to create its fortune, and nearly destroyed it. France and England fought over it during the Hundred Years' War, and Cardinal Richelieu was so upset with the city's support of England dur-ing the 17th-century invasion of the Ile de Ré that he besieged the town for 15 months, starving three quarters of its citizens. Oblivious to its rocky past, 20th-century vacationers flock to La Rochelle for its medieval architecture, its proxim-ity to some of the most perfect isles off the French coast, its quirky museums, and its superlative seafood restaurants.

▛ TRANSPORTATION

Trains: bd. Maréchal Joffre. Info office open 9am-6:45pm. To: **Bordeaux** (2hr., 5 per day, €21.10); **Nantes** (2hr., 5 per day, €19.80); **Paris** (3 hr. by TGV, 5 per day, €50.60); **Poitiers** (2hr., 8 per day, €17.10).

Ferries: Boats run to **Ile d'Aix** (**Interiles** ☎ 05 46 50 51 88; **Croisières Océanes,** office on cours des Dames; ☎ 05 46 50 68 44; see p. 344 for prices). **Bus de Mer** (☎ 05 46 34 02 22) shuttles between the old port and les Minimes (Apr.-June every 30min., July-Aug. every 15min.; €1.70).

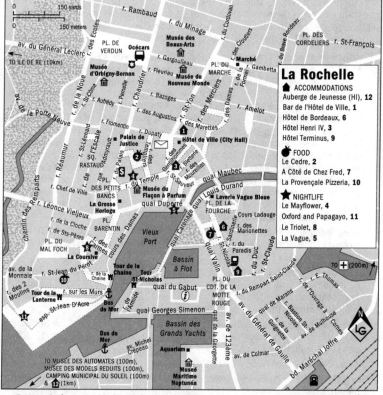

La Rochelle

ACCOMMODATIONS
Auberge de Jeunesse (HI), 12
Bar de l'Hôtel de Ville, 1
Hôtel de Bordeaux, 6
Hôtel Henri IV, 3
Hôtel Terminus, 9

FOOD
Le Cedre, 2
A Côté de Chez Fred, 7
La Provençale Pizzeria, 10

NIGHTLIFE
Le Mayflower, 4
Oxford and Papagayo, 11
Le Triolet, 8
La Vague, 5

Buses: Océcars (☎05 46 00 21 01) sends buses from pl. de Verdun to **Royan** (1¼hr.; 3 per day; €11) and **Saintes** (4 per day, 8:25am-7:15pm, €8.70) via Rochefort. Buy tickets from driver. Info office at pl. de Verdun open M-Tu and Th-F 8:15am-12:15pm and 1:30-6:30pm, W 8:15am-1pm and 2-6:30pm, Su 8:15am-1pm.

Public Transportation: Autoplus (☎05 46 34 02 22) serves the campgrounds, hostel, and town center (€1.20; buses run 7am-7:30pm). Pick up a schedule at the pl. de Verdun main office. Open M-F 8:30am-12:30pm and 2-6pm, Sa 8:30am-12:30pm.

Taxis: pl. de Verdun (☎05 46 41 55 55 or ☎05 46 34 02 22). €7 to hostel.

Bike Rental: Vélos Municipaux Autoplus (☎05 46 34 02 22), off quai Valin (open M-Sa 7:30am-7pm, Su 1-7pm) or in pl. de Verdun near the bus station (open May-Sept. 9am-12:30pm and 1:30-7pm, 9am-7pm July-Aug). Free with ID deposit for 2hr., €1 per hr. thereafter.

■ 🛈 ORIENTATION AND PRACTICAL INFORMATION

La Rochelle spreads out from the **vieux port,** where many cafés line **Quai Duperré,** to the boutique-filled **vieille ville** just inland. Opposite the *vieille ville,* to the south, lies the more modern area of **la ville en bois** ("Wooden Village"), which despite its name is actually a complex of industrial buildings, storage houses for boats, and several museums, including the excellent aquarium (see **Sights,** below). Still further to the south you can find a little strip of beachfront, **Les Minimes.** To get from the train station to the **tourist office,** head up av. du Général de Gaulle to the first square, pl. de la Motte Rouge, and turn left onto the quai du Gabut. The tourist office is on the left, in the Quartier du Gabut. (5min.)

Tourist Office: pl. de la Petite Sirène, quartier du Gabut (☎05 46 41 14 68; fax 05 46 41 99 85; www.larochelle-tourisme.com). Multilingual staff sells a useful brochure that includes maps and information in French (€0.50) and an abbreviated version in English (€0.15). Pick up the free entertainment magazines *Tenue de Soirée* and *Sortir* for current festivities. 2hr. walking tours of the **vieille ville** depart daily from the tourist office at 10:30am (€6, children €4). In July and August, you can also take 90min. tours by horse and carriage (depart daily from tourist office at 2:30pm; €7.50, children €5). Every Thursday July to mid-Sept., **night visits** led by costume-clad locals leave from the tourist office (8:30, 9, and 9:30pm; €7.50, students and children €5). Reservations are required for the carriage and night tours, and can be made by calling the tourist office. Most tours are in French, although English tours can sometimes be arranged in advance. Hotel **reservation service** €2. Open Oct.-May M-Sa 9am-6pm, Su 10am-1pm; June and Sept. M-Sa 9am-7pm, Su in June 11-5pm and Su in Sept. 10am-1pm; July-Aug. M-Sa 9am-8pm and Su 11am-5pm.

Money: Banque de France, on rue St-Come (☎05 46 51 48 00). Good rates. Open for exchange M-F 8:30am-noon. In a pinch, there are 24hr. **exchange machines** at **Crédit Lyonnais,** 19 rue du Palais.

Youth Center: Centre Départemental d'Information Jeunesse (CDIJ), 2 rue des Gentilshommes (☎05 46 41 16 36 or 05 46 41 16 99; fax 05 46 41 50 35). Boards list apartments and jobs. Open M 2-6pm, Tu-F 10am-12:30pm and 1:30-6pm. Closed Sa and Su. **Internet** €1.60, 1hr. use maximum.

Laundromat: Laverie Vague Bleue, 4bis quai Louis Durand, corner of rue St-Nicolas (☎05 46 50 67 91). Open daily 8:30am-8:30pm. Happy Hour W 8:30am-12:30pm with prices reduced by €0.70.

Police: 2 pl. de Verdun (☎05 46 51 36 36).

Hospital: rue du Dr. Schweitzer, 24hr. emergency entrance on bd. Joffre. (☎05 46 45 50 50).

Internet Access: Cyber Squat, 63 rue St-Nicolas (☎05 46 34 53 67). €0.75 connection fee, €0.10 per min., €4.60 per hr. Open M-Sa 11am-about midnight. The cheapest email in town is at the **Centre Departemental d'Information Jeunesse** (see above).

Post Office: 6 pl. de l'Hôtel de Ville (☎05 46 30 41 30). **Currency exchange.** Main office at 52 av. Mulhouse, by the train station. Open M-F 8am-7pm, Sa 8am-noon. For **Poste Restante:** "Hôtel de Ville, 17021 La Rochelle." Open M-F 8:30am-6:30pm, Sa 8am-12:30pm. **Postal code:** 17000.

▶ ACCOMMODATIONS AND CAMPING

Cheap beds in town are limited, especially in the summer; make reservations in early June for trips in July and August, when rates are higher. The rates listed below are for high season, and those hotels that offer better deals the rest of the year are noted.

Hôtel Terminus, pl. de la Motte-Rouge (☎05 46 50 69 69; Claude.LECORVIC@wanadoo.fr). Victorian wallpaper and furniture create a romantic ambience in this hotel, complete with a sunny lounge on the first floor and restaurant-like breakfast room. Breakfast €5.70. Singles and doubles with toilet €40-49, with shower, toilet, and satellite TV €49-60; triples and quads €64-70. MC/V. ❹

Centre International de Séjour, Auberge de Jeunesse (HI), av. des Minimes (☎05 46 44 43 11; fax 05 46 45 41 48). Take bus #10 (dir: Port des Minimes) from av. de Colmar, 1 block from the station, to "Lycell Hotelier" (M-Sa every 20min. until 7:15pm, €1.20). Continue walking in direction of bus up to traffic circle, and take left-most turn off traffic circle. Follow this road for about 15min. Hostel set back from road on the right-hand side. Or enjoy the view of the waterside walk. Keep to the port edges and watch for the hostel on your left, at the end of the boardwalk. (30min. from station.) Enormous, hospital-like hostel with dark 2- to 6-bunk dorms and sailboat-patterned blankets. Breakfast included. Restaurant overlooking the marina sells decent food at cheap prices (*plats* and *salades* €5 or less). Laundry. Reception July-Aug. 8:30am-11pm; Sept.-June 8am-12:30pm, 1:30-7:30pm, and 8:30-10pm. Lockout 10am-2pm. Code for entry after 11:30pm. Reserve ahead. Dorms €12.50; singles €18. ●

Hôtel Henry IV, 31 rue des Gentilshommes (☎05 46 41 25 79; fax 05 46 41 78 64), on pl. de la Caille off rue du Temple, in the heart of the *vieille ville*. Cozy wood-paneled floral rooms reminiscent of a bed and breakfast, 1970s tiled bathrooms in brown and orange, cheery dining room with a giant photograph of sunflowers. Breakfast €5.50. Singles and doubles with toilet €34-37, with toilet and shower €42-46; triples and quads €54-68. Rates are lower by about €5 in low season. MC/V. ●

Hôtel de Bordeaux, 43 rue St-Nicolas (☎05 46 41 31 22; fax 05 46 41 24 43; www.hotel-bordeaux-fr.com), right off quai Valin, 5min. from station. A great location, with 22 recently renovated rooms in bright shades of yellow and blue above a café. Breakfast €5.10. Reception 8am-9:30pm. Singles and doubles with toilet €29-34.80, with shower €33-44, with toilet and shower €37-48; extra person €10.70. Low-season rates lower, but all rates may rise next year. AmEx/MC/V. ●

Bar de l'Hôtel de Ville, 5 rue St-Yon (☎05 46 41 30 25). Hotel-bar in the center of town houses students during the year and offers its pastel rooms and linoleum floors to travelers mid-June to Aug. The cheapest rooms on the cramped top floor will make you feel like an impoverished, overworked French grad student, complete with the occasional smoky smell. Reception closed Su and after 8pm weeknights. Rooms €26-29, with shower and toilet €35. One studio apartment, complete with bathroom and fully equipped kitchenette (€54 per day, €305 per week). ●

Camping Municipal du Soleil, av. Michel Crépeau (☎05 46 44 42 53). A 10min. walk from the city center past the old port along the quai, following av. Marillac to the left at its junction with allée des Tamaris. Or catch bus #10 (dir: Port des Minimes). Crowded, friendly campground close to the port. Open mid-May to Sept. 15. Reservations suggested. One person and car €6.80; extra person €3.10. The tourist office has a list of more distant campsites and info on more beautiful but remote island camping. ●

🍴 FOOD

The *fruits de mer* are always ripe in La Rochelle; follow the fishy smell to the **covered market** at pl. du Marché for fresh seafood, fruit, and vegetables. (Open daily 7am-1pm.) **Monoprix**, on rue de Palais, near the clocktower, sells the usual (open M-Sa 8:30am-8pm, July-Aug. M-Sa 8:30am-9pm and Su 9am-noon), as do the **Co-ops** which have sprung up around town; two are at 41 rue Sardinerie and 17 rue Amelot. (Both open daily 9am-1pm and 3:30-8pm.) Restaurants crowd the *vieille ville* along **rue St-Jean** and the quai.

A Côté de Chez Fred, 30-32 rue St-Nicolas (☎05 46 41 65 76). This little seafood place physically surrounds its supplier, Poissonnerie Fred; you can watch the fish being prepared through an open window. *Plats* €7-13. Don't skip the fish soup (€5.80). Open M-Sa noon-2:30pm and 7-10:30pm. AmEx/MC/V. ●

La Provençale Pizzeria, 15 rue St. Jean du Perot (☎05 46 41 43 68). Despite its name, pizza is only a small part of the menu at this restaurant, which serves many local favorites including mussels, duck, and the ever-popular rabbit. 3-course *menu* €11. Open M-Sa noon-2pm and 7-9pm, Su 7-9pm. ❷

Le Cedre, 22 rue des Templiers (☎05 46 41 03 89). Like most French cities, La Rochelle is full of fast food places that sell kebabs, but fresh vegetables and quality bread at this Lebanese take-out separate it from the rest. Sandwiches €3-5 (kebabs, chicken, falafel, and good ol' hamburgers); fries €2-3. Open daily noon-2pm and 7-10pm. ❶

🔊 SIGHTS

THE OLD TOWN. The pedestrian *vieille ville*, dating from the 17th and 18th centuries, stretches beyond the whitewashed townhouses of the harbor to a glitzy inland shopping district sprinkled with museums. Stroll by the 14th-century **grosse horloge** (great clocktower), but skip the archaeological exhibit inside. Check out the Renaissance **Hôtel de Ville,** with its prominent statue of Henry IV, who built it. *(45min. French tours of the interior July-Aug. daily 3 and 4pm; June and Sept. daily 3pm, Oct.-May Sa-Su 3pm. €3, students €1.50.)*

TOUR ST-NICOLAS AND TOUR DE LA CHAÎNE. The 14th-century towers guarding the port guaranteed La Rochelle's safety from attack—essential in a city that served as a giant warehouse for both France and England. When hostile ships approached, guards closed the harbor by raising a chain between the two towers. Now unfit for such use, the 800-year-old chain lines the path leading from rue de la Chaîne to the tower. Today, La Rochelle's citizens are more worried about getting out than preventing others from getting in: the harbor has begun to silt up dangerously. Tour St-Nicolas, on the left as you face the harbor, has impressive fortifications and narrow, dizzying staircases; in the Tour de la Chaîne is a fascinating timeline of the city's history (text in French only) with a model of the town in Richelieu's day. *(St-Nicolas ☎05 46 41 74 13; Chaîne ☎06 46 34 11 81. Both towers open July-Aug. daily 10am-7pm; May 15-June and Sept. 1-15 daily 10am-1pm and 2-6pm; Sept. 16-May 14 Tu-Su 10am-12:30pm and 2-5:30pm. €4, ages 18-25 €2.50, under 18 free. Combined ticket including Tour de la Lanterne €7, ages 18-25 €4.50; Oct.-May free first Su of the month.)*

TOUR DE LA LANTERNE. Accessible from the Tour de la Chaîne by a low rampart, this 58m high tower was France's first lighthouse. The 15th-century tower has a morbid history—it became known as the **Tour des Prêtres** after 13 priests were thrown from the steeple during the Wars of Religion. In 1822, four sergeants were imprisoned here before being executed in Paris for conspiring against the monarch. The 162 steps to the top hold intricate graffiti carved into the stone by other 19th-century detainees, providing historical documentation of castles and shipwrecks. At the summit, only three inches of stone separate you from your own 45m free-fall, but you can see all the way to the Ile d'Oléron on sunny days. *(☎05 46 34 11 81. Same hours and prices as the Tour St-Nicolas.)*

🔊 AQUARIUM. The newly reopened aquarium is home to a whopping 10,000 marine animals, kept in habitats that simulate everything from the French Atlantic coast to the tropical rainforest. Audio tours in English (€3.50) are filled with fascinating fish tales, like that of chivalrous male jawfish who carries his eggs in his mouth for two weeks before they hatch, forgoing food for the sake of his offspring. The aquarium makes a perfect rainy day activity, but be prepared for the crowds of people with the same idea. *(Bassin des Grande Yacht, next to the Musée Maritime. ☎05 46 34 00 00. Open July-Aug. daily 9am-11pm; Apr.-June and Sept. 9am-8pm; Oct.-Mar. 9am-8pm. €10, students and children €7.)*

MUSÉE DU NOUVEAU MONDE. This museum explores France's political, social, and economic relations with the New World, a theme that is particularly relevant to La Rochelle, which once served as a major port. Exhibits of paintings, maps, and sculptures depict the New World from France's point of view. It's pretty clear that the French thought New-Worlders were bestial savages. *Plus ça change...* *(10 rue Fleuriau. ☎ 05 46 41 46 50. Open M and W-Sa 10:30am-12:30pm and 1:30-6pm, Su 3-6pm. €3.50, students and children under 18 free.)*

MUSÉE D'ORBIGNY-BERNON. The Musée holds a respectable collection of European and Chinese decorative arts and ceramics, including special exhibits on Japanese samurai and 17th to 19th-century Chinese life and ancient musical instruments from Southeast Asia. The museum also covers local history—they've got a wonderful display of 84 pharmaceutical vases from the old Aufredi hospital. *(2 rue St-Côme. ☎ 05 46 41 18 83. Open M and W-Sa 10am-noon and 2-6pm, Su 2-6pm. €3.50, students and under 18 free. €6.55 buys combined admission to the Musées d'Orbigny-Bernon, Nouveau Monde, and Beaux-Arts. Joint ticket available at tourist office, valid for one month.)*

MUSÉE DU FLAÇON À PARFUM. In the shopping district near la Grosse Horloge, a burst of sweet fragrances greets visitors to this tiny tribute to scent on the second floor of the Saponaire perfume shop. A private collector has amassed thousands of perfume bottles, including *crème parfum* flasks produced by the Ku Klux Klan in 1933, and bottles designed by Cocteau, Dali, and Mirò. One 1937 bottle is modeled on Mae West's torso. Descriptions available in English. *(33 rue du Temple. ☎ 05 46 41 32 40. Open M 2:30-7pm, Tu-Sa 10:30am-noon and 2-7pm; July-Aug. also open Tu-Sa noon-2pm. €4.30, students €3.80, under 10 free.)*

OTHER SIGHTS. The outdoor **Musée Maritime Neptunéa de la Rochelle** consists of seven decks's worth of exhibits on two large fishing boats; special exhibits include a wind tunnel (for storm simulations), a display on locals fishing techniques, and a submarine. *(Pl. Bernard Moitessier. ☎ 05 46 28 03 00. Open Apr.-Sept. daily 10am-6:30pm, closes at 7:30pm in July and Aug.; Oct-Mar. 2-6pm. Closed late Nov.-Jan. Last entry 1½hr. before closing. €7, students and children €5.)* There are paintings by Rembrandt and Delacroix in the **Musée des Beaux Arts,** along with a nice Fromentin series—the latter ones can be found on postcards all over town. Look for Signac's 18th-century painting of the bustling city harbor. *(28 rue Gargoulleau. ☎ 05 46 41 64 65. Open W-M 2-5pm. €3.35, students and children under 18 free.)*

🎵 ENTERTAINMENT AND FESTIVALS

La Coursive, 4 rue St-Jean-du-Perot, hosts operas, jazz and classical music concerts, traditional and experimental plays, dance performances, and art films. (☎ 05 46 51 54 02; fax 05 46 51 54 03. Open M 5-9pm, Tu-Sa 1-8pm, Su 2-6:30pm.) On summer evenings, **quai Duperré** and **cours des Dames** are closed to cars and open to mimes, jugglers, musicians, and an open market. (July-Sept.) For a cool place to hang out on a summer night, head to the **cour du Temple,** a lively square tucked away off rue des Templiers. **L'Academie de la Bière,** housed in a classic *vieille ville* white stone building, is the perfect place to learn about all the different brews they offer. (☎ 05 46 43 77 52. Open daily noon-2am.) Try relaxed **Le Mayflower** for its €3 rum concoction. (☎ 05 46 50 51 39. Open daily 6pm-late.) Along the waters of the old port, join the dressed-down folks at **La Vague,** 16 Quai Duperré, for a cocktail amidst the surf boards and sun umbrellas. (☎ 05 46 30 53 19. Open daily 7pm-3am.)

The crowd is young at the twin nightclubs **Oxford and Papagayo Discothèque,** plage de la Concurrence. Oxford offers a wild night of dancing under a giant disco ball while Papagayo is a fun-filled party complete with fake palm trees, 80's music, and karaoke. (☎ 05 46 41 51 81. Cover €5, €9.50 with drink. Open W-M 11pm-5am.)

Decked with mirrors, brass, and lacquer, **Le Triolet**, 8 rue des Carmes, gets a lot of yuppies very silly on 94 different kinds of whiskey. From 7 to 11pm, the mood is classy, with a piano providing jazz, but after 11pm things heat up as Le Triolet turns into a discotheque with an eclectic soundtrack. (☎ 05 46 41 70 16. Cover €16.50. Open July-Aug. daily 7pm-5am; low-season M-Sa 7pm-5am.)

La Rochelle's popular festivals attract art-loving, sun-seeking mobs like nowhere else. During the last week of June and the first week of July, the city becomes the Cannes of the Atlantic with its **Festival International du Film de La Rochelle.** French fans come from Paris to stay up all night watching films. If you get lucky, you might even spot Juliette Binoche in the crowd. (☎ 05 46 51 54 00. All 100 films €77; 3 films €15; one film €6; under 21, 10 films €29. For tickets, write to 16 rue St-Sabin, 75011 Paris.) Without batting an eyelash, La Rochelle turns around and holds its **FrancoFolies,** a massive six-day music festival in mid-July that brings francophone performers from around the world. (☎ 05 46 28 28 28; www.francofolies.fr. Event tickets €10-30.) And to round out the month, the end of July sees a 10-day **theater festival** on quai Simenon. (☎ 05 46 34 33 75.) During the 2nd week of September, hundreds of boats in the Port des Minimes open their immaculate interiors to the public for the **Grand Pavois,** a boat competition, known as "the foremost floating boat show in Europe." (☎ 05 46 44 46 39; www.grand-pavois.com.) The **marathon** runs through town at the end of November (☎ 05 46 44 42 19).

ISLANDS NEAR LA ROCHELLE

ILE DE RÉ

Ile de Ré, dubbed "Ré La Blanche" for its 70km of fine, white sand beaches, is a sunny paradise just 10km from La Rochelle. Connected by a bridge to the mainland, the 30km long island contains one of Europe's largest nature preserves, extensive paved bike paths, pine forests, farmland, vineyards, bustling towns, and huge stretches of untouched sand. Though only 15,000 lucky people live on the island year-round, July and August bring crowds to the beaches on the southern half and to the main town, **St-Martin-de-Ré,** in the middle of the north coast.

▣ **TRANSPORTATION.** The island is easily accessible by bus. Driving across **pont La Pallice** costs a ridiculous €18 round-trip in tolls from June to September. (Oct.-May €10; €3 for motorcycles and scooters.) **Walking** and **biking** are easy options, and the cycle from La Rochelle to Sablanceaux takes less than an hour. The ride is a bit tough going up the 4km long bridge, but once you get there, the trails on the island are marvelous, with great coastal views. From pl. de Verdun in La Rochelle, head west on av. Maréchal Leclerc and follow road signs to Ile de Ré until the bike path appears on the left. If that thought makes your calves quiver, city bus lines #1 and 50 (dir: La Pallice) go as far as Sablanceaux, the first beach on the island after the bridge. (20 min., July-Aug. 32 per day, €1.20; make sure the bus is going to Sablanceaux, some run on lines 1 and 50 stop before crossing the bridge.) If you'd like to venture beyond Sablanceaux, try **Rébus,** which runs between pl. de Verdun and village on Ré, including St-Martin (45min., 8 per day, €4.60) and Les Portes, at the northern tip (1½hr., 8 per day, €8). (☎ 05 46 09 20 15. Info office at the Gare Routière, av. Bouthilier in St. Martin. Open Tu-Sa 10-11:50am and 1-6pm.) Once you get to Ile de Ré, there are plenty of places to rent bikes in each village. **Cycland** has branches in Sablanceaux, La Flotte, St-Martin, Ars, Les Portes, St-Clément, and La Couarde. (☎ 05 46 09 08 66. Bikes €3-5 per hr., €7 per day. Deposit €200 by check or cash. Open July-Aug. daily 9am-7:30pm; Sept.-June 9:30am-1pm and 2:30-7pm. AmEx/MC/V.)

Ile de Ré

- Phare des Baleines
- St-Clement-des-Baleines
- Plage de la Conche des Balaines
- Ars-en-Ré
- Les Portes-en-Ré
- ATLANTIC OCEAN
- Plage des Prises
- Loix
- Plage du Peu Ragot
- La Couarde-sur-Mer
- Plage des Anerles
- Plage du Petit Sergent
- Le Bois-Plage-en-Ré
- St-Martin-de-Ré
- Plage des Gollandières
- Plage du Pas des Boeufs
- Plage de Gros Jonc
- La Flotte
- La Noue
- Abbaye des Châteliers
- Oyster beds (écluses)
- Ste-Marie-de-Ré
- Fort de la Prée
- FRANCE / Ile de Ré
- Rivedoux Beach
- Sablanceaux
- Plage Sud
- Pont La Pallice
- TO MAINLAND (4km)

0 — 2 miles
0 — 2 kilometers

🛈 PRACTICAL INFORMATION. The largest and most centrally located town on the island, **St-Martin-de-Ré** (pop. 2650) is the best starting place for exploring Ile de Ré. It's a good idea to pick up the free tourist booklet in La Rochelle, but you can get a free bike path map at St-Martin's **tourist office**, on quai Nicolas Baudin. (☎05 46 09 20 06; fax 05 46 09 06 18; ot.st.martin@wanadoo.fr. Open July-Aug. daily 10am-8pm; May-June and Sept. 10am-1pm and 2-7pm; Oct.-Apr. 10am-noon and 2-6pm, closed Su afternoon.) The best **currency exchange** rate, with a 1% commission, is at **Crédit Agricole**, 4 quai Foran, on the port. (☎05 46 09 20 14. Open Tu-F 9am-12:15pm and 1:30-6pm, Sa 9am-12:45pm.) The **post office** is on pl. de la République. (☎05 46 09 20 14.) **Postal code:** 17410.

🛏 ACCOMMODATIONS AND CAMPING. Prices go way up in the summer. St-Martin's **Hôtel Le Sully ❸**, 19 rue Jean Jaurès, has wood-paneled rooms with lace curtains a block up from the port on a busy pedestrian street. (☎05 46 09 26 94; fax 05 46 09 06 85. Breakfast €4.60. Singles or doubles with shower €29-37, with toilet and shower or bath €37-42; extra bed €7.60. Oct.-May prices lower. MC/V.) There are also places to stay in smaller towns. In **La Flotte**, 4km east of St-Martin and 9km north of Sablanceaux, is **l'Hippocampe ❸**, 16 rue Château des Mauléons, with small, comfortable rooms. (☎05 46 09 60 68. Breakfast €5. Shower €2.50. Reserve ahead. Singles and doubles €28, with bath €39. MC/V.) Campsites are plentiful on Ile de Ré, but those between the bridge and St-Martin-de-Ré are very crowded in July and August. One of the most popular sites is gorgeous **Camping Tamaris ❶**, 4 rue du Comte D'Hastre, right near **Rivedoux**'s center, a thickly forested site in one of the island's best spots. (☎05 46 09 81 28. Open Easter-Sept. 1-3 people €11.50, extra person €3.80, under age 7 €2. Electricity €3.20.) If you're seeking solitude head to beachside **La Plage ❶**, 408 rte. du Chaume, near St-Clément. (☎05 46 29 42 62. Open Apr.-Sept. 2 people with tent €12.50, €4 per extra person.)

🍴🎭 FOOD AND ENTERTAINMENT. Island restaurants are pricey, but most towns have pizzerias and *crêperies* as well as **morning markets,** which are listed in full in Ré's tourist packet. St-Martin's **market** is indoors off rue Jean Jaurès, by the port. (Open Tu-Sa 10am-12:30pm and 2-7pm.) Two supermarkets, **Intermarché** and **Super U,** are just east of St-Martin on the road to La Flotte. (Open July-Aug. M-Sa 8:30am-8pm, Su 8:30am-12:30pm; Sept.-June M-Sa 9am-noon and 3-7:30pm.)

IN RECENT NEWS

THE TRUE "SURVIVOR"

Off the coast of Poitou-Charentes, between the Ile d'Oleron and the Ile d'Aix, stands a remarkable fortification of stone, Fort Boyard. The fort was an idea long before it became a reality. During Louis XIV's time a royal engineer suggested building a fort in the sea to protect the islands from attack by the English, but he was scoffed at as a fanciful dreamer. Napoleon later seized this dream, which suited his ambitious attitude. Ironically, construction went so slowly that by the time it was completed in 1848 it was no longer needed for military defense. Instead, like many forts and châteaux in the 19th century, it was turned into a prison.

Recently, Fort Boyard's dramatic setting has been put to a very different use, as it has become the location for the TV game show *Les Clefs du Fort Boyard* (The Keys of Fort Boyard). Long before English-speaking folks were starving themselves and performing repulsive feats on reality TV shows, *Les Clefs* was putting 6-member teams through rigorous challenges. Contestants must face everything from swinging weapons to swarming insects in order to win gold coins. Through it all, they must avoid tigers lurking in the fort—a defense strategy Napoleon would be proud to call his own.

Apparently, this whole ordeal has a great deal of appeal to audiences, as the show is still a hit in France and spin-offs have sprung up in 8 other countries, including Britain and the US. *La Comédie Française*? Hardly. But entertaining? Most definitely.

St-Martin has a surprisingly good nightlife for its size. Port-side vendors stay open until 11pm or midnight during the summer to please the late-night tourists, and locals shuttle between the bars and discos all night. **Le Cubana** and **Boucquingham,** both on Venelle de la Fosse Bray, are intimate piano bars tucked behind the quai, across from the tourist office. (Cubana ☎ 05 46 09 93 49; Boucquingham ☎ 05 46 09 01 20. Both open M-Th 5pm-2am and F-Sa 5pm-3am. €8 cover with one drink most nights. MC/V.) **Le Bastion,** cours Pasteur, across town with a great view of the sea, is a wild all-purpose grill, pizzeria, nightclub, and disco. It hosts weekly theme nights in summer. (☎ 05 46 09 21 92. Open Tu-Sa 5:30pm-5am.) Farther down the island, on Rivedoux plage, **Le Réseu Club,** pl. de la République, cranks it out from 11pm to 5am every Friday and Saturday night. (☎ 05 46 09 30 90. €10 cover.)

🔾 **TOWNS AND SIGHTS.** Between Sablanceaux and beachy La Flotte are the ruins of the 13th-century **Abbaye des Châteliers.** First built in 1156, the abbey was destroyed during the Wars of Religion as Ré passed between Catholic and Protestant hands. The monks abandoned the abbey in 1574, and many of its stones were then taken in 1625 to build the Prée Fort. The ruins now stand in an isolated field, visible from the bus from Sablanceaux or Rivedoux to La Flotte. **La Flotte** (pop. 2700) is the island's most typical fishing town, with a very lively port and pedestrian area. It is home to the **EcoMusée La Maison du Platin,** av. du front de Mer, 4 cours Felix Fauré, devoted to the history of island's major industries: fish, salt, and wine. The museum hosts walking tours in French of the town, the Abbey des Chateliers, and nearby oyster farms (€3.80). Schedules vary; call for information. (☎ 05 46 09 61 39. Open Apr. to mid-Nov. M-F 10:30am-noon and 2:30-6pm, Su 2:30-5:30pm. Admission €3.50, ages 7-18 €2.) Learn more about the island's fishing traditions with a tour (90min.) of the **écluses à poissons,** medieval fishing devices. These stone walls, which lie along the southern coast's beaches near Sablanceaux, were erected so that fish would be trapped when the tide went out. (Call the tourist office in St-Marie for a schedule at ☎ 05 46 30 22 92. Wear boots!)

St-Martin holds a port built by Vauban and a citadel built by Louis XIV to protect Ré from the invading English; the citadel is now an active prison, with around 500 inmates. The 15th- to 17th-century Renaissance gallery of the **Hôtel Clerjotte,** on av. Victor-Bouthilier, houses the **Musée Ernest Cognac,** which is devoted to the history of the island, and filled with model ships, old paintings, and archaeological finds. (☎ 05 46 09 21 22. Open July-Sept. daily 10am-1pm and 2-7pm; Oct.-June W-Su 10am-noon and 2-5pm. €4, students €2.) Climb up the hill from the quai to the imposing 15th-century **Eglise St-Martin**, originally Romanesque but built and destroyed so many times in religious wars that its outside and interior now have no stylistic relation. From the top of the church's belltower you can take in a spectacular view of the entire island. (July-Aug. open daily 9:30am-11:30pm, Sept.-June 9:30am-sunset. Admission to church free; belltower €1.50, children €0.75.) On your way up the island, stop by **Ars** to admire its 17 windmills, dismantled in the 19th century when a phyloxera plague wiped out the island's chief crop. As you near **St-Clément-des-Baleines,** keep your eye out for the blinking red light of the 1854 **Phare des Baleines;** flashing once every 15 seconds, the lighthouse is watched by boats over 60km away. You can climb its 167 stairs for a view of the ocean. (Apr.-June 10am-7pm; July-Aug. 9:30am-7:30pm; Sept. 10am-6pm; Oct.-Mar. 10:30am-1pm and 2-5:30pm. €2, children €1.)

BIKES AND BEACHES. It's easy to rent a bike in any island town and pedal along the bike paths, coastal sidewalks, and wooded lanes spread out across the island. Although everybody and his grandmother bikes the southern half of Ile de Ré to St-Martin, crowds thin out as you travel north. The *Guide des Itinéraires Cyclables,* available from island tourist offices, describes five 10-22km paths. One of the island's best trails begins in Le Martray, just east of Ars, and runs along the northern coast through the island's trademark salt marsh and bird preserve, a wetlands sanctuary humming with the songs of the rare blue-throated thrush and heron. The marsh is worth visiting in the summer, but winter's really the time to see it—20,000 birds stop by on their migration from Siberia and Canada to Africa. Rent a bike in Ars to pedal this trail. Other bike paths lead you through forests, beside beaches, and past other island landmarks.

The major attraction of the island is, of course, its splendid beaches. Slather yourself with sunscreen and shake off all inhibitions at the **Plage du Petit Bec** in clothing-optional **Les Portes-en-Ré.** If you want to avoid that full-body glow, head to the pine-fringed dunes of **Plage de la Conche des Balaines,** near the lighthouse just off the Gare Bec. Both beaches, at the northern tip of the island, are huge and empty of the crowds that fill beaches on the western coast. The sea off the exposed north coast tends to be dangerous, and the shores rocky; for better swimming, try the long strip of beach along the southern shore, beginning at **La Couarde.**

ILE D'AIX

Smaller and less accessible than Ré, Aix (pop. 200) is almost entirely free of the souvenir shops and fast food stands that cover most towns in this region. Aix sees its fair share of visitors (250,000 a year), but this island maintains the feel of unspoiled wilderness. Just 3km long and barely 600m wide, the island has backwoods trails perfect for quiet hiking, and tiny coves set in the rocky, shell-covered coastline. The best beaches are along the southwest edge near the lighthouses. There are almost no cars on Aix, because it's one of the only coastal islands with no highway to the mainland. To get here, it's ferry or bust.

Once on the island, stop for a free map and brochure at the **Point Accueil** (☎ 05 46 83 01 82), on your right as you leave the port. The info center also organizes guided **historical tours** of the island in French (1hr.; 3 per day 11am-4:30pm; €3, under age 12 free). **Horse carriages** do the same number of rounds from one block farther up. (☎ 05 46 84 07 18. 50min.; €6, under age 10 €5.) To explore the island, **rent bicycles** from *crêperies* and snack shops in town. (Approx. €3.50 per hr., €8.50 per day.) Some of the most beautiful coastal spots on the island are accessible only by foot, and it takes only two hours to walk around the island.

This island's most famous visitor was Napoleon, who spent his last three post-Waterloo days here before he surrendered to the British, a fact celebrated in the island's two museums. The **Musée Africain** and **Musée Napoléonien** house their small but impressive collections in the island's tiny town center, surrounded by a sprinkling of public buildings, flower-laced bungalows, and little shops. The Musée Africain presents an ethnographical and zoological exhibition on Napoleon's Egyptian campaign. The Musée Napoléonien has a vast collection of portraits, bric-a-brac, and war memorabilia, including a facsimile of the emperor's totally illegible surrender to the British and 40 clocks with statues of Napoleon that were all stopped at 5:49, the time of his death. (☎05 46 84 66 40. Both open June-Sept. W-M 9:30am-6pm; Apr. and Oct. 9:30am-1pm and 2-6pm; Nov.-Mar. 9am-12:30pm and 2-5pm. Separate admission €3, ages 18-25 €2.30, under 18 free. Combined admission before 4:30pm €4, ages 18-25 €3.) Farther inland lies **Fort Liedoit,** built by Napoleon to protect this tiny but strategically located island off the coast of France. The fort housed German prisoners during World Wars I and II and was later turned into a summer camp for children until the government bought it and designated it as a historical monument in 1980. (July and Aug. tours available through the tourist office; 4 times a day 11am-4:30pm; €3.)

Ile d'Aix's only hotel, **Hôtel Napoleon ❹,** on rue Gourgaud, is expensive, but the hotel's spacious fresh rooms will provide a peaceful night. (☎05 46 84 66 02. Singles and doubles with shower €54, with shower and toilet €57-60; demi-pension for two people €93.) For an unique camping experience try the quiet **Camping le Fort de la Rade ❶,** which is inside a fort next to the port; stone walls and purple lilacs surround your tent. (☎05 46 84 28 28; fax 05 46 84 00 00. If you arrive after the reception is closed, you're welcome to enter on your own, as long as you pay in the morning. €5.50-7.50 per tent, €4 per person, €2.50 per child.) The few restaurants on Aix tend to be pricey. The **bakery,** on your right as you walk up rue Gourgaud, sells cheap sandwiches, and there's a little grocery store with all the essentials just across the street. The cheerful restaurant **Pressoir ❸,** in the middle of the island on rue Le Bois Joly, is run by a bunch of young fisherman types with perpetual five-o'clock shadows. Enjoy fresh *moules frites* on the terrace for €9.70. (☎05 46 84 09 37. Open daily noon-3pm and 7-11pm. *Menus* €10.50-23.)

In the summer, **ferries** link Aix to La Rochelle. **Inter Iles,** 14 cours des Dames, runs boats to the island via the fascinating Fort Bayard. (☎05 46 50 51 88. 1½hr.; round-trip €21, children €11; 2-4 ferries per day, July-Aug. 4 per day; half-day round-trip €17, children €9. MC/V.) Similar service is provided by **Croisières Océanes.** Their booth is on the cours des Dames in La Rochelle. (☎05 46 50 68 44. 1hr.; €21 round-trip, ages 4-12 €10. Ask about *Journées Promotion,* when prices dip to €12. MC/V.)

THE MARAIS POITEVIN

Stretching west from Niort to the Atlantic just north of La Rochelle, this natural preserve has been nicknamed *la Venise Verte* (the Green Venice) for the serene canals which wind through its wetlands and forests. Biking along the banks, or punting on the canals, you'll pass weeping willows, purple irises, herons, lots of cows, and the occasional rustic home. At its start by the Sèvre Niortaise river, graceful trees form a canopy overhead and duckweed carpets the water's surface, making the canals look like grassy paths. Toward the coast, the lush greenery gradually gives way to the dry marsh. The canals enhance agriculture and control flooding, ensuring that small-scale farming remains the region's primary industry.

Though well worth the trouble, the Marais is not a very convenient daytrip; consider spending a night if you come. Most towns are tiny and inaccessible by public transport, so the local hub of **Niort** is the best base from which to explore the region. From Niort it's easy to get to **Coulon,** where you can hire bikes or boats to get into the Marais. Both Niort and Coulon's tourist offices provide info and maps and sell an excellent walking and biking map, the *Pays du Marais Poitevin des Deux-Sèvres Carte Touristique* (€4.90).

NIORT

Niort's greatest attribute is its prime location, just a 20min. bus ride from Coulon, and an easy entrance to the Marais. Though Niort (pop. 16,000) does boast its own château, proximity to the Sèvre Niortaise River, and a fair number of restaurants and hotels, its quiet streets are at best peaceful, if not simply dull.

⑦ PRACTICAL INFORMATION. Trains run from Niort to Paris (2½hr., 11 per day, €45.20); La Rochelle (45min., 8 per day, €9.40); Poitiers (1hr., 8 per day, €12.40); Saintes (45min., 6-7 per day, €9.70); Royan (1¼hr., 5 per day, €13.40). Info open M-Th and Sa 6-11:45am and 12:50-7:30pm, F 6-11:45am and 12:50-9:40pm, Su 11am-noon and 1-8:30pm. Right next to the train station, at the **Gare Routière,** you can catch **CASA buses** to La Garette and Coulon (see the daytrip below). Niort has numerous **car rental** agencies all within one block of the train station. Choose from Budget, Hertz, Europcar, National, and Avis.

From the train station, follow the signs to the Centre Ville to get to the **tourist office,** which is at 16 rue du Petit St-Jean, next to the Hôtel de Ville. They can provide you with maps and info on the Marais and Niort. They also offer horse and boat rentals for visitors exploring the Marais. (☎ 05 49 24 18 79; fax 05 49 24 98 90; www.niortourisme.com. Open July-Aug. M-Sa 9:30am-7pm and Su 10am-1pm; Apr.-June and Sept.-Nov. M-Sa 9:30am-6:30pm; Dec.-Mar. M-F 9:30am-6pm and Sa 9:30am-12:30pm. Reservations required. Horse rental €93 for three days; boats €54 per day for 4-5 people.) The emergency number for the **police** is ☎ 17; the **hospital** is at 40 av. Charles de Gaulle (☎ 05 49 32 79 79). There's **Internet access** at **Medi@click,** 6 r. Porete St-Jean, near pl. St-Jean d'Angely. (☎ 05 49 28 31 31. Open Tu-Sa 9am-noon and 2-6pm.) The **post office** is at 4 rue Ernest Perochon. (☎ 05 49 24 38 15. Open M-F 8:30am-6:30pm, Sa 8:30am-noon.) **Postal code:** 79000.

⑦⑦ ACCOMMODATIONS AND FOOD. Just across from the train station, **Hôtel de L'Univers ❷,** 22 rue Mazagran, offers upscale carpeted rooms and a courtyard garden. (☎ 05 49 24 41 70; fax 05 49 77 09 52. Breakfast €4.50. Singles €25-35; doubles €29-40; triples €32-40.) Or try the **Hôtel St-Jean ❷,** 21 av. St-Jean d'Angely, halfway between the train station and the center of town. From the station, walk straight up rue de la Gare, which will change its name to rue du 24 Février. When you reach the place St-Jean turn left onto av. St-Jean (not to be confused with the rue Porte St-Jean, which is to the right); the hotel is one block up on the left. (8min.) Presided over by a cheery owner, the well-lit rooms have thin walls with printed floral wall paper that will remind you of your grandmother's house. (☎ 05 49 79 20 76; fax 05 49 35 03 27; hotelsaintJean@wanadoo.fr. Breakfast €3.50. Singles €18-24; doubles €20-27; triples and quads €27-33. MC/V.) **Camping Municipal ❶,** 21 bd. Salvador-Allende, is a grassy campsite along the river 2km from town. Take TAN bus #2 from pl. de la Breche to "Tour Chabut" (€1.15 per person, *carnet* of 10 €8.50). Reserve ahead in July and August. (☎ 05 49 79 05 06; fax 05 49 79 05 06. Campgrounds open April-Sept. Reception 7am-10pm. €2.75 per person, €1.65 per child; €1.40 per car. Tent rental €1.10. Electricity €2.45.)

Locals congregate in **rue Victor Hugo** and **rue Ricard,** and at the covered **market** in Les Halles. (Open Tu-Su 9am-1pm, larger version Th and Sa.) The **Marché Plus** supermarket, on rue Victor Hugo, is just past the Place Pilori. (Open M-Sa 7am-9pm.) Vegetarians and fans of organic food will find good choices including salads and steak at **Les Deux Chèvres ❸,** 19 rue Basse. (☎ 05 49 05 10 44. *Menu* €15. Open M 7-10pm, Tu-Sa noon-2pm and 7-10pm.)

◙ **SIGHTS.** The center of town lies on the banks of the Sèvre Niortaise, and several monuments from different periods in the town's history are strung out along the river. Look for the elegant Gothic **Eglise St-André**, the Renaissance **Hôtel de Ville** (also known as **Le Pilori**), the 14th-century **Eglise Notre-Dame,** and the bold 12th century **Donjon,** all that remains of Richard the Lionheart's former castle. The well-preserved towers in the latter hold an archaeological and historical museum, complete with pottery found in this region dating back to 2000 BC. The castle's battlements provide a remarkable view of Niort and the surrounding countryside. (☎05 49 78 72 00. Open May 2-Sept. 15 W-M 9am-noon and 2-6pm; Sept. 16-May 9am-noon and 2-5pm. €2.80, W free; students and seniors free.)

▓ **NIGHTLIFE.** Although most of Niort's streets are empty at night, the **rue St-Gelais** stays lively with its two discothèques: **Le Cubana** (☎05 49 17 17 25) a small club packed with a loud crowd of students; and **Le Mylord,** where a crazy color scheme of orange-painted walls and blue sofa-chairs provides the setting for an older crowd. (Open Th-Sa 11pm-5am.) To get to rue St-Gelais from the place de la Breche, head up rue Ricard and turn right onto rue J. J. Rousseau; rue St-Gelais will be straight ahead.

COULON

Tiny Coulon's (pop. 2200) winding streets and bridges run alongside the canals of the Marais, making it the ideal spot from which to take a boat into the Marais. **CASA Autocars,** 11-13 chemin du Fief Binard (☎05 49 24 93 47), come from Niort's Gare Routière (next to the train station) and its central pl. de la Brèche (30min.; M-Sa 6 per day, Su and holidays 2 per day 12:10 and 6:10pm, return 1:28 and 7:28pm; €1.80, students €1.60). Take bus #20 (dir: Coulon/Marais Poitvin).

Once here, the most practical way to get farther into the Marais is by boat or bike, though many hitch (not recommended by *Let's Go*). Head to the **tourist office,** rue Gabriel Auchier, for general info about the Marais's offerings; there are bike, canoe, and punt rental locations all over the town. (☎05 49 35 99 29. Tourist office open July-Aug. daily 10am-1pm and 2-7pm; call for off-season hours. Hotel and chambres d'hôtes reservation service €2.)

Though more expensive than bikes, boats are well worth the extra money and are the only way to truly experience the Marais. Guides will fill you in on the marsh's history and secrets. Stirring the waters also releases methane gas trapped below; your guide will prod the water to light a fire right on the surface. In Coulon, **Le Trigale,** 6 rue de l'Eglise (☎05 49 35 14 14), will set you up with a private boat and boatsman (1-2½hr., 1-7 people €26-64). You can also reserve a spot on a scheduled boat (1½hr.; €10 per person) or rent a boat and navigate yourself (1-7hr.; €13-48). There are also many other vendors offering similar deals, call the tourist office for details.

Hotels are expensive here. **Le Central ❹**, 4 rue d'Autre-mont, has singles and doubles beginning at €39.65. Campers should try the three-star **Camping de la Venise Verte ❶**, 2km outside of town, and embedded in luscious greenery. Follow the river west from Coulon to get to the campground. (☎05 49 35 90 36; fax 05 49 35 84 69. 50 canal-side sites, a pool, and canoe and bike rental. Open Apr.-Sept. June 23-Sept. 2 adults, car, tent, and electricity €16; low-season €13.50. 4 to 5-person bungalows €45 per night.) **L'Ilot du Chail ❶**, another well equipped campground, is found in the little village of **La Garette,** 3km south of Coulon. (☎05 49 35 00 33. Bike and canoe rentals available. Open May-Sept. €3 per person, €2 per child, €1.50 per car. Electricity €2.50.) Right next to the campsite is the starting point for an 8km hike through marshy forests, past the two-door houses (one for land, one for water) unique to the area. La Garette is just after Coulon on CASA bus #20. Get off at "La Garette—Centre des Loisirs." Continue walking in the direction of the bus, past the horse stables, until you get to the camp.

OTHER SIGHTS OF THE MARAIS

About 35km from Niort, the ruins of the 12th-century **Abbaye St-Pierre de Maillezais** peer out from among the trees. Within the crumbled walls, driven into uneven and shifting marshland, are the 13th-century monks's ruined kitchen and living quarters, as well as the tombs of several dukes of Aquitaine. The closest you can get to the abbey by public transportation is the train station in **Fontenay-le-Comte,** which is accessible by **SNCF buses** from the Gare Routière in Niort (45 min.; M-Sa 10 per day, Su 4 per day; €5.40). Once you get to Fontenay-le-Comte, you'll need to take a taxi the remaining 12km. Alternatively, you can rent a car in Niort and follow N148 (dir: Nantes). About seven minutes after you pass the town of Oulmes, signs point to the parking lot for the abbey on the left. (☎02 51 00 70 11 or 02 51 50 43 00. Open July-Aug. daily 10am-7pm; Sept.-June M-Sa 9:30am-12:30pm and 1:30-6pm, Su 10am-7pm. Free tours in French every hour.) Farther west, just north of La Rochelle, is the little inlet known as the **Baie de l'Aiguillon,** one of the largest shellfish-producing regions of France; oyster- and mussel-collecting are still its livelihood. Bordered on the east by a nature reserve and by sparkling water on the west, **Aiguillon-sur-mer** is a little vacation resort amid the salt marshes and the swamps. Aiguillon is serviced by **Sovetours** (☎02 51 95 18 71) and is accessible by bus from La Rochelle, although the schedule makes it impossible to take a daytrip, so you may have to camp out. (Bus 1¾ hr.; 1 bus per day 6:45pm, return 10:20am; €13). Just east of Aiguillon sits a **nature reserve** at St-Denis-du-Payre, with trails to the winter residence of greylag geese and wigeons, and the summer home of storks, redshanks, and the occasional spoonbill. Thousands of birds drop by in spring and autumn during the migratory periods. Aiguillon has several campsites, which can serve as a base both for the bay and the nature reserve. The **municipal campgrounds,** rte. de Lyon, are just outside of town on a lake. (☎02 51 56 40 70. Reception 8am-1pm, 2-7pm. Open Apr.-Sept. €4.20 per person, €2.90 per child, €4.40 per site, electricity €3.60.)

LES SABLES D'OLONNE

Les Sables d'Olonne was once a port outlet for Olonne, the region's capital. When its harbor silted up, it became useless for shipping, and Olonne abandoned it. Today, Les Sables's beautiful beaches, hotels, and restaurants attract hordes of French tourists on their summer vacations.

⚑🔁 ORIENTATION AND PRACTICAL INFORMATION. The station is on av. de Gaulle. (Open M 5:15am-8pm, Tu-Sa 6:30am-8pm, Su 7am-8:30pm.) **Trains** to: La Rochelle (2hr., 5 per day, €16.60) via La Roche-sur-Lyon; Nantes (1½hr., 6-7 per day, €14.20); Paris (5hr., 6 per day, €54.10). The bus station is next door. **Sovetours** sends buses to La Rochelle (3¼hr., 1 per day at 9am, €15) and Fromentine (2hr., 4 per day, €10. ☎02 51 58 28 51. Office open M-F 8:30am-12:30pm and 2:30-6:30pm, Sa 9:30am-noon.) **La Sabia,** 95bis rue de la Croix Blanche (☎02 51 23 54 88), runs **ferries** to l'Ile d'Yeu. (July-Aug. 3 departures daily 7:30am-7pm; call for exact times and off-season schedule. Round-trip €33, children €22.)

Local TUSCO **buses** go to several beaches in the area. (☎02 51 32 95 95. Buses run 7am-7pm. Ask at the tourist office for a bus map and schedule. €0.85.) For taxi service, call **Radiotaxi Sablais** (☎02 51 95 40 80). To rent **bikes,** visit the beachfront **Holiday Bikes,** 66 promenade Clemençeau. (☎02 51 32 64 15. Bikes €8-9 per day, scooters €38 per day, motorbikes €50-120 per day; €80 deposit. Open June-Sept. daily 9am-7pm.)

POITOU-CHARENTES

Les Sables d'Olonne

🏠 ACCOMMODATIONS   🍎 FOOD

Hôtel dé Depart, **3**   Le Port, **1**

Hôtel les Voyageurs, **4**   ⭐ NIGHTLIFE

                              Casino des Atlantes, **2**

The **tourist office** is a 15min. walk from the train station. The friendly staff has excellent regional and local maps. The *Randonées* brochure is full of info on hiking and bike excursions in the area. (☎ 02 51 96 85 85; fax 02 51 96 85 71; www.ot-lessablesdolonne.fr. Open July-Aug. daily 9am-7pm; Sept.-June daily 9am-12:15pm and 2-6:30pm; Oct.-Mar. M-F 9am-12:15pm and 2-6:30pm, Sa-Su 9:30am-12:30pm and 2-6pm.) **Banque de France**, 6 av. du Général de Gaulle, offers **currency exchange** at good rates. (☎ 02 51 23 81 00. Open M-F 8:45am-noon and 1:30-3:30pm.) The **police** are at 1 bd. Blaise Pascal. (☎ 02 51 21 19 91.) The **hospital** is at 75 av. d'Aquitaine (☎ 02 51 21 85 85).The **Centre Information Jeunesse,** in the Hôtel de Ville at pl. du Poilu, has everything from **Internet** access (with *télécarte*) to apartment listings. (☎ 02 51 23 16 83. Open M-F 9am-noon and 2-6pm, F 9am-noon and 2-5pm.) The **post office**, on av. Nicot, has **currency exchange.** (☎ 02 51 21 82 82. Open M-F 8:30am-5:45pm, Sa 8:30am-noon.) **Postal code:** 85100.

📞💻 **ACCOMMODATIONS AND FOOD.** As you exit the train station, the street running to your left hosts **Hôtel les Voyageurs ❸**, 16-17 rue de la Bauduere, at pl. de la Gare, which has modern, spacious rooms with wood floors and bright furniture. (☎ 02 51 95 11 49; fax 02 51 21 50 21. Breakfast €6. Singles and doubles with shower and toilet €33-36; triples with bath €44-50. MC/V.) The cheapest digs in town are the 14 simple, small, and comfortable rooms of **Hôtel de Départ ❸**, near the train station at 40 av. de Gaulle. (☎ 02 51 32 03 71; fax 02 51 32 03 71. Breakfast €5. Doubles €26; triples €34.) Ask the tourist office for a complete list of hotels. There are dozens of **campgrounds** in and around Les Sables, listed at the tourist office and easily accessible by public transportation.

There's a **covered market** in the 19th-century Art Nouveau **Les Halles,** between rue des Halles and rue du Palais. (Open June 15-Sept. 15 daily 8am-1:30pm; Sept. 16-June 14 Tu-Su 8am-1:30pm.) There are also two **Intermarché** supermarkets, a small one on bd. de Castelnau and a larger one on bd. de l'Ile Vertime. (Both open July-Aug. M-Sa 8:30am-8pm, Su 8:30am-1pm; Sept.-June daily 9am-6pm.) The *brasseries* and *crêperies* along the Plage du Remblai serve the cheapest food in town. For a more complete meal, try the quays near the Porte de Pêche, which overflow with restaurants serving whatever the boats bring in. **Le Port ❸**, at 24 Quai Georges V, specializes in grilled fish (€13 and up), and has affordable €7-15 *plats* as well. (☎ 02 51 95 25 81. Entrées €5-7, plats €7-15. Open daily noon-2pm and 7-10pm.)

◧ SIGHTS. There are a few interesting sights hidden among the postcard racks and bright plastic sea pails of les Sables, although they pale before the lure of the beach on a sunny day. The **Musée du Coquillage**, 8 rue du Maréchal Leclerc, near Porte de Pêche, is one of a kind in Europe. Its shelves are full of amazingly intricate and beautifully-colored shells and corals gathered by a local sea diver for his once private collection. (☎ 02 51 23 50 00. Open July-Aug. daily 9:30am-11pm; Sept.-June 9:30am-12:30pm and 2-6:30pm; Sept.-Apr. Su morning closed. €5, under age 12 €3.50). The **Musée de l'Abbaye Ste-Croix**, on rue de Verdun, occupies a wing of a restored 17th-century Benedictine abbey and presents a hodgepodge of regional prehistory, as well as folk and contemporary art, most notably the work of Victor Brauner and Gaston Chaissac. (☎ 02 51 32 01 16. Open June 15-Sept. Tu-Su 10am-noon and 2:30-6:30pm; Oct.-June 14 2:30-5:30pm. €4.60, children €2.30; first Su of every month free.) **La Chaume**, the promontory across the channel from the center of town, has two monuments on its *quais:* the 18th-century **Château St-Clair**, whose cloud-scraping Tour d'Arundel is visible from a distance; and the restored **Prieuré St-Nicolas**, a 17th-century priory, 18th-century fort, and contemporary art gallery. On the mainland, **Notre-Dame-de-Bon-Port**, pl. de l'Eglise, is a rare blend of Gothic and Baroque styles.

▶◀ EXCURSIONS AND BEACHES. Outdoor activities are not hard to find in Les Sables. **Sables Tours** books excursions, sports, and entertainment in the region. (☎ 02 51 96 85 71.) The tourist office distributes a free 5ft. foldout brochure of the area's hiking and biking trails *(randonnées)*, covering its dunes, forest, and beach. In July and August, they also post daily listings of local tennis tournaments, concerts, and organized beach volleyball. Guided boat trips, canoeing, surfing, sailing, diving, and other water sports are also available. The closest **hiking** trail to Les Sables starts about 1km north of the train station. From the station, follow rue Georges Clemenceau until it intersects rue du Doctor Charcot; signs will mark the beginning of an 18km trail that winds through the Vendée countryside and its tiny villages to a beautiful church at Olonne sur Mer.

You'd expect a place named Sables to have lots of beaches, and it doesn't disappoint. **Plage du Remblai** is the largest, most commercial, and most crowded of Les Sables's offerings. For solitude, take bus #1 or 2 to La Chaume's **Plage de la Paracou** nearby. Following the coastline north from Paracou, you'll reach two uncrowded beaches with great surf. **Plage de Sauveterre** is 1½km north of Paracou, **Plage des Granges** another kilometer further on. In between, there is nudity. ■Lots of nudity. Adventurers may enjoy the **Forêt Domaniale d'Olonne**, just east of these beaches, where huge dunes tumble from dry woodlands into the sea.

Nightly in the summer, **Les Remblais**, the widest strip of the boardwalk, becomes a pedestrian walkway with organized concerts, outdoor theater, jugglers, clowns, and marionette shows. The tourist office has the complete schedule of events. For the big spender, the nearby **Casino des Atlantes** features blackjack tables, slot machines, and a piano bar. (☎ 02 51 32 05. Open until 3am.)

NOIRMOUTIER AND ILE D'YEU

Noirmoutier and Ile d'Yeu are two pinprick islands just off the mainland between Nantes and Les Sables d'Olonne. Noirmoutier is beachy and touristy; Ile d'Yeu is the undiscovered treasure of the French coast, a wild expanse of woods, dunes, and rocky little inlets. Noirmoutier is linked to the mainland by bridge; you'll need a ferry to get to Yeu. Both bridge and ferries depart the mainland at **Fromentine,** where you'll probably stay unless you book well in advance.

▣▨ TRANSPORTATION. SNCF buses run from the south exit of the train station in Nantes to Noirmoutier (1¾hr., 6 per day 7am-7:30pm) via Fromentine (1½hr, €11.20). **Sovetours** buses run to Fromentine from Les Sables. (☎02 51 95 18 71. 2hr., 4 per day 8am-6pm, €10.50.) The buses to Fromentine drop you off at the Gare Routière, which is right next to the **tourist office,** where you can get information about accommodations in Fromentine and on the islands, as well as information about ferries to **Ile d'Yeu.** (☎02 51 68 51 83. Open M-Sa 10am-noon and 3-6pm, Su 10am-noon.) To get from the Gare Routière to the Gare Maritime, where ferries depart, cross the pl. de la Gare and turn left onto the av. de l'Estacade. The Gare Routière is at the end of this road.

Two ferry companies shuttle visitors from Fromentine to **Ile d'Yeu: Compagnie Yeu Continent,** stationed near the *gare maritime* (☎02 51 49 59 69; www.compagnie-yeu-continent.fr; 1hr.; 3 per day; roundtrip €26, students €21.10, children €18.60; AmEx/MC/V) and **Vedettes Inter-Iles Vendéenes (VIIV)** (☎02 51 39 00 00; 2 per day; roundtrip €27, students €22.50, children €19; MC/V.) VIIV also connects Noirmoutier to Ile d'Yeu, running from Fosse on Noirmoutier to Yeu. (45min., roundtrip €26, students €21.20, children €18.60.) **SABIA** boats leave les Sables from quai A. Gerbaud in Port de Plaisance for Ile d'Yeu. (☎02 51 23 54 88; fax 02 51 21 33 85. 1hr., 2 per day, 7-10am; round-trip €33, children €22.) Reservations should be made through the companies or the tourist offices in Fromentine and Les Sables.

▣ ACCOMMODATIONS. There are only two hotels in Fromentine, but they're decent and cheap. **Hôtel de Bretagne ❸,** 27 av. de l'Estacade, has spacious high-ceilinged rooms, many with views of the sea. (☎02 51 68 50 08; fax 02 51 68 20 18. Breakfast €5. Singles and doubles with shower €33; triples €39.65; quads €44.20. Extra bed €6.10. AmEx/MC/V.) Next door, **Hôtel du Cap de l'Arbre ❸,** 29 av. de l'Estacade, lets large, well-kept rooms with clean bathrooms and a small pool. (☎02 51 68 52 05; fax 02 51 68 46 87. Breakfast €6. Doubles €30-50, triples €40-65. MC/V.)

There are seven **campsites** in Fromentine; the tourist office has a list. **Camping la Grande Côte ❷,** on the Route de la Grande Cote only a few hundred meters from the beach, boasts a pool, bike rental, laundry, and food services. (☎02 51 68 51 89. Open mid-Apr. to October. Two people and car €16.50.)

NOIRMOUTIER

Noirmoutier's fortune has been made through salt farming and tourism. In the 16th and 17th centuries, the island was the salt capital of France, exporting the vital preservative and seasoning to all of Europe. Today, the saline industry has yielded to the sailing industry; Germans and Dutch flock to Noirmoutian waters to raise their sails. This island is divided into eight small villages, the largest of which is **Noirmoutier-en-l'Ile.**

NOIRMOUTIER-EN-L'ILE

Although this island's main attraction is its beaches, its capital, Noirmoutier-en-l'Ile, holds a couple of historic sites. One block away from the tourist office on rue du Gal Passaga lies a well-preserved 12th-century **château** which repelled foreign invaders for centuries. Today it welcomes them into an artifacts museum and invites them to enjoy a sweeping vista of the island's salt marshes. (☎02 51 39 10

42. Open June 17-Sept. 8 daily 10am-7pm; Feb. 9-June 16 and Sept. 9-Nov. 3 W-M 10am-12:30pm and 2:30-6pm. €3.65, children €2.) In the **Eglise St-Philbert,** rue de l'Eglise, two ornate 18th-century altars flank the main platform.

The small **Musée de la Construction Navale,** across the quai, explains ship-building methods and the town's seafaring history. (☎ 02 51 39 24 00. Hours same as château, except closed M rather than Tu. €3, children €1.50. Ticket to both château and museum €5.35, children €3.05.) Right next door is the **Sealand Aquarium,** where visitors watch seals play and marvel at the brightly colored tropical fish. Hikers and cyclists explore the salt puddles of the **Natural Bird Preserve,** marshlands just south of town. Guides from the **Maison de la Reserve** will turn your stroll through the bird sanctuary into an ornithology lesson. (☎ 02 51 35 81 16. Open June-Sept. daily 10am-1pm and 5-7pm. July-Aug. free guided bird observations. Tours €5, students €3.30, children €1.70.)

Buses from Fromentine drop you off at the Gare Routière in Noirmoutier-en-l'Ile. Right behind the Gare is the pl. de la République. The pedestrian streets behind the place form the center of town, where you'll find most shops and plenty of cheap restaurants and markets. For info about beaches and accommodations on the island, check out the **tourist office,** rue St-Louis, in the small square behind pl. de la République. (☎ 02 51 39 80 71. Open daily 9am-12:30pm and 2-6pm.) The best map of the island is the *Ile de Noirmoutier Pistes Cyclables et VTT,* which details streets, biking paths, museum locations, and accommodations. It's available at the *tabac* across the street from the tourist office. There are several **ATMs** at the pl. de la République, and you can **exchange currency** at a good rate at **Crédit Agricole,** 4 rue du Rosaire, along the quai on pl. de la République. (Open July to mid Sept. Tu-F 9am-12:30pm, Sa 9am-12:30pm; late Sept.-June Tu and W 9am-12:30pm, Sa 8:30am-12:30pm.) The **post office** is on rue du Puits Neuf. (☎ 02 51 39 02 36. Open M-F 9am-noon and 2-5pm, Sa 9am-noon.) **Postal code:** 85330.

There is a scarcity of cheap beds, especially in August. **Chez Bébert ❷,** 37 ave. Joseph Pineau, offers some of the least pricey beds in sunny, simple rooms. To get there from the pl. de la République, follow rue Piet away from the quai. This road will change its name twice, first to rue Richer and then to rav. Joseph Pineau. (☎ 02 51 39 08 97. Breakfast €5. Open June-Dec. 22. Singles €23-26; doubles €29-33; triples €38-44.) Several blocks down the road (which changes its name often) is the spacious **Hôtel du Bois de la Chaize ❸,** av. de la Victoire, which recently refinished its hardwood floors and repainted its fresh white walls. The rooms here are expensive, but the quality is worth the price. (☎ 02 51 39 04 62. Breakfast €6. Singles and doubles with shower and toilet €55-60; triples €70; quads €77.) **Hôtel Esperanza ❹,** 10a rue du Grand Four, lets plain rooms with a view of the courtyard garden. To get there from the tourist office, follow rue du Janvier to its end, turn right onto rue du Robinet, and go straight for one block. (☎ 02 51 39 12 07. Breakfast €4.90. Singles and doubles with toilet €37, with shower €41. Extra bed €10.70. MC/V.)

For travelers on a tight budget, camping is a good option on Noirmoutier. Two km east of town, the 600 sites of the two-star **Campsite La Vendette ❶,** rte. des Sableaux, spread along the beach. (☎ 02 51 39 06 24; fax 02 51 35 97 63. Reception daily 8am-8pm. Open Apr.-Sept. Two people and tent or caravan €14.60; €3.50 per extra person, €1.50 per extra child. Electricity €2.) A little farther away, **Le Caravan'ile ❷,** in the village of la Guerinière, runs three-star facilities bordering the beach. (☎ 02 51 39 50 29. Reception M-F 8:30am-12:30pm and 2-8pm, Sa and Su 8:30am-8pm. Open Feb.-Nov. Two people and car €19.50; €4 per extra adult, €2.50 per extra child.) When your stomach starts grumbling, the **Cours des Halles grocery store,** 3 rue de la Prée au Duc, competes for top budget choice with the **market** in pl. de la République. (Open F 9am-2 pm; July-Aug. also Tu and Su.)

THE REST OF THE ISLAND. Dovetours buses run from Noirmoutier-en-l'Ile to the other villages of the island three times a day (8:30am, 12:30, 4pm), but you'd do better to rent a **bike** in Noirmoutier-en-l'Ile. It's the only way to visit the island's marshy, salty center, which is closed to cars. Try **Le Temple des Loisirs**, at 18 rue de Rosaire. (☎02 51 39 80 71 or 02 51 39 12 42. €4-5.50 per hr., €9-12.50 per day. Credit card deposit. Open July-Aug. daily 8am-8pm; off-season M-Sa 9am-12:30pm and 2:30-7pm. Arrange in advance if you would like to return your bike after 7pm. MC/V.)

Noirmoutier's ancient **Passage du Gois** has attracted European tourists since its discovery in 1942. This 3km road connecting Noirmoutier to the continent is flooded with one to four meters of water during high tides, but becomes fully exposed and walkable twice daily during low tide. The passage is open to pedestrians and cyclists about one hour before and after low tide. Daredevils who get stuck can find safety in one of eight tall *refuges* along the path. The passage begins in the island's southern town, **Barbatre.** (Consult tourist office at ☎02 51 39 08 97 for low-tide times.)

A short pedal away from town down av. Joseph Pineau gets you to **plage des Dames,** the island's most popular beach. This beach serves as a gateway to the north coast's warmer beaches; turn left onto the labeled bike path next to plage des Dames and roll along the beach-view path until you find an inlet to your liking. Two kilometers from des Dames, you'll hit **plage de la Clère,** a lovely if slightly crowded beach overlooking a tranquil harbor.

Surrounding Noirmoutier-en-l'Ile are the sparkling white piles of the salt marshes, the island's most exotic biking terrain. West of the town you can ride around in the **salt mines.** East from Noirmoutier-en-l'Ile, in the direction of "Les Sableaux," is a marsh where bucket-toting locals and tourists search ankle-deep water for shellfish, mussels, and the occasional lobster. Potato farms and salt marshes line the path to the fishing village of **L'Herbaudière,** northwest of Noirmoutier-en-l'Ile. Thirty *saumiers* (salt farmers) have revitalized the long dormant industry. The island's southern beaches lie just beyond the inland forests that extend nearly to the sea. **Plage de l'Epine** in **La Bosse,** 4km southwest of Noirmoutier, is a pleasant spot to relax on the sand under the shadow of an evergreen.

ILE D'YEU

Ile d'Yeu (pop. 5000) is, in a word, idyllic. Bordered on all sides by the clear reflection of the water, the island has a vast array of landscapes—dense mini-forests, wide, flat beaches, stony paths, and thunderous oceanscapes. Since the island is not accessible by car, the wilderness is well preserved despite the abundance of tourists in July and August. Ferries unload passengers at Port Joinville, home of marine-wear boutiques, retiree-filled restaurants, and banks. The island's real charms, however, are outside of town.

Biking is the best way to explore the island; you can cover it all in four to five hours if you resist the temptation to stop and swim. The many paths range from sandy to boulder-strewn; fortunately, bikes in Port-Joinville are built for the back roads. Expect to pay €5 per hour and €8-12 per day. Most rental places will store your bags and give you a xeroxed map of suggested routes. Stop at the **tourist office,** on rue du Marché, before embarking. The office distributes biking and hiking itineraries of varying lengths, with extensive directions and descriptions of sights in English and French. (☎02 51 58 32 58. Open July-Aug. M-Sa 9am-6:30pm, Su 9am-12:30pm; Apr.-June and Sept. M-Sa 9am-12:30pm and 2-6:30pm, Su 9am-noon; Oct.-Mar. M-Sa 9am-12:30pm and 2-5:30pm, Su 9am-noon.)

Ile d'Yeu's rugged inland and beautiful beaches may well entice you to stay a night. Accommodations are expensive, but some are worth the price. **Hotel L'Escale ❸,** 14 rue de la Croix du Port, is about a 5min. walk from the quai at Port

Joinville, on a quiet street. Sunny rooms look out on a lovely flower-filled court-yard. Kids will love the family rooms with lofts. (☎ 02 51 58 50 28; yeu.escale@voila.fr. Singles and doubles with shower and toilet €32-45; triples and quads €45-55). The island's once-crowded **campground ❶** is near the beach at Pointe de Gilberge, 1km from the port. (☎ 02 51 58 34 20. 4 people and 2 tents €8.70-9.15; €1.40 per extra person; €2.45 per car.) In summer, many visitors camp illegally, though *Let's Go* does not recommend it. Fresh, cheap food is available at the **outdoor market** on quai de la Mairie. (Open M-Sa 9am-noon or 1pm.). The **Casino supermarket** is on rue Calypso, two minutes from the port. (Open Tu-Th 9am-1pm and 2:30-7pm, F until 7:30pm, M and Sa 9am-7:45pm, Su 9:30am-12:30pm. MC/V.)

There are four easy **bike circuits** of the island, all starting in Port-Joinville. The smallest takes you to the island's southern port and back in 2½ hrs.; its highlight is **Port Meule,** just south of Joinville, with its gorgeous sea cliffs and mossy and marshy inlets. The longest route (5½hr.) takes you all around the island, passing Renaissance churches and picturesque ports. One of the most popular bike itiner-aries (4½hr.) includes a stop 2km southeast of Port Joinville at the 18th-century church in **St-Sauveur**, where a yellow-green door and bright stained-glass windows illuminates a dark, musty interior. Working your way eastward and southward, you'll come across flat, sparkling **plage des Sapins,** which is very popular with windsurfers, followed by **plage de la Conche,** an impressively expansive stretch of beach. The route curves around to the south coast, where cliffs rise in all direc-tions. **Plage Anse des Soux,** surrounded by looming cliffs, is a great place for an early afternoon siesta. The 4½hr. path then leads back to Joinville, but you can continue west to the **Grand Phare,** a 20m lighthouse on the island's highest "hill," and get a birds-eye view of the island, and to the **Pointe du Châtelet,** a jutting cliff which bears a rusted commemorative cross built in 1934 for sailors lost at sea. (☎ 02 51 58 30 61. Open for climbing daily 9am-5pm.) Near the cross is the 14th-century **Vieux Château,** used as a fortress in the 16th century and later abandoned by Louis XIV. The remarkable remnants stand crumbling on the craggy coast, accessible by bike path alone. (Tours July-Aug. daily 9:30am-7:30pm; late June and Sept. 11am-5:30pm. €2.50, children €1.20.)

BERRY-LIMOUSIN

A landlocked position and lack of world-famous attractions has long left Berry-Limousin out of the limelight of French tourism. All the better, for this relatively untouched region offers peaceful countryside dotted with Limousin cattle, tiny villages between little valleys and woods of oak, and striking cities. The still-inhabited châteaux of the Route Jacques Cœur makes Berry a less stressful and more intimate version of the more famous Loire Valley châteaux.

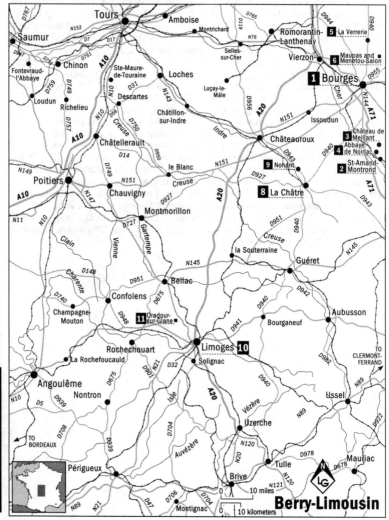

Berry-Limousin

In the 14th century, Limousin gave three popes to Avignon, the last of whom, Gregory XI, returned the papacy to Rome. During the same period, Berry was ruled by Jean de Berry, third son of King Jean le Bon, who is famous for commissioning an exquisite book of medieval miniatures, *Les Très Riches Heures du Duc de Berry*. While Paris was occupied by the English in the 15th century, Bourges served as France's capital and benefited from the lavish attention of the king's financier, Jacques Cœur, who built a string of châteaux through the heart of Berry. Later on, Berry-Limousin became an artistic breeding ground, home to novelist Georges Sand, painter Auguste Renoir, and dramatist Jean Giraudoux.

1	▨ **Bourges:** The area's largest city; has a justly famous Gothic cathedral **(p. 355)**
2	**St-Amand-Montrond:** A tiny medieval town close to several nearby châteaux **(p. 360)**
3	**Château de Meillant:** Best reached from St-Amand, a huge Gothic fortress **(p. 360)**
4	**Abbaye de Noirlac:** A 12th-century Cistercian abbey **(p. 360)**
5	**La Verrerie:** One of the most popular—and heavily decorated—châteaux around **(p. 360)**
6	**Maupas and Menetou-Salon:** Two eccentric, in-use châteaux bikeable from Bourges **(p. 361)**
7	**Château Charles VII:** Once the favorite residence of Charles VII, now crumbling **(p. 361)**
8	**La Châtre:** A quiet, peaceful little town, useful as a regional base; Chopin festival **(p. 361)**
9	**Nohant:** George Sand's childhood home, and Chopin's sometime hometown **(p. 362)**
10	**Limoges:** Porcelain capital of Europe; quiet medieval neighborhoods **(p. 363)**
11	▨ **Oradour-sur-Glane:** Site of France's worst Nazi massacre; untouched ever since **(p. 367)**

BOURGES

Bourges (pop. of 80,000 *bourgeois*) owes much of its popularity to the largesse of a corrupt politician. In 1433, Jacques Cœur, financier of Charles VII and all-around commercial genius, chose the humble city as the site for his personal mansion. Bourges now possesses a beautifully preserved medieval *vieille ville*, lying under the shadow of its majestic Gothic cathedral. Within a few blocks of the station is a fairy tale village of winding cobblestone streets, colorful half-timbered houses, and Gothic turrets.

▐ TRANSPORTATION

Trains: pl. Général Leclerc (☎02 48 51 00 00). Info office open M-F 9am-7pm, Sa 9am-6pm. To: **Nevers** (1hr., 12 per day, €9.40); **Paris** (2½hr., 5-8 per day, €24); **Tours** (1½hr., 10 per day, €16.80). Many trains require a change at **Vierzon.**

Buses: rue du Champ de Foire (☎02 48 24 36 42). Office open Sept.-June M-Tu and Th-F 8-9:30am and 4-6pm, W and Sa 8am-noon. Buses run to **Châteauroux** (1¾hr., 1-3 per day, €4.90); **Vierzon** (1¼hr., 3 per day, €3.80); nearby villages (tickets €1.35, *carnet* of 10 €11.43). The most popular nearby village is **St-Germain** (take bus #4 from "La Nation"; 2-4 per day), with its bowling alley and several pubs. Schedules vary they're posted outside the station.

Public Transportation: CTB (☎02 48 50 82 82) serves all areas of the city. Tickets €1.10, *carnet* of 10 €7.65. Schedules available at the tourist office.

Taxis: ☎02 48 24 50 00. 24hr. €5 from train station to tourist office.

Bike Rental: Narcy, 39 av. Marx-Dormoy (☎02 48 70 15 84; fax 02 48 70 02 61). €7.50-8 per day, €16 per weekend. Credit card deposit. Open M-F 9:30am-noon and 2-7pm, Sa 9am-noon and 2-6pm.

Car Rentals: Hertz, 4 av. Henri Laudier (02 48 70 22 92), near train station. Cars from €66 per day. 21+; under 25 €21.80 fee per day. Open M-F 8am-noon and 2-6pm. AmEx/MC/V. **Autop,** 21 av. Jean Jaurès (☎02 48 70 63 63). Cars from €45 per day. Open M-F 8am-noon and 2-6pm, Sa 8am-noon.

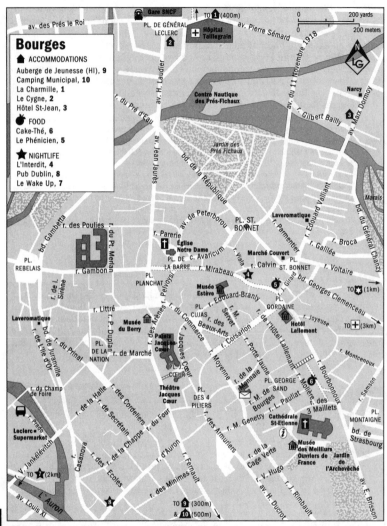

Bourges

♠ ACCOMMODATIONS
Auberge de Jeunesse (HI), **9**
Camping Municipal, **10**
La Charmille, **1**
Le Cygne, **2**
Hôtel St-Jean, **3**

🍴 FOOD
Cake-Thé, **6**
Le Phénicien, **5**

★ NIGHTLIFE
L'Interdit, **4**
Pub Dublin, **8**
Le Wake Up, **7**

🛈 PRACTICAL INFORMATION

Tourist Office: 21 rue Victor Hugo (☎02 48 23 02 60; fax 02 48 23 02 69; www.ville-bourges.fr), facing rue Moyenne near the cathedral. Cross the street in front of station and follow av. Henri Laudier as it becomes av. Jean Jaurès, into the *vieille ville*. Bear left onto rue du Commerce. Continue straight onto rue Moyenne, which leads to office. (15min.) Or catch bus #1 (dir: Val d'Auron, €1.10) to "Victor Hugo." Hotel reservations (€1). 1½hr. **walking tours** July-Sept. daily 2pm in English, 3pm in French; €5, students €3. Free night tours in English July 15-Aug. 15 Th-Sa 8pm. Office open Apr.-June and Sept. M-Sa 9am-7pm, Su 10am-7pm; July-Aug. M-Sa 9am-7:30pm, Su 10am-7pm; Oct.-Mar. M-Sa 9am-6pm, Su 2-5pm.

Laundromat: Laveromatique, 117 rue Edouard Valliant and 15 bd. Juranville (☎02 48 67 41 49). Open daily 8am-8pm.

Police: rue Mayet Genetry (☎02 48 75 55 20).

Hospital: 145 rue François Mitterrand (☎02 48 48 48 48).

Internet Access: Médiathèque, bd. Lamarck/Parc St-Paul (☎02 48 23 22 50). Free! On the third floor of the library; 30min. time limit. Open July-Aug. Tu-F 12:30-6:30pm, Sa 9am-noon; Sept.-June M-W 12:30-6:30pm, Th 12:30-8pm, F 12:30-6:30pm, Sa 10am-5pm. **Esprit Club,** 81 rue Gambon (☎02 48 24 71 12). €4.60 per hr. Open daily 11am-12:30am.

Post Office: 29 rue Moyenne (☎02 48 68 82 82). **Currency exchange.** Open M-F 8am-7pm, Sa 8am-noon. **Poste Restante:** 18012 Bourges Cédex. **Postal code:** 18000.

▐ ACCOMMODATIONS AND CAMPING

Bourges's cheapest hotels are outside the city center. Unoccupied beds may be hard to find during festivals and in the middle of the summer.

▨ Hôtel St-Jean, 23 av. Marx-Dormoy (☎02 48 24 70 45; fax 02 48 24 79 98). A lovely hostess lets plain, clean, carpeted rooms, only a 10min. walk from both the train station and the center of town. Amiable owners. Breakfast €4. Singles €22, with shower and toilet €27.45; doubles €26/€33.54; triples with shower and toilet €42.69. V. ❷

Auberge de Jeunesse (HI), 22 rue Henri Sellier (☎02 48 24 58 09; fax 02 48 65 51 46), 10min. from town center, far from train station. From station, take av. Henri Laudier onto av. Jean Jaurès to pl. Planchat. Follow rue des Arène as it becomes rue Fernault. At a busy intersection, cross to rue René Ménard. Turn left at rue Henri Sellier, and walk approx. one block. Hostel is on the right, set back from the street behind a brown and white building. (25min.) Or take bus #1 (dir: Val d'Auron; daily 6am-6pm) to "Conde." Cross parking lot to your right, take paved footpath to the left that crosses the park patch in front of you. Continue straight down rue Vieil Castel. Hostel is across street, 30m down a driveway slightly to right. Bar, laundry, kitchen, parking, and bare but clean 3- to 8-bunk rooms, some with showers. Grassy backyard overlooks a small river. Breakfast €3. Sheets €2.70. Reception daily 8-10am and 5-10pm. Beds €8. ❶

Centre International de Séjour: La Charmille, 17 rue Félix-Chédin (☎02 48 23 07 40; fax 02 48 69 01 21). From station, cross the footbridge over the tracks and head up rue Félix-Chédin. (5min.) La Charmille—half hostel, half *foyer*—is the skateboard mecca of Europe, with bowls and ramps. Skating classes in summer. Social atmosphere among the mostly teenage guests. Super-clean rooms, all with shower. Breakfast included. Meals €8.50. Laundry. Singles €15; two or more €11 per person. MC/V. ❶

Le Cygne, 10 pl. du Général Leclerc (☎02 48 70 52 05; fax 02 48 69 09 91). Across from the train station, but a 20min. walk from center of town. Rooms are cozy and well kept, though showing signs of age. Attached restaurant. Breakfast €5.35. Parking €3. Singles and doubles with shower €27.50-35; triples with shower and toilet €40; quads with shower and toilet €49; *demi-pension* €40 for one person; two people €52. ❸

Camping Municipal, 26 bd. de l'Industrie (☎02 48 20 16 85; fax 02 48 50 32 39). Follow directions to *auberge* (see above) but continue on rue Henri Sellier and turn right on bd. de l'Industrie. Landscaped 3-star campground in a pleasant riverside residential neighborhood, a 10min. walk from the city center. Swimming pool. Reception Sept.-June daily 8am-9pm; June-Aug. 7am-10pm. Open Mar. 15-Nov. 15. €3 per person, children €1.60; €3 per tent, €4.30 per car, €4.12 per caravan. Electricity €2.50. ❶

🍴 FOOD

The outdoor tables on **pl. Gordaine** and **rue des Beaux-Arts** fill with locals in spring and summer. For a touch of elegance, try regional cuisine at one of the restaurants in the old timber-framed houses on **rue Bourbonnoux** or **rue Girard**. Look for specialties such as *poulet en barbouille* (chicken roasted in aromatic red wine) and *oeufs en meurette* (eggs in red wine). The largest **market** is held on pl. de la Nation (Sa morning); another livens pl. des Marronniers. (Open Th until 1pm.) There is a smaller **covered market** at pl. St-Bonnet. (Open Tu-Sa 7:30am-1pm and 3-7:30pm, Su 7:30am-1pm.) Cheap sandwich shops line **rue Moyenne** and **rue Mirabeau**, while the huge **Leclerc supermarket**, rue Prado off bd. Juranville, provides the fixings for your own culinary experiments. (Open M-F 9:15am-7:20pm, Sa 8:30am-7:20pm.)

■ **Cake-Thé,** 74 prom. des Remparts (☎02 48 24 94 60). Beautiful little tearoom down a lavender-lined passage. Outdoor terrace in summer. Full of music, flowers, and lace. Tea €1.85-3; coffee €3. Open Sept.-July Tu-Sa 3-7pm.

Le Phénicien, 13 rue Jean Girard, off pl. Gordaine (☎02 48 65 01 37). Middle Eastern eatery makes peerless pita on the premises for the penniless. Vegetarian options. Sandwiches €3.70-4. Lunch *menu* €7.50-8.50. Open M-Sa 11am-11pm. ❶

👁 SIGHTS

■ **CATHÉDRALE ST-ETIENNE.** Built in the 13th century, St-Etienne is one of France's most magnificent cathedrals, comparable to Notre Dame in Paris. A stunning set of 13th-century stained glass illuminates the white marble interior in dark reds and blues; visit between 10 and 11am for the best light. One ticket allows you to visit the unspectacular cathedral crypt and climb St-Etienne's northern tower for a splendid view of the city. *(Cathedral open daily Apr.-Sept. 8:30am-7:15pm; Oct.-Mar. 9am-5:45pm. Closed Su morning. Crypt and towers May-June 15 daily 9:30am-12:15pm and 2-6pm; July-Aug. 9:30am-6pm; Sept.-Apr. 9:30am-12:15pm and 2-5:15pm. €5.50, students €3.50. Mass June-Aug. M-F 6:30pm; Sept.-May M 6:30pm, F 9am. Grand Mass Su 11am.)*

PALAIS JACQUES-CŒUR. This mansion was commissioned in 1443 by Jacques Cœur, finance minister of King Charles VII. Cœur was one of the earliest members of the wealthy middle class, and the palace was intended to entertain high society guests and flaunt his personal fortune. Jacques saw little of it, though; he was imprisoned for embezzlement in 1451, years before its completion. The palace is now unfurnished, but exquisite carved mantelpieces, gargoyles, sculpted ship galleys, and a heavily decorated chapel remain. *(10bis rue Jacques-Cœur. ☎02 48 24 06 87. Tours July-Aug. 9am-6pm every hr.; Apr.-June and Sept.-Oct. 9am-noon and 2-6pm; Nov.-Mar. 9am-noon and 2-5pm. English text available. €5.50, ages 18-24 €3.50, under 18 free.)*

MUSEUMS. Bourges has several small, free, unspectacular museums, most with explanations only in French, worth a short visit only if you have a lot of free time. The **Musée du Berry** showcases locally excavated prehistoric, Gallo-Roman, and medieval artifacts. *(4 rue des Arènes. ☎02 48 57 81 15. Open M and W-Sa 10am-noon and 2-6pm, Su 2-6pm.)* The **Musée Estève** displays oil paintings by the local contemporary artist of the same name. *(13 rue Edouard Branly. ☎02 48 24 75 38. Open M and W-Sa 10am-noon and 2-6pm, Su 2-6pm. English explanations.)* The **Musée des Meilleurs Ouvriers de France,** in the Hôtel de Ville, charts the work of artists and workers in the region. In 2003, the museum will host a temporary exhibit on hairstyling. *(Pl. Etienne Dolet. ☎02 48 57 82 45. Open July-Aug. daily 10am-6pm; Sept.-June Tu-Sa 10am-noon and 2-6pm.)*

OUTDOORS. The **Jardin de l'Archevêché,** behind the cathedral, has rows of perfectly manicured flowers and cone-shaped trees. *(Open June-July daily 8am-10pm; May and Aug. 8am-9pm; Mar. 8am-7pm; Apr. and Sept. 8am-8pm; Oct.-Feb. 8am-6pm.)* The **Jardin des Près-Fichaux,** off bd. de la République, adds a beautiful river to a similar scene. Stroll past Roman ramparts and back gardens on the **Promenade des Remparts,** between rue Bourbonnoux and rue Molière. The dirt pathway along the Marais is supremely tranquil, passing some of the more rural homes in Bourges.

ENTERTAINMENT AND FESTIVALS

Bars and cafés pepper the *vieille ville,* but the nightlife is pretty subdued. Crowds of locals gather nightly at **Pub Dublin,** 108 rue d'Auron, for pool and beer, from €3 a bottle. (☎ 02 48 26 38 33.) Electronic music sets the pulse of **L'interdit,** 5 rue Calvin, a small, social club frequented mainly but not exclusively by gay men. Knock or buzz to be let in through the locked door. (☎ 02 48 65 90 57. Open Th-Su 5pm-2am.) **Le Wake Up,** 147 chemin de Villeneuve, is a house of techno and pop rock where teens and early twenty-somethings dance to a live DJ. Play laser tag in the 500m labyrinth of ramps and walls. (☎ 02 48 67 90 46. Open daily 4pm-1am.)

End the evening with **Les Nuits Lumière de Bourges,** a lovely self-guided tour of Bourges. This tour begins with music and a slide-show about local history, then directs you to stops on a predetermined route along streets illuminated by blue lampposts. The 2hr. route begins at the Jardin de l'Archevêché. (June-Oct. Free.)

Over 200,000 ears perk up in April for the **Festival Printemps de Bourges.** Most tickets cost €7-28, but some informal folk, jazz, classical, and rock concerts are free. (Contact the Association Printemps de Bourges at ☎ 02 48 70 61 11.) June 21-Sept. 21 brings **Un Eté à Bourges,** a nightly conflagration of classical and rock concerts and theater. (Tickets €7.50-14, most events free.)

ROUTE JACQUES CŒUR

Jacques may have left his *cœur* in Bourges, but his ego spilled far into the surrounding countryside. The Route Jacques Cœur is the name of a string of 17 châteaux (plus one 12th-century abbey for good measure) that stretches from La Buissière in the north to Culan in the south. Less ostentatious than those of the Loire, these castles see much less tourism. Many are still inhabited by the families that made them famous, and you may find yourself getting your own personal tour.

Most of the châteaux listed in this section can be seen only by tour, and the tour guide often doubles as ticket seller. If you arrive while a tour is already in progress, wait at the ticket booth until the tour guide returns. Written English explanations are usually available, although tours in English are not.

Châteaux make relaxing daytrips, but most can be reached only by car or bike. Fortunately, the routes are typically very well marked. Arrange lodging in advance. The tourist offices in Bourges (p. 355) and St-Amand-Montrond (see below) have free maps of the route in English and have info on excursions.

SOUTH OF BOURGES

ST-AMAND-MONTROND

Forty-five kilometers south of Bourges, St-Amand-Montrond (pop. 12,000) is a good starting point for a day-trip from Bourges to explore the southern part of the route. Though the neighboring châteaux and hectares of hikeable forest have made it famous, the town itself deserves a few hours of your attention. A pedestrian tour organized by the tourist office walks you past the city's two medieval churches, **Paroisse de St-Amand** and **Eglise St-Roche.** You can also see the ruins of the ancient **Forteresse de Montrond.** (Call ☎ 02 48 96 79 64 to schedule a visit.) To get to St-Amand, take the **train** from **Bourges** (¾-1¾hr.; M-Sa 6 per day, Su 3 per day; €8.40). From St. Amand, it's a long walk (2hr.) or a short bike ride to each of the nearby châteaux. You can rent **bikes** at the municipal campgrounds. To get there from the train station, turn right off of av. Jean Jaurès onto rue Tissier and follow its continuation Chemin du Près des Joncs. The campgrounds will be to your left. (☎ 02 48 96 09 36. Open M-Sa 9am-noon and 2-7pm. Bikes €10 per day.) The **tourist office,** pl. de la République, sells maps indicating sights within the city and environs (€1). From the train station, follow av. de la Gare and its continuation, av. Jean Jaurès, which turns into rue Henri Barbusse, to the town center. After 20min., you will run right into pl. de la République; the tourist office is on your left. (☎ 02 48 96 16 86; fax 02 48 96 46 64. Open M-Sa 9am-noon and 2-6:45pm.)

CHÂTEAU DE MEILLANT

A beautiful 8km bike ride from St-Amand through the **Fôret de Meillant** ends at the foot of this imposing, heavily spired 15th- to 16th-century building. In the 15th century, it was bought by the Amboise family, who imported Italian architects, sculptors, and decorators. Its curious mixture of Gothic and Renaissance styles is especially visible in the **Tour du Lion,** the upper part of which was designed by none other than Leonardo da Vinci. Next to the château is a little building containing miniature renditions of life from the Middle Ages to the 18th century. To get to Meillant from **St-Amand,** take rue Nationale north out to the D10. (☎ 02 48 63 32 05. Open Apr.-Oct. 9-11:45am and 2-6:45pm; Feb.-Mar. and Nov. 9-11:45am and 2-5:30pm. Château and gardens €7, students €4, ages 7-15 €3.)

ABBAYE DE NOIRLAC

Just 4km west of St-Amand-Montrond, the **Abbaye de Noirlac** sits peacefully next to a field of grazing cows. The abbey is typically Cistercian, with spacious rooms, undecorated arches, and geometric stained-glass windows. Most of the monks's **chapter house** dates from the original 12th-century construction. Within the complex, the **Centre de l'Enluminure et de l'Image Médiévale** holds a collection of medieval art. In summer, the popular **L'Eté de Noirlac** fills the space with jazz and classical music. (☎ 02 48 48 00 10.) From St-Amand, take rue Henri Barbusse to the rue 14 Juillet. After crossing the river, turn left and follow the signs to N144 direction "Bourges." (☎ 02 48 62 01 01. Open July-Aug. daily 9:45am-6:30pm; Apr.-June and Sept. 9:45am-noon and 1:45-6:30pm; Oct.-Mar. 9:45am-noon and 1:45-5pm; Oct.-Jan. closed Tu. Ticket office shuts 1hr. before closing. French tours every hr. starting 10am; July-Aug. no tours noon-1:45pm. English explanations available; call ahead for a tour in English. €5.40, students €3.80, under 16 €3.10.)

NORTH OF BOURGES

LA VERRERIE

The 15th-century La Verrerie, set on a gorgeous lake in the Ivoy forest 45km north of Bourges, is one of the most elegant and popular châteaux on the Route. Like many of its Loire cousins, it has a long history of British control, but a refreshingly non-violent one. Inside are 18th-century Beauvais tapestries and hand-carved tables from the 16th and 17th centuries. To get to La Verrerie from Bourges, take N940 (dir: Montargis). At La Chapelle, turn right toward Auxerre on rte. 926. After 10km, signs for La Verrerie will appear. (☎ 02 48 81 51 60. Open Apr.-May and Oct.-Nov. 15 W-M 10am-6pm; June-Aug. daily 9am-6pm. €7, students €5, under 7 free.)

MENETOU-SALON AND MAUPAS

A bit closer to Bourges and easy to reach by bike, Maupas and Menetou-Salon make a perfect daytrip. **Menetou-Salon** lies 20km north of Bourges. Jacques bought the estate in 1448, but his imprisonment and the Revolution left the castle in ruins until the 19th century, when the Prince of Arenburg decided to finish it. Though the current prince lives in New York and only visits his hunting lodge four times a year, his personal touches make Menetou a treat. Along with antiques you'll also see the giant Land Rover the prince and his buddies drove from Alaska to the tip of South America to win a spot in the *Guiness Book of World Records* as the first to traverse the entire length of the Americas. To get to Menetou-Salon from Bourges, take D940 north to D11 and follow the signs to Menetou-Salon. (Estate ☎ 02 48 64 08 61. Open July-Aug. 15 daily 10am-6pm. Adults €9.50, students €5.50.)

To continue to **Maupas**, follow the signs to Parassy and Moroques. The château is on your left, about 1km before Moroques. Keep your eyes open for the white iron gates tucked away on the curbside. This 13th-century castle is decorated with antique furniture and faiences collected by Antoine Agard, whose family has lived there since 1686. The gardens are perfectly manicured in the shape of the *fleur de lys*. The 45min. tour leads you through bedrooms, playrooms, the dining salon, and kitchen of the Comte de Chambord, the last legitimate Bourbon pretender to the French throne. (Estate ☎ 02 48 64 41 71. Open July 14-Sept. 15 10am-noon and 2-7pm; Easter-July 14 and Sept. 16-Oct. 15 M-Sa 2-7pm, Su and holidays 10am-noon and 2-7pm. €6.50, students €4.50, ages 7-15 €4.)

CHÂTEAU CHARLES VII

Twenty kilometers northeast of Bourges, the village of **Mehun sur Yèvre** (pop. 7500) is an easy daytrip from Bourges, and worth visiting for the crumbling ruins of the **Château Charles VII.** Built in the 14th century for the Duke de Berry, this château was once called "the most beautiful house of the world." Later, the château was King Charles VII's favorite residence, and it was here that he conferred the status of nobility on Joan of Arc, who was his guest in Mehun sur Yèvre during the winter of 1430. The château has suffered from neglect, and all that remains are two towers. One houses a museum with fragments of statues salvaged from the ruins and pieces of local artwork; the other is half crumbled away. Next to the château, you can wander along the paths of the **Jardins du Duke de Berry.** Your ticket to the château includes admission to an exhibition of local works in the **Pôle de la Porcelaine.** (☎ 02 48 57 06 19. Open Mar.-Apr. and Oct. Sa-Su 2-6pm; May-June and Sept.-Oct. Tu-Su 2-6pm; July-Aug. daily 10am-noon and 2-6pm. €4.55.) **SNCF trains and buses** run from Bourges to Mehun sur Yèvre (20min., 8 per day 6am-7pm, return 6:30am-9pm). To get to the château from the train station, cross the street and head down the av. Jean Vacher to the pl. Claude Debussy. Cross the place and head down the rue Jeanne d'Arc, across several bridges. Turn left onto the rue Pasteur and the château will be right in front of you. For more info about Mehun sur Yèvre, contact the **tourist office,** pl. du 14 Juillet. (☎ 02 48 57 35 51.)

LA CHÂTRE

La Châtre (pop. 5500) is an exceptionally pretty base from which to visit the sights of Berry. The city hosts a lively Saturday market and a well-attended Chopin festival at the end of July. The tourist office's guide maps out a pedestrian tour of La Châtre; the walk takes visitors past 15th-century houses, the 12th- to 14th-century **Eglise St-Germain,** and the **Musée George Sand et de la Vallée Noire,** 71 rue Venose, housed in a square, 15th-century keep. The museum has plenty of Sand's souvenirs and drawings to pick over, as well as a large ornithological collection. (☎ 02 54 48 36 79. Open July-Aug. daily 9am-7pm; Sept.-Dec. and Feb.-Mar. 9am-noon and 2-

7pm; Apr.-Sept. 9am-5pm. €4, students and children €3.) The 4th week in July the town is taken over by the huge **Rencontre Internationale Frédéric Chopin,** with seminars and nightly recitals in the town and in nearby Nohant (tickets €16-31).

La Châtre no longer has a working train station; **bus** is the only way to get to town. **Voyages Michaut** (☎02 48 63 00 27) runs buses to La Chatre from **Châteauroux** (40min., 2-5 per day, €5.50) and **Montlucon** (1hr., 2-5 per day, €8.60). The **SNCF Info Boutique,** 142 rue Nationale, in the center of town, can help organize outbound journeys that connect the bus with trains at Châteauroux. (☎02 54 48 00 06. Open Tu-Sa 9am-noon and 2-6pm.)

The **tourist office** is in the park on av. George Sand. From the train station, leave the parking lot and head straight out on av. Aristide Briand. About four blocks past pl. Jules Neraud, turn left on av. George Sand; the office is ahead on your right, set back from the street. (☎02 54 48 22 64; fax 02 54 06 09 15; www.berry.tm.fr. Open July-Aug. M-Sa 9am-12:30pm and 2:30-7pm, Su 10am-noon and 2-6pm; Apr.-June and Sept. M-Sa 9:30am-12:30pm and 2:30-7pm, Su 10am-noon and 2-6pm; Oct.-Mar. M-F 9:30am-12:30pm and 2-6:30pm, Sa 9:30am-12:30pm and 2-5:30pm.)

If you call at least two days in advance, you can stay at the romantic, 52-bed **Auberge de Jeunesse (HI) ❶,** rue Moulin Borgnon (leave a message if no one picks up). To get to the hostel from the tourist office, continue down av. George Sand across pl. du Marché, then veer left on rue de St-Roche. Turn right and follow the road downhill. The hostel is on your right, behind a park overlooking a valley. (☎02 54 06 00 55; fax 02 54 48 48 10. Sheets €3.50. Bunks €9. **Non-members** €3 extra.) A large **STOC supermarket,** pl. du Général de Gaulle (☎02 54 48 05 24), sells the basics. The **market** is on pl. du Marché. (Open Sa 8am-noon.)

NEAR LA CHÂTRE: NOHANT

Tiny Nohant (pop. 481), 8km from La Châtre, consists of one unpaved square housing an ancient church beside George Sand's childhood home. It was here that Sand wrote her first novel, *Indiana,* and here that many great literary and artistic figures came to dine, among them Balzac, Delacroix, Flaubert, and Liszt. Chopin stayed 10 years here with Sand; the puppet theater he built with Sand's son is still in perfect condition, as is the study upstairs where the composer wrote over 15 of his pieces. (☎02 54 31 06 04. Open daily July-Aug. 9am-7pm; Sept.-June 10am-noon and 2-5pm. Last tour 30min. before closing. €5.50, students €3.50.)

To get to Nohant, take the **bus** (dir: Châteauroux; 10min., 3 per day, €1.20) from **La Châtre.** The square will be to your right when you get off. A good time to visit is the last weekend in July, when **La Fête au Village** puts a little more sparkle into the tiny town square, with outdoor dining, music, and market vendors.

THE ORIGINAL BOY GEORGE While most girls called Amandine-Aurore-Lucile might like to give themselves a snappier title, a boy's name wouldn't normally top the list—especially in the 19th century. But George Sand (1804-1876) never worried about convention. Prolific novelist, proto-feminist, and passionate lover, she achieved fame and notoriety that could scarcely be expected from a provincial *mademoiselle* from Nohant. After leaving her home and husband for the excitement of the capital in 1831, she embarked on a series of amorous adventures—her conquests included Alfred de Musset, Prosper Mérimée (the author of *Carmen*), and, most famously, Frédéric Chopin. Sand adopted male clothing as part of her protest against the social strictures of the day. She returned to Nohant in 1839 with the consumptive Chopin; while he composed some of his best-loved works, she celebrated the beauty of her homeland with novels such as *La Mare au Diable* and *La Petite Fadette.*

LIMOGES

Limoges (pop. 150,000) would be nothing without its crockery. For countless centuries, the peaceful city has manufactured porcelain and enamel for the upper classes. That trade, and its metallic proceeds, has given Limoges a graceful beauty; beautiful old architecture, an exquisite Gothic cathedral, and countless workshops and galleries with *émaux d'art* (enameled art) and *faiences* (glazed earthenware).

⌐ TRANSPORTATION

Trains: Gare des Bénédictins, pl. Maison-Dieu (☎05 55 11 11 88), off av. de Gaulle, restored to its 1920s Art Deco splendor. Info office open 5:15am-11pm. To: **Bordeaux** (3hr., 7 per day, €24.20); **Brive** (1hr., 5 per day, €12.80); **Lyon** (6hr.; 1:13am and 1:13pm; €37.70); **Paris** (3-4hr., 5 per day, €37); **Poitiers** (2hr., 3 per day, €16.80); **Toulouse** (3½hr., 3 per day, €30.90).

Buses: pl. des Bénédictins (☎05 55 04 91 95). The bus station is in the train station. **Jet Tours,** 3 rue Jean Jaurès (☎05 55 32 47 48), and **Bernis Tourisme,** 24 rue de la République (☎05 55 34 30 50), run buses to locations outside the city. Call for info.

Local Buses: TCL (☎05 55 32 46 46) runs buses around the city. Info office at 10 pl. Léon Betoulle, across from the town hall. Open M 1:30-6pm, Tu-F 8:30am-12:30pm and 1:30-6pm, Sa 8:30am-12:30pm. Ticket €1, *carnet* of 10 €8.50.

Taxis: Taxis Limoges (☎05 55 37 81 81 or 05 55 38 38 38). 24hr.

Car Rental: Europcar (☎05 55 77 64 52), in the train station. Open M-F 8am-6pm, Sa 9:30am-noon and 2-5:30pm. **Avis** (☎05 55 79 78 25) is also in the train station. Open M-F 9:45am-1:30pm and 4-7pm, Sa 9:45-1:30pm and 4-6pm.

✦ ┢ ORIENTATION AND PRACTICAL INFORMATION

Limoges was originally two different villages with separate medieval fortifications. This division continues unofficially today; the former villages represent Limoges's two principal *quartiers*. The **Cité,** which lies on the banks of the Vienne around the Cathédrale St-Etienne, the first village built, is now primarily a scenic area. **Le Château,** to the west, holds most of the shops and restaurants.

Tourist Office: 12 bd. de Fleurus (☎05 55 34 46 87; fax 05 55 34 19 12; ot.limoges.haute-vienne@en-france.com), near pl. Wilson. From the train station, keep left by the train tracks down av. du Général de Gaulle. Cut diagonally across pl. Jourdan onto bd. de Fleurus. English-speaking staff has maps and lists *chambres d'hôte*. **Currency exchange** with 4% commission. Themed **walking tours** of the city July-Aug.; in English on request; 1½hr.; €4.50, children €1.50. Open June 15-Sept. 15 M-Sa 9am-7pm, Su 10am-6pm; Sept. 16-June 14 M-Sa 9am-noon and 2-7pm.

Money: Banque de France, 8 bd. Carnot (☎05 55 11 53 00). No commission and good rates. **Exchange desk** open M-F 8:45am-noon.

Laundromat: Le forum des lavendières, 14 rue des Charseix. Open daily 8am-9pm. **Laverie,** 31 rue de François Chinieux. Open daily 7am-9pm.

Police: 84 av. Emile Labussière (☎05 55 14 30 00).

Hospital: 2 av. Martin Luther King (☎05 55 05 61 23).

Internet Access: Free at **Bibliothèque Francophone Multimédia de Limoges,** 2 rue Louis Longequeue (☎05 55 45 96 00), just beyond the Hôtel de Ville. Open W and Sa 10am-1pm and 2-6pm. Also **Planète Micro,** 5 bd. Victor Hugo (☎05 55 10 93 61). Open M-Sa 10am-2am, Su 2pm-2am. €2.94 per hr.

Post Office: av. Garibaldi near av. de la Libération. **Currency exchange** with no commission. Open M 2-7pm, Tu-Sa 10am-7pm. **Postal code:** 87000.

▐ ACCOMMODATIONS

■ **Hôtel de Paris,** 5 cours Vergnaud (☎05 55 77 56 96). With your back to the train station, walk up av. du Général de Gaulle for about 200ft., then veer right onto cours Bugeaud. Walk past the gardens on your right, and turn right onto cours Vergnaud. Recent renovations brought new wallpaper, furniture, and bathrooms, but retained a charming Victorian style. Most of the spacious rooms look out over the champs de Juillet. Breakfast €3.80. Singles €23-45; doubles €30-45; triples €54. MC/V. ❷

Foyer des Jeunes Travailleurs, 20 rue Encombe Vineuse (☎05 55 77 63 97). With your back to the train station, descend the stairs to the right. At the bottom, cut across the grass to the street, curving slightly to your right. Rue Théodore Bac is across the street on your left. Take this to pl. Carnot, turn left onto av. Adrien Tarrade, and take the first left onto rue Encombe Vineuse. (15min.) Simple singles and doubles with sinks. Long-term residents and friendly owners gather in the communal TV room every evening. Kitchen. Breakfast included. Reception 24hr. Singles €14; doubles €20. ❶

Hôtel de la Paix, pl. Jourdan (☎05 55 34 36 00; fax 05 55 32 37 06). From the train station, turn left and walk down av. Général de Gaulle. The hotel is on the far side of the pl. Jourdan. Oversized phonographs and art deco posters decorate the reception. Large rooms with slightly uneven floors, some with a view of the park outside. Breakfast €5. Single with shower €35; singles and doubles with shower and toilet €45-57. MC/V. ❸

Mon Logis, 16 rue du Général du Bessol (☎05 55 77 41 43). Descend the stairs to the right of the train station and take cours Gay Lussac. Turn left onto Gay Lussac and make a right onto rue du Général du Bessol. Guests are greeted by a large, loud German Shepherd—don't worry, he is harmless and friendly! Spacious, bright rooms lined with nature posters of Limoges and environs and blessed with lots of sunshine. Breakfast €4.70. Singles €21-31; doubles €34-48; extra bed €6.10. MC/V. ❷

Camping Municipal D'Uzurat, 40 av. d'Uzurat (☎05 55 38 49 43, fax 05 55 37 32 78). From the train station, take bus #20 (dir: Beaubreuil; M-Sa 6am-8:30pm) to "L. Armand." On Sundays, take bus #2 (dir: Beaubreuil) to "Uzurat." By foot, take av. Général Leclerc from pl. Carnot and follow signs to Uzurat. (1hr.) Walk down av. d'Uzurat until you reach the campground. 5km north of Limoges, this is the only site near town, right on the shore of Lake Uzurat. Grounds have tennis courts and minigolf and hiking trails nearby. €9 for two people and tent, €11.30 with caravan; extra person €2.75, children €1.70. Electricity €3.20. ❶

◖ FOOD

The central Les Halles **indoor market** faces pl. de la Motte (M-Sa); a larger market brightens pl. Carnot. (Sa mornings.) A **Monoprix supermarket** is at 11 pl. de la République (open M-Sa 8:30am-8pm) and a huge **Champion** is on av. Garibaldi in the Saint Martial shopping mall on the north side of town. (Open M-F 8am-8pm, Sa 9am-8pm.) Restaurants on and near the medieval rue de la Boucherie provide a chic (and expensive) dining experience. **L'Amphytron ❸,** 26 rue de la Boucherie, serves traditional French food in a converted 13th-century butcher's house. (☎05 55 32 36 39. Open M and Sa 7-10:30pm, Tu-F noon-2pm and 7-10:30pm. *Menus* from €16.) For a cheaper meal in an equally beautiful setting, head to **rue Haute-Cité** near the cathedral, which has *crêperies, brasseries,* and even an Indian restaurant.

🔍 SIGHTS

LA CITÉ. The oldest *quartier* of Limoges, this is also the most beautiful, as well as a peaceful retreat from the bustle of Le Château. After viewing the buildings here, walk along the tree-lined promenade that runs between the 12th- and 13th-century Pont St-Martial and the Pont St-Etienne on the far side of the Vienne river.

MUSÉE NATIONAL ADRIEN DUBOUCHE. This beautiful national museum houses the largest ceramics collection in Europe, spanning centuries. The large, blue-and-white Chinese plate (dating from 1345) with a dragon in its center, on the second floor, is one of the most valuable pieces of china in the world. *(8bis pl. Winston Churchill. ☎ 05 55 33 08 50. Open July-Aug. W-M 10am-5:45pm; Sept.-June W-M 10am-12:30pm 2-5:45pm. €4, ages 18-25 and Su €2.60; 1st Su of the month and under 18 free.)*

MAISON DE LA BOUCHERIE. Unique to Limoges, this district of narrow streets and medieval houses in the town center was for many centuries home only to the town's butchers. For a slice of their life, visit the **Maison Traditionelle de la Boucherie,** 36 rue de la Boucherie. Guides lead tours of a butcher's house. *(☎ 05 55 34 46 87. Open July-Sept. daily 9:30am-noon and 2:30-7pm. Free.)* Across the street, the 15th-century **Chapel St. Aurelien** is filled with statues of the patron saint of butchers.

CATHÉDRALE ST-ETIENNE. This impressively large structure is one of the few great Gothic constructions south of the Loire. The cathedral, which took 600 years to complete, was built on the remains of a 1013 Roman temple, whose crypt and bell tower porch remain intact. *(Pl. St-Etienne. Ask at the tourist office for directions. Open M-Sa 10am-noon and 2-6pm, Su 2:30-6:30pm. Free tours in French M-Sa 11am.)*

EVÊCHÉ BOTANICAL GARDENS. These gardens, which surround the cathedral, are a gorgeous and relaxing place to enjoy the view from the banks of the Vienne. The gardens double as a botanical museum. *(☎ 05 55 45 62 67. Tours by appointment.)*

MUSÉE MUNICIPAL DE L'EVÊCHÉ. Also known as the Musée de l'Email, this 18th-century bishop's palace is filled with the city's impressive collections of Egyptian art, Merovingian capitals, masonry, sarcophagi, local Roman artifacts, and the inevitable enamels and porcelain. There are also five paintings by Auguste Renoir, born in Limoges in 1841. *(Next to the cathedral in la Cité. ☎ 05 55 34 44 09 or 05 55 45 6 75. Open June W-M 10-11:45am and 2-6pm; July-Sept. 15 daily 10-11:45am and 2-6pm; Oct.-May W-M 2-5pm. Free.)*

OTHER SIGHTS. Limoges's famous ceramics decorate several remarkable structures, including Les Halles, the nearby Pavilion de Verdurier, and the fountain in front of the *mairie*. To learn more about porcelain production, take a tour of a factory at the **Manufacture Bernardaud.** *(27 av. Albert Thomas. ☎ 05 55 10 55 91. Tours June-Sept. 9-11am and 1-4pm; Oct.-May by reservation only. €4.)* Another part of the ceramics tradition thrives at **Atelier Mosaïque,** 17 rue Montmailler, one of the hidden treasures of Limoges. In his small shop, Mr. Soubeyrand de St-Exupery makes and sells delicately designed mosaics (see sidebar, **The Local Story**). Half-finished mosaics lie around his work area, while the finished products adorn the walls in the form of mirrors, portraits, jewelry boxes, clocks, and more. *(☎ 05 55 77 73 05. Open M-Sa 9:30am-10:30pm. 2-week seminars offered continuously.)* The **Crypte St-Martial** is all that remains of the medieval Benedictine Abbaye St-Martial, which was the heart of the **Château** *quartier*. Inside the crypt, you can see the ruins of the abbatial city, a 1st-century Roman necropolis, and the tombs of St-Valérie and St-Mar-

THE LOCAL STORY

MOSAICS

The Atelier Mosaique, a tiny workshop with the feel of a retiree's basement, is a world away from the businesslike Bernadaud factory nearby. M. Soubeyrand de Saint-Exupery was putting the final touches on a small mosaic of a landscape when Let's Go interrupted his meditation to ask him a few questions.

Q: How do you make a mosaic?

A: Ah, you should enroll in one of my classes [laughs]. We use the same technique of *kaolin* enamel on tiles as they do to make the famous Limoges porcelain. Once I have made several different types of tiles, I cut them into smaller pieces and fit them together on a base with cement, according to a design I've planned in advance.

Q: How are your mosaics different from traditional mosaics?

A: The most well-known mosaics come from ancient Rome, Greece, Pompeii, and North Africa. Many of these are extremely detailed and grid-like. Many have religious themes with gods and that sort of thing, while others are geometrical, for decorating pools and *hamams*. I learned my art in Italy and the Maghreb, so I feel they've influenced my technique.

Q: How did you choose to come to Limoges?

A: It was destiny. Well, more specifically, it's famous for being the land of porcelain, for the *arts de feu*. It is, in some ways, the natural extension of my mosaics to incorporate other kinds of influences. Mosaic is an art of assemblage. I combine different methods with different styles.

tial. (☎ 05 55 34 46 87. *Entrance on pl. de la République. Open July-Sept. 9:30am-noon and 2:30-7pm. Written English explanations available. Free.*) Of the 48 distilleries in Limoges at the turn of the century, only one remains: the **Musée des Distilleries Limougeaudes,** 54 rue de Belfort, which gives 30min. tours (including tastings) of their liquor works. Interesting *and* tasty! (☎ 05 55 77 23 57. *Open 10am-noon and 3-5pm. Free. English translations not available.*)

♫ ENTERTAINMENT AND FESTIVALS

At night the streets of Limoges empty out, but if you know where to look you can find a handful of small but popular bars and clubs in the center of town. The **Cheyenne Café,** 4 rue Charles-Michels, is usually the loudest and most crowded. (☎ 05 55 32 32 62. Open daily 10am-2am.) An unusually diverse crowd frequents **Café des Anciennes Majorettes de la Baule,** 27 rue Haute-Vienne; older people and young locals alike pack the spacious interior to socialize over French music. Local artists's paintings and shelves of used books decorate the walls. (Open Tu-Th 10am-1am, F-Sa 10pm-2am.) **La Bibliothèque,** 7 rue Turgot, is a cool bar. Mahogany stools, red carpeting, chandeliers in the shape of candelabras, and walls lined with shelves of leather-bound books help this place live up to its name, except the part about reading. (☎ 05 55 11 00 47. Open daily 11am-2am.) **Café Traxx,** 12 rue des Filles de Notre Dame, is a fairly small, social house/techno gay bar in a former medieval home. (☎ 05 55 32 07 55. Open daily 6pm-2am.)

The **Grand Théâtre,** 48 rue Jean Jaurès, presents 60 ballet, orchestral, operatic, and choral productions from September to early June. (Reservations ☎ 05 55 34 12 12. €5-35.) The **Théâtre de l'Union,** 20 rue des Coopérateurs, also has a season from September to May. (☎ 05 55 79 90 00.) On weekdays, the five **Centres Culturels Municipaux** put on a diverse array of concerts, theater productions, and films; contact the **Centre Culturel Jean-Moulin,** 76 rue des Sagnes (☎ 05 55 35 04 10), or **Centre Culturel Jean Gagnant,** 7 av. Jean Gagnant (☎ 05 55 34 45 49), for more info.

The **Fête de Ste-Jean,** at the end of June, brings diving, fireworks, water shows, dancing, and musical performances. The popular **Fête des Arts de la Rue** dominates the last three days in June with nightly fire shows and concerts. (☎ 05 55 45 63 85.) At the end of September, the **Festival International des Théâtres Francophones** features 15,000 French Canadians, French-speaking Africans, and francophones from all over the world. During the street banquet **La Frairie des Petits Ventres** (Festival of Small Stomachs), residents consume meat in mass quantities.

NEAR LIMOGES

ORADOUR-SUR-GLANE

On June 10, 1944, in a horrible act of brutality, Nazi SS troops massacred all of the inhabitants of the farming village **Oradour-sur-Glane** without warning or provocation. No one can explain the Nazis's decision, although one theory holds that they mistook the town for Oradour-sur-Vayres, a Resistance stronghold. The Nazis entered at two in the afternoon, and corralled the women and children into the church and the men into six barns. At four, a shot was fired, ordering the troops to begin the massacre. The women and children in the church were burned alive; the men were tortured, shot, and then burned. By seven o'clock, 642 people, including 205 children, had been slaughtered. Most of the SS troops participating in the attack were tried in 1953, found guilty, and then immediately freed as the result of a general amnesty by the French government; Heinz Barth, commander of the unit, is currently serving a life sentence in a German jail. Plaques with heartbreaking messages and pictures mark two glass tombs containing the bones and ashes of the dead. The town remains in ruins. Train wires dangle from slanting poles and 50-year-old skeletons of cars rust next to crumbling walls. You can walk freely along the main thoroughfare and peer into the remnants of each home. Signs indicate the name and profession of each person who lived there. A small memorial between the cemetery and town displays bicycles, toys, and watches, all stopped at the same moment by the heat of the fire. A museum, **Le Centre de la Mémoire,** places the massacre in the context of the Nazi regime. (☎ 05 55 43 04 30. Museum and town open July-Aug. daily 9am-8pm; Sept.-Oct. and Mar.-Apr. 9am-6pm; Nov.-Dec. 16 and Feb. 9am-5pm; May-June 9am-7pm. Museum €4.60, students and children €3.80. Free entry into town.)

Not without hesitation, a new Oradour (pop. 2000) has been built next to its obliterated precursor. Oradour is best reached by car. (45min.) Ask for a map at the Limoges tourist office.

PÉRIGORD

The name summons up an intoxicating set of images: green country-side splashed with yellow sunflowers, white chalk cliffs, plates of black truffles, and the smell of warm walnuts. The area around Les Eyzies-de-Tayac has turned up more stone-age artifacts—tools, bones, weapons, cave paintings, and etchings—than any other place on earth. The painted caves of Lascaux are the most extensive and best preserved in the world. While they were closed to the public in 1963, visitors can still experience their mysterious powers at Lascaux II, a replica located 150m from the original site. Today, the Grotte de Font de Gaume in Les Eyzies-de-Tayac and the Grotte du Pech-Merle, 25km from Cahors, contain extraordinary original paintings still accessible to the public. The caves open into spectacular countryside, including feudal châteaux, poplar-lined rivers, and valleys carpeted with sunflowers and wheat fields.

PÉRIGUEUX

Presiding high above the Isle River, the towering steeple and five massive cupolas of the Cathédrale St-Front dominate Périgueux from above the Isle River. Périgueux (pop. 32,300) arose from the 13th-century union of two rival towns: the abbey-centered Cité de Puy-St-Font and the Gallo-Roman Vésone. Despite barbarian invasions in the 3rd century, Huguenot attacks in the 16th century, and the Jacqueries peasant uprisings, the city has managed to preserve significant architecture in both halves of the town. The town center, paved in white cobble-stones, is quiet during the afternoon, but in the evening Périgueux's youth crawl out of its historic cracks and into the city's bars and clubs. Travelers with cars might consider daytripping from here to see the caves of the Périgord rather than staying in the more expensive Les Eyzies.

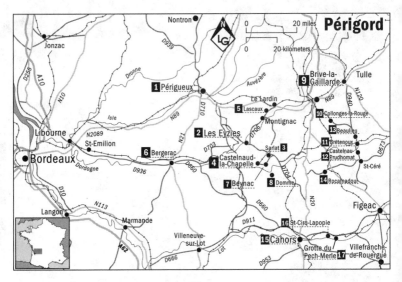

1	**Périgueux:** Small city with many ruins; good base for visits to prehistoric caves **(p. 368)**
2	**Les Eyzies-de-Tayac:** Close to most of the great Neolithic art, though not Lascaux **(p. 374)**
3	**Sarlat:** Beautifully restored, film-worthy medieval architecture **(p. 375)**
4	**Castelnaud-la-Chapelle:** Well-restored castle with 100 Years' War museum **(p. 377)**
5	▓**Lascaux:** Site of the most spectacular cave paintings—and their duplicates **(p. 379)**
6	**Bergerac:** Celebrated red and sweet white wines; village in fertile Dordogne valley **(p. 380)**
7	**Beynac:** A fortress sheathed in greenery above a stony ancient town **(p. 382)**
8	▓**Domme:** Walled village on a high rock dome; its towers imprisoned 70 Templars **(p. 383)**
9	**Brive-la-Gaillarde:** A major rail junction and solid base for exploring the Quercy region **(p. 384)**
10	▓**Collonges-la-Rouge:** Slow, exquisite red-rock village **(p. 386)**
11	**Bretenoux:** Base for two or three towns near the upper stretches of the Dordogne **(p. 387)**
12	**Castelnau-Prudhomat:** Triangular château with burnt-red ramparts; tapestries inside **(p. 388)**
13	▓**Beaulieu:** Medieval village with terrifying apocalyptic church sculpture **(p. 388)**
14	▓**Rocamadour:** Pilgrimage town built, astoundingly enough, into a cliff face **(p. 389)**
15	**Cahors:** Relaxed, remote isthmus town; monumental bridge; good stopover for cyclists **(p. 391)**
16	▓**St-Cirq-Lapopie:** Cliff-edge village on the Lot; full of artisans, flowers, and tourists **(p. 393)**
17	▓**Grotte du Pech-Merle:** Best-preserved of all the prehistoric caves; less accessible **(p. 394)**
18	**Château Cénevières:** Italianate castle with many quirky attractions **(p. 394)**

▐ TRANSPORTATION

Trains: rue Denis Papin. Info office open M 4:50am-8:50pm, Tu-Th 5:40am-8:05pm, F 5:40am-10:15pm, Sa-Su 6:15am-10:15pm. To: **Bordeaux** (1½hr., 7 per day, €15.40); **Brive** (1hr., 7 per day, €10); **Limoges** (1-1½hr., 6 per day, €12.80); **Lyon** (6-8hr., 5 per day, €43.80); **Paris** (4-6hr., 12 per day, €42.80) via Limoges; **Sarlat** (1½hr., 4 per day, €11.30); **Toulouse** (4hr., 8 per day, €26.80) via Agen.

Buses: pl. Francheville (☎05 53 08 43 13). Office open M-Th 8:30-11:30am and 2:30-5:30pm, F 8:30-11:30am and 2:30-4:30pm. To **Angoulême** (1½hr.; M-Sa 3 per day, 1 on Su; €14.03) and **Sarlat** (1½hr., F-Sa 2 per day, €7.62).

Taxis: Taxi Périgueux, pl. Bugeaud (☎05 53 09 09 09). 24hr.

▐ ORIENTATION AND PRACTICAL INFORMATION

To get to the *vieille ville* and tourist office from the train station, turn right on rue Denis Papin and bear left on rue des Mobiles-de-Coulmiers, which becomes rue du Président Wilson. On your right, you'll pass rue Ernest Guillier. Take the next right (just after the Monoprix) and walk down one block. The **tourist office** is on the left, beside the round stone **Mataguerre Tower.** (15min.)

Tourist Office: 26 pl. Francheville (☎05 53 53 10 63; fax 05 53 09 02 50). Free map; walking, *petit train,* and boat tours. Open July-Aug. M-Sa 9am-7pm, Su 10am-6pm; Sept.-June M-Sa 9am-6pm. The annex, **Point "i,"** pl. de Général de Gaulle, is a good source of assistance for late arrivals. Open June 15-Sept. 15 daily 9am-10pm.

Espace Tourisme Périgord, 25 rue Wilson (☎05 53 35 50 24). Info on Périgord, lists of campgrounds, *gîtes,* and *chambres d'hôte,* and excellent free topographic maps. Open M-F 8:30am-noon and 2-6pm.

Money: Banque de France, 1 pl. du Roosevelt (☎05 53 03 30 30), has **currency exchange.** Exchange desk open M-F 8:45am-12:15pm.

Laundromat: Lav'matic, 20 rue Mobiles de Coulmiers, near Rondpoint Lanxade. Open daily 8am-9pm.

Police: rue du 4 Septembre (☎05 53 08 10 17), near the post office.

Hospital: Centre Hospitalier, 80 av. Georges Pompidou (☎05 53 07 70 00).

Périgueux

🏠 ACCOMMODATIONS
Barnabé-Plage, **8**
Foyer des Jeunes Travailleurs, **3**
Hôtel des Voyageurs, **1**
Les Charentes, **2**

🍎 FOOD
Au Bien Bon, **7**
Chez Catherine, **5**

⭐ NIGHTLIFE
Zanzi Bar, **4**
Gordon Pub, **6**

Youth Center: Centre Information Jeunesse, 1 ave. d'Aquitaine (☎ 05 53 53 52 81). Finding short term jobs is difficult, but your best shot is here. Open M-Th 8:30am-noon and 1:30-5:30pm, F 8:30am-noon and 1:30-5pm.

Internet Access: Surf the net from a medieval mansion at **Arena Games,** 13 rue des Farges (☎ 05 53 53 75 21). Take a sharp left after the tourist office onto rue de la Bride, which becomes rue des Farges. €1 per 15min., €3 per hr. Open M-Th 11am-midnight, F 11am-1am, Sa 2pm-1am, Su noon-midnight.

Post Office: 1 rue du 4 Septembre (☎ 05 53 03 61 12), offers **currency exchange.** Open M-F 8am-7pm, Sa 8am-noon. **Poste Restante:** 24017. **Postal code:** 24070.

🏠 ACCOMMODATIONS AND CAMPING

▨ **Hôtel des Voyageurs,** 26 rue Denis Papin (☎/fax 05 53 53 17 44), right across from the train station. 15 clean, bright if well-worn rooms at great prices, tended by a friendly couple. The rooms that face the station can be noisy when windows are open. Breakfast €3.20. Singles €12.50; doubles €14, with shower €17. ❶

Les Charentes, 16 rue Denis Papin (☎ 05 53 53 37 13), facing the train station. Dark wood hallways papered with Victorian designs lead to slightly worn rooms with antique-like furniture. Breakfast €5. Reception 7am-11pm. Call ahead if arriving outside those hours. Closed 1st week of Nov. and Dec. 23-Jan. 4. Singles with shower €23, with TV €27, with toilet €32. Extra person €4.60. AmEx/MC/V. ❷

Foyer des Jeunes Travailleurs Résidence Lakanal, rue des Thermes (☎05 53 06 81 40; fax 05 53 06 81 49). Turn right from the train station onto rue Denis Papin and follow it as it becomes rue Chanzy. Turn left onto av. Cavaignac, and turn left again on rue Romain. Cross the roundabout to rue Mosaique and follow it until it hits rue de Themes. Walk along the train tracks; the hostel is at the end of the street. (25min.) The hostel, in an industrial section of town, is mostly a residence for young workers. Prepare to share a clean but cramped 2-bunk dorm room and small shower; spacious singles are not available until July 1. Reception 24hr., except Sa-Su 3-5pm. Reserve ahead. Dorms €11.50 with bedding and breakfast, with dinner €17.60; singles with bath €13.50. ●

Barnabé-Plage, 80 rue des Bains (☎05 53 53 41 45), 1.5km outside Périgueux in Boulazac. From cours Montaigne, take bus #8 (dir: "Cité Bel Air," roughly one per hour from 7am to 7pm, €0.75) to "Rue des Bains." It may be faster to walk if you miss the bus; from Cathédrale St. Front, walk downhill and cross the river on Pont des Barris. Turn left immediately after the bridge onto Rue des Prés. The street ends at Rue des Bains, right in front of the campground. (25min.) Riverside site packed in summer. Reception 11am-midnight. €2.85 per person, €2.70 per tent, €4.30 per camping car. MC/V. ●

FOOD

The labyrinth of narrow stone streets between cours M. Montaigne and rue Taillefer is lined with regional cusinary treasures: *foie gras,* walnuts, *cèpe* and *girolle* mushrooms, and fruit liqueurs. A stroll down rue Salinière and rue Limogeanne reveals a luxurious assortment of *chacuteries, pâtisseries, boulangeries* and *sandwicheries.* While restaurants in this area can be slightly pricey, the other side of rue Taillefer is more reasonable. **☒Au Bien Bon ❸,** 15 rue Aubergerie, serves cuisine at the forefront of regional cooking, and has design-your-own lunch *formules.* Try the *menu* with appetizer, main course and dessert for €13. (☎05 53 09 69 91. Open M 7:30-10pm, Tu-Sa noon-2pm and 7:30-10pm.) **Chez Catherine ❷,** 6 rue de Condé, resembles the offspring of an antique shop and a café; everything in this *petite restauration* is for sale! You can leaf through old magazines as you choose between three kinds of quiches for the €6.50 lunch. (☎05 53 35 40 78. Open Tu-Su 10am-7pm.) There's a morning **market** on pl. du Coderc, pl. de l'Hôtel de Ville and a larger one on pl. de la Clautre, near the cathedral (W and Sa 8am-1pm). The behemoth **Monoprix,** on pl. Bugeaud in the town center, is impossible to miss. (Open M-Sa 8:30am-8pm.)

SIGHTS

Gabarre de Périgueux offers 50min. **boat tours** of the city between June 15 and Sept. 15, departing from the base of Cathédrale St-Front (€6.50). The tourist office gives out an excellent walking-tour guide to medieval-Renaissance and Gallo-Roman Périgueux. To get inside the *hôtels particuliers* and monuments, you'll have to take one of their tours. (June 15-Sept. 15 M-Sa 10:30am, 2:30, and 4pm. Tours available in English. €4.60, Students €3.50. Reserve ahead.)

MEDIEVAL AND RENAISSANCE PÉRIGUEUX

Nearly 1500 years of rebuilding, restoration, and revision have produced **Cathédrale St-Front,** an ungainly edifice that dominates the skyline above the river with its five immense Byzantine cupolas in the shape of a cross. In the late 1800s, Paul Abadie took inspiration from it for an equally controversial project: the Basilique Sacré-Coeur in Paris. (Open daily 8am-noon and 2:30pm-7pm.)

Down the rue St-Front from the Maison and the cathedral, the **Musée du Périgord,** 22 cours Tourny, is home to one of France's most important collections of prehis**Foyer des Jeunes Travailleurs Résidence Lakanal,** rue des Thermes (☎05 53 06

81 40; fax 05 53 06 81 49). Turn right from the train station onto rue Denis Papin and follow it as it becomes rue Chanzy. Turn left onto av. Cavaignac, and turn left again on rue Romain. Cross the roundabout to rue Mosaique and follow it until it hits rue de Themes. Walk along the train tracks; the hostel is at the end of the street. (25min.) The hostel, in an industrial section of town, is mostly a residence for young workers. Prepare to share a clean but cramped 2-bunk dorm room and small shower; spacious singles are not available until July 1. Reception 24hr., except Sa-Su 3-5pm. Reserve ahead. Dorms €11.50 with bedding and breakfast, with dinner €17.60; singles with bath €13.50. ❶

🍴 FOOD

The labyrinth of narrow stone streets between cours M. Montaigne and rue Taillefer is lined with regional cusinary treasures: *foie gras*, walnuts, *cèpe* and *girolle* mushrooms, and fruit liqueurs. A stroll down rue Salinière and rue Limogeanne reveals a luxurious assortment of *chacuteries*, *pâtisseries*, *boulangeries* and *sandwicheries*. While restaurants in this area can be slightly pricey, the other side of rue Taillefer is more reasonable. **Au Bien Bon ❸**, 15 rue Aubergerie, serves cuisine at the forefront of regional cooking, and has design-your-own lunch *formules*. Try the *menu* with appetizer, main course and dessert for €13. (☎ 05 53 09 69 91. Open M 7:30-10pm, Tu-Sa noon-2pm and 7:30-10pm.) **Chez Catherine ❷**, 6 rue de Condé, resembles the offspring of an antique shop and a café; everything in this *petite restauration* is for sale! You can leaf through old magazines as you choose between three kinds of quiches for the €6.50 lunch. (☎ 05 53 35 40 78. Open Tu-Su 10am-7pm.) There's a morning **market** on pl. du Coderc, pl. de l'Hôtel de Ville and a larger one on pl. de la Clautre, near the cathedral (W and Sa 8am-1pm). The behemoth **Monoprix**, on pl. Bugeaud in the town center, is impossible to miss. (Open M-Sa 8:30am-8pm.)

👁 SIGHTS

Gabarre de Périgueux offers 50min. **boat tours** of the city between June 15 and Sept. 15, departing from the base of Cathédrale St-Front (€6.50). The tourist office gives out an excellent walking-tour guide to medieval-Renaissance and Gallo-Roman Périgueux. To get inside the *hôtels particuliers* and monuments, you'll have to take one of their tours. (June 15-Sept. 15 M-Sa 10:30am, 2:30, and 4pm. Tours available in English. €4.60, Students €3.50. Reserve ahead.)

MEDIEVAL AND RENAISSANCE PÉRIGUEUX

Nearly 1500 years of rebuilding, restoration, and revision have produced **Cathédrale St-Front**, an ungainly edifice that dominates the skyline above the river with its five immense Byzantine cupolas in the shape of a cross. In the late 1800s, Paul Abadie took inspiration from it for an equally controversial project: the Basilique Sacré-Coeur in Paris. (Open daily 8am-noon and 2:30pm-7pm.)

Down the rue St-Front from the Maison and the cathedral, the **Musée du Périgord,** 22 cours Tourny, is home to one of France's most important collections of prehistoric artifacts, including fossils from Les Eyzies, 2m long mammoth tusks, and an Egyptian mummy whose toes peek out from crusty coverings. It includes a small collection of fine arts. Placed alongside artifacts are works by local middle schoolers, the result of an ongoing educational project. (☎ 05 53 06 40 70. Open M and W-F 11am-6pm, Sa-Su 1-6pm. €3.50, students €1.75, under 18 free; Sept. 15-June 15 M-F noon-2pm free.) Retrace your steps to the tourist office, where you'll find the crumbling **Tour Mataguerre.** It takes its name from an English captain who was kept prisoner in its dungeons for 17 years during the Hundred Years' War.

GALLO-ROMAN PÉRIGUEUX

The few crumbling remains of Gallo-Roman Périgueux lie to the west of the *vieille ville,* down rue de la Cité from pl. Francheville. Perhaps the most impressive is the towering **Tour de Vésone,** built in the first century AD and once the centerpiece of a brilliant Roman colony. The tower itself was a *cella,* the center of worship in a Roman temple, though now it's little more than three-quarters of a crumbling stone tube. About a fourth of the weighty structure was knocked down completely, supposedly by the last fleeing demons of paganism, which was expelled by St. Front in the 5th century. (Park grounds open Apr.-Sept. daily 7:30am-9pm; Oct.-Mar. 7:30am-6:30pm.) Next door, the **Villa de Pompeïus,** currently under construction, was once the lavish home of a wealthy Roman merchant. Back across the bridge from the Tour de Vésone and to the left down rue Romaine, you'll find a cluster of architectural vestiges of the first century through the high Middle Ages. Unruly flowers sprout from the crevices of the **Château Barrière**, a four-storied late-Gothic castle. The Romanesque house next door is an example of the use of *spolia*—chunks of ruins incorporated decoratively into new buildings. Both buildings were constructed on the remains of the Roman wall which surrounded Vésone, built in AD 275 to protect the city against the first Norman and barbarian attacks. Just a couple of meters away rests the **Porte Normande,** a fragment of this wall.

Up rue Romaine, the 11th-century **Eglise St-Etienne-de-la-Cité** was the first Christian edifice in Vésone and the seat of the bishopric until Calvinist attackers in 1669 destroyed all but the choir and one-third of the nave. Barely 40m beyond the church, up rue de l'Ancien Evêché, the **Roman amphitheater** has been transformed into a public park, complete with sagging archways, palm trees, and an inviting fountain. (Garden open Apr.-Sept. daily 7:30am-9pm; Oct.-Mar. 7:30am-6:30pm.)

🎵 ENTERTAINMENT AND FESTIVALS

While the streets may be sleepy, the *places* jump with activity. **Place St-Silain** and **place St-Louis** are nightlife centers, while **place du Marché au Bois** hosts frequent concerts. On lively **rue de la Sagesse,** bars spill music out onto the cobblestone street. **Zanzi Bar,** 2 rue Conde, right next to Chez Catherine (see **Food,** p. 371), serves jungle-inspired cocktails (from €5) and exotic tapas (€6) in an *ambiance tropicale.* (☎ 05 50 50 28 99. Open Tu-Sa 6:30pm-1am, June-Aug. until 2am. MC/V.) **Gordon Pub,** 12 rue Condé, off rue Taillefer, is an Irish-style pub with a small terrace. (☎ 05 53 35 03 74. Beer €2. Open July-Oct. M-F 11am-2am, Sa 2pm-2am; Nov.-June M-F 11am-1am, Sa 2pm-2am.)

Macadam Jazz presents free outdoor jazz concerts on Tuesdays throughout July and August. **Son-et-Lumière de Périgueux: La Légende de Saint-Front** illuminates the Cathédrale St-Front every summer on Wednesday nights at 10:30pm from the end of July through the middle of August. (☎ 05 53 53 18 71. €13, students €10.) The town quiets down during the first week of August for **Mimos,** the best mime festival in the world. Mime companies from the far corners of the world come to give performances that push the boundaries of this art beyond the imagination. The big events cost money, but free performances and workshops all over town spread entertainment to everybody. (☎ 05 53 53 18 71. Ticketed events €10, students €8.)

LES EYZIES-DE-TAYAC

Les-Eyzies-de-Tayac (pop. 900) is the carless traveler's best base for a visit to the Vézère valley's famous cave paintings (although it is still a substantial trip from Lascaux). A huge number of the region's most stunning caves are less than a 20min. walk from the center of town. With two important museums and the official information center for the region's prehistoric sites, it's also a good place to start learning about Neolithic art. The village abounds with Neanderthal-themed hotels, duck-filled restaurants, fossils 'n *foie gras* knick-knack boutiques, and hordes of camcorder-toters who rush to see it all summer long. Arrive early if you want to get into the caves—visits are limited. If Les Eyzies is more than a daytrip for you, book your rooms even earlier or you'll be sleeping under a postcard rack.

⬛🛈 ORIENTATION AND PRACTICAL INFORMATION. Trains to: Paris (6-8hr.; 4 per day, €42.75); Périgueux (30min., 4-5 per day, €6.10); and Sarlat (1hr.; 3 per day, change at Le Buisson; €7.50). Open M-F 6:30am-6pm, Sa-Su 11am-6pm. (☎ 05 53 06 97 22.) With your back to the train station, turn right and walk 500m down the village's only street, av. de la Préhistoire, to reach its center. (5min.) The best resource for detailed information about the area's prehistoric sites is the **Point Accueil Préhistoire,** directly across from the post office on the main street through town. (☎ 06 86 66 54 43. Open daily 9:15am-1:30pm and 3-7pm.) But if you want to get out and see the caves yourself, head to the **tourist office** (www.leseyzies.com; contact@leseyzies.com) at pl. de la Mairie. It offers summer tours to sights outside of walking distance (call ahead), lists of caves and **gîtes d'étapes,** and **bike** and **canoe** rentals. (Bikes €8 per half-day, €14 per day. €20 deposit.) **Internet access** (€6 per hr.) and **currency exchange** without a commission. (☎ 05 53 06 97 05; fax 05 53 06 90 79. Open July-Aug. M-Sa 9am-7pm, Su 10am-noon, 2-6pm; Apr.-June and Sept. M-Sa 9am-noon and 2-6pm, Su 10am-noon and 2-5pm; Oct.-Mar. M-Sa 9am-noon and 2-6pm.) The **police** are in nearby St-Cyprien (☎ 05 53 30 80 00). The **post office** is on the main street, past the tourist office as you walk away from the train station. Provides **currency exchange.** (☎ 05 53 06 94 11. Open M-F 9am-noon and 2-5pm, Sa 9am-noon.) **Postal code:** 24620.

🛏🍴 ACCOMMODATIONS AND FOOD. Rooms tend to be expensive. The tourist office has a list of private B&Bs in the surrounding area (€25-32 for 1-2 people). Car travelers will notice signs along the main roads advertising *fermes* (farms) with camping space (€3-8). Some village homes rent rooms for €23-46 during the summer; look for *chambres* signs, especially on the east end of the town. In town, try the **Hôtel des Falaises ❸,** av. de la Préhistoire. Clean, soap-scented color-coordinated rooms with shower, sink, and toilet. Doubles come with a tub, larger rooms have a balcony overlooking the garden. (☎ 05 53 06 97 35. Breakfast €4. Reception in the bar downstairs 8am-8pm. Doubles with bath €28-31; twins €29; triples €39. MC/V.) The hotel offers more private and homey lodging in the **annex,** about 100m down the road toward Font-de-Gaume in a large half-timbered building. (One small single €23; doubles €28-31; triples €40-45.) For **Camping La Rivière ❶**, rte. de Périgueux, turn left as you step out of the tourist office toward Périgueux on av. de la Préhistoire. Follow the road straight for about five minutes, cross the bridge, and take another left when you reach the Citroën/Avia gas station. (☎05 53 06 97 14; fax 05 53 35 20 85; www.campings-dordogne.com/la-riviere; la-riviere@wana-doo.fr.) Snack bar, restaurant, bike rental, laundry, Internet, athletic facilities, kitchen, and a pool. Reception 8am-10pm. Open Apr. 6-Mar. 11. Apr. 6-June 29 and Sept. 1-Mar. 11. €3.45-4.30 per person; €1.90-4.20 per site; price varies with season. Electricity €3. Attached to the campsite is a small but luxurious **hotel** inside a 16th century Périgoridian home with fresh, well-furnished rooms. (Breakfast €4.30. Doubles with shower €30; quads with shower €43. MC/V.)

Most restaurants in Les Eyzies are expensive and extremely good. A **market** runs the length of town every Monday. (Open Apr.-Oct. 9am-1pm.) **Halle des Eyzies,** just past the center of town on rte. de Sarlat, is full of expensive boutiques hawking *foie gras* and walnut products. Here you can find wonderful local wines, oils, cookies, cakes, and every duck, goose, and pork product imaginable. (Open June 15-Sept. daily 9am-1pm and 2:30-7pm.) A large convenience store, **Relais de Mousquetaires,** sells groceries by the bridge on the Périgueux edge of town. (Open M-Tu, Th-F 9am-12:30pm and 3:30-7pm; Su 9am-noon.) **La Grignotière,** facing you as you step out of the tourist office, serves cheap drinks and sandwiches (€3-4) all day long, and regional, duck-filled three-course *menus* (€9.80) at mealtimes. (☎05 53 06 91 67. Open daily 7:30am-midnight. MC/V.)

◙ **SIGHTS.** The land beneath the **Musée L'Abri Pataud** was once the property of a local farmer, Monsieur Pataud, though the plot consisted of bones, stone tools, and precious little arable land. As it turned out, his farm had been built over an *abri* (shelter), where prehistoric human reindeer hunters had lived over a span of 20,000 years. The museum now gives an in-depth explanation of the archaeological techniques used in the Périgord region. The 18,600-year-old remains of a teenage girl found on the site may represent a transitional link between Neanderthal and Cro-Magnon man. (☎05 53 06 92 46; pataud@mnhn.fr. Open July-Aug. daily 10am-6:30pm; Sept.-June by reservation only—reserve well in advance. Visits every 30 min. €4.60.)

The **Musée National de Préhistoire,** on a cliff overlooking the village, is undergoing renovation until 2004; however, the open area of the old museum is still worth seeing, mainly for the 30,000 year-old petrified rhinoceros, lying in the exact position in which he died and was found. (☎05 53 06 45 45. Open July-Aug. daily 9:30am-7pm; Mar. 15-June and Sept.-Nov. 15 W-M 9:30am-noon and 2-6pm; Nov. 16-Mar. 14 9:30am-noon and 2-5pm. 1hr. tours: 3 per day in French; 1 per day in English 1:30pm. €4.50, 18-25 €3, under 18 free, free for all the 1st Su of the month.)

SARLAT

Until 1962, Sarlat (pop. 10,700) was a quiet hamlet with little to distinguish it from nearby towns. That's when Minister of Culture André Malraux, inspired by the old city's architectural unity and lack of modernization, chose it for a massive restoration project. Three years later, the new Sarlat emerged—handsomely restored and surprisingly medieval. Since then it has been the setting for films such as *Cyrano de Bergerac* and *Manon des Sources*. Flea markets, wall paintings, dancing violinists, acrobats, and the purveyors of *foie gras, gateaux aux noix*, and golden Monbazillac wines fill the narrow streets. Sarlat certainly merits a day's meandering, and it's the best base from which to explore the villages and châteaux of the Lower Dordogne and the prehistoric site of Lascaux (see p. 379).

☎☷ TRANSPORTATION AND PRACTICAL INFORMATION. Trains (☎05 53 59 00 21) rumble from av. de la Gare to Bordeaux (2½hr., 4 per day 6am-7:30pm, €18.60) and Périgueux (3hr., 2 per day M-F 6am and Sa 5:40pm, €11.40) via le Buisson. (Info booths open daily 6am-12:30pm and 1:15-7pm.) **CFTA,** 15 av. Aristide Briand (☎05 53 59 01 48), and **Trans-Périgord** run **buses** from the train station to Brive (1½hr.; 1 per day M-F 6:30am, July-Aug. Tu, Th, Sa noon; €6.10) and from the pl. Pasteur to Périgueux (1½hr.; 2 per day M-F 6am and 12:30pm; €9.76). **Sarlat Bus** runs locally on two almost identical routes that go around town, line A stops at the train station, and line B stops at the roundabout 1 block away, down rue Dubois. (☎05 53 59 01 48, M-Sa 8:30am-5pm.) For a **taxi** call ☎05 53 59 06 27 or 05 53 59 39 65. (24 hr.) **Car rental** is available from **Europcar** at pl. Tassigny, down the hill from the train station. (☎05 53 31 10 39. Open M-F 8am-noon and 2-6:30pm, Sa 8am-noon and 2-6pm.) To rent **bikes,** try **Cycles Sarlandais,** 36 av. Thiers. (☎05 53 28 51 87; fax 05 53 30 23 90. €11 per day. Open Tu-Sa 9:30am-7pm. MC/V.) Interestingly named **Cum's Bikes,** 8 av. de Selves, is a block from the youth hostel. (☎05 53 53 31 56. Open M-Sa 2-7pm; arrange in advance to return your bike on Sunday.)

To walk to the town center and the **tourist office,** rue Tourny, follow av. de la Gare downhill and turn right on av. Thiers, which becomes av. Général Leclerc. Past the small pl. du 14 Juillet, the road becomes rue de la République, which bisects the *vieille ville.* Bear right on rue Lakanal, past the church-turned-restaurant, and left onto rue de la Liberté, which leads to the Cathédrale St-Sacerdos. The tourist office is in the Ancien Evêché, just across from the cathedral. (15min.) The staff offers an accommodations service, **currency exchange** when banks are closed, and **tours.** (☎05 53 31 45 45; fax 05 53 59 19 44. Open Apr.-Oct. M-Sa 9am-7pm, Su 10am-noon and 2-6pm; Nov.-Mar. M-Sa 9am-noon and 2-7pm. 1-2 English **tours** weekly Apr.-Sept.; call in advance to arrange. 1-3 tours per day in French. €4, children €2.50.) There's an **ATM** just opposite the entrance to the Bishop's Palace on rue Tourny, and a **laundromat** at 24 av. de Selves. (Open daily 7am-9pm.) The **police** are at pl. Salvador Allende (☎05 53 59 10 17); and the **Centre Hospitalier** is on rue Jean Leclaire (☎05 53 31 75 75). Access the **Internet** at **France Télécom,** 41 av. Gambetta (€4.60 per hr.; open M-F 8am-noon and 2-6pm, Sa 8am-noon), or **Cyber-café,** 19 rue de la République (☎05 53 31 67 04; €5.30 per hr., students €4; open daily 10am-midnight). The **post office,** pl. du 14 Juillet, has **currency exchange.** (☎05 53 31 73 10. Open M-F 8:30am-6:30pm, Sa 9am-noon.) **Postal code:** 24200.

☷ ACCOMMODATIONS AND FOOD. Hotels are expensive (€35-60 per night), and the hostel is often filled in summer. There are *gîtes,* farms, and many campgrounds in the surrounding countryside, but you'll need a car to get to them. Ask the tourist office for a list. The **Hôtel des Récollets ❹,** 4 rue Jean-Jacques Rousseau, off rue de la République, is in a 14th- to 15th-century hillside house with bright and well-renovated rooms, some with a beautiful view of the *vieille ville.* (☎05 53 31 36 00; fax 05 53 30 32 62. Breakfast €5.80. Reception 8am-9pm. Reserve ahead. Singles and doubles with toilet and shower or bath €38-45; triples €59.50; quads €74.70. MC/V.) For tent-packers, there are countless campsites in the area. The small, laid-back **Auberge de Jeunesse ❶,** 77 av. de Selves, is 40min. from the station, but only five to ten minutes from the *vieille ville.* Follow rue de la République until it becomes av. Gambetta; go for another 100m, then bear left at the fork onto av. de Selves. To get to the auberge by bus from the train station, walk down the hill on rue Dubois and catch line B (dir: Hôpital) to "la Pologne." The auberge has 16 beds in three co-ed rooms, as well as a grassy yard for campers. (☎05 53 59 47 59 or 05 53 30 21 27. Kitchen access. Sheets included. Reception 6am-8:30pm. Reserve ahead. Open Mar. 15-Nov. Bunks €10 the first night, then €9 per night. Camping €6 the first night, then €5 per night.) The three-star campground **Le Montant ❶,** 4km from town on D57 toward Bergerac, has a bar, laundry and pool. (☎05

53 59 18 50 or 05 53 29 45 85; fax 05 53 59 37 73. Open Easter-Sept. Reception 9am-8pm. €4.30 per person, €5.50 per tent, including vehicle. Electricity €2.30.)

Meals here are marvelous but expensive. *Brasseries* on the rue de la République and at the pl. de la Liberté offer 3-course menus around €10-15, but you can get similar prices at the classier restaurants that crowd the narrow side streets. Most of the regional delicacies—*foie gras, confit de canard*, truffles, mellow red and sweet white Bergerac wines—can be bought directly at the farms for much less. *Pâtisseries* and *confiseries* sell decorated breads, walnut-and-chocolate tarts, *gateaux aux noix* (walnut cookies), and chocolate-dipped meringue *boules* the size of grapefruits. The city **market** takes over the city. (Open Sa 8:30am-6pm.) Wednesday mornings see a smaller version on pl. de la Liberté. **Champion supermarket** sits near the youth hostel on rte. de Montignac (D704); follow av. de Selves away from the town center. (Open M-Sa 9am-7:30pm, Su 9am-noon.) Stock up in the heart of the *vieille ville* at **Petit Casino,** 32 rue de la République. (Open M-Sa 8am-7:30pm, Su 8am-12:30pm.)

▣ SIGHTS AND ENTERTAINMENT. Malraux's little project in the 60s certainly did the trick; the spotless golden stone buildings of Sarlat's *vieille ville* are the most interesting aspect of the city. Most of the sights—and all of the tourists—are to the right off rue de la République as you enter the town from the station. The 16th-century neo-Gothic **Cathédrale St-Sacerdos,** to the right after you leave the tourist office, is newly renovated. Behind the cathedral, the conical **Lanterne des Morts** (Lantern of the Dead) has served as a chapel, charnel-house, a site for electing city consuls, and a powder magazine. Across the street from the bishop's palace, and similarly ornamented, is the **Maison de la Boétie,** a tall, gabled house with stone flourishes. Its carved pilasters and detailed window transoms are typical of the Italian Renaissance. The windows are intricately composed of hundreds of tiny panels of glass. The building was the birthplace of writer Etienne de la Boétie, Montaigne's friend and a key figure in late Renaissance efforts to reconcile Catholics and Protestants. The **public gardens** in pl. Maurice Albe are perfect for a picnic.

Every weekend, street performers and musicians converge on pl. de la Liberté, making cafés crowded and boisterous. Around 11pm, young locals meet in the well-polished **Le Bataclan,** 31 rue de la République, a boisterous, flashy bar that opens onto the street, with the standard techno and noisy rock in the background. (☎ 05 53 28 54 34. Open daily 7am-2am.) In the last two weeks of July and the first week of August, Sarlat hosts the well-attended **Festival des Jeux du Théâtre.** (☎ 05 53 31 10 83; fax 05 53 30 25 31. Tickets €15-26.)

▶ DAYTRIP FROM SARLAT

CASTELNAUD AND LES MILANDES

Ten kilometers southwest of Sarlat, the town of **Castelnaud-la-Chapelle** snoozes in the shadow of its pale yellow stone château. The largest castle in the region, it looks solid enough now, with its massive round towers and exterior wall; nonetheless, Castelnaud was won and lost seven times during the Hundred Years' War. To visit the castle, leave your car or bike at the foot of the hill in the post office parking lot, right by the bridge over the Dordogne, and mount the steep but much more direct path by foot through the village, following signs for *piétons*. (10min.) The castle now houses a collection of 13th- to 17th-century armory and a behemoth catapult. Videos in the museum demonstrate how these weapons were used, while full-scale replicas surround the castle outside. Friendly tour guides share gruesome tales of warfare in the middle ages, and in July and August audience members can dress in medieval garb during live demonstrations. (☎ 05 53 31 30 00. Open July-Aug. daily 9am-8pm; May-June and Sept. 10am-7pm; Feb.-Apr. and Oct.-Nov. 15 10am-6pm; Nov. 16-Jan. Su-F 2-5pm. July-Aug. 6 French tours a day, 2-3 English tours a day. Demonstration July-Aug. daily 11:30am-1pm and 2-6pm. Call in advance off-season for English tours. Château and museum €6.40, ages 10-17 €3.20, under 10 free; €3.20 for adults before 1pm.)

The elegant Renaissance **Château Les Milandes**, 5km from Castelnaud, was built by François de Caumont of Castelnaud in 1489 to satisfy his wife, who wanted a more stylish home than the outdated fortress of Castelaud. Centuries later, the cabaret singer Josephine Baker fell in love with the neglected château's steep pointed roofs and gables, bought the place, and created a "world village," to house and care for children she had picked up on her international tours. The tour through two floors of her homey living space includes a museum devoted to her life and times. A falconry show, complete with handlers dressed in medieval garb, takes place 2-4 times per day on the lawns outside. (☎05 53 59 31 21. Open July-Aug. daily 9:30am-7:30pm; Apr.-June and Sept. 10am-6pm; Oct.-Mar. 10am-noon and 2-5pm. Tours off-season only. Falconry show Apr.-Oct.; call for schedule. €7.30, students €6.10, ages 4-15 €5.30.)

CAVES OF THE VEZERES VALLEY NEAR SARLAT

LASCAUX

The most famous and spectacular prehistoric cave paintings yet discovered line the ceilings of **Lascaux,** aptly christened "the Sistine Chapel of prehistory." A couple of teenagers stumbled upon these "prehistoric frescoes" in 1940 while looking to retrieve their runaway dog. Lascaux was closed to the public in 1963—the humidity from millions of tourists's oohs and aahs bred algae, and micro-stalactites ravaged the paintings that nature had preserved for 17,000 years. Today, only five archaeologists per day, five days a week, are allowed into the original caves.

Instead, visitors queue Disney-style to see **Lascaux II,** which duplicates practically every inch of the original. The new paintings of 5m-tall bulls, horses, and bison are brighter than their ancient counterparts, yet were created with identical natural powders, taken from the soil in the original caves. While there is a distinct lack of ancient awe and mystery, Lascaux II does inspire a sense of wonder at prehistoric art and 20th-century tourism. Their guided tour is among the best cave tours in the valley, engagingly describing the figures that gallop and trot across the ceiling. You'll see a deer whose eyes appear to follow you, a horse sprawling on his back on a rock nearby, and a herd of galloping elk.

The Lascaux twins are 2km from the town of **Montignac** (pop. 3000), 25km north of Sarlat along D704 and 23km northeast of les Eyzies along D706. The Montignac **tourist office** (☎05 53 51 95 03), pl. Bertram-de-Born, shares a building with the **ticket office** (☎05 53 05 65 65) for Lascaux II. Tickets go fast—reserve a week or two ahead, or arrive at the ticket office early in the morning. Or, you can go to the ticket office in Montignanc and buy the tickets before proceeding to Lascaux (Lascaux ticket office open from 9am until tickets sell out. 40min. tours in French and English €7.70, ages 6-12 €4.50. Tickets by advanced booking ☎05 53 51 96 23. Open May-Aug. daily 9am-7pm; Sept.-Oct. and Apr. Tu-Su 9am-6pm; Nov.-Mar. Tu-Su 10am-12:30pm and 2-5:30pm. MC/V.)

The train station nearest Montignac is at **Le Lardin,** 10km away. From there, you can call a **taxi** (☎05 53 50 86 61). During the school year (Sept.-June), CFTA (☎05 55 86 07 07 for info office in Brive) runs buses from Brive (1½hr.; 1 per day; M-F 6pm, Sa 4:30pm; return M-Sa 6:50am; €5.35); Périgueux (1½hr.; 1 per day; M-Sa 12:10pm; return M-F 6:30am, Sa 1pm; €6.10), and most conveniently, from pl. Pasteur in Sarlat (20 min.; 3 per day; M-F 6am and 12:30pm, Sa 8am; return M-Sa 1:05pm and M-F 7:15pm; €4.60). In July and August, however, most CFTA run to Montignac from Sarlat and Périgueux W (W 7:30am and 9:15am, return 7:15pm and 5pm). The caves are 2km outside Montignac's city center and can be reached by foot or taxi. In July and

August, CFTA buses run only once a week. However, several other options are available for transport. **Découverte et Loisirs** in Sarlat runs a minibus tour to Lascaux, once a week. (☎ 05 65 37 19 00 for reservations and schedule. May-Sept. 1 per week. €40 includes admission to the cave). Renting a car in Sarlat is the easiest option, but the trip by bike isn't too steep, besides a sharp incline out of Sarlat (see **Transportation,** p. 376). The **Camping Municipal ❶,** with 91 spots, is just outside town on D65. (☎ 05 53 52 83 95. Open Apr.-Oct. 15. €3 per person, €2.30 per site, €2 per car.)

NEAR LES EYZIES-DE-TAYAC

CAVES WITHIN WALKING DISTANCE OF LES-EYZIES

The **Grotte de Font-de-Gaume,** on the D47 1km east of Les Eyzies (10min. by foot), has the most important paintings still open to tourists. The faded but spectacular 15,000-year-old friezes, completed over the course of hundreds of years, are technically advanced—for instance, they use the natural contours of the cave for relief. This is the last cave in the Aquitaine basin with polychrome (mixed-color) paintings still open to the public. Locals discovered the paintings in the 18th century, but did not realize their importance until two centuries later, by which time several murals had decayed or been defaced by graffiti. The most brilliant colors are consequently in the deeper areas of the cavern. The scene of a black reindeer licking the nose of a kneeling red cousin is amazingly expressive, but the *vôute* (vault), where 12 bison stampede across the ceiling, is the undisputed highlight. (☎ 05 53 06 86 00; fax 05 53 35 26 18; www.leseyzies.com/grottes-ornees; levy@monuments-France.fr. Open Apr.-Sept. Th-Tu 9am-noon and 2-6pm; Mar. and Oct. Th-Tu 9:30am-noon and 2-5:30pm; Nov.-Feb. Th-Tu 10am-noon and 2-5pm. Reservations required. July-Aug. reserve 15 days in advance; Sept.-June 1 week in advance. €5.50, ages 18-25 €3.50, under 18 free. 45min. tours available in English.)

The **Grotte des Combarelles,** 2km farther down the road, has lost its paintings to humidity, and only etchings remain. But the "Lascaux of engravings" is no less spectacular without color. More than 600 surprisingly realistic carvings depict a large variety of species, including donkeys, cave lions, and rhinos. Fifty human figures keep watch from the narrow halls of the cave. The small six-person tours are more personalized than the larger groups at Font-de-Gaume, and the tour-guides are wonderfully flexible. Reserve far in advance for the summer. (☎ 05 53 06 97 72. Tickets and reservations ☎ 05 53 06 86 00. Hours, prices, and website same as Font-de-Gaume; 1hr. tours in French only.)

The **Gorge d'Enfer,** just upstream from Grand Roc and 2km from Les Eyzies, is full of waterfalls, lagoons, and blooming flora. Inside is the **Abri du Poisson,** a shelter which contains the oldest drawing of a fish in France—a 25,000-year-old, meter-long "beaked" salmon. The rendering is so detailed that you can make out its upturned jaw, a sign of exhaustion after spawning. (☎ 05 53 06 86 00. Open Apr.-Sept. daily 9am-noon and 2-6pm; Mar. and Oct. 9:30am-noon and 2-5:30pm; Nov.-Feb. 10am-noon and 2-5pm. €2.29, under 18 free.)

NEARBY CAVES WITHOUT PAINTINGS

Many caves have natural decoration as fascinating as anything ancient man created. Most interesting is the **Grotte du Grand Roc,** 1.5km northwest of town along the road to Périgueux. A footpath by the road makes it easy to walk there. (10min.) The cave lies halfway up the chalk cliffs and commands a spectacular view of the valley and Tayac's fortified church. The cave is filled with millions of stalactites, stalagmites, and *eccentriques*—small calcite accretions that grow neither straight down nor straight up. The most eccentric of these are a vaguely ostrich-like form and an eroded column resembling Bigfoot's footprint. The cave is naturally a constant and pleasant 16°C and an unpleasant 95% humidity. (☎ 05 53 06 92 70. Open July-Aug. daily 9:30am-7pm; Apr.-June and Sept.-Oct. 10am-6pm; Nov.-Dec. and Feb.-Mar. 10am-5pm. Closed Nov. 11-Jan. 31, except school vacations. 30min. tour in French only, though many explanatory signs are in English. €6.10, children €3.20.)

Those interested in more recent cavemen should head for the **Musée Spéléologie,** 91 rue de la Grange-Chancel, 1km north of Les Eyzies. It's in the Fort de Roc, dug into a cliff above the Vézère Valley by English soldiers during the Hundred Years' War. The museum explains the region's cave history with models, documents, and equipment. (☎ 05 53 06 97 15. Open June 15-Sept. M-F 11am-6pm. €3, under 16 €1.50.)

CAVES ACCESSIBLE BY CAR OR BIKE

Fifteen kilometers northwest of Les Eyzies in Rouffignac, on the road to Périgueux, **La Grotte de Rouffignac,** also known as **La Grotte aux Cent Mammouths,** houses 250 engravings and paintings. Among etchings of rhinos and horses, the shaggy mammoths are most striking. This is one of the longest caves in the area. The guided tour (via train) lasts an hour. (☎ 05 53 05 41 71; fax 05 53 35 44 71. Handicapped accessible. Open July-Aug. daily 9-11:30am and 2-6pm; Mar. 24-June and Sept.-Oct. 10am-11:30am and 2-5pm. €5.70, children €3.40.)

Only 12 not-very-detailed figures are visible at the sculptured frieze **Abri du Cap-Blanc,** 7km northeast of Eyzies on D48, but they are outstandingly preserved. Fifteen thousand years ago, hunters drew horses, bison, and reindeer onto the thick limestone walls. The carvings are not as detailed as those in Font-de-Gaume. The exhibit's centerpiece is a 2m long herd of shuffling animals. Reservations necessary July-Aug. (☎ 05 53 59 21 74; fax 05 53 29 89 84; cap-blanc@wanadoo.fr; www.leseyzies.com/cap-blanc. Open July-Aug. daily 10am-7pm; Apr.-June and Sept.-Feb. 11 10am-noon and 2-6pm. 45min. tours in French. €5.40, children €3.20.)

Northeast of Les Eyzies on route D66, the **Roque St-Christophe** is the most extensive cave dwelling yet to be discovered. Its five floors of terraces stretch over 400m. From 40,000 BC until the Middle Ages, this fascinating sanctuary served as a defensive fort and home to over 3000 people. Visit the 11th-century kitchen and peer over the 60m high cliff where Protestants sought shelter from a Catholic army in 1580. A 45min. tour shows you the cave's ovens, monastic remains, and military defenses. (☎ 05 53 50 70 45; www.roque-st-christophe.com. July-Aug. daily 10am-7pm; Mar.-June and Sept.-Oct. 10am-6pm; Nov.-Feb. 11am-5pm. €5.50, students €4.50, ages 5-13 €3.)

BERGERAC

Until the early 20th century, when trains started rolling into Bergerac's newly built station, the Dordogne defined the town culturally and economically. Flat-bottomed boats, known as *gabarres,* departed from the Quai Salvete, trading lumber, wine, and all the other necessities of life with Bourdeaux and Libourne. The *vieille ville,* with its 14th- and 15th-century houses close to the docks, was the heart of town. Now the trade takes place in the fabulous town markets instead of on the river. Perfect produce is available every day, and the fertile land along the riverbanks yields red and sweet white wines. The chapels, vine-covered roofs, and winding streets of the now-quiet *vieille ville* perfectly accompany a Côtes de Bergerac or a golden Monbazillac.

■■ ■ **ORIENTATION AND PRACTICAL INFORMATION.** The train station on av. du 10, 8ème R.I., is a 10min. walk from the *vieille ville* along what is first rue Ste-Catherine and then cours Alsace-Lorraine. (☎ 05 53 63 53 81. Office open M-Sa 7am-7pm, Su 8:30am-12:30pm and 1:50-10:30pm.) Trains leave for Bordeaux (1½hr., 7 per day 6am-7pm, €12.20); Sarlat (1hr.; 5 per day 7:30am-7pm; €9.60); Périgueux via Buisson (1½-2hr., 3 per day, 7:30am-noon, €11.90) and via Libourne (2hr., 6 per day, €17.70). Two **car rental** agencies are on the same street as the train station: **Hertz** (☎ 05 53 57 19 27; open M-F 8am-noon and 2-6pm, Sa 8am-noon and 3-6pm) and **Budget.** (☎ 05 53 74 20 00. Open 8am-noon and 2-6:30pm, Sa 9am-noon and 2-6pm.) **Rent bikes** at **APOLO Cycles,** 31 cours Victor-Hugo, just between the train station and pl. de la République. (☎ 05 53 61 08 16; fax 05 53 57 72 48. €9 per day, €14 per weekend. Scooters €30-50 per day; motor bikes €55-175 per day. Open M-Sa 8am-noon and 2-7pm.) For **taxis,** call ☎ 05 53 57 17 06.

The main **tourist office,** 97 rue Neuve d'Argenson, has maps of the city and listings of area hotels, and gives 1hr. **tours** of town. (☎ 05 53 57 03 11; www.bergerac-tourisme.com. Tours 1 per day; €4, children €2. Open July-Aug. M-Sa 9:30am-7:30pm, Su 10am-1pm and 2:30-7pm; Sept.-June M-Sa 9:30am-7pm.) The **Police Nationale Commissariat** is on 37 bd. Chanzy (☎ 05 53 74 66 22); the **hospital** (☎ 05 53 63 88 88), 9 av. du Prof. Albert Calmette; the **post office,** 36 rue de la Resistance. (☎ 05 53 63 50 00. Open M-F 8:30am-5:30pm, Sa 9am-noon.) **Postal Code:** 24100.

⌂◲ ACCOMMODATIONS AND FOOD. Accommodations can be atrociously expensive, but **Hôtel Pozzi ❷,** 11 rue Pozzi, offers 11 adequate rooms at fair prices. Showers and toilets are in the hallway. (☎ 05 53 57 04 68. Breakfast €4.30. Reception 7am-midnight; closed Su. Reserve one week in advance. Singles €16; doubles €20; quads €30.) The best value in town can be found at **Hôtel Le Family ❸,** 3 rue du Dragon right next to the covered market. Family rooms with lofts for kids maximize space in this small hotel. Every room comes with A/C, TV, and a sparkling clean shower and toilet. (Breakfast €4.88. Single €34.61; doubles €34.61-36.59. Extra bed €9.13. Sept.-May prices €5 lower. MC/V.) Just a 10 min. walk from the center of town along the Dordogne, municipal **Camping La Pelouse ❶,** 8 bis. rue J. J. Rousseau, is a great spot to pitch your tent. (☎ 05 53 57 06 67. Open all yr. €2.62 per adult, €1.85 per child, €2 for electricity.) To get there, walk through the *vieille ville* to the river, cross the Pont Neuf, turn right, and walk along the river bank until you reach the campsite.

Restaurants, especially in the *vieille ville,* can be expensive. There is always plenty of cheap and tasty food in the bakeries, *pâtisseries,* and *charcuteries* which seem to line every street, and the **Marché Couvert** at pl. du Marché Couvert, a spectacular **market** spreads from the pl. du Marché Couvert to completely surround the Eglise de Notre Dame with fruit and wine vendors. (Open W and Sa mornings.) **La Hermine Blanche ❷,** 2 rue de la Brèche near the Marché Couvert, offers very affordable food in a brightly painted dining room. In the evenings, the standard menu of crepes and salads (€2-7) is accompanied by a selection of *hummos, tzatziki plats* (€5-10) and other Middle Eastern specialties. (☎ 05 53 57 63 42. Open Tu-Sa noon-2pm and 7-10pm.)

◉▣ SIGHTS AND ENTERTAINMENT. Get an introduction to wine at **La Maison du Vin,** 2 pl. du Docteur Cayla. (☎ 05 53 63 57 57. Open Sept.-June 15 Tu-Sa 10:30am-12:30pm and 2-6pm, June 16-Aug. 10am-7pm. Free; includes a movie explaining wine production and a wine tasting.) Just a few blocks away, in the stately Renaissance Maison Peyrarède, is the smoky smelling **Musée du Tabac.** The museum presents a 3000-year history of tobacco; don't miss the intricate ivory cigar holder on the top floor, containing a sculpted Sicilian wedding, complete with frolicking lovers, a horse-drawn carriage, and serenading musicians. (☎ 05 53 63 04 13. Open Tu-F 10am-noon and 2-6pm, Sa 10am-noon and 2-5pm, Su 2:30-6:30pm. €3, students free, children 10-17 without student card €1.50.)

La Fête des Vendanges, from the last week of September through the first week of October, celebrates Bergerac's vineyards and the crucial role that the Dordogne played in the 19th-century wine industry. An opening day parade kicks off the festivities as all the local wine makers converge on Vieux Pont, bearing their banners. Some arrive on foot, others by horse-drawn carriage. They pile into the *gabarres* and set off symbolically for a few hundred meters down the Dordogne toward Bordeaux. On the river banks, spectators cheer as the wine flows freely.

...AVING THE ROAD TO THE FUTURE

...isitors to the lower Dordogne Valley ...ome to see its sun-soaked chateaux, ...anoe along its meandering river, and ...aze upon spectacular views. Yet ...here's another integral element to ...acationing here that most tourist ...ffices manage to conceal– the auto-...nobile. With limited public transporta-...ion and hills steep enough to make ...ance Armstrong think twice, the car ...s man's best friend. Unfortunately, ...he winding country roads that con-...nect the Dordogne villages were not ...designed for modern car travel. Many ...oads are barely wide enough for two-...vay traffic, inevitably causing steamy ...summer jams. The government has ...proposed a wide, straight highway ...rom Sarlat to Bergerac. It would run ...along the Dordogne and pass by ...najor attractions like Les Milandes, ...Beynec and Castelnaud.

This seemingly simple solution, ...nowever, has sparked a tremendous ...debate. Groups affiliated with the his-...toric monuments and natural sights in ...he area (the *Associations de Patri-moine*) charge that the road would ...spoil the panoramic beauty of the ...Dordogne. They also fear that the road ...vould worsen the problem by encour-...aging more people to drive. Instead, ...he *Associations* favor a route north of ...Beynac that would not run through the ...Dordogne. In their fight, they have ...solicited the aid of tourists, posting ...petitions at major attractions. So far, ...he government has shown no signs of ...a change of heart, but also seems in ...no hurry to start its road. For now, ...expect sunny skies and crowded ...oads in the Dordogne.

THE LOWER DORDOGNE VALLEY

Steep cliffs and poplar thickets overlook the slow-moving waters of the Dordogne, which served in the Hundred Years' War as a natural boundary between France and English Aquitaine to the south. The châteaux, built to keep watch on the enemy, are numerous, if not as regal as those of the Loire. In summer the valley overflows with tourists in canoes, on bikes, and in cars. *Chambres d'hôte* provide cheap farmhouse rooms near the historic sites; ask at any tourist office for a list.

⌁ TRANSPORTATION. The valley stretches west from Bergerac, passing 15km south of Sarlat. To get there and get around you'll need to rent a car or be prepared for a good bike workout.

Car rentals are available in Perigueux, Brive, and Sarlat. For **bikers,** Sarlat is the best place to start from, as all of the villages and châteaux listed in this section are clustered in an area about 10km southwest of Sarlat. It's about 4-6km between each village, and once you get out of Sarlat the bike ride along the Dordogne is fairly level. Most villages are built on hills, with the châteaux at the top, so the easiest way to see them is to leave your bike at the bottom and walk. Hitching is reportedly easy, although it is never safe or recommended by *Let's Go,* and most family-filled cars have no room to spare. An alternative to renting a car is to take a minibus tour with **Découverte et Loisirs,** which tours the Dordogne valley several times a week from Sarlat. (☎ 05 65 37 19 00. €28-40 per person, call for schedule.)

Many outfits along the Dordogne rent **canoes** and **kayaks.** At the Pont de Vitrac, near Domme, you can find them at **Canoës-Loisirs** (☎ 05 53 28 23 43) and **Périgord Aventure et Loisirs** (☎ 05 53 28 23 82). **Canoës-Dordogne** (☎ 05 53 29 58 50) and **Canoë Vacances** (☎ 05 53 28 17 07) are at La Roque Gageac. **Le Sioux** is near Domme and Cénac. (☎ 05 53 28 30 81. Open July-Sept. 15.) Get schedules and info from tourist offices; prices average €11 per person for a half-day and €16 for a full day. When you finish your course down the river, many rental organizations will pick you up in a bus and bring you back to your starting point free of charge.

BEYNAC-ET-CAZENAC

The fortress at **Beynac** (pop. 516), 10km southwest of Sarlat and 4km from Castelnaud, perches 150m above the river. Sheathed in greenery, it overlooks a town of ancient stone houses decorated with wrought-iron balconies and flowered terraces. In 1214, when Simon de Montfort invaded the lower Dordogne, he sacked the castles of Domme, Castelnaud, and Beynac in turn, allegedly in pursuit of Cathar heretics and sympathizers. The lord of Beynac, a good Catholic and supporter of the French king, put up no resistance when Montfort decided to "humiliate" the castle by pruning the tops of the ramparts. Beynac has enjoyed a topsy-turvy history since then, with only one thing certain throughout: it was always at odds with its neighbor, siding with the French after Castelnaud sided with the English during the Hundred Years' War. (☎05 53 29 50 40. Castle open Mar.-Sept. daily 10am-6:30pm; Oct.-Nov. 10am-noon and 2pm-dark; Dec.-Feb. 11am-dark. €6.55, ages 5-11 €2.80.) The Gauls never left the **Parc Archéologique de Beynac**, just below the château. Thatch huts with mud walls, a 5000-year-old *dolmen* (sacrificial table), and many historic sheep are scattered throughout this mildly interesting reproduction of an ancient Gaulish village. (☎05 53 29 51 28. Open July 3-Sept. 15 Su-F 10am-7pm. €5, ages 6-16 €3.)

The **tourist office** sits by the river at the bottom of Beynac's steep hill. (☎05 53 29 43 08. Open July-Aug. daily 10am-noon and 2-6pm.) The 19 cheapest beds around are in two large dorm rooms at the **Gîte d'Etape de Beynac ❶**, at the pl. d'Alsace to the left as you leave town on the road to Castelnau. In July and August, reserve at least a week in advance. (☎05 53 29 40 93; if there's no answer, call the *mairie* at ☎05 53 31 34 00. €7.73 per person, €4.70 per child.) **Camping Le Capeyrou ❶** is just out of town on the riverbank, by the entrance to the city. (☎05 53 29 54 95. Open May-Sept. Reception daily 9am-12:30pm and 2:30-7:30pm. €4 per person, €2 per child, €5.50 per site. Electricity €2.50.)

DOMME AND LA ROQUE GAGEAC

Domme (pop. 1000) was built by King Philip the Bold in 1280 as a defensive stronghold. Although it is only about 13km from Sarlat, it is probably the hardest village to reach by bike thanks to the winding 4km ascent from the Dordogne up the hill to the village. Enter through any one of the three crumbling gates on the lower side of the town, and make your way up tiny alleys and past limestone homes and *foie gras* stores to the main square, pl. de la Halle. The **tourist office**, pl. de la Halle, lists *chambres d'hôte* (€23-35), and sells tickets for all the attractions in Domme, many of which are accessible only on guided tours. (☎05 53 31 71 00; fax 05 53 31 71 09. Open July-Aug. daily 10am-7pm; Sept.-June 10am-noon and 2-6pm; phone ahead for Jan.) Excellent guided tours in French take you into one of the towers guarding the town's main gate, the dilapidated **Porte des Tours**. Seventy Templar Knights were imprisoned there in 1307 and tortured for nearly 20 years by King Philip IV, who wanted the secret of their hidden treasure. The graffiti they scratched into the walls with their teeth, hands, and fingernails still remain; they combine Islamic and Jewish motifs encountered by the Templars in the Holy Land with an idiosyncratic Christian iconography. Astrological signs and images of stars abound, along with representations of Christ, the Virgin Mary, and the Templar cross. Their chief persecutors, Pope Clement V and Philip IV, appear as well, represented as monsters. (Consult tourist office for tours. 1hr.; 1 per day, July-Aug. 2-3 per day. €5.60, students €4.80, children €3.20.)

Back in the center of town, a **tour des grottes** (cave tour) descends from pl. de la Halle into the intricate cavern network of the stalagtite-bristling **Grottes de la Halle,** some of the largest caves in Europe. (☎05 53 31 71 00. Cave tours in French and English July-Aug. every 30min. 10:15am-7pm; Apr.-June and Sept. every 45min. 10:15am-noon and 2-6pm; Feb.-Mar. and Oct. every hr. 2-5pm. €5.60, students €4.80, children €3.20. Ticket includes entrance to the Musée des Arts et Traditions Populaires de Domme.) When you exit the caves, enjoy the view of the Dordogne from the **Promenade des Falaises**; the nearby **public gardens** offer a great spot for picnicking. At the other end of the pl. de la Halle, the uninspiring **Musée des Arts et Traditions Populaires de Domme** displays costumes and artifacts from 17th- to 19th-century Périgord. (☎05 53 31 71 00. Open July-Aug. daily 10:30am-7pm; Apr.-May and Sept. 2-5pm; June 10:30am-12:30pm and 2:30-6pm. €2.90, students €2.20, ages 5-14 €1.90. Free entrance if combined with the Grottes de la Halle.)

The **Nouvel Hôtel ❸**, rue Malville at pl. de la Halle, lets 14 comfortable rooms, all with toilet and shower or bath. (☎05 53 28 36 81. Reception 8am-10pm. Open Easter-Dec. Singles €30; doubles €42-62; triples €46-68. MC/V.) The **Camping Municipal Cénac St-Julien ❶** sits near the river 1½km out of Domme on the way to La Roque Gageac on D46. (☎05 53 28 31 91. Reception July-Aug. 8am-noon and 12:30-8pm; June and Sept. 9:15-11:45am and 1:30-8pm. Reserve ahead. Open June-Sept. 15. €3.50 per person, €4 per tent. Electricity €2.40.) **Canoë Cénac** rents kayaks near the campground. (☎05 53 28 22 01. €7 per hr., €14-22 per day. Buses bring you back to Beynec at the end of you downstream trip.)

After you pass the campsite and cross the river on D46, turn left onto D703. Four kilometers downstream, **La Roque Gageac** juts out from the base of a sheer cliff, its steep, twisting streets lined with medieval-style stone houses and decidedly untraditional vegetation, from bamboos to palm trees. For a perfect view of the many châteaux along the Dordogne, take a tour on a **gabare**, a large boat popular in this region. They leave from the dock beyond the town's big parking lot. (1hr.; every 15min. 10am-6pm. English-speaking guides available. €7.20, children €4.20.) The 12th-century **Fort Troglodytique Aérien**, high above La Roque, commands a spectacular view of the Dordogne river valley. Its height and position within the rock made it ideal; it withstood all British assaults during the Hundred Years' War, even outlasting the château it protected, until neglect felled it. It's accessible only by foot. (☎05 53 31 61 94. Open July-Aug. daily 10am-7pm; Apr.-June and Sept.-Nov. 11 Su-F 10am-6pm. €4, students €3, ages 10-16 €2.)

BRIVE-LA-GAILLARDE

Brive (pop. 50,000) received its nickname, *"la Gaillarde"* (the Bold), when its courageous citizens repelled English forces during the Hundred Years' War. Continuing this tradition, Brive was the first town in France to liberate itself from the German occupation in 1944. Apparently Brive reserves such outbursts for special occasions; the modern visitor will find it a quiet, unpretentious industrial city, free from the tourist crowds common to this area. Old 12th- to 19th-century houses mix with 1970s high-rises to create a pleasant if unspectacular cityscape. For travelers with a car, Brive is an inexpensive base for exploring the Quercy region.

▐ TRANSPORTATION

Trains: av. Jean Jaurès. Info office open M-F 9am-9:30pm and Sa 9am-6:30pm. To: **Bordeaux** (2½hr.; M-Sa 3 per day, Su 2 per day 7:38am and 9:17pm; €22.15); **Limoges** (1hr., 5 per day, €12.50); **Paris** (4hr.; 3 per day M-Sa 9:30am-2:30pm, Su 2:30-7:40pm; €44.10); **Sarlat** (1hr. including bus from Souillac to Sarlat, 3 per day, €9); **Toulouse** (2½hr., 5 per day, €22.50) via **Cahors** (1hr., 5 per day, €12.40).

Local and Intercity Buses: Office at pl. du 14 Juillet (☎05 55 74 20 13), next to the tourist office. Info desk open M-Sa 8:15am-12:15pm and 2-6:30pm. Buses also stop at the train station and in pl. de Lattre de Tassigny, next to the post office. **STUB** runs within the city; **CFTA** runs to surrounding areas, including **Collognes-la-Rouge** and **Beaulieu. Trans-Périgord** buses (☎05 53 09 24 08) go to **Sarlat** via **Souillac** (1½hr., 1 per day, €9). Buy tickets on board.

Taxis: ☎05 55 24 24 24. 24hr.

Car Rental: Avis, 56 av. Jean Jaurès (☎05 55 24 51 00). Open M-F 8am-noon and 2-6:30pm, Sa 9-11:30am and 2:30-5:45pm. **Hertz,** 54 av. Jean Jaurès (☎05 55 24 26 75). Open M-F 8am-noon and 2-6:30pm, Sa 8am-noon and 2-6pm. If closed, call the reservation center at ☎01 39 38 38 38. **Europcar,** 52 av. Jean Jaurès (☎05 55 74 14 41). Open M-F 8am-noon and 2-6pm, Sa 8am-12:30pm and 2-6pm.

Bike Rental: Sports Bike, 142 Av. Georges Pompidou (☎05 55 17 00 84), or **Belot Philippe,** 141 Av. Ribot (☎ 05 55 86 14 33).

⊞ 🛈 ORIENTATION AND PRACTICAL INFORMATION

Tourist Office: pl. du 14 Juillet (☎05 55 24 08 80; fax 05 55 24 58 24). From the train station, go straight down av. Jean Jaurès to the Collégiale St-Martin, cut diagonally across the courtyard of the Collégiale and veer left onto rue Toulzac, which becomes av. de Paris. The office is 100m up on the right through the large parking lot. Maps of the town and environs. Tours of Brive Tu and Th 10am, W 9:45am; €4. Open July-Aug. M-Sa 9am-noon and 2-7pm, Su 10am-1pm; Sept.-June M-Sa 9am-noon and 2-6pm.

Money: Banque de France, bd. Gén. Koenig (☎05 55 92 37 00), at pl. de la République, **exchanges currency.** Exchange counter open M-F 9:30am-noon.

Police: 4 bd. Anatole France (☎05 55 17 46 00).

Hospital: bd. Docteur Verlhac (☎05 55 92 60 00).

Internet Access: The best rates in town are at **Media Computer,** 46 av. du 11 Novembre (☎05 55 17 58 41). €3 per hr. Open daily 9:30am-noon and 2-7pm. **Ax'tion,** 33 bd. Koenig (☎05 55 17 14 15). €0.15 per min., €7.65 per hr. Open M-Sa 9am-7pm, closed Aug. 15-22.

Post Office: pl. Winston Churchill (☎05 55 18 33 10). **Currency exchange** with no commission on US dollars. Open M-F 8am-6:45pm and Sa 8am-noon. **Postal code:** 19100. **Poste Restante:** "Brive 19100."

🛏 ACCOMMODATIONS AND CAMPING

Auberge de Jeunesse (HI), 56 av. du Maréchal Bugeaud (☎05 55 24 34 00; fax 05 55 84 82 80; brive@fuaj.org). From the train station, walk the length of av. Jean Jaurès past the St-Sernin church, crossing the street at the bottom. Take rue de l'Hôtel de Ville straight into the old town, turn right just before you reach Eglise St-Martin, and follow rue du Docteur Massenat. Take a few steps left on bd. du Salan, and turn right onto av. du Maréchal Bugeaud. The hostel will be on your right. Small, bare, well-lit 2- to 4-bunk rooms with firm mattresses. A battered patch of grass outside is scattered with plastic yellow tables, full of lively twentysomethings. Breakfast €2.80. Sheets €2.70. Reception M-F 8am-noon, Sa-Su 9am-noon and 6-10pm. Members €8; non-members must buy membership. MC/V. ❶

Bar Hôtel de la Gare, 65 av. Jean Jaurès (☎05 55 74 14 49). Right next to the train station, this hotel offers small, recently renovated rooms in shades of pink, yellow, and blue. Sparkling clean hall showers. Singles and doubles with sink €19-21, with shower €26; triples €38. ❷

Hôtel-Restaurant l'Andréa, 39 av. Jean Jaurès (☎05 55 74 11 84; fax 05 55 17 25 73). Bright, newly renovated, spacious rooms. A little finery for a bigger price-tag. Breakfast €3.80. Reception 7am-midnight. Doubles with toilet €30.50, with bath €33.55; quads €45.75. MC/V. ❸

Camping Municipal des Iles (☎/fax 05 55 24 34 74), beyond the youth hostel on bd. Michelet, is crowded, but offers a view of the Corrèze river, and is a 5min. walk to the center of town. Reception 7am-9pm. €3 per person, €1.50 per child; €2.70 per tent. Electricity €2.60-3.80. ❶

🍴 FOOD

Food in Brive tends to be about €2 more expensive than fare in larger cities. Brive's **market** is on pl. du 14 Juillet, just outside the tourist office. (Open Tu, Th, and Sa 8am-noon.) There is a **Casino supermarket** at the intersection of bd. Gén. Koenig and av. de Paris. (Open M-Sa 9am-7:30pm.) The few cheap restaurants are concentrated around **pl. Anatole Briand** and the cathedral side of **pl. Charles de Gaulle.** Family-run **Le Corrèze** ❸, 3 rue Corrèze, in a narrow building in the old town, prepares gourmet regional fare at good prices. Four-course *menus* start at €11 with more extravagant options approaching €20. (☎05 55 24 14 07. 2- and 3-course meals €7-8.50. Open M-Sa noon-2pm and 7-10pm. MC/V.)

🔎 SIGHTS

From pl. de la République, rue Emile Zola leads to the **Centre National de la Résistance et de la Déportation Edmond Michelet,** 4 rue Champanatier, which honors the Brive native. Take bd. Koenig to the pl. de la République, turn right on rue Emile Zola, then left on rue Hue, and right onto rue Champanatier. Michelet, a Resistance leader, endured the concentration camp at Dachau for more than a year, surviving to become a minister under de Gaulle. Photos of women and children on their way to the gas chambers, heartbreaking last letters to loved ones, and other mementos tell the story of the French Resistance and the Nazi concentration camps. Free audioguides available in French and English. (☎ 05 55 74 06 08; fax 05 55 17 09 44. Open M-Sa 10am-noon and 2-6pm. Free.)

The 12th-century **Eglise Collégiale St-Martin,** pl. Charles de Gaulle, is named for the iconoclastic Spaniard who introduced Christianity to Brive in the 4th century. Its high crossed arches and pale, thin stone columns mark the center of town. Martin was beheaded after interrupting the feast of Saturnus by loudly proclaiming his faith and smashing idols; his sarcophagus can be seen in the crypt.

The **Musée Labenche,** 26bis bd. Jules Ferry, in a beautiful Renaissance building, daringly combines subjects most towns would separate into three museums: art, natural history, and interior decorating. Exhibits include ancient coins, a number of turn-of-the-century accordions, and 17th-century English tapestries. All explanations in French. (☎ 05 55 92 39 39. Open Apr.-Oct. W-M 10am-6:30pm; Nov.-Mar. daily 1:30-6pm. €4.50, students €2.50, free under 16 and last Su of the month.)

🎵 ENTERTAINMENT AND FESTIVALS

Brive is not exactly a center of nightlife, but it tries. After midnight, twenty-somethings fill **La Charette,** 33 av. Ribot, which plays techno and disco. (☎ 05 55 87 65 73. Cover €9.15, Th-F women free. Open Tu-Sa until 3am.) **Pub le Watson** livens the otherwise lukewarm rue des Echevins with boisterous beer-drinkers at its outdoor tables and indoor booths. (☎ 05 55 17 12 09. Open Tu-Sa 5pm-2am.) **Havane Café,** 9 rue des Cloutiers (pl. de la Jauberlie), offers sangría, salsa, posters of your favorite Cuban heroes, and a chance to practice your Spanish. (Beer €2. Open July-Aug. daily 1pm-2am; Sept.-June daily 6pm-2am. AmEx/MC/V.)

In mid-August, **Orchestrades Universelles** attracts young orchestras, bands, and choirs from all over the world to Brive for a celebration of classical, traditional, and jazz music. All performances are free until 9pm on the last evening, when a spectacular final gala featuring 750 young musicians fills l'Espace de Trois Provinces. (☎ 05 55 92 39 39. Tickets €3.05-15.25.) For three days during the first weekend in November, the pl. du 14 Juillet and Salle Georges Brassens swarm with authors, writers, and books from all over France for the **Foire des Livres.** (☎ 05 55 92 39 39.) Four times a year, from December to February, the streets of Brive host **La Fois Grasses,** a market with the delicacies that make Brive famous: *champignons* (mushrooms), truffles, chocolates, and foie gras.

▶ DAYTRIP FROM BRIVE: COLLONGES-LA-ROUGE

Twenty kilometers southeast of Brive, the exquisite red-rock village of Collonges-la-Rouge sends visitors home wondering if the place is real. Cylindrical towers dangle tangled grapevines as rolling pastures and orchards bask in the afternoon sunlight. There's nothing to do here but look, really, though one look is enough to understand why this town has been classified one of the most beautiful villages in France. If you're dead-set on visiting sights, the **Maison de la Sirène** displays a beautiful 18th-century painting of a blonde siren clutching a mirror in one hand and a comb in the other. The maison also contains a museum of local history that doesn't quite live up to the splendor of the town (€2). The 12th-century **church** in the town center received a facelift during the 16th-century religious wars; a Gothic steeple now rises majestically above 3m of thick fortressed walls. CFTA buses leave from pl. Thiers in Brive (M-F 4 per day, Sa 7:40am and 12:20pm; one-way €3.05, students under 26 €1.50).

THE UPPER DORDOGNE VALLEY

This fertile area south of Brive is home to hilltop châteaux, lazy rivers, and tiny hamlets that have never seen a tour bus. A world away from the lower reaches of the valley, its terrain ranges from deep valleys nestled between rolling hills, canopies of trees, towering cliffs of white rock, and fields of tall grass and rolls of hay. You can bike it, but you'll probably want to rent a car. Bretenoux, Rocamadour, Padirac, Gourdon, and Souillac, and Gramat are serviced by trains, but there are few buses, and the lines that do exist only run a few times a week. Sites of interest are invariably far from stations, so bring your hiking shoes.

▣ TRANSPORTATION. Trains run to Bretenoux from Brive (45min.; 4-5 per day; Su 2 per day 2:30pm and 6:10pm; €6.90). Castelnau, Montal, and Beaulieu are accessible by bike from Bretenoux, but visiting them all will take a day or two. The train station is 2km north of Bretenoux; shuttle buses run very infrequently from the train station to Bretenoux (10min.; W and Sa 3 per day 8:55am-3:20pm; Tu and Th 1 per day 9:10am) and St-Céré (15min., same schedule as buses to Bretenoux, €2.30). A schedule is posted outside the train station. (Call ☎ 05 65 38 08 28 or 05 65 38 24 18 for more info.) It's probably easier to make the clearly marked 25min. walk south to Bretenoux; from there it's a flat 3km southwest to Castelnau, 8km southeast, and to St-Céré. From the train station, Beaulieu is 6km north. ■

BRETENOUX

This 13th-century town is useful as a transportation hub from which to explore the upper valley, although the town itself (pop. 2000) lacks the charm of its neighbors, and offers but a few drab accommodations. The **tourist office,** in the Manoir du Fort on av. de la Libération, has maps and info on hiking. (☎ 05 65 38 59 53; fax 05 65 39 72 14. Open daily 9am-noon and 2-6pm.) An immense **supermarket** sits near the traffic light by the train station. (☎ 05 65 10 22 00. Open M-F 8:30am-7:30pm, Sa 8:30am-7:15pm.) A **Petit Casino** supermarket can be found one block down from the tourist office, av. de la Libération. (☎ 05 65 38 58 70. Open M 3-7:30pm, Tu-Sa 7:30am-12:30pm and 3-7:30pm, Su 9:30am-12:30pm.) An **open-air market** is held behind the tourist office (Tu and Sa 8am-noon).

Three-star **Camping de Bourgnatelle ❶** is a beautiful site along the river that runs through the town. (☎ 05 65 38 44 07 or 08 35 33 75 68; bougnatel@aol.com. Reception 9am-1pm and 3-8:30pm. Reserve in advance. July-Aug. €3.20 per person, children under 7 €1.80, €3.20 per site; May-June and Sept. €2.75 per person, children €1.15, €2.50 per site. Electricity €2.15. MC/V.) You can rent **bikes** in Bretenoux from **Cycles Bladier,** av. de la Libération. (☎ 05 65 38 41 56. Bikes €8 per day; mountain bikes €9 per half-day, €12.50 per day. Passport deposit. Open Tu-Sa 8am-noon and 2-7pm. Price lower for longer rentals.) There are numerous places to rent kayaks and canoes all along the Dordogne river, but the best bargains on rentals and lessons are at the non-profit **Canoe Kayak-Bretenoux,** right next to the bridge into town as you're coming from the train station. For half and full day rentals, you can drop the canoes off at towns down the river as you finish. (☎ 05 65 35 91 59. Open July-Aug. daily 9am-noon and 2-5pm. €8 per person for 90min., €11 per person per half-day, €14 per person per day. Lessons from €10 for 90 min.)

NEAR BRETENOUX
CASTELNAU-BRETENOUX AND ST-CÉRÉ

The burnt-red ramparts of Castelnau-Prudhomat, 3km southwest of Bretenoux, have guarded the valley below for 900 years. The château was built unusually in the shape of a triangle, flanked by three corner towers. In the central *cour d'honneur*, the medieval Tour Sarrazin commands a beautiful view of the rolling hills and villages of the Dordogne valley that extends for miles. Famed 19th-century opera singer Jean Mouliérat restored the château after an 1851 fire, poking large windows into the walls and filling the rooms with antiques. Today, Aubusson and Beauvais tapestries are displayed beside modern operetta scores and 15th-century stained glass in the cluttered oratory. The true charm of the castle comes from its dried moat and crumbling walls. (☎ 05 65 10 98 00. Open July-Aug. daily 9:30am-6:45pm; Apr.-June and Sept. 9:30am-12:15pm and 2-6:15pm; Oct.-Mar. W-M 10am-12:15pm and 2-5:15pm. Last entry 45min. before closing. French tours with English pamphlets every 30min.; €5.50, ages 18-25 €3.50, under 18 free.)

Château de Montal rests 8km southeast of Bretenoux and 2km from St-Céré. Follow the signs to St-Céré; the château will be on your right just before you enter the city. The biggest attraction is the carved staircase—the underside of each step is uniquely decorated. Otherwise, this château offers more of the same tapestries, wooden furniture, and renaissance fireplaces as others in the area. From 1941 to 1945, the artwork of the Louvre, including the *Mona Lisa*, was kept at Montal for safekeeping. (☎ 05 65 38 13 72. Open Mar.-Oct. Su-F 9:30am-noon and 2:30-6pm. Tours in French every 45min. €5, students €4, children 7-15 €2.50) The nationally acclaimed **Festival Saint-Céré** is a series of classical music and dance performances, including at least one full-fledged opera, that takes place from late July to August 14. Venues include the courtyard of the Château de Castelnau and the Théâtre de l'Usine, an old factory in St-Céré. (For tickets and info call ☎ 05 65 38 28 08. €15-40, students €11.)

About half-way between Rocamadour and St-Céré lie the mysterious caverns and subterranean river known as **Le Gouffre de Padirac**. The 90min. tour takes visitors first by boat and then by foot through the twisting caves and great domed rooms of gargantuan stalactites and stalagmites, formed by millions of years of calcium deposits carried by the water. Little English translation is available, but the natural grandeur of the 103m-underground formations transcends language barriers. (☎ 05 65 33 64 56. Open Apr.-July 8 and Sept. daily 9am-noon and 2-6pm; July 9-July 31 9am-6:30pm; Aug. 8:30am-6:30pm. €7.70, under 12 €5. Last tours leave 90min. before closing. Boats leave when they are filled.) The closest train station is in Gramat, 10km southeast of Le Gouffre.

BEAULIEU-SUR-DORDOGNE

Ten kilometers north of Bretenoux on Route D940, the medieval village of Beaulieu-sur-Dordogne (pop. 1330) offers several comfortable accommodations, making it a great stopover or base from which to explore the upper Dordogne.

Although Beaulieu is most conveniently accessed by car, **CFTA** buses run here almost every day from Brive. The headache it takes to figure out the irregular schedule is worth it. (☎ 05 55 86 07 07. 1hr.; 1-3 per day 7:50am-6:20pm; July-Aug. Su, W no service. €9.15.) Other transportation options for the carless include riding the train from Brive to Bretenoux, taking a taxi (☎ 05 55 91 02 83 or 05 55 91 00 76), and walking north 6km. Finally, the Auberge de Jeunesse will try to match you up with free space in a car if you call them in advance. Once you get to Beaulieu, bike rentals are available at **Beaulieu Sports**, on Av. Gen. de Gaulle (☎ 05 55 91 13 87). The **tourist office** is in the central square. (☎ 05 55 91 09 94; fax 05 55 91 10 97. Open daily 9:20am-12:30pm and 2-7pm.) Guided **tours** of Beaulieu leave once a week from the tourist office. (M 9:45am; July-Aug. 4 per day, 10:30am-6pm. €5 per person, students €3.50, under 12 free.) The **post office** is next door to the tourist office. (Open M-F 9am-noon and 2-5pm, Sa 9am-noon.) **Exchange currency** at Banque Populaire du Centre on rue Général de Gaulle. (Open Tu-F 8:30am-noon and 1:30-6pm, Sa 8:30am-12:30pm.)

Overlooking the river is the popular ▓**Auberge de Jeunesse (HI) ❶**, pl. de Monturu, the only inexpensive place to stay in the region. This charming 14th-century house, which feels more like a bed and breakfast than a hostel, has surprisingly modern facilities. (☎ 05 55 91 13 82; fax 05 55 91 26 06; beaulieu@fuaj.org. Kitchen access. Sheets €2.70. Breakfast €3.20. Reception 6-8pm. July-Aug. reserve 2-3 weeks in advance. Open Apr.-Sept. 2- to 6-bed dorms €8. **Members only.**) For a good deal more money, you can have your own room at **Les Charmilles ❹**, bvd. Rodolphe de Turenne. Spacious rooms with views of the river. (☎ 05 55 91 29 29. Doubles with shower and toilet €50; triples €60; quads €70; *demi-pension* €45 per person.) Campers can stay at three-star **Camping des Îles ❶**, a quiet spot on an island next to town with (yes, you guessed it) a great view of the river. (☎ 05 55 91 02 65; fax 06 55 9 05 19; JYCASTANET@aol.com. Open Apr. 15-Oct. 15. €5.80 per tent, €3.80 per person; electricity €2.75.) Meals in this town are quite expensive—from €16 for a three-course *menu*. Pick up supplies for a self-cooked meal at several bakeries in town and at the **Petit Casino** supermarket next to the tourist office. Your best bet for a filling meal is the **Crêperie Beau-lieu ❷**, rue Presbytère. (☎ 05 55 91 20 46. *Galettes* and salads €3-8. 3-course *menu* €12-17. Open M-Sa noon-2pm and 7-10pm.)

Beaulieu is home to the 13th-century **Abbaye Bénédictine St-Pierre.** The abbey is known for its medieval painting and sculpture, particularly the stone-carved tympanum above the south portal. A chillingly expressionless Jesus, arms spread wide, dwarfs the angels and apostles around him, while tiny condemned human beings and demons are crushed under the weight of heaven. Inside the abbey, a narrow room leads to the altar, above which the Virgin Mary appears to conduct a chamber orchestra of cherubs for an audience of the twelve apostles. (Open daily 8am-7:30pm.) All the way down rue de la Chapelle, along the banks of the river, is the 12th-century **Chapelle des Pénitents,** pl. de Monturu. The view of the river is the best part of the walk down.

The most popular way to view the river is by canoe or kayak. Rent from **Saga Team's Canoe Location.** They are stationed in 10 towns along the Dordogne; the station in Beaulieu is at the municipal campgrounds, under the bridge that leads into town. (☎ 05 55 28 84 84. €10 per half-day, €14 per day.)

ROCAMADOUR

The tiny town of Rocamadour (pop. 638) is a "verticity," built into the mountainside in three sections, one above the other. The private château at the peak of the cliff is connected to the village at the bottom by a winding road that runs through the *Cité Réligieuse.* The town was of no consequence until 1166, when the perfectly preserved body of St-Amadour was unearthed near the town's chapel. It is reputed that St-Amadour was actually the biblical Zacchaeus, a tax collector who changed his ways after dining with Jesus. As the story grew, so did the miracles, and the town became an important pilgrimage site. Today, Rocamadour's visual splendor rather than the hope of miracles draws day-trippers from Brive.

🔓 **PRACTICAL INFORMATION. Trains** run from **Brive** to Rocamadour, stopping at the old train station, 4km from town on route N140 (40min.; M-Sa 3 per day, 5:35am-1:35pm, Su at 1:35pm only; trains return to Brive M-Sa 8:50am-8:50pm, Su at 1:40pm and 7pm only; €9.30). The Rocamadour station has no ticket office or info booth. The tourist offices in Rocamadour have schedules and tickets; tickets can also be purchased on the train. From the station, a flat, winding road leads directly to the top of town. (45min.) Hitching, never safe or recommended by *Let's Go,* is difficult, as most passing cars are already full. For a **taxi,** call ☎ 05 65 33 63 10 or 05 65 33 73 31. Separate **tourist offices** serve the cliff's top (☎ 05 65 33 22 00; fax 05 65 33 22 01) and bottom (☎ 05 65 33 62 59; www.rocamadour.com). Each distributes a list of hotels and restaurants, books rooms, sells maps (€0.75), and

PÉRIGORD

exchanges currency at nefarious rates. The lower office is in the old Hôtel de Ville, the upper in l'Hospitalet, on rte. de Lacave. (Both open Sept.-June 10am-12:30pm and 1:30-6:30pm; July 9-Aug. 24 9:30am-7:30pm.) **Bikes** can be rented from the upper tourist office for €8.70 per day. The **police** (☎ 05 65 33 60 17) are around daily in July and August but only on weekends (and sometimes not at all) other months. The **post office** is near the lower tourist office. (☎ 05 65 33 62 21. Open M-F 9:30-11:30am and 2-4pm, Apr.-Oct. also Sa 9am-noon.) **Postal code:** 46500.

ACCOMMODATIONS AND FOOD. Prices at Rocamadour hotels make daytripping almost mandatory; if you're willing to pay the price, there are two moderately priced accommodations in prime locations with great views. **Relais de Remparts ❸**, next to the clifftop castle, caters mainly to pilgrims. Their simple rooms are available for private meditation or for a night's sleep, saggy mattresses notwithstanding. (☎ 05 65 33 23 23; fax 05 65 33 23 24; http://pro.wanadoo.fr/relais-desremparts. Breakfast €4.60. Lunch €13. Dinner €11.50. Reception M-F 9am-8pm and Sa-Su 10am-7pm. Singles with sink €26, doubles €42-45; **demi-pension** €39-44 per person. A bit pricier are the calm, elegant rooms of the formal **Hôtel du Roc ❸**, on the main street in the lower town. (☎ 05 65 33 62 43; fax 05 65 33 62 11; www.ver-thotel.fr. Reception 6am-midnight. Open mid-Feb. to Nov. Singles with shower and toilet €29-32, doubles €32-43. Discount on multi-day stays. AmEx/MC/V.)

Not surprisingly, all the restaurants in town have tourist-adjusted prices. Tiny stores line Rocamadour's main street, hawking *noix* (nuts), *truffes* (truffles), *foie gras*, and *cabécou* (a mild, nutty local goat cheese). Several stores at the far end of the pedestrian road give free tastings of a sweet walnut *apéritif*, a specialty of the Quercy region. Most stores also offer free samples of other nutty delights, such as grilled, caramel-coated walnuts and crumbly hazelnut cake. Bakeries and grocery stores are pricey; consider bringing groceries from elsewhere and picnicking in the great scenery. For the most reasonable prices around, try **Le Lion d'Or ❸**, on the main street in the lower town, where you can dine on regional specialties while enjoying a good view of the valley. Make sure you like walnuts—you'll find them in your salad, meat, and desserts. (☎ 05 65 33 62 04. Menus €10.50-25. MC/V).

SIGHTS. Millions of believers, kings and vagabonds alike, have crawled on their knees up the **Grand Escalier**, which rises steeply up the cliffside beside the town's main street. King Henry II of England visited in 1170, and Blanche de Castille dragged her son St-Louis (Louis IX) along in 1244, just before he led a crusading army into the Holy Land. Today some pilgrims still kneel in prayer at each step, but most of the kneeling is done by tourists retrieving film rolls. The Grand Escalier winds up to the 12th-century **Cité Réligieuse,** which is actually not a city but an enclosed courtyard that encompasses seven chapels, two of which can be visited without a guide. Its nucleus is the **Chapelle Nôtre-Dame,** a dark, quiet place of prayer. Within, the only visible object is a black model ship, honoring all shipwreck victims, under the watchful eye of a 12th-century Black Madonna. (Chapel ☎ 05 65 33 23 23. Cité open July-Aug. daily 9am-6pm and 6:30-10pm; Sept.-June daily 8am-6pm. Mass daily at 11am.) Under Notre-Dame lies the **Crypte St-Amadour,** where the saint's body rested undisturbed until a Protestant tried to set it ablaze during the Wars of Religion. Though apparently immune to fire, the Saint's body could not withstand the assailant's fallback weapon, an axe. What remains is preserved next door in the **Musée d'Art Sacré,** which also holds paintings, colorful statues, illuminated manuscripts, and other relics of religious art. (☎ 05 65 33 23 30. Open June 15-Sept. 15 daily 10am-7pm; Apr.-June 14 and Sept. 16-Nov. 11 daily 10am-noon and 2-6pm. €4.60, students €2.60.) Adjacent to the chapel, the **Basilique St-Sauveur** attracts visitors with a gilt wooden altar. (☎ 05 65 33 62 61. Open Apr.-Oct. M-Sa 9am-noon and 2-6pm. Free.) A **tour** takes visitors to the **Crypte St-Amadour** and the **Chapelle St-Michel** (45 min.; 3 French tours per day, 10:30am-2:30pm; English tours July-Aug. by phone reservation at ☎ 05 65 33 62 61; €5).

Next to the Cité is the zigzagging **Chemin de Croix,** which depicts the 14 stations of the cross in vivid relief. The weak-kneed will appreciate the elevator (roundtrip from the lower city to the top of the chemin €4, round trip from the lower city to the Cité Réligieuse €3). At the summit is the 14th-century **château,** inhabited by the chaplains of Rocamadour and closed to the public. You can walk along the **ramparts**—you'll feel as though you're floating in midair. (Open daily 8am-8pm. €2.50.)

Next to the upper tourist office is the **Grotte des Merveilles,** a cave of stalagtite formations and black smudges that are actually the remnants of prehistoric paintings. 45min. guided tours in French point out the paintings (☎ 05 65 33 67 92. Open Apr.-June and Sept.-Nov. daily 10am-noon and 2-6pm; July-Aug. daily 9am-7pm. Adults €5, children €3.) Signs from the upper tourist office point the way (300m) to **La Féerie du Rail,** a song- and dance-filled miniature world that is sure to delight kids. Every detail down to the last doorknob was constructed by one man in 45,000 hours. Go early as shows tend to sell out. The 45min. show is in French with English subtitles. (☎ 05 65 33 71 06; fax 05 65 33 71 37. April-Sept. 5-8 shows per day; Oct.-Nov. only 2 per day, at 2:45pm and 4:15pm. Tickets sold July 13-Aug. 22 daily 9am-noon and 2-7pm; Aug. 23-Nov. 11 and Easter-July 12 daily 10am-noon and 2-6pm. €6, children €4.) On the **Rocher des Aigles,** which shares the plateau with the castle, there's a 45min. show featuring trained birds of prey. (☎ 05 65 33 65 45. July-Aug. daily noon-6pm 5 shows; Apr.-June and Sept. M-Sa 1-5pm and Su 1-6pm 3 shows; Oct.-Nov. M-Sa 2-4pm and Su 2-5pm, one show at 3pm. €6, children €4.)

CAHORS

Cradled in the horseshoe-shaped curve of the Lot River, Cahors (pop. 20,000) is a budget-friendly base for daytrips into the scenic Lot Valley. The town itself, much of which is currently under construction, is a little too big to capitalize on the natural beauty of the surroundings and a little too small to have an urban appeal. There is enough in the town to fill a day, but you might get impatient for the villages, vineyards, cliffs, and caves of the surrounding Lot Valley.

🖪🖪 TRANSPORTATION AND PRACTICAL INFORMATION. Trains leave from av. Jean Jaurès. (Info booth open daily 6am-8:30pm.) To: Brive (1½hr., 10 per day, €12.70); Limoges (2½hr., 6 per day, €21.90); Montauban (45min., 10 per day, €8.60); Paris (5-7hr., 7 per day, €49.20); Toulouse (1½hr., 9 per day, €13.80). **Voyages Belmon Buses,** 2 bd. Gambetta, runs full-day **bus excursions** to nearby sights daily. (☎ 05 65 35 59 30; fax 05 65 35 22 55. €15.50-32.50). **Cycles 7,** 417 quai de Regourd, **rents bikes.** (☎ 05 65 22 66 60. €8 per half-day, €13 per day. Passport deposit. Open Tu-Sa 9am-noon and 2-7pm.) You can **rent cars** near the train station; **Avis** is at 512 av. Jean Jaurès. (☎ 05 65 30 13 10. Open M-F 8am-noon, 2-6pm; Sa 8am-noon. MC/V.)

To get to the **tourist office,** pl. Mitterrand, bear right on av. Jean Jaures (the street right in front of the station), cross the street, and head up rue Anatole France. At the end of the street, turn left onto rue du Président Wilson and then right onto **bd. Gambetta,** the main thoroughfare separating the *vieille ville* from the rest of Cahors. The office will be just around the corner on your right. (15min.) Do not be fooled by the inaccurate Office du Tourisme sign in pl. Emilien-Imbert. The staff finds rooms, gives outdoors advice, and offers **city tours** in French and English. (☎ 05 65 53 20 65; fax 05 65 53 20 74. Open July-Aug. M-F 9am-6:30pm, Sa 9am-6pm, Su 10am-noon; Sept.-June daily 9am-noon and 2-6pm. Tours Tu and Th 5pm, F 10:30am.) Do your **laundry** at **GTI Lavarie-Pressing,** 208 rue Clemenceau (open daily 7am-9pm) or at **Lavomatic,** in pl. de la Libération, right next to Hôtel aux Perdreaux. (Open daily 7am-9pm.) **Internet access** is at the **Bureau Information Jeunesse,** in the **Foyer des Jeunes,** 20 rue Frédéric Suisse (see below; €3 per hr., free on Sa; open M-F 9am-noon and 1-6pm, Sa until 5pm). The **post office,** 257 rue Wilson, has **currency exchange.** (☎ 05 65 23 35 00. Open M-F 8am-7pm, Sa 8am-noon.) **Postal code:** 46000.

ACCOMMODATIONS AND CAMPING. The hostel in Cahors is amenity-laden, but the rooms are unimpressive. There are a few budget hotels in the *vieille ville*. The **Foyer des Jeunes Travailleurs Frédéric Suisse (HI)** resides at 20 rue Frédéric Suisse. From the train station, ignore the Auberge de Jeunesse sign and bear right onto rue Anatole France, then turn left onto rue Frédéric Suisse (10min.) These streets are very dark at night. This 17th-century building contains co-ed rooms that host up to twelve guests. Amenities include TV, ping-pong, and laundry. (☎ 05 65 35 64 71; fax 05 65 35 95 92. Breakfast €3.20. Lunch or dinner €7.80 Sheets €3.20. Reception 24hr. except closed 12:30-2pm; call ahead if arriving late. 8- to 12-bunk dorms €8.50 for members; singles and doubles €8.50 per person.)

To get to **Hôtel Aux Perdreaux,** 137 rue de Portail Alban, from the train station, follow rue Joachim to bd. Gambetta. Cross the street and proceed down rue Portail Alban (15min.). Perdreaux has airy, linoleum-tiled rooms with showers and shared toilets, some with balconies. (☎ 05 65 35 03 50. Breakfast €4. Reception 8am-10pm. Reserve July-Aug. Singles €25; doubles €28; triples and quads €35. MC/V.) For easy access to the markets (and early morning noise), stay at the **Hôtel de la Paix,** 30 pl. St-Maurice, near the cathedral. Follow the directions to the hostel, but continue on rue Frédéric Suisse through the arch at the end of the street and turn right down rue Caviole. Turn left on rue du Président Wilson, cross bd. Gambetta and go downhill to rue Maréchal Joffre, which leads to the cathedral. The hotel is on the other side of the *place* (15min.). Basic, dim rooms with worn beds. (☎ 05 65 35 03 40; fax 05 65 35 40 88. Breakfast €5.50. Reception M-Sa. Singles €22.50; doubles with shower €33.60, with bath €36.60. MC/V.)

Camping "Rivière de Cabessut," rue de la Rivière, is an idyllic three-star campground, near the center of town on the riverbanks. Every amenity imaginable: bar, laundry, pool, athletic facilities, and mini-golf. Take city bus #5, direction "Terre Rouge" from the train station to the "Stade Lucien Desprats" (8min., €0.75) and walk the remaining 10 minutes along the riverbank. Buses run M-Sa. To walk the entire way, from pl. de la Liberation, take the second left to rue Pelegry, and turn right at rue du Pont Neuf, which will lead you to the bridge. Turn left on the other side of the bridge and continue along the riverbank. (30-35min.) (☎ 05 65 30 06 30; fax 05 65 23 99 46; camping-riviere-cabessut@wanadoo.fr. Reception 8am-10pm. Reserve ahead in summer. Open Apr.-Sept. €2 per person, €8 per site.)

FOOD. Open-air markets liven up pl. Chapou (W and Sa 8am-noon). On the first and third Saturdays of the month, produce and flowers swamp the *vieille ville*. The more modest **covered market** is just off the square. (Open Tu-Sa 8am-12:30pm and 3-7pm, Su 9am-noon). Two **supermarkets** compete for customers: **Casino,** pl. Gén. de Gaulle (open M-Sa 9am-12:30pm and 3-7:30pm, Su 9am-12:30pm; Sept.-June closed Su); and **Champion,** inside the shopping center at pl. Emilien-Imbert, just off bd. Gambetta. (Open M-Th 9am-12:30pm and 2:30-7pm, F-Sa 9am-7pm.) The classy *"bar à vins,"* **Le Dousil,** 124 rue Nationale, at the corner of rue Clemenceau, has an excellent €9 lunch *menu* with salad, bread and cheese, wine, dessert and coffee. Local wines go for €1.60 a glass. (☎ 05 65 53 19 67. Open Tu-Sa 11am-2am. AmEx/MC/V.)

SIGHTS AND ENTERTAINMENT. With its six massive stone arches and three towering turrets, the monumental 14th-century **Pont Valentré,** credited with repelling invaders during the Siege of Cahors in 1580, is the city's most impressive sight. Legend holds that its architect, dismayed by construction delays, bargained with the devil to exchange his soul for building materials. When it came time to give the devil his due, the architect slit the throats of all the town's roosters; the unannounced dawn took the devil by surprise, turning him to stone with the first rays of the sun. Today, if you look carefully, you can still see the devil clutching a corner of the central tower. The bridge will be under renovation for much of 2003—hopefully, the devil is not involved.

Like many other churches in Périgord, the 12th-century **Cathédrale St-Etienne,** pl. Chapou, is topped by three cupolas of Byzantine inspiration. The northern wall's sculpted 1135 tympanum depicts Christ's ascension. The cathedral now hosts frequent classical concerts. (☎ 05 65 35 27 80. Open Easter-Oct. daily 8am-7pm; Oct.-Easter 8:30am-6pm.)

The grim **Musée de la Résistance, de la Déportation, et de la Libération du Lot,** in the former Bessières barracks in pl. du Gén. de Gaulle, catalogues Cahors's role in France's shames and triumphs during WWII. The reams of newspaper clippings, transcripts of speeches, and photographs are well worth seeing. Each room is dedicated to a local resident who lost his life in the war. (☎ 05 65 22 14 25. Open daily 2-6pm. Free.) The **Musée Henri Martin,** 792 rue Emile Zola, has a number of small modern art exhibits, including Pointillist interpretations of Cahors by the Toulouse born student of Delacroix, Henri Martin. The rest of the museum is devoted to ultra-modern photography and video art on the theme of Cahors, its people and its history. (☎ 05 65 20 88 66. Open M, W, Sa 11am-6pm, Su 2-6pm. €3; ages 7-18 and 60+ €1.50, children under 6 free; free for all the first Sunday of the month.)

For one week at the end of July, Cahors taps its toes to American blues during the **Festival de Blues.** Afternoon and early evening blues "appetizers" in coffee shops and bars throughout town are free, as are many of the formal concerts. For big-name concerts, buy tickets in advance. (☎ 05 65 35 99 99; www.cahors.blues-festival.free.fr. Tickets €15-23, students €8. Available after July 3.)

THE LOT VALLEY

The emerald-green Lot Valley snakes its way from Cahors to Cajarc between steep cliffs, sheltering sunflowers and vineyards. Long a favorite of bikers and hikers, the river Lot has recently been opened to boaters for a 70km stretch near Cahors. Though buses pass through the valley on their way from Cahors to Figeac, stops are few and far between, and inevitably involve some hiking—often upwards of 5km. But roads shadow the river, making car rental an option. **Quercyrail,** pl. de la Gare in Cahors, also runs several tourist trains to various sights in the valley on day excursions, stopping by the chateau or St-Cirq-Lapopie depending on the day. (☎ 05 65 23 94 72. May-Jun., Sept.-Oct. Su; July-Aug. Sa-Su train and boat tour or train and visit to chateau; July-Aug. M, Th train to chateau; July-Aug. W train and hike to St-Cirq-Lapopie; July-Aug M, W-Th train and bus to St-Cirq-Lapopie.) The Cahors tourist office sells hiking maps for the entire Lot Valley for €4.60.

ST-CIRQ-LAPOPIE

St-Cirq-Lapopie...appeared to me like an impossible rose in the middle of the night. I succumbed to its singular enchantment...I no longer wished to be elsewhere.
   —André Breton

Breton rhetoric aside, many Frenchmen cite the tiny St-Cirq-Lapopie as one of the most beautiful villages in France. Built on a cliff ledge, along streets so steep that the roof of one house begins where its neighbor's garden ends, St-Cirq-Lapopie hangs high over the Lot valley, 36km east of Cahors. The picturesque stone houses along narrow streets date from the 17th century, and now the entire village is classified as a historical monument. Sadly, the village's renown has spread—you *will* be joined by carloads of tourists. The view from the ruins of **Château Lapopie,** the highest point in town, extends over the river, cliffs, and plains below. The village's cultural center, the **Maison de la Fordonne,** contains a museum chronicling the rocky history of St-Cirq, including a display devoted to Breton. (☎/fax 05 65 31 21 51. Open June-Sept. daily 10:30am-12:30pm and 1:30-7:30pm; Mar. 16-May 10:30am-noon and 2-6pm; Sept.-Nov. 14 2-6pm. €2.)

To get to St-Cirq-Lapopie by car, follow D653 out of Cahors; turn right on to D662 when you reach Vers. **SNCF buses** run past St-Cirq-Lapopie from **Cahors** on the way to Figeac (35min., 5 per day, €5). Ask to be let off at Tour de Faure, Gare. The town is across the bridge and a beautiful 2km walk uphill. (30min.) The **tourist office**, pl. de Sombral, in the main square, offers a self-guided tour in English and French walking tours. (☎05 65 31 29 06. Open June-Aug. daily 10am-1pm and 2-7pm; Sept.-May 10am-1pm and 2-6pm. Tours July-Aug. 1 per day F-Su; €3.50)

The best place to stay is the *gîte d'étape* ■**La Maison de la Fourdonne.** Spotless, pine-paneled 3- to 5-bed rooms all have baths; some have balconies. (☎/fax 05 65 31 21 51. Reservations obligatory July-Aug. Reception same as museum hours. Bring your own sheets or sleepsack. €9 per night.) Between the town and the bus stop is the riverside **Camping de la Plage,** with many opportunities for hiking or kayaking. (☎05 65 30 29 51; fax 05 65 30 23 30; camping.laplage@wanadoo.fr. €4.50 per person; July-Aug. €4.50 per site, Sept.-July €3 per site.)

GROTTE DU PECH-MERLE

A few kilometers past the turn-off for St-Cirq-Lapopie on the road from Cahors is the turn-off for D653 and the **Grotte du Pech-Merle,** one of the best-preserved prehistoric caves still open to the public. Unfortunately, the nearest bus stop is 7km away in Cabrerets. Discovered by local teenagers in 1922, the 4km-long gallery contains paintings from 18,000 to 30,000 years ago, and a natural sideshow of core mineral formations. Bring a jacket—it gets chilly 60m underground. The cave has a daily visitor limit of 700, so arrive early or call ahead to reserve. Admission includes the adjoining museum. English pamphlets are available at the entrance. (Grotte ☎05 65 31 27 05; www.crdi.fr/~a.lot.of.france/lp01.htm; pech@crdi.fr. Museum ☎05 65 31 23 33; fax 05 65 30 21 26. Both open Apr.-Oct. daily 9:30am-noon and 1:30-4:45pm. 50min. max. visit. French tours July-Aug. every 30min. €7, children €5.) *Gîtes d'étape* and campgrounds line the route to Pech-Merle. Hitching is said to be easy, though it's not recommended by *Let's Go.*

CHÂTEAU CÉNEVIÈRES

Flotard de Gourdon, a local 16th-century nobleman, traveled to Italy and returned eager to transform his castle. Today, elegant chimneys, classical columns, narrowing staircases that play with perspectival illusions, and a modest "alchemy room" attest to his success. The Château Cénevières, resting on top of a cliff barely 7km from St-Cirq-Lapopie, also displays a fascinating collection of correspondence from such notables as Henri IV and Talleyrand in the 13th-century **Tour de Gourdon.** The current owners of the château run excellent guided tours. Don't neglect the glorious views of the valley from the back. (☎05 65 31 27 33. Open Easter-Oct. daily 10am-noon and 2-6pm; Oct. 2-5pm. Admission and 1hr. tour €4.50, children €2.30.) The most convenient way to reach the château is by the **Quercyrail** excursion from the Cahors train station. (☎05 65 23 94 72. July-Aug. M and Th 1:30-6:30pm. €18, château tour included.)

AQUITAINE AND THE PAYS BASQUE

The southwest corner of France encompasses the most varied of all French cultures and landscapes. In Aquitaine, the sprawling vineyards of the Médoc surround Bordeaux, while below, the pine forest of Les Landes opens onto the windswept beaches of the Côte d'Argent. Further south, Bayonne's bilingual signs and red and green houses proclaim the city's status as the capital of the Pays Basque. France's border with Spain is a jumble of sensory impressions: the glitter and glitz of Biarritz's Casino, the baaas of sheep as they graze on the fields of St-Jean-Pied-de-Port, the sharp smell of the seafood market at St-Jean-de-Luz, the orange glow of the sun as it sinks behind the Pyrénées. This geographical extremity of France has long tugged away from the rest of the country. Aquitaine remained in English hands from the 12th to 15th century, while the Pays Basque was part of independent Basse-Navarre until its ruler inherited the French throne in 1598 as Henri IV. Today, a small minority of Basque separatists maintain that their *Euzkadi* homeland is independent, part of neither France nor Spain (see p. 414).

BORDEAUX

Bordeaux's aromatic wines, grown on the *bords d'eaux* (riverbanks) of the Garonne and Dordogne, are some of the best in the world. But wine is not a new obsession here—without it, Bordeaux (pop. 280,000) might never have thrived. The sandy, rocky land around the city was useless until someone, probably an ancient Roman, discovered that the soil was perfect for growing grapes. Today, the city provides a base for tours of the châteaux (here, the headquarters of a vineyard, not a castle) of legendary nearby vineyards like St-Emilion, Médoc, Sauternes, and Graves, and wine festivals fill its summer months. Finally, Bordeaux's

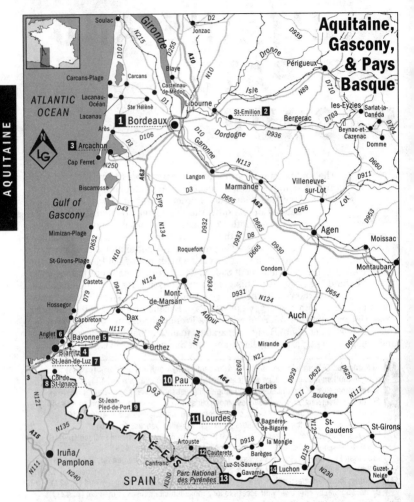

Aquitaine, Gascony, & Pays Basque

position as a university town makes for great nightlife. Bordeaux is currently undergoing extensive disruption as it constructs a new tramway system through the city's center. Construction is expected to be completed by 2004.

TRANSPORTATION

Flights: Airport 11km west of Bordeaux in **Mérignac** (☎05 56 34 50 00). A shuttle bus (☎05 56 34 50 50) connects the airport to the train station and tourist office (45min.; M-F every 30min. 6am-10:45pm, Sa-Su every 45min. 8:45am-10:45pm; €5.80, students €4.30). **Air France** (☎08 02 80 28 02) flies to **London** daily.

Trains: Gare St-Jean, rue Charles Domercq (☎05 56 33 11 83). To: **Lyon** (7-8hr., 4 per day, €50.60); **Marseille** (6-7hr., 12 per day, €53.70); **Nantes** (4hr., 4 per day,

€34.20); **Nice** (9-10hr., 5 per day, €66.90); **Paris** (TGV: 3-4hr., 15-25 per day, €55.10); **Rennes** (6hr., 1 per day, €44.20); **Toulouse** (2-3hr., 11 per day, €27.30).

Public Transportation: The **CGFTE bus system** (☎05 57 57 88 88) serves the city and suburbs. Maps at the train station and info offices at 4 rue Georges Bonnac and pl. Jean-Jaurès. Open M-Sa 9am-7pm. The *Carte Bordeaux Découverte* allows unlimited city bus use (1 day €3.75, 3-day €8.40); otherwise, fare is €1.15.

Taxis: Aquitaine Taxi Radio (☎05 56 86 80 30). About €17 to the airport.

Car Rental: Europcar, 35 rue Charles Domercq (☎05 56 31 20 30; fax 05 56 31 26 94), facing the train station. Open M-F 7am-10pm, Sa 7am-8pm, Su 10am-11:30pm. AmEx/MC/V.

Bike Rental: Free at the tourist office with ID deposit. (Call ☎05 56 10 20 30 for info. Open June-Sept. and the 1st Su of each month at pl. des Quinconces.) **Bord'eaux Vélos Loisir,** quai Louis XVIII (☎05 56 44 77 73), facing the pl. des Quinconces, rents bikes, in-line skates, and "talking bikes" that give directions to major landmarks in 4 languages. Bikes and in-line skates €8 per half day, €14 per day. Open May-Oct. daily 9:30am-8pm; Nov.-Apr. 2:30-6:30pm. MC/V.

ORIENTATION AND PRACTICAL INFORMATION

It takes about 30min. to walk from the train station to the *centre ville*, the oldest and most picturesque part of town. Follow **cours de la Marne** from the station. This busy thoroughfare will take you past the **Marché des Capucins** on your right and into the **pl. de la Victoire.** Nearby, the huge stone arch of the **porte d'Aquitaine** towers above the surrounding bars and clubs that serve crowds of students coming for nightcaps from the nearby **Domaine Universitaire.** From here, turn right under the arch of the *porte* onto the pedestrian **rue Sainte Catherine.** The patterned brick sidewalks bring you into *vieux Bordeaux*, the hub of the city, where shops and restaurants draw tourists and locals alike. After 10-15min., you'll cross the wide **cours de l'Intendance** and enter the **pl. Comédie** as the street you're on becomes the **cours du 30 juillet.** The **tourist office** is ahead on the right, just beyond the Grand Théâtre. The **bus depot** is right in front of the station. Buses #7 and 8 (dir: Grand Théâtre) run from the train station to pl. Gambetta (every 10min.; less frequently after 10pm, last bus 11:30pm; €1.15). **Pl. Gambetta,** a splash of greenery with park benches, lawns, and trees in the middle of the old town, is a good landmark and a point to catch the #7 or 8 bus back to the train station. Bordeaux is a big city; guard yourself and your wallet, especially at night.

Tourist Office: 12 cours du 30 juillet (☎05 56 00 66 00; fax 05 56 00 66 01; www.bordeaux-tourisme.com). Well stocked with maps and brochures. Open May-Oct. M-Sa 9am-7pm, Su 9:30am-6:30pm; Nov.-Apr. M-F 9am-6:30pm, Su 9:45am-4:30pm. **Branch** at train station (☎/fax 05 56 91 65 70). Open Nov.-Apr. M-F 9:30am-12:30pm and 2-6pm; May-Oct. M-Sa 9am-noon and 1-6pm, Su 10am-noon and 1-3pm.

City Tours: Several in French and English are given by the **tourist office.** Walking tours Nov. 16-Apr. 14 Su-Tu and Th-F 10am; July 15-Aug. 31 3pm. €6.40, students €5.60. Bus tours Apr. 15-Nov. 15 W and Sa 10am. €9.60, students €8.80.

Local Vineyard Tours: May-Oct. and Apr. 15-Nov. 15 half-day bus tour daily 1:30pm; Nov. 16-Apr. 14 W and Sa only. €26, students and seniors €22.50.

Budget Travel: Wasteels, 13 pl. de Casablanca (☎08 03 88 70 32; fax 05 56 31 91 48), across the street from the station, books charter flights. Open M-F 9am-noon and 2-7pm, Sa 9am-1pm and 2-6pm. MC/V.

Consulate: UK, 353 bd. du Président Wilson (☎05 57 22 21 10, emergency 06 60 28 21 10; fax 05 56 08 33 12). Open M-F 9am-12:30pm and 2:30-5pm.

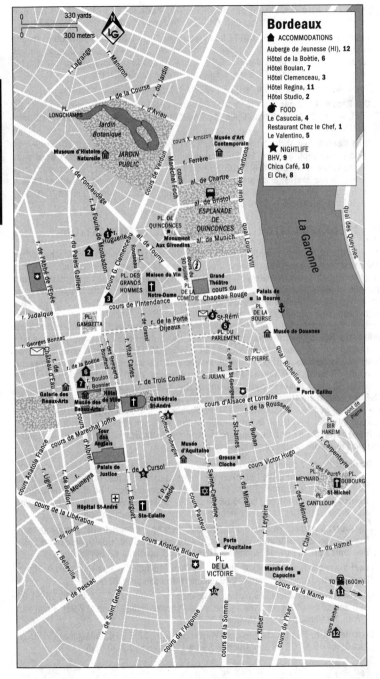

Bordeaux

🏠 **ACCOMMODATIONS**
Auberge de Jeunesse (HI), **12**
Hôtel de la Boètie, **6**
Hôtel Boulan, **7**
Hôtel Clemenceau, **3**
Hôtel Regina, **11**
Hôtel Studio, **2**

🍎 **FOOD**
Le Casuccia, **4**
Restaurant Chez le Chef, **1**
Le Valentino, **5**

⭐ **NIGHTLIFE**
BHV, **9**
Chica Café, **10**
El Che, **8**

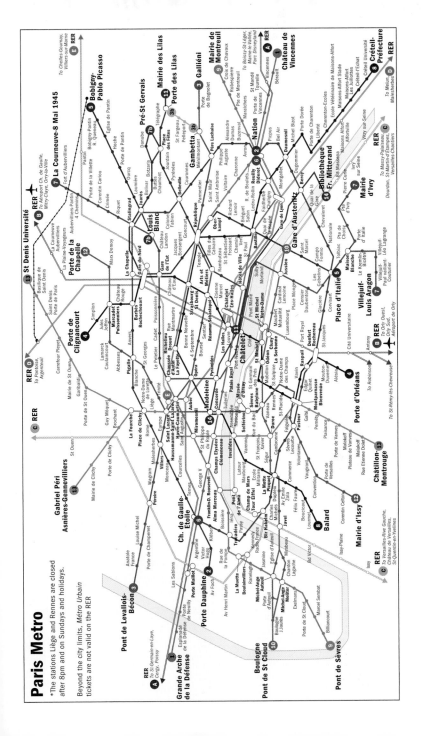

Paris Metro

*The stations Liège and Rennes are closed after 8pm and on Sundays and holidays.

Beyond the city limits, *Métro Urbain* tickets are not valid on the RER.

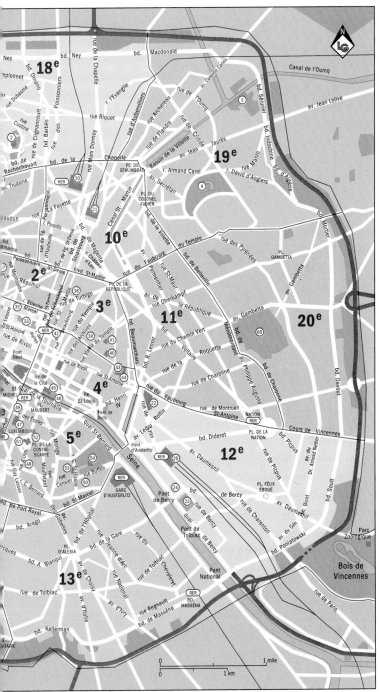

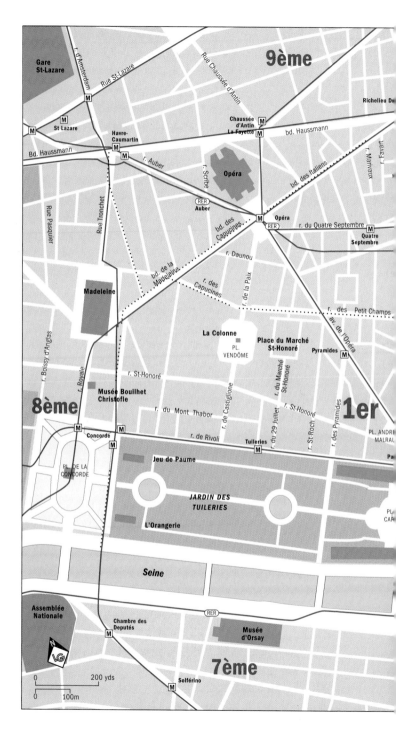

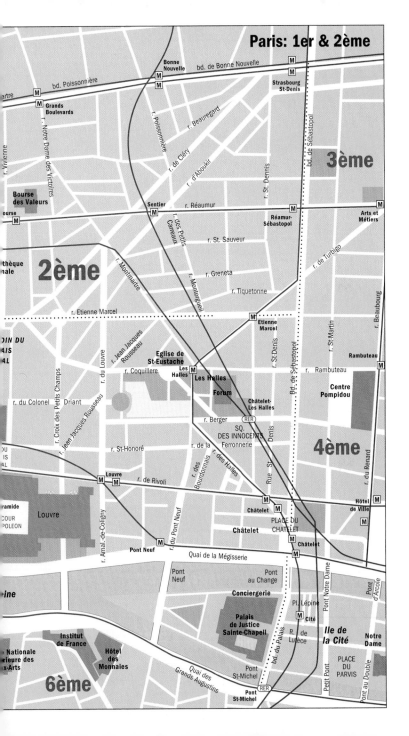

Paris: 1er & 2ème

3ème

2ème

4ème

6ème

Bonne Nouvelle
bd. de Bonne Nouvelle
bd. Poissonnière
Strasbourg St-Denis
artre
Grands Boulevards
r. Vivienne
r. Notre Dame des Victoires
r. Poissonnière
r. Beauregard
r. de Cléry
r. d'Aboukir
r. St. Denis
bd. de Sébastopol

Bourse des Valeurs
ourse
Sentier
r. Réaumur
Réaumur-Sébastopol
Arts et Métiers

thèque
nale
r. des Petits Carreaux
r. St. Sauveur
r. Montmartre
r. de Turbigo
r. Greneta
r. Montorgueil
r. Tiquetonne
r. Beaubourg

r. Etienne Marcel
Etienne Marcel
r. St-Martin

IN DU
AIS
AL
r. Jean Jacques Rousseau
r. du Louvre
Eglise de St-Eustache
r. Coquillère
Les Halles
Les Halles
r. St-Denis
Bd. de Sébastopol
r. Rambuteau
Rambuteau

r. du Colonel Driant
Forum
Centre Pompidou
Châtelet-Les Halles

r. du Colonel Driant
r. Croix des Petits Champs
r. Jean Jacques Rousseau
r. Berger
RER
SQ. DES INNOCENTS
Ferronnerie
4ème

r. St-Honoré
r. de la
r. des Halles
Rue St-Denis

U
IS
AL
Louvre
r. de Rivoli
r. des Bourdonnais
r. du Renard

ramide
COUR
POLEON
Louvre
r. Amal.-de-Coligny
r. du Pont Neuf
Châtelet
PLACE DU CHÂTELET
Châtelet
Hôtel de Ville

Pont Neuf
Châtelet
Quai de la Mégisserie
Châtelet

ine
Pont Neuf
Pont au Change
Conciergerie
Pl. Lépine
Cité
Pont Notre Dame
Pont d'Arcole

Institut de France
Palais de Justice Sainte-Chapell
R. de Lutèce
Ile de la Cité
Notre Dame

Nationale
rieure des
x-Arts
Hôtel des Monnaies
bd. du Palais
Quai des Grands Augustins
Pont St-Michel
Petit Pont
PLACE DU PARVIS
Pont au Double

Pont St-Michel
RER

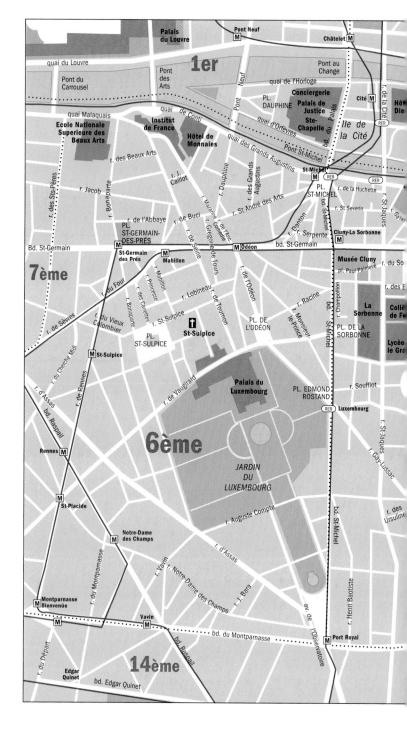

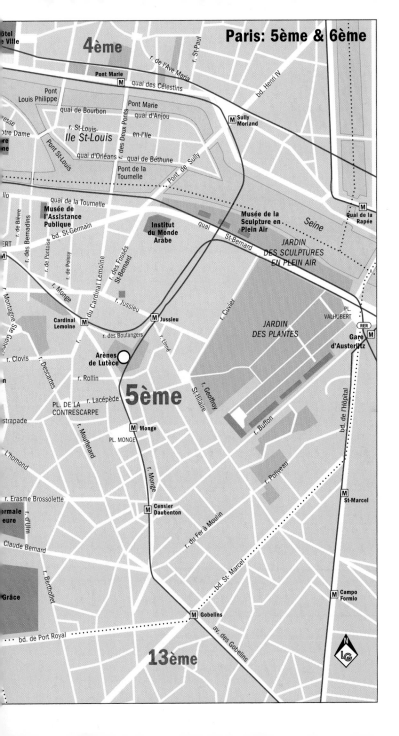

Paris: 5ème & 6ème

4ème

r. de l'Ave Maria

r. St-Paul

bd. Henri IV

Pont Marie M quai des Célestins

Pont Louis Philippe

quai de Bourbon

Pont Marie

quai d'Anjou

M **Sully Morland**

resse otre Dame re ne

r. St-Louis-
Ile St-Louis

r. des Deux Ponts

en-l'Ile

Pont St-Louis

quai d'Orléans

quai de Béthune

Pont de Sully

Pont de la Tournelle

llo

quai de la Tournelle

Musée de l'Assistance Publique

bd. St-Germain

r. de Bièvre

r. des Bernadins

ERT

M

r. de Pontoise

r. de Poissy

r. Monge

du Cardinal Lemoine

r. des Fossés St-Bernard

Institut du Monde Arabe

quai

St-Bernard

Musée de la Sculpture en Plein Air

Seine

JARDIN DES SCULPTURES EN PLEIN AIR

Quai de la Rapée M

r. Jussieu

Cardinal Lemoine

r. des Boulangers

M **Jussieu**

r. Cuvier

JARDIN DES PLANTES

PL. VALHUBERT

RER

Gare d'Austerlitz M

r. Montagne Ste Geneviève

r. Clovis

r. Descartes

Arènes de Lutèce

r. Linné

r. Geoffroy St-Hilaire

r. Rollin

r. Lacépède

5ème

PL. DE LA CONTRESCARPE

strapade

r. Mouffetard

M **Monge**

PL. MONGE

r. Buffon

r. Monge

L'homond

r. Erasme Brossolette

Censier Daubenton M

bd. de l'Hôpital

M **St-Marcel**

ormale eure

r. d'Ulm

Claude Bernard

r. du Fer à Moulin

r. Poliveau

r. Berthollet

Grâce

bd. St. Marcel

M **Campo Formio**

bd. de Port Royal

M **Gobelins**

av. des Gobelins

13ème

N L G

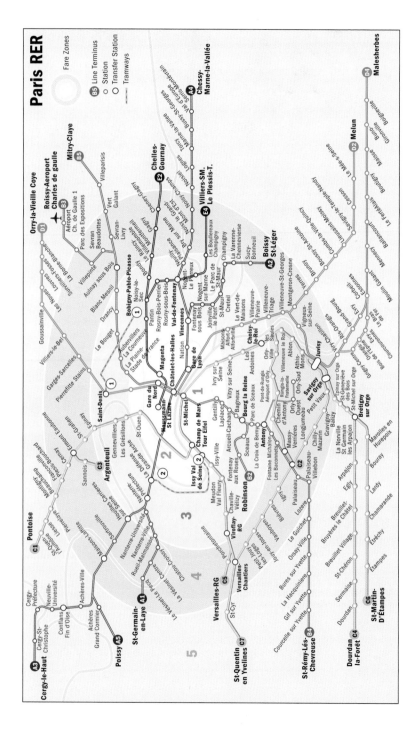

Paris RER

Legend:
- **B5** Line Terminus
- ○ Station
- ⊙ Transfer Station
- — Tramways
- Fare Zones

American Express: 14 cours de l'Intendance (☎05 56 00 63 36). Open M-F 8:45am-noon and 1:30-5:30pm. 24hr. refund assistance: ☎08 00 90 86 00.

Youth Center: Centre d'Information Jeunesse d'Aquitaine, 5 rue Duffour Dubergier (☎05 56 33 00 70). Information about activities and jobs. Open M-F 9am-6pm.

Laundromat: 203 cours de la Marne. Also at 27 rue de la Boétie and at 43 cours de la Libération. All open daily 7am-9pm.

Police: 87 rue de l'Abbé de l'Epée (☎05 56 99 77 77). Branch at train station.

Hospital: 1 rue Jean Burguet (☎05 56 79 56 79).

Internet Access: France Télécom, 2 rue Château d'Eau (☎08 00 35 23 19), near pl. Gambetta. Walk away from the river on rue Judaïque. €4.50 per hr., students €3. Open M-F noon-7pm. **Netzone,** 209 rue Ste-Catherine (☎05 57 59 01 25), near pl. de la Victoire. €5 per hr., students €4. Open M-Sa 10am-10pm, Su 2-7pm.

Post Office: 52 rue Georges Bonnac (☎05 57 78 88 88), off pl. Gambetta. **Currency exchange.** Open M-F 8am-7pm, Sa 8am-noon. **Postal code:** 33065.

AQUITAINE

▮ ACCOMMODATIONS AND CAMPING

Bordeaux's main hostel has recently reopened after a long renovation. Though in a somewhat unsavory area near the train station, and a long walk from the town center, it's convenient for those getting off a train with a heavy backpack. Private rooms in Bordeaux are numerous, but often expensive. A few deals can be found on the side streets around the pl. Gambetta and the cours d'Albret, but they fill up fast. Reserve at least a few days in advance in summer.

▨ **Hôtel Studio,** 26 rue Huguerie (☎05 56 48 00 14; fax 05 56 81 25 71; studio@hotel-bordeaux.com), is a backpacker favorite for good reason. Walk 1 block down rue Clemenceau from pl. Gambetta, and half a block left on rue Huguerie. The clean, sunny rooms have telephones and cable TV, at the lowest prices around. Rooms are a little dark on the lower floors, but with all the perks and the comfortable beds, you might not even notice. Internet access: hotel clientele €2.25 per hr., guests €4.50. Breakfast €4. Reception 8am-11pm. Reserve early. Small singles €16; small doubles €20; larger singles and doubles €24; triples €30.50; quads and quints €38. MC/V. ❷

▨ **Hôtel Boulan,** 28 rue Boulan (☎05 56 52 23 62; fax 05 56 44 91 65). Take bus #7 or 8 from the train station to cours d'Albret. Right around the corner from the Musée des Beaux Arts. 16 rooms with hardwood floors and cable TV; some with balconies overlooking quiet rue Boulan. Hotel is being renovated; ask to see your room first. Breakfast €3.50. Singles €17, with shower €20-23; doubles €20-25. MC/V. ❷

Auberge de Jeunesse (HI), 22 cours Barbey (☎05 56 33 00 70; fax 05 56 33 00 71). Friendly staff and spotless rooms compensate for the constantly slamming doors and user-unfriendly key system. Near the station, the hostel is in a neighborhood filled with seedy characters who can make the 30min. walk from the city center a harrowing experience at night. Breakfast €2.50. Curfew 3am. Dorms €13. Non-members can pay an extra €1.60 to stay 1 night. ❶

Hôtel de la Boétie, 4 rue de la Boétie (☎05 56 81 76 68; fax 05 56 81 24 72). Check-in is at Hôtel Bristol around the corner, 4 rue Bouffard. Run by the same family as Hôtel Studio, La Boétie offers similar amenities. Each plain white room comes with shower, cable TV, telephone, and nondescript prints of minor paintings. Reception 5:30am-11:30pm. Singles and doubles €20-24.50. Larger rooms available. MC/V. ❷

Hôtel Clemenceau, 4 cours Georges Clemenceau (☎05 56 52 98 98; fax 05 56 81 24 91). In the heart of old Bordeaux, barely 20m from where buses #7 and 8 stop in pl. Gambetta. This 2-star hotel is a bit expensive and impersonal, but has sizable rooms, views of pl. Gambetta, A/C, and small refrigerators. Breakfast €4.50. Reception until 1am; after-hours ask for code. Su-Th singles €26; doubles €31-35. F-Sa singles €23; doubles €26. MC/V. ❸

Hôtel Regina, 34 rue Charles Domercq (☎05 56 91 66 07, fax 05 56 94 32 88), opposite the train station. Perfect for late arrivals and passers-through, with pastel rooms. Noise from the street and the bus stop may be bothersome. Singles with shower €23, with toilet and bath €31; doubles €29/€35. MC/V. ❷

▮ FOOD

Center of the self-proclaimed *"région de bien manger et de bien vivre"* (region of fine eating and living), Bordeaux takes its food as seriously as its wine. Local specialties include oysters, *foie gras*, and beef braised in wine sauce. Most restaurants are scattered around the **rue St-Rémi** and **pl. St-Pierre.** Here, candlelit tables spill out of restaurants, filling the alleyways that converge on **pl. du Parlement.** For Middle Eastern specialties, try the area around **St-Michel.** Most *Bordelais* don't eat before 9pm in the summer, and restaurants usually serve until 11pm or midnight.

There's fruit at the **market** in pl. des Grands Hommes (open M-Sa 7am-7pm), fish at the **marché des capucins,** and organic food in the **marché biologique** on pl. St-Pierre. (Open Th 5am-5pm.) For prepackaged goods, try the enormous **Auchan supermarket,** near the Maison des Etudiantes at the huge Centre Meriadeck on rue Claude Bonnier. (Open M-Sa 8:30am-10pm.)

▨ **Restaurant Chez le Chef,** 57 rue Huguerie (☎05 56 51 92 71). This beautifully formal restaurant seats guests in a hidden garden. The traditional dishes are some of the best Bordeaux has to offer—fresh salmon with basil, cassoulet, duck preserve—at prices lower than many of Bordeaux's *sandwicheries.* Price *formules* from €9.50. Dress formally to fit in with the other diners. Open M-Sa noon-2pm and 7-10pm. MC/V. Attached **hotel:** doubles €30; special €5 reduction with *Let's Go* guide. MC/V. ❸

La Casuccia, 49 rue St-Rémi (☎05 56 51 17 70). Light, romantic restaurant, perfect for an intimate candle-lit *tête-a-tête* or an outing with friends. Especially good are their pizzas (€5.50-€10) and *gratin d'avocat au crabe* (€8.50). Filling *menus* start at €10. Open daily 11:30am-3pm and 7pm-midnight. MC/V. ❷

Le Valentino, 6 rue des Lauriers (☎05 56 48 11 56), is an oasis in the expensive quarter of Bordeaux. Beautifully presented cuisine tastes just as good as it looks. Three course lunch *menus* with wine and coffee for €9.50 are arguably the best deal in Bordeaux. Extensive international wine selection; sample 8-10 wines for €10. Dinner *menus* €11-28. Open M-Sa 11am-2:30pm and 7-11pm. AmEx/MC/V. ❸

◉ SIGHTS

Admission to all museums in Bordeaux is free on the first Su of every month.

CATHÉDRALE ST-ANDRÉ. Nearly nine centuries years after its consecration by Pope Urban II and one century since its renovation, this building is still the centerpiece of Gothic Bordeaux. On the facade of the church are statues of angels and apostles—many apparently deranged or deformed—surrounding reliefs from the life of Christ. Its bell tower, the **Tour Pey-Berland,** juts 50m into the sky, with a large statue of Notre-Dame d'Aquitaine on top for good measure. The tower was placed 15m away from the cathedral, Italian-style, because its masons feared that the vibrations of the massive bells might make the cathedral collapse. Climb the 229 spiraling steps for the view of your life. *(Pl. Pey-Berland. ☎05 56 52 68 10. Cathedral* *open Apr.-Oct. daily and Nov. M-F 7:30-11:30am and 2-6:30pm. June-Aug. free organ recital every other Tu at 6:30pm. Belltower open July-Aug. daily 10am-7pm; Sept. and Apr.-June 10am-6pm; Oct.-Mar. 10am-5pm. €4, under 25 and seniors €2.50.)*

EGLISE ST-MICHEL. The best cityscape of Bordeaux can be seen from the tower of the Eglise St-Michel. On ground level, you can see even more of the world sitting in one of the many cafés that surround the church or browsing the different markets that fill the courtyard each morning. (Open 9am-1pm daily.) As one local describes the area, "here we have a bit of Portugal, a bit of Morocco, a bit of Algeria, and a bit of Aquitaine." This is the most Bohemian district of Bordeaux, the place where students hang out and sip mint tea in the surrounding cafés with their friends. *(Tower open June-Sept. €2.50.)*

PALAIS DE LA BOURSE. The construction of the Palais de la Bourse, with its pillars and pilasters, fountain, and wrought-iron facades, was the most important step in the 18th-century modernization of Bordeaux. The town's grand buildings, squares, gardens, and promenades spread outward from this spot. The building on the left houses the surprisingly interesting **Musée National des Douanes,** or National Customs Museum. Come here to feed your budding obsession with tariffs and excise taxation. *(☎ 05 56 48 82 82. Open Apr.-Sept. daily 10am-noon and 1-6pm; Oct.-Mar. M-Sa 10am-noon and 1-5pm. €3, students and seniors €1.50.)*

MONUMENT AUX GIRONDINS. Several avenues in Bordeaux converge on pl. de Quinconces, at whose center is a much-adorned pole topped by a stone Lady Liberty. The monument commemorates a group of revolutionary leaders from towns bordering the Gironde river. The Girondins, as they were called, had the misfortune of being far more moderate than the deranged Montagnards, who ended up beheading them. Before losing their heads though, they produced the Revolution's most important document, the **Declaration of the Rights of Man** (see p. 9); the event is commemorated in the bicentennial date inscribed on the monument's side (1989). The hundred-year-old monument is filled with symbols: the three women on the side facing town represent Bordeaux, the Dordogne, and the Garonne, and empty pedestals facing the river remind us of the murdered Girondins—most famously poor Pierre Vergniaud, who argued so eloquently for the King's life.

GRAND THÉÂTRE. The colonnaded Neoclassical facade of this 18th-century opera house conceals a breathtaking interior. It's probably the most strictly classical opera house in the world, and one of the most impressive. Attend an opera, concert, or play, or take a daytime tour. *(On pl. de la Comédie. Tickets ☎ 05 56 00 85 95. Open daily 11am-6pm. Tours through tourist office ☎ 05 56 00 66 00. €4.80, students €4.)*

MUSÉE DES BEAUX ARTS. This small, unimpressive museum was originally used to display Napoleon's captured war booty; later additions, acquired through purchase rather than invasion, are mostly 17th- through 19th-century works by European artists, including Titian, Rubens, and Van Dyck. *(20 cours d'Albret, near the cathedral. ☎ 05 56 10 20 56. Open W-Su 11am-6pm. €4, students free.)*

VINORAMA DE BORDEAUX. Although this is the best of Bordeaux's wine museums, it may not be worth the trek from the city center to the Chartron district. Visitors carry around a tape recorder with the voice of Bacchus narrating the history of mannequins involved in the wine-making process. The tour ends with a brief wine-tasting session, including samples of wine made from an ancient Roman recipe, a wine from around 1850, and a modern wine. *(12 cours du Médoc. Near the river just off the quai des Chartrons. ☎ 05 56 39 39 20. Open June-Sept. Tu-Sa 10:30am-12:30pm and 2:30-6:30pm, Su 2-6:30pm; Oct.-May Tu-F 2-6:30pm, Sa 10:30am-12:30pm and 2:30-6:30pm. €5.50, children €2.50.)*

YOUR OWN WAY

MARATHON DU MÉDOC

The gunshot rings out and you're instantly part of a surging throng of costumed athletes. To your left, a woman is dressed as a pastry chef. To your right, a large man fills out the ample shape of his bumblebee costume. As you hit mile 3, you catch up to a can-can girl with rustling petticoats. Wait, make that a boy. His lipstick is smeared above his lip, covered with a 5 o'clock shadow.

As you run, there are children cheering by the side of the road. Further along the gravel road, tables are set outside châteaux, offering wine, cheese and fruits. The cheese is getting soft under the sun; the heavy smell mixes with the sharp wine and the steamy earth. You stop, catching your breath, drinking the wine as you would water. Other runners pass by. They look serious, some are dressed in running shorts. You remember your duty. But you're still clutching a glass of wine. And it's a Lafite Rothschild. You're torn. You begin to run with the wine. You lurch, trying not to spill, pausing to sip, stagger, and regain your rhythm. Lurch, sip, stagger.

If you find the finish line, you will have completed the Marathon du Médoc. Held in early September, it starts in Pauillac and winds through 52 vineyards. With wine stations, an oyster bar, and costumed runners, you'll hardly notice the hills. The winner gets his weight in grand cru wine. Register early in the year—7000 tickets are drawn in a lottery. *(To register online, visit www.marathondumedoc.com. For more info call Pauillac's Maison du Vin at ☎ 05 56 59 17 20.)*

OTHER SIGHTS. The grim, sooty Entrepôt Laine houses Bordeaux's **museum of contemporary art** and, upstairs, its **museum of architecture.** Exhibits in both rotate and are sometimes worth seeing; pick up a copy of *Dans les Musées de Bordeaux* at the tourist office or any museum to determine if you picked a lucky time. *(7 rue Ferrère, two blocks from cours de Maréchal Foch. ☎ 05 56 00 81 50; capc@mairie-bordeaux.fr. Both open Tu-Su 11am-6pm, W 11am-8pm. €4.80, students €4, seniors free.)* The **Musée d'Aquitaine** is a historic and ethnographic display of the classical and folk art of Aquitaine from prehistory to the present. Don't miss the giant Gothic rose window near the end of the exhibit. *(20 cours Pasteur. ☎ 05 56 01 51 00. Open daily 11am-6pm. Booklet and video presentations in English. €4.)* Near the **pont de Pierre,** the city's oldest bridge, stands the 15th-century slate-roofed **Porte de Cailhau.** A few blocks down cours Victor Hugo on rue St-James is the imposing 16th-century **Grosse Cloche.** Two angels preside over the Big Clock, whose golden hands still keep good time.

♫ ENTERTAINMENT

For an overview of nightlife, grab a free copy of *Clubs and Concerts* at the tourist office, or purchase the biweekly magazine *Bordeaux Plus* (€0.50) at any magazine stand. **Pl. de la Victoire** and **pl. Gambetta** are mobbed by 70,000 students during the school year, and continue to serve as the hotspots for entertainment during the summer. **St-Michel** has a more mellow atmosphere, with locals gathering at the café tables around 6pm and often staying until midnight. Closer to the train station, the pubs and dance clubs in **quai Ste-Croix** and **quai de Paludate** are always packed with leather-clad revelers. After the clubs close, you can eat and drink at **pl. Marché des Capucins** and hang out with early-morning market workers. Bordeaux's gay scene is second only to Paris.

El Che, 34 cours de l'Argonne (☎ 05 56 92 33 98). A funky Afro-Cuban *bar-rhumerie* near pl. de la Victoire. Sip on homemade rum cocktails (€4) in this bit of tropical Ile des Antilles transported to the gray streets of Bordeaux. Free salsa lessons W and F 8pm. Open Tu-Sa 7pm-2am. MC/V.

BHV (Bar de l'Hôtel de Ville), 4 rue de l'Hôtel de Ville (☎ 05 56 44 05 08), across from the Hôtel de Ville. Flashing lights spin off the mirrors in this small but fashionable gay bar, filled most nights of the week. Try the *pichet*—a bucket of beer with enough straws to serve the entire bar (€15). Theme nights W. Drag shows Sept.-June every other Su. Open daily 6pm-2am.

Chica Cafe, 3 rue Duffour Dubergier (☎06 82 86 45 37), in the shadow of the cathedral. This friendly, boisterous Latino bar is a pool hangout spot for older men during the day, and a student's dance venue at night. The bare concrete dance floor in the basement stages occasional concerts. Beer €2; margaritas €5.20. Happy Hour 6-8pm; nonbeer alcohol €1.50. Open M-Sa 7:30am-2am, Su 10:30am-2am.

◪ WINERIES AND VINEYARDS

A HISTORY OF CLARET

Bordeaux's reputation for wine is the product of 20 centuries of shameless (but justifiable) self-promotion. The wines were of variable color and quality until Louis IX snatched the port of La Rochelle from the English in 1226. Not to be deprived of his claret (as the English call red Bordeaux wine), King Henry II bestowed generous shipping rights on Bordeaux, making it England's wine cellar. At first the citizens simply shipped out wines produced farther up the River Garonne, but the money flowing in sparked a local planting mania. Soon Bordeaux's port began refusing to accommodate other wines. In the 18th century, the vineyards spread from the Médoc region to areas south of the Dordogne, including St-Emilion. Today, the wines of Bordeaux flow into 500 million bottles a year.

TASTING IN BORDEAUX

If you're just in town for a day or two and are desperate for the full wine experience, head to the **Maison du Vin/CIVB,** 1 cours du 30 juillet, where there's a wine bar, professionals on hand to tell you what you're drinking, and even a tasting course. The 2hr. "Initiation to Wine Tasting" program, available in English, teaches the subtle art of oenophilia through comparative tasting; you'll leave confident enough to waltz into any four-star restaurant. The staff can give you a list of local châteaux and recommend vineyards. Ask about a 15min. video on Bordeaux wines. (☎05 56 00 22 66; fax 05 56 00 22 82; www.vins-bordeaux.fr. Open M-Th 8:30am-6pm, F 8:30am-5:30pm. Wine-tasting course twice weekly; €16.) Locals buy their wine at **Vinothèque,** 8 cours du 30 juillet (☎05 56 52 32 05; open Tu-Sa 9:15am-7:30pm, M 1-7:30pm; MC/V), and classy **L'Intendant,** 2 allées de Tourny. (☎05 56 48 01 29. Open Tu-Sa 10am-7:30pm, M 2:30-7pm. MC/V.)

VISITING THE CHÂTEAUX

It's easiest to explore the area with a car, but some vineyards are accessible by train—St-Emilion and Pauillac in particular make good daytrips—and the tourist office gives afternoon **tours.** (Apr. 15-Nov. 15 daily 1:30pm, Nov. 16-Apr. 14 W and Sa 1:30pm. St-Emilion tours W and Su, Médoc tours Th and Sa, Graves and Sauternes F. €26, students and seniors €22.50.) Bring a good map if you're biking or walking, because local roads are hard to navigate. The owners of the châteaux are usually happy to give private tours, but call ahead or ask the tourist office to call for you. All of the châteaux sell wine directly.

ST-EMILION

The viticulturists of St-Emilion (pop. 2350), just 35km northeast of Bordeaux, have been refining their technique since Roman times; theirs is, not surprisingly, among the best appellations in France. Today they gently crush 12,850 acres of grapes to produce 23 million liters of wine annually. Quite apart from its wine, the medieval village's stone buildings, twisting narrow streets, and café-lined *places* are a pleasure to visit. Beneath the streets there is another part of St-Emilion, accessible only through a tour from the tourist office (see below). The **Eglise Monolithe,** carved by Benedictine monks over three centuries, is the largest subterranean church in Europe. The underground **catacombs** nearby served as the burial place for a series of Augustine monks when the cemetery became too small. The monks were lowered by rope through a conduit into the natural underground grotto. The tour also stops at the hermitage of **St-Emilion** himself, a Benedictine monk originally from Brittany who left for then-undeveloped Aquitaine when his miracles brought him unwanted celebrity status.

The **Maison du Vin de St-Emilion,** pl. Pierre Meyrat, offers a 1hr. course on local wines. Their wine shop has wholesale prices and a free exhibit. (☎05 57 55 50 55. Open Nov.-Mar. M-Sa 10am-12:30pm and 2-6:30pm, Su 10am-12:30pm and 2:30-6:30pm; Aug. daily 9am-7pm; Apr.-July and Sept.-Oct. daily 9am-12:30pm and 2:30-6pm. Wine course offered mid-July to mid-Sept. 11am. €17. MC/V.)

The **tourist office,** near the church tower at pl. des Créneaux, distributes the *Grandes Heures de St-Emilion,* a list of **classical concerts** and **wine tastings** hosted by nearby châteaux. (☎05 57 55 28 28; fax 05 57 55 28 29. Open July-Aug. daily 9:30am-8pm; Sept.-Oct. and Apr.-June 9:30am-12:30pm and 1:45-6:30pm; Nov.-Mar. 9:30am-12:30pm and 1:45-6pm.) In addition to renting **bikes,** they offer tours in English to local châteaux. (Bikes €9 per half-day, €14 per day. Tours July-Aug. M-Sa 2 and 4:15pm; May-June and Sept. 3:30pm. €8.) **Trains** come here from Bordeaux (30min., 2 per day, €10.10). Plan on spending the whole day; trains arrive in the morning and don't leave until 6:30pm. It's the second stop from Bordeaux and the tiny station is poorly marked—don't miss it! To get to the tourist office, take a right on the main road from the station; when you reach town, walk straight up rue de la Porte Bouqueyre toward the tower (2km) or take the bus.

MÉDOC, GRAVES, SAUTERNES

Though St-Emilion is probably the best vineyard for a first visit—it's accessible and attached to a beautiful village—there are other worthwhile regions near Bordeaux. The **Médoc** region lies north of Bordeaux, between the Gironde estuary and the ocean—its name comes from the Latin *medio-acquae,* meaning "between the waters." This area is home to some of the world's most famous red wines: Lafite-Rothschild, Latour, Margaux, Haut-Brion, and Mouton-Rothschild. Book an organized tour, or take the Citram bus 70S from the depot to Pauillac, the most renowned village of the region. The **tourist office** can rent bikes, suggest routes, and help make reservations to visit local châteaux. (☎05 56 59 03 08; fax 05 56 59 23 38. Open July 1-Sept. 15 9am-7pm; Sept. 16-Oct. and June M-Su 9:30am-12:30pm; Nov.-May M-Sa 9:30am-12:30pm and 2-6pm, Su 10am-12:30pm and 2:30-6pm.)

South of the Garonne is the **Graves** region, named for its gravelly topsoil. Graves's dry and semisweet wines were the drink of choice in the time of Eleanor of Aquitaine, before the reds of Médoc overtook them 300 years ago. In the southeastern end of Graves is the **Sauternes** region, celebrated for its sweet white wines.

The château **Smith Haut Lafitte** in the town of Martillac is less than a 20min. drive from Bordeaux. Proprietors Daniel and Florence Cathiard bought the crumbling vineyard in 1990 from corporate ownership. Now a small but luxurious château with peacocks strolling in its garden, Smith Haut Lafitte gives detailed tours and tastings by reservation. (☎05 57 83 11 22; cathiard@smith-haut-lafitte.com; www.smith-haut-lafitte.com.) Across the street from the vineyards is the four-star luxury hotel **Les Sources des Caudalie,** run by the Cathiard daughters, where you can join the ranks of Madonna and Princess Caroline of Monaco and indulge yourself in the revolutionary *vinotherapie* spa. (☎05 57 83 82 82; fax 05 57 83 82 81; info@caudalie.com; www.caudalie.com. Red wine barrel bath €45.70 for 30min. Bath, massage, jet shower, and honey and wine wrap €122.)

ROTTING TO PERFECTION A climatic quirk gives Sauternes wines their particular taste. When the weather cools here in September, a morning fog rises from the confluence of the Ciron and Garonne rivers, allowing a fungus—*Botrytis Cinerea* or "Noble Rot"—to breed on the grapes. Water evaporates as the grapes shrivel up, leaving a high concentration of sugar and a rich, complex taste. Each grape is picked only when it has been well covered in "rot;" the selection requires several careful harvests. Unlike other regional whites, these sweet wines take many years to reach their peak, and are only cultivated during years when the climate cooperates; vineyards here are famous for rejecting entire vintages that they consider below their standards.

ARCACHON

Arcachon (pop. 11,450) is one of the best in a chain of beach towns on the Côte d'Argent (Silver Coast), the thin strip of sand which runs along 200km of France's southern Atlantic seaboard. It's known in particular for two silicon landmarks: the **Dune du Pyla**, Europe's highest sand dune, and the **Banc d'Arguin**, a 1000-acre sand bar. Arcachon is a resort town at heart, full of vacationing families in summer and senior citizens and despondent hotel owners in the winter. During its high times, the town is a perfect daytrip; easygoing, unpretentious, and naturally beautiful.

▓▞ ORIENTATION AND PRACTICAL INFORMATION. Trains, pl. Roosevelt, go only to Bordeaux (45min.-1hr.; 10-20 per day, last train M-Sa 9:05pm, Su and holidays 9:50pm; €8.80.) **City bus** #611 runs from a stop in front of the train station to "Pyla-sur-Mer," site of the Dune (20 min.; July-Aug. 15 per day, Sept.-June 2 per day; €2.70). Sometimes the bus does not stop at Pyla; the Haitza stop is only a 10min. walk from the dune. Walk uphill between the two hotels; at the three-star hotel at the bend in the road, and take the wooden stairway down to the sea. **Locabeach 33,** 326 bd. de la Plage, rents two-wheeled transportation. (☎05 56 83 39 64. Open July-Sept. Tu-Sa 9am-midnight. Bikes €7.10 per half-day, €10-13 per day; deposit €125-150 or passport. Scooters and motorcycles €22.90 per day. MC/V.)

Arcachon's **tourist office,** pl. Roosevelt, is about three blocks left of the station. (☎05 57 52 97 97; fax 05 57 52 97 77; tourisme@arcachon.com. Open July-Aug. daily 9am-7pm; Oct.-May M-Sa 9am-12:30pm and 2-6pm; Apr.-May also Su 9am-1pm.) There's an **annex** on the corner of bd. Mestrezat and rue des Pêcheries. (Open July-Aug. daily 9am-7pm.) Wash beach towels at the **laundromat** on the corner of bd. Général Leclerc and rue Molière. The **police** (☎05 57 72 29 30) are on pl. de Verdun. The **hospital** (☎05 57 52 90 00) is on allée du Dr. Jean Hameau. The **post office,** 1 pl. Franklin Roosevelt, opposite the tourist office, has **currency exchange** and a **Western Union** desk. (☎05 57 52 53 80. Open July-Aug. M-F 8:30am-6pm, Sa 8:30am-noon; Sept.-June M-F 8:30am-6pm, Sa-Su 8:30am-noon.) **Postal code:** 33120.

▛ ACCOMMODATIONS. In the summer, rooms here start at €36 for a double; even in the off-season, the prices begin at €27. A mellow summer hostel, camping, or cheap bunks in Bordeaux are your best options. **The Auberge de Jeunesse (HI) ❶,** 87 av. de Bordeaux, is in Cap-Ferrat. To get there, take a ferry from Arcachon's Jetée Thiers on av. Gambetta. (☎05 56 54 60 32. At least 1 per hr. €5.50, round-trip €9.50.) From the Cap-Ferrat ferry pier, take av. de l'Océan and continue as it becomes rue des Bouvreuils after the roundabout. (15min.) Turn left onto av. de Bordeaux, and the hostel will be on your right after a few minutes. (☎05 56 60 64 62. **HI members only.** Reception 8am-1pm and 6-9pm. €7. Open July-Aug. only.) In Arcachon, the very social **Camping Club d'Arcachon ❷,** 5 allée de la Galaxie, 2km from the beach, has a two-tiered pool, billiards, and a bar-restaurant. (☎05 56 83 24 15; fax 05 57 52

28 51. Check-out noon. 1-3 people and car June-Sept. and Aug. 1-20 €22; Oct.-May €12. Extra person €4. Electricity €4. AmEx/MC/V.) There are five campsites within a few kilometers of each other in **Pyla-sur-Mer** along the rte. de Biscarrosse. It's quite a trek to any of these; the closest, for what it's worth, is **Camping de la Dune ❷**, 300m from the beach on rte. de Biscarrosse. Take bus #611 (dir: Biscarrosse; 1 per hr. 8:45am-7:45pm) from the SNCF station of Arcachon to "Camping de la Dune." (☎05 56 22 72 17; campingdeladune@wanadoo.fr; www.campingdeladune.fr. Open May-Sept. 2 people with car €24.40, extra person €3.35; off-season prices €6-10 lower.)

◘ **FOOD.** It would be a crime to leave Arcachon without savoring a few ounces of the 15,000 tons of oysters gathered here annually. Beach cafés line **av. Gambetta** and **bd. de la Plage,** offering copious seafood platters and €10 *moules frites* (mussels-'n'-fries). **Le Pavillon d'Arguin ❸**, 63 bd. du Général Leclerc across the street from the tourist office, offer fresh and plentiful seafood menu for €15 all day long. (☎05 56 83 46 96. Sa-Su reservations recommended. Open July-Aug. noon-2:30pm and 7-10:30pm; Sept.-June Tu-Sa noon-2:30pm and 7-10pm. V.) A cheaper option is to imitate the French tourists, most of whom load up on bread from one of the many *boulangers artisanals* and produce from the **Marché Municipal,** rue Jehenne. (Open June-Aug. daily 8am-1pm.)

◙ ◘ **SIGHTS AND ENTERTAINMENT.** Rising suddenly from the edge of a pine forest, the 117m ▓**Dune du Pyla** looks more like a transplanted section of the Sahara than a French beach. Wind and sand race across the face of the dune while smaller humps of sand provide some sheltered spots. For courageous souls who are willing to cross the entire dune, there is a protected area at the edge where wading is possible, although a fierce undertow makes deeper swims too dangerous. Farther along the water, there are separate beaches for the clothed and the nude. From the bus stop in Pyla-sur-Mer, head down bd. de l'Océan and take the first right. Follow the same road for about 20min.; the Dune area will be on your right. The **Ecole Professionnelle de Vol Libre du Pyla (EPVLP)** has **hang gliding** from the dune; ask at the tourist office. (☎05 56 22 15 02. €61 per flight, €400 per week.)

Arcachon's bird sanctuaries and nature parks attract flocks of tourists. **UBA boats** take 2hr. excursions to the **Arguin Sandbar** from the Jetée Thiers pier at 10:45am, 2:30, and 3pm, weather permitting. (☎05 56 54 60 32 or 05 56 54 83 01. €15, children €10.) The same company also offers trips to the oyster beds and around an island bird sanctuary. (Tour daily 2:30pm; €11.) About 15km out of town, the **Parc Ornithologique du Teich** shelters 260 species of birds in one of France's most important sanctuaries. (☎05 56 22 69 43. Open June-Aug. daily 10am-8pm; off-season 10am-6pm. €5.)

In the hilly town of Arcachon itself, **Ville d'Hiver,** an arboreal district of turn-of-the-century villas, lies across from the **Parc Mauresque** north of the beach. Doctors designed the neighborhood's curving streets to protect invalids from the ocean winds; this "winter village" is 2°C warmer on average than its beachfront counterpart. Now the fairy tale villas, which range in style from faux Swiss chalet to pseudo-Gothic castle, make up a quiet suburban neighborhood, removed from the tourist rat-race below. The village is accessible on foot or via **tours** in a shameful tourist office mini-train. (1½hr.; June-Sept. 3 per week 10:30am. Call for reservation. €4.) The **Ste-Cécile** observatory, across the park on the way back from the Ville d'Hiver, offers a stunning view of Arcachon. The spiral staircase is not easy to climb, and worse to descend. (Open 9am-7pm. Free.)

Arcachon's kids run to several beachfront discothèques as soon as night falls. There's also the **Casino d'Arcachon,** 163 bd. de la Plage, a fairy tale creation containing, besides the obvious, several bars and a nightclub. (☎05 56 83 41 44; fax 05 56 83 41 44. Open daily 10am-2am.)

BIARRITZ

Once a whaling village at the base of the Pyrénées, Biarritz became the playground of aristocrats in the mid-19th century. Napoleon III, Alphonse XIII of Spain, Nicholas of Russia, and the Shah of Persia all visited its shores, drawn by its natural beauty. Biarritz still glistens with money. Hardly a city at all in the traditional sense, it is a theme park for a select few and a museum of wealth and glamour for everyone else. Biarritz's beautiful beaches, however, attract a truly democratic mix of glitterati sunbathers and scraggly surfer bums.

TRANSPORTATION

Flights: Aéroport de Parme (☎05 59 43 83 83), 7 Esplanade de l'Europe. M-Sa take bus #6 from Hôtel de Ville to "Parme Aéroport" (every 30min. 7am-7pm), Su take bus B. **Ryanair** (UK ☎01 279 680 500) flies to **London.**

Trains: Biarritz-la-Négresse (☎05 59 23 04 84), 3km from town. To: **Bayonne** (10min.; 17 per day; €2; TGV €3.50); **Bordeaux** (2hr.; 7per day; €20.30, TGV €23.30); **Paris** (8hr., TGV 5hr.; 5 per day; €61.10, TGV €67.90); **Pau** (1½hr., 4 per day, €13.70); **Toulouse** (4hr., 5 per day, €31.10). **SNCF office,** 13 av. Foch (☎05 59 24 00 94). Open daily 8am-8pm.

Buses: ATCRB (☎05 59 26 06 99), main office in St-Jean de Luz. Bus stops on rue Joseph Petit, next to the tourist office. Buy tickets on the bus.

Local Transportation: STAB (☎05 59 52 59 52). Office with maps and schedules on rue Louis-Barthou, near the tourist office. 20min. to Bayonne (bus #1 or 2); 10min. to Anglet (bus #7, 9, or 4). 1 hr. tickets €1.15, *carnet* of 10 €9.50, students during school year €8.

Taxis: Atlantic Taxi Radio (☎05 59 03 18 18). 24hr.

Bike and Scooter Rental: SOBILO, 24 rue Peyroloubilh (☎05 59 24 94 47). Bikes €12.20 per day. Scooters €33 per day. Open daily 8am-7pm. MC/V.

Surfboard Rental: Rip Curl Surf Shop, 2 av. Reine Victoria (☎05 59 24 38 40), 1 block from Grande Plage. €10 per half-day, €15 per day; €300 and ID deposit. Open July-Aug. M-Sa 10am-8pm, Su 3-7pm; Sept.-June M-Sa 10am-12:30pm and 3-7pm. For **lessons,** contact **Rip Curl** at ☎05 59 24 62 86. 1 person for 2hr. €34, 3 people for 2hr. €84, 6 people €153.

ORIENTATION AND PRACTICAL INFORMATION

From most towns near Biarritz, buses are more convenient than trains. Even from farther away, the best option is a train to Bayonne and then a bus to Biarritz. Bus #2 runs to the city center, the tourist office, and the hostel. From farther away, trains only service **Biarritz-la-Négresse,** 3km from the center. To get to the center of Biarritz, take blue bus #2 (dir: Bayonne via Biarritz; June-Aug. every 20-40min. 6:30am-9pm) or green bus #9 (dir: Biarritz HDV; June-Aug. 6:30am-7pm). To walk into town from Biarritz-la-Négresse, turn left onto allée du Moura, which becomes av. du Président Kennedy. Turn left a few kilometers later onto av. du Maréchal Foch, which continues to **pl. Clemenceau,** Biarritz's main square. (40min.)

Tourist Office: 1 sq. d'Ixelles (☎05 59 22 37 00; fax 05 59 24 14 19), off av. Edouard VII. Staff tracks down same-night rooms or campsites for free. Pick up the free *Biarritzscope* for monthly events listings. Open July-Aug. daily 8am-8pm; Sept.-June 9am-6pm.

Money: Change Plus, 9 rue Mazagran (☎05 59 24 82 47). No commission. Open July-Aug. M-Sa 9am-8pm, Su 10am-1pm; Sept.-June M-F 9am-12:30pm and 2-7pm.

Laundromat: Le Lavoir, 4 av. Jaulerry, by the post office. Open daily 7am-9pm.

Beach Emergencies: Grande Plage ☎05 59 22 22 22. **Plage Marabella** ☎05 59 23 01 20. **Plage de la Milady** ☎05 59 23 63 93.

Police: rue Louis-Barthou (☎05 59 24 68 24).

Hospital: Hôpital de la Côte Basque, av. Interne Jacques Loëb (☎05 59 44 35 35).

Internet Access: Génius Informatique, 60 av. Edouard VII (☎05 59 24 39 07). €0.75 per min., €7.50 per hr. Open daily 9am-8pm.

Post Office: 17 rue de la Poste (☎05 59 22 41 10). **Currency exchange** open M-F 8:30am-7pm, Sa 8:30am-noon. **Postal code:** 64200.

ACCOMMODATIONS AND CAMPING

Bargains do exist, but you may want to plan a month ahead in July and August or enlist the help of the tourist office. The best priced hotels are off rue Mazagran, around rue du Port-Vieux. The youth hostel is newly-renovated but far from the city center; all other hotels listed are centrally located.

Hôtel Barnetche, 5bis rue Charles-Floquet (☎05 59 24 22 25; fax 05 59 24 98 71; www.hotel-barnetche.fr), in the center of town. From pl. Clemenceau, take rue du Helder through pl. Libération to rue Charles Floquet. 12-bed dorm room is the best deal in town; larger rooms great for families. No-nonsense, energetic owner keeps everything ship-shape. Obligatory breakfast (with homemade croissants) included. In Aug., obligatory (and tasty) *demi-pension* €20 extra. Reception 7:30am-10:30pm, July-Aug. until 11pm. Reservations by phone or web recommended. Open May-Sept. Dorms €17 per person. Doubles €58; triples and quads €25 per person. ❷

Auberge de Jeunesse (HI), 8 rue de Chiquito de Cambo (☎05 59 41 76 00; fax 05 59 41 76 07; www.hostelbooking.com), a 40min. walk or a 15min. bus ride to the center of town. Consider renting a bike or scooter. Take bus #2 to "Bois de Boulogne." Walking, take av. Maréchal Foch as it becomes av. du Président J.F. Kennedy. Turn right on rue Ph. Veyrin and the hostel is at the bottom of the hill on your right. Well-equipped, with Internet (€5 per hr.), ping-pong, surfboard rentals (€7.62 per day), and a bar. Breakfast included. Dinner €8. Main course €5. Sheets €2.70. Reception 8:30am-12:20pm, 6pm-10pm. Dorms €12.20 per person. **HI members only.** MC/V. ❶

Hôtel Palym, 7 rue du Port-Vieux (☎05 59 24 16 56; fax 05 59 24 96 12). Beautiful wood furnishings in clean, airy rooms. Some rooms are renovated, others, especially in the annex, are not. Bar and terraced pizzeria span 2 streets below. Some rooms come with TV. Breakfast €5. Reception 8am-midnight. Singles €28; doubles €37, with shower €46; triples €47, with shower €62. Sept.-June prices 10% lower. MC/V. ❸

Camping: Biarritz, 28 rue d'Harcet (☎05 59 23 00 12; www.biarritz.camping.fr). Calm and within 1km of Milady beach. A 45min. walk from town. Take the Navette-des-Plages bus (#9) or walk down av. Kennedy from the station following signs. (30min.) Caters to surfers, but not as exclusively as Anglet does. Open May-Nov., June, Sept. 2 people with tent €13.90; July 1-10 and Aug. 21-31 €17.40; July 10-Aug. 20 €19.40. ❶

FOOD

In dining, as with everything in Biarritz, style trumps substance. Expect impressive elegance and high prices around **Grande Plage** and **pl. St-Eugénie.** More mid-priced eateries can be found on **av. de la Marne** as it splits from av. Edouard VII. Prepare for €9-13 *menus* and oceans of chintz floral ruffles. Cheap crepes and sandwiches can be found along **rue du Port-Vieux** and **rue Mazagran.** The **Marché Municipal** on rue des Halles offers local produce and an abundance of specialties. (Open daily 7am-1:30pm.) Next door is a **Shopi supermarket,** 2 rue du Centre. (☎05 59 24 18 01. Open M-Sa 8:45am-12:25pm and 3-7:10pm.)

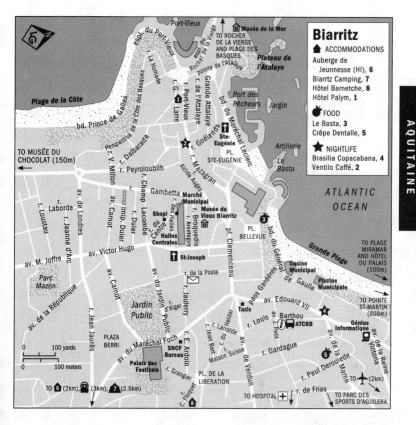

Biarritz

🏠 ACCOMMODATIONS
Auberge de
  Jeunnesse (HI), **6**
Biarrtz Camping, **7**
Hôtel Barnetche, **8**
Hôtel Palym, **1**

🍎 FOOD
Le Basta, **3**
Crêpe Dentalle, **5**

⭐ NIGHTLIFE
Brasilia Copacabana, **4**
Ventilo Caffé, **2**

A Q U I T A I N E

La Crêpe Dentelle, 6 av. de la Marne (☎05 59 22 28 29). Delicious and substantial crepes served with Breton cider. €9.90 lunch *menu.* Open daily noon-3pm and 7-11pm. MC/V. ❷

Le Basta, 31 blvd. du Général de Gaulle (☎05 59 22 22 58), under the pl. St-Eugénie. Enjoy a view of the Port des Pêcheurs and the Eglise St-Eugénie from the terrace of this café. *Moules frites* €8.20. Seafood and Basque *plats* for €12. Open daily noon-5pm and 7-11pm. ❸

🔵🔶 SIGHTS AND BEACHES

All of Biarritz is designed in consideration of its beaches. The **Grande Plage** is nearly covered in summer by thousands of perfect bodies and less perfect onlookers. This is also the beach of choice for the surfers. On the walkway behind the beach, is the immaculate, white **Casino Municipal.** Walk left along av. de l'Impératrice to reach the **Pointe St-Martin** and the tall lighthouse, **Le Phare de Biarritz.** From here, it is possible to see the sands of the Landes separating from the rocky coast of the Basque country. Inland, the **Hôtel Du Palais** sits overlooking the Plage Miramar. Constructed in 1845 by Emperor Napoléon III for Princess Eugénie, the E-shaped palace has since been converted into a hotel but retains all the luxury of the Napoleon III era. Rooms begin at €225 in high season, but you can stop at the terrace café for a cup of coffee to soak in the atmosphere of Biarritz's best four-star hotel. Across av. de l'Impératrice is the old **Hôtel Continental,** where Russian nobles fled after the Bolshevik Revolution in 1917.

On the other side of the Grande Plage, jagged rock formations provide a sheltered spot in the **Port des Pêcheurs** to harbor small fishing craft. **BASC Subaquatique,** near Plateau de l'Atalaye, organizes scuba excursions. (☎05 59 24 80 40. Open July-Aug. €17 on your own, €20 with guide, €28 for beginners. Diving excursions to sunken ships available.) Walk from the point out over the steel bridge and through the **Rocher de la Vierge,** a tooth-like rock with a statue of the Virgin Mary, to gaze at magical sunsets. The **Plage des Basques** stretches on the other side of the jetty. Endless paths cut into the flowered coast two minutes from the town center, but check the tides before traipsing onto the rocks. At low tide, this deserted beach has the cleanest water and sand in town.

Finally, trek out of town to the **Musée du Chocolat,** 14-16 av. Beaurivage, which contains the private collection of the proprietor of **Henriet,** the chocolate shop on pl. Clemenceau, where you can see elaborate chocolate sculptures being created and sample white, milk, and dark chocolate. (☎05 59 41 54 64. Open July-Aug. daily 10am-noon and 2:30pm-7pm; Sept.-June M-Sa 10am-noon and 2:30-6pm. €5, students €4.)

■ ENTERTAINMENT AND FESTIVALS

Casino Municipal gloats over the Grande Plage in all its art-deco glory. Curse Lady Luck as you and up to 700 of your friends blow a month's worth of baguettes on the greedy slot machines. (☎05 59 22 44 66. Open daily 10am-3am.) Jeans and sneakers are fine for slot machines, but you'll need to look snazzier to get upstairs. Hang out around the **Port des Pêcheurs** until 11pm or midnight, when the rich and reckless strap on their party boots. Things pick up early at the **Ventilo Caffé,** 30 rue Mazagran, a bar with a heavenly theme where young people drink and talk while sitting in exotic red velvet chairs. Sushi bar upstairs F-Sa. (☎05 59 24 31 42. Open July-Aug. daily 8am-3am; Sept.-June 8am-2am.) Dress up before heading to the **Brasilia Copacabana,** 24 av. Edouard VII and dance til dawn. (☎05 59 24 65 39. Cover €10.) On weekend nights, many head for cheaper, wilder **San Sebastian** just over the border in Spain.

The **International Festival of Biarritz** takes over the first week of October. Throughout September, **Le Temps d'Aimer** will please the culturally inclined with music, ballet, and art exhibits. (Tickets at the tourist office. €16-30; student discounts.) In July and August, *pelote* and Basque dancing hit **Parc Mazon** Mondays at 9pm. Two *cesta punta* tournaments animate the Fronton Euskal-Jai in the Parc des Sports d'Aguiléra: for two weeks in mid-July, Biarritz hosts the international **Biarritz Masters Jai-Alai** tournament; for three weeks in mid-August the town is taken over by the **Gant d'Or,** a tournament among big-name players. The winning teams of each tournament compete for the **Trophée du Super Champion** in September. (For all three, call tourist office at ☎05 59 22 37 00. Tickets €9.15-18.30.)

BAYONNE

Bayonne (pop. 43,000) is only a few kilometers from the center of Biarritz, it seems to be hundreds of years removed from its more fashionable neighbor. This is a city where the pace of life has not changed since the 17th century; here the verb for "walk" is *flâner* (meaning "stroll"), rather than *marcher* or *se promener*. Bayonne rises early, as lively markets crowd the banks of the Nive, but takes a long siesta when things heat up in the afternoon and life slows down as people retreat

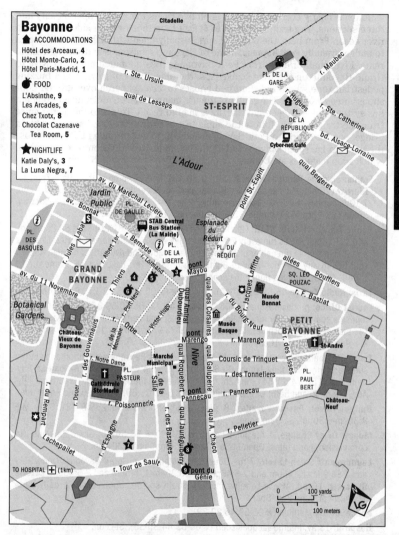

Bayonne

ACCOMMODATIONS
Hôtel des Arceaux, **4**
Hôtel Monte-Carlo, **2**
Hôtel Paris-Madrid, **1**

FOOD
L'Absinthe, **9**
Les Arcades, **6**
Chez Txotx, **8**
Chocolat Cazenave
 Tea Room, **5**

NIGHTLIFE
Katie Daly's, **3**
La Luna Negra, **7**

AQUITAINE

indoors behind exposed wooden beams and colorful shutters. Towering above it all, the grand Gothic cathedral marks the leisurely passing of time with the tolling of its bells. It is only in the middle of July and August that things pick up, when hurried tourists flock to Bayonne in droves to catch the traditional Basque festivals, bullfights, and sports matches.

ORIENTATION AND PRACTICAL INFORMATION

Ernest Hemingway, in a fit of wordy enthusiasm, once wrote that "Bayonne is a nice town. It is like a very clean Spanish town, and it is on a big river." His observation was nearly correct. Bayonne is on two rivers that join to split the city into three sections. The train station is in **St-Esprit,** on the northern side of the wide river **Adour.** From here, the pont St-Esprit, usually lined with fishermen, connects to budget-friendly **Petit-Bayonne,** home of Bayonne's museums and smaller restaurants. Five small bridges from Petit-Bayonne cross the much narrower Nive to Grand-Bayonne on the west bank. This, the oldest part of town, has a buzzing pedestrian zone where red-shuttered houses (*arceaux*) perch over ground floor shops and *pâtisseries.* The center of town is manageable on foot, and an excellent bus system makes Anglet and Biarritz a snap to reach. To get to the **tourist office** from the train station, follow the signs to the *centre ville,* crossing the main bridge, pont St-Esprit, to Petit-Bayonne, and continuing through pl. Réduit across the next bridge (pont Mayou) to Grand-Bayonne. Turn right onto rue Bernède, which soon becomes av. Bonnat. The tourist office is on your left. (10min.)

Trains: pl. de la République (☎05 59 50 83 42). Info office open daily 9am-7pm. To: **Biarritz** (10min., 11 per day, €2); **Bordeaux** (2hr., 9 per day, €19.90-21); **Paris** (5hr., 7 TGVs per day, €65.90); **Toulouse** (4hr., 5 per day, €30.50). Also to **San Sebastian, Spain** (1½-2hr.; M-F 6 per day, Sa-Su 5 per day; €23.50, under 26 €11.80).

Public Transportation: STAB, Hôtel de Ville (☎05 59 59 04 61). Open M-Sa 8am-noon and 1:30-6pm. Buses run every 20-30min. Lines #1, 2, and 6 serve **Biarritz.** Lines #1 and 2 also stop in the center of **Anglet.** Line #4 follows the river Adour through **Anglet.** Last bus in any direction around 8pm (7pm on Su). 1hr. ticket €1.15; *carnet* of 10 €9.45, €8 for students during the school year.

Taxis: Radio Taxi (☎05 59 59 48 48). **Taxi Gare** (☎05 59 55 13 15). Both 24hr.

Tourist Office: pl. des Basques (☎05 59 46 01 46; fax 05 59 59 37 55; www.bayonne-tourisme.com). Free city map, help finding rooms, and free *Fêtes en Pays Basque* and *Les Clés de la Ville* brochures. Open July-Aug. M-Sa 9am-7pm, Su 10am-1pm; Sept.-June M-F 9am-6:30pm, Sa 10am-6pm.

Tours: The tourist office organizes 2hr. walking tours of Bayonne's neighborhoods in the summer. (July-Aug. daily 10am, €4.60.) Tours given in English on Th. **Bateau Le Bayonne** (☎06 80 74 21 51) runs 2hr. boat trips along the Adour river. Departures July-Aug. 10am, 2, and 5pm; €12.20, children ages 5-12 €7.60, children 5 and under free.

Budget Travel: Pascal Voyages, 8 allées Boufflers (☎05 59 25 48 48). Open M-F 8:30am-6:30pm, Sa 9am-noon.

Money: Or et Change, 1 rue Jules Labat (☎05 59 25 58 59), in Grand-Bayonne. No commission, good rates. Open M-Sa 10am-12:30pm and 1:30-7pm.

Laundromat: Salon Lavoir, 7 rue Douer at pl. Montaut in Grand Bayonne. Open Tu-W and F-Sa 9am-12:45pm and 2-6:45pm, Th 10:30am-12:45pm and 2-6:45pm. **Laverie St-Esprit,** 16 bd. Alsace-Lorraine, near the train station. Open July-Aug. daily 8am-10pm; Sept.-June 8am-8pm.

Police: av. de Marhum (☎05 59 46 22 22).

Hospital: 13 av. Interne Jacques Loëb (☎05 59 44 35 35), St-Léon.

Internet Access: In St-Esprit, **Cyber-net Café,** 9 pl. de la République (☎05 59 55 78 98). €6.10 per hr. Open daily 7am-8:30pm.

Post Office: 11 rue Jules Labat (☎05 59 46 33 60), Grand-Bayonne. **Currency exchange.** Open M-F 8am-6pm, Sa 10am-noon. **Branch office,** bd. Alsace-Lorraine, has same hours. **Poste Restante** (at main branch): 64181. **Postal code:** 64100.

⛏ ACCOMMODATIONS AND CAMPING

In **St-Esprit,** reasonably-priced lodgings dot the train station area. The hotels in **Grand-Bayonne** are usually more expensive; in **Petit-Bayonne,** hunt around **pl. Paul**

Bert, but expect a noisy night near Basque bars. Hotels fill quickly during the festival season in July and August—reserve up to a month ahead. The closest hostels are in Anglet (see p. 415) and Biarritz (see p. 407), each a 20min. bus ride away.

Hôtel Paris-Madrid, pl. de la Gare, to the left of the station (☎05 59 55 13 98; fax 05 59 55 07 22), a 3min. walk from Petit-Bayonne. More like a home than a hotel, and a great base for getting to know the region. Large, individualized rooms; space for families. Gracious husband and wife speak excellent English and are more knowledgeable and forthcoming than 20 tourist offices. TV/reading room. Breakfast €4. Hall shower €1. Reception 6am-12:30am. Singles and doubles €15-20, with shower €22-25, with shower and toilet €26-28; triples and quads with bath €39-42. MC/V. ❶

Hôtel des Arceaux, 26 rue Port Neuf (☎05 59 59 15 53). Follow the directions to the tourist office, but turn left from rue Bernède onto rue Port Neuf at pl. de la Liberté in Grand-Bayonne. Unbeatable location and friendly reception in the center of Grand-Bayonne. Rooms are small but newly refurnished. Breakfast €4.60. Reception M-F 7:30am-10pm, Sa-Su 8:30am-10pm. July-Aug. singles and doubles €25.90, with TV and bath €26-38; larger rooms from €50.30 for two people. Extra person €6.10. MC/V. ❸

Hôtel Monte-Carlo, 11 rue Hugues, to the right of the train station (☎05 59 55 02 68). Check in at the lively bar/restaurant next door. Clean but absolutely bare rooms. Reception from 8am. Breakfast €4.50. Singles €20; doubles €23, with shower €26; quads with shower €40. MC/V. ❷

⚪ FOOD

The narrow streets of Petit-Bayonne and St-Esprit offer €8-10 *menus* of *jambon de Bayonne* (dry cured ham) and *poulet à la basquaise* (chicken wrapped in large peppers). Grand-Bayonne, the city's cloth-napkin zone, serves regional specialties in a less budget-oriented atmosphere. Vendors sell meats, fish, cheese, and produce at the **marché municipal,** on quai Roquebert. (Open Tu-Th 7am-1pm, F 7am-1pm and 3:30-7pm, Sa 6am-2pm.) There is a **Monoprix supermarket** at 8 rue Orbe. (☎05 59 59 00 33. Open M-Sa 8:30am-7:30pm. MC/V.)

L'Absinthe, 15 quai Jauréguiberry (☎05 59 25 60 13), has delicate cuisine in small, intensely tasty servings. Dinner (*menus* €20-24) served within the purple and yellow, art deco-ed room or on a terrace by the river. Absinthe €3.50. Open M-Sa noon-3pm and 7-11pm. MC/V. ❹

Chez Txotx, 49 quai Jauréguiberry (☎05 59 59 16 80). This bull-fight themed Spanish *brasserie* with a tapas bar (€1 per tartine) fills its seats on the dock and in the bar with a lively crowd. Fresh fish come directly from the covered market next door (€9.50-€13.50). Live music two days a week. Open daily noon-3pm, 6pm-2am. MC/V. ❸

Les Arcades, 40 rue Port Neuf (☎05 59 59 33 66). Outdoor tables on the popular rue Port-Neuf make a perfect spot for people-watching. Lunch from €10.40 includes a number of regional specialties. Open M-Sa 7:30am-7pm. MC/V. ❸

Chocolat Cazenave Tea Room, 19 rue Port Neuf (☎05 59 59 03 16). Since 1854, the Cazenave has served chocolate under the arches of the rue Port-Neuf, with a degree of luxury nearly unimaginable. Dark frothy hot chocolate with freshly whipped cream (€4.30) is served between mirrored walls. Open M-Sa 9am-noon and 2-7pm. MC/V.

⚪ SIGHTS

The 13th-century **Cathédrale Ste-Marie,** pl. Pasteur, whose spiny steeples pierce the sky above Bayonne, feels disproportionately tall in relation to the town it serves. Although the church has endured sporadic fires, weathered a brief stint as a cem-

IN RECENT NEWS

BASQUE CASE

In Bayonne, the capital of France's Basque region, restaurants post signs reading *Euskara badikigu*. Years of Latin lessons won't help you figure out this means "Basque spoken here," for Basque is the only non-Indo-European language spoken in Western Europe. Basque might not be the original language of Babel as 18th-century theologians believed it was, but Basques remain tied to an ancient past. Scientists recently found a genetic link between Basques and Celts; evidence that both are the closest ancestors to pre-farming communities in Europe.

Yet recent talk of Basque identity has not been about DNA but the ETA (Basque Homeland and Liberty), a radical movement based in Spain that organizes terrorist attacks in the name of independence. As violence continues in Spain, France has increased efforts to shut down the ETA. French police have cracked down on training cells, and ETA members have been imprisoned for acts of terrorism.

Yet only 10% of French Basques vote for Basque parties, and even fewer support the ETA's radical ideology. How has France escaped the problems of Spain? French Basques did not experience the cultural oppression as their Spanish counterparts did under Franco; and some scholars suggest that tolerance towards French Basques has actually aided in their assimilation with the larger nation. The Pays Basque remains the middle ground, literally and metaphorically, balancing its cultural identity between two extremes of terrorism and assimilation.

etery, and suffered massive destruction during the secularizing zeal of the Revolution, renovations have completely erased all traces of decay. (Church open M-Sa 7am-noon and 3-7pm, Su 3:30-10pm. Cloister open daily 9:30am-12:30pm and 2-5pm; Easter-Oct. 9am-6pm.) The prison block of the **Château-Vieux de Bayonne** on nearby rue des Gouverneurs has held such notorious villains as Don Pedro of Castille in 1367. The avenue continues to Bayonne's vast, grassy **fortifications,** where you can lose yourself among the shaded lawns. Around the corner on av. du 11 Novembre, Bayonne's refreshing **botanical gardens** flourish atop the battlements with 1000 species of Japanese flora, including a miniature bamboo forest. (Open Apr. 15-Oct. 15 daily 9am-noon and 2-6pm.)

The works of Bayonnais painter Léon Bonnat (1833-1922) are displayed along with his extensive art collection at the **Musée Bonnat,** 5 rue Jacques Laffitte. The walls are hardly large enough to hold all the paintings in this entertaining museum. Masterpieces by Degas, Darer, Ingres, and Goya comingle with racier exhibits like erotic paintings coyly hidden behind pink shower curtains. (Open W-M May-Oct. 10am-6:30pm; Nov.-May 10am-12:30pm, 2pm-6pm. €5.50, students €3.) The refurbished collection of the **Musée Basque,** 37 quai des Corsaires, has everything from traditional religious objects to fishing equipment. (Open May-Oct. Tu-Sa 10am-6:30pm; Nov.-Apr. 10am-12:30pm and 2-6pm. €5.50, students €3.) On Sundays at 11am, the **Eglise St-André** gives a traditional Basque mass with Basque chants.

For sandy and more secluded delights than you'll find on the crowded beaches of Anglet or Biarritz, try the **Metro plage** in Tarnos; take bus #10 from the train station. The water is only swimmable during July and August when coast guards line the beach, but the 2km walk is beautiful throughout the year.

🎵 ENTERTAINMENT AND FESTIVALS

In this quiet town of long afternoons and short evenings, nightlife is nearly nonexistent. The main bars that are grouped on the streets running between **pl. Paul Bert** and **quai Galuperie** in Petit-Bayonne cater mostly to aging local men. Travelers seeking a more lively atmosphere often take the ten-minute bus ride to Biarritz or even head for the border to San Sebastian, where the evening begins at midnight and doesn't end until around 8am. In Bayonne, the Irish pub **Katie Daly's,** 3 pl. de la Liberté, serves expensive pints to animated crowds on the weekends. Live music W-F. (☎05 59 59 09 14. Pints of Guinness €5.95, €4.45 from 7-9pm. Open M-Sa noon-2am, Su 6pm-2am.) **La Luna Negra,** in an alleyway between rue Poissonnerie and rue Tour de Sault, presents a cornucopia of music styles at its caba-ret-style bar and stage. W is blues night; Th-Sa entertainment ranges from mimes to storytellers to classical concerts. (Open W-Sa starting at 9:30pm. €5.) **L'Atalante,** 7 rue Denis Etcheverry, in St-Esprit, shows artsy international films in their original language. (☎ 05 59 55 76 63. €5.80, students €3.80; closed late July-early Aug.)

Preparation for Bayonne's festivals occupies most of the early summer, and at the end of June the season begins, lasting through September. June 21, the longest day of the year, brings the **Fête de la Musique.** Rock bands, jazz ensembles, breakdancers, and Basque crooners all contribute to this free concert and, for one night, there are no volume restrictions on live performances or radios. In mid-July, **Jazz aux Remparts** begins, with some of the world's most famous jazz artists flying in to play on Bayonne's battlements. (Contact the **Théâtre Municipale** at ☎ 05 59 59 07 27. Ticket office open Tu-Sa 1-7pm. €18-28 per night, students €15-22, under 15 €4-6.) The orchestra **Harmonie Bayonnaise** stages jazz and traditional Basque con-certs in the pl. de Gaulle gazebo. (July-Aug. Th 9:30pm. Free.) After the first Wednesday in August, unrestrained hedonism breaks out during the **Fêtes Tradi-tionelles,** as the locals immerse themselves in five days of concerts, bullfights, fire-works, and a chaotic race between junk heaps masquerading as boats. From July through September, Bayonne holds several bullfights or *corridas* in the **Plaza de Toros** (☎ 05 59 46 61 00). Seats (€12-76) sell out fast, but the cheap, nose-bleed sec-tion usually has seats available on fight days.

▶ DAYTRIP FROM BAYONNE OR BIARRITZ

ANGLET

Anglet is known as the surfing capital of France; the town's *raison d'être* is 4km of fine-grained white sand, parcelled out into nine beaches, each beach with its own name and personality. The waves are strongest at the **Plage des Cavaliers,** where most of Anglet's surfing competitions are held. The smaller **Plage des Sables d'Or** has beach volleyball and topless sunbathers. Swimmers should beware the strong cross-current undertow. When in doubt, swim near a lifeguard (they're on all the beaches except the Plage du Club and the Plage des Dunes). There are walking trails covered with pine needles at the **Forêt du Chiberta,** along with a newly constructed adventure and ropes course. Contact **Evolution 2 Pays Basque,** 33 rue de Madrid. (☎ 05 59 41 18 81. Open May 15-Nov. 1.) To get there, take STAB line #7 or 9 to "Pignada." Professional surf competitions are all free for spectators. In March, both surfers and skateboarders compete in the **Quik Cup.** Mid-August brings the three-day **France Championship,** while the traveling **O'Neill Surf Challenge** takes up residence for five days at the end of August, around the same time as the **Europe Bodyboard Championship.** The last major event of the year is the **WCT Quiksil-ver ProFrance,** which runs from the end of September into October. You can pre-pare for your title challenge by renting a board and taking lessons at one of the many surf shops along the beaches. The prices are all similar. Try **Rip Curl/Ecole Française de Surf,** av. des Dauphins. (☎ 05 59 23 15 31. Boards half-day €10, full-day €16; passport deposit required. 2hr. lessons €34 for 1 person; €84 for 3 people; €154 for 6 people.)

The well-equipped **tourist office,** 1 av. de la Chambre d'Amour in pl. Général Leclerc, is a good 10-15min. walk from the sea. (☎ 05 59 03 77 01; fax 05 59 03 55 91. Open July-Sept. M-Sa 9am-7pm; Oct.-June M-F 9am-12:45pm and 1:45-6pm, Sa 9am-12:15pm.) There is an **annex** closer to the shore on av. des Dauphins. (Open July-Sept. daily 10:30am-7:30pm.) **STAB** buses (€1.15) run about every 15min., but less frequently on Sundays and holidays. Get a map or schedule if you can. The #2 or "B" bus in Biarritz or Bayonne, the #7 in Bayonne, and the #9 or "C" from Biarritz

AQUITAINE

to La Barre all go to Anglet. (Aug. only.) The #2 and 9 buses stop near the youth hostel. You can rent **bikes** near the beach at **Sobilo**, pl. des Docteurs Gentille. (☎05 59 03 37 56. Open M-Sa 10am-7pm.)

ST-JEAN-DE-LUZ

The village of St-Jean-de-Luz (pop. 13,000; Basque name *Donibane Lohitzun*) has always lived off the sea. Its early wealth came from whaling and the Basque *corsaires* (pirates) who raided British merchants throughout the 1600s. These high-seas riches are responsible for the finest examples of Basque architecture, from the octagonal belltower above Maurice Ravel's birthplace to a church built like a fishing boat. St-Jean is one of the area's most perfectly Basque towns, worth a visit for its regional architecture and a nets-by-sunset port-town charm, although travelers on a budget may want to daytrip from the more affordable Bayonne.

■ TRANSPORTATION

Trains: bd. du Cdt Passicot. Info office open M-F 10am-12:30pm and 2-6:30pm. To: **Bayonne** (30min.; 7 per day; €3.80, TGV €5.40); **Biarritz** (15min.; 10 per day; €2.40, TGV €4.10); **Paris** (5hr.; 10 per day; TGV €70.40); **Pau** (2hr.; 5 per day; €14.90).

Buses: across from the station. **ATCRB** (☎05 59 26 06 99) runs to **Bayonne** (7-13 per day, €3.60) and **Biarritz** (7-13 per day, €2.80). Also to **San Sebastian,** Spain (1¼hr.; 2 per day June 16-Sept. 25 M-Sa and Sept. 26-June 15 Tu, Th, and Sa; €7). Buy tickets on bus. Office open M-Sa 9am-7pm. **Pullman Basque,** 33 rue Gambetta (☎05 52 24 06 97), runs excursions to St-Jean-Pied-de-Port, the Basque villages, Spain, and elsewhere. Half-day tours to La Rhune (F). Ticket office open July-Sept. daily 8:30am-12:30pm and 2:30-7:30pm; Oct.-June 9:30am-12:15pm and 2:30-7:15pm.

Taxis: at the train station (☎05 59 26 10 11).

Bike Rental: Sobilo (☎05 59 26 75 76), at the station. Bikes €18 per day. Scooters €31 per day. Open daily 8am-7pm. MC/V

■ ☷ ORIENTATION AND PRACTICAL INFORMATION

From the train station, bear left diagonally across the rotary onto bd. du Commandant Passicot. The **tourist office,** pl. Foch, is on your right, just past the second rotary. From pl. Foch, rue de la République runs two short blocks to **pl. Louis XIV,** the center of town. The beach is one minute farther, along a restaurant-studded alley, and the pedestrian **rue Gambetta** runs perpendicular to the right past the church and endless shops. **Ciboure,** the section of St-Jean-de-Luz on the other side of the river **Nivelle,** can be reached by crossing the pont Charles de Gaulle.

Tourist Office: pl. Foch (☎05 59 26 79 63; fax 05 59 26 21 47). Maps and info on accommodations, events, and excursions. English tours of the town July-Aug. Tu, Th, Sa at 10am; €5. Tours in French Sept.-June Tu 3pm.

Laundromat: Automatique, 3 rue Chauvin Dragon. Open daily 8am-10pm.

Surf shop: Le Spot, 16 rue Gambetta (☎05 59 26 07 95). 2hr. lesson €35. Wet-suit €10 per half-day, €16 per day; bodyboard €8 per half-day, €13 per day. Open Jan.-Oct. daily 9:30am-9pm; Nov.-Dec. Su 10am-8pm. MC/V.

Police: av. André Ithurralde (☎05 59 51 22 22).

Hospital: av. André Ithurralde (☎05 59 51 45 45). 24hr. emergency service at the private hospital **Polyclinique,** 10 av. de Layats (☎05 59 51 63 63).

Post Office: 44 bd. Victor Hugo (☎05 59 51 66 50) has **currency exchange.** Open July-Aug. M-F 9am-6pm, Sa 9am-noon; Sept.-June M-F 9am-noon and 1:30-5:30pm, Sa 9am-noon. **Postal code:** 64500.

ACCOMMODATIONS AND CAMPING

Hotels are expensive and fill up rapidly in summer. Arrive early, especially in August. You may do best to commute from Bayonne or Biarritz. However, if you do stay in St-Jean-de-Luz, you can expect nice rooms and service for the prices.

Hôtel Verdun, 13 av. de Verdun (☎05 59 26 02 55), across from the train station. Well-kept, pastel-colored rooms with huge bathrooms for what are sadly the lowest prices in St-Jean. July-Sept. singles and doubles €34, with shower €41, with toilet €48 (obligatory *demi-pension* adds €10); Jan.-Apr. and Oct.-Dec. €23; May-June €25. MC/V. ❸

Hôtel Bolivar, 18 rue Sopite (☎05 59 26 02 00; fax 05 59 26 38 28), on a central but quiet street near the beach. Sparkling rooms with shining floors, some with balconies. Breakfast €5.50. Reception 7am-9:30pm. Open May-Sept. Singles €30-32, with shower €42-46; doubles €31-37, with shower €46-56; triples with bathroom €55-61. AmEx/MC/V. ❸

Campsites: There are 14 sites in St-Jean-de-Luz and 13 more nearby. All are slightly separated from the city center, behind the plage Erromandi. The tourist office has info. To walk to most of the campsites, take bd. Victor Hugo, continue along av. André Ithurralde, then veer left onto chemin d'Erromardie. (20min.) Or take an ATCRB bus headed to Biarritz or Bayonne and ask to get off near the *camping*. For a quiet and sheltered location, continue 200m around the bend to **Camping Iratzia** (☎05 59 26 14 89), chemin d'Erromardie. Reception 9am-8pm. ❶

FOOD

St-Jean-de-Luz has the best Basque and Spanish specialties north of the border. The port's famous seafood waits on ice in every restaurant along the rue de la République and pl. Louis XIV. For these meals, expect to pay upwards of €13. There is a large **market** at pl. des Halles. (Open Tu and F-Sa 7am-1pm.) For groceries, stop at the **Shopi supermarket,** 87 rue Gambetta (open M-Sa 8:30am-12:30pm and 3-7:15pm, Su 8:30am-12:30pm), or **8 à Huit,** 46 bd. Victor Hugo (open M-Sa 8:30am-1pm and 3:30-8pm; July-Aug. also Su 8:30am-12:30pm).

Buvette de la Halle, bd. Victor Hugo-Marché de St-Jean-de-Luz (☎05 59 26 73 59), serves the freshest regional specialties for the best prices in St-Jean. At this café beside the marketplace, the staff chats with diners while serving grilled sardines for €6, *gambas* (large shrimp) for €12, *gâteaux Basques* for €4, and *apéritifs* of wild prune *Patxaran* for €3. Open June-Sept. daily noon-3pm and 7-11pm. ❷

Pil-Pil Enea, rue Sallagoity (☎05 59 51 20 80) near the post office, is a tiny restaurant serving the finest *merlu* fished by Europe's only female captain and cooked by her husband. The environmentalist fisher woman catches all her fish by line rather than inhumane net. *Menu* for two people €29.70. Open M-Sa noon-2pm, 8pm-10pm. ❸

Relais de St-Jacques, 13 av. de Verdun (☎05 59 26 02 55), in the Hôtel Verdun across from the train station, has an ever-changing €11 *menu* including soup, a main course, and an all-you-can-eat dessert tray. Open July-Aug. daily noon-2pm and 7-8:45pm; Sept.-June M-F noon-2pm and 7-8:45pm, Sa noon-2pm. MC/V. ❸

Herria Ostatua, 30 rue Chauvin Dragon (☎05 59 26 29 79), dishes away *menus ouvrier* (worker's menu) consisting of an entrée, a main course (all-you-can-eat buffet Sept.-June), dessert, wine, and coffee for a flat €10. During lunch time, the terrace and the dining room are filled with muscled workers and fisherman of the town. Open daily 9am-1:30am; meals served noon-2:30pm and 7:30pm-10pm. MC/V. ❷

Chez Etchebaster, 42 rue Gambetta (☎05 59 26 00 80), caters to sweet tooths with cherry jam (€6) and cream-filled *gâteaux basques* (€13). Open Tu-Sa 8am-12:30pm and 3-7:30pm, Su 8am-1pm and 4-7pm. MC/V.

AQUITAINE

FRONTON CENTER In the Pays Basque, the term *pelote basque* refers to a number of games. One of them, *cesta punta* (or *jai alai*), is the world's fastest ball game. Burly players hurl a hard ball at a wall at speeds of up to 200km per hour by means of a *chistera* (basket appendage) laced to the wrist. Outdoor *fronton* arenas and indoor *trinquets* bear witness to local players's speed and skill. Spreading beyond its homeland, *pelote basque* fever has caught on in such places as Cancun, Cuba, and Connecticut. Sorry, ladies: so far, only men have played.

◎ ♫ SIGHTS AND FESTIVALS

To see St-Jean-de-Luz at its most striking, follow the walkway on the beachfront away from the river Nivelle to the end of the Grande Plage. The path up toward the **Chapelle Van Bree** takes you on a *balade à pied* (footpath) along the edge of St-Jean's layered cliffsides. From the lookout points, gaze out across the river Nive and to Hendaye and the Spanish border beyond. In town, the 15th-century **Eglise St-Jean-Baptiste**, rue Gambetta, looks plain from the outside, but is filled within by elaborate gilt wood carvings of saints and apostles. (Open daily 8:30am-noon and 2-6:30pm.) This was the church where Louis XIV married the Spanish king's daughter Maria-Teresa, according to the terms of the 1659 Treaty of the Pyrénées. The treaty was worked out after months of negotiations by Cardinal Mazarin and the Spanish prime minister on the nearby *île des faisans* or "island of conferences," a "no man's land" jointly owned by France and Spain.

At the pl. Louis XIV, the **Maison Louis XIV** has inside decoration and furnishing frozen in time, seemingly awaiting the return of its most famous boarder. It was here that Louis XIV stayed while Mazarin negotiated, and here that he consummated his marriage with Maria Teresa. Unlike the average royal marriage, this one proved successful; upon the queen's death, the king lamented, *"C'est le premier chagrin qu'elle me cause"* ("this is the first sorrow she has caused me"). (☎05 59 26 01 56. Open July-Aug. M-Sa 10:30am-noon and 2:30-6:30pm, Su 2:30-6:30pm; Sept.-June until 5:30pm. €4.50, students €3.80. 30min. guided tour in French leaves every 30min. Written explanations in English upon request.)

▨ SWIMMING WITH THE FISHES

From 1954 to 1956, St-Jean-de-Luz was France's primary supplier of tuna. Fishing boats still leave regularly from quai de l'Infante and quai Maréchal Leclerc. To get in on the fun at sea level, stop by the docks, where **Mairie Rose** offers a four-hour fishing trip from 8am to noon. (☎05 59 26 39 84; www.bateau-marierose.com. €25.) If you prefer to leave the fish alive, **Promenade Jacques Thibaud,** sheltered by protective dikes, provides some of the best sailing and windsurfing in the Basque region. Farther on, the best surfing in St-Jean-de-Luz is beyond the more popular beaches on **Plage d'Erromardi.**.

♫ FESTIVALS

Summer is packed with concerts, Basque festivals, and a championship match of *cesta punta*, one of the many variations on the game of *pelote basque*, a game like jai alai or lacrosse. (*Cesta punta* July-Aug. Tu and F at 9pm. Tickets at the tourist office; €7.65-18.30.) The biggest annual festival is the three-day **Fête de St-Jean,** held the last weekend in June, when singing and dancing fill the streets. Nearly perpetual performances by amateurs and professionals alike liven the *fronton* (arena), with sangria and barbecued Basque dishes with names like *Taloak* and

Txartelak. **Toro de Fuego** heats up summer nights in pl. Louis XIV with pyrotechnics, dancing, and bull costumes. (July-Aug. W 10:30pm, Su 11pm.) At the **Fête du Thon** (the second Sa in July), the town gathers around the harbor to eat tuna, toss confetti, and pirouette (€9.50, pay at the harbour.). The madness continues the third Saturday of July with the all-you-can-eat **Nuit de la Sardine** at the Campos-Berri, next to the *cesta punta* stadium. The fabulous **Fête du Ttoro** features all manner of exciting activities involving *ttoro* (fish soup). The *fête* takes place on an early Saturday in September; the next day, residents can sheepishly confess to the priests whom they pelted with fish guts hours earlier

■ DAYTRIP FROM ST-JEAN-DE-LUZ

COL DE ST-IGNACE

Basque Bondissant (☎ 05 59 26 30 74) runs buses to Col de St-Ignace from the green-rimmed bus terminal facing the train station in St-Jean-de-Luz (30min.; July-Aug. M-F 2 per day, Sept.-June M-Tu and Th-F 1 per day; round-trip €4, including train to top €14.)

Ten kilometers southeast of St-Jean-de-Luz, the miniscule village of **Col de St-Ignace** serves as a gateway to the Basque country's loveliest vantage point. From here, an authentic 1924 *chemin de fer* (railroad) crawls at a snail's pace up the mountainside to the 900m summit of **La Rhune.** Each tortuous turn reveals a postcard-perfect display of forests hovering above sloping farmland, as *pottoks* (wild Basque ponies) return your curious stares and sheep bound down the mountainside. At the peak, chilling air and gusty winds prevail even in summer. (Trains operated by **SHEM.** ☎ 05 59 54 20 26; www.basque-explorer.com/rhune.htm. July-Oct. daily every 35min. from 9am; May-June and Oct.-Nov. 15 Sa-Su and holidays 10am and 3pm. €9.15 round-trip.) La Rhune *(Larun)* is Spanish soil; shop owners slip easily between French and their native tongue. If you decide to walk back down from La Rhune, safety warrants a longer, roundabout route; loose rocks on the path make for treacherous footing. Take the well-marked trail to the left of the tracks down to the village of **Ascain,** instead of trying to return directly to St-Ignace, and hike the remaining 3km on D4 back to Col de St-Ignace (1½hr.); or set out directly for St-Jean-de-Luz from Ascain along the busy highway (5km).

ST-JEAN-PIED-DE-PORT

St-Jean-Pied-de-Port is the last stop before the tortuous mountain pass of Roncevaux on the pilgrimage to the tomb of St. James in Santiago de Compostela, Spain. Pilgrims have been making the trek ever since the 10th century, their routes intersecting in this medieval village surrounded by the red Pyrenean hills. In the village, a single cobblestone street marks the steep ascent through the *haute ville* to the dilapidated fortress, offering ever expanding vistas of the rolling hills and red-tiled roofs of the surrounding villages. First built by Sancho the Strong in the 13th century, the walls of St-Jean-Pied-de-Port have withstood attack from Visigoths, Charlemagne's men, the Moors, and the Spanish army. Outside the walls, visitors can set off on numerous hikes into the French and Spanish mountains. The Fôret d'Iraty, a mecca for hikers and cross-country skiers, is only 25km away.

■ PRACTICAL INFORMATION. Trains leave for **Bayonne** (1hr.; 5 per day, last train July-Aug. 6:50pm; Sept.-June Su-Th 4:33pm, F 4:56pm, Sa 6:50pm; €7.20) from the station on av. Renaud (☎ 05 59 37 02 00; open daily from 5:40am, info office 6:45am-noon and 1pm-7pm). **Rent bikes** at **Garazi Cycles,** 1 pl. St-Laurent. (☎ 05 59 37 21 79. €8 per half-day, €18.50 per day, €23 per weekend, €60 per week. Passport deposit. Open M-Sa 8:30am-noon and 3-6pm.) From the station, turn left and then immediately right onto av. Renaud, follow it up the slope, and

turn right at its end to reach the **tourist office,** 14 av. de Gaulle, which gives out small hiking maps for the surrounding region. (☎05 59 37 03 57; fax 05 59 37 34 91; saint.jean.pied.de.port@wanadoo.fr. Open July-Aug. M-Sa 9am-12:30pm and 2-7pm, Su 10:30am-12:30pm and 3-6pm; Sept.-June M-F 9am-noon and 2-7pm, Sa 9am-noon and 2-6pm.) The **police** are on rue d'Ugagne (☎05 59 37 00 36). The **post office** (☎05 59 37 90 00), rue de la Poste, has **currency exchange.** (Open M-F 9am-noon and 2-5pm, Sa 9am-noon.) **Postal code:** 64220.

🄵🄲 ACCOMMODATIONS AND FOOD. St-Jean offers pretty rooms at unbecoming prices; you won't find much under €31 per night. The best option is to stay at Mme. Etchegoin's **gîte d'étape ❶,** a popular stopover for pilgrims following the chemin de St-Jacques. The lodging is just outside the city walls, 9 rte. d'Uhart. From the tourist office, walk downhill, cross the bridge, and take your first right on the opposite bank. The street becomes rte. d'Uhart after you pass through the city gates (5min., follow signs to Bayonne). Twelve spartan bunks, divided among three white rooms, await in an 18th-century house, as do six attractive well-worn *chambres d'hôte* with antique furnishings and hardwood floors. (☎05 59 37 12 08. Open Mar.-Nov. Breakfast €4. Reception 8am-10pm. Sheets or sleeping bag €2.80. Dorms €8. Doubles €32.) **Hôtel des Remparts ❸,** 16 pl. Floquet, has 14 large clean pastel rooms on the same road as Mme. Etchegoin's *gîte,* but inside the city walls. (☎05 59 37 13 89; fax 05 59 37 33 44. Breakfast €5.50. Reception Apr.-Sept. 9:30am-10pm; Oct.-Mar. M-F only. Singles €31; doubles €41; triples €47.40. MC/V.) A block uphill from the tourist office, opposite the old town wall, **Hôtel Itzalpea ❸,** 5 pl. du Trinquet, has ten box-like rooms, some without windows. (☎05 59 37 03 66; fax 05 59 37 33 18. Breakfast €6.10. Reception 8am-midnight. Singles and doubles with shower, TV, and telephone €35; triples and quads €45-53. MC/V.) Quiet **Camping Municipal ❶** rests against a low ivy-encrusted stone wall by the Nive, 5min. from the center of town. For its price, the campsite has the most central and convenient location of any lodging in St-Jean. From the porte St-Jacques, follow the river upstream 50m to the next bridge. When you cross the river, the site will be on your left on av. du Fronton. (☎05 59 37 11 19. Open Apr.-Oct. daily 7am-noon and 3pm-8pm. €2 per person, €1.50 per tent, €1.50 per car.)

Farmers bring *ardigazna* (tangy, dry sheep's-milk cheese) to the **market** on pl. de Gaulle. (Open M 9am-6pm.) In July and August, there are also local fairs that bring produce from all the villages nearby; ask for the dates at the tourist office. Bread, cheese and wine are all available at any one of the many small shops that line **rue d'Espagne.** For everyday food, there is the **Relais de Mousquetaires supermarket,** also on rue d'Espagne. (☎05 59 37 00 47. Open M, W, F-Sa 9:30am-12:30pm and 4-7:30pm.) None of the inexpensive restaurants in St-Jean-Pied-du-Port are spectacular, but there are several cafés and *crêperies* along the main strip past the tourist office are good for a cheap meal and refreshing sangría.

🄶🄻 SIGHTS AND ENTERTAINMENT. St-Jean's streets and mountain location make for wonderful explorations. The ancient *haute ville,* bounded by **Porte d'Espagne** and **Porte St-Jacques,** consists of one narrow street, **rue de la Citadelle,** bordered by houses made from regional crimson stone. The well-preserved remains of St-Jean-Pied-de-Port's **Citadelle de Vauban** lie at the top of narrow rue de la Citadelle, which originates in the trinket frenzy of the *haute ville.* Although the interior of this fortress is now an elementary school, visitors enjoy unlimited access to the fortified grounds. The present edifice, built by the knight Antoine Deville, dates back to 1628, but you'll also notice signs of renovations begun in 1680 by Vauban, chief military architect and planner under Louis XIV. Return to the *haute ville* by the partially concealed staircase that runs along the ramparts. It will be on your right as you complete a counter-clockwise tour of the grounds.

The staircase returns you to the steep main street, which takes you past the 13th-century **Prison des Evêques,** 41 rue de la Citadelle. Once a municipal prison, the building sat next to the medieval headquarters of local bishops. At some point, the names were combined and the "prison of the bishops" was born. The museum now documents information on the pilgrimage of St-Jacques and the game of *pelote basque.* (Open Apr.-Oct. 15 daily 10am-12:15pm and 3-6:15pm. €2.30.) Rue de la Citadelle returns you to the rear of the **Eglise Notre-Dame-du-Bout-du-Pont,** fused with the **Porte St-Jacques** on the banks of the Nive. Once a fortress, the church betrays its past with rocky, low-lit crevices instead of side chapels. Carefully patterned stained glass casts a mist of light over the rest of the simple edifice. (Open daily 7am-9pm.) A wooded walk to the left of the church along the river leads to the stone arches of the postcard-popular **Pont Romain.** (10min.)

In summer, *bals* (street dances) and concerts offer free frivolity, while Basque choirs and the Basque ballgame *pelote* add local color. (*Pelote* June-Sept. F at 5pm at the *fronton municipal* by the campground.) Thursday nights in July and August, traditional Basque folkdances are held in different locations around the town. Once on Bastille Day and once in mid-August, Basques get buff for the **Force Basque** competition, which includes gritty tug-of-war matches and the hoisting of 150-pound hay bales. Admission around €6.10, but you can peer through vines from the fence for free.

◙ **HIKE: THE PILGRIM'S ROUTE.** The Spanish border is only a four- to five-hour walk from St-Jean-Pied-de-Port along a clearly marked trail. The **GR65** leads you through the Pyrénées toward the Pass of Roncevaux and a quick 800km later to Santiago de Compostela and St. James's tomb. To get on the trail from St-Jean, take the rue d'Espagne out from the Porte de l'Eglise. Continue straight ahead as it becomes rte. de St-Michel and then rte. Napoleon. You will start to see painted red and white stripes on the telephone poles, the symbol of the GR65. The narrow paved road slopes up the mountainside, past family farms and then into the Pyrénées, where cows, sheep, and wild horses wander. The **Fontaine de Roland** and the **col de Bentarte** signal entry onto Spanish land. The round-trip hike takes about eight hours; if it becomes too late to turn back, there is lodging near the pass of Roncevaux, about a 2hr. walk past the Fontaine de Roland. **Amis du Chemin de Saint-Jacques de Pyrénées** Atlantiques, 39 rue de la citadelle, inside the old city, offers help, advice, and lodging to verified pilgrims. (☎ 05 59 37 05 09. Open March 15-Nov. daily 7:30am-8:30pm. Shelter €7 per night.)

PAU

Once the seat of the kings of Navarre, Pau (pop. 78,000) has retained little of its former grandeur. While the château of native son Henry "Edict of Nantes" VI remains in near-perfect condition, the surrounding city has begun to show some signs of wear. Thanks to the nearby Pyrénées, however, Pau benefits from good weather and close proximity to several centers of mountain sports. Pau's status as the capital of the Béarn region has also made it the capital of Béarnais cuisine—the city now holds more than 150 restaurants, each serving delicacies that 17th-century epicures agreed were the best in the kingdom.

■◙ **ORIENTATION AND PRACTICAL INFORMATION.** The **train station,** on av. Gaston Lacoste, is at the base of the hill by the château. Info open M-F 9:30am-6:40pm, Sa 9am-6pm. **Trains** go to: Bayonne (1¾hr., 7 per day, €12.50); Biarritz (2hr., 6-7 per day, €12.80); Bordeaux (2hr., 9 per day, €28.40); Lourdes (30min., 14 per day, €6.10); Paris (5hr., 8 per day, €71.10); St-Jean-de-Luz (1¾hr., 4 per day, €14.90). **CITRAM,** 30 rue Gachet (☎ 05 59 27 22 22), runs **buses** to Agen (1¾hr., 1 per day, €25). Office open M 2:30-6:15pm, Tu-F 8:40am-12:15pm and 2:30-6:15pm, Sa 8:40am-12:15pm. **Société TPR,** 2 pl. Clemenceau (☎05 59 82 95 85), heads to Bayonne (2¼hr., 2 per day, €12); Biarritz (2½hr., 2 per day, €13); Lourdes (1¼hr., 5 per day, €5.50). Office open M-F 8am-noon and 2-6pm. **STAP,** rue Gachet (☎05 59 14 15 16), runs **local buses** (tickets €0.90, *carnet* of 8 tickets, €5). For a **taxi,** call ☎05 59 02 22 22. (24hr.) **Pedegaye Cyclesport,** 3 chaussée de la Plaine, rents **bikes.** (☎05 59 77 82 30. €15.25 per day, €40 per week. Deposit €150. Open M 2-7pm, Tu-Sa 9am-noon and 2-7pm. MC/V.)

To get to the tourist office and town center from the station, ride the free **funicular** to bd. des Pyrénées (every 3min.; M-Sa 6:45am-12:10pm, 12:35-7:30pm, and 7:55-9:40pm; Su 1:30-7:30pm and 7:55-9pm), or climb the steep zigzagging path outlined in white fences to the top of the hill. At the top, the **tourist office** is at the far end of pl. Royale, across the tree-lined park from the funicular. Ask for their free map. They also have a free accommodations service, and give out copies of *Béarn Pyrénées*, with *gîtes* and camping info. (☎05 59 27 27 08; fax 05 59 27 03 21. Office open M-Sa 9am-6pm, Su 9:30am-1pm.) **Service des Gîtes Ruraux,** 20 rue Gassion, in the Cité Administrative, gives advice on mountain lodgings and makes reservations for a commission. (☎05 59 11 20 64. Open M-F 9am-12:30pm and 2-5pm.) Other services include: **police,** rue O'Quin (☎05 59 98 22 22); the **hospital,** 4 bd. Hauterive (☎05 59 92 48 48); and a **laundromat,** rue Gambetta. (Open daily 7am-10pm.) Access the **Internet** at **C Cyber,** 20 rue Lamothe, past the post office. (☎05 59 82 89 40. €0.75 per 10min. Open M-Sa 10am-2am, Su 2-11pm.) The **post office,** on cours Bosquet at rue Gambetta, has **currency exchange.** (☎05 59 98 98 98. Open M-F 8am-6:30pm, Sa 8am-noon.) **Postal code:** 64000.

⌐⌐ ACCOMMODATIONS AND FOOD. Hôtel de la Pomme d'Or ❷, 11 rue Maréchal Foch, between the post office and pl. Clemenceau, has bare, functional, but spacious rooms with wooden floors. Turn left out of the tourist office along rue Louis Barthou and left again on rue A. de-Lassence. Walk through pl. Clemenceau and turn right on rue Maréchal Foch. (☎05 59 11 23 23; fax 05 59 11 23 24. Breakfast €3.50. Reception 24hr. Singles €16, with shower €21; doubles €19/€25; triples €32/34; quads €35/38.) 3km from the train station, there's a **Logis des Jeunes** hostel ❶ outside Pau in Gelos. Take bus #1 (dir: Larrious Mazeres-Lezon) to "Mairie de Gelos." A limited number of frequently filled beds and kitchen facilities await. (☎05 59 06 53 02. No reservations; call from the train station to see if they have any vacancies. Dorms €13, HI members €8.50.) **Camping Municipal de la Plaine des Sports et des Loisirs ❶** is a 6km trek from the station. Take bus #7 from the station to pl. Clemenceau (dir: Trianon or Place Clemenceau) and switch to bus #4 (dir: Bocage Palais des Sports). Get off at the final stop. (☎05 59 02 30 49. Open May 5-Sept. 22. €3 per person, €5.50 per tent.)

The region that brought you tangy *béarnaise* sauce has no *paucity* of specialties: salmon, pike, *oie* (goose), *canard* (duck), and *assiette béarnaise*, a succulent platter that can include gizzards, duck hearts, and asparagus. The area around the château, including **rue Sully** and **rue du Château,** has elegant regional restaurants (*plats* for €9, *menus* for €16). Down the hill, the *quartier du hédas* offers more expensive fare in a fancier setting. Inexpensive pizzerias, kebab joints, and Vietnamese eateries can be found on **rue Léon Daran** and adjoining streets. The Olympic-sized **Champion supermarket** sits in the new **Centre Bosquet** megaplex on cours Bosquet. (Open M-Sa 9am-7:30pm.) The enormous **market** at **Les Halles,** pl. de la République, is a maze of vegetable, meat, and cheese stalls. (Open M-Sa 7am-1pm.) The **Marché Biologique,** pl. du Foirail, offers organic produce to the health-conscious. (Open Sa-M 7:30am-12:30pm.) Near Les Halles, the beautiful and modern **Le Saint Vincent ❷,** 4 rue Gassiot, serves €8 *moules frites* and €9 *escargots.* (☎05 59 27 75 44. Open M-Sa lunch noon-2:30pm, dinner 7-11pm. MC/V.) On a cobblestone street by the château, **Au Fruit Defondu ❸**, 3 rue Sully, serves 10 kinds of fondue—many including typical *béarnaise* fare (€9.50-€14.50). Don't forget to leave space for the divine chocolate fondue (€12.20 for two people) for dessert. (☎05 59 27 26 05. Open daily 7pm-12:30am. MC/V.)

◎� SIGHTS AND ENTERTAINMENT. Formerly the residence of *béarnais* viscounts and Navarrese kings, the 12th-century **Château d'Henri IV** is now a national museum. Glorious Gobelin tapestries, preserved royal chambers, and ornate ceilings and chandeliers grace a castle that doesn't seem to belong to any particular age—partly because Napoleon and Louis-Philippe remodeled it to suit their needs. Today, the military fortress of the 12th century seems lost among the long balconies and large windows that made life nicer for kings from the 15th century onward. Interminable-feeling French tours of the château leave every 15min. and last an hour. (☎05 59 82 38 00. Open daily 9:30am-12:15pm and 1:30-5:45pm. Last tour 1hr. before closing. English brochure available. €4.50, students €3, under 18 free.) It becomes clear that Henry IV is a local obsession when you visit the **Musée des Beaux-Arts**, on rue Mathieu Lalanne, where a marble staircase leads to an enormous tableau of his birth and then to a wall-length depiction of his 1598 coronation. The rest of this uneven museum contains a small collection of modern art and a more impressive collection of 17th- to 19th-century European paintings. (☎05 59 27 33 02. Open W-M 10am-noon and 2-6pm. €2, students €1.)

The mild climate makes Pau conducive to botanical flights of fancy, and for a good part of the year the town is covered in flowers and trees of every color and origin, from America to Japan. The best place to sample some of this biodiversity is around the pond in the **parc Beaumont.** Follow the bd. des Pyrénées away from the castle to the Palais Beaumont; the park is just behind the Palais.

Clubs in the town center cater to an older and more sedate crowd. A lively foreign bar scene illuminates the bd. des Pyrénées at night. **The Galway**, 20 bd. des Pyrénées, provides good old Irish folk music to a not-so Irish (but often Anglophone) crowd. (☎05 59 82 94 66. Pints of beer from €4. Live music on Fridays. Open July-Aug. 10am-3am, Sept.-Aug. 11am-2am.) Down the street, an Australian bar, an Irish *brasserie*, and a Russian café serve a stylish mixed crowd of youngsters and thirty-somethings. For those looking for more excitement, **Le Contretemps** has laser lights, a live DJ, and pounding techno music. (☎05 59 98 40 74. Open M-Sa 9am-2:30am; closed M nights. DJs Th-Sa.)

Cinéma le Méliès, 6 rue Bargoin, shows some artsy films, some in English. (☎05 59 27 60 52. Tickets €5.40, students €4.30. Closed Aug.) In mid-March, the **Festival d'Art e Flamenco** comes to town with an impressive array of dancers and musicians (Reservations ☎05 58 06 86 86; info at www.landes.org. Tickets €16-22, students €13-19.) Starting in mid-June, the **Festival de Pau** brings a month of theater, music, ballet, and poetry to the château courtyard and to the Théâtre St-Louis. (Reservations at the tourist office ☎05 59 27 27 08 or from FNAC ☎05 59 80 77 50.) A Formula 3 **Grand Prix de Pau** is held the weekend of Pentecost. In the first week of August, the **Festival International des Pyrénées**, 35km south of Pau in Oloron, brings in 45 folk ballet troupes from 25 countries (info and tickets ☎05 59 39 98 00 or 05 59 80 77 50). Trains and SNCF buses run to Oloron from Pau's train station (30-35min., 14 per day, €6.10).

LOURDES

In 1858, 14-year-old Bernadette Soubirous reported seeing the first of what would total 18 visions of the Virgin Mary in the Massabielle grotto in Lourdes (pop. 16,300). Over time, "The Lady" made a spring appear beneath Bernadette's fingers, told her to repent, drink, and wash in a nearby stream, and instructed her to "go

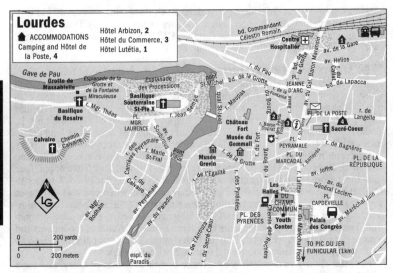

Lourdes

▲ ACCOMMODATIONS
Camping and Hôtel de la Poste, **4**

Hôtel Arbizon, **2**
Hôtel du Commerce, **3**
Hôtel Lutétia, **1**

tell the priests to build a chapel here so that people may come in procession." Bernadette may have gotten more than she bargained for. Today, over five million visitors from 100 countries come annually to this pilgrimage center, toting rosaries and hoping for miracles as they traipse to the Blessing of the Sick. But even pilgrims shouldn't miss Lourdes's secular wonders. The medieval fortress rising from the center of town and the panoramic views from the summit of nearby Pic du Jer rival any nearby city's attractions. Lourdes is also a gateway to the Pyrénées—the must-see town of Cauterets is just a 50min. bus ride away.

■ TRANSPORTATION

Trains: 33 av. de la Gare (☎05 62 42 55 53). Info office open daily 6am-8:50pm. To: **Bayonne** (2hr., 5 per day, €16.60); **Bordeaux** (3hr.; 7 per day; €26.90, TGV €28.50); **Paris** (7-9hr.; 5 per day, TGV €79.80); **Pau** (30min.; 16 per day; €6.10, TGV €7.70); **Toulouse** (2½hr., 8 per day, €19.50).

Buses: SNCF runs from the station to **Cauterets** (50min., 3-6 per day, €5.90).

Local Buses: Buses run from all points in the city to the Grotto. Buses also run to the Pic du Jer (from which the funicular departs) and to the Lac de Lourdes. Buses run about every 20min. Easter-Oct. daily 7am-6:30pm. Tickets €1.50.

Taxis: Taxi Lourdais at the train station (☎05 62 94 31 30) and grotto (☎05 62 94 31 35.) Easter-Oct.

Bike Rental: Cycles Antonio Oliveria, 14 av. Alexandre Marqui (☎05 62 42 24 24), near the train station. Open Tu-Sa 9:30am-7pm. €9.15 per half-day, €18.30 per day, €73 per week. MC/V.

■ ■ ORIENTATION AND PRACTICAL INFORMATION

The train station is on the northern edge of town, 10min. from the town center. To get from the station to the **tourist office,** turn right onto av. de la Gare, then bear left onto busy av. Maransin at the first intersection, cross a bridge above bd. du Lapacca, and proceed gently uphill. The office is in a modern glass complex on the right. (5min.) To get to the **grotto** and most other sights, follow av. de la Gare through the intersection, turn left on bd. de la Grotte, and follow it as it snakes right at pl. Jeanne d'Arc. Cross the river Gave to reach the Esplanade des Processions, the Basilique Pius X, and the grotto. (10min.)

Tourist Office: pl. Peyramale (☎05 62 42 77 40; fax 05 62 94 60 95; lourdes@sudfr.com). Friendly polyglot staff distributes maps, info on religious ceremonies, and a list of hotels. Open May-Oct. M-Sa 9am-7pm; Nov. 1-15 9am-noon and 2-7pm; Nov. 16-Mar. 15 9am-noon and 2-6pm; Mar. 16-Apr. 9am-noon and 2-7pm. Bernadette-related sights are managed by the Church-affiliated **Sanctuaires de Notre-Dame de Lourdes** (☎05 62 42 78 78), which has a **Forum d'Info** to the left, in front of the basilica. Open daily 8:30am-12:30pm and 1:30-7pm.

Youth Center: Forum Lourdes/Bureau Information Jeunesse, in pl. de Champ Commun beyond Les Halles (☎05 62 94 94 00). Open M-F 9am-noon and 2-6pm.

Laundromat: Laverie GTI, 10 av. Maransin. Dry-cleaning too. Open daily 8am-7pm.

Police: 7 rue Baron Duprat (☎05 62 42 72 72). Open daily 9am-noon and 3-8pm.

Hospital: Centre Hospitalier, 3 av. Alexandre Marqui (☎05 62 42 42 42). At the intersection of av. de la Gare, av. Marqui, and av. Maransin. **Medical emergency:** 2 av. Marqui (☎05 62 42 44 36).

Information for people with disabilities: A Catholically-inclined guide to facilities entitled *Guide de Lourdes* (€3) is available from the **Association Nationale Pour Integration Handicapés Moteurs,** on bd. du Lapacca. Call first (☎05 62 94 83 88).

Internet Access: In the social and cultural center in pl. du Champ Commun (☎05 62 94 94 00). €3 per hr. Open daily 9am-noon and 2-6pm.

Post Office: 31 av. Maransin (☎05 62 42 72 00). **Currency exchange** machine takes bills only. Open M-F 8:30am-6:30pm, Sa 8:30am-noon. **Postal code:** 65100.

ACCOMMODATIONS AND CAMPING

You should have no problem finding a room for €22 in Lourdes. Hotels of similar qualities cluster in the same neighborhoods—for cheap hotels head to rue Basse, for two star hotels head to av. de la Gare and rue Maransin. The city's massive healing industry has induced many proprietors to improve wheelchair accessibility as well as facilities for the visually and hearing impaired.

Hôtel Arbizon, 37 rue des Petits Fossés (☎/fax 05 62 94 29 36). Follow av. Helios away from the train station as it curves down the hill. Bear right and under the bridge in front of you on bd. du Lapacca. Take the first left uphill after the bridge onto rue Basse; rue des Petits Fossés is the first right. Centrally located, with small but sufficient rooms at low prices. Pleasant, welcoming owner. Breakfast €3.97. Reception 7am-midnight. Open Feb. 9-Nov. 11. Those without showers won't shower. *Demi-pension* €20.58-23.63. Singles €13.73; doubles €18.30; triples €22.87; quads €27.45. ❶

Hôtel Lutétia, 19 av. de la Gare, (☎05 62 94 22 85; fax 05 62 94 11 10; info@lutetia-lourdes.com). A mock-château near the train station. 51 clean, white, and flowered rooms with sink, table, chair and telephone are quickly filled in the summer; call ahead. Pricier rooms come with TV. Elegant restaurant on the first floor serves *menus* from €10. Elevator, free parking. Singles €17.25, with toilet €24, with shower €36, with bath €37; doubles €21.35/€28/€39/€40. MC/V. ❷

Hôtel du Commerce, 11 rue Basse (☎05 62 94 59 23; fax 05 62 94 89 56; hotel-commerce-et-navarre@wanadoo.fr). Faces the tourist office with a pizzeria on the first floor. Bright, newly renovated rooms all have showers and toilets. Rooms in back have a view of the château. Breakfast €3.80. July-Oct. 10 singles €31.20; doubles €37.40; triples €44.6. Oct.11-June Singles €27.20; doubles €32.40; triples €41.60. MC/V. ❸

AQUITAINE

Camping and Hôtel de la Poste, 26 rue de Langelle (☎05 62 94 40 35), has about 12 large spaces with grass and shade trees in a backyard 2min. beyond the post office. The campground also lets 8 pristine rooms in the attached hotel. Breakfast €4. Open Easter-Oct. 15. Hot shower €1.30. Doubles €22, with shower €25. €2.50 per person, €3.60 per site. Electricity €2.45. ❶

▐ FOOD

Find expensive groceries at **Casino supermarket,** 9 pl. Peyramale (☎05 62 94 03 87; open Tu-F 8:30am-1pm and 3:30-8pm, Sa 8:30am-1pm and 3-8pm, Su 8am-1pm), or at the bigger **Prisunic supermarket,** 9 pl. du Champ Commun. (☎05 62 94 63 44. Open M-Sa 8:30am-12:30pm and 2-7:30pm, Su 8am-noon.) Produce, flowers, second-hand clothing, books, and cheap pizza are all sold daily at the **market** at **Les Halles,** pl. du Champ Commun. (Open daily 8am-1pm, every other Th until 5pm.)

Restaurants not affiliated with hotels are few and far between in Lourdes. On the main strip of the **bd. de la Grotte,** many similar restaurants charge similar prices for similar meals. The meal, surrounded by religious souvenir shops selling Virgin Mary water bottles and toothbrushes, will cost from €10-15. Slightly lower priced *plats du jour* and *menus* can be found around the tourist office and on **rue de la Fontaine;** don't expect gourmet fare.

◉ SIGHTS

Passeport Visa Lourdes (€30, children €16) provides access to all seven activities: admission to four Bernadette-related museums, the Fortified Castle and its museum, the funicular to Pic du Jer, and a tourist train ride through town. Ask for details at the tourist office. **Carte Lourdes Pass,** free at the tourist office, gives entrance to two of the same activities after you visit the five others.

GROTTE DE MASSABIELLE. It was in this cavern at the edge of town that the Virgin Mary appeared to Bernadette. Visitors to Lourdes come for even just a glimpse of these holy rocks and the spring that flows beneath. In the afternoon rush, hundreds shuffle past this small dark crevice in the mountainside, touching its cold rock walls, whispering prayers, and waiting to receive a blessing from the priest on duty. Nearby, water from the spring where Bernadette washed her face is available for drinking, bathing, and bringing back home. The cave lies by the river on the right side of two superimposed churches, the Basilique du Rosaire and the upper basilica. *(No shorts, tank tops, or food. Fountain and grotto open daily 5am-midnight.)*

THE BASILICAS. The **Basilique du Rosaire** and **upper basilica** were built double-decker style above Bernadette's grotto. In the **Rosaire,** completed in 1889, an enormous Virgin Mary strikes a maternal pose. The **upper basilica,** consecrated in 1876 has a more traditional interior. If you're looking for **the Basilique St-Pius X,** you're probably standing on it. It's underground, in front of the other two basilicas and to the left of the Esplanade des Processions—a stadium-sized concrete echo chamber designed in the form of an upturned ship. It won an international design prize in 1958, despite closely resembling the parking garage of the Starship Enterprise. Covering 12,000 square meters, its concrete cavern fits 20,000 souls with room to spare. Super-electric stained-glass rectangles are placed at 10m intervals. *(All 3 open Easter-Oct. daily 6am-7pm; Nov.-Easter 8am-6pm, excluding masses at 11am and 5pm.)*

PROCESSIONS AND BLESSINGS. The **Procession of the Blessed Sacrament** and the **Blessing of the Sick** are huge affairs held daily at 5pm, starting in the Basilica St-Pius X; fight for bench space or watch from the upper basilica's balcony. As a one-day pilgrim, you can join the procession and march along the esplanade behind rolling ranks of wheelchairs. *(Meet other pilgrims July-Sept. at 8:30am at the "Crowned Virgin" statue in front of the basilica.)* A solemn **torchlit procession** in six languages blazes from the grotto to the esplanade nightly at 8:45pm. Light a candle, available for a few euros in booths by the river Gave. *(Mass in English Apr.-Oct. daily at 9am at the Hémicycle, just across the river from the cave in a cavernous concrete building.)*

MUSEUMS. The **Musée de Gemmail** reproduces famous works of art in the thick multi-layered stained-glass technique that gives the museum its name. If you like stained glass, check out the equally large annex near the pont St-Michel. *(72 rue de la Grotte. ☎ 05 62 94 13 15. Open Apr.-Oct. daily 9-11:45am and 2-6:45pm. Annex on bd. Père Rémi Sempe. Free.)* Down the street, the **Musée Grevin** is as close as you'll ever get to a Catholic Disneyland. 100 uncannily real figures act out the lives of Bernadette and Jesus. Most impressive is the life-size replica of Leonardo da Vinci's *Last Supper*. *(87 rue de la Grotte. ☎ 05 62 94 33 74. Open July-Aug. daily 9-11:30am, 1:30-6:30pm, and 8:30-10pm; Apr.-June and Sept.-Oct. 9-11:30am and 1:30-6:30pm. €5.50, students €2.70.)*

CHÂTEAU FORT. Practically the only sight in town without a religious connection, the feudal castle overlooks Lourdes from atop a rocky crag. A shuttlecock in territorial disputes between France and England during the Middle Ages, the current building dates principally from the 14th century. The high square tower and well-preserved walls of the château now offer unequaled panoramas of surrounding Lourdes, and guard the strange displays of the **Musée Pyrénéen.** The museum displays a series of regional objects including wine barrels, decorated plates, and butter churns. *(☎ 05 62 42 37 37. Enter by elevator. Open Apr. 15-Oct. 15 M-Sa 9am-noon and 1:30-6:30pm, Su 11am-6pm; Oct. 16-Apr. W-M 9am-noon and 2-6pm. €5.)*

FUNICULAIRE. From just outside of town, a track climbs 1000m up the **Pic du Jer.** Local buses lead to the bottom of the track. Take this six-minute ride and walk the extra way (10min.) up to the observatory at the summit for a stunning 360° view of the surrounding countryside and the town below. More energetic folk can hike up or down with a map available from the ticket booth. Beware of rapidly descending mountain bikers. *(☎ 05 62 94 00 41. Daily every 30min. 10am-6pm. €7.50, children €5.50. Depot on the southern edge of town, at the base of the mountain. Follow the main road (rue St-Pierre at first) 2km from the center of town by the tourist office. There's also a bus from the ticket booth at the intersection of rue de la Grotte and rue de la Tour de Brie. Round-trip bus ticket €3.)*

LAC DE LOURDES. Local bus #7 (July-Aug. 4 per day 8:25am-6:30pm; Sept.-June less frequently) runs to a large, peaceful lake 4km from the center of town, where locals flip off the dock or eat ice cream in the slightly overpriced waterside café. A blessed relief from the hectic town, the lake makes for a good follow-up to morning visits to the grotto and sanctuaries. By foot, take av. Maransin toward the train station and turn left on the bd. Romain. The street becomes av. Béguere and then rte. de Pontacq. Take a left on the chemin du Lac and you'll hit the water. (30min.)

THE WESTERN PYRÉNÉES

CAUTERETS

The people of tiny Cauterets (pop. 1300) seem friendlier than anywhere else in France. The explanation lies either in the sugared vapors of *berlingots* coming from the candy stores or simply in the soothing influence of the town's location. Nestled 930m up in a narrow, breathtaking valley among near-vertical peaks, sleepy Cauterets wakes up in May and June to the sounds of a turquoise river rushing beneath its bridges. The melting snows of early summer bring wilderness lovers here, to the edge of the Parc National des Pyrénées Occidentales. For serious hikers, the wildly contrasting French and Spanish sides of the Pyrénées are both accessible from Cauterets, but there are also several day hikes ranging from one and a half to eight hours. When hiking becomes overly taxing, the *thermes* offer a relaxation program of *remise en forme* to bring you back to your former self.

ORIENTATION AND PRACTICAL INFORMATION. Cauterets runs lengthwise along the river Gave and is small enough to walk across in three minutes. It is accessible only by bus from Lourdes. From the bus station, turn right and follow av. Général Leclerc up a steep hill to the tourist office at pl. Foch. **SNCF buses** (☎05 62 92 53 70) run from pl. de la Gare to Lourdes (1hr.; 6 per day; €5.90, students €4.60). Office open daily 9am-12:30pm and 3-7pm. You can rent **bikes**, as well as inline skates and ice skates, at **Skilys**, rte. de Pierrefitte, on pl. de la Gare. (☎05 62 92 52 10. Mountain bikes with guide €17-30 per half-day, €38-54 per day, €230-380 deposit; without guide €9.15 per half-day, €15.25 per day, ID deposit. Open daily 9am-7pm; in winter 8am-7:30pm. AmEx/MC/V.) **Bernard Sports-tifs**, 2 rue Richelieu, next to the tourist office, offers good prices on **alpine ski rentals** and discounts for American students. (☎05 62 92 06 23. €10.80-15.25 per day for boots, skis, and poles; €58-82 for six days.)

The **tourist office**, pl. Foch, has a list of hotels, a useful map, and a *Guide Pratique*. (☎05 62 92 50 27; fax 05 62 92 59 12; www.cauterets.com. Open July-Aug. daily 9am-12:30pm and 1:30pm-7pm; Sept.-June 9am-12:30pm and 2-6:30pm.) For hiking info, drop by the **Parc National des Pyrénées** office at pl. de la Gare. The **police** are on av. du Docteur Domer (☎05 62 92 51 13). For **medical emergencies**, call ☎05 62 92 14 00. Access the **Internet** at **Pizzeria Giovanni**, 5 rue de la Raillère (☎05 62 92 57 80; open July-Aug. daily noon-3pm and 7-11pm, Sept.-June Th-Su only), or at the basement of the public library, 2 esplanade des Oeufs. (☎05 62 92 52 45; www.infos@planeticj.com. €5 per hr. Open Tu-Sa 2-7pm.) The **post office**, at the corner of rue Belfort and rue des Combattants, has **currency exchange.** (☎05 62 92 53 93; fax 05 62 92 08 83. Open July-Sept. 12 M-F 9am-6pm, Sa 9am-noon; Sept. 13-June M-F 9am-noon and 2-5pm, Sa 9am-noon.) **Postal code:** 65110.

ACCOMMODATIONS, CAMPING, AND FOOD. For the real mountain traveler, the best accommodations in town are at the **Gîte d'Etape UCJG ❶**, av. du Docteur Domer, close to the center of town (200m). From the Parc National office, cross the parking lot and street and turn left uphill underneath the funicular depot. The *gîte* is just beyond the tennis courts. Gloriously located with welcoming hosts, this *gîte* has 60 beds in every sort of set-up, from a canvas barracks to the eaves of an attic, as well as leafy campsites. (☎05 62 92 52 95. Kitchen, shower, and sheets included. Reception daily, but hours vary. Open June 15-Sept. 15. Dorms €8; €6.50 for space in the *gîte*'s tent; €3.50 per bring-your-own tent; bed in bungalow €8.50.) **Hôtel Christian ❸**, 10 rue Richelieu, offers a view of the Pyrénées, darts, and *bocce* for somewhat high prices. Make sure to talk to the incredibly gracious owner, whose family has run the hotel for generations. Cheaper rooms on the top floor are smaller and darker than the others. Reception 7:30am-10pm. (☎05 62 92 50 04; fax 05 62 92 05 67; www.hotel-christian.fr. Breakfast included. Closed Oct. 10-Dec. 20. Singles €31.50, with shower €35.70, with TV €40.80; doubles €37.50/€44.50/€51.80; triples with shower and TV €67.50; quads with shower and TV €82. MC/V.) Every room at **Hôtel Bigorre ❷**, 15 rue de Belfort, has a balcony that looks out on the surrounding mountains. The rooms are spacious, but some have peeling wallpaper and cracking paint. Rue de Belfort runs between pl. de la Gare and pl. Foch (near the tourist office). (☎05 62 92 52 81; www.bigorrehotel.com; infos@bigorrehotel.com. Open May 20-Nov. 5; rest of year on weekends and school holidays. Breakfast included. Reception 7:30am-10pm. Singles €19.80, with shower €27.50; doubles €31.10/€39.70; triples or quads €43.80-61.10.)

The beautifully old-fashioned **Halles market,** a few doors down from the tourist office on av. du Général Leclerc, has fresh produce. (Open daily 2-8pm.) An **open-air market** is held in the parking lot at pl. de la Gare (June 15-mid Oct. F 8am-5pm). The local specialty is the *berlingot,* a hard sugar candy originally used by patients visiting the *thermes* to contribute to "the cure." You can watch 35 flavors of the candies being prepared by hand and cranked through a magical candy-making machine at **A la Reine Margot,** pl. de la Mairie Crown. (€1.40-1.55 per 100g. Open daily 10am-midnight.) The husband and wife team at **Chez Gillou,** 3 rue de la Raillère, specialize in blueberry and almond cakes known respectively as *tourtes myrtilles* and *pastis des Pyrénées.* (☎05 62 92 56 58. Cakes €5.40 each. Open July-Aug. and Feb.-Mar. daily 7am-1pm and 3:30-7:30pm; Sept., Dec., and Apr.-June Th-Tu 7:30am-12:30pm and 3-7pm.) Get regional jam (€2.90-5.80), *pâté,* Basque cider, and cheap quiche with local flavorings just up the street at **Au Mille Pâtes,** 5 rue de la Raillère. (☎05 62 92 04 83. Open daily 8am-12:30pm and 4-7:30pm.)

◼ **SIGHTS.** From av. du Docteur Domer, the **Téléphérique du Lys** cable car (☎05 62 92 03 59) races above the clouds every half-hour into the nearby mountains. From here, trails lead across the ridge and eventually to the breathtaking Lac d'Ilhéou. (1½hr.) In July and August and ski season, the **Télésiege du Grand Barbat** chairlift takes you onto the **Crête du Lys,** over 1000m above Cauterets. (€9 round-trip, €5 one-way to Crête du Lys.) You can hike back down from **Crête du Lys,** on a medium difficulty track, passing Lac d'Ilhéou on the way. (1½hr.)

Cauterets's natural sulfur springs have been credited over the years with curing everything from sterility to consumption. But it's no bubble bath—the doctors and nurses here have taken to heart the maxim of "no pain, no gain." Separate steril-ized rooms each offer different contraptions for "enjoying" the full effects of the water. You'll be given protective plastic covering for your shoes if you want to see the inhalation chambers and hosing rooms. The *thermes* also offer a relaxing pro-gram of massage for those who don't have what it takes to undergo the full process. For info on the *thermes,* contact **Thermes de Cesar,** av. Docteur Domer. (☎05 62 92 51 60. Aerobath-sauna-hydrojet pool €21.50, hydromassage jet showers €29. Open M-F 9am-12:30pm and 1:30-6pm, Sa 9am-12:30pm and 3-6pm.)

🎵 **ENTERTAINMENT.** Esplanade des Oeufs offers a casual **cinema** (☎05 62 92 52 14) playing French and foreign films (the latter are mostly popular American imports in their original language) and a **casino.** (☎05 62 92 52 14. Open May-Oct. daily 11am-3am.) The **patinoire** (skating rink) hosts skating nights year-round, mostly near the end of the week, according to an complicated schedule given out by the tourist office. The rink itself can be reached through the parking lot of the train station. (€5.50, children €3; skate rental €2.50.)

CURATIVE POWER Taking "the cure" in hot sulfur springs was done not for pleasure but for health, and the doctors who presided over the proceedings in the 19th century did little to make it easier. The cure included everything from having your sinuses cleaned with small brushes to taking the water up through the nose and expelling it out the mouth. Around the 1840s, some doctors decided that the healing process was helped along if the patient held a morsel of sugar in the mouth while gar-gling the hot water. The change stuck around, mostly as a way to make the cure more bearable, and France's *thermes* were surrounded by *confiseries,* turning out the hard sugar candies known as *berlingots.* The *thermes* have since refined their techniques so that the *berlingot* is no longer a necessary component, but the candies are now savored by many as a "cure" in their own right.

AQUITAINE

PARC NATIONAL DES PYRÉNÉES OCCIDENTALES

One of France's seven national parks, the **Parc National des Pyrénées** houses endangered brown bears and lynxes, 200 threatened colonies of marmots, 118 lakes, and 160 unique plant species in its snow-capped mountains and lush valleys. Punctuated with sulfurous springs and unattainable peaks, the Pyrénées change dramatically with the seasons, never failing to awe a constant stream of visitors. To get a full sense of the extent and variety of the mountain range, you really have to experience both the lush French and barren Spanish sides of the Pyrénées (a 6- to 7-day round trip hike from Cauterets). But there are plenty of more modest opportunities as well, in case you're just looking to get your feet wet in the wilderness.

AT A GLANCE

AREA: Narrow 100km-long swath along the Franco-Spanish border

CLIMATE: Misty in France, arid in Spain

GATEWAYS: Gavarnie (**p. 431**); Luz-St-Sauveur (**p. 431**); Ainsa, Spain (**p. 431**)

DAY HIKES: Turquoise Lac de Gaube (3.5hr. from Cauterets), the Chemin des Cascades (4hr. from Cauterets)

LONG HIKES: Cirque de Gavarnie, passing through waterfalls and lush forests (4-day hike from Cauterets), or continue on into Spain (6-7days from Cauterets)

ACCOMMODATIONS: *Gites* (around €11) are available in towns along the GR10; One-night camping permitted in areas at least an hour away from major highways

🛈 PRACTICAL INFORMATION AND SERVICES. Touch base with the friendly and very helpful staff of **Parc National Office**, Maison du Parc, pl. de la Gare, before braving the wilderness. They have free info on the park and 14 different trails beginning and ending in Cauterets. The trails in the park are designed for a range of aptitudes, from novices to rugged outdoor enthusiasts. The **Haute Randonnée Pyrénées (HRP)** trails offer a more challenging mountain experience. Talk with the folks at the Parc National Office before attempting them. Documentary films (in French) featuring aerial views of the local mountains, showing two to three times a week, can advise you on hikes. (☎05 62 92 52 56; fax 05 62 92 62 23; www.parc-pyrenees.com. €3.80, children and students €1.50. Open June-Aug. daily 9:30am-noon and 3-7pm; Sept.-May M-Tu and F-Su 9:30am-12:30pm and 3-6pm, Th 3-6pm.)

The **maps** sold at the Parc National office are probably sufficient. (Regional maps €6.40, day-hike maps €8.85.) For the Cauterets region, use the #1647 Vignemale map published by the Institut de Géographie Nationale. The **Bureau des Guides**, on tiny rue Verdun in Cauterets, runs tours and guides for rock-climbing, canyoning, hiking, and skiing. Medium-difficulty tours are €14-30.50 per person; harder ones €46-140. Tours leave from the Cauterets tourist office. (Summer ☎05 62 92 62 02, winter 05 62 92 55 06. Open daily 10am-12:30pm and 3:30-7:30pm.)

Gites in the park average €11 a night and are strategically placed in towns along the GR10. Reserve at least 2 days ahead, especially in July and August, when the mountains flood with hikers. The Parc National office in Cauterets will help you plan an itinerary while the **Service des Gites Ruraux** (☎05 59 80 19 13) in Pau will make *gite* reservations for you. The general rule is that you can camp anywhere in the wilderness for one night, provided you are more than an hour's hike from the nearest highway. Long-term camping in one place is not allowed. You can find a camp zone near a *refuge* if you want to stay in one place for a couple of days. Listen to **Météo-Montagne** for a weather forecast in French for nearby mountains (☎08 36 68 02 65; updated twice daily). For **Mountain Rescue**, call ☎05 62 92 41 41.

SKIING. The Cauterets tourist office has free *plans des pistes* (maps of ski paths for all skill levels). Many area resorts are accessible by **SNCF bus** from Cauterets or Lourdes. **Luz-Ardiden** offers downhill and cross-country skiing. (☎ 05 62 92 30 30; fax 05 62 92 87 19. €20.60, student reductions available.) Farther away are **Barèges** (☎ 05 62 92 16 01) and **La Mongie** (☎ 05 62 95 81 81), which offer joint tickets for €23.50 per day.

HIKING. The **GR10** meanders across the Pyrénées, connecting the Atlantic with the Mediterranean and looping through most major towns. Both major and minor hikes intersect with and run along it; for either level of trail, pick up one of the purple maps at the park office (€8.85). The most spectacular local hikes begin at the **Pont d'Espagne** (a 2½hr. walk or 20min. drive from Cauterets). Several **buses** run daily in July and August (every 2hr. 8am-6pm, €3.50, round-trip €5); inquire at **Bordenave Excursions** (☎ 05 62 92 53 68). The rest of the year, call a **taxi.** (☎ 06 12 91 83 19. Around €17.) One of the most spectacular and popular trails follows the GR10 to the turquoise **Lac de Gaube** (1hr.) and then to the end of the stony glacial valley (2hr. past the lake) where you can spend the night 2km in the air at **Refuge des Oulettes ❶.** (☎ 05 62 92 62 97. Open June-Sept. €12.50, €30.50.) A greener hike lies one valley over along the **Vallée du Marcadau,** which also offers shelter at the **Refuge Wallon Marcadau ❶.** (☎ 05 62 92 64 28. Open June-Sept. 15. Breakfast €2.29. €12.50, *demi-pension* €31.84.) Both hikes are popular as daytrips. In May or June, when the melting snow swells the streams, the **Chemin des Cascades** (waterfall trail), which leads from the Pont d'Espagne to La Raillère, is sensational. The 4hr. round-trip from Cauterets is a good, short hike—if you lose the path, keep the river on your left as you go up. The **Circuit des Lacs** is a marathon eight-hour hike that includes the Vallée du Marcadau as well as three beautiful mountain lakes.

THE CIRCUIT DE GAVARNIE. From Cauterets, the GR10 connects to Luz-St-Sauveur over the mountain and then on to Gavarnie, another day's hike up the valley; the round-trip from Cauterets to Gavarnie and back is known as the **"circuit de Gavarnie."** These towns are also accessible by **SNCF bus** (6 per day from Cauterets to Luz, 1hr., €5.90; 2 per day from Luz to Gavarnie, €5.30). The Luz tourist office is at pl. du 8 Mai 45. (☎ 05 62 92 30 30.) Circling counter-clockwise from Cauterets to Luz-St-Sauveur, the **Refuge Des Oulettes ❶** (see above) is the first shelter past the Lac de Gaube. Dipping into the Vallée Lutour, the **Refuge Estom ❶** rests peacefully near Lac d'Estom. (Summer ☎ 05 62 92 72 93, winter ☎ 05 62 92 75 07. €8.50 per night, *demi-pension* €26.) The **Refuge Jan Da Lo ❶** in Gavarnie, near the halfway mark of the loop. (☎ 05 62 92 40 66. €8.33 per night, €22.11 for *demi pension.*) From Gavarnie, you can hop on a horse offered by the refuge (€15 round-trip) for a two-hour trek to the grandiose, snow-covered **Cirque de Gavarnie** and its misty waterfall. During the third week in July, the **Festival des Pyrénées** animates the foot of the Cirque. Nightly performances begin as the sun sets over the mountains; afterwards, torches are distributed to light the way back to the village. (Tickets available from the tourist office in Gavarnie. €20, students under 25 €17.)

INTO SPAIN AND BACK. To get a full sense of the diversity of these mountains, you must experience both the Spanish and French sides of the range. The desiccated red rock of the Spanish side and the misty forests of the French side are accessible in a six- to seven-day hike from Cauterets. Confer with the tourist office in Ainsa, Spain (☎ 34 974 50 07 07), for reservations at the Spanish *refuges* before attempting this trek. A one- to two-day hike from Pont d'Espagne will take you up and over the Spanish border. Descend the far side of the Pyrénées to the village of Torla where you can hop on one of the buses to the *refuge de Goriz* (call ahead to reserve ☎ 34 974 34 12 01). A magnificent hike to **Brèche de Roland,** with its snow-capped mountain peaks, perched on the edge of the cirque de Gavarnie, will start your return to France the following day. You can cut your hike short here at four to five days and take a bus back from Gavarnie to Luz and then to Cauterets; otherwise, it's another rewarding two-day trek back to Cauterets. Climb from the Vallée d'Ossoue to camp among the clouds of the *Refuge de Bayssellance* in view of mount Montferrat, before returning to Cauterets along the Vallée de Lutour.

LUCHON

More grandiose and cosmopolitan than other Pyrenean mountain towns, Luchon (pop. 2900) has attracted the rich and famous to its celebrated *thermes* for over two centuries. The baths are the town's main attraction, and the number of senior citizens in the tourist population is correspondingly large. But you'll also find women in Chanel and cigarette-toting teenagers on the boulevards, all enjoying the same serene atmosphere. Hikers will appreciate that the numerous trails in the surrounding mountains are less crowded than those of the Parc National. A *télé-cabine* (gondola) ferries skiers and hikers from the town center to Superbagnères.

■ ▚ **ORIENTATION AND PRACTICAL INFORMATION.** The **train station**, av. de Toulouse, runs **trains** and **SNCF buses** to Montréjeau (50min., 4-5 per day, €5.60), from which you can connect to Bayonne, Paris, St-Gaudens, Toulouse, and other cities. Trains also run directly to Toulouse (2hr., 1-2 per day, €16). Info office open daily M-F 6am-8:15pm, Sa-Su 6am-9pm.

From the station, turn left on av. de Toulouse and then bear right at the fork to follow av. M. Foch. At the lions, cross the rotary and bear left, following signs for the *centre ville*. You will arrive at the main **allée d'Etigny**, which unfolds to your left. A few blocks down on the right is the **tourist office**, 18 allée d'Etigny, which offers lists of nearby hikes and mountain biking trails and a map of the town. (☎05 61 79 21 21; fax 05 61 79 11 23; www.luchon.com. Open M-F 9am-noon and 1:30-7pm, Sa-Su 9am-7pm.) For ambitious outdoor experiences, check in at the **Bureau des Guides,** next to the tourist office, which has info on biking, hiking, rock climbing, and canyon hiking nearby and in Spain. Guided hikes run around €137 per day for a group of 12; canyoning and climbing €228. (☎05 61 79 69 38; bureaudes-guides@free.fr. Open July-Sept. daily 10am-noon and 3-7pm; May-June M-Sa 10am-noon and 3-6pm.) Other town services include a **laundromat,** 66 av. M. Foch (open daily 8am-8pm); **police,** at the Hôtel de Ville (☎05 61 94 68 81); the **medical emergency center,** 5 cours de Quinconces (☎05 61 79 93 00); and **Internet access** at the **post office,** located on the corner of allée d'Etigny and av. Gallieni. (☎05 61 94 74 50. Open M-F 8:45am-noon and 2-5:45pm, Sa 8:45am-noon.) **Postal code:** 31110.

■ ▚ **ACCOMMODATIONS AND FOOD.** The closest *gîte*, **Gîte Skioura ❶,** is 3km uphill from the tourist office en route to Superbagnères. If you call ahead, they might pick you up. Otherwise, follow cours des Quinconces out of town and up the mountain. During the week, it's more convenient to catch the *car thermal* from the train station allée d'Etigny to the *thermes* and get off at the camping stop (15min., free). Five large rooms contain 40 beds and a fireplace big enough to heat a castle. Some privacy is afforded by cloth partitions between every two beds. During the high season, the *gîte* is dominated by groups. (☎05 61 79 60 59 or 06 81 34 76 10. Breakfast €3.95. Sheets €2.50. Open all year. Dorms €12.85.) **La Demeure de Venasque ❶,** 2km up the road from Gîte Skioura, offers more homey dorm accommodations in a large house in the middle of an open field along with every kind of facility, including a basketball court, foosball, and a music room. (☎05 61 94 31 96; fax 05 61 94 31 96. Breakfast €3.95. Dorms €11.) Across from the train station, the **Hôtel du Baliran ❸,** 1 av. de Toulouse, has first-rate rooms and ornate tiles in modern bathrooms. (☎ 05 61 79 27 95 or 06 15 41 22 40; fax 05 61 94 31 64. Breakfast €5. Reception 24hr. Singles and doubles with shower €30; triples €36; quads €50. MC/V.) There's a **Casino supermarket** at 45 av. M. Foch on the way from the train station. (Open M-Sa 8:30am-12:30pm and 3-7:30pm.) Inexpensive €8-12 *menus* can be found at any of the nondescript *brasseries* that line **allée d'Etigny.**

◪◪ SIGHTS AND HIKES. The tourist office can tell you about hiking paths (1-2½hr.) and mountain bike trails that leave from the **Parc Thermal,** just behind the *thermes* at the end of allées d'Etigny on Superbagnères. The **Altiservice** runs a **télé-cabine** transporting hikers and bikers to the top of Superbagnères. (05 61 79 97 00. One-way €4.60, round-trip €7. Open Apr.-Sept. Sa-Su 1:30-5pm; July-Aug. daily 9:45am-12:15pm and 1:30-6pm; ski season daily 8:45am-6pm.) The tourist office has two free hiking and biking maps that show the way back down. Also see the Bureau des Guides (above). Treat yourself to a soak in the **thermes,** housed in the appropriately lavish white marble building at the end of allées d'Etigny. 12 euros buys access to the 32°C pool and the **Vaporarium,** a natural underground sauna unique to Europe. For this and other programs, inquire at **Vitaline,** 66 allée d'Etigny. Tours of the adjacent 18th-century *thermes* leave June-Sept. Tu at 2pm. (Reservations and info ☎ 05 61 79 22 97; fax 05 61 79 72 41; www.luchon.com. €3.10, children €1.60. Open mid-Dec. to mid-Oct. daily 4-7pm.)

AQUITAINE

LANGUEDOC-ROUSSILLON

An immense region called Occitania once stretched from the Rhône valley to the foothills of the Pyrénées. Its people spoke the *langue d'oc*, a Romance language whose name comes from their word for "yes." While independent of France and Spain, the area was a fiefdom of the Count of Toulouse. In the mid-12th century, Occitania's nobles and peasants alike adopted the heretical Cathar brand of Christianity. Disturbed by the loss of Occitan believers—and revenues—the Church launched the Albigensian Crusade (named for the Cathar stronghold of Albi) against the "heretics"; the slaughter that followed resulted in Occitania's political and linguistic integration into France. Up to the Revolution, most of the population clung to their old language, but by the late 19th century it had all but died out. Roussillon, in the far southwest corner, was historically separated from France as a part of Catalonia—Perpignan even served as the capital of the Kings of Majorca. Today, Roussillon's cultural links across the Spanish border remain strong, and locals identify with Barcelona more than with Paris. Many here speak Catalan, a relative of the *langue d'oc* which sounds like a hybrid of French and Spanish.

TOULOUSE

Just when all French towns start to look alike, you discover Toulouse, or *la ville en rose* (the city in pink). The city's magnificent buildings, from the stately homes of 16th-century pastel merchants to the striped Capitole, are built of local rose-colored bricks, a distinctive shade lighter than the red ones of Albi and less ochre-tinged than those of Montauban. Many of them are trimmed with white marble, giving Toulouse a grandeur befitting the 4th-largest city (pop. 350,000) in France. Politically, Toulouse has always been a free-thinking, headstrong place. Its powerful counts made life miserable for French kings in the Middle Ages, and it wasn't until the Revolution that France finally got a firm grip on the *capitouls* (town

councillors) of its unique 12th-century government. Still pushing the frontiers of knowledge, this university town, where Thomas Aquinas made Aristotle palatable to medieval theologians, now serves as the capital of France's aerospace industry. During the school year, 100,000 students flood the pizzerias of rue du Taur, the city's countless museums, and the quays of the Garonne.

◤ TRANSPORTATION

Flights: Aéroport Blagnac (☎05 61 42 44 00). **Air France** (☎08 02 80 28 02) flies to **London** (2 per day, from €210 round-trip) and **Paris** (25 per day, from €115 round-trip). **Navettes Aérocar** (☎05 34 60 64 00; www.navettevia-toulouse.com) serves the airport from the bus station and allée Jean Jaurès (30min., every 20min.; €3.70, under 25 €2.90.)

Trains: Gare Matabiau, 64 bd. Pierre Sémard. To: **Bordeaux** (2-3hr., 14 per day, €26.10); **Lyon** (6½hr., 3-4 per day, €48); **Marseille** (4½hr., 8 per day, €38.50); **Paris** (8-9hr., 4 per day, €70.60); **Perpignan** (2½hr., 6 per day, €23.20). Tickets M-Sa 9am-7:30pm.

Buses: Gare Routière, 68-70 bd. Pierre Sémard (☎05 61 61 67 67), next to the train station. Open M-Sa 7am-7pm and Su 8am-7pm. To: **Albi** (1½hr., 4 per day, €11.20); **Carcassonne** (2¼hr., €10.60); **Foix** (2hr., 1 per day, €8.90); **Montauban** (70min., 4 per day, €6.50). Buy tickets on the bus. **Eurolines** (☎05 61 26 40 04; www.eurolines.fr) with an office in the station, runs buses to most major cities in Europe. Open M-F 9:30am-6:30pm, Sa 9:30am-5pm. Prices shift around, but there are usually worthwhile package deals to big traveler destinations. To: **Berlin** (3¼hr., F and Su 1 per day, €162); **Brussels** (21hr.; Tu-W, F, Su 2 per day; €119); **London** (20hr.; Tu-W, F, Su €135); **Barcelona** (6hr., M-Sa 1-2 a day, €56-88); **Casablanca** (32hr., W and Sa 1 per day, €210); **Amsterdam** (20½hr., Tu-W and F-Su 1 per day, €133); **Prague** (24hr., F and Su 1 per day, €137).

Metro: SEMVAT, 49 rue de Gironis (☎05 61 41 70 70 or 05 62 11 26 11). Buy tickets just inside the stations (€1.20 per ticket). Maps at ticket booths and tourist office. Open daily 8am-midnight.

Taxis: Taxi Bleu (☎05 61 80 36 36). Between the train and bus station. €16-20 to the airport. 24hr.

✦ 🛈 ORIENTATION AND PRACTICAL INFORMATION

Toulouse sprawls on both sides of the Garonne, but the museums and sights are mostly within a small section east of the river, bounded by rue de Metz in the south and by bd. Strasbourg and bd. Carnot to the north and east. The métro is useful for reaching your hotel from the train station, but after you've dropped off your pack, there should be no need to venture underground again. Even the walk from the train station to the main part of town takes only about 15 minutes. The center is the huge stone plaza known as the Capitole.

Tourist Office: Donjon du Capitole, rue Lafayette, sq. Charles de Gaulle (☎05 61 11 02 22; fax 05 61 22 03 63; www.ot.toulouse.fr; infos@ot.toulouse.fr), in the park behind the Capitole. From the station, take the *métro* to Capitole or turn left along the canal and then right onto allée Jean Jaurès. Walk two thirds of the way around pl. Wilson (bearing right), then take a right onto rue Lafayette. The office is in a small park on the left of the intersection with rue d'Alsace-Lorraine. Free **accommodations service.** City tours in English (July-Sept. Sa at 3pm, €7.70; in French M-F 3 per day). Office open June-Sept. M-Sa 9am-7pm, Su 10am-1pm and 2-6pm; Oct.-May M-F 9am-6pm, Sa 9am-12:30pm and 2-6pm, Su and holidays 10am-12:30pm and 2-5pm.

Budget Travel: OTU Voyage, 60 rue de Taur (☎05 61 12 54 54). Cheap fares for students. Open M-F 9am-6:30pm, Sa 10am-1pm and 2-5pm. **Nouvelles Frontières,** 2 pl. St-Sernin (☎05 61 21 74 14, national 08 25 00 08 25), has cheap flights for all. Open M-Sa 9am-7pm. MC/V.

Consulates: UK, c/o Lucas Aerospace, Immeuble Victoria Center, Bâtiment Didier Daurat, 20 chemin de Laporte (☎05 61 15 02 02). Open M-Tu and Th-F 10am-noon and 2-5pm. **US,** 25 allées Jean Jaurès (☎05 34 41 36 50).

Currency Exchange: Banque de France, 4 rue Deville (☎05 61 61 35 35). No commission, good rates. Open M-F 9am-12:20pm and 1:20-3:30pm.

English Bookstore: The Bookshop, 17 rue Lakanal (☎05 61 22 99 92). Extensive number of novels, French history books, and travel guides. Open M-Sa 10am-7pm. MC/V.

Youth Center: CRIJ (Centre Regional d'Info Jeunesse), 17 rue de Metz (☎05 61 21 20 20). Info on travel, work, and study. Open July 13-Sept. 16 M-Sa 10am-6pm; Sept. 17-July 12 M-Sa 10am-1pm and 2-7pm.

Laundromat: Laverie St-Sernin, 14 rue Emile Cartailhac. Open daily 7am-10pm.

Hospital: CHR de Rangueil, chemin de Vallon (☎05 61 32 25 33).

Police: Commissariat Central, bd. Embouchure (☎05 61 12 77 77).

Internet Access: Espace Wilson Multimédia, 7 allée du Président Roosevelt, at pl. Wilson (☎05 62 30 28 10). €3.05 per hr. Open M-F 10am-7pm, Sa 10am-6pm. Reserve ahead if possible. **Adéclik,** 5 pl. St-Pierre (☎05 61 22 56 48). €2 per hr.

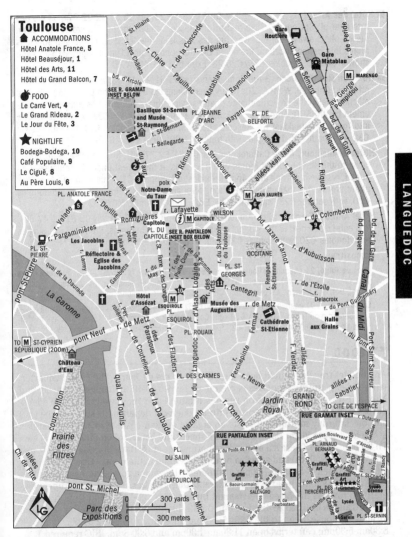

Toulouse

🏠 **ACCOMMODATIONS**
Hôtel Anatole France, **5**
Hôtel Beauséjour, **1**
Hôtel des Arts, **11**
Hôtel du Grand Balcon, **7**

🍴 **FOOD**
Le Carré Vert, **4**
Le Grand Rideau, **2**
Le Jour du Fête, **3**

⭐ **NIGHTLIFE**
Bodega-Bodega, **10**
Café Populaire, **9**
Le Cigüe, **8**
Au Père Louis, **6**

Post Office: 9 rue Lafayette (☎ 05 34 45 70 51). **Currency exchange** with good rates. Open M-F 8am-7pm and Sa 8am-noon. **Poste Restante:** "La Poste Capitole, Poste Restante, 9 rue Lafayette, 31049 Toulouse Cedex." **Postal code:** 31000.

🏠 ACCOMMODATIONS AND CAMPING

Hotels line the blocks near the train station, but most aren't worth staying in. Cheaper, more comfortable hotels can be found in the center of the city or away from the noise and traffic on the outskirts of town. Toulouse has no youth hostel, but the low-priced hotels are friendly and welcoming.

Hôtel des Arts, 1bis rue Cantegril (☎05 61 23 36 21; fax 05 61 12 22 37), off rue des Arts near pl. St-Georges. Take métro (dir: Basso Cambo) to "pl. Esquirol." Walk down rue de Metz, away from the river; rue des Arts is on the left. Low prices and spacious rooms in a perfect location. Breakfast €4. Reception 7am-11pm. Singles €15-21, with shower €23-25; doubles €25/€26-28. Extra bed €5. MC/V. ❷

Hôtel du Grand Balcon, 8 rue Romiguières (☎05 61 21 48 08; fax 05 61 21 59 98), off pl. du Capitole. Worn 1920s luxury overlooking the bustle of the pl. du Capitole. The official hotel of the French airborne postal service, this is classified as a historical monument by UNESCO; Antoine de St-Exupéry stayed in room #32 (€31) whenever he flew into Toulouse. Breakfast €5. Reserve ahead. Singles and doubles €24.40, with shower €32, with bath €35.10; triples with bath €41.20; quad €35.10. ❸

Hôtel Beauséjour, 4 rue Caffarelli (☎/fax 05 61 62 77 59), just off allée Jean Jaurès, close to the station. Bright rooms with new beds at the lowest prices in Toulouse. Call ahead; reserve if arriving after 4pm. Breakfast €4. Shower €1. Reception till 11pm. Ask about tiny singles that usually go to long-term guests (€14). Huge singles and doubles €20, with shower €23, with bath €25. Extra bed €8. AmEx/MC/V. ❷

Hôtel Anatole France, 46 pl. Anatole France (☎05 61 23 19 96; fax 05 61 21 47 66). In a calm *place* next to the student quarter. Airy and bright rooms. Breakfast €4. Singles and doubles €20, with shower €23, with TV and toilet €31. Extra bed €5. MC/V. ❷

Campsites:

Pont de Rupé, 21 chemin du Pont de Rupé (☎05 61 70 07 35; fax 05 61 70 00 71), at av. des Etats-Unis (N20 north). Take bus #59 (dir: Camping) from pl. Jeanne d'Arc to "Rupé." Restaurant, bar, and laundry. €9 per person, €8 with car, €3 per additional person. ❶

La Bourlette, 201 chemin de Tournefeuille (☎05 61 49 64 46), 5km outside Toulouse along N124 in St-Martin-du-Touch. Take bus #64 (dir: Colomiers) from métro stop "Arène" and ask for "St-Martin-du-Touch." €4 per person, €2.75-4 per site. Car included. Open year-round. ❶

🍴 FOOD

Any budget traveler should head directly to the **rue du Taur** in the student quarter, where cheap, spirited eateries serve meals for €5.50-10. Lebanese, Chinese, and Mexican restaurants coexist on rue des Filatiers and rue Paradoux. On Wednesdays, **place du Capitole** transforms into an open-air department store (6am-6pm) and on Saturday mornings it hosts an **organic market.** (6am-1pm.) Other markets are held at **place Victor Hugo, place des Carmes,** and **boulevard de Strasbourg.** (Open Tu-Su 6am-1pm.) There's a **Monoprix** supermarket at 39 rue Alsace-Lorraine (open M-Sa 8:30am-8:50pm) and a **Casino** near pl. Occitane at the Centre Commercie St-Georges. (Open M-Sa 9am-7:30pm.) Students who want a good, hot meal at student rates (€2.40) should head to the **Restaurants Universitaires.** The nearest student cafeteria to town is the **Arsenal Restaurant Universitaire,** 2 bd. Armand Duportal, near rue du Taur (☎05 61 23 98 48). For info on the 13 other student cafeterias scattered around Toulouse, head to the **CROUS,** 58 rue du Taur. (☎05 61 12 54 00. Open M-F 8:30am-5:30pm; cafeterias open 11:30am-1:30pm and 6:30-8pm. ISIC required.)

Le Grand Rideau ❸, at 75 rue du Taur, is a cross between a small restaurant, art gallery, and theatre, serving regional food in a three-course lunch (€8.90) and a generous evening *menu* (€14). Some concerts are planned, but impromptu performances spring up all the time. Animation on Th-F nights. (☎05 61 23 90 19. Open Tu-F noon-2pm and 7pm-midnight, M noon-2pm.) The *brasseries* that crowd busy pl. Wilson offer €8.50-15 *menus.* A good student hang-out for dinner is **Jour de Fête ❷,** 43 rue du Taur. This relaxed *brasserie* serves a large *plat du jour* for €6.50 and a salad for €4.50. (☎05 61 23 36 48. Open daily noon-midnight.) Seafood from nearby port towns is prepared in restaurants on either side of bd. Lazare Carnot as it leaves allée Jean Jaurès; expect to pay upwards of €14 for a full dinner. **Le Carré Vert ❸,** 3bis bd. de Strasbourg, on the corner of bd. Strasbourg and allée Jean Jaurès, serves a 3-course seafood lunch (€12.50) that includes wine. (☎05 61 21 25 79. Open M-Sa noon-2pm and 7-11:30pm. AmEx/MC/V.)

🅘 SIGHTS

From local artists to canonized painters, the diversity of Toulouse's art makes for a nice afternoon of museum-hopping. Toulouse is famous for the red-brick **stone mansions** of the town's wealthy 15th- and 16th-century dye merchants, which can be seen on the tourist office's 2hr. French **tour.** (July-Sept. M-Sa at 10am. €7.70.) Most of Toulouse's museums are free to students. Multi-sight passes are sold at all museums: €3 gives entry to any three museums, €4.50 to six.

LE CAPITOLE. The city's most prominent monument is this brick palace. The huge stone plaza in front is ideal for people-watching. The building was once home to the bourgeois *capitouls,* who unofficially ruled the city (technically controlled by counts) for many years. All marriages in Toulouse must pass through the **Salle des Illustres,** beside the Mairie. **La Salle Henri Martin,** next door, includes 10 post-Impressionist *tableaux* by Henri Martin representing Toulouse in all four seasons. *(Salles open M-F 8:30am-noon and 1:30-7pm, Sa and Su 10am-noon and 2-6pm. Free.)*

BASILIQUE ST-SERNIN. St-Sernin is the longest Romanesque structure in the world, but its most visible feature is an enormous brick steeple that rises skyward like a massive wedding cake in five ever-narrowing double-arched terraces. **St-Dominic,** head of the Dominican order of friars, made the church his base in the early 13th century, though he departed a bit from the ascetic monastic traditions. Behind the left side of the altar in the back of the church, the **crypt** conceals a treasure trove of holy relics, from engraved silver chests to golden goblets, some from the time of Charlemagne. *(☎05 61 21 70 18. Church open July-Sept. M-Sa 8:30am-6:15pm and Su 8:30am-7:30pm; Oct.-June M-Sa 8:30-11:45am and 2-5:45pm, Su 8:30am-12:30pm and 2-7:30pm. Tours in French July-Aug. 2 per day; €5.50. Crypt open July-Sept. M-Sa 10am-6pm, Su 11:30am-6pm; Oct.-June M-Sa 10-11:30am and 2:30-5pm, Su 2:30-5pm. €2.)*

EGLISE NOTRE-DAME-DU-TAUR. This unrestored church was originally named St-Sernin-du-Taur after Saturninus, the first Toulousian priest, martyred in AD 250. Legend has it that disgruntled pagans tied him to the tail of a wild bull that dragged him to his death, ending the wild ride at the site of this building. *(12 rue du Taur. Open July-Sept. daily 2pm-6:30pm; Oct.-June 2-6pm.)*

RÉFECTOIRE DES JACOBINS AND CHURCH. The final resting place of St-Thomas Aquinas is this 13th-century, Southern Gothic church. The ashes of St. Thomas Aquinas take center stage in an elevated, underlit tomb. *(Rue Lakanal. Open daily 9am-7pm. Weekly summer piano concert; €16-28, students €9; tickets at tourist office. Cloister €2.20.)* The Réfectoire des Jacobins presents regular exhibitions of archaeological artifacts and modern art. *(69 rue Pargaminières. ☎05 61 22 21 92. Open daily 10am-7pm during expositions; otherwise, same hours as church. €5.)*

MUSEUMS. The huge **Musée des Augustins** displays an unsurpassed assemblage of Romanesque and Gothic sculptures, including fifteen snickering gargoyles, in a gorgeous redone Augustine monastery. *(21 rue de Metz, off rue des Arts. ☎05 61 22 21 82. Free organ concert W 8:30pm. Open W-M 10am-6pm, W until 9pm. €2.20, students free.)* The striking **Hôtel d'Assezat** hosts the Fondation Bemberg, which displays 28 Bonnards, a modest collection of Dufys, Pissarros, and Gaugins, and the odd Picasso, Renoir, and Matisse. *(Pl. d'Assézat. ☎05 61 12 06 89. Fondation ☎05 61 12 06 89. Open Tu and F-Su 10am-12:30pm, 1:30-6pm, Th 10am-12:30pm and 1:30-9pm. Groups €2.75.)* The

L A N G U E D O C

Musée St-Raymond holds a decent collection of archaeological finds. Especially fascinating is a hall lined by the ominous sculptures of hundreds of Roman emperors. *(Pl. St-Sernin. ☎ 05 61 22 31 44. Open June-Aug. daily 10am-7pm; Sept.-May 10am-6pm. English text guide available. €2.20, students free.)*

CITÉ DE L'ESPACE. Opened in 1997, the fantastic **Cité de l'Espace** park is devoted to Toulouse's space program, complete with interactive games and a planetarium. *(Take A612 exit 17 to Parc de la Plaine, av. Jean Gonord or bus #19 (dir: pl. de l'Indépendance) and follow the signs. M-F the bus does not stop at the park; get off bus at "Ivoire," walk down the main street, and turn right at the roundabout. ☎ 05 62 71 64 80. Open July-Aug., Feb., and Apr. daily 9am-7pm; Sept.-Jan. Tu-F 9am-6pm, Sa-Su 9am-7pm; Mar. and May-June M-F 9am-6pm and Sa-Su 9am-7pm. Closed 2nd week of Jan. English audioguide available. €12, students €10, children 6-12 €9. Tickets to planetarium included.)*

🎵 📷 ENTERTAINMENT AND FESTIVALS

Toulouse has something to please almost any nocturnal whim, although the city is liveliest from October to May when the students come out in full force. The numerous cafés, *glaciers*, and pizzerias flanking **place St-Georges** and **place du Capitole** are open late, as are the bars off **rue St-Rome** and **rue des Filatiers.** During the school year, students head to the **place St-Pierre** to watch rugby in one of the small bars while drinking *pastis*. From September to June, the weekly *Flash* keeps up on the latest in restaurants, bars, and clubs (€1 at *tabacs*). The July-August issue *Flash Eté* is basically a festival listing. CD and book megalith **FNAC**, at the intersection of bd. Strasbourg and Carnot, has cultural pamphlets, club advertisements, and tickets to large concerts. (☎ 05 61 11 01 01. Open M-Sa 9:30am-7:30pm.)

The wine bar ⬛**Au Père Louis,** 45 rue des Tourneurs, is always packed by well-dressed crowds who drink the regional wines by the glass (€2.30) and bottle (€10). The *maison* (with a lunchtime restaurant) has been around since 1889. (☎ 05 61 21 33 45. Open M-Sa 8:30am-3pm and 5-10:30pm.) More informal evenings begin at the smoky **Café Populaire,** 9 rue de la Colombette. Groups come here for the cheapest beer in Toulouse. A box of 13 bottles of beer costs €19, and a mere €13 on Mondays. (☎ 05 61 63 07 00. Happy hour 7:30-8:30pm: buy one *pastis*, get one free. Open M-F 9pm-2am, Sa 2pm-4am.) **La Ciguë,** 6 rue de la Colombette, just off bd. Lazare Carnot, is a friendly gay bar and a great place to ask about the discos *du jour*. Every night, a different DJ plays the same hard rock. (☎ 05 61 99 61 87. Beer €3. Open daily 6pm-2am. MC/V.) The best dancing is at **Bodega-Bodega,** 1 rue Gabriel Péri, just off bd. Lazare Carnot. It's hard to guard your money when the poker chips they give as change make it so easy to buy another drink. (☎ 05 61 63 03 63. Beer €2.50. Margaritas €6. Tapas €7, until midnight. €6 cover Th-Sa 10pm-2am. Open Su-F 7pm-2am, Sa 7pm-6am. MC/V.)

Cave Poésie, 71 rue du Taur (☎ 05 61 23 62 00), hosts plays and performances. The full moon is the catalyst for an "open door" night (starting 9pm) of comedians, poets, musicians. **Cour de l'Ecole des Beaux Arts,** quai de la Daurade, stages classic plays with a modern twist. (☎ 05 61 23 25 49 or 05 61 23 25 45.) Most of Toulouse's **movie theaters** are around pl. Wilson. **UGC,** 9 allée du Président Roosevelt, plays mostly American new releases, some dubbed. (☎ 05 62 30 28 30.) Everything is shown in its original language at **Utopia Cinemas,** 23 rue Montardy, including artsy films from around the world (☎ 05 61 23 66 20).

From July to September, **Musique d'Eté** brings classical concerts, jazz, gospel, and ballet to a variety of outdoor settings. Tickets are sold at concert halls and the tourist office (€13). Traditional music and dance groups parade through the streets on the last Sunday in June for the festival known as the **Grand Fénétra**. (Info

☎05 61 49 18 36.) The **Festival International de Piano aux Jacobins** tickles Toulousian ivories every couple of days during September at the Jacobins cloister. (8:30pm. Tickets available at the tourist office or through the Bureau du Festival ☎05 61 22 40 05; www.pianojacobins.com. €16-28, students €9.)

🏛 DAYTRIPS FROM TOULOUSE: CASTRES

The city of Castres (pop. 48,000) rose from historical obscurity upon acquiring the 11th-century bones of St-Vincent. The holy relics made the town an essential stop for pilgrims en route to Santiago de Compostela, until his basilica was destroyed during the Wars of Religion. The city compensated by constructing two museums, each worth their own brief pilgrimages—the **Musée Goya** and the **Musée Jaurès.** Make Castres a daytrip from Toulouse, as hotels are exorbitantly priced.

In front of the shrubs of the perfectly-groomed **Jardin de l'Evêché,** the **Musée Goya** houses the world's 2nd-largest collection of Spanish painting, along with Catalan and Aragonese masters. The paintings inside the ancient Episcopal palace include four series of Goya's sardonic engravings, on subjects as diverse as the horrors of war and the humor of daily life. (☎05 63 71 59 27. Open July-Aug. M-Sa 9am-noon and 2-6pm, Su 10am-noon and 2-6pm; Sept.-June Tu-Sa 9am-noon and 2-5pm, Su 10am-noon and 2-5pm. €3, students €1.50, under 18 free.)

The **Centre National et Musée Jean Jaurès,** 2 pl. Pélisson, is packed with political cartoons, photographs, and newspaper articles that recount the spirited life and rhetoric of the man himself. A brilliant scholar and professor of philosophy, prominent socialist Jaurès led the striking glass-workers of Carmaux in 1896 and vehemently supported Alfred Dreyfus, a Jewish officer framed as a traitor by the army, before his own assassination in 1914. (☎05 63 72 01 01. Open July-Aug. daily 9am-noon and 2-6pm; Apr.-June and Sept. Tu-Su 9am-noon and 2-6pm; Oct.-Mar. Tu-Su 9am-noon and 2-5pm. €1.50, students €0.75.) For two weeks in mid-July, the **Festival de Dance** celebrates international Hispanic culture with concerts, exhibitions, flamenco and ballet performances. Many events are free; tickets to others are available at the tourist office or by calling the **Théâtre Municipale.** (☎05 63 71 56 57. Open M-F 10:30am-12:30pm and 3-6:30pm.)

When hunger strikes, try the **markets** on **pl. Jean Jaurès** (Tu and Th-Sa 7:30am-1pm) and **pl. de l'Albinque.** (Tu-Su 8:30am-1pm.) **Monoprix** is on rue Sabatier at pl. Jean Jaurès. (Open M-Sa 8:30am-7:30pm.) There are a few bakeries on **rue Gambetta** and **rue Victor Hugo** in the town center, while restaurants surround the **Pont Vieux, pl. Jean Jaurès,** and **rue Villegoudou.** For a sit-down meal, try **La Mandragore ❸,** behind pl. Jean Jaurès on rue Malpas. Regional French cuisine with an extra touch of herbs—try the *crème brulée* perfumed with lavender. 3-course *menu* with wine (€11.50) served M-F. (☎05 63 59 51 27. Open Tu-Sa.) Traditional *Nougatines Castraises* (€9 for 200g) is the specialty of **Cormary,** 13 rue Victor Hugo, which also sculpts fine chocolates, marzipan, and pastries into animal shapes. (☎05 63 59 27 09. Open M-F 6am-1pm and 1:30-7:30pm, Sa 6am-5:30pm, Su 6am-1pm. MC/V.)

The **train station,** av. Albert 1er (open M-F 6:30am-6pm, Sa-Su 6:30am-7pm), has service to Toulouse (1hr., 8 per day, €11.20). Though trains from Albi do eventually arrive in Castres, **buses** are cheaper and more direct. They run from the **bus station,** pl. Soult (☎05 63 35 37 31), to Albi (45-55min., 8 per day, €6) and Toulouse (1½hr., 7 per day, €10). In exchange for a photo ID, the **tourist office,** 3 rue Milhau Ducommun, loans **bikes** for up to two hours. To get there from the station, turn left onto av. Albert 1er and then bear right onto bd. Henri Sizaire. At pl. Alsace-Lorraine, continue straight over the bridge, ignoring signs for the *centre ville.* Turn left onto bd. Raymond Vittoz, then turn left onto rue Villegoudou and veer right onto rue Leris. It's on the right at the very end of the street. (20min.) From the bus station, walk across pl. Soult and continue straight on rue Villegoudou, then see above. (☎05 63 71 37 00; fax 05 63 62 63 60; www.ville-castres.fr. Open July-Aug. M-Sa 9am-12:30pm and 1:30-6:30pm, Su 10:30am-noon and 2:30-5pm; Sept.-June M-Sa 9:30am-12:30pm and 2-6pm, Su 2:30-4:30pm.)

MONTAUBAN

Montauban (pop. 55,000) sits on the river Tarn, 50km north of Toulouse, indifferent to the ebb and flow of the tourist industry. Its ochre-tinted medieval architecture dates back to a spat between the townspeople and the wealthy, oppressive abbey at Montauriol ("golden mountain"). The Count of Toulouse incited the enraged artisans to sack the abbey in 1144 and use its stones to start construction of present Montauban. Never on good terms with mainstream Catholicism, Montauban was one of the last bastions of Protestantism in France following the revocation of the Edict of Nantes in 1685. Today, Montauban's biggest claim to fame is as birthplace of the celebrated 19th-century painter Jean-Auguste Dominique Ingres (1780-1867). The impressive Musée Ingres merits an artlover's daytrip to Montauban, but better prices and entertainment can be found in Toulouse.

TRANSPORTATION. **Trains** roll from av. Chamier to: **Bordeaux** (2hr., 9 per day, €21.90); **Paris** (5½hr.; 7-9 per day; €52.90, TGV €67.10); **Toulouse** (25min., every hr., €7.30). Info office open M-Sa 7am-7:45pm. **Buses** leave from pl. Lalaque; **SNCF** goes to **Albi** (1¼hr., 2 per evening, €9.90) and **Jardel** (☎05 63 22 55 00) runs to **Toulouse** (1hr., 4 per day, €6.10). **Local buses** are run by **Transports Montaubanais**, bd. Midi-Pyrénées (☎05 63 63 52 52; €0.90, *carnet* of 10 €7).

PRACTICAL INFORMATION. To get to the tourist office, walk down av. Mayenne from the station, cross pont Vieux, and continue uphill on côte de Bonnetiers. On the far side of the Eglise St-Jacques, turn right on rue Princesse, which runs into the central **pl. Nationale.** Follow rue Fraîche out of the far corner and turn left two blocks later onto rue du Collège. The **tourist office,** 4 rue du Collège (main entrance on pl. Prax-Paris), gives out a free self-guided tour map in English and runs **tours** in French and English of the town and its museums. Ask for the free practical guides to Montauban and the entire area of the Tarn-et-Garonne. Reservations service €1.60. (☎05 63 63 60 60; www.officetourisme.montauban.com. Open July-Aug. M-Sa 9am-7pm, Su 10am-noon and 2-6pm; Sept.-June M-Sa 9:30am-noon and 2-6pm. Tours July-Aug. 2:30pm; €5, students €2.50.) **Crédit Mutuel,** 8 bd. Midi-Pyrénées, has **currency exchange.** (☎05 63 91 74 74. Open Tu-F 8:30am-noon and 1:30-5pm, Sa 8:30am-noon.) The **police station** is at 50 bd. Alsace-Lorraine (☎05 63 21 54 00), and the **hospital** at 100 rue Léon Cladel (☎05 63 92 82 82). **Internet access** is at **3D Gamma,** 103 fbg. Lacapelle. (☎05 63 91 00 91. €4.80 per hr. Open M-F 11am-midnight, Sa 2pm-midnight.) The **post office** is at 6 bd. Midi-Pyrénées. (☎05 63 68 84 84. Open M-F 8am-6:30pm, and Sa 8am-noon.) **Postal code:** 82000.

ACCOMMODATIONS AND FOOD. With Toulouse so close, there is little reason to stay the night in overpriced Montauban. If you choose to stay, hotels by pl. Nationale and on av. Mayenne, between the old town and the train station, are your best bet. The luxuriously comfortable **Hôtel du Commerce** ❹, 9 pl. Roosevelt, is worth the few extra euros. Cheerful yellow rooms come with new beds, TV, and polished, sparkling bathrooms (with shower and toilet). The obligatory but generous breakfast (€5.50) is served in a beautiful wooden country-style *salle à manger.* After Pont Vieux, turn right on rue de l'Hôtel de Ville. Follow it uphill to pl. Roosevelt, in front of the cathedral. (☎05 63 66 31 32. Singles €39-€55; doubles €40-55. MC/V.) One small **market** is held regularly on pl. Nationale (Tu-Su 8am-

12:30pm); another goes on at pl. Prax-Paris under the Halles Ligou (Sa 9am-1pm). A **Champion** supermarket is across pl. Prax-Paris from the tourist office in the *centre commercial*. (Open M-Th 9:15am-3:30pm, F-Sa 9am-7:30pm, Su 9am-12:30pm.) Sandwicheries, pizzerias, and a surprising number of Indian restaurants speckle the *vieille ville*. Sit-down restaurants are few in number, and rather pricey (3-course *menu* €11-15). **La Guelette ❷,** 12 rue d'Auriol, which intersects rue Fraiche at the corner of pl. Nationale, serves an extensive selection of salads, omelettes, and crepes. A 3-course lunch menu with salad, *plat*, and dessert (€11) is a good deal. (☎05 63 91 49 42. Open daily noon-3pm and 7:30-11pm. MC/V.)

◧ ◨ SIGHTS AND FESTIVALS. Overlooking the river and the Pont Vieux, the **Musée Ingres** occupies the Bishop's palace. While the museum is not exclusively devoted to the celebrated Neoclassical painter nor his predilection for nude female forms, its upper floors spotlight several hundred of his sketches and some minor paintings. Below, the excavated fort displays the town's archaeological finds. (☎05 63 22 12 91. Open July-Aug. daily 9:30am-noon and 1:30-6pm; Sept.-June Tu-Su 10am-noon and 2-6pm. €4; students free; 1st Su of every month free.) Just after revoking the Edict of Nantes, Louis XIV spitefully constructed Montauban's baroque cathedral, **Notre Dame de l'Assumption.** Four enormous sculptures of the Evangelists keep solemn watch over *Le Voeu de Louis XIII,* one of Ingres's largest and most impressive religious works. Commissioned by the Ministry of the Interior in 1820, the painting was part of an attempt to reforge the link between France and the Church after the Revolution. (Open daily 9am-noon and 2-6pm.)

Montauban has two annual music festivals. **Alors Chante** plays traditional French tunes, for one week at the end of May and beginning of June. (☎05 63 63 02 36. Tickets €10-32.) A **Jazz Festival** swings through town the third week of July. Concerts with big names (James Brown has appeared in the past) are all ticketed events, but between the 17th and 21st of July the streets of the *vieille ville* ring out with free concerts, usually at noon and 7pm. (Info ☎05 63 63 60 60; www.jazzmontauban.com. Tickets €16-39, students €11-14; available at tourist office.)

ALBI

Dominated by its magnificent Cathédrale Ste-Cécile, Albi (pop. 50,000) is a town of narrow cobblestone streets twisting down to the tree-lined river Tarn. Native son Henri de Toulouse-Lautrec left this town for the lights of Paris and the Moulin Rouge, a decision that seems unfathomable on a summer afternoon, when the setting sun sparkles off the brick tower of the cathedral and filters through into the maze of the city center. Next to the cathedral, the former Bishop's palace has been transformed into a museum in Toulouse-Lautrec's name. Albi remains relatively unfrequented by American tourists, although the English and the French flock here to savor the town's natural beauty. Those who come planning to see only the cathedral and museum often end up staying longer, entranced by the peaceful city.

☐ TRANSPORTATION. Trains run from av. Maréchal Joffre to: Castres (1½hr., 3 per day, €12.50) via St-Sulpice; Paris (7hr., approx. 8 per day, €63.90) via Toulouse; Toulouse (1hr., 15 per day, €10.10). Info office open M-F 5:30am-9:45pm, Sa 6am-9:45pm, and Su 6:50am-10:10pm. **Buses** leave from pl. Jean Jaurès (☎05 63 54 58 61) for Castres (1hr., M-Sa 8 per day, €5.30) and Toulouse (5 per day, 1 on Su; €10). **Local transportation** is provided by **Espace Albibus,** 14 rue de l'Hôtel de Ville. (☎05 63 38 43 43. Tickets €0.80. Buses run M-Sa roughly 7:30am-7:30pm.) **Albi Taxi Radio** (☎05 63 54 85 03) awaits at the station. **Rent bikes** at **Cycles Andouard,** 7 rue Séré-de-Rivières. (☎05 63 38 44 47. €13 per day, €75 per week. ID deposit. Open Tu-Sa 9am-noon and 2-7pm. MC/V.)

LANGUEDOC

🔃 PRACTICAL INFORMATION. To reach the **tourist office,** Palais de la Berbie, at pl. Ste-Cécile, turn left from the station onto av. Maréchal Joffre and left again onto av. du Général de Gaulle. Bear left over pl. Lapérouse to the pedestrian *vieille ville.* Rue de Verdusse leads toward pl. Ste-Cécile, from where signs point the way. (10min.) The office offers an accommodations service (€1.50); city tours in French (June 15-Sept. 15 M-Sa 12:15pm, €4). Provides **currency exchange** only on bank holidays. (☎05 63 49 48 80; fax 05 63 49 48 98; www.tourisme.fr/albi; accueil@albitourisme.com. Open July-Aug. M-Sa 9am-7:30pm, Su 10:30am-1pm and 2:30-6:30pm; Sept. and June M-Sa 9am-12:30pm and 2-6:30pm, Su 10:30am-12:30pm and 2:30-5:30pm; Oct.-May M-Sa 9am-12:30pm and 2-6pm.) There's a **laundromat** at 8 rue Emile Grand, off Lices Georges Pompidou. (☎05 63 54 51 14. Open daily 7am-9pm.) The **police** are waiting at 23 rue Lices Georges Pompidou (☎05 63 49 22 81). The **Centre Hospitalier** is on rue de la Berchère (☎05 63 47 47 47). Access the **Internet** at **Ludi.com,** 62 rue Séré-de-Rivière. (☎05 63 43 34 24. €4.60 per hr. Open M-Sa 11am-midnight.) The **post office,** pl. du Vigan, offers **currency exchange.** (☎05 63 48 15 63. Open M-F 8am-7pm, Sa 8am-noon.) **Postal code:** 81000.

🔃 ACCOMMODATIONS AND CAMPING. Arrive early or reserve ahead in Albi, especially for summer weekends. For info on *gîtes d'étape* and rural camping, call **ATTER** (☎05 63 48 83 01; fax 05 63 48 83 12). Even the budget hotels are expensive for solo travelers, but the antiquated ▨**Hôtel La Régence ❷,** 27 av. Maréchal Joffre, is a good deal. Near the train station, the bright-wallpapered hotel is close to the center of things. (☎05 63 54 01 42; fax 05 63 54 80 48. Breakfast €5. Singles €23; singles and doubles with shower €27-41. Extra bed €8. MC/V.) If La Régence is full, try the well-equipped **Hôtel du Parc ❸,** 3 av. du Parc. From the station, follow av. Maréchal Joffre, veering left as it becomes bd. Carnot. The hotel is on the left across from the beautiful Parc Rochegude. (☎05 63 54 12 80; fax 05 63 54 69 59. Breakfast €5.65. Reception 24hr. Singles €26; doubles with shower €35, with bath €40-45; quads with shower €51. AmEx/MC/V.)

You can **camp** near a pool at **Parc de Caussels ❶,** 2km east of the center of town, toward Millau on D999. To get there, take bus #5 from pl. Jean Jaurès to "Camping" (M-Sa every hr. until 7pm). To walk (30min.), leave town on rue de la République and follow the signs. (Reception 7am-10pm. Open Apr.-Oct. 15. €7.50 for 1 person, €10 for 2 people with car, extra person €3.)

🔃 FOOD. Near Albi stretches the vast region of **Gaillac,** where *vignoble* estates prepare some of the best wines of the Southwest. Red, white, and *rosés* are all available from the Gaillac estates, and can be tasted and bought in Albi at specialty shops and restaurants. Markets are held indoors at **pl. du Marché** near the cathedral (Tu-Su 8am-1pm), outdoors at **pl. Ste-Cécile** (Sa 8am-1pm), and organically at **pl. du Jardin National** (Tu and Th 5-7pm). Stock up on groceries at **Casino,** 39 rue Lices Georges Pompidou. (Open M-Sa 8:30am-7:30pm.) For a truly romantic dinner, descend the stairway by the Pont Neuf to ▨**Le Robinson ❹,** 142 rue Edouard-Branly. This elegant Eden, with draping vines, romantic lighting, and outdoor terraces, offers a peek at the Tarn as it flows under the bridge. Delicately flavored *menus* (€17-26) prepared by an international team of chefs. Vegetarian options. (☎05 63 46 15 69. Open Tu 7:30-10pm, W-Su noon-2pm and 7:30-10pm. MC/V.) Regional specialties are served with exquisitely fresh fruits and vegetable garnishes at **La Tête de l'Art ❸,** 7 rue de la Piale. Try the local tripe flavored with saffron. (☎05 63 38 44 75. *Menus* €13.50-26. Open July and Aug. daily and Sept.-June Th-M noon-2pm and 7:30-10pm. MC/V.) **Le Tournesol ❷,** rue de l'Ort en Salvy, is a popular vegetarian restaurant situated behind the pl. du Vigan, with healthy concoctions of grains (*plat du jour* €7.50) and heavenly homemade desserts. (☎05 63 38 38 14. Open Tu-Th and Sa noon-2pm, F noon-2pm and 7:30-9:30pm.)

◙ **SIGHTS.** The pride of Albi, eclipsing even the Lautrec museum, is the ▨**Cathédrale Ste-Cécile.** With its high stained-glass windows, lavish gold-and-blue walls and graphic frescoed representations of hell, it is the physical manifestation of the Catholic Church's power. It was built to enforce the "one true religion" after the Church's "Albingensian Crusade" wiped out the Cathar heresy that had taken root in Albi. Inside, magnificent stone carvings line the walls of the choir in patterns so intricate they almost look like lace. The enormous fresco of the Last Judgment that presides over the altar is thought to be the work of German painter Hieronymus Bosch, known for his nightmarish and fantastical visions. The church's **organ** bursts into song on Wednesdays at 5pm and Sundays at 4pm in July and August. (☎05 63 43 23 43. Open June-Sept. daily 9am-6:30pm; Oct.-May 9am-noon and 2-6:30pm. 11am services. Two tours July-Sept. 8 daily at 10am and 2:30pm. €5, English audioguide €3.)

Born to the Count of Toulouse and the Count's cousin and wife, **Henri de Toulouse-Lautrec** (1864-1901) suffered from a congenital bone disease that left him significantly shorter than average. "Whenever he appeared at a crowded dance hall or smoke-filled café, he caused a sensation," wrote Maurice Joyant. "Astonished, people stared at this dwarf with two deformed legs, his over-size head, his malicious eyes peering through spectacles astride his huge nose, his bulbous lips and tousled bushy black beard." Lautrec led a life of debauchery in the cafés, cabarets, and brothels of Paris, and with his keen sense of caricature, satiric wit, and accomplished brush, left behind a lasting homage to Parisian nightlife in oil paint and ink. The collection of works ferreted away by his mother and assembled in the ▨**Musée Toulouse-Lautrec,** in the 13th-century Palais de la Berbie, includes all 31 of the famous posters of Montmartre nightclubs. Upstairs, a fine collection of art includes sculptures and paintings by Degas, Dufy, Matisse, and Rodin. (☎05 63 49 48 70. Open July-Aug. daily 9am-6pm; June and Sept. 9am-noon and 2-6pm; Apr.-May 10am-noon and 2-6pm; Oct.-Mar. W-M 10am-noon and 2-5:30pm. €4.50, students €2.50. Tourist office gives **tours** June-Sept. 8 at 11am and 4pm. €8.50, students €6.50, audioguide in English available for €3.) Don't miss the **courtyard** behind the museum, with an ornamental garden and views of the river Tarn. Toulouse-Lautrec's family still owns his birthplace, the **Hôtel du Bosc,** 14 rue Toulouse-Lautrec in old Albi. You can visit the 12th-century **Château du Bosc,** where he spent childhood vacations, in a forest 45km northeast of Albi. Drive up the N88 toward Rodez or take the train to the **Naucelle** station, 3km from the château. (☎05 65 69 20 83; fax 05 65 72 00 19. Open daily 9am-7pm.)

◪ **ENTERTAINMENT AND FESTIVALS.** You'll have no problem finding a crowd along **pl. de l'Archevêché** in front of the Palais de la Berbie and at the late-night bar-restaurants on **Lices Georges Pompidou** near pl. du Vigan. Innovative plays organized by the **Théâtre de la Croix Blanche,** 14 rue de Croix Blanche (☎05 63 54 18 63 for schedules, tickets around €11) take place in various town centers during the first two weeks of July. **L'Athanor Scène Nationale,** on the felicitous pl. de l'Amitié Entre les Peuples, off bd. Carnot and opposite Parc Rochegude, often shows foreign art films in *v.o.* (☎05 63 38 55 56. Open Tu-F 2-7pm, Sa 10am-noon and 2-7pm. €6, students and seniors €4.) Albi brings in the noise with an abundance of celebrations, all listed in *Sortir à Albi,* available at the tourist office. In the last two weeks of May, **Jazz Balade** brings harmony to the streets, with paid performances (up to €13) and a variety of free shows. The **Festival Théâtral** takes place the first week of July. (Tickets €18, students €16.)

LANGUEDOC

NEAR ALBI

CORDES-SUR-CIEL

The traveler who looks at the summer night from the terrace at Cordes knows that
he need go no further, and that if he wishes it, the beauty of the place, day after
day, will banish solitude.
            —Albert Camus, 1954

Poking its church steeple above the morning mists and overlooking the far-off yellow valleys of St-Cérou, medieval Cordes-sur-Ciel often looks as good as its
name—a celestial city, perched among the clouds, where an alienated Camus
found the courage to believe that "estranged lovers would finally embrace, love
and creation achieve perfect equilibrium." Located 24km north of Albi, this fairy
tale of a city is bounded by a crumbling double wall that sprouts flowers and
sometimes entire gardens. The tiny city rises to a summit and descends the other
side by a single steep cobblestone street, twisting through multiple gates that have
regulated its commerce for the better part of a millennium.

Much of the town's medieval architecture, including its impressive stone gates,
is preserved thanks to archeologist Charles Portal. You can see his collection as
well as artwork of Cordes at the **Musée Charles Portal,** located in Portail Peint as
you first approach the upper town from pl. de la Bouteillerie. (Call tourist office
for info at ☎ 05 63 56 00 52. Open July-Aug. daily 11am-noon and 3-6pm; Apr.-June
and Sept.-Oct. Su and holidays 3-6pm. €2.50, students €1.25.) A few steps farther
down Grande Rue Raymond VII is the **Musée de l'Art du Sucre,** a sweet tooth's
dream, which sells all kinds of candied concoctions and intricate sugar models.
(☎ 05 63 56 02 40. Open Feb.-Dec. daily 10:30am-12:30pm and 2:30-6:30pm. €2.30.)

Across the street from the museums, elevated **place de la Bride** provides a panoramic view of the peaceful countryside. The extensive fortifications that ringed
medieval Cordes never included a central fort. Instead, pl. de la Bride served as a
platform from which siege weapons flung stones and other objects at invaders
below. At Cordes's summit is **Eglise St-Michel,** the highest point in town (open daily
3-5:30pm); right beside it is the site of the **Puits de la Halle,** a 114m long well constructed in 1222 along with the town. Formed by tunnelling through an entire
mountain, its only use was to supply Albi with water during sieges. Walking down
the far side of the hill on Grande Rue Raymond VII, take a moment to examine the
facade of **La Maison du Grand Ecuyer**, carved with snarling stone gargoyles and delicately wrought columns, pilasters, and foliage.

For four days surrounding the 14th of July, fire-eaters play to costumed crowds
at the medieval market during the **Fête du Grand Fauconnier,** which offers plays,
concerts, and magic shows within the *vieille ville.* Gnaw a drumstick at one of the
Fête's banquets. (Reservations and info ☎ 05 63 56 00 52. Entrance €7, children €3,
free if costumed. Costume rentals at **Ecole de la bouteillerie** in the lower town. (☎ 05
63 56 34 63. During *Fête* open 9am-1pm.)

The best transportation from Albi is the buses of **Sudcar Rolland** (☎ 05 63 54 11
93). Two buses run M-Sa from Albi's bus station to Cordes (€4.60, students €2.30;
last bus from Cordes to Albi 6:45pm). **Trains** from Albi go via Tessonnières to Vin-
drac (1 hr., 2 per day, €5.80), where you can call the **Barrois minibus** (☎ 05 63 56 14
80) to take you the 5km to Cordes (€3.80). If the minibus is unavailable, getting
from the train station to Cordes can be a nightmare of a 5km walk. Though it's not
recommended by *Let's Go*, many choose to hitch, but don't count on catching a
ride; the many vacationing families seldom pick up hitchhikers.

The **tourist office,** pl. de Halle in Maison Fontpeyrouse, can help find accommodations. (☎ 05 63 56 00 52; www.cordes-sur-ciel.org. Tours Tu-F 11am; €3.80. Open

July-Aug. Tu-F 10am-7pm, Sa-M 2:30pm-6pm; Sept.-June 10:30am-12:30pm and 2:30-6pm.) An **annex** in the lower city is in the Maison du Pays Cordais. (Open daily 10:30am-12:30pm and 2-6pm.) A **market** takes place at the bottom of the hill. (Sa 8am-noon) A **navette** shuttles between the annex in the *haute ville* and the lower part of Cordes. (Departs daily every 12min. €2, children €1.30.)

CARCASSONNE

Carcassonne from afar is eye-catching. Carcassonne up-close is breath-taking. This is where Cinderella lost her glass slipper, Beauty nursed the Beast, and Jack's giant lived a happy life until that whole beanstalk affair. Round towers capped by red tile roofs and an undulating double wall guard the approach to the city. As you walk through the stone portals, the ramparts still seem to resound with the clinking of armor and sharpening of steel. The dream fades fast once you clear the city walls. The 'battle sounds's are actually the screams of thousands of photo-taking visitors jostling for space on the narrow streets. Carcassonne has become one of France's top tourist traps, where families and school groups get their yearly fill of on cheap plastic swords and shields. The city should not be missed, but try to experience it late in the evening, when the streets are clear of crowds and the floodlit fortress echoes with free animations and concerts.

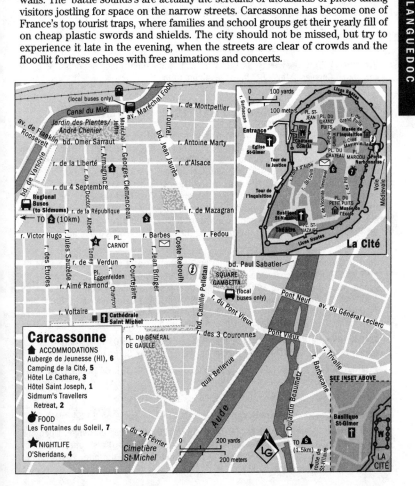

Carcassonne

▲ ACCOMMODATIONS
Auberge de Jeunesse (HI), **6**
Camping de la Cité, **5**
Hôtel Le Cathare, **3**
Hôtel Saint Joseph, **1**
Sidmum's Travellers
   Retreat, **2**

● FOOD
Les Fontaines du Soleil, **7**

★ NIGHTLIFE
O'Sheridans, **4**

LANGUEDOC

◪ TRANSPORTATION

Trains: ☎04 68 71 79 14, behind Jardin St-Chenier. Info office open M-Sa 9am-noon and 1:30-6:15pm. To: **Lyon** (5½hr., 2 per day, €41.35); **Marseille** (3hr., every 2hr., €31.40); **Montpellier** (2hr., 14 per day, €17.70); **Narbonne** (30min., 10 per day, €8.30); **Nice** (6hr., 5 per day, €46.80); **Nîmes** (2½hr., 12 per day, €21.90); **Perpignan** (2hr., 10 per day, €14.50); **Toulouse** (50min., 24 per day, €11).

Buses: Regional buses leave from the *gare routière* on bd. de Varsovie. From the train station, cross the canal, turn right on bd. Omer Sarrut, and left at the fork. Check schedules at the station and the tourist office. To: **Narbonne** (3hr., 1 per day, €7); **Toulouse** (2½hr., 3 per day, €8). **Cars Teissier** (☎04 68 25 85 45) runs to **Lourdes** (€23).

Public Transportation: A free **shuttle** *(navette)* takes you from sq. Gambetta (in the lower city) to the citadel gates. (☎04 68 47 82 22. June 15-Sept. 15 M-Sa, every 15min. 8:30am-12:30pm and 2-6pm.) **CART**, sq. Gambetta (☎04 68 47 82 22), runs **buses** throughout the city, including from the train station to the citadel gates and the campground. To get from the station to the *cité*, take bus #4 (dir: Gambetta) and then bus #2 (dir: La Cité. M-Sa every 20-40min. 7am-7pm. €0.90.)

Taxis: Radio Taxi Services (☎04 68 71 50 50). At the train station or across the canal by Jardin Chenier. 24hr. €6-7 from the station to the *cité*.

✴️ 🛈 ORIENTATION AND PRACTICAL INFORMATION

The **bastide St-Louis,** once known as the *basse ville* (lower town), recently changed its name to recruit daytrippers who might otherwise pass it over. Its main attractions are shops, hotels, the **train station,** and most importantly, the **shuttle** and **TOUC,** which both run to the citadel. Otherwise, it's a pleasant but steep 30 minute hike. To get from the station to the *cité*, walk straight down av. de Maréchal Joffre, which turns into rue Clemenceau. Just past the clearing of place Carnot, turn left onto rue Verdun, which leads to Square Gambetta and the **tourist office.** Bear right through the square and turn left up the narrow road that leads to Pont Vieux. Continue straight up the hill to the *cité*. The **tourist office annex** will be on the right as you enter the castle.

Tourist Office: 15 bd. Camille Pelletan, sq. Gambetta (☎04 68 10 24 30; fax 04 68 10 24 38; www.carcassonne-tourisme.com.). Open July-Aug. daily 9am-7pm; Sept.-June 9am-12:30pm and 1:30-6pm. Annex in the *cité's* porte Narbonnaise (☎04 68 10 24 36). Open July-Aug. daily 9am-7pm, Sept.-June 9am-1pm and 2-6pm. Also annex near the station on av. de Maréchal Joffre (☎04 68 25 94 81). Hours same as *cité* annex.

Money: Banque Nationale, 50 rue Jean-Bringer (☎08 02 35 01 03), **exchanges** currency at decent rates. Open M-F 8am-noon and 1:30-5pm, Sa 8am-noon.

Internet: Alerte Rouge, 73 rue de Verdun (☎04 68 25 20 39). €4 per hr. Open M-Sa 10am-11pm.

Police: La Comissariat, 4 bd. Barbès (☎04 68 11 26 00).

Medical Assistance: Centre Hospitalier, rte. de St-Hilaire (☎04 68 24 24 24).

Post Office: 40 rue Jean Bringer (☎04 68 11 71 00). **Currency exchange.** Open M-F 8am-7pm, Sa 8am-noon. **Branch office** (☎04 68 47 95 45) also offers currency exchange on rue de Comte Roger and rue Viollet-le-Duc in the *cité*. **Postal code:** 11000. **Poste Restante:** 11012.

ACCOMMODATIONS AND CAMPING

Carcassonne's comfortable hostel is a gift from above to budgeteers, with 120 beds right in the middle of the *cité*. Hotels in the Bastide St-Louis are surprisingly cheap; those in the *cité* are ferociously expensive. If you find crowds unbearable, the Sidmums hostel is in the beautiful countryside 10km outside the city.

Auberge de Jeunesse (HI), rue de Vicomte Trencavel (☎04 68 25 23 16; fax 04 68 71 14 84; carcassonne@fuaj.org), in the *cité*. The only place worth staying if you want to see the castle late at night. Bunked beds with shower and sink. Breakfast included. Kitchen. Sheets €2.70. Bike rental €8 per day. Laundry. Snack bar. Internet access €4.70 per hr. Lockout 10am-4pm. Reception 24hr. Reserve a few days ahead, earlier July and August. Bunks €12.50. **Members only.** MC/V. ❶

Sidmums Travellers Retreat, 11 chemin de la Croix d'Achille (☎04 68 26 94 49 or 06 16 86 85 00; www.sidmums.com). This 10-bed hostel will seem like paradise after the crowds in town, set in the countryside against the peaceful town of Preixan. Sid and his Mum will offer you advice on the best hikes in the area, drive you to nearby pubs, or serve you cool lemonade in the garden. Call for pick-up from the station (€5) or take the bus headed for Limoux from the canal side of the *gare routière* (ask for "Preixan;" 4-6 per day, last bus 6:15pm). Kitchen. Mini-store. Reception 24hr. Reserve ahead. Bikes €8 per day. Bunks €15; 1 double €30. ❶

Hôtel Le Cathare, 53 rue Jean Bringer (☎04 68 25 65 92; fax 04 68 47 15 02), near the post office in the lower town. 4 tiny, aging singles for €14; bright, well-renovated rooms are worth the extra money. Restaurant. Breakfast €4.50. Reception 8am-7pm. Singles and doubles €18, with shower €26; triples €46-53. MC/V. ❷

Hôtel Saint Joseph, 81 rue de la Liberté (☎04 68 71 96 89; fax 04 68 71 36 28). Take av. Maréchal Joffre across the canal and across bd. Omer Sarraut; continue for one block on rue G. Clemenceau before turning right onto rue de la Liberté. 37 rooms in a charming, bright building on a calm street near the train station. Breakfast €4. Reception 7am-11pm. 4 singles without shower €23; singles and doubles with shower and TV €28, with shower or bath and toilet €29.80-31; triples with shower and TV €37.70; quads with shower and TV €45.80. MC/V. ❸

Camping de la Cité, rte. de St-Hilaire (☎04 68 25 11 77), has plenty of wide open grassy space across the Aude; from the lower town, turn right immediately after you cross Pont Vieux down rue du Jardin and follow the footpath. (30min. from train station.) Or take the shuttle from the train station. (15min.) Pool, tennis, and a grocery store. Reception 8am-9pm. Open Mar. 15-Oct. 10. Mar. 15-June 15 and Sept. 15-Oct. 10 €12.20 per site and 1-2 people, €3.70 for each extra person. June 15-July 9 and Aug. 25-Sept. 15 €15 per site, €4.50 for each extra person. July 10-Aug. 24 €16.80 per site, €4.60 for each extra person. ❶

FOOD

Carcassonne's specialty is the inexpensive *cassoulet*, a stew of white beans, herbs, and meat (usually duck or pork, sometimes pigeon). There is a food **market** on pl. Carnot (open Tu, Th, and Sa 7am-1pm) and a **Monoprix** on rue G. Clemenceau at rue de la République. (Open M-Sa 8:30am-8pm.) Restaurants on **rue du Plo** offer €8.50-10 *menus;* save room for dessert at one of the outdoor *crêperies* on **pl. Marcou.** Restaurants in the *cité* tend to close in winter. Simple and affordable places line **bd. Omer Sarraut** in the lower city. **Les Fontaines du Soleil ❷,** 32 rue du Plo is one of Carcassonne's most popular restaurants, with a sunny garden courtyard and a fountain. The €9.50 weekly lunch *menu* includes a salad, *cassoulet*, and a pitcher of wine. (☎04 68 47 87 06. Open 11:30am-3pm and 7-10:30pm. MC/V.)

◉ SIGHTS

It's no surprise that Carcassone's **fortifications** date back to the first century; this hill above the sea road to Toulouse is a strategically valuable spot. An early Visigoth fortress here repelled Clovis in AD 506. The town was finally taken after many centuries of unsuccessful sieges, falling with Languedoc during the Albigensian Crusade. The *cité* eventually came under the control of the French crown. King Louis IX built the 2nd outer wall, copying the double-walled fortresses he had observed in Palestine during the Crusades. Untended, the city deteriorated during the 1700s until the architect Viollet-le-Duc restored it in 1844.

Intended at the time of its construction in the 12th century to be a palace, the **Château Comtal,** 1 rue Viollet-le-Duc, was transformed into a citadel when Carcassonne submitted to royal control in 1226. Entrance to the outer walls is free, but you can enter the château only on a paid tour. The **Cour du Midi,** a stop on the tour, holds the remains of a Gallo-Roman villa, once home to the troubadours for which Carcassone's court was famous. The **Tour de la Justice**'s treacherous staircase, which ends in a dead end, was a stairway to heaven (or hell) for ill-fated invaders who would rush upstairs and find themselves trapped. 30min. tours in French run continuously. English tours June 15-Sept. 15 daily at 11:15am and 2:15pm. (☎04 68 25 01 66; fax 04 68 25 65 32. Open daily June-Sept. 9am-7:30pm; Apr.-May and Oct. 9:30am-6pm; Nov.-Mar. 9:30am-5pm. €5.50, ages 18-25 €3.)

The *cité* of Carcassonne is filled with small museums, most of which can be skipped. An exception is **Le Musée de l'Ecole,** 3 rue du Plo, in the city's old schoolhouse, which holds a fascinating display of textbooks, certificates and letters from the late 1800s, when Jules Ferry was in the process of transforming the French education system. (☎04 68 25 95 14. Open July-Aug. daily 10am-7pm, Sept.-June daily 10am-6pm.) Outside the city walls, across the parking lot from the main entrance over the pont Levis, the **Musée Mémoires Moyen Age,** chemin des Anglais, combines a uninformative video presentation with an intricate model of Raymond de Trencavel's 1240 countersiege of Carcassonne, complete with battle towers, catapults, and grimacing soldiers. (☎04 68 71 08 65. Open June-Sept. daily 10am-8pm, off-season 9am-6pm. €4, students €3.50, children €2.50.)

The lower town—the **Bastide St-Louis**—was born when Louis IX, afraid enemy troops might find shelter close to his fortress, burned the houses that clung to the city's outside walls and relocated their residents, whom he gave their very own walled fortifications and church. Converted into a fortress after the Black Prince razed Carcassonne during the Hundred Years' War in 1355, the *basse ville*'s **Cathédrale St-Michel,** rue Voltaire, still sports fortifications on its southern side, facing bd. Barbès. Don't miss the gargoyles snarling down from their high perches. (Open M-Sa 7am-noon and 2-7pm, Su 9:30am-noon.)

♫ ◉ ENTERTAINMENT AND FESTIVALS

The evening is the best time for wandering the streets of the *cité* and relaxing in the cafés in **pl. Marcou.** Bars and cafés along **bd. Omer Sarraut** and **pl. Verdun** are open until midnight. Grab a Guiness (€5.50 a pint) at **O'Sheridans,** 13 rue Victor Hugo off Place Carnot, a friendly Irish pub filled with French and Anglo crowds. (☎04 68 72 06 58. Open daily 4pm-2am. Live music W and Th. AmEx/MC/V.) At the base of the *cité*, nocturnal locals dance the night away at **La Bulle,** 115 rue Barbacane. (☎04 68 72 47 70. €9 cover includes first drink. Open F-Sa until dawn.)

In July, the month-long **Festival de Carcassonne** brings dance, opera, theater, and concerts to the Château Comtal and the ancient amphitheater. (Info and reservations ☎04 68 11 59 15; www.festivaldecarcassonne.com. €21-42, most shows €10 for students.) The **Festival Off** showcases smaller bands as well as mildly alternative free comedy and dance performances in the *places* of the *cité* and in the Bastide St-Louis. On **Bastille Day,** deep red floodlights and smoke set the entire *cité* ablaze in remembrance of the villages ordered burned by the inquisitorial jury headquartered hear in the Tour de l'Inquisition. The firework display is the second best in France. For two weeks in early August, the entire *cité* returns to the Middle Ages for the **Spectacles Médiévaux.** Locals dressed in medieval garb talk to visitors, display their crafts, and pretend nothing has changed in eight centuries. Every afternoon at 5:30pm, there is an equestrian show with mock-jousting and pitched battles. Even non-French speakers will enjoy the nightly 9:30pm *spectacle*—a huge multimedia drama that brings the 13th century to life. For ticket info, contact Compagnie Mystère Baiffe. (☎06 86 86 31 33.)

FOIX

Il était une fois ("once upon a time"), as French fairy tales begin, a town grew up at the base of a large castle surrounded by mountains. Little has changed in Foix, neither the bad joke nor its fairy-tale atmosphere. The towers of the magnificent château look down on the busy marketplace below, cobblestone streets lead through a maze of red-roofed houses, and nearby caves and grottoes still bear the marks of the prehistoric peoples who first settled the Ariège region. In the summer, the whole town turns out for an enormous medieval spectacle to relive the days of yore. The city is a good base for hiking and kayaking nearby. Strongly consider renting a car—the Château de Montségur, prehistoric caves, and serene Ariège passes are poorly served by public transportation.

◪ PRACTICAL INFORMATION. The **train station,** av. Pierre Sémard (☎05 61 02 03 64), is north of town off the N20. (Info open M-Sa 8:10am-12:20pm and 1:25-8:30pm, Su 8:15am-1:55pm and 2:15-10:20pm.) Trains go to Toulouse (1hr., 10 per day, €10). By bus, **Salt Autocars,** 8 allées de Villote (☎05 61 65 08 40), also runs to Toulouse (1¼hr., 2 per day, €8).

To reach the **tourist office,** 29 rue Théophile Delcassé, leave the train station and turn right. Follow the street until you reach the main road (N20). Follow this highway to the second bridge, cross it, and follow cours Gabriel Fauré for about three blocks. Rue Théophile Delcassé is on your right. (☎05 61 65 12 12; fax 05 61 65 64 63; www.mairie-foix.fr. Open July-Aug. M-Sa 9am-7pm, Su 9am-noon and 2-6pm; June and Sept. M-Sa 9am-noon and 2-6pm, Su 10am-12:30pm; Oct.-May M-Sa 9am-noon and 2-6pm.) For **police,** call ☎05 61 05 43 00. The **hospital** is 5km out of town in St-Jean de Verges. (☎05 61 03 30 30.)

For **Internet** access, drop by the **Bureau d'Information Jeunesse (BIJ),** pl. Parmentier. (☎05 61 02 86 10. €2.50 per hr. Reserve ahead. Open M 1-5pm, Tu and Th-F 10am-5pm, W 10am-6pm.) There is a **laundromat** at 32 rue de la Faurie. (Open daily 8:30am-8pm.) The **post office,** 4 rue Laffont, has **currency exchange.** (☎05 61 02 01 02. Open M-F 8am-7pm, Sa 8am-noon.) **Poste Restante: 09008. Postal code: 09000.**

◪◪ ACCOMMODATIONS AND FOOD. The best option for budget travelers is unquestionably the **◪Foyer Léo Lagrange ❶,** 16 rue Peyrevidal. To get there, turn right onto cours Gabriel Fauré out of the tourist office and right again onto rue Peyrevidal just after the Halle Aux Grains; the *foyer* will be on your right. A cross between a nice hotel and a friendly hostel, it offers privacy and sociability in 22 clean 1- to 4-bedrooms, each equipped with a sink, closet, desk, and private shower. Rooms facing the street in back have impressive views of the château. (☎05 61 65 09 04; fax 05 61 02 63 87. Free **Internet** access. Kitchen available. Reception 8am-11pm; call ahead if arriving late. €14 per person.) Opposite the Foyer is **Hôtel Eychenne ❸,** 11 rue Peyrevidal, which rents large rooms above a smoky but lively bar in a central location. (☎05 61 65 00 04; fax 05 61 65 56 63. Breakfast €4.60. Reception 8am-8pm; call ahead if arriving late. Singles and doubles with shower €29, with toilet €37; triples or quads with shower €46. MC/V.) Classy **La Barbacane du Château ❸**, 1 av. de Lérida, is just past the flowered roundabout to the right on cours Gabriel Fauré from the tourist office. A reasonable price for the elegance of mahogany, large bed, sparkling bathrooms, and glossed tables. Several rooms have excellent views of the château. (☎05 61 65 50 44; fax 05 61 02 74 33. Elevator. Breakfast €7. Open Apr.-Oct. 7am-11:30pm. Singles and doubles €32, with bath €45. MC/V.) **Camping du Lac/ Labarre ❶** is a three-star site on a lake 3km up N20 toward Toulouse. Buses from Toulouse stop at the camp. From the train station, head left along N20 until you see the signs for the campground on your left. Rent canoes and kayaks from lakefront **Base Nautique** (half-day €8) down the street. (☎05 61 65 11 58; fax 05 61 05 32 62; www.campingdulac.com. Open July-Aug. €6.50 per person, €15 for 2 people, car, tent, and electricity. Oct.-May €3.50 per person, €10 for 2 people, car, tent, and electricity. June €5 per person, €12 for 2 people, car, tent, and electricity.)

Foix's restaurants serve specialties of the Ariège region. Try *truite à l'ariègeoise* (trout), *cassoulet* (white-bean and duck stew), or the wonderfully messy *écrevisses* (crayfish). Restaurants with moderately priced local specialties line **rue de la Faurie.** For regular supplies, head to **Casino** supermarket, rue Laffont. (Open M-Sa 9am-7pm.) On Fridays, **open-air markets** sprout up all over Foix, with meat and cheese at the Halle aux Grains, fruit and vegetables at pl. St-Volusien, and clothing along the allées de Villote. (Food 8am-12:30pm; clothes 8am-4pm.) For good prices on regional food, try the casual **Le Jeu de l'Oie ❷**, 17 rue de la Faurie. €6.90 will get you a generous *plat du jour;* the three-course lunch *menu* allows you to sample the taste of local cuisine. (☎05 61 02 69 39. Open July-Aug. M-Sa noon-2:30pm, 7-11pm; Sept.-June M noon-2:30pm, Tu-F noon-2:30pm and 7-11pm, Sa 7-11pm. AmEx/MC/V.) For those who want to escape the *cassoulet* glut, **l'Atlas ❸**, 14 pl. Pyrène, serves many varieties of couscous and *tagines* (a steaming casserole of lamb or chicken and vegetables) under vibrant Moroccan tapestries and a vine canopy. Three-course *menu* with wine for €10. (☎05 61 65 04 04. Open Tu-F and Su 11:30am-3pm and 7-10:30pm, Sa 11:30am-3pm.)

◑ ◪ SIGHTS AND EXCURSIONS. The fairy tale continues at **Château de Foix,** the prototypical medieval castle, with three stunning towers perched protectively on a high point above the city. Inside the well-preserved castle, the small **Musée de l'Ariège** displays a collection of armor, stone carvings and artifacts from the Roman Empire to the Middle Ages. Be sure to take the free tour in English. The towers of the castle offer an impressive panoramic view of the Pyrenean foothills. (☎05 34 09 83 83. Both open July-Aug. daily 9:45am-6:30pm; June and Sept. 9:45am-noon and 2-6pm; Oct.-May W-Su 10:30am-noon and 2-5:30pm. Tours in French every hr., 1 per day in English at 1pm. €4, students €2.)

The Ariège region boasts some of the most spectacular **caves** in France. The **Grotte de Niaux** would be a stunning cave in its own right, but it becomes spectacular when the guide's lantern illuminates the prehistoric wall drawings of bison, horses, and ibex that date from around 12,000 BC. Reservations are required to enter the cave. 20km south of Foix, the grotto is only accessible by car. (☎05 61 05 88 37. Open Apr.-Oct. daily; Nov.-Mar. Tu-Su. €9, students €5.50.) An hour-long boat ride navigates the **Rivière Souterraine de Labouiche,** the longest navigable underground river in Europe. The small metal boat cruises through galleries of stalagtites and stalagmites, pulled along by wisecracking guides who can give the tour in both French and English. There is no public transportation to this site. (☎05 61 65 04 11. Open July-Aug. daily 9:30am-6pm; Apr.-May 24 M-Sa 2-6pm, Su 10am-noon and 2-6pm; May 25-June and Sept. daily 10am-noon and 2-6pm; Oct.-Nov. 11 Su 10am-noon and 2-6pm. €7.10, children under €5.20.)

PRACTICE MAKES *PERFECT!* History is written by the victors, and the terms by which we now know the Cathars are those of their sworn enemies. "Cathar," derived from the Greek word for "purity," was meant as a mockery. The most powerful heretical sect in France, the Cathari reacted to the excesses and shallow spirituality of the Church. Cathari priests, called *Perfecti,* really did live up to their title: they diligently kept vows of chastity, poverty and obedience. Cathars rejected baptism as unfair for those too young to choose a faith, and viewed the Christian symbol of the cross as the glorification of a torture device. The Cathari were tolerated until the turn of the 12th century, when the Pope excommunicated them and sent Crusaders into Languedoc. Catholics and Cathars alike were killed in the conquest, following the Pope's dictate: "Kill them all, for God knows his own." The bloody conquest of Montségur wiped out the sect, though not its faith.

■ **FESTIVALS.** From the end of July though the middle of August, on weekends at 10pm, an extravagant medieval spectacle, **Il était une Foix...l'Arlège,** enlivens the area around Foix's château. Villagers wrestle bears, fight battles, and shoot off more fireworks than Bastille Day celebrations in some major cities. (For info and tickets call the Théâtre de Verdure de l'Espinet at ☎05 61 02 88 26. €10-22, students €5-11.) In the second week of July, the **Résistances** festival brings 100 art films—many of which premiere in Cannes—to Foix. (☎05 61 05 13 30; www.cine-resistances.com. €5 per film, €60 weekly; students half price.)

NEAR FOIX

CHÂTEAU DE MONTSÉGUR

Rocky Montségur was the final refuge of the Cathars. When the pope intensified his campaign against the Cathar sect in the early 13th century, the Cathar bishop of Toulouse, Guilhabert de Castres, chose to retreat to the security of Montségur ("Secure Mount"), perched on the highest point of a commanding spur of rocks known as "the pog." A bloody Cathar raid at Avignonet in retaliation for the Inquisition provoked an equally violent and final assault by the Catholic church. Montségur was besieged from May 1243 until March 1244. The Pope's forces slowly advanced up the *pog*, establishing footholds first at the **tower rock** and after a bloody confrontation at the **barbican** (outer tower). When the castle keep finally succumbed, the surviving Cathars were told to renounce their beliefs or burn at the stake. On March 16, 1244, 200 Cathars gave their answer, launching themselves onto a pyre at the base of the *pog*. The night before the mass suicide is shrouded in mystery and myth; allegedly, the Cathar bishop entrusted the sect's treasure to four *perfecti*, who escaped into the mountains and were never found. Today, massive, crumbling walls and a broken vault are the only evidence of the last bastion of Catharism. The setting, history, and archaeological still make for a breathtaking experience. (Tours in French; July-Aug. 4 per day, May-June and Sept. 2 per day. €3.80, ages 8-14 €2. Open May-Sept. daily 9am-7:30pm; Oct.-Mar. 10am-4pm. €3.50, students €2.) To view the results of archaeological excavations at Montségur, visit the small **Musée de Montségur** just down the street. (☎05 61 01 10 27. Open Feb.-Dec. 10am-12:30pm and 2-7:30pm. Free.)

Montségur is 35km southeast of Foix along the D9. During the school year (Sept.-June), five **Sovitour buses** (☎05 61 01 02 35) run from Foix's Centre Culturel Olivier Carol to Lavelanet. Ask the driver to drop you at the turn-off to Montségur, and follow the signs through Villeneuve d'Olmes to Montférrier (5km). From here it's another 5km uphill to Montségur. (July-Aug. daily; offseason 4 per day; €4.20.)

Montségur's **tourist office** distributes info on the château and various hiking and biking trails, including the **Massif de St-Barthélémy** and the **Massif de la Frau.** (☎ 05 61 03 03 03. Open July-Sept. daily 10am-1pm and 2-7pm.)

A **gîte d'étape ❶** in the center of the village offers the comfort of several small beds lined together. To get there, follow the signs to Hôtel Costes, and knock on Mr. Massera's door, 90 rue du Village. (☎ 05 61 01 08 57; maryluk@club-internet; frwww.montsegur.org/getape.htm. Reservations required. Bunks €10-11.) Next to the *gîte*, the two-star **Hôtel Costes ❸** has large, comfortable rooms. (☎ 05 61 01 10 24. Breakfast €5.80. Reception Apr.-Nov. 15 8am-8pm. Doubles with shower €31.25-35.85; triples €42. MC/V.) When Hôtel Costes is full, try **Hôtel Couquet ❸**, 51 rue Priucefale, which has six huge quads at good prices. (☎ 05 61 01 10 28. Rooms €27.45-30.50.) Also in the heart of the village, the Germa family's **chambre d'hôte ❹**, 46 rue du Village, offer a room for 2 to 5 people and homemade breakfast and baked bread for around €40 per night. (☎ 05 61 02 80 70.)

VILLEFRANCHE-DE-CONFLENT

Deep in the mountains of the Conflent range, hidden within the shadow of Vauban's military masterpiece, Fort Liberia, the miniscule Villefranche-de-Conflent (pop. 220) occupies a once-prized position. For almost 300 years, the walled city kept an active garrison to protect the borders arbitrated by Louis XIV in the 1659 Treaty of the Pyrénées. With the low red sun baking its cobblestone streets, Villefranche makes an ideal afternoon stopover for travelers en route from Perpignan to Toulouse via the scenic Train Jaune line.

🛈 **PRACTICAL INFORMATION.** The **train station** is just outside the town walls off the highway. From the station, take the only road to the highway and turn right toward Villefranche. (5min.) **Trains** (☎ 04 67 10 14 00) run to Perpignan (50min., 8 per day, €4.60). The station is also the terminus of the scenic **Train Jaune** route (see **Outdoors,** below). The **tourist office,** 32bis rue St-Jacques, has lodging info and sells IGN hiking maps for €9-12. (☎ 04 68 96 22 96; fax 04 68 96 07 24. Open July-Aug. daily 10am-6pm; Sept.-Dec. and Feb.-June 2-5pm.) **Hiking** info is also available through the **Direction Départementale de la Jeunesse et des Sports** (☎ 04 68 35 50 49).

Running 63km through the Pyrénées, the tiny **Train Jaune** links Villefranche to **Latour-de-Carol** (2½-3hr., 6 per day, €15). The train runs over deep mountain valleys on spectacular viaducts, stopping at many towns along the way. A trip to Latour and back will take a day and cost €30, or you can continue on to Toulouse (3hr. from Latour-de-Carol, 3 per day, €26). Shorter trips can be made (from €2.50). Get started early so as not to be caught unawares by the train schedule. (☎ 08 36 35 35 35; http://ter.sncf.fr/train-jaune/default.htm.) In winter (Nov.-Apr.), the Train Jaune hauls **skiers** to fashionable **Font-Romeu** (3-4 per day, €10.80). Equipped with snow machines and ski lifts, this resort offers first-rate skiing. Call the **tourist office** in Font Romeu at ☎ 04 68 30 68 30 for info.

🛈 **ACCOMMODATIONS.** Villefranche has few cheap hotels, and even the expensive ones fill quickly during the summer. **Hôtel Le Terminus ❸**, just to the right of the train station, offers six pastel rooms with wooden floors. (☎ 04 68 96 11 33. Breakfast €3.80. Reception 24hr. Call ahead. Singles and doubles €27.50, with shower €30.50, with bath €33.50-38.20. MC/V.) The *mairie* (town hall) on pl. de l'Eglise operates **gîtes communaux ❸**, but you must stay for a full week (Sa-Sa)—or at least pay the weekly rate. (☎ 04 68 96 10 78. Town hall open M-F 8am-noon and 2-6pm. July-Aug. €125-245, Sept.-June €150-305.) If you succumb completely to the lure of the Pyrénées and the tiny Train Jaune, continue on from Villefranche to the stop "Thues/Caranca" (30min., 7 per day, €4.90 from Villefranche). The *gîte-camping*

Mas de Bordes ❶ is perched beside a crumbling stone church in a canyon nook, right by a natural hot spring. (☎ 04 68 97 05 00. €9.15 with kitchen access; camping €4 per person, €1 per tent.) The *gîte* is a three-hour walk from an entrance to the **GR10,** the hiking trail which stretches from the Atlantic to the Mediterranean.

◙ ◨ SIGHTS AND OUTDOORS. Built into the mountainside high above the town, Vauban's masterpiece, the 17th-century **Fort Liberia,** takes the form of two overlapping hexagons. Buy tickets at the info office/shop inside the town, on the main street before the turn off to the tourist office. (☎ 04 68 96 34 01. €5.35, students €4.60. Open daily June-Sept. 9am-8pm; Apr.-May 10am-7pm; Oct.-Mar. 10am-6pm.) To reach its fortified heights, hike (20min.) or catch the *navette* from Porte de France (€2.30). Vaubon left towers to climb and passageways to navigate, but it is the view of the impossibly picturesque Villefranche from above that makes the trip worthwhile. There are actually only 832 steps in the subterranean "Staircase of 1000 Steps," which leads back down to the city, but you probably won't mind.

The walled fortifications of Villefranche offer more rock passageways in which you can lose yourself, but the **remparts,** accessible from the tourist office, look better from the outside. (☎ 04 68 96 22 96. Open July and Aug. daily 10am-7:30pm; June and Sept. 10am-6:30pm; Oct.-May 2-5pm. €3.50, students €2.30. Cassette tour in English or French available for €3.)

◙ FESTIVALS. On June 23, the **Fête des Feux de St-Jean,** celebrated throughout the Catalonian region, burns brightly in Villefranche. Torches lit on the Canigou mountain return sacred fire to the village, where locals dance the traditional *sardane,* drink wine, and leap over bonfires. People dressed as giants also appear in the village every Sunday in April in recognition of **Pâques.** Instead of Bastille Day, Villefranche-de-Conflent celebrates the **Fête de St-Jacques** from July 20-22.

The biggest festival in the area is in the nearby city of **Prades,** which for 23 years was home to the great Catalan cellist Pablo Casals during his political exile from Franco's Spain. The annual **Festival Pablo Casals,** from the last week of July through the middle of August, attracts an array of international musicians for three weeks of chamber music and workshops. Tickets (€23-30) are available after May 15 from the **Association Pablo Casals,** rue Victor Hugo. (☎ 04 68 96 33 07; fax 04 68 96 50 95. Open M-F 9am-noon and 2-6pm. MC/V.)

COLLIOURE

Collioure (pop. 2770) is nestled at the idyllic spot where the Pyrénées tumble through emerald vineyards and orchards to meet the shores of the Mediterranean. The rocky harbor of this small port captured the fancy of Greeks and Phoenicians long before it modeled for a then-unknown Matisse, who baptized the town an artists's mecca in 1905. He was soon followed by Dérain, Dufy, Dalí, and Picasso. You'll understand the town's draw after a glimpse at the expansive sea and stone lighthouse tower bathed in the late afternoon sun. On market days, fishermen and farmers sell products direct from the boat or the homestead. Apricots and peaches fresh from the orchards are sold alongside anchovies and regional Banyul wines.

⌂ PRACTICAL INFORMATION. The **train station** (☎ 04 68 82 05 89), at the top of av. Aristide Maillol, sends trains north to Narbonne (1hr., 12 per day, €11.50) and Perpignan (20min., 15 per day, €4.40). You can also go south to **Spain;** trains run to Barcelona (3½hr., 5 per day, €12.10) and Port Bou (6 per day, €2.90). For info on the coastal bus routes, call **Cars Inter 66** (☎ 04 68 35 29 02) or inquire at the **tourist office,** pl. du 18 Juin. They can help plan dayhikes. (☎ 04 68 82 15 47; fax 04 68 82 46 29; contact@collioure.com; www.collioure.com. Open July-Aug. daily 9am-8pm;

Sept.-June M-Sa 9am-noon and 2-6:30pm.) **X-Trem Bike,** 7 rue de la Tour d'Auvergne, keeps strange hours but has good prices on **bike rentals.** (☎06 15 97 83 74. Open daily 8:30am-12:30pm, 1:30-2:30pm, 6:30-7:30pm. Half-day rental €8, full day €14, week €60; €75 deposit.) **Exchange currency** at **Banque Populaire,** 16 av. de la République. (☎04 68 82 05 94. Open M-F 8am-noon and 1:30-5pm.) The **police station** is on rue Michelet. (July-Aug. ☎04 68 82 25 63; Sept.-June ☎04 68 82 00 60.) The **post office** is on rue de la République. (☎04 68 98 36 00. Open M-Tu and Th-F 9am-noon and 2-5pm, W 8:30am-12:30pm and 2-5pm; Sa 8:30-11:30am.) **Postal code:** 66190.

⌂ ☐ ACCOMMODATIONS AND FOOD. Collioure fills its hotels and beaches to the brim during July and August. **Hôtel Triton ❸,** 1 rue Jean Bart, is on the waterfront, five minutes from the center of town. The rooms have A/C, TVs, and showers, for comparably low prices. (☎04 68 98 39 39; fax 04 68 82 11 32. Breakfast €6. Reserve rooms as early as possible. Doubles €31, with toilet €44, with view of the sea €53. AmEx/MC/V.) The **Hostellerie des Templiers ❹** is on av. Camille Pelletan (mailing address: 12 quai de l'Amirauté), facing the château. Tiled stairways lead to hallways covered top to bottom with over a thousand original paintings, gifts of such lodgers as Matisse, Picasso, and Dalí (see **Sights,** below). The simple rooms come equipped with original works of art. The hotel also has two annexes in the back offering cheaper rooms. (☎04 68 98 31 10; fax 04 68 98 01 24; info@hotel-templiers.com; www.hotel_templiers.com. Breakfast €5.80. Reception 8am-11pm. June-Aug. doubles with bath €52-60; quads with bath €93. Low-season doubles with bath €45-54, quads with bath €76-79. Annex: in summer doubles with bath €48; in winter €38. AmEx/MC/V.) **Camping Les Amandiers ❷,** 28 rue de la Démocratie, Plage de l'Ouilla, is a 20-min. walk north of town on the N114 road, but only 150m from the beach. The campgrounds are crowded with cars and tents, but the price includes hot showers. (☎04 68 81 14 69; fax 04 68 81 09 95. Reception 8am-10pm. Open Apr.-Sept. €20 for 2 people and tent.)

Local produce is sold at a fantastic **market,** centered on pl. du Maréchal Leclerc and spilling out along the canal toward the Château Royal. (Open W and Su 8am-1pm.) Reasonably priced *créperies*, bakeries, and cafés crowd **rue St-Vincent** near the port. For the greatest selection, head to the **Shopi supermarket,** 16 av. de la République. (Open M-Sa 8:30am-12:30pm and 3:30-7pm.) The **Petit Casino** on pl. Maréchal Leclerc has more extensive hours. (Open mid-June to mid-Sept. M-Sa 7am-7:30pm, Su 7am-3pm; mid-Sept. to mid-June Tu-Sa 7:30am-12:30pm and 3:30-7pm, Su 7am-12:30pm.)

◎ SIGHTS. Extending from pl. du 8 Mai 1945 to the port, the hulking white stone **Château Royal** sheltered the kings of Majorca in the 13th century, and was later fortified by both French and Spanish kings during the unending border wars. The view of the brilliant blue harbor at the top of the chateau is spectacular. (☎04 68 82 06 43. Open June-Sept. daily 10am-5:15pm; Oct.-May 9am-4:15pm. €3, students and children €1.50.) The view encompasses the red-domed tower of the 17th-century **Notre-Dame-des-Anges,** whose tower rises majestically from foundations in the sea. The steeple was a fortified stone lighthouse in the Middle Ages. The tower is not open for climbing, and the inside of the church itself is much less impressive. (Open daily 7:30am-noon and 2-6pm.) A 30min. hike through the **Parc Pams,** behind the Musée d'Art Moderne off rte. de Port-Vendres, will give a good view of the 16th-century **Fort Saint Elme,** built by Spain's Charles V. Back across the bay, on the northern end of town, a walkway built into the bottom of the cliffs a few kilometers north to **Argelès** along the isolated coastline. Hikers can get info from the tourist office on these and other magnificent trails nearby.

To retrace the steps of Matisse and Dérain, follow the **Chemin du Fauvisme.** The *chemin* begins and ends in the "Espace Fauve" in front of the tourist office, where you can pick up a map and itinerary. Over a thousand of the artists's originals are displayed on the walls of the **Hostellerie des Templiers,** 12 quai de l'Amirauté (see **Accommodations,** above). Proprietor Jo Pous was only a child when Matisse and Picasso set up easels in the living room. Visitors who are not staying in the hotel are welcome to view the paintings. Less impressive is the small collection at the **Musée d'Art Moderne-Fonds Peské,** Villa Pams, rte. de Port-Vendres, which includes some paintings of Collioure and ceramics from the Hispano-Mauresque period. (☎04 68 82 10 19. Open July-Aug. daily 10am-noon and 2-7pm; Sept. and June 10am-noon and 2-6pm; Oct.-May W-M 10am-noon and 2-5pm. €2, students €1.50.)

Those with a taste for the harbor should stop by **Les Etablissements Desclaux,** 3 rte. d'Argelès. Besides selling anchovies, the store escorts visitors into the back where they can watch the salty product being prepared and taste a series of anchovies preserved in vinegar with flavors like lemon, curry, and pimento.

[icons] EXCURSIONS AND FESTIVALS. The **Centre International de Plongée,** 15 rue de la Tour d'Auvergne, provides numerous nautical services and entertainments, including windsurfing (2hr. rental or 1hr. mini-course €15), and scuba diving. (☎04 68 82 07 16; fax 04 68 82 44 74; www.cip-collioure.com. 8-session initiation course €237, per dive €25 with scuba card. Open Apr.-Nov.)

From August 14 to 18, the streets of Collioure fill with dance and music for the **Festival de St-Vincent.** Midway through the festival, on August 16th, a **corrida** (bullfight) at the arena (5pm) is followed by a **fireworks** display over the sea (10pm).

PERPIGNAN

The hot and crowded city of Perpignan (pop. 130,000) is only a few kilometers from the transparent waters of the Mediterranean, but the distance feels much larger when you're stuck in the midst of this congested city. Although the Catalan influence permeates the town, with brilliant "blood and gold" flags hanging everywhere, there is little to see or do in central Perpignan. Even the streets of the old city, heralded by the towers of the Castillet, are notable only for their restaurants. What makes Perpignan worthwhile are cheap hotels, a good transportation system, and friendly locals; the town provides a reasonably-priced home base for visits to the more expensive and beautiful towns of Collioure, Céret, or Canet-Plage.

[icon] TRANSPORTATION

Flights: Aéroport de Perpignan-Rivesaltes, 10km northwest of the town center, just outside of town along the D117 (info and reception desk ☎04 68 52 60 70). **Ryanair** (☎04 68 71 96 65; www.ryanair.com) offers the cheapest flights to **London** (from €115). **Hertz** rents **cars** at the airport (☎04 68 61 18 77). **Navette Aeroport** runs shuttles from the SNCF train station and the *gare routière* to the airport. (☎04 68 55 68 00. €4.50, children and groups €3. M-F 5 per day, Sa 6 per day, Su 4 per day.)

Trains: rue Courteline, off av. de Gaulle. Info open M-Sa 8am-6:30pm. To: **Carcassonne** (1½hr., change at Narbonne; 2 per day; 12.20); **Lyon** (4-5hr., 4-5 per day, €41.10); **Montpellier** (2hr., 8-10 per day, €18.30); **Nice** (6hr., 3 per day, €45.60); **Paris** (6-10hr., 4 per day, €78.20); **Toulouse** (2½-3hr., some change at Narbonne; 15 per day; €21.90).

Buses: 17 av. Général Leclerc (☎04 68 35 29 02). Office open M-Sa 7am-6:45pm. **Car Inter 66** (☎04 68 35 29 02) runs 4 buses to the beaches from **Le Barcarès** to the north for €5.35. Schedules at both tourist offices. They offer a **tourist pass** good for 8 days within the *département* (€22.90).

Local Transportation: CTP, pl. Gabriel-Péri (☎04 68 61 01 13). Tickets €1.05; *carnet* of 10 €7.50.

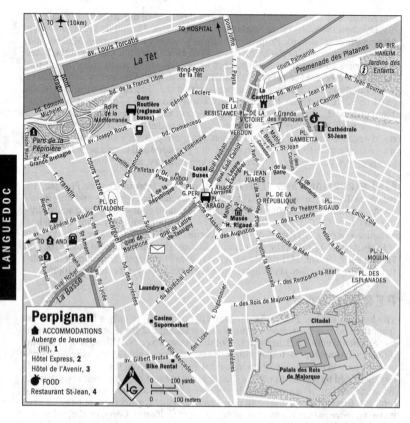

Perpignan

🏠 ACCOMMODATIONS
Auberge de Jeunesse
(HI), **1**
Hôtel Express, **2**
Hôtel de l'Avenir, **3**
🍴 FOOD
Restaurant St-Jean, **4**

Taxis: A.B.S. Taxi (☎06 14 55 84 36). Catch them at the train station. 24hr.

Bike Rental: Cycles Mercier, 20 av. Gilbert Brutus (☎04 68 85 02 71). €38 for 5 days.
€120 deposit. Open M-Sa 9am-12:30pm and 2:30-7:30pm.

➕🛈 ORIENTATION AND PRACTICAL INFORMATION

Perpignan's train station, once referred to as "the center of the world" by a rather
off-center Salvador Dalí, is almost constantly packed with weary travelers, making connections to Catalonia, Spain, 50km to the south, and to the Pyrénées,
whose foothills begin rolling 30km to the west. The city itself stretches out for a
long way from the station, but most of the action takes place in the small *vieille
ville* just past the tower of the red **Castillet**. The area makes a triangle, bounded
on the far side by the regional tourist office, the **pl. de la Victoire** up the canal
toward the train station, and the **Palais des Rois de Majorque.** Be thankful for the
bus shelters' useful maps, as the *vieille ville* is a labyrinth. Most of Perpignan's
gypsy population lives on the hilltop past the *vieille ville* in the **Quartier St-
Jacques,** near the intersection of bd. Jean Bourrat and bd. Anatole France. In the
daytime, this neighborhood's residents sit outside, chatting noisily—but it's better to avoid it at night.

Tourist Office: Palais des Congrès, pl. Armand Lanoux (☎04 68 66 30 30; fax 04 68 66 30 26; www.perpignantourisme.com), at the opposite end of the town center from the train station. Follow av. de Gaulle to pl. de Catalogne, then take bd. Georges Clemenceau across the canal past Castillet as it becomes bd. Wilson. Follow the signs along the park (promenade des Platanes) to the glass-paneled Palais des Congrès (20min. walk from train station). Multilingual staff offers comprehensive **tours** in French (2½hr., €4). For tours in English, call ☎04 68 22 25 96. Open June-Sept. M-Sa 9am-7pm, Su 10am-noon and 2-5pm; Oct.-May M-Sa 9am-noon and 2-6pm.

Laundromat: Laverie Foch, 23 rue Maréchal Foch. Open daily 7am-8:30pm.

Youth Center: Bureau d'Information Jeunesse, 35 quai Vauban (☎04 68 34 56 56), near the hostel. Open June-Aug. M-F 9:30am-12:30pm and 2-5pm; Sept.-May M-F 9:30am-12:30pm and 1:30-6pm, Sa 2-5pm.

Police: av. de Grande Bretagne (☎04 68 35 70 00).

Hospital: av. du Languedoc (☎04 68 61 66 33).

Internet Access: Cyber Espace, 45 bis. av. du Général Leclerc, across the street from the *gare routière* (☎04 68 35 36 29). €4.50 per hr., €8 for 3hr. daily 9-11am, 2-6pm, or 9pm-1am; Happy Hour 11am-2pm, €3 per hr. Open July-Aug. M-Sa 2pm-1am, Su 2-6pm; Sept.-June M-Sa 7am-1am, Su 2-8pm. **Hôtel Méditerranée,** 62bis av. de Gaulle (☎04 68 34 87 48). €6.10 per hr.; after 8pm or before noon €4.55 per hr. Open daily 7am-2am. **Arena Games,** 9bis rue Pous (☎04 68 34 26 22). €6.10 per hr., students €5.30. Open daily 11am-11:30pm.

Post Office: quai de Barcelone (☎04 68 51 99 12). **Currency exchange.** Open M-Tu and Th-F 8am-7pm, W 9am-7pm, Sa 8am-noon. **Poste Restante:** 66020. **Postal code:** 66000.

ACCOMMODATIONS AND CAMPING

The cheapest hotels are near the train station on av. Général de Gaulle. From these hotels, it's only about a 10min. walk to the city center. The bare Auberge de Jeunesse is also in this section of the city.

Hôtel de l'Avenir, 11 rue de l'Avenir (☎04 68 34 20 30; fax 04 68 34 15 63; avenirhotel@aol.com), off av. du Général de Gaulle. Colorful rooms with furnishings and wall decoration handpainted by owner. Hallways, terraces, and a rooftop garden give the feel of a beautiful summer home. The lowest-priced rooms fill quickly, so reserve ahead. Breakfast €4. Shower €2.75. Singles €15.25; doubles and larger singles €18.30-€19.90, with toilet €22.15-23.70, with shower €26.70-32; quads €38.15. Prices for everything except singles drop €1.50-2.30 in the off-season. AmEx/MC/V. ❷

Auberge de Jeunesse La Pépinière (HI), rue Marc-Pierre (☎04 68 34 63 32; fax 04 68 51 16 02), on the edge of town, between the highway and the police station. From the train station, take a few steps down av. de Gaulle and turn left onto rue Valette. Turn right onto av. de Grande Bretagne, left on rue Claude Marty (rue de la Rivière on some maps) just before the police station, and right onto rue Marc-Pierre. (10min.) Small metal bunks are crowded into each room of this barrack-like hostel. Squat toilets and trough sinks are nearby. Music begins playing at 8am and the no-nonsense proprietors run through the hostel calling everyone to breakfast. Small kitchen available 4-11pm. Breakfast included. Sheets €3. Check-out 11am; strictly enforced. Lockout 11am-4pm. Closed Dec. 20-Jan. 20. Bunks €11.60. **Members only. ❶**

Hôtel Express, 3 av. Général de Gaulle (☎04 68 34 89 96). A block from the train station. Clean, functional rooms include table and chair. Breakfast €3.05. Shower €2.30. Often full; call ahead. Singles and doubles €15.25, with shower €19; triples or quads €28-38.75. MC/V. ❷

Camping Le Catalan, rte. de Bompas (☎04 68 63 16 92). Take "Bompas" bus from train station and ask to be let out at "Camping Catalan" (15min., 2 per day, €1.80). Snack bar, pool, hot showers, and 94 spots. July-Aug. 2 people €14; Mar.-June 2 people €10. Extra person €2.50-4. ❶

🍴 FOOD

Perpignan's best culinary feature is its spread of reasonably priced restaurants serving Catalan specialties. If you've been waiting to try *escargots*, don't slither an inch farther; *cargolade* smothers your shell-wearing garden friends with garlic *aïoli*. The specialty *touron* nougat is available in many flavors. **Pl. de la Loge, pl. Arago,** and **pl. de Verdun** in the *vieille ville* are filled with restaurants that stay lively at night. For candle-lit tables, take the **rue des Fabriques Couvertes** from pl. de Verdun. Pricier options line **quai Vauban** along the canal. Try **av. de Gaulle,** in front of the train station, for cheaper alternatives. You'll find barrels and baskets of specialties that don't stick around long at the **open-air markets** on pl. de la République (open daily 6am-1pm) and pl. Cassanyes (open Sa-Su 8am-1pm). Pl. de la République also holds an assortment of fruit stores, *charcuteries,* and bakeries, as well as the **Marché République.** (Open Tu-Su 7am-1pm and 4-7:30pm.) **Casino supermarket** stockpiles food on bd. Félix Mercader. (☎04 68 34 74 42. Open M-Sa 8:30am-8pm.) The best location in the city is held by the ▓**Restaurant St-Jean** ❸, 1 rue Cité Bartissol, which sets its tables in the courtyard of the cathedral. Enjoy *pause terroir* (€9.20), grilled bread smothered with cheese and toppings such as onions, potatoes and anchovies. (☎04 68 51 22 25. Open daily noon-2:30pm and 7-10pm.)

👁 SIGHTS

A **museum passport,** valid for one week (€6), allows entrance to the Musée Hyacinthe Rigaud, the Casa Pairal, the Musée Numismatique Joseph Puig, 42 av. de Grande-Bretagne (☎04 68 34 11 70), and the Musée d'Histoire Naturelle, 12 rue Fontaine Neuve (☎04 68 35 50 87). Purchase at any of the listed museums. Entrance to each museum is €3.

An uphill walk across the *vieille ville* brings you to the sloping red-rock walls of Perpignan's 15th-century Spanish **citadel.** Concealed inside is the simple, square 13th-century **Palais des Rois de Majorque,** where the Majorcan kings used to breed lions. Its towers give an amazing view of the Mediterranean Sea and the Pyrénées. The courtyard now serves as a concert hall, sheltering plays and jazz and classical concerts in summer at 9pm; tickets at the door. (Enter from av. Gilbert Brutus. Palais ☎04 68 34 48 29. Open June-Sept. daily 10am-6pm; Oct.-May 9am-5pm. Tours every 30min. in French. €3, students €2. Ticket sales end 45min. before closing.)

Back in the *vieille ville,* the **Musée Hyacinthe Rigaud,** 16 rue de l'Ange, contains a small but impressive collection of paintings by 13th-century Spanish and Catalan masters; canvases by Rigaud, court artist to Louis XIV and one of the 17th century's great portraitists; and works by Ingres, Picasso, Miró, and Dalí. (☎04 68 35 43 40. Open W-M noon-7pm. €3, students €2.) Guarding the entrance to the city's center, **Le Castillet** holds the small **Casa Pairal,** a museum of Catalan domestic ware and religious relics. (☎04 68 35 42 05. Open June 15-Sept. 15 W-M 10am-7pm; Sept. 16-June 14 W-M 10am-5:30pm. €4, students €2.) A paragon of Gothic architecture, the **Cathédrale St-Jean** at pl. Gambetta is partly supported by a macabre pillar depicting the severed head of John the Baptist. (☎04 68 51 33 72. Open 9am-noon and 3-7pm.)

🎵 🔲 ENTERTAINMENT AND FESTIVALS

Perpignan is a big city that keeps small-town hours. Everything seems to shut down by 8pm, and even the restaurants usher out their last customers around 10:30pm. If you're looking for a night on the town, prepare yourself for a calm and café-centric experience. During the summer, traditional Catalonian dancing livens up pl. de la Loge (two per week 11am-1pm). The open-till-dawn clubs lining the beaches at nearby **Canet-Plage** (see p. 462) constitute the wildest nightlife, but unless you can make the night last until 6:25am (9:30am on Sunday morning), getting back to Perpignan will mean paying €14-17 for a taxi.

Procession de la Sanch takes over the streets of the *vieille ville* on Good Friday. Although the hooded, solemn ceremony feels a little like the rites of some secret society, everyone in town is welcomed to watch. As in most of southwestern France, sacred fire is brought down from Mt. Canigou on June 23 for the **Fête de St-Jean.** Dance the *sardana*, munch powdered-sugar *rouquilles*, and gulp down the sweet *muscat* wine. In July, the **Estivales de Perpignan** (www.estivals.com) brings world-renowned theater and dance to Perpignan. Get info about the 2002 acts to the right of the tourist office in the Palais de Congrès. During the first two weeks in September, Perpignan hosts **Visa Pour l'Image,** an international festival of photojournalism (www.visapourlimage.com).

🔲 DAYTRIP FROM PERPIGNAN: CÉRET

Car Inter 66 (☎ 04 6 8 39 11 96 in Céret; ☎ 04 68 35 29 02 in Perpignan; fax 04 68 87 00 56) *runs* **buses** *to Céret from Perpignan (45min., every hr., €5.90). From the bus stop on av. Clemenceau, the* **tourist office,** *1 av. Georges Clemenceau (☎04 68 87 00 53; www.ceret.fr.), is 2 blocks up the hill on the right. Make sure your bus stops in the town center. The office offers a free map of easy hikes and tours. (2hr.; tours €3.80. Open July-Aug. M-Sa 9am-12:30pm and 2-7pm, Su 10am-12:30pm; Sept.-Oct. M-F 10am-noon and 2-5pm, Sa 10am-noon.)*

Céret, in the foothills of the Pyrenées, blossoms in the spring—the first cherries of each season from Céret's prized orchards are sent to the President of France. The town square is not just known for its cherry markets but also for being the "Cubist Mecca," beloved by Chagall, Picasso, Manolo, and Herbin. Céret is now home to one of the best museums in southwestern France. Far enough into the hills to allow spectacular hiking, Céret has plenty to offer any naturalist or artist.

The **Musée d'Art Moderne,** 8 bd. Maréchal Joffre, is up the hill from the tourist office. The collections in this graffiti-covered building are composed primarily of personal gifts to the museum by artists including Picasso, Braque, Chagall, and Miró. (☎04 68 87 27 76. Open June 15-Sept. 15 daily 10am-7pm; May-June 14 and Sept. 16-30 10am-6pm; Oct.-Apr. W-M 10am-6pm. July-Sept. €7, students €5.50; Oct.-June €5.50, students €3.50, under 16 free.)

According to legend, the **pont du Diable** (Bridge of Satan), which links the town center to its outskirts, couldn't be successfully built until the devil agreed to aid in its construction. But he claimed the right to the first soul to cross the bridge, so the villagers sent a black cat across it. In the town center, admire the marble fountain in **pl. des Neuf Jets.** The Castilian lion was kept as a symbol of France's victory over Spain in taking Céret in 1659.

In late May, Céret celebrates the **Grande Fête de la Cerise** with two days of cherry markets and Catalan songs. The most raucous *fèria*, **Céret de Toros,** occurs every year over the second weekend in July. At 3:30pm, young cows are released into the crowd for anyone to wrestle to the ground. The street show serves as an appetizer for the grand performances, when two bullfights satisfy local bloodlust. A *novillada* without picadors lets young matadors practice on young bulls. Afterwards, music continues in the streets well into the night. (☎ 04 68 87 47 4; adac@ceret-de-toros.com; www.ceret-de-toros.com. Tickets €26-82 for one *corrida* or *novillada*, €91-214 for two *corridas* and one *novillada*.) In the last weekend in July, crowds gather for the **Festival de la Sardane,** commemorating the traditional Catalan folkdance. It includes a contest of Sardane groups as well as nearly continuous dancing in the streets. (Entrance to contest €12.)

NEAR PERPIGNAN

CANET-PLAGE AND THE CÔTE CATALANE

Perpignan residents commute to **Canet-Plage,** a 30min. bus ride from the main city. There are trampolines and miniature golf courses, and over 20 beach clubs cast their neon glow on the long sandy beaches of this rollicking town. Inland, the streets are lined with cafés and a daily market.

🖫 ⚡ TRANSPORTATION AND PRACTICAL INFORMATION. CTP Shuttles (☎ 04 68 61 01 13) runs **buses** to Canet-Plage; catch the #1 in Perpignan at pl. Catalogne (at the top of av. Général de Gaulle) or at prom. des Platanes on bd. Wilson. (30min.; every 30min.; last bus from Canet around 9pm, last from Perpignan around 8:30pm; round-trip €2.10.) In July and August, **Bus Interplages** connects the Côte Catalane resorts from Le Barcarès to Cerbère. (☎ 04 68 21 05 18; one-way €9, round-trip €16.50.) **Taxis** are on av. Méditerranée near the beach. (☎ 04 68 73 14 81. €20 to Perpignan, €26-€30 to the airport.) Rent **bikes** at **Sunbike,** 122 Promenade Côte Vermeille. (☎ 04 68 73 88 65. Bikes €8 for 2hr., €14 for 8hr., €45 per week. Open July 14-Aug. 20 daily 8am-midnight; June 13-July 13 and Aug. 21-Sept. 9am-8pm, Oct.-May Tu-Sa 9am-noon and 2-6pm.) The Canet-Plage **tourist office,** pl. de la Méditerranée, doles out free brochures and maps. (☎ 04 68 73 61 00. Open July-Aug. daily 9am-7pm; Sept. and June M-Sa 9am-noon and 2-6pm, Su 10am-noon and 2:30-5:30pm; Oct.-May M-Sa 9am-noon and 2-5pm, Su 10am-noon and 3-5pm.)

🖫 🗋 ACCOMMODATIONS AND FOOD. Unless you are camping or can claim one of the 24 rooms in the well-priced **Hôtel Clair Soleil ❸,** 26 av. de Catalogne, it's worth the trouble to commute from Perpignan. Internet access is free, and all rooms come with balconies. (☎/fax 04 68 80 32 06; clair-soleil@wanadoo.fr. Breakfast €4. Singles, doubles, or triples with shower €34.50, with toilet €40.50. Additional bed €8. 15% student discount. Prices lower Sept.-June. AmEx/MC/V.) Three-star **Camping Club Mar-Estang ❷,** a 25min. walk from the tourist office, hosts the most lively social scene in Canet-Plage. It has tennis courts, water-slides, and its own disco, which holds foam parties every Monday. They organize excursions to both Carcassonne (€24.50) and Figuères (€26), in Spain. (☎ 04 68 80 35 53; fax 04 68 73 32 94. Open Apr. 28-Sept. Reception 7am-midnight. July 28-Aug. 25 2 people and car €23; Apr. 28-July 27 and Aug. 26-Sept. 2 people and car €20. Electricity €4. 30% discount for 4 or more nights.)

On the beachfront, it's not hard to find a good, cheap meal. **Gallerie Cassanyes,** leading away from the Espace Méditerranée, is packed with sandwich shops and restaurants that improve in quality the farther you get from the plaza. Pizzerias have pizzas or pasta for around €7. The **market** near the beach on pl. Foment de la Sardane sells produce and cheap clothes. (Open Tu-Su 7:30am-12:30pm.) There is another **market** in the village, 45min. from the beach, at pl. St-Jacques. (Open W and Sa 7:30am-noon.) Pick up supplies at the **Petit Casino supermarket,** 12 av. de la Méditerranée. (Open July-Aug. daily 8am-12:30pm and 3:30-7:45pm; Sept.-June Tu-Sa 8am-12:30pm and 3:30-7:30pm, Su 8am-12:30pm.) Bakeries and *charcuteries* cluster along the same avenue toward the port.

ENTERTAINMENT. At night the beachfront shimmers with neon lights. Vendors line the boardwalk, children crowd onto the musical carousels in the Espace Méditerranée, and parents sit in one of the surrounding cafés, most of which bring in live music after 8pm. The **casino**, at the edge of the Espace Méditerranée, is a good place to lose your money. (☎04 68 80 14 12. Casino open July-Aug. daily 10am-4am; Sept.-June Su-Th 10am-2am, F-Sa 10am-4am.) A 20min. walk away from the beach toward Canet, the discothèque complex **La Luna**, in the Colline des Loisirs, is packed with people once the bars close around 2am. (☎04 68 73 31 01. Open July-Aug. daily midnight-6am; Sept.-June F-Sa midnight-6am. €12 for individual entrance to each of the three discos.) The most youthful disco scene is found at **Voice&BDF**—groups can call ahead for a bus from Perpignan. **Paradisco** draws a slightly older crowd, while **Full Moon** hosts a good variety of guests.

NARBONNE

Situated 30min. from the crowded sands of Narbonne-Plage and Gruisson-Plage, unremarkable Narbonne (47,000) was not always a minor city. As Rome's first colony in France, it was at one point the capital of a duchy that encompassed Nîmes, Toulouse, and four other cities. Narbonne fell off the map when its port silted up in 1340. Most of its fine Roman architecture subsequently deteriorated, leaving only the huge, unfinished cathedral as a reminder of what once was. Narbonne never really recovered; today its quiet provincial elegance hides few attractions. The city's crime rates are higher than would be imagined for such a peaceful-looking town; lock doors and try not to walk alone at night.

PRACTICAL INFORMATION

Trains: av. Carnot (☎04 67 62 50 50). Ticket office open daily 5:40am-8pm. To: **Béziers** (15min., 19 per day, €4.30); **Carcassonne** (30min., 15 per day, €8.30); **Montpellier** (1hr., 12 per day, €12.20); **Perpignan** (70min., 14 per day, €8.80); **Toulouse** (1½hr., 13 per day, €17.20).

Tourist Office: pl. Salengro (☎04 68 65 15 60; fax 04 68 65 59 12; www.mairie-narbonne.fr). Turn right onto av. Carnot, which becomes bd. F. Mistral, and then left up the stone staircase onto passage Rossell. Continue across rue de l'Ancienne Porte Neuve up the stone ramp and you will come out at pl. Salengro. (10min.) Free tourist guide in several languages. Open June 15-Sept. 15 M-Sa 8am-7pm, Su 9:30am-12:30pm; low season M-Sa 8:30am-noon and 2-6pm.

Tours: city tours (☎04 68 90 30 66) in French and English leave June 15-Sept. 15 every 30min. in front of the museums. €4.60, students and seniors €3.05; includes price of museum entry.

Police: bd. Général de Gaulle (☎04 68 90 38 50).

Internet Access: Versus, 73 rue Droite (☎04 68 32 95 27). €1 for 5min., €5 per hr. Open M-Th 8am-9pm, F 8am-midnight, Sa 10am-1am, Su 2-9pm.

Post Office: 19 bd. Gambetta (☎04 68 65 87 00). **Currency exchange.** Open M-F 8am-7pm, Sa 8:30am-noon. **Postal code:** 11100.

ACCOMMODATIONS

Centre International de Séjours, pl. Salengro (☎04 68 32 01 00; fax 04 68 65 80 20; cis.narbonne@wanadoo.fr), near the tourist office. This well-staffed hostel prioritizes groups that reserve ahead, but there's often extra space in the 3- to 5-bed dorm rooms.

Breakfast included. Restaurant. Night guard 24hr. Reception 8am-7pm. No reservations for individuals. 2nd-floor rooms with wooden bunks €11, bigger 3rd-floor rooms with showers €14; singles €19, with shower €23. ❶

Hôtel de France, 6 rue Rossini, off bd. du Dr. Ferroul near the pont de la Liberté (☎04 68 32 09 75; fax 04 68 65 50 30). This 2-star hotel has a calm atmosphere and an excellent location just off the canal. Bright, airy rooms with TV on the bottom floors; the small, charming singles on the attic floor have low ceilings and a sunroof. Breakfast €5.50. Reception 7:30am-10pm. Reserve July-Aug. Singles and doubles €25-27, with shower €40-45; triples and quads €48-63. MC/V. ❸

Hôtel de la Gare, av. Pierre Sémard, across from the train station (☎04 68 32 10 54). Dim and old but clean rooms with showers, and low prices. Friendly owner keeps many cats—avoid hotel if you have allergies. Reception 24hrs. Breakfast €3.60. Singles and doubles €20; quads €29, with bath €7. ❷

Hôtel de Paris, 2 rue du Lion d'Or (☎04 68 32 08 68). Follow the directions to the tourist office and turn onto rue Lion d'Or from rue Chennebier. Though the hotel's small, musty rooms are rather run-down, it is located in the town center. Breakfast €5. Reception 24hr. Singles and doubles €23, with shower €31; quads €46; quints €54. Prices lower Sept.-May. MC/V. ❷

Campsites: Narbonne has many beachside campgrounds. In July and Aug., 6 buses per day head to the campsites from Narbonne's train station (€2.50). **Camping des Côtes des Roses** (☎04 68 49 83 65) has tennis, horseback riding, and mini-golf near the Mediterranean. Open Easter-Sept. 2 people €12. Electricity €15. **Camping le Soleil d'Oc** (☎04 68 49 86 21) rents spots Apr.-Oct. 2 people €15. Electricity €17.50. ❶

▐ FOOD

Good restaurants are hard to find in Narbonne. Grab a bite from the canal-side vendors lining **cours de la République** or pick up picnic items at the **market** on plan (not *place*) St-Paul on Thursday mornings. (Open 9am-noon.) There is a covered market at **Les Halles,** along the canal on cours Mirabeau. (Open daily 6am-1pm.) **Monoprix,** pl. Hôtel de Ville, satisfies all other food needs. (Open M-Sa 8:30am-7:30pm.) For lunch, the best deals are at **Le Chat Botté ❸,** 72 rue Droite. The €11.20 *menu de meunier* gives unlimited access to an extensive buffet of *hors d'oeuvres,* two more courses, and a carafe of wine. In the evenings, enjoy an elegant three-course dinner menu for €16. (☎04 68 65 34 50. Open M-Sa noon-2pm and 7-10:30pm, Su 7-10:30pm. AmEx/MC/V.)

◒ SIGHTS

Narbonne's monuments are all either in or next to the cathedral, on rue Gauthier, near the tourist office. There are no individual entrance fees; a **pass** allows entrance into the three museums for three days (€5, students €3.50).

The **Cathédrale St-Just et St-Pasteur** is the city's most central and prominent landmark. The architecture inside is unusual. Flying buttresses encircle the massive walls of the choir, but end abruptly. The cathedral is only half as large as its architects intended, because a dispute between the archbishops and the city government stopped construction. Free summer concerts (Su 9pm) showcase the bombastic pipe organ. (Open July-Aug. daily 10am-7pm; low season 9am-noon and 2pm-6pm.) Accessible from the inside of the cathedral, the opulent and beautifully restored **Palais des Archeveques** testifies to the power of the former archbishops of Narbonne. (☎04 68 90 30 66.) Within its walls, the **Musée Archéologique** displays a full collection of Roman artifacts. Across the atrium in the **Musée d'Art et d'Histoire,** where French, Flemish, and Italian 17th-century paintings hang in the exquisite former apartments of the archbishops. In front of the palace, in pl. Hôtel de Ville, a little section of an exposed commercial Roman road built in 120 BC (but not discovered until 1997) points the way to **l'Horreum,** an unfortunately named Roman grain warehouse. (Museums and l'Horreum ☎ 04 68 90 30 54. Open Apr.-Sept. daily 9:30am-12:15pm and 2-6pm; Oct.-Mar. Tu-Su 10am-noon and 2-5pm.)

Le Coche d'Eau du Patrimoine covers 20 centuries of history in several hours on its **boat tour** of the Canal de la Robine. (☎ 04 68 90 63 98. Tours July-Aug.)

🎵 📷 ENTERTAINMENT AND FESTIVALS

Narbonne-Plage, the town's most valuable asset, lies 15km to the east. **Buses** (☎ 04 68 90 77 64) leave from the parking lot to the right of the train station or from the terminal on quai Victor Hugo (35min.; July-Aug. 8 per day, Sept.-June 2-4 per day; €2.50). **Nightlife** in Narbonne is almost nonexistent. One solution is to take the **Carte JINS** bus, which runs Friday and Saturday in July and August, to the town of **Gruissan,** which is known for its strip of energetic discothèques. (Discos ☎ 04 68 32 68 69. Cover €10, including first drink.) **Buses** leave Narbonne in front of the JINS office, 60 bd. Général de Gaulle, at 11:30pm, returning from Gruissan at 4am.

Narbonne's biggest event is the festival **Le Théâtre: Scène Nationale de Narbonne,** which keeps January to May filled with all kinds of cultural acts. (☎ 04 68 90 90 20; www.narbonne.com/letheatre. Performances at 2 av. Domitius; usually at 8:45pm. Tickets €13.70-24.40. Reserve early.) Free amateur performances are the staple of Narbonne's **18th Annual Amateur Theater Festival,** which lasts one week in early July. (☎ 04 68 32 01 00. No charge for most events.)

BÉZIERS

Béziers today (pop. 69,000) is a archetypal Languedoc city, though its past can hardly be called provincial. Celts, Iberians, Phoenicians, Greeks, Romans, Arabs, and Franks have all passed through and left their mark on this welcoming city. The monuments here aren't spectacular, but its diverse past has inevitably left a few pleasant historical surprises. Béziers is also the starting point of the man-made Canal du Midi, which links to the Garonne River and serves as a channel between the Atlantic and the Mediterranean—before the construction of the Suez canal, the only alternative to the Strait of Gibraltar.

🗷 PRACTICAL INFORMATION. Frequent **trains** leave from the station, bd. Verdun, for **Montpellier** (40min., 25 per day, €9.45); **Narbonne** (15min., 20 per day, €4.30); **Toulouse** (1½hr., 6 per day, €19.20). Station open M-Sa 6am-9:15pm. From in front of the station, take the underpass and climb the steep rue de la Rotonde to the top of the hill, where you'll find the long tree-lined allées Paul Riquet. A left on allées Paul Riquet, named for the 17th-century engineer of the Canal du Midi, leads to an immense statue of Riquet himself. Behind him is the **tourist office,** 29 av. St-Saëns. (15min.) The office can direct you to the local wineries or nearby beaches. (☎ 04 67 76 47 00; fax 04 67 76 50 80. Open July-Aug. M-F 9am-7pm, Su 10am-noon; Sept.-June M 9am-noon and 2-6pm, Tu-F 9am-noon and 2-6:30pm, Sa 9am-noon and 3-6pm.) **Banque Courtois,** 24 allées Paul Riquet, has **currency exchange.** (Open M-F 9am-12:45pm and 3:45-5pm.) Other services include: **police** at 14 bd. Maréchal Leclerc (☎ 04 67 35 17 17); the **hospital** at ZAC de Montimaran (☎ 04 67 35 70 35); and **Internet** access at **Cyberia,** 7 rue Solférino. (☎ 04 67 62 99 91. €0.75 per 15min. Open M-Sa 8am-midnight, Su 2pm-midnight.) The **post office** is on pl. de Gabriel Péri. (☎ 04 67 49 86 00. Open M-F 8am-7pm, Sa 8am-noon.) **Postal code:** 34500.

IN RECENT NEWS

DEATH IN THE AFTERNOON

Bullfighting is not just for hot-blooded Spaniards. It was a French writer, Prosper Merimée, who put the romance in bullfighting with his short story "Carmen," and a French composer, Georges Bizet, who gave it a lyrical beauty in his opera. Bullfights are still held in several cities in the south of France, including Céret, Beziers, Carcassonne, Nimes, and Arles. The majority of these fights are modeled after the Spanish competition, during which 6 bulls are killed.

All too often, French bullfights are derivative from the Spanish version in a less savory way. According to the Society for the Prevention of Cruelty to Animals, 90% of bulls used in French bullfights are imported from Spain, and many are sick animals that would not be allowed to fight in Spain. France has also gained the reputation for 'doctoring' bullfights—sawing off and rebuilding horns with resin to make them painful for the bull to use. As spectators to bullfights are seldom connoisseurs, they often unknowingly support such operations.

Today, polls indicate that roughly 30% of the French do not support bullfighting. The cultural capital of the south, Marseille, has been a no-bullfight zone since 1962, and protesters hope to make Marseille the rule rather than the exception. And in the meantime, a French tradition is slowly replacing the violent Spanish one. In the *cocarde camarguaise*, a provençal game, players distract the bull with mitted hands while swiping at pom-poms that are strung between the bull's horn.

⊠ ACCOMMODATIONS AND CAMPING. The **Hôtel Cécil ❷**, 5 pl. Jean Jaurès, at the center of town off allées Paul Riquet, has the cheapest prices around for small but cozy rooms. One room is rented to students for €14. (☎ 04 67 28 48 55. Breakfast €4.50. Reception 7am-1am. Curfew 1am. Reserve ahead July-Aug. Singles with sink €17, with shower €23; doubles €21.50/€28.) The **Hôtel D'Angleterre ❷**, 22 pl. Jean Jaurès, off allées Paul Riquet, rents 22 tastefully decorated, unique rooms with large windows. The hotel is close to the busy cafés. (☎ 04 67 28 48 42; fax 04 67 28 61 53. Breakfast €5. Reserve in summer. Singles €20-22; doubles €2 with shower €25; quads with bath €45. MC/V.) **Hôtel Le Revelois ❷**, 60 av. Gambetta, is a block past the train station above a bar on a noisy street. Large, renovated rooms (15 out of 17) are bright and have TVs; ask to see yours first to be sure. (☎ 04 67 49 20 78; fax 04 67 28 92 28. Breakfast €5. Reception until 1am. Reserve July-Aug. Singles and doubles €25, with shower €32, with toilet €36, with bath €40; doubles and triples with shower €45-50; prices lower in winter.)

Info on **beach camping** at Valras in July and September is available at the tourist offices in Béziers or Valras (☎ 04 67 32 36 04).

▣ ▣ FOOD AND ENTERTAINMENT. *Biterroise*, the sweet local specialty cake, is flavored with almonds and filled with a pâté of grapes and wine. There's an indoor **market** at **Les Halles**, pl. Pierre Sémard. (Open Tu-Su 8am-noon.) Across the street, on the corner of rue Paul Riquet and rue Flourens, the **Frio Supermarché** has a reasonable selection. (Open M-Sa 8am-8pm, Su 8am-1pm.) There is a larger **Monoprix** at 5 allées Paul Riquet. (Open M-Sa 8:30am-8pm.)

As rue Paul Riquet runs toward the Théâtre Municipal, its sides become a giant blur of restaurants and cafés. These are all reasonably priced and great for people-watching; unfortunately, many are open only for lunch. For dinner, elegant but surprisingly inexpensive restaurants line the small av. Viennet, which runs between pl. G. Péri and the Cathédrale St. Nazaire (pl. de la Révolution).

The biweekly magazines *Pau's Café* and *Olé* list clubs and bars, as well as upcoming concerts, exhibits, and spectacles in Béziers and the surrounding area. *Exit* magazine describes the disco scene. After 10pm, many of the cafés on allées Paul Riquet attract crowds with pounding music and small bar sections. The fashionable set that frequents the **Ness Café**, 36 allées Paul Riquet, is often treated to live music on summer nights. Wine from €2.50 and pizza starting at €6.50. (☎ 04 67 49 07 19. Open Su-F 9am-1am, Sa 9am-

2am.) **Le Dollar** draws a slightly older clientele to its friendly, American interior. (☎ 04 67 28 20 84. Open daily 7am-1am.)

In mid-August, a **féria** that has earned Béziers the nickname "the French Seville" fills the town with *corridas* (bullfights) and *flamenco* dancing for three days. Tickets to individual events are available at the arena on av. Emile Claparede (€25-81); reservations for the entire three days can be made by telephone or on the web. (☎ 04 67 76 13 45; www.arenes-de-beziers.com. €117-360.)

◪ SIGHTS. The four museums of Béziers can be accessed with one pass (€3.05) sold at all museums. Hours and individual entrance fees are the same for all four. **Le Musée du Biterrois**, pl. St-Jacques, pulls together regional objects and curios from the Roman Empire until WWII. These fascinating items include ancient farm instruments, a 1913 Renault driven by "the youngest driver in the world" (4-year-old Jean Lovign), and documents testifying to both French collaboration and resistance during WWII. The museum also contains **Musée d'Histoire Naturelle,** showcasing stuffed birds, pinned insects, and a small aquarium. (Both museums ☎ 04 67 36 71 01. Open July-Aug. Tu-Su 10am-6pm; Apr.-June and Sept.-Oct. Tu-Su 9am-noon and 2pm-6pm; Nov.-Mar. Tu-Su 9am-noon and 2-5pm. €2.30, students €1.55.) **Musée Fabregat**, 6 pl. de la Revolution next to the cathedral, displays three floors of paintings and sculptures of regional artists from 15th to the 20th century (☎ 04 67 28 38 78). **Musée Fayet**, 9 rue du Capus, near les Halles, is noted for its extensive collection of sculptures by Bézier native Jean-Auguste Injalbert (☎ 04 67 28 38 78).

The **Cathédrale St-Nazaire,** built on the ruins of a pagan temple in pl. de la Révolution, was destroyed with the rest of the city in 1209 but rebuilt in the 14th century. The best view in town is from atop the belltower, which overlooks the countryside and a gorgeous horizon. (Open M-Sa 9am-noon and 2:30-7pm.) Follow rue des Albigeois from the cathedral to bd. d'Angleterre, take a right onto rue St-Vincent, and walk around the Collège Ste-Madeleine to reach **l'Eglise de la Madeleine.** The Romanesque structure is supported by a pillar scorched when an earlier church, full of Cathar martyrs, was razed by Abbot Arnaud Amalric in 1209. (Open Tu-Sa 9am-noon and 3pm-6pm, M 3pm-6pm.)

Paul Riquet's **Canal du Midi,** which links the Atlantic to the Mediterranean via the river Garonne, lies at the base of the city, down quai Port Neuf. The canal still helps irrigate the town and guide tourists around the city.

◪ EXCURSIONS. 15km from Béziers, the one-time fishing village of **Valras** has become a family beach resort complete with water slide and Ferris wheel. To get there, take bus #401 from the autogare at pl. du Général de Gaulle. (☎ 04 67 36 73 76. 45min.; July-Aug. 12 per day, last return 8pm; Sept.-June M-Sa 9 per day, Su 6 per day, last return at 7pm; round-trip €5.30.)

For those blessed with their own transportation, most of the nearby private vineyards and *caves cooperatives*, central outlets for local wineries, give tours ending with wine-sampling. **Le Club des Grands Vins des Châteaux du Languedoc** provides info on *dégustations* of the region's acclaimed *appellations:* Minervois, St-Chinian, Faucères, and a spicy red Cabrières. Contact the club's offices at the Château du Raissac, 2km west of Béziers. The cellars of the château itself are open to visitors year-round. (☎ 04 67 49 17 60; www.raissac.com; info@raissac.com. Open M-Sa 9am-1pm and 2-6pm.)

SÈTE

Sète (pop. 42,000), strategically situated between the Mediterranean Sea and the Bassin Thau, was founded in 1666 as a port town. At the turn of the 20th century, most of the Italian village of Gaet immigrated to Sète to escape the depression in

Italy. The result has been a hybrid Italian-French culture with unusual maritime festivals and the charming *Sètois* accent made famous by folk singer Georges Brassens. Today, Sète is France's largest Mediterranean fishing town. Heavy machinery now blots the otherwise picture-perfect shoreline, though there is a certain industrial poetry to the rusty ships and screeching gulls—appropriately enough, since the town gave birth to Paul Valéry, one of France's greatest modern poets. Visitors will enjoy the two local beaches.

GETTING THERE. The **train station,** quai M. Joffre, sends trains to: Béziers (30min., 30 per day, €6.50); Montpellier (20min., 30 per day, €4.40); Narbonne (50min., 23 per day, €9.20); and Toulouse (2hr., 6 per day, €23.10). Info office open M-F 9am-noon and 2-5:50pm.

PRACTICAL INFORMATION. Sétoise local buses run until 8pm. (☎04 67 74 18 77; €0.95.) Bus #3 goes from the train station to the tourist office; bus #6 runs from quai de la Résistance to both beaches. Pick up taxis at the train station. (☎04 67 74 01 89. €8 from the train station to the hostel.)

Sète's **tourist office,** 60 rue Mario Roustan, behind quai Général Durand, has free, occasionally faulty maps. To take the 20min. walk from the station, go straight onto pont de la Gare, cross the canal, and turn right onto quai Pavois d'Or. Turn the corner and cross the first bridge on the right, then turn left and walk down quai de Lattre de Tassigny past Pont Virla and Pont de la Civette until rue Roustan veers off to the right. (☎04 67 74 71 71. Open July-Aug. daily 9am-8pm; Sept.-June M-Sa 9am-noon and 2-6pm; Apr.-May also Su 10am-noon and 2-6pm. Change **currency** here at no commission. Open M-F 10am-1pm and 3-7pm, Sa 9:30-noon.)

To reach the **hospital** on bd. C. Blanc (☎04 67 46 57 57), take bus #2, 3, or 5 to "Hôpital." The **police** are at 50 quai de Bosc (☎04 67 46 80 22). For **Internet** access, stop at **Le Cyber-Snack,** 10 av. Victor Hugo and try to appreciate the bovine motif. (☎04 67 46 14 36. Open M-F 10am-7pm and Sa 2-7pm. €6.10 per hr.) The **post office** is on bd. Danièle Casanova. (☎04 67 46 64 20. Open M-F 8:30am-12:30pm and 1:30-6pm, Sa 8:30am-noon.) **Poste Restante:** 34207. **Postal code:** 34200.

ACCOMMODATIONS. The **Auberge de Jeunesse "Villa Salis" (HI) ❶,** rue du Gén. Revest, is at the top of one of the steepest roads in France. Follow the directions to the tourist office, then at pont de la Civette turn right onto rue Gén. de Gaulle and follow the signs to the *auberge* around the Parc du Château d'Eau and up the steep hill to the coral-colored inn. (20min.) Or take the #1 bus from the Théâtre bus stop (across the bridge from the train station, on the right) to "La Caraussane." Go back up the road and rue du Général Revest will be the third on the right. You will be rewarded for all that exertion by 90 spartan beds in tight 4- to 5-bed single-sex rooms. A commanding view of the city and clean bathrooms and showers make up for occasional rude treatment by the staff. Be sure to lock up valuables. (☎04 67 53 46 68; fax 04 67 51 34 01. Breakfast included. Dinner required July-Aug. Sheets €2.70. Reception 8am-noon and 6-10pm. Check-out 10am. Reservations recommended. Bunks €11.90, with dinner €18. Camping with dinner €16.50. MC/V. **Members only.**) The inconspicuous **Hôtel Tramontane ❷,** 5 rue Frédéric Mistral, off the quai de la Résistance in the center of town, offers clean, cheery rooms and sparkling bathrooms. (☎06 07 83 49 55. Breakfast €4.60. Reception 8am-noon, 6-9pm. Singles and doubles €19, with shower €36; triples €31/€39; quads €36/€42. AmEx/MC/V.) Two-star **Hôtel le Valéry ❸,** 20 rue Denfert-Rochereau, is just minutes from the train station. Walk across the bridge and continue straight onto rue Victor Hugo and then left on rue Denfert-Rochereau. A wide staircase leads to large, light, airy rooms. (☎04 67 74

77 51; fax 04 67 46 12 84. Breakfast €4. Reception 8am-10pm. July-Aug. reserve week in advance. Singles and doubles €31, with shower €22; triples €31/€38; quads €36/€43. MC/V.)

⬛ **FOOD.** The food in Sète is not distinctive—touristy seafood places and stock Italian eateries dominate the options. A good bet is the **Monoprix supermarket** at 7 quai de la Résistance (☎04 67 74 39 38; open M-Sa 8:30am-9pm, Su 9am-noon) or the **daily market** at **Les Halles**, just off rue Alsace-Lorraine. (Open 6am-1pm.) Vendors on the canal hawk fresh *tielles* (squid and tomato pizzas) for €2, though inland bakeries sell less authentic versions for €1.50. The restaurants lining **Promenade J.B. Marty**, at the end of rue Mario Roustan near the *vieux port*, serve the catch of the day in unusual ways for €9 and up. Cheaper pizza, pasta, and seafood are the specialties of the less touristy eateries on **rue Gambetta** and its offshoots. In Sète, the old maxim holds true: low prices mean low quality.

⬛ **SIGHTS.** The **Société Nautique de Sète,** on Môle St-Louis, at the southern end of town, is one of France's oldest yacht clubs. Throughout the summer, yacht races, including the famed Tour de France à la Voile, sail by the Môle. The best place to watch is in front of the café **Les Jardins de L'America's Cup.** The **plage de la Corniche** in the southwest corner of town starts off a 12km stretch of sandy beaches, accessible by bus #6 or a summer shuttle from quai de la Résistance at stops marked "La Plage" (July 1-Aug. 30, both €0.95).

A walk to the *vieux port* and up the hill along rue Haute gets you to the **maritime cemetery** that inspired Valéry's poem *Le Cimetière Marin*. The poet himself is interred here. (Open dusk till dawn.) The modern building above the cemetery, the **Musée Paul Valéry,** rue François Desnoyer, displays a huge collection of model ships and exhibits on local archaeology, history, and even water-jousting. (☎04 67 46 20 98. Open July-Aug. daily 10am-noon and 2-6pm; Sept.-June W-M 10am-noon and 2-6pm. July-Aug. €4.60; Sept.-June €3.) On the other side of the city is **L'Espace Georges Brassens,** 67 bd. Camille Blanc, a multimedia museum that pays homage to the irreverent folk singer from Sète. (☎04 67 53 32 77. Take buses #2 and 3. Open July-Aug. daily 10am-noon and 2-7pm; Sept.-June 10am-noon and 2-6pm; Oct.-May. closed M. €5, students €1.50.)

If you're physically fit, climb chemin de Biscan-Pas from the hostel to the top of **Mont St-Clair** (183m) for a great view of Sète, its canals, and the sea. (15min.) The church **Notre Dame de la Salette,** with wall murals from the 1950s, is the destination of fishermen's wives on a pilgrimage in late September for the *Feu de la St-Jean*.

⬛⬛ **ENTERTAINMENT AND FESTIVALS.** Every evening the popular **La Bodega,** 21 quai Noel Guignon, plays live music of every variety. (☎04 67 74 47 50. Open daily 5:30pm-3am; Oct.-May closed Su.) In late August (typically the last Monday in August), locals celebrate **La Fête de St-Louis** and its animated **Tournois de Joutes Nautiques,** in which participants joust from oversized rowboats. Arrive early to secure a spot on quai de la Résistance for the competition. Most other summer weekends, at 2:30pm, gladiators stage exposition battles in preparation for the tournament. **La Fête de St-Pierre**, the first weekend in July, brings solemn religious rites in the morning and loud festivity at night. On Sunday morning, during the **Bénédiction de la Mer,** fishermen invite the crowds onto their decorated boats. They end the day by throwing flowers into the water to commemorate those lost at sea.

In the first weekend in August or the last in July (starting on Thursday), Sète hosts the annual jazz festival **Jazz à Sète,** which usually draws a few big names. (☎04 67 51 18 11 for info. Tickets €22-25, students €18-20.)

LANGUEDOC

MONTPELLIER

Montpellier (pop. 211,000), Languedoc's capital, behaves like the student town that it is, solidifying its reputation as the most light-hearted place in the south. Amateur theatrical performances sprout up on every street corner, academics and posers browse fabulous bookstores, and the city puts together a vibrant annual avant-garde dance festival. Cafés on pl. de la Comédie, fondly known as *l'Oeuf* (the egg), sell expensive coffee with complementary hours of five-star people-watching. The city is a shopper's paradise: stores on every street sell to the trendy and the retro alike. Come sundown, students put down the books and hit the bars around pl. Jean Jaurès. During the summer, the city floods with tourists, but the wide avenues and sunny streets maintain a relaxed and airy feeling.

▐▀ TRANSPORTATION

Trains: pl. Auguste Gibert (☎08 92 35 35 35). Info office open daily 6am-midnight. To: **Avignon** (1hr., 10 per day, €12.50); **Perpignan** (1½hr., 13 per day, €36.20); **Marseille** (1¾hr., 10 per day, €19.60); **Toulouse** (2½hr., 11 per day, €25.20); **Nice** (4hr., 2 per day, €36.40); **Paris** (3¼hr., 13 per day, €63.10).

Buses: rue du Grand St. Jean (☎04 67 22 87 87), on the 2nd floor of a parking garage next to the train station. Info office open M-Sa 9:30am-4:30pm, Su 2-7pm. **Les Courriers du Midi** (☎04 67 06 03 78) travel to **Béziers** (1¾hr.; M-Sa every hr., Su 4 per day; €10.70) and **Nîmes** (1¾hr., M-Sa 2 per day, €8.25).

Public Transportation: TAM, 6 rue Jules Ferry (☎04 67 22 87 87), operates the local buses and a tramway that connects the city center to its outskirts. Trams every 3-7min. 5am-1am; buses less regular and only until 9pm. 1hr. tickets for trams and buses €1.10, weekly pass €11.10. Buy bus tickets from the driver, tram tickets from automated dispensers in the trams. **Rabelais** connects the city center and the train station 9pm-12:30am. **L'Amigo** connects Corum (near the city center) to popular night clubs on the outskirts of town. Buses leave Corum Th-Sa at midnight, 12:45, 1:30am, and return at 2:30, 3:30, 5am.

Taxis: TRAM (☎04 67 58 10 10) and **Taxi A** (☎04 67 20 35 20). €11 from station to hostel. Both 24hr.

Bike Rental: Vill'à velo (TAM), 27 rue Magvelone (04 67 22 87 89), across from the bus station. €1.50 per hr., €6 per day. €150 deposit. ID required. Electric bicycles and tandem bicycles also available. Open M-Sa 9am-7pm; Su 9am-1pm, 2-7pm.

✚ ⓘ ORIENTATION AND PRACTICAL INFORMATION

Leaving the train station, **rue Maguelone** leads to fountain-filled **place de la Comédie,** Montpellier's modern center and a good starting point for your visit. To reach the tourist office from the *place*, turn right and walk past the cafés and street vendors. It's behind the right-hand corner of the Pavillon de l'Hôtel de Ville. (10min.) Continuing in this direction leads you to the huge shopping center. The *vieille ville* is bounded by bd. Pasteur and bd. Louis Blanc to the north, esplanade Charles de Gaulle and bd. Victor Hugo to the east, and bd. Jeu de Paume to the west. From pl. de la Comédie, **rue de la Loge** ascends to the center of the *vieille ville*, **place Jean-Jaurès.** Montpellier is a big place; renting a bike is recommended.

Tourist Office: 30 allée Jean de Lattre de Tassigny (☎04 67 60 60 60; fax 04 67 60 60 61; www.ot-montpellier.fr). Free maps and same-night hotel reservation service. Distributes the weekly *Sortir à Montpellier* and *L'INDIC*, a student guide published in October. **Currency exchange** with no commission. Wheelchair accessible. Open M-F 9am-

LANGUEDOC

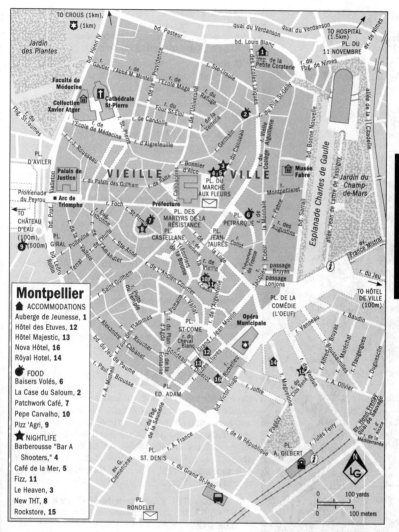

Montpellier

⌂ ACCOMMODATIONS
Auberge de Jeunesse, **1**
Hôtel des Etuves, **12**
Hôtel Majestic, **13**
Nova Hôtel, **16**
Rôyal Hotel, **14**

● FOOD
Baisers Volés, **6**
La Case du Saloum, **2**
Patchwork Café, **7**
Pepe Carvalho, **10**
Pizz 'Agri, **9**

★ NIGHTLIFE
Barberousse "Bar A
Shooters," **4**
Café de la Mer, **5**
Fizz, **11**
Le Heaven, **3**
New THT, **8**
Rockstore, **15**

6:30pm, Sa 10am-6pm, Su 10am-1pm and 2-5pm; July-Aug. M-F 9am-7:30pm, Sa 10am-6pm, Su 9:30am-1pm and 2:30-6pm. **Branch office** at the train station (☎04 67 92 90 03). Office open M-Sa 9am-7:30pm, Su 10am-6pm.

Tours: City tours in French July-Sept. €6.50, students €5.50. Tours in English can be arranged for groups of seven or more.

Budget Travel: Wasteels, 1 rue Cambacares (☎08 25 88 70 70) offers good plane, train, and bus prices. Open M and W 9:30am-noon, 2-6:30pm; Tu, Th, F 9:30am-6:30pm, Sa 9:30am-1pm and 2-5:30pm.

IN RECENT NEWS

PARADISE LOST

Sophocle's drama, *Antigone*, was hardly a tale of family tranquility—a king's son revolts against his father's rule and is killed by his brother, while his sister kills herself in protest. French urban development officials must have slept through that particular Greek literature class, because they still chose to give the play's name to the housing complex that opened in 1980 in Montpellier. Tempting fate, officials advertised the development as a utopian living environment for low-income families.

There was some method behind the madness. Many Montpellier residents were upset by a loud, ugly corporate and commercial center, called le Polygone, built under the mayorship of François Delmas in the 1970s. Courting the public's favor, Mayor Georges Frèche named his pet project "Antigone," intending it to be the correction to his predecessors's mistake.

Remembering that Antigone was set in ancient Thebes, the government decided that the housing complex needed a Greco-Roman flair. Architects attempted to recreate Athens on the outskirts of Montpellier, and the result was a cartoonish neighborhood, with exaggerated buildings and unusual colors. Perhaps realizing that their brainchild had an uncanny resemblance to Parc Astérix, developers added shops, corporate space, games, hotels, and a sports complex, ironically making it resemble le Polygone. The only thing missing is a roller-coaster. As for those low-income families—most of them have now moved out.

English Bookstore: BookShop Montpellier, 6 rue de l'Université (☎04 66 09 09 08). Browse bestsellers and language guides to complementary coffee. Open M-Sa 9:30am-1pm and 2:30-7pm.

IB News, 2 rue Fournarié (☎04 67 91 20 75). Will delightedly supply information about gay life in Montpellier and other towns in the South.

Laundromat: Lav'Club Miele, 6 rue des Ecoles Laïques. Open daily 9:30am-8pm.

Police: 13 av. du Prof. Grasset (☎04 67 22 78 22).

Hospital: 191 av. Doyen Gaston Guiraud (☎04 67 33 67 33).

Internet Access: Cybercafé www, 12 bis rue Jules Ferry (☎04 67 06 59 52), across from the train station. €1.50 per hr. Open daily 9:30am-1am. **FM,** 12 rue du Petit St Jean (☎04 67 91 24 98). €2 per hr. Open Tu-F noon-9pm and Sa noon-10pm. **Planète 2000**, 21 rue Verdun (☎04 99 13 35 15). €2 per hr. Open M-Sa 11am-midnight, Su 2pm-midnight.

Post Office: pl. Rondelet (☎04 67 34 52 40). From pl. de la Comédie, follow rue Jean Moulin, cross bd. Observatoire onto rue de Fbg de la Saunerie, then follow rue Rondelet. **Currency exchange. Western Union** office. Open M-F 8am-7pm, Sa 8am-noon. **Branch office** at pl. des Martyrs de la Résistance (☎04 67 60 03 60). Open M-F 9:30am-11:50pm and 1:30-5:30pm, Sa 8:30am-noon. **Postal code:** 34000 (central).

■ ACCOMMODATIONS AND CAMPING

Except for the campsite, all listings are in the large *vieille ville*. For group travelers, it is usually cheaper and more convenient (no curfew, private room), to stay in a hotel instead of the overcrowded youth hostel. Search **rue Aristide Olivier, rue du Général Campredon** (off cours Gambetta and rue A. Michell), and **rue A. Broussonnet** (off pl. Albert 1er) for other reasonably priced hotels. Hotels fill up very quickly.

Nova Hôtel, 8 rue Richelieu (☎04 67 60 79 85; fax 04 67 60 89 06; olivier.granier@wanadoo.fr). From the train station bear left on rue de la République. Turn right on bd. Victor Hugo, left on rue Diderot, and right on rue Richelieu. (5min.) Warm, comfortable rooms. 5% discount for students with a *Let's Go* guide. Breakfast €4.60. Reception 7am-11:30pm. Reserve a month in advance in the summer, earlier in festival season. Singles with shower but no toilet €28; doubles with shower €38.60; triples with shower €44.70; quads with bath €51. AmEx/MC/V. ❸

Hôtel Majestic, 4 rue du Cheval Blanc (☎04 67 66 26 85). From the train station, follow directions to Nova

Hôtel, then turn left off rue Richelieu onto rue du Cheval Blanc. Not exactly majestic, but with small, clean rooms (some with no window) in a quiet neighborhood. Breakfast €4. Shower €3. Reserve a month in advance. Reception 7:30am-11pm. Singles €18, with shower €29; doubles with shower €35; triples €46; quads €53. MC/V. ❷

Hôtel des Etuves, 24 rue des Etuves (☎/fax 04 67 60 78 19; hoteldesetuves@wanadoo.fr). From the train station, follow directions to Nova Hôtel. Turn left off rue Richelieu onto rue du Cheval Blanc, then right onto rue des Etuves. Personable atmosphere and 13 fresh, spacious rooms, all with showers, most with TV. Breakfast €4.10. Reception 7am-11pm, closed Su 3-6:30pm. Reserve one week in advance. Singles with shower €20-30; doubles with shower €30-37. ❷

Rôyal Hotel, 8 rue Maguelone (☎04 67 92 13 36), down the street from the train station. This upscale, somewhat haughty three-star hotel offers a few amenities for a little more money: a clean bathroom, television with satellite channels, mini bar, and cute (though small) rooms. Breakfast €6.10. Reception open 24hr. Reserve one week in advance. Doubles (for 1-2 guests) €59. Extra bed €15.50. ❺

Auberge de Jeunesse (HI), 2 impasse de la Petite Corraterie (☎04 67 60 32 22; fax 04 67 60 32 30). To walk to the hostel from the train station, walk straight out on rue Maguelone and continue across pl. de la Comédie onto rue de la Loge. Turn right onto rue Jacques Cœur and proceed straight to pl. Notre Dame. Bear left out of the *place* onto rue l'Aiguillerie and follow it until its name changes to rue des Ecoles Laïques. The hostel is on the right, just before bd. Louis Blanc. (20min.) Or take the tram towards Mosson to the Louis Blanc stop, then walk back up the street on rue des Ecoles des Laïques and take your first right. This hostel is understaffed, and the employees can be grumpy and inflexible. The 2am curfew will keep you from the lively nightlife. Call ahead to reserve, though it may not be worth the trouble. 80 beds in 4- to 9-person single-sex rooms. Co-ed, unappealing bathrooms. Breakfast €3.20. Sheets €2.70 per week. Reception 8am-10am and 1pm-midnight. Lockout 10am-1pm. Bunks €8. MC/V. ❶

L'Eden Campsite: 3km away in coastal Lattes, rte. de Palavas (☎04 67 15 11 05; fax 04 67 15 11 31). To reach L'Eden, take bus #17 from the bus station to "Oasis Palavasienne." (20min.) 4-star camping with tennis courts, pool, and restaurant. Free shuttle to the beach. (15min.) Open May-Aug. May-June 1-2 people €16, 3 people €19, 4 people €22; July-Aug. 1-2 people €28, 3 people €28, 4 people €31. ❷

■ FOOD

Montpellier caters to students and tourists with a number of reasonably priced restaurants. Standard French fare dominates the *places* of the *vieille ville*, but ethnic specialties have made footholds elsewhere. **Rue des Ecoles Laïques** in the old city has Greek, Egyptian, Italian, and Lebanese food. Students frequent the eateries on **rue de Fbg. Boutonnet.** Contact **CROUS,** 2 rue Monteils, for info about the four **university restaurants.** None are conveniently located, but €2.67 gets you a full meal. (☎04 67 41 50 00. Open Sept.-June M-F lunch and dinner, Sa one of the four is open on a rotating basis.) Unimpressive morning **markets** go up at pl. Cabane and bd. des Archeaux (daily) and pl. de la Comédie (M-Sa). The excellent **supermarket INNO,** in the basement of the Polygone commercial center, just past the tourist office, offers great bargains. (Open M-Sa 9:30am-8pm.)

Baisers Volés, 3 rue Embouque d'Or (☎04 67 63 04 43). A little *salon de thé* where you can grab a light meal or a cup of tea. Join the local college crowd and catch up on journal writing as movies play quietly in the modern background. Try their specialty, the *baisé volé,* a cake flavored with rose water and honey (€3.80). Open M-Sa 10am-7pm and Su 3-7pm (only if it rains). MC/V. ❶

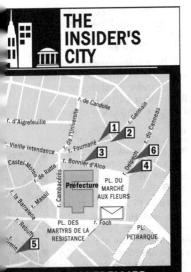

THE INSIDER'S CITY

GAY MONTPELLIER

With an ideal location near the shores of the Mediterranean, it's easy to see why Montpellier is one of France's unofficial gay capitals (geared more towards gay men than lesbians).

1 IB News writes a journal on the gay scene in southern France, and can answer any questions about the hottest beaches, bars, and bums.

2 Shop for club wear at Le Village, a hip boutique with upscale men's clothing. The friendly owner has posted info about local goings-on.

3 Bistro d'Alco serves upscale traditional French fare in a queer-friendly atmosphere.

4 The terrace of Café de la Mer is the perfect place to people-watch over a post-dinner coffee. This café is the unofficial gay rendez-vous point before going out for the night.

5 At New THT, a young chic crowd rocks to disco. Once known for public debauchery, the atmosphere now is a little more low-key.

6 Le Heaven serves the same clientele as THT, but with less talking and more of said debauchery.

La Case du Saloum, 8 rue École de Pharmacie (☎04 67 02 88 94). Cool, unassuming establishment serves Senegalese dishes and homemade fruit juice. Knock yourself out with their popular specialty, ginger punch, made from natural ginger, orange juice, and rum. *Plats* offered for €10 and €15. Open daily 11am-3pm and 7pm-1am.❷

Pizz'Agri, 60 ave de l'École de l'Agriculture (☎04 67 04 15 98). Take #6 bus towards J. Blayac and get off at Erables. This restaurant eschews traditions. It serves smoked duck pizzas (€9.90) and Moroccan and Indian food in unique ways and large portions. Show your *Let's Go* guide for a free *apéritif.* Open noon-3pm and 7-10:30pm. ❸

The Patchwork Café, 15 rue St-Firmin (☎04 67 60 75 35). This pizzeria hosts theme nights. Get your fortune told on Monday, your caricature drawn on Tuesday, and your arms tattooed on Wednesday. Pizza toppings range from cheese to kangaroo and ostrich meats. Open daily noon-3pm and 7pm-1am. ❷

Pepe Carvalho, 2 rue Cauzit (☎04 67 66 10 10), near pl. St-Ravy. Named after the Catalan hero of Manuel Vásquez Montalbán's detective stories. Enjoy the lively atmosphere and cheap tapas (€2.50, in 30 varieties). €9 *menu* includes 5 tapas. Three-person special gives you 15 tapas and a bottle of wine for €36. Sangría €1.80. Open M-Sa noon-3pm and 7pm-1am, Su 7pm-1am; July-Aug. open until 2am. AmEx/MC/V. ❷

🅢 SIGHTS

The gigantic **Musée Fabre,** 39 bd. Bonne Nouvelle, near the esplanade, holds one of the largest collections of fine art outside of Paris. The museum will be closed until late 2006 for renovations; the small pavilion annex will display a sample of the collection. (☎04 67 66 13 46. Open Tu-F 9am-5:30pm, Sa-Su 9:30am-5pm. €3, students €1.50.) The **Collection Xavier Atger,** 2 rue de l'Ecole de Médecine, donated by Jean François Xavier Atger, contains anatomical drawings, etchings, and sketches by Fragonard, Watteau, and Caravaggio. (☎04 67 66 27 77. Open Sept.-July M, W, F 1:30-5pm. Free.)

The old city's pedestrian streets and bookstores, as well as the sprawling pl. de la Comédie, have some of the best entertainment in Montpellier. Hidden behind grandiose oak doors are the secret courtyards and intricate staircases of 17th- and 18th-century *hôtels particuliers.* Particularly notable are the **Hôtel de Varennes,** 2 pl. Petrarque and the **Hôtel des Tresoriers de France,** rue Jacques Cœur. The tourist office distributes a walking guide; their tours pass some of the 100-odd *hôtels.* Rue Foch, off pl. des Martyrs in the northwest corner of the old city, leads to the **promenade du Peyrou.** The promenade links the **Arc de Triomphe,** erected in 1691 to honor Louis XIV, to the **Château d'Eau,** the arched terminal of an aqueduct. Locals may tell you it dates back to antiquity, but it only just turned 100. Bd. Henri IV leads to the **Jardin des Plantes,** France's first botanical garden. (☎ 04 67 63 43 22. Open Apr.-Sept. M-Sa 9am-noon and 2-7pm; Oct.-Mar. 10am-noon and 2-5pm. Free.)

If you're tired of culture, check out the sandy **plage de Palavas.** Take the #17 bus from Montpellier's bus station to "*gare routière*" in Palavas. (20 min.)

♫ NIGHTLIFE

The most animated bars are scattered along **place Jean-Jaurès.** At sundown, **rue de la Loge** fills with vendors, musicians, and stilt-walkers. The extremely popular **Barberousse "Bar A Shooters,"** 6 rue Boussairolles, just off pl. de la Comédie, sells 73 different flavors of rum for €1.50 each. (☎ 04 67 58 03 66. Open M-Sa 6pm-1am.) At the dance spot **Rockstore,** 20 rue de Verdun, teens and twenty-somethings grind to different styles of music each night. (Bar ☎ 04 67 06 80 00. No cover. Beer €3.50. Open July-Aug. M-Sa until 6am; Sept.-June M-Th until 4am, F-Sa until 6am.) **Fizz,** 4 rue Cauzit, is a hot live music dance club. Foreign students meet each other on the first floor and dance close on the second. (☎ 04 67 66 22 89. Cover €12.50 with 2 drinks; students €8 F-Su, €12.50 M-Th; women free Tu and Th. Beer €5.50, hard stuff €6.50. Open Tu-Su midnight-4am.)

There is vibrant **gay** nightlife in Montpellier. The best discos, such as **La Villa Rouge** (☎ 04 67 06 52 15) in Lattes, lie on the outskirts of town; the Amigo buses (see **Public Transportation,** p. 470) are a good way to get there. Gay bars are sprinkled throughout the *vieille ville* (see sidebar **Insider's City,** p. 474). Pre-party at **Café de la Mer,** 5 pl. du Marché aux Fleurs, known as the gay hub of Montpellier. (☎ 04 67 60 79 65. Open daily until 1am.) Try **New THT,** 10 rue St-Firmin, off rue Foch. (☎ 04 67 66 12 52. No cover. Beer €3.10, straight liquor €5.40. Happy Hour 8-10pm: buy one drink, get the next free. Open daily 9am-1am.) For a wilder time, try **Le Heaven,** 1 rue Delpech. (☎ 04 67 60 44 18. Beer €3, liquor €5. No cover.)

The **Corum,** at the far end of Esplanade Charles de Gaulle, showcases the philharmonic orchestra Oct.-June. (☎ 04 67 61 67 61. €12-23; student and senior discounts.) **Cinéma Le Diagonal,** 18 pl. St-Denis, shows modern foreign films in their original languages. (☎ 04 67 92 91 81. €5.80.) The *café-théâtre* **L'Antirouille,** 12 rue Anatole France, presents international music and rock concerts W-Sa nights. (☎ 04 67 60 07 40. €3-12.50. Open Apr.-Aug. M-Sa 9pm-2am; Sept.-Mar. daily 8pm-1am.)

In the last two weeks of June and the first week of July, the open-air festival **Printemps des Comédiens pac Euromédecine** arrives in Montpellier. For details, contact the Opéra Comédie, pl. de la Comédie. (Info ☎ 04 67 60 19 99, reservations 04 67 63 66 66. Tickets €6-21, under 25 and seniors €6-18.) In the first two weeks of July, the **Festival International Montpellier Danse** organizes performances, workshops, and films on local stages and screens. (Contact Hôtel d'Assas, 6 rue Vieille Aiguillerie. ☎ 04 67 60 83 60, reservations 04 67 60 07 40. Tickets €3.80-27.45.) The rest of July is taken up by the opera, jazz, and classical music performances of **Festival de Radio France et de Montpellier.** (Info and tickets ☎ 04 67 02 02 01. €10.50-33.50; student and senior discounts.)

PROVENCE

Carpets of olive groves and vineyards unroll along hills dusted with lavender, sunflowers, and mimosa, while the fierce winds of the *mistral* carry the scent of sage, rosemary, and thyme. Since Roman times, writers have rhapsodized about Provence's varied landscape—undulating mountains to the east, flat marshlands in the Camargue, and rocky cliffs in the Vaucluse. In more recent times, Provence has inspired the artistic sensibilities of Van Gogh, Cézanne, Gauguin, and Picasso.

Marseille, with 2600 years of history, is the second most populous city in France and serves as the linchpin for the area, linking Provence to the glitz and glamor of the Riviera. With their Roman remnants and cobblestone grace, Orange and Arles meet the Rhône as it flows to the Mediterranean. Briefly home to the medieval papacy, Avignon still holds the formidable Palais des Papes. Provence is perhaps most popular today for its festivals; in the summer, even the smallest hamlets in the Vaucluse whirl with music, dance, theater, and antique markets.

MARSEILLE

France's third-largest city, Marseille (pop. 800,000), is like the *bouillabaisse* soup for which it is famous: steamy and pungently spiced, with a little bit of everything mixed in. Unlike Provence and the Riviera, Marseille does not care if you visit. Even so, the city Alexandre Dumas called "the meeting place of the entire world" remains strangely alluring, a jumble of color and commotion. Whatever Marseille lacks in architectural unity or social sophistication is made up for by its vibrancy.

Provence

TO THE ARDECHE VALLEY
TO LYON

Highways
National Roads
Departmental Roads
(Routes Departementales)

0   10 miles
0   10 kilometers

Vaison-la-Romaine **26**

Séguret   DENTELLES DE MONTMIRAIL

Eygues

Bagnols

Orange **25**

Mt. Ventoux ▲

Carpentras

Châteauneuf-du-Pape

L'Isle-sur-la-Sorgue **7**

VAUCLUSE PLATEAU

Villeneuve-les-Avignon **6**

Uzès **24**

Pont du Gard **23**

Fontaine de Vaucluse **8**

Roussillon **13**

Avignon **5**

Gordes **14**

Lacoste **11**

Apt   Coulon

Cavaillon

Oppède-le-Vieux **9**

Ménerbes **10**

Bonnieux **12**

Nîmes **22**

Tarascon **18**

St-Rémy **19**

Les Baux-de-Provence **17**

Lourmarin

Durance

Abbaye de Montmajour **16**

Arles **15**

Salon-de-Provence

Vauvenargues

Aigues-Mortes **21**

THE CAMARGUE

Vaccarès Lagoon

Berre Lagoon

Aix-en-Provence **4**

Martigues   Marignane

Golfe du Lion

Stes-Maries-de-la-Mer **20**

Mediterranean Sea

Marseille **1**

Château d'If

Calanques **2**

Cassis **3**

TO NICE AND THE CÔTE D'AZUR

TO CORSICA

PROVENCE

A mix of wild nightclubs, beaches, islands, and urban adventure, Marseille resists categorization, a constantly changing city defiantly proud of its uniqueness.

Its beginnings date back to 600 BC, when Phoenician Greeks sought shelter in Marseille's port. The well-located city quickly grew into a trading center and an independent ally of Rome. In the first century BC, the city's neutrality policy during the Roman civil war vexed Julius Caesar, and so he came, saw, and conquered Marseille. The city has since found neutrality elusive—through centuries of warfare, plague, and immigration it has developed a reputation for roughness and danger. As a gateway to Europe, Marseille has welcomed waves of Spanish, Armenian and West African immigrants through the decades, and, since the 1960s, increasing numbers of Jews and Muslims from France's former colonies. Unfortunately, the underside of Marseille's cultural diversity is the occasional tension between ethnic groups, as witnessed by the burning of a Jewish synagogue in April 2002.

⚔ ORIENTATION

The city is divided into 16 *arrondissements*, referred to as "*quartiers*," with major streets as dividing lines. **La Canebière**, a street affectionately known to English sailors as the "can o' beer," divides the city into north and south, funneling into the **vieux port** (old port) to the west and becoming bland urban sprawl to the

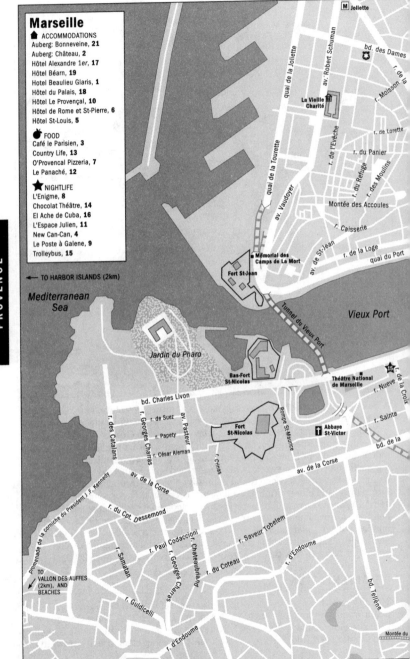

Marseille

🏠 ACCOMMODATIONS
Auberg: Bonneveine, **21**
Auberg: Château, **2**
Hôtel Alexandre 1er, **17**
Hôtel Béarn, **19**
Hotel Beaulieu Glaris, **1**
Hôtel du Palais, **18**
Hôtel Le Provençal, **10**
Hôtel de Rome et St-Pierre, **6**
Hôtel St-Louis, **5**

🍎 FOOD
Café le Parisien, **3**
Country Life, **13**
O'Provencal Pizzeria, **7**
Le Panaché, **12**

⭐ NIGHTLIFE
L'Enigme, **8**
Chocolat Théâtre, **14**
El Ache de Cuba, **16**
L'Espace Julien, **11**
New Can-Can, **4**
Le Poste à Galene, **9**
Trolleybus, **15**

← TO HARBOR ISLANDS (2km)

*Mediterranean
Sea*

PROVENCE

Ⓜ Joliette

bd. des Dames

quai de la Joliette

av. Robert Schuman

r. de la

r. Moisson

La Vieille
Charité

r. de Lorette

r. de l'Evêché

r. du Panier

r. du Refuge

r. des Moulins

quai de la Tourette

av. Vaudoyer

Montée des Accoules

r. Caisserie

r. de St-Jean

r. de la Loge

Mémorial des
Camps de La Mort

quai du Port

Fort St-Jean

av. de St-Jean

Vieux Port

Tunnel du Vieux Port

Jardin du Pharo

Bas-Fort
St-Nicolas

Théâtre National
de Marseille

r. Nueve

r. de la Croix

bd. Charles Livon

r. de Suez

r. Georges Charras

av. Pasteur

r. Papety

r. César Aleman

r. des Catalans

Fort
St-Nicolas

Rompe St-Maurice

r. Chras

Abbaye
St-Victor

r. Sainte

bd. de la

Promenade de la corniche du Président J. F. Kennedy

av. de la Corse

av. de la Corse

r. du Cpt. Dessemond

r. Paul Codaccioni

r. Chateaubriand

r. Saveur Tobelem

r. d'Endoume

TO
VALLON DES AUFFES
(2km), AND
BEACHES

r. Samatan

r. Georges Charras

r. du Coteau

bd. Tellene

r. Guidicelli

r. d'Endoume

Montée du

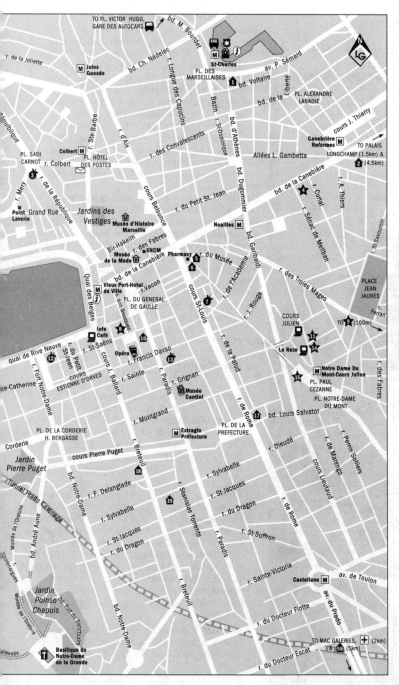

PROVENCE

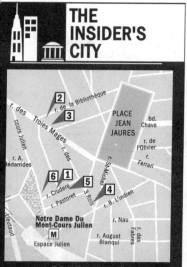

THE INSIDER'S CITY

COURS JULIEN

An eclectic collection of wall murals, vintage music and clothing shops, bookstores, comic book shops, theaters, and countless cafés and restaurants, cours Julien is one of Marseille's most interesting neighborhoods and the perfect place to stroll for a bargain. On Sundays and Mondays, many shops are closed.

1 Check out the impressive **murals** on **rue Vian**, which are filled with cartoonish humor and bright colors.

2 **Black Music**, 2 rue de la Bibliothèque, offers a wide collection of classical and contemporary black music. (☎04 91 92 07 14)

3 **Kaleidoscope**, 3 rue des Trois Mages, offers a sweet selection of used records. (☎04 91 47 48 56)

4 Tiny **Baluchon Boutique**, 11 rue des Trois Rois, features the best vintage digs. (☎04 91 48 14 26)

5 **Village Crudere**, on rue Crudere, is a larger used-clothing shop. (☎04 91 42 98 04)

6 Immerse yourself in a sea of paperbacks at **Le Plaisir de Lire** on cours Julien. (☎04 91 47 95 15)

east. North of the *vieux port* and west of bd. République, working-class residents of many ethnicities pile into the hilltop neighborhood of **Le Panier.** East of Le Panier, between cours Belsunce and bd. Athènes, and between cours St-Louis and bd. Garibaldi, the foreign-feeling **Quartier Belsunce**'s dilapidated buildings house the city's Arab and African communities. Use caution in this neighborhood at night and stay on major streets. Both the bus and train stations lie at the top of bd. Athènes, near this troublesome quarter. Upscale restaurants and nightlife cluster around the *vieux port*, on quai de Rive Neuve, cours Estienne d'Orves, and pl. Thiers. East of the *vieux port*, La Canebière, rue St-Ferreol, and rue Paradis contain the city's largest stores and fashion boutiques. The narrow streets past **rue de Rome** (near La Canebière) are full of colorful African markets. The areas in front of the **Opéra** (near the port) and around **rue Curiol** (near rue Sénac) are meeting grounds for prostitutes and their clients; be particularly cautious here after dark. A few blocks southeast, **cours Julien,** with funky shops and tiny concert spaces, has a countercultural feel. Marseille's two métro lines ("M" in this text) are clean and simple. The bus system is thorough but complex—a route map helps enormously. Use the buses to access the beach, which stretches along the coast southwest of the *vieux port*.

TRANSPORTATION

Flights: Aéroport Marseille-Provence (☎04 42 14 14 14). Flights to: **Corsica** (**Air Littoral,** ☎08 25 83 48 34; **Air Libe Express,** ☎08 25 805 805); **Lyon** (**Air France,** ☎08 20 820 820); **Paris** (Air France and Air Libe Express). Shuttle buses connect airport to Gare St-Charles 5:30am-11pm (3 per hr., €8). Taxis from the *centre ville* to the airport €36 during the day, €45 at night.

Trains: Gare St-Charles, pl. Victor Hugo. M: Gare St-Charles. Info and ticket counters open daily 4:30am-1am. To: **Lyon** (3½hr., 21 per day, €38.10); **Nice** (2¾hr., 21 per day, €23.50); **Paris** (4¾hr., 19 per day, €66.60). **Baggage service** open daily 7:15am-10pm; €3-6.10 per bag. **SOS Voyageurs** (☎04 91 62 12 80), in the station, helps tourists find lodgings. Open daily 9am-7pm. **Note:** While listed on train schedules, many trains to nearby cities, like Aix-en-Provence, may actually be buses, and thus will be marked as "car" on the schedule.

Buses: Gare des Autocars, pl. Victor Hugo (☎04 91 08 16 40), near the train station. M: Gare St-Charles. Ticket counters open M-Sa 6:30am-6:30pm, Su

7:30am-12:30pm and 1:30-6:30pm. **Cartreize** (☎04 42 96 59 00) is an organization of local operators. Buy tickets on the bus (except to Nice) with exact change. To: **Aix-en-Provence** (every 20min., €4.10); **Arles** (2-3hr., 7 per day, €13); **Avignon** (2hr., 5 per day, €15); **Cannes** (2¼-3hr., 4 per day, €21); **Nice** (2¾hr., 1 per day, €22.50). **Eurolines** also makes international trips to destinations in Western Europe. Open M-Sa 9am-6pm.

Ferries: SNCM, 61 bd. des Dames (☎08 91 70 18 01 for Corsica, Italy and Sardinia, ☎08 91 70 28 01 for Algiers and Tunisia; www.sncm.fr). M: Joliette. To: **Algeria** (20½ hr., €162-250 adult, €110-165 reduced price); **Corsica** (11½hr., €35-52/€26-40); **Sardinia** (17hr., €58-67/€41-50); **Tunisia** (20hr., €144). Prices vary according to season and port of arrival. Open M-F 8am-6:00pm, Sa 8:00am-noon and 2-5:30pm.

Public Transportation: RTM, 6-8 rue des Fabres (☎04 91 91 92 10). Office open M-Sa 8:30am-5:30pm. **Tickets** sold at bus and metro stations, or exact change (€1.40) on board. Day pass (€3.80) sold at tourist office, bus or metro stations. The **Carte Liberté** costs €6.50-13 for 6-12 voyages. **Métro** lines #1 and 2 stop at train station. Line #1 (blue) goes to *vieux port* (dir: Timone). Metro runs M-Th 5am-9pm, F-Su 5am-12:30am. Tourist office has map.

Taxis: (☎04 91 02 20 20). Several taxi stands surround the *vieux port*. €20-30 to hostels from Gare St-Charles. 24hr.

🔁 PRACTICAL INFORMATION

Tourist Office: 4 bd. de la Canebière (☎04 91 13 89 00; fax 04 91 13 89 20). Brochures of walking tours, free maps, accommodations service, excursions, and RTM day pass. City tours (€6.50) daily 10am and 2pm. Open July-Aug. M-Sa 9am-8pm, Su 10am-6pm; Oct.-June M-Sa 9am-7pm, Su and holidays 10am-5pm. **Annex** (☎04 91 50 59 18) at train station. Open daily 10am-6pm, Sa-Su closed 3-4pm.

Consulates: UK, 24 av. du Prado (☎04 91 15 72 10). Open M-F 9am-noon and 2-5pm. **US,** 12 bd. Paul Peytral (☎04 91 54 92 00). Open by appt. M-F 9am-noon and 2-4pm.

Money: La Bourse, 3 pl. Général de Gaulle (☎04 91 13 09 00). Good rates and no commission. Open M-F 8:30am-6:30pm, Sa 9am-5:30pm. **Comptoir Marseillais de Bourse,** 22 La Canebière (☎04 91 54 93 94). Again, good rates and no commission. Open M-Sa 9am-7pm. **American Express,** 39 La Canebière (☎04 91 13 71 21), located in Afat Voyages. Open M-F 9am-6pm, Sa 9am-noon and 2-5pm.

English Bookstore: Librairie Fueri-Lamy, 26 rue Paradis (☎04 91 33 57 03). Slim paperback selection. Open daily 9:30am-7:30pm. AmEx/MC/V.

Youth Information: Centre Régional Information Jeunesse, 96 La Canebière (☎04 91 24 33 50). Info on sports, short-term employment, leisure activities, and services for disabled persons. Open July-Aug. M-F 9am-1pm; Sept.-June M and W-F 10am-5pm, Tu 1-5pm. **CROUS,** 42 rue du 141ème R.I.A. (☎04 91 62 83 60), has info on housing, work, and travel. Open M-F 9am-12:30pm and 1:30-4:30pm.

Laundromat: Point Laverie, 56 bd. de la Libération and 6 rue Mery. Open daily 7am-8pm. Also on rue Bruetil. Open daily 6:30am-8pm.

Gay Support: Lesbian & Gay Pride, 8 bd. de la Liberté (☎04 91 50 50 12).

Rape Hotline: SOS Viols (☎04 91 56 04 10). 24hr.

Police: 2 rue du Commissaire Becker (☎04 91 39 80 00). Also in the train station on esplanade St-Charles (☎04 91 14 29 50). Dial ☎17 in emergencies.

Hospital: Hôpital Timone, bd. Jean Moulin (☎04 91 38 60 00). Take metro line #1 to "Castéllane," then take bus #54, which drops you off just behind the hospital. **SOS Médecins** (☎04 91 52 91 52) connects you with on-call doctors.

IN RECENT NEWS

SYNAGOGUE OR AVIV

On a pleasant morning in Marseille last June, the sun peeks out over a grove of tall pine trees in Les Caillols, a neighborhood in the northern part of the city. Nearby, there are sounds of children playing. Nothing seems out of the ordinary until one's gaze turns to the rubble and broken glass or the cracked, parched ground. Until the night of March 31, 2002, the Or Aviv Synagogue stood here. Nearly three months after it was set on fire, all that remains is a clearing, and a crater filled with stones, bricks, and other debris; the building is missing.

The attack, the first destruction of a synagogue in the West in recent memory, came amid a spate of violence against Jews and Jewish buildings in France last spring, as tensions between Israelis and Palestinians in the Middle East rose once more. But it was particularly striking for Marseille, France's 2nd-largest city, which has taken pride in the cohesiveness of its diverse population. The city's interfaith council, which has brought together Christian, Jewish, Muslim and Buddhist leaders for monthly meetings, is one of many similar groups in France.

And so, when Or Aviv was burned down, Marseille's "special spirit," as one religious leader described it, came into question. Samuel Perez, then-president of the synagogue, said he couldn't imagine such an attack ever taking place. "In Europe and in the United States, in 50 or 60 years, there have not been any synagogues that have burned completely," he said. "We suffered greatly."

24-Hour Pharmacy: Pharmacie le Cours Saint-Louis, 5 cours Saint-Louis (☎04 91 54 04 58). Open daily 8:30am-7:30pm. Serves as the *pharmacie de garde* along with four other pharmacies on a rotating basis; check *La Provence* for up-to-date info.

Internet Access: Info Café, 1 quai Rive Neuve (☎04 91 33 53 05). €2 per 30min. Open M-Sa 9am-10pm, Su 2:30-7:30pm. **Bug's café,** 80 cours Julien (☎04 96 12 53 43). €4.80 per hr. Open M-Sa 10am-11pm, Su 2-7pm. **Le Rezo,** 68 cours Julien (☎04 91 42 70 02). €4.60 per hr. Open M-W 9:30am-8pm, Th-F 9:30am-10pm, Sa 10am-10pm.

Post Office: 1 pl. Hôtel des Postes (☎04 91 15 47 20). Follow La Canebière toward the sea and turn right onto rue Reine Elisabeth as it becomes pl. Hôtel des Postes. **Poste Restante** and **currency exchange** at this branch only. Open M-F 8am-7pm, Sa 8am-noon. **Branch office** at 11 rue Honnorat (☎04 91 62 80 80), near the station. Open M-F 8am-6:45pm, Sa 8am-noon. **Postal code:** 13001.

ACCOMMODATIONS

Marseille has many cheap hotels, but few reputable ones. Resist the cheap accommodations in the Quartier Belsunce; the area may be dangerous after dark, and some hotels are fronts for brothels. Hotels listed here prioritize safety and location. Both hostels are far from the city center and offer an escape from the hubbub of the center without losing access to the city, but bus access is infrequent in summer (with buses generally every 45min.), so plan ahead. They usually have space year-round, but call a few days ahead.

Hôtel du Palais, 26 rue Breteuil (☎04 91 37 78 86; fax 04 91 37 91 19). Competent, kind owner runs a tight ship. Large, well-maintained, cheery rooms at a good value. Soundproofed rooms have A/C, TVs, and showers or baths. Breakfast €5. Singles €38, doubles €45, triples €53; students can get a triple for €38. Extra bed €8. MC/V. ❹

Hôtel Alexandre 1er, 111 rue de Rome (☎04 91 48 67 13; fax 04 91 42 11 14). Located right across from pl. Préfecture, this hotel is a high quality choice. Spacious rooms, all with showers. Breakfast €5. Reception 24hr. Singles €29; doubles €37-40; triples €48; quads €64. MC/V. ❸

Auberge de Jeunesse Bonneveine (HI), impasse Bonfils (☎04 91 17 63 30; fax 04 91 73 97 23), off av. J. Vidal. From the station, take metro line #2 to "Rond-Point du Prado," and transfer (keeping your ticket) onto bus #44 to pl. Bonnefon. At the bus stop, walk back toward the traffic circle and turn left at J. Vidal, then turn onto impasse Bonfils; the hostel is on the left. Swimming and sunbathing are just 200m away. A well-organized hostel full of a young, international crowd. Bonneveine's cement-block building houses a bar, restaurant, Internet access, pool table, video games, vending machines, and 150 beds. Rooms are basic but adequate. Breakfast included. Lockers €1.50. Laundry. July-Aug. 6-day max. stay. Reception 7am-1am. Curfew 1am. Reserve ahead in summer. Closed Dec. 22-Feb. Dorms Apr.-Aug. €13.60 1st night, €11.90 thereafter; doubles €16.40/€14.70. Feb.-Mar. and Sept.-Dec. dorms €12.80/€11.10; doubles €15.40/€13.70. **Members only.** MC/V. ❶

Auberge de Jeunesse Château de Bois-Luzy (HI), allée des Primevères (☎/fax 04 91 49 06 18). Take bus #6 from cours J. Thierry at the top of La Canebière to "Marius Richard." 10m up the hill from the bus stop, take a right onto bd. de l'Amandière and walk to the soccer fields. Follow the road down to the right and around the fields to reach the hostel. Or take bus #8 (dir: Saint-Julien) from "La Canebière" to "Felibres Laurient," walk up hill and make the first left, hostel will be on your left. Night bus "T" also leaves "La Canebière" for "Marius Richard." The big yellow tower-topped hostel used to house a count and countess, or so they say; those days are long gone now. Mostly 3- to 6-bed dorms and a few doubles. Breakfast €3. Dinner €7.50. Luggage storage €2 per bag per day. Sheets €1.80. Reception 7:30am-noon and 5-10:30pm. Lockout noon-5pm. Dorms €7.60; singles €11.50; doubles €8.40. **Members only.** ❶

Hôtel Béarn, 63 rue Sylvabelle (☎04 91 37 75 83; fax 04 91 81 54 98). On a quiet side street near the port, between rue Paradis and rue Breteuil. Large adequate rooms with high ceilings and inviting windows. Internet access €4 per hr. Breakfast (with homemade jam from a local monastery) €4. Reception 7am-11pm. Singles and doubles with shower €23-34, with bath €34; triples with bath €41-42. AmEx/MC/V. ❷

Hôtel Saint-Louis, 2 rue des Recollettes (☎04 91 54 02 74; fax 04 91 33 78 59). Pretty, high-ceilinged rooms painted in cheerful colors, just off La Canebière. Some with balcony, nearly all with satellite TV. Breakfast €4.60, €5.40 in bed. Reception 24hr. Singles €27.50, doubles with bath €38-45, triples €53. Extra bed €7. AmEx/V. ❸

Hôtel de Rome et Saint-Pierre, 7 cours St-Louis (☎04 91 54 19 52; fax 04 91 54 34 56). Decadent rooms (all with TV and A/C) are worth the splurge, if you can afford it. The cute old elevator and the expansive staircase fit well in this luxurious, centrally located hotel. Breakfast €8.50. Reception 24hr. Singles €69; doubles €74, with bath €84; triples €92-98. AmEx/MC/V. ❺

Hôtel Beaulieu Glaris, 1 pl. des Marseillaises (☎04 91 90 70 59; fax 04 91 56 14 04). Right at the foot of the staircases of Gare St-Charles, this comfortable hotel is perfect for late-night arrivals or early-morning departures. Rooms are cramped but clean. Though the surrounding noisy neighborhood has the reputation for late-night unsavoriness, the hotel is quite safe; room lock and keys must be left with desk attendant. Reservations are possible, though the cheapest rooms are often booked. Breakfast €4. Reception 6am-midnight. Singles €25, with TV €31; singles and doubles with shower and TV €39; triples with shower €49. MC/V. ❸

Hôtel Le Provençal, 32 rue Paradis (☎04 91 33 11 15; fax 04 91 33 47 08). The Provençal's small rooms are bare and clean. The hotel overlooks a bustling street around the corner from L'Opéra and is close to the *vieux port*. Breakfast €3.90. Reception 24hr. Singles €23; doubles €26, with shower €30.50; triples €34, with shower €39. AmEx/MC/V. ❷

⚑ FOOD

Marseille has the international restaurants fitting of an international hub. The North African places just above and below La Canebière stand out as a budget traveler's dream—they make excellent and filling dishes for under €6. The city's

restaurant density soars around the *vieux port*, peaking on pl. Thiers and the cours Estienne d'Orves, where you can eat outside for as little as €12. Once the staple of penniless fishermen, the city's trademark *bouillabaisse* (a full meal comprising various Mediterranean fish, fish broth, and a spicy sauce called "rouille" or "rust") has become high cuisine and is priced to match. Still, you can find a reasonably-priced *bouillabaisse* in many restaurants near the vieux port and on rue Fortia and rue St-Saens. For a more artsy crowd and cheaper fare, head up to cours Julien and take your pick from the restaurants lining the pedestrian mall. Locals stock up at the fish market, where ingredients for homemade *bouillabaisse* are sold inches from the fishing boats on quai des Belges. (Daily 8am-noon.) There is a vegetable market on cours Julien (M-Sa 8am-1pm) and an open-air market on cours Pierre Puget, beginning at rue Breteuil (M-Sa, starts at 8am). Before you head for the hostels, stock up on the second floor of Monoprix supermarket, on La Canebière, across from the AmEx office. (Open M-Sa 8:30am-8:30pm.)

O'Provençal Pizzeria, 7 rue de la Palud (☎04 91 54 03 10), off rue de Rome. Perfect portions, fast service, and A/C make the best pizza in town better. Try the lip-smacking Trois Fromages (chevre, roquefort, mozzarella; €8) or the Napolitane (€7). Open M-Sa 11:30am-2:15pm and 7:30-11pm. AmEx/MC/V. ❷

Country Life, 14 rue Venture (☎04 96 11 28 00), off rue Paradis. Tasty all-you-can-eat vegan food under a huge skylight and amid a near-forest of foliage. Big buffet plate €5.95; small plate €2.90. Open M-F 11:30am-2:30pm; health-food store open M-Th 9am-6:30pm, F 9:30am-3pm. MC/V. ❶

Le Panaché, 44 rue St-Saens (☎04 91 54 87 81). A relatively quiet, satisfying restaurant on a jam-packed street. €15 *menu* includes *bouillabaise,* octopus salad, and an excellent sorbet. Open Tu-Su 10am-2pm and 6-11pm. AmEx/MC/V. ❸

Café le Parisien, 1 pl. Sadi Carnot (☎04 91 90 05 77). Moneyed hipsters, local socialites, and card- and dice-playing old men sup at the city's most famous café. The stunning *trompe l'œil* interior recalls 1901, when the café first opened its doors. Decadent lunches are pricey, but coffee in all its incarnations is reasonably priced. Open Sa-W 4am-9pm. Tapas nights Th-F until midnight or 1am. ❹

👁 SIGHTS

A walk through the city's streets is more rewarding than any other sights-oriented itinerary, and trips are easily planned with maps from the tourist office. There's always the cheesy *Petit Train*, which departs from quai Belges about every hour on two different circuits. (☎ 04 91 40 17 75. 10:15am-5pm. €5, children €3.)

BASILIQUE DE NOTRE DAME DE LA GARDE. A clear, stunning view of the city, surrounding mountains, and stone-studded bay made this church's hilltop site strategically important for centuries. In WWII, during the liberation of Marseille, a fierce battle raged for days before FFI forces took back the intricately beautiful basilica. The east face of the church remains pocked with bullet holes and shrapnel scars. Towering nearly 230m above the city, the church's golden statue of Madonna bearing the infant Christ, known affectionately as *"la bonne mère,"* is regarded by many as the symbol of Marseille. *(Take bus #60 (dir: Notre Dame); or, from the tourist office, walk up rue Breteuil and turn left onto rue Grignon. It will become bd. de la Corderie. Turn left onto bd. André Aune and you will see a huge staircase. ☎ 04 91 13 40 80. Open in summer daily 7am-8:30pm; in winter 7am-6pm.)*

ABBAYE ST-VICTOR. St-Victor, an abbey fortified against pirates and Saracen invaders, is one of the oldest Christian sites in Europe. The eerie 5th-century catacombs and basilica contain pagan and Christian relics, including the remains of two 3rd-century martyrs. Sarcophagi are piled up along the walls; some, partially excavated, remain half-embedded in the building's foundations. The abbey hosts a concert festival each year from March to December. *(Perched on rue Sainte at the end of quai de Rive Neuve. Follow the signs from the quai. ☎ 04 96 11 22 60. Open daily 9am-7pm. €2 for crypt entrance. Call ☎ 04 91 05 84 48 for festival info. Tickets €26, €23 for students.)*

HARBOR ISLANDS. The **Château d'If,** sun-blasted, blunt, and bright, guards the city from its golden rock perch outside the harbor, looking vaguely like a little kid's sand castle come to life. Its dungeon, immortalized in Dumas's **Count of Monte Cristo,** once held a number of hapless Huguenots. While their cells were drafty and underdecorated, the view from their barred windows would have made a life sentence almost bearable. Nearby, the windswept **Ile Frioul** quarantined suspected plague infectees for two centuries, starting in the 1600s. It was only marginally successful, as an outbreak in 1720 killed half the city's 80,000 citizens. The **hospital** is now a public monument and holds occasional raves. The ride out to the islands takes you between the batteries of the **Fort St-Jean,** whose original tower guarded a giant chain that closed off the harbor in times of trouble.

possible for a prayer room, and this tent in front of me. We'll do this for about two more months, and then we're going to put a prefabricated foundation on the same ground where the synagogue burned, 200m squared. We're going to build, on this ground, a synagogue that will last, a true synagogue.

Q: What was the reaction of the Jewish community to the fire?

A: Well, in Marseille there are 70,000-80,000 Jews—that's important. In the fire, there were six or seven or eight important religious parchments that burned. When sacred things like that burn, you are obliged to bury them—you're burying something very dear. On the day of the burial, there were 15,000-20,000 people from Marseille who came to watch the burial. Never, in Marseille, were there so many people in a demonstration, never. It was enormous, enormous.

Q: Are you more of a cynic now, because of the fire?

A: No, we're not cynical, we're confident. We must fight to rebuild. We must not give up, we must not leave.

Q: In an article in *The New York Times* in April, Xavier Nataf (aide to Marseille's chief rabbi) said that Marseille has its own "special spirit." Do you agree?

A: In Marseille there are many religious communities, and there are is truly little racism between them. The former mayor of Marseille, over 20 years ago, created a particular Marseille spirit. The mayors since him have kept that same spirit, and have sought to bring together a wide range of different communities.

(Reserve in advance in the high season. Boats depart from quai des Belges for both islands. Call the Groupement des Armateurs Côtiers at ☎04 91 55 50 09. Round-trip 20min.; €8 for each island, €13 for both. Château ☎04 91 59 02 30. Boats leave for the château June-Aug. daily 9am-5pm; Sept.-May Tu-Su 9am-3:30pm. €4, under age 25 €2.50. Call the hospital at ☎04 91 57 00 73 for event info.)

LA VIEILLE CHARITÉ. The crowning achievement of the famous 17th-century local architect Pierre Puget, La Charité sheltered orphans, the elderly, and other undesirables. It broke new ground in the field of child abandonment; parents could leave their unwanted children in front, where a wooden turnstile near the gate kept the nuns inside from ever seeing their faces. Now home to many of Marseille's cultural organizations, it houses several of the city's museums, including Egyptian, prehistoric, and classical collections as well as temporary exhibits. The complex exhibits both grace and balance with high, blank, exterior walls facing the **Panier** district and a contrasting sunny interior with colonnades and a stunning Baroque chapel. *(2 rue de la Charité. ☎04 91 14 58 80. Open June-Sept. Tu-Sa 11am-6pm. Temporary exhibits €3, permanent €4.50, students with ID half-price.)*

PALAIS LONGCHAMP. Inaugurated in 1869, the palace was built to honor the completion of a canal which brought fresh water to alleviate Marseille's cholera outbreak. Endowed with towering columns and, shockingly, flowing water, the monument itself is only the center of the complex, which includes two museums, a park, and an observatory. The **Musée des Beaux-Arts** features dramatic Biblical works and paintings of 19th-century Provence. The **Musée de l'Histoire Naturelle** includes a ridiculous assortment of stuffed animals and temporary exhibits on subjects as diverse as the history of dinosaurs and milk. *(Take metro #1 to Cinq Avenues Longchamps. Art museum ☎04 91 14 59 30. Open June-Sept. Tu-Su 11am-6pm; Oct.-May Tu-Su 10am-7pm. €2, students €1. Natural history museum ☎04 91 14 59 50. Open Tu-Su 10am-5pm. €3.20.)*

LE JARDIN DES VESTIGES. The remains of the original port of Marseille rest peacefully in the quiet **Jardin des Vestiges.** The grassy harbor, full of limestone stacked like giant Legos, makes a good picnic stop. Your ticket to the garden also admits you to the **Musée d'Histoire de Marseille,** whose millennia-old artifacts, such as a nearly full-scale ancient boat model, are haphazardly displayed. *(Enter through the Centre Bourse mall's lowest level. Museum ☎04 91 90 42 22. Garden and museum open M-Sa noon-7pm. €2, students €1, over 65 and under 10 free.)*

OTHER SIGHTS. The memorable **Musée Cantini** chronicles the region's artistic successes of the last century, with major Fauvist and Surrealist collections. *(19 rue Grignan. ☎04 91 54 77 75. Open Tu-Sa 10am-5pm. €3, students €1.50, over 65 and under 10 free.)* The **Mémorial des Camps de la Mort** is a small but potent museum recalling the death camps of World War II, and Marseille's role in them: in 1943 nearly 2,000 buildings which were home to Jews were destroyed in the *vieux port.* Here you'll find sobering quotes by Primo Levi, Louis Serre, and Elie Wiesel, and a disturbing collection of ashes. *(Quai de la Tourette. ☎04 91 90 73 15. Open June-Aug. W-Su 11am-6pm; Sept.-May 11am-5pm. Free.)* The **Musée de la Mode** carries ever-changing exhibits of contemporary fashion. *(Espace Mode Méditerranée, 11 La Canebière. ☎04 91 56 59 57. Free tours in French W and Sa-Su 4pm. Open Tu-Su 11am-6pm. €2; students €1, over 65 free.)* The **MAC, Galeries Contemporaines des Musées de Marseille,** features art from the 1960s to today, including works by César and Wegman. *(69 av. d'Haifa. ☎04 91 25 01 07. Open Tu-Su 11am-7pm. €3, students €1.50.)*

◪ ALONG THE SHORE

From the Palais du Pharo to the av. du Prado, the **promenade de la corniche du Président J.F. Kennedy** takes you along Marseille's most beautiful stretch of beaches and inlets. Though traffic is usually heavy, you won't mind winding slowly past the luminous Mediterranean. Be sure to stop at the **Vallon des Auffes.** This hidden fishing port looks today much as it did 50 years ago, with rows of brightly painted, traditional fishing boats dipping and tucking at their moorings. Pedestrians take bus #83 from the *vieux port* (dir: Rond-Point du Prado) to "Vallon des Auffes."

Bus #83 continues on to Marseille's **public beaches.** Get off just after it rounds the statue of David and turns away from the coast. (20-30min.) Or take #19 (dir: Madrague) from M: Castellane or M: Rond-Point du Prado. Both **plage du Prado** and **plage de la Corniche** offer wide beaches, clear water, grass for impromptu soccer matches, good views of the cliffs surrounding Marseille, and less-than-ideal sand. **Supermarché Casino et Cafeteria,** across from the statue, will provide for your every need. (Open M-Sa 8:30am-8:30pm. cafeteria open daily 8:30am-10pm.)

🎵 🎬 ENTERTAINMENT AND FESTIVALS

Don't let Marseille's reputation for seediness keep you inside, but make sure to exercise caution. Try not to end up in far-flung areas of the city late at night, since night buses are scarce, taxis expensive, and the metro closes most days after 9pm. After dark, don't venture far from the busy streets near the *vieux port;* everyone should avoid the North African quarter, cours Belsunce, and bd. d'Athènes. People-watching and nightlife center around **cours Julien,** east of the harbor, and **pl. Thiers,** near the *vieux port.*

Theater buffs should check out the program at the **Théâtre National de Marseille La Criée,** 30 quai de Rive Neuve. (☎04 91 54 70 54. Tickets €9-25. Box office open by telephone Tu-Sa 10am-7pm, in person 1-7pm.) There's also **Théâtre Gymnase,** 4 rue du Théâtre Français. (☎08 20 00 04 27. Box office open Sept.-July M-Sa noon-6pm. Call from 11am-6pm. Tickets €20-28; students €12.) Unwind with the latest French and American films at **Le César,** 4 pl. Castellane. (☎04 91 37 12 80. €6.10.)

BARS AND CLUBS

▓Trolleybus, 24 quai de Rive Neuve (☎04 91 54 30 45; info 06 14 68 88 14). Has to be seen to be believed. This mega-club, occupying an 18th-century warehouse, has a room each for house-garage, rock, pop-rock, and soul-funk-salsa as well as a discothèque built around 2 regulation-size *boule* courts. A heavily local crowd gets down to French and international DJs, who have been playing here for 13 years. Beer from €5, drinks €6.50. Sa cover €10 includes 1 drink. Open July-Aug. W-Sa 11pm-7am, off-season Th-Sa 11pm-7am.

El Ache de Cuba, 9 pl. Paul Cézanne (☎04 91 42 99 79 or 06 88 21 19 52). A slice of Havana, with music blaring out of speakers and onto the sidewalk. Oct.-June weekly Latin dance and Spanish lessons. You must buy a card (€2) to order something, but it's a ticket into the community. After that, drinks are about €2.50, including the "House Punch." Open W-Sa 5pm-2am.

L'Enigme, 22 rue Beauvau (☎04 91 33 79 20), parallel to rue Paradis and pl. de Gaulle. This friendly spot, a popular gay bar, is frequented mostly by men, though women show up occasionally. House, techno, and disco DJs F-Sa nights. Drinks €2 7-9pm; from 9pm on €3-5. Open daily 7pm-5am.

New Can-Can, 3 rue Sénac (☎04 91 48 59 76). A perpetual weekend party for the city's gay/lesbian community. Cool discothèque setup, replete with red leather couches. Su-Th no cover; F free before midnight, then €13; Sa €8 before midnight, €14 after. Open 11pm-6am; 1hr. show Th-Su around 2-2:30am.

LIVE PERFORMANCE

For more info on performance or cultural activities, call **Espace Culture,** 42 La Canebière. (☎ 04 96 11 04 60. Open M-Sa 10am-6:45pm.)

> **L'Espace Julien,** 39 cours Julien (☎ 04 96 12 23 44). Nightly concerts (8:30pm) range from jazz to funk and reggae. Closed July-Aug. Concerts from €10-25. For info, call M-F 9am-noon and 2-6pm.

> **Chocolat Théâtre,** 59 cours Julien (☎ 04 91 42 19 29). Comic pieces and stand-up Tu-Sa at 9pm. Tickets Tu-Th €13.30, F €15, Sa €18. Dinner and show €23-39, students Tu-Th €11.

> **Le Poste à Galene,** 103 rue Ferrari (☎ 04 91 47 57 99), features both local groups and the cutting-edge of the world-famous. Techno and everything else. Tickets €5-17. Open M-F from 8:30pm, shows at 9:30pm.

FESTIVALS

Experience the **International Documentary Film Festival** in June and the **Lesbian and Gay Pride March** in late June and early July. The **Festival de Marseille Méditerranée** keeps Marseille full of music, dance, and theater in July. December brings the **Festival de Musique,** a week-long jubilee of jazz, classical, and pop music at l'Abbaye de St-Victor. Call the tourist office or **Espace Culture** (☎ 04 96 11 04 60) for info.

▶ DAYTRIP FROM MARSEILLE: LES CALANQUES

The Calanques (and **calanques** in general) are inlets of clear water surrounded by walls of jagged, blinding white rock. Stretching from Marseille to Toulon, their precipices and seas shelter a rare and fragile balance of terrestrial and marine plants and wildlife—pine, juniper, and wild asparagus, foxes, bats, owls, and peregrine falcons. Bleached white houses skirt the hills, looking down on swarms of scuba divers, mountain climbers, cliff divers, and nudists.

The **Société des Excursionistes Marseillais,** 16 rue de la Rotonde (☎ 04 91 84 75 52; call M-W and F 5:15-7pm, Sa 3-5pm) conducts walking tours of the Calanques. After paying the €72 membership fee, you can participate in their hiking expeditions. A far cheaper option is to take bus #21 to "Luminy" (€1.40); this leaves you near the calanques **Morgiou** and **Sormiou.** The first of the inlets, **Callelongue,** also lies at the farthest reaches of Marseille's bus line. Take #19 from M: Castellane to its terminus, "La Madrague de Montredon," then catch #20 and follow the coastal roads until its terminus. Service on #20 is sporadic (slightly more than one bus per hour from La Madrague, 6:57am-7:20pm), but you can kill time by exploring trails in the nearby hills. Line #20 often ends prematurely at **Goudes** (the town before Callelongue), which is a good base for trails to secluded inlets; ask the driver to take you all the way to Callelongue when you get on.

NEAR MARSEILLE

CASSIS

Twenty-three kilometers from Marseille, the sparkling resort town of Cassis clings to a hillside overlooking the Mediterranean. Immaculate white villas clump around the slopes above, and the town itself—a network of winding staircases, slender alleyways, and thick gardens—leads down to a jewel-green port. Unfortunately, during the summer, lines of honking cars mar this town's delicate beauty. Parking is a competitive sport, and the town takes on an unmistakable touristy feel. Luckily, the relative peace and unquestionable beauty of the *calanques* are nearby; follow the signs to the **Calanque de Port-Pin,** about an hour east of town. From there, it's a half-hour hike to the popular, otherworldly **Calanque En Vau** and beach.

E7 TRANSPORTATION AND PRACTICAL INFORMATION. Since the train station is 3km outside town, it's easiest to take a **bus** from Marseille (40-50min.; 4 per day, 8:45am-6pm; leaves from the bus station at M: Castellane) or Cassis (4 per day, 6:50am-4pm; €3.20; call ☎ 04 42 08 41 05 for info.) **Trains,** however, conveniently run at later hours. (21-22min.; 25 each day from Marseille, between 6am-11:06pm; 25 each day from Cassis, between 5:16am-10:04pm; €4.40.) For a **taxi** from the train station to town (about €7-8), call ☎ 04 42 01 78 96 or 06 81 60 48 51. From the bus stop, go right and walk for 5min. through the center of town. At the water, on the central Quai des Moulins, you will find the **tourist office,** whose maps are especially helpful when trekking to the hostel outside of town. (☎ 04 42 01 71 17; fax 04 42 01 28 31. Open June-Sept. M-F 9am-7pm, Sa-Su 9am-1pm and 3-7pm; Mar.-May and Oct. M-F 9:30am-6pm, Sa 10am-noon and 2-5pm, Su 10am-noon; Nov.-Feb. M-F 9:30am-12:30pm and 2-5pm, Sa 10am-noon and 2-5pm, Su 10am-noon.) The **police** can be reached at ☎ 04 42 01 17 17. A **pharmacy** can be found at 11 av. Victor Hugo. (☎ 04 42 01 70 03. Open Th-Tu 8am-12:30pm and 3-8pm. Cassis's **garde** pharmacy changes regularly; check the pharmacy's window for updated info.) Send your naked sunbathing pictures back home and **exchange currency** at the **post office,** in the public garden between the bus station and the port. (☎ 04 42 01 98 30. Open M and W-F 8:30am-noon and 2:30-5pm, Tu 9am-noon and 2:30-5pm, Sa 8:30am-noon.) There are several **ATMs** around the port.

[1][2] ACCOMMODATIONS AND FOOD. Cassis makes a terrific daytrip from Marseille, since hotels are expensive and fill up quickly. If you can't stand leaving, try the **Auberge de Jeunesse de la Fontasse (HI) ❶,** 20km from Marseille off D559, near En Vau. The hostel is a sweaty 4km climb from the Cassis tourist office (1hr.), but the gorgeous view makes it worthwhile. Start from Cassis's port and follow signs for the Calanques. When the road ends at two paths, take the steep right path and then watch closely for the signs printed on rocks. Flop onto one of 66 beds in 6- to 10-person dorms, powered by solar energy and irrigated with filtered rain water (from taps). There are no showers and light chores are required of all guests. (☎ 04 42 01 02 72. Reception 8-10am and 5-9pm. Closed Jan.-Mar. 15. Bunks €8.30. **Members only.**) If you have planned your trip in advance, stay at **Le Provençal ❹,** 7 av. Victor Hugo. The A/C, TVs, central location and soothing rooms make the stay worthwhile. (☎ 04 42 01 72 13. Breakfast €6. Reception 7:30am-10pm. Doubles with shower €43, with toilet €54, with bath €55; triples with shower €60, with toilet and bath €65-70. Extra bed €11. Prices lower in off-season. V.) The crowded **Camping Les Cigales ❶,** is 20min. away; take av. Agostina to av. Colbert, then turn right onto av. de la Marne. (☎ 04 42 01 07 34; fax 04 42 01 34 18. Bring your own toilet paper. Open Mar. 15-Nov. 15. Reception 8am-8pm. €4.95 per person, €2.60 per child, €4.60 per site, €9.70 for 1 person with tent, €14.85 for 2 people with tent. Cars and campers extra. Electricity €2.60. Bar on site. AmEx/MC/V.)

The roads right next to the beach are lined with reasonably priced *crêperies;* the small back streets around rue Icard are home to more expensive, yet intimate, restaurants. There is a **Petit Casino,** on av. Victor Hugo. (Open M-Sa 8am-12:30pm and 3:30-7:30pm, Su 8am-12:30pm and 4-7pm.) Cheap pizzas (€7.50-9) and monstrous plates of mussels and fries (€10.50) can be had at **Le Petit Cassis ❷,** 19 rue Michel Blanc. (☎ 04 42 01 17 32. Open F-W 11:45am-3pm and 6-11pm.)

[1][2] SIGHTS AND ACTIVITIES. You can explore the crystalline water with a kayak at **Kayak de Mer,** pl. Montmorin, on the beach. (☎ 04 42 01 80 01. Single kayak €25 per half-day, €40 per day; double kayak €40/€65.) Or see the cliffs on a **boat tour.** (☎ 04 42 01 90 83. 45-90min. Different tours bring you to *calanques.* Boats leave regularly from port Feb.-Nov. 15; Jan.-Feb. make reservations. €10-15.)

PROVENCE

AIX-EN-PROVENCE

Aix (pronounced "X," pop. 137,000) is one of those rare cities that caters to tourists without being spoiled by them. This is the city of Paul Cézanne, Victor Vasarely, and Emile Zola, and every golden facade or dusty café has had its brush with greatness. Aix's art is now preserved in its eclectic art collections; be sure to follow in the footsteps of Cézanne through his favorite haunts on the Chemin de Cézanne once you've explored the town's intimate tiny squares, twisty streets and flowing fountains. Aix's student population ensures a lively nightlife scene all year long and keeps it far in the cultural forefront of Provence. From the end of June through early August, dance, opera, jazz, and classical music take over the city.

▐▀ TRANSPORTATION

Trains: at the end of av. Victor Hugo, off impasse Gustave Desplace. Ticket window open M-F 5am-9:25pm, Sa-Su 6am-9:25pm. Reservations and info open M-F 8am-7:30pm, Sa 8am-7pm; be prepared for a long wait. Almost every train goes through Marseille. To: **Cannes** (3½hr., 8 per day between 5:10am-9pm, €25.10); **Marseille** (35min.; 21 trains per day, 5:10am-9:25pm; €5.70); **Nice** (3-4hr.; 8 per day, 5:10am-9pm; €27.60). Note: Some trains to and from Marseille are actually buses; check the departure info before leaving. If it says "car," your "train" is actually a bus.

Buses: av. de l'Europe (☎04 42 91 26 80), off av. des Belges. Info desk open daily 7:30am-7pm; tickets 6:30am-7pm. Companies compete for the heavy commuter traffic to **Marseille,** with buses almost every 10min. **RDT13** (☎04 42 93 59 00) serves **Avignon** (2hr.; M-Sa 5 per day, 1 on Su; €13.50). **Phocéens Cars** (☎04 93 85 66 61) goes to **Cannes** (1¾hr., 2 per day, €21) and **Nice** (2¼hr., 2 per day, €20.60). **Ceyte** (☎04 90 93 74 90) runs to **Arles** (1¾hr.; M-Sa 5 per day, 1 on Su; €11.40). Ask for under-26 student discounts for Nice or Cannes (ISIC required).

Public Transportation: Aix-en-Bus (☎04 42 26 37 28) runs buses around the city (€1.10, €7.30 for 10-pack *carnet*).

Taxi Radio Aixois: ☎04 42 27 71 11. €10 from train station to hostel 3km west of *centre ville.* 24hr.

Bike Rental: Cycles Zammit, 27 rue Mignet (☎04 42 23 19 53), between pl. des Prêcheurs and pl. Bellegarde. Bikes €9-10 per half-day, €12.20 per day, €61 per week. Passport deposit. Open Tu-Sa 9am-12:30pm and 3-7:30pm. AmEx/MC/V.

▚ ▐ ORIENTATION AND PRACTICAL INFORMATION

The cours **Mirabeau** sweeps through the center of town, linking **La Rotonde** (a.k.a. **place du Général de Gaulle**) to the west with **place Forbin** to the east. Fountain-dodging traffic along the cours separates cafés on one side from banks on the other. The mostly pedestrian *vieille ville* snuggles inside the **périphérique**—a ring of boulevards including bd. Carnot and cours Sextius. The **tourist office** and the central terminus for city buses are on **place du Général de Gaulle.** To reach them from the train station, go straight onto av. Victor Hugo and bear left at the fork, staying on av. Victor Hugo until it feeds into **La Rotonde.** (5min.) The tourist office is on the left, between av. des Belges and av. Victor Hugo. To get there from the bus station, go up av. de l'Europe, take a left onto av. des Belges and follow it to La Rotonde. The tourist office will be on the right.

Tourist Office: 2 pl. du Général de Gaulle (☎04 42 16 11 61; fax 04 42 16 11 62). Sells "Visa for Aix" card (€2) with reduced rate to museums, and provides city tours, some in English (€8, €4 with "Visa for Aix"). Hotel reservations service June-Aug. M-Sa

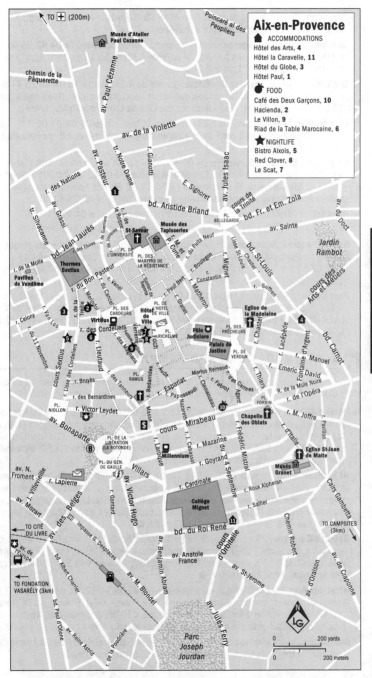

Aix-en-Provence

ACCOMMODATIONS
Hôtel des Arts, **4**
Hôtel la Caravelle, **11**
Hôtel du Globe, **3**
Hôtel Paul, **1**

FOOD
Café des Deux Garçons, **10**
Hacienda, **2**
Le Villon, **9**
Riad de la Table Marocaine, **6**

NIGHTLIFE
Bistro Aixois, **5**
Red Clover, **8**
Le Scat, **7**

PROVENCE

9am-7pm. Open July-Aug. M-Sa 8:30am-8pm, Su 10am-1pm and 2-6pm; Sept.-June M-Sa 8:30am-7pm, Su 8:30am-1pm and 2-6pm.

Currency exchange: L'Agence, in Afat Voyages, 5 cours Mirabeau (☎04 42 26 93 93; fax 04 42 26 79 03). Open July-Aug. M-Sa 9am-7:30pm, Su 10am-2pm; Sept.-June M-F 9am-6:30pm, Sa 9am-1pm and 2-5pm.

English Bookstore: Paradox Bookstore, 15 rue du 4 Septembre (☎04 42 26 47 99). New and used books. Also videos, CD-ROMs, and job listings. Open M-Sa 9am-12:30pm and 2-6:30pm. Also, check out the **Cité du Livre** (see **Sights,** below).

Laundromat: Lavomatique, 15 rue Jacques de la Iroquois (☎06 08 01 02 13). Open daily 7am-8pm. Also at 3 rue Fonderie (open daily 7am-8pm), and 3 rue Fernand Dol (open daily 7am-8pm).

Help Lines: SIDA Info Service (☎08 00 84 08 00) is an AIDS hotline. **SOS Viol** (☎04 91 56 04 10) is a rape hotline. Call **SOS Médecins** (☎04 42 26 24 00) for medical advice (24hr.). **Service des Etrangers** (☎04 42 96 89 48) helps out foreigners. To access Aix's rotating 24-hour **pharmacie de garde,** call ☎04 42 26 40 40.

Hospital: av. des Tamaris (☎04 42 33 50 00). **Ambulances:** ☎04 42 21 37 37.

Police: 10 av. de l'Europe (☎04 42 93 97 00), near the Cité du Livre.

Internet Access: Millennium, 6 rue Mazarine (☎04 42 27 39 11), off cours Mirabeau. €3 per hr. Open daily 10am-midnight. Also **Virtu@us,** 40 rue Cordeliers (☎04 42 26 02 30). €2.30 per 30min., €3.80 per hr. Open M-F 9am-1am, Sa 10am-1am, Su 2pm-1am.

Post Office: 2 rue Lapierre (☎04 42 16 01 50), just off La Rotonde. Open M-F 8:30am-6:45pm, Sa 8:30am-noon. **Currency exchange.** The **annex,** 1 pl. de l'Hôtel de Ville (☎04 42 63 04 66), has the same services. Open M, Th-F 8am-6:30pm, Tu-W 8:30am-6:30pm, Sa 8am-noon. **Postal code:** 13100.

⚑ ACCOMMODATIONS AND CAMPING

There are few inexpensive hotels near the city center, and during festival season they may be booked in advance. Reserve early or hope for cancellations.

Hôtel du Globe, 74 cours Sextius (☎04 42 26 03 58; fax 04 42 26 13 68). Spacious rooms with pristine bathrooms, oversize armchairs and TVs; some have balconies. Rooftop terrace. Breakfast €8. Reception 24hr. Singles €32, with shower €35; doubles with shower €48, with bath €53; 2 small beds with shower €53, with bath €57; triples with bath €66; quads with bath €77. Extra bed €9. AmEx/MC/V. ❹

Hôtel Paul, 10 av. Pasteur (☎04 42 43 23 89; fax 04 42 63 17 80; hotel.paul@wanadoo.fr), past the Cathédrale St-Sauveur. Spacious, simple, immaculate rooms in a bright and modern hotel; some with large bathrooms. Breakfast in garden €4.30. Reception 7:15am-10:30pm, closed Su noon-6pm. Singles and doubles with shower €31; triples €46; rooms facing garden €9 more. ❹

Hôtel La Caravelle, 29 bd. du Roy-René (☎04 42 21 53 05; fax 04 42 96 55 46). Cute, appealing, moderately sized rooms with cool lighting several blocks south of the *centre ville.* Breakfast €5.50. Reception 24hr. Singles €39; doubles €43-58; doubles on garden and quad €66. AmEx/MC/V. ❹

Hôtel des Arts, 69 bd. Carnot at rue Portalis (☎04 42 38 11 77; fax 04 42 26 77 31). Identical, compact, modern rooms. All rooms have shower, toilet, phone, and TV. Breakfast €4.30. Reception 24hr. Singles and doubles €30-35, depending on whether you face noisy bd. Carnot or the quiet rue de la Fonderie. MC/V. ❸

Campsites: Two campgrounds lie outside of town, accessible by bus #3 from "La Rotonde" at the "Trois Sautets" and "Val St-André" stops, respectively.

Arc-en-Ciel, rte. de Nice, is 2km from the city center (☎04 42 26 14 28). Small, comfortable campsite is divided by the Arc—several sites have a view of Cézanne's Pont des Trois Sautets. Pool, hot showers, and multilingual management who allege that this is the oldest continuously operated campsite in Europe. €5.20 per person, €5.80 per site, parking included. ❶

Chantecler, av. St-André, by rte. de Nice, is 2km from the city center (☎04 42 26 12 98; fax 04 42 27 33 53). Sites have views of Mont Ste-Victoire on a quiet, wooded hill. Pool, impeccable hot showers and restrooms, restaurant, and bar. Open year-round. Reception 8am-11pm. June-Aug. €11.95 per person, €15.45 with electricity; low season €11.05 and €14.25. ❶

FOOD

Aix's culinary reputation stands on its sweets. The city's *bonbon* is the **calisson d'Aix,** a small iced marzipan-and-melon treat created in 1473. Other specialties include soft nougat and hard praline candies. Check out the *pâtisseries* on rue Espariat or rue d'Italie; rue d'Italie also has bakeries, *charcuteries*, and fruit stands. The roads north of cours Mirabeau are packed with restaurants, as is **rue de la Verrerie,** off rue des Cordeliers. For the freshest fruits and vegetables, try the markets on pl. de la Madeleine (Tu, Th, Sa 7am-1pm) and pl. Richelme (daily, same times). Supermarket aficionados can choose from three **Petit Casinos,** at 3 cours d'Orbitelle (☎04 42 27 61 43; open M-Sa 8am-1pm and 4-7:30pm), 16 rue Italie (open Tu-Sa 8am-8pm, Su 8am-1pm), and 5 rue Sapora (open Tu-Sa 8:30am-7:30pm, Su 8:30am-12:30pm).

The Aixois like nothing better than to watch each other preen, and their cafés along **cours Mirabeau** encourage a polite voyeurism. Though eating on Mirabeau is generally more expensive, an espresso at the ancient gilt-and-mirrored **Café des Deux Garçons** won't kill you. The former watering hole of Cézanne and Zola, affectionately known as the "Deux Gs," charges only €1.50 for a coffee. (☎04 42 26 00 51. Open daily 7am-2am.) At lunch and dinner-time, little restaurants spill their colorful tables into the squares and side streets of Aix. **Le Villon ❸,** 14 rue Félibre Gaut, off rue des Cordeliers, has pleasant outdoor seating, friendly waitstaff, and an excellent *tarte citron* (€4.60). Inside there's candlelight and jazz, classical or French music, even at lunchtime. (☎04 42 27 35 27. Lunch *menu* €9.60. Dinner *menu* €11.50-18. Open M-Sa noon-2pm and 7-11pm. MC/V.) Another mouth-waterer is **Hacienda ❸,** 7 rue Mérindol, on pl. des Fontêtes off pl. des Cardeurs. (☎04 42 27 00 35. Lunch *menus* €10-12. Dinner *menu* €13. Reserve in advance at night. Open M-Th noon-3pm, F-Sa noon-10pm.) For tasty, if pricey, Moroccan fare at tables canopied by a huge tree, head to **Riad de la Table Marocaine ❹,** 21 rue Lieutaud. (☎04 42 26 15 79. Most couscous dishes €18 or less; *menus* €28-34. Open W-M noon-3pm and 7-11pm. AmEx/MC/V.)

SIGHTS

Every corner of Aix has some remarkable edifice and every *place* has its own museum. Individual exploration and discovery is the best way to experience Aix's languorous charm. The "Visa for Aix" (€2), sold at the tourist office or participating museums, gives you reduced price at museums, a free tour of Thermes Sextius, and half-price on the tourist office's town tour.

FONDATION VASARELY. This trippy black-and-white museum is an absolute must-see for both modern art fans and those who know nothing about the "plastic alphabet." Designed in the 1970s by Hungarian-born artist Victor Vasarely, famed for his eye-boggling geometrics and the development of "kineticism," the building contains some of the old man's most monumental and original work in eight huge hexagonal spaces. The entrancing audioguide probes Vasarely's attempts to create a "polychromatic city of happiness." *(Av. Marcel-Pagnol, Jas-de-Bouffan, next to the youth hostel; take bus #10 from near the bus station. ☎04 42 20 01 09. Open June-Sept. M-F 10am-1pm and 2-7pm, Sa-Su 10am-7pm; Oct.-May closes at 6pm. €7, students and ages 7-18 €4.)*

CHEMIN DE CÉZANNE. A self-guided 2hr. walking tour moves through the landmarks of Aix's most famous son, including his birthplace and hangouts. In his studio, the **Atelier Paul Cézanne,** the artist's beret still hangs in the corner of a room filled with paint-smeared palettes and the props he used for still-lifes, as though he might step inside from the overgrown garden at any moment and pick them up. *(9 av. Paul Cézanne. Take bus #21 north of Aix, or just walk 10min. up av. Paul Cézanne. ☎04 42 21 06 53. Open June 15-Sept. daily 10am-6:30pm; Apr.-June 14 10am-noon and 2:30-6pm; Oct.-Mar. 10am-noon and 2-5pm. €5.50, students €2, children under 16 and seniors free.)*

CATHÉDRALE ST-SAVEUR. A dramatic mix of Romanesque, Gothic, and Baroque naves built on (and with) stones from a preexisting Roman site, this church is pure architectural whimsy. Carved panels from the 15th-century main portal remain in mint condition. During the Revolution, the bas-relief representing a "transfiguration" was completely destroyed, leaving a blank space above the doors, and all the statues in the great front were decapitated. They were recapitated in the 19th century with disappointing new heads. *(Rue Gaston de Saporta, on pl. de l'Université. ☎04 42 23 45 65. Open daily 9am-noon and 2-6pm, except during services.)*

PAVILLON DE VENDÔME. In the winter, this 17th-century building houses paintings and furniture from the turn of the 18th century, as well as temporary exhibits in the summer. The glorious gardens are authentically Aix; soothing smells of boxwood and roses, a fountain, and neatly manicured shrubs. *(32 rue Célony. ☎04 42 21 05 78. Museum open Apr.-Sept. W-M 10am-noon and 2-6pm; Feb.-Mar. and Oct. 10am-noon and 1:30-5:30pm; Nov.-Jan. 10am-noon and 1-5pm. €2, under 26 free. Gardens open daily 9am-5:30pm. Free.)*

CITÉ DU LIVRE. This former match factory is now a cultural center with three major sections. The **Bibliothèque Méjanes** contains the largest library in the region and a gallery of contemporary art. Bookended by giant, rusty steel replicas of French classics, this bright library stocks current *Newsweeks* and a good collection of British and American literature. The **Discothèque** loans a wide selection of music from around the world. The air-conditioned **Videothèque d'Art Lyrique** shows operas, ballets, and concerts of past **Festivals d'Aix** for free. *(8-10 rue des Allumettes, southeast of La Rotonde. ☎04 42 91 98 88. Open Tu and Th-F noon-6pm, W and Sa 10am-6pm. While it's all open to the public, borrowing from the Bibliothèque requires a €20 membership.)*

OTHER SIGHTS. The **Musée Granet** contains several lesser-known Cézannes and a smattering of works by David, Ingres, and Delacroix, as well as archaeological finds. Only part of the full collection is accessible, and in early 2003 it will close completely for 3 years of renovation. *(Pl. St-Jean-Marie-de-Malte. ☎04 42 38 14 70. Open W-M 10am-noon and 2-6pm. Free.)* A fine collection of 17th- and 18th-century tapestries hangs in the **Musée des Tapisseries.** The highlight is the series depicting the story of Don Quixote. *(Palais Archiépiscopal, 2nd fl., 28 pl. des Martyrs de la Résistance. ☎04 42 23 09 91. Open W-M 10am-5pm. €2, under 25 free. July-Aug. free tours in French and English. Call ☎04 42 21 05 78 for info on tours.)*

■ NIGHTLIFE

Partying is a year-round pastime in Aix. Most clubs open at 11:30pm but don't get going until 2am. Pubs and bars hold earlier hours. **Rue de la Verrerie** has the highest concentration of bars and clubs; candlelit cafés line the **Forum des Cardeurs,** behind the *Hôtel de Ville.* House and club music prevails at **Le Richelm,** 24 rue de la Verrerie, literally an underground club and swanky bar. *(☎04 42 23 49 29. Cover includes 1 drink: Tu-Th €9.15, F €12.20, Sa €15.25. Women free Tu-Th. Open Tu-Sa 11:30pm-dawn.)* Get down to techno, dance, R&B, and house at **Le**

Mistral, a big dance club at 3 rue F. Mistral; don't show up here in shorts, jeans, or sandals. (☎04 42 38 16 49. €16 cover includes one drink. Tu women free with one drink. Open Tu-Sa 11:30pm-5am.) **Bistro Aixois,** 37 cours Sextius, packs loads of students and alcohol into a compact space with a Caribbean beach party motif. (☎04 42 27 50 10. Open daily 6:30pm-4am. MC/V.) **The Red Clover,** 30 rue de la Verrerie, is a lively bar with an overflowing international crowd. Happy Hour 6-8pm. (☎04 42 23 44 61. Open daily 8am-2am.) **Le Scat,** 11 rue Verrerie, is a happening jazz, rock, and dance club. (☎04 42 23 00 23. Nightly concerts 1am; free M-Th and F-Sa. €13 cover includes one drink. Open M-Sa 11pm-6am.) **Ciné Mazarin,** 6 rue Laroque, off cours Mirabeau, and **Renoir,** 24 cours Mirabeau, project French films and several foreign films, some in English. (Both ☎04 42 26 99 85; €7.50, students €6, under €4.50.)

■ FESTIVALS

Aix's overwhelming festival season kicks off in the beginning of June with the week-long **Cinestival.** With the free **"billet scoop"** from the tourist office, films cost €3. The **Festival d'Aix-en-Provence,** a famous series of operas and orchestral concerts, lasts from June to July. (Ticket office at 11 rue Gaston de Sapora. ☎04 42 17 34 34; www.festival-aix.com. Tickets €6 and much higher.) For two weeks at the end of July and the beginning of August, the city hosts **Danse à Aix,** which features ballet, modern, and jazz performances. (☎04 42 23 41 24. Call M-F 2-5pm. €11-38, students €11-30.) Tickets are available at the tourist office or at 1 pl. John Rewald. (M-Sa 9am-noon and 2-6pm.) For two weeks in early July, the city puts on a two-week **Jazz Festival** of salsa, big band, and, yes, jazz (€20). The **Office des Fêtes et de la Culture,** Espace Forbin, 1 pl. John Rewald (☎04 42 63 06 75), can fill you in on all the festivals. **Aix-en-Musique,** 3 pl. John Rewald (☎04 42 21 69 69), sponsors concerts year-round.

AVIGNON

The crooked rabbit-run of Avignon's streets is crowned by the unparalleled Palais des Papes, a sprawling Gothic fortress known in its time as "the biggest and strongest house in the world." Some 700 years ago, political dissent in Italy led the homesick French pontiff Clement V to shift the papacy to Avignon. During this "Second Babylonian Captivity of the Church," as it was dubbed by the stunned Romans, seven popes erected and expanded Avignon's Palais, making the city a "Rome away from Rome." Gregory XI returned the papacy to Rome in 1377, but his reform-minded Italian successor so infuriated the cardinals that they elected an alternate pope, who again set up court in Avignon, beginning the Great Schism. In 1403 the last "anti-pope" abandoned the luxurious ecclesiastical buildings, but the town remained Papal territory until the Revolution. Though the popes have gone, the city seems to carry on its role as a capital of Catholicism, the fervor of the papal courts spilling out of history into modern Avignon.

Avignon (pop. 100,000) is today chiefly known for its two theatre festivals—first and foremost, the famous **Festival d'Avignon,** a hugely popular theatrical celebration held since 1947, and also the younger, more experimental **Festival OFF.** For three weeks in July, performers, singers, and con men roam the streets, entertaining and pick-pocketing hordes of French tourists. Prices soar, accommodations fill up quickly, and authorities crack down on festival-induced vagrancy. Avignon quiets down after the festival, but its sights and performer-filled streets maintain their liveliness. The city is also a good base for trips to some of Provence's most beautiful villages: the hamlets of the Alpilles (p. 514) and of the Lubéron (p. 503).

PROVENCE

▐ TRANSPORTATION

Trains: porte de la République (☎04 90 27 81 89). Info desk and ticket counters open daily 4am-12:30am. To: **Arles** (30min., 19 per day, €5.50); **Lyon** (2hr., 7 per day, €23.90); **Marseille** (70min., 8 per day, €14.60); **Montpellier** (1hr., 11 per day, €12.50); **Nice** (3hr., 5 per day, €40.90); **Nîmes** (30min., 12 per day, €7.10); and **Toulouse** (3½hr., 6 per day, €30.50). TGV ticket counters open daily 5:40am-10pm. To: **Dijon** (2¾hr., 12 per day, €51); **Lyon** (1hr., 12 per day, €35.70); and **Paris** (3½hr., 13 per day, €79.20).

Regional Buses: bd. St-Roch, right of the train station. Info desk (☎04 90 82 07 35) open M-F 8am-6pm, and Sa 8am-noon. Buy tickets on bus. **CTM** goes to: **Arles** (45min., 5 per day, €7.80); **Les Baux** (1hr., 2 per day, €7.80); **Marseille** (2hr., 5 per day, €15.20); and **St-Rémy** (45min., 10 per day, €5.20). Buses are less frequent in the off-season.

Public Transportation: TCRA, av. de Lattre de Tassigny (☎04 32 74 18 32), near porte de la République. Office open M-F 8:30am-12:30pm and 1:30-6pm. Tickets €1, *carnet* of 10 €7.80.

Taxis: Radio Taxi, porte de la République (☎04 90 82 20 20). 24hr.

Bike Rental: Aymard Cycles Peugeot, 80 rue Guillaume Puy (☎04 90 86 32 49). Open Tu-Sa 8am-noon and 2-7pm. €9.15 per day, €36.60 per week. €120 deposit. MC/V.

▐✦▐ ORIENTATION AND PRACTICAL INFORMATION

Avignon's 14th-century ramparts enclose a labyrinth of alleyways, squares, and cramped little streets—stick to the main thoroughfares to avoid getting lost. To reach the tourist office from the train station, walk straight through porte de la République onto cours Jean Jaurès. The tourist office is about 200m uphill on the right. Cours Jean Jaurès becomes rue de la République and leads directly to **place de l'Horloge,** Avignon's central square. Just southeast of l'Horloge, little pedestrian streets glitter with boutiques. At night, lone travelers should stay on well-lit paths and avoid the area around rue Thiers and rue Philonarde. Avignon is a haven for car thieves and pickpockets, especially during festival time.

Tourist Office: 41 cours Jean Jaurès (☎04 32 74 32 74; fax 04 90 82 95 03). Open July M-Sa 9am-7pm and Su 10am-5pm; Apr.-June and Aug.-Sept. M-Sa 9am-6pm; Oct.-Mar. M-F 9am-6pm, Sa 9am-5pm, and Su 10am-noon. **Annex** at pont St-Bénezet. Open Apr.-Oct. daily 10am-7pm.

Train Tours: Les Trains Touristiques (☎06 11 35 06 66). Short tour of Rocher des Doms €2; longer city tour €6. Train tours leave from pl. du Palais des Papes every 15-35min. Trains run Mar. 15-Oct. 15 daily 10am-7pm, until 8pm July-Aug.; shorter train runs only from 1:30pm onwards.

Bus Tours: Autocars Lieutaud (☎04 90 86 36 75) runs excursions to **the Alpilles, La Camargue, Nîmes, Arles,** the **Luberon, Vaison-la-Romaine** and **Orange** for €15-28. (Apr.-early Nov.) **Les Provençals** (☎04 90 14 70 00) also tours many nearby locales; see **Sights,** p. 525. (€25-45. June-late Sept. Tu-F €5-9 discount with pass.)

English Bookstore: Shakespeare Bookshop and Tearoom, 155 rue Carreterie (☎04 90 27 38 50), down rue Carnot toward the ramparts. Paperbacks, English cream teas, and excellent homemade brownies (€1.25). Open Tu-Sa 9:30am-12:30pm and 2-6:30pm.

Youth Information: Espace Info-Jeunes, 102 rue Carreterie (☎04 90 14 04 05). Info on jobs, study, health care, housing, and work. Open M-F 8:30am-noon and 1:30-5pm.

Laundromat: 66 pl. des Corps Saints. Also 48 rue Carreterie. Both open daily 7am-8pm.

Police: bd. St-Roch (☎04 90 16 81 00), left of the train station.

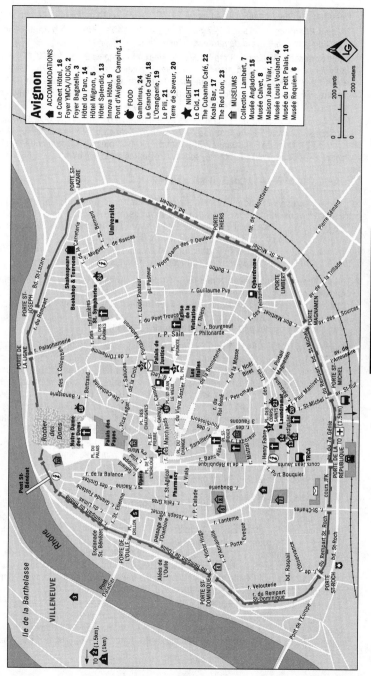

Avignon

▲ ACCOMMODATIONS
Le Colbert Hôtel, 16
Foyer YMCA/UCJG, 2
Foyer Bagatelle, 3
Hôtel du Parc, 14
Hôtel Mignon, 5
Hôtel Splendid, 13
Innova Hôtel, 9
Pont d'Avignon Camping, 1

♣ FOOD
Gambrinus, 24
Le Grande Café, 18
L'Orangerie, 19
Le Pili, 21
Terre de Saveur, 20

★ NIGHTLIFE
Le Cid, 11
The Cubanito Café, 22
Koala Bar, 17
The Red Lion, 23

🏛 MUSEUMS
Collection Lambert, 7
Musée Angladon, 15
Musée Calvet, 8
Maison Jean Vilar, 12
Musée Louis Vouland, 4
Musée du Petit Palais, 10
Musée Requien, 6

PROVENCE

Hospital: 305 rue Raoul Follereau (☎04 32 75 33 33), south of the town center. 24hr.

24-Hour Pharmacy: 11-13 rue St. Agricol (☎04 90 82 14 20). Open daily 8am-7:15pm. For the nightly *pharmacie de garde*, call the police.

Internet Access: Webzone, 3 rue St. Jean le Vieux, at pl. Pie (☎04 32 76 29 47). A fair number of computers and friendly, talkative, English-speaking staff. €3 per 30min., €4.50 per hr. Open M-F 9am-noon, Sa 11am-midnight, and Su noon-8pm. **Cyber-drome,** 68 rue Guillaume Puy (☎04 90 16 05 15). Hip café with 15 stations and games. €3.05 per 30min.; €4.60 per hr. Open daily 8am-1am.

Post Office: cours JFK, near porte de la République (☎04 90 27 54 00). **Currency exchange.** Open M-F 8am-7pm and Sa 8am-noon. **Branch office** on pl. Pie (☎04 90 14 70 70). Open M-F 8:30am-12:30pm and 1:30-6:30pm, Sa 8:30am-noon. **Postal code:** 84000. For **Poste Restante,** specify "Poste Restante: Avignon."

▐ ACCOMMODATIONS AND CAMPING

In general, Avignon's budget offerings are pleasant and plentiful. Unfortunately, unreserved beds vanish once the theater troupes hit town. All prices increase (often by €10 in a hotel) during July festival season. The tourist office lists organizations that set up cheap housing during the festival; you might also consider staying in Arles, Nîmes, Orange, or Tarascon, and commuting by train (between €5.50-7.10). All hotels and campsites sell reduced-price Palais admission tickets.

Hôtel Mignon, 12 rue Joseph Vernet (☎04 90 82 17 30; fax 04 90 85 78 46; hotelmignon@wanadoo.fr). Fashion-conscious hotel on a chic street near great shopping; original color schemes in each comfortable, sweet-smelling, well-equipped room. Sparkling dark blue tiled bathrooms. Breakfast included. Singles €30, with bath €41; doubles with bath €46; triples with bath €55.40; quads €72. MC/V. ❸

Foyer YMCA/UCJG, 7bis chemin de la Justice, Villeneuve (☎04 90 25 46 20; fax 04 90 25 30 64; info@ymca-avignon.com). From the train station, turn left and follow the city wall; cross the second bridge (pont Daladier) and the Ile Barthelasse and continue straight for 200m, then take a left onto chemin de la Justice; the foyer will be up the hill on your left. (30min.) From the post office, take bus #10 (dir: Les Angles-Grand Angles) to "Général Leclerc" or #11 (dir: Villeneuve-Grand Terme) to "Pont d'Avignon." Clean and sparsely decorated but cheerful rooms with terraces; great views of the Palais and surrounding countryside—or the inviting pool. Internet access €2.80 per hr. Breakfast €5. *Demi-pension* obligatory in July. Reception 8:30am-noon and 1:30-6pm. July-Aug. F-Su reception is at on-site restaurant. Reserve ahead. Apr.-Oct. singles €15 per person, with shower and toilet €30; doubles €13-20 per person; triples €10.30-17.30 per person. Rates drop 20% in other months. MC/V. ❶

Foyer Bagatelle, Ile de la Barthelasse (☎04 90 86 30 39 or 04 90 85 78 45; fax 04 90 27 16 23). Follow directions for the YMCA to pont Daladier; Bagatelle is just across it on the right. (10min. from the town center.) Or take bus #10 or 11 to "La Barthelasse." Incomparable view of the city from the banks of the Rhône. Simple 2-, 4-, 6-, or 8-bed rooms with softly colored walls. Internet access €4.60 per 30 min. Supermarket, 2 cafeterias, and bike rental (€16 per day with ID deposit). Breakfast priced *à la carte*. Reception 11am-8pm. Lockout 2-5pm. Beds €10.15; doubles €23-31. Excellent **camping** facilities available in the dense shade of plane trees. Reception 8:30am-8:30pm. 1 person and tent €7.40, 2 people and tent €10.20. Electricity €2.40. MC/V. ❶

Hôtel Splendid, 17 rue Agricol Perdiguier (☎04 90 86 14 46; fax 04 90 85 38 55), near the tourist office. Charming, recently redone rooms with new wooden furniture on a quiet street in a busy area; some rooms are quite small. Breakfast €5. Reception 7am-11pm. Singles with shower €30-34; doubles with shower €40-46. Extra bed €5. AmEx/MC/V. ❸

Hôtel du Parc, 18 rue Perdiguier (☎04 90 82 71 55; fax 04 90 85 64 86). Modern, understated rooms with a rustic feel. Right across from the Hôtel Splendid, and just as good. Breakfast €5. Reserve well ahead. Reception noon-10pm. Singles €29, with shower €36; doubles with bath €42; triples with bath €55. MC/V. ❸

Le Colbert Hôtel, 7 rue Perdiguier (☎04 90 86 20 20; fax 04 90 85 97 00; colbert.hotel@wanadoo.fr). An elegant staircase and colorful, well-decorated rooms with strong, sleep-inducing air-conditioning. Breakfast €5. Singles €45, doubles €58, triples €79. Closed Nov.-Feb. MC/V. ❹

Innova Hôtel, 100 rue Joseph Vernet (☎04 90 82 54 10; fax 04 90 82 52 39; hotel.innova@wanadoo.fr). Clean, spare, adequate rooms, some recently renovated; within footsteps of everything. Breakfast €5. Bike storage available. Singles €27; doubles with shower €30-50, quads €60. MC/V. ❸

Camping: Pont d'Avignon, 300 Ile de la Barthelasse, 10min. past Foyer Bagatelle (☎04 90 80 63 50; fax 04 90 85 22 12). Hot showers, laundry, restaurant, supermarket, pool, and tennis and volleyball courts in a four-star site that will knock your socks off. Reception July-Aug. 8am-10pm; June and Sept. 8:30am-8pm; Mar.-May and Oct. 8:30am-6:30pm. Open Mar.-Oct. July 1 person and tent €13.45; 2 people and tent €19.65; extra person €3.95. Electricity €2.35. Aug. same prices €12, €17, €2.35, and €3.50, respectively; prices significantly lower in mid- and low season. MC/V. ❷

◪ FOOD

There's a smattering of lively restaurants in crooked **rue des Teinturiers.** The cafés of **pl. de l'Horloge** are good for a drink after dinner, when mimes and street musicians milk the crowds for smiles and centimes. The Vietnamese restaurants scattered throughout the city on small impasses or in alleys off major thoroughfares are often great budget options. For those with midnight-snacking tendencies and few dietary scruples, **snack bars** line the boulevards and places of Avignon, serving up all manner of hot, greasy sandwiches as well as the occasional vegetarian option. **Parc de Rocher des Doms,** overlooking the Rhône, provides good picnic spots and has an outdoor café near the pond. **Les Halles,** the large indoor **market** on pl. Pie promises endless amounts of regional produce. (Tu-Su 7am-1pm.) The same fare may be less expensive at the **open-air markets** outside the city walls near porte St-Michel (Sa-Su 7am-1pm) and on pl. Crillon. (F 7am-1pm.) Go down to the basement for **Shopi** supermarket, rue de la République, about 100m from the tourist office. (Open M-Sa 8:30am-8pm.) Or try the reliable **Petit Casino** on rue St-Agricol (open M-Sa 8am-8pm and Su 9am-8pm) and at 3 rue Corps Saints. (Open July-Aug. M-Sa 8am-12:45pm and 4-7:45pm; Sept.-June M-Sa 8am-12:30pm and 3-7:30pm.) Most restaurants stay open an hour or two later during the festivals.

■ **Terre de Saveur,** 1 rue St-Michel (☎04 90 86 68 72), just off pl. des Corps Saints. Homey provençal restaurant serves hearty dishes with organic vegetables and rye bread on the side. Vegetarian *menu* €13; omnivore version €15. *Plats* €9-11.45. Open M-Sa 11:30am-2:30pm, F-Sa and nightly during festival 7-9:30pm. MC/V. ❸

Le Grand Café, 4 rue des Escaliers Ste Anne (☎04 90 86 86 77), behind the Palais. Excellent, pricey dishes served in a mirror-filled grand old room in partial disrepair. Mouthwatering *tajine d'agneau aux abricots* €15; most *plats* €15-18. Open Tu-Sa noon-2pm and 7-10pm; café open 11am-midnight. AmEx/MC/V. ❹

L'Orangaerie, 3 pl. Jérusalem (☎04 90 86 86 87), near pl. Carnot. In an expensive city, this restaurant is an exceptional find, offering fresh *provençal* specialities like *tagliatelles* and daily market selections. *Menus* €14 and €18. Open M-Sa noon-3pm and 7-11pm. Oct.-Feb. closed M, Tu, and W nights. MC/V. ❸

Le Pili, 34 pl. des Corps Saints (☎04 90 27 39 53). An intimate outdoor terrace is the perfect setting for sumptuous Mediterranean fare, and pizzas at unbeatable prices. €8 lunch *menu* includes wine. Dinner *menus* €13 and €20. Open M-Sa 11:30am-2pm and 7-11pm. Closed M dinner hours and Sa lunch hours. AmEx/MC/V. ❸

Gambrinus, 62 rue de la Carreterie (☎04 90 86 12 32), near porte St-Lazare. A speedy bar-restaurant specializing in huge portions of mussels, from traditional *moules marinières* with fries (€7.30) to *moules à la bière* (€8.70). Beer, you say? The bar has 6 on tap and 60 in bottles (drafts €2.20-3.10). Billiards €1.50. Open M-Sa 8am-1:30am. Closed Aug. 1-15 and Jan. 1-15. MC/V. ❷

👁 SIGHTS

*Avignon's sights, at least all those listed here, operate on a **Pass** system. At the first monument or museum you visit, you'll pay full admission (regardless of age or status); at sights visited for 15 days thereafter, you pay the reduced price.*

◪ PALAIS DES PAPES. This golden Gothic palace, the largest in Europe, launches gargoyles out over the city and the Rhône. Its sheer, battlemented walls are oddly pock-marked by the tall, ecclesiastical windows of the Grande Chapelle and the dark cross of arrow-loops. Begun in 1335 by the third pope of Avignon, Benoît XII, and finished less than twenty years later by his successor Clément VI, the papal palace is neatly divided into two sections with the contrasting styles of their builders: the strict, spare grandeur of the Cistercian Benoît and the astonishing scale and ostentation of the aristocratic Clément. Although Revolutionary looting stripped the interior of its lavish furnishings, the giant rooms and their frescoed walls are still spectacular—the dark, grand chapel makes the perfect setting for a climatic movie scene. But what dazzles the viewer most is the way the Palais unrolls almost endlessly, chamber after chamber. Try to comprehend the magnitude of the palace with the amazingly thorough and detailed audio-guide in eight languages, included in the tour. From May to September, the most beautiful rooms in the Palais are given over to diverse exhibitions, which have recently included Picasso and a first-ever look at the palace's own history. Call for details on the 2003 exhibition. *(☎04 90 27 50 74. Open July-Sept. daily 9am-8pm; Oct.-June 9am-7pm. Last ticket 1hr. before closing. Palace and exhibition €9.50, pass €7.50.)*

PONT ST-BÉNÉZET. This 12th-century bridge is known to all French children as the "Pont d'Avignon," immortalized in a famous nursery rhyme. In 1177, Bénézet, a shepherd boy, was commanded by angels to build a bridge across the Rhône. He announced his intentions to the population of Avignon, but the people, thinking he was "a man inhabited by fairies," laughed at him. The Archbishop, derisively pointing to a gigantic boulder in front of the cathedral, told Bénézet that he would have to place the first stone himself. Miraculously, the shepherd heaved up the rock and tossed it into the river. This holy shotput convinced the townspeople, allowing Bénézet to turn to equally miraculous fundraising efforts, which finished the bridge in 1185. Despite the divinely chosen location, the bridge has suffered a number of destructive incidents at the hands of warfare and the (until recently) turbulent Rhône. Today it stops partway across the river, as if Bénézet decided that four arches were enough to make his point. Perched precariously on the second arch is the **St-Nicolas Chapel,** dedicated to the patron saint of mariners. It costs €3.50 (with pass €3) to walk on the bridge, though watching from the riverbank is good enough. *(☎04 90 85 60 16. Includes a detailed audio-guide in 7 languages. Open daily Apr.-Nov. 9am-7pm, July-Sept. until 8pm; Nov.-Mar. 9:30am-5:45pm.)* Farther down the river, **Pont Daladier** makes it all the way across the river to the campgrounds, offering free views of the broken bridge and the Palais along the way.

COLLECTION LAMBERT. This new museum does a good job of engaging visitors with oft-confusing and oft-misunderstood contemporary art. Art critics will appreciate the emphasis on postmodernism's self-referential nature. Don't miss the short film of the verbal battle between a bare-chested woman and her father, to the tune of "Rocky." *(5 rue Violette. ☎04 90 16 56 20. Open July-Aug. Tu-Su 11am-7pm, Nov.-Feb. closes at 6pm. €5.50, pass €4.)*

MUSÉE DU PETIT PALAIS. The big "little" cardinal's palace on the pl. du Palais des Papes is crowded with local art, much of it religious, within view of the shores of Villeneuve. *(☎04 90 86 44 58. Open June-Sept. W-M 10am-1pm and 2-6pm; Oct.-May 9:30am-1pm and 2-5:30pm. €6, pass €3.)*

MUSÉE CALVET. This elegant 18th-century **hôtel particulier** exhibits a number of paintings and pieces by French artists, including Camille Claudel. It also boasts a hall's worth of alluring marble sculptures. *(65 rue Joseph Vernet. ☎04 90 86 33 84. Open W-M 10am-1pm and 2-6pm. €4.60, pass €2.30.)*

MUSÉE ANGLADON. Another recent addition to Avignon's museums, Angladon boasts works by Van Gogh, Picasso, Manet, Degas, and Modigliani, but is hardly tantalizing. *(5 rue Laboureur, just off Jean Jaures. ☎04 90 82 29 03. Open July-Aug. Tu-Su 1-6pm; low-season closed Tu. €5, pass €3.)*

OTHER SIGHTS. For those with a penchant for finer things, a 19th-century *hôtel* houses the small but intriguing decorative arts collection of the **Musée Louis Vouland.** *(17 rue Victor Hugo. ☎04 90 86 03 79. Visits available in English with reservation. Open May-Oct. Tu-Sa 10am-noon and 2-6pm, Su 2-6pm; Nov.-Apr. Tu-F 10am-noon and 2-6pm, Sa-Su 2-6pm. €4, pass €2.50.)* The **Musée Requien** may be interesting for budding paleontologists. Impressive fossils and the full skeleton of a 35 million-year-old horse make it potentially enjoyable. *(67 rue Joseph-Vernet. ☎04 90 14 68 56. Open Tu-Sa 9am-noon and 2-6pm. Free.)* Next to the Palais sits the 12th-century **Cathédrale Notre-Dame-des-Doms,** which contains the flamboyant and dramatically lit Gothic tomb of Pope John XXII. *(Open daily 10am-7pm.)* On the hill above the cathedral, the beautifully sculpted **Rocher des Doms Park** has vistas of Mont Ventoux, St-Bénézet, and the fortifications of Villeneuve. The **Maison Jean Vilar,** dedicated to the founder of the festival, celebrates the performing arts with recordings, workshops, lectures, exhibits, and free movies. *(8 rue de Mons. ☎04 90 86 59 64. Open Tu-F 9am-noon and 1:30-5:30pm, Sa 10am-5pm. Some exhibits €5, students and those with pass €3.)*

🎭 📷 ENTERTAINMENT AND FESTIVALS

Regular performances of opera, drama, and classical music take place in the **Opéra d'Avignon,** pl. de l'Horloge (☎04 90 82 81 40). **Rue des Teinturiers** is lined with theaters holding performances from the early afternoon through the wee hours of the morning. These include the **Théâtre du Chien qui Fume** at no. 75 (☎04 90 85 25 87), the **Théâtre du Balcon,** 38 rue Guillaume Puy (☎04 90 85 00 80), and the **Théâtre du Chêne Noir,** 8bis rue Ste-Catherine (☎04 90 82 40 57). The **Utopia Cinéma,** behind the Palais des Papes on 4 rue Escalier Ste-Anne, screens a wide variety of movies in *version original.* (☎04 90 82 65 36. €5, 10 showings €40.) The **Maison Jean Vilar** (see **Other Sights,** above) shows free videos.

Avignon has surprisingly little nightlife for a city of its size—until the festivals, when all bars listed here stay open until 3am. Brasseries on **cours Jean Jaurès** and **rue de la République** stay open late to entertain quiet crowds on their terraces. A few lively bars color **pl. des Corps Saints.** Cheap suds and a powerful sound system draw boisterous Australians and backpackers to the **Koala Bar,** 2 pl. des Corps Saints. (☎04 90 86 80 87. Beer from €2.50, drinks from €2. Happy hour daily 9-10pm. Open 8:30pm-1:30am, until 1am Nov.-Feb.) Avignon university students and

COOL BOULES The game of *boules*–that odd conjunction of steel balls, dirt courts and postgame drinking favored by aging men–is popular across France, particularly in cities in the south like Avignon. The popular *boule lyonnaise* has strict standards for the length of its courts–27.5 meters in total, with each section of the court having a specified length as well. Games can be played in singles or up to 4 on one team; in each round the player or team with balls inside *le rond* (a circle around the *cochonnet*, the little ball at the opposite end of the court which is the players's target) wins points, and the first to 11 wins the game. Though a game could continue forever, regulations mandate that games must end after 1½ to 2½ hours, depending on the number of players. While *boules* might seem like a relaxing way to spend an afternoon, the boules mini-universe is more intense than it first appears. World championships are held every two years, and great teams are remembered for years in Sport-Boules Magazine. In an Avignon court, a man raises his arms over his head in frustration when an opponent's ball knocks his out of the way: boules is a game to be taken seriously.

world travelers pack **The Red Lion,** 21-23 rue St-Jean Le Vieux, on pl. Pie. Live music three nights a week, Thursday theme nights twice a month, and beer from €2.50. (☎04 90 86 40 25. Happy hour daily 5-8pm. Open M-F 8am-1:30am and Sa-Su from 10am.) **Le Cid,** 11 pl. de l'Horloge, is a happening gay and lesbian bar with cool green lighting and red plush seating. (☎04 90 82 30 38. Open daily 7am-1:30am. Beers from €2.50.) **The Cubanito Café,** 52 rue Carnot, features nightly dancing to Cuban music, including salsa, in a boisterous, kick-back atmosphere. (☎04 90 27 90 59. Open daily 8am-1am. Beers from €2.20.) **Red Zone,** 25 rue Carnot, fulfills its role as a student club with later hours and music ranging from salsa to house to R&B. (☎04 90 27 02 44. Open daily 9am-3am; closed Su Nov.-Feb.)

July brings poster wars and more theater than imaginable—the definite highlight of Avignon's calendar. During the riotous **Festival d'Avignon,** which lasts most of July, Gregorian chanters rub shoulders with all-night *Odyssey* readers and African dancers. The official festival, also known as the **IN,** is the most prestigious theatrical gathering in Europe, appearing in at least 30 different venues, from factories to cloisters to palaces. (Info and tickets ☎04 90 14 14 14. Festival office ☎04 90 14 14 60; fax 04 90 27 66 83. Tickets €0-33. Reservations accepted after mid-June. Rush tickets at venue 45min. before the show; students and those under 25 get a 50% discount.) The cheaper and more experimental (although equally established) **Festival OFF** presents over 700 pieces, some in English, over the course of three weeks in July. (OFFice on pl. du Palais. ☎01 48 05 01 19; www.avignon-off.org. Tickets purchased at the venue or the OFFice; not available over the phone. Tickets €0-16.) You don't always need to buy a ticket to get in on the act—fun, free theater overflows into the streets during the day and particularly at night. The Centre Franco-Américain de Provence sponsors the **Euro-American Film Workshop** in late June at the Cinéma Vox. The festival showcases feature-length and short films directed by young French and American aspirants, with an occasional attention-grabbing name. Meals, parties, and lectures give an opportunity for hobnobbing and name dropping. Films are in *v.o.* with French or English subtitles. (☎04 90 25 93 23. Films €6, morning films €1.50, day pass €55.)

■ DAYTRIP FROM AVIGNON: VILLENEUVE-LÈS-AVIGNON

The **Bateau Bus** boat, allées de l'Oulle, near the Pont Daladier, cruises past Pont St-Bénézet and docks at Villeneuve. From there, a Petit Train (€1) will take you to the town center. (☎04 90 85 62 25. July-Aug. 6 per day 10:30am-7:20pm. Round-trip €7, children €4.50; 20% off with pass. Tickets on board or at tourist office in Avignon.)

Villeneuve-lès-Avignon ("new town by Avignon") sits on a hill overlooking Avignon. Founded in the 13th-century by the French to intimidate their provençal neighbors, it became the home of many of the dignitaries and attendants to the papal court, earning it the nickname "City of Cardinals." If you need some respite from the street performers during the festival in Avignon, take a short walk across the river to the much calmer Villeneuve and have a picnic here before the wide views of the hill of Fort St-André.

La Chartreuse du Val de Bénédiction, rue de la République, is one of the largest Carthusian monasteries in France. The six centuries or so since its construction have only improved it; the back wall of the church has collapsed, making its main highlight the glorious and unobstructed view of Fort St-André. The best visit here is an independent, ambling one; the church holds many delights, including a delightful rose-filled garden, cool little alleyways, and original staircases. (☎ 04 90 15 24 24. Open Apr.-Sept. daily 9am-6:30pm, Oct.-Mar. 9:30am-5:30pm. €5.50, students and pass €3.50.) Crowning Mont Andaon is the Gothic **Fort Saint-André.** Built by King Philip the Fair in the 14th century, its 750m fortified walls and double towers commanded the French side of the Rhône and protected an abbey and a little town. The towers served as prisons after losing their strategic value; the stone floors and walls still bear the marks of the prisoners's desperate carvings, including a dinner plate surrounded by cutlery, Christ, and a ship. (☎ 04 90 25 45 35. Open Apr.-Sept. daily 10am-1pm and 2-6pm, Oct.-Mar. 10am-noon and 2-5pm. €4, students and pass €2.50.) Housed within the confines of the fort is the 11th-century Benedictine **Abbaye St-André,** the first major construction on Mont Andaon. Its original buildings were mostly destroyed during the Revolution, but have been replaced with one of the most beautiful gardens in France, complete with purple lilies, gravel walks, branching olive trees, and the occasional live goat. Between the hidden fountains and arcades of cypresses are views of the Rhône valley and Avignon. (☎ 04 90 25 55 95. Open Apr.-Sept. Tu-Su 10am-12:30pm and 2-6pm; Oct-Mar. Tu-Su 10am-noon and 2-5pm. €4, pass €3.)

The most prominent monument in Velleneuve is the Gothic **Tour Philippe Le Bel,** at the intersection of av. Gabriel Péri and Montée de la Tour. It once guarded the French end of the Pont St-Bénézet. A climb of 125 steps takes you to a wind-whipped stone platform with a dizzying view. (☎ 04 32 70 08 57. Tower open Apr.-Sept. daily 10am-12:30pm and 3-7pm; Oct.-Mar. 10am-noon and 2-5:30pm. €1.60, students and pass €0.90.) Back up the hill a bit is the **Musée Municipal Pierre de Luxembourg,** on rue de la République, which displays a small collection of anonymous 15th-century religious works and 17th- and 18th-century provençal paintings; its claim to fame is the manic, epic *Coronation of the Virgin* by Enguerran Quarton, which takes up a whole room itself. (☎ 04 90 27 49 66. Open Apr. 15-Sept. 30 daily 10am-12:30pm and 3-7pm; Oct.-Apr. 14 Tu-Su 10am-noon and 2-5:30pm. €3, pass €1.90.) For a quick lunch, try **Café de l'Univers ❷,** on the central pl. Jean Jaurès. Their excellent *tartines*—the precursor to the pizza—run €7-9. (☎ 04 90 25 12 14. Open daily 6am-12:30am. V.) The **tourist office** is at 1 pl. Charles David. (☎ 04 90 25 61 33; fax 04 90 25 91 55. Open July M-F 10am-7pm, Sa-Su 10am-1pm and 2:30-7pm; Aug. daily 9am-12:30pm and 2-6pm, Sept.-June M-Sa 9am-12:30pm and 2-6pm.)

THE LUBÉRON AND THE VAUCLUSE

"No nature is more beautiful."
—Petrarch

Just when you thought that nothing could possibly be more picturesque than Arles or Avignon, you find a region of such stunning beauty that it leaves you gasping for breath. The Vaucluse, and the neighboring Parc Naturel Régional du Lubéron, fulfills every romanticized vision of a sunny idyllic afternoon in the French country-side. Tiny medieval villages perched on rocky escarpments, fields of lavender extending to the horizon, and ochre hills that seem to burn in the sunset are the backdrop for village squares filled with elderly men drinking *pastis* and playing *pétanque*. For centuries, this mini-Eden has been a home and inspiration to writers, from Petrarch to the Marquis de Sade to Samuel Beckett. Although we list a few famous beauties here, you will find this region at its untainted best on your own. Your guidebook should only be a starting point.

⬛ TRANSPORTATION. A good chunk of the Lubéron could easily be covered in two days by **car,** by far the easiest option. Pick one up in Avignon, which is filled with rental companies. N100 blows right through the middle of the Lubéron park and branches off to the smaller towns, but the twisting, narrow roads from one town to the next are often more picturesque. Expect to pay €2-3 for parking in most villages. However, combining occasional bus trips with walks or bike rides between towns (usually 7-15km) will let you experience Provence at its pristine finest, albeit in more time. Locals sometimes choose to hitch, but rides for tourists are difficult to come by and *Let's Go* does not recommend hitchhiking at any rate. Avignon buses leave from the central bus terminal. **Voyages Arnaud** (☎ 04 90 38 15 58) runs buses from **Avignon** to **Isle-sur-la-Sorgue** (40min., 8 per day, €3.10); **Fontaine de Vaucluse** (55min., 4 per day, €3.90); and **Bonnieux** (70min., 1 per day, €3). **Les Express de la Durance** (☎ 04 90 71 03 00) buses head to **Cavaillon** (40min., 12 per day, €3.10). **Autocars Barlatier** (☎ 04 90 73 23 59) goes to the train station at **Bonnieux** (1hr., 5 per day, €5.30), sometimes via Oppède-le-Vieux (1 per day, €5). The woman at the Avignon bus station will answer your questions helpfully and accurately. The regional **tourist office** is in **Bonnieux** (see p. 507). However you travel, good walking **shoes** are a must in the hilly and often unpaved roads.

L'ISLE-SUR-LA-SORGUE

L'Isle-sur-la-Sorgue (pop. 18,000) is the first step from Avignon and into the true Vaucluse countryside. Entangled in the green ribbon of its river, this quiet town surrenders itself to the rush of water. The clear, shallow waters of the Sorgue are split into numerous channels to the east of the city, surrounding and running beneath the town center, aptly nicknamed "Venice." These waters are the lifeblood of the city; their harvest of crayfish and trout once fed a hundred families. The mossy spokes of waterwheels turn everywhere you look, occasionally disrupting the path of the traditional three-plank low fishing boats (called *Nego-Chin* or "Drowning Dog"). For travelers, the river is an excellent spot for a picnic lunch, especially in the Jardin Public, but not much else.

The town's main attraction is its **open-air market**. (Th and Su 8am-1pm.) On the first Sunday of August, the **water market** crowds the Sorgue with boats and *Nego-Chins* full of hawkers's wares. In July, the city and its neighbors host the **Festival de la Sorgue,** celebrating the river with water jousting and concerts.

The easiest way to L'Isle-sur-la-Sorgue is by **train** from Avignon (about 20min.; 14-15 per day; €3.60). Cheap accommodations are hard to find in town, but **La Gueulardière ❹,** 1 rte. d'Apt. near the rotary, offers five quiet, well-kept rooms in a dignified old hotel where tree leaves flutter in the breeze and old paintings decorate the walls. (☎ 04 90 38 10 52; fax 04 90 20 83 70. Breakfast €4. Reception 8am-9pm. Rooms €53. AmEx/MC/V.) Camping at **La Sorguette ❶,** on rte. d'Apt (RN100), along the river 2km north of the town center, is a great base for exploring the Vaucluse. (☎ 04 90 38 05 71; fax 04 90 20 84 61; www.camping-sorguette.com. July-Aug. kayaks €8 per hr., €16 per half-day. Reception 8:15am-7:30pm. Open Mar. 15-Oct. 15. July-Aug. 24 two people with car €15; Mar.-July 6 and Aug. 24-Oct. €13.50. Extra person and child under 7 €4.50-5.15. Electricity €3-3.50.) **Isle 2 Roues (Cycles Peugeot),** on av. de la Gare right outside the train station, rents **bikes.** (☎04 90 38 19 12. Open Tu-Sa 8am-noon and 2-7pm. €13 per day. Passport deposit.) Or try **Provence Vélos Location,** a family-run, friendly, English-speaking rental place. (☎/fax 04 90 60 28 07. Check www.guideweb.com/provence-velos for their four locations in Provence, including Isle-sur-la-Sorgue. €13.50 per day. All offices open daily 7am-7pm.) The **post office,** across from the Jardin Public, has no commission on **currency exchange.** (☎04 90 21 28 22. Open M-F 8:30am-noon and 1:30-5:30pm, Sa 8:30am-noon. Postal code: 84803.) For a **laundromat** (rare in these parts!), go to L'Impasse de la République. (Open daily 8am-8pm.) For a **taxi,** call ☎06 08 09 19 49. For the **police,** quai Jean Jaurés, call ☎04 90 20 81 20. The **tourist office,** in the church on pl. de l'Eglise, supplies info on festivals, markets, and hiking. (☎04 90 38 04 78; fax 04 90 38 35 43. Open July-Aug. M-Sa 9am-1pm and 2:30-6:30pm, Su 9am-1pm; Sept.-June M-Sa 9am-12:30pm and 2-6pm, Su 9am-12:30pm.)

FONTAINE DE VAUCLUSE

Both hope and chilly water spring eternal in spectacular Fontaine de Vaucluse (pop. 500). The Sorgue rushes full-speed here from **Le Gouffre,** one of the largest river sources in the world. At its spring peak, Le Gouffre pours 90 cubic meters of water per second into the Sorgue. This pool at the base of an immense stone cliff defies understanding; its depth is immeasurable and its wetness incomprehensible, even to Jacques Cousteau, who probed the Gouffre but never hit bottom. Equally fruitless were the quests of Petrarch, who pined on the banks of the lake after "Laura," the lovely wife of a Marquis de Sade. After spotting Laura in an Avignon church on April 6, 1327, Petrarch spent two decades composing sonnets in Fontaine, a melancholy time recounted in *De Vita Solitaria.* In July and August, tourists swarm into Fontaine only a little less ferociously than its river does.

The 10m **Colonne** in the center of town commemorates Petrarch's life and labor, as does the small, unexceptional **Musée Petrarque** across the bridge. (☎04 90 20 37 20. Open June-Sept. W-M 9am-noon and 1:30-6pm; Apr. 3-May 31 and Oct. 1-15 daily 10am-noon and 2-6pm; Mar. 1-Apr. 2 and Oct. 16-31 Sa-Su 10am-noon and 2-6pm; Nov.-Mar. closed except to groups. €4.60, students €2.80.) The town side of the river is scattered with several small museums, including the **Musée d'histoire 1939-1945,** which painstakingly reconstructs daily life under the *anneés noires* (*"dark years"*) of Vichy and the Occupation, with an obvious Gaullist-mythic perspective. (☎04 90 20 24 00. Open June-Sept. W-M 10am-6pm; Apr. 10-May W-M 10am-noon and 2-6pm; Oct. 1-15 W-M 10am-noon and 2-5pm; Oct. 16-Dec. Sa-Su 10am-noon and 2-5pm; Mar.-Apr. 14 Sa-Su 10am-noon and 2-6pm. €3.50, students €1.50, under 12 free.) There's also the surprisingly interesting **Le Monde Souterrain,** which offers spellbinding underground tours through slightly hackneyed reconstructed caverns. (☎04 90 20 34 13. Open June-Sept. daily 9:30am-7:30pm; Feb.-May and Oct.-Nov. 9:30am-noon and 2-6pm. Last tour 1hr. before closing. Tours €5, under age 18 €3.25.) If you need more info, stop at the **tourist office,** about 200m to the left of the Colonne. (☎04 90 20 32 22; fax 04 90 20 21 37. Open daily M-Sa 9am-1pm and 2-7pm.)

Surprisingly inexpensive lodgings can be found at the ▨**Hôtel Font de Lauro ❸,** 1½km from Fontaine de Vaucluse, right off the road to l'Isle-sur-la-Sorgue. Rooms have a quiet *provençal* feel and views of vineyards. A pool ties the bow on this bargain package. The sign is small, so be on the lookout. (☎/fax 04 90 20 31 49. Breakfast €5.70. Gate closes at midnight. July-Aug. reservations required. Doubles with shower €27, with bath €37.50; one triple with bath €50. MC/V.) The rural **Auberge de Jeunesse (HI) ❶,** chemin de la Vignasse, is 1km. from town. Follow signs from the Colonne or ask the bus driver to let you off near the *auberge*. Wake to a chorus of roosters in this idyllic, spacious stone country house. (☎04 90 20 31 65; fax 04 90 20 26 20. Breakfast €3.20. Kitchen access. Sheets €2.70. Laundry. Reception 8-10am and 5:30-11pm. Curfew 11pm. Open Feb.-Nov. 15. Bunks €8, camping €4.80. **Members only.**) The hostel also offers suggestions for **hiking** in the Lubéron, especially on the nearby national hiking trails GR6 and GR91.

La Cigalière ❷, av. Robert Garcin, is a friendly new *saladerie* and *crêperie* run by a young couple in a warm, colorful atmosphere; the full plate "La Lorraine" (€8.50) is particularly good. (☎04 90 20 21 79. Crepes €4.30-6.10, salads €2.75-6.10. Open July-Aug. daily 11am-midnight, low-season Th-Tu 11am-10pm.)

Kayak Vert, about 500m from Fontaine on the road to l'Isle-sur-la-Sorgue, rents kayaks for the 8km trip down to L'Isle-sur-la-Sorgue. A friendly mandatory guide escorts you down and a minibus takes you back up to Fontaine. The Sorgue is a Class 1 river, meaning it's safe and suitable for all skill levels. (☎04 90 20 35 44; fax 04 40 20 20 28; www.canoefrance.com. 2-person canoes €36; 1-person kayak €17; university students with ID €14. Open mid-Apr.-Oct., weather permitting. Reserve ahead.) There is a **post office** with a rare **ATM** up the street from the Colonne, away from the river. (Open M-F 9am-noon and 2-5pm, Sa 8:30-11:30am.) A **mini-market** is across the street. (Open July-Aug. Tu-Su and holidays 8:15am-8pm; low-season daily 7:15am-12:30pm and 3:30-7pm, except closed W afternoon.)

OPPÈDE-LE-VIEUX

The mysterious ghost town of Oppède-le-Vieux (pop. 0) clings to the mountainside below an exquisitely ruined château and above gardened terraces of lavender and olive groves. This medieval village was slowly abandoned in the 16th century for the *hameau* (hamlet) in the plain, becoming deserted by the early 20th century. The only hints of the once-bustling market town are sun-baked stone buildings, a couple of artists's studios, and a tiny square. This town is so deserted that tourists's cars are not allowed in, and must be parked below the hills near the modern town (€2). Following signs from the parking lot on foot, you will reach the square. (10min.) From there, wander up to the 11th century **Eglise Notre-Dame d'Alidon,** next to the **château.** Private property signs around the ruined castle are largely unenforced, but the warning signs should be heeded: overhanging arches and cliff-top towers have been known to drop loose stones on unaware trespassers. The risk may be worth it, since the sight of the valley at the top and along the way is breathtaking.

MÉNERBES

This is the town made (in)famous by Peter Mayle's *A Year in Provence*. Apparently, the popular author left because he kept finding fans swimming in his pool. He is believed to have moved to southern Lubéron, but his book has continued to make Menerbes a tourist haven, with a little help from the magnificent views of the valley and neighboring stone quarries from the church at the top of the village. Just outside town, about 1km in the direction of Cavaillon, on the road leading to Menerbes, is the **Domaine de la Citadelle,** a vineyard and home of the **Musée du Tire-Bouchon.** It has collected 1000 unique corkscrews and a few dirty ones; several corks shaped like men boast strategically-placed screws. The self-guided visit is appropriately topped off with a *dégustation.* (☎04 90 72 41 58. Open Apr.-Oct. daily 10am-noon and 2-7pm; Nov.-Mar. M-F 9am-noon and 2-6pm. €4, students €3.50, children under 15 free.) **Taxis** can be reached at ☎04 90 72 31 41 or 06 07 86 23 88. The town is even big enough to have a **post office.** Or maybe it's just there to handle fan Mayle. (Open M-F 9am-noon and 2:30-5pm, Sa 9-11am.) **Postal code:** 84560.

LACOSTE

You'd expect Lacoste (pop. 440) to be haunted by the demons of its past—the picturesquely ruined château perched above the village was home from 1774 to 1778 to the **Marquis de Sade,** who abducted local peasants to satisfy his sexual needs before being arrested and imprisoned. On the contrary, this sleepy town is nowadays as restrained as the notorious château, which is boarded up and closed. The raciest thing left in the village is a group of American art students who rush around trying to capture the beauty of the site.

Lacoste is home to one of the few affordable accommodations in the valley. The **Café de Sade ❶,** a giant, camp-style dormitory, has unbelievable views and welcoming hotel rooms. (☎04 90 75 82 29; fax 04 90 75 95 68. Breakfast €5.50. Sheets €4. Closed Jan.-Feb. Bunks €12.50, *demi-pension* €28; doubles €36-37, with bath €42-46.) A **market** is held on Tuesday mornings (7am-1pm) in the tiny square next to the **post office.** (Open June 15-Sept. 15 M-F 9am-noon and 2:30-4:30pm, Sa 9-11am; Sept. 16-June 14 M-F 9-11am and 2:30-4:30pm except closed W afternoon, Sa 9-11am). **Postal code:** 84480.

BONNIEUX

Flowers burst from the balconies and windows of the well-restored houses that clutter the hillside of Bonnieux (pop. 1420). This *village perché* is the capital of the Lubéron, blending its postcard-perfect lavender fields with the real world. The **market** on pl. du Terrail sells regional specialties, including crusty cheese and barbarous *saucisson* (F mornings). Atop the town, on a windswept cedared ledge, the Templar knights's 12th-century **Eglise Haute** offers a panorama that redeems the hard climb up. The **Musée de la Boulangerie,** 12 rue de la République, which traces the history of French bread-making in a 17th-century bakery, is a must-see for baguette-lovers, if no one else. (☎04 90 75 88 34. Open July-Aug. W-M 10am-1pm and 3-6:30pm; Apr.-June and Sept.-Oct. W-M 10am-12:30pm and 2:30-6pm. €3.50, students €1.50.) The **tourist office** is responsible for all the villages in the Lubéron, and has piles of pamphlets and other info, as well as a currency **exchange.** (☎04 90 75 91 90; fax 04 90 75 92 94. Open M 2-6pm, Tu-Sa 9:30am-12:30pm and 2-6pm.) Stock up on groceries at the **Relais des Mousquetaires,** off pl. Carnot (open M-Sa 8:30am-12:30pm and 3:45-7pm, Su 8:30am-12:30pm, closed W afternoon). Rent **bikes** at **Mountain Bike Luberon,** rue Marceau, which organizes free delivery within 15km of Bonnieux, including Lacoste. (☎04 90 75 89 96, mobile 06 83 25 48 07. €8 per half day, €14 per day, week €74. Open Mar.-Nov. 8:30am-noon and 1:30-6:30pm.) Call a **taxi** at ☎04 90 72 31 41 or 06 07 86 23 88. **Café Clérici-La Flambée ❸,** pl. du 4 Sept., will rejuvenate you with delightful, simple blue and yellow rooms with names like "Josephine" and "Emmanuelle." (☎04 90 75 82 20. Doubles €30-38, triples €46, studio €50-64. Reception 8am-9:30pm. AmEx/MC/V.) Next door, the same owners run a pleasing pizzeria and provençal **restaurant ❷** with a spectacular panoramic view. (Pizzas €7-9. Open daily noon-2pm and 7-9:30pm, closed Su afternoon.) You can also camp at **Le Vallon ❶,** 1km from town toward Ménerbes. (☎/fax 04 90 75 86 14. Open mid-Mar. to mid-Nov. €2.20 per person, €1.40 per car, €2.50 per tent. Electricity €2.50.)

ROUSSILLON

This is the most famous of the ochre villages, for good reason. The site itself can be seen from as far away as Gordes—a wild, red-orange incision in the lush, green countryside. The village (pop. 1200), built on and of the world's largest vein of natural ochre, is a wonderland of reds. Every doorway, windowsill, and wall is tinted with the warm and vibrant shades of the earth. Be sure to explore the *Sentier des Ochres*, where you can walk through a vast, dusty ochre deposit between stunning

PROVENCE

wind-sculpted cliffs. White shoes and clothing are a bad choice here. (Open July-Aug. daily 9am-7:30pm; Mar.-mid-Nov. M-Sa 9:30am-5:30pm, Su 9:30am-6pm. €2. Closed on rainy days for safety's sake.) To feed your appetite for a hike, stop at the **bakery,** av. de la Burlière. (Open F-W 7am-12:45pm and 3:30-7pm.) The **tourist office,** on pl. de la Poste, has hotel listings. (☎04 90 05 60 25; fax 04 90 05 63 31. Open June-Aug. daily 9am-noon and 1:30-6:30pm, Sept.-May M-Sa 10am-noon and 2-5:30pm.) There's currency **exchange** and a 24-hour **ATM** at the **post office** next door. (Open Apr.-mid-Nov. M-F 9am-noon and 2-5pm, Sa 9am-noon; mid-Dec.-Feb. closes at 4:30pm).

GORDES

Perhaps the most picturesque of the hillside towns, Gordes (pop. 2050) is known for its **bories,** drystone huts and dwellings built through the skillful placement of stone upon stone without the use of mortar. Often seen in the middle of fields or lost in the tangled undergrowth of the hills, they predate the Romans but continued to be built and used by the locals until quite recently. The **Village des Bories** outside town is a unique hamlet of *bories* inhabited until the mid-19th century. These giant mounds of local stone serve as complete and self-sustaining dwellings, with their own chimneys, wine cellars, bread ovens, and space for livestock. (☎04 90 72 03 48. Open daily 9am-around sunset. €5.50, ages 10-17 €3.) **Sénanque Abbey,** an active Cistercian community surrounded by exquisite fields of lavender, is 4km away from Gordes. The exceedingly touristy site was occupied by monks from AD 1148 until the Revolution, then repopulated and restored in the mid-19th century. Today it sells honey, lavender products, and *sénacole,* a liqueur produced by the local monks. (☎04 90 72 05 72. Abbey open Feb.-Oct. M-Sa 10am-noon and 2-6pm, Su 2-6pm; Nov.-Jan. M-F 2-5pm, Sa-Su 2-6pm. €5, under 18 €2.) The **château** in the middle of town, originally a fortress, houses the Hôtel de Ville and a collection of 200 vibrantly sensual paintings in the **Musée Pol Mara.** (Open daily 10am-noon and 2-6pm. €4, ages 10-17 €3.) An enormous **market** surrounds the château on Tuesday mornings, selling everything from pottery to paintings, sausage to socks.

Hordes of tourists inflate restaurant prices in Gordes, but the small, agreeable **Cannelle ❷,** rue Baptistin Picahas is shockingly immune. (☎04 90 72 07 86. Open July-Aug. daily 9am-8pm; Sept.-Dec. and Feb.-June daily 9am-8pm except closed. Salads from €5.50, pizzas from €7, sandwiches €4.) The **tourist office** is also in the château. (☎04 90 72 02 75. Open daily 9am-noon and 2-6pm.) There's even a 24-hour **ATM** in the *place* in front of it. The **post office** is in the center of town. (Open May-Sept. M-F 9am-noon and 4-7pm, Sa 9-11:30am; Oct.-Apr. M-F 9-11:30am and 2-5pm, Sa 9-11:30am).

ARLES

Each street in Arles (pop. 35,000) seems to run into or out of the great Roman arena, which binds together the distant past and bustling present. The city's historical wealth and relative intimacy have always made it a favorite among visitors to Provence. Van Gogh lost two years and an ear here, and Picasso loved Arles's bullfights enough to donate 70 of his drawings to the city. Today, Arles's international photography festival attracts both amateurs and professionals, and transforms each hall, museum, nook, and cranny into an exhibit. As a plus, the hills of the Alpilles and the Camargue marshlands are an easy daytrip away.

■ ■ 🖪 ORIENTATION AND PRACTICAL INFORMATION

Northwestern Arles touches the Rhône River. The train station is in the north, the tourist office in the south, and the heart of the old city lies in between.

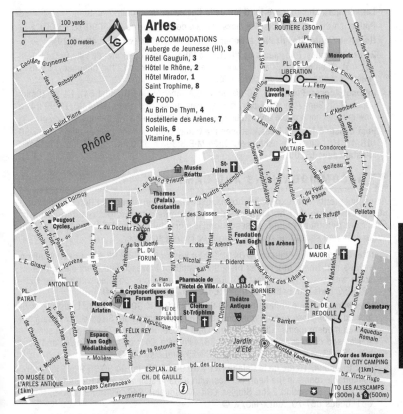

Arles

⌂ ACCOMMODATIONS
Auberge de Jeunesse (HI), **9**
Hôtel Gauguin, **3**
Hôtel le Rhône, **2**
Hôtel Mirador, **1**
Saint Trophime, **8**

🍎 FOOD
Au Brin De Thym, **4**
Hostellerie des Arènes, **7**
Soleilis, **6**
Vitamine, **5**

PROVENCE

Trains: av. P. Talabot. Ticket counters open M-Sa 5:50am-9:50pm, Su 5:50am-9:40pm. To: **Avignon** (30min., 17 per day, €5.50); **Marseille** (1hr., 23 per day, €11.20); **Montpellier** (1hr., 6 per day, €11.80); **Nîmes** (30min., 8 per day, €6.30).

Buses: av. P. Talabot (☎04 90 49 38 01), just outside the train station. Info desk open M-F 9am-4pm. **Les Cars de Camargue,** 24 rue Clemenceau (☎04 90 96 36 25). Info desk open M-Th 8:15am-noon and 2-5:30pm, F 8:15am-noon and 2-4:30pm. To **Nîmes** (1hr., M-Sa 4 per day, €5.20). **Cars Ceyte et Fils** and **CTM,** 21 chemin du Temple (☎04 90 93 74 90), go to **Avignon** (45min.; M-Sa 7 per day, Su 2 per day; €8.10).

Taxis: A.A.A. Arles Taxis (☎04 90 93 31 16); **Arles Taxis Radio** (☎04 90 96 90 03).

Bike Rental: Peugeot Cycles, 15 rue du Pont (☎04 90 96 03 77). €14 per day. Open Tu-Su 8am-noon and 2-7pm.

Tourist Office: Espl. Charles de Gaulle, bd. des Lices (☎04 90 18 41 20; fax 04 90 18 41 29). Turn left outside the station and walk to pl. Lamartine; after the Monoprix turn left down bd. Emile Courbes. Continue to the big intersection by the southeast old city tower, then turn right onto bd. des Lices. Accommodations service €1 plus down payment. Open Apr.-Sept. daily 9am-6:45pm; Oct.-Mar. M-Sa 9am-5:45pm, Su 10:30am-2:30pm. **Branch** in the train station (☎04 90 18 41 20. Open M-Sa 9am-1pm.)

Money: Arène Change, 22bis rond-point des Arènes (☎04 90 93 34 66). No commission on US dollars. Open W-M 9am-12:30pm and 2-6:30pm; Apr.-Sept. closes Su 1pm.

Laundromat: Lincoln Laverie, 6 rue de la Cavalerie. Open daily 7am-9pm.

Police: on the corner of bd. des Lices and av. des Alyscamps (☎04 90 18 45 00).

Hospital: Centre Hospitalier J. Imbert, quartier Fourchon (☎04 90 49 29 29).

24-hr. Pharmacy: Pharmacie de l'Hotel de Ville, 34 rue de l'Hotel de Ville (☎04 90 96 01 46). Open M-Sa 8:30am-7:30pm. Arles's **garde de ville** (24hr. pharmacy) changes each weekend; call the police for info.

Internet Access: Point Web, 10 rue du 4 Septembre (☎04 90 18 91 54). €1 for 10min. Open M-Sa 9am-7pm. **PC Futur,** Internet café on av. Stalingrad (☎04 90 18 99 24) a few minutes north of the train station. €4 per hr. Open Tu-Sa 10am-noon and 2-7pm.

Post Office: 5 bd. des Lices, between the tourist office and the police station (☎04 90 18 41 10). **Currency exchange.** Open M-F 8:30am-6:30pm, Sa 8:30am-12:30pm. **Postal code:** 13200.

▌ ACCOMMODATIONS AND CAMPING

Arles has plenty of inexpensive hotels, especially around **rue de l'Hôtel de Ville** and **pl. Voltaire.** Note that hotel prices do not include a municipal residency tax of €0.77 per person per night. Reservations are crucial during the photography festival in July and should be made a month or two in advance.

■ **Hôtel Gauguin,** 5 pl. Voltaire (☎04 90 96 14 35; fax 04 90 18 98 87). Cheerful saffron yellows and smells of lavender bring the warmth of Provence into every elegant room; some with balcony. Breakfast €5. Reception 7am-10pm. Doubles with shower €29-33.50; 2 beds with bath €36; triples €42. Extra bed €8. MC/V. ❸

Hôtel Mirador, 3 rue Voltaire (☎04 90 96 28 05; fax 04 90 96 59 89). Unusually well-located hotel, close to both transportation and the *centre-ville.* Sleep cozily in salmon-colored modern rooms, all with TV. Breakfast €4.30. Reception 7am-11pm. In summer singles and doubles with shower €30-38, with bath €41; off-season singles and doubles €30-33, with bath €36. Extra bed €9.15. AmEx/MC/V. ❹

Saint Trophime, 16 rue de la Calade (☎04 90 96 88 38; fax 04 90 96 92 19). Stately, comfortable rooms in the heart of Arles, with a grand staircase entrance and TV. Breakfast €5.65. Reception 24hr. Singles €34-37; doubles €47, with bath €50-5; triples €61; quads €67-70. AmEx/MC/V. ❹

Hôtel le Rhône, 11 pl. Voltaire (☎04 90 96 43 70; fax 04 90 93 87 03). Eager owners and an adorable breakfast room. Smaller than average, these pink rooms with modern bathrooms have the premium location. Breakfast €5. Singles and doubles €26, with shower €30-33; triples with shower €36, with toilet €40.50. AmEx/MC/V. ❸

Auberge de Jeunesse (HI), 20 av. Maréchal Foch (☎04 90 96 18 25; fax 04 90 96 31 26), 10min. from the town center and 20min. from the station. From the station, take the "Starlette" bus to "Clemenceau," and then take the #4 bus (dir: L'Aurelienne) to "Foch" (€0.80). There are no Starlette buses on Su, and the last bus from the station that connects at Clemenceau leaves Clemenceau at 6:34pm. To walk from the station, follow directions to the tourist office, but instead of turning on bd. des Lices, cross it and continue down av. des Alyscamps; follow the signs. Modern, with a quiet garden and ramshackle toilets. Fickle staff can be unhelpful at times. Near the municipal pool and cinema. Personal lockers. Breakfast and sheets included. Dinner €8 on nights when there are groups eating. Bar open until midnight. Reception 7-10am and 5-11pm. Lockout 10am-5pm. Curfew 11pm in winter, midnight in summer. Reservation (by letter or fax) recommended Apr.-June. Bunks €13.50; €11.50 after first night. MC/V. ❶

Camping: City, 67 rte. de Crau (☎04 90 93 08 86), is the closest site to town. 2-star site, with pool, snack bar, and laundry. Take bus #2 from station ("Starlette" bus to "Clemenceau"). Then take bus #2 (dir: Pont de Crau) to "Hermite" (€0.80). Reception 8am-8pm. Open Apr.-Sept. €6.20 per person, €2.80 per child under 7; €16.20 for person, child, and site, €2.80 more for car. ❶

🟦 FOOD

Bargains still exist here, though locals are rapidly discovering what foreigners will pay for their food. The cheapest bites are found in the many cafés and *brasseries* in the small squares. Local specialties are seasoned with thyme, rosemary, and garlic, all of which grow in the region. Other regional produce fills the **open-air markets** on bd. Emile Combes (W 7am-1pm) and bd. des Lices (Sa 7am-1pm). There are two **supermarkets** in town: **Monoprix** on pl. Lamartine, close to the train station and the city gates (open M-Th 8:30am-7:30pm, F-Sa 8:30am-8pm), and **Petit Casino,** 26 rue Président Wilson, off bd. des Lices toward the center of town. (Open M-Sa 7:30am-12:30pm and 3:30-7:30pm, Su 8:30am-12:30pm; July-Aug. also open M 8:30am-12:30pm.) The cafés on **pl. Voltaire** are strung with colored lights and animated by a jovial international crowd. On summer evenings the **pl. du Forum** bustles as much as it ever did in Roman days.

▧ **Soleilis,** 9 rue Docteur Fanton (☎04 90 93 30 76). After dinner, find room for the best ice cream in Arles, and possibly in Provence, made with freshly-picked fruits. A must, especially for the unusual flavors, such as pear. €1.80 for one scoop and homemade waffle cone, €1 for regular cone. Mountainous sundaes €5.20. Open July-Aug. daily 2-7pm and 8:30-10:30pm or later; Mar.-June and Sept.-Oct. 2-7pm. ❶

Vitamine, 16 rue du Docteur Fanton (☎04 90 93 77 36). Chic, and heaven-sent for vegetarians. Pasta and 38 salads (€4.60-7.65). Try the €5.50 *nougat glacé.* Reserve for terrace seats. Open M-Sa noon-3pm and 7-10:30pm or midnight. Closed Jan. MC/V. ❷

Au Brin de Thym, 22 rue Docteur Fanton (☎04 90 49 95 96). Outdoor terrace on a lively street, with delectable dishes, including the *ailes de raie au beurre blanc* (a light fish, €13), and goat cheese salad (€8). Open daily noon-2pm and 7-9:30pm. MC/V. ❸

Hostellerie des Arènes, 62 rue Refuge (☎04 90 96 13 05). While a little more pricey than the places next door, the mouth-watering homemade plates, including an excellent lasagna (€9), are worth it. €13.50 *menu.* Open W-M noon-2pm and 7-11pm. MC/V. ❸

🔘 SIGHTS

Every snack bar and café in Arles has a Roman ruin beneath it. Get an English copy of *Arles et Vincent* (€1 from the tourist office), which explains four sets of ground markers that crisscross the city in an attempt to organize its monuments. The city's **"Pass Monuments"** (€12, students and under 18 €10) will give you access to all the major sights, including Les Arènes, Cryptoportiques, Musée Réattu, Muséon Arlaten, Musée d'Arles Antique, Théâtre Antique, Les Alyscamps, and Cloître St-Trôphime. The times here listed indicate the last chance to purchase tickets; most sights close 30min. later. For info, call the **Régie des Monuments** at ☎04 90 49 36 74.

LES ARÈNES. It's always a surprise to emerge from the medieval network of streets here and meet the high, layered arches of a Roman amphitheater. Built in the first century AD, this structure—the largest of its kind surviving in France— was so cleverly designed that it could evacuate all 25,000 spectators in five minutes. In the 8th century, homes were built on and in the original structure, converting it into a fortified village, and two towers built during that era still remain. The highest (and inaccessible) tower bears witness to a thousand years of vandalism, including names scratched in by WWII American GIs. The smaller tower, however, offers a nice view of all of Arles—and a heavenly breeze on hot summer days. *Corridas* staged here from Easter through September are as bloody as anything the Romans watched. (*Arenas ☎04 90 49 36 86. Open May-Sept. daily 9am-6:30pm; Mar.-Apr. and Oct. 9am-5:30pm; Nov.-Feb. 10am-4:30pm. Without Monument Pass €4, children and students €3. Corridas and cocardes ☎04 90 96 03 70. Bullfights from €14, children €7.*)

CRYPTOPORTIQUES DU FORUM. A visit inside this former Jesuit chapel is an unforgettable experience. Dating from the first century BC, the gloomy underground galleries provided the foundations for the Roman forum. Hold your breath and walk into the darkness. *(Rue Balze. Open May-Sept. daily 9am-6:30pm; Mar.-Apr. 9-11:30am and 2-5:30pm; Oct. 9-11:30am; Nov.-Feb. 10-11:30am and 2-4:30pm. €3.50, students and under age 18 €2.60.)*

MUSÉE RÉATTU. Once a stronghold of the knights of St-John, this spacious museum now houses a collection of captivating contemporary art, watercolors, oils of the Camargue by Henri Rousseau, and two rooms of canvases by the Neoclassical artist Réattu. Its pride and joy are the 57 drawings with which Picasso honored Arles in 1971; most attempt to capture the many "faces" (literally) of the town. One of the great pleasures here is the building itself, with gargoyled rooftops, courtyards, and a view of the broad Rhône. *(Rue du Grand Prieuré. ☎ 04 90 49 37 58. Open May-Sept. daily 10am-noon and 2-6:30pm; Mar.-Apr. and Oct. 10am-12pm and 2-5pm; Nov.-Feb. 1-5pm. €4, students €3.)*

MUSÉON ARLATEN. Various provençal artifacts attempting to recreate a vision of 19th-century daily life are brought together in a superb folk museum founded by turn-of-the-century poet Frédéric Mistral, who dedicated his life to reviving local traditions. Staffers are even clothed in traditional garb. Items range from parasols, hairpieces and drawings to an oddly appealing, childlike recreation of a legendary regional dragon. *(29 rue de la République. ☎ 04 90 93 58 11. Open June-Aug. daily 9:30am-1pm and 2-6:30pm; Apr.-May and Sept. Tu-Su 9:30am-12:30pm and 2-6pm; Oct.-Mar. Tu-Su 9:30am-12:30pm and 2-5pm. €4, students €3.)*

MUSÉE D'ARLES ANTIQUE. This ultramodern blue building contains a well-assembled set of Roman tools, mosaics, sarcophagi, and other local artifacts. Ponder how much wine can fill one of the immense jugs. The museum also includes spectacular, almost complete, mosaics dating from the 2nd century, and large to-scale models of Roman architecture, including the ingenious pontoon bridge that was once the symbol of Arles. *(Av. de la 1ère D.F.L. ☎ 04 90 18 88 88. 10min. from the center of town. With your back to the tourist office, turn left, walk along bd. G. Clemenceau to its end, and follow the signs. Open Mar.-Oct. daily 9am-7pm; Nov.-Feb. 10am-5pm. €5.35, students €3.80. Tours in French by reservation.)*

FONDATION VAN GOGH. You'll find no Van Goghs here—only tributes to him by other artists. Though the museum houses some big names and frequent special exhibits, some of the most interesting work is by relative unknowns: Alain Clement's "Pour Vincent," for example, which shows a masked figure from a psychiatric ward "dynamiting himself to regain the lemon-yellow sun." *(26 rond-point des Arènes. ☎ 04 90 49 94 04. Open daily 10am-7pm. €5, students and children age 8 and up €3.50.)*

THÉÂTRE ANTIQUE. Squeezed between the amphitheater and the gardens, this partially ruined theater is a reminder of the refined side of Roman culture, save for the superimposed modern seating. Seemingly random capitols lie around the flower-filled backstage, and only two columns of the stage wall stand, but enough remains for modern productions to take advantage of the theater's magnificent acoustics. *(Rue de la Calade. For reservations call the Théâtre de la Calade at ☎ 04 90 93 05 23 or the tourist office. Open May-Sept. daily 9am-6:30pm; Mar.-Apr. 9-11:30am and 2-5:30pm; Oct. 9-11:30am; Nov.-Feb. 10-11:30am and 2-4:30pm. €3, students and children €2.20.)* Just behind the theater, the shady **Jardin d'Eté** is a great place to picnic, eavesdrop on concerts, or cuddle with your *cherie*. Wander through to notice the bizarrely morbid head of Van Gogh mounted on a large stone. *(Open May-Sept. daily 7am-8:30pm; Oct.-Apr. 7am-5:30pm.)*

LES ALYSCAMPS. This cemetery was one of the most famous burial grounds of the ancient world, even meriting a mention in Dante's *Inferno;* its name is a twist on Champs-Elysées, or "Elysian Fields." Consecrated by St-Trôphime, first bishop of Arles, it now holds 80 generations of locals. The most elaborate sarcophagi have been destroyed or removed, but the atmosphere here is intact; a sense of overpowering quiet and unbreakable peace hangs heavily in the poplared avenues and the 12th-century abbey at their end. Explore the deathly cool lower level of the abbey, where one cough brings an otherworldly echo. *(10min. from the center of town. From the tourist office, head east on bd. des Lices to its intersection with bd. Emile Courbes. Turn left onto av. des Alyscamps and cross the tracks. ☎04 90 49 36 87. Open May-Sept. daily 9am-6:30pm; Mar.-Apr. 9-11:30am and 2-5:30pm; Oct. 9-11:30am; Nov.-Feb. 10-11:30am and 2-4:30pm. €3.50, students and children under 18 €2.60.)*

CLOÎTRE ST-TRÔPHIME. The city's famous medieval cloister is an oasis of calm and shade. Each carved column in its arcades is topped by lions in brushwood, saints in stone leaves, and the occasional fluttering bird. Adjoining the cloister is the Eglise St-Trôphime, built between the 11th and 15th centuries. Its elaborate facade deserves a place in art-history books: in a chapel inside are the reliquaries and remnants of some 30 saints—you can observe the sturdy shinbones of St-Roch, and ogle the skulls of Saints Genes and Innocent. *(Pl. de la République. ☎04 90 49 33 53. Open May-Sept. daily 9am-6:30pm; Mar.-Apr. and Oct. 9am-5:30pm; Nov.-Feb. 10am-4:30pm. €3.50, students €2.60. Church free.)*

◘ FESTIVALS

The major cultural event of the year in Arles is the **Rencontres Internationales de la Photographie,** held in the first week of July. Undiscovered photographers from around the world court agents by roaming around town with portfolios under their arms. More established photographers present their work in 15 locations (including the Abbaye de Montmajour), conduct nightly slide shows (€6.50-8), participate in debates, and offer colloquia with artists, some free. When the festival crowd departs, the remarkable exhibits are left behind. (€3.25-5 per exhibit, all exhibits €18.50, under 25 free.) For more info, visit the tourist office or contact **Rencontres,** 10 Rondpoint des Arènes (☎04 90 96 76 06). During the festival, tickets can be bought in the Espace Van Gogh.

Of more interest to the casual tourist are Arles's many colorful *provençal* festivals. On May 1, the ancient Confrèrie des Gardians ("brotherhood of herders" of the Camargue's wild horses) parades through town and gathers in the arena for the **Fête des Gardians.** On the last weekend in June and the first in July, bonfires blaze in the streets and locals wear traditional costume for the beautiful **Fêtes d'Arles.** Halfway through the festival, bareback riders race through the bd. des Lices on white *camarguais* horses for the **course de Satin,** while every three years, at its end, the city crowns the *Reine d'Arles* (Queen of Arles), a young woman chosen to represent the region's language, customs, and history. Traditional ceremonies, dance performances, and fireworks occur in the arena at midnight (free). The next day brings the **Cocarde d'Or,** when the new queen crowns the winning *rasateur;* bulls are then run through the streets between the horses of the shepherds. **Bullfights** are more common, occurring at Easter and in early September. (Tickets €12-83. For more info, call the Bureau des Arènes at ☎04 90 96 03 70; fax 04 90 96 64 31; www.label-camargue.com.)

▨ DAYTRIP FROM ARLES: ABBAYE DE MONTMAJOUR

M-Sa, 8 buses per day run from Arles, 2 run on Su (€2). Abbey (☎/fax 04 90 54 64 17) open Apr.-Sept. daily 9am-7pm, Oct.-Mar. 10am-1pm and 2-5pm. €5.50, ages 18-25 €3.50, children free.

Grim, stony Montmajour Abbey dominates the fields just 7km from Arles. Though the monastery never had more than 60 monks, it was old (founded AD 948) and rich enough to possess a huge architectural complex, including a 26m fortified tower (with forboding gaps in the rooftop terrace near the edge) and the 10th- and 11th-century **Chapelle St-Pierre.** The empty nave of the abbey church is stunningly large. The stonework conserves a human touch in its details: the light, arched ceilings in the crypt's rotunda and five radiating chapels are laced with distinctive worker's marks that ensured the builders's pay. Medieval sailors's graffiti, discovered in the cloister in 1993, is evidence that the abbey has also served as a popular gathering place from time to time over the centuries. The abbey's appeal is augmented by its rotating, extensive photo exhibits.

THE ALPILLES

Provence is at its best in small towns. The quiet, castle-strewn, sleepy hills of the Alpilles, north of Arles and south of Avignon, shelter some of the area's finest.

LES BAUX-DE-PROVENCE

"There is nothing terrible and savage belonging to feudal history of which an example may not be found in the annals of Les Baux." ·
—John Addington Symonds

Les Baux-de-Provence is known for its medieval ruins, demolished castle, and gracefully restored Renaissance homes. The village sits 245m up on a defensively strategic rocky spur of the Alpilles. The Baux lords plundered medieval Provence from this eagle's nest of a town, managing at one point to hold 72 towns in the region. Even Dante came to their court—it's thought that he found inspiration for his *Inferno* in the twisted, tortured Val de l'Enfer ("Valley of Hell") below the castle. The Baux line died out in the 14th century, and Louis XIII humiliated the town by destroying its castle and ramparts in 1632. You can still see the spectacular ruined château and poke around a few of the town's medieval streets. The only downside to a visit here is the phenomenal number of tourists; over a million come to Les Baux annually, and the tiny town center that Louis XIII demolished has been rebuilt with souvenir shops and cafés.

The ruined halls and towers of the mountaintop **Château des Baux** cover an area five times that of the village below. Private apartments, once the seats of courtly love, are cracked open to the wind, their windows gaping over empty air. Slim limestone stairs climb into the blue sky, while a giant *trébuchet*, the biggest medieval siege warfare engine, stands out on the plateau. Those who arrive early will enjoy the eerie treat of having the mountaintop, valley, and distant Mediterranean all to themselves. Hold on to children and lighter possessions, as gusts of wind are strong on the unprotected cliff. Housed in a cool Romanesque chapel inside the château's gates, the tiny **Chapelle St-Blaise** has a delightful slideshow of van Gogh and Cézanne's paintings of olive trees. (☎04 90 54 55 56. Open July-Aug. daily 9am-8:30pm; Dec.-Feb. 9am-5pm; Sept.-Nov. and Mar.-May 9am-6:30pm. Thorough audio guide in 7 languages. €6.50, students €5, under 18 €3.50.) Les Baux is known for its limestone quarries, one of which has been converted into the fantastic, awe-inspiring **Cathédrale d'Images.** From the bus stop, continue down the hill, turn right at the crossroads, and follow the sign. (7min.) Dozens of projectors splash 3000 images from above into gigantic man-made subterranean galleries to the accompaniment of mysterious and booming music. 2003 will bring a show with scenes of the Renaissance Flemish painters Hieronymous Bosch and Pieter Bruegel. (☎04 90 54 38 65. Open daily 10am-7pm, last show at 6:15pm. €7, ages 8-18 €4.10.) Walk down the hill to the **Fondation Louis Jou,** rue Frédéric Mistral, which commemorates Les

Baux's favorite son with major works by the printmaker himself as well as engravings by Dürer and Goya. If it seems shut down, continue 50m and inquire at the small shop; it may not really be closed. (☎04 90 54 34 17. Open Apr.-Oct. F-M 2-5pm and Tu-Th by reservation; Nov.-Mar. by reservation. €3, students €1.50.)

▓Mas de la Fontaine ❹, at the foot of the village in the Val d'Enfer, offers seven elegant and fashionably decorated rooms in a traditional *mas* (provençal farm) with a garden and pool. This place is worth the splurge and travelers know it, so make reservations. Follow signs to the Gendarmerie, from where the hotel is two minutes downhill on your right. (☎04 90 54 34 13. Breakfast €6. Open Mar. 15-Oct. 30. Doubles with shower €40-47, with bath €51-55; triples €6. Extra bed €10.) Most backpackers bring picnics to the Cité Morte, but you can buy supplies at the small **bakery** in the parking lot. (Open Mar.-Dec. daily 8:30am-8pm; Jan.-Feb. 10:30am-5pm.) Otherwise, there are plenty of sandwich stands and *crêperies* to be found.

The **tourist office** in the Hôtel de Ville, about halfway up the hill between the parking lot and the Cité Morte, gives out a free map. (☎04 90 54 34 39. Open Apr.-Sept. daily 9am-7pm; Oct.-Mar. 9am-12:30pm and 1:30-6pm.) **CTM buses** from Les Baux run to **Arles** (☎04 90 93 74 90; 30min., M-Sa 4 per day 11:45am-6:45pm; €4.80). **Taxis** can be obtained at ☎06 80 27 60 92.

TARASCON

The small city of Tarascon (pop. 13,000) is intimately linked to provençal folklore. According to legend, in the first century AD the Tarasque, a monster bred in the pathless swamps of the Rhône, began to devour local livestock and children at night. St. Martha, armed only with a wooden cross and her rope belt, domesticated the beast. For four days over the last weekend of June, during the **Fête de la Tarasque,** a replica of the monster is paraded through the town, accompanied by concerts, bullfights, horse shows, and folkloric events. Tarascon's proximity to Arles (17km), Avignon (23km), and Nîmes (24km) make it an easy daytrip or a good fallback if festivals clog the bigger cities's lodgings. Tarascon, when not *en fête*, has few attractions; imagining Martha's battle with the beast on your own is as adventurous as it'll get.

The prize of Tarascon is the imposing 15th-century **Château de Tarascon,** perched above a wedge of the Rhône. This luxurious fortress, built by Louis II of Anjou, saw few years of warfare, serving mainly as a prison; it is, therefore, in unbelievable condition. Surrounded by a now-dry grassy moat, it boasts a lovely provençal garden, medieval graffiti, an apothecary, and stunning tapestries. The climb to the roof will give you a picture-perfect view of Tarascon's rival château, the ruined Château de Beaucaire, across the river. (☎04 90 91 01 93. Open daily 10am-7pm. €5.50, ages 18-25 €3.50, under 18 free.)

> ## QUIT HOGGING THE TRUFFLES! If you see a group of
> diners in a French restaurant with their napkins over their heads, don't be alarmed.
> They're merely savoring the delicate aroma of the most sought-after mushroom in the
> world—the *truffe noir,* or black truffle. Not to be confused with the Belgian chocolate
> blobs that bear a minimal visual resemblance to them, the real, honest-to-goodness
> truffle grows in the roots of oak and hazelnut trees. Picked fresh, a truffle is worth its
> weight in gold to the gastronomically obsessed. Why so dear? The truffle hides under-
> ground and defies systematic cultivation. Fortunately, nature has blessed the French
> with the truffle-hunter *par excellence.* Pigs, which are attracted to the truffle's sexy
> odor, can snuffle out these delicacies in no time. The biggest obstacle is making off
> with the treasured *truffe* with a greedy pig in hot pursuit.

Whatever Tarascon lacks in activities, it makes up for in accommodations. To reach the **Auberge de Jeunesse (HI) ❶**, 31 bd. Gambetta, from the train station, turn right and follow the tracks until you reach bd. Victor Hugo. Cross the street and follow the path between the tracks and the wall for 20m, turning left on the next major road. The hostel is another five minutes farther, on your left near a phone booth. It has comfortable beds in 8- to 12-bed dorms, kitchen facilities, a secure bike area, and free parking. Reservations are accepted by email (tarascon@fuaj.org), but this gem of a hostel is rarely full. (☎ 04 90 91 04 08. €3.20 breakfast obligatory first morning. Reception 7:30-10am and 5:30-10:30pm. Lockout 10am-5:30pm. Sheets €2.70. Beds €8.) **Hôtel du Viaduc ❷**, 9 rue du Viaduc, has clean, cozy, comfortable rooms, some of them newly renovated. From the train station, cross under the tracks and head left. (5min.) Popular with cyclists, it maintains a locked bike area and free parking. Jovial, partially English-speaking proprietors generate a convivial atmosphere. (☎ 04 90 91 16 67. Breakfast €5, *petit dejeuner* €2.50. Doubles €20, with shower €25, with toilet €28-34. Internet access €3 per 30min.) **Camp** at **Tartarin ❶**, bd. du Roy René, behind the château on the Rhône, a simple site with bar, snack stand, free showers, and lots of shade. The ground, unfortunately, is hard with spotty grass. (☎ 04 90 91 01 46; fax 04 90 91 10 70. Reception 9am-noon and 3-7pm; after-hours until 11pm try the bar. Open Apr.-Oct. €3.40 per person, €3 per tent, €1.70 per car. Electricity €2.70.)

Bistrot des Anges ❸, pl. du Marche, serves up daily provençal menus (€16) and extraordinary chocolate cake in a hip, relaxed setting. (☎ 04 90 91 05 11. Open M-Th 9am-6pm, F-Sa 9am-6pm and 8-10pm. MC/V.)

Trains from Tarascon go to **Arles** (10min., 7 per day, €2.60) or **Avignon** (10min., 16 per day, €3.50). Ticket window open M 6:10am-7pm, Tu-F 6:20am-7pm, Sa 6:40am-7pm, Su 9:35am-noon and 1:25-6pm. **Cevennes Cars** (☎ 04 66 29 27 29) sends **buses** from the train station to **Avignon** (35min.; M-Sa 4 per day 6:50am-7pm, €7.60) and **St-Rémy** (25min.; M-F 3 per day 7:55am-6:05pm, 2 on Sa, €3.10). In a pinch, call **Espace Taxi** (☎ 06 08 40 75 31 or 04 90 91 34 50). For the **24-hour pharmacy**, call the **police**, 3 rue du Viaduc (☎ 04 90 91 52 90). The wonderful women of the **tourist office**, 59 rue des Halles, provide free guides and maps. From the train station, walk across the common and turn left on cours A. Briand; walk for two minutes, and rue des Halles will be on your right. (☎ 04 90 91 03 52. Open M-Sa 9am-noon and 2-6pm.) There are no currency exchange bureaus in town, but a **24-hour ATM** lies just to the left of the tourist office. The **post office** is to the left of the train station. (☎ 04 90 91 52 00. Open M-F 8:30am-5:30pm, Sa 8:30am-noon.) **Postal code:** 13150.

ST-RÉMY

A little town approached through luminous arcades of plane trees, the highlight of St-Rémy is a small group of Roman remnants; the ruins of ancient Glanum were Vincent van Gogh's favorite destination when the asylum let him out for good behavior.

The sights of St-Rémy are concentrated in two areas. The town center has several worthy museums, including the **Centre d'Art Présence van Gogh** in the 253-year-old Hôtel Estrine, 8 rue Estrine. Although it lacks original van Gogh paintings, the mid-sized museum has rotating exhibits on the master's work and on contemporary artists. (☎ 04 90 92 34 72; fax 04 90 92 36 73. Open Tu-Su 10:30am-12:30pm and 2:30-6:30pm. €3.20, students and seniors €2.30.) The 15th-century **Hôtel de Sade**, rue de Parage, holds all the best finds from nearby Glanum, including amazingly well-preserved glasswork and pottery. (☎ 04 90 92 64 04; fax 04 90 92 64 02. Open July-Aug. daily 11am-6pm; Apr.-June and Sept. 10am-noon and 2-6pm; Jan.-Mar. 10am-noon and 2-5pm. €2.50.)

Glanum, a settlement from the 7th century BC, lies nearly 1km south of the town center, past the tourist office on av. Vincent Van Gogh. (15min.) Discovered eighty years ago, the sprawling collection of houses, temples, springs, and sacred wells unearthed here seem more recent than AD 100. Dedicated to Cybele, the Roman Mother Goddess, the town once prospered as a stop on the main road from Spain to Italy (the *Via Domitia*); it now gives fascinating insights into the hybrid Gallo-Roman culture that emerged in Provence. (☎ 04 90 92 23 79. Open Apr.-Sept. daily 9am-7pm; Oct.-Mar. 9am-noon and 2-5pm. €5.50, ages 12-25 €3.50.) Standing in solitary splendor across the street are the well-preserved **Antiques,** a commemorative arch and mausoleum built during the reign of Augustus. You can check out or into the nearby monastery and invalids's home of **Saint-Paul de Mausole,** chemin des Carrières. Van Gogh interned here himself and spent the last year of his life above the flowered cloister (he was given three rooms, including one just for his materials), which now shows very creative exhibits by current patients. (☎ 04 90 92 77 00. Open Apr.-Oct. daily 9:30am-7pm; Nov.-Mar. 10:30am-1pm and 1:30-5pm. €3, students €2.20, under 12 free.) The Monday after Pentecost brings a veritable stampede of farm animals—mostly sheep—through the town center during the **Fête de la Transhumance,** a celebration of the traditional migration of provençal flocks from the plains to the Alpine pastures. The **Carreto Ramado,** a pagan festival dedicated to field work, in which 50 horses draw an enormous cart of fruits and vegetables, and the big **Féria Provençale,** in which bulls are teased but not killed, take place in mid-August. The tourist office distributes the free *Patrimoine* handbook, with tons of cultural info.

Restaurants are almost all pricey, but you can eat a decently-priced lunch at the simple **Le Saint-Remy-de-Provence ❸,** 48 av. Durand Maillane, to the left of the parking lot in front of the tourist office. (☎ 04 90 92 36 58. *Menus* from €11. Open July-Aug. daily noon-2:30pm and 6:30pm-midnight; Mar.-June and Sept.-Dec. closed Tu nights. Closed Jan.-Feb. MC/V.) Near the statue of Nostradamus are a handful of good *brasseries* and a **Petit Casino** supermarket on rue de la Résistance. (Open M-W and F-Sa 7:30am-12:30pm and 3:30-7:30pm, Su 7:30am-12:30pm.) To take in the vistas that Vincent loved, get the pamphlet that includes the *Promenade sur les lieux peints par Van Gogh* from the **tourist office,** pl. Jean Jaurès. From the bus stop, walk up av. Durand Maillane; the office will be on the left, in a parking lot, next to the **police station** (☎ 04 90 92 00 47). Ask about group tours in English, German and Spanish from late Apr. to Sept. 15. (☎ 04 90 92 05 22; fax 04 90 92 38 52. Free map. Tours of old St-Rémy, the Alpilles, and Vincent's sights €6.10-6.40, not including St-Paul entrance fee. Open early Apr.-Oct. daily 9am-12:30pm and 2-7pm; Nov.-early Apr. 9am-noon and 2-6pm.) **Buses** (☎ 04 90 14 59 00) come from **Avignon** (45min.; 8 per day 7:15am-5:15pm, €5.20).

THE CAMARGUE

In stark contrast to the *provençal* hills to the north, the Camargue is a vast delta lined with tall grasses and prowled by all manner of wildlife. Pink flamingos, black bulls, and the famous local white horses roam freely across the flat expanse of wild marshland, protected by the confines of the national park. The human inhabitants include **gardians,** rugged herders from a 2000-year-old line of cowboys, and the gypsies who have made the area a stopping point for 500 years. The Camargue is anchored in the north by Arles and in the south by Stes-Maries-de-la-Mer and Aigues-Mortes; Stes-Maries serves as the best base for excursions into the region.

STES-MARIES-DE-LA-MER

According to legend, in AD 40 Mary Magdalene, Mary Salomé (mother of the Apostles John and James), Mary Jacobé (Jesus's aunt), and their servant Sara were put to sea to die. Their ship washed ashore here; Stes-Maries's dark, fortified church (its only noteworthy sight) was built to house their relics. The tourist traffic it occasions has made Stes-Maries into a sort of monster, a honky-tonk collection of overpriced snack trailers and stores willing to cast anything *provençal* in plastic. The town is still worth a visit, though; besides possessing the aforementioned church, Stes-Maries is the unofficial capital of the Camargue, and most expeditions into that strange wilderness start from here. The town is also dear to gypsies, who come here as pilgrims every May.

ORIENTATION AND PRACTICAL INFORMATION. The town is wedged between untouched conservation land to the north, sea to the south, and marshes to the east. **Buses** leave from Arles (50-55min., between 7:50am and 6:10pm daily; M-Sa 5 per day, Su 4 per day; €6); contact **Les Cars de Camargue** (☎ 04 90 96 36 25) for info. The bus stop in Stes-Maries-de-la-Mer lies just north of pl. Mireille. Once here, **rent bikes** at **Le Vélo Saintois**, 19 rue de la République. (☎ 04 90 97 74 56. €6.50 for 2hr., €8 per half-day, €14 per day; passport or ID deposit. Open July-Aug. daily 8am-7pm; Sept.-Nov. and Feb.-June 9am-6:30pm.) A few minutes up the road away from town, **Le Vélociste** offers the same prices for rentals. (☎ 04 90 97 83 26. Route d'Arles. Passport or ID deposit. Open W-M 9am-12:30pm and 2-7pm.) If you get stuck in the Camargue's mud, call **Allô Taxi** at ☎ 04 90 97 83 83 or ☎ 06 18 63 08 59.

To get to the **tourist office,** 5 av. Van Gogh, walk toward the ocean down rue de la République from the bus station or down rue Victor Hugo from the church. They give out a free guide to the region, which lists biking, hiking, boating, and horseback tours in the area, and provides a helpful list of the area lodgings. (☎ 04 90 97 82 55. Open July-Aug. daily 9am-8pm; Apr.-June and Sept. 9am-7pm; Oct.-Feb. 9am-5pm.) **Crédit Agricole**, on pl. Mireille, has an ATM outside the tourist office. (☎ 04 90 97 81 17. Open Tu-W and F 9am-4:30pm, Th 10am-12:30pm and 1:45-4:30pm, Sa 9am-12:15pm.) **Pharmacie Cambon-Neuville-Corus** is on 18 rue Victor Hugo. (☎ 04 90 97 83 02. Call for urgent service during off-hours. Open M-Sa 9am-12:30pm and 3-7:30pm, Su 10am-12:30pm.) The **police** are on av. Van Gogh, right next to Les Arènes. (☎ 04 90 97 89 50.) The **post office** is on 6 av. Gambetta. (☎ 04 90 97 96 00. Open M-F 9am-noon and 1:30-4:30pm, Sa 8:30am-11:30pm.) **Postal code:** 13460.

ACCOMMODATIONS AND CAMPING. Hotels fill quickly in summer, and rooms under €35 are scarce. You can base yourself in Arles and make the town a daytrip; many choose instead to sleep illegally on the beach, though *Let's Go* does not recommend it. The **Hôtel Méditerranée ❹**, 4 bd. Frédéric Mistral, is a pretty, quiet hotel blooming with flowers; some of the beautiful rooms have little terraces. (☎ 04 90 97 82 09; fax 04 90 97 76 31. Breakfast €5. Reception 24hr. Reserve ahead in summer. Closed for part of Jan. Doubles €38.50-43; triples €58; quads €64. About €4 cheaper off-season. MC/V.) North of Stes-Maries, in the heart of the Camargue, is the **Auberge de Jeunesse (HI) hameau de Pioch Badet ❷**. To get there, take the bus that runs between Stes-Maries and Arles to "Pioch Badet" (15min., 6 per day, €1.90 from Stes-Maries; 40min., €4.50 from Arles). The quiet, camp-style hostel fills early in summer, so take the first bus you can. (☎ 04 90 97 51 72. Kitchen. Bike rental €10 per day, passport deposit. Horse tours €11.50 per hr., €53.50 per day. Obligatory *demi-pension* €20.59. Picnic lunch €6.90. Sheets €2.75. Reception 7:30-10:30am and 5-11pm; call ahead if you plan to arrive later. Lockout 10:30am-5pm. July-Aug. curfew midnight; extended during festivals. Reserved primarily for groups from Nov.-Jan.)

If you're in the mood for a big splurge, a night at the three-star **Mangio Fango ❺**, on the rte d'Arles 10 min. from the center of town, will allow you to live in splendor. Enjoy the excessively large, exquisite rooms, the heated pool, outdoor terrace and garden—at a price. (☎ 04 90 97 80 56. Breakfast €9.15. Reception 9am-11pm.

Doubles €84-107, €58-88 off-season. AmEx/MC/V.) The starry sky of the Camargue may beat having roof over your head; **camp** at **La Brise ❶,** an expansive site crossed by watery ditches and stands of reeds and dotted with purple-pink trees. It's five minutes east of the city center and has a pool and laundry. Be warned: the Camargue breeds mosquitoes. (Take the bus from Arles to "La Brise." ☎ 04 90 97 84 67. Reception 8:30am-8:30pm. July-Aug. 1 person with tent €9.70, 2 people with car €17.60, €6.50 per person; Apr.-June 1 person with tent €9.20, 2 people with car €16.80, €6.10 per person; significantly lower in off-season. Electricity €4.)

🛈 FOOD. The Camargue's main crop is a sweet, fat-grained rice; you will find it in gelatinous cakes sold at *pâtisseries*, at local restaurants, and on the shelves of **supermarkets** like the **Petit Casino** on av. Victor Hugo. (☎ 04 90 97 90 60. Open in summer daily 8am-8pm; in winter 8am-noon and 4-8pm.) A **market** fills pl. des Gitanes on Mondays and Fridays. (Open 7am-noon.) Restaurants cluster away from the waterfront around **rue Victor Hugo**, especially on **pl. Esprit Pioch**, where they serve seafood, the ubiquitous paella, *pavé de taureau*, and refreshing sangría. Most *menus* start around €12, but €9 is reasonable for lunch.

🄢 SIGHTS. The only major sight in town, and the focus of Stes-Maries, is the gray 12th-century **fortified church** looming high above the town's menagerie of snack bars. Up a vertigo-inducing staircase, these grim parapets guard a startling view of sea, sunset, and marshland; the dark Romanesque interior offers a cool respite from the shadeless town, as well as an uneasy collection of gaudy, bizarre artifacts and a church mini-book vending machine. In the crypt, the relics of the saints are displayed, and a statue of Ste-Sara glimmers in the corner, almost obscured by her layers of gilt and brocaded cloaks. The saints's power supposedly has cured the blind, healed the lame, and halted the harsh *mistral* winds of 1833. (☎ 04 90 97 87 60. Church open daily 8am-12:30pm and 2-7pm. Roof and tower open in summer daily 10am-8pm; in winter 10am-12pm and 2-5pm. €2.)

🄵 FESTIVALS. According to legend, the family chief of the region's native gypsies, Sara, welcomed the Stes-Maries and asked that she and her people be baptized into Christianity. The **Pèlerinage des Gitans** is a yearly event uniting gypsy pilgrims from all over Europe (May 24-25). A costumed procession from the church to the sea bears statues of the saints and reenacts their landing. A **festival** on the weekend around October 22 honors the Maries, with similar ceremonies for non-Roma pilgrims. In the second week of July, the **Féria du Cheval** brings horses from around the world for shows, competitions, and rodeos at the Stes-Maries and Méjanes arenas. (Call the Arènes de Méjanes at ☎ 04 90 97 10 60 for details. €24-70.) During July, August, and September, **bullfights** and horse shows occur regularly at the modern arenas. (Call the Arènes at ☎ 04 90 97 85 86. Tickets from €14.)

🄴 EXCURSIONS. Stes-Maries is undoubtedly the capital of the Camargue, and most organized visits to the region leave from here. While some tours are listed here, the tourist office is teeming with brochures with more info. The best way to see the Camargue is on **horseback,** and the region is dotted with stables offering tours throughout the park on horses. The beautiful beasts can go far into the marshes, wading through deep water into the range of birds and bulls inaccessible by any other means. Most rides are oriented toward novices, so don't be afraid if you've never saddled up before. Do, however, wear tennis shoes or boots and long pants. The stables are all united under a single association, the **Association Camarguaise de Tourisme Equestre,** and their prices remain within a few euros of one another. (☎ 04 90 97 10 10; fax 04 90 97 70 82. €12 per hr., €23 for 2hr., €33 per half day; picnic usually included on day trips.) For **jeep safaris,** contact **Le Gitan,** 13 av. de la Plage, in Stes-Maries. Safaris explore the banks of the Grand and Petit Rhône.

P R O V E N C E

The jeeps hold 7-8 people. (☎04 90 97 89 33. 2hr. trips €31 per person; 4hr. trips €37 per person. July-Sept. trips depart between 10am-6pm; off-season the last trip leaves at 4pm. Open daily 9am-8pm.) **Camargue**, 5 rue des Launes, sends **boats** from Port Gardian deep into the Petit Rhône for up-close bird- and bull-watching. (☎04 90 97 84 72; fax 04 90 97 73 50. Open Mar.-Nov. 1½hr., 3-4 per day until Oct., when there are 2 per day. July-Aug. first departure 10:30am, last departure 5:55pm; Sept.-May last departure 4:10pm. €10, children €5.)

Although most of the trails are open only to horseback riders, **bicycle touring** is a great way to see much of the area. Keep in mind that bike trails may be sandy and difficult to ride. Trail maps indicating length, level of difficulty, and danger spots are available from the Stes-Maries tourist office. Bring an ample supply of fresh water—it gets hotter than Hades. A 2hr. pedal will reveal some of the area, but you'll need a whole day if you plan to stop along the wide, deserted white-sand beaches that line the trail. Aspiring botanists and zoologists should stop at the **Centre d'Information de Ginès**, on the bus line between Stes-Maries and Arles, which distributes info on the region's unusual flora and fauna. ("Pont de Gau," 10min. from Stes-Maries. ☎04 90 97 86 32. Open Apr.-Sept. daily 10am-6pm; Oct.-Mar. Sa-Th 9:30am-5pm.) Next door, the **Parc Ornithologique de Pont de Gau** provides several kilometers of paths through the marshes and offers views of birds and grazing bulls. (☎04 90 97 82 62. Park open Apr.-Sept. daily 9am-sunset; Oct.-Mar. 10am-sunset. €6, under age 17 €3.)

AIGUES-MORTES

This curiously inland port city, whose name means "Dead Waters," is home to salt marshes spotted with herons, egrets, and flamingos, surrounding the thick defensive wall of the city. In summer, the water around Aigues-Mortes takes on a purplish hue as it evaporates to create its famous salt formation, the *fleur du sel de Camargue*. Aigues-Mortes's primary attractions are history and scenery; inside its slow-paced walls, boutiques and restaurants sell the specialty foods of the Camargue while tourists stroll along the towered battlements.

⚹⚹ TRANSPORTATION AND PRACTICAL INFORMATION. SNCF **trains** and **buses** run to Nîmes (50min.; daily 4 per day 6:40am-7pm; €6), as do **STDG** buses (1hr., 5 per day, €5.70). Les Courriers du Midi run **buses** to Montpellier (1½hr., M-Sa 2 per day, €6). It is not easy to get to Aigues-Mortes from the east; from **Arles** a train or bus to Nîmes will get you within shouting distance, and there is no public transportation from Stes-Maries-de-la-Mer to here. If you are really desperate, call Aigues-Mortes Taxi (☎06 11 56 20 12). The **tourist office**, porte de la Gardette, is in the dark tower on the inside of the main gate to the left; from the train station cross the bridge and follow the boulevard into town. (☎04 66 53 73 00; fax 04 66 53 65 94. Open July-Aug. M-F 9am-8pm, Sa-Su 10am-8pm; June and Sept. M-F 9am-6pm, Sa-Su 10am-6pm; Oct.-May 9am-noon and 1-6pm.) The **post office** is several blocks east on rue Baudin. (☎04 66 53 60 02. Open M-F 8:30am-noon and 2:30-5pm, Sa 8:30-11:30am.) The **police** are at 1 bd. Gambetta. (☎04 66 53 69 73.) The most convenient pharmacy is **Pharmacy Cathala**. (5 rue J. Jaurès. ☎04 66 53 68 00. Open M-Sa 8:45am-12:15pm and 2:30-7:15pm.) In urgent cases at night, call Cathala or the other two pharmacies (☎04 66 53 61 30 or ☎04 66 53 83 09). **Crédit Agricole**, 6 rue A. Courbet, exchanges currency for a commission charge (open M-F 8:45am-12:30pm and 1:30-5pm), and there are several ATMs around the central **pl. St-Louis**.

⚹⚹ ACCOMMODATIONS AND FOOD. The cheapest option in town is the **Hôtel L'Escale ❸**, 3 av. Tour de Constance, directly across the street from the tower, whose white walls and wooden furniture retain the appealing scent of the sea. (☎04 66 53 71 14; fax 04 66 53 76 74. Reception 6:30am-11pm. Reservations usually required July 15-Aug. 15. Singles and doubles with sink and shower €26, with toilet €30; triples €29; €40; one quint €57. AmEx/MC/V.) The **Hôtel Tour de Constance ❹**, 1 bd. Diderot, is slightly more expensive with sparkling, swirling tile floors. (☎ 04 66 53 83 50. Breakfast €5. Reception until 10pm. Doubles with shower €32, with TV €35-39; triples with shower €46; quads with shower €54. MC/V.)

Fast food and small **boutiques** can be found on **rue Jean Jaurès**, while lively, well-priced eateries fill **pl. St-Louis**. A **market** often spans the length of the wall just outside the city's fortifications. (Open W and Su 8am-12:30pm.) **Le Moulin de Pauline**, 22 rue Emile Zola, sells a huge selection of Camargue specialties including fleur du sel, jams, dry bull sausage, wines, and *apéritifs*, which customers can taste. (☎ 04 66 51 97 67. Open July-Sept. Tu-Su 10:30am-9:30pm; Feb.-June 10:30am-12:30pm and 2-7:30pm; Oct.-Feb. 10:30am-12:30pm and 2:30-6:30pm.)

🔲 🔳 SIGHTS AND ENTERTAINMENT. Louis IX (St-Louis) built this *bastide* as a springboard from which to reconquer the Holy Land; he launched the Seventh and Eighth Crusades from here in 1248 and 1270. Though the crusades were fatal for St-Louis—he was captured on the first and died on the second—the town has succeeded marvelously, its planned grid still enclosed by 13th-century walls. The **Tour de Constance**, keystone of the city's defensive fortifications, has been perfectly preserved, probably as a result of its impenetrable 6m-thick walls. An optional tour in French takes you to the top of the tower, which offers a picturesque view of the densely packed town and of the reddish water around it, and through the vaulted prison on the way down. (☎ 04 66 53 61 55. 9 daily 40min. tours in French. Tower and ramparts open July-Sept. daily 10:30am-7:30pm; mid-May to June 10am-7pm; Mar. to mid-May 10:30am-6pm; Jan.-Feb. and Oct.-Dec. 9:30am-5pm. All times include a 1-2pm lunchtime closing. €5.50, under 26 €3.50.) **Place St-Louis** honors the town's founder with a statue. On the corner of the *place* is the 13th-century **Notre Dame des Sablons**, St-Louis's final stop in France before his first crusade. St-Louis turned the church from one of wood into fortified stone; it now features modern painted-glass windows, childlike and not too appealing. (Open daily 8:30am-noon and 2-6pm.)

L'Aventure runs daily **boat tours** into the Camargue. (☎ 06 03 91 44 63. €7 for 1½hr., €8.50 for 2hr.) If time is short or the sun too hot, let the images of the Camargue drift by in the **3-D Cinéma** across the canal—the somewhat hackneyed version of the idyllic French pastoral life you've always dreamed of. (Open Feb.-Nov. Sa-Su and daily during school vacations. Shows every hr. July-Aug. 3-10pm, Feb.-June and Sept.-Nov. 3-7pm. €5.70, children 12 and under €3.40.) The first week in August brings Mediterranean singers to the town for the **Festival des Nuits d'Encens.** (Info ☎ 04 66 73 90 95. Concert tickets €14-23, students €11-18). The second weekend of October sees the **Fête Votive's** *Course Camarguaise.* In this Camarguaise tradition, a bull is released into an arena with a tassel attached to his horns. A prize is awarded to the *raseteur* who can detach the tassel. On the last weekend of the month, the **Fête de St-Louis** recreates the past with historical pageants, jousting, and a medieval market.

NÎMES

It is the Spanish feel of Nîmes (pop. 132,000) that draws the vacationing French. They flock here in particular for the *férias*, with their bull runs, bullfights, flamenco dancing, and lots of other hot-blooded activity. It is a pity, however, that Nîmes doesn't merit a long-term stay. The city has adequate nightlife and some nice metropolitan features, but lacks both the intimacy of other provençal cities and the glitz of the Côte d'Azur. In fact, Nîmes remains a top tourist destination for one reason only: its incredible Roman structures. The arena, the Maison Carré, and the exceptional Pont du Gard aqueduct are must-sees.

PROVENCE

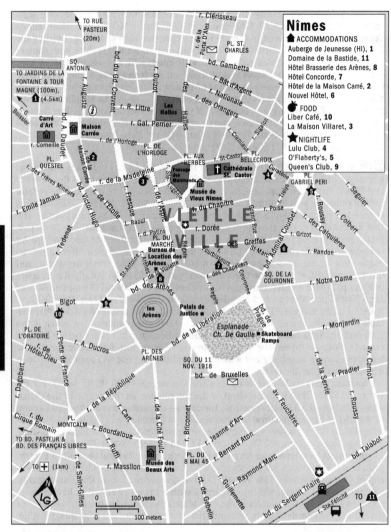

Nîmes

🏠 **ACCOMMODATIONS**
Auberge de Jeunesse (HI), **1**
Domaine de la Bastide, **11**
Hôtel Brasserie des Arènes, **8**
Hôtel Concorde, **7**
Hôtel de la Maison Carré, **2**
Nouvel Hôtel, **6**

🍎 **FOOD**
Liber Café, **10**
La Maison Villaret, **3**

★ **NIGHTLIFE**
Lulu Club, **4**
O'Flaherty's, **5**
Queen's Club, **9**

▸ TRANSPORTATION

Trains: bd. Talabot. Info office open M-F 5:45am-9:30pm, Sa 6:45am-9:45pm, Su 6:45am-10pm. To: **Arles** (25min., 8 per day, €6.30); **Bordeaux** (5hr., 4 per day, €46.40); **Marseille** (1¼hr., 11per day, €15.30); **Montpellier** (30min., 50 per day, €7.20); **Orange** (1½hr., 3 per day, €10.30); **Paris** (3hr., 10 per day, €75.90); **Toulouse** (3hr., 8 per day, €29.30).

Buses: rue Ste-Félicité (☎04 66 29 52 00), behind the train station. Info office open M-F 8am-noon and 2-6pm. **Société des Transports Départementaux du Gard (STDG)** (☎04 66 29 27 29) runs to **Avignon** (1½hr.; M-F 8 per day, 6 on Sa, 2 on Su; €6.70).

Cars de Camargue (☎04 90 96 36 25) serves **Arles** (M-F 5 per day, 3 on Sa; €5.40) and **Montpellier** (M-Sa 2 per day; €8.40).

Public Transportation: T.C.N. (☎04 66 38 15 40). Buses stop running at 8pm. Tickets good for 1hr. Ticket €0.95, *carnet* of 5 €3.75.

Taxis: TRAN office (☎04 66 29 40 11) in train station. Base €1.80; €0.58 per km until 7pm, €0.83 per km after 7pm. 24hr.

ORIENTATION AND PRACTICAL INFORMATION

Nîmes's shops, museums, and cafés cluster in the *vieille ville* between bd. Victor Hugo and bd. Admiral Courbet. To get there from the train station, follow av. Feuchères, veer left around the park, and scoot clockwise around the arena. To reach the tourist office, go straight on bd. Victor Hugo for five blocks until you reach the Maison Carré, a Roman temple in the middle of pl. Comédie, whose facade looks out upon rue Auguste and the tourist office.

Tourist Office: 6 rue Auguste (☎04 66 58 38 00; fax 04 66 58 38 01; www.ot-nimes.fr). Free accommodations service, detailed map, and festival info. The free *Nimescope* lists events. Info on bus and train excursions to Pont du Gard, the Camargue, and nearby towns. Open July-Aug. M-F 8am-8pm, Sa 9am-7pm, Su 10am-6pm; May and Sept. M-F 8am-7pm, Sa 9am-7pm, Su 10am-6pm.

Tours: Le Petit Train (☎04 66 70 26 92). Leaves almost every hr. from espl. Charles de Gaulle in front of the Palais de Justice. Open July-Aug. daily 9:30am-7:30pm; Apr.-June and Sept.-Oct. 9:30-11:30am and 2:30-5:30pm. €4.60, ages 3-12 €1.50.

Budget Travel: Nouvelles Frontières, 1 bd. de Prague (☎04 66 67 38 94; fax 04 66 78 38 62). Open M-F 9am-7pm, Sa 9pm-6pm.

Money: Banque de France, 2 sq. du 11 Novembre (☎04 66 76 82 00), offers **currency exchange** with no commission. Exchange desk open M-F 8:30am-12:15pm.

Laundromat: Lavomatique, 5 rue des Halles. Open daily 7am-8pm. **Laverie Libre Service,** 22 rue de Vérone. Open daily 7am-9pm.

Police: 10 rue de la Tresorerie (☎04 66 67 84 29).

Hospital: Hôpital Caremeau, rue Professeur Robert Debré (☎04 66 68 68 68).

Internet access: Net's Games, 22 rue de l'Horloge, pl. de la Maison Carré (☎04 66 36 36 16). €3.80 per hr. Open daily 10am-midnight. **PC Gamer,** 2 rue de Nationale (04 66 76 27 85). €3.80 per hr. Open M-Sa 10:30am-1am, Su 2pm-1am.

Post Office: 1 bd. de Bruxelles (☎04 66 76 69 50), across from the park at the end of av. Feuchères. **Currency exchange** with no commission. Open M-F 8am-7pm, Sa 8am-noon. **Branch offices:** 19 bd. Gambetta and 11 pl. Belle Croix. **Postal Code:** 30000 and 30900. **Poste Restante:** 30006.

ACCOMMODATIONS AND CAMPING

The *vieille ville* is dotted with pricey hotels. If you are up for a long walk or bus ride every morning, the hostel is unquestionably the best option. Reserve a couple of weeks in advance during festivals and summer concerts.

Auberge de Jeunesse (HI), 257 chemin de l'Auberge de la Jeunesse (☎04 66 68 03 20; fax 04 66 68 03 21), off chemin de la Cigale, 4½km from quai de la Fontaine. On foot, pass the Maison Carré on bd. Victor Hugo and continue straight on bd. A. Daudet. Go left at sq. Antonin onto quai de la Fontaine. The Jardins de la Fontaine will be on your right; continue alongside the garden straight on av. Roosevelt. Follow the signs for the Auberge; they will lead you right onto rte. d'Alès and left onto chemin de la Cigale.

(40min.) Or take bus #2 (dir: "Alès" or "Villeverte") to "Stade, Route d'Alès" and follow the signs. After buses stop running at 8pm, the hostel minibus (call ahead to arrange) will pick you up at the station for free. It will also bring you back to the station in the morning for €1.30. This delightfully modern and welcoming hostel is well worth the difficult trek. 4- to 6-bed dorms with bath and magnetic key-card access. Some family rooms available. Ping-pong, *pétanque*, foosball, laundry, kitchen, and bar until 1am. **Internet** access €3.80 per hr. Bikes €8 per day. Scooter €20 per day. May-Oct. bike/kayak tour combo to Pont du Gard €20. Breakfast €3.20. Dinner €8.50. Sheets €2.70 per week. Individual, locking cupboards for luggage. Reception Mar.-Sept. 24hr. (night guard). No curfew. Lockout 10am-5pm. Reservations advised. Bunks €8.65. **Camping** €4.95. MC/V. **Members only. ❶**

Hôtel Brasserie des Arènes, 4 bd. des Arènes (☎04 66 67 23 05; fax 04 66 67 76 93; hotel@brasserie-arenes.com). Perfect location, facing the arena, with big, well-kept rooms. Breakfast €4.60. Singles €19; doubles with shower €23; triples with shower €31; quads €45. MC/V. ❷

Hôtel Concorde, 3 rue des Chapeliers (☎/fax 04 66 67 91 03), off rue Regale. A friendly staff cares for clean but cramped rooms in this small hotel. If you get a room with a toilet, don't expect privacy—a small and ineffective barrier separates the toilet from the bedchamber. Breakfast €4. Singles €17.50, with shower €23.50; doubles €23, with shower €26.50; triples with shower €38. MC/V. ❷

Hôtel de la Maison Carré, 14 rue de la Maison Carré (☎04 66 67 32 89; fax 04 66 76 22 57). Once the dirty carpets are replaced in 2003, visitors will fully appreciate this hotel's brightly lit, cutely decorated rooms. Shower and TV in all but the smallest single. Breakfast €5. Reservations recommended. Singles €30-35; doubles €40-45; triples €55; quads with bath €55. MC/V. ❹

Nouvel Hôtel, 6 bd. Admiral Courbet (☎04 66 67 62 48), along the major boulevard that leads from the amphitheater. A big hotel with an institutional feel. TV in all rooms. Breakfast €4.60. Shower €3. Singles and doubles €24, with shower and toilet €36; triples with shower and toilet €36; quads with shower but no toilet €39. AmEx/MC/V. ❸

Campsite: Domaine de La Bastide (☎/fax 04 66 38 09 31), rte. de Générac, 5km south of the train station. Take bus D (dir: "La Bastide," last bus 7:30pm) to its terminus. By car, drive towards to Montpellier and get off at rte. de Générac. Three-star site with grocery store, laundry, and recreational facilities. €7.30 per person, €11.60 for two. Caravan with electricity €10.40 per person, €14.65 for two. ❶

🍴 FOOD

Local chefs employ generous amounts of *herbes de Provence* (a mixture of local herbs) and *aïoli* (a thick sauce of garlic and olive oil). Nîmes specializes in *la brandade de morue*, dried cod crushed with olive oil and packed in a turnover, pastry, or soufflé. Unfortunately, even the more expensive restaurants in Nîmes are unspectacular. If a kitchen is available, you can probably cook better, and certainly cheaper, meals. Stock up at the **open-air market** on bd. Jean-Jaurès (F 7am-1pm), the **market** in Les Halles (daily 6am-1pm), or the large **Marché U,** 19 rue d'Alès, just down the hill from the hostel. (Open M-Sa 8am-12:45pm and 3:30-8pm.) The terraced herb gardens and ponds on the back slopes of the **Jardins de la Fontaine** are great places to bring a picnic basket.

Caladons, honey cookies sprinkled with almonds, are Nîmes's favorite sweet. Cafés and bakeries line the squares in the center of town; *brasseries* dominate **bd. Victor Hugo, bd. Admiral Courbet,** and the Arena. Terraced **Place du Marché,** with its crocodile fountain, reverberates with chatter late into the night. The boulangerie and *pâtisserie* **La Maison Villaret ❶**, 13 rue de la Madeleine, has guarded the secret of its *croquants Villaret*—dry biscuits made of crushed almonds and baked in the same wood-burning ovens—since their invention in 1775. (☎ 04 66 67 41 79. Open M-Sa 7am-7:30pm.) **Liber Café ❷**, 34 rue Porte de France, is another diamond in the rough. The meals (€7) are not extraordinary, but the intellectual European and North African crowd comes for the books, guitars, art, and cheap prices. (☎ 06 09 67 12 75. Open daily 3pm-2pm.)

👁 SIGHTS

A three-day pass to all sights is sold at each sight (€9.15, students €4.57).

LES ARÈNES. The city's pride and joy is also the best-preserved Roman amphiteater in France. Impressive when empty, the amphitheater is awesome when packed with screaming crowds for the concerts and bullfights that it still hosts. The elliptical stone arena, built in AD 50, seats 23,000 people. *(☎ 04 66 76 72 77; ticket office ☎ 04 66 02 80 80. Open M-F 10am-6pm. €4.30, students €3.)*

MAISON CARRÉ AND CARRÉ D'ART. The long, rectangular temple known as the **Maison Carré** was dedicated to Caius and Lucius Caesar, the grandson and adopted son of the emperor Augustus. The temple's purity of form and exquisite carvings have always arrested the eye; Louis XIV liked it so much that he almost ordered it brought to Versailles to be a lawn ornament. *(☎ 04 66 36 26 76. Open June-Sept. daily 9am-7pm and 2:30-7pm, Oct.-May 10am-6pm. Free.)* The Maison Carré is gracefully counter-balanced from across the square by Norman Foster's ultra-modern **Carré d'Art,** which displays a beautiful collection of contemporary art on huge white walls. *(☎ 04 66 76 35 70. Open Tu-Su 10am-6pm. €4.30, students €3.)*

JARDINS DE LA FONTAINE. At the end of the quai de la Fontaine, the ruined Temple de Diane has been improbably converted into a formal garden, complete with lush flora and marble sculptures. Its gorgeous fountains and reflecting pools sparkle with crystal-clean water from the Nemausus spring. You might imagine yourself on another world except for the shouts of the old men who use the shady sands as *boule* courts. *(Off pl. Foch to the left along the canals from the Maison. Garden open Apr.-Sept. 15 daily 7:30am-10pm; Sept. 16-Nov. 7:30am-6:30pm; Nov.-Mar. 8am-7pm. Free.)* Rising majestically above the park is the **Tour Magne.** Built in the Iron Age and modified by Augustus in 15 BC, this massive tower, essentially a blunt stone spike, once represented a corner of the Roman empire. Now the eroded ruins offer an exhilarating view of Nîmes and the surrounding countryside. *(☎ 04 66 67 65 56. Open July-Aug. daily 9am-7pm; Sept.-June 9am-5pm. €2.40, students €1.90.)*

MUSÉE DES BEAUX ARTS AND MUSÉE DU VIEUX NÎMES. Nîmes's two major museums are small and not particularly interesting. The **Musée de Beaux-Arts,** a Neoclassical building accented with marble pillars and Roman mosaic floors, features paintings of the French, Italian, Flemish, and Dutch schools from the 15th to 19th centuries as well as temporary exhibits. The **Musée du Vieux Nîmes,** in a 17th-century palace, displays 17th-century clothing in meticulously reconstructed, somewhat mundane period rooms. *(Beaux-Arts: rue de la cité Foule. ☎ 04 66 67 38 21. Vieux Nîmes: pl. aux Herbes, next to the cathedral. ☎ 04 66 36 00 64. Both open July-Aug. Tu-Su 10am-6pm; Sept.-June 11am-6pm. €4.30, students €3.)*

🎵 💬 ENTERTAINMENT AND FESTIVALS

Nîmes is a pretty lousy place to party outside of the festival season. Bars are lively during the *férias* (see below), but otherwise they shut down relatively early. Check out the cafés along the pl. du Marché. Bustling **O'Flaherty's,** 21 bd. Amiral Courbet, has €3.50-5 pints of beer and live music on Thursday nights in winter.

PROVENCE

The dart-filled, Guinness-sloppy bar is a favorite of anglophones, anglophiles, and just plain Englishmen. (☎04 66 67 22 63. Open M-F 11am-2am, Sa-Su 5pm-2am.) **Queen's Club,** 1 rue Jean Reboul, is trendy, but not uncomfortably so. Thirty-somethings drink €3.30-5 pints of beer and €2 glasses of wine before heading out to the clubs. (☎04 66 67 13 93. Open daily 5pm-1am.) **Lulu Club,** 10 impasse de la Curaterie, off rue de la Curaterie, is a gay dance bar. (☎04 66 36 28 20. €8 cover includes 1 drink. Mixed drinks €4; straight alcohol €8. Open Tu-Sa 11pm onward.) **Cinéma Le Sémaphore,** 25 rue Porte de France, plays non-French films in their original languages. (☎04 66 67 83 11. €5.20, under 25 €4.30, noon shows €4.)

The new Nîmes hot spot is the beach, where temporarily constructed restaurant-bars open in June and entertain till early September. Local students flock there to forget their semesters with drinking and dancing. Take bus #6 to the Plage de la Corniches and get off at "Les Passantes" or "Les Amours d'Antan."

Concerts, movies, plays, and operas take place at *les arènes* throughout the year (€9-46). Summer acts have included Ray Charles and Ben Harper; David Bowie visits in 2003. For info and reservations, contact the **Bureau de Location des Arènes,** 4 rue de la Violette. (☎04 66 02 80 80. Open M-F 10am-6pm.)

It is worth changing travel plans to see one of the famous *férias*. In all, Nîmes holds four important *férias:* the **Féria d'Istres** in late June, the **Féria de Primavera** in mid-February, the **Féria des Vendages** in mid-September, and the most boisterous, the **Féria de Pentecôte** (during Pentecost). For five days, the streets resound with the clattering of hooves as bulls are herded to the *arènes* for combat. The nights are full of revelry in the streets, the bars, and homes.

The **Courses Camarguaises,** held at varying dates in June, July, and August, provide more humane entertainment. Fighters strip decorations from the bulls's horns, narrowly avoiding the lethal points, and then vault over barriers to safety. (Tickets €10.50-53.50. Purchase at the Arena ticket office, 4 rue de la Violette. Cheap seats usually available on the day of the event.) During **les Marchés du Soir** (a.k.a. **Jeudis de Nîmes**), the city center fills with local painters, artists, and musicians late into the night (July-Aug. Th 7-11pm). Performances at the Théâtre de la Mer are the focus of the **Fiesta Latina.**

▶ DAYTRIP FROM NÎMES: PONT DU GARD

The Pont du Gard is the centerpiece of a Roman aqueduct that once supplied Nîmes with water. Its three dizzying, diminishing levels of arches bridge the 275m-wide gorge of the roaring Gordon River at a height of 50m. The bridge was built in 19 BC by Agrippa, a close friend of Emperor Augustus, to transport water from the Eure springs near Uzès to the baths and fountains of Nîmes. The bridge is an engineering *coup de grace*. The covered canal carries water 50km despite falling only 17m. in altitude during the trip. That means an average gradient of only 0.34 degrees, which is only feasible with near-perfect construction. Visitors can walk through the bridge's huge water channels and swim in the cool river below.

If you have a whole day to spare, the best way to experience the Pont du Gard is to start from **Collias,** 6km toward Uzès. Here **Kayak Vert** rents two-person canoes, kayaks, and bikes. The pleasant two- to three-hour paddle takes you down river past the Château de St-Privat (sight of a famous treaty signing) to the Pont du Gard, where a bus shuttles you back to Collias. (☎04 66 22 80 76. Kayak/canoe rental and shuttle €16; bikes €17 per day, €15 per half-day; canoes and kayaks €14 per day. 15% discount for students or guests of the hostel in Nîmes.)

The **Société des Transports Départementaux du Gard** (STDG ☎04 66 29 27 29) runs daily buses from the bus station to the Pont du Gard (30min.; M-Sa 5 per day, 2 on Su; €4.75). Buses also leave for the Pont du Gard from Avignon (45min., 7 per day, €5). The bus will drop you off and pick you up at the roundabout by the Hôtel L'Auberge

Blanche—a.k.a., the middle of nowhere. The Nîmes tourist office leads tours to the Pont-du-Gard every Tuesday during July and August, from 2:30-7:30pm, meeting at the main entrance of the Jardins de la Fontaine at 2:30pm. €13, students €9.)

Camping le Barralet, rue des Aires in Collias, offers a pool and hot showers in addition to river bathing. A grocery store is 200m away. (☎ 04 66 22 84 52; fax 04 66 22 89 17. Open Mar.-Sept. 1 person €6-7.40, 2 people €11-13.50, 3 people €13.50-16.50. Lower prices Apr.-June and Sept. MC/V.)

UZÈS

26km north of Nîmes, in lush, rolling countryside, lies the small town of Uzès (pop. 5000). Along the pristine boulevards, bakeries and *brasseries* bathe in the sunlight filtering through giant plane trees. The pl. aux Herbes, identified by its ancient stone fountain and arching buildings, was the backdrop for *Cyrano de Bergerac* and *Le Jour de Gloire*.

TRANSPORTATION AND PRACTICAL INFORMATION. STDG (☎ 04 66 29 27 29) runs buses to Uzès from Avignon (1hr., 3 per day, €7.30) and Nîmes (1hr.; M-Sa 9 per day, Su 2 per day; €5). During the week, buses run from Uzès to the Pont du Gard (20min., 6 per day, €3). There are fewer buses on weekends and holidays. The **tourist office,** pl. Albert 1er, northeast of the bus station on the bd. Gambetta, provides a free booklet on Uzès and a tourist-friendly map. (☎ 04 66 22 68 88; fax 04 66 22 95 19. Open June-Sept. M-F 9am-6pm, Sa-Su 10am-1pm and 2-5pm; Oct.-May M-F 9am-noon and 1:30-6pm, Sa 10am-1pm.)

ACCOMMODATIONS AND FOOD. Most accommodations are expensive. One exception is **Le Prieuré du Christ Roi,** av. de la Garebut, which offers a pool and sturdy bare-mattressed bunks in rooms for 2 to 14 people. This ancient converted farm is frequented mainly by religious groups but happily accommodates backpackers as well. To get there from the bus station, walk down av. de la Libération, cross the rotary road, and take the Anduze direction. The *prieuré* is just past the Peugeot garage on the right, after 10min. (☎ 04 66 22 68 67; fax 04 66 03 35 42. Dinner €9 for groups. Sheets €3. Pool €2.30. Beds €12.) Another good option is the three-star **Camping La Paillote** north of town, which manages wooded sites with hot showers, a pool, a bar, and laundry. From the tourist office, take rue Cigalon north to rue Masbourguet, which becomes rue St-Firmin. Take a left in front of the cemetery, then on the far side take a right onto the little road marked "Chemin de Grezac." La Paillote is 200m down on the right. Reserve far in advance. (☎ 04 66 22 38 55; fax 04 66 22 26 66; dr.nicolae@freesbee.fr. Two people with car €16. Extra person €4.80. Electricity €3.)

The boulevards surrounding the *vieille ville* are lined with bakeries and cafés. Restaurants dominate pl. aux Herbes. Wednesday and Saturday mornings bring a **market** in pl. aux Herbes and on the surrounding boulevards. A **Petit Casino** supermarket lies on the corner of bd. Gambetta and av. Général Vincent. (Open Tu-Sa 7:30am-12:30pm and 3:30-7:30pm, Su 8am-12:30pm.)

SIGHTS AND ENTERTAINMENT. Dominating the city with its gigantic medieval tower is **Le Duché,** pl. du Marché. Built in the 11th century and never challenged, the fortress has been continuously renovated for seven centuries. The resulting structure is an intriguing blend of period styles, with a gothic chapel and delicately carved and columned Renaissance facades. The palace remains home to the family of Crussol d'Uzès, descendants of the first duke and duchess of France. The spirit evident in their family motto, *ferro non auro* ("by iron, not gold") was embodied in the late Duchesse Anne, the first French woman to get her driver's license (and also a fine for speeding) in 1898. Admission to the entire palace includes a tour in French with a written English translation. For a lower price you are allowed to climb the tower and survey the town of Uzès. (☎04 66 22 18 96. Open July 15-Sept. 15 daily 10am-1pm, 2-6:30pm; Sept. 16-July 14 10am-noon, 2-6pm. Tour €10, students €6.50, ages 7-11 €4. Tower €5.)

The **Cathédrale St-Théodorit,** pl. de l'Evêché, has been burned, rebuilt, and restored many times during its turbulent history. A mishmash of Renaissance, Baroque, and neo-medieval style, the cathedral features a remarkable 17th-century, 2772-pipe organ with delicately carved, gold-trimmed shutters. (Open daily 9am-6:30pm. Free organ concerts in Oct. and July.) Next door is the 12th-century **Tour Fenestrelle,** the belltower of a cathedral destroyed in the 16th century. Its magnificent arched windows and tiled roof are Uzès's most beautiful sights. To the cathedral's left, a stone balcony offers a magnificent view of the countryside.

Bulls stampede through the streets and cascades of *pastis* flow freely during the **Fête Votive** that lasts for a week after the first Friday in August. Truffle buffs hit cloud nine on the third Sunday of January during **la Journée de la Truffe,** a celebration of the elusive mushroom. Restaurants throughout Uzès create special truffle-influenced menus. The second half of July sees the **Nuits Musicales d'Uzès.** Ancient chants, religious music, and even opera are performed in Uzès's historical landmarks. Tickets (€11-34 per performance) are available at the tourist office. Contact the tourist office for information about all the festivals.

ORANGE

Despite its name, this northern provençal town hasn't tended a single citrus grove in its two millennia; "Orange" is a perversion of the name of the Roman city "Arausio." Orange's juice, the Côtes du Rhône vintage, originates in its renowned vineyards. *Caves* scattered throughout the region offer *dégustations* of the fine liquid, for a price. The immense theater and elaborate triumphal arch, astonishingly well-preserved, are the chief reasons for visiting Orange. Beyond that, and barring a festival, there's nothing much to keep you here.

■ ⁊ ORIENTATION AND PRACTICAL INFORMATION

The center of Orange is the neighborhood of **pl. Clemenceau, pl. République,** and **pl. aux Herbes.** To reach the main tourist office from the train station at the eastern edge of town, follow the signs to the *centre ville*, walking away from the station along **av. Frédéric Mistral,** and keep left as it becomes rue de la République. Continue through pl. République, go around the right side of the building at the far end, and go straight on rue St-Martin, which becomes av. Charles de Gaulle. The tourist office is across cours Aristide Briand, and to your right. (15min.)

Trains: av. Frédéric Mistral. Info office open daily 7:30am-7:45pm. To: **Avignon** (20min.; M-Sa 19 per day, Su 13 per day; €4.70); **Marseille** (1¼hr., 5 per day, €17.10); **Lyon** (2½hr.; M-Sa 7 per day, Su 4 per day; €21.60); **Paris** (3½hr., 2 TGV per day, €62.50).

Buses: (☎04 90 34 15 59), on cours Pourtoules. Ticket office open M-Tu and Th-F 8am-12:30pm and 3-5pm, W 8am-noon and 3-5pm. To **Avignon** (55min.; M-Sa about every hr., Su 4 per day 7:45am-6:25pm; €4.70).

Taxi: Taxi Monge (☎04 90 51 00 00).

Tourist Office: 5 cours Aristide Briand (☎04 90 34 70 88; fax 04 90 34 99 62), near the *autoroute*. Staff will help you in English and make last-minute reservations with €16 deposit. Lists of daytrips. Paid tours of Théâtre Antique in English (July-Aug. 1 per day, price varies). Open Apr.-Sept. M-Sa 9:30am-1pm and 2-7pm, Su 10am-12:30pm and

2:30-6pm; Oct.-Mar. M-Sa 10am-1pm and 2-5pm. **Branch office,** pl. des Frères Mounet, opposite Théâtre Antique. Open Apr.-Sept. M-Sa 10am-1pm and 2:15-7pm.

Laundromat: 5 rue St-Florent, off bd. E. Daladier. Open daily 7am-8pm.

Police: 427 bd. E. Daladier (☎04 90 51 55 55).

Hospital: Louis Giorgi, chemin de l'Abrian, on av. H. Fabré (☎04 90 11 22 22).

24-hr. Pharmacy: Changes each night; call the police for schedule.

Internet Access: Planet Game, 78 av. Charles de Gaulle (☎04 32 81 05 27), near the tourist office. €5 per hr. Open July-Aug. daily 9am-midnight; Sept.-June M-F 9am-8pm, Sa-Su 9am-2pm.

Currency exchange: Crédit Agricole, on cours Aristide Briand across from the tourist office (☎04 90 11 49 00). Open M-Tu and Th-F 8:30am-4:45pm, W 9:15am-8:45pm.

Post Office: 679 bd. E. Daladier (☎04 90 11 11 00), on cours Pourtoules. **Currency exchange.** Open M-F 8am-6:30pm, Sa 8am-noon. **Postal code:** 84100.

▐ ACCOMMODATIONS AND CAMPING

Decent, cheap rooms should not be hard to find in Orange, as long as you book ahead in late July and early August.

Hôtel St-Florent, 4 rue du Mazeau (☎04 90 34 18 53; fax 04 90 51 17 25), near pl. aux Herbes. Jovial family owners have painted frescoes on every wall of their brightly colored, lovely small hotel. Antique wooden bed frames compensate for some small rooms. Breakfast €6. Closed Dec.-Feb. Singles with shower €25-34; doubles with shower €34, with bath (some with TV) €40-65; triples with bath and TV €50; family suites with bath €60-70. Extra bed €8. July-Aug. prices slightly higher. MC/V. ❸

Arcôtel, 8 pl. aux Herbes (☎04 90 34 09 23; fax 04 90 51 61 12). Simple, cheery, comfortable rooms, close to both the central *place* and the Roman theater. Some triples and quads are huge. Buffet breakfast €5.50. Reception 7am-11pm. Singles €16.80; doubles €24.40; triples with bath €39.65; quads with bath €47.30. Prices a little higher Apr.-Sept. 15. AmEx/MC/V. ❷

Hôtel Arène, pl. de Langes (☎04 90 11 40 40; fax 04 90 11 40 45). A centrally located, upscale hotel, each room decorated in a different style; 12 have balconies, and all have soundproof doors. Breakfast €8. Reception 24hr. Singles and doubles €56-91.50. AmEx/MC/V. ❺

Camping: Le Jonquier (☎04 90 34 49 48; fax 04 90 51 16 97), on rue A. Carrel. A hike. From the tourist office, walk toward the *autoroute* and turn right after the school onto av. du 18 Juin 1940. Take a left onto rue H. Noguères, and after 5min. go right on rue A. Carrel; take the middle road through the rotary, and the site will be up on your left. (15min.) 3-star site with pool, tennis and mini-golf, hot showers, and mini-mart. High bushes offer some privacy in grassy sites. Reception 8am-8pm. Open Apr.-Sept. 1 or 2 people, car and tent €20.50; €4 per additional person. Electricity €1. MC/V. ❶

▐ FOOD

During the nights of the **Chorégies** (see **Entertainment,** below), the cafés on pl. aux Herbes and pl. de la République raise prices and keep concert-goers up until 3am. Many restaurants serve *pan bagna,* the traditional salad-filled sandwich of the south. For groceries, head to the **Petit Casino,** 16 rue de la République. (Open M-Sa 7:30am-12:30pm and 3:30-7:30pm.) Every Thursday an **open-air market** is held on pl. République, pl. Clemenceau, and cours A. Briand, selling everything from produce to handmade jewelry. (Open 7am-1pm). On Saturdays, there is also a *provençal* market, without food, in the same square. (Open 10am-3pm).

For an all-around pleasing, if pricey meal, head to **Le Forum ❸,** 3 rue du Mazeau. Try the delicately prepared gazpacho of cold cucumber soup or any number of *provençal* dishes. (☎ 04 90 34 01 09. *Menus* from €15. Open Tu-F and Su 12-1:30pm and 7-9:30pm, Sa 7-9:30pm. Closed parts of Feb. and Aug. MC/V.)

🔵 🎵 SIGHTS AND ENTERTAINMENT

Built in the first century, Orange's striking **Théâtre Antique** is the best-preserved Roman theater in Europe. Its 3811 sq. ft. stage wall is one of only three left in the world; Louis XIV is said to have called it the most beautiful wall in his kingdom. The theater originally held 10,000 spectators and was connected to a gymnasium complete with running tracks, combat platform, sauna, and temple. After the fall of Rome, this house of pagan entertainment fell into disrepair and became a house of peasant containment, as local homes sprung up in and around its walls. In the mid-19th century, engineers rediscovered its great acoustics and used the three remaining rows as a template for rebuilding the seating area. The best way to discover the theater for yourself is to explore its nooks and crannies; when you arrive at the ancient concession stand, the audioguide will explain in detail the various kinds of ancient Orange's *bière.* Above the theater, the overgrown park **Colline St-Eutrope** features a panoramic view and free, though acoustically poor, concert standing room amid the few ragged remnants of the Prince of Orange's castle.

Across the street from the theatre is the mildly interesting **Musée Municipal,** which exhibits many antique objects found in excavations around Orange, as well as rooms dedicated to the more recent history of the Orange family and to the fabrication of *provençal* cloth. (☎ 04 90 51 17 60 for both theater and museum. Open daily June-Aug. 9am-8pm; Apr.-May and Sept. 9am-7pm; Mar. and Oct. 9am-6pm; Jan.-Feb. and Nov.-Dec. 9am-5pm. Combined ticket €7. Students €5.50.)

Orange's other major monument, the **Arc de Triomphe,** stands on the ancient via Agrippa, which once connected Arles to Lyon. To get there, follow rue Victor Hugo north from rue St-Martin. Built during Augustus's time, the arch, dedicated to Tiberius in AD 25, is now slightly bedraggled, its stones stained and faded with time. Eight Corinthian columns adorn this three-arched monument, whose facades depict Roman victories over the Gauls on land and sea. During the Middle Ages, it was filled in to create a defensive tower, the Tour de l'Arc. A **Petit Train** visits these sites from June-Sept., embarking from near the tourist office in front of the Théâtre Antique. (☎ 04 90 37 28 68. 30min. €5, under age 10 €2.50.)

From July 6 to August 3, the **Théâtre Antique** returns to its original function with the Chorégies, a series of grand opera and choral productions. Info available from the Maison des Chorégies, 18 pl. Sylvain, next to the theater. (☎ 04 90 34 24 24; fax 04 90 11 04 04. Open June-Aug. M-Sa 10am-7pm; Feb.-May M-F 11am-1pm and 2-5pm. Tickets run €4-160; students under age 28 can buy tickets for as little as €2, and get up to 50% off on all other seats.) In August, more laid-back rock concerts, films, and variety shows take the stage. For info, call the **Service Culturel,** located next door to Maison des Chorégies, where you can also inquire about other performances, including several small arts festivals in Orange in mid-late June. (☎ 04 90 51 57 57. Open M-Th 8:30am-noon and 1:30-6pm, F 8am-noon and 1:30-4:30pm, on the nights of performances.)

NEAR ORANGE: VAISON-LA-ROMAINE

A drive through seemingly endless vineyards and past cozy hamlets brings you to Vaison-la-Romaine (pop. 6000). This once-wealthy Roman town still appeals, even if it requires a touch of imagination to conjure up lavish villas and luxurious baths amid the sprawling rubble. The dream houses of wealthy Romans were followed by a 12th-century defensive fortress and its accompanying medieval village; the

Ouvèze river now conveniently divides the cobblestoned, ivy-covered *haute ville* from the Roman excavations and the modern town. Every Tuesday the new quarter is overrun by vendors's carts piled with *provençal* crafts, honey, lavender, olives, cheese and wine. Do not linger past 4pm if you don't plan on staying in Vaison for the night—transportation to and from the town is spotty.

⚏ PRACTICAL INFORMATION. Buses run to Avignon (1¼ hr.; M-F 7:50am and 12:30pm, Sa 7:40am and 12:30pm, Su 7:40am and 4pm; €6.60) and Orange (50min., 11:25am and 4pm, €4.30). Call **Voyages Lieutard** for details (Avignon ☎04 90 86 36 75; Vaison ☎04 90 36 05 22). To reach the **tourist office**, pl. du Chanoine Sautel, from the bus station, cross the parking lot of the gas station and turn right on av. Victor Hugo to pl. Monfort. Continue past the *place* for a block and turn right onto Grande Rue. The tourist office is two blocks down on the right. (☎04 90 36 02 11; fax 04 90 28 76 04. Open July-Aug. daily 9am-12:30pm and 2-6:45pm; times vary widely the rest of the year.) Rent a **bike** at **Peugeot Motos Cycles,** 17 av. Jules Ferry. (☎04 90 36 03 29. €6.10-9.20 per day, passport deposit. Open Tu-Sa 8am-noon and 2-7pm.) The Internet-dependent will be pleased with the **Carte Cyber Café** at 30 ZA de L'Ouvèze. (☎04 90 28 97 41. €6 for 1hr., €11 for 2hr. Open M-F 9am-6:30pm, Sa 9am-noon.) Air your dirty **laundry** at 48 cours Tauligan (open daily 8am-10pm). The **police** can be reached at 04 90 36 04 17; call a **taxi** or **ambulance** at ☎04 90 36 00 04. The town's **24hr. pharmacy** changes each week, between Pharmacie Connu et Fabre, 38 Grand Rue, (☎04 90 36 00 66), Pharmacie Monfort, pl. Montfort (☎04 90 36 37 88), and Pharmacie Victor Hugo, 32 rue Victor Hugo (☎04 90 36 14 06). The **post office** is at pl. du 11 Novembre and has a **currency exchange.** (☎04 90 36 06 40. Open M-W and F 8:30am-noon and 1:30-5:15pm, Th 8:30am-noon and 1:45-5:15pm, Sa 8:30am-noon.) **Postal code:** 84110.

⚏⚏ ACCOMMODATIONS AND FOOD. Most hotels are pricey. **Hotel Burrhus ❹,** 1 pl. Montfort, has the cheapest rooms in town, and feels like a country home, with spacious wooden floors and dressers and a breezy breakfast patio. (Breakfast €6. Reception 24 hr. Closed Dec.-Jan. Singles from €38; doubles €44-69; prices a few euros higher in summer. AmEx/MC/V.) The best budget lodgings here belong to the 4-star **Camping Théâtre Romain ❶,** chemin du Brusquet, a 10min. walk from the town center. From the tourist office, take the road between the office and Puyamin. At the traffic circle, follow signs for "camping" and walk down chemin du Brusquet. Lots of shade under rows of vibrantly colorful, leafy trees. (☎04 90 28 78 66; fax 04 90 28 78 76. 74 tent sites. Bar, pool, and laundry. Reception 8am-12:30pm and 2-8pm. Open Mar. 15-Nov. 15. July-Aug. €7.10 per tent or car, €5.10 per additional person, electricity €2.60-3.60. Mar.-June and Sept.-Nov. €4.60 per tent or car, €4.50 per additional person, electricity €2.60-3.60.)

The best sources of inexpensive food are the **markets** in the town center. (Open Tu and Sa 8am-1pm.) **Super U supermarket,** is at the intersection of av. Choralies and av. Victor Hugo, right after the bus stop. (☎04 90 10 06 00. Open M-Sa 8:30am-8pm.) Most cafés and *brasseries* in Vaison have *menus* starting at around €11. A beacon in this expensive town shines in the form of **Le Vieux Port ❸,** 43 cours Tauligan, off Grande Rue. The formule *panisse* (€11.80)—mussels and fries, a pichet of wine, and creme caramel—is a popular favorite. (☎04 90 28 76 36. *Menus* €14.90-25.90. Open Tu-Sa noon-2:30pm and 7-9:45pm, Su noon-2:30pm. MC/V.)

⚏⚏ SIGHTS AND FESTIVALS. A **passport,** good for the duration of your stay, allows access to all the sites (€7, students under age 25 €3.50, ages 12-18 €3). The passport also includes tours in French (daily in summer) and English (2 per week to the Puymin site). Ask at tourist office for times. The tourist office divides the

Roman city into the **Quartier de Puymin** and the **Quartier de la Villasse,** where still-stately ruins of houses, baths, and mosaics stretch over hills carpeted with pines and cypress trees. Although few traces are left of the ancients, the excellent city guides will engagingly recreate the Roman way of life. The Puymin excavation includes a reconstruction of the **Roman theater,** which regularly hosts events in the summer and offers a beautiful view of the surrounding vineyards. Also in Puymin is the small **Musée Theo Desplans,** which houses the best-preserved sculptures, mosaics, and ceramics from the excavations. (Puymin open July-Aug. daily 9:30am-6:45pm; June and Sept. 9:30am-6:15pm; Mar.-May 10am-12:30pm and 2-6pm; Feb. and Oct. 10am-12:30pm and 2-5:30pm; Nov.-Jan. 10am-noon and 2-4:30pm. Villasse has same schedule, though closed June-Sept. 12:30-2pm. Oct.-May the museum closes 15min. earlier than the archaeological sites.)

Included in the passport is the 12th-century **cloister** near the Quartier de la Villasse. Head to the river; the cloister will be on your right. With its columns and stylized capitals perfectly intact, the gallery has become a display case for remnants of the 6th-century Merovingian church. Connected to the cloister, the eerie and yet soothingly calm 11th- to 13th-century **Cathédrale de Notre-Dame** sits on a foundation of recycled Roman columns. (Both open July-Aug. daily 9:30am-12:30pm and 2-6:45pm, June and Sept. 9:30am-12:30pm and 2-6:15pm. From Oct.-May, they follow the same schedule as the museum. Cloister €1.50 without pass.)

Across the well-preserved **Pont Romain** and up the hill is the medieval *haute ville,* where lush, flowery gardens spill over walks and wooden gates. The 12th-century **fortress** (known locally as the "château"), built under Count Raymond V of Toulouse, still fends off invaders—including you. The only way to visit is by taking one of the tourist office's tours (Apr.-Sept. only), but this may not be much fun since the ones to the old village are given in French. Even with the pass, they cost €3. The stronghold is locked up for safety reasons, but the climb will give you a great view of the town below, the wine-covered Ouvèze valley, and **Mont Ventoux's** fabled peak (1912m). The tourist office in nearby **Malaucène** organizes **night hikes** for the intrepid up to the Mont at 9pm on Fridays in July and August. (☎ 04 90 65 22 59. €8, ages 12-16 €5. Call before Friday at noon for reservations.)

In July the city puts on an impressive **festival d'été,** which brings ballet, opera, drama, and classical music to the Roman theater almost nightly. (For reservations and info, call the Service Culturel, rue Bernard Noel, at ☎ 04 90 28 74 74. English spoken. Tickets €15-38; student rates available.) Also in July and August is the short **Festival des Choeurs Lauréats,** in which professional choral groups come and perform in Vaison. (For info and reservations, call the tourist office or Centre à Coeur-Joie at ☎ 04 90 36 00 78. Tickets €15.25.) **Les Journées Gourmandes,** a celebration of the food of Provence, takes place in early November.

THE CÔTE D'AZUR

A sunny place for shady people.
—Somerset Maugham

 Between Marseille and the Italian border, the sun-drenched beaches and warm waters of the Mediterranean form the backdrop for this fabled playground of the rich and famous. Sunbathers bronze *au naturel* on pebbly beaches, high rollers drop millions in casinos, cultural types wander in abandoned coastal fortifications, and trendy youth swing until dawn in Europe's most exclusive nightclubs.

One of the most touristed parts of France, the Côte d'Azur began as a Greco-Roman commercial base. Forts, ports, and prosperous villages sprang up here around 600 BC, only to be razed by barbarian invaders toward the middle of the first millennium. The region didn't see any prolonged stability until the 16th century, when the French monarchy managed to assimilate it for good. The Riviera's resort status is a comparatively recent phenomenon. English and Russian aristocrats of the late 18th century started it all, wintering here to avoid their native countries's abominable weather. Soon Nice was drawing a steady crowd of the idle rich. In the 1920s, Coco Chanel popularized the *provençal* farmer's healthy tan among her society customers; parasols went down, hemlines went up, and the upper class's ritual sun-worship began.

Like a beautiful and unscrupulous woman, the Riviera has been the passion and the death of many a famous artist, including F. Scott Fitzgerald, Picasso and Renoir. Most towns along the eastern stretch of the Côte now lay claim to a chapel, room, or wall decorated by Matisse or Chagall. Modern celebrities sport the ultimate accessory—a vacation home in St-Tropez while high society steps out yearly for the Cannes Film Festival and the Monte-Carlo Grand Prix, both in May. Less exclusive are Nice's raucous *Carnaval* (early February) and various summer jazz festivals. Penny-pinching travelers can soak up the spectacle as well plenty of sun, sea, and crowded sand.

⬛ BEACHES

In summer, the best time to swim is from 7pm to 9pm, just before sunset. Bring a beach mat (€3.50 at supermarkets); even the sand beaches are a bit rocky. Since almost all the towns on the Côte lie along one local rail line, just hop off and on to see what you can find. The largest cities have the worst beaches: Marseille's are artificial, Nice's rocky, Cannes's private, and St-Tropez's remote. Smaller beaches between towns, like Cap Martin (between Monaco and Menton), St-Jean-Cap-Ferrat (between Monaco and Nice), and St-Raphaël-Fréjus (between Cannes and St-Tropez), are better options. Nearly all beaches are topless or top-optional, and it's seldom hard to find a private little spot if you want to go bottomless, too. Nudity is the norm at the astounding Héliopolis on the Ile du Levant (see p. 582), and in the *calanques* between Eze-sur-Mer (see p. 550) and Cap d'Ail (see p. 551). Don't neglect less-frequented islands: Porquerolles, the Ile du Levant, and the Iles des Lérins off Cannes all have fine rock ledges and secluded coves.

Many travelers used to sleep on the beaches here, but the practice seems to be dying out. Nice's beach is notoriously unsafe—don't take the risk. In some of the classier towns (Cannes, Cap d'Ail), beaches are a nighttime hangout for local drug dealers and riffraff; many respectable-looking kids earn their summer salaries in tourists's jewelry, mopeds, and cash. If you decide to bed down on the beach, choose populated, well-used beaches that attract neither thugs nor cops—St-Raphaël-Fréjus is one of the better options. In the daytime, a number of beaches provide showers, toilets, and towels for a small fee (€1.50-2.50).

1	**Nice:** Budget mecca; Anglophone party town; you *will* come here **(p. 534)**	
2	**Vence:** Ancient hilltop village near Nice with ruins and a chapel designed by Matisse **(p. 546)**	
3	▓**St-Paul:** The quintessential Côte d'Azur medieval hilltop village—art galleries, too **(p. 548)**	
4	▓**Villefranche:** Coastal jewel of a village, now more "discovered" than others **(p. 549)**	
5	**Beaulieu-sur-Mer:** Seaside resort with an amazing faux-Greek villa **(p. 549)**	
6	▓**St-Jean-Cap-Ferrat:** Serene, secluded village with a treasure-chest mansion **(p. 550)**	
7	**Eze:** Three-tiered, cliff-clinging corniche town survived Moors but fell to tourists **(p. 550)**	
8	**Cap d'Ail:** Not the best corniche village, but it has an amazing waterfront villa hostel **(p. 551)**	
9	**Monaco and Monte-Carlo:** Mini-state oozes money; the place to gamble yours away **(p. 552)**	
10	**Menton:** Genuine Riviera charm—no glitz, flash, or noise; draws seniors, Cocteau fans **(p. 557)**	
11	▓**Antibes:** Exclusive town with room for all; sandy beaches, superior Picasso museum **(p. 560)**	
12	▓**Juan-les-Pins:** Young and hedonistic—your best bet for late-night action **(p. 563)**	
13	**Cannes:** World-famous film festival in an accessible (but still expensive) glam-town **(p. 564)**	
14	▓**Iles de Lérins:** Respite from the city; lush pine forests and an active monastery **(p. 570)**	
15	**Mougins:** Village turned affluent suburb; boutiques and expensive cafés **(p. 570)**	
16	▓**Grasse:** Where perfume comes from. No, really. The *air* smells! **(p. 571)**	
17	▓**Canyon du Verdon:** Deep hikeable canyon channels whitewater to immense lake **(p. 572)**	
18	**Castellane:** Out of the way, but best base for Canyon visits and adventure sporting **(p. 573)**	
19	**St-Raphaël:** Beach-town base for visits to St-Tropez; no class, but no affectation either **(p. 575)**	
20	**Fréjus:** 20min. from beaches; has a Roman amphitheater and a Vietnamese pagoda **(p. 576)**	
21	▓**St-Tropez:** Ultimate Riviera—sun, sex, and celebrities; golf tournaments, regattas **(p. 578)**	
22	**Iles d'Hyères:** Exotic golden landscape flecked with exotic golden nude bathers **(p. 582)**	

NICE

Sun-drenched and sizzling, Nice (pop. 380,000) is the unofficial capital of the Riviera. This former vacation haunt of dukes and czarinas continues to seduce tourists with its non-stop nightlife, extreme shopping, and first-rate museums. No matter the season, the old town's maze of pedestrian streets fills with colorful markets by day and lively bar-goers by night. With excellent transportation and budget lodgings, the 5th-largest city in France serves as an inexpensive base for sampling the Côte d'Azur's pricier delights. Prepare to make new friends, hear more English than French, and have more fun than you'll be able to remember—literally.

✈ INTERCITY TRANSPORTATION

Flights: Aéroport Nice-Côte d'Azur (☎08 20 42 33 33). **Air France,** 10 av. Félix-Faure (☎08 20 82 08 20). Open M-Sa 9am-6pm. Sunbus #23 goes to the airport from the train station (☎04 93 13 53 13, every 15min., 6am-8:30pm, €1.30). The pricier **ANT** airport bus runs from the bus station (☎04 93 21 30 83; M-Sa every 20min., Su every 30min.; €3.50). Outbound flights to **Bastia** in **Corsica** (€93.14; under 25, over 60, and couples €64.15) and **Paris** (€283.15; under 25, 60+, and couples €40.15). **EasyJet** flies to **London** (see **Budget Airlines,** p. 64).

Trains: There are two primary train stations in town:

    Gare SNCF Nice-Ville, av. Thiers (☎04 92 14 81 62). To: **Cannes** (45min., every 15-45min., €5); **Marseille** (2½hr., every 30-90min., €24); **Monaco** (15min., every 10-30min., €2.90); **Paris** (5½hr., 6 per day, €75.30-91). Open daily 5am-12:15am.

    Gare du Sud, 4bis rue Alfred Binet (☎04 93 82 10 17), 800m from Nice-Ville. Private outbound trains to **Plan-du-Var** and **Digne-les-Bains.**

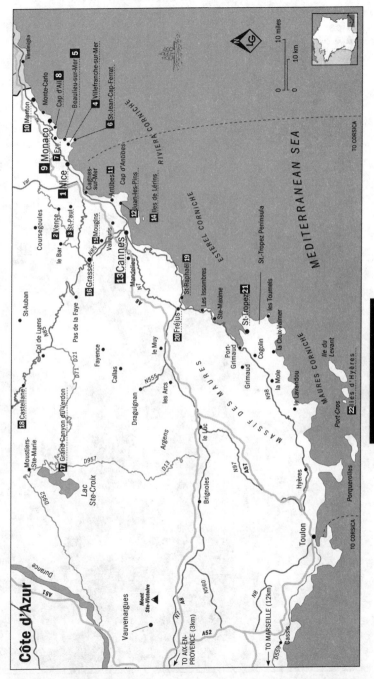

Côte d'Azur

C Ô T E   D ' A Z U R

MEDITERRANEAN SEA

RIVIERA CORNICHE

ESTEREL CORNICHE

MAURES CORNICHE

MASSIF DES MAURES

10 Menton
9 Monaco
8 Cap d'Ail
5 Beaulieu-sur-Mer
Monte-Carlo
Villefranche-sur-Mer
4 Villefranche-sur-Mer
6 St-Jean-Cap-Ferrat
7 Èze
1 Nice
11 Cagnes-sur-Mer
2 Vence
3 St-Paul
15 Mougins
Vallauris
16 Grasse
13 Cannes
Mandelieu
19 St-Raphaël
20 Fréjus
12 Juan-les-Pins
14 Îles de Lérins
Cap d'Antibes
Antibes
Cannes
Les Issambres
Ste-Maxime
21 St-Tropez
St-Tropez Peninsula
les Tournels
la Croix-Valmer
Port-Grimaud
Grimaud
Cogolin
la Môle
le Lavandou
Port-Cros
22 Îles d'Hyères
Île du Levant
Île de Porquerolles

TO CORSICA
TO CORSICA

18 Castellane
17 Grand-Canyon du Verdon
Moustiers-Ste-Marie
Lac Ste-Croix
St-Auban
Col de Luens
Pas de la Faye
Fayence
Callas
le Bar
Coursegoules
Vauvenargues
Mont Ste-Victoire
Draguignan
les Arcs
le Muy
le Luc
Brignoles
Hyères
Toulon
Cassis

TO AIX-EN-PROVENCE (3km)
TO MARSEILLE (12km)

10 miles
10 km

Var
Durance

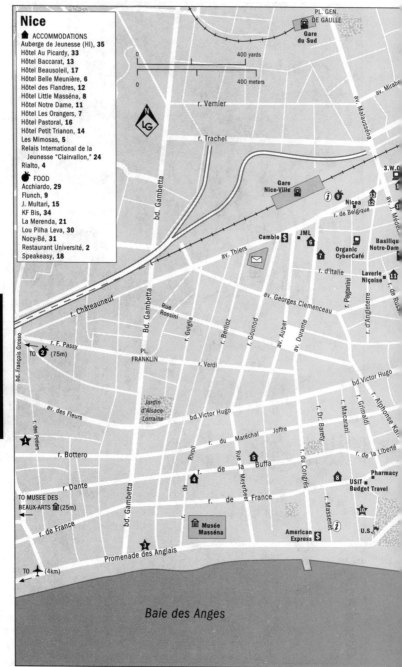

Nice

ACCOMMODATIONS
Auberge de Jeunesse (HI), **35**
Hôtel Au Picardy, **33**
Hôtel Baccarat, **13**
Hôtel Beausoleil, **17**
Hôtel Belle Meunière, **6**
Hôtel des Flandres, **12**
Hôtel Little Masséna, **8**
Hôtel Notre Dame, **11**
Hôtel Les Orangers, **7**
Hôtel Pastoral, **16**
Hôtel Petit Trianon, **14**
Les Mimosas, **5**
Relais International de la
  Jeunesse "Clairvallon," **24**
Rialto, **4**

FOOD
Acchiardo, **29**
Flunch, **9**
J. Multari, **15**
KF Bis, **34**
La Merenda, **21**
Lou Pilha Leva, **30**
Nocy-Bé, **31**
Restaurant Université, **2**
Speakeasy, **18**

COTE D'AZUR

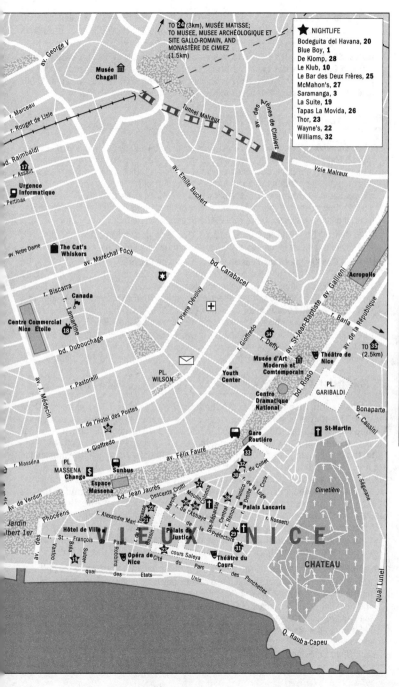

TO 24 (3km), MUSÉE MATISSE;
TO MUSÉE, MUSÉE ARCHÉOLOGIQUE ET
SITE GALLO-ROMAIN, AND
MONASTÈRE DE CIMIEZ
(1.5km)

★ NIGHTLIFE
Bodeguita del Havana, 20
Blue Boy, 1
De Klomp, 28
Le Klub, 10
Le Bar des Deux Frères, 25
McMahon's, 27
Saramanga, 3
La Suite, 19
Tapas La Movida, 26
Thor, 23
Wayne's, 22
Williams, 32

av. George V

r. Marceau

r. Rouget de Lisle

Musée
Chagall

Tunnel Malraux

av. des Arènes de Cimiez

Voie Malraux

bd. Raimbaldi

r. Assalit

17

Urgence
Informatique
Pertinax

av. Emile Buchert

av. Emile Bieckert

The Cat's
Whiskers

av. Notre Dame

av. Maréchal Foch

bd. Carabacel

Acropolis

r. Biscarra

Lamartine

Canada

r. Pierre Dévoluy

r. Gioffredo

r. Defly

av. St-Jean-Baptiste av. Galliéni

r. Barla

av. de la République

Centre Commercial
Nice Etoile

18

bd. Dubouchage

PL.
WILSON

Youth
Center

Musée d'Art
Moderne et
Comtemporain

34

Théâtre de
Nice

TO 35
(2.5km)

r. J. Médecin

r. Pastorelli

Centre
Dramatique
National

bd. Risso

PL.
GARIBALDI

Bonaparte
r. Cassini

r. de l'Hotel des Postes

r. Gioffredo

20

Gare
Routière

St-Martin

r. Masséna

PL.
MASSENA
Change

Sunbus

av. Félix Fauré

33

r. du Collet

r. Séguranne

Espace
Massena

bd. Jean Jaurès

30

r. de la Loge

Cimetière

Av. de Verdun

Phocéens

Descente Crotti

27

Droite

Bunico

Marché Crotti

26

r. Alexandre Mari

Moulin

Jourua

Ste-Réparate

Palais Lascaris

Jardin
Albert 1er

Hôtel de Ville

r. St-François

r. Droite

Centrale

r. Benoît

r. Rossetti

21

r. de l'Abbaye

r. de
la Préfecture

Palais de
Justice

29

Sulter

Robbins

Paule

Opéra de
Nice

Théâtre du
Cours

31

VIEUX NICE

CHATEAU

Vanloo

r. St- Béa

cours Saleya

r. du Parc

r. des Ponchettes

quai des Etats

Unis

quai Lunel

Q. Rauba-Capeu

19

COTE D'AZUR

Buses: 5 bd. Jean Jaurès (☎ 04 93 85 61 81), left at the end of av. Jean Médecin. Info booth open M-Sa 8am-6:30pm. If booth is closed, buy tickets on the bus. To **Cannes** (1½hr., 3 per hr., €6) and **Monaco** (40min., 4 per hr., €3.50).

Ferries: SNCM (☎ 04 93 13 66 66; reservations ☎ 04 93 13 66 99; fax 04 93 13 66 89) and **Corsica Ferries** (☎ 04 92 00 42 94; fax 04 92 00 43 93) operate out of the port. Take bus #1 or 2 (dir: "Port"). Service to **Corsica** (€35-45; under 25 €20-30; bikes €14; small cars €45). See **Corsica:** p. 584, for more info.

▐▬ LOCAL TRANSPORTATION

Public Transportation: Sunbus, 10 av. Félix Faure (☎ 04 93 13 53 13), near pl. Leclerc and pl. Masséna. Info booth open M-F 7:15am-7pm, Sa 7:15am-6pm. Buses generally operate daily 7am-8pm, but schedules vary; the tourist office provides the **"Sunplan"** bus map and the **"Guide Infobus."** Individual tickets run €1.30, but worthwhile passes are available (day pass €4, 5-day pass €13, weeklong pass €16.80, 8-ticket *carnet* €8.30). Buy passes at info or on board. **Noctambus,** aptly named, operates 4 routes when the sun goes down, daily 9pm-2:40am. Inquire at the tourist office for info.

Taxis: Central Taxi Riviera (☎ 04 93 13 78 78). Get a price range before boarding and make sure the meter is turned on. To airport from train station costs €24.40.

Bike and Car Rental: Nicea Location Rent, 12 rue de Belgique (☎ 04 93 82 42 71; fax 04 93 87 76 36), around the corner from the station. Scooter €49.50 per day, €167 per week; deposit from €600. Also rents bikes, in-line skates, and motorcycles. 5-10% discount for students, 10% if you reserve by e-mail. Open Dec.-Sept. daily 9am-6pm. AmEx/MC/V. **JML Location,** 34 av. Auber (☎ 04 93 16 07 00; fax 04 93 16 07 48), opposite the station. Bikes €11 per day, €42 per week. Scooters €37 per day, €196 per week. €228 credit card deposit for bikes, €914 for scooters. Cars €45 per day, €0.12 each km over 200. Minimum age 23. Open June-Sept. daily 8am-6:30pm; Oct.-May M-F 8am-1pm and 2-6:30pm, Sa 8am-1pm, Su 9am-1pm and 4-6:30pm.

◪ ▱ ORIENTATION AND PRACTICAL INFORMATION

The train station, **Nice-Ville,** is next to the tourist office on **av. Thiers** in the north of the city. The station is surrounded by cheap restaurants, budget hotels, and triple-X video stores. Exiting the station, to the left is **av. Jean Médecin,** a main artery that meets the water at **place Masséna.** (10min.) Heading right, you'll run into **bd. Gambetta,** the other main water-bound thoroughfare. Hugging the coast, the **promenade des Anglais** (which becomes **quai des États-Unis** east of av. Jean Médecin) is a people-watcher's paradise, as are the cafés, boutiques, and overpriced restaurants west of bd. Jean-Medecin in the **rue Masséna** pedestrian zone. Below and to the left of Jean Médecin lies the pulsating **Vieux Nice.** Continuing in this direction past the old city, you'll discover **Port Lympia,** a warren of alleyways, *brasseries*, and tabacs.

Unfortunately, Nice's big-city appeal comes hand-in-hand with big-city crime. Women should avoid walking alone at night. Everyone should **exercise caution** around the train station, in Vieux Nice, and on the Promenade des Anglais.

Tourist Office: av. Thiers (☎ 08 92 70 74 07; fax 04 93 16 85 16; www.nicetourism.com), beside the train station. Makes same-day reservations for hotels in Nice. Ask for the English-language *Nice: A Practical Guide* and a map (essential in Vieux Nice). The *Semaine des Spectacles* (€1 at tabacs), published every Wednesday, lists entertainment for the entire Côte. Open June-Sept. M-Sa 8am-8pm, Su 9am-7pm; Oct.-May M-Sa 8am-7pm. **Branches:** 5 prom. des Anglais (fax/☎ 04 92 14 48 03); same hours as above, but closed on Su Oct.-May. Also at airport terminal 1 (☎/fax 04 93 21 44 50). Open June-Sept. daily 8am-10pm; Oct.-May closed Su.

Budget Travel Offices: USIT, 15 rue de la France (☎04 93 87 34 96; fax 04 93 87 10 91), near pl. Masséna. Books cheap international flights and bus and train trips within France, and arranges excursions and camping trips. Open M-Sa 9:30am-6:30pm.

Consulates: Canada, 10 rue Lamartine (☎04 93 92 93 22). Open M-F 9am-noon. **UK,** 26 av. Notre Dame (☎04 93 62 13 56). Open M, W, and F 9:30-11:30am. **US,** 7 av. Gustave V (☎04 93 88 89 55; fax 04 93 87 07 38). Open M-F 9-11:30am and 1:30-4:30pm.

Currency Exchange: Cambio, 17 av. Thiers (☎04 93 88 56 80), opposite the train station. 5% commission on Euro traveler's checks. Open daily 7am-9pm. **Change,** 10 av. Félix Faure (☎04 93 80 36 67). Open M-Sa 9:30am-12:30pm and 2-5:30pm. **American Express,** 11 prom. des Anglais (☎04 93 16 53 53; fax 04 93 16 51 67), at the corner of rue des Congrès. Open daily 9am-8:30pm.

English Bookstore: The Cat's Whiskers, 30 rue Lamartine (☎04 93 80 02 66). Great selection, from bestsellers to cookbooks. Open July-Aug. M-Sa 10:30am-12:30pm and 3:30-7pm; Sept.-June M-F 9:30am-noon and 2-6:45pm, Sa 9:30am-noon and 3-6:30pm. Sometimes closed M morning. AmEx/MC/V.

Youth Center: Centre d'Information Jeunesse, 19 rue Gioffredo (☎04 93 80 93 93; fax 04 92 47 86 79; www.crij.org/nice), near the Museum of Contemporary Art. Helps with long-term stays, job hunts, excursions, culture, and nightlife. Posts student summer jobs. Most useful if you speak some French. Open M-F 10am-7pm, Sa 10am-5pm.

Laundromat: Laverie Niçoise, 7 rue d'Italie (☎04 93 87 56 50), beside the Basilique Notre-Dame. Open M-Sa 8:30am-12:30pm and 2:30-7:30pm.

Police: 1 av. Maréchal Foch (☎04 92 17 22 22). At the opposite end of bd. M. Foch from bd. Jean Médecin.

Hospital: St-Roch, 5 rue Pierre Devoluy (☎04 92 03 33 75).

24 hr. Pharmacy: 7 rue Masséna (☎04 93 87 78 94; open daily 7:30pm-8:30am); 66 av. Jean Médecin (☎04 93 62 52 44).

Internet Access: Organic CyberCafé, 16 rue Paganini (☎04 93 16 97 82); the sign on the door says "CyberCafé Bio." Drink organic coffees while you type. €1.60 per 15min., €2.60 per 30min., €4.50 per hr. Mention *Let's Go* for these prices. Open daily 9am-9pm. Nearby **3.W.O.,** 32 rue Assalit (☎04 93 80 51 12), boasts 12 computers with American keyboards. €2 per 15min., €3 per 30min., €5 per hr. Open daily 10am-8pm. Around the corner, **Urgence Informatique,** 26 rue Pertinax (☎04 93 62 07 60) offers friendly service and late summer hours. €2 per 15min., €3 per 30min., €5 per hr. Open M-Sa 9am-9pm and until midnight in July and Aug.

Post Office: 21 av. Thiers (☎04 93 82 65 22; fax 04 93 88 78 46), near the station. Open M-F 8am-7pm, Sa 8am-noon. **Postal code:** 06033 Nice Cédex 1.

ACCOMMODATIONS

Nice's hostels are remote and busy. Call three to five days in advance. The city has two clusters of budget hotels. Those by the train station are new but badly located; those closer to Vieux Nice and the beach are well situated but tend to be less modern. The hostels are often full; call three to five days in advance and reserve at least two to three weeks ahead in the summer.

HOSTELS

Relais International de la Jeunesse "Clairvallon," 26 av. Scudéri (☎04 93 81 27 63; fax 04 93 53 35 88; clajpaca@cote-dazur.com), in Cimiez, 4km out of town. Take bus #15 to "Scudéri" (dir: Rimiez; 20min., every 10min.) from the train station or pl. Masséna; after 9pm, take the N2 bus from pl. Masséna. Get off the bus, turn right, head

COTE D'AZUR

uphill, and take the first left. To walk from the station, turn left and left again on av. Jean Médecin, then right before the overpass on bd. Raimbaldi. Go 6 blocks and turn right on av. Comboul, then left on bd. Carabacel. Follow it up the hill as it becomes bd. de Cimiez. Turn right before the hospital onto av. de Flirey, and keep trudging uphill until you reach av. Scudéri. Turn left and follow the signs. (30min.) You and 150 new friends will enjoy a mini-football field, lovely dining room, garden with fountain, swimming pool (open 5-7pm), and TV access in the luxurious villa of a deceased marquis. 4- to 10-bed rooms. Breakfast included. 5-course dinner €8.50. Laundry €4, dryer €2. Check-in 5pm. Lockout 9:30am-5pm. Curfew 11pm. No reservations. Dorms €13. ●

Auberge de Jeunesse (HI), rte. Forestière du Mont-Alban (☎04 93 89 23 64; fax 04 92 04 03 10), 4km from it all. From the bus station, take #14 (dir: Mont Boron) to "l'Auberge" (every 30-45min.; last bus 7:50pm). From the train station, take #17 and switch to #14. By foot, from the train station, turn left and then right on av. Jean Médecin. Follow it through pl. Masséna and turn left on bd. Jaurès. Turn right on rue Barla, following the signs up the hill. (50min.) Ultra-clean hostel draws a cool, friendly crowd. 6- to 10-bed dorms. Kitchen. Lockers in dorms. Internet with phone card. Breakfast included. Sheets €2.70. Laundry €6. Lockout 10am-5pm. Curfew 12:30am. Dorms €13.40. ●

NEAR THE TRAIN STATION

🖼 **Hôtel Belle Meunière,** 21 av. Durante (☎04 93 88 66 15; fax 04 93 82 51 76), directly across from the train station. Birds chirp in the courtyard of this converted mansion and backpackers become friends over free breakfast and nighttime imbibing. 4- to 5-bed co-ed dorms. Showers €2. Luggage storage €2. Laundry €5.50-9.50. Reception 7:30am-midnight, access code after hours. €13 per person, with shower and toilet €18; doubles with shower €45.50; triples €40.50, with shower and toilet €54. MC/V. ●

🖼 **Hôtel Pastoral,** 27 rue Assalit (☎04 93 85 17 22), on the far side of av. Jean Médecin near the train station. Elegant furniture, spacious hardwood rooms, and a caring owner create a comfortable atmosphere. Breakfast €4. Free luggage storage. Singles €20; doubles €25, with shower and toilet €30; triples and quads €12.50 per person. ❷

Hôtel Les Orangers, 10bis av. Durante (☎04 93 87 51 41; fax 04 93 82 57 82), across from the station. Beautiful exterior, bright and airy co-ed dorms with close-packed beds, showers, and fridges (hot plate on request). Friendly English-speaking owner loans beach mats and stores luggage for free. Reserve long ahead for singles. Closed Nov. Dorms €14, singles €16-25, doubles €36-38, triples €46-48, quads €60. MC/V. ●

Hôtel des Flandres, 6 rue de Belgique (☎04 93 88 78 94; fax 04 93 88 74 90), 100m from the train station and 800m from the beach. With an imposing entrance, large rooms with shower, and high ceilings, this hotel appears more expensive than its prices. Friendly owner. Breakfast €5. Reception 24hr. Singles €35-45; doubles €45-51; triples €60; quads €67. Extra bed €12. MC/V. ❹

Hôtel Beausoleil, 22 rue Assalit (☎04 93 85 18 54; fax 04 93 62 49 14; www.beausoleil-hotel.com), a 5min. walk from the train station. Specializes in pastels—pink doors, gray floral sheets, blue and white walls—as well as providing attentive service and a modicum of luxury to the budget traveler. Spacious rooms come with A/C, shower, toilet, TV, telephone, and sound-proofed walls. Breakfast €5. Reception 24hr. Singles €46-53; doubles €61-70; triples €73-81. July-Aug. prices €10 higher. AmEx/MC/V. ❹

Hôtel Baccarat, 39 rue d'Angleterre (☎04 93 88 35 73; fax 04 93 16 14 25; www.hotel-baccarat.com), 2nd left off rue de Belgique. Large rooms with floral bedspreads, pastel trimmings, and clashing furniture. Secure atmosphere. All rooms with shower and toilet. 3- to 5-person dorms. Free beach mat loan. Breakfast €3.80. Reception 24hr. Dorms €14; singles €29; doubles €36; triples €44; quads €66. MC/V. ●

Hôtel Notre Dame, 22 rue de Russie (☎04 93 88 70 44; fax 04 93 82 20 38; jyung@caramail.com), at the corner of rue d'Italie, 1 block west of av. Jean Médecin. Friendly owners rent fresh-scented rooms in Grecian white and blue and protect guests with an intimidating dog. Breakfast €4. Free luggage storage. Reception 24hr. Singles €31; doubles €42; triples €54; quads €67. Extra bed €9.15. MC/V. ❸

NEAR VIEUX NICE AND THE BEACH

Hôtel Petit Trianon, 11 rue Paradis (☎04 93 87 50 46), left off pedestrian rue Masséna. A budget oasis in a pricey part of town. Elegant chandeliers, tasteful wallpaper, pastels, and firm beds create a soothing rooming experience. Friendly and helpful new owner. Reservations essential (10 rooms available). Free beach towel loan. Singles €15.25; doubles €31, with shower and toilet €39; triples €50, with shower and toilet €55; quad with shower and toilet €65. Extra bed €8. MC/V. ❶

Hôtel Little Masséna, 22 rue Masséna (☎/fax 04 93 87 72 34). Small, worn, and clean rooms with TV and kitchenette in a boisterous and touristy part of town. Owners are young and friendly. Breakfast €4.50. Reception daily 8am-noon and 2-9pm. Singles and doubles €28, with shower €38, with shower and toilet €48. Extra person €6.10. Oct.-May prices €2-5 lower. MC/V. ❸

Hôtel Au Picardy, 10 bd. Jean Jaurès (☎/fax 04 93 85 75 51), across from the bus station. Ideally located near Vieux Nice. An apparent fascination with brown paint and a lack of natural light keep the rooms dark. Street-side chambers can be noisy, but the windows are soundproofed. You'll want to go straight to sleep—fortunately, the beds are firm. Breakfast €3. Showers €1.50. Singles €19, with shower €28; doubles €24-27, with shower and toilet €33; triples €34-38; quads €38-48. Extra bed €5. ❷

Les Mimosas, 26 rue de la Buffa (☎04 93 88 05 59; fax 04 93 87 15 65). Near the beach and lively rue Masséna. An impressive staircase leads to small but newly renovated, air-conditioned rooms that fill up quickly with backpackers in the summer. Laid-back owner places bows on doors and soap on beds. 1 apartment for longer stays; inquire for details. Free coffee, beach towel loan. Singles €30.50; doubles €37-45.75; triples €45.75-53.35; quads €53.75-64. Oct.-Mar. prices €5 lower. MC/V. ❸

Rialto, 55 rue de la Buffa (☎/fax 04 93 88 15 04). A little farther from the big show. More apartment than hotel. 8 bright and spacious rooms boast baths and sizeable kitchens. Doubles €45; triples €57; quads €72; 6-8 person studios €84-102. ❹

◪ FOOD

Nice is, above all, a city of restaurants, from four-star establishments to pungent holes-in-the-wall. *Pâtisseries* and bakeries sell inexpensive local specialties flavored with North African spices, herbs, or olives. Try the round, crusty *pan bagnat* with tuna, sardines, and vegetables; *pissaladière* pizza topped with onions, anchovies, and olives; *socca,* thin, olive oil-flavored chickpea bread; and *bouilla-baisse,* a hearty stew of mussels, potatoes, and fish. The famous *salade niçoise* combines tuna, potatoes, tomatoes, and a spicy mustard dressing.

Cafés and food stands along the beach are expensive. The fruit, fish, and flower **market** at cours Saleya is a good place to pick up fresh olives, cheeses, and melons (T-Su 6am-1:30pm). A fruit and vegetable **market** also appears daily on av. Maché de la Libération. (T-Su 6am-12:30pm.) Dozens of cheap Chinese and Indian joints surround the train station. Expensive gourmet establishments lines rue Masséna; a €9.15 pizza is the cheapest food you'll get. Av. Jean Médecin features reasonable *brasseries* and *panini* vendors. Vieux Nice hides gems as well as tourist traps. The generic but cheap **Flunch ❶,** av. Thiers, next to the train station, caters to tight budgets and easy-to-please taste buds. A main dish, dessert, drink, and surprise

gift costs only €3.95. (☎04 93 88 41 35. Open daily 7:30am-10:30am, 11am-9:15pm.)
Retain some semblance of literacy at **Restaurant Université ❶**, 3 av. Robert Schumann, which serves students filling meals for €5, with student ID €3. (☎04 93 97
10 20. Open Sept.-June daily 11:30am-1:30pm.)

▨ **Lou Pilha Leva,** 13 rue du Collet (☎04 93 13 99 08) in Vieux Nice. Tourists and locals
pack the outdoor wooden benches of this favorite. Tasty local food at acceptable prices.
Pizza slice €3; socca €2; pissaladière €2; moules €5. Open daily 8am-11pm. ❶

▨ **La Merenda,** 4 rue de la Terrasse. Those lucky enough to get a table can savor the work
of a culinary master who turned his back on a 4-star hotel to open this 12-table gem.
Nothing about the menu is constant, except its exotic flair—stuffed sardines, fried zuc-
chini flowers, oxtail, tripe, and veal head. Reserve in person. Amazing value, all things
considered. Menu €7-12. Open M-F noon-1:30pm and 7-9:30pm. ❷

Speakeasy, 7 rue Lamartine (☎04 93 85 59 50). Alas, there's no illicit liquor here. But
there are delectable and affordable vegetarian and vegan lunch options, prepared by
an American chef/animal-rights activist in a cozy, intimate setting. Organic bean pat-
ties, couscous, and daily specialties satisfy even the staunchest carnivores, and convert
some along the way. €10 for 2 courses. Open M-Sa noon-2:15pm. ❸

Acchiardo, 38 rue Droite (☎04 93 85 51 16), in Vieux Nice. Simple but appetizing Italian and French dishes served amidst a farm scene complete with hanging corn husks,
grape vines, and bronze pans. Pastas (€6) and classic French meats (house escallop
specialty €11.50) are popular with a local clientele loyal to the family-run business.
Open M-F noon-1:30pm and 7-10pm. No credit cards. ❶

J.Multari, 58bis av. Jean Médecin (☎04 93 92 01 99). This graceful salon de thé, bakery and sandwich shop serves excellent reasonably priced fare. Try a goat cheese,
chicken, or ham sandwich on fresh baguette (€3.10), salad (€3), pizza (€1.45), or a
mouth-watering pastry (€1-2). 4 other locations in Nice: 2 rue Alphonse Karr (☎04 93
87 45 90), 22 rue Gioffredo (☎04 93 80 00 31), 8 bd. Jean Jaurès (☎04 93 62 10
39), and 13 cours Saleya (☎04 93 62 31 33). Open M-Sa 6am-8:30pm. ❶

Nocy-Bé, 4-6 rue Jules Gilly (☎04 93 85 52 25). Chill out at this mellow tearoom,
adorned with low-hanging lamps and comfortable floor rugs. Choose from 45 teas
(€2.29-3.80) or relax to the max with a narguilé (water pipe) with one of 14 fruit fragrances (€7.60). Open daily 4pm-12:30am; July-Sept. daily 5pm-12:30am. ❷

KF Bis, 8 rue Delfy (☎04 93 80 02 22), the neighbor of the Musée d'Art Moderne, is
local and chic. Low lighting, sisel carpet, enormous wine glasses, and copies of Warhol's Monroe foster a feel of cool sophistication. You won't be disappointed by the
salmon, corn, and blini salads (€9), the many croques and tartines (€8.50), and main
dishes such as beef in a tomato, aubergine, and mozzarella fondue (€10-13). Good
wine selection (€15.50-28). Open June-Aug. Tu-F 11:30am-3pm and 5:30-11:30pm,
Sa-Su 5:30-11:30pm; Sept.-May Tu-Su 11:30am-3pm and 5:30-11:30pm. AmEx/V. ❸

◉ SIGHTS

Many visitors stay at the beaches from sundown to sunset (or later). Contrary to
popular opinion, however, there are activities in Nice aside from naked sunbathing. Nice's scattered museums are impressive, and they'll keep your clothes on.
Trust us, that's in all of our best interests.

▨ **MUSÉE NATIONAL MESSAGE BIBLIQUE MARC CHAGALL.** Chagall founded
this extraordinary concrete and glass museum in 1966 to showcase his 17 Message
Biblique paintings. These huge, colorful canvases are complemented by a cursory
photobiography of Chagall, a wonderful garden, and a small stained-glass-encir-
cled auditorium decorated by the artist himself. (Av. du Dr. Ménard. 15min. walk north of

the station or take bus #15 (dir: "Rimiez") to "Musée Chagall." ☎ 04 93 53 87 20. Open July-Sept. W-M 10am-6pm; Oct.-June W-M 10am-5pm. Last tickets sold 30min. before closing. €5.50, under age 26 and Su €4, under 18 free.)

■ **MUSÉE MATISSE.** No one contributed more to Nice's fame than Henri Matisse. Upon his first visit to the city in 1916, the artist decided to live and work there until his death. Originally a 17th-century Genoese villa, the museum contains a disappointingly small collection of paintings, but a dazzling exhibit of Matisse's three-dimensional work, including bronze reliefs and dozens of cut-and-paste tableaux. (164 av. des Arènes de Cimiez. Take bus #15, 17, 20, 22, or 25 to "Arènes." ☎ 04 93 81 08 08. Open Apr.-Sept. W-M 10am-6pm; Oct.-Mar. W-M 10am-5pm. €3.80, students €2.30. Call for info on lectures.)

MUSÉE D'ART MODERNE ET D'ART CONTEMPORAIN. In the vein of modern art museums, this one is all concrete, glass, steel, and marble. The minimalist galleries showcase European and American avant garde pieces from the last four decades. French New Realists and American Pop Artists, like Lichtenstein, Warhol, and Klein are emphasized. (Prom. des Arts, at the intersection of av. St-Jean Baptiste and Traverse Garibaldi. Take bus #5 (dir: St-Charles) to "Musée-Promenade des Arts." The museum is behind the bus station. ☎ 04 93 62 61 62. Open W-M 10am-6pm. €3.80, students €2.30.) Across from the museum sits another example of modern architecture, the conspicuous gold eyesore known as the **Acropolis.** Nothing like the Athenian version, it looks like it was meant for the set of Star Trek. It now serves as conference center, office space, and auditorium.

■ **VIEUX NICE.** Sprawling southeast from bd. Jean Jaurès, this quarter is the colorful center of Nice's nightlife. Tiny pansy-filled balconies, fountains, public squares, hand-painted awnings, and pristine churches crowd Vieux Nice's labyrinthine streets. In the morning, the charming area hosts some bustling **markets,** including a fish frenzy at **Place St-François** and a flower market on **Cours Salaya.** In the evening, knick-knack stands supplement the cafés and restaurants. (Fish frenzy Tu-Su 6am-1pm; flower market Su 6am-noon, Tu-Sa 6am-5:30pm, W and Sa 6am-6:30pm.)

CATHÉDRALE ORTHODOXE RUSSE ST-NICOLAS. Also known as the **Eglise Russe,** this cathedral—the first christened outside of Russia—was commissioned by Empress Marie Feodorovna, widow of Tsar Nicholas I. Modeled after St-Basil's in Moscow, the onion-domed structure quickly became a spiritual home for exiled Russian nobles. In contrast to French cathedrals, the altar is hidden behind a gilded screen. There's one hint that the cathedral is influenced by the Riviera: its dominant colors are Mediterranean light blue and yellow rather than dark and somber blues and grays. (17 bd. du Tsarevitch, off bd. Gambetta. ☎ 04 93 96 88 02. Open June-Aug. daily 9am-noon and 2:30-6pm; Sept.-May daily 9:30am-noon and 2:30-5pm. €1.80.)

LE CHÂTEAU. At the eastern end of the promenade, Le Château—that is to say, the remains of an 11th-century cathedral—sits in a pleasant green hillside park crowned with an artificial waterfall. Don't be fooled: there hasn't been a château here since an (apparently unsuccessful) 8th-century battle. The top does, however, give a spectacular view of the rooftops of Nice and the sparkling Baie des Anges. The vista can be reached by climbing 400 steps or catching an elevator at the Tour Bellanda. (Park open daily 7am-8pm. Elevator runs 9am-7:30pm. €1.)

MUSÉE DES BEAUX-ARTS. The former villa of Ukraine's Princess Kotschoubey has been converted into a celebration of French academic painting and Van Dongen and Raoul Dufy. Dufy, Nice's second greatest painter, celebrated the spontaneity of his city with sensational pictures of the town at rest and play. (33 av. Baumettes. Take bus #38 to "Chéret" or #12 to "Grosso." ☎ 04 92 15 28 28. Open Tu-Su 10am-noon and 2-6pm. €3.80, students €2.30.)

ONE EARL GREY AND ONE HOOKAH, PLEASE

Though it resembles and could be used as a bong, the *narguilé*, or water pipe, can be legally used to inhale a wide variety of nicotine-enhanced fruit fragrances. The popularity of the *narguilé* is surging in France; a burst of water-pipe-oriented bars have recently opened in Paris, Lyon, Marseilles, and Nice. Scholars debate the origin of the pipe, supporting alternate theories of a South African, Ethiopian, Persian, or European origin. The 400-year-old hookah has hit a mass audience with the rise of tobacco use and public coffee houses. With a smoke cooling and purification system, the pipe can reach 2m in length.

The water pipe has fascinated numerous literary figures, including Lewis Carroll and France's own Honoré de Balzac. Alice gazed in awe at the large blue caterpillar smoking a hookah in her *Adventures in Wonderland* as the caterpillar recited hallucinogenic poetry. Balzac was no less intrigued by the water pipe's potential for literary inspiration. He once wrote, "The hookah, like the *narguilé*, is an elegant instrument; it creates bizarre and disturbing visions which give its user a sort of aristocratic superiority."

Strange visions AND social climbing—who knew the water pipe could be so multipurposed? So if you walk into a *narguilé* bar in Nice, don't think you took a wrong turn into an opium den. Today's addiction is just as exotic, but far less harmful, using a special tobacco that doesn't contain tar.

MONASTÈRE DE CIMIEZ. This monastery has housed Nice's Franciscans since the 13th century, and a few still call it home. Their former living quarters are now the **Musée Franciscain**, which exhibits illuminated manuscripts, medieval crosses, and a Giotto painting of St. Francis. The complex also includes a church, lovely surrounding gardens, and a large cemetery where Matisse and Dufy are buried. *(Pl. du Monastère. Take bus #15 (dir: "Rimiez") or #17 (dir: "Cimiez") to "Monastère" from the station, or follow the signs and walk from the Musée Matisse. ☎04 93 81 55 41. Museum open M-Sa 10am-noon and 3-6pm. Church open daily 8:30am-12:30pm and 2:30-6:30pm. Gardens open summer 8am-7pm, winter 8am-6pm. Cemetery open daily 8am-6pm. Free.)*

MUSÉE ARCHÉOLOGIQUE ET SITE GALLO-ROMAIN. Adjacent to the site of ancient Gallo-Roman baths, this museum displays artifacts discovered in the Côte from the Bronze through the Middle Ages, including excavated coins, jewelry, and sarcophagi. *(160 av. des Arènes de Cimiez. ☎04 93 81 59 57. Take bus #15, 17, 20, 22, or 25 to "Arènes." Next to Musée Matisse. Open Apr.-Sept. Tu-Su 10am-noon and 2-6pm; Oct.-Mar. 10am-1pm and 2-5pm. €3.80, students €2.30.)*

JARDIN ALBERT IER AND ESPACE MASSENA. Jardin Albert 1er is the central city park. In addition to the usual repertoire of benches and fountains, it boasts the outdoor Théâtre de Verdun, which presents jazz and plays in summer. *(Between av. Verdun and bd. Jaurès, off prom. des Anglais and quai des États-Unis. Box office open daily 10:30am-noon and 3:30-6:30pm.)*

OTHER SIGHTS. Named by the rich English community that commissioned it, the **Promenade des Anglais,** a posh palm-lined seaside boulevard, is Nice's answer to the great pedestrian thoroughfares of Paris, London, and New York. Today the promenade is lined by luxury hotels like the stately **Négresco** (toward the west end), where the staff still don top hats and 19th-century uniforms. Just east of the Négresco, the **Espace Masséna** belies its mundane name ("public space"): romantic picnickers woo each other in the shade beside lavish fountains. **Musée Masséna,** 35 promenade des Anglais, is nearby, though temporarily closed for renovation. **Private beaches** crowd the seashore between bd. Gambetta and the Opéra, but public strands west of bd. Gambetta compensate for the exclusivity. Many travelers are surprised when they actually see Nice's beaches, which are no more than stretches of rocks smoothed by the sea. Bring a beach mat.

🎵 💡 ENTERTAINMENT AND FESTIVALS

Nice guys really do finish last—the party crowd is still swinging when revelers in St-Tropez and Antibes have called it a night. The bars and nightclubs around rue Masséna and Vieux Nice pulsate with dance, jazz, and rock. For more info pick up the free brochure *l'Excés* (www.exces.com) at the tourist office and in some bars. To experience Nice's nightlife without spending a euro, head down to the **promenade des Anglais**, where street performers, musicians, and pedestrians fill the beach and boardwalk. Local men have a reputation for harassing people on the promenade; lone women in particular should be aware.

The dress code at all bars and clubs is simple: look good. Some places (pubs) let patrons dress sloppily (i.e., not perfectly), but almost all will turn away people in shorts, sandals, sneakers, or baseball caps. For men, grays and blacks are fashionable; for women, hot neon would be acceptable if it were tight. One warning: the French are known for dressing *classé* ("in good taste"). Don't go over the top—you'll stick out like a sore *Let's Go* thumb.

BARS

De Klomp, 6 rue Mascoinat (☎04 93 92 42 85). Anything goes in this friendly Dutch pub, where a diverse crowd mingles to live music nightly. Sample one of their 40 whiskeys (from €6.50), 18 beers on tap (pint €7), or 50 bottled beers. Happy Hour 5:30-9:30pm with €4 pints. Open M-Sa 5:30pm-2:30am, Su 8:30pm-2:30am.

McMahon's, 50 bd. Jean Jaurès (☎04 93 13 84 07). Join the locals and expats who lap up Guinness at this friendly Irish pub. Karaoke on Tu, drink promos on Th, and dancing barmaids nightly. Happy Hour daily 4-9pm with €4 pints and €2 wine. Open daily 8am-2am.

Wayne's, 15 rue de la Préfecture (☎04 93 13 46 99). The common denominators in this wild, crowded bar: young, anglo, and on the prowl. Live music daily in the summer. Happy Hour daily 6-9pm with €3.50 pints and cocktails. Open Su-Th noon-1am, F-Sa noon-1:30am.

Thor, 32 cours Saleya (☎04 93 62 49 90; www.thor-pub.com). Svelte blonde bartenders pour pints for a youthful crowd in this raucous Scandinavian pub. Backpackers and locals alike let loose to live music starting at 10pm in the Nordic-inspired interior. Happy hour 6-9pm with €4 pints. Open daily 6pm-2am.

Le Bar des Deux Frères, 1 rue du Moulin (☎04 93 80 77 61). This hip local favorite is hidden behind the facade of an old restaurant. A young, crazy crowd throws back tequila (€3.10) and beer (€5) amid red curtains and smoky tables. Happy hour T-Sa 6:30-10pm with all drinks €1.60-4. June-Sept. Live DJ daily. Open T-Sa 6pm-2:30am, Su-M 10pm-2:30am.

Bodeguita del Havana, rue Chauvain (☎04 93 92 67 24), just above rue Gioffredo. A re-creation of 1940s Havana. Castro might be coming but Guantanamera is king. Late 20s-early 30s crowd. Live salsa daily. Salsa lessons Su-W 8-10pm (€8). Cuban cocktails €8.50. Open daily 8pm-2:30am.

Tapas la Movida, 2 bis rue de l'Abbaye (☎04 93 62 27 46), resembles a revolutionary secret meeting spot, but the only plotting you'll do is figuring out how to crawl home after braving the bar-o-mètre (€15), a meter-long wooden box of shots. Live reggae and rock concerts M-Th (€1.50). Open M-Sa 8pm-12:30am.

Williams, 4 rue Centrale (☎04 93 62 99 63). When the other bars have called it a night, Williams keeps the kegs flowing for an Anglo crowd. Make a spectacle of yourself with karaoke nights M-Th. Live music F and Sa. Open daily 9pm-7am.

NIGHTCLUBS

Nice's nightclubs can quickly drain your funds. Going on Thursdays, Sundays, before midnight, or being female are all good ways to reduce the impact on your wallet. Cover usually includes the first drink. The scene in Nice is in constant flux, with new clubs replacing old ones almost daily and the It spot shifting rapidly.

Saramanga, 45-47 prom. des Anglais (☎04 93 96 67 00). Nice's hottest club. Hawaiian-shirted bartenders pour exotic drinks, showgirls play with fire, and "little people" dance on platforms. Cover €15. Open F-Sa 11pm-6am.

La Suite, 2 rue Bréa (☎04 93 92 92 91). This small club attracts a funky, well-dressed, moneyed crowd. Velvet theater curtains drape the walls and go-go dancers show some skin on weekends. Cover €13. Open T-Su 11:00pm-2:30am.

Blue Boy, 9 rue Jean-Baptiste Spinetta (☎04 93 44 68 24), in west Nice. Though far from town, Blue Boy remains Nice's most popular gay club. Men and women free M-F, Su; cover €9 on Sa. Don't miss the foam parties on W, June-Sept. Open daily 11pm-6am.

Le Klub, 6 rue Halévy (☎06 60 55 26 61). This oft-frequented gay club caters to a gorgeous, well-tanned crowd, with a cocktail lounge and video projections on the dance floor. Cover €11 on Sa. Open July-Aug. T-Su 11:30pm-6am; Sept.-June open W-Su.

CULTURE

The **Théâtre du Cours,** 5 rue Poissonnerie in Vieux Nice, stages traditional drama. (☎04 93 80 12 67. €12.20, students €9.15.) The grand **Théâtre de Nice,** on the promenade des Arts, hosts all sorts of theatrical performances, concerts, and marionettes (☎04 93 13 90 90. €10-30, students €7-25.) The **Opéra de Nice,** 4-6 rue St-François de Paule, hosts visiting symphony orchestras and soloists. (☎04 93 13 98 53 or 04 92 17 40 00. €8-40.) The **FNAC,** 24 av. Jean Médecin in the Nice Etoile shopping center, sells tickets for virtually every musical or theatrical event in town. (☎04 92 17 77 77. www.fnac.com.)

FESTIVALS

In mid-July, the **Nice Jazz Festival** attracts 45,000 visitors, who enjoy over 500 musicians in 75 concerts over an 8-day period. The 2002 lineup included B.B. King, George Clinton, and Ani Defranco. Concerts nightly 7pm-midnight. (Arènes et Jardins de Cimiez. ☎08 20 80 04 00; www.nicejazzfest.com. Tickets €30 per night; 3-day pass €76; 8-day pass €152.) During the ■**Carnaval** in Lent (Feb. 21-Mar. 5), Nice gives Rio a run for its money with two weeks of parades, fireworks, outlandish costumes, and, of course, partying. Call the tourist office for more info.

NEAR NICE

Inland from Nice, the small towns of St-Paul and Vence hide their art treasures removed from the mania of the coast.

⌐ TRANSPORTATION. SAP Buses (☎04 93 58 37 60) sends buses #400-410 to Vence and St-Paul from **Nice** (60min.; 28 per day; €4.10 to **St-Paul,** €4.50 to **Vence**). To get to St-Paul from **Cannes,** take the train to Cagnes-sur-Mer and change to bus #400-410 (€1.50). The last #400-410 leaves St-Paul for Nice and Cagnes-sur-Mer at 7:20pm from the stop just outside the town entrance. The trip from Vence to St-Paul costs €1.20.

VENCE

The former Roman market town of Vence (pop. 17,000) snoozes in the green hills above Nice. The medieval village and modern surrounding town, with its marketplaces and fountains, provide a picturesque break from the coastal crowds.

There are lots of sights in the old town, and it's fun getting lost in it, though you can pick up a walking tour map at the tourist office. Stroll through the **Château de Villeneuve,** a grand 17th-century villa filled with religious works by Matisse and others. (☎04 93 58 15 78. Open Nov.-June Tu-Su 10am-12:30pm and 2-6pm; July-Oct. Tu-Su 10am-6pm. Adults €5, students €2.50.) The central **cathedral** proudly displays a paintbox-bright mosaic of *Moses in the Bulrushes* by Chagall (open daily 9am-6pm). Henri Matisse designed Vence's architectural masterpiece, the **Chapelle du Rosaire,** from the multi-colored stained-glass windows down to the sacerdotal robes. From the bus stop, facing the tourist office, turn left and walk up av. de la Résistance. Take a right on rue Elise and a left on av. des Poilus; at the roundabout go right onto av. de Matisse, cross the bridge, and follow the little brown sign to the left, staying on av. de Matisse for 1½km. (☎04 93 58 03 26. Open Tu and Th 10-11:30am and 2-5:30pm, M, W, and F 2-5:30pm. Mass on Su at 10am. €2.50.)

A few kilometers from Vence is a dazzling art gallery, the **Galerie Beaubourg** (see sidebar, **The Local Story**). This 19th-century château displays—and will sell—the big modern names, from César to Dado to Stella to Arman. Prices range from a budget-friendly €300 to the spectacular €700,000. (☎04 93 24 52 00; fax 04 93 24 52 19; www.galeriebeaubourg.com. Open July-Aug. daily 11am-7pm, Sept. M-Sa 11am-7pm, Oct. and Dec.-Mar. T-Sa 2-6pm, Apr. M-Sa 2-6pm, May-June M-Sa 2-7pm. Closed Nov. €5, students €2.50.) From in front of the tourist office, take bus #14 (dir: "Bergerie") to "Notre Dame des Fleurs" (11 per day, €0.95). A **taxi** (☎04 93 58 11 14) from in front of the tourist office to the gallery costs about €10.

You'll sleep like a cherub at **La Closerie des Genets** ❹, 4 impasse Marcellin Maurel, just off av. Maurel outside the *vieille ville.* Lovingly-decorated rooms have blue shutters, light yellow walls, and new beds, as well as private baths. A lucky few have views of the sea. New friendly owners have renovation plans. (☎04 93 58 33 25; fax 04 93 58 97 01. Breakfast €6. Reservations. Singles €33.50; doubles €47-57; triples-quints €69-122; prices €5 cheaper in Oct.-May. AmEx/MC/V.) **La Victoire** ❸, pl. du Grand Jardin, offers less luxurious rooms, but a convenient location next to the bus stop. (☎04 93 58 61 30; fax 04 93 58 74 68. Breakfast €5.50. Singles with bath €27-32; doubles with bath €32-36. Extra bed €14. MC/V.)

For food, sample local produce on pl. du Grand Jardin (daily market). On Tuesday and Friday mornings, check out the markets in the Cité Historique.

THE LOCAL STORY

PIERRE NAHON, OWNER OF GALERIE BEAUBOURG

Q: What type of art do you look for?
A: We look for what we like. We have followed several artists for many years: César, Arman, Warhol, etc.

Q: What is the composition of your clientele?
A: 90% foreigners. Many Americans, Germans, Belgians.

Q: Has there ever been a piece of art that was difficult for you to part with?
A: Of course. As the proverb goes, you sell now and regret after; what you don't sell, those pieces of art are your true *richesse.*

Q: When did you first become interested in art?
A: I am 65 years old. When I was 15, I loved Picabia. I opened my first gallery in Paris in the 1960s. Art was always my passion.

Q: Do you have a private collection?
A: I have a very important collection. I want to buy and conserve works of art, but all is for sale. Occasionally, you're obligated to separate with something you love.

Q: Is there a piece of art that you wish you could have right now, if money were not an issue?
A: Warhol. I consider him the *plus grand* American artist and the only American artist. He represents the best of America; he was an amazing innovator. I never hesitate to buy a Warhol.

Q: What do you like most about your work?
A: I don't work. I live a very nice life in the middle of artists.

The **tourist office** lies at pl. du Grand Jardin, across from the bus stop. (☎04 93 58 06 38; fax 04 93 58 91 81; www.ville-vence.fr. Open July-Aug. M-Sa 9am-7pm, Su 9am-1pm; Sept.-June M-Sa 9am-12:30pm, 2-6pm. 90 min. tours by reservation; 5-person min.; €3).

ST-PAUL

If you visit one medieval village on the Côte D'Azur, make it St-Paul. Ever since Chagall discovered St-Paul's colors and light and called it home, the clifftop village has been an art lover's paradise. 80 galleries sell local paintings, pottery, handcrafts, and works by the likes of Léger and Ernst. As you stroll through the well-trampled village, stop at Chagall's gravestone (cemetery open daily 8am-6pm) and the exquisite *eglise collégiale*, home to the mounted skull of St. Etienne. (Open daily 8am-8pm.)

Much of St-Paul's art is in nearby **Fondation Maeght,** 1km from the town center. From the "St-Paul" bus stop, take a right onto chemin de St-Claire, passing Chapelle St-Claire on your right, and you will see blue signs for the foundation. Designed by Joseph Sert, the foundation is part museum and part park, with shrubs and fountains mixed in with works by Miró, Calder, Arp, and Léger. Maeght, an art dealer, commissioned a small, somber chapel in memory of his lost son. Filled with stained glass by Braque and Ubac, the chapel is now part of the museum. (☎04 93 32 81 63. Open July-Sept. daily 10am-7pm; Oct.-June 10am-12:30pm, 2:30-6pm. €8, students €6.50. Photography permit €2.50.)

The **tourist office,** 2 rue Grande, just inside the walls of St-Paul, dispenses free maps and info on galleries and exhibitions. (☎04 93 32 86 95; fax 04 93 32 60 27; artdevivre@wanadoo.fr. Open June-Sept. daily 10am-7pm; Oct.-May 10am-6pm.) They also give personal one-hour tours of the medieval city at request in English. (10am-5:30pm. €8 per person.) You can also rent a set of bowls for a game of pétanque for €3 per person or schedule a game with an inhabitant of the village (€61 for 60min. plus €3 per person).

THE CORNICHES

Rocky shores, pebble beaches, and luxurious villas dot the coast between hectic Nice and high-rolling Monaco. More relaxing and less touristed than their glam-fab neighbors, these tiny towns sparkle quietly with interesting museums, architectural finds, and breathtaking countryside. The train offers an exceptional glimpse of the coast up close, while buses maneuvering along the high roads of the *corniches* provide a bird's-eye view of the steep cliffs and crashing sea below. Take one mode of transport out and the other back and you'll get to experience both.

▐ **TRANSPORTATION.** Trains and buses between Nice and Monaco serve most of the Corniche towns. With a departure about every hour, **trains** from **Nice** to **Monaco** stop at **Villefranche-sur-Mer** (7min., €1.30), **Beaulieu-sur-Mer** (10min., €1.70), **Eze-sur-Mer** (16min., €2), and **Cap d'Ail** (20min., €2.40).

Numerous numbered **RCA buses** (☎04 93 85 64 44; www.rca.tm.fr) run between Nice and Monaco, making stops along the way. **#111** leaves Nice, stopping in **Villefranche-sur-Mer** (9 per day). Two buses continue on to **St-Jean-Cap-Ferrat** (M-Sa 9:10am and 12:15pm). **#100** runs between Nice and **Villefranche-sur-Mer** 11 times daily. **#112** runs 7 times per day (3 on Su) between Nice and Monte-Carlo, stopping in **Eze-le-Village.** RCA and Broch (☎04 93 85 61 81 or 04 93 07 63 28; daily every hr.) run between Nice and **Villefranche-sur-Mer** (15min., €1.60), **Beaulieu-sur-Mer** (20min., €2), **Eze-le-Village** (25min., €2.40), **Cap d'Ail** (30min., €3.20), **Monaco-Ville** (40min., €3.70), and **Monte-Carlo** (45min., €3.70). Most tickets include free same-day return, though you should make sure.

VILLEFRANCHE-SUR-MER

The stairwayed streets and pastel houses of Villefranche-sur-Mer have earned the town a reputation as one of the Riviera's most photogenic gems. The backdrop for dozens of films (from a James Bond installation to *Dirty Rotten Scoundrels*), the town has enchanted artists and writers from Aldous Huxley to Katherine Mansfield. Tina Turner makes an annual pilgrimage to her hillside villa here. Despite the celebrity presence, Villefranche remains an authentic *provençal* town, with an excellent beach and some interesting sights.

As you walk from the station along quai Courbet, a sign for the *vieille ville* directs you along the 13th-century **rue Obscure,** the oldest street in Villefranche. A right at the end of rue Obscure takes you to the **Church of Saint Michel,** which contains an impressive wooden statue of a martyred Christ sculpted by an anonymous slave. At the end of the quai stands the pink and yellow 14th-century **Chapelle St-Pierre,** decorated from floor to ceiling by Jean Cocteau, former resident, filmmaker, and jack-of-all-arts. (☎04 93 76 90 70. Tu-Su. Hours fluctuate—call ahead. €2.) The rather dull 16th-century **Citadelle** houses three small museums, the most interesting of which is the rustic **Musée Volti,** dedicated to Antoniucci Volti, who created curvaceous female forms out of bronze, clay, canvas, and copper. (☎04 93 76 33 27. Open July-Aug. W-Sa and M 10am-noon and 2:30-7pm, Su 2:30-7pm; June and Sept. W-Sa and M 9am-noon and 2:30-6pm, Su 2:30-7pm; Oct.-May W-Sa 9am-noon and 2-5:30pm, Su 1:30-6pm. Free.)

If you're dead-set on spending a night in the Corniches rather than the nearby budget-friendly Nice, Villefranche has few options. **La Régence ❹,** 2 av. Maréchal Foch, offers carpeted rooms on top of an all-night bar along the main drag. (☎04 93 01 70 91; laregence@caramail.com. Internet access. Breakfast €5. All rooms have shower and toilet. Singles €40; doubles €44; triples €49.)

To reach the **tourist office** from the train station, exit on quai 1 and head inland on av. G. Clemenceau. Continue straight as it becomes av. Sadi Carnot. The office is at the end of the street in the Jardin François. It distributes a walking tour of the town and suggests excursions to nearby villages. (☎04 93 01 73 68; fax 04 93 76 63 65; www.villefranche-sur-mer.com. Open July-Aug. daily 9am-7pm; June and Sept. M-Sa 9am-noon, 2-6:30pm; Oct.-May 9am-noon and 2-6pm.)

BEAULIEU-SUR-MER

Reportedly named by Napoleon, who called it a *"beaulieu"* (beautiful place) upon his visit, this seaside resort has a ritzy past. Belle Epoque villas, a classy casino, and ornate four-star hotels along the waterfront attest to town's previous status as *the* place to winter for Europe's elite. The big money has since moved to quieter mansions in nearby St-Jean-Cap-Ferrat, but Beaulieu still attracts a few stars. For those of lesser means, the only justification for a visit to this relatively uninteresting town is its spectacular villa.

On a plateau overlooking the sea, Renaissance man Theodore Reinach built his dream villa **▨Kérylos,** which today stands as proof that money can buy happiness. This home perfectly imitates an ancient Greek dwelling: columns, mosaics, and marble sculptures are all copied from original specimens, and the frescoes in the foyer have been artificially aged. Even the piano was fashioned to seem less than anachronistic. On one of the coast's prettiest terraces, the villa is encircled by gardens with statues of the Olympian gods. (Tours only. Free 90min. audioguide. Open July-Aug. daily 10am-7pm; Feb. 8-June and Sept.-Nov. 3 daily 10am-6pm; Nov. 4-Feb. 7 M-F 2-6pm, Sa-Su 10am-6pm. €7, students €5.50.)

A promenade along the waterfront passes by the major hotels. If you'd rather walk than gawk, the **tourist office,** pl. Georges Clemenceau, suggests scenic routes to nearby towns. (☎04 93 01 02 21; fax 04 93 01 44 04; tourisme@ot-beaulieu-sur-mer.fr; www.ot-beaulieu-sur-mer.fr. Open July-Aug. M-Sa 9am-12:30pm and 2-7pm, Su 9am-12:30pm; Sept.-June M-F 9am-12:15pm and 2-6pm, Sa 9am-12:15pm and 2-5pm.)

ST-JEAN-CAP-FERRAT

As if the *Riviera* needed a trump card! St-Jean-Cap-Ferrat is a haven for the upper-class—the King of Belgium still makes a yearly appearance. The town is serviced by **bus #111,** but nothing compares to the 40-minute ◼seaside walk from Beaulieu (access the path in front of the Beaulieu casino). Passing lavish villas, rocky beaches, and once-beautiful docks, it could take up to an hour with all the photo opportunities.

The **Fondation Ephrussi de Rothschild** is just off av. D. Semeria, in between the tourist office and the Nice-Monaco road. The foundation holds the furniture and art collections of the eccentric Baroness de Rothschild and her famous father, encompassing Monet canvases, Gobelins tapestries, Chinese vases, and a stunning tea room. Outside, each of seven lush gardens reflects a different part of the world, including Spain, Japan, and, *bien sûr*, France. The villa can be accessed directly from Beaulieu. Follow the shore path toward St-Jean, turning right after the three-pronged tree and before the pink villa that separates the path from the Mediterranean. From the top of this walled shore access, turn left and follow the road uphill, turning right at the sign to the Fondation. (☎04 93 01 45 90; message@villa-ephrussi.com; www.villa-ephrussi.com. Guided tour in French is the only way to see the first floor: 11:30am, 2:30pm, 3:30pm, and 4:30pm; €2. Tea salon open 11am-5:30pm. Open July-Aug. daily 10am-7pm; Sept.-Nov. 1 and Feb. 15-June daily 10am-6pm; Nov. 2-Feb. 14 M-F 2-6pm, Sa-Su 10am-6pm. €8, students €6.)

St-Jean's **beaches** have earned the area the nickname *"presqu'île des rêves,"* peninsula of dreams. Mainly attracting locals, who descend from their villas to bask in the sun, the beaches feel secluded and peaceful. With so many options, you'll want to pass on the aptly named **plage Passable,** just down the hill from the tourist office, and hit Cap's best beach, the wide **plage Paloma,** past the port on av. Jean Mermoz. For a more solitary sunbath, make a right off av. Mermoz at the junction of pl. Paloma and try **Les Fossettes** and, farther on, **Les Fosses.** These beautiful rocky stretches look out on a quiet and unpopulated bay. You should also consider walking around Pointe de St-Hospice. The 30min. walk offers secluded sunbathing spots and stunning vistas.

The tiny **tourist office,** 59 av. Denis Séméria, is half-way along the winding street that runs from Nice and Monaco to the port. It distributes free maps, free walking tours of the peninsula's 14km of trails, and directions to hidden beaches. (☎04 93 76 08 90; fax 04 93 76 16 67. Open July-Aug. M-Sa 8:30am-6:30pm; June 10-30 and Sept. 1-7 M-Sa 8:30am-6pm; Sept. 8-June 9 M-Sa 8:30am-noon and 1-5pm.)

EZE

Eze (pop. 2,700) is a three-tiered city; each level has a distinctive character. The seaside town, **Eze Bord-de-Mer,** (also called **Eze-sur-Mer**) includes the train station and a stretch of pebble beach popular with windsurfers, kayakers, and sailors. The upper tier, **Col d'Eze,** is mostly residential. It is the middle tier, **Eze-le-Village,** that makes Eze famous. This Roman village-turned-medieval citadel has been occupied by everyone from the Moors to Piedmontese, but has been conquered only once—by the thousands of tourists who now invade it every week.

Photo-snapping tourists aside, Eze-le-Village is living testament to the Riviera's past. The **Porte des Maures,** erected in remembrance of a devastatingly successful surprise attack by the Moors, dates to the tumultuous 10th century, when much of the Côte was in Moorish hands. The **Eglise Paroissial** is decorated by sleek Phoenician crosses trimmed with Catholic gilt (☎ 04 93 41 00 38; open daily about 9am-7pm). The **Jardin Exotique,** which offers fabulous views of the sea and the Cap d'Antibes, is planted around a Savoy fortress that was razed in 1706 by the invading armies of Louis XIV. (☎ 04 93 41 10 30. Open daily Sept.-June 30 9am-noon and 2-6pm; July-Aug. 31 9am-8pm. €2.50, students €1.60.)

Eze-le-Village offers more than narrow streets and nice vistas—the second-largest factory of the **Fragonard Parfumerie** is located here. Free 15min. tours explain the perfume-making process and sell perfumes at warehouse prices. (☎ 04 93 41 05 05; www.fragonard.com. Open daily 8am-6:30pm.) The more intimate **Parfumerie Galimard** has a free **museum** and guided visits. (☎ 04 93 41 10 70. Open daily 9am-6pm.)

The best views are awarded to travelers who venture 1 hour up or 40 minutes down the **Sentier Friedrich Nietzsche,** a winding trail that inspired its namesake to finish the third part of *Thus Spake Zarathustra*. The trail begins in Eze Bord-de-Mer, 100m east of the train station, and ends at the base of the medieval city, near the parfumerie. Be warned—unless you're a serious athlete, the hike may be too much for your lungs. If you give it a go, wear hiking shoes and bring a camera.

Eze annually hosts two major festivals, each attracting about 4,000 people. In early July, the **Festival Latino** fetches salsa, theater, and art notables from Latin America. In late July, the **Eze d'Antan** festival illuminates the history of Eze in the Middle Ages. For details on both, call the tourist office.

The **tourist office,** pl. de Gaulle, has free maps and info. (☎ 04 93 41 26 00; fax 04 93 41 04 84; www.eze-riviera.com; eze@webstore.fr. Open Apr.-Oct. daily 9am-7pm; Nov.-Mar. 9am-6:30pm.) Guided tours of the medieval village and exotic garden are offered daily by request (€5 per person; try to call 1 day in advance to make a reservation). To get there, take the Navette mini-bus from the train station. There's an **annex** right next to the train station. (☎ 04 93 01 52 00. Open May-Oct. 10am-1pm and 3-6:30pm.)

To get to Eze, take the train from **Nice** (14min., €2). From May 1-Sept. 30, a **Navette** mini-bus connects Eze's three tiers, stopping in **Eze Bord-de-Mer** in front of the tourist office annex and in **Eze-le-Village** where the main road meets the path to the medieval city (8 per day 9:35am-6:45pm; one way €3.80, round trip €6.85). If you miss the bus, a **taxi** ride (☎ 06 18 44 77 93) to the top costs about €20.

CAP D'AIL

If it's a provincial flavor you want, villa-strewn Cap d'Ail (pop. 5000) will leave a bitter taste in your mouth. But three kilometers of cliff-framed, foamy seashore, a hostel that's actually a waterfront villa, and numerous airy footpaths make it a great place for sunbathing—especially *sans clothing*. Dozens of illegal naturists keep the moon full over the Cap at **Les Pissarelles.** To get there, walk 15 minutes along av. du 3 Septembre, the town's main thoroughfare. To find the sun on the more modest **plage Mala,** turn left from the train station and make another left into a stone tunnel that leads down to the mansion-lined av. R. Gramaglia. Then head straight for to the sea and jump onto the **sentier du bord de mer,** which winds along cliffs all the way to Mala. The path can be identified by its ultramarine guardrail.

The **Relais International de la Jeunesse "Thalassa"❶,** on av. R. Gramaglia, can be reached by following the signs from the train station. (7min.) Plutocrats would love its waterfront location, but a friendly, fun-loving crowd is instead the main guest of its single-sex dorms. (☎ 04 93 78 18 58; fax 04 93 53 35 88; clajpaca@cote-dazur.com. Breakfast, sheets, and lockers included. Satellite TV. Dinner €8.50. Free luggage storage. Lockout 9:30am-5:30pm. Curfew July-Aug. midnight; Apr.-June and Sept.-Oct. 11pm. Open Apr.-Oct. Dorms €13.) Hostelers who miss the curfew sometimes take their chances and illegally bed down on plage Mala. Admittedly, Cap d'Ail's police are not always enthused about descending 152 steps just to oust sleeping backpackers. However, as is the case throughout the Riviera, the sand may also be the nighttime haunt of pickpockets and drug addicts. *Let's Go* strongly recommends a legal bed and a roof over your head.

The **tourist office,** 87bis av. du 3 Septembre, has free maps and info on daytrips. Walk uphill, keeping left until you leave the residential area. Continuing on av. de la Gare, turn right onto rue des Combatants de l'Af. du N. Turn left on av. du 3 Septembre; the office will be on your right. (20min.) (☎04 93 78 02 33; fax 04 92 10 74 36; www.monte-carlo.mc/cap-d'ail. Open July-Aug. M-Sa 9am-noon and 2-6pm, Su 9am-noon; Sept.-June M-F 9am-noon and 2-6pm, Sa 9am-noon.)

MONACO AND MONTE-CARLO

This tiny principality (native pop. 7160) is, square inch for square inch, probably the wealthiest place in the world. The rest of the Côte may be glamorous, but Monaco doesn't need glamor: its wealth is proven aptly enough by its ubiquitous surveillance cameras and security officials, high-speed luxury cars, and sleek multi-million dollar yachts. At Monaco's spiritual heart, provided it has one at all, is its famous casino, located in the capital city, Monte-Carlo. The sheer spectacle of it all, along with the tabloid allure of Monaco's royal family, is definitely worth the daytrip from Nice.

▐ TRANSPORTATION

Trains: av. Prince Pierre. Station open 5:20am-12:20am. Info desk and ticket window open daily 5:45am-8:30pm. To: **Antibes** (60min., every 30min., €6.40); **Cannes** (65min., every 30min., €7.10); **Menton** (11min., every 30min., €1.70); **Nice** (23min., every 30min., €2.90).

Buses: Buses leave from pl. d'Armes and pl. du Casino (☎04 93 85 61 81 in Nice). Two lines: **E. Broch** (☎04 93 31 10 52) and **RCA** (☎04 93 85 64 44). To **Menton** (20min., every 15min., €2) and **Nice** (45min., every 15min., €3.70).

Public Transportation: 6 bus routes (☎97 70 22 22) serve the entire town (every 11min. 7am-9pm, every 20 min. Su and holidays 7:30am-9pm). Bus #4 links the train station to the casino; bus #2 connects the *vieille ville* and *jardin exotique* via pl. d'Armes. Tickets €1.30, *carnet* of 4 €3.30, *carnet* of 8 €5.25. Tickets on board.

Taxis: ☎93 15 01 01 (24 hr). 11 taxi stands. Around €8 from pl. du Casino to the hostel, €12.20-15.25 to the Relais de Jeunesse in Cap d'Ail.

Car rental: Avis, 9 av. d'Ostende (☎93 30 17 53). Open M-Sa 8am-noon and 2-7pm; Su 9am-noon. AmEx/MC/V. **Hertz,** 27 bd. Albert 1er (☎93 50 79 60; fax 93 25 47 58). Open M-Sa 8:30am-noon and 2-7pm; Su 8:30am-1pm. AmEx/MC/V.

Scooter Rental: Auto-Moto Garage, 7 rue de Millo (☎93 50 10 80). Open M-F 8am-noon and 2-7pm, Sa 8am-noon. €23 for 9am-7pm, €26 for 24hr., €145 per week. Credit card deposit. AmEx/MC/V.

✦ ▐ ORIENTATION AND PRACTICAL INFORMATION

Though small, this jam-packed principality is difficult to navigate. In the center of town, Monaco's new four-story train station lacks a principal entrance. The site of the former station, at **av. Prince Pierre,** serves as one entrance to the new one, via marble walkway. To exit to av. Prince Pierre, follow signs for "Le Rocher" and "Fontvieille." You'll come out near pl. d'Armes and **La Condamine,** Monaco's port, restaurant, and nightlife center. To the right of La Condamine, the old city **(Monaco Ville)** rises fortress-like over the harbor; below and behind, you'll find the museum-laden **avenue de Fontvieille.** Leaving the station in the opposite direction (bd. Prin-

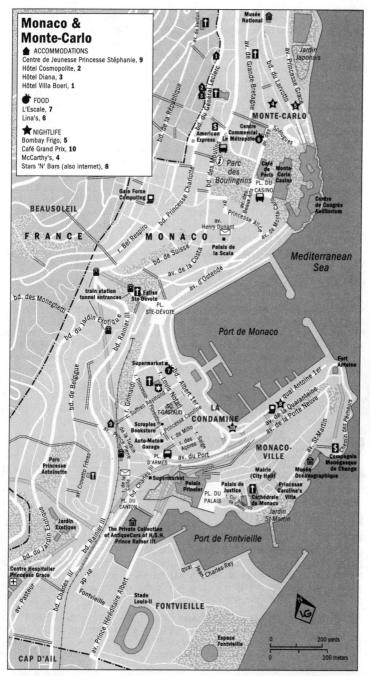

Monaco &
Monte-Carlo

🏠 ACCOMMODATIONS
Centre de Jeunesse Princesse Stéphanie, **9**
Hôtel Cosmopolite, **2**
Hôtel Diana, **3**
Hôtel Villa Boeri, **1**

🍎 FOOD
L'Escale, **7**
Lina's, **6**

⭐ NIGHTLIFE
Bombay Frigo, **5**
Café Grand Prix, **10**
McCarthy's, **4**
Stars 'N' Bars (also internet), **8**

Musée National

Jardin Japonais

av. de Verdun
av. de Grande-Bretagne
bd. du Princesse Grace
av. Princesse Grace
av. de Lavrotto

bd. du Général Leclerc

MONTE-CARLO

bd. de la République

American Express

Centre Commercial Le Métropole

Café de Paris

Monte-Carlo Casino

Parc des Boulingrins

PL. DU CASINO

Centre de Congrès Auditorium

BEAUSOLEIL

Gale Force Computing

bd. Princesse Charlotte

r. Bel Respiro

FRANCE

MONACO

av. Henry Dunant

Palais de la Scala

bd. de Suisse

av. de la Costa

av. d'Ostende

Mediterranean Sea

bd. des Moneghetti

train station tunnel entrances

Église Ste-Dévote
PL. STE-DÉVOTE

bd. Rainier III

bd. du Jardin Exotique

bd. de Belgique

Port de Monaco

Fort Antoine

Supermarket

bd. Albert 1er

Louis Notari

SQ. T-GASTAUD

LA CONDAMINE

quai Antoine 1er

av. de la Quarantaine
av. de la Porte Neuve

Fort St-Martin

Scruples Bookstore

Auto-Moto Garage

PL. D'ARMES

av. du Port

MONACO-VILLE

Chemin des Pêcheurs

Compagnie Monégasque de Change

Parc Princesse Antoinette

av. Crovetto Frères

Supermarket

Palais Princier

PL. DU PALAIS

Mairie (City Hall)

Palais de Justice

Musée Océanographique

Cathédrale de Monaco

Princesse Caroline's Villa

Jardin St-Martin

Jardin Exotique

The Private Collection of AntiqueCars of H.S.H. Prince Rainer III

Port de Fontvieille

Centre Hospitalier Princesse Grace

av. Pasteur

bd. Charles III

av. de Fontvieille

quai Jean Charles-Rey

Stade Louis-II

FONTVIEILLE

av. Prince Héréditaire Albert

Espace Fontvieille

CAP D'AIL

0   200 yards
0   200 meters

C O T E   D ' A Z U R

cesse Charlotte) or below (pl. St-Dévote) will put you on the other side of the port, closer to the fabled tables of **Monte-Carlo.** Up the hill from the casino and technically across the border is "down-to-earth" (comparatively) **Beausoleil,** France. Be economical with your money by shopping at **Carrefour** in Fontvielle; throw it all away at the 80 luxurious boutiques along **Le Métropole.**

Tourist Office: 2a bd. des Moulins (☎92 16 61 16; fax 92 16 60 00; www.monaco-tourisme.com), near the casino. A friendly, English-speaking staff provides city plans, a monthly events guide, and hotel reservations free of charge. Open M-Sa 9am-7pm, Su 10am-noon. There are **annexes** in the train station at the av. Prince Pierre exit and in the port June 15-Sept. 1.

Tours: Mini-train tours depart from the Oceanography Museum (June-Sept. 10:30am-6pm; Oct.-May 11am-5pm; closed Jan. and Nov. 15-Dec. 26). Tickets €6.

Currency Exchange: Compagnie Monégasque de Change, parking du chemin des Pêcheurs (☎93 25 02 50), near Fort Antoine at the end of the port, has reasonable rates and no commission. Open Su-F 9:30am-5:30pm. Closed Nov. 5-Dec. 25. **American Express,** 35 bd. Princesse Charlotte (☎97 70 77 59). Open M-F 9:30am-noon, 2-6:30pm. **Monafinances,** 17 av. des Spélugues (☎93 50 06 80).

Police: 3 rue Louis Notari (☎93 15 30 15).

Hospital: Centre Hospitalier Princesse Grace, av. Pasteur (☎97 98 99 00 or emergency 97 98 97 95), off bd. Rainier III, which runs along the train tracks.

24 hr. Pharmacy: There is always a pharmacy open all night. Call the police station or look in "Monaco-Matin," the daily newspaper.

Internet Access: FNAC, in "Le Métropole" (☎93 10 81 81; www.fnac.com). Free Internet access on 2 computers. Open M-Sa 10am-7:30pm. **Stars 'N' Bars,** 6 quai Antoine 1er (☎97 97 95 95; www.starsnbars.com). 4 computers, €6 for 30min. Open daily 10am-midnight. **Gale Force Computing,** 13 av. St-Michel (☎93 50 20 92; gfc@monaco.mc). €4.50 for 30 min. Open M-F 9am-12:30pm and 2-6pm (5pm on F). **Dito,** 20 av. de Fontvielle (☎93 10 11 60). €0.15 per minute. Open M-F 9am-6pm.

Post Office: Palais de la Scala (☎97 97 25 25). Monaco issues its own stamps; French stamps cannot be used in Monaco. **Branch office** across from Hôtel Terminus at the av. Prince Pierre train station exit. 5 additional branches. All offices open M-F 8am-7pm, Sa 8am-noon. **Postal code:** MC 98000 Monaco.

| **PHONING TO AND FROM MONACO** | Monaco's country code is 377. To telephone Monaco from France, dial 00377, then the 8-digit Monaco number. To call France from Monaco, dial 0033, and drop the first zero of the French number. |

⌐ ACCOMMODATIONS

If you choose to stay within a stone's throw of the casino, forget those college plans for your children. Unless you're James Bond, your best bet is bargain-filled **La Condamine,** near the old train station. Alternatively, cross the street to **Beausoleil,** France, where prices are nearly halved. Consider staying just outside of Monaco—the hostel in Cap d'Ail is a reasonable option, since transport to the golden city is typically very good.

Centre de Jeunesse Princesse Stéphanie, 24 av. Prince Pierre (☎93 50 83 20; fax 93 25 29 82; www.youthhostel.asso.mc). Take the av. Prince Pierre exit from the train station. Turn left and walk straight ahead uphill 100m to the hostel, a pink building. Though a bit sterile for a princess's namesake, this hostel has an excellent location, 4-

bed rooms, and a small backyard with a view of the port. Breakfast included. Lockers in rooms with €5 deposit. Sheets free with ID deposit. Laundry €5. Reception July-Aug. daily 7am-1am; Sept.-June daily 7am-midnight. Check-out 9:30am. Enforced curfew: Su-F 11:45pm and Sa 12:45am. Reservations required. **Ages 16-31.** 7-day max. stay, July-Aug. 5 days. Closed Dec. Beds €16; July-Aug. 10- and 12-bed dorms €14. ❷

Hôtel Villa Boeri, 29 bd. du Général Leclerc (☎04 93 78 38 10; fax 04 93 41 90 95), in Beausoleil, France, 300m from the casino. Leave the train station at bd. Princesse Charlotte and keep to the left. Walk about 15min. Bd. de France on the Monaco side changes to bd. du Général Leclerc. Floral patterns, mirrored hallways and plastic furniture recall the days of disco at this genial new hotel. A/C and TV. Breakfast €5. Reception 24 hr. Singles and doubles €34-43; triples €69; quads €81; more luxurious rooms €46-60. Prices rise 10-25% June-Sept. AmEx/MC/V. ❹

Hôtel Diana, 17 bd. du Général Leclerc (☎04 93 78 47 58; fax 04 93 41 88 94; hotel.diana.beausoleil.monte.carlo@wanadoo.fr), in Beausoleil, France. Follow directions for Hôtel Villa Boeri. A marble staircase and wood panelling contrasts with the rooms's 1970s decor. Breakfast €6. Reception 24hr. Reservations required. Singles €29, with shower, €46; doubles €46-58; triples €61. AmEx/MC/V. ❸

Hôtel Cosmopolite, 19 bd. du Général Leclerc (☎04 93 78 36 00; fax 04 93 41 84 22), next door to Hôtel Diana. Amiable Italian owners recently opened this simple but clean hotel. A/C and TV. Breakfast €7. Reception 24hr. Singles €34, with toilet €51-66; doubles €54-69; triples €77. AmEx/MC/V. ❹

🖪 FOOD

Not surprisingly, Monaco has little budget fare. Fill a picnic basket from the fruit and flower **market** on pl. d'Armes at the end of av. Prince Pierre (open daily 6am-1pm), the huge **Carrefour** in Fontvieille's shopping plaza (☎92 05 57 00; open M-Sa 8:30am-10pm), the **Casino** supermarket on bd. Albert 1er (☎93 30 56 78; open M-Sa 8:30am-8pm), or **Marché U** at 30 bd. Princesse Charlotte. (☎97 97 14 01. Open M-Sa 8:30am-7:15pm.) **L'Escale ❷,** 17 bd. Albert 1er, offers first-class dining at coach prices. Pizzas and pastas run €8. Filet of *loup* (wolf) and *steak au poivre* will cost you €7 and €13. (☎93 39 13 44. Open daily noon-3pm and 7-11pm. MC/V.) **Lina's ❶,** in *Le Métropole* shopping center, offers tasty sandwiches of all kinds. (☎93 25 86 10; www.linascafé.com. €4-7. Open M-Sa 9:15am-7:30pm.)

🖪 SIGHTS

🖪 **MONTE-CARLO CASINO.** This is the home of the famously alluring gambling house where Richard Burton wooed Liz Taylor and Mata Hari shot a Russian spy. Its position along the rocky coast is convenient for suicide, an end once sought by as many as four bankrupts per week. Even if you despise gambling, the extravagant, red-curtained, gilt-ceilinged interior is worth a peak. The lucky can try their hand at **slot machines** (M-F from 2pm, Sa-Su from noon) and **blackjack** and **roulette** (daily from noon). While all casinos have **dress codes** (no shorts, sneakers, sandals, or jeans), the exclusive *salons privés*, host to elite games like *chemin de fer* and *trente et quarante*, require coat and tie and charge a €10 cover. The more relaxed **Café de Paris** next door opens for gambling at 10am. The 21+ rule is strictly enforced—bring a passport. The Monte-Carlo casino also boasts the ornate Atrium du Casino theater. (☎92 16 20 00; www.casino-monte-carlo.com. €10.)

🖪 **PALAIS PRINCIER.** Perched on a cliff above the casino, the palace is the occasional home of Prince Rainier and his tabloid-darling family. The Grimaldis have ruled their small but doggedly independent state since 1297, when François Grimaldi of Genoa captured Monaco with a few men disguised as monks. Monaco's tiny military is ever-vigilant for future renegade monks; the palace guard changes with great fanfare (daily 11:55am). In their white summer uniforms (black in winter) and fashionable gun holders, the soldiers appear as useful as the cannon strategically aimed at the shopping district. When the prince is away, the flag lowers and the doors open to tourists. Tours show off the small but lavishly decorated palace, including a hall of mirrors, Princess Grace's official state portrait, Prince Rainier's throne, and the chamber where King George III of England died. *(☎ 93 25 18 31. Open June-Sept. daily 9:30am-6pm; Oct. daily 10am-5pm. €6, students and children 8-14 €3.)*

MUSÉE OCÉANOGRAPHIQUE. An educational break from Monaco's excesses, the oceanographic museum was founded by Jacques Cousteau and prince-cum-marine biologist Albert I. The main attraction is a 90-tank aquarium, filled with seawater pumped in directly from the Mediterranean. Kids will enjoy the shark lagoon and 1.9m green moray eel, the largest on display in the world. *(Av. St-Martin. ☎ 93 15 36 00. Open Apr.-Sept. daily 9am-7pm; Oct.-Mar. daily 10am-6pm. €11, students and children 6-18 €6. Audioguide €3.05.)*

CATHÉDRALE DE MONACO. This white neo-Romanesque-Byzantine church holds the tombs of 35 generations of Grimaldis and played host to the 1956 wedding of Prince Rainier and Grace Kelly. The victim of a tragic car accident, Princess Grace lies in a tomb behind the altar marked with her Latin name "Patritia Gracia." To the right of Grace's tomb, encased in glass, is a newly restored and much-ballyhooed painting of Monaco's patron saint, Nicolas, by *niçois* painter Louis Brea. *(Pl. St-Martin, near the Palais. ☎ 93 30 87 70. Mass Su 10pm, Sa 6pm. Open Mar.-Oct. daily 7am-7pm; Nov.-Feb. 7am-6pm. Free.)*

JARDIN EXOTIQUE. Designed as a photo-op, this meticulous garden offers sweeping views of the old city as well as an extensive cactus collection. Free tours (on the hour) explore stalagmites and stalactites in the park's dungeon-like grottoes. *(62 bd. du Jardin Exotique, up the public elevators on bd. de Belgique. ☎ 93 15 29 80; www.monte-carlo.mc/jardinexotique. Open May 15-Sept. 15 daily 9am-7pm; Sept. 16-May 14 daily 9am-6pm or until sundown. €6.45, students and children 6-18 €3.20, under 6 no charge.)*

CAR COLLECTION. Most of us would be content with a quality automobile. The **Private Collection of Antique Cars of H.S.H. Prince Rainier III** (translated, that's the Prince's car collection), on the other hand, includes 105 of the sexiest cars in the world. Gawk at the fun-loving Prince Albert's toy race cars, the 1956 Rolls Royce Silver Cloud that carried Prince Rainier and Grace Kelly on their wedding day, and the auto that captured the first Grand Prix de Monaco in 1929. *(Terrasses de Fontvieille. ☎ 92 05 28 56. Open daily 10am-6pm. €6, students and children 8-14 €3.)*

OTHER SIGHTS. Napoleonophiles and war enthusiasts will appreciate the **Collections des Souvenirs Napoléonais et des Archives Historiques du Palais,** just to the left of the palace entrance. The small museum houses Napoleon paraphernalia and attempts to explain the history of Monaco with coins, documents, and paintings. *(Next to the Palais Princier entrance. ☎ 93 25 18 31. Open June-Sept. daily 9:30am-6:30pm; Oct. daily 10am-5pm; Dec.-May Tu-Su 10:30am-12:30pm and 2-5pm. €4, students €2.)* Take a stroll along the seaside **Jardin St-Martin,** off the avenue of the same name, which has a dramatic statue of Albert I and good views of the coast. *(Open Apr.-Sept. daily 7am-10pm; Oct.-Mar. daily 7am-6pm.)* Keep your eyes peeled for **Princess Caroline's villa,** a pink oasis just outside the gardens between the cathedral and the oceanography museum. Guards are forbidden to disclose the location, but the armed monk insignia on its gates should tip you off. If you've come to Monaco for enlightenment, question your sanity and then sip tea among cherry trees and tiny brooks in the **Jardin Japonais.** *(Open daily 9am-sunset. No charge.)*

🎭 🍷 NIGHTLIFE AND FESTIVALS

Though some still frequent Monte-Carlo's old-school clubs like the Vegas-style discos on the **av. des Spélugues,** most now head to the bar-restaurants at the port in **La Condamine. Stars 'N' Bars,** 6 quai Antoine 1er, is trafficked mostly by locals and American-loving European tourists. A restaurant by day, its dance floor fills with tight clothes and slick hair at night. (☎97 97 95 95. Restaurant open daily 10am-11pm. Disco open Sept.-June F-Sa midnight-5am; July-Aug. daily midnight-5am. 21+. Cover €8.) The cooler crowd strolls up the port to **Café Grand Prix,** 1 quai Antoine 1er, the place to be. A mixed group grooves to live music in the cozy, streamlined interior. (☎93 25 56 90. Open daily 10am-5am. Live music kicks off at 12:30pm. Happy hour daily 6-9pm with all drinks half-price). **McCarthy's,** 7 rue du Portier in Monte-Carlo, may have a ritzy address and mahogany paneling, but it encourages you to kick back leprechaun-style and let the Guinness flow. (☎93 25 87 67. 18+. Open daily 6pm-dawn. Live music begins at 11:30pm June-Aug. daily and Sept.-May Th-Sa.) Do as the *monégasques* do and splurge at **Bombay Frigo,** 3 av. Princesse Grace, on the waterfront, west of the Jardin Japonais. A trendy mélange of Mediterranean and Indian influences, this resto attracts the upwardly mobile or those already there. Top DJs spin on weekends. Sharp dress is a must, unearthly beauty a plus. (☎93 25 57 00. Open June 15-Sept. 15 M-Sa 6pm-3am.)

From May 29-June 1, the best race car drivers in the world compete for the prestigious **Formula One-Grand Prix.** Unless you like the bustle of mass sporting events, this is not the time to visit. Most tourist attractions are closed and access to the waterfront is limited to paying spectators. Then again, the Grand Prix attracts the international jet-set; for a week you can goggle at the endless parade of Jaguars and yachts. For details, contact the tourist office or Service Municipal des Fêtes. (☎93 10 12 10.) Lurking in the Grand Prix' shadow, the **Festival International du Cirque** (☎92 05 26 00), Jan. 17-24, featuring the world's top circuses, and the **Flower-Arranging Competition** in mid-May (☎93 30 02 04) are unique in their own right.

MENTON

Menton (pop. 30,000) is often called the "Secret Riviera." Though removed from the glitter and glare of nearby tourist traps, Menton offers the picturesque white-sand beaches, lush gardens, and medieval alleys that made the Riviera famous in the first place. On France's eastern border, it also is a gateway to Italy.

🚌 TRANSPORTATION

Trains: pl. de la Gare (☎08 36 35 35 35). Trains operate 5am-11:45pm. Reservations 5am-noon and 12:45-7:35pm; self-serve machines at other times. Trains leave every 30min. to: **Cannes** (1¼hr., €7.70); **Monaco** (11min., €1.70); **Nice** (35min., €3.80). Also to: **Ventimiglia** (10min., €1.20) and **Genoa** (2½hr., 8-12 per day, €16.60) in Italy.

Buses: prom. Maréchal Leclerc (☎04 93 35 93 60); walk straight and to the left of the train station. Open M-F 8am-noon and 1-5pm, Sa 9-11am. Buses operate 7am-8pm. **Autocars Broch** (☎04 93 31 10 52) and **Rapides Côte d'Azur** (☎04 97 00 07 00) run buses every 15min. to **Monaco** (€2) and **Nice** (€4.30).

Taxis: (☎04 92 10 47 02). 5 central taxi stands serve the city from 5am-11pm; for other times reserve in advance by phone. Taxi from the train station to the hostel costs €7.

Bike Rental: L'escale du 2 Roues, 105 av. de Sospel (☎04 93 28 86 05). €13 per day. **Holiday Bikes,** 4 espl. G. Pompidou (☎04 92 10 99 98; www. holiday-bikes.com; hb.menton@club-internet.fr). €12.20 per day, €60 per week, and €230 deposit. Scooters and motorcycles also available.

✈ 🛈 ORIENTATION AND PRACTICAL INFORMATION

Menton is divided into the *vieille ville*, the new town, and the beach. **Av. du Verdun** or **av. Boyer** (depending on the side of the street) is the main thoroughfare of the new town, ending at a casino. A left turn at the casino takes you to the crowded pedestrian **rue St-Michel** and the heart of the *vieille ville*, an untouristed but intriguing tangle of serpentine streets and stairwells. The liveliest beach is **plage des Sablettes,** a wide stretch of chalky pebbles below the Basilique St-Michel.

Tourist Office: 8 av. Boyer (☎04 92 41 76 76; fax 04 92 41 76 78; www.villedementon.com; ot@villedementon.com). From the station, walk straight out onto av. de la Gare. After a block, you'll hit a boulevard; cross to the far side and turn right onto av. Boyer. The friendly, English-speaking staff provides free maps and practical guidebooks. Open July-Aug. M-Sa 9am-7pm, Su 9:30am-12:30pm; Sept.-June M-F 8:30am-12:30pm and 1:30-6pm, Sa 9am-noon and 2-6pm.

Garden Tours: Service du Patrimoine, 5 rue Ciapetti (☎04 92 10 33 66). Tours begin at 10am and 2:30pm and take about 2½hrs. Call ahead for English tours.

Currency Exchange: Crédit Lyonnais, 4 av. Boyer (☎04 92 41 81 11). Open M-F 8:30am-noon and 1:30-5:15pm, Sa 8am-1pm.

Internet Access: Le Café des Arts, 16 rue de la République (☎04 93 35 78 67). €6 per hr. Open M-F 7:30am-8pm, Sa 7:30-2pm

Post Office: cours George V (☎04 93 28 64 84), across from the tourist office. Offers **currency exchange.** Open M-W and F 8am-6:30pm, Th 8am-6pm, Sa 8am-noon.

Postal code: 06500.

🏠 ACCOMMODATIONS AND CAMPING

Auberge de Jeunesse (HI), plateau St-Michel (☎04 93 35 93 14; fax 04 93 35 93 07; menton@fuaj.org). Head straight from the train station along av. de la Gare and cross the first boulevard you hit, taking a left onto the far side. Take the first right, following the sign for "Camping St-Michel." Continue straight ahead on rue des Terres Chaudes, with the train tracks on your lower right. Turn left at Escalier des Rigaudis. At the level point, turn right up the steep stair section. At the top of the stairs, turn left and follow the path to a clearing. The hostel is on your left, 60m past the campsite. If you don't feel like burning a thousand calories, take bus #6 (8:40, 11:10am, 2, 5pm; €1.10). This hostel compensates for its remoteness with friendly atmosphere, fabulous vistas, and free breakfast served on a terrace overlooking the bay. Dinner €8. Sleepsack €2.70. Laundry €6. Reception 7am-noon and 5pm-midnight. **Strictly enforced** curfew at midnight. Open Mar.-Oct. Beds €11.35. ❶

Hôtel Beauregard, 10 rue Albert 1er (☎04 93 28 63 63; fax 04 93 28 63 79; beauregard.menton@wanad+oo.fr). Take an immediate right out of the train station and go down the steps behind Le Chou Chou *brasserie.* Turn right and the hotel is 80m down on the left. A friendly staff lets airy, spacious rooms with rich peach walls and blue carpet. TV. Breakfast €4.90. Reserve 1-2 months in advance July-Aug. Singles and doubles €29, with toilet and shower €34-39; triples with toilet and bath €45. Extra bed €8. ❸

Hôtel de Belgique, 1 av. de la Gare (☎04 93 35 72 66; fax 04 93 41 44 77; perso.wanadoo.fr/hotel.de.belgique). Attractive rooms with floral wallpaper. Singles €27; doubles €34, with toilet and shower €48; triples €52. Extra bed €10. MC/V. ❸

Hôtel Richelieu, 26 rue Partouneux (☎04 93 35 74 71; fax 04 93 57 69 61; hotelrichelieu.menton@wanadoo.fr). Take a left turn off av. Boyer just before the tourist office; it is 3 blocks down to the right. A marble staircase and upholstered walls give this hotel a downtown feel. Breakfast €5.50. Singles with shower and toilet €32-42; doubles €43-83; varies with season. Extra bed or person €15. AmEx/MC/V. ❹

Camping Municipal du Plateau St-Michel, rte. des Ciappes de Castellar (☎04 93 35 81 23; fax 04 93 57 12 35), 50 steps shy of the hostel. A quiet, adult crowd enjoys free hot showers, an affordable restaurant-bar, and a panoramic sea view in this isolated spot. Reception M-Sa 8:30am-noon and 3-6:30pm, Su 8:30am-noon and 3:30-6:30pm. €2.90 per person, €3.20 per small tent, €4 per large tent, €3.20 per car. Electricity €2.10 per day. Prices €0.30-0.60 higher June 15-Sept. 15. MC/V. ●

▐ FOOD

Get fresh food at the small **Marché Carëi,** on av. Sospel at the end of av. Boyer (open daily 7am-12:30pm) or the **Shopi** supermarket, 35 av. Félix Faure (☎04 93 57 56 56; open July-Sept. M-Sa 8:30am-8pm; Oct.-June 8:30am-7pm). Restaurants dot the waterfront and the pedestrian **rue St-Michel** in the *vieille ville,* including some good Italian places in bustling **pl. du Cap.** Street vendors in this Italian-influenced town sell *panini* (Italian-style sandwiches) and *glace italienne.*

Le Café des Arts, 16 rue de la République (☎04 93 35 78 67). True to its name, this cafe provides Internet access and delicious food in the midst of an airy art gallery. Large salads run €7, daily specials €10. Open M-F 7:30am-8pm, Sa 7:30am-2pm. ●

Le Petit Anjou, 14 rue Partouneaux (☎04 93 28 88 60). From av. Boyer, turn onto rue Partouneaux and walk two blocks. Mix with locals at this 16-table nook decorated with rock slabs and colorful oil paintings. Wide selection of salads (€8.50), meat (€8.50-17.50), and pasta (€7.50-9). The classic filet of beef (€16) is tasty. Open June-Aug. M-Sa noon-2:30pm, 8-10:30pm; Sept.-May lunch hours M-Sa and dinner hours Th-Sa. ●

◢ SIGHTS

Menton's main attraction is the **Musée Jean Cocteau,** quai Napoléon III, on prom. du Soleil. Best known for his work in film and drama, Cocteau experimented in the studio arts, and this 17th-century building showcases the interesting results. (04 93 57 72 30. Open M and W-Su 10am-noon and 2-6pm. €3.05, students under 25 €2.29, 18 and under free.) Cocteau fans will also appreciate the **Salle des Mariages** in the Hôtel de Ville, the only marriage site sanctioned by the state. Cocteau decorated this wonderfully odd, windowless room as a Greek temple and then added Vegas-esque touches like leopard rugs and red velvet chairs. (☎04 92 10 50 00. Open M-F 8:30am-12:30pm and 1:30-5pm. €1.50, students €1.15, under 18 no charge.)

The bell-tower of the **Basilique St-Michel** rises majestically above rue St-Michel in the *vieille ville.* Go to rue St-Michel, take a left onto rue des Logettes, and then ascend the steps of rue des Ecoles Pie. Despite undergoing many renovations since the first stones were laid in 1619, the church's Italianate facade remains distinctly Baroque. Twelve side-chapels exhibit crimson tapestries donated by the princes of nearby Monaco. (Open Su-F 10am-noon and 3-5:15pm. Su mass 10:30am.) Next door is the charming **Chapelle des Pénitents Blancs,** unconventionally decorated with shellfish. The sea-stone mosaic of **pl. St-Michel,** between the two churches, sets the stage for an incredible vista of the plage des Sablettes and the coastline of the Italian Riviera.

The **Monastère Annonciade,** site of the original Menton, overlooks the town from the lofty height of 225m. Take the **Chemin de Rosaire** (just west of the bus station, before the police station), which passes 15 chapels built by Princess Isabelle of Monaco to thank the Virgin of the Annonçiade for curing her leprosy. If the 30min. climb is rough on your legs, imagine the pilgrims who did it on their knees. The small monastery at the top is eerily beautiful, decorated with a set of femurs, some bones of unknown origin, and a gift shop. (☎04 93 35 76 92. Open daily 8am-6:30pm; mass M-Sa 11:15 am, Su 10am.)

ANTIBES

While most Riviera towns flaunt sun and sand like cheap costume jewelry, Antibes (pop. 73,000) relaxes demurely as the undisputed gem of the coast. Though blessed with beautiful beaches, a charming *vieille ville*, and the renowned Picasso museum, the city is less touristy than Nice and more relaxed than St-Tropez. Nearby **Juan-les-Pins** (see p. 563) is well-known for its debaucherous summer nightlife. Adding yet more flavor, Antibes has recently been inundated by thousands of young Anglophones looking for work on the luxury yachts in the harbor. These globe-trotting "yachtees," along with theater, music festivals, and a seaside hostel, make Antibes one of the most youth-oriented beach towns around.

⌐ TRANSPORTATION

Trains: av. Robert Soleau (☎08 36 67 68 69 and ☎08 36 35 35 35). Open daily 5:25am-12:05am. To: **Cannes** (15min., every 60min., €2.10); **Nice** (30min., every 60min., €3.30); **Marseille** (2¼hr., every 60min., €21.80).

Buses: Pl. de Gaulle (☎04 93 39 11 39). **RCA/TAM** sends buses #200 to: **Cannes** (25min., every 20min., €2.40); **Nice** (60min., every 20min., €4.10); and the **Nice airport** (40min., every 40min., €6.90).

Public Transportation: For info on the public bus service in Antibes, call ☎04 93 34 37 60. (Open M-F 8am-noon and 2-6pm; Sa 9-noon and 2-5pm.)

Taxi: Allô Taxi Antibes (☎04 93 67 67 67).

Bike and Scooter Rental: ScootAzur, 43 bd. Wilson (☎04 93 67 45 25; fax 04 93 67 45 26). Bikes from €12 per day, €56 per week; €150 deposit. Scooters from €33 per day, €175 per week; deposit €900. Open M-Sa 9am-noon and 2-7pm. AmEx/MC/V.

⚋ ✠ ORIENTATION AND PRACTICAL INFORMATION

Av. Robert Soleau connects the train station and **pl. de Gaulle**, center of the new town and home to the tourist office. From here, a short walk along rue de la République passes the bus station and heads into the heart of **Vieux Antibes**. Following tree-lined bd. Albert 1er from pl. de Gaulle and turning right at the water leads you to a long stretch of beach and the beginning of **Cap d'Antibes** (15min.), though the hostel and the tip of the peninsula are 30 minutes from there.

Tourist Office: 11 pl. de Gaulle (☎04 92 90 53 00; fax 04 92 90 53 01; accueil@antibes-juanlespins.com; www.antibes-juanlespins.com). Free maps and info on accommodations, camping, and festivals. The staff helps with reservations. Open July-Aug. daily 9am-7pm; Sept.-June M-F 9am-12:30pm and 1:30-6pm, Sa 9-noon and 2-6pm. **Branch** at the train station. Open July-Aug. M-F 7:30am-7pm.

Currency Exchange: Bureau de Change, 17 bd. Albert 1er (☎04 93 34 12 76). **No commission** on foreign currencies. Open daily 9am-noon and 2-7pm. **Eurochange,** 4 rue G. Clemenceau (☎04 93 34 48 30). Open M-Sa 9am-7pm.

English Bookstore: Heidi's English Bookshop, 24 rue Aubernon (☎/fax 04 93 34 74 11). Largest English bookshop on the Côte. Friendly staff knows a lot about the area. Open daily 10am-7pm. MC/V.

Laundromat: Pressing Wilson, 103 bd. Wilson (☎04 93 61 22 16). Open Tu-Sa 8:15am-noon and 2:30-7pm. **Laverie,** on rue Thuret, just off of bd. d'Aguillon. Open daily 8am-8pm.

Police: 5 rue des Frères Oliviers (☎04 92 90 78 00).

Hospital: Rue de la Fontaine (☎04 92 91 77 77).

Internet: Xtreme Cyber, Galérie du Port, 8 bd. d'Aguillon (☎04 93 34 36 34; xtremecyber@yahoo.fr). €0.12 per min., €5 for 50min. Open M-F 9am-7pm, Sa 10am-2pm.

Post office: Pl. des Martyrs de la Résistance (☎04 92 90 61 00), between the park and parking lot. Open M-F 8am-7pm, Sa 8am-noon.

Postal code: 06600.

ACCOMMODATIONS

Antibes lacks the budget hotels of Nice and Cannes, but there are a few hostels your wallet will appreciate. Accommodations in the *vieille ville* are good for sight-seers; Juan-les-Pins's hotels better suit those interested only in beach and nightlife. Reserve one to two weeks in advance in summer.

Relais International de la Jeunesse (Caravelle 60), 25 av. de l'Antiquité, at the intersection of bd. de la Garoupe and av. de l'Antiquité (☎04 93 61 34 40; fax 04 93 61 71 53; www.riviera-on-line.com/caravelle), is a 40min. walk along the shore. From Juan-les-Pins, walk south on bd. Edouard Baudoin, which becomes bd. du M. Juin, and cross the peninsula on chemin des Ondes. Turn right on bd. Francis Meillard, then left on bd. de la Garoupe, following signs for Juan-les-Pins Bord de Mer. Or take bus #2A from the bus station at pl. Guynemer in Antibes (every 40min., 7:05am-7:45pm, €1.10). High-ceilinged dorms, spectacular views of the sea, and a party-inducing yard make this hostel a backpacker's favorite. Breakfast included. Dinner €8. Luggage drop-off all day. Sheets €3. Reception 5:30-10:30pm. Lockout 10am-5:30pm. No curfew. Dorms €14. **Camping** €8 per person, without breakfast. ❶

The Crew House, 1 av. Saint Roch (☎04 92 90 49 39; fax 04 92 90 49 38; crewhouse_fr@yahoo.com). From the train station, walk down av. de la Libération until it turns into av. de Verdun, then make a right onto av. Saint Roch. A yachtee's paradise, this centrally-located hostel attracts a fun Anglo crowd. Backpackers are very welcome in the clean dorms and lively central courtyard. Internet €0.12 per min. Lockers; bring your own lock. Reception Apr.-Oct. 7:30am-9pm; Nov.-Mar. 8am-6pm. Dorms Apr.-Oct. €20, €100 per week; Nov.-Mar. €15, €75 per week. AmEx/MC/V. ❷

Hôtel Jabotte, 13 av. Max Maurey at the base of Cap D'Antibes (☎04 93 61 45 89; fax 04 93 61 07 04; www.jabotte.com; info@jabotte.com), is 2min. from the sea in a happening beach area. Helpful managers preside over cabana-style rooms. Central courtyard provides a respite from sun and sand. From pl. de Gaulle, follow bd. Albert 1er to its end, turn right on av. Maréchal Leclerc, and take a left onto bd. James Wyllie; av. Max Maurey is a right turn off the beach. Or take the free navette bus, which leaves from the train and bus stations every hr. M-Sa 7am-7pm. Breakfast €5.50. Check-in M-Sa before 7pm, Su before 1pm or after 6pm. Reception 8am-7:30pm. Singles and doubles €34-67; triples €69-87; quads €99-128. AmEx/MC/V. ❹

CÔTE D'AZUR

THE YACHTEE MYTH
If you want to join the "yachtee" population of Antibes, think twice before you buy your plane ticket. Thousands of anglo sun-worshippers head for the town every summer hoping to find work in the port, but most have no luck. The infiltration began in the early 1990s, when a binge of 18-26 year-old Australians, New Zealanders, and Americans came to Antibes seeking dockhand jobs. While walking down to the local Irish pub may have been enough for a job in the beginning, now most boats want qualified and stable help. Resident anglos say the yachtees usually run out of money and have to head elsewhere. The seasonal inundation seems to be on the decline, however, with the word spreading that yachtees are jobless.

Stella's, 5 av. Paul Arène (☎04 93 34 12 14; mobile 06 03 16 34 54). From the station, cross the street and take av. de la Libération toward the port. Av. Paul Arène is the third right after the roundabout. 16 tightly-packed beds in two coed rooms fill the top floor of Stella's beautiful, well-located Mediterranean home. Call between 9am-8:30pm. Dorms €20, €120 per week. ❷

🍴 FOOD

Vieille Antibes is loaded with restaurants adored by locals and tourists alike. The narrow streets behind **rue de la République** have particularly tasty options. The **Marché Provençal,** on cours Masséna near the Picasso museum, is considered one of the best on the Côte d'Azur. (Open June-Aug. daily 6am-1pm; Sept.-May Tu-Su.) The largest local supermarket is **Intermarché,** 1 bd. Albert 1er. (☎04 93 34 19 10. Open M-Sa 8:15am-7:30pm.)

🏅 **Le Broc en Bouche,** 8 rue des Palmiers, off of rue Aubernon (☎04 93 34 75 60), is the perfect place to shop and dine—everything, from the inventive dishes (€10) to the eclectic furniture (tables €300), is on sale. Open July-Aug. daily 7-11pm; Sept.-June Tu-Sa noon-2pm and 7-11pm. ❸

La Toscana, on the corner of av. Meissonier and av. du 24 Aout (☎04 93 34 54 77), might have a generic interior, but locals love its large selection of pastas (€7-9), pizza (€6-8), meats (€10-15), and fish (€12.50-16). Open Tu-Su noon-2:30pm and 7-11pm; F-Sa until midnight). ❸

Le Brulot, 3 rue Frédéric Isnard, right off av. G. Clemenceau (☎04 93 34 17 76; www.brulot.com), is the hot local place for sit-down meals. Specializing in Provençale cuisine *au feu de bois* (wood-fired), this 2-level restaurant serves delicious meats (€13-21) and fish (€8.50-20). Try the enormous *côte de boeuf* for two (€37.50). The €10 lunch menu is a good deal. Bring a date to the intimate basement, hollowed out of a cave. Reservations necessary. Open June-July 7pm-midnight; Sept.-May M-W 7pm-midnight, Th-Sa noon-2:15pm and 7pm-midnight. AmEx/MC/V. ❸

🔵 SIGHTS

Once home to Pablo Picasso, Graham Greene, and Max Ernst, Antibes takes great pride in its resident artists. **Musée Picasso,** pl. Mariejol, in the Château Grimaldi, hosted Picasso for a productive five months in 1946 and has been rewarded with an excellent collection of his paintings and sculpture. (☎04 92 90 54 20. Open Tu-Su June-Sept. 10am-6pm; Oct.-May 10am-noon and 2-6pm. €4.60, students €2.30. Audioguide €3.) **Musée Peynet,** pl. Nationale, known affectionately as the "Museum of Love," displays over 300 colorful drawings and cartoons by local artist Raymond Peynet, who enjoys something of a cult following. (☎04 92 90 54 30. Open June-Sept. Tu-Su 10am-6pm; Oct.-May 10am-noon and 2-6pm. €3, students €1.50.) The **Musée Archéologique,** on the waterfront in the Bastion St-André-sur-les-Remparts, displays archaeological finds and exhibits on the history of ancient Antibes. (☎04 93 34 00 39. Open June-Sept. Tu, Th and Sa-Su 10am-6pm, W and F 10am-8pm; Oct.-May Tu-Su 10am-noon and 2-6pm. €3, students €1.50.) The attractive **Musée Napoléonien,** av. Kennedy in Cap d'Antibes, contains Bonapartist paraphernalia such as Canova's bust of the Emperor. (☎04 93 61 45 32. Open M-F 9:30am-noon and 2:15-6pm, Sa 9:30am-noon. €3, students €1.50.) Take a walk through the lobby and grounds of the renowned **Hôtel du Cap-Eden-Roc** next door. Spending the night will cost you a pretty penny (☎04 93 61 39 01. Reserve for July-Aug. in Apr. Closed mid-Oct. to mid-Apr. Singles €280-infinity.) The largest private marina on the Mediterranean, **Port Vauban** harbors some spectacular sleek white yachts, guarded vigilantly by the 16th-century **Fort Carré.** (☎06 14 89 17 45. Tours only. Open June-Sept. Tu-Su 10:15am-5:50pm; Oct.-May Tu-Su 10:15am-4pm. €3.)

🎵 ENTERTAINMENT AND FESTIVALS

Juan-les-Pins is the place to be at night, though you can have a good time in the Antibes bars before the clubs in the neighboring town open. The bars and pubs along boulevard d'Aguillon hold Happy Hours (6pm) for a cosmopolitan crowd of yachtees. During the first two weeks of July, the **Festival d'Art Lyrique** brings world-class soloists and orchestras to the old port (☎ 04 92 90 53 00; €13-62).

> **La Gaffe,** 6 bd. d'Aguillon, is where the cool Anglo kids head, and they are joined at night by beautiful, bikini-clad barmaids. Fruity "alco-pops" go for €5-6. (☎ 04 93 34 04 06. Live rock bands June-Sept. W and F-Sa. Happy hour: June-Sept. Th-Tu 11pm-midnight, W 9-10pm and F from 6-7pm.; Oct.-May Th-Tu 6-7pm; W 9-10pm: 2 for 1. Open daily 8am-2:30am.)

> **Le Blue Lady,** rue Lacan, across the street, is a low-key, Anglo bar with pool tables and a popular outdoor terrace. (☎ 04 93 34 41 00. Open M-F 7:30am-12:30am, Sa 8:30am-12:30am.)

> **The Hop Store,** 38 bd. d'Aguillon, a little more sedate, has all the trimmings of an Irish pub. (☎ 04 93 34 15 33. Happy hour noon-1pm and 7-8pm with €3.40 pints. Live music on weekends. Open daily 8:30am-2:30am.)

> **Xtreme Café,** 6 rue Aubernon, is a classy wine bar with a funky purple and stone interior, draws a good-looking crowd. (☎ 04 93 34 03 90. Open June-Sept. Tu-Su 10am-2:30am; Oct.-May Tu-Su 10am-12:30am.)

NEAR ANTIBES: JUAN-LES-PINS

Officially one city, Antibes and Juan-les-Pins are 2km apart and have separate train stations, post offices, and tourist offices. They also move to different beats. Younger and more hedonistic, Juan-les-Pins is packed with seekers of sun, sea, and sex (not necessarily in that order). In the summer, boutiques stay open until midnight, cafés until 2am, and nightclubs until the dancers return to the beach.

🚆 **PRACTICAL INFORMATION.** The **train station** is on av. l'Estérel, where it joins av. du Maréchal Joffre. (Open daily 6:40am-9:40pm.) Trains leave for **Antibes** (5min., until 11:58am, €1.20), **Cannes** (10min., €1.90), and **Nice** (30min., €3.60) on a variable schedule. By **bus** from pl. Guynemer in Antibes, take Sillages #1A (15min.; every 20min., 7am-7:40pm; €1.10). For a **taxi,** call ☎ 04 92 93 07 07. To **walk from Antibes,** follow bd. Wilson from pl. du Général de Gaulle for 1½km and turn left onto av. Dautheville. To get to the **tourist office,** 51 bd. Guillaumont, walk straight out on av. du Maréchal Joffre from the train station and turn right onto av. Guy de Maupassant; the office is two minutes away on the right, at the intersection of av. Amiral Courbet and av. Guillaumont. (☎ 04 92 90 53 05. Same email and website as Antibes tourist office. Open Sept.-June M-F 9am-noon and 2-6pm, Sa 9am-noon; July-Aug. daily 9am-7pm.)

🏠🍴 **ACCOMMODATIONS AND FOOD.** Juan-les-Pins has very little budget lodging. The friendly manager of **Hôtel Trianon ❸,** 14 av. de l'Estérel, caters to backpackers with free Internet access and well-furnished rooms. (☎/fax 04 93 61 18 11. Breakfast €4. Singles €24.50; doubles €30-37; triples €40-45. AmEx/MC/V.)

Next door, **Hôtel Parisiana ❹,** 16 av. de L'Estérel, has more expensive and better-looking rooms with rich carpets, firm beds, and fresh flowers. (☎ 04 93 61 27 03; fax 04 93 67 97 21. All rooms with fridge, shower, and TV. Breakfast €5. Reception 8am-10pm. Singles €35; doubles €49; triples €59; quads €67. Prices €10 lower

Sept.-May. The price is lower for stays of more than four nights during low season. MC/V.) Though illegal, dangerous, and not recommended by *Let's Go*, some carousers seem to mistake the beach's sand for a mattress.

Juan-les-Pins's restaurants are virtually indistinguishable, although **La Bamba ❷**, 18 av. Dautheville, seems to be the most popular. This airy restaurant bakes hot pizzas (€8-10.50), pastas (€7.50-10.50), and meats and fishes (€11-22) from its wood-burning oven. (☎04 93 61 32 64. Open daily 5:30pm-midnight. AmEx/MC/V.)

The **Casino supermarket** is on av. Admiral Courbet, across from the tourist office and the beach. (☎04 93 61 00 56. Open M-Tu and Th-Sa 8am-12:30pm and 3:30-7pm; Su 8am-12:30pm.)

🎷 **ENTERTAINMENT AND FESTIVALS.** The heart of Juan-les-Pins nightlife is the Casino area, where cruising the strip is entertainment in itself. Discothèques open around 11pm and close around 5am, with cover charges about €15.25. The flavor of the moment is 🎵**Pulp**, av. Gallice, where a hip crowd beautifies the dance floor and plush red sofas. (☎04 93 67 22 74. Cover €15.25. F ladies free. Open July-Sept. daily midnight-5am; Oct.-June F-Sa midnight-5am.) **Le Village**, 1 bd. de la Pinède, accomplishes its Mexican theme with pueblo facades and life-size burros. (☎04 92 93 90 00. Cover €16. M disco, Tu ladies night, Th latino, Su house. Low season F ladies free. Open daily July-Aug. midnight-5am, Sept.-June F-Sa midnight-5am.) **Kelly's Irish Bar**, 5 bd. de la Pinède, is a new kid on the block, targeting the ubiquitous anglo population. (☎06 20 20 17 49. Pints €5.40-6.70. July-Aug. live music daily from 11pm. Open July-Aug. 6pm-4am; Sept.-June 6pm-2am.) In psychedelic **Whisky à Gogo**, 5 rue Jacques Leonetti, a young crowd dances to house, hiphop, and Latino beats amid water-filled columns. (☎04 93 61 26 40. Cover €15.25. Open July-Aug. daily midnight-6am; Sept.-June F-Sa midnight-6am.)

Most discothèques are only open on weekends in the off-season. Fortunately, bars pick up the slack. At the tropical-themed **Pam Pam Rhumerie**, 137 bd. Wilson, bikinied showgirls vibrate to drumbeats and down flaming drinks like the Waikiki. (☎04 93 61 11 05; www.pampam.fr. Open Mar. 25-Nov. 11 daily 3pm-4am.)

The jointly owned **Ché Café**, 1 bd. de la Pinède (open daily July-Aug. 4pm-5:30am; Sept.-June daily 5pm-3:30am and until 5am F-Sa), and **La Réserve** (open July-Aug. daily 8am-5am; Sept.-June 8am-2am), across the street, host pre-clubbing crowds on their large patios (☎04 93 61 20 06). Across from Ché, **Zapata's** lassos, sombreros, and jalapeno pepper lights take you to Mexico. (Open daily 5pm-5am.) If you have any money left, lose it at the cave-like **Eden Casino**, bd. Baudoin. (☎04 92 93 71 71. 18+. No shorts or sneakers. No cover. Open daily 10am-5am.)

In mid-July, Juan-Les-Pins puts on the massive **Festival International de Jazz (Jazz à Juan)**. In 2002, Joe Cocker and Wynton Marsalis made appearances. (jazzajuan@antibes-juanlespins.com. Tickets €20-59, available at tourist offices in Juan-les-Pins and Antibes.)

CANNES

The name Cannes (pop. 70,000) conjures up certain images: Catherine Deneuve sipping champagne by the pool, Marilyn posing red-lipped on the beach, and countless other celebrities fighting for camera time. With its renowned annual film festival, these associations are not at all inaccurate. But the festival happens only once a year, and Cannes has to do *something* with itself in between. That something is being the most accessible of the Riviera's glam-towns, without the wealth of Monte-Carlo or the exclusivity of St-Tropez. The palm-lined boardwalk, gorgeous sandy beach, and innumerable boutiques are open to anyone, and if your legs are bronze, your sunglasses stylish, and your shopping bags full, you belong.

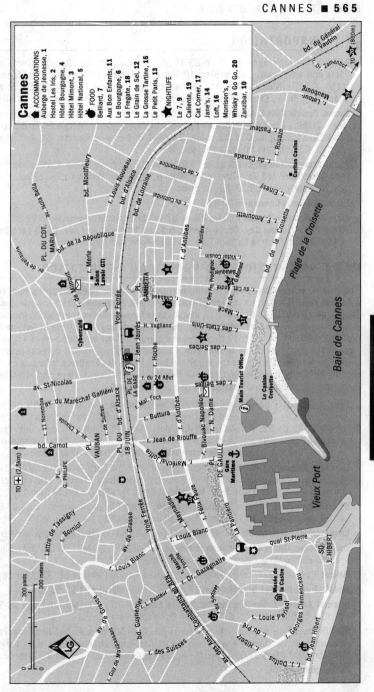

COTE D'AZUR

Cannes

▲ ACCOMMODATIONS
Auberge de Jeunesse, 1
Hostel Les Iris, 2
Hôtel Bourgogne, 4
Hôtel Mimont, 3
Hôtel National, 5

● FOOD
Belliard, 7
Aux Bon Enfants, 11
Le Bourgogne, 6
La Fregate, 18
Le Grain de Sel, 12
La Grosse Tartine, 15
Le Petit Paris, 13

★ NIGHTLIFE
Le 7, 9
Caliente, 19
Cat Corner, 17
Jane's, 14
Loft, 16
Morrison's, 8
Whisky à Go Go, 20
Zanzibar, 10

☞ TRANSPORTATION

Trains: 1 rue Jean-Jaurès (☎08 36 35 35 35). Station open daily 5am-12:30am, info desk and ticket sales daily 5:30am-10:30pm. To: **Antibes** (15min., €2.10); **Monaco** (1hr., €7.10); **Nice** (40min., €5); **Marseille** (2hr., 6:30am-11:05pm, €15.25); **St-Raphaël** (25min., €5.30); and other coastal towns. TGV to **Paris** via Marseille €75-91.

Buses: Rapide Côte D'Azur, pl. de l'Hôtel de Ville (☎04 93 39 11 39). To: **Nice** (1½hr., every 20min., €5.70) and **Nice airport** (60min.; every 40min. M-Sa 5:50am-8:30pm, Su 8:30am-8:30pm; €12.20, under 25 €9.15). Buses to **Grasse** (50min., every 30min., €3.66) leave from the train station.

Public Transportation: Bus Azur (☎04 93 45 20 08), at pl. de l'Hôtel de Ville. Info desk and ticket sales M-F 7am-7pm, Sa 8:30am-6:30pm. Bus tickets €1.25; carnet of 10 €8.30, weekly pass €9.20. Buy on board.

Taxis: Allô Taxis Cannes (☎04 92 99 27 27).

Bike and Scooter Rental: Holiday Bikes, 32 av. du Maréchal Juin (☎04 93 94 30 34). Bikes from €11 per day, €53 per week; scooters from €36 per day, €145 per week. €450 deposit. Open M-Sa 9am-7pm, Su 10am-noon and 7-8pm. AmEx/MC/V.

✦🛈 ORIENTATION AND PRACTICAL INFORMATION

The *centre ville*, between the station and the sea, is the city's shopping hub; **rue d'Antibes** runs through its center. If you head right from the station on rue Jean-Jaurès, you'll end up in the old city, known as **le Suquet**, where there's flea-market-style shopping on **rue Meynadier** by day and upscale dining on tiny **rue St-Antoine** by night. Star-gazers or tourist office-seekers should follow rue des Serbes (across from the station) to **bd. de la Croisette,** Cannes's long and lavish coastal promenade. The tourist office is on the left in the huge **Palais des Festivals,** which is encircled by celebrity handprints. Cannes's beautiful **beach** begins here and stretches along the peninsular land of clubs known as **Palm Beach.**

Tourist Office: 1 bd. de la Croisette (☎04 93 39 24 53; fax 04 92 99 84 23; www.cannes.fr). 2½hr. guided tours every 2nd and 4th Saturday of the month 2pm (☎04 92 99 84 22; €7). Open July-Aug. daily 9am-8pm, Sept.-June daily 9am-7pm. **Branch** office at train station (☎04 93 99 19 77). Open M-Sa 9am-7pm. For hotel reservations, call town's **centrale de reservation** (☎04 93 99 99 00) daily 9am-7pm.

Currency Exchange: Office Provençal, 17 rue Maréchal-Foch (☎04 93 39 34 37), across from train station. Open daily 8am-8pm. **American Express,** 1bis rue Notre Dame (☎04 93 99 05 45). Open M-F 9am-5:30pm; May-Sept. open Sa 9am-noon.

English Bookstore: Cannes English Bookshop, 11 rue Bivouac Napoléon (☎04 93 99 40 08; fax 04 93 66 39 72). Open M-Sa 10am-1pm and 2-7pm. AmEx/MC/V.

Laundromat: Salon Lavoir GTI, 26 rue Merle (☎06 62 84 00 20). Open daily 7am-9pm.

Youth Center: Cannes Information Jeunesse, 5 quai St-Pierre (☎04 93 06 31 31). Info on jobs and housing. Open M-F 8:30am-12:30pm and 2-5pm.

Police: 1 av. de Grasse (☎04 93 06 22 22) and 2 quai St-Pierre (☎08 00 11 71 18).

Hospital: Hôpital des Broussailles, 13 av. des Broussailles (☎04 93 69 70 00).

Internet Access: CyberCafé Institut Riviera Langues, 26 rue de Mimont (☎04 93 99 14 77). €1.50 for 15min., €4.60 per hr. Open daily 9am-10pm.

Post Office: 22 rue Bivouac Napoléon (☎04 93 06 26 50), off allée de Liberté near Palais des Festivals. Open M-F 8am-7pm, Sa 8:30am-noon. **Branch office** at 37 rue de Mimont (☎04 93 06 27 00). Open M-F 8:30am-noon and 1:30-5pm, Sa 8:30am-noon.

Postal code: 06400.

ACCOMMODATIONS AND CAMPING

You should be able to get a good night's sleep at reasonable prices. During the film festival, hotel rates triple and rooms need to be reserved at least a year in advance. Also plan early for high season, particularly August.

Hostel Les Iris, 77 bd. Carnot (☎/fax 04 93 68 30 20 or 06 09 45 17 35; lesiris@hotmail.com). Take a right onto rue Jean Jaurès and another right onto bd. Carnot. The hostel is on the left, about 50m before Hôtel Amarante. (7min.) Young, friendly, Englishspeaking owners converted a hotel into this clean, bright hostel. Light blue doors and yellow hallways lead to rooms of 2-6 with firm beds. Breakfast €4.50. Dinner €7-8. Sheets €4 per week; towels €4. Reception 10am-9pm, key code access after-hours. All rooms have keys. Beds €16. MC/V. ❷

Auberge de Jeunesse: Le Chalit, 27 av. du Maréchal Gallieni (☎/fax 04 93 99 22 11 or 06 03 40 70 86). Take stairs to a passage that goes under the train station; signs will point you to the hostel. (5min.) At night, travelers should avoid the dark tunnel; instead, turn right on bd. Carnot as you exit the station and follow it straight until av. 11 November. Take a right on 11 Nov. and a left onto av. Gallieni. Movie posters adorn the light-filled rooms. Restaurant in basement. Sheets €3. Reception May-Sept. 8:30am-1pm and 5-8pm; Oct.-Apr. 8:30am-3pm and 5-7pm. Lockout 10:30am-5pm. 24hr. access with door code. 4- to 8-bed dorms €20-22. Reservations May-Sept. ❷

Hôtel Mimont, 39 rue de Mimont (☎04 93 39 51 64; fax 04 93 99 65 35). Rue de Mimont is two streets behind the train station. Either take the infamous underground passage (see hostel directions above) for two blocks or leave the train station to your left, turn left on bd. de la République, and then make another left on rue de Mimont. The best budget hotel in Cannes. Clean, spacious rooms have new beds with thick duvets, TVs, and direct-line telephones. Breakfast €5.50. Reception 8am-11pm. Singles €29, with toilet €36; doubles €36.50, with toilet €42; triples with toilet €51—a real steal. Extra person €10. Prices 10% higher July and Aug. AmEx/MC/V. ❸

Hôtel National, 8 rue Maréchal Joffre (☎04 93 39 91 92; fax 04 92 98 44 06; hotelnationalcannes@wanadoo.fr). Bland white rooms (all with TV) just steps away from the lively rue Meynadier and the *vieille ville.* Friendly, 18-year British owner. Breakfast €5. Reception 8am-10pm. Singles with shower and toilet €30-42; doubles €30-42, with shower and toilet €40-55; triples €45-70. AmEx/MC/V. ❹

Hôtel de Bourgogne, 11 rue du 24 août (☎04 93 38 36 73; fax 04 92 99 28 41), off rue Jean-Jaurès. Well-maintained rooms in muted shades of red. Not bursting with charm, but in the heart of the town. Breakfast €5. Reception 24hr. Singles €28, with shower €35, with shower and toilet €45; doubles €37, with shower €39, with shower and toilet €53; triple €55. AmEx/MC/V. ❸

Camping:

Le Grand Saule, 24 bd. Jean Moulin (☎04 93 90 55 10; fax 04 93 47 24 55; www.legrandsaule.com), in nearby Ranguin. Take bus #9 from pl. de l'Hôtel de Ville toward Ranguin (20min., €1.15). 3-star site with swimming pool, snack bar, billiards, and pinball machine feels more like a resort than the great outdoors. Sauna €5; table tennis €8. Open May-Sept. July-Aug. 1 person €16, 2 people €22; May-June and Sept. 1 person €11, 2 people €16. Car €3. Electricity €3. Laundry €3. MC/V. ❶

Parc Bellevue, 67 av. M. Chevalier (☎04 93 47 28 97; fax 04 93 48 66 25), in La Bocca, an enormous and daunting suburb. Take bus #2 to "Chevalier" and walk straight for 500m, following signs for the campground. Large 211-spot campground with beautiful views and trails. As many mobile homes as tents. Reception 8am-7pm. July-Aug. 1 person with tent €13, 2 people with tent €17; Apr.-June and Sept. 1 person with tent €10, 2 people with tent €13. Car €2. ❶

THE BIG SPLURGE

LA GROSSE TARTINE

Surrounded by the rich, the famous, and the devestatingly well-dressed, you will doubtlessly get the urge to experience the high life in Cannes during your visit. For a wonderful meal, pass on the tourist-saturated rue du Suquet and head over to **La Grosse Tartine ❹**. The friendly manager will greet and usher you to a table on the sunny terrace or in the cozy yellow interior with tropical hints and vintage French posters.

Though the restaurant offers a budget-oriented selection of *tartines* (open-faced sandwiches), including lamb *confit*, chicken, goat cheese and *oie gras poêlé* (€11-18.50), you should consider splurging on three courses from the main menu. To begin, try the house speciality: homemade warm *foie gras* (€17), accompanied by grapes and figs. For a main course, the chef suggests fish dishes (€16-30) from *saumon tartare* to royal king prawns, and a varied listing of meats (€18-30), including beef, lamb, steak tartare, and duck. For dessert (€8-9), do not miss the to-die-for *gateaux fondant au chocolat*, a rich dark chocolate cake with a molten chocolate center.

Three courses and wine may force you to ration your funds for the next few days, but the generous portions of rich cuisine will ensure that your empty stomach has good memories. (☎04 93 68 59 28. *9 rue du Bamidnight. AmEx/MC/V.*)

◘ FOOD

Though dominated by higher-end restaurants, Cannes offers good food for the budget-oriented. There are **markets** on pl. Gambetta and on pl. du Commandant Maria, but even better is the **Forville** market on rue Meynadier and rue Louis Blanc, which offers a large selection of fruit, vegetables, fish, and flowers. (All open Tu-Su 7am-1pm.) You can also try **Champion supermarket,** 6 rue Meynadier. (☎04 93 39 62 13. Open M-Sa June-Aug. 8:30am-7:30pm; Sept.-May 8:30am-7:45pm.)

There are tasty and reasonably priced restaurants throughout the pedestrian zone, especially **rue Meynadier.** Farther along, the narrow streets of **le Suquet** beckon; the extra ambience will cost you.

- ▧ **La Grosse Tartine,** 9 rue du Bamidnight (☎04 93 68 59 28), is a glamorous dining experience. (See sidebar, **The Big Splurge.**) ❹

- ▧ **Aux Bons Enfants,** 80 rue Meynadier, offers 3 savory courses for €15.50. This 3rd-generation restaurant will not disappoint. The menu changes nightly, according to what catches the chef's eye at the nearby Marché Forville. Open May-July and Sept. M-Sa noon-2pm and 7-9:30pm; Oct.-Apr. M-F noon-2pm and 7-9:30pm; Sa noon-2pm. No credit cards. ❹

- **La Fregate,** 26 bd. Jean Hibert (☎04 93 39 45 39). This large *brasserie,* popular with local youth, serves big portions of Italian-inspired cuisine in a nice interior and a seaside terrace. Enormous selection of pizzas (€8-12), pastas (€6.50-10), and meats (€13-20), and non-stop summer service make this a reliable pleasure. Open June-Sept. daily 24hr.; Oct.-May daily 6am-1am. AmEx/MC/V. ❷

- **Belliard,** 1 rue Chabaud (☎04 93 39 42 72; fax 04 93 38 96 62; gbelliard@aol.com). Belliard has been pleasing locals since 1930. This nationally-recognized bakery, pastry shop, *salon de thé,* and restaurant offers a gourmet €7 plate. Choose from 3-4 meat/fish options and 7-8 *legumes.* Open M-Sa 7am-8pm. ❷

- **Le Petit Paris,** 13 rue des Belges (☎04 93 38 88 60), is a good deal in an otherwise expensive area. Salads (€9-11), pastas (€8.40-10), meats and fishes (€10.50-16), omelettes (€6.90-8.90), and sandwiches (€3-9.50) are served until 5pm. Don't let the trite name turn you away. Open M-Sa 7am-midnight. AmEx/MC/V. ❸

- **Le Grain de Sel,** 28 rue du Suquet, has a good deal (though a bit of a splurge) in its €14.95 *menu.* Enjoy beautifully-presented provençal dishes in the warm yellow interior or on the romantic outdoor terraces. (☎04 93 39 21 24. Open Th-Tu 7pm-midnight. MC/V). ❸

Le Bourgogne, 13 rue de 24 août, run by a friendly chef, concocts delicious French-Italian dishes in a rustic interior. (☎04 93 38 33 27. €12 *menu*. Open daily 11am-2:30pm and 7-11pm.) ❸

SIGHTS AND SHOPPING

Perched at the top of the Suquet, **L'Eglise de la Castre** and its shady courtyard give an excellent view of the bustling city below. Inside, the **Musée de la Castre** displays weapons, masks, and instruments from Ghana, the Congo, and Nigeria. (☎04 93 38 55 26. Open Tu-Sa June-Aug. 10am-1pm and 3-7pm; Sept. and Apr.-May 10am-1pm and 2-6pm; Oct.-Mar. 10am-1pm and 2-5pm. €3, students €2.)

Blessed with tons of boutiques, Cannes has the best window shopping on the Riviera. **Boulevard de la Croisette,** along the waterfront, is ruled by high-end names like Cartier, Chanel, and Dior. The (barely) less pricey **rue d'Antibes** and its environs mix high-end brand names and funky independent boutiques. Go to **Rue Meynadier,** a carnivalesque street market, if you're in the mood for dirt-cheap duds.

ENTERTAINMENT AND FESTIVALS

The world of cinema arrives with pomp and circumstance in Cannes for the ☒**Festival International du Film** from May 15-26. The festival is invite-only, though the sidewalk show is free. July 4 and 14 bring the **Fête Américaine** and **Fête Nationale,** particularly boisterous versions of festivals held throughout France.

Cannes's three casinos give you multiple options to blow your money. The least exclusive, **Le Casino Croisette,** 1 espace Lucien Barrière, next to the Palais des Festivals, has slot machines, blackjack, and roulette. (☎04 92 98 78 00. Cover €10. No jeans, shorts, or T-shirts; jacket necessary for men. 18+. Gambling daily 8pm-4am, slots open at 10am.)

NIGHTLIFE

If you want to get into one of Cannes's elite nightspots, dress to kill. Just as fun and half the price, cafés and bars near the waterfront stay open all night. Nightlife thrives around **rue Dr. G. Monod.**

Morrison's, 10 rue Teisseire (☎04 92 98 16 17; info@morrisonspub.com). Guinness posters, mahogany walls, and a massive Irish flag please pub-lovers from France and abroad. Beer from €2.80. Live music from 10pm W-Th. Happy Hour daily 5-8pm. Open daily 5pm-2:30am.

Jane's, 38 rue des Serbes (☎04 92 99 79 59). Cannes's favorite discothèque, in the Hôtel Gray d'Albion, features go-go dancers, an active dance floor, and a massive lounge area. Cover Th €10, F-Sa €15, or €10 before midnight; Su €10 for men, women free (all include first drink). Open Th-Su 11pm-dawn.

Loft, 13 rue du Dr. G. Monod (☎04 93 39 40 39). A mellow crowd fills this dimly-lit lounge and sips cocktails to the beats of the live DJ. Downstairs, the Asian-French restaurant **Tantra** morphs into a club on weekends, and tables become dance floors. No cover. Open daily 10:30pm-2:30am.

Cat Corner, 22 rue Macé (☎04 93 39 31 31). Plush velour sofas, funky lighting, and a central location attract Cannes's coolest and wealthiest. DJs spin house, R&B, and funk. Cover €16 (includes 1 drink). Open daily 11:30pm-5am.

Caliente, 83 bd. de la Croisette (☎04 93 94 49 59.) With its blaring neon sign and loud Latin beats, you can't miss this sizzling nightspot. The raucous crowd loves the live salsa music and unpretentious atmosphere. No cover. Open daily 6pm-3am; until 5am Th-Sa.

Whisky à Go Go, 115 av. de Lérins (☎04 93 43 20 63), by Palm Beach. Torches guide the way to this flaming nightspot, packed with men on the prowl and the ladies who love them. Cover €15.25 (includes 1 free drink); F ladies free, men's cover includes 4 free drinks. Open F-Sa 11pm-dawn; July-Aug. daily.

Le 7, 7 rue Rougières (☎04 93 39 10 36). Guaranteed to give you a fun night, Le 7 is known for the nightly drag shows in its catwalk-like, intimate interior. Cover €16 (includes one drink). Drag shows start at 1:30am. Open daily 11:30pm-dawn.

Zanzibar, 85 rue Félix Faure (☎04 93 39 30 75). Europe's oldest gay bar, serving drinks since 1885. Intimate patio and candle-lit cavern, with a marine theme: silver Poseidons, boat parts, the works. Open daily 6pm-dawn.

◪ DAYTRIPS FROM CANNES

ILES DE LÉRINS

Société Planaria, across from the Palais des Festivals on the port, sends boats to St-Honorat nearly every hr. (☎/fax 04 92 98 71 38. May-Sept. daily 8am-5:30pm; Oct.-Apr. 8am-4:30pm. €8 round-trip.) Compagnie Esterel Chanteclair, around the corner, provides the cheapest fare to Ste-Marguerite. (☎04 93 39 11 82; fax 04 92 98 80 32; www.ilesdelerins.com. Around every 30min., from 7:30am-6:15pm; round trip €9.) No ferry service between the islands.

Just a 15min. ferry ride from Cannes, the Iles de Lérins provide a welcome break from the city. If you're pressed for time, visit the smaller island, **St-Honorat,** home to pine forests and an active monastery **(Abbaye de Lérins).** Saint Honorat settled there in the 5th century and was joined by other famous early Christians. Together they founded Lérins, one of Europe's most celebrated monasteries. Today, the order shares the land with tourists who love the homemade honey and wine at their gift shop. (☎04 92 99 54 00. Mass M-Sa 11:25am, Su 9:50. Open June-Sept. daily 9:30am-4:30pm; Oct.-May 10:40am-3:30pm. Free.) On the south side of the island, the **original monastery** stands broken and deserted, waiting to be explored. Wonderful views await at the top (open daily 10:30am-4pm).

Four times the size of its neighbor, the park island **Ste-Marguerite** is densely forested by eucalyptus and parasol pines. Once home to St. Honorat's equally holy sister Margaret, its main attraction is **Fort Ste-Marguerite,** a fearsome, star-shaped, thankfully inactive prison that once held the Man in the Iron Mask. **Le Musée de la Mer** displays the masked man's cell, a bare rectangle with a small hole in the corner—guess its use if you can. (☎04 93 43 18 17. Open Apr.-Sept. 10:30am-1:15pm and 2:15-5:45pm; Oct.-Mar. 10:30am-1:15pm and 2:15-4:45pm. €3, students €2.)

MOUGINS

You can reach Mougins by bus #600 from Cannes's train station (direction "Grasse" or "Val du Mougins;" 17min.; every 30min., M-Sa 6am-12:40am; every hr., Su 8:30am-12:40am; €1.60). From there, walk 25m back down the road and take a left, following signs and passing magnificent estates on the way to Mougins (25min.).

The village of Mougins (pop. 19,500), 8km from Cannes, has been elevated (260m above sea level, in fact) to affluent suburbia. The narrow stone streets, art galleries, and charming (though pricey) cafés are definitely worth a visit. The **Musée de la Photographie,** Porte Sarrazine, off rue Maréchal Foch, includes a collection of old cameras and photos of a trendy, stripe-shirted Picasso at work and play. (☎04 93 75 85 67. Open July-Sept. daily 10am-8pm; Oct.-June W-Sa 10am-noon and 2-6pm, Su 2-6pm. €2; students €1.) The **tourist office,** 15 av. Jean-Charles Mallet, provides plenty of info on the area, including excursions to the enormous **Parc de la Valmasque.** (☎04 93 75 87 67; www.mougins-coteazur.org. Open July-Aug. daily 10am-8pm; Sept.-June M 2:30-5:30pm, Tu-Sa 10am-5:30pm.)

GRASSE

You'll know you're in Grasse (pop. 45,000) when the smell of sea foam turns to citronella and tanning oil to tea rose. Capital of the world's perfume industry for 200 years, Grasse is home to France's three largest, oldest, and most distinguished *parfumeries*. The town is also near the GR4 trail, and an excellent springboard for exploration of the Grand Canyon du Verdon (see p. 572). If you're not a fan of *eau de toilette* or cologne, though, stick to the sunny beaches of the coast.

■ **ORIENTATION AND PRACTICAL INFORMATION.** Grasse's proximity to Cannes (15km) makes it a pleasant afternoon excursion. Although the town spreads into the valley below, most tourist destinations are concentrated in the *vieille ville* and on the south-facing hillside. As you face the sea, the bus station is to the immediate left of the old city; **bd. de Jeu de Ballon** is the thoroughfare just above the station, home to the **tourist office annex** and, farther down, to the casino. A few steps more and you'll reach **place du Cours,** a large plateau overlooking the valley and within easy reach of the Fragonard perfumery and several museums.

The **bus station,** pl. de la Buanderie, has service daily to Cannes (40min.; every 30min., Su every hr.; €3.70) and Nice (1hr., every 40min., €6.10), through the **RCA** (☎04 93 36 08 43) and **SOMA** (☎04 93 36 49 61) bus lines, respectively. (Open M-Th 8am-5pm, F 8am-4pm.) No trains stop at Grasse, but there's an **SNCF info office** (☎08 36 35 35 35) across the *place*. (Open M-F 8:50am-5:30pm, Sa 8:50am-noon and 1:30-5pm.) The **tourist office** is near the casino on cours Honoré Cresp in the Palais des Congrés. Pick up a map with a 1½hr. long annotated walking tour of the city. (☎04 93 36 66 66; fax 04 93 36 86 36. Open July-Sept. M-Sa 9am-7pm, Su 9am-1pm and 2-6pm; Oct.-June M-Sa 9am-1pm and 2-6pm.) Cash in at **Change du Casino,** 6 cours Honoré Cresp, near the casino. (☎04 93 36 48 48. Open Tu-Su 9am-12:30pm and 1:30-5:30pm.) The **post office** is in the parking garage under the bus station. (☎04 92 42 31 11. Open M-F 8:30am-6pm, Sa 8:30am-noon.) **Postal code:** 06130.

■ **ACCOMMODATIONS AND FOOD.** Grasse has several low-cost, no-frills hotels. To get to **Hôtel Ste-Thérèse ❸,** 39 bd. Y.E. Baudoin, climb the street behind the tourist office annex, keeping left and continuing uphill on bd. Y.E. Baudoin. (15min.) Friendly owners maintain a clean hotel with beautiful views. Though once a church, recent renovations have eliminated most signs of this past, save for a few remaining stained glass windows. (☎04 93 36 10 29; fax 04 93 36 11 73; hotelstetherese@wanadoo.fr. Breakfast €4.60. Singles €26, with shower and toilet €35; doubles €36-44.50; triples €59.50. MC/V.) **Hôtel Les Palmiers ❸,** 17 bd. Y.E Baudoin, on the way to Hôtel Ste-Thérèse, has colorful rooms with high ceilings and slightly weak bedsprings in a large house overlooking a fragrant garden. (☎/fax 04 93 36 07 24. Breakfast €5. Singles €27, with shower and toilet €35; doubles €36; triples €45; quads €54. AmEx/MC/V.) **L'Oasis ❸,** near the bus station, lacks charm, but is well-located near major sights. Lower-level chambers are dark and small. (☎04 93 36 02 72; fax 04 93 36 03 16. Reception 7am-10pm. Breakfast €3.50-4.50. Singles with shower €26.70; doubles with shower €30, shower and toilet €38; quads €43-48.50. AmEx/MC/V.)

There are dozens of specialty food stores, *crêperies*, and little cafés in the *vieille ville*. Stock up on groceries at the **Monoprix** supermarket, rue Paul Goby, under the bus station. (☎04 93 36 40 56. Open M-Sa 8:45am-7:30pm.) Or visit the morning **market** on pl. aux Aires (Tu-Su 8am-noon). Grasse's most affordable restaurants also have the best ambience, centering around the cobblestone **pl. aux Aires.**

◙ **SIGHTS AND SMELLS.** Follow the aromas of musky cologne and flowery eau de toilette to Grasse's three largest *parfumeries*. The best of the bunch, ▓**Fragonard,** 20 bd. Fragonard, gives free tours of its 220 year-old factory, still in

A NOSE BY ANY OTHER NAME What does it take to make it in the perfume world? The celebrities of the scent industry are known as "noses"—the trade name for the master olfactors who produce haute couture's most famous fragrances. The best noses train for 15 years before ever extracting an essence; by the time they're ready to mix a scent, the snuffling students have memorized around 2000 smells. Mixing new scents is no less of an arduous process—it can take up to two years for a nose to mix the *key note* (the most perceptible scent of the perfume) with the *core note* (the central character of the perfume) and the *base note* (which blends the rest of the scents together). Noses are hot commodities—there's only a handful in the world—and are required by contract to protect their precious snouts.This means an almost monastic lifestyle: alcohol, cigarettes, and spicy foods are strictly forbidden.

use today; on display upstairs is the world's largest collection of perfume bottles ranging from Ancient Egyptian to the minimalist chic of Calvin Klein. (☎ 04 93 36 44 65; www.fragonard.com. Free 20min. tours in English. Open June-Sept. daily 9am-6:30pm; Oct.-May daily 9am-12:30pm and 2-6pm.) **Molinard,** 60 bd. Victor Hugo, 5min. down av. Victor Hugo, has a newer factory and a small museum dedicated to *provençal* furniture. Concoct your own *eau de parfum* at the 1½hr. "Sniffer Workshop" for €38. (☎ 04 93 36 01 62; www.molinard.com. Free tours in English. Open June-Sept. daily 9am-6:30pm; Oct.-May daily 9am-12:30pm and 2-6pm.) **Galimard,** 73 rte. de Cannes, well out of town, also offers 2hr. sessions with one of their professional "noses," who'll help you create a personal fragrance for €34. (☎ 04 93 09 20 00; www.galimard.com. Free tours daily. Open June-Sept. daily 9am-6:30pm; Oct.-May M-Sa 9am-12:30pm and 2-6pm.) To make sense of all these scents, head to the superb **Musée International de la Parfumerie,** 8 pl. du Cours, Grasse's best museum. The 2nd floor displays a 3000-year-old mummy's scented hand and foot, and you can sniff the basic components of perfume in the 4th floor greenhouse. (☎ 04 93 36 80 20. Audioguide €1.50. Open June-Sept. daily 10am-7pm; Oct. and Dec.-May W-M 10am-12:30pm and 2-5:30pm. €4, students €2.)

Housed in his 17th-century villa, the **Musée Jean-Honoré Fragonard,** 23 bd. Fragonard, features originals and reproductions of the libertine painter's work. Keep on the look-out for a startling number of sexual acts and organs concealed in the paintings. Or don't. (☎ 04 93 36 01 61. Open June-Sept. daily 10am-7pm; Oct.-May W-M 10am-noon and 2-5:30pm. €4.) In Grasse's *vieille ville*, the Romanesque **Cathédrale Notre-Dame-du-Puy,** displays three works by Rubens, as well as Jean-Honoré Fragonard's only religious painting, *Lavement des Pieds*, commissioned especially for the lavish Baroque chapel inside. (☎ 04 93 36 11 03. Open June 19-Aug. daily 9am-6pm; Sept.-June 18 M-Sa 9:30-1:30am and 3-5pm.)

■ **FESTIVALS.** In early May, **Expo-Rose** attracts rose growers from around the world for the largest exhibition of its kind (€7.70). The *Grassois* put down their eyedroppers again in the beginning of August for the fragrant **Fête du Jasmin.**

GRAND CANYON DU VERDON

Sixty kilometers off the coast in Provence's rocky interior is the Grand Canyon du Verdon, Europe's widest and deepest gorge. Its plunging cliffs and topaz streams are especially worth a visit if you like water sports; the nearby town of Castellane is home to a micro-industry of adventure outfits. The canyon is also a memorable (if slow) way to move between the Riviera and the Alps; Napoleon himself did it in 1816. **Castellane,** 17km east of the canyon and the largest village in the area, is, unfortunately, a bit of a pain to reach from the coast. The canyon itself can be nearly inaccessible from Castellane outside of July and August.

CASTELLANE

The sleepy little town of Castellane (pop. 1500) is the best place from which to visit the canyon. **Autocars Sumian** (☎ 04 42 67 60 34) sends buses to Marseille (3½hr.; July-Sept. 15 M, W, Sa; Sept. 16-June Sa only; €19.80), and from Aix-en-Provence (3hr.; 15 M, W, Sa; Sept. 16-June Sa only; €15.80). **VFD** (☎ 08 20 83 38 33) runs from Grasse (70min., 1 per day, €11.60), Nice (2¼hr., 1 per day, €17.20), and Digne (70min., 1 per day, €10.80). They give a 20% discount to students. For the more convenient timing of the **Chemins de Fer de Provence** (☎ 04 97 03 80 80 in Nice, ☎ 04 92 31 00 67 in Digne), take the little train from Nice (2¼hr., 4 per day M-Sa, €13.20) or Digne (50min., 4 per day, €6.60) to St-André les Alpes, then continue by bus to Castellane (bus departures matched with train arrivals, €3.20).

The friendly staff of the **tourist office,** straight on rue Nationale from the bus stop, gives out hotel and campsite listings as well as €1.50 maps of the canyon. (☎ 04 92 83 61 14; fax 04 92 83 76 89; office@castellane.org; www.castellane.org. Open July-Aug. M-Sa 9am-12:30pm and 2-7pm, Su 10am-12:30pm; May, June, and Sept. M-F 9am-noon and 2-6pm, Sa 10am-noon and 3-6pm; Oct.-Apr. M-F 9am-noon and 2-6pm.) There's **Internet** at **Le Web du Verdon,** rue du 11 Novembre (☎ 04 92 83 66 24). The **police** (☎ 04 92 83 60 08), bd. F. Mistral, are at the end of town on the road to the Canyon. For the **hospital,** call ☎ 04 92 83 98 00; to get there, continue on bd. St-Michel from the tourist office. The **post office** is on pl. Marcel Sauvaire. (☎ 04 92 83 99 80. Open M-F 9am-noon and 2-5pm, Sa 9am-noon.) **Postal code:** 04120.

Rooms fill quickly in summer. The following accommodations are in Castellane itself, not near the canyon; if none of these pans out, try the tourist office's list of dorm-style *gîtes d'étape* closer to town. The cheapest beds are at the **Gîtes d'Etape L'Oustaou ❷,** a backpacker-friendly hostel with light-filled 4- to 6-bed dorms and doubles, triples and quads off a twisty hallway. The area feels rural yet is 3min. from town. To get there, take chemin des Listes next to pl. M. Sauvaire behind the Credit Agricole, turn right and follow the road along the river (☎ 04 92 83 77 27; fax 04 92 83 78 02. Sheets €1.50. Lockout 10:30am-4:30pm and curfew 11pm for dorms, no curfew or lockout for private rooms. Bed and breakfast €17, with dinner €28. Doubles with shower and toilet €48.50; extra person €21.30. MC/V.) **Le Verdon ❸,** bd. de la République on pl. M. Sauvaire, has orange rooms, some overlooking a garden. (☎ 04 92 83 62 02; fax 04 92 83 73 80. Reception 7am-10:30pm. Breakfast €6. Singles €25, with shower €27, and toilet €40; doubles €33-40. MC/V.)

There are a number of campsites and hostels closer to the canyon. Near the canyon entrance, actually within the gorge, is **Chalet C.A.F. Refuge de la Maline ❶,** the last canyon bus stop. By car, follow D952 toward the canyon to La Palud-sur-Verdon. Then continue on D23 and follow signs for the chalet. The large dorms here are quite cramped but the view of the gorge is mind-boggling, and the restaurant downstairs is a popular stopping point for people heading in and out of the canyon. (☎ 04 92 77 38 05. Breakfast €4.15. Dinner €13. Sleepsack €1.60. Open Apr.-Nov. Beds €11.65. Electricity and hot water included. **Camping** €4.) The strip between Castellane and the Canyon is dotted with campsites. The small, unexceptional **Camping Frédéric Mistral ❶** is usually overcrowded, but has the advantage of being a 2min. walk down D952 from pl. M. Sauvaire toward the canyon. (☎ 04 92 83 62 27. Reception 9am-1pm and 2-9pm. 2 people with tent and shower €11. Electricity €14. Extra person €4.) About ½km farther is **Nôtre Dame ❶,** a greener and more spacious campsite with friendly managers. (☎/fax 04 92 83 63 02. Open Apr.-Oct. 15. 2 people with tent and car €9; €13 in July-Aug. Electricity €3.)

For quick groceries, visit **Casino** supermarket, 1 pl. de l'Eglise. (☎ 04 92 83 63 01. Open July-Aug. M-Sa 8am-7:30pm, Su 8am-1pm and 4-7pm; Sept.-June Tu-Sa 8am-12:30pm and 3:30-7:30pm, Su 8am-12:30pm.) For a sit-down meal after a long day of hiking, relax on the terrace of **La Main à la Pâte ❷,** 5 rue de la Fontaine. The Ital-

COTE D'AZUR

ian-oriented restaurant features salads (€3-8.50), pizzas (€7-8.50), and pastas (€7.50-8). (☎04 92 83 61 16. Open Th-Tu noon-2pm and 7-11pm. MC/V.)

Getting to the **canyon** from Castellane is difficult without a car. The **Navette Gorges du Verdon** sends free buses to **Point Sublime, La Palud,** and **La Maline,** the entrance to the gorge. (July-Aug. 2 per day; Apr.-June and Sept. 2 per day on weekends and holidays.) Outside of these times, your best bet is the kindness of strangers (not recommended by *Let's Go*) or a taxi (☎04 92 83 68 06; €50 from Castellane to La Maline; consider carpooling). Some dynamos even **cycle** the mountainous 30km to the gorge. To give it a try, rent a **bike** at **Aboard Rafting,** 8 pl. de l'Eglise. (☎04 92 83 76 11; €10 per half-day, €20 per day.)

THE CANYON

Although the tree-speckled, chalky canyon is itself appealing, most people come here for the Verdon River and the immense Lac de Ste-Croix into which it flows. The canyon's most beaten track is **Sentier Martel,** a.k.a. the **GR4** trail. The six- to eight-hour hike traces the river from La Maline east to Point Sublime as the gorge widens and narrows, passing through tunnels and caves rumored to have once hidden fugitives. Flashlights are useful for the tunnels.

The Verdon River's water ends up in **Lac de Ste-Croix,** a mellow emerald lake at the mouth of the gorge that's perfect for canoeing and kayaking. The GR4 trail past La Palud-sur-Verdon will eventually take you there by foot. By car, take D952 past La Palud to Moustiers and then follow signs to Ste-Croix-de-Verdon, or take D957 before Moustiers to Les Salles-sur-Verdon.

Before venturing into the canyon, stock up on hiking gear at **L'Echoppe,** rue Nationale, Castellane's only outdoor outfitter. (☎/fax 04 92 83 60 06. Open Apr.-May M-Sa 9:30am-noon and 3-7pm; June and Sept. M-Sa 9am-12:30pm and 2:30-7:30pm; July-Aug. daily 8:30am-8pm. Closed Oct.-Mar. MC/V.)

A number of **water sport** outfits run trips through the canyon. **Aboard Rafting,** 8 pl. de l'Eglise (☎/fax 04 92 83 76 11; www.aboard-rafting.com), offers all types of trips with an anglophone staff; **Acti-Raft,** rte.des Gorges du Verdon (☎04 92 83 76 64; fax 04 92 83 76 74; www.actiraft.com); **Aqua Viva Est,** 12 bd. de la République (☎/fax 04 92 83 75 74; www.aquavivaest.com); and **Aqua Verdon,** 9 rue Nationale (☎/fax 04 92 83 72 75; www.aquaverdon.com), all run comparable outfits. Though **rafting** is the most conventional way to go down the river, summer water levels are only high enough about twice a week. (Usually Tu and F; for information on water levels call ☎04 92 83 69 07. 1½hr. trip €28-30, half-day trip €37-55, day trip €59-75. Reserve ahead.) The adventurous can try a number of other water sports, including **aquarando, canyoning, hydrospeeding,** and **water rambling** (call companies for descriptions and rates). Equestrian types can trot their way through the canyon on **horseback** with **Les Pionniers** in La Palud-sur-Verdon. (☎/fax 04 92 77 38 30. €25 for 2hr., €34 per half-day, €61 per day. Make reservations in advance.)

ST-RAPHAËL AND FRÉJUS

Situated along the Estérel Hills, the tightly linked cities of St-Raphaël and Fréjus provide an excellent base for a visit to St-Tropez. Package tourists flock to the beach town of St-Raphaël for its inexpensive accommodations, rollicking nightlife, and proximity to the sea. More independent tourists also find it invaluable for its train and bus stations, which provide convenient springboards for exploring the area. For those more keen on charm and history than golden sand, the nearby city of Fréjus is riddled with a Roman and Episcopal past, and is home to what is perhaps the Riviera's best hostel. Though both towns may play second fiddle to St-Tropez, they are far more friendly to budget travelers.

ST-RAPHAËL

St-Raphaël (pop. 32,000) is basically defined by its beach. The boardwalk turns into a carnival midway through summer evenings, packed with vendors, gaming booths, and flirting teenagers. Though St-Raph certainly isn't the place to go for a quiet time, it isn't artificial, either, and the tourists here are real people looking for a good time. Cheap beds mean that you may end up staying in St-Raphaël if you're visiting St-Tropez or Fréjus. If so, stick to the beach and avoid the town itself, which is devoid of charm or interest.

■■ ⊠ **ORIENTATION AND PRACTICAL INFORMATION.** St-Raphaël is a major stop on the coastal train line, separated from Cannes by the **Massif de l'Estérel,** 40km of red volcanic rock and dry vegetation. There are hotels and restaurants in between the train station and the waterfront, a few blocks straight out of the rue Waldeck Rousseau exit.

Trains run from pl. de la Gare to: Cannes (25min., every 30min., €55.30); Marseille (1¾hr., every hr., €18.20); Nice (50min., every 30min., €8.80). Info office open daily 6:30am-9:30pm. Buses leave from their own station behind the train station. **Estérel Bus** (☎ 04 94 95 16 71) serves Forum Fréjus (30min., every 30min., from 7am-8:50pm, €1.10). **Sodetrav** (☎ 04 94 95 24 82) goes to St-Tropez (1½hr., 14 per day, €8.30). **Beltrame** (☎ 04 94 95 95 16) goes to Cannes (70min., 8 per day, €5.50). **Phocéens** (☎ 04 93 85 66 61) heads to Nice (2¼hr., 2 per day, €8.80). **Taxis** (☎ 04 94 83 24 24) wait outside the train station. **Les Bateaux de St-Raphaël** ferries at the old port go to St-Tropez. (☎ 04 94 95 17 46; fax 04 94 83 88 55. 1hr.; July-Aug. 5 per day, otherwise 2 per day; €10 one-way, €19 round-trip. If you're staying at the hostel in Fréjus, ask about 10% fare reductions.)

The **tourist office,** opposite the train station on rue Waldeck Rousseau, books accommodations. (☎ 04 94 19 52 52; fax 04 94 83 85 40; www.saint-raphael.com. Open July-Aug. daily 9am-7pm; Sept.-June M-Sa 9am-12:30pm and 2-6:30pm.) The **police** are on rue de Châteaudun. (☎ 04 94 95 24 24) Get info about jobs, housing, French courses, and cheap travel at **Information Jeunesse,** 21 pl. Gallieni, on the main thoroughfare between the train station and the beach. (☎ 04 94 19 47 38; open M-Th 8am-noon and 1:30-5pm; F 8am-noon and 1:30-4:30pm.) For laundry, check out **Top Pressing,** 34 av. Général Leclerc (Open M and Tu, Th-F 8am-12:15pm and 2:30-7pm; W and Sa 8am-12:15pm.) There's **Internet access** at the overpriced **Cyber Bureau,** 123 rue Waldeck Rousseau, beside the train station. (☎ 04 94 95 29 36. Open July-Aug. M-F 8am-7pm, Sa 8am-12:30pm; Sept.-June M-F 8am-noon and 2-7pm, Sa 8am-12:30pm. €1.55 for 10min., €7.75 per hr.) The **post office** is on av. Victor Hugo, behind the station. (☎ 04 94 19 52 00. Open M-F 8am-6:30pm, Sa 8am-noon.) **Postal code:** 83700.

⌐ **ACCOMMODATIONS AND CAMPING.** St-Raphaël's intense package tourism can make you feel like the only person in the world traveling independently, but accommodations are more plentiful here than in Fréjus, and cheaper than in St-Tropez. Be sure to book ahead in July and August. Fréjus's fun hostel is a short ride away (see p. 577). If you like sleeping under the stars, St-Raph is the place to do it—discreet beach-bivouacking is relatively safe and usually ignored by authorities, although *Let's Go* does not recommend it. The best deal in town is **Hôtel les Pyramides ❸,** 77 av. Paul Doumer. You can relax in the large green-and-white-rooms (all with TV, toilet, and shower) or the spacious lounge and outdoor patio. Rooms in the back overlook the train station and can be a bit noisy with an open window. To get there, leave the station to the left, make a right onto av. Henri Vadon, and take the first left onto av. Paul Doumer. (☎ 04 98 11 10 10; fax 04 98 11 10 20; www.saint-raphael.com/pyramides. Breakfast €6. Open Mar. 15-Nov. 15. Reception 7am-9pm; July-Sept. 24hr. Reservations necessary. Four singles €25 each; doubles €35-54; triples €55; quads €65. Extra bed €12. MC/V.) Right on the waterfront, **Le Touring ●**, 1 quai Albert 1er, has cushioned furniture, firm beds, welcoming rooms in every shade of brown, and its own bar and *brasserie*. Exit the station on the right; Albert 1er is your third left at the water. (☎04 94 95 01 72; fax 04 94 95 86 09; letouring@wanadoo.fr. Breakfast €4. Reception 24hr. Closed Nov. 15-Dec. 15. Singles and doubles with one bed and shower €32-41, with toilet €44 or €58 in summer; triples €58-68. AmEx/MC/V.) Near the train tracks, **La Bonne Auberge ❷**, 54 rue de la Garonne, has colorful rooms of varying quality, as well as a restaurant. (☎04 94 95 69 72. Breakfast €5. Dinner menus €11, €15, and €23. Open Feb.-Nov. Singles €21-35; doubles €31-55; triples and quads €38-80. MC/V.)

◗◖◗ FOOD AND NIGHTLIFE. It's hard to come by interesting dining spots in a town where most people's meals are packaged with their rooms. The most lively and affordable restaurants are near the **old port**, quai Albert 1er. The **Monoprix** supermarket is at 14 bd. de Félix Martin, off av. Alphonse Karr near the train station. (☎04 94 19 82 82. Open M-Sa 8:30am-7:30pm.) **Morning markets** color pl. Victor Hugo, down the hill from the bus station, and pl. de la République, and fresh fish can be bought at the old port (All markets daily 7am-12:30pm.) For a good dependable meal from a friendly staff, try **Le Grillardin ❸**, 42 rue Thiers. Salads (€5.50-9.90), tasty pizzas (€6.40-9.90), meats *au feu de bois* (€10.65-21.05), and fresh fish (€9.90-18.30). There are also €15.10 and €22.90 *menus*. (☎04 94 40 46 14. Open July-Sept. Tu and Th-Sa noon-2pm, daily 7pm-1am; Oct.-May Th-Tu noon-2pm and 7-11pm. MC/V.) For a cheap and satisfying meal, **Le Mille Pâtes ❷**, 138 rue J. Barbier off quai Albert 1er, serves pizzas and pastas (from €7) on a bright floral tablecloth, plus a €12 and €14 *menu*. (☎04 94 83 94 10. Open daily 9:30am-3pm and 5:30pm-midnight. AmEx/MC/V.) At night, sunbathed clubbers head to **La Réserve**, promenade René Coty. (☎04 94 95 02 20. Cover €13, with first drink included. Open Th-Sa 11pm-5am.)

◗◙ BEACHES AND FESTIVALS. Thirty kilometers of golden sand run along the coast from St-Raphaël west through Fréjus and east through Boulouris, which is more isolated and consequently less crowded. Most of the beach is public and dotted with snack stands. The first weekend in July is the free **Competition Internationale de Jazz New Orleans** in St-Raphaël. Hundreds of musicians face off in the streets and around the port. Call the cultural center (☎04 98 11 89 00) for details.

FRÉJUS

The charming town of Fréjus will inject any sun-soaked traveler with a welcome dose of culture. Founded by Julius Caesar in the first century BC, the town's many Roman ruins have given it the nickname "Pompeii of Provence." Although Fréjus is far from the beach and surrounded by an oppressive sprawl of high-rises, its varied sights, adorable center, and superb hostel make it well worth a visit.

◰ TRANSPORTATION

Fréjus is connected to St-Raphaël by regular **buses** until around 7pm. Fréjus's **train** station on rue Martin Bidoure (☎08 36 35 35 35) is little used—St-Raphaël processes most of the town's traffic. Limited service goes to St-Raphaël (5min., 8 per day, €1.20), Cannes (45min., 8 per day, €5.30), Nice (1½hr., 8 per day, €8.80), and Marseille (2hr., 2 per day, €18.20). **Local buses** (€1.10) connect the *vieille ville* with the beach, daytrips, and St-Raphaël. The **bus station**, pl. Paul Vernet (☎04 94 53 78 46), is next to the tourist office. (Open M-F 9:15am-12:15pm and 2:30-5:30pm, Sa 9:15am-12:15pm.) For **taxis**, call ☎04 94 51 51 12; there's a stand in pl. Vernet.

◼◼ 🔼 ORIENTATION AND PRACTICAL INFORMATION

Fréjus's seven-kilometer beach, a 20min. walk from the town center, is closer physically and spiritually to St-Raphaël than to Fréjus; visitors should stick to the *vieille ville* here and its surrounding sights. To get to the **tourist office**, 325 rue Jean Jaurès, from St-Raphaël, take bus #6 to pl. Paul Vernet. In June-Sept., the office offers guided tours in English every Wednesday from 10am-noon. (☎04 94 51 83 83; fax 04 94 51 00 26; www.ville-frejus.fr; frejus.tourisme@wanadoo.fr. Tours €5, €3 for students. Office open July-Aug. M-Sa 9am-7pm, Su 10am-noon and 3-6pm; Sept.-June M-Sa 9am-noon and 2-6pm, Su 10am-noon and 3-6pm.) The **Hôpital Inter-communal** (☎04 94 40 21 21) is on the corner of av. André Léotard and av. de St-Lambert. The **police** are on rue de Triberg (☎04 94 51 90 00). The **post office**, av. Aristide Briand, is just down the hill from the tourist office. (☎04 94 17 60 80. Open M-F 8am-6:30pm, Sa 8am-12:30pm.) **Postal code:** 83600.

🔼 ◖◗ ACCOMMODATIONS AND FOOD

One of the best hostels on the Côte (although a hike from St-Tropez) is the ◼**Auberge de Jeunesse de St-Raphaël-Fréjus (HI) ❶**, chemin du Counillier. From the Fréjus tourist office, take av. du 15ème Corps d'Armée, then turn left on chemin de Counillier after the 2nd roundabout. (20min.) From St-Raphaël, a shuttle bus (€1.10) leaves quai #14 of the bus station for the hostel at 5:45pm; return buses leave the hostel at 8:50am and 6:30pm. Local buses run every hour from 7:20am to 7pm; get off at "Les Chênes" (or "Paul Vernet," a farther but more frequent stop), and walk up av. Jean Calliès to chemin du Counillier. Charles and Chantal will make you feel right at home at this peaceful, secluded hostel (1km off the freeway), complete with wooden dining rooms and a lovely 170-acre spread of tree-shaded parkland. They are very knowledgeable about the area and maintain an ultra-clean hostel. Four- to eight-person single-sex dorms have beautiful views of the inland valley. Ask about discounts on bike rentals, canoes, and St-Tropez ferry tickets. (☎04 94 52 93 93; fax 04 94 53 25 86; youth.hostel.frejus.st.raphael@wanadoo.fr. Breakfast included. Kitchen. Sheets €2.70. Reception 8-10am and 6-8pm; reservations by telephone during these hours. Lockout 10am-6pm. Curfew July-Aug. midnight, Sept.-June 10pm. Closed Nov.-Feb. Dorms €12. Quads with shower and toilet €14 per person. **Camping** €8 per person with tent.)

In the center of town, **La Riviera ❸**, 90 rue Grisolle, has simple, functional light-green rooms and a friendly, English-speaking staff. To get there from pl. Paul Vernet, walk straight down rue Jean Jaurès past pl. de la Liberté, and turn left on rue Grisolle. (☎04 94 51 31 46; fax 04 94 17 18 34. Breakfast €5. Singles and doubles €27-29, with shower €36-39; triples €39.50-47.10; quads €47.60-55.20. MC/V.)

Budget restaurants cluster around **place de la Liberté**. Nearby, the unassuming **Faubourg de Saigon ❷**, 126 rue St-François de Paule, off rue Jean Jaurès, serves excellent Vietnamese dishes (around €7) in its fan-and-lantern-filled interior. (☎04 94 53 65 80. *Menu* €14. Open daily noon-2pm and 7-10pm, but no lunch service on M. AmEx/V.) Or try the restaurant at **La Riviera ❷**, 90 rue Grisolle, for simple, but tasty dishes. Salads (€2.75-7.60), pasta (€5.80-7.30), meat (€7.95-14.50), and fish (€5.80-13). *Menus* for €11.45 and €14.50. (☎04 94 51 31 46. Open Tu-Su noon-2pm and 7-10pm). The **Marché Provençal** fills **rue de Fleury** and **place Formigé** on Wednesday and Saturday mornings. If you're coming from the hostel, ask the bus driver to drop you off directly. There's an **Intermarché** supermarket, av. de l'Europe, at the second roundabout on the way to the hostel. (☎04 94 53 30 70. Open M-Th 8:30am-12:30pm and 3-7:30pm, F-Sa 8:30am-7:30pm, Su 9am-12:30pm.)

CÔTE D'AZUR

👁 SIGHTS

◼ THE FRÉJUS EPISCOPAL BUILDINGS. In the middle of the *vieille ville* is the remarkable product of 2000 years of building and rebuilding. Visible from a side entrance on pl. Formigé, the octagonal **baptistry**, dating back to the 5th century, is one of France's oldest buildings. The spectacular 12th- to 14th-century **cloisters** feature marble columns culled from Roman ruins. Wooden-beamed ceilings are decorated with over 1200 miniature paintings depicting fantastical beasts, human-animal hybrids, and bawdy medieval scenes. Look carefully for a woman lifting her skirt, a man riding a pig, and a backflipping village acrobat. Far less riotous (and less interesting) is the austere Gothic **cathedral**, whose walnut doors were sculpted in 1530. *(Pl. Formigé. ☎04 94 51 26 30. Cloister open Apr.-Sept. 15 daily 9am-7:30pm; Sept. 16-Mar. Tu-Su 9am-noon and 2-5:30pm. €4, students €2.50. Doors and baptistry accessible only by guided tour in French. Cathedral open daily 8am-noon and 2:30-7pm.)*

ROMAN RUINS. Built in the first and second centuries to entertain rowdy, home-sick soldiers, the **Roman Amphitheater** lacks the embellishments of those in Nîmes or Arles, which were designed for more discerning patrician eyes. The former stomping ground of gladiators now hosts rock concerts and two bullfights a year. *(☎04 94 51 34 31. From the tourist office, take rue Jean Jaurès to pl. de la Liberté, then turn right on rue de Gaulle. Open Apr.-Oct. M and W-Sa 10am-1pm and 2:30-6:30pm; Nov.-Mar. M and W-F 10am-noon and 1-5:30pm, Sa 9:30am-12:30pm and 1:30-5:30pm. Free. Bullfights July 14 and Aug. 15; €22-61.)* The original wall of Fréjus's other ancient forum, the **Roman Theater**, remains intact; the rest of the structure now hosts concerts and plays. *(☎04 94 53 58 75. From the roundabout at the tourist office, go about 250m on rue G. Bret. Open July-Aug. M and W-Sa 10am-1pm and 2:30-6:30pm, Su 7am-7pm; Apr.-Oct. M and W-Sa 10am-1pm and 2:30-6:30pm, Su 8am-5pm; Nov.-Mar. M and W-F 10am-noon and 1-5:30pm, Sa 9:30am-12:30pm and 1:30-5:30pm, Su 8am-5pm. Free.)* Pillars and a few arches are all that's left of a 40km **aqueduct**, past the theater along av. du 15ème Corps d'Armée.

OTHER SIGHTS. Fréjus has an assortment of sights neither medieval nor ancient, which you can probably do without visiting if you're pressed for time. **Villa Auréli-enne**, on the hill next to the hostel, is an elegant 19th-century private home featuring art exhibitions and surrounded by an immense park. *(Av. du Général d'Aimée Calliès. Call the tourist office for info.)* **The Pagode Hong-Hiên** was built in part by Vietnamese soldiers who fought for France during WWI and settled in Fréjus. Surrounded by noisy freeways, this is the closest Buddhism gets to kitsch: a weird assemblage of large plaster figures recounting the life of Buddha. *(13 rue H. Giraud, 10min. up av. Jean Calliès from the hostel. ☎04 94 53 25 29. Open daily 9am-noon and 2-7pm. €1.50.)* Two minutes farther up av. Jean Calliès is the **Memorial des Guerres en Indochine**, a stone monument to the French who were killed in the Indo-Chinese war as well as a one-room photographic history display. *(☎04 94 44 42 90. Open daily 10am-5pm. Museum closed Tu. Free.)* Diehard fans of the film director, artist, and poet can visit the circular **Cocteau Chapel**, which he designed and built, although it was left unfinished upon his death in 1963. *(Av. Nicola on the RN7 to Cannes. Bus #3/13 from "pl. Paul Vernet," 11 per day. ☎04 94 53 27 06. Open Apr.-Oct. M and W-F 2:30-6:30pm, Sa 10am-1pm and 2-6:30pm; Nov.-Mar. M and W-F 1:30-5:30pm, Sa 9:30am-12:30pm and 1:30-5:30pm.)*

ST-TROPEZ

Nowhere is the glitz and glamour of the Riviera more apparent than in St-Tropez (pop. 5400). The town is named after Torpes, the highest steward of the Roman emperor Nero. In AD 68, Torpes's profession of Christianity angered Nero sufficiently that he decapitated the steward. However, its modern devotion is to sun, sand, and big boats. Originally a small fishing hamlet, St-Tropez first came into public view in 1892 with the arrival of Paul Signac and other Post-Impressionist artists. Sixty-four years later, Brigitte Bardot's nude bathing scene in *Et Dieu Créa la Femme (And God Created Woman)* sealed the town's celebrity status. Today, the former village's sleek yachts, exclusive clubs, and nude beaches continue to attract Hollywood stars, corporate giants, and daytripping backpackers, all trying to get a piece of the action.

⚄ 🛂 ORIENTATION AND PRACTICAL INFORMATION. Reaching the "Jewel of the Riviera" requires some effort, as it lies well off the rail line. Once you get here, it's another hassle altogether to leave town for the outlying beaches and villages. Hitchers say that thumbing for lifts won't get you far, but often try to get motorists's attention and trust by approaching them as they leave campsites or parking lots. That said, *Let's Go* does not suggest or recommend hitchhiking, which is a dangerous and foolhardy thing to do. The town itself is condensed and walking-friendly, with constant activity between the **port** and **place des Lices.**

The fastest, and cheapest way to get here is by **boat. Les Bateaux de St-Raphaël** (☎ 04 94 95 17 46; fax 04 94 83 88 55), at the old port, sail in from St-Raphaël (1hr.; July-Aug. 5 per day, otherwise 2 per day; €10 one-way, €19 round-trip). Otherwise, **Sodetrav buses** (☎ 04 94 97 88 51) leave from av. Général Leclerc, across from the ferry dock and public parking, for St-Raphaël (1½-2¼hr.; July-Aug. 14 per day, off-season 8 per day; €8.30) and Toulon (2¼hr., 8 per day, €15.90). Bus station open July-Aug. M-Sa 8:15am-8pm, Su 10:15am-1:30pm; Sept.-June M-F 9:30am-noon and 2-6pm, Sa 10am-noon. You can rent a **bike** or **moped** at **Louis Mas,** 3-5 rue Quarenta. (☎ 04 94 97 00 60. Bikes €8-12 per day; deposit €153-229. Mopeds €20 per day; deposit €382. Open Easter-Oct. 15 M-Sa 9am-7pm, Su 10am-1pm and 4-7pm.) For **taxis,** call ☎ 04 94 97 05 27, or hail one from the Musée de L'Annonciade.

The **tourist office** is on quai Jean Jaurès. After arriving by bus or ferry, walk into town along the waterfront for about 10 minutes until you hit a series of cafés. The tourist office is the one without outdoor seating. The tan and well-dressed staff gives out schedules for the municipal system of *navette* (shuttle) transport, and also the *Manifestations* event guide. (☎ 04 94 97 45 21; fax 04 94 97 82 66; www.saint-tropez.st; tourism@saint-tropez.st. Open daily June 29-Sept. 1 9:30am-8:30pm; Sept. 2-Oct.6 and May 16-June 28 9:30am-12:30pm and 2-7pm; Mar. 30-May 15 9:30am-12:30pm and 2-6:30pm; Nov. 4-Jan. 5 and Jan. 7-Mar. 29 9am-noon and 2-6pm.) **Master Change,** 18 rue Allard, is at the old port. (☎ 04 94 97 80 17. Open Mar.-June and Sept.-Oct. daily 8am-8pm; July-Aug. 8am-10pm.) There's **Internet** access for a hefty sum at **FCDCI,** 2 av. Paul Roussel. (☎ 04 94 54 84 81. Open June-Sept. M-Sa 9:30am-9pm; Oct.-May M-Sa 9:30am-12:30pm and 2:30-7:30pm. €5.50 for 30min.; €9 per hr.) If you need to clean your clothes before you hit the clubs, head over to **La Bugade,** 3 rue Quaranta. (Open daily 7am-8pm.) The **police** are on rue François Sibilli, near the church, and on av. Général Leclerc by the new port. (☎ 04 94 56 60 30) The **hospital** is on av. Foch, off pl. des Lices. (☎ 04 94 79 47 30) There is a **post office** on pl. A. Celli between the new and old ports. (☎ 04 94 55 96 50. Open M-F 8:30am-noon and 2-5pm, open at 9:30am on the 2nd and 4th Th of every month; Sa 8:30am-noon.) **Postal Code:** 83990.

🛏 ACCOMMODATIONS AND CAMPING. Hotels are scarce and expensive in St-Tropez, and it's not rare to get here and find no accommodations available at all. A stay in St-Raphaël or Hyères is easier on the wallet but forces you to limit your time here—though staying up all night in St-Tropez and heading out the next day may be an option. The closest **hostel** is in Fréjus. **Camping** is the best and cheapest option. Though no sites are within walking distance of the town, a frequent ferry connects the large campsite at Port Grimaud with the peninsula (see below). The campgrounds flanking St-Tropez's famous beaches are smaller and often full; book them months in advance. If you haven't reserved, the tourist office can tell you which ones have space. Camping on the beach is actively prohibited.

One of the most budget-friendly and central hotels is **Lou Cagnard ❹**, 18 av. Paul Roussel, about a 3min. walk from pl. des Lices. Well-maintained rooms overlook the avenue or peaceful garden in the back. All rooms have a shower. Reservations are essential. (☎04 94 97 04 24; fax 04 94 97 09 44. Closed Nov. 3-Dec. 27. Reception 8am-9pm. Breakfast €7. Singles and doubles €43-50, with toilet €53-66. MC/V.) Another good option is **La Belle Isnarde ❹**, rte. de Tahiti, about a 15min. walk from the tourist office. From the pl. des Lices, take a right on av. du Marechal Foch, a quick right onto rue de la Resistance, and a left onto av. de la Resistance, which turns into Chemin des Belles Isnarde. From there, the hotel is 2min. up on the left. Spacious rooms in a calm setting with pleasant garden. (☎04 94 97 13 64 and 04 94 97 57 74. Closed Oct. 15-Apr. 15. Breakfast €6. Singles and doubles with shower €45-50, with shower and toilet €57-59. Cash only)

Campazur runs three campsites close to St-Tropez. Campers have it lucky at **Les Prairies de la Mer ❶**, Port Grimaud. The huge, very social site is near a white beach and the canals of Port Grimaud, "France's Venice." Amenities include hot showers, tennis, and water sports. (☎04 94 79 09 09; fax 04 94 79 09 10; prairies@campazur.com; www.campazur.com. Open Apr.-Oct. July-Aug. 2 people, tent, and car €20; off-season €15.) The **MMJ ferry** leaves the *capitainerie* three minutes away for St-Tropez once an hour. (☎04 94 96 51 00; €9 round-trip.) The smaller **Kon Tiki ❶** has a choice location near the northern stretch of Pampelonne beach. Campers can soak up sun by day and the beach's wild nightlife (including Kon Tiki's own bar) by night. (☎04 94 55 96 96; fax 04 94 55 96 95; kontiki@campazur.com. Same dates and prices as above.) Next door is **Toison d'Or ❶**, the smallest of the three sites. (☎04 94 79 83 54; fax 04 94 79 85 70; toison@campazur.com. Same dates and prices as above.) In July and August, Sodetrav sends a bus from the St-Tropez station to both sites daily. (11:35am, 2:10pm, 4pm, and 5:40pm; €1.60.) Otherwise, take the free municipal shuttle (four a day) from pl. des Lices to "Capon-Pinet" and walk along the beach until you reach the site. (30-40min.)

◘ **FOOD.** St-Tropez's vibrant restaurant and café scene lies along the old port and the narrow streets behind the waterfront. Of course, like everything else, eating is a glamorous and costly affair. Budget travelers will do best to forgo the swanky restaurants and grab paninis from the snack shops. **La Tarte Tropezienne ❷**, pl. des Lices, allows you to dine in a sophisticated, air-conditioned room with a chic local clientele. The simple but excellent cuisine is the best option for a budget-oriented gourmand in St-Tropez. Salads (€6.95-8.50), *tartines* (€7.50-8.50), club sandwiches with salad and potatoes (€8-10.50), delicious omelettes (€4.30-6), and pastries. (☎04 94 97 04 69. Open daily 6:30am-9pm.) For a slice of Americana, head to **Basilic Burger ❷**, pl. des Remparts, where fresh salads and juicy hamburgers (€5-9) complement Coca-Cola memorabilia. (☎04 94 97 29 09. Open July-Aug. daily 9am-11:30pm; Sept.-June 9am-9pm. Cash only.) The popular **Délice des Lices ❶**, pl. des Lices, is *the* place to go for a late-night snack. (☎04 94 54 89 84. Hot and cold sandwiches €3.10-4.60. Open 24hr.) Check out the fabulous **grand marché** on **place des Lices** (Tu and Sa 7:30am-1pm), or the **morning market** on place aux Herbes, behind the tourist office. There's a **Monoprix** supermarket, 9 av. Général Leclerc (☎04 94 97 07 94. Open July-Aug. daily 8am-10pm; Sept.-June daily 8am-7:50pm) and a **SPAR** market, 16 bd. Vasserot, on pl. des Lices. (☎04 94 97 02 20. Open Apr.-Sept. M-Sa 7:30am-8pm, Su 8am-1pm and 4-8pm; Oct.-Mar. M-Sa 7:30am-1pm and 3:30-7:30pm, Su 8am-1pm and 4-7:30pm)

◉ SIGHTS. Most travelers don't come to St-Tropez for the museum scene. Nevertheless, **Le Musée de l'Annonciade,** pl. Grammont, is a good break from the sun. This converted chapel houses Fauvist and neo-Impressionist paintings. (☎04 94 97 04 01. Open June-Sept. W-M 10am-noon and 3-7pm; Oct.-May W-M 10am-noon and 2-6pm. €5.35; Dec.-Mar. €4.60; students €2.30.) **The Citadel** above the port contains the **Musée Naval,** which follows St-Tropez's interesting military history through WWII. (☎04 94 97 59 43. Open Apr.-Sept. daily 10am-12:30pm and 1:30-6:30pm; Oct. and Dec.-Mar. 10am-12:30pm and 1:30-5:30pm. €4, students €2.50.)

◪ BEACHES. St-Tropez's pride and joy is its white, sandy, endless coastline. Unfortunately, the beaches are not conveniently reached. The *navette* municipal shuttle (leaves from pl. des Lices; 4 per day; ask the tourist office for the variable schedule) runs to **Les Salins,** a rather secluded sunspot. Another line stops near **plage Tahiti** ("Capon-Pinet"), the first stretch of the famous Pampelonne beachline, where exclusive beach clubs alternate with public sand. To find a beach that suits your style, try taking the *navette* to Les Salins and exploring the beaches to the left; you can follow the beautiful, rocky **sentier littoral** (coastal path) along the coast to the right until it melds with the Pampelonne beachline, passing a handful of unpopulated swimming spots and celebrity villas on the way. (1hr.) Fifteen kilometers along the peninsula, great swimming and good rock climbing await at **plage de L'Escalet,** but you can only get there by foot or private car. If you don't have the time or inclination to seek out a better beach, there's a decent spot only 10 minutes from the old port. Follow chemin des Graniers, which curves around the citadel and the water, to the small, uncrowded **plage des Graniers.** Most spots allow or expect you to sun *au naturel*—in St-Tropez, tan lines mean you just got here.

♫▣ ENTERTAINMENT AND FESTIVALS. At the height of St-Tropez's excess and exclusivity is its wild nightlife. When the sun sets, the port and the streets behind the waterfront become a playground for the tanned and glam. One nighttime locus is the beachfront, which is not so convenient for travelers without cars or coastal villas of their own. **Les Caves du Roy,** av. Paul Signac and within Hotel Byblos, wins the prize for the most elite club. Try a €23 vodka and tonic or the €20,000 Methusalem Cristal Roederer White while hobnobbing with celebrities. (☎04 94 56 68 00; www.lescavesduroy.com. Open July-Aug. daily 11:30pm-4am; June and Sept. F-Sa 11:30am-4am.) Restaurant-bar **Bodega de Papagayo** (☎04 94 97 76 70), on the old port, and its accompanying nightclub **Le Papagayo** (☎04 94 97 20 01), attract moneyed youth and soccer stars. (Open June-Sept. daily; May and Oct. F-Su 11:30pm-5am. Club cover €25 includes first drink; €21 thereafter. No cover if you "look good.") One of the hippest bars in St-Tropez, and the least frequented by tourists, is **Le Loft,** 9 rue des Remparts. The small candlelit space is adorned with carpets, cushions, and plush chairs. (☎04 94 97 60 50. Open daily 10pm-3am.) A down-to-earth Anglo crowd frequents **Kelly's Irish Pub,** a pretension-free joint toward the end of the old port. You can order a beer (€3) or listen to live music here even if you're not wearing designer duds. (☎04 94 54 89 11. Open daily 10:30am-3am.) The epitome of sedentary style is the **Café de Paris,** a gold, velvet, and crystal-chandeliered café with an enormous patio in the center of the port. (☎04 94 97 00 56; www.cafedeparis.fr. Beer and wine from €4.50. Open daily 7am-3am.) **Le Pigeonnier,** 13 rue de la Ponche, is a casual nightclub catering to both gays and straights. (☎04 94 97 84 26. Open daily 11:30pm-5am. No cover, but drinks cost a good €13.)

St-Tropez celebrates its historic ties to the idle rich with a yearly string of golf tournaments and yacht regattas. Every May 16-18, during **Les Bravades,** locals pay homage to their military past and patron saint with costumed parades. June 29 brings **St-Peter's Day** and a torch-lit procession honoring the saint of fishermen.

🔀 DAYTRIPS FROM ST-TROPEZ

*Sodetrav (☎ 04 94 97 88 51) sends **buses** from St-Tropez (30min., M-Sa 7 per day, €3.10). Or take the **ferry** to Port Grimaud (see **St-Tropez: Accommodations,** p. 579), and catch the **petit train** at the top of the Prairies de la Mer campsite (every hr.).*

Less ritzy than the city but more endearing, the inland villages of the St-Tropez peninsula make excellent daytrips. These hilltop villages, with their picture-perfect settings and memorable views, are becoming highly desirable real estate. As tour groups have started to want a piece of the charm, they have begun to lose their status as secret gems; come quickly, before the bottled water prices double.

The best of the peninsula is adorable **Grimaud.** One gets the sense that any adjustment here would be a mistake. Remarkable stone houses line the meandering, fountain-filled streets of the town, with a church in the middle and a castle on top. The narrow streets by pl. Neuve are home to boutiques and some expensive restaurants. Above pl. Neuve, signs point to the simple, Romanesque **Eglise St-Michel.** (Open daily 9am-6pm.)

Grimaud has to be a daytrip unless you're camping; it has no budget hotels. The **tourist office** is at 1 bd. des Aliziers, a few doors down from the museum. (☎ 04 94 43 26 98; fax 04 94 43 32 40; www.grimaud-provence.com. Open July-Aug. M-Sa 9am-12:30pm and 3-7pm, Su 10am-1pm; Apr.-May, June, and Sept. M-Sa 9am-12:30pm and 2:30-6:15pm; Oct.-Mar. M-Sa 9am-12:30pm and 2:15-5:30pm.)

ILES D'HYÈRES

*Ferries to the island depart from the town of Hyères, to the east of Toulon. **Trains** run from Toulon (9 per day, €7) and Marseille (6 per day, €10). Sodetrav **buses** (☎ 04 94 12 55 00) run to Toulon (1hr., every 15min., €5.70) and St-Tropez (1½-2hr., 8 per day, €13), while Phocéens-Cars (☎ 04 93 85 66 61) go to Cannes (1½hr., 2 per day, €18.30) and Nice (2hr., 2 per day, €19.82). To get to the ferry ports, catch Sodetrav local bus #67 to "Port La Gavine" (€2.10) or "La Tour Fondue" (€2.80).*

These exotic, underpopulated islands lie off the coast somewhere between St-Tropez and the grimy metropolis of Toulon. Nicknamed the "Iles d'Or" or "Golden Islands" by Henry II, the islands draw tourists for three main reasons: nature, *natation* (swimming), and, of course, the nudity.

TLV Ferries (☎ 04 94 58 95 14; www.tlv-tvm.com) run to Porquerolles from Tour Fondue (20min.; July-Aug. 20 per day, low-season 6-16 per day; round-trip €14.) Ferries (☎ 04 94 57 44 07) also run to **Port-Cros** (1hr.) and **Ile du Levant** (1½ hr.) from **Port D'Hyères** (July-Aug. 4 per day, Sept.-June 2 per day; round-trip €20). In July and August, a boat from Hyères connects Port-Cros with **Ile du Levant** (round-trip €23). If you'd like to see both islands in the off-season, **Le Lavandou** shuttles between the two, but be prepared for hostile faces when you admit another company got you to the mainland. (☎ 04 94 71 01 02. Boats depart Port-Cros for Le Levant at 12:15, 3:15, and 5:15pm, though schedule varies. One-way ticket €6.50.)

The largest of the three islands and the one most easily accessed from the coast, **Porquerolles** (pop. 342), has the most colorful history. It was home to a religious order until François I, in a stroke of genius, declared it an asylum for convicts who had received clemency for agreeing to defend the mainland against pirates. The criminals promptly transformed the island into a base for their own piratical activities. A century later, Louis XIV, put a violent stop to their raiding. Today, mainlanders and tourists seek respite from the hectic Riviera in the island's rugged cliffs and small, hidden coves. On Porquerolles, the Hyères **tourist office,** 3 av. Ambroise Thomas, below the Casino, supplies free maps and ferry schedules. (☎ 04 94 01 84 50; fax 04 94 01 84 51; www.ot-hyeres.fr. Open July-Aug. daily 8am-8pm; Sept.-June M-F 9am-6pm, Sa 10am-4pm.)

Like its neighbor, the **Ile du Levant** was originally settled by monks. Its former inhabitants would be shocked if they could see it today, a haven for asceticism in one regard only: clothing. Home to **Héliopolis,** Europe's oldest nudist colony, islanders go *au naturel* on the beaches and wears the legal minimum (not much) in the port and village. If nudity is not your cup of tea, try the narrow, windy hiking trails within the **Domaine des Arbousiers,** a substantial natural reserve. The Héliopolis map includes 7 trails. Walking straight uphill from the port, you'll eventually reach what passes for a town square, with restaurants, hotels, and a nightclub. (15min.) If you would like to spend a night, try **Hôtel La Source ❷,** about 5min. from the port. The garden setting is calm and peaceful, with the exception of the chirping cigales that will greet you in the summer. Simple rooms get the job done. (☎04 94 05 91 36; fax 04 94 05 93 47. Open Mar.-Oct. Breakfast €6. Singles €21, with shower €40; doubles with shower €49-54. Extra bed €16. MC/V). For camping, try **Colombero ❶,** just 2min. from the port. (☎04 94 05 90 29. €7 per person.)

The smallest and most rugged of the three islands, **Port-Cros,** is a stunning national park that offers hours of fun for hikers. Its mountainous terrain is home to 114 species of migratory birds, 602 indigenous plants, and 48 non-indigenous human beings. The well-trodden **sentier des plantes** (plant trail) passes by several forts and the beautiful but crowded **Plage de la Palud.** To find a more solitary swimming hole, continue on the **sentier de Port Man,** reached by a 4hr. hike that circles the north end of the island and penetrates its jungly, unpopulated interior. A national park info booth on the port provides maps of the island (€1.50) and suggests activities. (☎04 94 01 40 70. Open July-Aug. daily 10am-6pm; Sept.-June whenever boats arrive and depart.) **Scuba dive** in the clear water off Port-Cros to see the area's many wrecks and search for the 40lb. brown *mérou,* a massive grouper once thought to be extinct. **Sun Plongée,** beside the Sun Bistro, runs openwater dives. (☎04 94 05 90 16; www.sun-plongee.com. With equipment €34.)

If you need an island-hopping base, **Hôtel du Portalet ❷,** 4 rue de Limans, lets tasteful pastel rooms with TV, high ceilings, and firm beds in a nice part of the *vieille ville.* The friendly owners are experts on the town. (☎04 94 65 39 40; fax 04 94 35 86 33; chbenit@oreka.com. Breakfast €4.60. Free luggage storage. Reception 7am-10pm. Singles €24-29, with shower and toilet €29-38, with bath €35-39; doubles €26-41, with bath €38-54. AmEx/MC/V.)

If you get hungry, there's a **Casino** supermarket on av. Gambetta, across from the McDonald's. (Open Tu-Sa 7:30am-12:30pm and 4-7:30pm, Su 8am-noon.) For a sitdown meal, try **La Brasserie ❸,** 2 rue Leon Gautier, within la Coupole. The large outdoor terrace, good variety, and excellent service are matched with reasonable prices. (☎04 94 12 88 00. Salads €4.50-8, pastas €8, fish €11.50-16.50, meat €11-14.50. Open Su-Th noon-10pm and F-Sa noon-11pm. MC/V.)

COTE D'AZUR

CORSICA
(LA CORSE)

Plunging out of the turquoise waters of the Mediterranean is the island paradise of Corsica (pop. under 250,000), dubbed *Kallysté* (the most beautiful) by the Greeks. In the north, deep-green scrub is fringed with rocky outposts and fishing hamlets; in the south, white cliffs dive into a pristine sea; to the west, towering red mountains are shingled with pines; and in Corsica's interior lie glacial lakes and gorges.

The snootiness for which the mainland French are famed is nowhere to be seen on Corsica; you'd never guess that this little island has spent the past thousand years being exploited by foreign powers. By the ninth century, Corsica was under Pisan control, and for the next five centuries Genoa fought Pisa for ownership of the island. The legacy of this imperial quarreling is a ring of over 300 rounded Genoese watchtowers, built to protect the coastal cities from pillaging Saracens.

The Corsican War of Independence, also known as the Forty Years' War, began as a series of rebellions in 1729. By 1755, the revered general Pasquale Paoli had declared the island autonomous, created a university, and drafted the island's— and the world's—first modern constitution. Among the Corsican officers who quickly swore allegiance to France was a certain Carlo Buonaparte. On August 15, 1769, his son Napoleon was born in Ajaccio, and the rest is history. Despite Napoleon's lack of support for the ideals of his father's generation, Corsican independence has remained an issue in the modern era. Today, the Front de Libération National de la Corse (FLNC) continues to try bombing its way to independence. Most Corsicans deplore this sort of extremism and question the wisdom of independence, for France directly provides 70% of Corsica's GNP.

Corsica's main industry is tourism and, from mid-June to August, flocks of mainland French retreat to the island's renowned beaches and pricey resorts. The summer climaxes in a double-barreled blast on August 15, when France celebrates the Fête de l'Assomption, and Corsicans observe **Napoleon's birthday.** Tourists depart by September, when the weather is at its best and the waters their warmest. Winter visitors can visit sleepy coastal towns or head inland to ski.

Corsican tourist offices have free guides to all of Corsica's accommodations, published by Agence du Tourisme de la Corse, 17 bd. du Roi Jérôme, Ajaccio (☎04 95 51 00 00; www.visit-corsica.com). There are very few budget hotels, and they often fill weeks ahead in summer. If you can't plan far in advance, it's worth calling a day or two before you need a room in case rooms open up. Campsites lie close to most cities; a ban on unofficial camping is strictly enforced. Inland, *refuges* provide little more than a roof over your head; they don't take reservations, but you can usually pitch a tent outside. *Gîtes d'étape* allow you to reserve ahead, offering more comfortable surroundings that include electricity and homemade cuisine.

✈ INTERCITY TRANSPORTATION

BY PLANE. Air France and its subsidiary **Compagnie Corse Méditerranée (CCM)** fly to **Bastia** and **Ajaccio** from **Paris** (round-trip from €170, students €140); **Nice** (€120, students €98); and **Marseille** (€128, students €104). In Ajaccio, the Air France/CCM office is at 3 bd. du Roi Jérôme (☎08 20 82 08 20). As with all airfares, you can get significant reductions if you hunt around; ask a budget travel agency in France.

BY BOAT. Ferry travel between the mainland and Corsica can be a rough trip, and not always much cheaper than a plane. High-speed ferries (3½hr.) run between Nice and Corsica. Overnight ferries from Toulon and Marseille take upwards of 10 hours. The **Société National Maritime Corse Méditerranée** (**SNCM** ☎ 08 91 70 18 01; fax 04 91 56 35 86; www.sncm.fr) sends ferries from **Marseille** (€43-60, under 25 €34-48); **Nice** (€38-48, under 25 €23-33); **Toulon** (43-60, under 25 €34-48) to **Bastia, Calvi, Ile Rousse, Ajaccio, Porto Vecchio,** and **Propriano.** It costs €45-315 to take a car, depending on the day and the car. In summer, nine boats cross between Corsica and the mainland, and only three out of season. SNCM schedules and fees are listed in a booklet available at travel agencies and ports. **Corsica Ferries** (see below) has similar destinations and prices.

SAREMAR (☎ 04 95 73 00 96; fax 04 95 73 13 37) and **Moby Lines** (☎ 04 95 73 00 29; fax 04 95 73 05 50) run from **Santa Teresa** in Sardinia to **Bonifacio.** (3-10 per day depending on the season, €6.71-15 per person and €19.61-51.50 per car one way.) **Corsica Ferries** (☎ 08 25 09 50 95; fax 04 95 32 14 71; www.corsicaferries.com) crosses from **Livorno** and **Savona** in Italy to **Bastia** (€22.50-37.50).

▐▀ LOCAL TRANSPORTATION

ON WHEELS. Rumor has it that Machiavelli and the Marquis de Sade collaborated on the design for Corsica's transportation system. **Train** service in Corsica is slow and limited to the half of the island north of Ajaccio—and it doesn't accept rail passes. Not for the faint of stomach, the antiquated trains are terrifying (or exciting) to travel on in windy mountainous areas. Buses are more comprehensive than trains and serve the greater part of the island, but also be prepared for very twisty roads. If you are prone to motion sickness, bring medicine. Call **Eurocorse Voyages** (☎ 04 95 21 06 30) for further info. Though *Let's Go* doesn't recommend it, **hitchhiking** on the island is possible for patient travelers, who often carry a sign displaying both their destination and their willingness to pay for gas: *"Je vous offre l'essence."* Ten liters of gas (about €10.10) usually covers 100km on flat roads, but buses are safer and about as cheap, though they're not always on time.

Corsica allegedly has the most dangerous roads in Europe, but if you're foolhardy enough to rent a **car,** expect to pay at least €44-81 per day or €227-305 per week. The unlimited mileage deals are best. Gas stations are scarce; the police will sometimes help if you run out. **Bicycle** rental can be pricey, as can **mopeds** *(mobilettes)* and scooters. Narrow mountain roads and high winds make cycling difficult and risky; drivers should honk before rounding mountain curves.

Hiking may be the best way to explore the island's mountainous interior. The longest marked route, the **GR20,** is an extremely difficult 200km, 14- to 15-day trail that takes hikers across the island from Calenzana (southeast of Calvi) to Conca (northeast of Porto-Vecchio), requiring a maximum of physical fitness and endurance. Do *not* tackle this trail alone, and be prepared for cold, snowy weather, even in early summer. For shorter and less challenging routes, try the popular **Mare e Monti,** a 10-day trail from Calenzana to Cargèse, and the easier **Da Mare a Mare Sud,** which crosses the southern part of the island between Porto-Vecchio and Propriano (4-6 days). All major trails are administered by the **Parc Naturel Régional de la Corse,** 2 Sargent Casalonga, in Ajaccio (☎ 04 95 51 79 00; fax 04 95 21 88 17; www.parc-naturel-corse.com), whose jurisdiction encompasses most of the Corsican heartland. For any route, a *topo-guide* (€13.72; €15.25 with shipping), available for purchase at a Parc Naturel office in person, by fax, or over the phone, is essential. The guide includes trail maps, listings of *gîtes* and *refuges,* and other important practical information. Prospective GR20 trekkers will want to consider buying *Le Grand Chemin* (€14.94), a more complete guide that includes elevations and sources of potable water. For more info, contact the Parc Naturel.

C O R S I C A

AJACCIO (AIACCIU)

The largest town in Corsica and its departmental headquarters, Ajaccio (pop. 60,000) nevertheless calls to mind a resort town on the Riviera. With its palm trees and yachts, yellow sunlit buildings and lively club scene, Ajaccio is a haven for wealthy, well-tanned tourists. Although beaches here don't match those elsewhere on the island, Ajaccio is one of the few Corsican towns with significant museums and considerable urban energy. While Napoleon's birthplace has no end of monuments commemorating the little dictator's exploits, Ajaccio's true cultural treasure is the preeminent Renaissance Italian art collection of the Musée Fesch.

▣ TRANSPORTATION

Flights: Aéroport Campo dell'Oro (☎04 95 23 56 56), 5km away. Office open M-F 8:30am-12:30pm and 2-6pm, Sa 8:30am-noon. TCA bus #8 shuttles to and from the bus station (€4). Flights to **Nice, Marseille,** and **Paris.** For info call **Air France,** 3 bd. du Roi Jérôme, or **Compagnie Corse Mediterranée** (☎08 20 82 08 20 for both).

Ferries: Gare maritime (☎04 95 51 55 45). Open June-Aug. daily 6:30am-8pm; Sept.-June M-Sa 6:30am-8pm and for departures and arrivals. **SNCM,** quai l'Herminier (☎04 95 29 66 99; fax 04 95 29 66 77), across from the bus station, goes to **Marseille** (8½hr., 6 per week); **Nice** (4hr. by day, 10hr. overnight; 1-2 per day); **Toulon** (7hr., 1 per week). Approximate prices: €40-62, ages 12-25 €25-50. Office open M-F 8am-8pm and Sa 8am-1pm. MC/V. **Corsica Ferries** (☎04 95 50 78 82) runs to **Toulon** (5¾hr., 1 per day on T, W, F, and Su at 3pm). Adult €38.20; students €23.20.

Trains: pl. de la Gare, (☎04 95 23 11 03), off bd. Sampiero, 400m from the gare maritime (toward the airport, away from the city center). Open daily 6:20am-8:20pm. To: **Bastia** (4hr., 4 per day, €23.10); **Calvi** via **Ponte Leccia** (4½hr., 2 per day, €26.90); and **Corte** (2hr., 4 per day, €12.30).

Buses: quai l'Herminier (☎04 95 51 55 45), at the gare maritime. Open June-Aug. daily 6:30am-8pm; Sept.-May M-Sa 6:30am-8pm. **Luggage storage** open daily 7am-7pm; €1.50 per bag. **Eurocorse Voyages** (☎04 95 21 06 30) goes to **Bastia** (3hr., M-Sa 2 per day, €19) via **Corte** (1½hr., €10.50); **Calvi** (3½hr., M-Sa 1 per day at 3pm, €23); **Bonifacio** (3½hr.; July-Sept. 14 daily, low-season M-Sa 2 per day; €19.50) via **Porto Vecchio** (3hr.; July-Sept. 14 daily, low-season M-Sa 2 per day; €19.50). **Autocars SAIB** (☎04 95 22 41 99) go to **Porto** (2hr.; July-Sept. daily 8:45am and 4pm, Oct.-June M-Sa 7:20am and 4pm; €11).

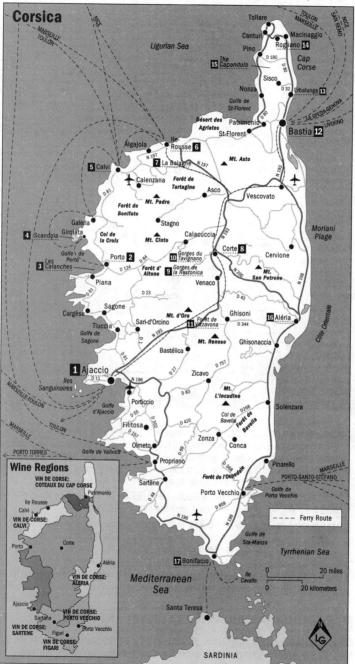

Corsica

MARSEILLE TOULON

NICE

Ligurian Sea

Tollare

Centuri

Macinaggio

Pino

Rogliano **14**

15 The Capandula

Cap Corse

D 180

D 80

Sisco

Nonza

Erbalunga **13**

Golfe de St-Florent

Patrimonio

St-Florent

Désert des Agriates

Ile-Rousse **6**

Bastia **12**

D 80

LA SPEZIA-GENOVA

LIVORNO

Algajola

7 La Balagne

N 197

5 Calvi

N 197

▲ Mt. Asto

Calenzana

Forêt de Tartagine

Asco

▲ Mt. Padro

Forêt de Bonifato

Stagno

Calacuccia

Vescovato

Moriani Plage

Galéria

Girolata

4 Scandola

Col de la Croix

▲ Mt. Cinto

10 Gorges du Tavignano

Corte **8**

Cervione

Golfe de Porto

Porto **2**

D 84

Forêt d'Altone

9 Gorges de la Restonica

▲ Mt. San Petrone

3 Les Calanches

D 124

D 23

Venaco

Piana

▲ Mt. d'Oro

N 200

Côte Orientale

Cargèse

Sagone

Sari-d'Orcino

Forêt de Vizzavona

11

Ghisoni

D 43

N 193

Aléria **16**

Tiuccia

Golfe de Sagone

N 193

Bastélica

▲ Mt. Renoso

D 344

Ghisonaccia

1 Ajaccio

N 196

D 27

Zicavo

D 757

Iles Sanguinaires

D 11

Porticcio

D 83

▲ Mt. L'Incudine

Solenzara

Golfe d'Ajaccio

Filitosa

D 302

D 420

Zonza

Conca

Col de Bavella

Forêt de Bavella

Olmeto

D 157

D 69

Propriano

D 268

Pinarello

Golfe de Valinco

Sartène

Forêt de l'Ospedale

D 368

MARSEILLE

PORTO-SANTO-STEFANO

Porto Vecchio

Golfe de Porto Vecchio

D 859

N 196

N 198

Tyrrhenian Sea

MARSEILLE-TOULON

MARSEILLE

TOULON

PORTO TORRES

- - - - Ferry Route

17 Bonifacio

Mediterranean Sea

Golfe de Sta-Manza

Ile Cavallo

0 ____ 20 miles

0 ____ 20 kilometers

Santa Teresa

SARDINIA

Wine Regions

VIN DE CORSE:
COTEAUX DU CAP CORSE

Patrimonio

Ile Rousse

Calvi

**VIN DE CORSE:
CALVI**

Porto

Corte

Aléria

**VIN DE CORSE:
ALÉRIA**

Ajaccio

Sartène

Figari

Porto Vecchio

**VIN DE CORSE:
PORTO VECCHIO**

**VIN DE CORSE:
SARTENE**

**VIN DE CORSE:
FIGARI**

CORSICA

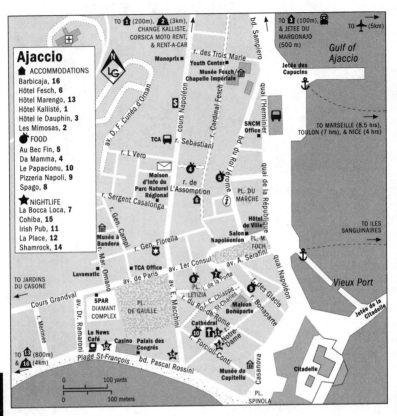

Ajaccio

🏠 ACCOMMODATIONS
Barbicaja, **16**
Hôtel Fesch, **6**
Hôtel Marengo, **13**
Hôtel Kallisté, **1**
Hôtel le Dauphin, **3**
Les Mimosas, **2**

🍴 FOOD
Au Bec Fin, **5**
Da Mamma, **4**
Le Papacionu, **10**
Pizzeria Napoli, **9**
Spago, **8**

⭐ NIGHTLIFE
La Bocca Loca, **7**
Cohiba, **15**
Irish Pub, **11**
La Place, **12**
Shamrock, **14**

Public Transportation: TCA, 77 cours Napoléon (☎04 95 23 67 70; fax 04 95 50 15 06). Buses run every 30min. Tickets €1.15, *carnet* of 10 €9; available at several *tabacs*. Buses #1, 2, and 3 go from pl. de Gaulle to the train station or down cours Napoléon. Bus #5 from av. Dr. Ramaroni and bd. Lantivy stops at Marinella and the beaches on the way to the **Iles Sanguinaires.**

Taxis: Accord Ajaccio Taxis, pl. de Gaulle (☎04 95 25 06 18) or **Jean-Marc Poli** (☎06 07 25 21 46). About €20 to airport from the city center. 24hr.

Car Rental: Ada (☎04 95 23 56 57), at the airport. Open daily 8am-11pm. AmEx/MC/V. **Rent-a-Car,** 51 cours Napoléon (☎04 95 51 34 45), in the Hôtel Kallisté, and at the airport (☎04 95 23 56 36). Open daily 8am-8pm. MC/V.

Scooter Rental: Corsica Moto Rent, 51 cours Napoléon (☎04 95 51 34 45), in the Hôtel Kallisté. Motorbikes from €31 per day, €157 per week. Deposit from €800. 18+. Open daily 8am-8pm. MC/V.

✈🛈 ORIENTATION AND PRACTICAL INFORMATION

Cours Napoléon, which runs from pl. de Gaulle past the train station, is the city's main thoroughfare. The pedestrian **rue Cardinal Fesch** starts at pl. Maréchal Foch and runs roughly parallel to cours Napoléon. Both are thick with cafés and boutiques. **Pl. de Gaulle, pl. Foch** with its Napoleonic fountain, and the **citadel** (still an active military base) enclose the *vieille ville*. The seaside **bd. Pascal Rossini** begins near pl. de Gaulle and runs next to **plage St-François**.

Tourist Office: 3 bd. du Roi Jérôme (☎04 95 51 53 03; fax 04 95 51 53 01; www.tourisme.fr/ajaccio), pl. du Marché. Free maps and bus schedules. June-Aug. theme tours in French (€6-13). Open July-Aug. M-Sa 8am-8:30pm, Su 9am-1pm and 4-7pm; Apr.-June and Sept.-Oct. M-Sa 8am-7pm and Su 9am-1pm; Nov.-Mar. M-F 8am-6pm, Sa 8am-noon and 2-5pm. **Agence du Tourisme de la Corse**, 17 bd. du Roi Jérôme (☎04 95 51 00 00; www.visit-corsica.com). Open M-F 8:30am-12:30pm and 1:30-6pm.

Hiking Info: Maison d'Info du Parc Naturel Régional, 2 rue Sergent Casalonga (morning ☎04 95 51 79 00, afternoon 04 95 51 79 10; fax 04 95 21 88 17; www.parc-naturel-corse.com), across from the *préfecture*. Topo-guides for sale and multilingual pamphlets for free. Open July-Aug. M-F 8am-6pm and Sa 8am-3pm; Sept.-June M-F 8am-noon and 2-5pm.

Money: Change Kallisté, 51 cours Napoléon (☎04 95 51 34 45), in the Hôtel Kallisté, changes at 2-3% below the fixed rate. Open daily 8am-8pm.

Laundromat: Lavomatic, 1 rue Maréchal Ornano (☎06 09 06 49 09), behind the *préfecture* and near pl. de Gaulle. Open daily 7am-9pm.

Youth Center: 52 rue Fesch (☎04 95 50 13 44; josephcorsica@hotmail.com). The center provides info on jobs and housing, as well as free **Internet access.** Open July-Aug. M-F 8am-6pm and Sa 1:30-7pm; Sept.-June M-F 8:30am-9pm and Sa 1:30-7pm.

Police: rue Général Fiorella (☎04 95 11 17 17), near the *préfecture*.

Hospital: 27 av. Impératrice Eugénie (☎04 95 29 90 90).

Internet Access: Free at the **Youth Center. Le News Café,** bd. Rossini, Diamant II (☎04 95 21 81 91). €2 for 15min., €2.50 for 30min., €4 per hr. Open daily 9am-2am.

Post Office: 13 cours Napoléon (☎04 95 51 84 65). Open M-F 8am-6:45pm and Sa 8am-noon. **Postal code:** 20000.

ACCOMMODATIONS AND CAMPING

Ajaccio has many hotels, but brace yourself for prices that rival those in Paris. Call far in advance from June to August, when rates soar and vacancies plummet. Ask hotels for their absolute cheapest room, and then ask if there's anything even cheaper; some hotels keep a couple of older rooms they don't initially list.

■ **Hôtel Kallisté,** 51 cours Napoléon (☎04 95 51 34 45; fax 04 95 21 79 00; www.cyrnos.com); follow the signs from quai l'Herminier. Well-designed rooms all have shower or bath, cable TV, and fan or A/C. Firm beds, a friendly staff, and central location make this your best option. Breakfast €6.50. Free luggage storage. Reception 8am-8pm. Mar.-July and Sept.-Oct. singles €45, doubles €52, triples €69; Aug. singles €56, doubles €69, triples €86; Nov.-Feb. singles €42, doubles €45, triples €58. Closed for renovations Nov. 10, 2002-Feb. 2003. MC/V. ❹

Hôtel Marengo, 2 rue Marengo (☎04 95 21 43 66; fax 04 95 21 51 26). From the city center, walk along the boardwalk with the sea to your left for about 25min., then make a right on bd. Madame Mère, and a left onto rue Marengo. Or, take bus #1 or 2 to "Trottel." Charming rooms by the beach, all with shower and A/C. The friendly, 18-year manager will usher you up a marble staircase to firm beds in a tranquil setting. Breakfast €5.80. Reception 9am-10pm. Open Apr.-Oct. July-Sept. singles and doubles €59, triples €69; Apr.-June and Oct. singles and doubles €52, triples €60. 4 rooms with toilet in the hallway €44-46.50. MC/V. ❺

Hôtel le Dauphin, 11 bd. Sampiero (☎04 95 21 12 94 or 04 95 51 29 96; fax 04 95 21 88 69), between the train station and ferry port. Light, modern, sky-blue rooms have shower, toilet, and TV, some with sea views. A/C €8. Breakfast included. Reception 5am-midnight. May-Oct. singles and doubles €49-60, triples €69; Mar.-Apr. singles and doubles €43-54, triples €66; Nov.-Feb. singles and doubles €38-49, triples €56. Extra bed €8. AmEx/MC/V. ❹

Hôtel Fesch, 7 rue Cardinal Fesch (☎04 95 51 62 62; fax 04 95 21 83 36), just off pl. Foch. In the heart of Ajaccio, this 3-star hotel offers spacious rooms with shower or bath, A/C, TV, and mini-bar. Dark wood and spotted faux fur chairs are the staple of the '70s art-deco design. 77 rooms mean you'll get a reservation. Breakfast €6.80. Reception 24hr. Closed Dec. 15-Jan. 15. July 13-Sept. singles €65, doubles €73; Apr. 13-July 12 and Oct. singles €57, doubles €64; Jan. 16-Apr. 12 and Nov.-Dec. 14 singles €51, doubles €55. Rooms with bathtub extra €3-7. Extra bed €18-22. AmEx/MC/V. ❹

Les Mimosas, rte. d'Alata (☎04 95 20 99 85; fax 04 95 10 01 77). Follow cours Napoléon away from the city center and turn left on montée St-Jean, which becomes rue Biancamaria and then rte. d'Alata. Continue walking straight on the other side of the roundabout, taking an immediate left onto chemin de la Carrossacia; follow the signs 600m inland to the site. (20min.) Or take bus #4 from cours Napoléon to "Brasilia" and walk straight to the roundabout, following the above directions. Close to town. Laundry €4. July-Aug. €4.80 per person, €2 per tent or car. Electricity €2.80. Prices 10% lower Apr.-June and Sept.-Oct. 15. ❷

Barbicaja, (☎04 95 52 01 17; fax 04 95 52 01 17), 4km away. Take bus #5 from av. Dr. Ramaroni just past pl. de Gaulle to "Barbicaja" and walk straight ahead (last bus at 7:30pm). Very close to the beach. Laundry €7.60. Open May-Sept. €5.70 per person, €2.30 per tent or car. Electricity €2.40. ❷

■ FOOD

The ■**morning market** on pl. du Marché sells Corsican specialties like chestnut biscuits and sheep cheese. A smaller market operates near the train station at pl. Abbatucci, on cours Napoléon. (Both Tu-Su 8am-noon.) There's a **Monoprix supermarket** at 31 cours Napoléon. (☎04 95 51 76 50. Open July-Sept. M-Sa 8:30am-7:40pm; Oct.-June M-Sa 8:30am-7:15pm.) There's also a **SPAR supermarket** at 1 cours Grandval, within the Diamant complex. (☎04 95 21 51 77. Open M-Sa 8:30am-12:30pm and 3:15-7:30pm, Su 8:30am-12:30pm.) Head to the pedestrian streets off **pl. Foch** towards the citadel for dozens of restaurants serving local dishes. Pizzerias, bakeries, and one-stop panini shops can be found on **rue Cardinal Fesch;** at night, patios on the festive quai offer affordable seafood and pizza.

■ **Au Bec Fin,** 3bis. bd. du Roi Jérôme (☎04 95 21 30 52), offers an amazing €12.50 menu. Start with smoked salmon or *foie gras,* and then try the roast veal or *filet de rascasse.* Open M-Sa noon-2pm and 7:30-10:30pm (until 11:30pm F-Sa). MC/V. ❸

Da Mamma, passage Guinguetta (☎04 95 21 39 44), off cours Napoléon. Try the *truite aux amandes* (trout with almonds) on the €15 menu. Friendly service on a secluded terrace. Open Tu-Sa noon-2pm and 7:30-10:30pm, Su-M 7:30-10:30pm. MC/V. ❸

Le Papacionu, 16 rue St-Charles (☎04 95 21 27 86), next to the cathedral. Friendly staff serves fresh pizzas (€9-11) and salads (€4-12.50) in a warm, colorful setting to a chic local crowd. Go early or late on weekends to avoid waiting. Open May-Oct. M-Sa 8-11:30pm and Nov.-Apr. W-Sa 8-11:30pm. AmEx/MC/V. ❷

Pizzeria Napoli, rue Bonaparte (☎04 95 21 32 79), will appease your midnight rumblings. Pizzas €7.30-9.30; pastas €7-9.80. Open July-Aug. daily 6:45pm-6am; Sept.-June Su-Th 6:45pm-4am and F-Sa 6:45pm-6am. ❷

Le Spago, rue Emmanuel Arène (☎04 95 21 15 71), off av. du 1er Consul. Smooth young crowd, engaging menu, and a club feel. Pastas €12.50-18; meats €13-16. Open M-F noon-2pm and 7:30-11pm, Sa 7:30-11pm. MC/V. ❸

🄢 SIGHTS

If you are a Napoleonophile, you'll find Ajaccio's sights better than another 100 days. Even for tall anti-imperialists, this capital of Corsican museums offers chances to learn about the island's culture and history. No one leaves Ajaccio without visiting the first home of the ubiquitous megalomaniac, the **Musée National de la Maison Bonaparte,** rue St-Charles, between rue Bonaparte and rue Roi-de-Rome. It is now a veritable warehouse of memorabilia, including the smaller-than-average bed in which the future emperor slept on his return from Egypt—the last time he would touch Corsican soil. (☎04 95 21 43 89. Open Apr.-Sept. M 2-6pm, Tu-Su 9am-noon and 2-6pm; Oct.-Mar. M 2-4:45pm, Tu-Su 10am-noon and 2-4:45pm. €4, students €2.60, under 18 free.) The glittering **Salon Napoléonien,** pl. Foch, in the Hôtel de Ville, displays Napoleon's portraits, sculptures, medals, and death mask. (☎04 95 51 52 53. Open June 15-Sept. 15 M-Sa 9-11:45am and 2-5:45pm; Sept. 16-June 14 M-F 9-11:45am and 2-4:45pm. €2.30).

Napoleon's uncle Fesch piled up a stash of money as a merchant during the Revolution, before leaving commerce for the cloth. His worldly wealth went into the 🄢**Musée Fesch,** 50-52 rue Cardinal Fesch, a premier collection of 14th- to 19th-century Italian paintings including Titian's sensual *Man with a Glove* and Veronese's equally erotic *Leda and the Swan.* Also within the complex is the **Chapelle Impériale,** the final resting place of most of the Bonaparte family—though Napoleon himself is buried in a humble 6-coffined tomb at Les Invalides in Paris. (☎04 95 21 48 17. Open July-Aug. M 1:30-6pm, Tu-Th 9am-6:30pm, F 9am-6:30pm and 9pm-midnight, Sa-Su 10:30am-6pm; Apr.-June and Sept. M 1-5:15pm, Tu-Su 9:15am-12:15pm and 2:15-5:15pm; Oct.-Mar. Tu-Sa 9:15am-12:15pm and 2:15-5:15pm. Museum €5.35, students €3.80; chapel €1.55, students €0.80, under 15 free. Tours mid-July to Aug. F 9:15pm; €9.15, students €7.60; price includes museum admission.)

The **Musée à Bandera,** 1 rue Général Levie, provides a comprehensive digest of Corsican history, from Corsu to Paoli to Resistance hero Scamaroni. It's incomprehensible without a good understanding of French. (☎04 95 51 07 34. Open July-Sept. 15 M-Sa 9am-7pm and Su 9am-noon; Sept. 16-June M-Sa 9am-noon and 2-6pm. €3.85, students €2.30.)

🄢 🄞 NIGHTLIFE AND FESTIVALS

Unlike most Corsican cities, Ajaccio can make for a wild night. Ajaccio's major clubs are out of town and can be reached by car or motorbike. **La Cinquième Avenue** is 5km away on rte. des Sanguinaires (☎04 95 52 09 77. Open daily midnight-5am.) **Le Blue Moon** is farther away in Porticcio. (☎04 95 25 07 70. Open July-Aug. daily 11:30pm-5am; Apr.-June and Sept. F-Sa 11:30pm-5am.) **La Place,** Résidence Diamant II, in town on bd. Lantivy caters to an older crowd in a modern setting of blue-velvet lounges and stainless-steel bars. (☎06 09 07 03 53. Open F-Sa 11pm-5am.) Clubs tend to have no cover but a one-drink minimum. If you've still got some cash to lose, head to the **Casino,** bd. Pascal Rossini (☎04 95 50 40 60. 18+. Open daily 1pm-4am.) For the latest, check out *Le Rendez-Vous* and *Sortir,* both available at the tourist office.

Cohiba, Résidence Diamant II, bd. Lantivy (☎04 95 51 47 05), is the hottest *avant boîte* (pre-club scene). A well-dressed crowd fills a sumptuous interior of red velvet chairs and dark wood. DJ plays house F and Sa. Open daily 7:30am-2am.

La Bocca Locca, 4 rue de la Porta (☎06 07 08 68 69), entertains a wild, fun-loving bunch with live salsa and tasty tapas in a red room with bull-fight posters on the walls. The large, mellow terrace is tastefully decorated with palm trees and colorful paintings. Open Tu-Sa 7pm-2am.

Shamrock, 3 rue Forcioli Conti, off pl. de Gaulle (☎06 09 97 24 82), is a Corsican-Irish pub. Low-key lounging in the green leather interior. Karaoke night W from 9pm. Happy hour daily 5-7pm: 2 draft beers for the price of 1. Open daily 5pm-2am.

Irish Pub, 4 rue Notre Dame (☎04 95 21 63 22), just down the street from Shamrock, gives a livelier pub experience. Loud music is played in a warm setting of rich green walls and wooden tables designed like beer bottle caps. Drafts €3-3.50; bottles €4-5. July-Aug. F-Sa live international music after 11pm. Open daily 6pm-2am.

Ajaccio often hosts a summer theater or music festival (call the tourist office for details). August 15 brings the three-day **Fêtes Napoléon,** commemorating the emperor's birth with plays, a parade, ceremonies, and a huge final *pyrosymphonie* (fireworks display) in the bay. But Ajaccio's real mania becomes apparent in the July and August **Shopping de Nuit,** when stores stay open until midnight on Friday as musicians, dance groups and circus performers liven the streets.

▶ DAYTRIP FROM AJACCIO: ILES SANGUINAIRES

The vertiginous Iles Sanguinaires, southwest of Ajaccio at the mouth of the gulf, bare their black cliffs to the sea. **Nave Va,** at a kiosk on the port, runs excursions to the largest of the islands. (☎04 95 51 31 31. Open Apr.-Oct. daily. €20.) On the island is the **Tour Mezza Mare,** immortalized in the love letters of romance writer Alphonse Daudet. Visible from this tower is the corresponding **Tour de la Parata** on the mainland. Bus #5, which leaves from av. Dr. Ramaroni (1 per hr. 7am-7pm, €1.75), stops at Parata and numerous beaches, the most popular being the golden **Marinella.** To get to the more remote **Capo di Feno,** drive in the direction of the Sanguinaires, taking a right after "Week End" beach onto **Chemin de la Corniche à la plage de Capo di Feno,** and continue till you see the beach. (20min.)

PORTO

A hiking paradise, the gulf of Porto combines all of the natural spectacles that make Corsica unique. Jagged volcanic mountains tower above a crystalline sea; lush pine groves nuzzle bridges as waterfalls pour into pools; to the north, a marine reserve conceals grottoes and rare species of plants and birds. The ove-touristed town of Porto (pop. 432) is no more than an extended souvenir shop, but lodgings are cheap and transportation convenient by Corsican standards.

▶▶ ORIENTATION AND PRACTICAL INFORMATION

Porto is split into an upper town, **Haut Porto** or **Quartier Vaita,** and a coastal area, **Porto Marina,** where some 15 hotels and restaurants jostle for space. D81 connects Haut Porto to Calvi in the north and leads to Ajaccio in the south; the unnamed main road leads from D81 to the port.

Buses: Autocars SAIB (☎04 95 22 41 99), in Ajaccio. To **Ajaccio** (2hr.; July-Sept. daily 2 per day, low-season M-Sa 2 per day; €11) and **Calvi** (3hr.; July-Aug. daily 1 per day, low-season M-Sa 1 per day; €16). **Autocars Mordiconi** (☎04 95 48 00 04) to **Corte** (July-Sept. 15 M-Sa 1 per day, €19).

Car, Bike, and Scooter Rental: Porto Locations (☎/fax 04 95 26 10 13), opposite the supermarkets in Haut Porto. **Cars** €60 per day, €305 per week. 18+. **Scooters** €46 per day, €230 per week. **Bikes** €15 per day, €68 per week. Credit card deposit €305 for cars, €610 for scooters. Open Apr.-Oct. daily 8:30am-7:30pm. AmEx/MC/V. **Hertz** (☎06 08 69 75 20), by the mini-golf sign on the left bank. Open daily 8am-8pm. AmEx/MC/V.

Taxis: Taxis Chez Félix (☎04 95 26 12 92).

Tourist Office: (☎04 95 26 10 55; www.porto-tourisme.com), near the marina on the main road. Bus schedules; info on water sports, boat trips, lodging. Topo-guide for local hikes (€2.30). Open June-Sept. daily 9am-7pm; Apr.-May M-F 9am-noon and 2-6pm, Sa 9am-noon; Oct.-Mar. M-F 9am-noon and 2-5pm.

Laundromat: Lavo 2000 (☎04 95 26 10 33), on the main road. Open daily 8am-9pm.

Post Office: (☎04 95 26 10 26), midway between the marina and Haut Porto. Open July-Aug. M-F 9am-12:30pm and 2-5pm, Sa 9-11:30am; Sept.-June M-F 9am-12:15pm and 2-4pm, Sa 9-11am. **Postal code: 20150.**

▚ ACCOMMODATIONS AND CAMPING

Porto's abundance of hotels makes the town more affordable than most of the island, although prices rise dramatically in July and peak in August.

Le Panorama (☎04 95 26 10 15), on the main road near the port, is the best value in town. Functional rooms with huge terraces overlooking marina and beach. All rooms with shower, some with toilet. Reception 8am-noon and 3-9pm. July-Aug. singles and doubles €26-28, Apr.-June and Sept.-Oct. €20-23. Extra bed €3. ❸

Bon Accueil (☎/fax 04 95 26 19 50; jesaispas@net-up.com), on the main road. Simple rooms, all with shower and toilet, get the job done, even if the mattresses are a little soft. Reception 7am-2am. Breakfast €5.50. July 15-Aug. €43 per person with *demi-pension*; Sept.-July 14 singles and doubles €29-35, triples €40-44. MC/V. ❹

Le Lonca (☎04 95 26 16 44; fax 04 95 26 11 83), right next to the post office, offers spacious rooms in a quiet area overlooking the hills. All rooms have shower or bath, toilet, and TV. Reception 7am-11pm. Breakfast €6.50. Open Apr.-Oct. July singles and doubles €38-50, triples €60; Aug. singles and doubles €54-69, triples €79; Apr.-June and Sept. singles and doubles €35-50, triples €56-60. MC/V. ❹

Camping: Three-star **Le Sole e Vista** ❷ (☎04 95 26 15 71; fax 04 95 26 10 79), on your right before the supermarkets as you enter Porto, has shady hillside plots and a rockin' bar. Reception 9am-10pm. Open Apr.-Oct. €5 per person, €2 per tent, €2 per car. Electricity €3.30. Three-star **Les Oliviers** ❷ (☎04 95 26 14 49; fax 04 95 26 12 49; guy.lannoy@wanadoo.fr), 200m toward Ajaccio on D81, has a similar arrangement. Reception open 8am-9pm. Open Apr.-Oct. €5-6 per person, €2.50 per tent or car. Electricity €3. 4- to 8-person fully equipped bungalows €305-793 per week. MC/V. **Camping Municipal** ❷ (☎04 95 26 17 76), straddling D84 in lower Porto, resembles a poorly planned parking lot, but always has vacancies. Reception 8am-9:30pm. Open June 15-Sept. 30. €4.70 per person, €2 per tent or car. Electricity €3. MC/V.

HOME ON THE RANGE The last thing you'd expect to encounter on a hike through a pine forest is a brood of squealing pigs, but around Porto, roaming snouts are everywhere. Corsican farmers take free-range herding to an extreme; their porkers fend for themselves for years, leading a semi-nomadic existence in the wild. Unfortunately for the oinkers, their absentee owners never forget a face—the animals are recognized on appearance alone. When it comes time for the slaughter, their meat is tender enough to earn Corsican *charcuterie* a reputation as the best in France.

Gîtes in Ota: Some of the cheapest accommodations in Corsica are available in the pleasant village of Ota, 5km inland and northward, a starting point for many hikes. The bus from Ajaccio to Porto stops at Ota (15min., 2 per day, €3.05). To walk from Porto, veer right and head uphill at the fork after the supermarkets; follow the signs to D124 and Ota. (1hr.) **Chez Felix ❶** (☎04 95 26 12 92; fax 04 95 26 18 25) has pleasant 4- to 8-bed dorms. Kitchen access. Breakfast €6. Sheets €2. €11 per person; *demi-pension* €28, doubles with bath and demi-pension €38. AmEx/MC/V. **Chez Marie ❶** (☎/fax 04 95 26 11 37) has more modern, spartan dorms with 6- to 12-beds. Kitchen access. Breakfast €4.60. Beds €11, demi-pension €27.60; doubles with demi-pension €27.60. MC/V.

🍴 FOOD

Rule of thumb: avoid hotel restaurants, where prices are high and food mediocre. **La Marine ❶**, on the main road near the marina, is one of the better eateries in town. Enjoy tasty pizzas (from €5.50) and affordable *menus* (from €9). (☎04 95 26 10 19. Open Apr.-Oct. daily 11:30am-2:30pm and 6:30-10:30pm.) If you would prefer more traditional Corsican dishes and fresh fish, try **La Tour Génoise ❹**, behind the aquarium in the marina. There are three menus (€15.10, 16.60, 19.70) with options to please any palate. (☎04 95 26 17 11. Open Apr.-Oct. daily noon-2pm and 7-10pm. Handicap access. AmEx/MC/V.) The *gîtes* in Ota (see **Accommodations,** above) have delicious Corsican specialties (menus €17-19), though the 1hr. walk from Porto may be too long for your taste. The two supermarkets are next to each other in Haut Porto on D81: **SPAR** (☎04 95 26 11 25; open July-Aug. M-Sa 8am-8pm, Su 8am-noon and 5-8pm; Sept.-June M-Sa 8:30am-noon and 3-7pm, Su 8:30am-noon) and **Supermarché Banco.** (☎04 95 26 10 92. Open July-Aug. M-Sa 8am-8pm, Su 8am-12:30pm and 4-8pm; Apr.-June and Sept.-Oct. M-Sa 8am-noon and 3-7pm).

🏔 HIKES AND SIGHTS

GORGES, POOLS, AND PINES. The old mule-track from Ota to Evisa is perfect for hikers of all levels. Rugged yet accessible, this 3-hour trail winds through the deep **Gorges de la Spelunca**, passing by 15th-century bridges and plenty of picnicking and swimming spots. The trail begins on the stairway to the left of the Mairie (see **Gîtes in Ota,** above, for buses); follow the painted orange rectangles. The most spectacular scenery lies near the beginning of the trail, from the first two Genoese bridges to the **Pont de Zaglia.** (45min.) To walk only this shorter section, follow the main road from Ota to the first Genoese bridge and pick up the original orange-rectangle trail. (25min.) There are no afternoon return buses from Ota or Evisa. Hitching is reportedly easy during high season, but as always, *Let's Go* does not recommend hitchhiking.

Chestnut trees and 50m pines fill the mountainous **Fôret d'Altone** between Evisa and Col. de Vergio. This trail, part of the **Tra Mare e Monti,** is famous for its **piscines naturelles,** impromptu swimming holes formed by pooling waterfalls. The pools are an hour or so from Evisa; beyond them is a more difficult and secluded trail to Col. de Vergio (6-7hr.), where a *gîte d'etape* marks its intersection with the **GR20.**

LES CALANCHES. The most astounding scenery on the entire island may be south of Porto, where the geological formations of the Calanches resemble, in the words of Guy de Maupassant, a "menagerie of nightmares petrified by the whim of some extravagant god." Hikes here range from easy-as-pie to do-or-die. The **Château Fort,** in the former category, begins 6km south of Porto on D81; ask the Ajaccio-Ota bus driver to let you off at **Tête de Chien.** (30min.) A more masochistic alternative awaits 2km farther south off D81; the marked trail, which begins near the stadium, climbs 900m to spectacular 1294m **Le Capo d'Orto.** (3hr. one-way.) From the top of the summit, you can join a trail heading back to Porto.

SCANDOLA. Totally off-limits to hikers and divers, the caves, grottoes, and wild terrain of the **Reserve Naturelle de Scandola** can only be explored by **boat tours** from Porto. The reserve's most celebrated inhabitants are falcon-like buzzards, whose wailing call is immediately recognizable. **Porto Linea,** next to Hôtel Monte Rosso, sends a 12-person boat into hard-to-reach caves and coves. *(☎ 04 95 26 11 50; available Apr.-Oct., reserve ahead; 3hr.; €35.)* Less intimate but equally spectacular, **Nave Va,** near Hôtel Le Cyrnée, tours Scandola with 50- to 180-person boats. *(☎ 04 95 26 15 16; Apr.-Oct. reserve ahead; 3hr.; €32.)*

SIGHTS IN PORTO. Guarding Porto's strip of hotels and postcard shops is one of Corsica's oldest Genoese towers, the 1549 **Tour Génoise.** After a 15min. climb, enjoy spectacular views of the windswept cliffs dropping majestically to the sea. *(Open Apr.-Sept. daily 10am-12:30pm and 3-7pm. €2.50.)* See what's for dinner at the one-room **Aquarium de la Poudrière,** on the marina. The cave-like space holds a giant stingray and other aquatic creatures from the Gulf of Porto. *(☎ 04 95 26 19 24. Open daily 10am-7pm. €5.50. Ticket for both the aquarium and Tour Génoise €6.50.)*

CALVI

Calvi (pop. 5700) is sometimes called Corsica's Côte d'Azur, and it shares some of that coastline's best and worst traits. It's yacht-bound and café-ridden, full of souvenir shops and the idle rich. It's also stunningly beautiful, with a star-shaped citadel above town and a long, sandy beach below it, all against a backdrop of snow-capped mountains. Even if Calvi isn't the top Corsican destination, two hostels and an accessible beach make it the most backpacker-friendly town on the island.

▐▀ TRANSPORTATION

Flights: Aéroport de Calvi Ste-Catherine, 7km southeast of town; a taxi ride there costs €16.80 (☎ 04 95 65 88 88). **Air France** and subsidiary **Air Littoral** (☎ 08 02 82 08 20) fly to **Lille, Lyon, Marseille, Nice,** and **Paris.**

Ferries: For info and tickets call **Agence TRAMAR** (☎ 04 95 65 01 38), quai Landry, in the Port de Plaisance. Open M-F 8:30am-noon and 2-5:30pm, Sa 8:30am-noon. Both **SNCM** (☎ 04 95 65 17 77) and **Corsica Ferries** (☎ 04 95 65 43 21) send high-speed boats to **Nice** and have offices near the Capitainerie du Port de Commerce. Open 2hr. before boat arrivals.

Trains: pl. de la Gare (☎ 04 95 65 00 61), on av. de la République near the Port de Plaisance. To: **Bastia** (3hr., 2 per day, €17.50); **Corte** (2½hr., 2 per day, €14.60); **Ile Rousse** (45min., 2 per day, €4). **Tramways de la Balagne** also sends trains to **Ile Rousse** (50min.; June-Sept. 10 per day, Apr.-May and Oct. 4 per day; €4). Open daily June-Sept. 5:45am-9:30pm; Oct.-June 14 5:30am-7:30pm.

Buses: Autocar SAIB buses (☎ 04 95 22 41 99) leave from in front of the Super U and head to **Porto** (3hr.; May-June and Sept.-Oct. M-Sa 1 per day, July-Aug. daily 1 per day; €16). **Les Beaux Voyages,** on av. Wilson (☎ 04 95 65 11 35), leaves from in front of the agency at pl. Porteuse d'Eau, where you can buy tickets. Open M-Sa 9am-noon and 2-7pm. Buses to: **Ajaccio** (4hr., M-Sa 1 per day, €22); **Calenzana** (July-Aug. M-Sa 2 per day, Sept.-June M-Tu and Th-Sa 1 per day; €5.30), where the **GR20** begins; and **Bastia** (2¼hr., M-Sa 1 per day, €12.50) via **Ile Rousse** (25min., €3.50).

Car Rental: Europcar, av. de la République (☎04 95 65 10 35, airport ☎04 95 65 10 19). €77 per day, €270 per week. Deposit €400. 21+. Open M-Sa 8am-1pm and 2:30-7:30pm, Su 8am-noon. MC/V. **Hertz,** 2 rue Maréchal Joffre (May-Sept. ☎04 95 65 06 64; airport ☎04 95 65 02 96). From €66 per day, €239 per week. Deposit €600. 21+. AmEx/MC/V. Open M-Sa 8am-8pm.

Bike Rental: Garage d'Angeli, pl. Christophe Colomb (☎04 95 65 02 13 and 06 19 09 28 36). €17 per day, €94 per week. Deposit €300. Open Apr.-Oct. daily 8:30am-noon and 1:30-7pm; Nov.-Mar. Tu-Sa 9am-noon and 2-6pm. **Oxy Bike** (☎06 86 48 28 96), in a field across from Super U on av. Christophe Colomb. €12 per half-day, €17 per day. Deposit €150. Open Apr.-Oct. daily 8:30am-7pm.

Scooter Rental: Tra Mare è Monti (☎04 95 65 21 26; red.calvi@wanadoo.fr), Port de Plaisance, next to *le cap-itainerie*. From €40 per day, €200 per week. Deposit €760. 18+. Open Apr.-Oct. daily 9am-8pm. MC/V.

Taxi: ☎04 95 65 03 10 or 04 95 65 03 10. Stand right by the train station. 24hr.

⚔ 🛈 ORIENTATION AND PRACTICAL INFORMATION

The city is manageable in size and easy to walk, threaded by one main road following the curve of the coast, called **bd. Wilson** between the citadel and the post office, then **av. de la République,** and finally **av. Christophe Colomb** as you leave the city. The lovely pedestrian **rue Clemenceau** runs below bd. Wilson, parallel to the port.

Tourist Office: Port de Plaisance (☎04 95 65 16 67; fax 04 95 65 14 09; omt.calvi@wanadoo.fr; www.tourisme.fr/calvi). Exit from back of train station, facing the beach, turn left, and it's on the second floor of the first building on the right. Friendly staff makes on-the-spot hotel reservations (€3). 90min. audioguide of the citadel available for €6. Open June-Sept. 15 daily 8:30am-1pm and 2:30-7pm; May M-Sa 9am-6:30pm; Sept. 16-Apr. M-F 9am-5:30pm.

Police: ☎04 95 65 44 77. On Port de Plaisance, to the right of the tourist office.

Laundromat: Laverie, in Super U Plaza, av. Christophe Colomb. Open daily 8am-10pm. Also **Calvi Clean,** bd. Wilson, which has new machines. Open daily 7am-10pm.

Internet Access: Calvi 2B Informatique (☎04 95 65 19 25), on av. Santa Maria, above the BVJ hostel. €1.25 per 15min. Open daily 9am-10pm. **Café de**

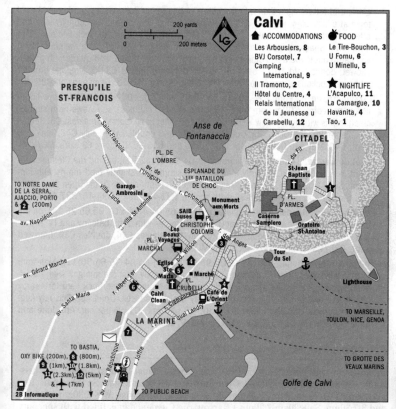

Calvi

⌂ ACCOMMODATIONS
Les Arbousiers, **8**
BVJ Corsotel, **7**
Camping International, **9**
Il Tramonto, **2**
Hôtel du Centre, **4**
Relais International de la Jeunesse u Carabellu, **12**

🍴 FOOD
Le Tire-Bouchon, **3**
U Fornu, **6**
U Minellu, **5**

★ NIGHTLIFE
L'Acapulco, **11**
La Camargue, **10**
Havanita, **4**
Tao, **1**

L'Orient (☎04 95 65 00 16), on the port, in the middle of quai Landry. €1 flat fee, plus €0.10 per min. Open Apr.-Oct. daily 8am-2am.

Post office: (☎04 95 65 90 90), on bd. Wilson. Open M-F 8:30am-6pm and Sa 8:30am-noon. **Postal code:** 20260.

◤ ACCOMMODATIONS AND CAMPING

With two of the only hostels in Corsica, Calvi is a haven for backpackers. There are also plenty of hotels, which get cheaper the farther from the center of town you look. Reserve ahead in the summer, especially July. Weekly rentals are often cheaper; ask about *tarifs dégressifs* at the tourist office.

BVJ Corsotel "Hôtel de Jeunes," av. de la République (☎04 95 65 14 15; fax 04 95 65 33 72), across from train station parking lot. 2- to 8-bed dorms with blankets, shower, and sink have high ceilings and plenty of space. Seaside rooms have excellent views. Friendly staff and ideal location near the center of Calvi make this your best budget option. Reception 7:30am-1pm and 5-10pm. Check-out 10am. Open Apr.-Oct. Beds €22, with breakfast €24. ❷

Relais International de la Jeunesse U Carabellu (☎04 95 65 14 16). Leave the station, turn left on av. de la République, pass the Super U, turn right at rte. de Pietramag-

CORSICA

giore, and follow signs 5km into the hills. Continue past Bella Vista camping until road forks at a stop sign; veer left and continue. (45min.) The route is exceedingly long and often deserted—women may not want to walk alone. On a beautiful, secluded spot 5km from town. Spacious rooms in a classic chalet. Incredible views of Calvi. The staff will let you camp out if you ask. Families get their own doubles, triples, and quads with private shower; dorms hold 10-11 beds. Breakfast included. Sheets €3.05. Luggage drop-off all hours. Lockout 10am-5pm. Open Mar.-Sept. Bunks €15.25. *Demi-pension* €25. ❷

Il Tramonto, rte. de Porto R.N. 199 (☎04 95 65 04 17; fax 04 95 65 02 40; www.hotel-iltramonto.com), 800m from town, past the citadel. Fabulous sea views from simple, clean rooms with light yellow walls. Shower and toilet in all rooms. Breakfast €5. Reception 7am-midnight. Open Apr.-Oct. Aug. singles and doubles €49; July €46; June and Sept. €40; May and Oct. €34; Apr. €31. Extra bed €13-16. Balcony €3 extra. MC/V. ❹

Hôtel du Centre, 14 rue Alsace Lorraine (☎04 95 65 02 01), behind rue Clemenceau. Right in heart of Calvi. Friendly manager lets simple but slightly tired rooms with firm beds. Breakfast €4.50. Free luggage storage. Reception 8am-9pm. Open June-early Oct. Singles and doubles €28-35, with shower €31-42; triples €34-46/€37-49. ❸

Les Arbousiers, rte. de Pietramaggiore (☎04 95 65 04 47; fax 04 95 65 26 14), on the beach 800m from town, past Super U. Eclectic rooms with bath, balcony and TV. Breakfast €5. Reception 24hr. Open May-Sept. July-Aug. singles €44; doubles €50. June and Sept. €35/€38; May €33/€35. AmEx/MC/V. ❹

Camping International, RN 197 (☎04 95 65 01 75; fax 04 95 65 36 11), 1km from town. Walk past Super U and Hôtel L'Onda; immediately past the minigolf sign, take a right. Relaxed atmosphere and friendly managers. Young people flock here for nearby beach and on-site bar. July-Aug. bands play 5 nights a week. Open Apr.-Oct. July-Aug. €5 per person, children under 8 €2.50; €3 per tent; €1.50 per car. Apr.-June and Sept.-Oct. €3.70/€1.85/€2.30/€1.25. MC/V. ❶

🍴 FOOD

Pickings are slim for cheap food in Calvi. Try the **Super U Supermarché,** av. Christophe Colomb. (☎04 95 65 04 32. Open July-Aug. M-Sa 8am-9pm, Su 8am-1pm; June and Sept. 1-15 M-Sa 8am-8pm and Su 8am-1pm; otherwise M-F 8:30am-12:30pm and 3-7:30pm, Sa 8:30am-7:30pm.) Narrow rue Clemenceau is filled with specialty food shops and groceries and hosts a **covered market** beside the Eglise Ste-Marie. (Open daily 8am-noon.) Cheap pizzerias line rue de la République and stylish port restaurants offer great views, but you'll want to stick to the pedestrian alleys for the best food and local ambience.

🍴 **U Minellu,** traverse de l'Eglise (☎04 95 65 05 52), prepares an excellent €16 menu filled with Corsican specialties. Begin with the *assiette du Minellu,* a medley of fresh Corsican ham and cheese, tomatoes, beets, chick peas, and hard-boiled eggs. Then try the *sanglier* (wild boar) or delicious *cannelloni au brocciu* (pasta with country cheese). The hearty servings will leave you sated, and the secluded terrace area will let you escape from the tourist-infested rue Clemenceau. Open July-Aug. daily 7pm-midnight; Apr.-June and Sept.-Oct. 15 W-M noon-2:30pm and 7-11pm. ❹

Le Tire-Bouchon, 15 rue Clemenceau (☎04 95 65 25 41), a wine bar, offers 35 Corsican wines by the glass (€1.60-6) or bottle, and simple local cuisine. Portions, starting at €5.40, are of medium size. Open June-Sept. M-Sa noon-2pm and 7-11pm, Su 7-11pm; Apr.-May and Oct.-Nov. Th-Th noon-2pm and 7-11pm. MC/V. ❷

U Fornu, bd. Wilson (☎04 95 65 27 60). This local staple, off the beaten track, has a good €14 *menu,* including *soupe corse* and *raie à la grenobloise* (stingray). The bread and desserts are all homemade. There's also a wide selection of *entrées* (€8-13) and main dishes (€11-20). Open daily noon-2pm and 7-11pm, closed for lunch on Su. ❷

◎ 🏖 SIGHTS AND BEACHES

Driven to desperation by invasions from the south, 13th-century Calvi asked the protection of nearby Genoa—and for five centuries remained Corsica's most unshakable Italian stronghold. In recognition of Calvi's loyalty, the Genoese crowned the entrance to the **citadel** with an inscription reading *civitas Calvi semper fidelis* ("the city of Calvi is always faithful"). Just beyond the entry portal, a welcome center distributes a useful free map and a self-guided audio-tour of the citadel (90min., €6), which covers some of the lesser monuments. (☎04 95 65 36 74. Open W-M 10am-12:30pm and 4-7:30pm.) Round the first corner and climb the stairs to reach the citadel's center, dominated by the austere **Palais des Gouverneurs** (now—not without irony—the mess hall of France's foreign legion) and the 16th-century **Cathédrale St-Jean Baptiste.** The church's Baroque domes belie an unusually sparse interior; the 15th-century blue-clad Madonna to the left of the choir, brought from Peru by a wealthy emigré, is the pride and joy of the town's religious element. (Open daily 9am-7pm.) The **Oratoire St-Antoine,** tucked into the citadel's port-side wall, is largely abandoned, but you should take a look at a decaying 1530 fresco in the upper left corner, showing Christ accompanied by St-Sebastian.

Like several other Mediterranean towns, Calvi claims to be the birthplace of **Christopher Columbus.** The local theory is that a certain Calvi expatriate, Antonio Calvo, returned to his hometown sometime in the 15th century to enlist new recruits for the Genoese navy. The talents of his nephew Christophe caught his eye, so Calvo adopted the young man and returned with him to Genoa. The scenario has its share of skeptics, but the tourist office claims it can produce conclusive evidence. In any case, a **plaque** in the north end of the citadel marks the ruins of the house where Columbus may have been born. The citadel's other famous house tells a more likely story: Napoleon and his family sojourned here in 1793 when fleeing political opponents in Ajaccio. Visit at the end of the day, since it's something of a tradition to watch the sunset at the far end of the citadel.

Calvi and the surrounding area abound with gorgeous sandy beaches and a clear turquoise sea. Shallow water allows you to tiptoe many meters into the ocean; strong winds make for great windsurfing. If the 6km expanse of **public beach** gets too windy, the rocks surrounding the citadel provide secluded and sun-drenched shelter. The **Tramways de la Balagne** (see **Transportation,** above) can take you to more remote coves further out of town.

🎵 🎤 ENTERTAINMENT AND FESTIVALS

The bars on the **Port de Plaisance** sparkle with excitement and finery in the summer night. Signs posted all over town advertise party nights on different spots along the northern coast. Locals come from far and wide to the two open-air nightclubs on the road to Ile Rousse.

Tao, on the Port de Plaisance (☎04 95 65 00 73), caters to an older crowd with a mellow atmosphere. Try the piano bar and French/Asian restaurant in the citadel overlooking the sea. Open June-Sept. daily 8pm-6am.

Havanita is the funkiest bar on the Port de Plaisance (☎04 95 65 00 37). Loudly dressed bartenders serve Cuban cocktails amid straw huts and palm trees. Happy Hour daily 6-8pm: drinks from €6. Open Apr.-Oct. daily 6pm-2am.

La Camargue, 25 minutes up N197 by foot (☎04 95 65 08 70). Scantily clad youth bump 'n' grind in one of several discos and around outdoor pools, while an over-30 crowd swings in the piano bar. Free shuttles for La Camargue leave from the port parking lot near the tourist office. €10 cover, includes first drink. Open July-Aug. daily 11pm-6am; June and Sept. Sa-Su only; piano bars open year-round.

L'Acapulco, on D151, also known as rte. de Calenzana (☎04 95 65 08 03). L'Acapulco, a right-turn ten minutes after La Camargue, is a near-twin to La Camargue, enhancing the tropical mood with flaming torches and waterfalls. L'Acapulco shuttles pick up at the Tour de Sel. €10 cover, includes first drink. Open July-Aug. daily 11pm-6am; June and Sept. weekends only; piano bar open all year.

Calvi hosts several festivals, including the **Festival du Jazz** in the last week of June, during which over 150 musicians give impromptu performances. (☎04 95 65 00 50. M-F €11, Sa €15.) In mid-September, the **Rencontres Polyphoniques** draw international singers. (☎04 95 65 23 57. Tickets €15-20.) And in late-October or early-November, the week-long **Festival du Vent** brings together a smorgasbord of artists, scientists, athletes, actors, and human rights activists to celebrate the mystical and omnipresent wind of Calvi and Corsica. For more information, call the tourist office at ☎04 95 65 16 67.

ILE ROUSSE

Stretching east from Calvi to the town of Ile Rousse (pop. 3000), Corsica's northern coast is lined with unblemished beaches and out-of-the-way coves. The scenery is at its best in Ile Rousse itself; with its powdery beach and clear, opalescent waters, the scenic train ride from Calvi alone justifies the trip. Ile Rousse was founded in 1759 by Pascal Paoli, the leader of independent Corsica, in an effort to divert trade from Genoese-dominated Calvi. Today, Ile Rousse remains the perfect hub for hikes into the breathtaking countryside of the Balagne.

SNCM sends **ferries** to Nice (3-10hr. depending on the boat; 2-7 per week; €35-40, students €30-35). Call **Agence CCR** on av. J. Calizi, for more info. (☎04 95 60 09 56; fax 04 95 60 02 56. Open M-F 9am-noon and 2-5:30pm, Sa 9am-noon.) The **train station** provides service to Calvi, Bastia, and Ajaccio. (☎04 95 60 00 50. Open July-Sept. daily 6am-8pm; low-season 6am-noon and 2-7pm.) **Tramways de la Balagne** trains hug the coast on the way to Calvi. (50min.; June-Sept. 10 per day, Apr.-May and Oct. 4 per day; €4.) Several beaches and campsites lie along the route—just ask the ticket collector in your carriage to let you off when you see one that looks particularly enticing. Few can resist the charms of **Aregno Plage** and its accompanying campsite, three stops from Ile Rousse.

No more than 2km across, Ile Rousse is easy to navigate. The town center lies to the right of the train station, while the *gare maritime* and tower-topped peninsula are to the left. To get to the **tourist office** from the train station or ferry depot, walk right for about five minutes; it's in a small office on the opposite side of pl. Paoli. The staff will give you a practical guide and information on nearby villages. (☎04 95 60 04 35; fax 04 95 60 24 74; info@ot-ile-rousse.fr; www.ot-ile-rousse.fr. Open July-Aug. M-Sa 9am-7pm, Su 10am-12:30pm and 5-7pm; June and Sept. daily 9am-noon and 2-7pm, closed Su afternoon; Oct.-May M-F 9am-noon and 2-6pm.)

Leader's Sport, av. Paul Doumer, rents high-quality mountain **bikes.** (☎04 95 60 15 76. Open July-Aug. daily 7am-8:30pm; June M-Sa 8am-7:30pm and Su 8am-12:30pm; Sept.-May M-Sa 9am-noon and 2:30-7pm. €16 per day, €77 per week; €229 deposit. MC/V.) There's **Internet** access at **Cyber One Café,** 15bis. av. Paul Doumer (☎04 95 62 72 91; www.cyberonecafe.com). As you surf, you can drink and eat. (€1.15 for 15min., €2.25 for 30min., €4.50 per hr. Drinks €1-3.50, sandwiches €2.50-4. Open M-Sa 10am-2am, Su 2pm-midnight.) The **post office** is on rte. de Monticello (☎04 95 63 05 50. Open M-F 8:30am-5pm, Sa 8:30am-noon.) **Postal code:** 20220.

The city's signature **covered market** off pl. Paoli is filled with local fruits, the tentacled and finned catch of the day, and 10 different types of honey. (Open daily 7am-1pm.) The local **Casino supermarket** on allée Charles de Gaulle takes up where the market leaves off. (☎04 95 60 24 23. Open July-Aug. M-Sa 8:30am-8pm and Su 8:30am-1pm; Sept.-June M-F 8:30am-12:30pm and 3-7:30pm, Sa 8:30am-7:30pm.)

Inexpensive pizza and sandwiches are the specialties of the *brasseries* along pl. Paoli. **U Fuccone ❷**, on rue Paoli, offers an excellent 3-course, €12 menu with warm goat cheese salad, *entrecôte au poivre*, and a *tarte au chocolat*. The friendly staff also serves pizzas (€7-8) and pastas (€7.50-11.50) on the terrace (☎ 04 95 60 16 67. Open May-Sept. daily 11:30am-3pm and 6:30pm-1am; low-season hours vary. AmEx/MC/V.) For a taste of Corsican cuisine, indulge at **U Spuntinu ❹**, on rue Napoléon. The 3-course *menu* (€17.80) includes *cannelloni au broccio* and *veau corse*. The 28-year-old, family establishment will not disappoint. (☎ 04 95 60 00 05. Open Mar. 16-Nov. 14 daily noon-1:30pm and 7:30-11pm; Nov. 15-Dec. 14 and Mar. 1-Mar. 15 M-Sa same hours; closed Dec. 15-Feb. V.)

Since Ile Rousse tends to attract moneyed Frenchmen, there's only one budget hotel in town. To find **Hôtel le Grillon ❸**, 10 av. Paul Doumer, go straight on av. Piccioni, beside the tourist office, and take a left. The friendly owners will usher you into light orange hallways and soft pink rooms, all with shower, toilet, TV, and telephone. (☎ 04 95 60 00 49; fax 04 95 60 43 69. Breakfast €5.20. Dinner menus for €12.50 and €15.70. Reception 6:30am-10pm. Open Mar.-Oct. Singles €30.40-46.45; doubles €32-51.80; triples €38.40-57.60. Aug. obligatory *demi-pension* for singles €65.40; doubles €89.80; triples €114.60. MC/V.) You'll have more luck camping; sites appear fairly regularly all along the Balagne coast, so just hop off the train when you see one that you like. **Les Oliviers ❶** in Ile Rousse is 800m from the town center on av. Paul Doumer, the road to Bastia. The congenial, coastal site offers a snack bar and tiny wooden chalets for two. (☎ 04 95 60 19 92 or 04 95 60 25 64; fax 04 95 60 30 91. Laundry €5. July-Aug. closed to cars after 11pm. Open Apr.-Oct. €5 per person, €3 per tent, €2 per car. Electricity €3.50. Chalet doubles €25. MC/V.)

NEAR ILE ROUSSE: LA BALAGNE

La Balagne, the inland stretch between Calvi and Ile Rousse, is dotted with olive trees and pristine mountain villages, many of which are accessible by foot. **Lumio** is 15min. by train from Calvi (€1.50) or 30min. from Ile Rousse (€3). Here, on the mountain that the Romans called *Ortus Solis* ("Where the sun rises"), the modern village lies meters away from its ancient counterpart Occi, mysteriously abandoned one morning in 1852. Not far off is the **Site archéologique du Monte Ortu,** where Neolithic artifacts have recently been discovered. Farther south, accessible by bus from Calvi and on the famous **GR20** trail, lies **Calenzana**, known as "the garden of the Balagne," where a 17th-century Baroque church overlooks the peaceful **Cimetière des Allemands.** On May 21, local Catholics make a pilgrimage to the **Sanctuaire de Ste-Restitude,** 1½km from town, named for the regional patron saint.

Stone-roofed **Sant'Antonino** lies to the east toward Ile Rousse. The highest village in the Balagne, it was built on a peak by the Moors in the 9th century, and its narrow streets remain accessible only by foot. Home to the renowned music school **Bartimore,** the village hosts musical concerts throughout the year, as well as local craftsmen who make traditional Corsican instruments. (Call ☎ 04 95 61 77 31 for concert info.)

Autocars Mariani, bd. Wilson in Calvi, will take you to these sleepy old villages in a comfortable tour bus. Buy tickets for their once-a-week excursion in the bureau beside the Ile Rousse tourist office. (Half-day tour €13. Calvi branch ☎ 04 95 65 00 47. Open M-Sa 9am-noon and 2-7pm. Ile Rousse branch ☎ 04 95 60 11 19. Open May-Sept. M-Sa 9am-12:30pm and 2:30-7pm; Oct.-Apr. M-Sa 9am-noon and 2-6:30pm.) If your boots are made for walking, you can hike to Sant'Antonino in less than two hours on a trail that starts immediately after Pub's Discothèque. From the Casino supermarket, head inland on rte. de Calvi for about 10 minutes until you see the discothèque on your left. At Sant'Antonino, the trail doubles back and passes by the peaceful village of **Corbara,** the home of a Franciscan monastery built in 1456.

CORTE (CORTI)

The most dynamic of Corsica's inland towns, Corte melds breathtaking natural scenery with an intellectual flair. Sheer cliffs, snow-capped peaks, and magical gorges are a dramatic backdrop for the island's only university, whose students (2600 of its 6000 residents) keep prices low. Known to natives as "the heart of Corsica," the town gave birth to Pasquale Paoli's national constitution in 1731. A majority of residents now subscribe to the continent's more moderate politics, but it is still the center of the Corsican cause. To show solidarity, most native-born locals speak the island's dialect, Corse, and sometimes give icy receptions to mainland French. Those not flying a *fleur-de-lys* will be delighted by Corte's friendly people, authentic cuisine, and singular hikes.

▐ TRANSPORTATION

Trains: at the rotary where av. Jean Nicoli and the N193 meet (☎04 95 46 00 97). To: **Ajaccio** (2hr., 4 per day, €12.30); **Bastia** (1½hr., 4 per day, €10.80); **Calvi** via **Ponte-Leccia** (2½hr., 2 per day, €14.60).

Buses: Eurocorse Voyages (☎04 95 31 73 76). To **Ajaccio** (1¾hr., M-Sa 2 per day, €11.50) and **Bastia** (1¼hr., M-Sa 2 per day, €10).

Autocars Mordiconi, just below pl. Paoli off av. Xavier Luciani (☎04 95 48 00 04), off the Tuffelli parking lot. To **Porto** (2½hr., July-Sept. M-Sa 1 per day, €19).

Taxis: Taxis Salviani (☎04 95 46 04 88 or 06 03 49 15 24). **Taxi Feracci** (☎04 95 61 01 17 or 06 12 10 60 60).

Car Rental: Europcar, 2 pl. Paoli (☎04 95 46 06 02). 21+. From €81 per day, €282 per week. Deposit €400. Insurance included. Open M-Sa 9am-noon, 3-7:30pm. MC/V.

▟ ▐ ORIENTATION AND PRACTICAL INFORMATION

To reach the center of Corte from the station, turn right on D14 (alias av. Jean Nicoli), cross two bridges, and follow the road until it ends at **cours Paoli,** Corte's main drag. A left turn here leads to **pl. Paoli,** the town center; at the top-right corner, climb the stairwayed **rue Scolisca** to reach the citadel and the **tourist office.**

Tourist office: (☎04 95 46 26 70; fax 04 95 46 34 05; www.corte-tourisme.com). Useful bus schedule and bilingual brochure with popular hikes. **Parc Naturel Régional** expert available June-Sept. M-F 9am-noon and 2-6pm. Open July-Aug. M-Sa 9am-8pm, Su 10am-1pm and 4-8pm; May-June and Sept. M-Sa 9am-1pm and 2-7pm; Oct.-Apr. M-F 9am-noon and 2-6pm.

Youth Center: Bureau Information Jeunesse de Corte, rampe Ste-Croix (☎04 95 46 12 48). Open M-Th 9am-noon and 2-6pm, F 9am-noon and 2-5pm.

Laundromat: Speed Laverie, allée du 9 Septembre (☎06 82 56 08 31), next to the Casino supermarket. Open daily 8am-9pm.

Police: (☎04 95 46 04 81), southeast of town on N200.

Hospital: (☎04 95 45 05 00), allée du 9 Septembre.

Internet Access: Grand Café du Cours, 22 cours Paoli (☎04 95 46 00 33). €1 for 15min., €2 for 30min., €3 per hr. Open daily 7am-2am. **Syndrome-Cyber,** 3 av. du Président Pierucci (☎04 95 47 13 32), just before the SPAR supermarket. €1.50 for 15min., €2 for 30min., €3 for 1hr. Open July-Aug. daily 2pm-2am; Sept.-June M-F 7:30am-2am, Sa-Su 10am-2am.

Post office: av. du Baron Mariani (☎04 95 46 08 20). Open M-F 8am-12:30pm and 1:30-5pm, Sa 8am-noon. **Postal code:** 20250.

▗ ACCOMMODATIONS AND CAMPING

Hôtel-Residence Porette (H-R), 6 allée du 9 Septembre (☎04 95 45 11 11; fax 04 95 61 02 85). Head left from station towards the stadium for 100m. Functional rooms with pastel walls. Sauna (€4), weight room, and restaurant. Breakfast buffet €5. Reception 24hr. Reservations required June and Aug.-Sept. Singles €21, with shower and toilet €24-31; doubles €23-25/€27-35; singles and doubles facing garden €5-19 extra; triples €51; quads €54. AmEx. ❷

Hôtel de la Poste, 2 pl. du Duc de Padoue (☎04 95 46 01 37), off cours Paoli. Near town center; renovated bathrooms, firm beds, and high ceilings. Breakfast €5. Reception 7am-10pm. Singles and doubles €43-46; triples €48; quads €51. ❹

Hôtel de la Paix, av. Générale de Gaulle (☎04 95 46 06 72; fax 04 95 46 23 84), past Hôtel de la Poste on the left. Modern, spacious rooms with pink walls and shower or bath and toilet. Breakfast €5.50. Restaurant with a 3-course menu €13. Aug. singles and doubles €50-57; triples €62-66. May-July singles and doubles €46-53; triples €54-61. Sept.-Apr. singles €35; doubles €35-46; triples €45. ❹

U Tavignanu, chem. de Balari (☎04 95 46 16 85; fax 04 95 61 14 01). Turn left out of station and right when the road forks, first following allée du 9 Septembre and then signs at the base of the Citadel; ends with a steep climb up a dirt trail. (20min.) Salt-of-the-earth owners. Converted hilltop farmhouse and shaded campsite. Inaccessible to cars. Breakfast included with *gîte*. Reception 7am-10:30pm. Breakfast €3.50. Dinner €14. *Gîte* €14, July-Aug. obligatory *demi-pension* €27. Camping: €3.80 per person, €1.90 per tent. ❶

Camping:

U Sognu, on D623 (☎04 95 46 09 07; fax 04 95 61 00 76). From top of pl. Paoli, follow rue Prof. Santiaggi around the bend, turn left and cross the bridge. At the fork, follow the sign and turn right. From train station, follow directions to Restonica; after the first bridge, take a left onto D623. Little shade but offers easy access to the nearby stream and scenic views of the mountains and *haute ville.* Breakfast €4.60. Restaurant meals €6.40-10.50. Reception 8am-noon and 3-11pm. Closed to cars after 11pm. Open Mar. 28-Oct. 15. €5 per person, €2.50 per tent or car. Electricity €3. ❶

Restonica (☎/fax 04 95 46 11 59; vero.camp@worldonline.fr). Follow directions from station to H-R Porette until a sign on the right points downhill to campsite. Crowded site, but good location. Breakfast €6. Pizzas €8. Laundry €7. Reception 7:30am-10pm. Open Apr. 15-Oct. 15. €5 per person, €2.50 per tent or car. Electricity €3.50. ❶

▗ FOOD

Place Paoli is the spot to find sandwiches and pizza; **rue Scolisca** and the surrounding citadel streets abound with inexpensive local cuisine, with most menus around €9-12. **SPAR,** 5 av. Xavier Luciani, is in the town center. (☎04 95 46 08 59. Open July-Aug. M-Sa 7:30am-8pm, Su 9am-noon and 5-7:30pm; Sept.-June M-Sa 8am-12:30pm and 3-8pm, Su 9:30am-noon; Jan.-Feb. closed Su.) The mammoth **Casino** is near the train station on allée du 9 Septembre. (☎04 95 45 22 45. Open June 15-Aug. daily 8:30am-7:45pm; Sept.-June 14 M-F 8:30am-12:30pm and 3-7:30pm, Sa 8:30am-7:30pm.) ▨**A Scudella ❷,** 2 pl. Paoli, cooks up unbeatable regional cuisine, with meaty standouts. The €9 menu includes double portions of an entrée and dessert; the €11 menu lets you choose a main dish and dessert. (☎04 95 46 25 31. Open M-Sa noon-2pm and 7-11pm. AmEx/MC/V.)

▗ SIGHTS

The *vieille ville* of Corte, with its steep, barely accessible streets and stone **citadel** peering over the Tavignano and Restonica valleys, has always been a bastion of Corsican patriotism. The route up is dedicated to the town's two heroes: **Pascal Paoli,** who drafted Corsica's famous constitution, proclaimed Corte the island's

IN RECENT NEWS

MUDDLE *CORSE* POLITICS

The Corsican political scene is about as accessible as quantum mechanics, and even Corsicans find it difficult to make sense of their politics. Today, 20% of Corsicans support nationalist parties. Though there are ten major nationalist parties, only one favors immediate independence: the **FLNC,** the political wing of *Indipendenza*, a secret organization that has been linked to terrorism. The other nationalist parties believe Corsica must experience political and economic autonomy before complete independence.

If the FLNC has any center of support, it is Corte. The maverick spirit of hometown hero Paoli lingers in the Cortenais, but political realities have changed. Since 1983, the mayor of Corte has been affiliated with the RPR, not known for warmth towards the independence cause. And on the local level, interactions between aspiring politicians and powerful men are much more influential than political affiliations. Corte's current mayor received overwhelming support from the right, left, *and* nationalists. The Cortenais fully admit the contradictions of their politics, which is captured in their idiom "Cortenais politics are not understood by the Cortenais."

Regardless of individual relations and party affiliations, Corsicans are anxious to see how the new Interior Minister, Nicolas Sarkozy, will treat the island. Thus far, he seems more Corsica-friendly than his predecessor, and has praised Corsica's "exceptional qualities." The question is whether he wishes to promote these qualities in the name of France or of Corsica.

capital, and led the free state until Corsica lost the war with France in 1769; and **Jean Pierre Gaffori,** who preceded Paoli as governor until his assassination by Genoese agents in 1753. In a plain-looking dwelling across from pl. Gaffori, a plaque honors the apartments where Charles Bonaparte, Napoleon I's father, lived for two years in the 1760s while serving the Paolian cause.

Rather than focusing on politics, the **Musée de la Corse,** at the top of rue Scolisca, provides an exclusively ethnographic history of Corsica. The thoughtful museum moves beyond regional costumes and handicrafts to contemplate issues such as the role of tourism on the island. The exhibits are in French and Italian; consider the 90min. English audio-guide (€1.50). Admission includes a visit to the only inland **citadel** in Corsica, built in 1419. Visitors can wander through the dungeon, kitchens, and bathrooms as sheep watch lazily. (☎04 95 45 25 45; fax 04 95 45 25 36. Museum open June 20-Sept. 20 daily 10am-8pm; Sept. 21-Nov. Tu-Su 10am-6pm; Dec.-Mar. Tu-Sa 10am-6pm; Apr.-June 19 Tu-Su 10am-6pm. Citadel closes 1hr. earlier than museum. English tours July-Aug. M-Sa 10:30am and 3:30pm; €1.50. Admission €3-5.30, students €2.30-3.) Trek uphill from pl. Paoli and take a left at the Eglise de l'Annonciation to reach a 360° **Belvedere** (viewpoint) on the oldest portion of the 15th-century city walls.

Corte's surrounding mountains and valleys host countless trails. There's **hiking** (call the tourist office for maps and trail info, ☎08 92 68 02 20 for weather conditions) and **horseback riding.** Try the **Ferme Equestre Albadu,** 1½km from town on N193 toward Ajaccio. (☎04 95 46 24 55. Reserve at least one day in advance. €14 per hr., €38 per half-day, €61 per day including picnic.)

⚡ DAYTRIPS FROM CORTE

GORGES DE LA RESTONICA

Southwest of Corte, the tiny D623 trail stretches 16km through the Gorges de la Restonica, a high-altitude canyon fed by glacial lakes. The hot-blooded can venture a swim in the gorge's icy rivers and tributaries. To get to the gorge, descend rue Prof. Santiaggi at the back of pl. Paoli and cross the bridge at the right; head right again on D623 at the ensuing fork. Walk 2km, following the signs for Restonica, until you get to the Parc Naturel Régional info office, where a free shuttle *(navette)* whisks hikers 13km up along a twisting and narrow road to the gorge's summit. (Open July-Aug. daily 8am-1pm, return 3-5pm. Call ☎04 95 46 02 12 for detailed schedules.)

If you have time for only one hike, make sure you tour the **glacial lakes** at the top of the gorge, one of the island's loveliest and least-populated areas, where hikers of all levels can enjoy the magnificent scenery. Take the *navette* to the Grotelle parking lot. To the right, a trail clearly marked in yellow leads to a sheep-pen-turned-snackbar, then crosses the river and steadily ascends to the "most visited lake in Corsica," circular **Lac de Melo.** (1hr.) This snow-fed beauty lies at 1711m, near the foot of Mont Rotondo (2622m), and is ringed by peaks including Corsica's highest Mont Cinto (2710m). The trail is marked *facile* (easy), but the climb is steep, rocky, and slippery when wet. Also, temperatures at the top can reach well below zero even when it's 25°C in town. From Melo, the trail continues, marked in yellow, to one of Corsica's largest and deepest lakes, the austere **Lac de Capitellu.** (1930m; 45min.) From here, the trail meets the red-and-white marked **GR20,** Corsica's island-spanning path.

To turn your mountain stroll into a full-day adventure, you can follow the GR20 to the left until it intersects with a trail that leads to the **Refuge de Petra Piana,** where you can spend the night or continue to the Lac de Rotondo. (4½hr.) Less trodden but equally spectacular is the hike to **Lac de l'Oriente.** Take the free *navette* to **Pont de Tragone** and then follow the marked trail that passes shepherd's houses until you reach the photogenic lake. (3hr.) For more info on Restonica's offerings, consult the French-language *Tavignano-Restonica topo-guide* (in bookstores for €11.45) or the tourist office hiking expert and their €5 map with 26 labeled hiking trails.

GORGES DU TAVIGNANO

Less rugged than Restonica, though equally physically demanding, the Tavignano gorges are filled with waterfalls, natural pools, and picturesque hiking trails. With no road access, Tavignano is likely to be less crowded than its better-known counterpart. A west-bound trail leaves directly from town at the base of the backside of the citadel, indicated by signs and marked in orange. The first 2½hr. of hiking along the Tavignano river lead to the **Passerelle du Russulinu** (902m), a suspension bridge surrounded by a picnic-friendly plain. Another three hours along the same trail leads to the **Refuge de la Sega** (1166m), where you can spend the night. There, two roads diverge. To the left, a well-traveled trail passes by ancient *bergeries* (sheep pens) and abandoned shepherd huts, crossing the **Plateau d'Alzo** and ending at the **Pont de la Frasseta,** 8km up on D623 in the heart of the Restonica. (4hr.) To the right, a trail less traveled leads to the heartland village of **Calacuccia,** on D84 45min. by car from Corte. (4hr.)

FORÊT DE VIZZAVONA

The forests surrounding the town of Vizzavona have some of the most accessible hiking trails on Corsica. Get to Vizzavona by a beautiful train ride (1hr.; 4 per day, July 10-Aug. 25 5 per day; €5.70). Outside the station, a billboard lists hiking routes. The plunging falls and clear lagoons of the **Cascades des Anglais** provide the most inspiring scenery, about 45min. southwest of town along the red-and-white GR20. You can picnic on the cascade's flat rocks and shaded coves.

BASTIA

Bastia (pop. 40,000), Corsica's second largest city, can feel impersonal and industrial. With ships constantly arriving and departing from its huge new port, it may seem that the entire city is just a waiting area for moving elsewhere. Bastia's well-serviced harbor and airport do indeed make it a convenient starting point for an excursion, particularly to the must-see Cap Corse (p. 610). However, its neither cosmopolitan nor over-touristed core, crumbling *vieille ville*, and exquisite Baroque churches often keep travelers here longer than expected.

⌐ TRANSPORTATION

Flights: Bastia-Poretta, 23km. away (☎04 95 54 54 54). An airport bus (☎04 95 31 06 65), scheduled to coincide with departing flights, leaves from pl. de la Gare, by the *préfecture* (30min., €8). Compagnie Corse Méditerranée (☎08 20 82 08 20) flies to **Marseille, Nice,** and **Paris.**

Trains: pl. de la Gare (☎04 95 32 80 61), to the left of the roundabout at the top of av. Maréchal Sebastiani. Station open M-Sa 6:10am-8:45pm, Su 6:30am-8:45pm. To: **Ajaccio** (4hr., 4 per day, €23.10); **Calvi** (3hr., 2 per day, €17.50); **Corte** (1½hr., 5 per day, €10.80); **Ile Rousse** (2½hr., 2 per day, €14.50).

Buses: Ask the tourist office for a bus schedule. **Eurocorse,** rue du Nouveau Port (☎04 95 21 06 30), runs to **Ajaccio** (3hr., M-Sa 2 per day, €17). **Rapides Bleus,** 1 av. Maréchal Sebastiani (☎04 95 31 03 79), sends buses to **Porto Vecchio** (3hr.; M-Sa 2 per day, June 15-Sept. 15 daily; €18) via Aléria (1½hr., €11), from across from the post office.

Ferries: quai de Fango, next to pl. St-Nicolas; turn left from av. Maréchal Sebastiani just past pl. St-Nicolas. **SNCM** (☎04 95 54 66 30; fax 04 95 54 66 39), by the quai de Fango, sails to **Marseille, Nice,** and **Toulon. Corsica Ferries,** 5bis rue Chanoine Leschi (☎04 95 32 95 95), float to **Nice** and **Toulon,** and to **Livorno** and **Savona** in Italy. **Moby Lines,** 4 rue Commandant Luce de Casablanca (☎04 95 34 84 94; fax 04 95 32 17 94), services **Genoa** and **Livorno** in Italy. For details on air and ferry connections to mainland France, see **Getting There,** p. 584.

Car Rental: ADA, 35 rue César Campinchi (☎04 95 31 48 95; fax 04 95 34 96 95), with a 2nd location at the airport (☎04 95 54 55 44). Open M-F 8am-noon and 2-7pm, Sa 8am-noon. AmEx/MC/V.

Scooter Rental: Toga Location Nautique, port de Plaisance de Toga (☎04 95 34 14 14), near the north quai. Scooters €61 per day, €288 per week; €1220 deposit. Open M-F 9am-noon and 2-7pm, Sa 9am-noon. AmEx/MC/V.

Taxis: (☎04 95 32 24 24, 04 95 36 04 05, or 04 95 32 70 70). 24hr. €32-33 to airport.

⊞ 🛈 ORIENTATION AND PRACTICAL INFORMATION

Find your bearings and the tourist office on the rectangular **pl. St-Nicolas.** The main thoroughfares are **bd. du Général de Gaulle,** which runs along the inland length of the *place,* and the parallel **bd. Paoli** and **rue César Campinchi.** As you face the mountains, the old port and citadel are to the left and the ferry docks are to the right.

Tourist Office: pl. St-Nicolas (☎04 95 54 20 40; fax 04 95 31 81 34; ot-bastia@wanadoo.fr), has numerous maps of the city and Cap Corse. Ask for a copy of their indispensable bus schedule. Open July-Sept. daily 8am-8pm, Oct.-June M-Sa 8:30am-6pm.

Centre Information Jeunesse: 9 rue César Campinchi (☎04 95 32 12 13; fax 04 95 32 50 77; www.crij-corse.com). Friendly staff provides info on work, housing, and leisure activities. Also free Internet access for up to 40min. Open M-F 8am-6pm, Sa 8am-noon. Closed July 26-Aug. 19.

Laundromat: Lavoir du Port, 25 rue Luce de Casabianca (☎04 95 32 25 51), just past the gas station. Open daily 7am-9pm.

Police: rue Commandant Luce de Casablanca (☎04 95 55 22 22).

Hospital: rte. Impériale (☎04 95 59 11 11).

Internet Access: free for up to 40min. at the **Centre Information Jeunesse** (see above). **Cybercafé,** 6 rue des Jardins (☎04 95 34 30 34), in the old city. €1.60 per 30min., €3.10 per hr. Open M-Sa 9am-11pm, Su 3:30-11pm.

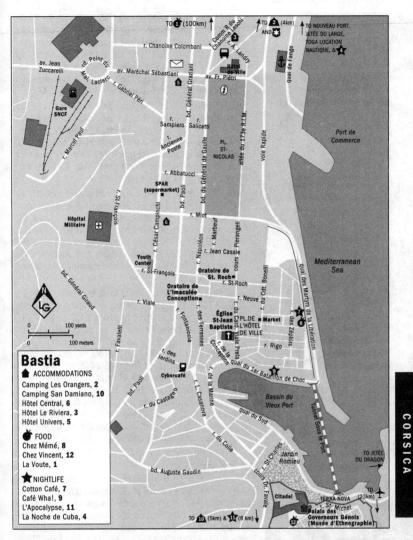

Bastia

⬆ ACCOMMODATIONS
Camping Les Orangers, **2**
Camping San Damiano, **10**
Hôtel Central, **6**
Hôtel Le Riviera, **3**
Hôtel Univers, **5**

🍖 FOOD
Chez Mémé, **8**
Chez Vincent, **12**
La Voute, **1**

⭐ NIGHTLIFE
Cotton Café, **7**
Café Wha!, **9**
L'Apocalypse, **11**
La Noche de Cuba, **4**

Post Office: at the intersection of av. Maréchal Sébastiani and bd. Général Graziani (☎ 04 95 32 80 70). Open M-F 8am-7pm; closed W 12:30-1:30pm, Sa 8am-noon. **Postal code:** 20200.

🏠 ACCOMMODATIONS AND CAMPING

Bastia's hotels are cheaper than those in Corsica's more popular resort towns. Off-season discounts and vacancies are common, but from June to September, call ahead. Campsites are far from town but well serviced by local buses.

THE HIDDEN DEAL

U TIANU

On the second floor of a generic building on a dark, tiny street behind the vieux port, U Tianu ❸ is not love at first sight. Ascend the steep red staircase and the first thing you'll notice is the broken-in kitchen that has been serving a loyal local clientele for 21 years. Passing a small, smoky bar area, you will encounter the first of two intimate dining rooms. Here, the anonymity of the exterior begins to fade. Old Corsican pictures and posters grace the white stucco walls. Wooden ceiling beams make the rooms feel more like converted barns than old apartments.

With one €19 *menu*, the "deal" of U Tianu may not be as immediately apparent as its seclusion and authentic, unpretentious atmosphere. Your €19, however, will go an incredibly long way: an *apéritif* of your choice, an *entrée*, main dish, cheese course, dessert, coffee, and *digestif*, in addition to as much red or rosé wine as you can drink. You will probably be unable to finish it, though not because it lacks in taste. The *menu* is full of down-to-earth but delicious Corsican specialties, including an *entrée* of *charcuterie corse*, main dishes of *veau au corse* (Corsican stewed veal) and *cannelloni au brocciu* (a Corsican pasta with local cheese). The friendly owners will make sure you are completely satisfied, offering with unusual readiness to remake any meal that is not excellent. *(4 rue Mgr. Rigo, ☎ 04 95 31 36 67. Open M-Sa 7pm-2am. Closed Aug. Cash and traveler's checks only.)*

Hôtel Central, 3 rue Miot (☎ 04 95 31 71 12; fax 04 95 31 82 40; www.centralhotel.fr). The hotel *is* central; it has large, well-kept, tastefully decorated and renovated rooms, all with toilet and shower or bath. Breakfast €5.50. Reception 24hr. Singles €35-50; doubles €40-68. Extra bed €15. For longer stays, there are fully equipped apartments for €330-610 per week. AmEx/MC/V. ❹

Hôtel Univers, 3 av. Maréchal Sebastiani (☎ 04 95 31 03 38; fax 04 95 31 19 91). Clean and modern rooms with yellow and blue bedspreads. All with A/C, shower, and toilet. Reception 24hr. Breakfast €5. Singles €45; doubles €55; triples €75; quads €90. Apr.-July prices for singles and doubles €5 higher; Aug. €15 higher. AmEx/MC/V. ❹

Hôtel Le Riviera, 1bis rue Adolphe Landry (☎ 04 95 31 07 16; fax 04 95 34 17 39), aptly lies near the new port and offers floral bedspreads and high ceilings. All rooms have shower, toilet, and TV. Reception 7am-midnight. Breakfast €4. July-Sept. singles and doubles €58; triples €68; Apr.-June singles and doubles €49; triples €59; Jan.-Mar. singles and doubles €43; triples €53. MC/V. ❺

Camping: San Damiano ❶, Lido de la Marana (☎ 04 95 33 68 02; fax 04 95 30 84 10; www.campingsandamiano.com), is 5km south of Bastia. **S.T.I.B.** (☎ 04 95 31 06 65) sends buses there from the station near pl. St-Nicolas (June-Aug. daily 8 per day). €6.10. Open Apr.-Oct. €5-6 per person, €4.50-5.50 for tent and car. Electricity €3. **Les Orangers ❶,** (☎ 04 95 33 24 09 or 04 95 33 23 65). To get there, take bus #4 from the tourist office to "Licciola-Miomo" (M-F every 30min., Sa-Su every hr.; €1.15), or follow bd. de Toga parallel to the sea. This small, basic site lies 30 seconds from a popular pebble beach. Open May-Oct. 15. €4 per person, €2 per tent, €1.60 per car. Electricity €3.20.

🍴 FOOD

Inexpensive cafés crowd **pl. St-Nicolas.** The best food and most scenic views can be found at the **citadel,** along the **Vieux Port,** and on the broad terraces of the **quai des Martyrs de la Libération** along the boardwalk. Early birds hit the **market** on pl. de l'Hôtel de Ville. (Open Tu-Su 6-11am.) **SPAR supermarket** is at 14 rue César Campinchi. (☎ 04 95 32 32 40. Open M-Sa 8am-12:30pm and 4-8:30pm, Su 8am-noon.) **U Tianu ❸,** 4 rue Mgr. Rigo, is a true hidden deal (see sidebar, **The Hidden Deal**). Just inside the citadel, ⬛**Chez Vincent ❸,** 12 rue St-Michel, serves delectable pizzas (€6.40-8.40) on a lovely terrace overlooking the sea. The friendly staff also serves pastas (€7-8.40), meats (€10.40-16), and a good selection of local wines.

(☎04 95 31 62 50. Open M-Sa 10am-2:30pm and 6:30pm-midnight. AmEx/MC/V.)
The seaside **Chez Mémé ❸**, at the north end of quai des Martyrs de la Libération,
offers a 3-course Corsican menu for €14. (☎04 95 31 44 12. Open daily noon-
2:30pm and 7-11:30pm. AmEx/MC/V.) The more formal **La Voute ❸**, 6 rue Luce de
Casablanca, near the new port, offers a wide variety of fish (€13.70-19.80),
including grilled *fillet de loup* (€16.90), and meats (€12.20-19), such as beef,
duck, and veal. They also serve pizzas (€6.10-8.90) and pastas (€8.40-14) in the
cave-like interior with yellow walls. (☎04 95 32 47 11. Open daily noon-2pm and 7-
11pm. AmEx/MC/V.)

◉ ◕ SIGHTS AND BEACHES

A walk through Bastia's *vieille ville* reveals the town's former time of glory as the
crown jewel of Genoese-ruled Corsica. To the north, the 1380 **citadel**, also called
Terra Nova, was the Genoese center of power on the island. The town's first building, the massive 1530 **Palais des Gouverneurs Génois**, lie inside the fortified walls.
Unfortunately, it is currently closed for renovations.

Walking toward the citadel from pl. St-Nicolas on rue Napoléon, you'll stumble
across the **Oratoire de St-Roch**, a jewel-box of a church with crystal chandeliers. A
few blocks down, the 18th-century **Oratoire de L'Imaculée Conception,** houses an
organ that once spent two years thumping out "God Save the Queen" daily: during
Corsica's brief stint as a joint Anglo-Corsican kingdom from 1794-1796 the British
puppet parliament was housed in the oratory. The Neoclassical towers of the
Eglise St-Jean Baptiste, pl. de l'Hôtel de Ville, cover an immense interior with gilded
domes and *trompe l'œil* ceilings.

Beaches in Bastia are dominated by hard-core sun-worshippers. If you don't
feel like sharing a beach with the masses, head north to the pebbly turf of **Miomo,**
and, farther on, the beautiful sands of the **Cap Corse.** Bus #4 leaves every 30min.
from pl. St-Nicolas, sometimes traveling as far as Macinaggio; the closest sandy
beach lies between **Erbalunga** (€2) and **Sisco** (€2.30). One and a half kilometers in
the opposite direction, at Montesoro, is **L'Arinella**—2km of smooth, gray sand
marred by freeway noise and barbed wire. To get there, follow the road that
leaves Bastia just beyond the citadel, or take bus #1, which leaves every 15min.
from pl. St-Nicolas and the citadel's entrance (€1.15), get off at "Montesoro," and
walk for 10min.

◖ NIGHTLIFE

Bastia is quiet come sunset, with the exception of the nightlife concentrated in the
vieux port. Large and airy, the seaside **Cotton Café,** 22 quai des Martyrs de la
Libération, serves tropical cocktails (€5.50) among plush sofas and palm trees.
(☎04 95 32 36 18. Live music July-Aug. daily; Sept.-June F-Su. Open daily 10am-
2am.) **La Noche de Cuba,** 5 rue Chanoine Leschi, near the north quai, is a laid-back
Latin bar with one of Bastia's few dance floors. (☎04 95 31 02 83. Open daily 6am-
2am.) At the old port, **Café Wha!,** quai du Premier Bataillon de Choc, stands out
with its bright neon sign and memorable name. A hip, young crowd drinks €6.40
margaritas on the outdoor patio. (☎04 95 34 25 79. Live music July-Aug. Th-Sa from
9pm. Open daily 11am-2am.) Bastia's hottest nightlife option is the faraway **La
Marana** area, home to beachside bars and open-air dance clubs like trendy **L'Apocalypse.** (☎04 95 33 36 83. Cover €10 with one free drink. Open F-Sa 11:30pm-5am;
July-Aug. also M and W.)

◪ DAYTRIP FROM BASTIA: ALÉRIA

*Autocars Rapides-Bleus (☎04 95 31 03 79) run from Bastia (1½hr.; M-Sa 2 per day, July-Sept. 15 daily; €11) and Porto Vecchio (1½hr.; M-Sa 2 per day, July-Sept. 15 daily; €10) to Aléria's post office. Farther down the road is the **tourist office**. (☎04 95 57 01 51; fax 04 95 57 06 26. Open July-Aug. M-Sa 9am-1pm and 2-7pm; June and Sept. M-Sa 9:30am-12:30pm and 3:30-6:30pm; Oct.-May M-F 9:30am-noon and 2-6pm.)*

Present-day Aléria (pop. 2500), halfway down Corsica's uninspiring eastern coastline, pales in comparison to the city's previous incarnations. This choice spot—parallel to Carthage and opposite Rome—has witnessed five major civilizations rise and fall: the Phoenicians, Etruscans, Greeks, Carthaginians, and Romans. The ancient center of Aléria is a mound about 1km south of the city. The summit has exceptionally long views in both directions, a fact which induced the Greeks to build a settlement there. Now the fort holds the **Musée Jérôme Carcopino**. (☎04 95 57 00 92.) The exhibit of Etruscan pottery, Roman artifacts—including a cosmetic kit that rivals Marie Antoinette's—and an extensive Greek collection are all interesting. Just past the museum is the **Roman city** itself. After passing the ruins of the Greek acropolis, enter the middle of the Roman forum; to the left is a temple to Jupiter, to the right, the extensive baths. Under Augustus, the population of the city swelled to 20,000, almost ten times that of present-day Aléria. Archaeologists have only begun to uncover the city's network of bedrooms and shops. (Museum open May 16-Sept. daily 8am-noon and 2-7pm; Oct.-May 15 M-F 8am-noon and 2-5pm, Roman city closes 30min. earlier. €2 for both, students €1.)

CAP CORSE

Stretching north from Bastia, the Cap Corse peninsula holds a string of former fishing villages connected by a narrow road of perilous curves and breathtaking views. The 18 multi-village *communes* of Corsica's wildest frontier have largely resisted over development. The Cap is also a hiker's dream, with every jungle-like forest and *maquis*-covered cliff laying claim to a decaying Genoese tower or hilltop chapel. Every town is an access point for some great trail. Unfortunately, there are few budget hotels, and most require you to pay for dinner with your room. Camping is a better option; a handful of sites sit around the Cap.

☰ TRANSPORTATION. The best way to visit the Cap is to drive around the entire peninsula, which takes about a day; consider renting a **car** in Bastia (see p. 606) or Calvi (see p. 596). Be alert and cautious: roads are narrow and winding, and Corsican drivers are fearless. It's best to drive on a weekend, when traffic on D80 thins out; you might also consider starting the trip from the St-Florentine area (the west side of the peninsula), where your vehicle hugs the mountainside rather than the sea below. To start on the west side from Bastia, take bd. Paoli, then bd. Auguste Gaudin past the citadel onto N199 (dir: St-Florentine). For the east-to-west route, follow the coastal bd. north from pl. St-Nicolas, following signs for the Cap.

A **bus tour** is cheaper than a car but far less flexible is. **Transports Micheli,** in Ersa at the top of the peninsula, offers full-day tours of the Cap leaving from 1 rue de Nouveau Port in Bastia, stopping at villages and for lunch (not included) at the glorious blue slate beach at Albo. (☎04 95 35 64 02. Tours Aug. Tu, Th, Sa 9am, return 5pm; €22.90.) From Calvi, **Autocars Mariani** runs excursions. (☎04 95 65 04 72. Tours F 7:30am, return 6:30pm. Apr. 15-Sept., €26.) Individual destinations such as **Centuri, Rogliano,** and **St-Florent** are served by several companies. Updated schedules and phone numbers for buses can be found in *Découverte Cap Corse,* an indispensable guide provided for free at tourist offices. The cheapest and most convenient way to see the eastern side of Cap Corse is to take public **bus #4** from pl. St-Nicolas in Bastia. The bus leaves for Erbalunga (20min.; M-F every 30min., Sa-Su every hr.; €2) and Marina di Siscu (30min., every hr., €2.30); it also goes all the way to Macinaggio (50min., M-Sa 3 per day, €6.40). Ask nicely and the driver will drop you off wherever you feel the urge to explore. But keep in mind that most buses serve only the coast; you'll have to hike to the nearest inland village. (☎ 04 95 31 06 65. Service generally daily 6:30am-7:30pm.)

You can also see the Cap by boat with **Compagnie Saint Jean**, Old Port. A fun-loving staff gives 1½hr. tours of the coast in July and August. (☎ 04 95 54 20 40 or 06 09 53 55 03. 4 per day, €10.) For updates on Cap tourism, contact the **Communauté de Communes du Cap Corse**, Maison du Cap Corse, 20200 Ville di Pietra Bugno (☎ 04 95 31 02 32; cc.capcorse@wanadoo.fr; www.internetcom.fr/capcorse).

ERBALUNGA

The most accessible of Cap Corse's villages, Erbalunga makes a relaxing afternoon excursion from nearby Bastia. This tiny fishing hamlet, where fishermen drop lines from their sea-hugging houses, shows few signs of the 21st century. Crystal blue waters, white pebble beaches and flat, secluded rocks seduce sunbathers to the beaches.

In the hills above, Benedictine monks observe a vow of silence at the **Monastère des Benedictines du St-Sacrement,** which you can pass by on a short hike that begins to the right of the restaurant **La Petite Auberge ❸.** M. and Mme. Morganti serve Corsican specialties including seafood (€17), pastas (€8.50-11), and a *menu* for €16.50; to get there, follow the main road three minutes north of the bus station. (☎ 04 95 33 20 78. Open daily noon-2pm and 7-9pm. MC/V.)

A supermarket, **SPAR,** is across from the bus station. (☎ 04 95 33 24 24. Open M-Sa 8am-12:30pm and 4-7:30pm, Su 9am-noon.) Two and a half kilometers south, **Lavasina** holds the famous **Eglise de Notre-Dame des Graces,** where thousands make a candlelit pilgrimage on Sept. 8 to celebrate the miracle that gave the church its name. Legend has it that a disabled nun from Bonifacio was miraculously granted the use of her legs after praying to an image of the Virgin that hangs in this church.

🔲 HIKE: SISCO

The *Découverte Cap Corse* guide, free at tourist offices, comes with a map listing 21 possible itineraries; hike #9, from **Sisco** (2hr.), is one of the best. Take bus #4 from pl. St-Nicolas to Marina di Sisco (30min., every hr., €2.30) and walk straight on route D32. From Marina di Sisco, follow the painted orange rectangles for a journey that penetrates deep into dense forests and expansive valleys, where a few tiny villages are the only trace of civilization. The path ultimately leads to **Petrapiana,** the intersection of several other routes, but make sure to take a break at **Barriggioni,** just 300m before Petrapiana, and admire the grandiose elegance of the **Eglise St-Martin,** which houses the eerie, bronzed remains of St-John Chrysostomos. From here, you can also take a detour to the 11th-century **Chapelle St-Michel,** perched precariously on a hilltop promontory; just follow the signs from the first church. You can advance farther in to the **Eglise St-Michel;** you'll see signs to the left of a grove of ferns near the second church. Though you can't enter the chapel, the striking, panoramic view of the bowl-shaped valley below, sprinkled with Renaissance bell towers, is definitely worth the 1hr. climb. Note that this demanding hike requires a good pair of hiking boots.

Make sure you have water and food to last you for your whole route, because the villages on the way do not sell provisions. The tiny village of **Petrapiana** has only 3 houses. On many routes, there are several variations of the trail marked by tangential orange rectangles, though the vegetation may be too dense, depending upon the season.

ROGLIANO

This hilltop village's crumbling monuments seem to defy both gravity and time. At the heart of the village is the 16th- to 17th-century **Eglise St-Agnellu,** with its three-story bell tower and Carrara marble altar, the latter a gift from emigrants who made their fortunes in Puerto Rico. Around the bend to the right of the church, turn left on chemin du Couvent and climb up to the impressive ruins of the **Château de la Mare,** a monumental Genoese fort that remains remarkably intact. If these buildings seem unduly numerous for a town of Rogliano's size, there's a reason: at 300 residents, the town has only a tenth of its original population. Before heading back to Macinaggio, treat yourself to an ice cream and breathtaking panoramic views at **Le Brasier.** To reach this architecturally superb little town, take **bus** #4 to Macinaggio (M-Sa 2 per day, €6.40) and walk; or drive inland on route D353, which starts in front of the church, for about 5km.

MACINAGGIO TO CENTURI: THE CAPANDULA

Crystal-clear waters, white sandy beaches, and deep-green escarpments characterize the "cap of the cap," the arid and windy extreme tip of Cap Corse. Inaccessible to cars, the Capandula is a protected national reserve since it serves as the last stop for African migratory birds heading north. Camping is thus forbidden, but hikers and bikers are blessed by the *sentier de Douaniers,* an extraordinary coastal trail named after the customs officials who first walked it. Beginning in **Macinaggio** or **Centuri,** the 8hr. hike passes by Genoese towers, secluded beaches, dramatic cliffs, and two villages. There are no amenities en route; bring lots of water, durable shoes, and sunscreen.

From the east coast, the trail takes off from **Macinaggio,** Rogliano's beachside sister, the spot to which Corsican leader Paolo Paoli returned in 1790 after 20 years of exile from his beloved home island. Forty kilometers from Bastia, this port town is one of the few port towns where you can find supplies and services. The **tourist office,** above the Capitainerie, has small maps of the trail. (☎04 95 35 40 34; sc.macinaggiorogliano@wanadoo.fr. Open July-Aug. daily 9am-noon and 4-8pm; June and Sept. 1-15 daily 9am-noon and 3-6pm, closed Su morning; Sept. 16-May M-F 9am-noon and 2-5pm.) The camping is good at **U Stazzu ❶,** just steps from the beach. To get there, follow the signs on the road by the church; the campsite is at the beginning of the sentier de Douaniers. (☎04 95 35 43 76. Open Apr.-Sept. €5 per person, €2.50 per tent.) Enjoy Cap Corse cuisine at **Ostéria di u Portu ❸,** right on the waterfront. Hearty €13 menu includes entrée, salad, ravioli, veal dish, and dessert. (☎04 95 35 40 49. fish menu €20. Open daily noon-2:30pm and 7-10:30pm.)

The miniature port of **Centuri** at the other end of the trail is one of the Cap's most picturesque spots, a place to sit at sunset and watch the boats bring in their daily haul of lobsters, mussels, and fish. On calm days, you can swim out from the rocky shores to a small nearby island. **Camping Caravaning L'Isulotto ❶,** just south of the town, has lots of amenities, including a bar and restaurant with a €9 *menu,* 200m from the sea. (☎04 95 35 62 81; fax 04 95 35 63 63. €4.50 per adult, €2.45 per tent, €1.55 per car. Electricity €3.30.)

BONIFACIO (BONIFAZIU)

The fortified city of Bonifacio (pop. 3000) rises like a Genoese sandcastle atop steep limestone cliffs. Both the landscape and the settlement, the sheltered port and the magical *haute ville* to the crescent-moon beaches, seem carved by a master sculptor. While these spectacular vistas are not to be missed, they come with astronomical price tags and hordes of tourists.

▐ TRANSPORTATION

Buses: Eurocorse Voyages (Ajaccio ☎04 95 21 06 30, Porto Vecchio ☎04 95 70 13 83) stops by the small ticket and info office in the port parking lot. To: **Porto Vecchio** (30min.; 1 per day, July-Sept. 4 per day; €6.50); **Propriano** (1½hr., €11.50); **Ajaccio** (3½hr.; July-Sept. 15 M-Sa 2 per day; €20.50) via **Sartène** (1¾hr., €11).

Ferries: *gare maritime* at the far end of the port. **SAREMAR** (☎04 95 73 00 96; fax 04 95 73 13 37) runs to **Santa Teresa**, Sardinia (1hr.; July-Aug. 4 per day, Apr.-June and Sept. 3-Oct. 14 3 per day, Oct. 15-Mar. 2 per day; €6.70-8.50, cars €19.65-27.90). **Moby** is more expensive but has later departure times in summer. (☎04 85 73 00 29; fax 04 95 73 05 50. July-Aug. 10 per day, Apr.-June and Sept.-Oct. 4 per day. €11-15, cars €22.50-51.50. Office open daily 7am-10pm.)

Taxis: at the port (☎04 95 73 19 08; 06 62 35 79 50; or 06 15 44 31 54).

Bike and Scooter Rental: Corse Moto Services, quai Nord, on the port (☎04 95 73 15 16). Scooters €40 per day, €245 per week, €1525 deposit. 18+. Open July-Aug. daily 9am-1pm and 3-7pm. MC/V. **Tam Tam,** rte. de Santa-Manza (☎04 95 73 11 59), 200m from the port on D58, veering away from the citadel. Bikes €12 per day, €75 per week. Open July-Aug. M-Sa 9am-1pm and 3:30-8pm, Su 9am-1pm; Apr.-June and Sept.-Oct. M-Sa 9:30am-12:30pm and 3:30-7:30pm, Su 9:30am-12:30pm. MC/V.

Car Rental: Europcar, av. Sylvère Bohn (☎04 95 73 10 99), at Station Esso just before the port. Cars from €73 per day, €254 per week; credit card deposit. Unlimited mileage and insurance included. 21+. Open Apr.-Oct. daily 8am-7pm. AmEx/MC/V. **Hertz,** on the port (☎04 95 73 06 41), near the stairs to the haute ville. Cars from €81 per day, €272 per week; deposit €800-1120. 21+. Open July-Aug. daily 8am-8pm; Sept.-June M-Sa 8:30am-1pm and 3:30-6:30pm. AmEx/MC/V.

▐▐ ORIENTATION AND PRACTICAL INFORMATION

Bonifacio is divided by a steep climb into the **port** and the **haute ville**. The major highway **N198** becomes **av. Sylvère Bohn** near the entrance to the town. Coming in that way, you'll see the port on your right and the *haute ville* looming above it. The main road veers left to become **D58**, which leads to nearby beaches. To reach the tourist office, walk along the port and up the stairs before the *gare maritime*.

Tourist Office: corner of av. de Gaulle and rue F. Scamaroni (☎04 95 73 11 88; fax 04 95 73 14 97; www.bonifacio.com). Friendly staff gives out free maps and guides, and helps with hotel reservations. Open May-Oct. 15 daily 9am-8pm; Oct. 16-Apr. M-F 9am-noon and 2-6pm, Sa 9am-noon. **Annex** on the port. Open July-Aug. daily 9am-7pm.

Money: If you can, exchange currency elsewhere. **Societe Générale,** rue St-Erasme, next to the stairs to the *haute ville* (☎04 95 73 02 49), charges €5.30 commission. Open M-F 8:15am-noon and 2-4:50pm.

Laundromat: Le Lavoir de la Marine, 1 quai Comparetti (☎04 95 73 01 03 or 06 85 43 91 29), on the port. Open daily 7am-7pm.

Police: at the start of rte. de Santa Manza (D58), just off the port (☎04 95 73 00 17).

Hospital: on D58 toward the beaches (☎04 95 73 95 73).

Internet Access: Cybercafé, on the port. €2.50 for 15min., €8 per hr. Open daily 8am-2am.

Post Office: pl. Carrega (☎04 95 73 73 73), uphill from pl. Montepagano in the *haute ville*. Open M-F 8:30am-5:15pm, Sa 8:30am-noon. **Postal Code:** 20169.

CORSICA

■ ACCOMMODATIONS AND CAMPING

Finding a room in the summer is virtually impossible. Camping is by far the cheapest option; many sites also offer affordable lodging in bungalows or chalets. Porto Vecchio has some economy-priced hotels, if you don't mind daytripping.

Hôtel des Etrangers, av. Sylvère Bohn (☎04 95 73 01 09; fax 04 95 73 16 97), on the road to Bonifacio. Spare, white rooms with shower and toilet, some with A/C and TV. Nothing incredible, but cheapest place to stay in town. Breakfast included. Reception 24hr. Closed Oct. 30-Mar. 25. July 16-Aug. singles and doubles €40-71; triples €62; quads €74. May 16-July 15 and Sept. €35-55/€58/€68. Apr.-May 15 and Oct. €38-43/€50/€60. Extra bed €10. MC/V. ❹

Hôtel Le Royal, pl. Bonaparte (☎04 95 73 00 51; fax 04 95 73 04 68), in the *haute ville*. Modern blue-and-white rooms, all with shower, toilet, A/C, and TV, some with sweeping views of the sea. Reception 24hr. Breakfast €6.10. Singles €32; doubles Nov. 8-Mar. and Mar. 21-May €44.30-53.40, June and Oct.-Nov. 7 €49-59.50, July and Sept. €68.60-79.30, Aug. €91.50-105. Extra bed €15.30. MC/V. ❹

Campsites:

L'Araguina, av. Sylvère Bohn (☎04 95 73 02 96; fax 04 95 73 57 04; www.corse.sud/camping.araguina), at the entrance to town between Hôtel des Etrangers and the port. Makes up for unceremonious, crowded setup with its proximity to beaches and town. Reception 8am-9pm. 5-person bungalows €351-793 per week. Open Mar. 15-Oct. €5.25-5.55 per person, €1.90 per tent or car. Electricity €2.80. ❶

Campo di Liccia, 4km from the beach and town (☎04 95 73 03 09; fax 04 95 73 19 94). The cheapest in a cluster of campsites on the road to Porto Vecchio. Pool. Open Apr.-Oct. Reception 8am-10pm. €4.45-5.80 per person, €1.85-2.45 per tent or car. Electricity €2.45-2.60. Cash or traveler's checks. ❶

◖ FOOD

Bonifacio's port is packed with mundane, tourist-trapping restaurants. Make the climb to the *haute ville* for more authentic Corsican cuisine. For an excellent, filling meal, **Cantina Doria** ❸, 27 rue Doria, in the *haute ville*, serves hearty regional specialties on wooden picnic tables in a Corsican-themed interior. Their best deal is the €13.50 menu, which includes a plate of *charcuterie, soupe corse* and *lasagnes au fromage,* or the *plat du jour.* (☎04 95 73 50 49. Open June-Sept. daily; Apr.-May and Oct. F-W noon-2:30pm and 7-11pm. MC/V.) Alternatively, a couple of **supermarkets** line the port, including **SPAR** at the start of rte. de Santa Manza. (☎04 95 73 00 26. Open July-Aug. M-Sa 8am-8:30pm, Su 8am-1pm; Sept. and June M-Sa 8am-8pm; Oct.-May M-Sa 8am-12:30pm and 3:30-7:30pm.)

◑ SIGHTS

Maintaining 3km of fortifications above curvy white cliffs, Bonifacio is a marvel of human and natural architecture. Make sure to take a **boat tour** of the city from the port. The friendly staff at **Marina Croisières** tours coves and limestone grottoes with an optional detour to the **Iles Lavezzi.** (☎04 95 73 09 77 or 06 82 66 35 02. Grottes-falaises-calanques tour Apr.-Sept. daily every 30min. 9am-6:30pm. €12. Iles Lavezzi-Cavallo tour 5 times per day; €25.)

To explore the *haute ville* from the inside, head up montée Rastello, the steep, wide staircase halfway down the port, which gives excellent views of the harsh cliffs stretching east from Bonifacio. Continue up montée St-Roch to the lookout at **Porte de Gênes.** It was constructed with a drawbridge in 1588 to be the town's only entrance. Eager to overthrow the colonizing Italians, Corsican nationals joined forces with King Henri II to besiege the town. After successfully destroying the Genoese fortress, the triumphant rebels rebuilt a more elaborate one on the ruins of the original. The Porte de Gênes and the **Bastion de L'Etendard** next door are built in French military style rather than that of the hated Genoese—the first hint of Corsica's future encroachers. Though once a prison, the Bastion is now a trap for tourists; the hokey historical displays inside the fortress are not worth €2.

After soaking up all this history, head left to pl. du Marché for the best views of Bonifacio's cliffs and limestone formation, **Grain de Sable.** The little mound just out of reach is Sardinia, 12km away. Turn right on rue Cardinal and then left on rue du Sacrement to reach the **Eglise Ste-Mairie-Majeure,** Bonifacio's oldest building. This 12th-century church guards one of the town's most important objects: a morsel of the **true cross,** stripped from a shipwreck. Continue through Bonifacio's tiny, winding streets to reach the **cemetery** at the southern tip of the *haute ville.* Like all Corsican burial grounds, it marks the dead with elaborate miniature mausoleums rather than stones. On Corsica, it's said that even death is beautiful.

⛱ BEACHES

Bonifacio's beaches are hard to get to and harder to leave. The only ones within walking distance of town are intimate but uninspiring; a path leads from Camping l'Araguina to **plage de la Catena** (30min.) and the cleaner and prettier **plage de l'Arinella.** (45min.) The peninsula east of Bonifacio is filled with good beaches, but you'll need a car to reach them. From the port, take D58 towards the water; virtually every turn-off leads to a beach. Isolated **Cala Longa** is 8km away; **plage Maora,** a large beach in a calm natural harbor, is 6km away. The turn-off for camping Rondinara, 17km away, leads to **plage de Rondinara,** one of Corsica's most famous beaches. You'll recognize its dunes and lagoons from postcards.

Even more impressive than the mainland beaches are the pristine sands of the **Iles Lavezzi.** All of the companies on the port run frequent ferries (30min.) to this nature reserve, where rock formations and expansive fields meet calm turquoise waters. Just off the island, there is great **scuba diving** along the beautiful reefs. **Atoll,** on the port, past the stairs to the *haute ville,* arranges dives for beginners and experts. (☎04 95 73 53 83; fax 04 95 73 17 72; www.atoll-diving.com. Open Apr.-Nov. daily 8am-7:30pm. Dives for beginners €60, for experts €37-59. MC/V.)

CORSICA

THE ALPS
(LES ALPES)

Natural architecture is the Alps's real attraction. The curves of the Chartreuse Valley rise to rugged crags in the Vercors range and ultimately crescendo into Europe's highest peak, Mont Blanc. Skiers enjoy some of the most challenging slopes in the world; in the summer hikers take over the same mountains for their endless vistas of flowery meadows and icy lakes. With two high seasons a year, you'll have to choose between the dependable crowds, dependable prices, and dependable weather of summer and winter, and the quieter but less predictable months between them. Skiing arrangements should be made a couple of months in advance; Chamonix and Val d'Isère are the easiest bases.

The Alps are split between two historical provinces, Savoy and Dauphiné. The Dauphiné includes the Chartreuse Valley, Vercors regional park, Ecrins national park, the Belledonne and Oisans mountains. Grenoble, its largest city, has a hearty student population, lively bars, and cuisine ranging from cheese fondues to couscous. The region first became independent in the 11th century, under Guiges I. His great-grandson Guiges IV took the surname "Dauphin" (dolphin); in time the name acquired the status of a title. In the 14th century, when the last independent Dauphin sold his lands to France, the French monarchs adopted the practice of ceding the province to the heir to the throne, the Dauphin. In the 15th century, Louis XI established a permanent *parlement* (court) in Grenoble, which has since been the region's cultural and intellectual capital. Savoy, which includes the peaks of Haute Savoie, Olympic resorts in the expansive Tarentaise valley, and the awe-inspiring Vanoise park, bears the name of the oldest royal house in Europe.

1	**Grenoble:** Dynamic university city near snow-capped peaks and ice-blue lakes **(p. 616)**
2	◾**Hauterives:** Surreal, arabesque fortress made from pebbles by a local postman **(p. 625)**
3	**Chambéry:** Adorable gateway to the high Alps; Rousseau's happiest home **(p. 626)**
4	**Aix-Les-Bains and Lac du Bourget:** France's largest natural lake, plus sulfur springs **(p. 629)**
5	◾**Annecy:** Flower-filled, fairy-tale city on a crystalline lake; near dozens of alpine hikes **(p. 631)**
6	◾**Chamonix:** Famous mountain-sports town within ski range of Italy and Switzerland **(p. 637)**
7	**Val d'Isère:** Small, pricey ski town with great off-trail skiing **(p. 646)**

GRENOBLE

Every September, 55,000 students descend on Grenoble (pop. 156,000). It's easy to see why so many students choose to live in the unofficial capital of the Alps. The city has the eccentric cafés, dusty bookshops, shaggy radicals, and earnest politics of any university town, but it is also near the snow-capped peaks and sapphire-blue lakes cherished by hikers, skiers, bikers, aesthetes, and set designers alike. The influx of immigrants to France in the 1960s gave Grenoble a sizable North and West African population, which accentuates this dynamic city's cosmopolitan feel.

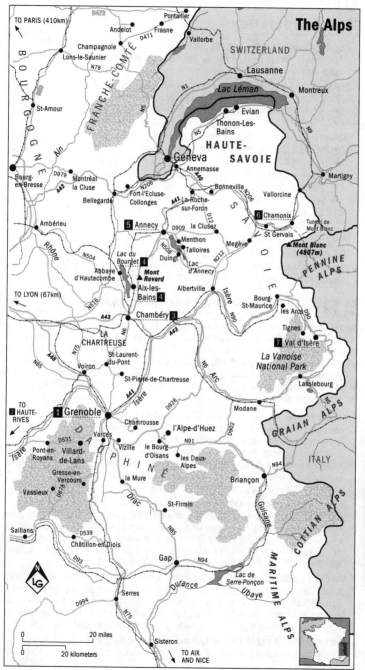

The Alps

TO PARIS (410km)

Andelot
Frasne
Pontarlier
Vallorbe
SWITZERLAND
Champagnole
Lons-le-Saunier
N78
Lausanne
Lac Léman
Montreux
St-Amour
Evian
Thonon-Les-Bains
Montréal la Cluse
Bellegarde
Fort-l'Ecluse-Collonges
Geneva
Annemasse
Bonneville
Vallorcine
Martigny
HAUTE-SAVOIE
Bourg-en-Bresse
Ambérieu
La-Roche-sur-Foron
la Clusaz
Megève
St-Gervais
Chamonix
Tunnel de Mont Blanc
5 Annecy
Menthon
Talloires
Duingt
Lac d'Annecy
Mont Blanc (4807m)
PENNINE ALPS
TO LYON (67km)
Lac du Bourget 4
Abbaye d'Hautecombe
Mont Revard
Aix-les-Bains 4
Albertville
Bourg-St-Maurice
les Arcs
Tignes
Chambéry 3
7 Val d'Isère
LA CHARTREUSE
Voiron
St-Laurent-du-Pont
St-Pierre-de-Chartreuse
La Vanoise National Park
Lanslebourg
GRAIAN ALPS
TO HAUTE-RIVES
1 Grenoble
Chamrousse
l'Alpe-d'Huez
Modane
ITALY
Varces
Vizille
le Bourg d'Oisans
Pont-en-Royans
Villard-de-Lans
Gresse-en-Vercours
les Deux-Alpes
Briançon
Vassieux
la Mure
St-Firmin
COTTIAN ALPS
Saillans
Châtillon-en-Diois
Gap
Lac de Serre-Ponçon
Serres
Sisteron
TO AIX AND NICE

MARITIME ALPS

ALPS

0   20 miles
0   20 kilometers

⌐ TRANSPORTATION

Flights: Aéroport de Grenoble St-Geoirs, St-Etienne de St-Geoirs (☎04 76 65 48 48), 41km away. Buses leave 1¼hr. before each flight from bus station (€13). Domestic flights only.

Trains: Gare Europole, pl. de la Gare. Ticket booth open daily 6am-9pm. To: **Annecy** (2hr., 18 per day, €14.10); **Chambéry** (1hr., 30 per day, €8.70); **Lyon** (1½hr., 27 per day, €15.40); **Marseille** (2½-4½hr., 15 per day, €32.30); **Nice** (5-6½hr., 5 per day, €47.20); **Paris** (3hr., 6 per day, €58.80-73.60).

Buses: Left as you exit the train station. Open M-Sa 6:15am-7pm, Su 7:15am-7pm. **VFD** (☎08 20 83 38 33; www.vfd.fr) runs to **Geneva** (3hr., 1 per day, €25.50) and **Nice** (10hr., 1 per day, €52.40). Frequent service to ski resorts and outdoor areas.

Public Transportation: Transports Agglomeration Grenobloise (TAG) (☎04 76 20 66 66). Info desk in the tourist office open Sept.-June M-F 8:30am-6:30pm, Sa 9am-6pm; July-Aug. M-Sa 9am-6pm. Ticket €1.10, *carnet* of 10 €8.90. Day pass €3, week pass €10.60. Two tram lines run July-Aug. about every 5-10min. 5am-midnight; Th-Sa, 4 lines run 6am-8:30pm and 9pm-midnight.

Taxis: (☎04 76 54 42 54). 24hr. To airport (gulp!) €55.

Car Rental: Self Car, 24 rue Emile Gueymard (☎04 76 50 96 96), near the train station. Insurance included. 21+. Open July-Aug. M-F 8am-noon and 2-6pm, Sa 8am-noon; Sept.-June 7:30am-noon and 1:30-6:30pm; Sa 8am-noon. AmEx/MC/V.

◣◪ 7 ORIENTATION AND PRACTICAL INFORMATION

To get to the tourist office and the center of town from the station, turn right onto pl. de la Gare and take the third left onto av. Alsace-Lorraine, following the tram tracks. Continue along the tracks on rue Félix Poulat and rue Blanchard; the tourist complex will be on your left, just before the tracks fork. (15min.) The *vieille ville*, primarily a pedestrian area, stretches from the tourist office to the river, bounded by the Jardin de Ville and Musée de Grenoble. The Bastille is across the river, looming ominously above the town.

Tourist Office: 14 rue de la République (☎04 76 42 41 41; fax 04 76 00 18 98; www.grenoble-isere.info). From the train station, tram lines A and B (dir: Echirolles or Universités) run to "Hubert Dubedout-Maison du Tourisme". The complex is the center of a visitor's universe, complete with **SNCF** counter, local **bus** office, and **post office.** Good map, hotel info, and train and bus schedules. Free copies of every local tourist publication. **Tours** of the old city July-Aug. daily Sept.-June 2 per month. €6.50. Office open M-Sa 9am-6:30pm, Su 10am-1pm and 2-5pm.

Hiking Information: Bureau Information Montagne, 3 rue Raoul Blanchard (☎04 76 42 45 90; fax 04 76 44 67 03; infos.montagne@grande-traversee-alpes.com), across from the tourist office. An indispensable source for info on hiking, mountaineering, biking, and cross-country skiing trails. Free brochures and expert advice. Detailed guides and maps for sale. Open M-F 9am-noon and 2-6pm, Sa 10am-1pm and 2-5pm. **Weather:** ☎08 36 68 02 38. **Snow Info:** ☎08 92 68 10 20.

Ski and Climbing Equipment Rental: Borel Sport, 42 rue Alsace-Lorraine (☎04 76 46 47 46; fax 04 76 46 00 75). Skis, boots, and poles €10-18 per day. Snowboard package €15.50 per day. Cross-country package €8-11 per day. Via Ferrata climbing ensemble (harness, cord, helmet) €11 per day. Snowshoes €4-6 per day. Open Sept.-May daily 9am-noon and 2-7pm; June-Aug. Tu-Sa 10am-noon and 2-6pm. MC/V.

Budget Travel: Voyages Wasteels, 7 rue Thiers (☎0 825 88 70 39; www.wasteels.fr). Cheap student travel packages. Open M-F 9am-noon and 2-6pm, Sa 9am-1pm and 2-5pm. MC/V.

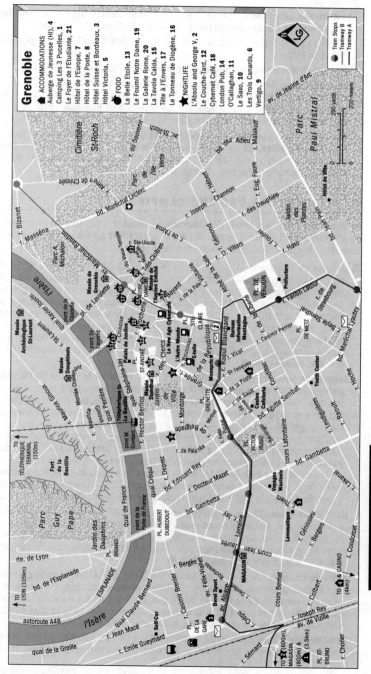

Grenoble

♦ ACCOMMODATIONS
Auberge de Jeunesse (HI), 4
Camping Les 3 Pucelles, 1
Le Foyer de l'Etudiante, 21
Hôtel de l'Europe, 7
Hôtel de la Poste, 8
Hôtel Suisse et Bordeaux, 3
Hôtel Victoria, 5

● FOOD
La Belle Etoile, 13
Le Fournil Notre Dame, 19
La Galerie Rome, 20
La Tavola Calda, 15
Tête à l'Envers, 17
Le Tonneau de Diogène, 16

★ NIGHTLIFE
L'Absolu and George V, 2
Le Couche-Tard, 12
Cybernet Café, 18
London Pub, 14
O'Callaghan, 11
Le Saxo, 10
Les Trois Canards, 6
Vertigo, 9

Tram Stops
Tramway B
Tramway A

ALPS

Laundromat: Lavomatique, 14 rue Thiers (☎04 76 96 28 03). Open daily 7am-10pm. **Très-Cloîtres,** 5 rue Très-Cloîtres (☎04 76 96 28 03). Open daily 7am-8pm.

Police: 36 bd. Maréchal Leclerc (☎04 76 60 40 40). Take bus #31 (dir: Malpertuis) to "Hôtel de Police."

Hospital: Centre Hospitalier Régional de Grenoble, La Tronche (☎04 76 76 75 75).

Internet Access: E-toile, 15 rue Jean-Jacques Rousseau (☎04 76 00 13 60), is your cheapest bet. €1.50 per 15min., €2 per 30min., €3.50 per hr. Open M-F 10am-11pm, Sa-Su 10am-midnight. **L'Autre Monde,** 4 rue Jean-Jacques Rousseau (☎04 76 01 00 20). €2.25 per 30min., €4.50 per hr. Open M-F 10am-1am, Sa 1pm-1am, Su 1-10pm.

Post Office: 7 bd. Maréchal Lyautey (☎04 76 43 51 39). Open M-F 8am-7pm, Sa 8am-noon. **Branch office,** 12 rue de la République (☎04 76 63 32 70), inside the tourist complex. Open July 15-Aug. M-F 9am-noon and 2-5:30pm, Sa 9am-noon; Sept.-July 14 M 8am-5:45pm, Tu-F 8am-6pm, Sa 8am-noon. **Postal code:** 38000.

▐ ACCOMMODATIONS AND CAMPING

A smattering of budget hotels dot downtown Grenoble. They tend to be crowded, so it's wise to call ahead. The student guide, aptly titled *Le Guide de l'Etudiant,* free at the tourist office, has info on long-term stays.

■ **Le Foyer de l'Etudiante,** 4 rue Ste-Ursule (☎04 76 42 00 84; fax 04 76 42 96 67; stud.feg@wanadoo.fr; www.multimania.com/foyeretudiante). From the tourist office, follow pl. Ste-Claire to pl. Notre-Dame and take rue du Vieux Temple on the far right. Your best bet during the summer. Stately old building encloses a frieze-lined courtyard where backpackers and students mix. Spacious rooms with desks and high ceilings. Kitchen, piano, free **Internet** access. Sheets €8. Laundry €2.20. Reception 24hr. July-Sept. 3-night min. for room; 5-night max. for dorm. Oct.-June 6-month min. stay. Dorms €8 per person. July-Sept. singles €14; doubles €22. Oct-June singles €243; doubles €364. **Oct.-Apr. women only. ❶**

Auberge de Jeunesse (HI), 3 av. Victor Hugo (☎04 76 09 33 52; fax 04 76 09 38 99; grenoble-echirolles@fuaj.org), about 4km from Grenoble in Echirolles. From the train station, take Tram A (dir: Echirolles) to "La Rampe." (30min.) Then, turn around and take the first left onto av. de Grugliasco, just before McDonald's. Passing the bowling alley, take the first right onto rue Fernard Pelloutier. Follow it past the Stade Nautique and take a right onto av. Victor Hugo. (12min.) Alternatively, you can take bus #16 from "Docteur Martin" in the *centre-ville* (dir: Le Canton; 8am-8pm) to "Monmousseau." Turn around and walk along av. Victor Hugo for about 50m. This is a temporary location for 2003 as a new hostel is being built for 2004. Two buildings with an industrial feel with functional rooms for 2 overlooking a quiet green space. Sheets €2.70. Reception M-Sa 7:30am-11pm, Su 7:30-10am and 5:30-11pm. Lockout 10am-5:30pm. €9 per night. MC/V. ❶

Hôtel de la Poste, 25 rue de la Poste (☎/fax 04 76 46 67 25), in the heart of the pedestrian zone. Amazingly priced rooms with antiquated charm at this homey refuge for budget travelers. Get friendly with the 26-year owner—the only shower is four feet from the reception desk. Reception 24hr. Singles €22, with shower and TV €26; doubles €28/€35; triples €32; quads €37. ❷

Hôtel de L'Europe, 22 pl. Grenette (☎/fax 04 76 46 16 94; hotel.europe.gre@wanadoo.fr). Dating from the 18th century, this hotel's gorgeous facade is a landmark. Well-renovated rooms in the *centre ville.* Small gym. Breakfast €5.50. Reception 24hr. Singles €26-29, with shower €35, with shower or bath and toilet €45; doubles €28-31/€38/€48-59; triples with bath €54-65; quads with bath €65-68. AmEx/MC/V. ❸

Hôtel Victoria, 17 rue Thiers (☎04 76 46 06 36; fax 04 76 43 00 14). 27-year, friendly owner creates a familial atmosphere at this super-clean, well-maintained hotel. Though a bit dark, rooms are spacious and have firm beds. Breakfast €5.50. Reception 7am-11:30pm. Curfew 11:30pm. Closed Aug. Singles with shower €29, with toilet €34; doubles with shower €34/€40-45; triples €48; quads €51. AmEx/MC/V. ❸

Hôtel Suisse et Bordeaux, 6 pl. de la Gare (☎04 76 47 55 87; fax 04 76 46 23 87), is across from the train station. Spacious, modern rooms with loud floral curtains and bedspreads. All rooms have shower or bath, toilet, and TV. Reception 24hr. Breakfast €5.40. Singles €39; doubles €45.60; triples €54.20; quads €55.80. AmEx/MC/V. ❹

Camping: Les 3 Pucelles, 58 rue des Allobroges (☎04 76 96 45 73; fax 04 76 21 43 73), in Seyssins, just on the southwest corner of Grenoble. Take tram A (dir: Fontaine-La Poya) to "Louis Maisonnat", then take bus #51 (dir: Les Nalettes) to "Mas des Iles"; turn left and the site is a couple of blocks down. Small and suburban, this is the closest campsite to town and the only one open all year. 70 sites and a swimming pool. Reception 7:30am-11pm. Laundry €2.15. Call ahead June-Aug. One person, tent, and car €7.50. Extra person €2.80. Electricity €2.20. MC/V. ❶

🍴 FOOD

Grenoble has many affordable restaurants, and some have discounts or student *menus.* Given the number of students, cafeteria food is almost a local specialty. **University Restaurants (URs)** open during the school year, and meal tickets are sold in *carnets* of 10 during lunch to student ID holders. (☎04 76 57 44 00. Ticket €2.40.) The two URs in Grenoble *ville* are **Restaurant d'Arsonval,** 5 rue d'Arsonval (open M-F 11:30am-1:30pm and 6:30-7:45pm), and **Restaurant du Rabot,** rue Maurice Gignoux. (Open daily noon-1:15pm and 6:30-7:50pm.) **Monoprix** is across from the tourist office (open M-Sa 8:30am-8pm); **Casino** is at 46 cours Jean Jaurès, about 10min. from the youth hostel. (Open M-Sa 8:30am-8pm.) There's also a **Casino Cafeteria** on rue Guetal with cheap, fast service. (Salads €2.15-4.45. Entrees €1-3.75. Hot dishes €3.50-6.40. Open daily 11am-9:30pm.) Grenoble hosts 16 **markets,** the most lively on pl. St-André, pl. St-Bruno, pl. Ste-Claire, and pl. aux Herbes. (All open Tu-Su 6am-1pm; pl. St-Bruno also F 6am-1pm; pl. Ste-Claire also F 3-8pm.)

Regional restaurants cater to locals around **pl. de Gordes,** between pl. St-André and the Jardin de Ville. Asian eateries abound between pl. Notre-Dame and the river and virtually own **rue Condorcet.** *Pâtisseries* and North African joints congregate around **rue Chenoise** and **rue Lionne,** between the pedestrian area and the river. Cafés and restaurants cluster around **pl. Notre-Dame** and **pl. St-André,** in the heart of the *vieille ville.* Lively, cheap pizzerias line quai Perrière across the river.

▨ **Tête à l'Envers,** 12 rue Chenoise (☎04 76 51 13 42). This 7-table gem specializes in a *mélange* of international cuisine. The menu changes daily, depending upon what's fresh at the market and in the creative mind of the expert chef. Even loyal locals agonize over the choice between 4 *entrées* (€7), *plats du jour* with seasoned vegetables (€8.30), and an exquisite plate of 6 desserts (€7). If you guess the identity of 5 of the 6 desserts, you win a prize. There are wonderful lunch menus as well (€11-12.20). Mention *Let's Go* for a free coffee or *digéstif.* Reservations recommended. Open Tu-F noon-3pm and 7:30pm-1am, Sa 7:30pm-1am. MC/V. ❷

▨ **La Galerie Rome,** 1 rue Très-Cloîtres (☎04 76 42 82 01). A gourmand owner presides over traditional French cuisine, including the delicious, artery-clogging *gratin dauphinois* (€8.40). *Plats* feature fish (€12.20-13), duck, veal, and beef (€13.70-22). Art is taken as seriously as food here; the restaurant is also a gallery where paintings hang on a centuries-old wall. Open Tu-Sa noon-2:30pm and 7-11pm. AmEx/MC/V. ❷

La Belle Etoile, 2 rue Lionne (☎04 76 51 00 40), specializes in Tunisian cuisine, with some of the best *couscous* in Grenoble (€7.40-13). This 20-year family establishment offers warm service and hearty portions. Large salads (€2.30-8.40), omelettes (€2.60-

HE *PENSÉES* OF PASCAL

.et's Go sat down to chat with Pascal, chef-owner of Tête à l'Envers ❷ over a fresh salad of the day.

Q: What is the philosophy of your restaurant?

A: We bring together the cuisine of the world: South American, African, Oriental, Chinese, spices from everywhere.

Q: What inspires your cooking?

A: This morning at the market I thought of an *entrée*, a confiture of onion with lemon juice. Products at the market stir ideas in our head.

Q: So how do you decide your menus? *Humeur* of the chef?

A: If we did the same plates every day, every year, it would be barbaric. We don't want to do a *steak frites* every day...we would need to make it very different. Why not put a vegetable in a dessert? In *entrées*, add fruit? In a salad, put some ice cream? We throw out the cookbook.

Q: Do you remember the first plate you were proud of?

A: *Salade verte*, tomato, shrimp, vinagrette of olive oil and martini rouge.

Q: In what direction do you think French cuisine is going?

A: I am by no means a pioneer in my style; there are many who do a *mélange*. The main problem with French cuisine is that it's too expensive. Why shouldn't everybody be able to eat well? Yes, *foie gras* itself is very expensive, but you can replace it with a little *pâté campagne*...It's not *foie gras*, but it's good. I prefer to be able to provide a *plat* for 10 euros. This is hard in a country where every thing you need to make food is *cher*.

5.60), *tagines* (€9.50), and fresh pastries (€2.30). Closed July 15-Aug. 20. Open Tu-Su noon-2pm and 7-11pm. AmEx/MC/V. ❷

La Tavola Calda, 10 rue Brocherie (☎04 76 54 67 25). Enter this smoky, hot den with off-white stucco walls if you're tired of gratin and would prefer large portions of tasty Italian cuisine. The amiable staff serves *entrées* (€2.45-9.50), pizzas (€5.95-8.25), meats (€10.40-13.60), and homemade pastas (€5.65-11.50) to a local crowd. Open Tu-Sa noon-1:30pm and 7:30-10:15pm. AmEx/MC/V. ❷

Le Tonneau de Diogène, 6 pl. Notre-Dame (☎04 76 42 38 40). Nothing beats Thursday nights (Sept. to mid-July), when local intellectuals discuss the weekly philosophical topic posted out front. While you ponder, munch on salads (€2.30-6.90), omelettes (€3.50-5), and meats (€2.90-9.40). 3-course menu €6.50. Open daily 8:30am-1am. A set of back stairs leads to **Le Sphinx** (☎04 76 44 55 08), Grenoble's finest philosophy library/bookstore. Open M-F noon-8:30pm, Sa 10am-7pm. AmEx/MC/V. ❶

Le Fournil Notre Dame, 2 pl. Notre Dame (☎04 76 42 12 42). Grenoble's *vieille ville* overflows with bakeries, but this is the place to go for utterly transcendent treats. Try the enormous *pain aux raisins* (€0.90), the *tarte aux noix* (€1.50), or a *croissant amandes* (€1). Open Tu-Su 7am-8pm. Closed Aug. 1-20.

👁 SIGHTS

THE VIEILLE VILLE. Built over 17 centuries, Grenoble's *vieille ville* is a motley but charming collection of squares, fountains, and parks. Vestiges of the Roman ramparts are most visible near the town's historic center, **pl. St-André,** now Grenoble's most popular student hangout. The 13th-century **Collegiale Saint-André** was the traditional burial place for Dauphins before the French crown acquired both land and title in 1349. *(Open 8am-5pm.)* Directly across, you can't miss the flamboyant Gothic **Palais de Justice,** built by Dauphin prince and future king Louis XI in 1453 to house the Dauphiné region's parliament. *(Tours depart from the tourist office Su-F 10:15am. €6.50, students €5.20.)* The **Café de la Table Ronde,** built in 1739, is the 2nd-oldest coffee spot in France. *(☎04 76 44 51 41. Open M-Sa 9am-1am. Café €1.)*

TÉLÉPHERIQUE GRENOBLE-BASTILLE. The icons of Grenoble, these gondolas emerge from the city every 10 minutes and head for the **Bastille,** a 16th-century fort perched ominously 475m above. From the top, on the rare clear day, you can look north toward the Lyon valley and its two converging rivers; the big peaks lie to the south, over the ridge of snow-capped mountains on the other side of Grenoble. Sporty types continue 1hr. up to **Mont-Jalla** but the views don't improve much. Back at the cable station, practice your alpine skills on the **via ferrata**, the first urban climbing site in the world, or walk down via the **Parc Guy Pape**, which descends through the other end of the fortress and deposits you in the Jardin des Dauphins. (1hr.) Be cautious: the trail is isolated and passes through several long, dark tunnels. *(Téléphérique: quai Stéphane-Jay. ☎04 76 44 33 65; www.telepherique-grenoble.com. Open July-Aug. M 11am-12:15am, Tu-Su 9:15am-12:15am; Nov.-Feb. M 11am-6:30pm, Tu-Su 10:45am-6:30pm; Mar.-May and Oct. M 11am-7:25pm, Tu-Sa 9:15am-11:45pm, Su 9:15am-7:25pm; June and Sept. M 11am-11:45pm, Tu-Sa 9:15am-11:45pm, Su 9:15am-7:25pm. Closed Jan. 7-18. One-way €3.80, students €3; round-trip €5.50, students €4.40.)*

MUSÉE DAUPHINOIS. Situated on the north bank of the Isère in a beautiful 17th-century convent, this regional museum boasts multimedia extravagance, futuristic exhibits, and sound effects. The two permanent exhibits have explanations in English. The museum's highlight is "Gens de l'Alpe" (People of the Alps), which explores the history of the hearty souls who carved out a livelihood in the mountains. Check out "La Grande Histoire du Ski" (The Great History of Skiing), featuring a vast collection of early and modern skis. *(30 rue Maurice Gignoux. Cross the Pont St-Laurent and go up Montée Chalemont. ☎04 76 85 19 01; www.musee-dauphinois.fr. Open June-Sept. W-M 10am-7pm; Oct.-May 10am-6pm. €3.20, under 25 free.)*

MUSÉE DE GRENOBLE. The sleek Musée de Grenoble houses one of France's most prestigious collections of fine art. Its masterpieces include larger-than-life canvases by Rubens, de la Tour, and Zubararàn, as well as a top-notch 20th-century collection with an entire room devoted to Matisse. *(5 pl. de Lavalette. ☎04 76 63 44 44; www.ville-grenoble.fr/musee-de-grenoble. Open July-Sept. Th-M 10am-6pm, W 10am-9pm; Oct.-June Th-M 11am-7pm, W 11am-10pm. €4, students €2; temporary and permanent collections €6, students €4. Guided 1½hr. visits in French Sa-Su 3pm; €4.)*

OTHER MUSEUMS. In a former warehouse built by Gustave Eiffel, **Centre National d'Art Contemporain (MAGASIN)** is an exhibition center for cutting-edge contemporary art. Find out what's showing in *Le Petit Bulletin*. *(155 cours Berriat. Take tram A (dir: Fontaine-La Poya) to "Berriat." ☎04 76 21 95 84. Open Tu-Su noon-7pm during exhibitions. €3.50, students €2.)* On the north bank of the river and below Eglise St-Laurent, the **Musée Archéologique Saint-Laurent** contains the remaining Roman vestiges in Grenoble. All explanations are in French, but you can purchase a general brochure in English for €0.75. *(Pl. St-Laurent. ☎04 76 44 78 68. Open W-M 9am-6pm. €3.20, students €1.60, under 25 free.)* Flanking pl. Notre-Dame, the **Musée de l'Ancien Evêché**, is built around Grenoble's 4th-century baptistery, but the museum's beautiful retrospective of the region through art and artifacts is more interesting. A Roman mosaic and 20th-century time capsule are worth your attention. *(2 rue Très-Cloîtres. ☎04 76 03 15 25. Open M and W-Sa 9am-6pm, Su 10am-7pm. €3.20, students €1.60, under 25 free. English audioguide free.)* Next to the Jardin de Ville, the old Hôtel de Ville is now home to the elegant **Musée Stendhal**, which investigates Grenoble's most eminent 19th-century citizen through a small collection of portraits, documents, and an informative 20min. video. *(1 rue Hector Berlioz. ☎04 76 54 44 14. Open July 15-Sept. 15 Tu-Su 9am-noon and 2-6pm; Sept. 16-July 14 2-6pm. Free.)*

🎵 🎭 ENTERTAINMENT AND FESTIVALS

Grenoble has the funky cafés and raucous bars of a true college town. Most lie between **pl. St-André** and **pl. Notre-Dame.** Covers range €8-10 and drinks nearly as

ALPS

much. Hours listed here are for the school year; most places have more limited hours in summer. The **Maison de la Culture** in the tourist office is so hip it calls itself **Le CARGO.** (☎04 76 01 21 21. Open Sept.-June Tu-Sa 9am-6:30pm.)

Le Couche-Tard, 1 rue du Palais (☎04 76 44 18 79), a small bar with graffiti-covered walls, neon lights, and a dance area, is where drunken scholars mix it up. Happy Hour M-Sa 7-10:30pm; cocktails €2. Open M-Sa 8pm-2am.

Les Trois Canards, 2 av. Felix Viallet (☎04 76 46 74 74), by the Jardin de Ville, has €1.60 shooters and a mind-boggling selection of flavored vodka (€2) for students and 20-somethings. Relax in the spacious interior with a live DJ, seahorses, disco ball, and various Budweiser paraphernalia. Open daily 8am-1am; July-Aug. closed Su.

Le Saxo, 5 pl. Agier (☎04 76 51 06 01), is a Grenoble institution; a well-dressed, chic crowd fills its spacious terrace and two small dance floors. Open daily 7pm-2am.

Cybernet Café, 3 rue Bayard (☎04 76 51 73 18), has **Internet** access but you won't find a single e-mail addict here. A funky but cool crowd loves this mellow, artfully decorated, bric-a-brac-filled spot. Happy hour 6-8:30pm with drinks €2-4. Internet €3 per 30min., €5 per hr. Open Tu-Sa 3pm-1am.

London Pub, 11 rue Brocherie (☎04 76 44 41 90), is a home-away-from-home for expats. This two-floor establishment has friendly staff and flag-adorned interior. After a few drinks, the bar area morphs into a de facto dance floor with a loud and happy crowd. Happy Hour daily 6-9pm: drafts from €1.60. Open M-Sa 6pm-1am.

O'Callaghan, 2 pl. de Bérulle (☎04 76 01 05 66), is an Irish oasis in the Alps, offering a secluded terrace and spacious interior with dart board and Guinness posters. Happy Hour 4:30-8pm: beer €3.10-4. Open daily 4:30pm-1am; Sept.-June Sa-Su from 3pm).

Vertigo, 18 Grande Rue (☎04 76 15 27 95), is where the crowds head when the bars wind down. Local DJs spin for a large dance floor with disco ball. Open Tu-Sa 1-5:30am. Cover Th-Sa €8, includes first drink; Th women free.

L'Absolu and George V, 124 cours Berriat (☎04 76 84 16 20), are two of the surprisingly few gay clubs in Grenoble. Intimate red lounge area, dance floor, and theme nights twice a month. Cover €10; includes one drink. Open Th-Su midnight-5:30am.

Grenoble is ablaze July 14 with fireworks over its very own (and still standing) Bastille. The **Festival du Court Métrage** (short films) takes place in early July. Contact the **Cinémathèque,** 4 rue Hector Berlioz (☎04 76 54 43 51). The **Festival de Théâtre Européen** hams it up in July. (☎04 76 44 60 92 for info. Shows free-€16.) In late November, the two-week **Festival 38ème Rugissants** brings contemporary music to Grenoble. (☎04 76 51 12 92.) For info and tickets on most events in Grenoble, visit the Billetterie, right next the tourist office. (☎04 76 42 96 02. Open M-Sa 9am-noon and 1:30-6pm.) The weekly *Le Petit Bulletin,* free in cinemas and some restaurants, has movie schedules.

🎿 SKIING

The four slopes around Grenoble aren't the only source of daytrips in the area. The Dauphiné region is proud of its *"Huit Merveilles"* (Eight Wonders), which include elaborate natural caves. The tourist office carries information on excursions to towns such as **Pont-en-Royans** and other natural beauties.

That said, you'd be nuts not to go **skiing** here. Rent equipment in Grenoble to avoid high prices at the resorts. The biggest ski areas are to the east in **Oisans.** The **Alpe d'Huez,** rising above one of the most challenging legs of the Tour de France, boasts an enormous 3330m vertical drop and sunny south-facing slopes; 220km of trails cover all difficulty levels. (Tourist office ☎04 76 11 44 44; fax 04 76 80 69 54; ski area ☎04 76 80 30 30. €33 per day, €171.50 per week.) Popular with advanced skiers, **Les Deux Alpes** has the biggest skiable glacier in Europe, limited summer skiing, and a slope-side youth hostel. Its lift system, including two gondolas, will whisk you up the 2000m vertical. (Tourist office ☎ 04 76 79 22 00; fax 04 76 79 01 38. Ski area ☎ 04 76 79 75 00. Youth hostel ☎ 04 76 79 22 80; fax 04 76 79 26 15. Lift tickets €32 per day, €137.70-153 per week.)

The **Belledonne** region, northeast of Grenoble, lacks the towering heights and ideal conditions of the Oisans but compensates with lower prices. **Chamrousse** is its biggest and most popular ski area, offering a lively atmosphere and a youth hostel. If conditions are right, there's plenty of good alpine and cross-country skiing at great value, especially for beginners. (Tourist office ☎ 04 76 89 92 65; fax 04 76 89 98 06. Youth hostel ☎ 04 76 89 91 31; fax 04 76 89 96 66. Lift tickets €23 per day, €79-113 per week.) Only 30min. from Grenoble, the resort makes for an ideal daytrip in the summer (bus ride €8.70). Chamrousse maintains four **mountain bike** routes of varying difficulty as well as a 230km network of **hiking** trails. In January, the town hosts a renowned comedy film festival.

The neighborly slopes and affordable prices of the **Vercors** region, south of Grenoble, are popular with locals. In traditional villages with small ski resorts, such as **Gresse-en-Vercors,** vertical drops range around 1000m. Rock-bottom prices make the area a stress-free option for beginners or anyone looking to escape the hassles of the major resorts. The drive from Grenoble takes about 40min. (Tourist office ☎ 04 76 34 33 40; fax 04 76 34 31 26. Tickets €8.80-12.20 per day, €52.90-72.10 per week.) Infested by ibex and saturated with quaintness, Vercors and its regional park have plenty of great **hikes,** as well as **mountain bike** circuits in and around the villages of **Autrans** and **Meaudre,** just outside of Grenoble. Contact **Bureau Info Montagne** (see p. 618) for maps and details. **Mountain climbers** should ask specifically for the free *Carte des Sites d'Escalade de l'Isère* or purchase a comprehensive topo-guide for about €16.

▓ HIKING

If you want to stay near town, a number of popular hikes are just a short bus ride away. In Vercors, views from the top of **Le Moucherotte** (1901m) are unparalleled. Take VFD bus #510 (dir: Plateau du Vercors) to "St-Nizier du Moucherotte" (40min., 2 per day, €4.40) and head to the center of town. In front of the church, an easy trail starts to the right of the orientation table and quickly joins the **GR91,** which passes the remains of an old *téléphérique* before reaching the mountain's summit via a former ski trail. Descend along the same route. (Round-trip 4hr.) A steeper trail reaches the summit of the **Chamechaude** (2082m) in the heart of the Chartreuse natural park. Take VFD bus #714 to "Col de Porte." Then follow the dirt trail that leads from behind Hôtel Garin to the right until you reach the middle of a field; to the left, a second trail leads into the forest where it joins the main path, a zig-zag ascent up to the **source des Bachassons.** From here you can admire the view or continue to the top of the mountain. Before ascending, you may want to pick up the free trail map *La Carte des Sentiers des Franges Vertes*, at the Bureau Info Montagne (see p. 618).

▓ DAYTRIP FROM GRENOBLE

HAUTERIVES

The village of Hauterives has put itself on the map with a whimsical palace and the intriguing story behind it. In 1879, the local postman, Ferdinand Cheval, tripped over an oddly shaped rock as he was making his daily rounds. One pebble led to another, and soon he was taking a wheelbarrow into the fields every evening to

ALPS

collect piles of odd little rocks. Over the next 33 years, he shaped his stones into a fantasy palace just outside the village. Rock by rock, it grew into an unbelievably detailed world of grimacing giants, frozen palms, and swirling staircases. When the postman finally laid down his trowel, the ◙**Palais Idéal** (Ideal Palace) was almost 80m long and over two stories high. The palace, an indescribable mix of Middle Eastern architecture and hallucinatory images, has become a national monument. You can climb all over it and explore its caves and crevices, mottoes and mysteries sculpted by two hands and the postman's unshakable faith. (☎ 04 75 68 81 19; www.facteurcheval.com. Open daily July-Aug. 9am-12:30pm and 1:30-7:30pm; Sept. and Apr.-June 9am-12:30pm and 1:30-6:30pm; Oct.-Nov. and Feb.-Mar. 9:30am-12:30pm and 1:30-5:30pm; Dec.-Jan. 9:30am-12:30pm and 1:30-4:30pm. €4.80, students €3.80, under 16 €3.30.)

You can take the **train** from Grenoble to **Romans** (1hr., 11 per day, €10.50). Switch to a **La Régie Drôme bus** to Hauterives (☎ 04 75 02 30 42; 30min.; July-Aug. W 8am and 4pm, F 7:15am, 8am, 11:30am, and 4pm; Sept.-June M-Tu and Th 6:15pm, F 9:30, 11:30am, 4, 6:15pm; €4.40). **Driving** from Grenoble, take A48 north; at Voreppe, switch to A49 toward Romans. At Romans, take D538 north to Hauterives. (1hr.) From Lyon, head south on A7 and change to D538 at Vienne. Hauterives's **tourist office**, rue du Palais Idéal, provides info on the palais and surrounding region. (☎ 04 75 68 86 82; fax 04 75 68 92 96. Open daily Apr.-Sept. 10am-12:30pm and 1:30-6pm; Oct.-Nov. and Feb.-Mar. 10am-12:30pm and 1:30-5:30pm; Dec.-Jan. 10am-12:30pm and 1:30-4:30pm.)

CHAMBÉRY

The main attraction of Chambéry (pop. 57,000) is its magnificent château, settled by the savvy counts of Savoy in 1232. All traffic through the Alps passed through their stronghold, bringing the counts great influence and wealth. Today the château is run by the no-less-powerful French bureaucracy. Slightly off the beaten track, Chambéry is a good base for exploring the Lac du Bourget.

⌦ TRANSPORTATION

Trains: pl. de la Gare. Open daily 5am-10pm. To: **Annecy** (45min., 29 per day, €7.60); **Geneva** (1¼hr., 14 per day, €12.60); **Grenoble** (1 hr., 20 per day, €8.70); **Lyon** (1½hr., 20 per day, €13.30); **Paris** (3hr., 6 per day, €55-70.74). **Luggage storage** €4.50 per bag. Available M-F 8:30am-noon and 2-6pm.

Buses: Several companies run from the bus station (☎ 04 79 69 11 88), across from the train station. Slow option for visiting Alpine villages. To **Annecy** (1hr., 7 per day, €8) and **Grenoble** (1¾hr., 5 per day, €8.50). Office open M-F 6:15am-7:15pm, Sa 6:30am-12:30pm and 2:30-5:30pm.

Public Transportation: STAC, bd. de la Colonne (☎ 04 79 68 67 00). Runs daily 7:30am-7:30pm. Nearly all buses leave from the ticket and info kiosk at bd. de la Colonne, also bus stop "Eléphants." A bus leaves from the train station for **Aix-les-Bains** and the lakes (5 per day, July-Aug.; €1). Ticket €1, *carnet* of 10 €5.85, students €4.30. Kiosk open M-F 7:15am-12:15pm, Sa 8:30am-12:15pm and 2:30-5:30pm.

Taxi: Taxi Allô (☎ 04 79 69 11 12). 24hr.

Car Rental: Europcar, 21 av. Maréchal Leclerc (☎ 04 79 62 05 62), opposite the train station. Open M-F 8am-noon and 2-6:30pm, Sa 8am-noon and 2-6pm. AmEx/MC/V.

Bike Rental: Vélostation, 217 rue de la Gare (☎ 04 79 96 34 13 or 06 82 92 75 45; fax 04 79 96 36 85), just out of the train station. Amazingly cheap rentals: €2 per half-day, €4 per day, and €10 for 5 days. Open M-F 6:30am-8pm, Sa-Su 9am-7pm.

🔢 🛈 ORIENTATION AND PRACTICAL INFORMATION

Chambéry's *vieille ville* lies below and to the left of the train station, with the châteu in its bottom right corner. To reach the tourist office from the station, walk left on rue Sommeiller for one long block and cross the busy pl. du Centenaire to bd. de la Colonne. (5min.)

Tourist Office: 24 bd. de la Colonne (☎04 79 33 42 47; fax 04 79 85 71 39; www.chambery-tourisme.com). Maps (€3.10-8.90) and a brochure of numerous guided tours (€4-5, students €2.50-3.50). La Savoie booklets detail hiking, biking, mountain climbing, fishing, and skiing itineraries for the region. Wheelchair access. Open June 15-Sept. 15 M-Sa 9am-12:30pm and 1:30-7pm, Su 9:30am-12:30pm; Sept. 16-June 14 M-Sa 9am-noon and 1:30-6pm. In the same building, the **Agence Touristique Départementale** (☎04 79 85 12 45) distributes practical info on regional tourism.

Youth Center: Savoie Information Jeunesse, 79 pl. de la Gare (☎04 79 62 66 87; fax 04 79 69 98 48; www.infojeunes73.org), in front of the bus station. Staff can provide information on study, jobs, practical questions, housing, and leisure activities. There's also cheap **Internet** access. Open July and late Aug. M-F 9am-5pm; Sept.-June M-Th 9am-6pm, F 10am-5pm.

Laundromat: Laverie Automatique, 1 rue Doppet (☎04 79 25 18 33), across from the Musée des Beaux Arts. Open daily 7:30am-7pm. **Lavomatique,** 37 pl. Monge (☎04 79 62 02 00), across from sq. Jacques Lovie. Open daily 7am-10pm.

Police: 585 av. de la Boisse (☎04 79 62 84 00).

Hospital: Centre Hospitalier, pl. François-Chiron (☎04 79 96 50 50).

Internet Access: At the **Youth Center** (see above). €1.50 per hr. **Cyberarena,** 5 rue St-Barbe (☎04 79 68 90 93), close to the château. €2 per 15min., €3 per 30min., €5 per 1hr. Open July-Aug. M-F noon-11pm, Sa 1pm-midnight, Su 2-11pm; Sept.-June M-W and F 11am-11pm, Th 11am-7pm, Sa 1pm-midnight, Su 2-11pm.

Post Office: sq. Paul Vidal (☎04 79 96 69 14). **Currency exchange** with no commission on small sums. Open M-F 8am-7pm, Sa 8am-noon. **Poste Restante:** 73000 Chambéry Verney. **Postal Code:** 73000.

🛏 ACCOMMODATIONS AND CAMPING

The town center is packed with budget hotels, most in varying states of decay. Consider staying at the hostel in Aix-les-Bains, 30min. away by train and bus.

Hôtel du Château, 37 rue Jean-Pierre Veyrat (☎04 79 69 48 78). From the train station, cross the street and walk down rue de la Gare, passing the Musée des Beaux Arts, and continue down rue J.P. Veyrat. Homey rooms with curiously low beds, dim lighting, linoleum floors, and hardwood furniture. Shower and toilet in the hallways. Excellent location. Breakfast €3.80. Reception 7am-8pm. Singles and doubles €20; triples €30. ❶

Hôtel du Lion d'Or, 13 av. de la Boisse (☎04 79 69 04 96; fax 04 79 96 93 20), across from the station. Not the best neighborhood, but rooms have modern amenities. Breakfast €6. Reception 24hr. Singles €22, with shower and toilet €32; doubles €26/€37-42; triples €38/€49-54. MC/V. ❷

Hôtel Savoyard, 35 pl. Monge (☎04 79 33 36 55; fax 04 79 85 25 70; savoyard@noos.fr), on the southern end of the *vieille ville*. This small, 10-room hotel offers a calm atmosphere and modern bathrooms. All rooms with shower, toilet, and TV. Reception 7am-11pm. Reservations suggested July-Aug. and Sept. Singles €34; doubles €44; triples €55; quads €65. MC/V. ❸

Hôtel des Voyageurs, 3 rue Doppet (☎04 79 33 57 00). Hardwood floors and mushy mattresses. Breakfast €4.60. Reception 7am-11pm. Singles and doubles €19.90, with shower €23; quads €37/€43. ❷

Camping Le Savoy, Parc des Loisirs (☎/fax 04 79 72 97 31), in Challes-Les-Eaux, 6km away. From the station, take bus #8 (dir: Chignin) to "Aviation." Turn right; the site is 6min. up the road on your left. Next to a park and lake. Laundry €1.50. Reception 9am-noon and 2-10pm. Reservations suggested July-Aug. Open May-Sept. €3.05 per person, €2.30 per tent, €1.25 per car. Electricity €2.45. AmEx/MC/V. ❶

⚑ FOOD

Budget meals are easy to find around the once-rich **rue Croix d'Or** in the *vieille ville*. The town's market is held in **Les Halles,** pl. de Genève. (Open Sa 7am-noon.) A **Monoprix supermarket** is on pl. du 8 Mai. (☎04 79 33 01 09. Open M-Sa 8:30am-7:30pm.) The cheapest meals in town are at the **Casino Cafeteria ❶,** 1 rue Claude Martin, where €6 will get you a 3-course menu. (☎04 79 33 46 98. Entrees €1-4. Hot plates €4-7. Open M-Th and Su 11:30am-9pm, F-Sa until 9:30pm.) 🗷**Le Bistrot ❸,** 6 rue du Théâtre, serves well-priced, delicious Savoyard specialties beneath antique mirrors and chandeliers. Try their signature *rebluchonade des alpages* (€14), a *fondue* served with a heaping ham-and-bacon salad, and endless amounts of potatoes. (☎04 79 75 10 78. *Entrée*, main dish, and dessert €22. Open Tu-Sa noon-2pm and 7-10pm.)

◎ SIGHTS

CHÂTEAU DES DUCS DE SAVOIE. For three centuries, Savoy's power emanated from this 13th-century château. At their height, the dukes commanded a realm that stretched from Neufchâtel to Nice and from Turin to Lyon. Enter through the intimidating 15th-century **Porte de l'Eglise St-Dominique.** The chapel has a two-faced exterior, the result of an 18th-century fire and its subsequent rebuilding and repainting in a *trompe l'œil* style. Invasions by French kings eventually convinced the dukes to transfer their capital, and Jesus's alleged burial cloth (kept in the chapel from 1453-1578), to Turin, Italy, where the shroud has remained since. In the absence of this famous relic, Ste-Chapelle's largest attraction is its set of 70 bells, the largest and loveliest in all of Europe. The interior of the chapel, the underground rooms, and the Préfecture can only be visited on a guided tour. *(Concerts every Sa 10:30am and 5:30pm. 1hr. tours in French July-Aug. M-Sa 10:30am, 2:30, 3:30, 4:30pm; May-June and Sept. Sa-Su 2:30pm. €4, students €2.50. Oct.-Apr. 2hr. tours, Sa-Su 2:30pm; include a visit of the vieille ville. €5, students €3.50. Call ahead for tours in English.)*

MUSÉE DES CHARMETTES. This museum was once the summer house of Jean-Jacques Rousseau, who sojourned here from 1736 to 1742 in semi-debauchery with the older and wiser Mme. de Warens, the divorcée entrusted to convert J-J to Catholicism. In *Confessions*, Rousseau recounts the episode as the happiest time of his life. The little house, surrounded by reconstructions of 18th-century gardens, later became a place of pilgrimage for 19th-century writers. The scenic route up makes reaching the peak all the more enjoyable. From pl. de la République, follow rue de la République, which becomes rue Jean-Jacques Rousseau and eventually chemin des Charmettes. From there, it's a 15min. walk uphill along a bubbling brook. Turn right after the museum sign. You can get there by bus, which leaves 30min. before the shows from in front of the tourist office (round-trip €4); reservations are necessary for transport and recommended for the shows. *(☎04 79 33 39 44. Shows W and F July 17-31 9pm; Aug. 8:30pm; 2hr.; €17, students €15. Musée open Apr.-Sept. W-M 10am-noon and 2-6pm; Oct.-Mar. W-M 10am-noon and 2-4:30pm. €3.10, students €1.50.)*

MUSÉE SAVOISIEN. Housed in a 13th-century Franciscan monastery, this museum is an ethnography of the Savoy region, with crafts, maps, ecclesiastical paraphernalia, and the like. The exhibits move chronologically from prehistoric pottery to the present, highlighting château life and the pivotal role of Savoy during WWII. To get there, leave the tourist office by the back door, turn left on bd. de la Colonne and walk past the Fontaine des Eléphants. *(Sq. de Lannoy de Bissy. ☎ 04 79 33 44 48. Open W-M 10am-noon and 2-6pm. €3.10, students €1.50.)*

MUSÉE DES BEAUX ARTS. This small museum displays a representative collection of Italian and other European paintings from the 17th to 19th-centuries. *(Pl. du Palais de Justice. ☎ 04 79 33 75 03. Open W-M 10am-noon and 2-6pm. €3.10, students €1.50.)*

LA FONTAINE DES ELEPHANTS. The best-known monument in Chambéry was erected in 1838 to honor the Comte de Boigne. After leading military expeditions in India, the Count returned with the spoils to his beloved Chambéry and spent most of it on public works for the city. True to its city's history, the fountain fuses East and West. Elephants stand in the traditional form of the Savoy cross, spouting showers of water and carrying de Boigne on their back. Locals call them "les quatre sans culs," the buttless four. *(From the tourist office, take a left on bd. de la Colonne.)*

THE VIEILLE VILLE. Chambéry's *vieille ville*, with its sober facades, arcades, and courtyard porticos, has a distinctly Italian flavor; it is painted in the colors of Sardinia, once a Savoy holding. A number of trans-alpine *hôtels particuliers* line rue Croix-d'Or, pl. St-Léger, and rue Basse du Chateau, a tiny 11th-century alley overhung by a modest bridge. Take a look at the courtyard of **#70 rue Croix d'Or;** built in the early 16th century, the hybrid dwelling has Gothic windows, Renaissance door-frames, and a spiral staircase. The **rue de la Juiverie** is lined with stately onetime residences of dignitaries and ambassadors. Their elegance conceals a gruesome past. Accused of poisoning the town's water fountains when the Black Death broke out in 1349, Chambéry's Jewish population was confined to this street while awaiting trial. Angry townspeople massacred the community before they ever got a trial; the survivors were blamed for the incident and killed.

AIX-LES-BAINS AND LAC DU BOURGET

Colonized by the Romans for its sulphurous hotsprings, the thermal station and spa extraordinaire Aix-les-Bains (pop. 26,000) is like a voyage in time—forward about forty years or so, to your own Golden Years. Virtually the only tourists here are aching arthritics undergoing treatment at the largest medicinal baths in France. These *curistes* keep prices happily low, and make Aix-les-Bains a pleasant base for visiting France's other premier bath, along the Lac de Bourget, a château-lined lake just 2km away favored by sunbathers and windsurfers.

🚆 PRACTICAL INFORMATION. Trains leave from pl. de la Gare. (Station open daily 5am-11pm; info and reservations open M-Sa 5:15am-9:30pm, Su 7am-9:30pm.) To: Chambéry (10min., 44 per day, €2.60); Annecy (40min., 32 per day, €6); Grenoble (1hr., 16 per day, €10.30); Lyon (1½hr., 7 per day, €14.60); Paris (3½hr., 9 per day, €55-70). **Buses** (☎ 04 79 69 11 88) leave from the train station. To Annecy (45min., 7 per day, €6.80) and Chambéry (20min., July-Aug. 7 per day, €2.70). There's a **taxi** stand at the train station (☎ 04 79 35 08 05; €6-7 to lake).

Aix's center is 5min. east of the station; the lake is a 40min. walk in the opposite direction. To get to the **tourist office,** pl. Maurice Mollard, cross bd. Wilson, head down av. de Gaulle, cross pl. Moulin, and walk along the park's edge for one block; it will be on your left next to the *Hôtel de Ville.* The friendly, English-speaking staff makes hotel reservations. (☎ 04 79 88 68 00; fax 04 79 88 68 01; www.aixlesbains.com. Open June-Aug. daily 9am-6:30pm; Apr.-May and Sept. 9am-12:15pm and 2-6pm; Oct.-Nov. and Mar. M-Sa 9am-noon and 2-6pm; Dec.-Feb. closes 5:30pm.) **Annex** at Grand Port, pl. Herriot. (☎ 04 79 34 15 80. Open June-Sept. daily 10am-12:30pm and 2-6:30pm; May Sa-Su 10am-12:30pm and 2-6pm.) Access the **Internet** at **Brasserie le Pavillon**, 35 bd. Wilson. (☎ 04 79 61 66 10. €4.50 per 30min. Open M-Sa 8am-1:30am, Su 8am-1pm.) The **post office,** av. Victoria, **exchanges currency.** (☎ 04 79 35 15 10. Open M-F 8am-7pm, Sa 8am-noon.) **Postal code:** 73100.

⌐⌐ ACCOMMODATIONS AND FOOD. The **Auberge de Jeunesse (HI) ❶**, prom. de Sierroz, is by the lake. Take bus #2 from the station (dir: Plage d'Aix; €1; last bus 7pm) to "Camping," and walk 3min. along the stream away from the lake. A taxi there costs €6. The hostel accommodates large groups in its 4-bed dorms and huge backyard. Simple but functional rooms off retro, multicolored stairways. (☎ 04 79 88 32 88; fax 04 79 61 14 05; aix-les-bains@fuaj.org. Kitchen and Internet. Breakfast included. Dinner €8.40. Sheets €2.90. Laundry €3. Reception July-Aug. daily 7-10am and 2-10pm; Sept.-June 7-10am and 6-10pm; call ahead to leave baggage earlier. Lockout 10am-2pm. Closed Nov. to early Feb. Bunks €13. MC/V.) **Hôtel Broisin ❷**, 10 ruelle du Revet, in a quiet courtyard off rue des Bains, charms guests with its ideal location and friendly 18-year owner. Simple rooms with TV. (☎ 04 79 35 06 15; fax 04 79 88 10 10. Breakfast €4. Reception 6:30am-8pm. Reservations recommended. Open Mar.-Nov. Singles €21.65, with toilet and shower €28.20; doubles €24.70/€31.25. Extra bed €10.65. AmEx/MC/V.) **Hôtel Central Clementine ❷**, 6 rue Henri Murger, has large rooms with TVs and firm beds. Hall shower. (☎ 04 79 88 14 10; fax 04 79 88 55 25. Breakfast €4.27. Reception 7:30am-2:30pm and 6:30-9:30pm. Singles and doubles €20, with toilet €23. Extra bed €6. MC/V.) **Camping International du Sierroz ❶**, next to the hostel. Cheerful Anglophone staff runs a lakeside site with volleyball, ping-pong, and play rooms. (☎/fax 04 79 61 21 43. Reception M-Sa 8am-12:30pm and 2-6:30pm, Su 8am-noon and 3:30-6:30pm. Open Mar. 15-Nov. 15. No reservations. €2.60-3.15 per person; €3.70-6.75 for tent and car, €6.70-10.40 with electricity; €0.80 per extra tent. MC/V.)

The **Monoprix supermarket** is at 179 rue de Genève, near the *centre ville*. (☎ 04 79 35 22 15. Open July-Aug. M-Sa 8:30am-7:30pm, Su 9-11:45am; Sept.-June M-Sa 8:30am-12:30pm and 2:30-7:30pm, Su 9-11:45am.) **Marché Plus** is at 19 sq. Alfred Boucher, a bit closer to the lake. (☎ 04 79 35 02 69. Open M-Sa 7am-9pm, Su 8am-noon.) Morning **markets** are held on pl. Clemenceau. (Open W 8am-5pm, Sa 8am-1pm.) **Grand Port** is dotted with restaurants with lake views and meals of the lake's scaly inhabitants. For a sit-down meal near *centre ville*, try **Le Passé ❶**, 6 rue de Dauphin, just off rue des Bains. Enjoy a wide selection of pizzas (€5.50-9), pastas (€5-8), and meats (€8-17) in the light-yellow fresco interior or on the calm terrace. (☎ 04 79 88 30 88. Menus €11-18. Open May-Oct. daily noon-2pm and 7-11pm; Dec.-Feb. M-Sa noon-2pm and 7-11pm. MC/V.)

◪ SIGHTS. In its heyday, Aix's **Thermes Nationaux** (☎ 04 79 35 38 50) was a luxury spa known the world over; its guests included Queen Victoria and Lamartine. Nowadays, just about any invalid (with necessary medical forms) can take a dip in the *piscine thermale* (thermal pool). Non-seniors can only experience the modern baths and the **Thermes Romains** with a rather dry tour in French. (1½hr.; Tu-Sa 3pm, buy tickets on the 3rd floor by 2:30pm; €4.) Much more appealing is the **Musée Faure**, 10 bd. des Côtes, devoted to impressionist art. This 19th-century Genoese villa has ballerinas sketched by Degas, a large room devoted to Rodin, and several Pissarro landscapes. (☎ 04 76 61 06 57. Open M and W-F 10am-noon and 1:30-6pm, Sa-Su 10am-noon and 1:30-6pm. €3.50, students €2, under 16 free.)

The *thermes* may be inaccessible to some, but the **Lac du Bourget** welcomes all. France's largest natural lake is twice as cold as the thermal baths, but its mountainous scenery is more pleasant than their wrinkled vistas. To get there from town, follow av. de Genève as it turns into av. du Grand Port, or take bus #2 from the baths or the train station (dir: Plage d'Aix; €1). There are two beaches at opposite ends of the Grand Port, **plage Municipale** (€2.30) and **plage de Mémars** (free). The **Centre Nautique**, pl. Daniel-Rops, has a heated pool on its private beach. (☎04 79 61 48 80. €4.40, under 18 €3.30. Open daily 10am-7:30pm.) **Nautis-Aix**, in Grand Port, rents **motorboats**. (☎04 79 88 24 34. €35-70 per hr. Open daily 9am-7pm. MC/V.) The opposite side of the lake has fewer swimming spots, but is more scenic and great for **biking.** Rent high quality, dual-suspension bikes from **Sports Aix-treme,** 60 av. Franklin Roosevelt, off av. de Grand Port, 20min. by foot from the town center. (☎04 79 88 38 82. €18 per half-day, €29 per day. Open Tu-Sa 9am-noon and 2-7pm. MC/V.) The Aix-les-Bains tourist office distributes rough maps of the lake.

⬛ DAYTRIP FROM AIX-LES-BAINS

ABBAYE D'HAUTECOMBE

Give or take a few counts, the entire House of Savoy is entombed in the Abbaye d'Hautecombe. The only part of this former Benedictine abbey open to visitors is its flamboyant Gothic **church,** the lavish result of eight centuries of necropolistic excess. Poor, exiled Umberto II, the last Savoy king, was the most recent occupant; he was stuffed inside in 1983, among 200 statues and 40 other tombs. One masterpiece is a marble statue of Marie Christine de Bourbon, who oversaw the church's restoration; the intricate sculpture, taken from a single block of stone, was eight years in the making. A marble *pietà*, the church's prized possession, is given pride of place in the chapel to the left of the choir. The exuberant interior can only be visited with an audioguide. (☎04 79 54 26 12; www.chemin-neuf.org/hautecombe. Open M and W-Sa 10-11:30am and 2-5pm, Su 10:30am-noon and 2-5pm. English by request. Free.) The abbey is an ideal biking daytrip; follow the Tour du Lac signs north to Groisin, where you'll see signs for the abbey. (Round-trip 3hr.) There's also a **boat** from Grand Port. (☎04 79 88 92 09; www.gwel.com. Round-trip 2½hr. July-Aug. W-M 4 per day, Sept.-June W-M 1-2 per day; €10.10.)

ANNECY

You may forget Annecy is a real town when you walk through its *vieille ville*. With its narrow cobblestone streets, winding canals, turreted castle, and overstuffed flower boxes, Annecy looks more like a fiberglass fairy-tale fabrication than a modern city with a metropolitan population of 50,300. Bordering these man-made charms are massive mountains and the purest lake in Europe, which together provide a stunning sight for both windsurfers below and paragliders above.

▭ TRANSPORTATION

Trains: pl. de la Gare. Station open daily 5am-10:30pm. Ticket window open M 4:45am-9:15pm, Tu-Sa 6:10am-9:15pm, Su 6:40am-10:40pm. **Luggage storage** open July-Aug. daily 8am-7:15pm; Sept.-June M-Sa 8am-noon and 2-5pm (€4.50). To: **Chambéry** (45min., 25 per day, €7.50); **Chamonix** (2½hr., 7 per day, €16.70); **Grenoble** (2hr., 12 per day, €14.10); **Lyon** (2hr., 9 per day, €18); **Nice** (7-9hr., 2 per day, €54.20); **Paris** (4hr., 8 per day, €57.60-72.40).

Buses: adjacent to the train station. Office open M-F 7:45-11am and 2-7:15pm, Sa 7:45-11am. **Autocars Frossard** (☎04 50 45 73 90) runs to **Chambéry** (1¼hr., 6 per day, €8.50); **Geneva** (1¼hr., 6 per day, €9); **Lyon** (3½hr., 2 per day, €16.40).

ALPS

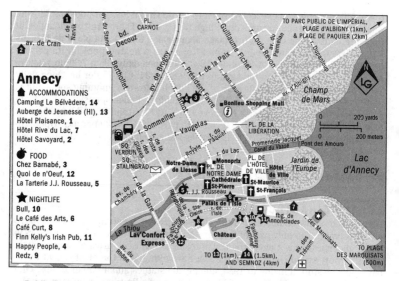

Annecy

🏠 ACCOMMODATIONS
Camping Le Bélvèdere, **14**
Auberge de Jeunesse (HI), **13**
Hôtel Plaisance, **1**
Hôtel Rive du Lac, **7**
Hôtel Savoyard, **2**

🍎 FOOD
Chez Barnabé, **3**
Quoi de n'Oeuf, **12**
La Tarterie J.J. Rousseau, **5**

⭐ NIGHTLIFE
Bull, **10**
Le Café des Arts, **6**
Café Curt, **8**
Finn Kelly's Irish Pub, **11**
Happy People, **4**
Redz, **9**

Public Transportation: SIBRA (☎ 04 50 10 04 04). Tickets €1, *carnet* of 8 €6.50. Info booth across from the train station open M-F 8:30am-7pm, Sa 8:30am-6pm. Extensive service; July-Aug. summer line stops at the hostel.

Bike, Ski, and In-line Skate Rental: Little Big Shop, 80 rue Carnot (☎ 04 50 67 42 13). Bikes €10.50 per half-day, €15 per day. Ski, boot, and pole packages €14.50-25.50 per day. Open M 9am-noon, Tu-Sa 9am-noon and 2-7pm. MC/V.

Golf Miniature de l'Imperial, 2 av. du Petit Port (☎ 04 50 66 04 99), beside plage de Paquier. In-line skates €5 per hr., €8 per half-day, €9 per day. Bicycles €8 per half-day, €15 per day. Open daily 9am-7pm.

Taxis: at the station (☎ 04 50 45 05 67). 24hr.

🔧 🚻 ORIENTATION AND PRACTICAL INFORMATION

Most activity centers around the lake, southeast of the train station. The canal runs east-west through the old town; the elevated château is on one side and the main shopping area, closer to the center of Annecy, is on the other. To reach the tourist office from the train station, take the underground passage to rue Sommeiller. Walk straight to rue Vaugelas, turn left, and follow rue Vaugelas for four blocks. The tourist office is straight ahead, in the large Bonlieu shopping mall.

Tourist Office: 1 rue Jean Jaurès (☎ 04 50 45 00 33 or 04 50 45 56 66; fax 04 50 51 87 20; ancytour@noos.fr), at pl. de la Libération. Detailed maps and info on hiking, hotels, campgrounds, rural lodgings, excursions, and climbing. Ask for the bilingual Annecy Guide, which describes nearby sights. The Sentiers Forestiers guide (€3.05) details hiking paths in the Semnoz forest. Comprehensive French topo-guide of the region is available (€9.60). **Tours** of the *vieille ville* (2hr.; July-Aug. French tours M-Sa 3:30pm, English tours M and F 4pm; €5.20). Office open July-Aug. M-Sa 9am-6:30pm, Su 9am-12:30pm and 1:45-6:30pm; Sept.-June daily 9am-12:30pm and 1:45-6pm.

Youth Center: Bureau Information Jeunesse, 1 rue Jean Jaurès (☎ 04 50 33 87 40; fax 04 50 33 00 87; infojeunes@ville-annecy.fr), in the Bonlieu center. The staff has info on study options, housing, jobs, practical issues, and leisure activities. Free **Internet** access. Open M 3-7pm, Tu-F 12:30-7pm, Sa 10am-noon.

Laundromat: Lav'Confort Express, 6 rue de la Gare, across the canal. Open daily 7am-9pm.

Internet: Youth Center (free; see above). **Syndrome Cyber-café,** 3bis av. de Chevenes (☎04 50 45 39 75), near the train station. €2 per 15min., €6 per hr. Open July-Aug. daily noon-10pm; Sept.-June M-W noon-7:30pm, Th-Sa noon-10pm. **L'Emallerie,** fbg. des Annonciades (☎04 50 10 18 91), in the *vieille ville*, has American keyboards. €1.50 per 15min., €6 per hr. Open June-Aug. daily 10am-8pm; Sept.-May M-Sa 10:30am-12:30pm and 2:30-7:30pm.

Hospital: 1 av. de Trésum (☎04 50 88 33 33).

Police: 17 rue des Marquisats (☎04 50 52 32 00).

Post Office: 4bis rue des Glières (☎04 50 33 68 20), off rue de la Poste, down the street from the train station. **Currency exchange** at good rates, no commission. Open M-F 8:30am-6:30pm, Sa 8am-noon. **Poste Restante:** 74011. **Postal code:** 74000.

⚑ ACCOMMODATIONS AND CAMPING

Annecy's priciest accommodations lie in the charming *vieille ville* and by the lake. Budget travelers should ascend to the top-notch, hillside hostel. A couple of budget hotels behind the train station have excellent value but dull scenery. Reservations are recommended, especially during ski season and the summer months.

▓ **Auberge de Jeunesse "La Grande Jeanne" (HI),** rte. de Semnoz (☎04 50 45 33 19; fax 04 50 52 77 52; annecy@fuaj.org). The summer line (dir: Semnoz) leaves the station and drops you off at the hostel (daily 7am-6:30pm; July-Aug. 6 per day, June and Sept. Sa-Su 6 per day; €1). Or take bus #1 (dir: Marquisats) from the station to "Hôpital," in front of the police station. Walk straight on av. de Tresum, away from the lake, and follow the signs pointing to Semnoz. Take a left onto bd. de la Corniche and a right onto chemin du Belvédère for a steep ascent to the hostel. (15min.) Beautiful modern building perched between the forest and the lake fosters a fun-loving atmosphere. 4- to 5-bed dorms are tiny but all have shower. Single-sex rooms available. Game room, kitchen, TV room, small bar, and laundry. Breakfast included. Dinner €8. Sheets €2.70. Reception Apr.-Nov. 8am-noon and 3-10pm; Jan. 15-Mar. 8am-noon and 5-10pm. Reservations suggested June-Aug., but require you to pay half in advance; reserve via the Internet (www.iyhf.net). Closed Dec.-Jan. 14. Bunks €12.70. MC/V. ❶

Hôtel Savoyard, 41 av. de Cran (☎04 50 57 08 08), in a pretty Savoyard mansion with courtyard. From the train station, exit left, walk around the station to av. Berthollet, and turn left again on av. de Cran; it will be on your left. Caring managers let rustic, spacious rooms with grandmotherly floral wallpaper and wooden floors. Reception 7am-10pm. Breakfast €4. Open May-Oct. Singles and doubles €20, with shower and bath €27-35; triples €25/€31-41; quads with bath €41. ❷

Hôtel Plaisance, 17 rue de Narvik (☎/fax 04 50 57 30 42), a right off av. de Cran (see above directions to Hôtel Savoyard). Charming manager caters to international clientele with intimate rooms, woodsy breakfast and TV salon. Ultra clean and calm. Reception 7am-midnight. Breakfast €3.90. Showers €2. Singles and doubles €23, with shower and toilet €32; triples €38.20; quads €45.80. MC/V. ❷

Hôtel Rive du Lac, 6 rue des Marquisats (☎04 50 51 32 85; fax 04 50 45 77 40). Dark rooms and sinking beds yearn for renovations, but the location right across from the lake and *vieille ville* is ideal. Reception 7am-9pm. Breakfast €3.85. Showers €1, free for longer stays. Singles and doubles €24.40; triples and quads €38.15. MC/V. ❷

Camping le Bélvèdere, 8 rte. de Semnoz (☎04 50 45 48 30; fax 04 50 51 81 62; camping@ville-annecy.fr), just above the youth hostel. Pretty site by the woods. TV, ping-pong, pétanque, and forested hiking trails nearby. Reception July-Aug. 8am-9pm; Apr. 15-June and Sept.-Oct. 15 8am-8pm. July-Aug. reserve via email or fax. Open Apr. 15-Oct. 15. Sept.-June 1-2 people, tent, and car €9.90-10.70, July-Aug. €13. Extra person €3.80-4.60; extra tent €1.55-2.30. Electricity €2.30. Laundry €5.35. MC/V. ❶

ALPS

◘ FOOD

Annecy's *vieille ville* is lined with affordable restaurants, each one more charming than the next. Fill your picnic basket with the soft local *reblochon* cheese at the morning **markets** on pl. Ste-Claire (Tu, F, Su 8am-noon) and on bd. Taine. (Open Sa 8am-noon.) Grocery stores line av. de Parmelan. A **Monoprix supermarket** fills the better part of pl. de Notre-Dame. (☎04 50 45 23 60. Open M-Sa 8:30am-7:30pm.) There's a **Casino** supermarket at 10 rue des Glières, across from the post office. (☎04 50 51 38 31. Open M-F 8am-12:15pm and 3-7:30pm, Sa 8am-12:15pm and 3-7pm.) The cleverly-named and popular ▧**Quoi de n'Oeuf ❸**, 19 fbg. Ste-Claire, serves plentiful portions on an adorable terrace in the *vieille ville*. Eggheads jump at the €10.50 *tartiflette*, salad, and dessert. (☎04 50 45 75 42. Open M-Sa noon-2pm and 7-9:45pm. MC/V.) For an escape from fondue, try **La Tarterie J.J. Rousseau ❷**, 14 rue J.J. Rousseau. The €9.10 menu includes *tarte salée* (including salmon, chicken, vegetarian, and cheese creations), *tarte sucrée*, and drink. (☎04 50 45 36 25. Open M-Tu noon-2pm, W-Sa noon-2pm and 7-9pm. MC/V.) With so many lovely gardens around, picnics here are a great option. Paper-bag it at **Chez Barnabé ❶**, 29 rue Sommeiller. (☎04 50 45 90 62. Salad bar €2.70-5.30. Homemade hot dishes €2.10-5.30. Sandwiches €2.50-3.10. Pizzas €1.60-2. Open M-Sa 10am-7:15pm.)

◔ SIGHTS

VIEILLE VILLE. A stroll through the *vieille ville* will cost you several rolls of film and a hundred sighs. **The Palais de l'Isle**, a 13th-century château first occupied by the counts of Geneva when their hometown came under Episcopal control, is a beautiful turreted building. Located strategically on a narrow island in the canal, it served as a prison, last used to jail Resistance fighters during WWII, whose impassioned carvings dot the walls. (*☎04 50 33 87 30. Open June-Sept. daily 10:30am-6pm; Oct.-May W-M 10am-noon and 2-5pm. €3.10, students €0.80.*) Straddling the town's narrowest canal, the large and bare **Eglise St-Maurice**, consecrated in 1442, is well-known for the rare 15th-century painting on the choir's left wall, which marks the tomb of Philibert de Monthoux, one-time Annecy noble. This macabre mural of a decomposing corpse—finished two years before its patron's death—is thought to reflect anxiety over the Hundred Years' War. Beneath the towers of the castle on the opposite side of the canal, **quai Perrière, rue de L'Isle**, and **rue Ste-Claire** are some of Annecy's most charming streets, despite their abundant arcades.

CANARD! Lac d'Annecy is the purest lake in Europe. Well, except for that recent infestation of the *puce du canard* (duck flea). If you notice little red, itchy bumps on your skin after a swim, blame the *puces*, who penetrate human skin in search of a warm home. Mosquito bite-like symptoms appear in affected individual for 4-5 days, occasionally causing fever. Eventually, the parasite dies, without long-term consequences.

The duck flea became a problem in 1996, when local ducks stopped migrating in the winter, choosing to settle year-round in Annecy because of higher global temperatures and artificial feeding by humans. The parasite originates within the ducks, whose infested eggs are often eaten by snails. Adult parasites re-enter the water to find a warmer home, namely your arm.

Infestation is worst from June to September, when warm temperatures are ideal for parasitic growth and survival. In summer 2002, cases were reported at every beach around the lake; especially Plage d'Albigny. Locals have noticed a decline in beach crowds and overall tourism. Avoid your chance of meeting the survivors by: (1) not swimming when it's very hot; (2) staying within 2m of shore; (3) using sunscreen and (4) showering after swimming.

GARDENS. Graced by manicured hedges, fountains, and the occasional long-necked swan, the shaded **Jardin de l'Europe** is Annecy's pride and joy. At its north side, the **Pont des Amours** (Lover's Bridge) connects the European gardens to the **Champ de Mars,** a grand esplanade frequented by picnickers, sunbathers, and frisbee-throwers. Annecy isn't one to gloat, but such gardens have led it to victory in the national *Ville Fleurie* (Flower City) contest three times in the last decade.

THE LAKE. After a stroll through the bustling streets, you may want to swim in Annecy's cold, crystalline lake. In summer, free **Plage d'Albigny,** two to three kilometers up av. d'Albigny, draws tourists and locals for windsurfing, sailing, and kayaking, as well as eating at trendy coastal restaurants. The smaller and more crowded **Plage des Marquisats,** south of the city down rue des Marquisats, permits swimming. The Club de Voile Française on the lake rents a limited selection of watercraft. Rent **Pedal boats** at one of the numerous companies along the port or, for better deals, on the south side of the Champ de Mars. *(€8 per 30min., €12 per hr.; lake tours €6-14.)* For €3.50, you can frolic in the **Parc Public de l'Impérial,** an aquatic wonderland with waterslides, sailing, tennis, swimming, and a casino. *(20min. up av. d'Albigny beside plage d'Albigny. ☎ 04 50 23 11 82. Open May-Sept. daily 11am-7:30pm.)* The lake is most breathtaking from above. Annecy is one of the best places in the world for **paragliding** *(parapenting)*, and there are plenty of companies to fuel the hobby (most have comparable prices). With **Takamaka,** little Daedali run off cliffs and fly above the crystal-blue lake waters. *(Tandem €80; 5-day course €427.)*

CHÂTEAU. The 12th-century château towers over Annecy, a short but steep climb from the *vieille ville.* Once a stronghold of Genevan counts, the castle and its imposing parapets now contain slightly dull archaeological and artistic exhibits. Inside the main building, the museum welcome desk occupies an enormous hearth that once fed a lively court. The 15th-century wooden statuary in the next room is interesting, as is the original ceiling of the banquet hall upstairs, the lone survivor of a 1952 fire. The **Observatoire Régional des Lacs Alpins,** in the rear of the castle, has exhibits about lake ecosystems, an aquarium, and a view that trumps every other attraction. *(☎ 04 50 33 87 30. Open June-Sept. daily 10:30am-6pm; Oct.-May W-M 10am-noon and 2-5pm. Château €4.60, students €1.50; entrance to grounds free.)*

█ HIKING

Although it may be hard to tear yourself away from Annecy's man-made charms, the nearby Alpine forests shelter excellent hiking and biking trails. Dozens of breathtaking hikes begin on the **Semnoz,** a limestone mountain south of the city. The **Office National des Forêts** (☎ 04 50 23 84 10) distributes a color map, *Sentiers Forestiers,* with several routes (€3.05 at the tourist office or hostel). The *Guide Pratique* also has lots of info on outdoor recreation. One of the best hikes begins at the **Basilique de la Visitation,** close to the hostel. If you're staying in town, take bus A to its terminus, "Visitation." From the basilica, continue along the road until you reach a small parking lot. Follow signs for "la Forêt du Crêt du Maure." Take the easy Ste-Catherine trail in a meandering circle around the Semnoz forest and past breathtaking views. (2hr.) After about an hour, the trail intersects with the red-and-yellow-marked **GR96,** on which long-haulers sometimes opt for a 38km circuit of the lake. An exquisite, scenic 16km *piste cyclable* (bike route) hugs the eastern shore of the lake. At the end of the piste, the entire loop can be completed on the main road (D909a), where you should be wary of traffic. The tourist office has a free lake map that includes the bike route and some departure points for hikes. The **Bureau des Guides** and **Takamaka,** 17 fbg. Ste-Claire, run excursions for all mountaineering activities, including hiking, biking, rock-climbing, ice-climbing, paragliding, and canyoning. (☎04 50 45 60 61; www.takamaka.fr. Open July-Aug. daily 9am-7pm; Sept.-June M-F 9am-noon and 2-6pm. Hikes €20 per half-day, €30 per day. Canyoning €45-80. Sign up the night before. MC/V.)

🎵 🎭 ENTERTAINMENT AND FESTIVALS

After a hard day shooting the rapids or gliding through the sky, relax at the bars lining the canal in the *vieille ville* or the lake.

Le Café des Arts, 4 pass. de l'Isle, is an artsy bar with a choice spot opposite the illuminated island castle. (☎04 50 51 56 40. Beer €1.10-3.90. Open daily 8:30am-2am.)

Café Curt, 35 rue Ste-Claire, is typically crowded with students and backpackers, who create an easy-going atmosphere. Wine €1.30-3. Kronenbourg €2. A fine selection of cognac €5-55. Open June-Sept. daily 10am-2am; Oct.-May daily 10am-1am.

Finn Kelly's Irish Pub, 10 fbg. des Annonciades (☎04 50 51 29 40), is another example of the great Irish bars of southern France. Spacious, well-decorated interior with a giant TV, pool table, dart board, books, and the requisite James Joyce picture. Happy Hour 6:30-8pm with buy one drink, get one free. Draft beer €3. Open daily 3pm-3am.

Redz, 14 rue Perrière (☎04 50 45 17 13), is the flashy sports car of bars, drawing an older clientele with various theme nights and DJs nightly June-Aug. Beers €2.40-6. Cocktails €9-16. Open Apr.-Oct. daily 11am-3am; Nov.-Mar. 5pm-3am.

Bull, 8 fbg. des Annonciades (☎04 50 45 32 89), centrally-located, is a late-night local hangout. Cover F-Sa €8, includes one drink. Karaoke W. Open Tu-Sa 10:30pm-5am.

Happy People (☎04 50 51 08 66), 48 rue Carnot, is a gay and lesbian disco that lives up to its name. Wild nights are the norm, perhaps because of the pitch-black sex room out back. Alcohol €9-12. Cover F-Sa €12; includes one drink. Open daily 11pm-5am.

Performing arts and films are the realm of the **Théâtre d'Annecy,** in the Bonlieu Mall across from the tourist office. (☎04 50 33 44 11. Tickets €15-23, students €11.50-20.) *Fête* fetishists can pick up schedules at the tourist office. The granddaddy of them all is the **Fête du Lac,** the first Saturday in August, with fireworks and water shows (€6-41.50).

AROUND LAC D'ANNECY

A sumptuous 12th-century **château** across the lake from Annecy marks the birthplace of St. Bernard de Menthon, who made his name in the business of dog-breeding. His ridiculously wealthy descendants still live in the castle, but the lower floors—including a walnut-paneled library, music salon, and 14th-century bedroom—are open to the public. (☎04 50 60 12 05. Open July-Aug. daily noon-6pm; May-June and Sept. F-Su 2-6pm. €5.50. Weekend tours in period dress, €6.)

Ten kilometers west of Annecy is the spectacular **Gorges du Fier,** a canyon etched by water erosion. You can explore the area on a 256m long suspended walkway. (Info ☎04 50 46 23 07. Open June 15-Sept. 10 daily 9am-7pm; Mar. 15-June 14 and Sept. 11-Oct. 15 9am-noon and 2-6pm. €4.20.) The trip is worthwhile mainly if you check out the **Château de Montrottier,** 5min. from the canyon entrance. The castle, formerly owned by the region's foremost art collectors, displays centuries-old Asian costumes, armor, and pottery. (☎04 50 46 23 02. Open June-Aug. daily 10am-1pm and 2-7pm; Mar. 15-May and Sept. W-M 10am-1pm and 2-6pm; Oct. 1-15 W-M 2-6pm. €5.35, students €4.60.) To get there, take **SIBRA** minibus A from the train station to "Poisy-Moiry" (30min., 5 per day, €1), and follow signs for **Lovagny** to the gorges. (3km.) If you would rather avoid the walk, **Voyages Crolard** runs a bus tour that includes admission to the gorges and the château (☎04 50 45 00 56. July-Aug. W 2pm, return 7pm; €18).

Talloires, 13km from Annecy, is a good starting point for the 1hr. hike to the impressive waterfalls at **La Cascade d'Angon** and to the beautiful gardens of the **Ermitage de St-Germain.** To reach the waterfalls, take the Closettaz path out of the village and follow the signs. The trail passes under the raging 100m high torrent and then climbs to the top. (1½hr.) Ask the tourist office in Annecy or Talloires about boat rides from Annecy to Talloires. (Talloires tourist office ☎04 50 60 70 64; fax 04 50 60 76 59.) South of Annecy, **Doussard** is notable for being the better-known lake's source and for its surrounding nature preserves. (Tourist office ☎04 50 44 30 45; fax 04 50 44 81 75.) Nearby **St-Jorioz** is known for its great mountain views. (Tourist office ☎04 50 68 61 82; fax 04 50 68 96 11.)

The smaller villages on the Lac d'Annecy, within 20km of Annecy and accessible by bus, make for excellent daytrips. **Voyages Crolard** buses depart from the train station, the bus stop in front of the tourist office, and near plage d'Albigny, and circle the lake. (☎04 50 45 08 12; www.voyages-crolard.com; 10 per day, Su less frequently; tickets €2.65-3.05.) D909 also circles the lake, intersecting N508 at Doussard on the southern point of the lake.

The nearest **skiing resort** is **La Clusaz,** 32km away, with 130km of trails and 56 lifts. Contact the **tourist office** in La Clusaz for info. (☎04 50 32 65 00; fax 04 50 32 65 01; www.laclusaz.com.) There is a decent **youth hostel ❶** outside La Clusaz on rte. du Col de la Croix Fry, which has mostly rooms of four with showers. (☎04 50 02 41 73; fax 04 50 02 65 85. Reception 8am-noon and 5-8pm. Open Dec. 15-Sept. 15. Breakfast included. May 15-Sept. 15 dorms €15. Dec. 15-May 14 weekly stays only; *demi-pension* €289; full *pension* €329. MC/V.)

CHAMONIX

Chamonix (pop. 10,000) hosted the first Winter Olympics in 1924, but never extinguished the torch; it remains one of the premier world destinations for skiers. Its slopes, hiking paths, and rock walls are among the toughest in the world. Seven *téléphériques* and 42 other lifts serve the nearby ridges and peaks, ferrying up skiers in winter, hikers and cyclists in summer, and climbers in all seasons. Those who glance away from the blinding snow for just a second will notice a pleasing and exciting town that combines the natural majesty of nearby Mont Blanc (4810m), the tallest in Europe, the lighthearted spirit of Anglos who come for ski season and never leave, and the antics of raucous *après-ski* spots.

▚ TRANSPORTATION

Trains: av. de la Gare (☎04 50 53 12 98). A special local train runs from **St-Gervais** to **Martigny,** stopping at Chamonix. Ticket sales daily 6:10am-8:10pm. Info kiosk July-Aug. daily 9:20am-noon and 1:15-6:18pm. **Luggage storage** €3 for 1st bag, €1.50 every additional. Open daily 6:30am-8:10pm. To: **Annecy** (2½hr., 7 per day, €16.80); **Geneva** (2½hr., 7 per day, €20.80); **Grenoble** (4hr., 4 per day, €26.20); **Lyon** (4hr., 6 per day, €29.60); **Paris** (6-7hr., 9 per day, €50-70).

Buses: Société Alpes Transports, at the train station (☎04 50 53 01 15). Ticket office open July-Aug. M-Sa 7:45-8:15am, 9:30am-12:15pm and 1:20-6:30pm, Su 8-8:30am, 9:30am-12:15pm, and 2-6:15pm. Call for office hours for other periods. To: **Courmayeur,** Italy (50min.; July-Aug. 6 per day, Sept.-June M-Sa 2 per day; €9.50) and **Geneva,** Switzerland (1hr.; July-Aug. M-Sa 3 per day, Su 1 per day; Sept.-Nov. and May-June M-Sa 1 per day; Dec.-Apr. M-F 4 per day, Sa-Su 5 per day; €29 to town, €32 to airport). **Voyages Crolard** (☎04 50 45 08 12) runs to **Annecy** (2¼hr., M-F 1 per day, €14.95).

Public Transportation: Chamonix Bus (☎04 50 53 05 55) runs to ski slopes and hiking trails. Follow signs from pl. de l'Eglise to the main bus stop. Chamonix hotels and *gîtes* dispense the **Carte d'Hôte,** which gives free travel on all buses. Tickets €1.50.

Taxis: at the station (☎04 50 53 13 94). **Alp Taxi Rochaix,** ☎04 50 54 00 48. 24hr. About €12 to the Auberge de Jeunesse.

■ 🛈 ORIENTATION AND PRACTICAL INFORMATION

The center of town is the intersection of av. Michel Croz, rue du Docteur Paccard, and rue Joseph Vallot, each named for a past conqueror of Mont Blanc's summit. Chamonix is divided into two halves by the **Arve** river. South of the river is the train station. Most everything else is on the other bank (closer to the slopes), including the tourist office; from the station, follow av. Michel Croz through town, turn left onto rue du Dr. Paccard, and take the first right to the pl. de l'Eglise. (5min.)

Tourist Office: 85 pl. du Triangle de l'Amitié (☎04 50 53 00 24; fax 04 50 53 58 90; www.chamonix.com). Knowledgeable, English-speaking staff. Lists of hotels and dorms, campgrounds map, hiking map *Carte des Sentiers d'Eté* (€4), and *Chamonix Magazine* (free). Info on area cable cars. Weather conditions in English. **Internet** access with a télécarte. Open July-Aug. daily 8:30am-7:30pm; June, Sept. 1-15 and mid-Dec. to Apr. 8:30am-12:20pm and 2-7pm; mid-Dec. to Apr. also Sa-Su 8:30am-7pm; May, Sept. 16-30, and Oct. to mid-Dec. daily 9am-12:30pm and 2-6pm. **Centrale de Reservation** (☎04 59 53 23 33) books apartments or hotels for stay of 2 nights or more.

Currency Exchange: Comptoir de Change, 21 pl. Balmat (☎04 50 55 88 40), has the most competitive rates. 24hr. exchange machine. Also changes AmEx traveler's cheques for €4.90 commission and sells cheap **film.** Open daily 8am-8pm.

Laundromat: Cham'Laverie, 98 via d'Aoste, just off of av. de l'Aiguille du Midi. Open M-Sa 9am-7pm, Su 2-6pm. Also **Laverie Automatique,** 65 av. du Mont Blanc, within the Galerie Commerciale Alpina. Open M-Sa 8:30am-7pm, Su 10am-5pm.

Hospital: Centre Hospitaller, 509 rte. des Pèlerins (☎04 50 53 84 00).

Police: 48 rue de l'Hôtel de Ville (☎04 50 55 99 58).

Internet Access: Plenty of downtown bars have web access. The best deal is **Cybar,** 80 rue des Moulins (☎04 50 53 69 70). €1 per 10min. Open June-Nov. daily 11am-1:30am; Dec.-May daily 10am-1:30am. **I-Guest** (☎04 50 55 98 58), in the Galerie Blanc Neige, off rue du Dr. Paccard, is cheaper for longer periods: €7.50 per hr., €20.50 for 3½hr., using a divisible card. Open daily 10am-1pm and 4-8pm. MC/V.

Post Office: pl. Jacques-Balmat (☎04 50 53 15 90), below the tourist office. Open M-F 8:30am-noon and 2-6pm, Sa 8:30am-noon. **Postal code:** 74400.

SKIING, BIKING, AND HIKING RESOURCES
Hiking Information:

Office de Haute-Montagne (☎04 50 53 22 08; fax 04 50 53 27 74; www.ohm-chamonix.com), on the 3rd floor of the Maison de la Montagne, across from the tourist office. The ultimate resource. An expert staff helps plan your adventures, gives info on weather conditions, and sells detailed maps (€4-9). Open July-Aug. daily 9am-noon and 3-6pm; closed Sept.-June Su and Oct.-Nov. Sa.

Club Alpin Français, 136 av. Michel Croz (☎04 50 53 16 03; fax 04 50 53 82 47; infos@clubal-pin-chamonix.com). Best source of info on mountain refuges and road conditions. Guides available; register 6-7:30pm the day before hikes. Bulletin board matches drivers, riders, and hiking partners; hikers from far and wide convene in the office to plan the weekend's trips and excursions (F 7pm). **Members only;** email to inquire about membership. Open July-Aug. M-Sa 9:30am-noon and 3:30-7:30pm, W morning closed; Sept.-June M-Tu and Th-F 3:30-7pm, Sa 9am-noon.

Skiing and Hiking Lessons and Info: Ecole du Ski (☎04 50 53 22 57), on the 2nd floor of the Maison de la Montagne. Half-day group lessons €42; 2hr. private lesson

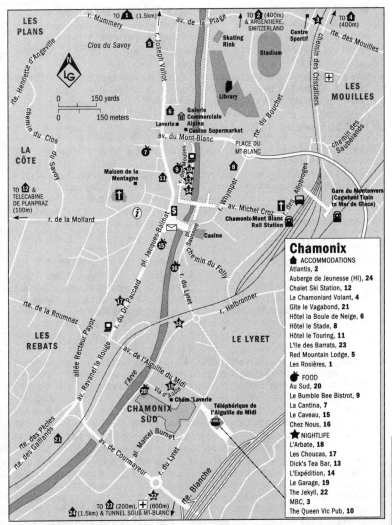

Chamonix

⌂ ACCOMMODATIONS
Atlantis, **2**
Auberge de Jeunesse (HI), **24**
Chalet Ski Station, **12**
Le Chamoniard Volant, **4**
Gîte le Vagabond, **21**
Hôtel la Boule de Neige, **6**
Hôtel le Stade, **8**
Hôtel le Touring, **11**
L'Île des Barrats, **23**
Red Mountain Lodge, **5**
Les Rosières, **1**

🍎 FOOD
Au Sud, **20**
Le Bumble Bee Bistrot, **9**
La Cantina, **7**
Le Caveau, **15**
Chez Nous, **16**

★ NIGHTLIFE
L'Arbate, **18**
Les Choucas, **17**
Dick's Tea Bar, **13**
L'Expédition, **14**
Le Garage, **19**
The Jekyll, **22**
MBC, **3**
The Queen Vic Pub, **10**

ALPS

€95; guided group descent of Vallée Blanche €58. Open Dec.-Apr. daily 8:15am-7pm. On the main floor, the **Compagnie des Guides** (☎04 50 53 00 88; www.cieguides-chamonix.com) gives skiing and climbing lessons and leads guided summer hikes and winter ski trips. Group ski excursions €56 per person. Register 5:30pm the evening before. Open Jan.-Mar. and July-Aug. daily 8:30am-noon and 3:30-7:30pm; Sept.-Dec. and Apr.-June Tu-Sa 10am-noon and 5-7pm.

Cycling Information: Pick up the free, invaluable map/guide *Itinéraires Autorisés aux Vélos Tout Terrain*, at the tourist office or at mountain biking rental shops.

Weather Conditions: at Maison de la Montagne, Club Alpin Français, and the tourist office. Call ☎08 92 68 02 74 for a French recording of road and weather conditions.

Mountain Rescue: PGHM Secours en Montagne, 69 rte. de la Mollard (☎04 50 53 16 89). 24hr. emergency service.

Hiking Equipment: Sanglard Sports, 31 rue Michel Croz (☎04 50 53 24 70). Boots €7-8 per day, €43-50 per week. Open July-Aug. daily 9am-7:30pm; Sept.-June 9am-12:30pm and 2:30-7:30pm. Closed Oct. 1-21. AmEx/MC/V.

Bike and Ski Rental: Dozens of places rent skis, snowboards, bikes, and climbing equipment. Skis should not be more than €8-16 per day or €40-65 per week, depending on quality. Snowboards should not exceed €16 per day and €80 per week.

▐ ACCOMMODATIONS AND CAMPING

Chamonix's hotels are expensive, but the more basic *gîtes* and dormitories are quite cheap. Hotels and *gîtes* are packed in the winter and summer—reserve up to six weeks in advance, but ease up in autumn and spring. The hardest time to get a room is early February, when the city hosts a car race. Call the tourist office for available places; the accommodations listed by *Let's Go* fill up fast, and there are other options out there. Mountain *refuges* tend to be remote and have few facilities, and are often unattended. For info on mountain *refuges*, see **Hiking,** below.

GÎTES AND HOSTELS

▨ **Red Mountain Lodge,** 435 rue Joseph Vallot (☎04 50 53 94 97; fax 04 50 53 82 64; www.redmountainlodge.co.uk; redmountainlodge@yahoo.com). From the train station, walk down av. Michel Croz and take a right onto rue Joseph Vallot. One of the best lodges in France, this is more home than hostel. The fun-loving Aussie owner and friendly, knowledgeable Anglo staff keep guests beaming with plush furnishings, views of Mont Blanc, and prizeworthy barbecues (2-3 per week; €12). Breakfast and sheets included. Reception 8am-noon and 5-7pm. Reserve ahead. Dorms €16; doubles and triples €20 per person, with shower €25. ❶

Atlantis, 788 rte. du Bouchet (☎04 50 53 74 31), 15min. out of town in a more natural setting, is a second gem of the Red Mountain owner. Follow directions for Chamoniard Volant, below, and take a left on the train track by rte. de la Frasse. Luxurious accommodations, a small bar, jacuzzi, sauna, tanning bed, and top-quality **mountain bike** rental (€15 per half-day, €30 per day). All-inclusive ski packages in-season. Breakfast and sheets included. Reserve ahead. Week packages only. €30 per person per day. ❷

Auberge de Jeunesse (HI), 127 montée Jacques Balmat (☎04 50 53 14 52; fax 04 50 55 92 34; www.aj-chamonix.fr.st), in Les Pélerins, at the foot of the Glacier de Bossons. Take the bus from the train station or pl. Mont-Blanc (dir: Pélerins) to "Pélerins Ecole" (€1.50), and follow the signs uphill to the hostel. On the special train, get off at "Les Pélerins" and follow the signs. By foot, walk down rte. des Pélerins. (30min.) A beautiful modern chalet practically on top of a glacier. Many groups fill 2- to 6- person bunks in a separate building. Reductions on practically everything in town. All-inclusive winter ski packages €389-481 per week. Breakfast included. Dinner €7.93. Sheets €2.90. Reception 8am-noon, 5-7:30pm, and 8:30-10pm. Dorms €13; singles and doubles €15.25 per person, with shower €16. MC/V. ❶

Gîte le Vagabond, 365 av. Ravanel le Rouge (☎04 50 53 15 43; fax 04 50 53 68 21; gitevagabond@hotmail.com). An easygoing Anglo staff runs this friendly *gîte* near the center of town. Popular bar, **Internet,** climbing wall. Breakfast €5. Dinner €10.50. Kitchen. Luggage storage. Laundry €7.70. Reception 8-10:30am and 4:30pm-1am. 4- to 8-bunk dorms €12.50. Credit cards MC/V. ❶

Le Chamoniard Volant, 45 rte. de la Frasse (☎04 50 53 14 09; fax 04 50 53 23 25; www.chamoniard.com), 15min. from the center of town. From the station, turn right, go under the bridge, and turn right across the tracks, left on chemin des Cristalliers, and right on rte. de la Frasse. Popular *gîte* has a decidedly rustic flavor and lots of ski para-phernalia. **Internet.** Breakfast €4. Dinner €10. Kitchen. Sheets €4. Reception 10am-10pm. Reservations required. 4- to 8-person dorms €12. ❶

Chalet Ski Station, 6 rte. des Moussoux (☎ 04 50 53 20 25), near télécabine Brevent. From the tourist office, follow signs to Les Moussoux up a steep hill; take a left at the top, and it will be on your right. Friendly wooden *gîte* with simple rooms and thin mat-tresses. Shower €0.75 for 5min. Sheets €2.50-5. Reception 8am-1pm and 4-11pm. Open Dec. 20-May 10 and June 25-Sept. 20. 4- to 9-bunk dorms €11. ❶

HOTELS

Hôtel la Boule de Neige, 362 rue Joseph Vallot (☎ 04 50 53 04 48; fax 04 50 55 91 09; laboule@claranet.fr). Cute 3rd-generation Alpine chalet with small but spotless rooms and firm beds, above a bar in a busy part of town. Breakfast €6. Reception 7am-noon and 5-7pm. Dec.-Feb. reserve 2 months in advance. Singles €26-34, with bath €40-50; dou-bles €31-39/€40-50; triples €43-51/€53-63; quads with bath €65-75. MC/V. ❸

Hôtel le Touring, 95 rue Joseph Vallot (☎ 04 50 53 59 18; fax 04 50 53 97 71; www.hoteltouring-chamonix.com; ngulliford@aol.com). Large English-run hotel with charming alpine decor and spacious rooms. From December to April it's almost always packed with groups and unavailable. Breakfast €6. Reception 8am-10pm. Singles with shower €36, with bath €56-60; doubles €44-47/€56-60, 3rd bed €10, 4th bed €6. July 12-Aug. 28 prices drop €10-15. MC/V. ❹

Hôtel le Stade, 79 rue Whymper (☎ 04 50 53 05 44; fax 04 50 53 96 39). From the train station, exit straight and take the first right. Downtown hotel offers good value with large and simple rooms. Breakfast included. Reception 8am-9pm. Singles €27.50; doubles €45, with shower and toilet €57; triples €65/€85. ❸

CAMPING:

Several sites lie near the foot of the Aiguille du Midi cable car. It's illegal to pitch tents in the Bois du Bouchet.

L'Ile des Barrats, 185 chemin de l'Ile des Barrats (☎/fax 04 50 53 51 44), off rte. des Pèlerins, has great views and crowds. Friendly manager keeps a well-maintained site. With your back to the cable car, turn left, pass the busy roundabout, continue 5min., and look right. Luggage storage. Reception July-Aug. 8am-10pm; May-June and Sept. 9am-noon and 4-7pm. Open May-Sept. Laundry €5. €5 per person, €4.60 per tent, €2 per car. Electricity €2.80. ❶

Les Rosières, 121 clos des Rosières (☎ 04 50 53 10 42; fax 04 50 53 29 55; www.campinglesrosieres.com), off rte. de Praz, is close to Chamonix Sud and often has room. Follow rue Vallot for 1.5km or take a bus to "Les Nants." Reception July-Aug. 8am-9pm; Sept.-June 9am-noon and 2-7pm. Open early Feb.-Oct. 15. €4.70-5.50 per person, €2.20-2.50 per tent, €2.10-3 per car. Electricity €2.70-3.20. ❶

▐ FOOD

The Chamonix tourist machine produces better restaurants than you might expect. Bars and ski lodges serve good meals as well. Regional fare like fondue and *raclette* shares menu space with international ski staples. The **Super U,** 117 rue Joseph Vallot, is the cheapest place for groceries. (☎ 04 50 53 12 50. Open M-Sa 8:15am-7:30pm, Su 8:30am-noon.) A **Casino** supermarket is at 17 av. du Mont Blanc, inside the Galerie Commerciale Alpina. (☎ 04 50 53 11 85. Open M-Sa 8:30am-7:30pm; July-Aug. also Su 8:30am-12:30pm). A morning **market** is held on pl. du Mont Blanc. (Open Sa 7:30am-1pm.) The **Jekyll** (see **Nightlife,** below), a popular bar, serves excellent food.

THE HIDDEN DEAL

THE JEKYLL

Irish Pubs are not known for fine cuisine. Patrons usually avoid food in favor of a pint of Guinness, whose heartiness makes it a meal itself. **The Jekyll ❶** is a clear exception to the rule.

Whereas the bland, harmless appearance of Dr. Jekyll hid the monstrous Mr. Hyde, The Jekyll hides a much more pleasant surprise behind its generic chalet exterior. While the the Jekyll's decor is filled with the usual pub-like odes to Guiness and photographs of James Joyce, the menu itself is an excellent, eclectic assortment, prepared by a Norwegian chef.

An initial scan of the *menu* may make you hold your wallet a little closer, but keep in mind that portions are so generous that two main dish and one entrée or dessert will satisfy two or three people. Entrées (€5.20-3) include a delicious goat cheese and fresh fig plate (€7.90). The creative menu offers thai coconut soup with chicken and rice (€11.90), cabbage rolls with feta and hummus €11.30), panfried sardines €10.60), seared tuna with risotto €17.70), fish and chips (€11), and of course, Irish lamb and Guinness stew (€12.90). A small dessert list €5.30-6.40) is headlined by apple crumb and fried camembert.

The friendly staff, mellow setting, *Ulysses* portions, and tasty cooking make *The Jekyll* a great deal. (*71 rte. des Pèlerins. From the town center, take rue du Lyret past two roundabouts. 10min.* ☎ *04 50 55 99 70. Open Dec.-Apr. daily 4pm-2am; July-Oct. M-Sa 6pm-2am; July-Aug. closed Su. MC/V.*)

Au Sud, 67 prom. Marie Paradis (☎04 50 53 42 97), offers a mix of regional specialities and traditional cuisine under a ceiling of hanging baskets. Try the excellent *entrecôte au poivre* (€12) or the *menu* (€14.50), which includes salad and *jambon cru, fondue savoyard,* and *sorbet* or *dessert du jour.* Th nights, there's *couscous royal* (€13.50). Open June-Sept. and Dec. 15-Mar. daily noon-2pm and 6pm-midnight; Apr.-May and Oct.-Nov. 15 W-M noon-2pm and 6-midnight. ❸

Le Bumble Bee Bistrot, 65 rue des Moulins (☎04 50 53 50 03), has a creative menu featuring such diverse dishes as *falafel, tandoori chicken,* steak, ale pie, and marsala duck (€9.30-13.80). There's a good selection of vegetarian options and delicious desserts. Light-yellow walls and soft tunes keep patrons mellow. Open Dec. to mid-May daily 6:30pm-2am; late May-Oct. M-Sa noon-3pm and 6:30pm-2am. MC/V. ❸

Chez Nous, 76 rue Lyret (☎04 50 33 91 29). This riverside locale specializes in *savoyarde* cuisine. Dip bread into the assorted, highly-praised fondues (from €11.50). 3-course *menu* €15. Open daily noon-2:30pm and 7-11:30pm. MC/V. ❸

Le Caveau, 13 rue du Docteur Paccard (☎04 50 55 86 18). This 300-year-old former wine and cheese cellar and disco is a local legend. Slow service and unusually high tables are balanced out by tasty pizzas and pastas (€6.70-12.50), vegetarian options (€8.50-9.50) and Mexican and Swedish specialties (€11-12). Open Dec. to mid-June and mid-July to Sept. daily 6:30pm-2am; Oct.-Nov. W-M 6:30pm-2am. MC/V. ❷

La Cantina, 37 impasse des Rhododendrons (☎04 50 53 83 80), off rue Joseph Vallot, is a funky Mexican restaurant popular with French natives. Diverse selection of vegetarian cuisine (€9.60-15.70), *Tex-Mex* (€9.15-13.10), and fajitas (€15.70-17.50). Open daily 7:30-11pm, Sa-Su until 2am. Bar open Dec. 20-May 12 daily 6pm-2am; July-Aug. Th-Sa 10pm-2am. MC/V. ❸

🎵 NIGHTLIFE

Chamonix's nightclubs are popular in the winter, when people shake what's left of their ski-weary bodies after the bars shut down. During the summer, they can be painfully empty. However, Chamonix is a serious bar town all year. You won't have to crawl far between drinks on bar-filled **rue des Moulins.**

▧ **The Jekyll,** 71 rte. des Pèlerins (☎04 50 55 99 70). (See sidebar, **The Hidden Deal.**)

▧ **The Queen Vic Pub,** 74 rue des Moulins (☎04 50 53 91 98). Energetic English pub draws a young, mixed, easygoing crowd. Pool tables and loud music in an elegant, 2-floor chalet. Happy Hour 6-9pm; beer €2.50. Open daily 6pm-2am.

L'Expédition, 26 rue des Moulins (☎04 50 53 57 68). This new local favorite draws a chic crowd to its small, intimate interior. Dec.-Apr. Tu and Th theme nights, including comedy, graffiti, and gangsta. Draft beer €5.50. Cocktails €4.20-7.80. Open June-Oct. daily 5:30pm-4am; Nov.-May 4pm-4am.

MBC Micro Brasserie de Chamonix, 350 rte. du Bouchet (☎04 50 53 61 59). A 10min. walk from the center of town, just across from the Centre Sportif. This first and only micro-brewery in Chamonix has quickly established a loyal following. Spacious and mellow interior. An international crowd chooses from 3 permanent brews and a beer of the month. Pints €4.50, pitchers €12. Open daily 4pm-2am.

Les Choucas, 206 rue du Dr. Paccard (☎04 50 53 03 23). Alpine swank in a revamped chalet. Cow-skin lounges and giant TV screen showing extreme skiing. Beer €3.40 before 10pm. Cocktails €7-10.50, including "Multiple Orgasm up Against the Wall." Open daily 4pm-4am; Oct.-Nov. Th-Sa 4pm-4am.

Dick's Tea Bar, 80 rue des Moulins (☎04 50 53 19 10), is the flagship of a bar-saturated street. London DJs keep the dance floor thumping at this hotspot, one of three Dick's in the Alps. Shots €3-6. Open Dec.-Apr. daily 10pm-4am; July-Aug. F-Sa midnight-4am. Dec.-Apr. cover €11, includes one drink.

L'Arbate, 80 chemin du Sapi (☎04 50 53 44 43), draws live music acts and an older, French crowd to its two-floor bar. Happy hour July-Aug. 8-9pm and mid-Dec. to mid-May 5-9pm with 2 for 1 draft beers. Music Dec.-Apr. daily 11:30pm; May-June and Sept. to mid Dec. F-Sa. Cover €10 for bands, includes one drink. Dec.-Apr. London DJ plays house techno. Cover €15-20. Open daily 5pm-4am.

Le Garage, 200 av. de l'Aiguille (☎04 50 53 64 49), is generally considered the best Chamonix disco. Caters to Anglos and Scandinavians. Stainless steel, neon-blue lights, and lots of booze. Party doesn't start till 1am. No cover, but one drink required (€3.50-10). Open Dec.-Apr. 10pm-4am; July-Aug. 11pm-4am; low-season Th-Sa 10pm-4am.

🏔 OUTDOORS

Whether you've come to climb up mountains or ski down them, expect a challenge. Steep grades, potential avalanches, and unique terrain make this area ill-suited for beginners to the world of ice. A classic introductory trip is an excursion on France's largest glacier, 7km long **La Mer de Glace,** in Montenverse. Get there on a special train that departs from a small station next to the main one. (☎04 50 53 12 54. July-Aug. daily every 20min. 8am-6pm; May-June and Sept. 1-15 daily every 30min. 8:30am-5pm; Sept. 16-Apr. daily every hr. 10am-4pm. €10, round-trip €13.) From the Mer, a cable car runs to an **ice cave** that is carved afresh every year—the glacier slides 30m per year, so last year's cave is farther down the wall of ice (car descent €2.10; cave admittance €3). Consider riding the train to the Mer and taking the downhill hike back. Just as you get out of breath on the way down, the **Luge d'Eté,** a concrete chute, will whisk you to the bottom. (☎04 50 53 08 97. Open July-Aug. daily 10am-7:30pm, also M and Th 8:30-10:30pm; Sept. and June daily 1:30-5:30pm; Oct.-Nov. Sa-Su 1:30-6pm. €5.)

TÉLÉPHERIQUES. Whether you're hiking or skiing, you will probably need to take a *téléphérique* (cable car) for part of the journey. Even if you plan to do neither of the above, the cable car can be an awe-inspiring experience. A board on pl. de l'Eglise lists the lifts that are currently open.

The **Aiguille du Midi** runs all year. (☎04 50 53 30 80, reservations 08 92 68 00 67.) Those with acrophobia (fear of heights) or argentophobia (fear of expenditure) might avoid the pricey and potentially frightening ride, which rises above towering forests and rocky, snow-covered cliffs to a needlepoint peak. Among the brave and well-to-do, few are disappointed. Go early, as clouds and crowds gather by mid-morning. The first stop, **Plan de l'Aiguille** (€12, round-trip €14), is a starting point for hikes (see **Hiking,** below) but otherwise not worthwhile. For great views, continue to **l'Aiguille du Midi** ("Needle of the South"), which is nearly twice as high. At the Aiguille, the panorama is breathtaking, as is the head-lightening 3842m air. Bring warm clothes and attend to your body. Walk and talk at the same time to make sure you are ok. For an additional €3, an elevator goes right to the summit, where there's a glorious 360-degree view (round-trip €33).

High-altitude escapades don't end with a view of Europe's tallest peak; from the Aiguille du Midi summit, you can take a trip to **Helbronner,** where you can straddle the French-Italian border (May-Sept. only; round-trip €17). You can eat a picnic lunch on the "Glacier Géant" here. The four-person gondolas run into the glacial heart of the Alps, passing within viewing distance of the Matterhorn and **Mont Blanc.** From Helbronner, a final *téléphérique* descends into Italy to **La Palud,** near the resort town of **Courmayeur.** Bring a passport and cash—the Italian side doesn't accept credit cards for the cable car. Check at the tourist office that the entire *téléphérique* route is in operation before setting out for this trip. (*Téléphérique* open Sept.-June daily 8am-3:45 or 4:45pm; July-Aug. 6am-5:40pm.)

Several *téléphériques* run year-round to the opposite side of the valley (away from Mt. Blanc), which is known for popular hiking trails and panoramic restaurants. **Le Brévent** (2525m) leaves from the corner of rte. Henriette and La Mollard, up the street from the tourist office. (☎04 50 53 13 18. Open July-Aug. daily 8am-6pm; Sept.-June 9am-5pm. One-way €12, round-trip €15.) Another great is **La Flégère,** 2km east of the city in Les Praz, on rue Joseph Vallot. It stops at an eponymous plateau on the way to **l'Index** (2595m), a starting point for the hike to Lac Blanc. (☎04 50 53 18 58. One-way €12, round-trip €15. Open July-Aug. daily 7:40am-5:50pm; June and Sept. 8:40am-4:50pm.)

SKIING. If you plan to ski for only a few days, buy daily lift tickets at the different ski areas—one area is more than enough for each day. If your trip plans extend to a week, buy a **Cham'Ski** pass, available at the tourist office or major *téléphériques* (Brevent, Flégère, Aiguille du Midi). The ticket gives unlimited access to the Chamonix Valley, excluding the small Les Houches area, and one day in Courmayeur-Val-Veny, Italy (€171; passport photo required).

Chamonix is surrounded by skiable mountains. The **southern side** of the valley opposite Mont Blanc, drenched in sunlight during the morning, offers easy to challenging terrain. In the afternoon, the sun and extreme skiers head over to the death-defying **north face,** which has mostly advanced, off-*piste*, and glacial terrain. Public buses, free to Cham'Ski holders, and the trains of the Mont Blanc tramway connect the valley's string of resort villages, from Les Bossons to Le Tour.

At the bottom of the valley, near the Swiss border, **Le Tour-Col de Balme** (☎04 50 54 00 58), above the village of **Le Tour,** is the first of Chamonix's ski areas. Its sunny trails are ideal for beginner to intermediate skiers (day-pass €24.60). More dramatic runs for the non-expert can be found around the **Brévent** and **Flégère** *téléphériques,* closer to town. Connected by a cable car, Brévent and Flégère together constitute Chamonix's largest ski area; located steps from the tourist office, the Brévent *téléphérique* is particularly convenient. Note, however, that the terrain at the top of the Brévent gondola is advanced; less confident skiers should get off at the middle stop **Planpraz,** the starting point for several easier trails. (Brévent and Flégère day pass €26.)

Extreme skiers have plenty of opportunities for off-*piste* near-death experiences on the opposite side of the Chamonix valley, starting with **Les Grands Mon-**

tets (☎ 04 50 54 00 71; 3275m), in Argentière (8km from Chamonix). The *grande dame* of Chamonix's ski spots is virtually all advanced terrain. With a remodeled half-pipe, les Grands Montets is now also geared toward **snowboarding.** (Day pass €31.80). Directly above Chamonix, the infamous **Vallée Blanche** requires a healthy dose of courage and insanity. From the top of the Aiguille du Midi *téléphérique* (€28), the ungroomed, unmarked, unpatrolled 20km trail cascades down a glacier to Chamonix. Despite their appearance from below, glaciers are more icefield than snowfield. Stay within sight of trail markers, or you may end up at the bottom of a crevice. Check conditions before venturing out. All *off-piste* skiers should check their route with the **ski patrol** or the **Office de Haut Montagne.** Skiing with a guide who knows the terrain is highly recommended. Never ski alone. Try the **Compagnie des Guides** (see p. 638; from €55 per person). English-speaking guides tailor the itinerary to your desires and ability, and make all the necessary arrangements, from equipment rental to lift reservations. Otherwise, you'll need to reserve a spot on the *téléphérique* in high season. (☎ 08 92 68 00 67.) If you don't want to ski on a glacier, you can ski beside one at the **Glacier du Mont Blanc** in Les Bossons, even at night. (☎ 04 50 53 12 39. Day pass €14. Night skiing W-F; €10.)

HIKING. Chamonix has 350 kilometers of hikes in terrain ranging from forests to glaciers. The town is surrounded by a web of trails, each marked by signs. A map, available at the tourist office, lists all the mountain refuges and gives departure points and estimated lengths for all the trails (€4). Climbers should buy the **IGN topographic map** (see p. 638), available at the **Office de Haute Montagne** and local bookstores (€9). Many trails begin in the far reaches of the Chamonix valley, but a handful of excellent ones are near town.

If you're an experienced mountain climber, you can ascend **Mont Blanc** (4810m), a two- or three-day climb. Don't try it solo. You can be caught by vicious blizzards, even in August. The Maison de la Montagne, the Compagnie des Guides, and the Club Alpin Français all have info (see **Skiing, Biking, and Hiking Resources,** p. 638).

Amateur hikers will enjoy the two ridges along the valley wall, called *balcons* or "balconies." The trails there start at medium altitudes and are accessible either by téléphérique or steep climbs out of Chamonix. On the south side of the valley, the **Grand Balcon Sud** is a picturesque, wildflower-studded trail linking the Brévent and Flégère téléphériques. From the Flégère cable car station, descend slightly and join the path that heads right toward a chimney. After two hours, the trail meets the Planpraz cable car station (2000m; the middle station of Brévent), where you can hike or ride back to town or embark on a difficult, scenic ascent to the **Col de Brévent** (2368m), the top of the Brévent lift. (1¾hr.) At the Flégère end of the Balcon Sud, another classic hike embarks for **Lac Blanc.** From the station, take the path that starts to the left near the stables and snakes its way up the hill. After passing by the tiny Lac de la Flégère (2027m), the trail flattens out and continues to the Lac Blanc (1¾hr.), a beautiful glacial lake with the expensive **Refuge du Lac Blanc** nearby. (☎ 04 50 53 49 14. Breakfast and dinner required. Reservations required. €44.50 per person.) Intermediate hikers can spare themselves the cable-car fees by taking the steep trail originating at the bottom of the Flégère téléphérique in **les Praz** and ascending 800m to the middle station. (3hr.) The Chalet de la Flégère **refuge** welcomes you up top. (☎ 04 50 53 06 13. June to mid-Sept. breakfast included; €29 per person. Low-season breakfast €6; €13 per person.)

The **Grand Balcon Nord,** on the opposite side of the valley, at a higher altitude, passes by dramatic scenery of jagged ice cascades and peaks. Take the Aiguille du Midi cable car to the first stop, Plan de l'Aiguille, and descend to the Refuge du Plan de l'Aiguille. (☎ 06 65 64 27 53. Open June 15-Sept. 15. Breakfast and dinner

€19. Rooms €10.) Keep to the trail that heads horizontally to the right and after 2½ unforgettable hours, you'll hit the **Hôtel Montenvers,** at the foot of the Mer de Glace glacier. Mountaineers use the refuge as a base for ice climbing. (☎ 04 50 53 87 70. Breakfast and dinner included. Open June 15-Sept. 15. €35.) Hôtel Montenvers is also accessible by an intermediate hike 900m up from the Montenvers train station, marked by signs. (2½hr.) The Refuge Plan de l'Aiguille can be reached by a difficult 1300m climb up one of the steep trails that begin at the Aiguille cable-car parking lot. (all 3½hr.)

VAL D'ISÈRE

Though named for the river that flows through the town, Val d'Isère (pop. 1750; 1850m) makes its livelihood on the peaks above. This world-class ski resort's main occupation is worshipping the mountains, the snow, and native son Jean-Claude Killy, who won gold in every single men's downhill event in the 1968 Grenoble Winter Olympics. But that's not the only reason he's a hero here; Killy brought Olympic events to Val d'Isère in 1992, and helped turn its main street into a tourist-laden strip of expensive hotels, restaurants, and ski boutiques. In summer, snow and prices melt, bikers and climbers fill the open hotels, and skiers retreat to the Glaciers du Pissaillas, where slushy white stuff persists until mid-August. A particularly crazy time is Dec. 11-15, when the Criterium de la Première Neige, one of the first international competitions of the season, comes to Val.

▐▀ TRANSPORTATION

Trains: pl. de la Gare in Bourg St-Maurice. Open daily 5am-10:30pm. To: **Annecy** (3hr., 6 per day, €21.30); **Grenoble** (3hr., 6 per day, €19.80); **Lyon** (3-4hr., 10 per day, €25.70). **Luggage storage** €4.50 per item. Available July-Aug. and Dec. 15-Apr. daily 10am-6pm; after-hours inquire at ticket window.

Buses: Autocars Martin (reservations ☎ 04 79 06 00 42), at the bus station by the roundabout 150m below the tourist office. Open July-Aug. M-Tu and Th-F 10-11am and 1:45-8:15pm, Sa 7-10am and 1:15-7:30pm; Dec.-Apr. M-F 9-11:30am and 1:30-7:45pm, Sa 6:30am-8:30pm, Su 7:30-11:30am and 1:30-7:45pm. **Main office** at pl. de la Gare in Bourg St-Maurice (☎ 04 79 07 04 49). Open daily 8am-noon and 2-6pm. Dec.-Apr. buses to **Geneva,** Switzerland (4-4½hr.; M-Th 3 per day, F-Su 4 per day; €48) via **Annecy** (3½hr., €40.40) and **Lyon airport** (4hr.; M-F 2 per day, Sa-Su 3 per day; €50.30). Also to the hostel in **Les Boisses** (15min.; Dec. 2-May 5 M-F 4 per day, Sa 1 per day, Su 2 per day; May 6-Dec. 3 M-F and Su 3 per day, Sa 4 per day; €2.80). **SNCF** info and reservation desks (☎ 04 79 06 03 55) are in the same building. Open July-Aug. Tu-Sa 9am-noon and 2-6pm; Dec.-Apr. M-Sa 9am-noon and 3-6:30pm.

Public Transportation: Val d'Isère runs **free shuttles** (navettes) around town. **Train Rouge** runs between La Daille and Le Fornet (Dec.-Apr. 8:30am-5:30pm and 5:30pm-2am, every 5-30min.), while **Train Vert** runs from the tourist office and the bus station up to le Manchet Sports complex and the entrance to the Vanoise national park (July-Aug. only). Both shave time off trips to the refuges.

Taxis: ABC (☎ 04 79 06 19 92); **Altitude Espace Taxi** (☎ 04 79 41 14 15). €46-68 to the train station in Bourg St-Maurice.

Bike and Ski Rental: About 30 spots in town offer rental; ask at the tourist office.

Hitchhiking: Bad transport and sympathetic locals make hitching a popular mode of transport, although Let's Go does not recommend it under any circumstances. Those hitching from the hostel to Val d'Isère usually cross the dam and wait by the highway. **No one hitches after dark.** Not even you.

■■ 🛈 ORIENTATION AND PRACTICAL INFORMATION

Val d'Isère has no train station—getting here takes time and money. The nearest station is in **Bourg-St-Maurice**, 30km to the north; a bus leaves there for Val d'Isère (M-F and Su 3 per day, Sa 8 per day; Apr.-Nov. last bus 6:35pm; Dec.-Mar. extended hours; €10.50). If you're going to the hostel, get off at **Tignes-Les Boisses,** 7km short of Val d'Isère (€9.40). The Val d'Isère mega-resort comprises three villages, all in a line: **Le Fornet** at the top, **La Daille** below at the entrance to the valley, and **Val Village** right in the middle, home to most accommodations and the **tourist office.** Unless otherwise stated, everything listed below is in Val Village, the most substantial of the three. Although Val d'Isère's street names are neither used nor clearly indicated, the town is navigable with the map in the tourist office's *Practical Guide.*

Tourist Office: in Val Village (☎04 79 06 06 60; fax 04 79 06 04 56; www.valdisere.com; info@valdisere.com). Distributes practical guides, available in 6 languages. Supplementary summer and winter guides detail prices and schedules. The staff can suggest where to hike and ski. Open May-June and Sept.-Nov. daily 9am-noon and 2-6pm; July-Aug. 8:30am-7:30pm; Dec.-Apr. Su-F 8:30am-7:30pm, Sa 8:30am-8pm. **Annex** at the town entrance (☎04 79 06 19 67); it's a small wooden hut on the right as you make your way up from La Daille. Open July-Aug. daily 9am-noon and 3-6pm; Dec.-Apr. Sa-Su 9am-noon and 2-7pm.

Laundromat: Laverie Automatique, just above the Casino supermarket, on your way up the roundabout. Open daily 8am-9:30pm. **Laverie Linge** (☎06 11 84 29 33), on your right about 300m down from the bus station.

Weather, Ski, and Road Info: Call tourist office or listen to **Radio Val** (96.1FM; ☎04 79 06 18 66). **Weather forecast:** ☎08 36 68 02 73. **Ski Lifts:** ☎04 79 06 00 35. **Ski Patrol:** ☎04 79 06 02 10.

Police: ☎04 79 06 03 41; above the tourist office and across from Casino supermarket.

Hospital: in Bourg St-Maurice (☎04 79 41 79 79).

Internet Access: Lodge Bar (☎04 79 06 19 31). Turn right at the roundabout above the bus station. Low ceilings, mosaic columns and mood lighting. Internet €3 for 15min.; €5.50 for 30min.; €9 per 1hr. Open Nov. 15-Apr. daily 4:30pm-1:30am; July-Aug. 6pm-1:30am. Also **Dick's Tea Bar** and **Café Fats** (see **Entertainment, p. 649**).

Post Office: Across from the tourist office (☎04 79 06 06 99) in "Vieux Val." **Currency exchange** with good rates and no commission. Open July-Aug. M-F 9am-noon and 1:30-4:30pm, Sa 8:30-11:30am; Dec.-Apr. M-F 8:30am-noon and 2-6pm, Sa 8:30am-noon; Sept.-Nov. and May-June M-F 10am-noon and 1:30-3:30pm, Sa 9:30-11am. **Postal code:** 73150.

🛈 ACCOMMODATIONS AND CAMPING

The world-class slopes only feet away make it very tough to find a room here in winter. During the off-season many hotels close, but the ones that don't maintain very reasonable prices. The cheapest beds are at the two *refuges,* **Le Prariond** and **Le Fond Des Fours,** each at least a 2hr. hike from downtown (see **Hiking,** p. 650, for directions and prices). Cheaper **gîtes** in Le Fornet offer an alternative to downtown hotels; the tourist office has a complete list. During the ski season, **Moris Pub,** 75m up from the tourist office, rents bright rooms upstairs for super-cheap prices. (☎04 79 06 22 11. Breakfast included. €22.90 per person. MC/V.)

Auberge de Jeunesse "Les Clarines" (HI) (☎04 79 06 35 07; reservations ☎04 79 41 01 93; fax 04 79 41 03 36; tignes@fuaj.org), in the village of **Les Boisses**. From Val d'Isère, a pleasant, well-marked trail begins at La Daille. Follow the river down to the lake and bear left along the shore until you ford a cascading creek. Turn right, cross the bridge, and take the small, unmarked path ascending to the right until it meets the road. To the right is Les Boisses and the hostel. (1½hr.) Or take the "Tignes/Val Claret" bus to "Les Boisses" from Bourg-St-Maurice (€9.40) or Val d'Isère (€2.80). A free shuttle runs between Tignes and Les Boisses (4 per day, Dec.-Mar. more). Wooden rooms off of bright orange hallways for 4-6 people, all but 3 with toilets, overlooking the Lac du Chevril. Friendly staff. Safe atmosphere. Discounts on rentals. **Skiing, hiking, biking,** and **water sports** packages (from €9-30 per day). **Paragliding** excursions (€90) and **horse riding, biking,** and **rock-climbing** trips. Reception 7:30-9am and 5-10pm. Entry code after 10pm. Reserve far in advance. Closed May-June 25 and Sept.-Nov. June-Aug. bed and breakfast €13, with dinner €20.30; week with *demi-pension* €120. Dec.-Mar. bunks with breakfast €13, with dinner €21, with alpine day pass €38. MC/V. ❶

Gîtes Bonnevie (☎04 79 06 06 26; fax 04 79 06 16 65), in Le Fornet. Cross the bridge and it's the 1st building on the right. Gorgeous wooden chalet-style studios for 2 or 10 people, all with bathroom, kitchen, TV, and splendid views. About as cheap as it gets. Apr.-Nov. €20 per person. Dec.-Mar. weekly rentals only: doubles €310, 10-man €1448. Winter prices fluctuate; call to verify. ❷

Hôtel Sakura (☎04 79 06 04 08; fax 04 79 41 10 65; sakura7@club-internet.fr; www.sakura7.com). Turn right at the roundabout above the bus station. Spacious, fully-equipped rooms with handmade wood furniture. All with shower or bath, toilet, TV, telephone, kitchen. Breakfast €6. Reception 8am-8pm. Open July-Aug. and Dec.-May. July-Aug. singles €43; doubles €49; triples and quads €95; quints €110. Dec.-May singles and doubles €99; triples and quads €169; quints €184. MC/V. ❹

Le Relais du Ski (☎04 79 06 02 06; fax 04 79 41 10 64; lerelaisduski@valdisere.com), 500m up from the tourist office, on the left. Small, wood-panelled rooms with hall showers. Breakfast €9; speak up if you don't want it. Dinner €17. Reception 24hr. June-Sept. singles €25-49; doubles €32-56; triples €39-60; quads €44-64. Dec.-Apr. singles €40-53; doubles €50-74; triples €66-84; quads €76-100. AmEx/MC/V. ❸

Le Chamois d'Or (☎04 79 06 00 44; fax 04 79 41 16 58; www.hotelchamoisdor.com). From the bus station, turn right at the roundabout and continue uphill, walking past the tennis courts and indoor swimming pool; the hotel will be on your right. (10min.) Wonderful views and firm beds at this 60-year old establishment. All rooms with shower or bath, toilet, and TV. Breakfast included. Reception Apr.-Nov. 8am-9pm; Dec.-Mar. 7:30am-10pm. Reserve in Sept.-Oct. for winter. July-Aug. singles and doubles €33.60-41.20; triples €87-109.80; quads €104-134.40. Dec.-Apr. singles €71-107; doubles €104-166; triples €135-219; quads €168-272. AmEx/MC/V. ❹

Les Crêtes Blanches (☎04 79 41 14 43; fax 04 79 06 17 22; www.cretes-blanches.com). Turn right at the roundabout above the bus station. Friendly, English-speaking manager presides over cozy rooms with wonderful views. All rooms with shower or bath, toilet, and TV. Plans to become a three-star hotel in 2003. Breakfast included. Reception 8am-8pm. July-Aug. singles €45-68; doubles €52-74; triples €84-90. Dec.-Apr. singles €71-176; doubles €96-182; triples €132-228. AmEx/MC/V. ❺

Camping les Richardes (☎/fax 04 79 06 26 60), 1km up from the tourist office. The free Train Rouge shuttle stops here. Plain campground in a beautiful valley, close to town. Crowded mid-Aug. during the 4x4 competitions. Reception June and Sept. 9am-noon and 5-8pm; July-Aug. 7:30am-12:30pm and 2-8pm. Open June 15-Sept. 15. €2.40 per person, €1.50 per tent, €1.40 per car. Electricity €1.90-3.80. Shower €1. MC/V (€15 minimum). ❶

🔾 FOOD

Perhaps someday Jean-Claude Killy will bring budget-oriented dining to Val d'Isère; until then, the supermarkets will have to do. There are two **Casino's.** One is in the *centre-ville*, just up the roundabout by the bus station. (☎ 04 79 06 02 66. Open July-Aug. daily 7:30am-1pm and 3:30-8pm; Dec.-Apr. daily 7:30am-1pm and 2:30-8:30pm.) The other is in the **Les Hameaux** store, 500m up from the tourist office. (☎ 04 79 06 12 24. Open July-Aug. and Dec.-Apr. daily 7:30am-1pm and 3:30-8pm; May-June and Sept.-Nov. M-W, F, Su 9am-12:30pm and 4-7:30pm.)

▨ Le Bananas (☎ 04 79 06 04 23) is up the roundabout and near the base of the téléphériques. Ski instructors and wannabes pack this rockin' chalet for bites and beers just inches from the slope. Delicious dishes with a *Tex-Mex* theme include quesadillas (€15) and a variety of salads (€4-12). Menus €17 and €20. Happy Hour Dec.-Apr. 7-8pm. Open daily noon-1:30am. MC/V. ❸

La Casserole (☎ 04 79 41 15 71) is just up the roundabout. In a dark wood chalet hung with animal skin, you can enjoy *savoyard* specialties like *fondues* and *tartiflettes* (€13-20). Meats €14-22. Salads €3.50-11.50. Open July-Aug. Tu-Sa noon-1:45pm and 6:30-10pm, Su noon-1:45pm; Nov.-Apr. daily 6:30-10:30pm. AmEx/MC/V. ❸

Café Fats (☎ 04 79 41 93 06) is to the right and behind the bus station. This popular anglo locus prepares down-to-earth cuisine in a relaxed atmosphere. Try the hearty English breakfast with homemade sausages (€11) or hamburgers (€7-8.40). At night, the place transforms into a bar, serving draft beers (€3-6) and 12 varieties of house vodka shots (€2.50). There's also **Internet** access; €5 per 30min. Open July-Aug. M-F 5pm-1am, Sa-Su noon-1am; mid-Oct. to early May daily 9am-1am. ❸

Maison Chevallot (☎ 04 79 06 02 42) is 20m up from the bus station. Your best bet for a delicious lunch or early dinner. Homemade *tourte au beaufort, quiche lorraine, tartiflette, fougasse,* and sandwiches are served with a salad (€4-5). For dessert, don't miss the excellent pastries, including nut cake (€2.29) and *fondant chocolat* (€2.30). Open daily 6:30am-8pm, May and Oct.-Nov. closed 1-3pm. ❶

🎵 ENTERTAINMENT

In addition to being a haven for pizzerias, the roundabout above the bus station serves as Val d'Isère's unofficial nightlife strip. Start your drinking at **Lodge Bar.** (See **Internet Access,** above. Cocktail *du jour* €5. Happy Hour 4:30-7pm: beer €1.50-3. Live music Tu and F during ski season.) Then stumble up the block to **Café Face,** filled with DJs and sax players. (☎ 04 79 06 29 80. Open Dec.-May daily 4pm-2am; July-Aug. 10pm-2am.) Across the street, **Dick's Tea Bar** is the best late-night option. An Anglo crowd packs the dance floor of this Val mainstay. (☎ 04 79 06 14 87; www.dicksteabar.com. Happy Hour during ski season 3-9pm: beer €3. Paninis €3-4. Shooters €6-8. Cocktails €13-19. **Internet** access €5 for 30min. Open Dec.-Apr. daily 3pm-4am; July-Aug. Tu-Su 10:30pm-4am). And don't forget **Café Fats** or **Le Bananas,** busy long into the night (see **Food,** p. 649).

🏔 OUTDOOR ACTIVITIES

SKIING. Skiing is king in Val d'Isère. Over 100 lifts provide access to 300km of trails. You can ski for a week without repeating a run. Lifts are valid on the entire Espace Killy, which includes every lift and run from Val d'Isère to Tignes, a ski station 7km away. The mountains are generally skiable from the end of November through the beginning of May, with optimum conditions in mid-winter. (Lift tickets €26 per half-day, €36.50 per day, €196 per week.)

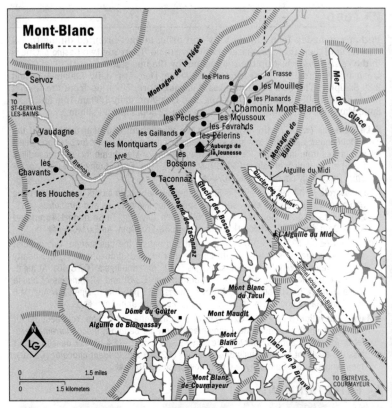

Mont-Blanc

Chairlifts - - - - - - -

Servoz

TO
ST-GERVAIS-
LES-BAINS

Montagne de la Flégère

les Plans

la Frasse

les Mouilles

les Moussoux

les Planards

Chamonix Mont-Blanc

les Pécles

les Favrands

Vaudagne

les Gaillands

les Pélerins

les Montquarts

Arve

les
Bossons

Auberge de
la Jeunesse

Montagne de
Blaitière

Aiguille du Midi

les
Chavants

Route Blanche

Taconnaz

Glacier des Pélerins

les Houches

Montagne de Taconnaz

Glacier des Bossons

L'Aiguille du Midi

Mer
de
Glace

Tunnel sous Mont-Blanc

Mont Blanc
du Tacul

Dôme du Goûter

Mont Maudit

Aiguille de Bionnassay

Mont
Blanc

N
LG

0   1.5 miles
0   1.5 kilometers

Mont Blanc
de Courmayeur

Glacier de la Brenva

TO ENTRÈVES,
COURMAYEUR

Most good beginner runs are at higher altitudes, around the Marmottes and Bor-sat lifts on the south side of Bellevarde (that's the back side; take the Bellevarde lift up) and in the super-scenic Pissaillas area (take the Solaise cable car, then the Glacier and Leissier lifts). Intermediate and advanced skiers like the slopes sur-rounding Tignes, while the north side of Bellevarde is known for expert runs. There's a giant **snow park** between Val and Tignes; a classic border run starts at the top of the Mont Blanc lift and whirls its way through the park to La Daille, where a Funival car whisks boarders back to the Bellevarde summit for an encore.

Val d'Isère is most proud of its glorious off-*piste* opportunities. Skiers of the **col Pers** region, accessible from the Pissaillas glacier, speed past wildlife as they pass through the Gorges de Malpassaet. Never ski off-*piste* alone, check weather condi-tions before you go, and let the ski patrol know your itinerary. Non-experts and those unfamiliar with the area should hire a **guide** (call ☎ 04 79 06 02 34).

From the end of June to mid-July, Pissaillas offers **summer skiing.** Lift tickets are available at the Le Fornet cable car, from where a free bus heads to the top. Con-ditions deteriorate and prices drop after 11am; there's no skiing after 1:30pm. (€16.50 per half-day, €21 per day. Lifts open at 7:30am.)

HIKING. Before hiking around Val, check the weather report and bring warm clothing—snowstorms and winter weather strike even in summer. Some interme-diate trails are suitable only for those with the proper equipment and experience.

Trails around the Val are well-marked with blazes and signs, but hikers should buy the detailed *Val d'Isère—Balades et Sentiers* (€3.80) and a **hiking map** in English at the tourist office (€6.90), which describe over 40 routes spanning 100km.

Until the construction of modern ski areas in the 60s, **Le Fornet** (1950m) was the highest year-round inhabited village in the French Alps. It can be reached by an easy 4km hike. (1½hr.) Starting from the church in Val Village, follow the sign for Le Fornet. The trail leads through the Vieux Val to a small pedestrian road and then briefly joins up with the GR5 before forking again toward Le Fornet. Just before the village, the trail gives the option of doubling back via the beautiful 45min. **sentier écologique** to meet up with the GR5 once again and return to town.

Val d'Isère's classic **intermediate** hikes lead through the Vanoise National Park, France's premiere wildlife reserve, to the two closest *refuges*. The trail to the **Refuge de Prariond** (one-way 3km; 1¾hr.; 300m vertical) begins in Le Fornet. It is a must for animal lovers; acrobatic *bouquetin* (ibex), *chamois* (the antelope's little cousin), and furry marmots roam the land around the trail. From the center of Le Fornet, cross the bridge and follow the signs to **pont St-Charles.** After the bridge, the marked trail switchbacks several times out of the far end of the parking lot before beginning a steep ascent to the **Gorges du Malpasset.** The trail then plateaus and continues gently to the *refuge.* (*Refuge* ☎ 04 79 06 06 02. Staffed Mar. 31-May 10 and June 15-Sept. 15. Otherwise, there is wood, gas, utensils, covers, and a tin box for your money. Breakfast €5.60; *à la carte* lunch €14; dinner €14. Shower €2. Animal-skin sleeping sacks €2.30. Reserve and get directions at the tourist office. €11.50 per person, students €8.50.) From Prariond, you can climb for another two hours and 600 vertical meters to the **Col de la Galise** pass (2987m) and the source of the Isère river, one of the most stunning panoramas in the region. Coming out of the *refuge*, take the trail to the right. At the **Roche des Coses** (2750m), you can branch right for a 45min. excursion into Italy and more stupendous vistas. Take care; this trail is usually snow-covered year-round.

The second *refuge* hike leads through alpine meadows to the **Refuge des Fours,** in the Vanoise National Park. Take the free shuttle to **le Manchet** (see **Local Transportation,** p. 646), and continue up the road to the trailhead near a cluster of old stone farmhouses. Take the trail on your right marked "refuge des fours." From there, it's a steady climb to the hut in a high valley across from the Méan Martin glacier and alpine lakes. (One-way 1¾hr.; 560m vertical. *Refuge* ☎ 04 79 06 16 90; same staffing months as Fornet. Breakfast €5.50. Lunch €14. Dinner €9.60. Sleeping sack €2.60. Showers €2.50. €11.50 per person, students €8.50.) There are numerous ways to return to Val without retracing your steps. One option is to cross the **Col des Fours** pass and head back to town via the **GR5.** Continue along the trail that took you to the *refuge*, and turn left onto the path that ascends the neckline between the 3135m Pelou Blanc and the 3072m Pointe des Fours. (1¼hr.; 450m vertical). Where the trail ends, hang a left on the red-and-white marked **GR5** for a gloriously scenic descent to town on the **Col d'Iseran,** a favorite leg of the Tour de France (6km; 1½-2hr.; 900m vertical descent).

An **advanced** full-day trek heads from le Fornet to the **Lac de la Sassière.** From the *téléphérique*, descend slightly and turn right at the trail marker for the Balcon des Barmettes. At the Balcon, head right on Trail #36, the **Bailletta,** which climbs steeply for 800m to the small **Lac de la Bailletta** (2½hr.), where it reaches a pass and descends gradually to the larger **Lac de la Sassière.** This man-made lake is crammed with trout and surrounded by *chamois*, ibex, and marmots. To return, retrace your steps for several hundred meters until the sign for **Picheru,** a steeper path than the *Bailletta* route. Picheru passes over several exposed knife-edge ridges before crossing just to the right of **Le Dome** and descending gradually into town. (Round-trip to Lac de la Sassière 12.2km; 7hr.; 940m vertical.) Another advanced trek heads from the *Camping les Richardes*; grab the man-killing **GR5** (marked with red and white) and hold on tight for a harrowing ascent to the **Col de l'Iseran** (2770m). About halfway up, you'll cross the RD902. From the top you can see a different glacier in every direction. (One-way 6km; 3hr.; 914m vertical.)

OTHER OUTDOOR ACTIVITIES. **Mountain Guides** (☎ 04 79 06 06 60) teach **ice climbing** (morning session €76) and **rock climbing** (afternoon session €28), and lead full-day **canyoning trips** (€64). They also lead nature expeditions for all levels.

For a relaxing trip to Val d'Isère's summit, let a *téléphérique* (cable car) whisk you up to the peak, over peaks, glaciers, and valleys. Cable cars run to **Solaise**, a small summit surrounded by a lake and easy hiking trails, and the higher **Bellevarde,** site of the 1992 Olympic downhill. (To Solaise Dec.-Apr. every 10min. 8:45-5pm; July-Aug. every hr. 9am-noon and 2-4:50pm. To Bellevarde Dec.-Apr. every 10min. 9am-4:45pm; July-Aug. every hr. 9:30-11:30am and 2:30-4:30pm. Cable cars €7, round-trip €8.) You can also hike up or down Solaise on trail #17, Chemin de l'Ouillete (round-trip 2½hr.), which starts near Chapelle St-Jean at the base. It's an accessible trail for all experience levels and provides wonderful views. From Bellevarde, you can descend a steep trail on the front of the mountain to return to Val d'Isère or a trail on the back that heads to La Daille, but think twice, since most of the terrain has been sliced and ground by **mountain bikers** and 4x4's.

For uncharted mountains, advanced **climbers** should call the Bureau des Guides ☎ 04 79 06 06 60). Beginners will appreciate **Via Ferrata's** in La Daille. The 2- to 3-hr. climb (360m vertical) via metal footholds and ropes hugs the side of the mountain facing the valley; there is also a more demanding four- to six-hour climb that requires a guide. Signs at the La Daille chapel indicate the way to the climbing site.

LYON AND THE AUVERGNE

If they manage to escape Paris, France's visitors descend upon popular Provence and the ritzy Riviera. Few, however, penetrate the Auvergne, the country's interior. The lucky adventurer who does will find rugged beauty without mobs of tourists. Giant lava needles, extinct volcanic craters, and verdant pine forests rise out of the Massif Central. The mineral waters of Vichy, Le Mont Dore, and Volvic attract both *curistes* (those who believe in the healing powers of thermal spring water) and bottling entrepreneurs. During World War II, the region achieved infamy as the empty hotels of Vichy became the headquarters for the collaborationist French government headed by Maréchal Pétain. Now it is a quiet, beautiful, mostly rural area, headlined by the welcoming, big-city vibrancy of Lyon.

1	**Lyon:** A cosmopolitan city, less rude and rushed than Paris; Lyon has it all **(p. 653)**
2	**Pérouges:** Tiny village, cobblestone streets, preserved 15th-century houses **(p. 667)**
3	**The Beaujolais:** Best known for cool, fruity wine; terraced hills and sleepy villages **(p. 667)**
4	**Clermont-Ferrand:** Dark stone and smoke-spitting factories; a base for regional hiking **(p. 668)**
5	**Puy de Dôme:** Massive, flat-top volcanic dome with views to remember **(p. 673)**
6	**Le Mont Dore:** Ski, spa, and hiking mecca near a cratered string of dormant volcanoes **(p. 674)**
7	**Le Puy-en-Velay:** Pilgrimage site with immense cathedral and volcanic tower **(p. 677)**
8	**Vichy:** Healing springwater; nostalgic city that would rather forget the recent past **(p. 681)**

LYON

World-renowned culinary capital, former center of the silk trade and the French Resistance, and ultramodern city, Lyon (pop. 1.2 million) is friendlier and more relaxed than Paris, with a few centuries's more history. Augustus ordered roads connecting this provincial capital of Gaul to Italy and the Atlantic, permanently establishing Lyon's status as a major crossroads and cultural capital. During the Renaissance, the city's tax-free permanent markets encouraged foreign merchants and bankers to set up shop here, and in the 15th century, Lyon became Europe's printing house. Silkworms imported from China in the 16th century also contributed to the city's rise to economic power. Spared from urban renewal's path of destruction in the early 1960s, the ornate facades and elegant courtyards of 16th-century townhouses in *Vieux Lyon* attest to this period of wealth. These buildings played a major role in the city being named a UNESCO World Heritage sight in 1998. Today Lyon is the stomping ground of world-renowned chefs Paul Bocuse, Georges Blanc, and Jean-Paul Lacombe, as well as the breeding ground for new culinary genius. There's no doubt you can eat *really* well at one of the masters's spin-off restaurants and just about anywhere in the city.

✈ INTERCITY TRANSPORTATION

Flights: Aéroport Lyon-Saint-Exupéry (☎04 72 22 72 21). Various airlines fly within France and around Europe, North Africa, and the Middle East. The TGV, which stops at the airport, is cheaper and more convenient than the 50 daily flights to Paris. **Satobuses/**

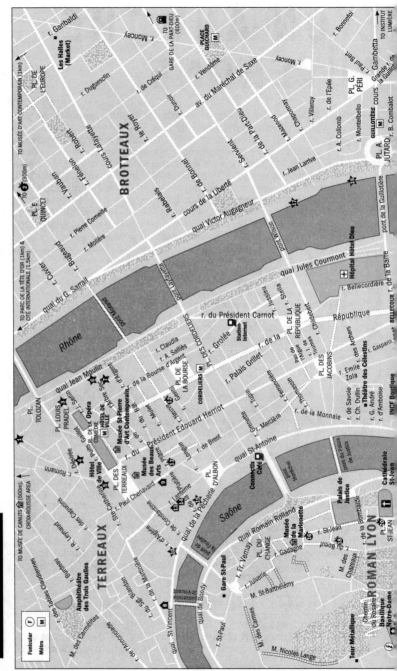

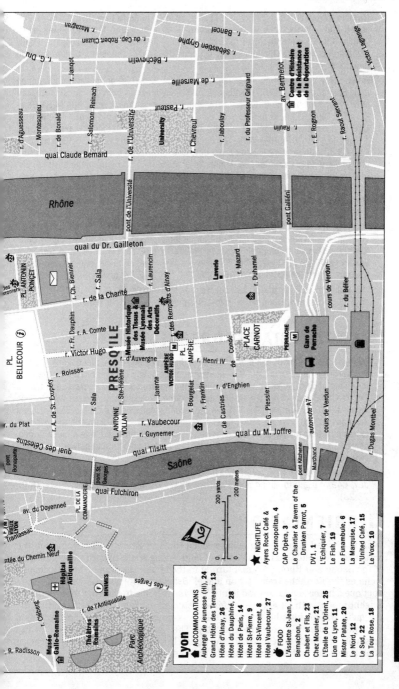

Navette Aéroport (☎04 72 68 72 17) shuttles to **Gare de la Part-Dieu, Gare de Perrache** and subway stops **Grange-Blanche, Jean Mace,** and **Mermoz Pinel** (every 20min., €8.20). **Air France,** 17 rue Victor Hugo, 2ème (☎0 820 820 820), has 6 daily flights to both Paris's Orly and Roissy airports (€101-207, depending on how close to departure you buy your ticket).

Trains: SNCF info desk open M-F 9am-7pm and Sa 9am-6:30pm; ticket windows open daily 5am-11pm. The **SNCF Boutique,** 2 pl. Bellecour across from the tourist office, can solve your traveling quandaries in a slighter calmer atmosphere. Open M-Sa 9am-7pm.To: **Dijon** (2hr., 6 per day, €21.20); **Geneva,** Switzerland (2hr., 13 per day, €18.80); **Grenoble** (1¼hr., 21 per day 6:10am-12:20am, €15.40); **Marseille** (3hr., 17 per day, €32.90); **Nice** (6hr., 12 per day, €47.70); **Paris** (2hr., 26 TGVs per day, €53-63.70); **Strasbourg** (5½hr., 5 per day, €38.40). Trains passing through Lyon stop only at **Gare de la Part-Dieu,** bd. Marius Vivier-Merle (M: Part-Dieu), in the business district on the east bank of the Rhône. SNCF info desk open M-F 9am-7pm and Sa 9am-6:30pm; ticket windows open M-Th and Sa 5:15am-11pm, F and Su 5:15am-midnight. There are lockers and **baggage storage** (open daily 6am-midnight; €4.50 for 2 bags). Trains terminating in Lyon continue to **Gare de Perrache,** pl. Carnot (M: Perrache).

Buses: On the lowest level of the Gare de Perrache, at the train station, and at "Gorge de Loup" in the 9ème (☎04 72 61 72 61 for all three). Perrache station open daily 5am-12:30am. Domestic companies include **Philibert** (☎04 78 98 56 00) and **Transport Verney** (☎04 78 70 21 01), but it's almost always cheaper, faster, and simpler to take the train. **Eurolines** (☎04 72 56 95 30; fax 04 72 41 72 43) travels out of France.

Bike Rentals: Holiday Bikes, 199 rue Vendôme, 3ème (☎04 78 60 11 10). €12 per day. €250 deposit. Open M-Sa 9am-12:30pm and 3-7pm, Su 9am-noon and 6:30-7pm. AmEx/MC/V.

▮ LOCAL TRANSPORTATION

TCL (☎04 78 71 70 00) has info offices at both stations and major metro stops. *Plan de Poche* (pocket map) available from the tourist office or any TCL branch. Tickets are valid for all methods of mass transport, including the **métro, buses, funiculars,** and **trams.** Tickets €1.40; *carnet* of 10 €10.60, student discount includes 10 passes valid for one month €9.10. One pass is valid 1hr. in 1 direction, connections included. *Ticket Liberté* day pass (€3.80) is a great deal for short-term visitors. The fast, frequent, and efficient **métro** runs 5am-midnight, as do **buses** and **trams,** which have 2 different lines; T1 connects Part-Dieu to Perrache directly. **Funiculars (cable cars)** swing between the Vieux Lyon métro stop and pl. St-Jean, the top of Fourvière and St-Just until midnight.

Taxis: Taxi Radio de Lyon (☎04 72 10 86 86). To airport from Perrache €36 during the day, €49 at night; to airport from Part-Dieu €31/49. 24hr. Also **Allô Taxi** (☎04 78 28 23 23).

▮ ORIENTATION

Lyon is divided into nine **arrondissements;** the 1er, 2ème, and 4ème lie on the **presqu'île** (peninsula), a narrow strip of land jutting south toward the confluence of the Saône and Rhône rivers. Starting in the south, the 2ème (the city center) includes the Perrache train station and **pl. Bellecour,** as well as most of the city's boutiques, hotels, and fast-food joints. The 1er is home to the nocturnal Terreaux neighborhood, with its sidewalk cafés and student-packed bars. Farther north, the presqu'île widens into the 4ème and the Croix-Rousse, a residential neighborhood that once housed Lyon's silk industry. The main pedestrian arteries of the presqu'île are **rue de la République,** affectionately known as "la Ré," to the northeast of pl. Bellecour, and **rue Victor Hugo,** to the south of Bellecour.

To the west is the oldest part of the city: Vieux Lyon, with narrow streets and traditional restaurants, and the **Fourvière** hill, with a Roman theater, a basilica, and fabulous views. Most people live east of the Rhône (*3ème* and *6-8ème*), also home to the **Part-Dieu** train station and modern commercial complex. Orient yourself with Fourvière and its **Tour Metallique,** a mini-Eiffel Tower, in the west and the **Tour du Crédit Lyonnais,** a reddish-brown "crayon" towering over Part-Dieu, in the east.

Most trains terminating in Lyon stop at both the **Gare de Perrache** and the **Gare de la Part-Dieu.** Perrache is more central and considered safer at night, but both are connected to Lyon's highly efficient **métro,** which is the fastest way to the tourist office in the **tourist pavilion** on pl. Bellecour. To walk from Perrache, head straight onto rue Victor Hugo and follow it until it ends at pl. Bellecour; the tourist office will be on the right. (15min.) From Part-Dieu, leave the station by the fountains and turn right, walk for three blocks and turn left onto cours Lafayette, cross the Rhône on pont Lafayette and continue as the street changes to pl. des Cordeliers, then turn left on rue de la République and follow it to pl. Bellecour. (30min.) Lyon is a reasonably safe city. Watch out for pickpockets inside Perrache, at pl. des Terreaux, and in pl. Bellecour's crowds.

◪ PRACTICAL INFORMATION

TOURIST AND FINANCIAL SERVICES

Tourist Office: In the Pavilion, at pl. Bellecour, 2ème (☎04 72 77 69 69; fax 04 78 42 04 32). M: Bellecour. Incredibly efficient, and hungry for your tourism. Brochures and info on rooms and restaurants. Hotel reservation office. Free, indispensable **"Map & Guide"** in 7 languages has museum listings, a subway map, and a blow-up of the city center. Ask about the wide range of excellent **city tours** in French (and English during the summer). Tours €9, students €6.50. 3hr. audio-tours of the city are available in 4 languages (€6.10). Also available is an insightful, anecdotal book that describes walking tours through the five quarters included in the UNESCO World Heritage list (€5.35), which humbles even the best of guidebook writers (i.e., *Let's Go* researchers). Equally invaluable is the **Lyon City Card,** which authorizes unlimited public transportation along with admission to the 14 biggest museums, tours, audio-tours, and boat tours. Valid for 1, 2, or 3 days. €15, €25, and €30, respectively. **Internet access** available but expensive. Office open May-Oct. M-Sa 9am-7pm; Nov.-Apr. daily 10am-6pm. For info on entertainment and cinema, try the weekly *Lyon Poche* (€1) or seasonal *Lyon Libertin* (€3) and *Guides de l'été de Lyon: Restaurant Nuits* (€2), all available in *tabacs*. For longer stays, get the free gold mine of all goings-on, *Le Petit Paumé.*

Bus Tours: Philibert (☎04 78 98 56 00; fax 04 78 23 11 07; webescapes@philibert.fr). 1½hr. tour of Lyon, with audio-guides in 6 languages. Tour starts at Perrache. You can get on or off at any point and reconnect later on. Mar. 30-Oct. daily. €17.

Consulates: Canada, 21 rue Bourgelat, 2ème (☎04 72 77 64 07), 1 block west of the Ampère-Victor Hugo métro. Open M-F 9am-noon. **Ireland,** 58 rue Victor Lagrange, 7ème (☎06 85 23 12 03). Open M-F 9am-noon. **UK,** 24 rue Childebert, 2ème (☎04 72 77 81 70). M: Bellecour. Open M-F 9am-noon and 2-5pm. **US,** in the World Trade Center, 16 rue de la République, 2ème (☎04 78 38 33 03). Open by appointment only 10am-noon and 2-5pm.

Money: Currency exchange in the tourist office, or for no commission at **Goldfinger S.A.R.L.,** 81 rue de la République (☎04 72 40 06 00). Bond? Perhaps. Open M-Sa 9:30am-6:30pm.

LOCAL SERVICES

English Bookstore: Decitre, 6 pl. Bellecour, 2ème (☎04 26 68 00 12). Fantastic selection and English-speaking salespeople to advise. Open M-Sa 9:30am-7pm. MC/V.

Bureau d'Informations de Jeunesse (BIJ), 9 quai des Célestins (☎04 72 77 00 66), lists jobs and more. Open M noon-6pm, Tu and Th-F 10am-6pm, W 10am-7pm, Sa 10am-1pm and 2-5pm. Closed Sa July-Aug.

Women's Center: Centre d'Information Féminine, 18 pl. Tolozan, 1er (☎04 78 39 32 25). Open M-F noon-1pm and 1:30-5pm.

Gay Support: Maison des Homosexualities, 16 rue St-Polycarpe (☎04 78 27 10 10). Social and cultural center, with library. Call for schedule of events.

24hr. Pharmacy: Pharmacie Blanchet, 5 pl. des Cordeliers, 2ème (☎04 78 42 12 42). Opens Su at 7pm.

Laundromat: Lavadou, 19 rue Ste-Hélène, north of pl. Ampère, 2ème. Open daily 7:30am-8:30pm. **Laverie,** 51 rue de la Charité, 2ème. Open daily 6am-10pm.

EMERGENCY AND COMMUNICATIONS

Police: 47 rue de la Charité (☎04 78 42 26 56). **Emergency:** ☎17.

Crisis Lines: SOS Amitié (☎04 78 29 88 88). **SOS Racisme** (☎04 78 39 24 44). Tu 6-8pm. **AIDS** info service, 2 rue Montebello, 3ème (toll-free ☎0800 840 800).

Hospitals: All hospitals should have English-speaking doctors on call. **Hôpital Edouard Herriot,** 5 pl. Arsonval. M: Grange Blanche. Best for serious emergencies, but far from the center of town. More central is **Hôpital Hôtel-Dieu,** 1 pl. de l'Hôpital, 2ème, near quai du Rhône. The central city hospital line, ☎08 20 08 20 09, will tell you where to go. There's also **Hôpital Antiquaille,** rue de l'Antiquaille, in Roman Lyon.

SOS Médecins, 10 pl. Dumas de Loire (☎04 78 83 51 51), arranges home visits.

Internet Access: Station-Internet, 4 rue du President Carnot, 2ème (☎08 00 69 20 01). €7 per hr., students €5. Open M-Sa 10am-7pm. **Connectix Café,** 19 quai St-Antoine, 2ème (☎04 72 77 98 85). €7 per hr. Open M-Sa 11am-7pm.

Post Office: pl. Antonin Poncet, 2ème (☎04 72 40 65 22), next to pl. Bellecour. **Currency exchange.** Open M-F 8am-7pm, Sa 8am-12:30pm. **Poste Restante:** 69002. **Postal Codes:** 69001-69009; last digit indicates *arrondissement.*

▛ ACCOMMODATIONS AND CAMPING

France's second financial center (after Paris, *bien sûr*) is filled on weekday nights with businessmen who leave by the weekend. Fall is the busiest season; it's easier and cheaper to find a place in the summer, but is still prudent to get reservations. Budget hotels cluster east of pl. Carnot. Prices rise as you approach pl. Bellecour, but there are some inexpensive options north of pl. des Terreaux. Vieux Lyon tends to break budgets, unless you stay in the hostel.

■ **Hôtel de Paris,** 16 rue de la Platière, 1er (☎04 78 28 00 95; fax 04 78 39 57 64). This hotel bursts with color and character in a way hardly imaginable considering the less Technicolor street outside. Comfortable lobby adorned with black-and-white Impressionist drawings of Lyon. Ranging from classic to futuristic, rooms have beautiful curtains and big, clean bathrooms. Breakfast €6.50. Reception 24hr. Singles €42; doubles €49-75; triples €78; quads €81. AmEx/MC/V. ❹

■ **Hôtel St. Vincent,** 9 rue Pareille, 1er (☎04 78 27 22 56; fax 04 78 30 92 87), just off quai Saint-Vincent. Simple, elegant rooms, within stumbling distance of much nightlife. Breakfast €5.50. Reception 24hr. Reserve ahead. Singles with shower €31, with toilet €38; doubles €38-47; triples €50-53. MC/V. ❸

Auberge de Jeunesse (HI), 41-45 montée du Chemin Neuf (☎04 78 15 05 50; fax 04 78 15 05 51). M: Vieux Lyon. On the west bank of the Saône, turn left onto montée du Chemin Neuf and prepare for a good 7min. climb. The hostel is a 15min. walk from pl. Bellecour, 25min. from Perrache. Or take the funicular from Vieux Lyon to Minimes, walk down the stairs and go left down the hill for 5min. Sure, the bathrooms might smell, and the showers only leave you with one free hand, but this outgoing, rocking hostel with stunning views of the city below is the place to meet fellow travelers in Lyon. Helpful staff. Bar, laundry, Internet access (a *chère* €2.25 per 15 min.), and kitchen. Modern, split-level 4- to 8- bunk rooms can be hot in summer. Breakfast included. Sheets €2.70. Reception 24hr. Reservations recommended. Bunks €12.20. **Members only.** V. ❶

Hôtel Vaubecour, 28 rue Vaubecour, 2*ème* (☎04 78 37 44 91; fax 04 78 42 90 17). Somewhat mysteriously hidden away on the third floor of an antique building with gorgeous high ceilings. Breakfast €3.85. Reception 7am-10pm. Reserve June-Aug. Singles from €22.90; doubles from €25.95; triples and quads from €54.15. Extra bed €12.20. MC/V. ❷

Grand Hôtel des Terreaux, 16 rue Lanterne, 1*er* (☎04 78 27 04 10; fax 04 78 27 97 75). Tastefully decorated, plush chambers with oversized bathrooms. The lobby and dining room, with a solid black stained-glass ceiling and overhanging wire lights, border on the postmodern. Buffet breakfast €8.50. Reception 24hr. Singles €72.50-125; doubles €82-125; triples €92-136. AmEx/MC/V. ❺

Hôtel d'Ainay, 14 rue des Remparts d'Ainay, 2*ème* (☎04 78 42 43 42; fax 04 72 77 51 90). M: Ampère-Victor Hugo. Basic, cheap, and sunny rooms. Breakfast €4. Shower €2.50. Reception 6am-10pm. Singles €22.50-26, with shower €32-37; doubles €27.50, €34-38.50. MC/V. ❷

Hôtel du Dauphiné, 3 rue Duhamel, 2*ème* (☎04 78 37 24 19; fax 04 78 92 81 52). Plain, comfortable rooms with showers; watch out for the massive plants on your way in the building. Rooms over €33 have TV. Breakfast €4.20. Reception 24hr. Check-out 11:30am. Singles €23-43; doubles €36.50-45; triples and quads €54-56. MC/V. ❷

Hôtel St-Pierre des Terreaux, 8 rue Paul Chenavard, 1*er* (☎04 78 28 24 61; fax 04 72 00 21 07). M: Hôtel de Ville. While it emits a certain 1970s vibe, this cheery, often-crowded hotel is well situated. All rooms have baths or showers. Breakfast €5.50. Reception 24hr. Reserve 10 days ahead. Singles €30-39; doubles €40-43; triples €54. MC/V. ❸

Camping Dardilly, 10km from Lyon in a dull suburb (☎04 78 35 64 55). From the Hôtel de Ville, take bus #19 (dir: Ecully-Dardilly) to "Parc d'Affaires." Pool, TV, and restaurant. Reception 8am-10pm. €3.05 per person; tent €6.10, caravan €7.60, car free. Electricity €3. MC/V. ❶

⛶ FOOD

The galaxy of Michelin stars adorning the city's restaurants confirms what the locals proudly declare—this is the gastronomic capital of the Western world. *Lyonnais* food is as bizarre as it is elegant and as creative as it is delicious. A typical delicacy consists of an unusual cow part (their feet) prepared in a subtle, creamy sauce. For dessert, finish off with *tarte tatin,* an apple tart baked upside-down and then turned over. Luckily, the tradition is an intrinsic part of the city's fabric; you can sample fine food even in inexpensive restaurants.

THE PRIDE OF LYON

The pinnacle of the *lyonnais* food scene is ▓**Chez Paul Bocuse** ❺, 9km out of town, where meals cost approximately the equivalent of Andorra's GNP. (See sidebar, **The Big Splurge.**) For *lyonnais* master Jean-Paul Lacombe's cuisine, head to **Leon**

THE BIG SPLURGE

CHEZ PAUL BOCUSE

Named the best restaurant in the world, **Chez Paul Bocuse ❺** is worth the indulgence at least once in your life—taking out a second mortgage has never been quite so delicious!

As the valet opens the door, you'll enter an exquisite set of dining rooms decorated with gold chandeliers and large mirrors. A fleet of attentive waiters appearing on cue, bearing the first plate of a 5- to 7-course meal. The dishes—rich, creamy, and enjoyable beyond description—follow centuries of traditional French cooking. Finish off with an extravagant dessert from the selection of gourmet treats lined up in front of you. If Bocuse isn't off on one of his international voyages, he'll likely come by himself to ask you how your meal is.

Appetizers include *foie gras de canard* (duck liver pâté, €32) and *soupe aux truffes noires* (black truffle soup, €72). Fish dishes include *filets de sole aux nouilles Fernand Point* (filet of sole in the style of Bocuse's mentor, Fernand Point; €42.50). For meat, try the *filet de boeuf du Charolais poelé au poivre* (pepper steak, €38.50) or *fricasse de volaille de Bresse à la crème aux morilles* chicken with mushrooms, €40). Bon appetit! *(50 rue de la Plage in Collonges-au-Mont-d'Or. By bus: take #40 "Neuville" (€1.40). Tell the driver you are going to "Bocuse" and he will tell you where to get off the bus.* ☎ 04 72 42 90 90; fax 04 72 27 85 87. *Individual dishes €12-72; menus €104, €136, and €139. Open daily noon-2pm and 8-9:30pm, F-Sa until 10 pm. AmEx/MC/V.)*

de Lyon ❺, 1 rue Pléney, 1er (☎ 04 72 10 11 12; *menus* €55, €86, and €135. Open Tu-Sa noon-2pm and 7:30-10pm). To savor the creations of yet another superchef, try Philippe Chavent's **La Tour Rose ❺**, at 22 rue du Boeuf, 5ème. (☎ 04 78 92 69 11; *menus* €53, €91, and €106; open M-Sa noon-1pm and 7-9:30pm.) You need not sell your inner organs to enjoy Bocusian cuisine, however—the master has several spin-off restaurants in Lyon with scrumptious yet affordable food. At **Le Nord ❹**, 18 rue Neuve, 2ème, Bocuse's traditional food graces the €18 *menu* in a famed century-old *brasserie*. (Extravagant desserts €5-6. ☎ 04 72 10 69 69; fax 04 72 10 69 68. Open daily noon-2:30pm and 7pm-midnight. AmEx/MC/V.) Bocuse's kitchens serve up more Mediterranean fare at the appropriately named **Le Sud ❸**, 11 pl. Antonin Poncet, 2ème, which has a €18 *menu*, plus pizzas and pastas from around €10.80, in a formal, beautiful setting. (☎ 04 72 77 80 00. Open noon-2:30pm and 7pm-midnight. AmEx/MC/V.) Whether you're heading north or south, reserve a few days ahead.

Locals take pride in their *cocons* (chocolates wrapped in marzipan), made in Lyon's grandest *pâtisserie*, **■Bernachon**, 42 cours F. Roosevelt, 6ème. Their chocolate is made entirely from scratch, starting with the bean. The showcases sparkle with pastries and the ambrosial *palets d'or*, which are recognized as the best chocolates in France—and not only because they're made with gold dust. (☎ 04 78 24 37 98. Individual delicacies €1-3. Open M-F 9am-7pm, Sa 8:30am-7pm and Su 8:30am-5pm in winter. Closed in Aug.)

OTHER FLEURS-DE-LYON

If *haute cuisine* doesn't suit your wallet and university canteens don't suit your palate, try one of Lyon's many **bouchons,** descendants of the inns where travelers would stop to dine and have their horses *bouchonné* (rubbed down). These cozy restaurants serving local fare can be found along **rue Mercière** and **rue des Marronniers** in the 2ème. Most places in Vieux Lyon are sure to feed you very well; try the *bouchons* along rue St-Jean, which have *menus* from €12-13. Also consider the cheaper Chinese restaurants or *brasseries* on the wide streets off **rue de la République** (2ème) or the kebab joints around the Hôtel de Ville.

■ **Chez Mounier,** 3 rue des Marronniers, 2ème (☎ 04 78 37 79 26). Delicious and generous traditional specialties in a sparingly decorated but exceedingly warm setting, with unendingly cheerful waitstaff. 4-course *menus* €9.60, €13.60, and €15.10. Open Tu-Sa noon-2pm and 7-10:30pm, Su noon-2pm. ❸

■ **Chabert et Fils,** 11 rue des Marronniers, 2ème (☎04 78 37 01 94). One of the best-known *bouchons*. *Museau de bœuf* (snout of cattle) is only one of many strange, typical *lyonnais* concoctions on the €16 *menu*. For dessert, try the indescribable, creamy *guignol* (€5.40), but plan to take an after-dinner nap. Lunch *menus* €8-12.50, dinner *menus* €16-27.50. Open daily noon-2pm and 7-11pm, F-Sa until 11:30pm. MC/V. ❸

L'Assiette St-Jean, 10 rue Saint Jean, 5ème (☎04 72 41 96 20). An excellent *bouchon*, with unusual, somewhat archaic decor. House speciality *gateau de foies de volaille* (chicken liver) €6.60; *menus* €13-27.50. Open June-Aug. Tu-Su noon-2pm and 7-10:30pm; rest of year W-Su 7-10:30pm. AmEx/MC/V. ❸

L'Etoile de l'Orient, 31 rue des Remparts d'Ainay, 2ème (☎04 72 41 07 87). M: Ampère-Victor Hugo. Be sure to have some tea at this intimate Tunisian restaurant, run by an exceedingly warm couple. Tajine lamb €11.50, couscous dishes €11-13. *Menus* €10-25. Open M noon-2pm, Tu-Su noon-2pm and 7-11pm. ❸

Mister Patate, pl. St. Jean, 5ème (☎04 78 38 18 79). All potatoes, all the time, with *plats* from €6.80-8.10. Some vegetarian options. Open Tu-Sa 11:30am-2pm and 6:30-11pm, Su 11:30am-3pm and 6:30-10pm. ❷

SUPERMARKETS

Supermarkets include a **Monoprix** on rue de la République at pl. des Cordeliers, 2ème. (Open daily 8:30am-8:30pm.) If you're craving a more gourmet experience, shop at **Maréchal Centre,** rue de la Platière at rue Lanterne, 1er. (☎04 72 98 24 00. Open M-Sa 8:30am-8:30pm.) You won't find any culinary masterpieces in Lyon's many university restaurants, but they're sure to please your wallet. One is **Résidence la Madeleine,** 4 rue Sauveur, 7ème. (☎04 78 72 80 62. Meals about €2.50. Open M-F 11:30am-1pm and 6:30-8pm, Sa 11:30am-1pm. Closed Aug.)

◎ SIGHTS

VIEUX LYON

Stacked up against the Saône at the bottom of the Fourvière hill, the narrow streets of Vieux Lyon wind between lively cafés, tree-lined squares, and magnificent Medieval and Renaissance houses. The colorful *hôtels particuliers*, with their delicate carvings, shaded courtyards, and ornate turrets, sprang up between the 15th and 18th centuries when Lyon controlled Europe's silk and publishing industries. The regal homes around rue St-Jean, rue du Bœuf, and rue Juiverie have housed Lyon's elite for 400 years—and still do.

TRABOULES. The distinguishing feature of Vieux Lyon townhouses is the **traboules** (see **Insider's City,** p. 664), tunnels leading from the street through a maze of courtyards, often with vaulted ceilings and statuary niches. Although their original purpose is still debated, later **traboules** were constructed to transport silk safely from looms to storage rooms. During WWII, the passageways proved invaluable as info-gathering and escape routes for the Resistance (though some *résistants* found their way blocked by Germans on the way out). Many are open to the public at specific hours, especially in the morning; get a list of addresses from the tourist office or, better yet, take one of their tours. *(Tours in English everyday at 2pm and in French at 2:30pm in summer, irregular hours during rest of year, consult tourist office. €9, students €4.50.)*

CATHÉDRALE ST-JEAN. The southern end of Vieux Lyon is dominated by the Cathédrale St-Jean, with its soaring columns and multicolored stained glass windows, some of which are relatively new replacements, due to the shattering debris of Lyon's exploding bridges during the Nazis's hasty retreat in 1944. Paris might

THE LOCAL STORY

CHEF OF THE CENTURY

Let's Go was about to interview world-renowned lyonnais chef **Paul Bocuse** from a telephone booth in Lyon when Bocuse suggested that Let's Go come out to his place for lunch, at Collonges-au-Mont-d'Or. Let's Go obliged, rushing back to the hostel to put on something approaching its Sunday best.

Paul Bocuse is, in four words, the original celebrity chef. The very top of his exhausting list of awards includes Commander of the National Order of Merit (one of France's highest honors). The prestigious international culinary competition named in his honor, the Bocuse d'Or (the Bocuse Gold medal), reflects the luster of his international reputation.

Let's Go found Bocuse to be warm, direct and assured. An imposing man in his mid-70s who recovered from a World War II wound under American care (he has frequently said he has American blood in his veins), Bocuse sat very close to the table, decked out in a trademark chef's hat.

Q: The title "Chef of the Century," the sculpture of you in the Musée Grevin, international fame and success—did you ever think all this was possible?

A: [chuckles softly] "Chef of the Century" is not a big deal...I think that we have a craft, a manual craft, and I believe it is important to work well. Above all, it is necessary to pass on our craft to future generations. That is what's most important.

Q: Can you explain to me your cooking philosophy?

A: The most important thing in cook-

have been worth a mass, but Lyon got the wedding cake; it was here that Henri IV met and married Maria de Medici in 1600. Inside, every hour between noon and 4pm, automatons pop out of the 14th-century astronomical clock in a charming reenactment of the Annunciation. The clock can calculate Church feast days until 2019. _(Cathedral open M-F 8am-noon and 2-7:30pm, Sa-Su 8am-noon and 2-7pm.)_

MUSEUMS. Down rue St-Jean, turn left at pl. du Change for the **Hôtel de Gadagne,** a typical 16th-century Vieux Lyon building, and its relatively minor museums. The better of the two is the **Musée de la Marionette,** which displays "skeptical" puppets from around the world, including models of **Guignol,** the famed local cynic, and his inebriated friend, Gnaffron. _(Pl. du Petit College, 5ème. M: Vieux Lyon. ☎ 04 78 42 03 61. 1hr. tours on request. Open W-M 10:45am-6pm. €3.80, students €2, under 19 free.)_

FOURVIÈRE AND ROMAN LYON

From the corner of rue du Bœuf and rue de la Bombarde in Vieux Lyon, climb the stairs heading straight up to reach **Fourvière Hill,** the nucleus of **Roman Lyon.** From the top of the stairs, continue up via the rose-lined **Chemin de la Rosaire,** a series of switchbacks that leads through a garden to the **espl. Fourvière,** where a model of the city points out local landmarks. Most prefer to take the less strenuous **funicular** (known as _la ficelle_) to the top of the hill. It leaves from the head of av. A. Max in Vieux Lyon, off pl. St-Jean. The **Tour de l'Observatoire,** on the eastern edge of the hilltop basilique, offers a more acute angle on the city. On a clear day, scan for Mont Blanc, about 200km to the east. _(Jardin de la Rosaire open daily 6:30am-9:30pm. Tour open W-Su 10am-noon and 2-6:30pm. €2, children under 15 €1.)_

■ BASILIQUE NOTRE-DAME DE FOURVIÈRE.

Lyon's archbishop vowed to build a church if the city was spared attack during the Franco-Prussian War. His bargain was met, and the bishop followed through. The basilica's white, meringue-like exterior is gorgeous from a distance. The low, heavy crypt, used for mass, was conceived by the architect Pierre Bossan to contrast with the impossibly high and golden Byzantine basilica above. Here, the walls are decked with gorgeous, gilded, gigantic mosaics depicting religious scenes, Joan of Arc at Orléans, and the naval battle of Lepante. _(Behind the Esplanade at very top of the hill. Chapel open daily 7am-7pm; basilica open 8am-7pm.)_

MUSÉE GALLO-ROMAIN. Circling deep into the historic hillside of Fourvière, this brilliant museum holds a collection of arms, pottery, statues, and jewelry, including six large, luminous mosaics, a bronze tablet inscribed with a speech by Lyon's favorite son, Emperor Claudius, and a huge, half-cracked eggshell pot. Artifacts are well-labeled in English and French. *(Open Mar.-Oct. Tu-Su 10am-6pm; Nov.-Feb. 10am-5pm. €3.80, students €2.30. Free Th.)*

PARC ARCHÉOLOGIQUE. Just next to the Minimes/ Théâtre Romain funicular stop, the Parc holds the almost too well-restored 2000-year-old **Théâtre Romain** and the smaller **Odéon,** discovered when modern developers dug into the hill. Both still function as venues for shows during the **Nuits de Fourvière** (see **Festivals,** p. 666). *(Open Apr. 15-Sept. 15 9am-9pm; Sept. 16-Apr. 14 7am-7pm. Free.)*

LA PRESQU'ILE AND LES TERREAUX

Monumental squares, statues, and fountains are the trademarks of presqu'île, the lively area between the Rhône and the Saône. At its heart is **pl. Bellecour,** from which pedestrian **rue Victor Hugo** strolls quietly south, lined with boutiques and bladers. To the north, crowded **rue de la République,** or "la Ré," is the urban aorta of Lyon. It runs through **pl. de la République** and ends at **pl. Louis Pradel** in the 1er, at the tip of the Terreaux district. Once a marshy wasteland, the area was filled with soil, creating dry terraces *(terreaux)* and establishing the neighborhood as the place to be for chic locals. Now bars, clubs, and sidewalk cafés fill up after 8pm and keep this area hopping late into the night. Across the square at **pl. Louis Pradel** is the spectacular 17th-century facade of the **Hôtel de Ville,** framed by an illuminated cement field of miniature geysers. The **Opéra,** pl. Louis Pradel, is a 19th-century Neoclassical edifice supporting what looks like an airplane hangar, alluringly lit in dark red at night.

■ MUSÉE DES BEAUX-ARTS. This unassuming, excellent museum includes a comprehensive archaeological wing, a distinguished collection of French paintings, works by Dutch and Spanish masters (including Picasso), a section devoted to the Italian Renaissance, and a lovely sculpture garden. Even the more esoteric works mixed into all-star pre-, post-, and just-plain-Impressionist collections are delightful. Explore, and a few nice surprises await: a Rodin bust of national hero Victor Hugo at the end of his life (1883), and an unbelievably large French coin collection. *(20 pl. des Terreaux. ☎04 72 10 17 40. Open W-Th and Sa-M 10am-6pm, F 10:30am-8pm. Sculptures closed noon-1pm; paintings closed 1-2pm. €3.80, students with ID €2.)*

ing is first to use good products. It's also important to have a team that understands my craft. We are a craft that requires companions.

Q: Do you feel that a high level of creativity is essential to contemporary cuisine?

A: Here, we do *la cuisine classique.* Yes, there is much creativity—I believe that's an important part of the craft. But our cuisine is, how shall I say, that of the old style. We do not seek out new influences. *Bien sur,* there are many restaurants that are very interesting, but we do not seek out Japanese influences, Asian influences, Californian influences. We remain within the cuisine of the region, as we have done for fifty years. We do not do *cuisine fusion.* That is a cuisine of confusion.

Q: What is your advice for travelers who don't have a lot of money?

A: *Alors,* the *brasseries*—one can eat much cheaper there.

Q: What do you think of patrons who drink Coca-cola with their meals?

A: I believe that in life people must remain free. If you drink Coca-cola, well, why not? It's perhaps not the...ideal...drink for a *repas* in France, but *pourquoi pas?*

Q: One last question: for the grand dinners at big international conferences—for example, the G7 summit conference of 1997—are you ever nervous a bit before dinners like that? Stage-fright, so to speak?

A: No, no, no [chuckling]. It's exactly like here. *Et maintenant,* [pointing to the first course, which is already sitting on the table], leave this and eat. Eat that there.

THE INSIDER'S CITY

TRABOULES IN VIEUX LYON

One of Lyon's most celebrated sights is its *traboules*—long passageways through buildings and courtyards used in the silk trade and the Resistance. *Traboules* are generally open daily 7am-8pm, some only in the morning.

1 The smallest traboule in Vieux Lyon, this one has a huge wooden door and a courtyard with flowers.

2 This short traboule leads to a spacious courtyard with pink houses. La Tour Rose—a spiraling Rapunzel-like tower—sits above the greenery.

3 This *traboule* leads to a tall, graceful courtyard, complete with a 16th century galleria.

4 Covered with graffiti, this shady golden courtyard is guarded by a gargoyle dog on the second floor.

5 For a change in pace, try the Petit Musée Fantastique de Guignol, a comic assortment of puppets. (☎04 78 37 01 67. Open M 2:30-7pm, Tu-Su 11am-12:30pm and 2:30-7pm, Su 11am-1pm and 3-6:30pm. €5, children €3.)

6 The Maison Thomassin features an overhanging ceiling dating to 1295—one of the oldest in France.

LA CROIX-ROUSSE AND THE SILK INDUSTRY

Lyon is proud of its historical dominance of European silk manufacture. The 1801 invention of the power loom by *lyonnais* Joseph Jacquard intensified the sweatshop conditions endured by the *canuts* (silk workers). Unrest came to a head in the 1834 riot in which hundreds were killed. Mass silk manufacturing is based elsewhere today, and Lyon's few remaining silk workers perform delicate handiwork, reconstructing and replicating rare patterns for museum and château displays.

■ **MUSÉE HISTORIQUE DES TISSUS.** It's not in the Croix-Rousse quarter, but textile and fashion fans—along with anyone else who's ever worn clothes, maybe even men—will have a field day here. This world-class collection includes examples of 18th-century elite garb (such as Marie-Antoinette's Versailles winter wardrobe), scraps of luxurious Byzantine textiles and silk wall-hangings that look like stained glass windows. Included with admission is the neighboring **Musée des Arts Décoratifs,** housed in an 18th-century **hôtel.** (*34 rue de la Charité, 2ème.* ☎04 78 38 42 00. Tissus open Tu-Su 10am-5:30pm. Arts Décoratifs open Tu-Su 10am-noon and 2-5:30pm. Maps in English. Tour in French Su 3pm. €4.60, students with ID €2.30.)

LA MAISON DES CANUTS. Some old silk looms in a tiny back room are all that remain of the weaving techniques of the *canuts* (silk weavers.) The Maison's shop sells silk made by its own *canuts.* Though a scarf costs €30 and up, you can take home a silkworm cocoon for €7 or less, and a handkerchief for €7. (*10-12 rue d'Ivry, 4ème.* ☎04 78 28 62 04; fax 04 78 28 16 93. Tours by arrangement. Open M-F 9am-noon and 2-6:30pm, Sa 9am-noon and 2-6pm. €4, students €2.30.)

EAST OF THE RHÔNE AND MODERN LYON

Lyon's newest train station and monstrous space-age mall form the core of the ultra-modern Part-Dieu district. Locals call the commercial **Tour du Crédit Lyonnais** *"le Crayon"* for its unwitting resemblance to a giant pencil standing on end. Next to it, the shell-shaped **Auditorium Maurice Ravel** hosts major cultural events.

CENTRE D'HISTOIRE DE LA RÉSISTANCE ET DE LA DÉPORTATION. The center is in a building in which Nazis tortured detainees during the Occupation. Here you'll find an impressive collection of assembled documents, photos, and films of the Resistance, which was based in Lyon; you'll also learn that media-savvy martyr Jean Moulin set up an official Resistance press agency. *(14 av. Bertholet, 7ème. M: Jean Macé. ☎04 78 72 23 11. Open W-Su 9am-5:30pm. €3.80, students €2. Admission includes an audio-guide in French, English, or German.)*

MUSÉE D'ART CONTEMPORAIN. In the futuristic **Cité International de Lyon,** a super-modern complex with offices, shops, theaters, and Interpol's world headquarters, you'll find this extensive, wholly entertaining mecca of modern art. All the museum's exhibits are temporary; the walls themselves are built anew for each installation. *(Quai Charles de Gaulle, next to Parc de la Tête d'Or, 6ème. Take bus #4 from M: Foch. ☎04 72 69 17 17. Open W noon-10pm and Th-Su noon-7pm. €3.80, students €2, less than 18 free.)*

INSTITUT LUMIÈRE. A visit to Lyon would somehow be incomplete without a stop at this museum, which chronicles the exploits of the brothers Lumière, inventors of film in 1895. It is a relatively small museum, but full of intriguing factoids: the brothers also invented postsychronisation, and Louis in 1920 created a forerunner to holograms. The Institut's complex also includes a movie theater, "Le Hangar du Premier-Film," and a park. *(25 rue du Premier-Film, 8ème. M: Monplaisir Lumière. ☎04 78 78 1895. Open Tu-Su 11am-7pm. €5.50, students €4.50.)*

PARC DE LA TÊTE D'OR. This massive and completely free park, one of the biggest in Europe, owes its name to a legend that a golden head of Jesus lies buried somewhere within its grounds. The park sprawls over 259 acres; you can rent paddle boats to explore its artificial green lake and island. Reindeer, elephants, and a thousand other animals fill the zoo; giant greenhouses encase the botanical garden. The 60,000-bush rose gardens are magnificent. *(M: Charpennes or Tram T1 from Perrache, dir: IUT-Feyssine. ☎04 78 89 02 03. Open Apr. 15-Oct. 14 6am-11pm; Oct. 15-Apr. 14 6am-9pm.)*

▓ NIGHTLIFE

Nightlife in Lyon is fast and furious; the city is crawling with nightclubs. There is a row of semi-exclusive joints off the Saône, on quais Romain Rolland, de Bondy, and Pierre Scize in Vieux Lyon *(5ème)*, but the city's best and most accessible late-night spots are a strip of riverboat dance clubs by the east bank of the Rhône. Students congregate in a series of bars on **rue Ste-Catherine** *(1er)* until 1am before heading to the clubs. More suggestions can be found in *Lyon Libertin* (€3) and *Guides de l'Eté de Lyon: Restaurant/Nuits* (€2), available at *tabacs.*

▓ **Le Fish,** across from 21 quai Augagneur (☎04 72 87 98 98), plays salsa, jungle, hip-hop, disco, and house in a swank boat with a packed dance floor; this club is chic nightclub royalty. Say hi to Dai, a veteran *lyonnais* bouncer, and he might give you a tour too. €11-13 F-Sa cover includes 1st drink, free before 11pm. Open W-Th 10pm-5am, F-Sa 10pm-6am. **Students only.**

Ayers Rock Café, 2 rue Desirée (☎04 78 29 13 45), and the **Cosmopolitan** (☎04 72 07 09 80), right next door. If you can still walk, be sure to stumble over, as both places are usually packed with students. Both have shooters for €3. Ayers has fabulous bartenders who put on as much of a show as those scandalous people in the corner. Cosmo is a little darker, a little less international, a little more restrained in its coolness. Ayers open daily 6pm-3am; Cosmo open M-Sa 8pm-3am.

Le Voxx, 1 rue d'Algérie (☎04 78 28 33 87), packed with stylish French and almost-stylish exchange students, is the latest in a series of hotspots radiating off pl. des Terreaux. Open M-Sa 8pm-2am and Su 10pm-2am.

Le Funambule, 29 rue de l'Arbre Sec (☎04 72 07 86 70), is a darkly lit, hip bar for the late-20s crowd. Open Tu-Th 7pm-1am and F-Sa 7pm-3am.

Le Chantier, 20 rue Ste-Catherine (☎04 78 39 05 56), has 12 tequila shots for €15.25. You have to slip down a spiral slide to reach the dance floor downstairs, which is filled with a crowd of students and locals. Open Tu-Sa 9pm-3am, sometimes later.

Tavern of the Drunken Parrot, next door to Le Chantier (☎04 78 28 01 39), serves homemade, extremely potent rum drinks (€2); the dark-and-dirty ship motif is certainly interesting. Open daily 6pm-3am.

La Marquise (☎04 78 71 78 71), next door to Le Fish, spends less on the boat but more on big-name jungle and house DJs. Cover €6 for occasional *soirées à thème*. Open W-Sa 11pm-dawn.

GAY AND LESBIAN NIGHTLIFE

The tourist office's city guide lists spots catering to Lyon's active gay community, and *Le Petit Paumé* offers superb tips. The most popular gay spots are in the 1er.

L'United Café, impasse de la Pêcherie (☎04 78 29 93 18), in an alley off quai de la Pêcherie. The weekend club circuit normally starts here around midnight, with American and Latino dance hits. Theme nights throughout the week range from the post office to beach party—and there are lip-shaped urinals to boot. No cover; drinks €3-6. Open daily 10:30pm-5am.

DV1, 6 rue Violi (☎04 72 07 72 62), off rue Royale, north of pl. Louis Pradel. Drag queens nightly, with a huge dance floor. A mostly male, mid-20s to mid-30s crowd. Drinks €3.50-4. Open W-Th and Su 10pm-3am, F-Sa 10pm-5am.

CAP Opéra, 2 pl. Louis Pradel (☎04 72 07 61 55), is a popular gay pub, with red lights to match the Opéra next door. Occasional *soirées à thème*. Open daily 2pm-3am.

L'Echiquier, 38 rue de l'Arbre-Sec (☎04 78 29 18 19). Mixed gay/lesbian crowd. Karaoke steals the show on Tu and W nights. Cover €7.65. Open W-M 10pm-dawn.

🎭 ENTERTAINMENT

LIVE PERFORMANCE AND CINEMA

Lyon's major stage theatre is the **Théâtre des Célestins,** pl. des Celestins, 2ème (☎04 72 77 40 00; box office open Tu-Sa noon-7pm; tickets €8-29, discounts for under 26 and over 65). The **Opéra,** pl. de la Comédie, 1er (☎04 72 00 45 45), has pricey tickets (€10-72), but €8 tickets for those under 26 and over 65 go on sale 15 minutes before the show. (Reservations office open M-Sa noon-7pm.) The acclaimed **Orchestre National de Lyon** plays a full season. (☎04 78 95 95 95. Oct.-June. Tickets €12-45.) The **Maison de la Danse,** 8 av. Jean Mermoz, 8ème (☎04 72 78 18 00; tickets €12-38), keeps pace with the dance scene. Lyon, the birthplace of cinema, is a superb place to see quality film. The **Cinéma Opéra,** 6 rue J. Serlin (☎04 78 28 80 08), and **Le Cinéma,** 18 impasse St-Polycarpe (☎04 78 39 09 72), specialize in black and white undubbed classics (€5.20-6.10).

FESTIVALS

In summer, Lyon has a festival or special event nearly every week. The **Fête de la Musique** (June 21) and **Bastille Day** (July 14) engender major partying. The end of June sets off the two-week **Festival du Jazz à Vienne,** welcoming jazz masters to Vienne, a medieval town south of Lyon, accessible by bus or train. (☎04 74 85 00 05 or Vienne's tourist office, 11 cours Brillier, ☎04 74 53 80 30. Tickets €26, students €24, children 12-16 years €17, under 12 free.) The **Pavillon de Tourisme** may provide special festival buses, as parking in Vienne is difficult. **Les Nuits de Fourvière** is a three-month summer festival held in the ancient Théâtre Romain and Odéon, from mid-June through mid-Sept. Popular artists are interspersed with classical concerts, movies, dance, and plays. (☎ 04 72 32 00 00. €10-35 tickets and info at the Théâtre Romain or the FNAC shop on rue de la République.)

The biennial **Festival de Musique du Vieux Lyon**, 5 pl. du Petit Collège, 5ème, brings artists from around the world to perform in Lyon's old town in early and mid-December. (☎ 04 78 38 09 09. Tickets €15-36.) Every December 8, locals place candles in their windows and ascend with tapers to the basilica for the **Fête des Lumières.** The celebration (which turns into a city-wide block party) honors the Virgin Mary for protecting Lyon from the Black Plague.

🔲 DAYTRIP FROM LYON: PÉROUGES

This tiny hamlet is such a source of history and pride for Europe that it was the site of the G-7 summit in 1996. Pérouges's streets, affectionately called **"galets,"** are made with rounded stones collected from nearby rivers, and their shape and color blend into the structure of the homes. While legend has it that Pérouges was built by a tribe of Gauls coming from Italy, the town has changed nationalities many times due to its location between feuding dukes and kings. Most of the buildings in the town date to the 15th century, a period of prosperity during which weaving was preeminent. Exquisitely preserved, the castles, caves, and plentiful, draping flora invoke romantic associations of royalty. The town's culinary specialty is **galette de Pérouges** (a doughy pastry made with sufficient amounts of sugar and butter), which is served with *cerdon*, a magnificent wine.

A superb way to see the evolution of the area's history is to stop in at the **Musée de Vieux Pérouges,** in the Maison des Princes, to which citizens have donated ancient wares. (Open M-F 10am-noon and 2-6pm, Sa-Su 10am-7pm. Closed Nov.-May. €3, children €2.) The **tourist office** can help with getting around. (☎ 04 74 61 01 14. Open May-Sept. M-F 9am-noon and 2-5pm. During off-season, call ahead.)

Pérouges is only 35km outside of Lyon. **Trains** run from **Lyon** (30min., M-Sa 16 per day, Su 7 trains per day, €5.60). From the train station, make a left onto rue de Verdun. At the fountain, make another left and then take your second right onto rue Pérouges. After 10 minutes, make a right onto a steep road which brings you uphill to town. Or take a **Philibert Tour** from Lyon with commentaries in English. (Tours leave Apr.-Oct. Sa from Part-Dieu at 1:15pm, Bellecour at 1:30pm, and Perrache at 1:45pm, returning by 6pm. €32.)

🔲 NEAR LYON: THE BEAUJOLAIS

The very mention of Beaujolais provokes a thirst for the cool, fruity wine that is one of this region's main exports. The Beaujolais lies between the Loire and the Saône, with Lyon at its foot and Mâcon at its head, and is home to an important textile and lumber industry, especially in the more mountainous areas to the west. The tourist offices dotting the countryside can give you suggested bike or car routes that wind through endless vineyards, sleepy villages, and medieval châteaux, with a couple of *dégustations* (tastings) thrown in for good measure.

The most beautiful areas in the Beaujolais are difficult to access by public transportation; trains run between Mâcon and Lyon, but stop mostly in uninteresting industrial towns like Villefranche. The best option is to rent a car in Lyon or Mâcon or venture in by bike, though bike rental places in the region itself are tough to find. In Lyon, try **Holiday Bikes** (☎ 04 78 60 11 10). In Mâcon, try **Pro' Cycles** (☎ 03 85 22 81 82). **Bus tours** from Lyon in English are available through the tourist office with **Philibert,** which leads a tour of the Beaujolais culminating in a *dégustation* in Le Hameau. (☎ 04 78 98 56 98. Apr.-Oct. Th-F and Su around 1:15pm; return to Lyon at 7pm. €34.)

THE AUVERGNE

CLERMONT-FERRAND

During the Middle Ages, Clermont-Ferrand (pop. 137,000) was two distinct cities, Clermont and Montferrand. A deep economic and political rivalry festered between the two cities until Louis XIII ordered their merger in 1630. Clermont got the better end of the deal; the "combined" city's walls excluded Montferrand. Forty minutes away by foot, Montferrand is now forgotten. For most of this century, Clermont was synonymous with Michelin tires. Mme. Daubrée, niece of the Scottish scientist Macintosh (whose experiments with rubber led to the invention of the famous rainproof coat), designed rubber balls to entertain her children. The balls caught on, and in 1886 her Michelin relatives used the rubber to make bicycle tires. Despite its colorful history and youthful feel, the city is not itself an appealing destination, serving better as a base for trips to the surrounding mountains.

▐ TRANSPORTATION

Trains: av. de l'Union Soviétique. Info open M-F 4:45am-11:15pm and Sa-Su 7am-11:15pm. To: **Le Puy** (2½hr., 9 per day, €17.10); **Lyon** (3hr.; 14 per day, €21.80); **Paris** (3½hr., 6 per day, €37.50).

Buses: 69 bd. F. Mitterrand (☎04 73 93 13 61), near the Jardin Lecoq. Buses to destinations throughout the Auvergne, including **Vichy** (1¾hr., 2 per day, €9). Office open M-Sa 8:30am-6:30pm.

Public Transportation: 15-17 bd. Robert Schumann (☎04 73 28 56 56). Service 5am-10pm. Buses cover the city. Ticket €1.20, day pass €4.15.

Taxis: Taxi 63 (☎04 73 31 53 15) or **Allô Taxi** (☎04 73 19 53 53).

▐ ▐ ORIENTATION AND PRACTICAL INFORMATION

Buses #2, #4, and #14 go from the station downtown to the lively **pl. de Jaude.** Bounded on either end by statues of local hero Général Desaix and the valiant Vercingétorix, the *place* is lined with cafés, a theater, and the modern shopping complex, **Centre Jaude.** If you'd rather make the 25min. walk, go left from the station onto av. de l'Union Soviétique, left again onto bd. Fleury, and take a quick right onto av. Carnot. Continue straight on this road through several name changes and bends to reach pl. de Jaude. Get a map at the tourist office in the train station.

Tourist Office: pl. de la Victoire (☎04 73 98 65 00; fax 04 73 90 04 11; www.ot-clermont-ferrand.fr). From the train station, make a left onto av. de l'Union Soviétique. Take a left at pl. de l'Esplanade and a quick right onto av. Carnot (changes names several times), walk about 10min. and make a right onto rue M. de lattre de Tassigny. The office will be on your right, before the cathedral. (20min.) Excellent map, bus schedules, and competent staff. In its basement, **L'Espace Massif Central** has further info on natural spaces in the Auvergne. Walking tours mid-June to early Oct. Office open June-Sept. M-F 9am-7pm and Sa-Su 10am-6pm; Oct.-May M-F 9am-6pm, Sa 10am-1pm and 2-6pm, Su 9:30am-12:30pm and 2-6pm. **Annex** at the train station. (☎04 73 91 87 89). Open M-Sa 9:15am-1:15pm and 2:15-5:15pm; Sept.-Apr. closed Su.

Budget Travel: Voyages Wasteels, 11 av. des Etats-Unis (☎08 25 88 70 34). Open M-F 9:30am-noon and 2-6pm, Sa 9:30am-noon.

Youth Centers: Espace Info Jeunes, 5 av. St-Genès (☎04 73 92 30 50). Open M-F 10am-6pm, Sa 10am-1pm.

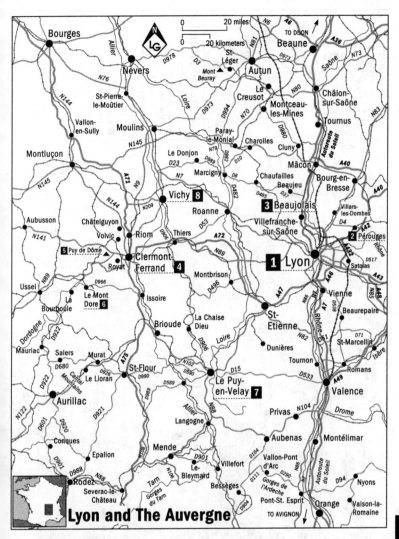

Lyon and The Auvergne

Laundromat: 6 pl. Hippolyte Renoux. Open daily 7am-8pm.

Police: 2 rue Pélissier (☎04 73 98 42 42).

Hospital: Centre Hospitalier Universitaire de Clermont-Ferrand, rue Montalembert (☎04 73 75 07 50). 24hr. **SOS Médecins,** 28 av. Léon Blum (☎04 73 42 22 22).

24-Hour Pharmacy: Pharmacie Ducher, 1 pl. Delille (☎04 73 91 31 77).

Internet Access: Virtua Network, 5 bd. Trudaine (☎04 73 91 65 53). €3 per hr. Open M-F noon-midnight and Sa 2pm-midnight. **Cyber Arena,** 14 rue Pascal (☎04 73 92 94 37). €3.05 per hr. Open daily 11am-11pm.

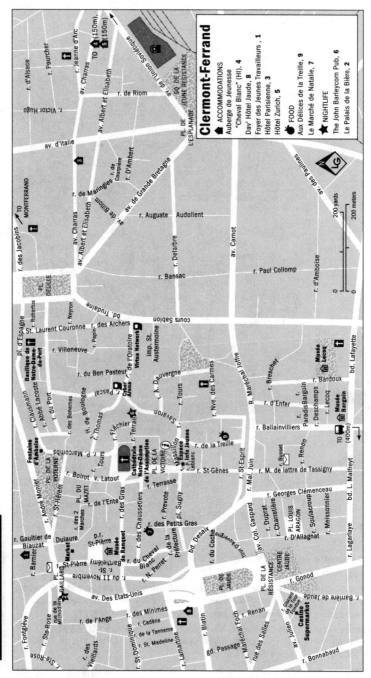

Clermont-Ferrand

ACCOMMODATIONS
Auberge de Jeunesse
"Cheval Blanc" (HI), 4
Dav' Hôtel Jaude, 8
Foyer des Jeunes Travailleurs, 1
Hôtel Parisienne, 3
Hôtel Zurich, 5

FOOD
Aux Délices de la Treille, 9
Le Marché de Natalie, 7

★ **NIGHTLIFE**
The John Barleycorn Pub, 6
Le Palais de la Bière, 2

200 yards
200 meters

Post Office: 1 rue Busset (☎04 73 30 65 00). **Currency exchange** and **Cyberposte.** Open M-F 8am-7pm, Sa 8am-noon. **Branch** at 2 pl. Gaillard (☎04 73 31 70 00). Open M-F 9am-7pm, Sa 8:30am-12:30pm. **Postal code:** 63000.

ACCOMMODATIONS AND CAMPING

There are a couple of inexpensive hotels conveniently clustered near the train station. Cheap rooms in the center of town are much rarer.

Foyer des Jeunes Travailleurs (Corum Saint Jean), 17 rue Gauthier de Biauzat (☎04 73 31 57 00; fax 04 73 31 59 99), off pl. Gaillard. From the station, take bus #2 or #4 to "Gaillard." Modern complex offers adequately-furnished rooms (some with private showers), a bar, and laundry facilities. Great location near the *vieille ville*. Breakfast included. Meals €5-8. Reception 9am-7pm. Often full during the school year; call 2-3 days ahead. Singles or doubles €16-22 per person. ❷

Hôtel Parisienne, 78 rue Charras (☎04 73 91 52 62), about 50m directly in front of train station. This calm hotel, with flowered wallpaper, squeaky floors and light-filled rooms, is a spectacular bargain. Reservations not accepted. Reception 8am-8pm. Singles and doubles €14-17, with shower €20. ❶

Dav'Hôtel Jaude, 10 rue des Minimes (☎04 73 93 31 49; fax 04 73 34 38 16). Freshly scented, brightly-decorated rooms, on a somewhat quiet street a few minutes from the cathedral. Reception 24hr. Breakfast €6.10. Singles €41.20-45.75, doubles €42.70-48.80. AmEx/MC/V. ❹

Auberge de Jeunesse "Cheval Blanc" (HI), 55 av. de l'Union Soviétique (☎04 73 92 26 39; fax 04 73 92 99 96). Across from and to the right of the station. Windows in character-less rooms look onto concrete. Squat toilets only. Kitchen. Breakfast included. Sheets €2.70. Reception 5-11pm. Lockout 9:30am-5pm. Curfew 11pm. Open Apr.-Oct. 1- to 8-bunk rooms €11.20 per person. **Members only.** ❶

Hôtel Zurich, 65 av. de l'Union Soviétique (☎04 73 91 97 98), right of the train station past the hostel. Homey rooms with plush red window curtains, golden bedspreads, and a grandmotherly *patronne*. Call ahead for reception. Singles and doubles €27-30. ❸

Camping: Le Chancet, av. Jean-Baptiste Marrou (☎04 73 61 30 73). 6km outside Clermont, on the Nationale 89 (dir: Bordeaux). From the station, take bus #4C (dir: Ceyrat) to "Préguille." 3-star site has sports, activities, and biking and hiking excursions in summer. Laundry. Reception July-Aug. 8am-10pm. €2.50 per adult, ages 4-10 €1.70; €5 per tent; €1.40 per car. Caravan site with electricity €9. ❶

FOOD

Though Michelin created the most influential restaurant guide in France, Clermont-Ferrand is not known for its food. Tasty restaurants are rare, but cheap ones are everywhere, like the Chinese, Italian, and Tunisian eateries around **rue St-Dominique,** off av. des Etats-Unis. There are a number of fast food joints along **av. des Etats-Unis** and some *brasseries* near the tourist office and cathedral. **Av. Charras,** right near the train station, offers Indian and Chinese restaurants and kebab stands.

There is a **Champion** supermarket on rue Giscard de la Tour Fondue. To get there, make a left at pl. de la Résistance and a right onto rue Giscard. (Open M-Sa 8:30am-8:30pm, Su 9am-12:30pm.) Local fruits, veggies, and cheese can be found at the **Marché Couvert/Espace St-Pierre,** off pl. Gaillard, a huge covered market with hundreds of regional specialties. (Open M-Sa 7am-7:30pm.)

Aux Délices de la Treille ❸, 33 rue de la Treille, prepares delicious regional *menus* (€11-22) in an intimate, plant-filled atmosphere on a quietly chic side street. Make sure to strike up a conversation with Yannick, the charismatic and omnipresent owner. (☎04 73 91 26 90. Open daily 11:30am-2:30pm and 6-11pm.) The freshest lunch place is **Le Marché de Natalie ❷**, 6 rue des Petits Gras, near the cathedral. (☎04 73 19 12 12. €11.50 *menu* and €4.50 cheeses. Open M and W-Sa 11:30am-4pm, Th, F, Sa also 7:30-10:30pm. MC/V.)

🜄 SIGHTS

The *vieille ville* of Clermont, called the **Ville Noire** (Black City), is one of the best-known districts in France; the buildings are made of black volcic stone, contrasting with their bright red roofs. The Roman ruins on nearby **Puy de Dôme** (see p. 673) and the relics in the city's museums are well-preserved. The **Passe Découverte** (€9) is accepted at the city's five major museums. All museums give free admission the first Sunday of each month.

CATHÉDRALE NOTRE-DAME DE L'ASSOMPTION. First built in 450, this massive church was completely reconstructed in the Gothic style between 1248 and 1295 and now commands attention from miles away. The strength of the lava-based material allowed the architects to elongate the graceful, jet-black spires to a height of 100m; you can ascend the seemingly insurmountable, 252-step tower for a panoramic view. In the dark, airy interior three massive rose windows gleam brilliantly. *(Pl. de la Victoire. Open June-Sept. 15 M-Sa 8am-noon and 2-6pm, Su 9:30am-noon and 3-7pm; Sept. 16-May 20 8am-noon and 2-6pm. €1.50 for tower.)*

BASILIQUE DE NOTRE-DAME-DU-PORT. This 11th- to 12th-century church built in the local Auvergnat Romanesque style boasts a particularly beautiful choir, surrounded by an ambulatory and radiating chapels. It was probably here that Urban II first preached the First Crusade. On the first Sunday after May 14, pilgrims stream in to see the icon of the Black Virgin. The ex-voto plaques in the crypt attest to recent miracles. *(Pl. Notre-Dame-du-Port. ☎04 73 91 32 94. Tours July-Aug. W and F at 3pm. Open daily 8am-7pm.)*

MUSÉE BARGOIN AND MUSÉE DES TAPIS ET DES ARTS TEXTILES. Undoubtedly the most interesting museum in Clermont, the Musée Bargoin is devoted to prehistoric and Gallo-Roman archaeology. It displays artifacts recovered from the Temple of Mercury on the Puy de Dôme, as well as Pompeiian wall paintings, mosaics, tapestries, and mummified infants. Most striking are the 3500 Gallo-Roman votive offerings found near a local spring in 1968. The **Musée des Tapis et des Arts Textiles** lays out a beautiful collection of rugs from around the world. Panels in French and English help decode the symbolism of the rugs—you can find out whether you're treading near the female sex organ or the oldest representation of the tree of life. *(45 rue Ballainvilliers. Bargoin ☎04 73 91 37 31; Tapis ☎04 73 90 57 48. Both open Tu-Su 10am-6pm. Each museum €4, students €2.)*

MONTFERRAND. Most of Montferrand's best sights are inconspicuous **hôtels particuliers,** private mansions which date from the Middle Ages and the Renaissance. The best way to visit the town, which rises above an unattractive commercial district 40min. away up av. de la République, is on a two-hour **walking tour** given by the tourist office. (Tu, Th, Sa from pl. Louis Deteix 3pm; €5.20, students €2.60.) Take bus #17 (dir: Blanzat or Cébazat) or bus #10M (dir: Aulnat) from the train station. Like Clermont, Montferrand is dominated by a (less magnificent) volcanic stone church. **Notre-Dame-de-Prospérité** stands on the site of the long-demolished château of the *auvergnat* counts. The 18th-century convent on rue du Seminaire is now the **Musée d'Art Roger-Quillot,** pl. Louis Deteix, exhibiting 14 centuries of art. *(Musée ☎04 73 16 11 30. Open Tu-Su 10am-6pm. €4, students €2, free the first Su of each month.)*

🎵 ENTERTAINMENT

Clermont's students complain that the city's nightlife is sluggish, but they struggle valiantly to fix that at a few popular nightspots. Check *Le Guide de l'Etudiant Clermont-Ferrand* (available at the tourist office) for complete listings. All types play pool and drink cheap beer in the many bars across from the train station. **Le Palais de la Bière**, 3 rue de la Michodière, on the corner of pl. Galliard and av. des Etats-Unis, lacks a little in ambience, but compensates with unusual Swedish and *framboise* beers and late-night *brasserie* fare. (☎ 04 73 37 15 51. Open Tu-Sa 7:30pm-1:30am. Closed Aug.) Imbibe with students and townies at **The John Barley-corn Pub**, 9 rue du Terrail. The bearded bartender will entertain you with stories of his travels across the world as a sailor. (☎ 04 73 92 31 67. Open daily 5pm-2am.)

The first week of February, European filmmakers gather for Clermont-Ferrand's annual **Festival International du Court Métrage** (International Festival of Short Films), considered the "Cannes du Court." Contact La Jetée, 6 pl. Michel de l'Hospital, 63058 Clermont-Ferrand Cédex 1 (☎ 04 73 91 65 73. Pass for 5-6 films €2.50.)

NEAR CLERMONT-FERRAND

PUY DE DÔME

Clermont-Ferrand's greatest attraction is its proximity to a hinterland of extinct volcanoes, crystalline lakes and pristine mountains. Puy de Dôme, the mountain in the middle, is part of the **Parc Naturel Régional des Volcans d'Auvergne**, which is west of Clermont-Ferrand. (☎ 04 73 65 64 00; fax 04 73 65 66 78.) Hikers, bikers, and skiers enjoy the unspoiled terrain of France's largest national park. A booklet available at the Clermont-Ferrand tourist office marks hiking paths. There are three main sections to the protected area: the **Mont-Dore**, the **Monts du Cantal**, and the **Monts Dômes**—the last of which is the best base for exploring the mountains.

From the top of the massive, flat-topped **Puy de Dôme** (1465m), you can see across the teacup-shaped **Chaine des Puys**, a green ridge of extinct volcanoes which runs north-south from Clermont-Ferrand. If you scale the Dôme in late autumn, you may behold the wondrous *mer de nuages* (sea of clouds), a blanket of clouds that obscures the plains below and from which only isolated peaks protrude into the clear blue sky. (Puy-de-Dôme open Mar.-Oct. daily 7am-10pm, weather permitting. Call ☎ 04 73 62 12 18 to see if the road to the top is open.) If you want to join the paragliders in the air, contact **Volcan Action** (☎ 04 73 62 15 15). A 15min. flight with an instructor will cost you €70 (all gear provided). At the peak, the **Centre d'Accueil de Puy de Dôme** has regional info, maps, informative displays on volcanoes, and free, geologically-rich tours of the summit nearly every hr. (☎ 04 73 62 21 46. Open July-Aug. daily 9am-7pm; Oct. daily 10am-6pm; May-June and Sept. M-F 10am-6pm and Sa-Su 10am-7pm.) The **Comité Départemental de Tourisme du Puy de Dôme**, pl. de la Bourse in Clermont-Ferrand, has reams of pamphlets and a guide with historical info on the area. (☎ 04 73 42 22 50. Open M-F 8:30am-6pm.)

Although Puy de Dôme is only 12km from Clermont-Ferrand, getting there takes planning. The Clermont tourist office's **Espace Massif Central** desk has info on how to get there. **Voyage Maisonneuve**, 24 rue Clemenceau, organizes infrequent **bus excursions** to the summit and other parts of the Auvergne. (5hr. Available July-Aug.; see tourist office for details. €13 to Puy de Dôme. Office ☎ 04 73 93 16 72. Open M-F 8:30am-noon and 2-6:30pm, Sa 9am-noon.) Your best bet, though, is to hike or drive. Hitching is a possibility, though not recommended by *Let's Go*. Hikers take bus line #14 to "Royat;" from there it's about a three-hour hike along the PR Chamina to the summit. Hitchers head out of town on av. du Puy de Dôme and follow the signs for about 8km to the base of the mountain. It's illegal to walk up the road that cars take up the mountain, and the rule is heavily enforced. Stand at the toll for an easy hitch, or follow the D941 a few kilometers west to the Col de Ceyssat, where you can grab the **sentier des muletiers,** a Roman footpath that leads to the top in an hour. Buy a good map (such as the IGN *Chaîne des Puys,* available in Clermont-Ferrand tabacs) and listen to the weather forecast for the day, as conditions change rapidly—hailstorms on the summit are not uncommon, even in June. Bring warm clothes and rain gear. From 10am to 6pm in July and August, and weekends and holidays in May, June, September, and October, drivers must leave their cars at the base and take a bus (round-trip €3.50, with last bus descending at 7pm; free parking at base and summit); otherwise, the toll is €4.50.

LE MONT-DORE

Ski resort and hiking mecca Le Mont-Dore (pop. 1700) lies at the highest point of an isolated valley, right at the foot of the largest volcano in a dormant range. The odd rock phenomena, deep craters, craggy peaks and ridges, and varying shades of green give the place a primordial feel; elephants, rhinos, and tigers once roamed through bamboo forests here, and their fossils remain encrusted in volcanic rock. Pine trees and meadows now cover the slopes, populated with *curistes* seeking good health in the warm waters that seep up through cracks in the lava. In the winter, skiers flock to Puy de Sancy, the highest peak in the Auvergne.

🚆 **PRACTICAL INFORMATION. Trains** run from pl. de la Gare (☎04 73 65 00 02) to Clermont-Ferrand (1½hr., 6 per day, €10.40). Info desk open M-Th 5:50am-9pm, F until 9:40pm, Sa until 7:45pm, Su 9:30am-noon and 2-7pm. **Taxis** are operated by **Claude Taxi** (☎04 73 65 01 05) and **Taxi Sepchat** (☎04 73 65 09 38). Rent **bikes** and **skis** at **Bessac Sports,** rue de Maréchal Juin. (☎04 73 65 02 25. Bikes €12 per half-day, €15 per day. Passport deposit. Skis €7-24 per day. Snowboards and hiking equipment also available. Open July-Aug. daily 9am-noon and 2-7pm; low-season Sa-Su 8:30am-7pm during school vacations. MC/V.)

From the train station, head up av. Michel Bertrand and follow the signs to the **tourist office,** av. de la Libération, behind the ice-skating rink on the other side of the Dordogne. It distributes a practical guide to the city, helps find accommodations (for stays over 3 days) and organizes hikes and bike circuits in the summer. **Internet access** on France Telecom cards is also available here. (☎04 73 65 20 21; fax 04 73 65 05 71. Open July-Aug. daily 9am-noon and 2-7pm; Sept.-June 9am-12:30pm and 2-6:30pm. Hikes €5.50.) **Voyages Maisonneuve** runs 5hr. **bus excursions** to regional lakes, volcanoes, and châteaux. (☎04 73 69 96 96. July-Aug. almost daily, €16. Reserve at the tourist office.) The **police station** is on av. M. Bertrand (☎04 73 65 01 70 or 17); the **hospital** is at 2 rue du Capitaine-Chazotte (☎04 73 65 33 33), off pl. Charles de Gaulle. **Pharmacie du Parc** is at 17 rue Meynadier (☎04 73 65 02 86 or 06 03 78 20 93. Open M-Sa 9am-12:30pm and 2:30-7:30pm.) The town's **pharmacie de garde** is either **Parc** or **Pharmacie de l'Etablissement,** 1 pl. du Panthéon. (☎04 73 81 08 98.) The **post office,** pl. Charles de Gaulle, **exchanges currency.** (☎04 73 65 02 47. Open M-F 8:30am-noon and 1:30-5:30pm, Sa 8:30am-noon.) **Postal code:** 63240.

🏠 **ACCOMMODATIONS AND CAMPING.** Le Mont-Dore is blessed with over a dozen hotels with rooms starting in the low €20s, so finding a cheap one, even if you have to reserve ahead, isn't difficult. Turn off your engines at **Hôtel Le Parking ❷,** 19 av. de la Libération, right behind the tourist office. Complete with turret, this sparkling, partially pink-interiored hotel has sizable, comfortable rooms, many with spectacular views. (☎04 73 65 03 43. Breakfast €3.90. Reception 7am-9pm. Closed Nov. Singles and doubles €21.40-24.50, with shower €26-29, with bath

€30.50-37.50; triples with bath €38.10-45. MC/V.) Modern wood paneling gives **Castel Medicis ❷**, 5 rue Duchatel, right at the top of the main part of town, a clean, bright feel. (☎ 04 73 65 30 50. Breakfast included. Reception 8:30am-8pm. Singles and doubles €20, with shower €28, with bath €31. Extra bed €8. MC/V.) The **Auberge de Jeunesse "Le Grand Volcan" (HI) ❶**, rte. du Sancy, is 3km from town. From the station, climb av. Guyot-Dessaigne, which becomes av. des Belges. Continue on D983 (which changes names several times) into the countryside. When you see ski lifts, the hostel will be on your right. The train station has info on local buses that run near the hostel. This chalet's spartan 1- to 6-bed rooms are not very appealing, but its idyllic setting near a cow pasture at the foot of Puy de Sancy makes up for it. Avoid the cramped loft singles. (☎ 04 73 65 03 53; fax 04 73 65 26 39. Kitchen, bar, and laundry facilities. Breakfast and bunk €11.30. Lunch and dinner €8. Reception June-Aug. 8am-noon and 6-11pm; low-season 8am-noon and 6-9pm. **Members only.**)

There are four **campsites** in and around town. The most convenient is **Des Crouzets ❶**, av. des Crouzets, across from the station in a pleasant, crowded hollow along the Dordogne. You can set up first and pay later. (☎/fax 04 73 65 21 60. Office open M-Sa 9am-noon and 3-6:30pm, Su 9:30am-noon and 4-6:30pm. Open mid-Dec. to mid-Oct. Reservations not accepted. €2.50 per person, €2.30 per site; car included. Electricity €2.50-5.) One kilometer behind the station is **L'Esquiladou ❶**, rte. des Cascades. The gravelly sites are better suited to caravans, but it feels less crowded than Des Crouzets. (☎/fax 04 73 65 23 74. Reception July-Aug. 9am-noon and 3-7pm; May-June and Sept.-Oct. 9am-noon and 3-6pm. €2.60 per person, €2.40 per tent. Electricity €2.50-5.)

◖ FOOD. It's difficult to find a restaurant in Le Mont-Dore that isn't attached to a hotel; these *pensions* serve everyone, but usually give discounts to guests. Most *menus* in town begin at €11, and good ones run €13-15. For a tasty pizza at an unbeatable price, try **Le Tremplin ❷**, 3 av. Foch. This cozy family owned joint will make you feel welcome. (☎ 04 73 65 25 90. Pizzas €6.50-8.70. MC/V.) For an unexpected bit of Mark Twain in this corner of France, head to **Le Louisiane ❸**, 2 rue Jean Moulin. This elegant steamboat-themed restaurant serves fish and regional plats *du terroir*; try *la Parillada*, an assortment of salmon, mussels, and other fish, for €13. (☎ 04 73 65 03 14. *Menus* €17-20. Open daily noon-2pm and 7-9:30pm. MC/V.) Still, the cheapest and most scenic meals are mountaintop picnics. The streets are full of boutiques hawking delicious regional specialties—wedges of soft, sweet St-Nectaire cheese and lengths of juicy sausage. A **Utile supermarket** is on rue du Cap-Chazzotte. (Open July-Aug. M-Sa 7am-7:30pm, Su 7am-12:30pm and 3-7:30pm; Sept.-June M-Sa 7am-12:30pm and 3-7:30pm.)

◖ SIGHTS. There's not a whole lot to do in the town, but you can become acquainted with the *curiste* tradition at the ornate **Etablissement Thermal**, pl. du Panthéon. Five of the springs used today were first channeled by the Romans, who found that the pure water did wonders for their horses's sinuses. The curious can visit the *thermes* on French tours; the visit ends with a dose of the *thermes*'s celebrated *douche nasale gazeuse*, a tiny blast of carbon and helium that evacuates sinuses more effectively than any sneeze. (☎ 04 73 65 05 10. Tours M-Sa, every hr., 2-5pm. €2.70.) Down the hill on av. Michel Bertrand, the **Musée Joseph Forêt** honors the celebrated art editor, a Mont-Dore native who left much of his collection to the town in 1985. For his grand finale, Forêt recruited seven painters and seven writers to collaborate in the publication of the largest book in the world. *Le Livre de l'Apocalypse*, weighing a quarter-ton, incorporates works by Dalí and Cocteau. The original was sold in bits to pay for its printing, but a facsimile sits in the back. (☎ 04 73 65 00 9. Call 12:30-3pm to set up a visit time. €2.)

■ **HIKING AND BIKING.** Trails through these volcanic mountains cover dense forests, crystal-clear waterfalls and cascades, and bizarre, moon-like rock outcroppings. Scaling the peaks is relatively easy—the summit of Puy de Sancy (1775m) is attained on a languorous six-hour hike. Nevertheless, if you plan on taking an extended hike, review your route with the tourist office, which has fantastic maps and will help you plan. For multi-day routes, leave an itinerary with the **peloton de montagne** (mountain police), on rue des Chaussers at the base of Puy de Sancy (☎ 04 73 65 04 06). All hikers should acquire maps and weather reports—mist in the valley often means hail or snow in the peaks. The tourist office sells the pocket-sized *Massif du Sancy* (€6.90), with hiking and biking circuits. You may also want their *Massif du Sancy et Artense* guide (€14.35), which covers 38 hikes originating in all areas of Le Sancy. An **IGN map** (either Massif du Sancy or the larger Chaîne des Puys) is necessary for any serious trek (€4.90).

To get all the views without all the exertion, take the **téléphérique** from the base station by the hostel to the Puy de Sancy. (☎ 04 73 65 02 73. July-Aug. daily every 10 min. 9am-6pm; Oct.-Apr. daily 8:45am-4:45pm, Oct.-Nov. only Sa-Su; May-June and Sept. daily 9am-12:30pm and 1:30-5pm. €4.90 one-way, €6 round-trip.) The oldest electric **funicular** in France runs from near the tourist office up to the 1245m-high Salon des Capucins. (July-Aug. every 20min. 9am-6:40pm, May and Sept. daily 10am-12:10pm and 2:10-6:40pm. €3.30 one-way, €4.20 round-trip.)

If you have a car or a bike, don't miss the chance to visit one of the many volcanic lakes, like **Lac Servière** (20km northeast), which fill in the craters of the Mont-Dore region. Most of the lakes are suitable for windsurfing, sailing, fishing, and swimming. **Lac d'Aydat**, to the northeast, offers pedal-boats and other amusements, as does **Lac Chambon**, 20km east of Le Mont-Dore via D996E, near Murol, where actors fill a château with 13th-century repartee. (Lac Chambon ☎ 04 73 88 62 62. Open Su-Tu and Th-F 10am-6pm. €6.90, ages 5-15 €4.60.)

Most hikes are marked by yellow trail signs, often accompanied by detailed maps of the surrounding area. For an **easy hike** (1½hr., 3½km round-trip), try the **Grande Cascade** waterfall. From the *thermes*, follow rue des Desportes a few meters to the right and climb the stairs on your left to join the chemin de Melki Rose, which then leads into the rte. de Bresse and the chemin de la Grande Cascade. After crossing a road, the trail runs through birch woods and winds up a narrow, pine-covered gorge. From there it's a quick climb on the metal stairway to the top of the waterfall. Another easy option is the **Salon du Capucin** (4½km round-trip, 1½hr.). From the tourist office, take av. Jules Ferry and follow the signs.

A low-grade **intermediate hike** (1½hr., 6km round-trip) starts at the Salon du Capucins trail convergence point, near the funicular drop-off point. From the lodge, head along the wide trail toward Le Bourgeat. Keep going straight, and after 5min. of moss-covered slopes you will emerge into a soft shrub-filled meadow with a great view of the surrounding mountains. Traverse the off-trail meadow until you find a yellow sign, and head toward Creve-Coeur; after 5 more minutes, a wondrous chasm view will suddenly appear. Heading toward Rigolet-Haut and Choucailles and then coming back along a paved road to Creve-Cœur will take you past cute rural houses, cows, and countless mountain views. From Creve-Cœur, it's an easy 0.9km walk back to Salon du Capucins.

A great **intermediate hike** begins at the base of the Puy de Sancy, near the hostel. (3-4hr., 8km round-trip.) Ascend the mountain via the Val de Courre, clearly labeled with yellow markers. At **Puy Redon**, you join the GR30, which climbs to the summit of Puy de Sancy. Summer snow patches are not uncommon, and on clear days the Alps are visible to the east. On the south side of the peak, wildflowers and other rare vegetation carpet the immense **Vallée de la Fontaine Salée**. Smart hikers who don't want to follow the GR4 all the way back (see below) retrace their steps along the Val de Courre instead of suffering through the marked ski trails of the GR4e. Another **half-day hike** starts just off the D996, a few hundred meters west of **le Marais.** (5-6hr. round-trip.) Follow the yellow-marked PR as it curves right and ascends through a thick wood. At the juncture of the GR30 you can turn left and follow a 2km detour to climb the Puy Gros. Otherwise, continue right for several kilometers, passing by another yellow-marked PR, and on to the Lac de Guerey.

The most ambitious, **advanced full-day hike** follows a series of trails that make a complete loop around the town and hit all of the major natural attractions along the way. (6hr.) Start from the tourist office and follow the signs to the Salon du Capucin, a towering mass of rocks overlooking town. Another vertical 200m takes you to the **Pic du Capucin,** where the trail hooks up with the GR30, marked with parallel red and white lines. The GR30 follows a narrow ridge, then skirts the summit of **Puy Redon,** hovering over the spectacular Val de Courre, and ascends another 100m to the summit of **Puy de Sancy,** the highest peak in the Massif Central. From there, follow the GR4 as it loops back north and descends a series of ski trails before climbing back into the trees. The weary should take the GR4e, which descends straight to the base of the ski mountain.

LE PUY-EN-VELAY

Jutting crags of volcanic rock pierce the sky near Le Puy (pop. 20,500), punctuating an horizon dominated by gentle green hills. A pilgrimage site since the first churches were built atop these natural skyscrapers, Le Puy has always received a burst of life from its visitors. But despite a good ratio of bars and a never-ending festival season, Le Puy is at heart a sleepy small town.

▛ TRANSPORTATION

Trains: pl. Maréchal Leclerc. Info and ticket offices open M 4:25am-7pm, Tu-Sa 5:40am-7pm, Su 10:05am-8:10pm. To: **Clermont-Ferrand** (2½hr.; M-F 6 per day; €17.10) sometimes via **Brioude** or **Arvant; Lyon** (2½hr., M-F 8 per day, €17.10); **St-Etienne-Châteaucreux** (1¼hr., M-F 10 per day, €11.40). Trains marked "car" are buses.

Buses: pl. Maréchal Leclerc, next to the train station (☎04 71 09 25 60). Open M-F 8am-noon and 2:30-6:30pm. **Chavanelle** goes to **St-Etienne** (2¼hr., M-Sa 3 per day, €8.80). Those traveling into the *midi* should bus to **Langogne** (2hr., M-F 2 per day at 7:50am and 4:15pm, €7.30) to catch a train. Buy tickets on bus.

Public Transportation: S.A.E.M. TUDIP, pl. du Breuil. Info at the tourist office. Individual tickets on bus, €0.95. *Carnet* of 10 at the tourist office, €6.90.

Taxis: Radio-Taxis, pl. du Breuil (☎04 71 05 42 43). 24hr.

▟ ▛ ORIENTATION AND PRACTICAL INFORMATION

Most trains arriving from the south or Clermont-Ferrand require a change at Brioude; trains from Lyon or Paris change at St-Etienne-Châteaucreux. From the station, walk left along av. Charles Dupuy, cross sq. H. Coiffier, and turn left onto bd. Maréchal Fayolle. After 5min. you'll reach two adjacent squares, **pl. Michelet** and **pl. du Breuil.** The tourist office and most hotels are here and on nearby bd. St-Louis; the cathedral, hostels, and *vieille ville* are way uphill to the right.

Tourist Office: pl. du Breuil (☎04 71 09 38 41; fax 04 71 05 22 62). Free accommodations service. Free, well-marked map with 3 different walking tours. Open July-Aug. M-Sa 8:30am-7:30pm, Su 9am-noon and 2-6pm; Sept.-June M-Sa 8:30am-noon and 1:30-6:15pm, Su 9am-noon and 2-6pm; Oct.-Mar. Su 10am-noon only.

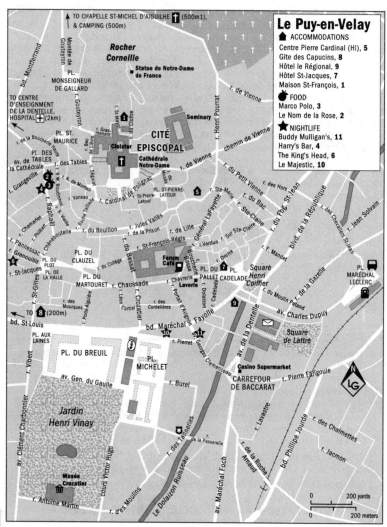

Le Puy-en-Velay

🏠 ACCOMMODATIONS
Centre Pierre Cardinal (HI), **5**
Gîte des Capucins, **8**
Hôtel le Régional, **9**
Hôtel St-Jacques, **7**
Maison St-François, **1**

🍎 FOOD
Marco Polo, **3**
Le Nom de la Rose, **2**

⭐ NIGHTLIFE
Buddy Mulligan's, **11**
Harry's Bar, **4**
The King's Head, **6**
Le Majestic, **10**

Laundromat: 12 rue Chèvrerie. Open M-Sa 7:45am-noon and 1-7pm. **Lav'Flash,** 24 rue Portail d'Avignon. Open M-Sa 8am-8pm and Su 9:15am-6:30pm.

Police: rue de la Passerelle (☎04 71 04 04 22).

Medical Assistance: Centre Hospitalier Emile Roux, bd. Dr. Chantemesse (☎04 71 04 32 10). 24hr. **Clinique Bon Secours,** 67bis av. M. Foch (☎04 71 09 87 00). For the rotating **pharmacie de garde,** call ☎04 71 04 04 22.

Internet Access: Forum Café, 5 rue Général LaFayette (☎04 71 04 04 98), is dirt cheap (€1.50 per hr.) but has only two computers. Open Tu-Sa 1-6pm.

Post Office: 8 av. de la Dentelle (☎04 71 07 02 05). **Currency exchange.** Open M-F 8am-7pm and Sa 8am-noon. **Branch office:** 49 bd. St-Louis (☎04 71 09 77 61). Open M-F 9am-noon and 2-5:30pm, Sa 9am-noon. **Postal code:** 43000.

ACCOMMODATIONS AND CAMPING

Reserve ahead in summer, especially for the mid-June pilgrimage.

Gîte des Capucins, 29 rue des Capucins (☎04 71 04 28 74), off bd. St-Louis. Small, extremely friendly and multilingual place with immaculate 4-6 bed dorms, each with private bath. Kitchen facilities and quaint garden in back. Breakfast €4.60. Sheets €1.55. Reception until late; there is usually someone around if you call. Beds €12.20. Well furnished, colorful 2-person apartments €51.80; 4-person apartments €64. ●

Hôtel St-Jacques, 7 pl. Cadelade (☎04 71 07 20 40; fax 04 71 07 20 44). Snazzily decorated, vibrantly bright orange-colored rooms with nice views of the *place*. Parking €4. Breakfast €5. Reception 24hr. Singles and doubles €40-48. MC/V. ●

Centre Pierre Cardinal (HI), 9 rue Jules Vallès (☎04 71 05 52 40; fax 04 71 05 61 24). 72 beds in numerous quads and one 18-bed dorm in a clean and beautiful former barracks. Excellent kitchen. Breakfast €3.20. Sheets €3.50. Reception 7:30am-8:30pm. Lockout Su 10am-8pm. Curfew 11:30pm. Closed holidays, Christmas vacation, and during the July Festival des Musicales. Bunks €7. **Members only.** ●

Maison St-François, rue St-Mayol (☎04 71 05 98 86; fax 04 71 05 98 87). Simple, adequate peach- and white-colored rooms, practically *in* the cathedral. Kitchen, convent garden, and joy-inducing common room. Caters primarily to pilgrims in summer, but there is often room in winter. Breakfast included. Meals €9.50. No sheets available. Reception 2-8pm. Check-out by 8:30am. Call a few days ahead. Beds €12.50. ●

Hôtel le Régional, 36 bd. Maréchal Fayolle (☎04 71 09 37 74), near pl. Michelet. Clean, large and colorful rooms in a noisy area with sound-proofed windows. Breakfast €4.50. Reception 7am-10pm. Singles and doubles €21.50, with shower from €26; triples from €34; quads €47.50. AmEx/MC/V. ●

Camping du Puy-en-Velay, chemin de Bouthezard (☎04 71 09 55 09), in the northwest corner of town, near the Chapelle St-Michel and the river. Walk up bd. St-Louis, continue on bd. Carnot, turn right at the dead end onto av. d'Aiguille, and look to the left. (15min.) Or take bus #6 (dir: Mondon) from pl. Michelet (10min., 1 per hr., €0.95). Grassy, but not very private. Reception 8am-noon and 2:30-9pm. Open Easter-Oct. 1 €2.20 per person, €2.40 per tent, €1.60 per car, €7.80 for 2 people, site, and car. ●

FOOD

In 1860, Rumillet Charnetier created **Verveine,** an alcoholic *digestif* of local herbs and honey with a sweet mint flavor (€10-22 per bottle). Speaking of things green, Le Puy is known for its **lentils,** which you'll find everywhere in local food. Inexpensive restaurants are on the side streets off **pl. du Breuil.** There is a **Casino supermarket** on the corner of av. de la Dentelle and rue Farigoule (open M-Sa 8:30am-8pm), with a **cafeteria** above. (Meals €4.60-7.30. Open daily 11:30am-9:30pm.) On Saturdays, farmers set up fresh produce **markets** in practically every square. (Open 6am-12:30pm.) The market in pl. du Plot throws in cheese and mushrooms, not to mention a few live chickens, rabbits, and puppies (not for consumption); the adjacent pl. du Clauzel hosts an antique market. (Open Sa 7:30am-1pm.) At pl. du Breuil, the biggest spread of all includes clothing, hardware, toiletries, and shoes.

Le Nom de la Rose ❷, 48 rue Raphael, presents an odd but eminently satisfying combination of French-cooked Mexican food, although it's a lot spicier on the other side of the Atlantic. (☎04 71 05 90 04. Menu €14.80, *chili con carne* €7.20, *quesadilla* €5.35. Open noon-3pm and 7pm-midnight. MC/V.) **Marco Polo ❸,** 46 rue Raphael, shows an Italian influence in its sizeable 3-course *menus* (€14-20). Specialties include an *osso bucco* (€11.50) that could slay an ox. (☎ 04 71 02 83 11. Reserve for Sa. Open June-Aug. Tu-Sa noon-midnight; Sept.-May until 10:30pm. V.)

◉ SIGHTS

The **billet jumelé** (sold Feb.-Oct.; €7) provides admission to all the sights in the Cité Episcopale, as well as the Musée Crozatier, Chapelle St-Michel, and Rocher Corneille. Sold at tourist office and all sites. Pick up the English-language **guide pratique.**

CATHÉDRALE NOTRE-DAME. Towering over the lower city, the **Cité Episcopale** has attracted pilgrims and tourists for over 1000 years. It was built on a rock, known as "le puy," where legend has it the Virgin appeared and healed a woman in the 5th century. Though designed as a Christian cathedral, many of its workers were Muslim, and their influence can be seen on the doors to either side of the entrance, where "There is only one true God" is written in Arabic. At the altar, a copy of Le Puy's mysterious **Vierge Noir** (Black Virgin) smiles enigmatically. A side chapel displays the celebrated Renaissance mural *Les Arts Libéraux*. It is thought to be unfinished—of the seven arts, only Grammar, Logic, Rhetoric, and Music are represented. (☎ 04 71 05 98 74. Open daily 7am-8pm. July-Aug. free tours after 2:30pm.)

CLOISTER. The most remarkable of the sights near the cathedral, its black, white, and peach stone arcades reflect an Islamic influence from Spain. Beneath flame-red tiling and black volcanic rock is an intricate frieze of grinning faces and mythical beasts. Amid the Byzantine arches of the **salle capitulaire,** a vivid and well-preserved 13th-century fresco depicts the Crucifixion. The same ticket allows a look at the **Trésor d'Art Religieux,** which contains walnut statues and jeweled capes. (☎ 04 71 05 45 52. Both open July-Sept. daily 9:30am-6:30pm; Apr.-June 9:30am-12:30pm and 2-6pm; Oct.-Mar. 9:30am-noon and 2-4:30pm. €4, ages 18-25 with ID €2.50.)

STATUE DE NOTRE-DAME DE FRANCE. At the edge of the *vieille ville* is the **Rocher Corneille,** the eroded core of a volcano. The summit looks out over a dreamscape of jagged crags and manicured gardens. For a windy view through Winnie the Pooh-type door-windows, clamber to the top of the cramped 16m **Notre-Dame de France,** a statue cast from cannons captured during the Crimean war. Notre-Dame earned national fame in 1942, when 20,000 young people came here to pray for the liberation of France. (Open July-Aug. daily 9am-7:30pm; Mar. 16-Apr. 9am-6pm; May-June and Sept. 9am-7pm; Oct.-Mar. 15 10am-7pm. €3, students €1.50.)

CHAPELLE ST-MICHEL D'AIGUILHE. Just outside the old city, this primitive chapel crowns an 80m spike of volcanic rock. Its rustic stained glass barely illuminates a fading 12th-century fresco and the almost voodoo-like 10th-century woodcut crucifix uncovered during excavations here. The chapel was built in 950 by the first pilgrim to complete the Chemin de St-Jacques, a trail from Le Puy to Spain still trod by the pious. (☎ 04 71 09 50 03. Open May-Sept. daily 9am-6:30pm; Feb.-Mar. 29 2-4pm; Mar. 30-Apr. 30 and Oct.-Nov. 12 9:30am-noon and 2-5pm. €2.50, under age 14 €1.)

🎭 🎵 NIGHTLIFE AND FESTIVALS

The most memorable of Le Puy's many bars is ▨**The King's Head,** 17 rue Grenouillit, a relaxed English pub that serves beer and fish and chips, as well as curries and whatever else friendly Dave concocts. (☎ 04 71 02 50 35. Open M 4pm-1am, Tu-Th noon-1am, F-Sa noon-2am, Su 5pm-1am.) **Harry's Bar,** 37 rue Raphael, cultivates a chic, low-key, dimly-lit environment, where locals chat away with

Harry and listen to jazz. (☎ 04 71 02 23 02. Beers €2-2.50, drinks €4. Open M-Th 5pm-1am and F-Sa 5pm-2am.) Another popular watering hole for locals is **Buddy Mulligan's,** 13 av. Georges Clemenceau, packed with a young crowd and home to wild Halloween and St-Patrick's Day celebrations. (☎ 04 71 02 52 17. Pints from €3.20. Open M-Tu 5pm-1am, W-Th 11am-1am, F 11am-2am, Sa 10am-2am, and Su 10am-1am.) **Le Majestic,** 8 bd. Maréchal Fayolle, is a *brasserie* by day, but spills out onto a terrace at night. (☎ 04 71 09 06 30. Techno F-Sa. Open M-Sa 7am-1am, Su 10am-1am.)

Le Puy likes to party, and hosts seven different festivals, ranging from music to theater, beginning in early July. There's a different one each week until they culminate in mid-September at the **Fête Renaissance du Roi de L'Oiseau.** Locals dress in costume, jugglers and minstrels wander the streets, and food and drink are purchased with specially minted festival currency. A tunnel system carved centuries ago into the rock below the *vieille ville* is opened up and turned into one great party hall, where beer and wine flow freely. (☎ 04 71 02 84 84. €2-5, depending on activity. Free to those in costume. For costume rentals call ☎ 04 71 09 16 53.)

VICHY

Vichy immerses itself in the days when its history recorded the comings and goings of Napoleon III, and prefers to forget its position as the capital of France from 1940 to 1944. Forced by the occupying German troops to leave Paris, the French administration (which was by then a Nazi puppet government) set up shop in this central spa town. Maréchal Philippe Pétain, a WWI hero, was elected as the leader of the new state (see **History,** p. 11). Understandably, today's Vichy chooses to preserve its memories of the Belle Epoque, rather than recall its part in the darkest days of the 20th century. Still, the absence of major WWII monuments, museums acknowledging Vichy's role in the war, or plaques marking the buildings used by Pétain's government, creates an eerie historical gap.

🛈 **PRACTICAL INFORMATION.** The **train** station on pl. de la Gare services Clermont-Ferrand (35min., 11 per day, €7.80); Nevers (1hr., 15 per day, €13.60); Paris (3hr., 6 per day, €33.80). Ticket counters open 5:30am-10pm; info desk open M-Sa 9:40am-5:50pm and on Su June-Aug.) The **bus station** is in a brick building next to the train station. (Office open M-F 8am-noon and 2-6pm.) **Public buses** run around town from 6:30am to 8pm (€1). Schedules are available at the tourist office and at Bus Inter (☎ 04 70 97 81 29), on pl. Charles de Gaulle near the post office.

Vichy's sleek and well-managed **tourist office,** 19 rue du Parc, as well as the most popular *sources,* lies in the **Parc des Sources.** From the station, walk straight on rue de Paris; at the fork turn left onto rue Clemenceau and then right onto rue Sornin. The tourist office is straight ahead across the park, in the Hôtel du Parc that once housed the Pétain leadership. (10min.) The staff gives away a good map, a list of hotels and restaurants, and has a free **accommodations service.** Ask for the booklet of suggested tours in Vichy and the region, or take a **walking tour** (€3.80-4.60) with them. Find out about operas, concerts, and other events in town from the free, French-language *Vichy Quinzaine* or the free, English-language *Vichy Guide.* (☎ 04 70 98 71 94; fax 04 70 31 06 00; www.ville-vichy.fr. Office open July-Aug. M-Sa 9am-7:30pm, Su 9:30am-12:30pm and 3-7pm; Apr.-June and Sept. M-Sa 9am-12:30pm and 1:30-7pm, Su 9:30am-12:30pm and 3-7pm; Oct.-Mar. M-F 9am-noon and 2-6:30pm, Sa 9am-noon and 2-6pm, Su 2:30-5:30pm.) The **police** are at 35 av. Victoria (☎ 04 70 98 60 03). The **Centre Hospitalier** is at 15 bd. Denière. (☎ 04 70 97 33 33, emergency ☎ 15.) **La Grande Pharmacie** is at 46 rue de Paris (☎ 04 70 98 23 01. Open M 2:30-7:15pm, Tu-Sa 9:30am-

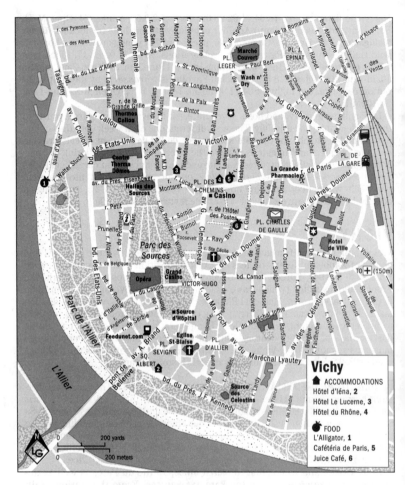

Vichy

🏠 ACCOMMODATIONS
Hôtel d'Iéna, **2**
Hôtel Le Lucerne, **3**
Hôtel du Rhône, **4**

🍎 FOOD
L'Alligator, **1**
Cafétéria de Paris, **5**
Juice Café, **6**

12:15pm and 2:30-7:15pm.) For the town's **pharmacie de garde**, dial ☎15. Bring coins for the **Wash'n Dry** at 3 bd. Gambetta. (☎06 78 78 08 92. Open daily 7am-9pm.) For a taxi, call **Taxi Radio Vichyssois** (☎04 70 98 69 69). For **Internet**, head to **Feedunet.com**, 21 av. Briand. (☎04 70 96 24 88. €4.60 per hr. Open M-Th 11am-11pm, F-Sa 11am-midnight, Su 2-9pm.) The **post office** at pl. Charles de Gaulle has **currency exchange** at a 1.5% commission. (☎04 70 30 10 75. Open M-F 8am-7pm, Sa 8am-noon.) **Postal code:** 03200.

🏠🍎 **ACCOMMODATIONS AND FOOD.** In keeping with Vichy's longstanding mission to pamper, even its budget hostels are deluxe. On rue de Paris, hotels jostle for business, with rooms starting around €20. The **Hôtel du Rhône ❸**, 8 rue de Paris, between the train station and the *thermes*, offers delightful, well-designed and -decorated doubles and triples and an air-conditioned salon, managed by the friendly multilingual owner. The restaurant downstairs offers regional specialties. *Let's Go* readers who stay over 2 nights receive a free breakfast. (☎04 70 97 73 00; fax 04 70 97 48 25. Breakfast €3, buffet €6. *Menus* €12-39. Reception 24hr. Singles and doubles with shower €25-46; deluxe rooms with bath €54-68. Extra bed €5. AmEx/MC/V.) **Hôtel Le Lucerne ❷**, 8 rue de l'Intendance, is centrally located, with well-maintained rooms, new friendly owners, and an old-fashioned elevator. (☎04 70 98 24 46; fax 04 70 31 71 61. Breakfast €4.50. Reception 7am-9pm. Open Apr.-Oct. Singles €20-23, with shower €25-26; doubles and triples €32-35. MC/V.) **Hôtel d'Iéna ❷**, 56 bd. John Kennedy, right across from the Parc d'Allier. A friendly hotel with small, not exquisite but comfortable rooms, and good views of the park. (☎04 70 32 01 20. Breakfast €4. Singles €20; doubles with bath €25. MC/V.) The riverside four-star **Camping Les Acacias ❷** has a grocery store, pool, and laundry. Take bus #7 from the train station (dir: La Tour) to "Charles de Gaulle" and transfer to bus #3 to "Les Acacias;" it's 3.5km by foot. (☎04 70 32 36 22. Open Apr. to mid-Oct. Reception 8am-10pm. €4.50 per person, €4.50 per tent. Electricity €2.50.)

There is a **Casino supermarket** on pl. Charles de Gaulle and l'Hôtel des Postes. (Open M-Sa 8:30am-12:30pm and 2:30-7:30pm, Su 9am-noon.) There's a covered **morning market** on pl. Léger where rue Jean Jaurès and bd. Gambetta intersect. (Open Tu-Sa.) Restaurants in Vichy, most affiliated with hotels, are usually expensive. There are bars, pubs, and cheap pizzerias on **rue de Paris**. The neon red-lit **Cafétéria de Paris ❶**, 13 rue de Paris, which looks like it belongs in the southern US, has hot dishes for €3.50-12 and a *menu* for €5.50. (☎04 70 97 81 26. Open Su-F 11am-9:30pm, Sa 11am-10pm.) Stroll along the river and sample more Americana at **L'Alligator ❷**, 1 quai d'Allier. (☎04 70 98 30 47. *Menus* €15-20; entrées €8.50-14. Open Mar.-Oct. noon-2pm and 7-10:30pm.) For a satisfying smoothie amid sunny orange and yellow walls, join students at the **Juice Café ❶**, 16 rue Ravy Breton. (☎04 70 97 93 86. Smoothies €4-4.50. Open Tu-Sa noon-7pm and Su-M 3-7pm.)

◙ ◗ SIGHTS AND ENTERTAINMENT. The only way to see Pétain's Vichy is to take a French **tour** from the tourist office—significant buildings of the World War II era are not marked, so you won't notice them otherwise. (Tours July-Aug. W and Sa 3:30pm; June and Sept. W. €3.80.)

Take a sip of Vichy's nectar, and you'll wonder how the town ever made it big—the water tastes disgusting. The *sources* bubble free of charge at the cold springs of **Sources des Célestins** on bd. Kennedy.

THE LOCAL STORY

VICHY'S WILLFUL AMNES

Until the late 1970s, the details o Vichy's *"années noires,"* or blac years, were largely swept aside by his torians and politicians alike in favor o heroic tales of the Resistance champi oned by Charles de Gaulle. Today Vichy's residents today are curiousl silent about their town's past.

"They prefer to forget that era," says Priscille Bonnefoy, a discoun clothing store employee. "It's not ver pleasant." Ann Auguste, a British native and owner of the Juice Café agrees. "It's a bit of a taboo. There' no museum, no monument. People start to wonder, why isn't there?"

When asked about the apparen absence of WWII-era monuments, a representative at the city hall deflect the questions. Instead, she carefull notes the distinction between the *Vichysstes* (Pétain supporters) and the *Vichyssois* (normal Vichy citizens)

Longtime residents interviewed a a local *boulodrome* defended the Vichy people, some blaming Pétain' top aide Pierre Laval for the regime' actions. Paul Deschamps, 86, a ve eran, says that Vichy's residents "ar not responsible for the *bêtises* of the Vichy government."

Two other aging *Vichyssois*, Andr Heitzmann and Henri Fournier, tal vividly about the Pétain propaganda films of the time and of how th Gestapo tortured resisters in the smal casino in town. "I find it even mor frustrating that they don't just let i go—there's a monument, there' everything you need to know, Auguste says. "And that way peopl won't bother about it anymore."

(Open Apr.-Sept. M-Sa 7:45am-8:30pm, Su 8am-8:30pm; Oct.-Mar. daily 8am-6pm.) The heart of the action, though, is the **Halle des Sources** at the edge of the **Parc des Sources.** Anyone can drink for €1.50. (☎04 70 97 39 59. Open M-Sa 6:15am-8:30pm, Su 7:45am-8:30pm.) If you go, take small swigs—it looks like plain water, but it's powerful stuff. **Célestins** is easiest to digest and was proven to relieve arthritis in a 1992 study by the Hôpital Cochimin in Paris. **Parc** is tougher on the stomach, and **Lucas** is chock-full of sulphur, hence the rotten-egg smell. Still thirsty? The **hot springs** are even more vile. Try the nauseating ones in the rotunda of the **Source d'Hôpital,** behind the **Grand Casino.** (Open M-Sa 6:30am-8:30pm, Su 7:45am-8:30pm.) **Chomel** is the most popular; **Grand Grille** is the most potent. Recover in the beautiful Parc des Sources. Surrounded by a wrought-iron Art Nouveau gallery and Opéra, it is Vichy elegance at its height.

A wide array of flora and fauna fall within the confines of the English-style gardens in the elegant riverside **Parc de l'Allier,** commissioned by Napoleon III. Across the river and a brisk 20-25min. walk along the promenade to the right of Pont de Bellerive lies Vichy's ultimate recreational facility. The sprawling **Centre Omnisports** offers sailing, wind-surfing, archery, canoeing, kayaking, rafting, tennis, swimming, and mountain biking. (☎04 70 59 51 00. Open daily 8am-9pm. Half-day activities pass for children 10-18 €5.45, full day €8.80, week €31.25.)

The tourist office posts a daily list of upcoming events in Vichy. There are cheap thrills at the **Grand Casino** in the Parc des Sources. (Open daily noon-4am.) **Operas** and **concerts** take place during the summer in the beautiful **Opéra,** 1 rue du Casino. (☎04 70 30 50 30. Open Tu-Sa 1:30-6:30pm, until curtain time on performance nights; by phone only Tu-F 10am-12:30pm. Operas €27-59, under 25 €24-53; concerts €17-40, under 25 €8-21, a few concerts are free.)

BURGUNDY (BOURGOGNE)

Ranging from the Côte d'Or, the Plateau de Langres, and the wild, forested Morvan, Burgundy is largely a rural and small town region with a quiet beauty. Known for its wine (Beaune and the Côte d'Or), mustard (Dijon), and rich cuisine (just about everywhere), Burgundy is also home to a wealth of famous Romanesque churches and stately renaissance homes.

A battleground for Gallic border wars in the first century BC, Burgundy was a major player in the Roman conquest; Autun was founded as a Roman capital. In the 5th century, the Burgundians, one of many Germanic tribes to pour across the Empire's borders during its final years, settled on the plains of the Saône and modestly named the region after themselves. During the Middle Ages, the duchy of Burgundy built magnificent cathedrals, and Cluny's powerful abbey governed over 10,000 monks. During the Hundred Years War, the Burgundians allied with the English to betray young Joan of Arc.

1	**Dijon:** Smart, modern Burgundian capital renowned for its snobbery and mustard **(p. 685)**
2	**Gevrey-Chambertin:** Château surrounded by France's arguably best vineyards **(p. 692)**
3	**Clos de Vougeot:** Gothic frat-castle owned by an association of alcoholic knights **(p. 692)**
4	**Beaune:** Ridiculous amounts of wine and a stunning 15th-century hospice **(p. 692)**
5	**Château de Rochepot:** Fairy-tale pointed turrets, slate roof, wooden drawbridge **(p. 697)**
6	**Mâcon:** Once-populous town with carved houses; not much to see or do **(p. 697)**
7	**Cluny:** Once the most powerful abbey in Europe, now ruined and dismantled **(p. 699)**
8	**Val Lamartinien:** Evergreen valley peppered with châteaux and Romantic poetry **(p. 701)**
9	**Paray-le-Monial:** Huge pilgrimage site; otherwise, its merit for travelers is debatable **(p. 702)**
10	**Autun:** Quiet town with old hilltop quarter, medieval ruins, serpentine streets **(p. 703)**
11	**Nevers:** Leafy provincial city at the confluence of two rivers; known for fine porcelain **(p. 706)**
12	**Auxerre:** Mid-sized, skippable city which retains some of its medieval charm **(p. 708)**
13	**Avallon:** Sensible base from which to approach the forest of the Morvan; little else **(p. 710)**
14	**Vézelay:** One of the most beautiful villages in France; its cathedral is legendary **(p. 711)**
15	**Semur-en-Auxois:** Lovely, typical Burgundian town; ramparts, mossy gargoyles **(p. 713)**

DIJON

The regional capital of Burgundy and—more importantly—the tangy hub of French mustard production, Dijon (pop. 160,000; annual mustard produced 84,000 tons) has all the attractions of a mid-sized provincial city. In the late Middle Ages, the powerful Dukes of Burgundy wielded a prestige and influence the weak Parisian monarchy could not hope to match. While Dijon is clearly speeding along into the 21st century as both an industrial and administrative center, the *vieille ville* seems comfortably frozen in the past with its plethora of *maisons en bois*, *hôtels particuliers*, and colorful tiled roofs. Host to a large student population and backpacker set, Dijon can ignite sparks lasting until the wee hours of the morning.

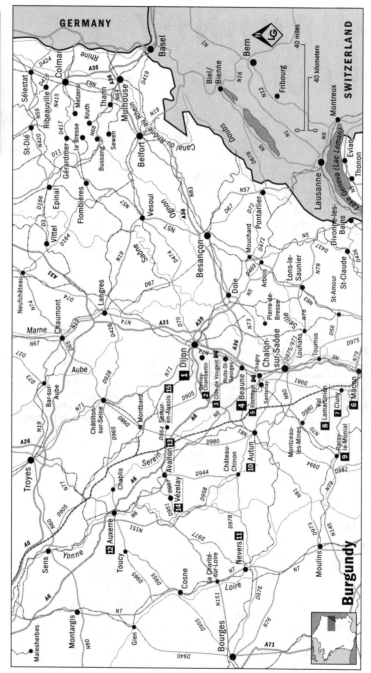

Burgundy

▐ TRANSPORTATION

Trains: cours de la Gare, at the end of av. Maréchal Foch. Info office open M-F 9am-7pm, Sa 9am-6pm. To: **Beaune** (30min., 27 per day, €5.70); **Clermont-Ferrand** (4hr., 5 per day, €29.70); **Lyon** (2hr., 5 trains and 2 TGV per day, €21.20); **Nice** (6-8hr., 4 trains and 2 TGV per day, €56.90); **Paris** (1¾-3hr., 7 trains and 13 TGV per day, €25.80). **SOS Voyageurs** (☎03 80 43 16 34). Open M-F 8:30am-7pm, Sa 8:30am-5pm. **Luggage storage** open M-F 8am-7:15pm, Sa-Su 9am-12:30pm and 2-6pm; July-Aug. M-F 8am-7:15pm; €3 per bag, €5 for two.

Buses: TRANSCO, av. Maréchal Foch (☎03 80 42 11 00), connected to the train station, to the left as you exit. Ticket and info office open M-F 5:30am-8:30pm, Sa 6:30am-12:30pm and 4-8:30pm, Su 9:30am-12:30pm and 4:40-8:30pm. Otherwise, buy tickets on the bus or at the *chef de gare's* office near the bus terminal. Service to: **Beaune** (1hr.; 9 per day 6:35am-7:25pm, Su only 11:10am; €5.74), **Chalon-sur-Saône** (2½hr.; 2 per day M-Sa 12:15 and 6:10pm; €10.43), **Autun** (2¼hr.; M-Sa 12:15pm, Su 11:10am; €12), and various stops in the **Côte d'Or.**

Public Transportation: STRD (☎03 80 30 60 90), pl. Grangier. Office open M-F 7:15am-7:15pm, Sa 8:30am-noon and 2-7:15pm. Map at the tourist office. Tickets €0.80; 12-trip pass €7; 1-day pass €2.70; 1-week pass €7.30; all available on board. Buses run 6am-8pm; limited evening service until 12:30am, Su morning until 1am.

Taxis: Taxi Dijon (☎03 80 41 41 12). 24hr.

Car Rental: Avis, 7bis cours de la Gare (☎03 80 42 05 99). Open M-F 8am-12:30pm, 2-8pm, and 8:30-9:30pm; Sa 8am-12:30pm and 2-6pm; Su 5:15-9:15pm.

Bike Rental: EuroBike, 4 rue du fbg. Raines (☎03 80 45 32 32), rents bikes, scooters, motorcycles, and in-line skates. Bikes €9.15 per half-day, €15.24 per day, €69.36 per week. Open Apr.-Oct. M-Sa 8am-noon and 2-6:30pm, Su 9:30-10:30am and 6:30-7pm; Nov.-Mar. M-Sa 9am-noon and 2-6pm. Off-season prices lower.

▐▐ ORIENTATION AND PRACTICAL INFORMATION

Dijon's *centre ville* is easy to navigate. Its main east-west axis, the pedestrian **rue de la Liberté,** runs roughly from **pl. Darcy** and the tourist office to **pl. St-Michel.** From the train station, follow av. Maréchal Foch straight to pl. Darcy. (5min.) The *vieille ville* and most of Dijon's sights are on the small streets radiating north and south from rue de la Liberté. The **pl. de la République,** northeast of pl. Darcy, is the central roundabout for roads leading out of the city.

Tourist Office: pl. Guillame Darcy (☎03 80 44 11 44). Gives free map, and sells a more heavy-duty version for €4.75. Organizes daily themed **city tours** July-Aug., some in English (€6, students €3; reserve ahead). **Accommodations service** €2.30 plus 10% deposit. **Currency exchange.** Open May-Oct. 15 daily 9am-8pm; Oct. 16-Apr. M-Sa 10am-6pm, Su 10am-noon and 2-6pm. **Branch** at 34 rue des Forges (☎03 80 44 11 44). Open May to Oct. 15 M-Sa 9am-1pm and 2-6pm; Oct. 16 to Apr. M-F 9am-noon and 2-6pm. **Branch** in the Palais des Ducs. Open M-F 8am-7pm, Sa 8am-12:30pm and 1:30-6pm, Su 9am-12:30pm and 1:30-6pm.

English Bookstore: Librairie de l'Université, 17 rue de la Liberté (☎03 80 44 95 44). Thriller paperbacks and erotic novels on 2nd floor. Open M 1-7pm, Tu-Sa 9:30am-7pm.

Youth Information: Centre Régional d'Information Jeunesse de Bourgogne (CRIJ), 18 rue Audra (☎03 80 44 18 44). Info on lodging, classes, grape-picking jobs, and travel. Open M-Tu and Th-F 10am-1pm and 2-6pm, W 10am-6pm.

Laundromats: 36 rue Guillaume Tell. Open daily 6am-9pm. Also at 28 rue Berbisey. Open daily 7am-9pm. Also at 8 pl. de la Banque. Open daily 7am-8:30pm.

Internet: Multi Rezo, cours de la Gare (☎03 80 42 13 89). Open M-Sa 9am-midnight, Su 2-10pm. €1 for 12min., €5 per hr., €15.20 for 5hr. **Reveil Informatique,** 38 rue Planchettes (☎03 80 63 89 71). Open M-F 9:30am-noon and 2-6:30pm. €9 per hr.

Police: 2 pl. Suquet (☎03 80 44 55 00).

Medical Assistance: Centre Hospitalier Regional de Dijon, 3 rue fbg. Raines (☎03 80 29 30 31). **SOS Médecins** (☎03 80 59 80 80) has doctors on call. For the rotating *pharmacie de garde,* call ☎03 80 44 55 00.

Post Office: pl. Grangier (☎03 80 50 62 19), near pl. Darcy. **Currency exchange.** Open M-F 8am-7pm, Sa 8am-noon. **Poste Restante:** 21031. **Postal code:** 21000.

🏠 ACCOMMODATIONS AND CAMPING

🏨 **Hôtel Victor Hugo,** 23 rue des Fleurs (☎03 80 43 63 45; fax 03 80 42 13 01). Quiet and convenient, Hugo's immaculate, spacious rooms, with shower or bath and toilet, make it worth every penny. Try to get a room next to the tall pine trees outside. Breakfast €4.80. Reception 24hr. Singles €28-35.50; doubles €42-43. MC/V. ❸

🏨 **Hôtel Montchapet,** 26-28 rue Jacques Cellerier (☎03 80 53 95 00; fax 03 80 58 26 87; www.Hotel-Montchapet.com). In a quiet neighborhood 10min. from the station, north of av. de la Première Armée Française off pl. Darcy. Kind proprietors let bright, comfortable rooms, many to students. Breakfast €5. Reception 7am-10:30pm. Check-out 11am. Singles €24, with toilet €30, with shower €39; doubles with toilet €36, with shower €36-46; triples and quads with shower €54-59. Extra bed €5. AmEx/MC/V. ❷

Hôtel des Ducs, 5 rue Lamonnoye (☎03 80 67 31 31; fax 03 80 67 19 51). In the center of town lies this find, with a stylish lobby, well-decorated, cheery rooms, and amazing bathrooms, including the occasional jacuzzi. Breakfast €7.50. Reception 6:30am-1:30am. Singles with shower €55, with bath €60-69; doubles €75; triples and quads €82.50. Low-season prices about €10-15 lower. AmEx/MC/V. ❹

Foyer International d'Etudiants, 6 rue Maréchal Leclerc (☎03 80 71 70 00; fax 03 80 71 60 48). Since it is a very long walk (30-40min.), take bus #4 from pl. Darcy (dir: St-Apollinaire) to "Parc des Sports." From av. Paul Doumer, turn right onto rue du Stade, then take the first left. A very international crowd. TV rooms, ping-pong and tennis courts, laundry, kitchen, and a lawn for sunbathing. Cafeteria open daily. Reception 24hr. Huge singles €14. AmEx/MC/V. ❶

Auberge de Jeunesse (HI), Centre de Rencontres Internationales, 1 av. Champollion (☎03 80 72 95 20; fax 03 80 70 00 61), 4km from the station. Take bus #5 (or night bus A) from pl. Grangier to "Epirey," right in front of this concrete megahostel with very dark hallways. **Internet access** €2.29 per 15min. Laundry. Breakfast included. Lunch or dinner from €4. Lockers €2. No keys before midday. Reception 24hr. Reservations recommended. Dorms €15; singles with shower €27.50-29.50; doubles and triples with shower €16-19; prices slightly lower for 2- to 3-night stays. MC/V. ❶

Hôtel du Sauvage, 64 rue Monge (☎03 80 41 31 21; fax 03 80 42 06 07). In a 15th-century post office. Half-timbered facade opens onto a flower-strewn courtyard and a canopy of greenery below. Breakfast €5.50. Reception 7am-11pm. June-Aug. reserve 2 weeks in advance. Flawless singles with shower €34-43, with bath €39-57; doubles €35-64. Huge 5-person loft €80. Extra bed €10. MC/V. ❸

Camping Municipal du Lac, 3 bd. Kir (☎03 80 43 54 72). Exit the back of the station and turn right on av. Albert 1er. After 1km, turn left on bd. Kir and follow the signs; if you cross a bridge, you've gone too far. Or take bus #12 from pl. Darcy (dir: Fontaine d'Ouche) to "Hôpital des Chartreux." Park and canal nearby. Grassy and calm; crowded in summer. Reception Apr.-May and Oct. daily 8:30am-noon and 2:30-7pm; June and Sept. 8:30am-noon and 1:30-5pm; July-Aug. 8:30am-8pm. Open Apr.-Oct. 15. €2.60 per person, children under 7 €1.40; €1.40 per car; €2 per site. Electricity €2.60. ❶

BURGUNDY

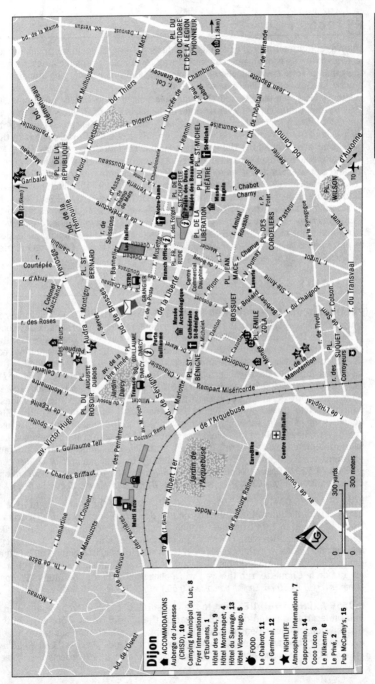

Dijon

▲ ACCOMMODATIONS
Auberge de Jeunesse (CRISD), 10
Camping Municipal du Lac, 8
Foyer International d'Etudiants, 1
Hôtel des Ducs, 9
Hôtel Montchapet, 4
Hôtel du Sauvage, 13
Hôtel Victor Hugo, 5

● FOOD
Le Chabrot, 11
Le Germinal, 12

★ NIGHTLIFE
Atmosphère International, 7
Cappuccino, 14
Coco Loco, 3
Le Kilkenny, 6
Le Privé, 2
Pub McCarthy's, 15

BURGUNDY

🍴 FOOD

Dijon's reputation for high cuisine is well deserved—and restaurant prices reflect it. *Charcuteries* provide an economical way to sample local specialties such as the popular **tarte bourguignonne** (creamy meat and mushroom pie), mushroom quiche, and **jambon persillé** (ham with parsley).

Rue Berbisey, rue Monge, and **pl. Emile Zola** host a wide variety of reasonably priced restaurants. There's a **supermarket** in the basement of Galeries Lafayette, 41 rue de la Liberté (open M-Sa 8:15am-7:45pm), and within **Monoprix,** 11 rue Piron, off pl. Jean Macé. (Open M-Sa 9am-8:45pm.) There is a colorful **market** in the pedestrian area around Les Halles. (Open Tu and Th-F mornings; all day Sa.)

Light green decor, an aquarium underfoot, display cases full of frog paraphernalia, and a menu listing *jambes de grenouille* are all symptomatic of a full-fledged croaker fetish at **Le Germinal ❷,** 44 rue Monge. (☎ 03 80 44 97 16. Lunch *menu* €10; dinner *plats* from €9.50. Reserve ahead. Open Tu-Th noon-2pm and 7-10:30pm, F-Sa noon-2pm and 7-11pm. MC/V.) **Le Chabrot ❸,** 36 rue Monge, serves a mouthwatering *crème de concombres glacée à la menthe* (fresh cucumber cream with mint) and chicken filet, as well as an exquisite gingerbread ice cream concoction as part of its €19 *menu affaire.* (☎ 03 80 30 69 61. Lunch *menu* €11; larger dinner *menu* €27. Open M-Sa 10am-10:30pm. MC/V.)

👁 SIGHTS

PALAIS DES DUCS DE BOURGOGNE (MUSÉE DES BEAUX-ARTS). The Dukes of Burgundy (1364-1477) were the best sort of rulers: fearless (Jean sans Peur), good (Philippe le Bon), and bold (Philippe le Hardi and Charles le Téméraire). At the center of the *vieille ville,* the 52m **Tour Philippe le Bon** is the most conspicuous vestige of ducal power. The palace and its semicircular arcade were designed in the late 17th century by the royal architect Jules Hardouin-Mansart. (☎ 03 80 74 52 71. *Tours Easter to mid-Nov. daily every 45min. 9am-5:30pm; mid-Nov. to Easter W afternoon, Sa-Su 9-11am and 1:30-3:30pm. €2.30, students €1.20.)* Most of the buildings currently house administrative offices, but the elegant **Musée des Beaux-Arts,** pl. de la Ste-Chapelle, occupies the palace's east wing. In its courtyard is the 15th-century kitchen, whose six gigantic hearths feed into one giant flue. The highlight of the museum is the section dedicated to "modern" art, which includes a Cezanne, modern abstract painters, and 20th-century Technicolor paintings by Lapicque. (*Pl. de la Libération.* ☎ 03 80 74 52 70. Open May-Oct. W-M 9:30am-6pm; Nov.-Apr. 10am-5pm. Modern art wing closed 11:30am-1:45pm. €3.40; groups and seniors €1.60; students with ID free; Su free.)

EGLISE NOTRE-DAME. The 11th-century cult statue of the Black Virgin here is credited with the liberation of the city on two desperate occasions: in 1513 from a Swiss siege and in 1914 from the German occupation. Two sumptuous tapestries depicting the miracles were commissioned for the Virgin in gratitude. The **Horloge à Jacquemart** clock, which ticks above the church's tower, was hauled off as plunder by Philippe le Hardi after his 1382 victory over the Flemish. Leaving the church via rue de la Chouette, rub the well-worn **chouette** (owl) for good luck. (*Pl. Notre Dame.* ☎ 03 80 74 35 76. English pamphlet €0.50.)

MUSÉE ARCHÉOLOGIQUE. Next to the cathedral, the Musée Archéologique, in a half-underground grand cave-hall, unearths the history of the Côte d'Or. In the former cloisters of St-Bénigne's abbey, it displays Gallo-Roman sculpture, medieval statuary and arms, and prehistoric jewelry. (*5 rue Dr. Maret.* ☎ 03 80 30 88 54. Open June-Sept. Tu-Su 9am-6pm; Oct.-May 9am-noon and 2-6pm. €2.20, students free; Su free.)

EGLISE ST-MICHEL. Begun at the end of the 15th century, this church changed in style from Flamboyant to Renaissance during its construction, resulting in a Gothic interior and colonnaded exterior. Like the Eglise Notre-Dame, it suffered severe damage during the Revolution, but was lovingly restored by Abbé Deschamps, who put his heart and soul into the job—he's buried in one of the chapels. The revamped gray Renaissance facade sparkles above the buildings in the old city. *(Pl. St-Michel. ☎03 80 63 17 84.)*

CATHÉDRALE ST-BÉNIGNE. Recently renovated, this Gothic cathedral commemorates a 2nd-century missionary whose remains were unearthed nearby in the 6th century. Its brightly tiled roof makes it one of Dijon's most prominent landmarks. Don't miss the 18th-century organ designed by Charles Joseph Riepp and the unusual (and spooky) circular crypt, pitch-black in places; flowers indicate Bénigne's grave. *(Pl. St-Bénigne. ☎03 80 30 39 33. Open daily 9am-7pm. Crypt €1.)*

MUSÉE MAGNIN. The elegant 17th-century Hôtel Lantin now houses this extensive collection of 16th- to 19th-century paintings. Though most of the art is obscure, the ensemble is well worth a visit for its furnishings, rich wallpaper, and intimate works. *(4 rue des Bons Enfants. ☎03 80 67 11 10. Open Tu-Su 10am-noon and 2-6pm; June-Aug. 10am-12:30pm and 2-6pm. €3, students €2.30.)*

OTHER SIGHTS. The **Jardin de l'Arquebuse** boasts reflecting pools, an arboretum, and 3500 species in a meticulously laid-out botanical garden. A giant sequoia tree makes for a grand entrance. *(1 av. Albert 1er. ☎03 80 76 82 84. Open July-Sept. daily 7:30am-10pm; Oct.-Feb. 7:30am-5:30pm; Mar.-June 7:30am-7pm.)* No trip to Dijon would be complete without a stop at the source of **Grey Poupon**, the **Maille Boutique**, 32 rue de la Liberté, where *moutarde au vin* became chic. It sells twenty different mustards, from €1.30. *(☎03 80 30 41 02. Open M-Sa 9am-7pm. MC/V.)*

🎵 📺 ENTERTAINMENT AND FESTIVALS

The city's best nightspot is ▪**Le Privé**, 20 av. Garibaldi, just north of pl. de la République, which pulses with energy from students and 20-somethings hanging out in leopard-skin booths or dancing to techno, house, and hip-hop under golden palm trees and in steel cages. Show up before midnight and you will dance alone. *(☎03 80 73 39 57. F-Sa cover €8; includes one drink. Su-Th cover €5, with one drink €8. Open Tu-Sa 10pm-5am, Su-M 11pm-5am.)* Next to Le Privé is **Coco Loco**, 18 av. Garibaldi, a bar/cantina full of 20-somethings. *(☎03 80 73 29 44. Open Tu-Sa 5pm-2am.)* At **Atmosphère Internationale**, a large complex at 7 rue Audra, students grind during the week and local youth relax on weekends in the bar/pool hall/nightclub. The party starts late. Wednesday and Thursday nights are *soirées internationales*. *(☎03 80 30 52 03. Open daily 5pm-5am. No cover for international students with ID; Su-W free for everyone; Th-Sa cover €5 includes a drink. MC/V.)* **Le Kilkenny**, 1 rue Auguste Perdrier, provides a relaxed mid-summer atmosphere. Kick back in dimly lit booths in this cellar bar, plastered with Guinness memorabilia. *(☎03 80 30 02 48. Open June-Aug. daily 7pm-3am; Sept.-May 6pm-3am. Draft beers €3.90-5.95, Irish specialty beers €4.25-7.50.)* **Rue Berbisey** is lined with bars and cafés. At **Cappuccino**, 132 rue Berbisey, the sometimes-boisterous clientele mingles to rock, jazz, hip-hop, and even heavy metal. *(☎03 80 41 06 35. Open M-Sa 3pm-2am.)* Stop across the street at **Pub McCarthy's**, 93 rue Berbisey, to schmooze with trendy locals. *(☎03 80 44 96 54. Open M-Sa 5:30pm-2am. Closed Aug.)*

The beautiful 18th-century **Théâtre de Dijon**, pl. du Théâtre, puts on operas from mid-October to late April. *(☎03 80 68 46 40. Tickets €21.35-42.69, students €9.15; 1hr. before curtain. Office open M-F 1-7pm and Sa 4-7pm during production months.)* Check out the shows (both classic and contemporary) at the **Nouveau**

Théâtre de Bourgogne, Théâtre du Parvis St-Jean, rue Danton. (☎03 80 30 12 12. Open Oct.-June M-F 1-7pm, Sa 4-7pm; performances M, F, Sa 8:20pm and W 7:30pm. Bar open 1hr. prior to performance.) Dijon's **Estivade** brings dance, music, and theater to the streets and indoor venues from late June to mid-July. Pick up a program at the tourist office. (☎03 80 30 31 00. Tickets free-€8.) The city devotes a week in late summer to the **Fêtes de la Vigne** and the **Folkloriades Internationales,** a celebration of grapes accompanied by over 20 foreign dance and music troupes. (☎/fax 03 80 30 37 95. Tickets €10-46, most €10-15; ask about youth discounts.)

▶ DAYTRIPS FROM DIJON

GEVREY-CHAMBERTIN

Perhaps the finest vineyards in all of France are 10km south of Dijon around Gevrey-Chambertin. Nine of the Côte's 29 *grands crus* are grown here, all with "Chambertin" in their name. Perched atop the vineyards, the **Château de Gevrey-Chambertin** is a perfect place to unwind, especially after a long bike ride. The gracious proprietress will take you through her 10th-century château, built to protect the wine and the villagers (in that order). The tour ends with a taste of the prized vintages, which cost €14 and up. (☎03 80 34 36 13. Get off at the bus stop at the entrance to the village, go left up the hill, left again, and the château will be on your left. Open Apr. 16-Nov. 18 daily 10am-noon and 2-6pm; Jan.-Apr. 15 and Nov. 19-Dec. 22 10am-noon and 2-5pm. Tour €4.50, including tasting.)

The Gevrey-Chambertin **tourist office** is small, but very helpful. (☎03 80 34 38 40. Open M and Sa 9:30am-12:30pm and 1:30-5:30pm, Tu-F 9am-12:30pm and 1:30-6pm, Su 10am-12:30pm and 1:30-5pm; July-Aug. M and Sa open until 6pm.) Bunk down in rural easy living at the **Marchands ❸,** 1 pl. du Monument aux Morts. (☎03 80 34 38 13; fax 03 80 34 39 65. Singles €28; doubles €39-43; triples €54-59; quads €69-74. MC/V.) Or call ahead to the tourist office for names of other bed and breakfasts, and reserve early in summer.

CHÂTEAU DU CLOS DE VOUGEOT

The D122 turns back southward from Gevrey-Chambertin, passing just to the east of minor châteaux in Morey-St-Denis and Chambolle-Musigny before arriving at the **Château du Clos de Vougeot,** a few kilometers north of Nuits-St-Georges (where the bus stops from Côte d'Or). Built in 1098, it was renovated to its present state in the 15th century by Louis XI, who regarded it as one of his greatest conquests. Today, it stands sentinel over a 125-acre vineyard, which its owners lease to several different *vignerons* (vintners). It is these vintners who give the château its spark: the **Confrérie des Chevaliers du Tastevin** (Brotherhood of the Knights of the Tastevin) was founded in 1934 to promote the sale of Burgundian *crus* during a slump in sales brought on by Prohibition and the Depression in the US. The 12,000 members hold frequent parties at the château as part of their duty to spread the gospel of Burgundian wine: *"Jamais en vain, toujours en vin"* ("Never in vain, always in wine"). They may have their fun here, but there's no wine tasting or buying at the château for the plebeians. (☎03 80 62 86 09. Open Apr.-Sept. Su-F 9am-6:30pm, Sa 9am-5pm; Oct.-Mar. daily 9-11:30am and 2-5:30pm. 1hr. tours depart every 30min. €3, students and children €2.50, under 8 free. AmEx/MC/V.)

BEAUNE

The puns are easy enough to make: *le vin de Beaune, c'est du bon vin.* But the throngs of dapper 40-somethings and red-faced septuagenarians who come to this viticulture hotspot (pop. 24,000) often don't speak enough French to get them.

While Beaune is hardly French, the crowds of visitors unite with the locals in their deep love of the liquid that Louis Pasteur called "the healthiest and most hygienic drink." Nestled along the Côte d'Or, 40km south of Dijon, the town serves as a base for shippers and wineries. Meandering along the maze of Beaune's cobblestone streets or through its medieval hospice with the recent memory of a (free!) fine vintage on the palate, you'll never want to leave.

TRANSPORTATION

Trains: av. du 8 Septembre (☎03 80 22 13 13). Info office open M-F 10am-noon and 2-7pm. To: **Chalon-sur-Saône** (25min., 23 per day, €4.90); **Dijon** (25min.; 33 per day, 4 TGV; €5.70); **Lyon** (1½hr., 11 per day, €18.10); **Paris** (2hr., 11 per day, €38.40).

Buses: TRANSCO (☎03 80 42 11 00) leaves from rues Buttes, Clémenceau, Jules Ferry, Pasteur, and St-Nicolas. To: **Autun** (80min.; M-Sa 1:10pm, Su 12:05pm; €6.40); **Châlon-sur-Saône** (1hr.; 1:30 and 7:05pm; €5.51); **Dijon** (1hr., 10 per day, €5.74). Stops along the **Côte d'Or**. Schedule at tourist office.

Car Rental: ADA, 26 av. du 8 Septembre (☎03 80 22 72 90; fax 03 80 22 72 92), across from the train station. Open M-Sa 8am-noon and 2-6pm. MC/V.

Bike Rental: Bourgogne Randonnées, 7 av. du 8 Septembre (☎03 80 22 06 03), near the station. Rents bikes and gives free maps with routes and itineraries. English-speaking staff. €3 per hr., €15 per day, €28 for 2 days, €65 per week. Credit card deposit. Open M-Sa 9am-noon and 1:30-7pm, Su 10am-noon and 2-6pm. MC/V.

Taxis: Allo Beaune Taxi (☎06 09 42 36 80). 24hr.

ORIENTATION AND PRACTICAL INFORMATION

Almost everything there is to see lies within the circular ramparts enclosing Beaune's *vieille ville*. To get to the town center from the station, head straight on av. du 8 Septembre, which becomes rue du Château. Once through the city walls, turn left onto rempart St-Jean, following it up and down the stairs as it crosses rue d'Alsace and becomes rempart Madeleine. The fourth right is **rue de l'Hôtel-Dieu,** which leads to the Hôtel-Dieu and the **tourist office.** (15min.) The streets of the town center run in concentric rings around the **Basilique Notre-Dame.**

Tourist Office: 1 rue de l'Hôtel-Dieu (☎03 80 26 21 30; fax 03 80 26 21 39). Free maps and lists of *caves.* **Hotel reservations** with 10% deposit. **Tours** of the *vieille ville* (July-Sept. 15 daily noon; €6.50 per person, €10.50 per couple). €14.50 *Pass Beaune* to 3 sights of choice. **Currency exchange** Sa-Su. Open Jan.-Mar. M-Sa 10am-6pm, Su 10am-12:30pm and 2-5pm; Mar. 29-June 20 M-Sa 9:30am-7pm, Su 10am-12:30pm and 2-5pm; June 21-Sept. 22 M-Sa 9:30am-8pm, Su 10am-12:30pm and 2-6pm; Sept. 23-Nov. 14 M-Sa 9:30am-7pm, Su 10am-12:30pm and 2-5pm; Nov. 15-17 9am-8pm; Nov. 18-Dec. M-Sa 10am-6pm, Su 10am-12:30pm and 2-5pm.

Laundromat: 19 rue fbg. St-Jean (☎03 80 24 09 78). Open daily 6:30am-9pm.

Police: 5 av. du Général de Gaulle (☎03 80 25 09 25, emergency ☎17).

Hospital: Centre Hospitalier, 120 av. Guigone de Salins, northeast of the town center (☎03 80 24 44 44). **24hr. ambulance:** ☎03 80 20 20 09.

Youth Center: Point Information Jeunesse, 8 av. de Salins (☎03 80 22 44 95). Info on work, study, and sports. Open M-Th 1:30-6pm, F 1:30-5pm.

Internet Access: Diz, 28 rue de Lorraine (☎03 80 26 36 01). Open M-Sa 11am-9pm. €5.50 per hr. 10min. minimum (€1).

Post Office: bd. St-Jacques (☎03 80 26 29 50). **Currency exchange, Internet,** and **Poste Restante.** Open M-F 8am-7pm, Sa 8am-noon. **Postal code:** 21200.

ACCOMMODATIONS AND CAMPING

Visitors swarm to Beaune from April to November; reserve at least a week in advance. For cheaper accommodations, base yourself in Dijon.

Hôtel Rousseau, 11 pl. Madeleine (☎03 80 22 13 59). From the station, head straight down av. du 8 Septembre, take a left on bd. Jules Ferry and another on ruelle Madeleine. 5min. from the town center at the end of a little gravel walk in the corner of the *place.* Comfortable rooms that open onto a secluded, lush courtyard. Plenty of company from early-morning pigeons and the owner's tropical birds. Breakfast included. Shower €3. Curfew 11:30pm. Singles €23-39; doubles €29-46, with shower €50-53.50; triples and quads €46-72.50. ❷

Beaun'Hôtel, 55 fbg. Bretonnière (☎03 80 22 11 01; fax 03 80 22 46 66). Southwest of the center, off bd. Clémenceau. Pretty, bright rooms in yellow, blue, and purple; many are quite large. Buffet breakfast €6.50. Reception 8am-6pm. Doubles €52.50-58; triples €60; family suite €78. Closed Dec.-Feb. MC/V. ❹

Hôtel le Foch, 24 bd. Foch (☎03 80 24 05 65; fax 03 80 24 75 59). Take av. de la République from the tourist office and turn right on bd. Foch. Pleasant rooms with lots of colors—some of them pretty, some not. Breakfast €5.34. Reception 7am-9pm. Singles and doubles €25.15, with shower €33-54; triples €38.11. Extra bed €6. MC/V. ❷

Stars Hôtel, rue Ampère (☎03 80 22 53 17; fax 03 80 24 10 14). From train station, walk up rue Château and make a left onto rue Jules Ferry. Head left onto rue Charles de Gaulle, and the hotel is 15min. down on the right. Prim and proper blue rooms, all with shower and toilet, in this futuristic cookie-cutter chain hotel. **Internet** access. Buffet breakfast €5.50. Reception 7am-11pm. Rooms €34; off-season €29. AmEx/MC/V. ❸

Camping: Les Cent-Vignes, 10 rue Dubois (☎03 80 22 03 91), 500m from the town center off rue du fbg. St-Nicolas. Head north on rue Lorraine from pl. Monge. Arrive early in summer. Graveled or grassy sites made pleasant and private by hedges. Laundry, restaurant, and grocery store. Open Mar. 15-Oct. 30. Reception 8am-9:30pm. €3 per person. Site €4, car included. Electricity €4. MC/V. ❶

FOOD

Food is expensive here. The restaurants around **pl. Madeleine** and **pl. Carnot** serve the least exorbitant *menus,* but even here prices for the local wine are uniformly high. There are three **Casino supermarkets,** at 28 rue du fbg. Madeleine (open M-Sa 8:30am-8pm); rue Carnot (open M 3-7pm, Tu-Sa 7:30am-12:30pm and 3-7:30pm, Su 8:30am-noon); and 15 rue Maufoux. (Open M-Sa 7:30am-12:30pm and 3-7:30pm.) A large **market** on pl. de la Halle livens up Wednesday and Saturday mornings, and on Monday afternoon from June to September 15. If you're willing to dispense with formality, you can eat a full meal for under €9 at the locally popular cafeteria **Crescendo** ❷, Stoc Centre Commercial, av. Charles de Gaulle, 12min. from the center. (Open daily 11:30am-2:30pm and 6:30-9:30pm; tea 9am-10pm.)

Monsieur Neaux, chef of **Relais de la Madeleine** ❷, 44 pl. Madeleine, wants you to try everything he cooks—your only regret will be that your belly isn't large enough. House specialties like duck *pâté,* a wondrous *mousse au chocolat,* and peppered trout are haute cuisine. (☎03 80 22 07 47. *Menus* €11.50, €14.50, and €23. Open Th-Tu noon-2pm and 7-10pm. AmEx/MC/V.) For pricier fare at a large plaza in the heart of the *centre ville,* take a seat at **Les Chevaliers** ❸, 3 Petite pl. Carnot, which has an extensive wine list. (☎03 80 22 32 26. *Menu* with *escargot,* delicious *poulet à la crème,* and dessert of the day €18.50. Other *menus* €22.50, €25.80, and €33.80. Open daily 10am-midnight. AmEx/MC/V.)

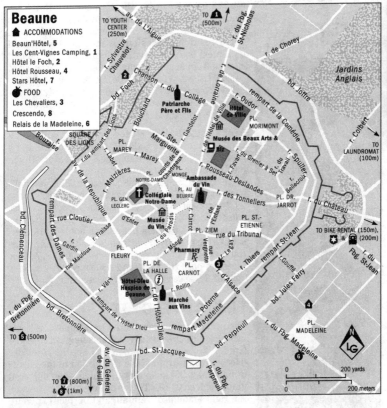

Beaune

⌂ **ACCOMMODATIONS**

Beaun'Hôtel, **5**
Les Cent-Vignes Camping, **1**
Hôtel le Foch, **2**
Hôtel Rousseau, **4**
Stars Hôtel, **7**

🍎 **FOOD**

Les Chevaliers, **3**
Crescendo, **8**
Relais de la Madeleine, **6**

👁 🏃 SIGHTS AND SIPS

■ **HÔTEL-DIEU.** In 1443, Nicolas Rolin, chancellor to the Duke of Burgundy, built this hospital to help the city recover from the ravages of war, poverty, and famine. Patients were treated here until 1971; the building is now the town's best non-potable tourist attraction. The hospital has held onto 143 acres of the area's finest vineyards; each year, on the third Sunday of November, the most recent vintages are sold at a charity auction. The courtyard is an excellent point from which to admire the magnificent tiled roofs that make this building one of France's architectural icons. From there, enter into the Salle des Poïvres, an exquisite communal patients' room. The *Hôtel's* great treasure, however, is the polyptych **The Last Judgment** by Roger van der Weyden. The exquisite details of the blessed and the damned are fully appreciated only with a giant magnifying glass. *(Open daily 9am-6:30pm. €5.10, students €4.10. Tour €1.60.)*

PATRIARCHE PÈRE ET FILS. The largest *cave* in Beaune is reached via the altar of an 18th-century chapel. Over 4 million bottles currently mature in these endless dark corridors of wine (actually 5km). In the final *caves*, a *dégustation* of 13 different wines is led by expert sommeliers. *(5-7 rue du Collège. ☎03 80 24 53 78. Open daily 9:30-11:30am and 2-6pm; arrive at least 1hr. before closing. €9; all proceeds to charity.)*

IN RECENT NEWS

PARENTS 1, KIDS 0

For millions of French schoolchildren, summer vacation isn't all fun and games. Parents, worried that a summer spent sunning on the beaches of Provence or hiking in the Alps will erase everything their budding scholars learned during the school year, flock to bookstores every June to stock up on *cahiers de vacances*. These "vacation notebooks" contain a series of educational activites, each designed to take no more than half an hour away from a little vacationer's day. There are *cahiers* specializing in every imaginable subject and for kids in every grade. Children of the digital age can complete their cahiers on CD-ROMS or online websites.

It's no wonder that these books have become a multi-million euro industry. Over 4.5 million are sold every year, at around €7 a piece. Altogether, it's estimated that around 80% of French children complete some kind of study over the summer, whether with *cahiers* or more traditional techniques.

Some parents and officials have questioned whether students actually benefit from their work, or whether the half-hour would be better spent at the pool. The *Institute de Recherches sur L'Economie de l'Education* (IREDU) recently studied the performance of students before and after vacation, concluding that students who use *cahiers* tend to do better after vacation, but also tend to be higher-performing students in the first place. Whatever their merits, you're sure to find them on the beaches of France this summer.

MUSÉE DU VIN. Inside the 15th-century Hôtel des Ducs de Bourgogne, the Musée du Vin shows visitors its wine cellar, vats, and immense presses for free. Other exhibits, occasionally modeled by clothed dummies, trace the evolution of wine bottles and carafes from ancient Roman times. (*Rue d'Enfer, off pl. Général Leclerc.* ☎ *03 80 22 08 19. Open Apr.-Nov. daily 9:30am-6pm; Dec.-Mar. W-Su 9:30am-5pm; Jan.-Mar. 9:30am-5pm. €5.10, students €3.10. Includes Musée de Beaux-Arts and Musée Etienne-Jules Marey.*)

OTHER SIGHTS. The **Musée des Beaux Arts** has a small collection of Gallo-Roman sculpture and a cache of paintings by 15th- and 16th-century Dutch and Flemish artists and 18th- and 19th-century French artists. (*Rue de l'Hôtel de Ville.* ☎ *03 80 24 56 92, weekends 03 80 24 98 70. Open Mar. daily 2-5pm; Apr.-Sept. 29 2-6pm; Sept. 30-Dec. 10am-5:30pm. For admission, see Musée du Vin.*) The somberly lit Burgundian-Romanesque **Collégiale Notre-Dame** holds a priceless set of 15th-century tapestries behind its altar, illustrating the life of the Virgin. (*Open daily 8:30am-7:30pm. Tapestries open M-Sa 9:30am-12:30pm and 2-7pm, Su 1-7pm. €2.30, students €1.50. Tours on request.*)

THE CÔTE D'OR

The nectar fastidiously stored in Beaune's dark cellars began its life basking on the sunny acres of the Golden Slopes to the north and south. The Côte d'Or—a 60km strip of land from Dijon to the village of Santenay, 20km south of Beaune—has nurtured grapes since 500 BC. Traces of limestone in the soil, the right amount of rainfall, and perfect exposure and soil drainage make it a godsend for viticulturists, and therefore among the most valuable real estate in the world.

The Côte d'Or is divided into two regions. The **Côte de Nuits,** stretching south from Dijon through **Nuits-St-Georges** to the village of **Corgoloin,** produces red wines from the Pinot Noir grape. Running from Corgoloin south to **Santenay,** the **Côte de Beaune** produces great white wines from Chardonnay grapes. The aptly-named **Route des Grands Crus** ("great wine route") winds through the region, passing through famous vineyards and wine-producing villages. Without a car and plentiful funds, the villages are hard to get to and stay in. Tastings are free, but most winemakers will expect you to buy something.

While the region's wines are superlative, the methods of transportation around the vineyards can't claim the same. If you're up for adventure, the best way to get to the vineyards near either **Beaune** or **Dijon** is to rent a mountain bike and pedal down the

Route de Grands Crus. Bike rental shops in both cities arrange tours of differing lengths that can get you where you want to go. If you have a little more cash, renting a car in **Dijon** or **Beaune** (around €70 per day including tax, insurance, and gas) is the easiest way to the grapes, but if you are planning on taking part in your fair share of wine tasting, this might not be the best option. **TRANSCO** buses (☎03 80 42 11 00) will also get you from Dijon to **Beaune** (1hr.; 9 per day, Su only 11:10am; €5.74); **Gevrey-Chambertin** (30min., 19 per day, €2.40); **Nuits-St-Georges** (45min.; 11 per day, Su only 12:34 and 6:24pm, €4). TRANSCO will take you from Beaune to **Château de Rochepot** (5 per day, Su only 12:05 and 6:05pm; €3.20).

Lodging on the Côte is expensive; some reasonable options are given below, but your best bet is to reserve a room days in advance at one of the many *chambres d'hôte* dotting the villages. The tourist office in Beaune or Gevrey-Chambertin will supply you with a copy of *Chambres et Tables d'hôte*, a comprehensive list of bed and breakfasts along the Côte d'Or and throughout France.

CHÂTEAU DE ROCHEPOT

The **Château de Rochepot,** 15km southwest of Beaune, springs straight out of a fairy tale, with its wooden drawbridge, slate roof, and pointed turrets. "To enter, knock three times," declares the ancient sign. The 45min. tour includes a peek at the Guard Room, the ingenious kitchens, the dining room, the old chapel, and the "Chinese" room, a gift of the last empress of China. (☎03 80 21 71 37. Open Apr.-June Su-F 10:30-11:30am and 2-5:30pm; July-Aug. 10am-6pm; Sept. 10-11:30am and 2-5:30pm; Oct. 10-11:30am and 2-4:30pm. €5.50.)

While lodging is scarce in this tiny town, ■**Le Relais du Château ❸**, rte. de Nolay, has a friendly, English-speaking proprietor, and the bright, clean rooms are a fantastic deal. (☎03 80 21 71 32. Breakfast €5.60. Restaurant *menus* €16.50-26. Doubles with shower €28, with shower and toilet €41. MC/V.)

MÂCON

Balanced between Burgundy and the Beaujolais, Mâcon (pop. 40,000) is a crossroads between the north and south. Laid against the right bank of the Saône, "Matisco" was an important Roman colony and later became a frontier city between French lands and the Holy Roman Empire. Romantic poet, politician, and ladies' man Alphonse de Lamartine (1790-1869) was *mâconnais*, but his fame and fervor far outstripped his quiet birthplace. For those with transportation, Mâcon is an ideal base for exploring the Beaujolais vineyards, as well as taking daytrips to Cluny and Paray-le-Monial. Otherwise, there's not much to keep you here.

◢◪ ORIENTATION AND PRACTICAL INFORMATION

The town center is a fairly compact area framed by rue Gambetta, rue Victor Hugo, cours Moreau, and the Saône. To reach the **tourist office,** pl. St-Pierre, from the rue Bigonnet station, go straight down rue Gambetta and take a left onto rue Carnot.

Trains and Buses: rue Bigonnet. Info desk open M-F 9am-noon and 1:20-6:30pm, Sa 9am-noon and 1:20-5:30pm. To: **Dijon** (1¼hr., 19 per day, €14); **Lyon** (1hr.; 20 per day; €9.80); **Paris** (2hr., 6 TGVs per day, €58.90). **TGVs** stop at **Mâcon-Loche,** 6km away. Hop on SNCF bus #7 (dir: Chalon-sur-Saône) for a quick ride to the TGV station (12min., 4 per day, €1.80).

Taxis: ☎06 07 36 57 06. 24hr. About €15 from Mâcon-Loche to Mâcon.

Bikes: Pro' Cycles, 45 rue Gambetta (☎03 85 22 81 83). Bikes €14 per day, €70 per week. Open M 3-7pm, Tu-Sa 9am-noon and 2-7pm.

Tourist Office: 1 pl. St-Pierre (☎03 85 21 07 07; fax 03 85 40 96 00). **Accommodations service** €2.30 with 10% down payment. The office gives 6 different themed visits in French. (July-Sept. Sa 2:30pm; €5.50, under age 12 free. July-Aug. tours in English. Ask for schedule.) Open June-Sept. M-Sa 10am-7pm, Su 3-7pm; Mar.-May and Oct. M-Sa 10am-12:30pm and 1:30-6pm; Nov.-Feb. M-Sa 10am-12:30pm and 2-6pm.

Laundromat: 20bis rue Gambetta (☎06 15 31 68 68). Open daily 7am-10pm.

Police: 36 rue Lyon (☎03 85 32 63 63). Emergency ☎17.

Hospital: Centre Hospitalier, bd. de l'Hôpital (☎03 85 20 30 40). Emergency ☎15.

Pharmacy: Pharmacie de la Pyramide, 362 rue Carnot (☎03 85 38 04 99). Open Tu-Sa 8:30am-12:30pm and 1:45-7:30pm, M 1:45-7:30pm. For the *pharmacie de garde,* call the police.

Internet Access: Le Victor Hugo Café, 37 rue Victor Hugo (☎03 85 39 26 16). €4 per hr. Open M-Sa 8am-1am and Su 3pm-midnight.

Post Office: 3 rue Victor Hugo (☎03 85 21 05 50). **Currency exchange** and **Poste Restante.** Open M-F 8:30am-7pm and Sa 8:30am-noon. **Postal code:** 71000.

ACCOMMODATIONS

Reasonably priced rooms are common in Mâcon, though you should reserve in July and August. **Hôtel Escatel ❶,** 4 rue de la Liberté, is a bit out of the way but extremely well priced. From the station turn left onto rue V. Hugo and follow it past pl. de la Barre as it flows into rue de l'Héritan. The hotel is to the right across from the intersection of rue de l'Héritan and rue de Flace. (15min.) The hum of traffic from the intersection fills its long college-dorm hallways and modern, cheerful rooms. (☎03 85 29 02 50; fax 03 85 34 19 97. Breakfast €5.80. Reception 24hr. Check-out noon. Singles €15.10, with shower €25.95, with bath €33.55; doubles €26/€30.50/€39.65. Extra bed €7.65. AmEx/MC/V.) If you want something in the *centre ville,* stay at **Le Promenade ❷,** 266 quai Lamartine. From the station, walk straight down rue Gambetta and make a left onto quai Lamartine. A neat, accommodating, sometimes crowded hotel provides rooms of varying quality, all with toilet and shower; treat yourself to a heavenly blue skylight room if you can. (☎03 85 38 10 98; fax 03 85 38 94 01. Reception 10am-3:30pm and 6:30-midnight. Singles and doubles €20-31; triples €32.50-34. AmEx/V.)

FOOD

Situated between Burgundy and the Beaujolais, Mâcon enjoys the best of both wine worlds, and it also produces its own Chardonnays, *Pouilly Fuissé* and *Mâcon Clessé,* which go well with *quenelles* (smooth, creamy fish dumplings) and *coq au vin.* A small **market** is held daily on pl. aux Herbes; a larger one is held on espl. Lamartine. (Open Sa 7am-1pm.) There's also a **Marché Plus** on 18 rue Lacretelle off rue V. Hugo. (Open M-Sa 7am-9pm, Su 9am-1pm.)

It's not difficult to find reasonably priced restaurants in Mâcon, but much of the budget eating is located on the *quais* in busy brasseries next to the noisy highway. For a night on the town, start off with an *apéritif* at **La Maison de Bois ❶,** 13 pl. aux Herbes, a friendly bar specializing in champagne, located in a 15th-century monastic house with grotesque carvings. (☎03 85 38 03 51. Beer €2.15-5.35. Open M 3-9pm, Tu-Sa 7am-2am.) **Restaurant Soukhothai ❷,** 51 rue Gambetta, serves delicately prepared Chinese, Thai, and Vietnamese food. Try the curried Thai chicken (€5.65) or the steamed prawns (€3.80). (☎03 85 39 48 10. Lunch *menus* €8.70 and €11, dinner *plats* €12.50 and €14.80. Open M 7-10pm, Tu-Sa noon-2pm and 7-10pm. MC/V.) For quality regional food in a traditional *brasserie* setting, head to **Le Lamartine ❸,** 259 quai Lamartine. (☎03 85 38 97 01. *Menu Lamartine* €14.80. Open Th-Su noon-2:30pm and 7-11pm, M noon-2:30pm, W 7-11pm. AmEx/MC/V.)

👁 SIGHTS

Students and those under 26 have free entry to the sights listed below.

MUSÉE DES URSULINES. Among the slim pickings of Mâcon's sights, this museum is by far the best, with a diverse collection ranging from ancient chess pieces and arresting paintings to a history of the Saône. Its archaeological exhibits include the occupied stone coffin of a Frankish warrior, opened to reveal the bones and possessions of the original tenant. The second floor is devoted to the ethnology and traditions of the *mâconnais*. The third floor has aristocratic paintings and some choice furniture, including a chair used to carry Louis XIV. *(Rue des Ursulines. ☎ 03 85 39 90 38. Open Tu-Sa 10am-noon and 2-6pm, Su 2-6pm. €2.30.)*

RESIDENCE SOUFFLOT. This hospital, designed in 1752 by Soufflot, architect of the Panthéon in Paris (see p. 137), continues to serve. Its centerpiece is an oval multi-level Italianate chapel, which let the sick join in mass without descending to the ground floor, and a *tonneau tournant* (revolving cupboard), where mothers once orphaned children anonymously. *(249 rue Carnot. Ask for the chapel key at the tourist office; hospital open only to groups during 2003 renovations. Open M-F 10am-7pm.)*

MAISON DE BOIS. Rue Carnot and rue Dombey have a number of late medieval houses, the most famous being the Maison de Bois (see **Food**, above), on the corner of rue Dombey and pl. aux Herbes. Built between 1490 and 1510, the facade has a marvelous array of carvings, with naughty monkeys and other animals. The house is one of only four of its kind left in France. At rue du Pont, turn right and walk across the **Pont St-Laurent** for a good view of the city and its characteristic old buildings. Though the bridge itself is unremarkable, the view shows how Mâcon, being a border town, was built up almost exclusively on the west bank.

🎵 🖼 ENTERTAINMENT AND FESTIVALS

Cafés on the *quais* are full all day long and well into the evening. Just behind quai Jean Jaurès are lively concert-bars, like **Bar l'Insolite,** 65 rue Franche, specializing in nightly karaoke. (☎03 85 38 07 63. Open Tu-Sa 10am-2am.) The big summer event is the four-week festival **L'Eté Frappé,** which features a variety of free shows at indoor and outdoor venues around Mâcon, with films, jazz, classical music, comedians, and dancing, from early July to mid-August. For goings-on in the region, ask the tourist office for the free annual *Les Rendez-vous* or *L'Eté Bleu.*

CLUNY

Cluny's population of 5000 has not grown since the 11th century, when a select few thousand controlled 10,000 monks, 1200 monasteries, and more than a few kings. Its once enormous abbey, which produced almost a dozen popes, faded into obscurity following the Wars of Religion and was sold and largely destroyed during the Revolution. Cluny now exports mustard jars and top-notch engineers from the *Ecole Nationale Supérieure d'Arts et Métiers* (ENSAM), but it is the town's rich medieval heritage that draws pilgrims from all over Europe.

📧 🔡 TRANSPORTATION AND PRACTICAL INFORMATION

Cluny has no train station; buses are tortuously routed and irritatingly infrequent. To get from the bus stop to the **tourist office,** walk against the traffic on rue Porte de Paris, turn right at pl. du Commerce, and continue for 5min.

Buses: SNCF goes to **Châlon-sur-Saône** (80min.; 5 per day 5:21am-6:13pm; €7.20); **Mâcon** (40min.; 7 per day; €3.81); and **Paray-le-Monial** (1½hr.; 6 per day; €23.30). The **Boutique SNCF,** 9 rue de la République (☎03 85 59 07 72), can help you through the connection maze. Open Tu-F 9am-noon and 1:30-5:30pm, Sa 9am-12:30pm.

Taxis: ☎03 85 59 04 87.

Bike Rental: Ludisport, 3 allée de la Teppe (☎06 62 36 09 58). €10 per 4hr., €18 per day. ID deposit. Open daily 9am-noon and 2-6pm.

Tourist Office: 6 rue Mercière (☎03 85 59 05 34; fax 03 85 59 06 95), in the Tour des Fromages. Helpful map and a free *guide pratique.* Open July-Aug. daily 10am-7pm; Apr.-June 10am-12:30pm and 2:30-7pm; Sept. 10am-12:45pm and 2-7pm; Oct. M-Sa 10am-12:30pm and 2:30-6pm; Nov.-Mar. until 5pm. **Tours** mid-July to Aug.; inquire at the Cluny Abbey info desk (open May-Aug. daily 9:30am-6pm; Sept.-Apr. 9:30am-noon and 1:30-5pm).

Laundromat: 2 rue de Merle (☎06 07 26 57 26). Open daily 7am-10:30pm.

Police: rte. de la Digue (☎17 or ☎03 85 59 06 32).

Hospital: 13 pl. de l'Hôpital (☎03 85 59 59 59). 24hr.

Pharmacy: Pharmacie de l'Abbaye, 6 rue Municipals (☎03 85 59 09 85). Open Tu-Sa 8:30am-12:30pm and 1:45-7:30pm. *Pharmacie de garde* info is posted on the doors of the town's pharmacies.

Internet Access: Point Accueil Jeune (☎03 85 59 25 36). €3 per hr. Open Tu and Th 2-7pm, W and F 10am-noon and 2-7pm, Sa 10am-7pm.

Post Office: off chemin du Prado (☎03 85 59 86 00), near pont de la Levée. Open M-F 8am-noon and 2-6pm, Sa 8am-noon. **Currency exchange** and **Poste Restante. Postal code:** 71250.

⚑ ACCOMMODATIONS AND CAMPING

Budget lodgings fill quickly in summer; reserve early or daytrip from Mâcon.

Cluny Séjour (☎03 85 59 08 83; fax 03 85 59 26 27), rue Porte de Paris, behind the bus stop. This converted 18th-century chandlery was once inhabited by Cluny's monks; the bright, clean rooms could be interpreted as unfurnished or austere. Breakfast included. Reception Jan.-Feb. M-Sa 9am-noon and 3-7pm; Mar. and Nov.-Dec. 9am-noon and 3-7pm; Apr.-May and Oct. 7am-noon and 3-8pm; June and Sept. 7am-noon and 3-8pm; July-Aug. 7am-noon and 3-10pm. 2- to 4-bed dorms €12.50. MC/V. ❶

Hôtel du Commerce, 8 pl. du Commerce (☎03 85 59 03 09). The rooms here are rather nondescript, but they are clean, with big wooden dressers and windows. Breakfast €4.60. Reception 6:30am-noon and 4:30-10:30pm. Singles €18; doubles €23-27, with shower €32, with bath and toilet €37.40. Extra bed €6.10. AmEx/MC/V. ❷

Camping St-Vital, rue de Griottons (☎/fax 03 85 59 08 34). A grassy, open three-star site with some shade next to the municipal swimming pool; stay on "Allée Claude Monet" or "Allée Auguste Renoir." Reception July-Aug. 7am-10pm; May-June and Sept. 9am-noon and 3-9pm. Reservations recommended. €3.80 per person, €1.80 per child under 7; €1.90 per tent or car; electricity €2.50. ❶

🍴 FOOD

Auberge de Cheval Blanc ❸, 1 rue Porte de Mâcon, serves up a tasty *coq au vin* and *boeuf bourguignon* (each €14.80). The *menus* (€14-34) are pricey, but the setting is very relaxed. (☎03 85 59 01 13. Open Su-Th noon-2pm and 7-9pm, F noon-2pm. MC/V.) **La Petite Auberge** ❷, pl. du Commerce, has piping hot oversized pizzas for €5.80-7.65 and salads for €2.95-6.10. (☎03 85 59 02 96. Open Th-M noon-1:30pm and 7:15-10pm, Tu noon-1:30pm. MC/V.) There is a **Casino supermarket** at 29 rue Lamartine. (Open M 9am-noon and 3-7pm, Tu-Sa 8am-12:15pm and 3-7:15pm, Su 8:30am-noon.) The **local market** is held every Saturday morning near the abbey.

BURGUNDY

🕐 🎵 SIGHTS AND FESTIVALS

Begin your tour with a great view of town and the green slopes around it from atop the 120 steps of the **Tour des Fromages,** right next to the tourist office. The tower was part of the abbey until the Revolution, when it was bought by a woman who used it to dry her cheeses. (Tour €1.25, students €0.80.) Then follow rue Mercière one block and turn right onto rue de la République. This area, particularly rue d'Avril and rue Lamartine, is home to the best of the well-preserved **Maisons Romanes** (medieval houses) which dot the city. The path leads straight through the **Porte d'Honneur,** which frames the remaining abbey spires. The Romanesque **abbey church,** dedicated to St-Pierre and St-Paul, is the third church on the site and goes under the imaginative name of **Cluny III.** The order of the Cluniacs was founded in the 10th century in an effort to reform monastic life. They quickly traded in their credo for influence, prestige, and wealth, attracting some of the brightest minds of the 11th and 12th centuries. At its height, Cluny and its nearly omnipotent abbot controlled a vast network of daughter abbeys and, by virtue of the order's unique charter, escaped the control of every ruler except the pope. Cluny III was the largest church in the world until the construction of St. Peter's in Rome. During the Wars of Religion, the Revolution, and its aftermath, the abbey was looted, sold, and used as a quarry. A mental reconstruction of the abbey's scale requires some effort, but its former wealth is apparent in the ornamentation of the Gothic **Pope Gelasius** facade. What remains is now home to the **Ecole Nationale Supérieure d'Arts et Métiers,** whose central cloister is surrounded by student rooms.

Buy your tickets to the abbey as well as to the **Musée d'Art et d'Archéologie** in the building on the left. The museum houses a reconstruction of the abbey and some religious art which escaped destruction, plus an imposing 15th-century library with 1800 musty books. (☎03 85 59 12 79. Abbey and museum open May-Aug. 9:30am-6pm; Sept.-Apr. 9:30am-noon and 1:30-5pm. Abbey tours in English July-Aug. W and F 10:15am, 2:15, 4:15pm; tours also available in French. €5.50, under 26 €3.50. Ask about night tours July-Aug.)

The yearly festival **Les Grandes Heures de Cluny** in July and August mixes classical music with Bacchic encounters. Concerts in venues throughout Cluny are followed by local *dégustations* and viticulture luncheons in Val Lamartinien. (Contact the tourist office for tickets. Concerts €19, students €15; *dégustations* €10.)

NEAR CLUNY

VAL LAMARTINIEN

The sights and roadsides of the area around Cluny are splashed with signs bearing verses by Romantic poet Alphonse de Lamartine (1790-1869). Twelve kilometers north of Cluny is the **Château de Cormatin,** complete with moat, formal gardens, aviary, and maze. The monumental open-well staircase in the north wing was the height of sophisticated engineering at the time of its construction (1605-1616). The Italian-style rooms, though unrestored, are well preserved. The tour features a plethora of interest-piquing historical details—once the Marquis died, the Marquise, then 22, lived the rest of her life in black—and even a brief meditation "session." You can **bike** by taking the car-free **la Voie Verte,** a 44km stretch of road devoted to bikers and bladers, which covers a good deal of fairly flat countryside near Cluny. The **SNCF bus** from **Cluny** (25min., 8 per day 5:20am-8:13pm, €2.40) or

Mâcon (1hr., 7 per day 7:58am-7:40pm, €5.60) will take you to the château. (☎ 03 85 50 16 55; fax 03 85 50 72 06. Open Apr.-Nov. 11 daily 10am-noon and 2-5:30pm. Tours in French with written English translation every 30min. €6.50, students ages 18-26 with ID €5, ages 10-17 €4. Park only €4.)

PARAY-LE-MONIAL

Paray-le-Monial (pop. 10,000) owes its fame to a 25-year-old nun. It was here, in 1673, that Christ appeared before Sister Marguerite-Marie Alacoque, revealing his identity with the words, "Here is the heart that so loved mankind." The adoration of the Sacred Heart caught on in the late 19th century, and Paray gained fame throughout the Christian world. The growing cult received a visit by Pope Pius IX in 1850, who elevated the town's simple cathedral to the status of basilica. Sister M-M was canonized in 1920. Since then Paray has been second in France only to Lourdes as a pilgrim magnet. For the non-fervent, it merits only an afternoon visit.

TRANSPORTATION. Trains are infrequent; check times or risk getting stuck. (☎ 03 85 81 13 25. Ticket counter open M 4:45am-noon and 12:30-8pm, Tu-F 5:30am-noon and 12:30-8pm, Sa 7:30am-noon and 2:30-5:30pm, Su 10:10am-noon and 2:30pm-8pm.) To: **Dijon** (2hr., 5 per day, €15.60); **Lyon** (2hr., 4 per day); **Moulins** (80min., 11 per day, €9.30); **Paris** via Moulins (3½hr. from Moulins; 17 per day from Moulins; €34.90). **SNCF buses** go to **Cluny** (2½hr., 4 per day, €23.30), where you can change for **Mâcon** (€11 by train, €3.81 by bus), and to local hubs **Roanne** (45min., 4 per day, €6) and **Le Creusot,** which has a TGV terminal (40min., 6 per day, €9.50). For a **taxi,** call ☎ 03 85 88 24 30.

PRACTICAL INFORMATION. To get to the **tourist office,** 25 av. Jean-Paul II, leave the station to the left and turn right on av. de la Gare. Cross the canal bridge and veer right onto av. de Gaulle. At the end of the street, turn left on rue des Deux Ponts, continue straight until you cross the bridge over the Bourbince, and then turn right on av. Jean-Paul II. When the road forks, after 15min., you'll be in front of the office, next to the basilica. (☎ 03 85 81 10 92; fax 03 85 81 36 61. Open July-Aug. daily 9am-7pm; mid-Nov. to Easter M-Sa 9am-noon and 1:30-6pm; Easter-June and Sept. to mid-Nov. daily 9am-noon and 1:30-6:30pm.) For **Internet access,** crash at **Centre-Com,** 20 rue du 8 Mai. (☎ 03 85 81 69 73. Open M 9am-noon and 2-6:30pm, Tu-F from 8:30am, Sa 9am-noon only; Aug. M-F 9am-noon and 2-6:30pm. €6 per hr.) If you're really about to crash, stop by **Pharmacie de la Basilique,** 26 rue Victor Hugo. (☎ 03 85 81 11 23. Open M 2:15-7pm, Tu-F 9am-12:15pm and 2:15-7pm, Sa 9am-12:15pm.) For the **pharmacie de garde,** call the **police,** 13 bd. Henri de Regnier (☎ 03 85 81 11 05). The **post office** is on rue du Marché. (Open M-F 8am-12:15pm and 1:15-6pm, Sa 8am-noon.) **Postal code:** 71600.

ACCOMMODATIONS AND CAMPING. Paray draws pilgrims year-round, and rooms are difficult to find during religious sessions (mostly in July and August); 1-2 months's advance reservation is strongly recommended. Cheap, comfortable rooms can be found in the Christian *foyers* near the basilica. The **Foyer du Sacré-Cœur ❷,** 14 rue de la Visitation, is a charming, quiet place with great wooden floors in the center of town. Rooms are tastefully decorated, some with crucifixes hovering protectively over the bed. Pilgrims predominate, but secular visitors are welcome. (☎ 03 85 81 11 01; fax 03 85 81 26 83. Breakfast €4, lunch €12.50, dinner €11.50. Reception July-Aug. Su-Th 8am-noon and 2-5:50pm, F 8am-noon; Sept.-June daily 9am-noon and 1:30-6:30pm. Singles from €18; doubles from €32; triples from €43.05.) The **Hôtel du Nord ❷,** 1 av. de la Gare, offers comfortable rooms amid very colorful decor, including leopard-print carpets. (☎03 85 81 05 12. Showers €4.30. Breakfast €4.80. Reception 6:30am-10:30pm. Singles €25, with shower €30; doubles with bath €39; quads €36.50. Free parking. MC/V.) In town is **Hôtel du Champ de Foire ❷**, 2 rue Desrichard, with clean, simple rooms with showers, and unique if sometimes oddly colored walls. (☎03 85 81 01 68; fax 03 85 88 86 30. Breakfast €3.95. Singles €23; doubles €30.50; triples €37.35; quads €43.45. MC/V.) **Camping de Mambré ❶** is on route du Gué-Léger. From the end of av. de la Gare, turn left and walk for 25min. This bustling campsite has a pool and laundry. (☎03 85 88 89 20; fax 03 85 88 87 81. Reception 8am-11pm. Open for camping and bungalows June-Sept. July-Aug. €6 per site, €3 per person, electricity €2.76; June and Sept. €5.18/€2.13/€2.29. Bungalows €52 per night; 3-night min. stay.)

◖ FOOD. Markets are held on bd. du Collège. (Open F 8am-12:30pm.) A string of cheap eateries are on **rue Victor Hugo** off pl. Guignault, but a prettier spot for lunch is one of the cheap brasseries on the south side of the Bourbince, in view of the basilica. A **8-Huit** grocery store is on the corner of rue Victor Hugo and rue du Marché. (Open M-Sa 8am-12:30pm and 2:30-8pm, Su 8:30am-12:30pm.) For a full meal, try the tasty **La Taïga ❷**, 9 rue Victor Hugo. (☎03 85 81 21 66. *Menus* €8-13. Salads under €6.50. Open July-Aug. daily 9am-midnight; Sept.-June 9am-10pm.)

◙ SIGHTS. The spire of **Basilique du Sacré-Cœur** is visible throughout town. Although Paray didn't emerge as a religious center until the first pilgrimage in 1873, the basilica, aging and not particularly attractive, dates from the 11th century. This production of the Cluny architectural workshop is brought to you by the number three (the Trinity), with a tripartite elevation and division on the facade, three major towers, and three radiating chapels. (Open daily 9am-7pm.)

Rue de la Visitation leads from the basilica to the other religious sights. The **Parc des Chapelains,** behind the church, is a peaceful spot for reflection in the outdoor chapel, whose nave is formed by tall, graceful plane trees. The **Accueil Pèlerinage de Paray** next door welcomes the curious with a multilingual video and info on religious sessions. (Pilgrimage Center ☎03 85 81 62 22. Open daily 9:30am-noon and 2-6pm.) Continue along rue de la Visitation to the **Monastère de la Visitation,** sometimes referred to as *la Chapelle des Apparitions*, where Jesus is said to have revealed himself to Marguerite-Marie and where her relics are now kept. (Open daily 7:30am-7:30pm.) At the end of rue de la Visitation, turn left to get back to the town center. On **pl. Guignault,** the sand-colored facade of the early 17th-century **Maison Jayet** (now the **Hôtel de Ville**) is adorned with pint-sized portraits of French royalty. The **Tour St-Nicholas,** also 17th-century, stands guard over pl. Guignault. Once the belfry of the long-gone St-Nicholas church, it is now just another worn facade and home to a beautiful wooden staircase; the rest of the church burnt down long ago. Art exhibits are held inside regularly, mostly during the summer.

AUTUN

Around 15 BC, Emperor Augustus founded Augustodunum to create a "sister and rival of Rome." The name was later shortened to Autun. The result of Augustus's grand plan is now an impressive collection of rubble. Stirred by civic jealousy of nearby Vézélay's success, the town erected the Cathédrale St-Lazare (1120-1146) and tried to grab market share in the lucrative medieval pilgrimage business. Despite the ravages of eight none-too-kind centuries, the cathedral still boasts some of the finest Romanesque sculpture in the world. Though a recent lack of pilgrims has pushed Autun (pop. 18,000) off the beaten path, its serpentine streets, cathedral, and Roman ruins make it a compelling stop.

■ ■ **ORIENTATION AND PRACTICAL INFORMATION.** The main street, **av. Charles de Gaulle,** connects the station to the central **pl. du Champ du Mars.** To get to the *vieille ville* from the *place,* follow the signs from rue aux Cordeliers or rue Saint-Saulge. The **tourist office** is off pl. du Champ du Mars.

Trains run from pl. de la Gare on av. de la République, but Autun is far from any major railway line and thus difficult to get to. Most journeys to and from Autun require a change at regional stops Châlon-sur-Saône or Etang, and many involve tortuous connections. It is possible to get to Dijon almost directly by train (2hr., 8 per day, €15.10) via Etang. **TGVs** leave Gare Le Creusot for Paris (1½hr., 5 per day, €41.90-55.30). The quickest way to get to Lyon is to catch a bus to regional transport hub Gare Le Creusot (45min., 5 per day, €5.40) and take the TGV from there (50min., 3 per day, €22.40). **SNCF buses** leave from outside the Autun station for Chalon-sur-Saône (2hr., 3 per day, €8.80). Helpful station office is open M-F 7:05am-7:10pm, Sa 9:05am-12:30pm and 2:30-6:30pm, Su 12:05-7:30pm. **TRANSCO buses** (☎ 03 80 42 11 00) leave for Dijon from pl. de la Gare (2¼hr.; daily 5:10pm, €12). For a **taxi,** call ☎ 03 85 52 04 83. (24hr.)

The **tourist office,** 2 av. Charles de Gaulle, offers various themed city **tours** and nocturnal tours in summer that mix music and historical sketches in the *vieille ville.* (☎ 03 85 86 80 38; fax 03 85 86 80 49. City tours €5.45, children €2.35. Night tours July-Aug. 9:30pm; €7.60, under age 12 free. Bike tours €9.90. Office open May-Oct. daily 9am-7pm; Nov.-Apr. 9am-noon and 2-6pm.) There's an **annex** at 5 pl. du Terreau, next to the cathedral. (☎ 03 85 52 56 03. Open May-Sept. 9am-7pm.) The **hospital** is at 9 bd. Fr. Latouche (☎ 03 85 52 09 06). The **police** (☎ 03 85 52 14 22) are at 29 av. Charles de Gaulle; call them for **pharmacie de garde** info. The **Cybercafé Explorateur,** 17 rue Guerin, caters to **Internet** addicts. (☎ 03 85 86 68 84. €6.10 per hr. Open Tu-Sa 10am-7:30pm.) Do your **laundry** at **Salon Lavoir,** 1 rue Guerin. (☎ 03 85 86 14 12. Open daily 6am-8pm.) You can **exchange currency** and pick up mail through **Poste Restante** at the **post office,** 8 rue Pernette. (☎ 03 85 86 58 10. Open M-F 8:30am-6:30pm, Sa 8:30am-noon.) **Postal code:** 71400.

■ ■ **ACCOMODATIONS AND FOOD.** Most cheap hotels are across from the train station. Make reservations a couple of weeks in advance during the summer. **Hôtel de France ❷,** 18 av. de la République, is a comfy, modern hotel across from the train station and over a quiet bar and restaurant. The little rooms under the slope of the roof are charming but warm in summer. (☎ 03 85 52 14 00; fax 03 85 86 14 52. Breakfast €4.70. Reception daily 8am-11pm. Singles and doubles €20-22, with toilet €24, with shower €26; triples €33-39; quads €39-46; quint €54. MC/V.) Right next door is the **Hotel of Commerce and Touring ❷,** 20 av. de la République. Pleasant, inviting rooms have raspberry and pink accents, at a good deal. (☎ 03 85 52 17 90; fax 03 85 52 37 63. Breakfast €5. Reception 6:30am-11pm. Closed Jan. Singles and doubles €25, with shower €30-38, with shower and toilet €33-39. MC/V.) The **Camping Municipal de la Porte d'Arroux ❶,** an easy 20min. walk from town, rides the soft banks of a river in the fields. From the train station, turn left on av. de la République, left on rue de Paris, and go under the Porte d'Arroux. Cross the bridge and veer right on rte. de Saulien; the campground is on your left. There is a restaurant and a grocery store; fishing and swimming are a few feet away. (☎ 03 85 52 10 82; fax 03 15 52 88 56. Open Apr.-Oct. Office open July-Aug. daily 7am-8pm; Apr.-June and Sept.-Oct. 9-11am and 6-9pm. Check-out noon. €2.50 per person; €3.45 per tent, €1.30 per car. Electricity €2.50.) Autun's ruins are prime picnicking territory. Prepare your feast at **Intermarché,** pl. du Champs de Mars. (Open M-Th 8:30am-12:45pm and 2:30-7:30pm, F-Sa 8:30am-7:30pm.) Champs de Mars is the *place* for markets. (W and F mornings.) Bright little restaurants line the cobblestone streets of the upper city. **Le Petit Rolin ❷,**

12 pl. St-Louis, serves simple light fare in the shadow of the cathedral, with romantic terrace seating at night. (☎ 03 85 86 15 55. *Menu* €15-25. Open daily 11am-3pm and 6-11pm. MC/V.)

■ SIGHTS. At the top of the upper city, the **Cathédrale St-Lazare** rises above the Morvan countryside. During a clerical quarrel, one group objected to the marvelous tympanum above the church doors and covered it in plaster, unwittingly protecting the masterpiece from the ravages of the Revolution. Today, Jesus still presides over the Last Judgment as Satan tinkers with the weighing of the souls. The artist's name, **Gislebertus**, is visible below Jesus' feet. In the dimly lit nave, intricately carved capitals illustrate biblical scenes; to see them at eye level, climb up to the *salle capitulaire* above the sacristy. Beware the basilisk, an imaginary serpent whose gaze reputedly turns humans into stone. (Open daily 8am-7pm.)

The **Musée Rolin**, 3 rue des Bancs, next to the cathedral, has a diverse historical collection in the 15th-century mansion of Burgundian chancellor Nicolas Rolin. It includes a Roman helmet shaped like a leafy human face, Gislebertus's poignant sculpture of Eve at the Fall, the noseless man of Nazareth, a magnificent collection of Gothic tableaux, and a room full of headless sculpted men. (☎ 03 85 52 09 76; fax 03 85 52 47 41. Open Apr.-Sept. W-M 9:30am-noon and 1:30-6pm; Oct.-Mar. M, W-Sa 10am-noon and 2-5pm, Su 10am-noon and 2:30-5pm. €3.10, students €1.55.)

There are a few signs that Autun was once the largest city in Roman Gaul. The cushy way to see them is on the **Petit Train,** which leaves from pl. du Champs de Mars and from the tourist office annex near the cathedral (45min.; June-Aug. 7 French tours per day 10am-6pm; €5, children €3). If you plan to ruin-hunt solo, be sure to arm yourself with a free map from the tourist office. Standing in the fields behind the train station, across the river Arroux, is the huge brick first-century **Temple de Janus.** The two remaining walls tower over cow pastures, white clouds drifting through their eroded, gaping windows, hinting at their former grandeur. To reach them from the train station, walk northeast along av. de la République and take a left onto rue du fbg. d'Arroux, passing under one of the city's two remaining Roman gates, the still-impressive, double-decker **Porte d'Arroux,** conveniently located near an idyllic river park. These two large arches for vehicles and two smaller ones for pedestrians led to the **Via Agrippa,** the main trade road between Lyon and Boulogne. Better preserved, the other gate, **Porte St-André,** at the intersection of rue de la Croix Blanche and rue de Gaillon, is more impressive still.

The **Théâtre Romain,** near the lake to the northeast of the *vieille ville,* is delightfully unrestored. Its stones, vivid and fresh, emerge from a grassy hillside, and picnickers relax where 12,000 enthralled spectators once sat. The amphitheater whimpers back to life during the first three weekends in August, when 600 locals bring chariot races and Roman games to life in the **Augustodunum** show. (Info ☎ 03 85 86 80 13. €12, children under 12 €8. Tickets sold at tourist office.) From the rear of the amphitheater, you can see the 30m pyramidal pile of bricks which is the **Pierre de Couhard.** The purpose of this heap remained unknown until excavations unearthed a 1900-year-old plaque that cursed anyone who dared to disturb the eternal slumber of the man buried inside. *Let's Go* does not recommend incurring dormant wrath. To reach the site, leave the *vieille ville* through the Porte de Breuil southeast of the cathedral and climb into the hills.

Autun's ramparts and towers are best seen from the hills above; to get there, take the path from near the cathedral to the Pierre de Couhard. Or rent a **bike** from the **Service Du Sports** on the far side of the lake. (☎ 03 85 86 95 80. €8.55 per half-day, €14.50 per day. Open July-Sept. 8:30am-6pm.)

BURGUNDY

NEVERS

Although this city (pop. 55,000) in western Burgundy was one of the settings for Marguerite Duras' novel and screenplay *Hiroshima Mon Amour*, its original claim to fame is its status as the final resting place of St-Bernadette de Lourdes. Bernadette Soubirous, a young girl who reported conversing with the Virgin Mary in Lourdes (see p. 423), came to Nevers in July of 1866 to enter the Couvent St-Gildard. Despite having some of the bustle of a modern industrial city, Nevers is a town of green parks, cobblestone streets, exquisite medieval and Renaissance architecture, and a long tradition of decorative arts. If at first you aren't impressed by this shy city, remember Duras's admonition: "Saying that Nevers is a tiny town is an error of both the heart and the mind."

☎⚡ TRANSPORTATION AND PRACTICAL INFORMATION. Trains go through Nevers to: Bourges (38-55min., 16 per day, €9.60); Clermont-Ferrand (1½hr., 13 per day, €19); Dijon (2¾hr., 5 per day, €22.50); Moulins (30-60min., 16 per day, €8.30); and Paris (2½hr., 7 per day, €25.46). (Ticket windows open daily 6am-9pm.) **Local buses** leave from rue de Charleville, left of the train station as you exit. (☎03 86 57 16 39. €1 to city center.) For a **taxi,** call ☎03 86 57 19 19 (7am-11pm) or 03 86 59 58 00. **Rent bikes** at **Belair,** 31bis rue de la Préfecture. (☎03 86 61 24 45. €15.20 per day, €69 per week. €300 deposit. Open M-Sa 8:30am-12:30pm and 1:30-7pm.) The town center is an easy 8min. walk away. From the station, head four blocks up av. Général de Gaulle to Nevers's main square, **pl. Carnot.** Diagonally across the square from av. de Gaulle is rue Sabatier, where the multilingual **tourist office** has taken over the Palais Ducal, 4 rue Sabatier. The office offers free maps of the city and a self-guided walking tour in several languages. (☎03 86 68 46 00; fax 03 86 68 45 98; www.ville-nevers.fr. Open Apr.-Sept. M-Sa 9am-7pm, Su 10am-7pm; Oct.-Mar. M-Sa 9am-noon and 2-6pm; Oct. and Mar. Su also open 9:30am-12:30pm. July-Aug. city tours in French daily 10am and 3pm; €5.) The **police** are at 6bis av. Marceau (☎03 86 60 53 00); the **Centre Hospitalier** at 1 av. Colbert (☎03 86 68 30 30). For **Internet access,** try **Pain et Friandaises,** 5 rue de la Pelleterie (☎03 86 59 26 69; open M-Sa 8am-7:30pm; €0.06 per min.) or **Forum Espace Culture,** at the corner of rue du Nièvre and rue de la Boucherie. (☎03 86 59 93 40. Open M 2-7pm, Tu-Sa 10am-7pm. €2.29 per 30min., €3.05 per hr.) There's **currency exchange** at **Crédit Municipal,** on pl. Carnot (M-F 8:15-11:45am and 1:15-5:15pm, Sa 8:15-11:45am), and at the **post office,** 25bis av. Pierre Bérégovoy. (☎03 86 21 50 21. Open M-F 8am-6:30pm, Sa 8am-noon.) **Poste Restante:** 58000. **Postal code:** 58019.

⚓ ACCOMMODATIONS AND CAMPING. Rooms near the station and the city center start around €20. Several blocks left of the train station and opposite the convent, **Hôtel Beauséjour ❷,** 5bis rue St-Gildard, has a lovely garden and tidy rooms with firm beds and wooden furniture decorated with stencils. (☎03 86 61 20 84; fax 03 86 59 15 37; hbeausejour@wanadoo.fr. Breakfast €5.50. Reception 7am-10pm. Singles and doubles with sink €23.50, with shower €29.50, with shower and toilet €31-38. Extra bed €8. MC/V.) To reach the friendly **Foyer Clairjoie ❷,** 2 rue du Cloître St-Cyr, walk up av. Général de Gaulle to the pl. Carnot, and cross the *place* to the right to the rue de Doyenné. Turn right onto rue du Cloître St-Cyr. The *foyer* caters mostly to long-term residents under the age of 30; it feels like a college dormitory and has laundry facilities. Inside its stone wall is a beautiful garden where residents chat and play ping-pong at night. Even when other hotels are booked solid, there are usually rooms available here. (☎03 86 59 86 00. Singles €23. MC/V.) **Hôtel de Verdun ❸,** 4 rue de Lourdes, across from the Parc Salengro, has spacious newly renovated rooms and owners who speak impeccable English. (☎03 86 61 30 07; fax 03 86 57 75 61; hotel.de.verdun@wanadoo.fr. Breakfast €2.30. Reception M-

Sa 7am-9pm, Su 7am-noon. Singles €30-40; doubles €40-50. MC/V.) **Camping Municipal ❶** surveys the *vieille ville* from across the Loire. To get there, follow rue de la Cathédrale down to the river, cross the bridge, and turn left. (15min.) Along with the view come showers and toilets. (☎ 03 86 37 56 52. Reception 7am-10pm. Open May to late Sept. €3 per person, €3 per tent, €1.50 per car.)

⬛ FOOD. Nevers's *vieille ville* is studded with pricey brasseries, but there are less expensive spots in all directions from pl. Carnot. **Rue du 14 juillet,** between pl. Carnot and the cathedral, has many decent, inexpensive restaurants. They are mostly grills and *pâtisseries*, although there are a few Greek and Chinese restaurants. **Marché Carnot** hosts a covered **market** with fresh fruits, cheeses, and meats on av. du Général de Gaulle and rue St-Didier. (Open M-F 7am-12:40pm and 3-6:55pm, Sa 6:30am-7pm.) A **Champion supermarket,** 12 av. du Général de Gaulle, is half a block from pl. Carnot. (Open M-F 9am-7:30pm, Sa 8:30am-7:30pm, Su 9am-noon.) **Le Goemon Crêperie ❶,** 9 rue du 14 juillet, makes handmade omelettes and crepes of all flavors (€2.29-5.49) in a wooden interior. (☎ 03 86 59 54 99. Open daily noon-2pm and 7-10pm.) **Pizzeria San Rémo ❶,** 12 rue du 14 juillet, indulges those Italian cravings with large portions and lively music. (☎ 03 86 36 74 55. Pizzas, pastas, salads, and meat dishes €6-12. Open daily noon-2:30pm and 7-11:30pm. MC/V.) **Restaurant La Tour ❶,** 2 pl. du Palais, has a public cafeteria connected to the inner courtyard of the Foyer Clairjoie. Selection is slim, but you'll get a full meal for €8. (☎ 03 86 59 86 07. Open M-F 11:30am-2pm and 7-8:30pm.)

⬛ SIGHTS. The most visible structure in Nevers is the Renaissance **Cathédrale St-Cyr et Ste-Juliette,** off pl. Carnot and up rue du Doyenné. St-Cyr's charm is in its unusual double-heeled arrangement—to the west is an enormous Romanesque apse with a fresco of Christ Pantokrator, while to the east is the 14th-century Gothic response. Be sure to notice the modern stained glass, fashioned by five different artists between 1977 and 1983 to replace the original windows, which were blown out during the bombing of Nevers in World War II. (☎ 03 86 59 06 54. Open June-Sept. Tu-Sa 10am-noon and 2-7pm. Free tours 11am, 3, 6pm.)

Opposite the cathedral, fairy tale turrets cap the 15th-century **Palais Ducal,** once the seat of regional government. There is a modest museum of local porcelain inside, but you're better off admiring the exquisite exterior. (☎ 03 86 68 46 00. Enter from tourist office. Free.) From the tourist office, go down the hill to the pl. Carnot, turn right onto the rue des Ourses, and follow it to the pedestrian rue François Mitterrand, lined with classy stores. Venture out toward rue Ste-Etienne to see a neighborhood that flourished in the 11th century's monastic boom. Almost one millennium old, the **Eglise Ste-Etienne** stands remarkably well preserved.

Across town, the peaceful **Couvent St-Gildard,** on the corner of rue Jeanne d'Arc and rue St-Gildard, houses the Sisters of Charity of Nevers and the body of St. Bernadette (1844-1879). Every year thousands of pilgrims visit this spiritual center, where St. Bernadette spent her last 13 years in seclusion at the Virgin Mary's personal urging. (☎ 03 86 57 79 99. Open Apr.-Oct. daily 7am-12:30pm and 1:30-7:30pm; Nov.-Mar. 7:30am-noon and 2-7pm. Free. Mass M-F 8 and 11:30am, Su 10am.)

A walk in the gardens lining the **Promenade des Remparts,** from the Loire to av. Général de Gaulle, follows the crumbled remains of 12th-century Nevers. Along the promenade is the **Musée Municipal Frédéric Blandin.** Installed in the 7th-century Abbaye Notre-Dame, the museum houses a modest collection of the blue, white, and yellow ceramics for which Nevers is famous. While they aren't as elegant as the products of Limoges, Nevers's glass, enamel, and porcelain have a distinct style. (☎ 03 86 71 67 90. Open Oct.-Apr. M and W-Sa 1-5:30pm, Su 10am-noon and 2-5:30pm; May-Sept. W-M 10am-6:30pm. €2, under 18 and students free.) Just outside the museum gardens, the imposing 14th-century **Porte du Croux** now houses an archaeology museum with local Gallo-Roman artifacts. (☎03 86 21 51 75. Open Tu, Th, and F 2-5pm.) Before leaving Nevers, cross over the **Pont de Loire** for a last view of the gentle green slopes and blue water of the Loire river and its banks.

AUXERRE

Auxerre (pop. 40,000) began its days as Autessiodrum, a Roman hub along the via Agrippa. Converted early, Auxerre's monastic community blossomed in the 5th century under the learned bishop Germain (AD 378-448) and his successors. The monasteries surrounding the city were referred to as the city's "sacred walls." These defenses were humbled or destroyed in war, but Auxerre was saved from obscurity by its Chablis wine, supplied en masse to an insatiable Parisian market. Today Auxerre, a bustling small town with scores of businesses, is unobscured by tourists, with a *vieille ville* that rises beautifully from the Yonne river.

ORIENTATION AND PRACTICAL INFORMATION

Trains: Gare Auxerre-St-Gervais, rue Paul Doumer, east of the Yonne. Info office open M-F 5:15am-8:30pm, Sa 6:15am-8:30pm, Su 6:45am-9:30pm. To: **Avallon** (1hr., 9 per day, €7.90); **Dijon** (2½hr., 10 per day, €20.20); **Lyon** via Dijon (3-5hr., 19 from Dijon per day, €35.70); **Paris** (2hr., 11 per day, €20).

Public Transportation: Le Bus runs around town M-Sa 7am-7:30pm. Tickets €1.05, *carnet* of 10 €8.30. Schedules at tourist office.

Taxis: ☎03 86 52 30 51 or 03 86 46 78 78. (24hr.)

Tourist Office: 12 quai de la République (☎03 86 52 06 19; fax 03 86 51 23 27). From the station, veer left and cross onto rue Jules Ferry. Turn right onto av. Gambetta, and cross the river on pont Bert. Take a right—the office is 2 blocks down quai de la République. (12min.) Accommodations service (€2.30), **currency exchange** Su, biking and **walking tours,** and **bike rental** (€8 per half-day, €13 per day; €150 and ID deposit; electric bikes at same prices). Open mid-June to mid-Sept. M-Sa 9am-1pm and 2-7pm, Su 9:30am-1pm and 3-6:30pm; mid-Sept. to mid-June M-F 9am-12:30pm and 2-6pm, Sa 9:30am-12:30pm and 2-6:30pm, Su 10am-1pm.

Police: 32 bd. Vaulabelle (☎03 86 51 85 00). Call for the **pharmacie de garde.**

Hospital: 2 bd. de Verdun (☎03 86 48 48 48). 24hr.

Laundromat: Lav-o-Clair, 138 rue le Paris.

Internet Access: Cyber Espace, 20 rue Fécauderie (☎03 86 51 53 78). €4.50 per 30min., €7 per hr. Open Tu-Su 11am-8pm. **Infonet,** 13 rue Cochois (☎03 86 52 15 96). €4.57 per hr. Open M-Th 8:30am-12:30pm and 2-6pm, F until 5pm.

Post Office: pl. Charles-Surugue (☎03 86 72 68 60). **Currency exchange, Poste Restante** and **Cyberposte.** Open M-F 8:30am-7pm, Sa 8:30am-noon. **Postal code:** 89000.

ACCOMMODATIONS AND CAMPING

■ **Hôtel le Seignelay,** rue du Pont (☎03 86 52 03 48; fax 03 86 52 32 39; contact@leseignelay.com). Rooms in this 18th-century inn are well-lit, tidy, and uniquely designed; some have recently been renovated. Hotel restaurant serves Burgundy specialties. Large buffet breakfast €6. Reception 7am-10pm. Closed Feb. June-Aug. reserve ahead. Singles €25-31.50, with bath €38-41.50; doubles €38-45/€50.50; triples and quads with bath €58-64.50. AmEx/MC/V. ❸

Foyer des Jeunes Travailleurs (HI), 16 bd. Vaulabelle (☎03 86 52 45 38). Follow the signs from the train station to the *centre ville*, cross pont Bert, and turn left on quai de la République; the first right is rue Vaulabelle. The *foyer* is in an apartment building back from the street, immediately past a gas station. (15min.) Clean hallways and neat rooms, though dark and bland. Amazing, out-of-place gilded lobby. Breakfast included. Meals €6.80. Reception 2-8pm. Singles €13. ❶

Hôtel Saint Martin, 9 rue Germain Benard (☎03 86 52 04 16). Sober, clean, dirt-cheap rooms with hall bathrooms, above a *bar-tabac* off bd. Davout. Breakfast €4. Reception M-Sa 6:30am-9pm. Closed Aug. Singles €17; doubles €20-26; triple €38; 5-person suite €40. V. ❷

Camping, 8 rte. de Vaux (☎03 86 52 11 15), south of town on D163. Reception 7am-10pm. Open Apr.-Sept. €2.30 per site, €2.60 per person. Electricity €2.10. ❶

⚡ FOOD

The **Monoprix supermarket**, 10 pl. Charles Surugue in the heart of the old town, also operates a cheap cafeteria, with a 3-course *formule* for €5.99. (Supermarket open M-Sa 8:30am-8pm. Cafeteria open M-Sa 11:30am-2pm.) **Markets** are held on pl. de l'Arquebuse (Tu-F) and on pl. Dégas, on the outskirts. (Open Su morning.) There are pizza joints all over the city. For slightly better fare, **La Marmite ❷**, 34 rue du Pont, serves a mixture of local and Italian recipes under the time-blackened timbers of an ancient house. The 3-course *menu* (€13) includes *escargot*. (☎03 86 51 08 83. Tasty salads €3.05-7.20; pasta dishes €6.85-10.65. Reserve for Sa evening. Open M 7-10:30pm, Tu-Sa noon-2pm and 7-10:30pm. Closed July 16-31. MC/V.)

👁 SIGHTS

From Pont Paul-Bert, there's a lovely view of the city and its churches. The **Quartier de la Marine**, around pl. St-Nicolas, is lined with the old wooden houses formerly occupied by rivermen. From the Yonne, wander up to the **Cathédrale St-Etienne**, begun in 1215, whose wounded facade still displays statuettes decapitated by Huguenots when they occupied the city in 1567. The iconoclasts also smashed much of the stained glass, but didn't get to the 13th-century windows in the ambulatory. The Gothic structure sits on top of an 11th-century Romanesque **crypt**, which preserves an ochre fresco of Christ on horseback. The **treasury** on the south wall guards relics, illuminated manuscripts, and St-Germain's 5th-century tunic. (Cathedral open M-Sa 9am-6pm, Apr.-Sept. 15 Su 2-6pm. Crypt €2.50; treasury €1.50; students who pay for crypt get into treasury for free. *Son-et-lumière*, with performance translated through audioguides into English, June-Aug. nightly 10pm and Sept. 9:30pm; €5. Call ☎03 86 52 23 29 for more details.)

The Gothic **Abbaye St-Germain**, 2 pl. St-Germain, attracts pilgrims to the tomb of the former bishop of Auxerre and medieval scholars to the attached ecclesiastic college. The cool underground chapel holds the oldest frescoes in France, some well-preserved. (Open June-Sept. W-M 10am-6:30pm; Oct.-May 10am-noon and 2-6pm. Crypt tours; €5.60 including Musée Leblanc, students under 26 free.) Toward pl. de l'Hôtel de Ville, the **Tour de l'Horloge**, a turreted 15th-century clock tower in white and gold, is the gateway to the *vieille ville*. The **Musée Leblanc-Duvernoy**, 9bis rue d'Egleny, between rue Gaillard and rue de l'Egalité, contains painting, pottery, and elegant 18th-century Beauvais tapestries. (☎03 86 52 44 63. Open W-M 2-6pm. €2, students under 26 free.) The **Société Mycologique Auxerroise**, 5 bd. Vauban, organizes mushroom-hunting expeditions in spring and autumn. (☎03 86 46 65 96.)

AVALLON

The tiny *vieille ville* of Avallon (pop. 8560) peeks over medieval walls high on a granite hill; its ramparts were designed by the prolific military architect Sébastien "The Fortifier" Vauban. Although the outskirts of town haven't quite held off waves of urban development, the center still reflects small-town charm. Poor on museums and monuments, Avallon is most useful as a base for exploring the Morvan or nearby Vézelay.

◪ PRACTICAL INFORMATION

Trains: ☎03 86 34 01 01. Station open M-F 5:30am-12:15pm and 1:15-8pm, Sa 5:30am-7:30pm, Su 8:30am-2pm and 3-8pm. Routes marked "car" on SNCF's schedule are serviced by buses. To: **Autun** (1¾hr.; 2 per day 10:10am and 3:25pm, Su 1 per day 6:42pm; €11.50); **Auxerre** (1½hr., 7 per day, €7.90); **Dijon** (2-3hr., M-Sa 2 per day at 6:12am and 5:48pm, Su 2 per day 11:42am and 5:48pm, €14.90); **Paris** (2½-3hr., 4 per day, €24.60).

Buses: TRANSCO (☎03 80 42 11 00) rolls from the train station to **Dijon** (2½hr.; M-Sa 3 per day, Su 1 per day 5:05pm; €15.18) via **Semur-en-Auxois.** Tourist office has schedules.

Taxis: Taxi Avallon (☎03 86 34 09 79).

Bike Rental: M. Gueneau, 26 rue de Paris (☎03 86 34 28 11). €16 per day. Open Tu-Sa 8am-noon and 2-6pm.

Tourist Office: 6 rue Bocquillot (☎03 86 34 14 19). Next to the Eglise St-Lazare. Head straight onto av. du Président Doumer and turn right onto rue Carnot. At the large intersection, turn left onto rue de Paris, which passes a large parking lot, becomes the pedestrian Grande Rue A. Briand, passes through the Tour de l'Horloge, and lands you at the office. (15min.) Map in English €0.50. **Accommodations service** €2.30. **Internet** access €3.05 per 15min. Open July-Aug. daily 9:30am-7:30pm; Sept.-June 10am-noon and 2-6pm; Nov.-Mar. closed Su.

Laundromat: Les Pros du Propre, 8 rue du Marché (☎06 14 93 24 86), off pl. de Gaulle. Open daily 7am-9pm.

Hospital: 1 rue de l'Hôpital (☎03 86 34 66 00), down the street from the post office. 24hr. The phone number for the town's *pharmacie de garde* is always marked on the window of **Pharmacie Rauscent Maratier,** 4 Grande Rue.

Gendarmerie: 2 av. Victor Hugo (☎03 86 34 17 17). **Local Police:** Small office at 37 Grande Rue (☎03 86 34 98 22).

Post Office: 9 rue des Odebert (☎03 86 34 91 08). Open M-F 8am-12:30pm and 1:30-6pm, Sa 8am-noon. **Currency exchange** and **Poste Restante. Postal code:** 89200.

⌂ ACCOMMODATIONS AND CAMPING

Hôtel du Parc, across from the station (☎03 86 34 17 00). Well-maintained and very affordable rooms in a 17th-century hotel with a nice terrace bar. Those without showers in rooms will not shower. Breakfast €3.60. Reception 7am-11pm. Closed late Dec. to mid-Jan. Singles and doubles €18-20, with shower €23-33. MC/V. ❷

Les Capuchins, 6 av. Paul Doumer (☎03 86 34 06 52; fax 03 86 34 58 47). Lively colored rooms with great baths and a nice garden are the mark of this dignified hotel. Restaurant downstairs. Breakfast €5.50. Reception 8am-10pm. Closed Tu-W, and for two weeks at Christmas. Doubles €48; triples €57; quads €65. AmEx/MC/V. ❹

Camping Municipal de Sous-Roche, 3km away (☎ 03 86 34 10 39). Walk straight from the train station onto av. du Président Doumer, left onto rue Carnot, then straight through the big intersection. Head along rte. de Lourmes, make a left onto rte. de Lourmes and then veer left on rue de Sous Roche. Quiet riverside campground. Reception 9am-10pm. Open Apr.-Sept. €3 per person, €2 per site, €2 per car. Electricity €3. ●

FOOD

At the top of town, **La Tour ❷,** 84 Grande Rue A. Briand, cooks up Italian and regional food in a warm, half-timbered 15th-century house behind the Tour de l'Horloge. (☎ 03 86 34 24 84. Big salads €4-8.50; pizzas €5.50-8.50; pastas €7.50-8. Open daily June-Aug. noon-2:30pm and 7-10:30pm, Sept.-May noon-2pm and 7-10pm. AmEx/MC/V.) There's also **Le Palais de Pékin ❷,** 8 rue de Odebert, which serves Chinese, Vietnamese, and Thai *menus.* (☎ 03 86 34 51 24. *Menu* €11.80, €12.80, and €14.80. Lunch *menu* €8. Open Th-Tu noon-3pm and 7-11pm. MC/V.) For groceries, the **Petit Casino supermarket,** rue de Paris, is a block past the intersection with rue Carnot toward town. (Open Tu-Sa 8:30am-12:30pm and 3-7:15pm, Su 8:30-10:30am.) Morning **markets** are held on pl. du Marché (Sa morning) and in the pl. du Général de Gaulle, a small square. (Open Th morning.)

SIGHTS

The countryside around Avallon is undeniably beautiful, and more compelling than anything within the town itself. A walk along the narrow paths of the western and southern ramparts reveals an excellent view of the dense forests, verdant pastures, and crumbling châteaux of the Vallée du Cousin. The tourist office can give you a free map of an 8km walk that covers the area's highlights.

The charming **Musée du Costume,** 6 rue Belgrand, off Grande Rue A. Briand, fills the rooms of the prince of Condé's 17th-century house with bustles and *bijoux* each summer as mannequins get all gussied up from a wide period of dress (18th-20th century) for the museum's exhibition, which changes annually. Superb for fashion or history lovers. (☎ 03 86 34 19 95. Open Easter-Nov. daily 10:30am-12:30pm and 1:30-5:30pm. Tours in French. €4, students €2.50.)

Two prominent remnants of days past stand side by side at the southern end of the *vieille ville.* The 15th-century slate **Tour de l'Horloge** straddles Grande Rue A. Briand. Down the street, the noticeably dark **Eglise Collégiale St-Lazare** gained its present name in AD 1000 when Henri Le Grand, Duke of Burgundy, donated a part of St-Lazare's skull to the church. The main Romanesque portal is ornamented with recessed arches, adorned by carvings of cherubim, the Zodiac, and the Elders of the Apocalypse carrying musical instruments. Note the spiraling colonnades to the sides of the doors. (Open daily 9am-noon and 2-6pm; Dec.-Feb. closed.)

VÉZELAY

High up a hillside 15km from Avallon, the village of Vézelay (pop. 492) watches over dense forest, golden wheat, and the white flecks of cattle in distant pastures. Vézelay is considered one of the most beautiful villages in France; most people, however, visit the town for its famous basilica, which has contained the relics of Mary Magdalene since the 11th century.

■ ☎ **ORIENTATION AND PRACTICAL INFORMATION.** There's no train station in Vézelay; **trains** run from Paris via Auxerre to Sermizelles (2½hr., 5 per day, €12.60). From here you can take **Taxi Vezelay** (☎ 03 86 32 31 88 or 06 85 77 89

36; 24hr.). An easier excursion is to take the **SNCF bus,** which leaves the train station at Avallon for Vézelay (June-Aug. daily 9:37am and 10:46am, return 5:24pm.) You might prefer to **bike** or take a **taxi** (from Avallon about €20). Vézelay's tiny **tourist office,** rue St-Pierre, just down the street from the church, has free maps and a *guide pratique* with accommodations listings. (☎03 86 33 23 69; fax 03 86 33 34 00. Office open May-Nov. 1 daily 10am-1pm and 2-6pm; Nov. 2-Apr. Th closed.) For the **pharmacie de garde,** check the window of the pharmacy on rue St-Etienne, or call the **police** (☎17). Renting **bikes** at **A.B. Loisirs,** Route du Camping in nearby Saint-Père, requires a short 2km downhill walk on D957, heading toward Avallon. (☎03 86 33 38 38. Bikes €16 per half-day, €23 per day. Open daily 9:30am-7pm.) The **post office,** rue St-Etienne, has an **ATM** and **currency exchange.** (☎03 86 33 26 35. Open June-Aug. M-F 8:30am-12:30pm and 1:30-5pm, Sa 8:30am-noon; Sept.-May M-F 9am-noon and 2-5pm, Sa 8:30-11:30am.) **Postal code:** 89450.

ᏝᏝ ACCOMMODATIONS AND FOOD. An option used primarily by pilgrims is the *maisons* run by the Fraternité Monastique de Jerusalem, which organize days of prayer, silence, and study. Contact the tourist office for info, or call the Fraternité at €03 86 33 39 53. Right by the bus stop, **Le Cheval Blanc ❷** has nine quaint rooms. Attached to the hotel is a restaurant which serves up salads (€8-8.25) and three *menus*. (☎03 86 33 22 12. Breakfast €6. *Menus* €14-22.50. Reservations required. Closed Dec.-Jan. Singles and doubles with shower and toilet €19-38.) In Saint-Père, the *bar-tabac-hôtel* **A la Renommée ❸** has large rooms decorated in tranquil blues, yellows, and mauves. Ask for a room with *"tout confort"* for a real treat. (☎03 86 33 21 34; fax 03 86 33 34 17. Breakfast €5.80. Open Mar.-Dec. Doubles with toilet €30-32, with bath €34-52; quads €65. Extra bed €13. MC/V.)

With its ruddy tile floor and smoky fireplace, the rustic **Auberge de la Coquille ❷,** 81 rue Saint-Pierre, perfectly suits the local specialties it serves—spicy *escargots* and crumbling rounds of *fromage epoisses,* among others. The *menu bourguignon* (€10.50)—a *galette bourguignon,* crepe *miel* (honey), and a glass of red wine—is a perfect light lunch. (☎03 86 33 35 57. 3- and 4-course *menus* €7.50-23. June-Aug. reservations suggested. Open Apr.-May and Sept.-Oct. noon-2:30pm and 6:30-9:30pm; June-Aug. 11:45am-3pm and 6:30-10pm. Open Dec.-Feb. Sa-Su and holidays.) Buy your own food at Vival supermarket, near the bottom of rue St. Etienne. (Open M-Sa 8:15am-8pm, Su 9am-8pm.)

◘ SIGHTS. St-Bernard of Clairvaux, one of medieval France's greatest theologians, launched the Second Crusade with an impassioned speech here in 1146. The **basilica** he spoke in—and the one that still stands today—was rebuilt after a fire in 1120 destroyed the Carolingian original. The real star here is the array of grotesque and expertly sculpted column capitals, depicting Biblical monsters and various hellbound unfortunates. The second column on the right features a fire-fed demon impaled on his own sword and a waifish woman whose insides are being devoured by a serpent. The chapel itself, in a nice contrast, is full of light; take a moment to bask in the warm sunlight. **Mary Magdalene's relics** have been somewhat less visited since the 13th century, when another set was discovered near where she reputedly landed in AD 40. They're still sanctified by the Church, though, and you can visit them in the rough crypt below. Above ground, a little bit of saintly bone wrapped in pearls and gold has been embedded in a column. (☎03 86 33 39 50. Open June-Aug. daily 7am-8:30pm, though hours vary; Sept.-May 7am-8pm. Tours in English with reservation; pamphlets in English.)

SEMUR-EN-AUXOIS

Although legend attributes the founding of Semur-en-Auxois (pop. 5100) to Hercules, the written record indicates that a group of monks from the Abbaye de Flavigny were responsible for erecting the first walls. The *vieille ville*'s towers and ramparts now crown an unspoiled provincial town of cobblestones and archways that overlook a bend in the Armençon river—but don't come here if you're looking for anything more than a quiet, relaxing night.

⊠ PRACTICAL INFORMATION. TRANSCO (☎03 80 42 11 00) runs **buses** from Semur to Avallon (45min.; 3 per day, €6.40); Dijon (1½hr., 3 per day, €9.60); Montbard (25min., 6 per day, €2.40). For a **taxi**, call ☎03 80 97 34 67 or 06 07 91 24 93.

The **tourist office**, pl. Gaveau, where rue de la Liberté meets the gates of the *vieille ville*, has bus schedules, free maps, and a list of hotels. The staff runs **tours** in English and French. (☎03 80 97 05 96. Tours June-Aug., by reservation and for groups; €3.05. Office open Oct.-June 15 M 2-6pm, Tu-Sa 9am-noon and 2-6pm; June 15-Sept. 30 M-Sa 9am-7pm, Su 10am-noon and 2-6pm.) You can find bikes for use in the countryside at **R.D.X.**, 2ter rue du Bourg Voisin. (☎03 80 97 01 91. €7 per half-day, €11 per day. Open June-Aug. Su-F 9am-noon and 2-7pm, Sa 1:30-7pm; Sept.-May hours vary.) The tourist office also includes a **SNCF info and reservation office.** (Open Tu-F 9am-noon and 2-6pm, Sa 9am-noon and 2-5pm.) Most businesses in Semur are closed on Monday. The **police** (☎03 80 97 11 17) and the **hospital** (☎03 80 89 64 64; open 24hr.) are on av. Pasteur, east of the center. The rotating **pharmacie de garde**'s phone line is ☎03 80 97 11 42. **Laundromat La Buanderie** is at the Centre Commercial Champlon. (Open daily 9am-7pm.) **ATMs** cluster around pl. de l'Ancienne Comédie, which also has a **post office** with **Poste Restante.** (☎03 80 89 93 06. Open M-F 8:30am-noon and 1:30-5:30pm, Sa 8:30am-noon.) **Postal code:** 21140.

⌂ ACCOMMODATIONS AND CAMPING. The **Hôtel des Gourmets ❷,** 4 rue Varenne, offers large, beautifully furnished rooms in an old house in the heart of the *vieille ville*. (☎03 80 97 09 41; fax 03 80 97 17 95. Breakfast €5.34. Free parking. Closed Dec. and year-round M-Tu. Singles and doubles €24.39-35.86, with bath €38.11; triples and quads €38.44; 6-person room €54.88. Extra bed €4.57. AmEx/MC/V.) **Hôtel du Commerce ❸,** 19 rue de la Liberté, is also right in the middle of the (overwhelming) action, and lets spotless, spacious rooms. An **Internet café** is open to the public on the ground floor. (☎03 80 96 64 40; fax 03 80 97 00 18. Breakfast €5. Reception 7am-9pm. Most singles and doubles €31, some €45-55. AmEx/MC/V.) **Camping Municipal du Lac de Pont ❶** offers a spot in the sun 3km south of Semur on a scenic lake with a beach, tennis courts, and bike rental, laundry, and a mini-mart. (☎03 80 97 01 26. Reception 9am-noon and 4-8pm. Open May-Sept. 15. €3.05 per person, €1.80 per site or individual child, €1.60 per car. Electricity €2.50.)

◖ FOOD. For groceries, stop at **Intermarché**, av. du Général Maziller, a few minutes past the end of rue de la Liberté. (Open M-Th and Sa 8:45am-7:15pm, F 8:45am-7:45pm.) Small **markets** take place at pl. Charles de Gaulle (Th morning), and on pl. Notre Dame (Su morning). **Le Sagittaire ❷,** 15 rue de la Liberté, has inexpensive, tasty dishes and a 3-course weekday lunch *menu* including wine and coffee for €9. (☎03 80 97 23 91. Open daily noon-2:30pm and 7-11pm. AmEx/MC/V.)

◷ SIGHTS. The tourist office schedules walking tours, offers free brochures with self-guided itineraries, and runs a 45min. **petit train** in summer. (July-Aug. Tu-Su 3 per day, Sept.-June schedules vary, for groups only, reservations only. €4, children €2.50.) Walk around the ramparts and the orchard-lined river Armençon. The *vieille ville* is illuminated nightly (mid-June to Sept. 10pm-midnight).

In the medieval town, down rue Buffon, lean, mossy gargoyles menace the *place* from the 15th-century facade of the **Collégiale Notre-Dame**. The 13th-century tympanum on the **porte des Bleds** faces rue Notre-Dame, while on the skinny left pillar, two sculpted snails slime their way to St. Thomas's feet—no doubt seeking divine intervention from their likely fate in a tasty butter-and-garlic sauce. The church is wonderfully bright inside when the sun is shining; otherwise it holds few surprises, one of them being a memorial to fallen American WWI soldiers. (Open daily 9am-noon and 2-6:30pm; Dec.-Feb. closes 5:45pm. English pamphlet available.) Check out the light show. (July-Aug. F-Sa 10:30pm. Rest of year by reservation.)

ALSACE, LORRAINE, AND FRANCHE-COMTÉ

As first prize in the endless Franco-German border wars, France's northeastern frontier has had a long and bloody history. The area has been trampled by invaders since the 3rd century, when barbarian tribes first swept westward into Roman Europe. Alsace-Lorraine was ravaged during the Franco-Prussian War of 1870-1871, when it was ceded to Germany, then devastated during the French reoccupation in WWI and blitzed once again when the Germans retook it in WWII. Just south of Alsace, Franche-Comté was often the pawn of its powerful neighbors. While the Franche-Comtois violently opposed France's final 1674 conquest of their land, they staunchly defended France against the invading Prussians in 1871.

Alsace and Lorraine are far less similar than their hyphenated twinship leads most people to believe. In Alsace's Vosges, wooded hills slope down to sunlit valleys and deep blue lakes perfect for hiking, camping, and cross-country skiing. On the eastern foothills lie the striped vineyards of the Route du Vin, and Alsace's well-preserved towns offer geranium-draped, half-timbered houses flanking tiny crooked streets and canals. In contrast, Lorraine unfolds to the west among wheat fields and gently undulating plains, and a few pock-marked fields outside Verdun are the only signs of a former No Man's Land. Lorraine's serenely elegant cities feature broad, tree-lined boulevards and stately Baroque architecture. Franche-Comté is mercifully untouristed in a region overpopulated by German visitors. The Jura mountain range provides lush, seemingly endless forests, and is home to some of France's finest cross-country skiing in the winter.

ALSACE

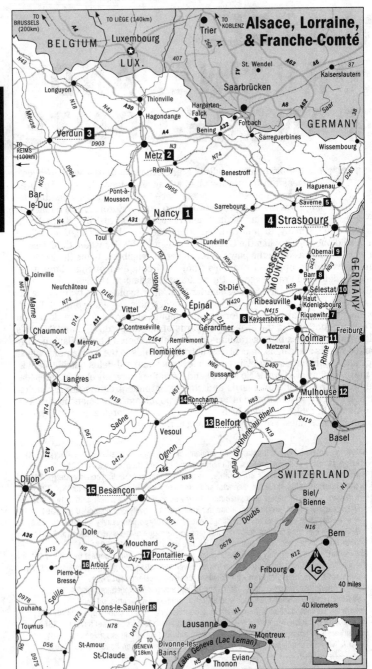

Alsace, Lorraine, & Franche-Comté

TO BRUSSELS (200km)
TO LIÈGE (140km)
TO KOBLENZ
BELGIUM
Luxembourg
LUX.
Trier
St. Wendel
Kaiserslautern
Saarbrücken
Longuyon
Thionville
Hargarten-Falck
Hagondange
Forbach
GERMANY
Verdun 3
Bening
Sarreguerbines
TO REIMS (100km)
Metz 2
Remilly
Benestroff
Wissembourg
Bar-le-Duc
Pont-à-Mousson
Haguenau
Sarrebourg
Saverne **5**
Nancy 1
Toul
Lunéville
Strasbourg 4
Joinville
Obernai **9**
VOSGES MOUNTAINS
Neufchâteau
St-Dié
Barr **8**
Sélestat **10**
Vittel
Épinal
Ribeauville
Haut Koenigsbourg
Contrexéville
Gérardmer
Kaysersberg 6
Riquewihr **7**
Chaumont
Merrey
Remiremont
Metzeral
Colmar 11
Freiburg
Flombières
Langres
Bussang
Mulhouse 12
Ronchamp 14
Vesoul
Belfort 13
Basel
Dijon
Besançon 15
SWITZERLAND
Biel/Bienne
Dole
Bern
Mouchard
Pontarlier 17
Arbois 16
Pierre-de-Bresse
Fribourg
Louhans
Lons-le-Saunier 18
Tournus
St-Amour
St-Claude
Lausanne
Montreux
Divonne-les-Bains
Lake Geneva (Lac Leman)
Evian
Thonon

0   40 miles
0   40 kilometers

NANCY

Nancy (pop. 100,000) owes its gilded beauty to the good Duke Stanislas, whose passion for urban planning transformed the city into a model of 18th-century classicism, with broad plazas, wrought-iron grillwork, and cascading fountains. Nancy has always been immersed in beauty. A hundred years ago, the Nancy School inspired art-nouveau sculptors and designers; today Nancy's symphony, opera, jazz, and ballet companies and avant-garde scene make it a cultural center. Even if it weren't so lovely to walk around, Nancy's outgoing natives and nighttime *joie de vivre* would make it one of the most enjoyable cities in northeastern France.

▐ TRANSPORTATION

Flights: Aéroport de Metz-Nancy Lorraine (☎03 87 56 70 00). Flights leave for **Lyon, Marseille, Nice, Paris,** and **Toulouse.** Shuttle to the train station (35-40min.; 7 per day; €6.10, students €4.60).

Trains: pl. Thiers (☎03 83 22 12 46). Ticket office open M-Sa 5:40am-10pm, Su 6:30am-10pm. To: **Metz** (40min., 24 per day, €8); **Paris** (3hr., 14 per day, €35); **Strasbourg** (1hr., 17 per day, €19).

Buses: Rapides de Lorraine, 52 bd. d'Austrasie (☎03 83 32 34 20), leave from in front of the train station. Open M-F 9am-noon and 2-6pm.

Public Transportation: STAN. Free bus maps at tourist office or at **Agence Bus,** 3 rue Dr. Schmitt (☎03 83 30 08 08). Open M-Sa 7am-7:30pm. Most buses stop at Point Central on rue St-Georges. Buy tickets on board, at the train station, or from machines. Tickets €1.20, *carnet* of 10 €8. Buses run 5:30am-8pm, some lines until midnight.

Taxis: Taxi Nancy, 2 bd. Joffre (☎03 83 37 65 37).

Bike Rental: Immense Michenon, 91 rue des 4 Eglises (☎03 83 17 59 59). Bikes €16.80 per day. Open M-Sa 9am-noon and 2-7pm. MC/V. **Cyclotop** (☎03 83 22 11 63), in the train station near the baggage deposit. €1.55 per hr., €3.80 per half-day, €5.35 per day. Motorbikes €4.60 per hr., tandems €7.65 per day. €45.75 deposit for bike or tandem, €76.25 for motorbike. ID required. Open daily 6:45am-9:30pm.

Car Rental: Avis, pl. Thiers (☎03 83 35 40 61). **Loca Vu,** 32 rue des Fabriques (☎03 83 35 15 05).

◢◣ ▐ ORIENTATION AND PRACTICAL INFORMATION

The heart of the city is **pl. Stanislas.** As you leave the station to the left, take your first right on rue Raymond Poincaré (not to be confused with the parallel rue Henri Poincaré), which turns into rue Stanislas once you pass through the stone archway. Several blocks down, the street opens onto pl. Stanislas and the tourist office. Be careful around the train station at night.

Tourist Office: pl. Stanislas (☎03 83 35 22 41; fax 03 83 35 90 10; www.ot-nancy.fr). Ask for a map and *Le Fil d'Ariane,* a French student guide. **Currency exchange** only when banks are closed. Hotel reservation service €2, plus partial deposit. Open Apr.-Oct. M-Sa 9am-7pm, Su 10am-5pm; Nov.-Mar. M-Sa 9am-6pm, Su 10am-1pm.

City Tours: Tourist office leads 1½hr. tours. July-Aug. Sa 2:30pm, Su 10:30am; Sept.-Oct. and Mar.-June Sa 4pm. €5.35. Call ahead for English tour, or rent an audioguide (€5.35). Ask about train tours, tours led by actors, and a self-guided walking tour of *art nouveau* buildings in Nancy.

Laundromat: Self Lav-o-matic, 107 rue Gabriel Mouilleron. Open daily 8am-8pm. **Le Bateau Lavoir,** 125 rue St-Dizier (☎03 83 35 47 47). Open daily 7:45am-9:30pm.

Police: 38 bd. Lobau (☎03 83 17 27 37), near the intersection with rue Charles III.

Hospital: CHU Nancy, 29 av. de Lattre de Tassigny (☎03 83 85 85 85).

Internet Access: Surf 'n Shoot, 3 rue Guerrier de Dumast (☎03 83 30 38 57). €4.20 per hr. Open M-F 10am-midnight, Sa 10am-2pm, Su 3pm-midnight. **E-café,** rue des 4 Eglises (☎03 83 35 47 34). €5.40 per hr., students €4.80 per hr. Open M 11am-9pm, Tu-Sa 9am-9pm, Su 2-8pm. **Musée du Téléphone.** €4 per hr., €2.30 per 30min. Open Tu-F 10am-7pm, Sa 2-7pm, 1st Su of the month 2-6pm.

Post Office: 10 rue St-Dizier (☎03 83 39 75 20). Open M-F 8am-6:30pm and Sa 8am-noon. **Branch:** 66 rue St-Dizier (☎03 83 17 39 11). Open M-F 8am-6:30pm, Sa 8am-4pm. **Postal code:** 54000.

☀ ACCOMMODATIONS AND CAMPING

CROUS, 75 rue de Laxou, helps students find summer accommodations in university dorms. Call **Foreign Student Services** at ☎03 83 91 88 26. (Open M-F 9am-5pm.) There are several budget hotels all around the train station, especially rue Jeanne d'Arc; all are a 10-15min. walk from pl. Stanislas. The hostel is lovely but far.

Centre d'Accueil de Remicourt (HI), 149 rue de Vandoeuvre (☎03 83 27 73 67; fax 03 83 41 41 35), in Villers-lès-Nancy, 4km southwest of town. From the station, take bus #122 to "St-Fiacre" (dir: Villiers Clairlieu; 2 per hr., last bus 8pm; St-Fiacre is not always a stop—check with the driver). Just downhill from the bus stop, turn right onto rue de la Grange des Moines, which bends uphill and turns into rue de Vandoeuvre. Look for signs to "Château de Remicourt." Hilltop views, a garden, and the location in a château make up for an institutional interior. Breakfast included. Reception 9am-9pm. 3- and 4-bed dorms €12.50; doubles with bath €30. MC/V. ❶

Hôtel Flore, 8 rue Raymond Poincaré (☎03 83 37 63 28; fax 03 83 90 20 94). Jovial owners let bright and homey rooms within spitting distance of the train station. Cool bar downstairs attracts young people. All rooms have shower. Sept.-June reserve ahead. Breakfast €4.20. Reception M-Sa 7:30am-2am, Su 11am-11pm. Singles €26-32; doubles €37-40; triples €43. MC/V. ❷

Hôtel Carnot, 2 cours Léopold (☎03 83 36 59 58). Quiet and bright hotel, with view of the peaceful pl. Carnot or a nice interior courtyard. Slightly worn, but new owner has renovation plans. Breakfast €5. Reception 24hr. Singles and doubles with shower €26, with shower and toilet €31-39; triples with shower €48. Extra bed €10. MC/V. ❸

Camping de Brabois, av. Paul Muller (☎03 83 27 18 28), near the Centre d'Accueil. Take bus #125 or 122 to "Camping" (dir: Villiers Clairlieu). Sweeping, spacious hilltop site overlooks the town. Showers, mini-tennis court, volleyball, playground, and grocery store make this more a resort than a campground. Access to woodland trails. Reception June-Aug. 7:30am-12:30pm and 1:30-10pm; Apr.-May and Sept.-Oct. 7:30am-12:30pm and 1:30-9pm. Open Apr.-Oct. 15. July-Aug. two people with tent €10.40, Apr.-June and Sept.-Oct. two people with tent €9.15. Extra adult €3.35, children 2-7 €1.75. Electricity €3.10. ❶

☕ FOOD

Nancy's signature *bergamote* is a bitter hard candy flavored by the orange spice used in Earl Grey tea. Off rue St-Dizier in pl. Henri Mengin is the covered **marché central.** (Open Tu-Th 7am-6pm, F-Sa 7am-6:30pm.) There is a **Shopi supermarket** at 26 rue St-Georges (☎03 83 35 08 35; open M-F 9am-8pm, Sa 9am-7:30pm) and a larger **Casino** in the Centre Commercial St-Sebastian on rue Notre-Dame. (Open M-Sa 8am-8:30pm.) Restaurants pack **rue des Maréchaux,** spilling over onto pl. Lafayette and up along Grande Rue to pl. St-Epvre. For afternoon snacks, there are waffle and crêpe stands behind pl. Stanislas on the **Terrace de la Pépinière.** You might

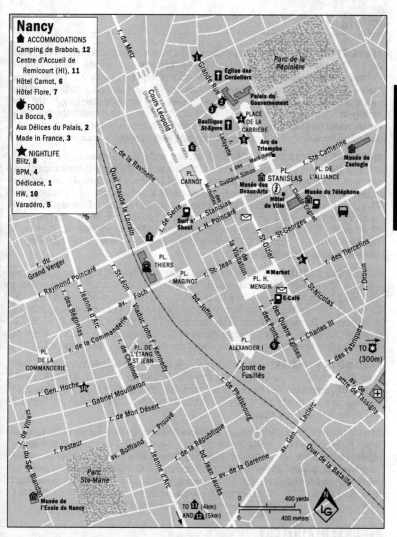

Nancy

🏠 ACCOMMODATIONS
Camping de Brabois, 12
Centre d'Accueil de Remicourt (HI), 11
Hôtel Carnot, 6
Hôtel Flore, 7

🍎 FOOD
La Bocca, 9
Aux Délices du Palais, 2
Made in France, 3

⭐ NIGHTLIFE
Blitz, 8
BPM, 4
Dédicace, 1
HW, 10
Varadéro, 5

want to reserve ahead or come early to ▧**Aux Délices du Palais ❶**, 69 Grande Rue. Locals love this hip sandwich joint. Swivel on a cowprint stool and munch on meat- or veggie-packed monsters. (☎ 03 83 30 44 19. Monsters €4.50-6. Open Tu-Sa noon-2:30pm and 7-9:30pm.) If you like huge sandwiches, try **Made in France ❶**, 1 rue St-Epvre, which prides itself on the fresh bread and vegetables of its monumental sandwiches. (☎ 03 83 37 33 38. Sandwiches €4.15-5.20. Open M-Sa 11:30am-9pm.) **La Bocca ❸**, 33 rue des Ponts, is a trendy Italian restaurant with intentionally kitschy decorations like heart-shaped red booth seats and zebra print lamp shades. (☎ 03 83 32 74 47. Menu €9.50. Open M and W-F 11:30am-2:30pm and 7-11pm, Sa 11:30am-2:30pm and 7pm-midnight, Tu 11:30am-2:30pm.)

ALSACE

🔍 SIGHTS

PLACE STANISLAS. If you see nothing else in Nancy, see this. Its three neoclassical pavilions were commissioned in 1737 by Stanislas Lesczynski, former king of Poland and then-duke of Lorraine, to honor his nephew, Louis XV. On summer nights, light from the balconies and fountain pools illuminates the curlicues of the moldings and statues lining the roofs. *Son-et-lumière* spectacles gild the lily nightly at 10pm in July and August. From pl. Stanislas, pass through the five-arch **Arc de Triomphe** to the tree-lined **pl. de la Carrière,** a former jousting-ground refurbished by Stanislas with Baroque architecture and wrought-iron ornaments.

MUSÉE DE L'ECOLE DE NANCY. This striking collection illustrates the development of the Nancy School, the city's contribution to the turn-of-the-century art nouveau movement. Sculpture, glasswork, and furniture by Emile Gallé (creator of the Paris Métro signs) and his contemporaries leave you itching to redecorate. There are many other buildings in Strasbourg with art nouveau elements; the tourist office distributes a guide with a walking tour. *(36-38 rue du Sergent Blandan. ☎ 03 83 40 14 86. Take bus #123 (dir: Vandoeuvre Cheminots) to "Nancy Thermal." Open W-Su 10:30am-6pm. €4.60, students €2.30. Students free W, everyone free 1st Su of each month 10am-1:30pm. Tours F-Su 3pm; €6.10.)*

MUSÉE DES BEAUX-ARTS. This excellent museum is housed in a stately Baroque building. The collection of paintings and sculptures dates from 1380 to the present, including gems by Rubens, Delacroix, Monet, Modigliani, Rodin, and Picasso. Especially noteworthy are the fantastical sculptures by Lipchitz and the exhibit of *art nouveau* Daum glasswork. *(3 pl. Stanislas. ☎ 03 83 85 30 72; fax 03 83 85 30 76. Open W-M 10am-6pm. €4.60, students and children €2.30, combined with Musée de l'Ecole de Nancy €6.10. Students free W and first Su of each month 10:30am-1:30pm. Tours €6.10.)*

PARC DE LA PÉPINIÈRE. Peacocks preen in the zoo as people pose in the outdoor café. Portals of pink roses lead into the deliciously aromatic **Roseraie,** a collection of vibrant blooms from around the world. *(Just north of pl. de la Carrière. Open June-Aug. daily 6:30am-11:30pm; May and Sept. 1-14 6:30am-10pm; Mar.-Apr. and Sept. 15-Nov. closes 9pm; Dec.-Feb. closes 8pm. Free.)*

OTHER SIGHTS. The 19th-century **Basilique St-Epvre,** known for its brilliant windows from around the world, hosts free evening concerts of classical and organ music. *(Off Grande Rue at pl. St-Epvre. Open daily 2-6pm.)* The innovative little **Musée du Téléphone,** on a quiet street off pl. Stanislas, traces the history of man's quest to reach out and touch someone, from telegraph stations to today's cordless wonders. Surf the web for €3.80 per hr. *(11 rue Claude Erignac. ☎ 03 83 86 50 00. Open Tu-F 10am-7pm, Sa 2pm-7pm, 1st Su of the month 2-6pm. Admission €3.50, students €1.50.)*

🎭 ENTERTAINMENT

In summer, the sound of nightly concerts emanates from the Roseraie at **parc de la Pépinière.** In mid-October, the **Jazz-Pulsations** festival lasts from dusk to dawn in the park. **Pl. Stanislas** is lit up on summer evenings for a free historical sound-and-light show. *(July-Aug. daily 10pm.)* The respected **Opéra de Nancy et de Lorraine** resides in one of the three big buildings on the *place.* (☎ 03 83 85 33 11. Open M-F 8am-noon and 1-7pm; tickets available Tu-F 1-7pm. Tickets €3.80-48.80, student discounts.) Every two years, the **Festival International de Chant Choral** brings 2000 singers from France and around the world. (Check in tourist office for details. Next concert in mid-May 2004. Concerts free.) The big **CCN Ballet de Lorraine,** 3 rue Henri

Bazin, holds performances at the opera house throughout the year. (☎ 03 83 36 72 20. Ticket office open M-F 10am-1pm and 2-6pm.)

For more frivolous fun, soak up the evening beauty of illuminated pl. Stanislas in one of its ritzy cafés, or grab a cheaper drink on rue Stanislas. Check out www.nancybynight.com for updates on bars, clubs, concerts, and theater events. Trendy 20-somethings head to **Varadéro,** 27 Grande rue, a Cuban-style bar playing mainly Latin music. (☎ 03 83 36 61 98. Shots €1.50; cocktails €4.50. Open M-Sa 6pm-2am.) **Blitz,** 76 rue St-Julien, equally trendy, has a fire-and-brimstone theme, with cauldrons hanging from the red walls. (☎ 03 83 32 77 20. Sake €2; cocktails €3.50. Open M-Sa 11am-2am). **Dédicace,** 9 rue Jean Lamour, is a gay bar, but everybody comes to play on Tu for *poste-éclair,* a mature version of spin-the-bottle. (☎ 03 83 36 95 52. Beer €2.50. Cocktails €3-7. Open daily 6:30pm-2am.) The hottest nightclub in town is **HW,** 1*ter* rue du Géneral Hoche. Young people dance on bars under the lofty ceilings and chandeliers of this converted warehouse. (☎ 03 83 40 25 13. Beer €3. Open daily midnight-6am.) **BPM,** 90 Grand rue N33, is a gay-friendly bar/club that plays techno and house music. (☎ 03 83 30 36 01. Beer €2.50-3. Cocktails €6-7. Happy Hour daily 8-9pm: buy one, get one free. Open daily 6pm-2am.)

METZ

Metz (pop. 127,000; pronounced "mess") is a stroller's heaven, with fountains, cobblestones, canals, and a fabulous cathedral. The Esplanade, a huge, impressive walkway normally packed with tourists and locals, extends to the river Moselle and is surrounded by immaculately clipped bushes and flowers in large patterns. A major university adds some life and noise, but Metz on the whole is refreshingly calm and slow for a city of its size.

▢ TRANSPORTATION

Trains: pl. du Général de Gaulle. Info office open Sept. to mid-June M-F 8:30am-7pm, Sa 8:30am-6pm; mid-June to Aug. M-F 8:30am-7:30pm, Sa 8:30am-6pm. **Luggage storage** €4.50 per day. To: **Luxembourg** (45min., every hr., €10.20); **Lyon** (5hr., 4 per day, €43.60); **Nancy** (40min., 15 per day, €8); **Nice** (10-12hr., 2 per day, €85.10; night train €91.10); **Paris** (3hr., 8 per day, €33); **Strasbourg** (1½hr., 12 per day, €18).

Buses: Les Rapides de Lorraine, 2 rue de Nonnetiers (☎ 03 87 75 26 62, schedules 03 87 36 23 34). Take the underpass to the right of the station, below the tracks, and then go left. Ticket window open M-Th 8am-noon and 2-5pm, F until 4pm. To **Verdun** (1hr., 2-3 per day, €11) and tiny regional towns. **Eurolines** travels all over Europe.

Public Transportation: TCRM, 1 av. Robert Schumann (☎ 03 87 76 31 11). Office open July-Aug. M-F 9am-12:15pm and 1:45-6:30pm; Sept.-June M-F 7:30am-7pm, Sa 8:30am-5:30pm. Tickets €0.90, *carnet* of 6 €4, day pass €3. Most lines run M-F 5:30am-8pm, Sa-Su less often. Line #11 runs 10pm-midnight.

Taxis: (☎ 03 87 56 91 92), at the train station.

Car Rental: Avis (☎ 03 87 50 60 30), at the train station. Open M-F 8am-12:15pm, 1:30-7pm, and 8-9:30pm; Su 4:30-8:30pm; Sa closed. AmEx/MC/V. **Europcar, Budget, National,** and **Hertz** are also at the station.

Bike Rental: Vélocation, at the train station and on the Esplanade. €3.50 per half-day, €5 per day. ID deposit. Open daily 10am-6pm.

✦ ▢ ORIENTATION AND PRACTICAL INFORMATION

The honey-colored *vieille ville* is mostly off-limits to cars. The cathedral dominates the skyline of the **pl. d'Armes;** the tourist office is just across the street in the

Hôtel de Ville. To get there from the station, take a right, then a left onto rue des Augustins. At pl. St-Simplice, turn left onto the pedestrian rue de la Tête d'Or, then right onto rue Fabet. You can also take bus #11 (dir: St-Eloy) or #9 (dir: J. Bauchez) from pl. Charles de Gaulle to pl. d'Armes. Metz is a big city; though it's safe and clean, you should always be cautious.

Tourist Office: pl. d'Armes (☎ 03 87 55 53 76; fax 03 87 36 59 43; tourisme@ot.mairie-metz.fr), facing the cathedral. **Currency exchange.** English-speaking staff makes hotel reservations in person (July-Aug.; €2) and distributes maps. *Metz en Fête* lists musical, artistic, and theatrical activities in detail. **Internet access.** Open July-Aug. M-Sa 9am-9pm, Su 11am-5pm; Mar.-June and Sept.-Oct. M-Sa 9am-7pm, Su 11am-5pm; Nov.-Feb. M-Sa 9am-6:30pm, Su 11am-5pm.

City Tours: Given by the tourist office M-Sa 3pm in French; €6.90, under 10 €3.45. English audioguides €6.90. **Taxi tours** (1hr., 3-4 people, €23.65).

Budget Travel: Agence Wasteels, 3 rue d'Austrasie (☎ 08 03 88 70 47). Student rates and passes. Open M-Th 9am-noon and 2-6pm, F 9am-noon and 2-7pm, Sa 9am-noon.

Youth Center: Centre Régional d'Information Jeunesse, 1 rue de Coëtlosquet (☎ 03 87 69 04 50). Open M and W 10am-6pm; Tu, Th-F 10am-noon and 1:30-6pm. Info on hiking, religious organizations, concerts, travel, and employment.

Laundromat: 22 rue du Pont-des-Morts (☎ 03 87 63 49 57). Open daily 7am-7pm.

Police: 45 rue Belle Isle (☎ 03 87 16 17 17), near pl. de Pontiffroy.

Hospital: Centre Hospitalier Regional Metz-Thionville, 1 pl. Phillipe de Vigneulles (☎ 03 87 55 31 31), near pl. Maud Huy.

Internet Access: Espace Multimédia, 6 rue Four de Cloître, near the cathedral (☎ 03 87 36 56 56). Open M 1-6pm, Tu-F 9am-6pm. Must fill out free membership form and then reserve a computer before beginning. Free. **Microludique,** 18 rue du Pont des Morts, 57000 Metz. Open M-Sa 11am-1pm and 2-9pm. €4.50 per hr.

Post Office: 9 rue Gambetta (☎ 03 87 56 74 23). **Currency exchange.** Open M-F 8am-7pm and Sa 8:30am-12:30pm. Central **branch** in Centre Commercial, pl. St. Jacques. (☎ 03 87 37 99 00). Open M-F 9am-7pm, Sa 9am-noon and 1:30-5pm. **Poste Restante:** 57037. **Postal code:** 57000.

▄ ACCOMMODATIONS AND CAMPING

Hotels in the heart of the pedestrian district are expensive and hard to come by. Turn left from the train station onto **rue Lafayette** and you'll find several large, impersonal hotels in the €23-27 range.

Auberge de Jeunesse (HI), 1 allée de Metz Plage (☎ 03 87 30 44 02; fax 03 87 33 19 80), by the river. The 30min. walk is tricky and tiring. Instead, take bus #3 (dir: Metz-Nord; last bus 8:30pm) or #11 (dir: St-Eloy; last bus midnight) from the station to "Pontiffroy." Small, cozy rooms and friendly staff, but no locks on doors. Free **bike loans.** Kitchen. Breakfast included. Sheets €2.70. Laundry service €7. Small lockers for luggage. Reception 7:30-10am and 5-10pm. Reservations suggested. 2- to 6-bed dorms €11.30 per person. **Non-members** €2.90 extra per night. MC/V. ❶

Hôtel Métropole, 5 pl. du Général de Gaulle (☎ 03 87 66 26 22; fax 03 87 66 29 91). Pleasant and classy stationside behemoth with spacious, elegant rooms. Breakfast €5. Reception 24hr. Singles from €27; singles and doubles with shower €32-45. Extra bed €6. DC/MC/V. ❸

Association Carrefour/Auberge de Jeunesse (HI), 6 rue Marchant (☎ 03 87 75 07 26; fax 03 87 36 71 44). From the station, turn right onto rue Vauban, which becomes av. Jean XXIII, and follow it around as it becomes bd. Maginot and bd. Paixhans. Rue

ALSACE

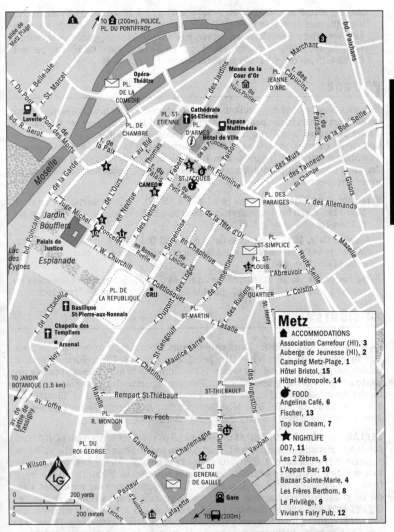

Metz

♠ ACCOMMODATIONS
Association Carrefour (HI), 3
Auberge de Jeunesse (HI), 2
Camping Metz-Plage, 1
Hôtel Bristol, 15
Hôtel Métropole, 14

🍎 FOOD
Angelina Café, 6
Fischer, 13
Top Ice Cream, 7

★ NIGHTLIFE
007, 11
Les 2 Zèbras, 5
L'Appart Bar, 10
Bazaar Sainte-Marie, 4
Les Frères Berthom, 8
Le Privilège, 9
Vivian's Fairy Pub, 12

Marchant will be on your left after 20min. Or take minibus line "B" from the station to "Ste-Ségolène" (every 15min. 7:30am-7:15pm), and take a left up the hill. Mostly locals in serviceable but Spartan digs. Larger, more central, but less congenial than the other hostel. Breakfast included. Meals €7.50. Laundry €3.30. Paper sheets €3.05, cloth sheets €4.05. Reception 24hr. 3- and 4-bed dorms €11.55 per person. Singles and doubles €13.30. **Non-members** €2.90 extra first 6 nights. MC/V. ❶

Hôtel Bristol, 7 rue Lafayette (☎03 87 66 74 22; fax 03 87 50 67 89), a small, adequate place near the train station. Retro 70s look. The larger rooms—some with minibar—are cheerier. Breakfast €5.50. Reception 24hr. Singles €26, with shower €28; doubles with shower €29-45; triples and quads with shower €51. DC/MC/V. ❸

Camping Metz-Plage, allée de Metz-Plage (☎03 87 68 26 48; fax 03 87 32 61 26), lining the river. Enter from rue de la Piscine, behind the hospital on rue Belle Isle. Caravans everywhere. Beautiful views, but very little privacy. Showers, grocery store, laundry, TV room, and fishing. Reception 7am-10pm. €2.45 per person, €2.20-2.45 per tent, €3.82-4.25 per car, €5-11.45 per trailer. Electricity included. ❶

◪ FOOD

Bakeries, sandwich shops, and other cheap eateries cluster near the hostel on **rue du Pont des Morts,** in the **pedestrian district,** toward the station on **rue Coislin.** The **Centre St-Jacques,** a mall off pl. St-Jacques, contains a number of specialty stores and cheap eateries, as well as an **ATAC supermarket.** (Open M-Sa 8:30am-7:30pm.) The biggest **markets** (Th and Sa 7am-1pm) are next to the cathedral or on pl. St-Jacques. (Open Oct. to mid-Apr.) €3.50 kebab shops sprout like mushrooms on every street corner.

▨ **Fischer,** 6 rue François de Curel (☎03 87 36 85 97). Prepares sandwiches on store-baked bread with fresh ingredients. Sandwiches €3.05. Salads €4.10-4.40. Open M-F 6:45am-7pm, Sa 7am-6pm. ❶

Angelina Café, 18 pl. St. Jacques (☎03 87 37 32 00). Serves American-style food as MTV plays on the big-screen TV in the faux-tacky interior. Pizza €7-8. Menu €7-11. Open daily 11am-10pm. ❷

Top Ice Cream, 35 pl. St. Jacques (☎03 87 74 70 03). Serves great homemade ice cream. 1 scoop €1; 2 scoops €2. Open M-Sa 9am-11pm, except Su 2pm-11pm.

◉ SIGHTS

CATHÉDRALE ST-ETIENNE. Thirteenth-century Metz sought to increase its prestige by erecting this church, with spectacular success. The golden cathedral, called the "lantern of God" by locals, is the third tallest in France and boasts the world's largest stained glass collection. The most spectacular examples are in the modern section; several in the western transept were designed by Chagall. *(Pl. d'Armes. ☎03 87 75 54 61. Open M-Sa 9am-7pm, Su 1-7pm. Tours in French 10:30am and 3pm. €4, with visit to crypt €5. Tours of the Mutte Tower 2, 4:30, 5:30pm; €7.)*

ESPLANADE AND GARDENS. At the other end of rue des Clercs from pl. d'Armes lies the Esplanade, an expansive formal garden overlooking the Moselle Valley. A surprise in the middle of the city, its greenery is possibly Metz's best feature. The tourist office has a map of trails here, which range up to 10km. Down the steps from the Esplanade, paths circle the shady, forest-surrounded **Lac aux Cygnes.** Paddle or pedal your way across the lake with rentals from **La Flotille.** *(4 quai des Régates. ☎03 87 66 89 14. Rowboats €9.20, motorboats €15 for 30min.)* In summer, the fountains spurt in tune to music, from J.S. Bach to Louis Armstrong. *(Mid-June to Aug. F-Su nightfall. Free.)* Swans preen at the **Jardin Botanique,** a taxonomist's heaven packed with flowerbeds and tagged trees. In the center, a greenhouse nurtures ferns and palm trees. *(☎03 87 55 54 00. Greenhouse open Apr.-Sept. M-F 9am-6:45pm, Sa-Su 9-11:30am and 2-6:45pm; Oct.-Mar. M-F 9:30am-6:45pm, Sa-Su 9-11:30am and 2-6:45pm.)*

BASILIQUE ST-PIERRE-AUX-NONNAINS. This tiny ancient church, the oldest in France, is half hidden in the greenery beyond the Esplanade. It was erected by the Romans in the year AD 380, intended to accommodate large baths and a sports arena. The dream of an expansion team ended in the 7th century, when it became a chapel. The sprawling pavilion next door hosts temporary exhibits and good monthly concerts. *(☎03 87 74 16 16. Open Tu-Su 2-6:30pm; Dec.-Feb. Sa-Su closed.)*

MUSÉE DE LA COUR D'OR. This huge collection of historical artifacts, from old surgical tools to Renaissance fireplaces, is so poorly lit that you'll have difficulty examining the exhibits even if you don't fall flat on your face. Bring a helmet and compass. The top two floors are dedicated to the less comprehensive **Musée des Beaux-Arts,** which highlights local works. Napoleonophiles might like the even smaller military history museum. *(2 rue du Haut-Poirier, in the Cour d'Or. ☎ 03 87 68 25 00. Open M and W-F 10am-5pm, Sa-Su 11am-5pm. €4.60, under 25 €2.30, under 12 free, everyone free Su 11-1pm and W 10am-1pm. Audioguide in 5 languages €2.40.)*

PLACE DE LA COMÉDIE. Built over a former swamp, the *place* served a less-than-comedic function during the Revolution—the guillotine was its main attraction. Its centerpiece is the 1751 Opéra-Théâtre, the oldest functioning theater in France. *(4-5 Pl. de la Comédie. ☎ 03 87 55 51 71. For tickets, call the Bureau de Location at ☎ 03 87 75 40 50. Open M-F 1-6pm. Ticket office open M-F 9am-12:30pm and 3-5pm.)*

🎵 ENTERTAINMENT AND NIGHTLIFE

At night, students pack the bars and cafés at **pl. St-Jacques,** the central gathering point. Metz has an amazing set of bars, and some good clubs.

🍺 Les Frères Barthom, rue du Palais en Nexirue (☎ 03 87 75 25 52). Maintains a silly, fun atmosphere in what seems like a gnome village. Beer made by monks €3.80-5. Open daily 4pm-1am. AmEx/MC/V.

Vivian's Fairy Pub, 15-17 pl. St Louis (☎ 03 87 18 95 01). A bar decorated *à la* Knights of the Round Table, with round wooden tables and French Celtic music playing. Beer on tap €4.60-5. Open M-Th 5pm-1am, F-Sa 5pm-3am.

Les 2 Zèbres, on pl. St-Jacques (☎ 03 87 76 24 00). Hip bar that draws a young, chic crowd to its packed see-and-be-seen terrace and its cozy cellar. Open Su-Th 8am-2am, F-Sa until 3am. MC/V.

Bazaar Sainte-Marie, 2bis-4 rue Ste-Marie. A quirky place, full of the sort of furniture you might find, well, at a bazaar. DJ on weekends plays house, groove, funk, and disco. Open July-Aug. M-Th 10am-2pm, F-Sa 10am-3pm; Sept.-June M-Th 8am-2am, F-Sa 8am-3am. AmEx/MC/V.

L'Appart Bar, 2 rue Haute Pierre (☎ 03 87 36 94 17). A gay and lesbian bar. Every Su brings a lively drag show. Beer €2.30. Cocktail €5.70. Open Sept.-June Tu-Th and Su 5pm-2:30am, F-Sa 5pm-3:30am; July-Aug. closed Tu.

007, 7 rue Poncelet (☎ 03 87 37 09 38). Nightclub with an Aztec decor. DJ every night plays only groove music. Cocktails €10. Cover F-Sa €10. Bar open Tu-Su 10pm-6am, disco Tu-Sa 11pm-5am.

Le Privilège, 20 rue de l'Ours (☎ 03 87 36 29 29), right across from L'Appart. Known among locals as the best gay nightclub in Metz. Open F-Su 11pm-5am.

After dark, be sure to stop by the cathedral to see the glowing stained-glass windows. In summer, a free **sound and light show** (see **Sights,** p. 724), complete with Vegas-style colored lights, fountains, and assorted tunes by Wagner, Elvis, and *Les Beatles,* is held at dusk on the pond at the foot of the Esplanade. (July-Sept. F-Su and holidays.) **Arsenal,** av. Ney, is a beautiful modern concert hall and exposition space hosting classical music performances and dance. (☎ 03 87 39 92 00; reservations ☎ 03 87 74 16 16.) For bargain shoppers, Metz's monthly **marché aux puces** (flea market) is France's second largest outside of Paris. (Ask tourist office for a brochure or call ☎ 03 87 55 66 00. Open Sa 6am-1pm, Su 7am-6pm.)

VERDUN

France and Germany each lost nearly 400,000 soldiers in the Battle of Verdun (1916). That conflict, undeniably the worst of WWI and perhaps of human history, has left its mark on everything in and around the town of Verdun. Eerie reminders surround the city: 15,000 marble crosses in the National Cemetery; the Trench of Bayonets, where almost all of France's 137th Regiment perished; and the symbol Verdun chose for itself, a dove above a pair of clasped hands. Verdun (pop. 20,000) has painstakingly rebuilt itself since the war, refurbishing commercial streets and adding modern buildings. Its tourist literature even refers to it as a "city in the country," but its main draw will always be its tragic past.

TRANSPORTATION

Trains: pl. Maurice Genovoix. Ticket booth open M-F 5:45am-7pm, Sa 9:45am-12:15pm and 2:15-7pm, Su 12:30-7:30pm. To **Metz** (1½hr., 5 per day, €11) and **Paris** (4 per day, €27.80).

Buses: pl. Vauban (☎03 29 86 02 71), at the end of av. Garibaldi. To **Metz** (2hr., 8 per day, €11). Open M-F 6am-8pm, Sa 6am-noon.

Car Rental: Grand Garage de la Meuse, 6 av. Colonel Driant (☎03 29 86 44 05). 21+. Open M-F 8am-noon and 1:30-7pm.

Bike Rental: Flavenot Damien, 1 rond-point des Etats-Unis (☎03 29 86 12 43), near station. €16 per day; passport deposit. Open M 2-7pm, Tu-Sa 9am-noon and 2-7pm.

ORIENTATION AND PRACTICAL INFORMATION

Verdun is split in two by the **Meuse river,** with the train station, cathedral, and hostel on one side, and the tourist office and war memorials on the other. To reach the **tourist office** from the station, walk straight ahead on av. Garibaldi (the street to the left) until you reach the bus station. Then turn right onto rue Frères Boulhaut and continue until you reach the Port Chaussée. Turn left and cross the bridge onto pl. de la Nation; the tourist office will be on your right.

Tourist Office: pl. de la Nation (☎03 29 86 14 18; fax 03 29 84 22 42). This privately-run office offers a free map of the city center, a larger fold-out map (€1), info on the memorials, and larcenous **currency exchange.** As information may be less than objective, travelers may want to ask locals about sights and activities. The office leads a daily 4hr. **tour** in French of major battlefields and monuments (May-Sept. daily 2pm; €24.50, under 16 €16.50; call before noon to reserve a seat). Open Dec.-Apr. M-Sa 9am-noon and 2-5pm, Su 10am-1pm; May-Aug. M-Sa 8:30am-6:30pm, Su 9:30am-5pm; Sept.-Nov. M-Sa 9am-noon and 2-6pm, Su 10am-1pm.

Laundromat: av. de la Victoire (☎03 29 86 60 43). Open daily 6:30am-11pm.

Police: pl. du Gouvernement.

Hospital: 2 rue d'Anthouard (☎03 29 83 84 85).

Post Office: av. de la Victoire (☎03 29 83 45 58). Better **currency exchange** rate than the tourist office. Open M-F 8am-7pm, Sa 8am-noon. **Poste Restante:** 55107 Verdun, B.P. 729. **Postal code:** 55100.

ACCOMMODATIONS AND CAMPING

■ **Auberge de Jeunesse (HI),** pl. Monseigneur Ginisty (☎03 29 86 28 28; fax 03 29 86 28 82), in the "Centre Mondial de la Paix," next to the cathedral. From the train station, cross to the island, keeping the Match supermarket in front of the station. Head right to rue Louis Maury. When you reach the square, continue up on rue de la Belle Vierge. The hostel is beyond the cathedral. Take the stairs in the corner of the parking lot in front of the cathedral down the hill into the city center. Simple, renovated rooms in a converted seminary, with great views and a valuable collection of stained glass. 4- to 16-bed dorms, most with bath and dim lighting. Breakfast €3.20. Sheets €2.70. Reception M-F 8am-1pm and 5-11pm, Sa-Su 8-10am and 5-9pm. Lockout 10am-5pm. Bunks €8.85, ages 4-10 €4.12. **Non-members** €2.90 extra 1st six nights. MC/V. ❶

Le Montaulbain, 4 rue de la Vieille Prison (☎03 29 86 00 47; fax 03 29 84 75 70), in the heart of the *vieille ville*. Fairly large, colorful rooms. Breakfast €5. Reception daily 7:30am-10pm. July-Aug. reservations recommended. Singles and doubles €24, with shower €25-35; triples with shower €38; quads with shower €42. MC/V. ❷

Hôtel Les Colombes, 9 av. Garibaldi (☎03 29 86 05 46), around the corner from the train station. Cheery, comfy rooms, some family-size. No access to showers in shower-less rooms. Breakfast €6. Reception 9am-10:30pm. Singles €26, with bath €30-34; doubles with shower €34-40; triples and quads with shower €29-40. MC/V. ❸

Camping Les Breuils, allée des Breuils (☎03 29 86 15 31; fax 03 29 86 75 76), past the Citadelle Souterraine on av. du Cinquième R.A.P., 1km from town. Take a right onto av. Général Boichut and then the 1st left. You'll be hemmed in by caravans, but tall bushes offer some privacy. Pleasant spots by the river. Bar, grocery store, showers, and pool. Reception 7:30am-10pm. Open Apr.-Oct. 15. July-Aug. €3.70 per person, €3.05 per site; Apr.-June and Sept.-Oct. 15 €3.36/€3.05. Electricity €3.20. MC/V. ❶

🍴 FOOD

Verdun's contribution to confection is the *dragée*, almonds coated with sugar and honey. First engineered by an apothecary in the 13th century to ward off sterility, it is today appropriately served at weddings and baptisms. Otherwise, Verdun cuisine doesn't offer much. Verdun's main **covered market** is on rue de Rû. (Open Tu 7:30am-noon, F 7:30am-12:30pm.) Stock up at the **Match supermarket,** in front of the train station on Rond-Point des Etats-Unis. (Open M-Sa 9am-7:30pm.) Restaurants and cafés are in the pedestrian area along **rue Chaussée** and **rue Royeurs,** and by the canal along **quai de Londres.** You'll get a tasty and substantial meal at **Pile ou Face ❶,** 54 rue des Royeurs, of massive crêpes (€3.05-5.95) and meal-worthy galettes (€5.18-8.38), on the terrace or in the bustling dining room. (☎03 29 84 20 70. F nights all you can eat. Open Tu-Su 10am-11pm. MC/V.)

👁 SIGHTS

Built in 1200, the **Porte Chaussée,** quai de Londres, has been a prison, guard tower, and exit for WWI troops. At the other end of rue Frères Boulhaut, Rodin's bronze **Victory** guards the Port St-Paul. The **Monument à la Victoire** rises above a flight of 72 granite steps at the edge of the *haute ville;* a metal soldier on top aims bronzed cannon at the German front. The monument stands on an old chapel, the last remains of the Eglise de la Madeleine, bombed beyond repair in 1916. Inside the chapel, three volumes record the names of soldiers who fought here. (Open daily 9am-noon and 2-6pm.) A few blocks away, the oft-bombed **Cathédrale Notre-Dame** retains a fine set of stained-glass windows. (Open Apr.-Sept. daily 8am-7pm; Feb.-Mar. and Oct.-Nov. 8am-6:30pm; Dec.-Jan. 8am-6pm.) **Parc Municipal Japiot,** across from the tourist office, rolls out the green carpet on the shady banks of the Meuse. (Open Apr.-Sept. daily 8:30am-8pm; Oct. and Mar. 9am-6pm; Nov.-Feb. 9am-5pm.)

The massive cement-and-stone **Citadelle Souterraine,** down rue de Rû, sheltered groups of 10,000 front-bound soldiers in its 4km of underground galleries.

Today, an official tour visits a small, chilly section of the tunnels. Realistic talking holograms depict the underground lives of hungry soldiers and worried generals. (30min. tours in French or dubious English every 5min. Open July-Aug. daily 9am-6:30pm; Oct.-Nov. 9:30am-noon and 2-5pm; Dec.-Mar. 10am-noon and 2-4:30pm. Adults €5.40, children €2.30.) Verdun hosts a yearly **sound and light show** in June and July, recreating the battle with a cast of 300 actors and special effects from over 1000 projectors. (Info ☎ 03 29 84 50 00. €16, ages 12-18 €2.30, children free.)

MEMORIALS NEAR VERDUN

Many sites to the east of Verdun commemorate the ten-month battle of 1916. Most are 5-8km away and difficult to reach without a car. The 4hr. tourist office tour (see p. 726) visits all of the memorials mentioned below in rapid French. Those who want to spend a little more time may want to rent a car; a complete circuit is around 25km.

After Alsace and parts of Lorraine were annexed by Germany in 1871, Verdun was thrust within 40km of the German border. France decided to build 38 new forts to protect Verdun and the surrounding area. These fortifications were the targets of German General von Falkenhayn's 1916 offensive. The first fort to fall was also the strongest: the immense concrete **Fort de Douaumont,** covering 3km of passageways, which was guarded by only 57 soldiers after most of its force was foolishly transferred to weaker areas. The fortress was captured in February 1916, much to the surprise of the French, who shelled it for the next eight months in an attempt to dislodge the German garrison. In October 1916, a fire broke out after heavy shelling, and the Germans fled; a detachment of French-led Moroccan troops retook the fort. The assault of this strategically useless building caused over 100,000 French deaths; a sealed gallery serves as the tomb for 679 German soldiers killed when a flame thrower set fire to a pile of grenades. (☎ 03 29 84 41 91. Open July-Sept. daily 10am-6:30pm. €2.50, under age 16 €1.25.)

The central and most powerful monument on the battlefields is the austere **Ossuaire de Douaumont,** a vast crypt crowned by a 46m granite tower that resembles a cross welded to an artillery shell. You can peer into the small windows of the vault at the base of the ossuary to see the remains of some 130,000 unknown French and German soldiers. Another 15,000, whose remains were identifiable, lie buried in the nearby military cemetery. Christian graves are marked by rows of white crosses; Muslims lie beneath gravestones pointing toward Mecca. There is a small monument to Jewish volunteers 300m west of the building. (Open May-Aug. daily 9am-6:30pm; Sept. 9am-noon and 2-6pm; Mar. and Oct. 9am-noon and 2-5:30pm; Apr. 9am-6pm; Nov. 9am-noon and 2-5pm. Ossuary free; film and tower €3, children €2.) Nearby, the **Tranchée des Baïonettes** holds the bodies of a detachment of France's 137th infantry regiment, buried alive while taking cover from heavy enemy fire. After the battle ended, the only visible sign of the men was the points of their bayonets protruding from the ground.

Fort de Vaux, the smallest of the fortifications, surrendered in June 1916 after seven days and nights of murderous hand-to-hand combat in its narrow passageways. In the dark (there was no electricity), the French defenders, who had no water and were forced to drink their own urine, fended off attacks with gas, grenades, and flamethrowers. Numerous appeals were made to the Verdun garrison for reinforcements, to no avail; inside the fort stands the statue of a carrier pigeon named Valiant, who carried out the last plea. The Germans were so impressed with the resistance they encountered that they awarded the French commander a saber of honor. (Open Apr.-Aug. daily 9am-6pm ; Oct.-Dec. 15 9:30am-noon and 1-5pm; Feb. 17-Mar. 9:30am-noon and 1:30-5pm. €2.50, children under 15 €1.25.)

The little town of Fleury stood at the epicenter of the battle of Verdun, changing hands 16 times during the war. The fighting left not a single trace of habitation or vegetation in the once-quaint town. The former site of the village's railway station is now the grim **Musée de Fleury,** built by Verdun veterans to honor their dead comrades. (Open Apr.-Sept. 16 daily 9am-6pm; Feb.-Mar. and Sept. 17-Dec. 9am-noon and 2-6pm. €5, under 16 €2.50.)

STRASBOURG

A few kilometers from the Franco-German border, cosmopolitan Strasbourg (pop. 450,000) occupies a unique international position. Politically, it has cast its lot with the République ever since its annexation by France in 1681—even the national anthem, *La Marseillaise*, was composed here. Culturally, it belongs to both countries, with tavern-like *winstubs* competing for street space with traditional *pâtisseries* and a host of international restaurants. As an administrative center for the European Union, Strasbourg hosts the European Parliament, the Council of Europe, and the European Commission for the Rights of Man. The University of Strasbourg, home to 40,000 students, keeps the town energetic and youthful. While tourists are quick to recognize the city's attractions, Strasbourg's international nature and abundance of cultural activities dilute their effect.

ALSACE

TRANSPORTATION

Flights: Strasbourg-Entzheim Airport (☎03 88 64 67 67) is 15km from Strasbourg. **Air France,** 15 rue des Francs-Bourgeois (☎03 88 15 19 50) and other carriers fly to **London, Lyon,** and **Paris.** Shuttle **buses** (☎03 88 77 70 70) run from the airport to the Strasbourg tram stop "Baggarsee" (12min., 3-4 per hr., one-way €4.20).

Trains: pl. de la Gare (☎03 88 22 50 50, reservations 03 36 35 53 35). Ticket office open M 5am-9pm, Tu-Sa 5:30am-8:50pm, Su 6am-8:50pm. To: **Frankfurt,** Germany (3hr., 18 per day, €36.60); **Luxembourg** (2½hr., 14 per day, €25.20); **Paris** (4hr., 16 per day, €34.50); **Zurich,** Switzerland (3hr., 3-4 per day, €39).

Public Transportation: Compagnie des Transports Strasbourgeois (CTS), pl. Kléber (☎03 88 77 70 70). Open M-F 7:30am-6:30pm, Sa 9am-5pm. Also at the central train station. Open M-F 7:15am-6:30pm. Extensive bus service. A single north-south tram line runs every 5-8min. (7am-7pm; less frequently 4:30-7am and 7pm-midnight). Tickets €1.10, *carnet* of €4.70, day pass €3; available at *tabacs.*

Taxis: Taxi 13, pl. de la République (☎03 88 36 13 13). 24hr. Also gives city tours (1-4 people €32) and service to the Route du Vin.

Car Rental: Europ'Car, 13 pl. de la Gare (☎03 88 15 55 66). From €71.70 per day, €82.40 for weekends. 21+. Open M-F 8am-noon and 3-8pm, Sa 8am-noon and 2-5pm. **Garage Sengler** (☎03 88 30 00 75), rue Jean Giradow in Hautepierre. €30.40 per day, plus €0.20 per km over 50km; €83.90 for weekend. 21+. Open M-F 8am-12:30pm and 2-6:30pm.

Bike Rental: Vélocation, at 4 locations: 4 rue du Maire Kuss (☎03 88 43 64 30), near the train station. Open M-F 6am-7:30pm, Sa 8am-noon and 2-7pm, Su 9am-noon and 2-7pm. 10 rue des Bouchers (☎03 88 43 64 40), in the town center. Open M-F 8am-7pm, Sa-Su 9am-noon and 2-7pm. On pl. du Château (☎03 88 21 06 38). Open Tu-F 9am-noon and 1:30-7pm, Sa-Su 9am-noon and 2-7pm. 1 bd. de Metz (☎03 88 32 20 11). Open M-F 7:30am-7pm. Bikes €3 per half-day, €4.50 per day. €45 deposit with check and photocopy of ID card.

✚ 🔢 ORIENTATION AND PRACTICAL INFORMATION

The **vieille ville** is an eye-shaped island in the center of the city, bounded to the north by a large canal and to the south by the river Ill. To get there from the train station, go straight down rue du Maire-Kuss, cross pont Kuss, and make a quick right and then left onto **Grande Rue,** which becomes rue Gutenberg. Turn right at **pl. Gutenberg** and head down rue Mercière toward the cathedral. A right turn after the bridge from the station leads to **La Petite France,** a neighborhood of old Alsatian houses, restaurants, and narrow canals.

Tourist Office: 17 pl. de la Cathédrale (☎03 88 52 28 28), next to the cathedral. **Branches** at pl. de la Gare (☎03 88 32 51 49) and pont de l'Europe (☎03 88 61 39 23). Good free map. Hotel reservations €1.60 plus deposit. Pick up the free guides *Shows and Events, Strasbourg Actualités,* or the informative French student guide *Strassbuch.* Open June-Sept. M-Sa 9am-7pm, Su 9am-6pm; Oct.-May daily 9am-6pm.

Tours: The **tourist office** organizes themed tours of the *vieille ville* and the cathedral: July-Aug. daily 10:30am, Sa also 3pm; May-June and Sept.-Oct. Tu-W and F-Sa 3pm; Dec. daily 3pm, Su also 4:30pm. Architectural, historic, and neighborhood theme tours Apr.-June and Sept.-Nov. Sa 2:30pm; July-Aug. M-Sa 6:30pm. 1½hr. €6, students €3. English audio-guides available year-round.

Budget Travel: Havas Voyages, 29 rue de la Nuée Bleue (☎03 88 52 89 00). Open M-F 9am-noon and 1:30-6:30pm, Sa 9am-noon.

Consulates: US, 15 av. d'Alsace (☎03 88 35 31 04, cultural services 03 88 35 38 20), next to pont John F. Kennedy. Open M-F 9am-noon and 2-5pm.

Money: 24hr. automatic currency exchange at **Crédit Commerciale de France,** pl. Gutenberg at rue des Serruriers (☎03 88 37 88 00). **American Express,** 19 rue du Francs-Bourgeois (☎03 88 21 96 59). Open M-F 9:30am-noon and 2-5:45pm.

English Bookstore: Librairie Bookworm, 3 rue des Pâques (☎03 88 32 26 99), off rue du Fbg. de Saverne. Everything from science fiction to grammar guides, with a good second-hand selection. Open M 1:30-6:30pm, Tu-F 10am-6:30pm, Sa 10am-6pm.

Youth Center: CROUS, 1 quai du Maire-Dietrich (☎03 88 21 28 00; fax 03 88 36 77 79). Meal vouchers for international student identity card holders M-F 9am-1pm; during school vacations M-F 10am-noon. €2.40 per meal. **Centre d'Information Jeunesse (CIJA),** 7 rue des Ecrivains (☎03 88 37 33 33), has info about jobs and lodging. Open M-Th 10am-noon and 1-6pm, F 10am-noon and 1-5pm.

Laundromat: Lavomatique, 10 rue de la Nuée Bleue (☎03 88 75 54 18). Open daily 7am-9pm. Also at 2 rue Deserte, near the train station.

Police: 11 rue de la Nuée Bleue (☎03 88 15 37 37).

Hospital: Hôpital Civil de Strasbourg, 1 pl. de l'Hôpital (☎03 88 11 67 68), south of the *vieille ville* across the canal.

Internet Access: Net.sur.cour, 18 quai des Pêcheurs (☎03 88 35 66 76). €2 per hr. Open M-F 11:30am-9pm, Sa-Su 2:30-7:30pm. **Net computer,** 14 quai des Pêcheurs (☎03 88 36 46 05). €3.05 per hr. Open M-F 9am-10pm, Sa 10am-11pm, Su 11am-10pm. **Best Café,** 10 quai des Pêcheurs (☎03 88 35 10 60). No cover, but one drink required. Open M-F 8am-7pm, Sa 12:30-5pm. Also at **Centre International d'Accueil** (see **Accommodations,** below) for €2.25 per 15min.

Post Office: 5 av. de la Marseillaise (☎03 88 52 31 00). Open M-F 8am-7pm, Sa 8am-noon. **Branches** at cathedral (open M-F 8am-6:30pm, Sa 8am-5pm) and at 1 pl. de la Gare. (Open M-F 8am-7pm, Sa 8am-noon.) All have **currency exchange. Poste Restante:** 67074. **Postal code:** 67000.

ALSACE

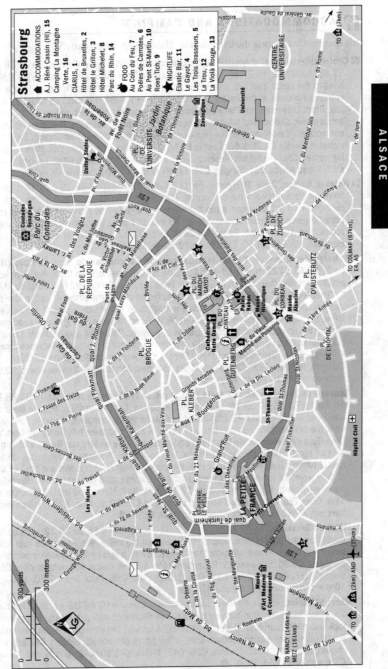

Strasbourg

ACCOMMODATIONS
A.J. Réné Cassin (HI), 15
Camping La Montagne
 Verte, 16
CIARUS, 1
Hôtel de Bruxelles, 2
Hôtel le Grillon, 3
Hôtel Michelet, 8
Parc du Rhin, 14

● **FOOD**
Au Coin du Feu, 7
Poêles de Carrotes, 6
Au Pont St-Martin, 10
Roes Tich, 9

★ **NIGHTLIFE**
Elastic Bar, 11
Le Gayot, 4
Les Trois Brasseurs, 5
Le Trou, 12
La Viola Rouge, 13

![] ACCOMMODATIONS AND CAMPING

Inexpensive hotels ring the train station. Make reservations early.

■ **Centre International d'Accueil de Strasbourg (CIARUS),** 7 rue Finkmatt (☎03 88 15 27 88; fax 03 88 15 27 89; ciarus@ciarus.com). From the station, take rue du Maire-Kuss to the canal, turn left, and follow quais St-Jean, Kléber, and Finkmatt. Take a left onto rue Finkmatt at the Palais de Justice; it is on the left. (15min.) Or take bus #10 (dir: Brant Université) to "Place de Pierre." Large, spotless facilities and an international atmosphere. Shower and toilet in all rooms. TV, ping-pong, cafeteria, laundry, and **Internet** access. "Disco" and "make-your-own-crêpes" nights. Wheelchair access. Breakfast included. Meals €4.30-8.50. Towels €1.50-2.50. Check-in 3:30pm, call ahead if arriving earlier. Check-out 9am. Reservations advised. 6-8 bed dorms €16; 3-4 bed dorms €18; 2-bed rooms €21. Singles €38. Family rooms €16 per person. MC/V. ❷

■ **Hôtel le Grillon,** 2 rue Thiergarten (☎03 88 32 71 88; fax 03 88 32 22 01), 1 block from the station toward the city center. This 2-star hotel has spacious rooms reminiscent of an ski lodge, above a hip bar where you'll get a free drink upon showing your *Let's Go* guide. **Internet** access free for 15 min., €1 per 15min. thereafter. TV in some rooms. Breakfast €6.50. Reception 24hr. Singles €29, with shower €38-53.50; doubles €36.50/€44-59.50. Extra bed €10.70. DC/MC/V. ❸

Auberge de Jeunesse, Centre International de Rencontres du Parc du Rhin (HI), (☎03 88 45 54 20; fax 03 88 45 54 21), on rue des Cavaliers, on the Rhine. 7km from station, but less than 1km from Germany. From station, take bus #2 (dir: Pond du Rhin) to "Parc du Rhin." (30min.) At the bus stop, facing the tourist office, go to the left; rue des Cavaliers is the street with flashing red lights on either side and with willow trees lining the right side. Deserted streets at night. Good facilities and great location overlooking the Rhine. Fills with school groups in summer. Volleyball and basketball courts, pool tables, disco and bar—all usually mobbed by hysterical teenagers. **Internet** access €1 per 10min. Breakfast included. Sheets €3. Reception daily 7am-12:30pm, 2-7:30pm, 8:30pm-1am. Check-out 10am. 3-5 bed dorms €13. **Non-members** €2.90 extra up to first six nights. MC/V. ❶

Auberge de Jeunesse René Cassin (HI), 9 rue de l'Auberge de Jeunesse (☎03 88 30 26 46; fax 03 88 30 35 16), 2km from the station. Catch a bus just outside the train station to the right; take #2 (dir: Illkirch) to "Auberge de Jeunesse." To walk, turn right from the station onto bd. de Metz and follow it as it becomes bd. Nancy and bd. de Lyon. Turn right onto rue de Molsheim and go through the underpass. **Be careful** in this area at night. Follow rte. de Schirmeck 1km to rue de l'Auberge de Jeunesse, on the right. (30min.) The setting by the canal and park is beautiful, but rooms are box-like and slightly worn. TV room, video games, kitchen, cafeteria, and bar with music. Breakfast included. Sheets €3. Reception 7am-12:30pm, 1:30-7:30pm, and 8:30-11pm. Curfew 1am. Open Feb.-Dec. 3-6 bed dorms €13; singles €25.50; doubles €24.50. **Non-members** pay €2.90 extra. Campground next door. MC/V. ❶

Hôtel de Bruxelles, 13 rue Kuhn (☎03 88 32 45 31; fax 03 88 32 06 22), just up the street from the train station, across the canal from the *vieille ville*. Ask to see your room before you take it—some are nicer than others. Lovely, bright breakfast nook downstairs. Breakfast €5.30. Showers €3. Reception 24hr. 4-5 bed rooms €53, with shower €65; singles €27/€41; doubles €27/€44; triples €44/€58. Extra bed €7.50. Jan.-Apr. 10% reduction on some prices. MC/V. ❸

Hôtel Michelet, 48 rue du Vieux Marché-aux-Poissons (☎03 88 32 47 38). Dim hallways lead to equally dim but very clean rooms decorated with some care. Many rooms look out onto courtyard. Great location right around the corner from the cathedral. Breakfast €4. Reception 7:30am-8pm, other hours call ahead. Singles €22.50, with shower and toilet €35; doubles €26/€42; triples €41.80/€48; quads with shower €53, with toilet €54. MC/V. ❷

Camping la Montagne Verte, 2 rue Robert Ferrer (☎03 88 30 25 46), just down the road from the René Cassin hostel. Spacious and shady riverside campsite. Reception July-Aug. 7am-12:30pm, 1:30-7:30pm, 8:30-10:30pm; Apr.-June, Sept.-Oct., and Dec. 8am-noon and 4:30-9:30pm. Car curfew 10pm. €4.30 per site. €3.30 per person, €1.60 per child under 7. Electricity €2.50-3.50. ❶

🍴 FOOD

The streets around the cathedral are filled with restaurants—particularly **pl. de la Cathédrale, rue Mercière,** and **rue du Vieil Hôpital.** A little farther away, off pl. Gutenberg, pretty cafés line **rue du Vieux Seigle** and **rue du Vieux Marché-aux-Grains.** Smaller restaurants can be found on and around **rue de la Krutenau.** All sorts swarm the cafés and restaurants of tiny **pl. Marché Gayot,** hidden off rue des Frères. In **La Petite France,** especially along rue des Dentelles and petite rue des Dentelles, you'll find small **winstubs** (VIN-shtoob)—classic Alsatian watering holes, traditionally affiliated with individual wineries, with timber exteriors and checkered tablecloths. Unfortunately, these *winstubs* have taken advantage of their tourist popularity to raise their prices. Local restaurants are known for *choucroute garnie,* sauerkraut served with meats, but you also can find delicious €4.50 sausages at many stands throughout the city. Swiss, German, Indian, Italian, French, and Turkish restaurants reflect Strasbourg's international character. **Markets** are held at bd. de la Marne (open Tu and Sa 7am-1pm), pl. de Bordeaux (open Tu and Sa 7am-1pm), pl. de la Gare (open M and Th 10am-6pm), and at many other places in town. Several **supermarkets** are also scattered around the *vieille ville,* including **ATAC,** 47 rue des Grandes Arcades, off pl. Kléber. (☎03 88 32 51 53. Open M-Sa 8am-8pm.)

🏵 **Au Coin du Feu,** 10 rue de la Râpe (☎03 88 35 44 85), between rue des Ecrivains and Place du Château, prepares spectacular food in beautiful arrangements. Funky but traditional Alsatian interior. Buy a glass of wine for €3-3.80 or get a free *kir* if you show your *Let's Go* guide. 2-course dinner menu €19.50, 3-course menu €23. Open daily noon-2pm and 7-11:30pm. Closed M and Tu lunch. MC/V. ❹

Roes'Tich, 6 rue du Bain aux Roses (☎03 88 36 25 59). Family-style local favorite serves Swiss specialties, in particular *Roesti,* grated potatoes with a topping (€9.20-10.20). Reservations recommended. Open daily noon-2pm and 6:30-10:30pm; July-Aug. closed Su and M. ❷

Au Pont St-Martin, 13-15 rue des Moulins (☎03 88 32 45 13), lets you peer down at canal locks over huge servings of seafood, salads (€7.20), and sauerkraut. This is a popular, consummately German triple-decker *winstub* in La Petite France. Midweek lunch *menu* €9.15. Open June-Aug. daily noon-11pm; low-season noon-2:30pm and 7-11pm. AmEx/MC/V. ❸

Poêles de Carrotes, 2 pl. des Meuniers (☎03 88 32 33 23), a vegetarian place, gives a break from oily meats. The lunch *menu* runs €9. Dinner is actually a little cheaper: hearty salads €7; vegetable *gratins* €7.30-8.55; pizzas €6.70; pastas €6-7.50. Open M-Sa noon-2pm and 7-10:30pm. MC/V. ❷

🔆 SIGHTS

CATHÉDRALE DE STRASBOURG. The ruddy, majestic Cathédrale de Strasbourg thrusts 142m into the sky from the belly of the city. Victor Hugo's favorite "prodigy of the gigantic and the delicate" took 260 years to build (completed in 1439) and remains outstanding in form, decoration, and size. **Reliefs** around the three portals on the façade depict the life of Christ; the left portal shows the Virtues stabbing the Vices with lances. Inside the southern transept, the massive wooden **Horloge Astronomique** is a testament to the wizardry of 16th-century Swiss clockmakers. At

12:30pm, tiny automated apostles march out of the face and a clockwork rooster greets a mechanical St. Peter. The tiny automata inside an organ chest in the nave, with movable joints and stern expressions, once ranted at the minister during services, much to the amusement of medieval parishioners. The cathedral's central spire, the **Piller des Anges**, depicts the Last Judgment. Goethe scaled the 332 steps of the tower regularly to cure his fear of heights. (☎ *03 88 24 43 34. Cathedral open M-Sa 7-11:30am and 12:40-7pm, Su 2:40-7pm. Tours July-Aug. M-F 10:30am, 2:30, 3:30pm; Sa 10:30am and 2:30pm; Su 2 and 3pm. €3. Horloge tickets (€0.80) on sale at the postcard stand inside the cathedral 9-11:30am, at the south entrance 11:50am-12:20pm. July-Aug. arrive 30min. early. Choral rehearsals Th 8-10pm; madrigals F 8-10pm; Gregorian chants Su 8:45am. Tower open for climbing July-Aug. 8:30am-7pm; Apr.-June and Sept. 9am-6:30pm; Mar.-Oct. 9-5:30pm; Nov.-Feb. 9am-4:30pm. €3, children and students €1.50.)*

PALAIS ROHAN. This magnificent 18th-century building houses an excellent trio of small museums. The **Musée des Arts Décoratifs,** once a residence for cardinals, was looted during the revolution and then refurbished for Napoleon in 1805. Rooms don't get any more stylishly imperial than these—gold-encrusted ceilings, immense monochrome expanses of marble, and the bedroom of the Emperor himself. Upstairs, the **Musée des Beaux Arts** boasts a solid collection of art from the 14th to the 19th centuries, mostly by Italian and Dutch painters like Giotto, Botticelli, Raphael, Rubens, El Greco, and Goya. Hans Memling's polyptych *Vanity* shows a gruesome Death, entrails askew, beside a beautiful woman admiring herself in a mirror. The unusually appealing, comprehensive, and well-organized **Musée Archéologique** illustrates the history of Alsace from 600,000 BC to AD 800. *(2 pl. du Château. ☎ 03 88 52 50 00. Open Tu-Su 10am-6pm. Museums €3 each, students €1.50.)*

MUSÉE D'ART MODERNE ET CONTEMPORAIN. Opened in 1998, this steel and glass behemoth holds a small but impressive collection of late 19th-century Impressionism, Cubism, and 20th-century painting. Monet, Gauguin, Picasso, Dufy, Kandinsky, and Ernst are featured; one room is devoted to regional artists Hans Jean Arp and Sophie Täuber. *(1 pl. Hans Jean Arp. ☎ 03 88 23 31 31. Open Tu-Su 10am-6pm. €4.50, students and seniors €3, children under 15 free. Audio guide €3.50.)*

LA PETITE FRANCE. This lovely old tanners' district, tucked away in the southwest corner of the city center, is characterized by slender steep-roofed houses with carved wood facades. Locals flock to this pretty and relaxed neighborhood, chatting in sidewalk cafés over accordion music and the gurgle of river water.

PALAIS DE L'EUROPE AND THE PARLIAMENT. The Palais is the home of the Council of Europe and the European Parliament, EU's governing bodies. The two lie side-by-side on av de l'Europe, at the northwest edge of the Orangerie. Due to the events of September 11, the buildings are indefinitely closed to the public.

OTHER SIGHTS. The 14th- to 16th-century mansion housing the **Maison de l'Oeuvre Notre-Dame** exhibits a dry collection of Rhenish art from the 11th to the 17th centuries and various wonderful cathedral-related artifacts. Of particular note are statues originally from the cathedral's facade and some 12th- to 14th-century stained glass. A recreated Gothic garden caps off the visit. *(3 pl. du Château. ☎ 03 88 52 50 00. Open Tu-Su 10am-6pm. €3; students, seniors, and large families €1.50.)* **L'Orangerie,** Strasbourg's largest and most spectacular park, was designed by Le Nôtre in 1692 after he cut his teeth on Versailles. It has all the attractions of a good municipal park: plenty of picnic room, ponds and waterfalls waiting to be explored by rowboat, a stork-frequented mini-farm, go-carts, and Le Nôtre's original skateboard park. The **Pavillon Joséphine** holds free concerts on summer evenings. *(Take bus #23, 30, or 72 to "l'Orangerie." Concerts Th-Tu 8:30pm.)* The **Kronenbourg brewery** gives visitors a taste of Germany in France, with free tours in French, English, or German, a look at the different stages of brewing, and a tasting session. (68 rte. d'Oberhausbergen. ☎03 88 27 41 59. Take tram to "Ducs d'Alsace." Tours M-Sa 9-10am and 2-3pm; June-Aug. also 11am and 4-5pm. Available in English.) **Heineken** offers free tours of its brewery in French, English, and German, but only for groups and by advance reservation. (4-10 rue St-Charles, Schiltgheim. ☎03 88 19 59 53. Call to schedule, M-F 8am-noon and 1:30-4:30pm.)

🍸 NIGHTLIFE

Strasbourg has bars everywhere. **Pl. Kléber** and **pl. Maréchal** attract a student crowd. The area between **pl. d'Austerlitz** and **pl. de Zurich**, across the canal from the *vieille ville*, is slightly seedy but certainly lively. Numerous bars and cafés cluster there, particularly around the tiny **pl. des Orphelins.** You may want to travel in a group. Grab a free copy of Le *Strasbuch* from the tourist office (in French).

▨ **Elastic Bar,** 27 rue des Orphelins (☎03 88 36 11 10). One of the most energetic scenes in the city. Students and regulars fill an interior decorated in "grunge" style—graffiti, winding steel staircases, and metal stickers plastered on the walls. Open M-Th 11am-3am, F 11am-4pm, Sa 6pm-4am.

▨ **Les 3 Brasseurs,** 22 rue des Veaux (☎03 88 36 12 13). This micro-brewery serves four home brews for €4.30 a glass, as well as good food (salad €6.10). Dark red and wood interior. Happy hour daily 5-7pm with 2 drinks for price of 1. Open daily 11:30am-1am.

Le Trou, 5 rue des Coules (☎03 88 36 91 04), entertains raucous students and other youths people in a crowded cellar surrounded by dark brick walls and curved ceilings. Feels like a 40s speakeasy. Beer €2.50-3.50. Open daily 8:30am-4am.

Le Gayot, 18 rue des Frères (☎03 88 36 31 88). Its squished terrace opens onto lively pl. Maréchal; the bar draws a young crowd during the school year, when students frequently play jazz piano. Live music Sept.-June W-Sa. Open daily 10:30pm-2am. MC/V.

La Voilà Rouge, quai Mathis (☎03 88 36 22 90), one of the few gay and lesbian nightclubs in Strasbourg, has outfitted a large barge (with a red sail) with a lounge and dance floor. Beer €5, liquor €8. Open Th-Su 11pm-5am.

🎵🎭 ENTERTAINMENT AND FESTIVALS

Summer in Strasbourg is all about the **pl. de la Cathédrale,** the stage every afternoon and evening for a troupe of musicians, flame-eaters, acrobats, and mimes. The **cathedral** itself hosts organ concerts in summer. (Free concerts June-Sept. Su 5:30pm. Organ recitals W 8:30pm. €10, students €5.) Also on summer nights, pl. du Château hosts the **Nuits de Strass,** a funny and free projection show, and **water-jousters** match weapons on the river Ill outside the Palais Rohan.

From October through June, the **Orchestre Philharmonique de Strasbourg** performs at the Palais de la Musique et des Congrès, behind pl. de Bordeaux. (Tickets ☎03 88 15 09 09, info 03 88 15 09 00. Students half-price.) The **Théâtre National de Strasbourg,** 1 av. de la Marseillaise, performs from September to May. (☎03 88 24 88 24. €15.25-21.35, students €11.45-15.25. Th shows €7.65.) The **Opéra du Rhin,** 19 pl. Broglie, features opera and ballet in its 19th-century hall. (☎03 88 75 48 23. Tickets €11-53, students under 26 half-price; rush tickets from €15, students €11.)

June brings the **Festival de Musique de Strasbourg,** a two-week extravaganza attracting some of Europe's best classical musicians. The **Festival de Jazz,** spanning the first two weeks of July, draws giants of the jazz world to Strasbourg. (Tickets €15, students €11.50, under 5 €5.50.) For info on both festivals, contact **Wolf Musique,** 24 rue de la Mésange (☎03 88 32 43 10). **Musica,** a contemporary music festival from mid-September to early October, includes concerts, operas, and films. (☎03 88 23 47 23.) For info on exhibitions, concerts, and films, visit www.musees-strasbourg.org.

ALSACE

NEAR STRASBOURG

SAVERNE

The 3rd-century Roman travel guide *Itinerarium Antonin* recommended Saverne (pop. 12,700) as a "good place to rest." This 21st-century guidebook agrees. The town is located on a narrow pass through the Vosges mountains, a position coveted by eight centuries of generals. Today the fat green mountains surrounding Saverne give visitors an indescribably soothing sense of physical isolation. There exists no better place for a morning stroll, a pastry and a coffee in the fountained square, and a walk beside the town's canals and gardens.

■ ☎ ORIENTATION AND PRACTICAL INFORMATION. Trains leave from pl. de la Gare. (☎ 03 88 91 33 66. Ticket office open M-F 6:30am-7:30pm, Sa 8:30am-6pm, Su 10am-8:30pm.) To: Metz (1hr., 5 per day, €13.90); Nancy (1hr.; July-Aug. 4 per day, Sept.-June 5 per day; €13.20); and Strasbourg (30min., 29 per day, €6.70). To get to the **tourist office**, 37 Grande Rue, from the train station, cross the square and turn right onto rue de la Gare. Cross the Zorn River and take a left onto Saverne's main street, **Grande Rue**; continue past the château on pl. de Gaulle and you'll find the office on your left. A helpful staff dispenses town and trail maps, along with information on local sights and hiking. (☎ 03 88 91 80 47; info@ot-saverne.fr. Open M-Sa 9am-noon and 2-6pm; May-Sept. also Su 10am-noon and 2-5pm.) **Rent bikes** at 7-9 rue du Griffon. (☎ 03 88 03 19 91. Open M-Sa 9am-noon and 2-6pm. Half-day €7.50, full day €15, weekend €21. MC/V.) The **police** are at 29 rue St-Nicolas, on the street veering right off the end of Grande Rue. (☎ 03 88 91 19 12.) **Hôpital Ste-Catherine** is at 19 côte de Saverne, east of the town center, near the forest. (☎ 03 88 71 67 67.) **Post office** is at 2 pl. de la Gare. (☎ 03 88 71 56 40. Open M-F 8am-noon and 1:30-6:30pm, Sa 8am-noon.) **Postal code:** 67700.

☎ ☎ ACCOMMODATIONS AND FOOD. The **Auberge de Jeunesse ❶** occupies the 4th floor of the Château des Rohan, right in the center of town. Recently renovated rooms have amazing views, some over the statues and rose garden of the château's courtyard. Despite its incredible location, the interior lacks charm and has an institutional feel. (☎ 03 88 91 14 84; fax 03 88 71 15 97; aj.saverne@wanadoo.fr. Internet. Breakfast €3.20. Sheets €2.70. Reception 8-10am and 5-10pm; ask for a key and code if you plan to be out late. Lockout 10am-5pm. Curfew 10pm. 8-bed dorms €8 per person; €2.90 extra for **non-members** the first 6 nights.) **Camping de Saverne ❶**, rue du Père Libermann, is a rose-flowered three-star campground near tennis courts, trails to the Vosges, and good views. (☎ 03 88 91 35 65. Reception Apr.-Sept. 7am-10pm. Tax and insurance €0.30 extra. €3 per person, children €1.50; €2 per tent, €2.70 with car. Electricity €2.50.)

The Romans called Saverne "Tres Tabernae" (Three Taverns) for its hospitality and gut-warming cuisine. **S'zawermer Stuebel ❷**, 4 rue des Frères, heir to this tradition, serves filling pasta (€6.90-7.40), pizzas (€6-9.20), and *Rapzepfles* (potatoes with flour, €7.80-13.20) on a shady terrace and in a tiny converted wine cellar with vaulted ceilings. (☎ 03 88 71 29 95. Open daily 11:30am-2:30pm and 6:30-10:30pm. MC/V.) **Muller Oberling ❶**, 66-68 Grande Rue, is a locally popular tea room in a good locale that offers quiche (€2.30), *tarte à l'oignon*, pizza (€3), an exceptional range of baked goods, and great views of the *place*. (☎ 03 88 91 13 30. Open M-F 7am-7pm, Sa 7am-6pm, Su 8:30am-12:30pm and 1:30-6pm; July-Aug. Su no break for lunch. MC/V.) There are kebab stands on the Grande Rue, and a **Match supermarket** at 8 rue Ste-Marie, a 10min. walk from the town center. (☎ 03 88 91 23 63. Open M-Th 8:30am-7:30pm, F 8:30am-8pm, Sa 8am-6:30pm.) Look for **market** at pl. de Gaulle. (Open Th mornings.)

ALSACE

⬛ **SIGHTS.** "Oh! What a lovely garden!" exclaimed Louis XIV upon visiting Saverne. The town's pride and joy is its **Roseraie,** a botanical garden that sprawls out to the left of Grande Rue, along the Zorn. Over 8500 blooms shimmy their pretty heads, giving Saverne a reputation as the "City of Roses." The first Saturday in August sees the **Cours de Greffe,** a contest for the most exquisite hybrid rose, while an exposition of new rose varieties takes up the last Sunday of August. (Open June-Aug. daily 10am-7pm; Sept. 10am-noon and 2-4pm. €2.50, students €2.) The **Château des Rohan,** home to the bishop-princes of Strasbourg from the 15th century to the Revolution, spreads its elegant Neoclassical arms along pl. de Gaulle in the center of town. The château now contains the **Musée du Château des Rohan.** (☎ 03 88 91 06 28.) The archaeology wing holds the requisite unspectacular Gallo-Roman remnants; and some interesting carved toads once given as offerings at the Grotte St-Vic by woman suffering gynecological problems (the toad was meant to represent a uterus). In the same building, the slick, self-important **Musée de Louise Weiss** is dedicated to the local feminist, journalist, and Resistance fighter. (Both open June 15-Sept. 15 W-M 10am-noon and 2-6pm; Mar.-June 14 and Sept. 16-Nov. 30 W-M 2-5pm; Dec.-Feb. Su 2-5pm. €2.45, students €1.70.)

🥾 **HIKES.** Saverne's greatest asset is its endless network of forested **hiking** and **biking** trails. **Club Vosgien** maintains phenomenal trails and also runs hikes in the area; ask the tourist office for info. Bikers can pick up the free brochure *Cyclo Tourisme,* which includes a map and suggested routes, from the tourist office. Even if you're not up for a long hike, try the 45min. jaunt through shaded woods to the lovely 12th-century castle **Le Haut Barr;** pick up a map at the tourist office and follow rue du Haut Barr (D17) southwest. Nearby is the **Tour du Télégraphe Chappe,** the first telegraph tower along the Paris-Strasbourg line. (☎ 03 88 52 98 99. Open June to mid-Sept. Tu-Su noon-6pm. €2, children €1.50.)

🏁 LA ROUTE DU VIN (THE WINE ROUTE)

The vineyards of Alsace flourish along a 170km corridor known as the Route du Vin that stretches along the foothills of the Vosges from Strasbourg to Mulhouse. The Romans were the first to ferment Alsatian grapes, but the locals, knowing a good thing when they taste it, have enthusiastically continued the tradition. Today they sell over 150 million bottles yearly. Hordes of tourists are drawn to the medieval villages along the route, with their picture book half-timbered houses and numerous wineries giving free *dégustations* (tastings).

The Route includes nearly 100 towns—a lot of ground to cover. **Accommodations** tend to be expensive, so consider staying in Colmar (p. 742) or Sélestat (p. 740), larger towns which anchor the Route. Buses run frequently from Colmar to towns on the southern part of the Route, but smaller northern towns are poorly served by public transportation. **Car rental** from Strasbourg or Colmar is practical but pricey. **Biking** is a viable alternative, especially from Colmar. The gently persistent hills may challenge novices, but trails and turn-offs are very well marked. Trains connect Sélestat, Molsheim, Barr, Colmar, and Mulhouse. Walking is not an option—country roads have minimal sidewalks. The best source of info on regional *caves* is the **Centre d'Information du Vin d'Alsace,** 12 av. de la Foire aux Vins, at the Maison du Vin d'Alsace in Colmar. (☎ 03 89 20 16 20; fax 03 89 20 16 30. Open M-F 9am-noon and 2-5pm.) Tourist offices in Strasbourg (p. 729) dispense regional advice, including the excellent *Alsace Wine Route* brochure.

If you only have the time or interest to cover one destination, *Let's Go* advises that you take the bus from the Colmar train station to **Kaysersberg** (see below), perhaps the Route's prettiest and most characteristic town.

DÉGUSTATION MADE EASY So you've taken a discerning sniff, sipped it with noisy flair, and finally nodded to the *garçon* in haughty approval. And still you have no idea if the wine you're drinking is a *premiere cuvée* or if it just has a *bouquet* of walnuts and old socks. Here's the low-down on Alsace's best wines:

Gewurztraminer: Fermented from a rosy grape introduced by the Romans, this dry, aromatic white wine has been called "The Emperor of Alsatian wines." Drink it as an *apéritif*, or with *foie gras*, Indian, Mexican, or Asian cuisine, and smelly cheeses.

Riesling: Considered one of the world's best white wines, Riesling is very dry and somewhat fruity. Drink it with white meats, *choucroute*, and fish.

Sylvaner: From an Austrian grape variety, Sylvaner is a light, fruity, and slightly sparkling white wine that goes well with seafood, *charcuterie*, and salads.

Muscat: A sweet and highly fruity white wine often drunk as an *apéritif*.

The **Pinot** family: **Pinot Blanc** is an all-purpose white wine for chicken, fish, and all sorts of appetizers. **Pinot Gris** is a "smoky" strong white wine that can often take the place of a red wine in accompanying rich meats, roasts, and game. **Pinot Noir** is the sole red wine of the Alsatian bunch, tasting of cherries and complementing red meats.

KAYSERSBERG

The exceptionally charming and relatively untouristed Kaysersberg (pop. 2755) is a little town with a lot of history. Its name, from the Latin *Cæsaris Mons* (Caesar's Mountain), dates to Roman times, when it commanded one of the most important passes between Gaul and the Rhine Valley. More recently, Albert Schweitzer was born here and went on to win the Nobel Peace prize. His home has since been converted into the pastel-green **Musée Albert Schweitzer**, 126 rue Général de Gaulle, which contains memorabilia retracing the life and works of the good doctor. African art is a welcome surprise in this rural Alsatian town. (☎03 89 78 22 78. Open May-Oct. daily 9am-noon and 2-6pm. €2, students €1.) Clamber up the hill above town to see the ruined castle, now privately owned and not open to visitors.

The **tourist office,** 39 rue Général de Gaulle, is in the Hôtel de Ville; cross the bridge behind the bus stop and walk straight up the road to a little square with a fountain. (☎03 89 78 22 78; fax 03 89 78 27 44; www.kaysersberg.com. Open July to mid-Sept. M-Sa 9am-12:30pm and 1:30-6:30pm, Su 10am-noon and 2-4pm; mid-Sept. to June M-Sa 8:30-noon and 1-5:30pm.) Kaysersberg has no train station, but **buses** run to **Colmar** (20min., M-Sa 1 per hr., €2).

RIQUEWIHR

Certainly the most visited village along the Route, the 16th-century walled hamlet of Riquewihr (pop. 1200) is the headquarters of a number of Alsace's biggest wine-shipping firms—you may want to ship yourself somewhere less zoo-like in the summer months. The beautiful **Tour des Voleurs** (Thieves' Tower) contains a grisly torture chamber with audio commentary in English for those with shackled imaginations. (Open Apr.-Oct. daily 10:15am-12:30pm and 2-6:30pm. €2, under 10 free.) The 13th-century **Tour du Dolder,** rue du Général de Gaulle, once a sentinel post, is a museum of local heritage. (Open July-Aug. daily 10am-noon and 1:30-6:15pm; Apr.-June and Sept.-Oct. Sa-Su only. €1.50, children under 10 free.) Riquewihr celebrates a number of alcohol-related holidays. The **Foire Aux Vins** takes place in nearby **Ribeauvillé** on the second-to-last weekend in July. On the first Sunday of September, music accompanies the clink of glasses during the **Minstrel's Festival.**

The **tourist office,** 2 rue de la Première Armée, leads free walking tours. (☎03 89 49 08 40. Tours July-Aug. W-M 5pm. Open Apr.-Oct. M-Sa 9am-noon and 2-6pm, Su 10am-noon and 2-6pm; Nov.-Mar. M-Sa 9am-noon and 2-6pm.) Pitch a tent at the small **Camping Intercommunal ❶**, 1.5km from the town center. (☎ 03 89 47 90 08. Reception July-Aug. 8:30-11am and 2:30-8pm; Apr.-June and Sept.-Oct. 8:30-11am and 3-7pm. Open Apr.-Oct. €1.70-3.70 per person, €4 per site. Electricity €4.10.)

BARR

On the slopes of Mont Ste-Odile, Barr (pop. 6000) rests peacefully beneath vineyards and the gentle Vosges foothills. Of the Route du Vin towns, Barr seems most tied to its grapes; two minutes from the town center, you can sip a glass of white wine while strolling between the rows of vines that created it. To reach the narrow, winding **vieille ville** from the industrial area around the train station, turn right onto the street just in front of the station (rue de la Gare) and take your first left onto av. des Vosges. Follow this past the roundabout, and for several more blocks until you reach rue St-Marc. Take a right here, walk two winding blocks and turn right onto rue des Bouchers. From the pl. de l'Hôtel de Ville, a right on rue du Dr. Sultzer leads to several *caves*. To the left is the massive, unornamented **Eglise Protestante,** starting point for the **sentier viticole** (vineyard trail). Walkable alone or in a tour organized by the tourist office, the path winds 2km through fields of glistening grapes. The second week of July sees the **Foire aux Vins**, the first weekend in October the **Fête des Vendanges** (Grape Harvest Festival).

Trains to Barr run from Sélestat (25min., 11 per day, €4.20) and Strasbourg (50min., 13 per day, €6.10). The **tourist office** is at pl. de L'Hôtel de Ville. (☎ 03 88 08 66 65; fax 03 88 08 66 51. Open Sept.-June M-Sa 9am-noon and 2-6pm; July-Aug. M-F 9am-12:30pm and 1:30-7pm, Sa 9am-noon and 2-6pm, Su 10am-noon and 2-6pm.)

OBERNAI

Obernai's lack of important sights is perhaps its biggest draw. The pleasures here are simple, and the town is best enjoyed in a twilight stroll around the 14th-century ramparts. The town (pop. 11,077) maintains a pristine Alsatian beauty despite a steady influx of tourists. Near where the ramparts meet rue Chanoine Gyss stands the Neogothic **Eglise Sts- Pierre et Paul,** the largest church in Alsace after the Strasbourg Cathedral. In the pl. du Marché behind the town hall, the **Fontaine de Ste-Odile** honors the patron saint of Alsace. The **Hôtel-de-Ville,** first constructed in 1370, was decorated in 1610 with murals illustrating the Ten Commandments. The first weekend after July 14th brings the **Hans Im Schnokeloch** festival, in which costumed locals act out Alsatian legends. A **Foire Aux Vins** (wine fair) takes place the second

THE LOCAL STORY

NATZWEILER-STRUTOF

Over the course of 5 years, over 10 million men, women, and children were brutally murdered by a Nazi regime bent on power and racial dominance. Most of these murders were committed in concentration camps in Poland and Germany, but the Nazis spread as far west as Natzweiler-Strutof (30km from Obernai), the only concentration camp on French soil.

Ten to twelve thousand Jews and French resistance fighters were massacred at Natzweiler. In one of the most horrific acts of the Holocaust, hundreds of prisoners met their dooms in twisted scientific experiments on chemical warfare and diseases like hepatitis and typhus. Some prisoners were killed solely to provide skeletons for anatomical and anthropological research.

The remains of the Natzweiler camp are open to the public, continuing to stand as a frightening reminder of the brutal capacity of human cruelty. Visitors can see the guard towers, four crematoria, and the gas chamber. A museum converted from a barracks displays pictures, diagrams, and items that tell the intensely human side of the story of inhuman deportation and execution. It is simple but powerful; if you doubt that, consider that it had to be rebuilt after being fire-bombed in 1976 by a neo-Nazi group.

(Natzweiler-Strutof can only be reached by car: from Obernai, take D426, D214, and D130, and then follow signs for Camp du Strutof. Admission is €2.50.)

THE BIG SPLURGE

WELL DONE

After a day spent exploring the rolling hills of nearby vineyards, Sélestat's **Au Bon Pichet** ❸ is the perfect place to unwind with hearty Alsatian fare and a bottle of the local's finest. Au Bon Pichet's owner, a butcher and Alsatian to the bone, can tell you everything you always wanted to know about meat but were afraid to ask. He has been a butcher for 20 years, 11 of which have been spent at this restaurant.

Au Bon Pichet's interior is a far cry from the dark smoky *winstubs* serving greasy fare to a boisterous crowd. A light, cheerful interior is decorated with white pine panelling and red-checkered tablecloths. Alsatian favorites are the specialities here: large salads with *foie gras*, duck, or smoked salmon (€7.40), homemade *spaetzle* noodles, amazing *tarte à l'oignon* (onion tart), *magret de canard* (tender duck breast; €15.25), and the classic bistro dish *tête de veau* (calf's head; €13). The subtly-flavored meat dishes are perfectly cooked to your liking, and the butcher is especially proud of his *choucroute*. Be sure to take advantage of the regional wine list. The dessert *Kugelhopf Glace au Marc de Gewurst* (Alsatian cake with raisins and almonds) is sweet and satisfying. The owner has been so successful at his restaurant that he has decided to try his hand at the hostelling business, opening Hotel St-Quirin. (*10 place du Marché-aux-Choux (☎03 88 82 96 65). Open Su-M 10am-2pm, Tu-Sa 10am-3pm and 6-10pm. AmEx/MC/V.*)

weekend in August. The **Wine Harvest Festival,** during the third week in October, culminates in the election of a Grape Harvest Queen.

Trains run from Sélestat (35min., 9 per day, €4.10) and Strasbourg (45min., 20 per day, €4.80). To get to the **tourist office** from the station, follow rue du Général Gouraud to pl. du Beffroi. The office has info on beer and wine tastings, festivals, and over 200km of marked trails. (☎03 88 95 64 13; fax 03 88 49 90 84; www.obernai.fr. Open June and Sept. daily 9am-noon and 2-6pm; July-Aug. daily 9:30am-12:30pm and 2-7pm; Oct.-May M-Sa 9am-noon and 2-5pm.)

SÉLESTAT

Halfway between Colmar and Strasbourg, Sélestat (pop. 17,200) has avoided acquiring the craziness of some of the Route du Vin's more frequented towns. Once part of the Holy Roman Empire and a center of Renaissance humanism, Sélestat has painstakingly preserved its cultural heritage, including the ultimate source of Rhineland bragging rights: the first-recorded Christmas tree. The town is beautifully situated, surrounded by the sloping wine country of the Route du Vin, and near to the Reid, a fertile and oft-flooded plain.

■ 🔃 ORIENTATION AND PRACTICAL INFORMATION. From pl. de la Gare, **trains** run to Colmar (15min., 20 per day, €3.60) and Strasbourg (30min., 20 per day, €6.40). The **tourist office,** 10 bd. Général Leclerc, in the Commanderie St-Jean, is north of the town center, a 10min. hike from the train station. Go straight on av. de la Gare, through pl. Général de Gaulle, to av. de la Liberté. Turn left onto bd. du Maréchal Foch, which veers right and becomes bd. Général Leclerc after pl. Schaal. Continue on bd. du Général Leclerc; the office is a few blocks down on your right. The efficient staff **changes currency** and rents **bikes.** (☎03 88 58 87 20; fax 03 88 92 88 63; www.selestat-tourisme.com. Open July-Aug. M-F 9:30am-12:30pm and 1:30-6:45pm, Sa 9am-12:30pm and 2-5pm, Su 11am-3pm; Sept.-June M-F 9am-noon and 2-5:45pm, Sa 9am-noon and 2-5pm. Bikes €5.50 for 2hr., €8 per half-day, €12.50 per day, €55 per week. €150 deposit.) Access **Internet** at **Bazook'kafé,** 3 rue St-Foy. (☎03 88 58 47 59. Open Tu-Th 2-7pm, F-Sa 2-11pm, Su 2-7pm. €5.50 per hr., students €3.90 per hr.) The **police** are at bd. du Général Leclerc. (☎03 88 58 84 22.) The **hospital** is at 23 av. Pasteur, behind the train station. (☎03 88 57 55 60.) The **post office** is on rue de la Poste, near the Hôtel de Ville. (☎03 88 58 80 10. Open M-F 8am-noon and 1:30-6pm, Sa 8am-noon.) **Postal code:** 67600.

ACCOMMODATIONS AND FOOD. The ▓**Hôtel de l'Ill ❷** lies at 13 rue des Bateliers, sandwiched on a peaceful residential street in the *vieille ville*. From the train station, take av. de la Gare, turn right onto the large av. de Gaulle, and continue straight as it becomes av. de la Liberté, rue du 4e Zouaves, and rue du Président Poincaré. At the large intersection just before the river, veer to the left onto bd. Thiers; rue des Bateliers will be the second left. The hotel packs 15 cozy, colorful, and modern rooms onto three floors presided over by a purring tabby cat. All rooms have shower, toilet, and TV. (☎03 88 92 91 09. Breakfast €4.60. Reception 7am-3pm and 5-11pm. Singles €22.90; doubles €36.60; triples with bath €53.40.) **St-Quirin ❹**, on 20 rue Dorlan, is a pricier, but worthwhile, option. Though built in a convent, St-Quirin has all the modern amenities—cable TV, minibar, and colorful spacious rooms. Live like the Sun King in the "Louis XIV" rooms. (☎03 88 92 68 00; fax 03 88 92 68 19. Cold breakfast €4; buffet €10. Reception open 8am-noon and 2:30-10pm. When reception is closed, go to Au Bon Pichet. Singles from €52; doubles from €72; Louis' room from €107. AmEx/MC/V.) The small, shaded **Camping Les Cigognes ❶** is outside the ramparts on the southern edge of the *vieille ville*, near public tennis courts, parks, and a lake. (☎03 88 92 03 98. Reception July-Aug. 8am-noon and 3-10pm; May-June and Sept.-Oct. 8am-noon and 3-7pm. Open May-Oct. €7.70-9.15 per person, €10.70-12.20 for 2-3 people.)

Bakeries, grocery stores, and the like are scattered throughout the *vieille ville*, especially on rue des Chevaliers and rue de l'Hôpital. Every Tuesday morning, a **market** fills the town center from 8am to noon with breads, meats, and produce. There's a Saturday morning market for **regional specialties.** In a quiet square around the corner from the churches, ▓**Au Bon Pichet ❸,** is by far the best food option around (see sidebar **Well Done,** p. 740).

SIGHTS AND FESTIVALS. According to legend, Sélestat was founded by a giant. His massive thigh bone (a mere mammoth tusk, some claim) occupies Sélestat's extraordinary ▓**Bibliothèque Humaniste,** 1 rue de la Bibliothèque, a storehouse for the products of Sélestat's 15th-century humanistic boom. There's a truly wonderful collection of ancient documents in this library, from Renaissance anatomy texts to 13th-century students' diligently annotated translations of Ovid, to the 16th-century *Cosmographiae Introductio*, the first book to mention "America" by name. (☎03 88 58 07 20. Open M and W-F 9am-noon and 2-6pm, Sa 9am-noon; July-Aug. also Sa-Su 2-5pm. €3.50, students and seniors €2. Audioguide €1.50.)

Surrounded by ivy-covered homes, the 12th-century **Eglise Ste-Foy** rises above the *vieille ville* and the pl. Marché-aux-Poissons. Constructed by Benedictine monks but later taken over by Jesuits, Ste-Foy is one of the most beautiful Romanesque churches in the area. Hints of the imperial Hohenstaufen family (look for their insignia, a grimacing lion) contrast with striking floor mosaics of the Ganges and Euphrates, rivers key to man's earliest civilizations, and the signs of the zodiac. Resentful of the monastery's power, the townspeople responded with the 13th- to 15th-century **Eglise St-Georges** across the square. Max Ingrand's vibrant 1960s stained glass complements the frescoes of the essentially Gothic church. The religious and political disorder of the 15th to 17th centuries have produced a more disturbing monument. The **Maison de Pain,** rue du Sel, appropriately located in the former seat of the breadmakers' guild, illustrates the history of breadmaking from 12,500 BC to the present, and even allows you to taste some of the leavened delight. (☎03 88 58 45 90. Open Jan.-June and Sept.-Nov. M-Tu and Th-F 10am-noon and 2-6pm, Sa-Su 2-6pm; July-Aug. Tu-F 10am-12:30pm and 1-6pm, Sa-Su 10am-5pm; Nov.-Dec. daily 10am-7pm. €4.60, under 12 free.)

Sélestat's major festival is the **Corso Fleuri,** or flower festival, on the second Sunday in August. Street artists perform, wine is tasted left and right, and wackily-clad gnomes invade the streets on floral floats. It all ends in a giant fireworks display. (Info at corso@ville-selestat.fr or call the Service Culturel. €6, under 12 free.)

COLMAR

Colmar (pop. 65,000) feels distinct from most French towns, a reminder that it hasn't always been a part of France. The largest town on the Route du Vin, Colmar has the charm of a sleepy Alsatian hamlet with a surprisingly sophisticated culture. The city's main attractions are two superb pieces of German Renaissance art—Grünewald and Haguenauer's *Issenheim Altarpiece* and Schongauer's *Virgin in the Rose Bower.* While the summertime can be overrun with shameful *trains touristiques* and scads of elderly tourists, Colmar's modern Alsatian character—stubby pastel houses, *choucroute,* and all—is anything but fake.

█ TRANSPORTATION

Trains: pl. de la Gare. Info office open M-F 9am-7pm and Sa 8:30am-6pm. To: **Lyon** (4½-5½ hr., 7 per day, €34.30); **Mulhouse** (19min., 43 per day, €34.30); **Paris** (5 hr., 21 per day, €39.70, only one is direct); **Strasbourg** (40min., 43 per day, €9.10).

Buses: on pl. de la Gare, to the right of the station exit. Open hours vary. Numerous companies run to small towns on the Route du Vin, including **Kayersberg** (9 per day) and **Riquewihr** (10 per day). The tourist office has a bus schedule (in *Actualities Colmar*).

Public Transportation: Allô Trace on rue Unterlinden, (☎03 89 20 80 80), in a covered *galerie* to the right of the tourist office. Open M-F 8:30am-12:15pm and 1:30-6:15pm, Sa 8:30am-12:15pm. Tickets €0.90, *carnet* of 10 €6.40. Buses run 6am-8pm, night *Somnabus* M-Sa 9pm-midnight.

Taxis: pl. de la Gare (☎03 89 41 40 19 or 03 89 80 71 71). 24hr.

Bike rental at **Colmar À Bicyclette,** a little stand-alone orange building in the Place Rapp. near av. de la République (☎03 89 41 37 90). €3 per half-day, €4.50 per day; €45 cash deposit and ID required. Helmets not rented. Open Apr.-May and Oct. daily 9am-noon and 2-7pm; June-Sept. M, Tu, Th, F 8:30am-noon and 2-8pm; W, Sa, Su 8:30am-8pm. Also at **La Cyclothèque,** 31 rte. d'Ingersheim (☎03 89 79 14 18). €7.60 per half-day; M-F €15.70 per day, Sa-Su €22.80 per day; €45 per week. Open M-Sa 8:30am-noon and 2-6:30pm.

█ █ ORIENTATION AND PRACTICAL INFORMATION

To get from the station to the tourist office, take the first left onto av. de la République. Follow it as it becomes rue Kléber and curves right through pl. du 18 Novembre into the main pl. Unterlinden; the tourist office is straight ahead.

Tourist Office: 4 rue des Unterlinden (☎03 89 20 68 92; fax 03 89 20 69 14; info@ot-colmar.fr). Map is free but faulty. The staff offers cash-only **currency exchange** and makes hotel reservations with a night's deposit. The free *Actualités Colmar* lists events and bus schedules. **City tours** Apr. to Oct. €4, children 12-16 €2.60. Office open July-Aug. M-Sa 9am-7pm, Su 9:30am-2pm; Apr.-June and Sept.-Oct. M-Sa 9am-6pm, Su 10am-2pm; Nov.-Mar. M-Sa 9am-noon and 2-6pm, Su 10am-2pm.

Police: 6 rue du Chasseur (☎03 89 24 75 00).

Hospital: Hôpital Pasteur, 39 av. de la Liberté (☎03 89 12 40 00).

Internet Access: Infr@réseau, 12 rue du Rempart (☎ 03 89 23 98 45). €3.50 per hour. Open M 2-9pm, Tu 10:30am-2pm and 3-9pm, W 10:30am-9pm, Th-F 10:30am-2pm and 3-9pm, Sa 10:30am-9pm, Su 2-8pm.

Post Office: 36-38 av. de la République (☎ 03 89 24 62 00), across Champs-de-Mars. **Currency exchange.** Open M-F 8am-6:30pm, Sa 8:30am-noon. **Postal code:** 68000.

ACCOMMODATIONS AND CAMPING

Colmar offers precious little in the budget range. The smattering of half-timbered one- and two-star hotels in the center of town are perfectly located but overpriced.

Auberge de Jeunesse (HI), 2 rue Pasteur (☎ 03 89 80 57 39). Take bus #4 (dir: Europe) to "Pont Rouge." To walk, take the underground passage in the train station and exit to the right onto rue du Tir; follow it until it merges with av. du Général de Gaulle, bearing left when av. du Général de Gaulle bridges the railroad tracks. Follow the street you're on, rue Florimont, as it curves left into rue du Val St-Grégoire. Take a right on rue du Pont Rouge; continue through the intersection on the rte. d'Ingersheim to rue Pasteur. (20min.) Plain, crowded rooms and common hallway showers. A little run-down. Kitchen. Breakfast included. Sheets €3.50. Reception Apr.-Sept. 7-10am and 5pm-midnight; Oct.-Mar. 7-10am and 5-11pm. Lockout 10am-5pm. Curfew midnight. June-Aug. reserve in advance. Closed Dec. 15-Jan. 15. 6- to 8-bed dorms €11.50; singles €16.50, doubles €28.50. **Members only.** MC/V. ❶

Hôtel Kempf, 1 av. de la République (☎ 03 89 41 21 72; fax 03 89 23 06 94; http://hotel.kempf.free.fr). Large, simple rooms with a homey atmosphere in a perfect location. All rooms with shower. Breakfast €5.50. Reception 8am-midnight. Singles €26-28; doubles €35-45; triples €55. €0.45 tax per person per night. MC/V. ❸

La Chaumière, 74 av. de la République (☎ 03 89 41 08 99), around the corner from the train station, a 5min. walk from the center of town. Kind hostess lets pleasant, clean, and simple rooms, some set around a cement balcony overlooking an inner courtyard. Breakfast €5. Reception 7am-11pm. 4-6 people with bath €80-86. Singles and doubles €28-30, with shower €37-40; triples €43. Jan.-Feb. prices €2 lower. MC/V. ❸

Camping de l'Ill, rte. Horbourg-Wihr (☎ 03 89 41 15 94), is two laurel-scented kilometers from town on a wooded river in view of the Vosges. Take bus #1 (dir: Horbourg-Wihr) to "Plage d'Ill." Reception July-Aug. 8am-10pm; Feb.-June and Sept.-Nov. 8am-8pm. Fills quickly in summer. Open Feb.-Nov. €2.90 per person, under 10 €1.70; €3.05 per site. Electricity €2.40. ❶

FOOD

There is a **Monoprix supermarket** at pl. Unterlinden. (Open M-F 8am-8pm, Sa 8am-8pm.) **Markets** are set up in pl. St-Joseph (Sa morning) and pl. de l'Ancienne Douane (Th morning), a popular café spot. Colmar boasts a number of viticulturists. A friendly welcome, a great selection of local wines (€3.80 and up), and a 400-year legacy await at **Robert Karcher et Fils,** 11 rue de l'Ours, in the *vieille ville.* (☎ 03 89 41 14 42. Open daily 8am-noon and 2-6pm. MC/V.) **La Cassolette ❷,** 70 Grand'Rue, serves large salads (€8.60-9) and delicious goat-cheese sandwiches (€3.50) in a cute, flower-filled interior. (☎ 03 89 23 66 30. Open M-Th 8am-7pm and F-Sa 8am-9:30pm.) **Brasserie Schwendi ❷,** 23-25 Grande Rue, offers *tartes flambées* and other hearty Alsatian fare, as well as a great selection of local beers and wines. Meals (*plats* €8.60-13) are served late on a pleasantly vacant pedestrian street. (☎ 03 89 23 66 26. Open daily 10am-1am, hot food served 11:45am-11pm. MC/V.)

ALSACE

👁 SIGHTS

The city's restored Alsatian houses glisten in fresh pastels; the best specimens are in the **quartier des Tanneurs** and down rue des Tanneurs, over a small canal, in **la petite Venise** (little Venice). Geraniums cluster in window boxes above cobblestone streets lining the canal. 105 grotesque stone heads adorn the 1609 **Maison des Têtes,** rue des Têtes, crowned with a 1902 statue of Bartholdi. The **⬛Musée d'Unterlinden,** 1 rue d'Unterlinden, converted from a 13th-century Dominican convent, holds an eclectic collection highlighted by Mathias Grünewald and Nikolaus Haguenauer's *Issenheim Altarpiece* (1500-1516), depicting the Crucifixion and other scenes from Christ's life in such complete iconographic detail that it has been said: "Near Grünewald, all collapses." (☎ 03 89 20 15 50. Open Apr.-Oct. daily 9am-6pm; Nov.-Mar. W-M 10am-5pm. €7, students €5, under 12 free.)

The **Eglise des Dominicains,** pl. des Dominicains, is now little more than a showroom for Martin Schongauer's exquisite *Virgin in the Rose Bower* (1473), a lushly colored panel overwhelmed by an outrageous neo-Gothic frame. Delicate 14th-century stained glass lights up the artwork with a golden glow. The German-captioned paintings on the wall date back to the German occupation of Alsace during the Franco-Prussian War; their return was a provision of the Treaty of Versailles. (Open Apr.-Dec. daily 10am-1pm and 3-6pm. €1.30, students €1.) The **Collégiale St-Martin,** pl. de la Cathédrale, feels more like a museum than a church. Despite its nondescript exterior, the church is actually full of interesting art, including a massive altarpiece transplanted from the convent that houses d'Unterlinden. (Open Tu and Th 8am-6:30pm, F-M and W 8am-6pm.)

Frédéric Auguste Bartholdi (1834-1904), best known for a 47m statue of his mother entitled *Liberty Enlightening the World* (known to some as the Statue of Liberty), has been memorialized in the engaging **Musée Bartholdi,** 30 rue des Marchands. The museum displays his personal art collection, drawings, and models. Also here is a giant plaster ear, a full-scale study for Ms. Liberty's *oreille.* (☎ 03 89 41 90 60. Open Mar.-Dec. W-M 10am-noon and 2-6pm. €4, students €2.50.)

🎵 👁 ENTERTAINMENT AND FESTIVALS

The 10-day **Foire aux Vins d'Alsace** in mid-August is the region's largest wine fair. Popular French and European musicians hold concerts in the evenings at 9pm. (☎ 03 90 50 50 50; www.foire-colmar.com. Festival entrance until 5pm €2, after 5pm €5. Concerts €10-23.) In the first two weeks of July, the **Festival International de Colmar** features two dozen classical concerts. (☎ 03 89 20 68 97; festival-internation@ot-colmar.fr. Tickets €10-50, under 25 €5-18. For more info call.) The Collégiale St-Martin's organists play on Tuesdays at 8:45pm for the **Heures Musicales** during July and August. (€8, students €6.50.)

MULHOUSE

While this bustling town of 110,000 may not have Nancy's architecture or Metz's gardens, Mulhouse atones for its indifferent buildings and occasional kitschy facades with a slew of fabulous museums. Once an industrial powerhouse for both mechanical and domestic goods, Mulhouse is today content with exploiting its productive past in the name of a more powerful industry: tourism.

TRANSPORTATION AND PRACTICAL INFORMATION

Trains run from bd. Général Leclerc to Basel, Switzerland (20min., 7 per day, €6); Belfort (30min., 32 per day, €8.20); Paris (4½hr., 10 per day, €43); and Strasbourg (1hr., 16 per day, 13.50). Local **buses** run from Porte Jeune, north of the pedestrian district. (☎ 03 89 66 77 77. Most services 7am-7pm; evening routes 8:30-11:30pm. Tickets €1.10, *carnet* of 10 €8, day pass €2.80. Tickets available at the train station or on the bus.)

The **tourist office,** 9 av. Foch, lies two blocks straight ahead from the right-most edge of the train station, across from a park. They make hotel reservations, and provide walking-tour maps. (☎ 03 89 35 48 48; www.tourism-mulhouse.com. Tours in French and English on request July-Aug. M, W, Sa 10am. €4, under 12 free. Main office open M-F 10am-7pm.) **Annex** in the Hôtel de Ville. (Open M-Sa 10am-7pm, Su 10am-noon and 2-7pm.) Rent **bikes** at **Cycles Beha,** pl. de la Concorde. (☎ 03 89 45 13 46. Open M 2-7pm, Tu-Sa 9am-noon and 2-7pm. €16 per day.) For a **taxi,** call ☎ 03 89 45 80 00. (24hr. €10-16 from train station to hostel.) The **police** are at 12 rue Coehorn (☎ 03 89 60 82 00), off bd. de La Marseillaise, in the north of the city; and the **hospital** is behind the train station at 20 rue du Dr. Laënnec (☎ 03 89 64 64 64). **Internet** access is at **Noumatrouff,** 57 rue de la Mertzau (☎ 03 89 32 94 17; free with reservation) or **La Filature,** 20 allée Nathan Katz. (☎ 03 89 36 28 28. €1.50 per hr. Open Tu-Sa 11am-6:30pm, Su 2-6pm.) The central **post office,** 3 pl. de Gaulle, offers **currency exchange.** (☎ 03 89 66 94 00. Open M-F 8am-7pm, Sa 8am-noon.) **Poste Restante:** 68074. **Postal code:** 68100.

ACCOMMODATIONS AND FOOD

Dirt-cheap rooms in town are elusive, but an assortment of comfortable two-stars compete for clients. Rates may drop on weekends. The newly refurbished **Auberge de Jeunesse (HI) ❶,** 37 rue d'Ilberg, offers 4- and 6-bed rooms with coed bathrooms. Take bus #2 (dir: Coteaux; bus #S1 after 8:30pm) to "Salle des Sports." Institutional and sparse, but cheap. (☎ 03 89 42 63 28. Breakfast €3.50. Linen €2.70. Reception 8am-noon and 5-11pm, July-Aug. until midnight. No entrance after reception is closed. €8 per person. MC/V. **Members only.**) Homey, family-run **▧Hôtel St-Bernard ❸,** 3 rue des Fleurs, conveniently located near the center of town, maintains bright, immaculate rooms. Included are showers, 32-channel TVs, free Internet and bikes, access to a small library, and, most importantly, a cute slobbery St. Bernard. (☎ 03 89 45 82 32; fax 03 89 45 26 32; stbr@evhr.net. Breakfast €6. Reception 7am-9:30pm. Singles with shower €28; doubles with shower €35-46. AmEx/D/MC/V.) **Hôtel de Bâle ❸,** 19-21 Passage Central, is a decent back-up. The common spaces are elegant and comfortable, but the same can't be said for all of the adequate rooms. (☎03 89 46 19 87. Breakfast €6. Reception 24hr. Singles €27, with shower and toilet €40; doubles €30, with shower or bath and toilet €42-49. MC/V.) **Camping de l'Ill ❶**, rue Pierre de Coubertin, has its own grocery store. (☎03 89 06 20 66. Reception 9am-1pm and 3-8pm. Open Apr.-Sept. €3.20 per person, €3.20 per lot. Electricity €3.10. Tax €0.15 per person per day.)

Mulhouse tries to price like the Swiss (steeply), but the student community brings costs down on **rue de l' Arsenal.** A **Monoprix supermarket** lies on the corner of rue du Sauvage and rue des Maréchaux. (Open M-F 8:15am-8pm and Sa 8:15am-7pm.) A few doors down, **Le Globe** grocery sells delicacies from *pâté* to handmade marzipan animals. (☎03 89 36 50 50. Open M-Sa 9am-6:45pm.) *Crêperies* and Middle Eastern restaurants of varying quality abound. Get super-cheap gyros (€2.50-4), salads (€2.50-4), cold sandwiches (€2.50 tuna, cheese, or shrimp), and desserts (€2.50) at **Le Bosphore ❶**, 13 av. de Colmar, the prettiest quick-service joint in town. (☎03 89 45 16 00. Open daily 10am-1am.) **Crampous Mad ❶**, 14 impasse des Tondeurs, serves crêpes (€2.10-7.25) and galettes (€2.00-7.90) on a bright terrace beneath a typical Alsatian facade. (☎03 89 45 79 43. Open M-F 11:30am-10pm and Sa 11:30am-11pm. MC/V.)

ⓖ SIGHTS

Mulhouse's historical district centers around the festive **pl. de la Réunion,** named for the joyful occasions in 1798 and 1918 when French troops reunited the city with distant Paris. On the edge of town, a set of worthwhile museums focuses on the technology of the city's past and present, from textile production to trains.

MUSÉE NATIONAL DE L'AUTOMOBILE. The brothers Schlumpf once owned the 500-plus mint-condition autos of this gas-guzzling museum. The staggering collection ranges from an 1878 steam-driven *Jacquot à Vapeur* to the bubbly electric cars of the future. Cars once owned by celebrities like Charlie Chaplin and Emperor Bao Dai are prominently displayed. *(192 av. de Colmar. Take bus #1, 4, 11, 13, or 17 north to "Musée Auto." ☎03 89 33 23 23. Open July-Aug. daily 9am-6:30pm; Apr.-Oct. 9am-6pm; Nov.-Mar. 10am-6pm. €10, students €7.50, ages 7-18 €5, under 7 free.)*

MUSÉE FRANÇAIS DU CHEMIN DE FER. A stunning collection of slick, gleaming engines and railway cars is kept in this warehouse-like museum. Peer into the perfectly restored compartments of such legends as the Orient Express. Every hour a massive 1949 steam engine (the last of its kind) chugs away in place for your viewing delight. Awesome metal sculptures of rail-layers hug the walkway to the one-room **Musée du Sapeur-Pompier.** *Sapeurs-Pompiers*, France's heroic firemen-*cum*-medics, consider themselves part of a grand tradition. *(2 rue Alfred de Glehn. ☎03 89 42 25 67. Take bus #17 (dir: Musées) from Porte Jeune Place, or #18 (dir: Technopole) from the train station; 1 per hr. On Su, use line "M." Open May.-Sept. daily 9am-6pm; Oct.-Apr. 9am-5pm. €7.60, students and children 6-18 €4, children under 6 free.)*

ELECTROPOLIS. This zippy new museum introduces kids to the wonderful world of energy with hands-on exhibits, films, and historical collections. It's the material you slept through in high school, only interesting. *(Next to the railway museum. ☎03 89 32 48 60. Open July-Aug. daily 10am-6pm; Sept.-June Tu-Su 10am-6pm. €7.30, students and children 6-18 €5.80; children under 6 free; combined ticket with railroad museum €12.20.)*

TEMPLE DE ST-ETIENNE. One of France's few Protestant Gothic cathedrals, St-Etienne casts a long shadow across the carousel and cafes on pl. de la Réunion. If the church seems distinctly modern, it's because the Protestants acquired it from its Catholic owners in 1890, then tore the place down and built it back up again.

The original stained-glass windows, some up to seven centuries old, were preserved and now line the galleries. (*☎03 89 66 30 19. Open May-Sept. W-M 10am-noon and 2-6pm, Su 2-6pm. Free.*)

OTHER SIGHTS. Around the corner from the train station is the incongruously grand home of the **Musée de l'Impression sur Etoffes.** This happy marriage of technology, history, and aesthetics details the softer side of industry in Mulhouse, featuring miles of textile swatches from the last 250 years and from innumerable textile printers—everything from Indonesian scarves to *Back to the Future* t-shirts. (*14 rue J. J. Henner. ☎03 89 46 83 00. Open daily 10am-noon and 2-6pm. €5.50, students €2.75, children 12-18 €2.30, under 12 free.*) To escape the ubiquitous machinery of Mulhouse, stop in the **Parc Zoologique et Botanique,** a collection of rare animals and plant life. (*Take bus #12 (dir: Moenschsberg) to "Zoo." ☎03 39 31 85 10. Open May-Aug. 9am-7pm; Apr. and Sept. 9am-6pm; Mar. and Oct.-Nov. 9am-5pm; Dec.-Feb. 10am-4pm. Mar.-Oct. €7.40; Nov.-Mar. €4; year-round students and children ages 6-16 €4.*)

BELFORT

Occupying a valley between the Vosges mountains to the north and the Jura to the south, Belfort (pop. 50,000) has been a favorite target of invading armies for centuries. Rather than dwelling on its impressive past, the old town has become an industrial powerhouse; Belfort is the home to the factories that produce TGV trains and Peugeot automobiles. It has retained some military presence, however: an infantry base lies outside of town, and men and women in uniform are often seen in town. Don't miss the Chapelle de Notre-Dame-du-Haut in nearby Ronchamp, one of Le Corbusier's masterpieces.

▉▉ TRANSPORTATION AND PRACTICAL INFORMATION. Trains run to Besançon (1hr., 20 per day, €12.30); Mulhouse (30min., 20 per day, €7.30); Paris (4hr., 9 per day, €39); and Strasbourg (1½hr., 8 per day, €17.70). **CTRB,** pl. Corbis, sends buses around Belfort. (*☎03 84 21 08 08. Office open M-F 9am-noon and 1:45-5:45pm. Lines run 6am-8pm. Tickets €1, carnet of 10 €7.80.*) Taxis Radio Belfortains are at 44 rue André Parant. (*☎03 84 22 13 44. Base €1.25, €1.25-1.60 per km.*)

To get from the station to the **tourist office,** 2bis rue Clemenceau, head left down av. Wilson and then bear right on fbg. de France. When the river comes into sight, turn left on fbg. des Ancêtres and follow it to rue Clemenceau; the office is the unexpectedly large building to the right across rue Clemenceau, to the right of the mammoth Caisse d'Epargne, set back from the road. Here, a young staff will outfit you with free maps, hotel and restaurant listings, and info on excursions. Ask for *Le Petit Geni,* a comprehensive guide to Belfort that provides discounts at local stores and restaurants, or *Spectacles,* a free guide to restaurants and clubs. (*☎03 84 55 90 90; fax 03 84 55 90 99. Open late June-Aug. M-Sa 9am-12:30pm and 1:30-6:30pm; Sept.-late June M-Sa 9am-12:30pm and 1:45-6pm.*) There is an automatic **currency exchange** machine at **Caisse d'Epargne,** pl. de la Résistance (*☎03 84 57 77 77*). A **laundromat** is at 60 fbg. de Montbeliard. (*☎03 84 21 84 10. Open daily 7am-9pm.*) The **police** are at 1 rue du Monnier (*☎03 84 58 50 00*) and the **hospital is** at 14 rue de Mulhouse (*☎03 84 57 40 00*). Access the **Internet** at **Belfort Information Jeunesse,** 3 rue Jules Vallés. (*☎03 84 90 11 00. Open M-Sa 10am-noon and 1:30-6pm. Closed Tu and Sa mornings.*) The **post office** is at 19 fbg. des Ancêtres. (*☎03 84 57 67 56. Open M-F 8am-7pm, Sa 8am-noon.*) **Postal code:** 90000.

▉ ACCOMMODATIONS AND CAMPING. Belfort has a smattering of one- and two-star hotels that are rarely full in summer, but few truly budget places. Fortunately, there is one gem. Kim and George, the owners of ▉**Hôtel Au Relais d'Alsace**

THE HIDDEN DEAL

HÔTEL AU RELAIS D'ALSACE

It would be impossible to find a warmer welcome than at the **Hôtel au Relais d'Alsace ❸**. Kim and Georges, the Franco-Algerian couple who owns and runs the hotel, just might be the sweetest people on the planet. Kim has limitless amounts of motherly enthusiasm for her guests, while Georges gives better advice than the tourist office about trails to take around town. Attracting families, backpackers, architecture students, and traveling musicians from all over the world, the lobby is perpetually filled with lively conversation and souvenir pictures drawn for the owners by past guests.

Kim and Georges offer spacious rooms, all with phones and TVs, which they decorated by hand in bright cheerful blocks of pastel color. The top floor gives a prized view of the nearby Château de Belfort. At breakfast, drink fresh-squeezed orange juice as you sign your name in the guest book. *(5 av. de la Laurencie. ☎ 03 84 22 15 55; fax 03 84 28 70 48; www.arahotel.com. From the station, take Faubourg de France on the right to the* vieille ville. *Pass through the Porte de Brishac (an old gate) and continue straight. Av. de la Laurencie will be on the left. Breakfast €5. Washer and dryer available. Singles with shower €25; doubles with shower €37; triples with shower €43; quads with shower €51.)*

❸, 5 av. de la Laurencie, offer a backpackers' dream (see sidebar **Hôtel Au Relais d'Alsace**, p. 748). **Résidence Madrid ❶**, 6 rue Madrid, is a cheap option near the station. Dorm-style facilities are serviceable, and the residents are a lively international bunch. There are sinks in every room, and co-ed toilets and showers on each floor. From the train station, turn left on rue Michelet, crossing over the railroad tracks. Take your second right onto rue Parisot which soon becomes av. Général Leclerc; rue Madrid will be on your left after about seven minutes. Be careful in this neighborhood at night. (☎ 03 84 21 39 16. Breakfast €2.40. Full meal €6.60, main course €4.20. Reception 8:30am-12:30pm, 1:30-7:30pm, 10:30pm until the morning. €13.50, €11.70 with youth hostel card.) **Hôtel St-Christophe ❹**, pl. d'Armes, wins the prize for best location—right across from the cathedral in the heart of the *vieille ville*. The main hotel offers large, comfortable rooms with TV; the annex across the square is a better deal. (☎ 03 84 55 88 88; fax 03 84 54 08 77. Breakfast €6.50. Reception 6am-10pm. Singles with shower €49; doubles with bath €56. Annex: singles €39; doubles €50. MC/V.)

The three-star **Camping International de l'Etang des Forges**, 4 rue du Général Bethouart, enjoys an ideal location on the Etang des Forges, a sparkling lake 10 minutes from the *centre ville*. The grounds offer little privacy but plenty of space, good views, and squeaky-clean bathrooms. (☎ 03 84 22 54 92; fax 03 84 22 76 55. Reception 8am-12:30pm and 2:30-10pm. Open May-Sept. 2 people with tent €13; €2 for children 5-10. Electricity €2.50.)

🍴 **FOOD. Faubourg de France**, which cuts from the river to the train station, is packed with cafes, bakeries, and whatever else your rumbling stomach might desire. Cafes and restaurants, most in the €12 and above range, also cluster thickly in the old town, especially near **pl. des Armes**. The local pastry is the *belflore*, a rather generic raspberry pastry covered with almond paste. A **Petit Casino** is by the hostel at rue Léon Blum. (Open 7am-noon and 3-7pm.) Couscous (€8.50-13) is a specialty at ⓩ**Gazelle d'Or**, 4 rue des 4 vents, a Moroccan restaurant. (☎ 03 84 58 02 87. Open M-Sa noon-1:30pm and 7-11pm.) **La Bella Ciao ❸**, 29 Grande Rue, is a veritable Little Italy, serving ravioli (€8.40-13), eggplant, and noodles (€8.40-13) as Italian music echoes between yellow, photo-strewn walls. (☎ 03 84 22 62 73. Open Tu-Su noon-2pm and 7-11pm.) **Aux Crêpes d'Antan ❶**, 13 rue du Quai, presents a formidable selection of creamy, aesthetically folded crepes and galettes (€3.80-7.60) in a *provençal*-themed shop just around the corner from the cathedral. (☎ 03 84 22 82 54. Open noon-2pm and

7pm-midnight.) If you've overdosed on the French pancake, try a potato. **La Patate Gourmande ❷**, (☎ 03 84 21 88 44), 12bis rue des Ancêtres, resembles a cabin in the woods transplanted to a tiny alley off the bustling street; their garnished baked and *au gratin* potatoes (€7.50-14) and elaborate salads (€4.50-9.50) fill the stomach. (Open daily noon-2pm and 7-9:30pm.)

◪ **SIGHTS.** Fortunately, Belfort's **château** has not yet become a tourist playground. A circuit of the grounds gives a lesson in military history, as well as incomparable views of the countryside. The château, originally a medieval fortress, was expanded and refortified by the prolific Vauban when the French laid claim to Belfort after the Thirty Years War. Orange arrows direct you along a tour of the fort that leads up passageways, over walls, and through a cool, dank tunnel. The château lies above the *vieille ville* and can be reached by the winding road from pl. des Bourgeois. (☎ 03 84 54 25 51. Free tours July-Aug. 10am-5pm.)

A passageway on one of the lower levels leads to the viewing platform of the **Belfort Lion,** Bartholdi's monument to those who fell during the 1870 siege. Carved entirely of red sandstone, the Sphinx-like reclining beast is both Belfort's most important monument and a symbol of national pride and resolve. (Platform open July-Sept. daily 9am-7pm; Apr.-June 9am-noon and 2-7pm, Oct-Mar. 10am-noon and 2-5pm. €0.90, under 18 free. Ticket €5.35, students €3.80; includes the Musée d'Art et d'Histoire and the Donation Jardot.) The château at the heart of the fortifications houses the **Musée d'Art et d'Histoire.** There's something here for everyone, from nostalgia-loving domestics to grenade-pin-spitting alpha males. (Open Oct.-Mar. 10am-noon and 2-5pm, Apr.-Sept. only W-M. €2.80, students €2.30.) The **terrace** above the museum is the best place for a view of the land below; diagrams at the northern, southern, and eastern sides point out landmarks. Along the route back into town, remnants of the octagonal fortifications that once surrounded the *vieille ville*, including several guard towers, are still intact. **Tour 46,** on the corner of rue Bartholdi and rue Ancien Théâtre, presents a variety of special exhibitions by great modern artists. (Open W-M 10am-6pm.) The **Donation Maurice Jardot,** 8 rue de Mulhouse, has an impressive collection of sketches and paintings by modern greats like Picasso, Braque, Léger, Chagall, and the architect Le Corbusier. Jardot donated them in 1997 to this beautifully renovated 19th-century house, once property of the poet Deubel. (☎ 03 84 90 40 70. Open Apr.-Sept. W-M 10am-6pm, Oct-Mar. W-M 10am-noon and 2-5pm. €3.80, students €2.30.)

Back in the *vieille ville*, on rue des Mobiles, just on the other side of the ramparts of rue des Bons Enfants, Vauban's perfectly preserved 1687 **Porte de Brisach** bears the motto of the ever-humble Louis XIV: *Nec Pluribus Impar* ("Superior to all others"). The **Cathédral St-Christophe** presides over pl. des Armes in the heart of Belfort. Made of the same sandstone as the château, its graceful classical facade shelters a chilling transept with paintings by Belfort native G. Dauphin.

◪ **ENTERTAINMENT AND FESTIVALS.** While its dance clubs are relegated to the suburbs, central Belfort has a number of fun bars. ◪**Farlo,** 14 rue des Capucins, attracts students with alternative rock, salsa, and Latino music, cages to grind behind, waitresses dancing on bars, and cocktails invented on-the-spot by the barmaids. (☎ 03 84 26 07 07. Beer €2.60, cocktails €6.50. Open Tu-F 5pm-12:30am, Sa 5pm-1am). **Bistro des Moines,** 22 rue Dreyfus Schmidt, is a bar-restaurant that specializes in beer of all kinds, as well as some lunch foods. (☎ 03 84 21 86 40. Beer €4.30-4.90; meals €13. Open M-F 10:30-1am, Sa 10:30-2am.) A good place for people-watching is **Café Bruxelles,** pl. des Armes. (Open M-Sa 10am-1pm. Beer on tap €2-3.15, coffee €1.25.) Numerous **concerts** are held around town in July and August. The château hosts free jazz on Wednesdays at around 8:30pm; the cathedral hosts cheap classical concerts on Thursdays—the tourist office has details.

ALSACE

In the first weekend in July, 80,000 enthusiastic music fans from all over Europe descend upon Belfort for **Les Eurockéennes,** France's largest open-air rock festival. A recent lineup, spread over three days, featured Ben Harper, Wyclef Jean, Deftones, Iggy Pop, and 41 other acts from the entire spectrum of rock, rap, and any hybrid thereof. (☎ 08 92 69 23 92; www.eurockeennes.fr. €0.35 per min. Tickets sold at FNAC stores.) At the end of May, musicians from around the world hit town for the **Festival International de Musique Universitaire,** a three-day extravaganza that offers over 200 concerts, many of them free, running the jamming gamut from classical and jazz to rock and world. Reserve accommodations well in advance; rooms are next to impossible to find during the event. The last week of November brings the film festival **Entrevues,** which showcases fresh, young directors and retrospectives. (For info on all festivals call Cinema d'Aujourd'hui ☎ 03 84 54 24 43.)

■ **EXCURSIONS.** With the Jura on one side and the Vosges on the other, Belfort is an ideal base for outdoor activity. The tourist office has many pamphlets listing nearby walks, hikes, and biking trails. *Country Walks* (available in English) includes a map and descriptions of hikable regions near the city. Bessoncourt, 4km to the east, is the departure point for the daunting E5 trail that stretches from the Adriatic to the Atlantic and for many *petites randonnées* (short rambles). Kids and the elderly should be able to handle the fairly flat 10-14km circuit (3-5hr.). To the north, the towering summit of the Ballon d'Alsace (1247m) is a meeting point for three major long-distance trails, the GR5, GR7, and GR59. The 7km hike to the peak is taxing and suitable only for the fit, but the panoramic view of the glacial Doller valley and the Rhine and Saône valleys is spectacular.

The warm **Lac de Malsaucy,** just west of Belfort, offers swimming, sunning, and outdoor performances. Throughout the summer, puppeteers, acrobats, comedians, and musicians perform here. In July, **Les Eurockéennes** (see above) makes the trek. Outdoor movies are shown on Thursday nights in late July and August.

Small boats, nautical bicycles, and mountain bikes can all be rented from the **Base de Loisirs du Malsaucy,** rue d'Evette. The nearby Maison Départmentale de l'Environnement (☎ 03 84 29 18 12) offers expositions on everything from frogs to weather. Free outdoor movies are shown on Tuesday nights.

■ **DAYTRIP FROM BELFORT: RONCHAMP**

*To reach Ronchamp, hop on an SNCF **bus** or **train** at the SNCF station in **Belfort** (20min.; M-F 9 per day, 6 on Sa, 2 on Su; €4). The **tourist office** (☎ 03 84 63 50 82) is off rue le Corbusier, behind the church. (Open July-Aug. M-Sa 9:30am-noon and 2-5:30pm; Sept.-June M-F 9am-noon and 2-5pm.) To reach the chapel from the train station, follow rue de la Gare, turn left onto rue le Corbusier, turn left again onto rue de la Chapelle, and lug yourself up the steep, winding road for 1½km. If you are without a car, a bike, or legs of steel, Hôtel Pomme d'Or near the base of the hill will call a **taxi** for you (about €5 roundtrip). ☎ 03 84 20 65 13. Open Apr.-Sept. daily 9:30am-6:30pm; Oct.-Mar. 10am-4pm. €2, children 5-12 free, students €1.5.*

Hidden in the hills to the west of Belfort, tiny Ronchamp (pop. 3000) would have lived out its life in provincial anonymity were it not home to one of the most unusual and striking buildings in all of France. Built on the site of a disastrous German attack in 1944, Le Corbusier's 1954 **Chapelle de Notre-Dame-du-Haut** was meant to be a testament to hope in the wake of World War II. From afar, the chapel seems to sprout like an overgrown mushroom from the Bourlemont Hill, 472m above the town. Up close, its typically Corbusierian elements are obvious: thick slabs of concrete, receding walls, and small glass panes. With a sparsely decorated candle-lit interior worship space and an exterior altar and pulpit, the chapel serves as shelter from and communion with the outside world. Next to the door, Le Corbusier put down his intentions for the chapel: "I wanted to create a space of silence, prayer, peace, and interior joy."

BESANÇON

Surrounded by the river Doubs on three sides and by a steep bluff on the fourth, Besançon (pop. 120,000) has baffled military strategists from Julius Caesar to the great military engineer Vauban 1800 years later. Today, the city is known for its delightful setting, fine parks, and relative freedom from tourists. The home of a major university and an international language center, Besançon boasts a sizable student population, including a surprisingly diverse international contingent, and an impressive number of museums and discos.

▉ TRANSPORTATION

Trains: av. de la Paix. Office open M-F 9am-6:30pm, Sa 10am-5:20pm. To: **Belfort** (1hr., 20 per day, €12.30); **Dijon** (1hr., 25 per day, €11.70); **Lyon** (2½hr., 11 per day, €20.40); **Paris** (2hr., 8 per day, €42.50-50.80) via **Dole** (33 per day); **Strasbourg** (3hr., 10 per day, €25.70). Minor station at av. de Chardonnet.

Buses: Monts Jura, parking lot behind 9 rue Proudhon (☎03 81 63 44 44). To **Pontarlier** (1hr., 6 per day, €7.80). Office open M-Sa 8-10am and 4-6:30pm.

Public Transportation: CTB, 4 pl. du 8 Septembre (☎08 25 00 22 44). Open M-Sa 10am-12:45pm and 1:15-7pm. Night buses run sporadically until midnight. Tickets €0.90, *carnet* of 10 €7.80, 24hr. pass €3. Buy on bus.

Taxis: (☎03 81 88 80 80). Minimum charge €4.60. 24hr. service.

Bike Rental: Cycles Pro Shop, 18 av. Carnot (☎03 81 47 03 04). Rentals €13 per day, €9 per half day; helmet €3. Deposit €150-300. ID required. Open M-Sa 9am-noon and 2-7pm.

▉ ▉ ORIENTATION AND PRACTICAL INFORMATION

Everything of interest in Besançon lies within a thumb-shaped turn of the Doubs River. To reach the tourist office, cross the train station's parking lot and head down the stairs. Follow the street in front of you heading downhill (**av. de la Paix,** which quickly turns into **av. Foch**), but stay to the right. At the corner of av. Foch and **av. Edgar Faure,** cross the street and continue to your right down av. Foch. When you reach the river it will continue to veer left and will turn into **av. de l'Helvétie,** which you should follow to **pl. de la Première Armée Française.** The office is in the park to your right, and the **vieille ville** is across the bridge. (10min.)

Tourist Office: 2 pl. de la 1ère Armée Française (☎03 81 80 92 55; fax 03 81 80 58 30; www.besancon.com). Free accommodations service; lists hotels and restaurants; provides info on excursions and festivals. Ask for a free copy of the student guide *La Besace* or audioguides (€4). May-Sept. **tours** available for individuals (in French; €6, students €4) and groups (in French, English, or German). Provides **currency exchange.** Open Apr.-Sept. M 10am-7pm, Tu-Sa 9:30am-7pm, Su 10am-noon; Oct.-Mar. M 10am-5:30pm, Tu-Sa 9:30am-5:30pm, Su 10am-noon.

Laundromat: Blanc-Matic, 54 rue Bersot, near the bus station. Also 57 rue des Cras, near the Foyer Mixte. Both open daily 7am-8pm.

Youth Center: Centre Information Jeunesse (CIJ), 27 rue de la République (☎03 81 21 16 16; www.top-jeunes.com). Info on internships, jobs, events, and apartments. HI and ISIC cards. Free **Internet** access. Open M 1:30-6pm, Tu-F 10am-noon and 1:30-6pm, Sa 1:30-6pm.

Police: 2 av. de la Gare d'Eau (☎03 81 21 11 22). Near pl. St-Jacques.

Hospital: Centre Hospitalier Universitaire, 2 pl. St-Jacques (☎03 81 66 81 66).

Internet Access: Free at the CIJ and the post office (see above). **Cyber Espace,** 18 rue de Pontarlier (☎03 81 81 15 74). €4.60 per hr. Open M-Sa 11am-midnight, Su 2-

8pm. **Passage Clouté,** 8 ave. Carnot (☎03 81 53 42 37). €4.60 per hr. Open M-Th 5pm-1am, F-Sa 5pm-2am, Su 6pm-1am.

Post Office: Main office at 4 rue Demangel (☎03 81 53 81 12), in the new town. **Postal code:** 25000. Convenient **branch** at 23 rue Proudhon (☎03 81 65 55 82), off rue de la République. **Currency exchange.** Open M-F 8am-7pm and Sa 8am-noon. **Postal code:** 25019. **Poste Restante:** "25031 Besançon-Cedex."

♠ ACCOMMODATIONS AND CAMPING

Hostels here are a bargain and offer excellent facilities, but are quite a trek from the *vieille ville*. Buses run to both hostels, but daytime lines run only 6am-8pm, after which you'll have to find a different nighttime line, take a taxi or burn a lot of shoe rubber. Besançon's central hotels are closer to the action, but require reservations ahead of time and usually don't justify their prices.

Foyer Mixte de Jeunes Travailleurs (HI), 48 rue des Cras (☎03 81 40 32 00; fax 03 81 40 32 01). Cross the parking lot of the train station and head down the stairs. Take the road in front of you that heads down slightly to the left (av. de la Paix), and keep to the left as the road bends and turns into rue de Belfort. After 10min., turn left on rue Marie-Louise, which becomes rue des Cras as you cross over the railroad tracks. Follow rue des Cras up a large hill and over a smaller one; the hostel entrance is just after rue Resal on your right. (30min.) Locals refer to it as "Foyer Les Oiseaux." Or for a mere €0.90, take bus #7 from pl. Flore (from rue de Belfort, turn right onto av. Carnot, walk for a block until you see the green lights of the pharmacy in pl. Flore; take a sharp left onto rue des Chaprais. The stop is on the same side of the street as a Casino grocery). Take the bus from pl. Flore to "Oiseaux" (dir: Orchamps; 3 per hr.). Large, bright, new white-washed rooms with private bathrooms. Concerts, movies, and other special events. Caters more to students than tourists. Breakfast included. Good 5 course meal €6.40. Reception 8:30am-8pm. No reservations. Dec.-Feb. only two rooms. Singles €17, €15 the 2nd night; doubles €25/€23. MC/V. ❷

Centre International de Séjour, 19 rue Martin-du-Gard (☎03 81 50 07 54; fax 03 81 53 11 79). Take bus #8 (dir: Campus) from the Foch stop near the station to "Intermarché." To get to Foch from the station, cross the parking lot, go down the stairs, and head down the road that leads downward at a slight diagonal to the left (av. de la Paix, which turns into av. Foch). The stop is half a block down on the left. A large, institutional hostel with many non-backpackers. Restaurant, TV room, and foosball. Breakfast €4.30. Meals €6.20-10. Reception 7am-1am. Check-in 3pm; check-out 9am. Singles €17.50, with shower and TV €26.60; doubles €22/€30; triples €24.90. MC/V. ❷

Hôtel du Nord, 8 rue Moncey (☎03 81 81 35 56; fax 03 81 81 85 96), on a quiet but centrally located sidestreet in the heart of the old town. Attentive reception and clean, full-sized rooms with cable TV—the lap of budget-travel luxury. Breakfast €4.60. Reception 24hr. Check-in and check-out noon. Reserve ahead. Singles and doubles with shower €29.80-52, triples and quads with shower €53.40. AmEx/D/MC/V. ❸

Hôtel du Levant, 9 rue des Boucheries (☎03 81 81 07 88), on pl. de la Révolution. An old hotel with clean, minimalist, somewhat run-down rooms. Good location. Breakfast €3.80. Reception 9am-3pm and 6:30-8pm. Singles €18, with shower €23; doubles €23/€33; triples with shower €45; quads with shower €52. MC/V. ❷

Camping de la Plage, rte. de Belfort in Chalezeule (☎03 81 88 04 26; fax 03 81 50 54 62), northeast of the city. Take bus #1 (dir: Palente) to the terminus. (5min.) Shuttle bus *(navette)* leaves site 5 times per day (June 23-Sept. 2). Otherwise it's a 35min. walk down rte. de Belfort. 4-star campground with free access to a pool from June 24-Aug. 9. Near a highway, but retains a certain rural charm. Breakfast €4. Reception open 9am-7pm. Open Apr.-Sept. €3.20 per person; €4.70 per car or tent. Electricity €3.50. ❷

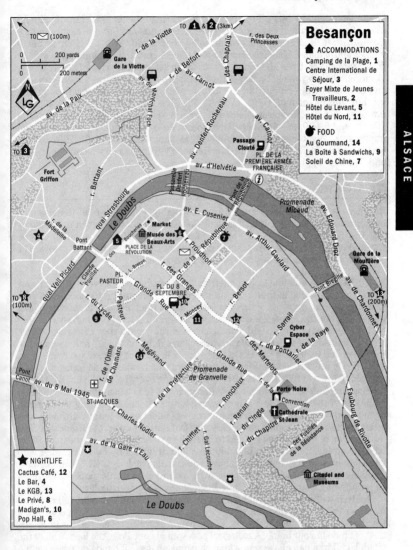

Besançon

⌂ **ACCOMMODATIONS**
Camping de la Plage, **1**
Centre International de
    Séjour, **3**
Foyer Mixte de Jeunes
    Travailleurs, **2**
Hôtel du Levant, **5**
Hôtel du Nord, **11**

🍴 **FOOD**
Au Gourmand, **14**
La Boîte à Sandwichs, **9**
Soleil de Chine, **7**

★ NIGHTLIFE
Cactus Café, **12**
Le Bar, **4**
Le KGB, **13**
Le Privé, **8**
Madigan's, **10**
Pop Hall, **6**

🍴 FOOD

Restaurants along **rue Claude Pouillet** cater to Besançon's cosmopolitan students, while **rue des Boucheries** targets tourists. Pl. de la Révolution stages outdoor and covered **markets.** (Open Tu and F 6am-12:30pm, Sa 6am-7pm.) Buy groceries at **Monoprix,** 12 Grande Rue. (Open M-Sa 8:30am-8pm.) Sharp **comté cheese** is Besançon's speciality. Wash it down with **vin jaune,** one of the more famous Arbois wines. Charcuteries along rue des Granges sell *jambon de Haut Doubs,* a regional smoked ham. 🍴 **La Boîte à Sandwichs ❶,** 21 rue du Lycée, is near a popular student nightlife area off rue Pasteur. Exotic ingredients like heart of palm fill over 50 wittily named sandwiches like *La Geisha, La Bohémienne,* and *Le Communiste,* and every conceivable salad concoction. (☎03 81 81 63 23. Sandwiches and salads €2.30-5.40. Open M-Sa 11:30am-2pm and 7pm-midnight. MC/V.) ◼**Au Gourmand ❶,** 5 rue Megevand, serves up an astonishing array of hearty dishes at incredibly low prices. Canary-yellow walls, vintage chocolate advertisements, and collections of teapots and cat figurines bring to mind the eccentric grandmother you never had. (☎03 81 81 40 56. Rice and pasta dishes €5.40-7.70; omelettes €3.10-5.35; warm salads with potatoes €4.60-6.10. Open Tu-F 11:30am-1:45pm and 6:45-9pm.) **Soleil de Chine,** 28 rue de la République, puts together an impressive all-you-can-eat buffet, as well as karaoke. (☎03 81 81 28 97. Lunch €8.85; dinner Su-Th €11.90, F-Sa €15. Karaoke F-Sa nights. Open daily noon-2pm and 7-10.30pm.)

🄖 SIGHTS

Besançon's *vieille ville* is graced by remarkably well-preserved Renaissance buildings, and actually visiting Vauban's Renaissance citadel is even more engaging. The citadel, built during the reign of Louis XIV, sits high on the hill above the city and offers stunning views, several excellent museums, and zoos galore. The citadel is at the end of rue des Fusillés de la Resistance.

THE CITADEL. A grueling trek uphill from the town, but worth every stitch in your side. While the Citad'in tour bus confirms this 17th-century stronghold as a conspicuous tourist spot, its status confers one great advantage: detailed English translations of the extensive collections. The free first level encompasses a deer park, picnic lawns arrayed with cookie-cutter shrubs, and a view of the city below. Museums inside include the **Salle de Vauban,** an exhibit on the life and times of the Sun King, and the **Musée Comtois,** a historical collection of folk art and crafts from Franche-Comté. Consider taking the **Petit Train,** which rides to the top and gives a tour along the way. (Pick up at pl. du 8 Septembre; every hr. on the hr.; €5.15.)

Of special note is the ◼**Musée de la Résistance et de la Déportation.** One hundred members of the French Resistance were shot at the citadel during the German occupation of Besançon. The comprehensive collection of letters, artifacts, and often graphic photographs, chronicles the Nazi rise to power, the Holocaust, and the invasion of France. Ask a guard to open the exhibition room on the third floor, which contains a collection of sculptures and drawings by two local men who were deported to concentration camps. You can also pick up a €1.60 audio guide, available in English, which plays survivors' recorded accounts. (☎03 81 65 07 55. Open July-Aug. 9am-6pm; Sept.-June 10am-5pm. No children under 10.)

Children will surely be delighted by the **Musée d'Histoire Naturelle,** full of mammals, birds, and fish that fell victim to the taxidermist's tools. Next door are a small **aquarium** and the **insectarium,** where a mock kitchen reveals all the little nasties that hide in your home. A **zoological park** sprawls out along the back wall of the citadel; children can chase squawking chickens on a small hands-on farm. On the other side of the zoo, raccoons and nighttime creepy-crawlies lie in wait to scare kiddies in the pitch-black **noctarium.** *(Citadel ☎03 81 87 83 33. Open July-Aug. daily 9am-7pm; Apr.-June and Sept.-Oct. 9am-6pm; Nov.-Mar. 10am-5pm. €7, students €6, under 14 €4, includes entrance to every museum and facility. Audio guide €1.60.)*

CATHÉDRALE ST-JEAN. Perched beneath the citadel, this cathedral's highlight is an interior that mixes architectural styles from the 12th to the 18th centuries. Look for the beautiful **Rose de St-Jean,** a circular altar of white marble dating from the 11th century, and the **Horloge Astronomique,** a 30,000-part clock housed within the cathedral and visible only by tour. Walking back into town on rue de la Convention, you pass through the **Porte Noire** (Black Gate), a stern if tarnished triumphal arch built during the reign of Marcus Aurelius. *(Cathedral ☎ 03 81 83 34 62. Open W-M 9am-6pm. Free. Horloge ☎ 03 81 81 12 76. Open Oct.-Mar. Tours Th-M at 9:50, 10:50, 11:50am, 2:50, 3:50, 4:50, 5:50pm. €2.50, under 18 and students free.)*

MUSÉE DES BEAUX-ARTS ET D'ARCHÉOLOGIE. France's oldest public museum exhibits Egyptian mummies and statuettes, and an exceptional collection of more than 6000 works by Ingres, Van Dyck, Rubens, Matisse, Picasso, Renoir, and other masters. *(Pl. de la Révolution. ☎ 03 81 87 80 49. Open June-Oct. W-M 9:30am-6pm, Nov.-May W-M 9:30am-noon and 2-6pm. €4, free for students and all on Su and holidays.)*

MUSÉE DU TEMPS. Avoiding abstract Proustian philosophy, this brand-new museum—appropriately situated in the watch-making capital of France—takes a concrete approach to the grand question of time. The collection of the Musée du Temps explores cogs-and-gears conceptions of time (i.e. clocks), as well as ancient understandings deduced from anthropology and archeology. The museum itself has a slightly relaxed notion of time; it opened two years behind schedule and is closed on Mondays and Tuesdays. *(Palais Granvelle, 96 Grande Rue. ☎ 03 81 87 81 50. Open W-Su May-Sept. 1-7pm; Oct.-Apr. 1-6pm. €3, students €1.50, ticket valid 2 days.)*

BOAT TRIPS. Les Vedettes Bisontines runs boat cruises on the Doubs and the citadel canals from pont de la République, near the tourist office. *(☎ 03 81 68 13 25. Available June-Sept., 3 per day; 100min.; €8.50, children €6.)* Or cross rue de la République to **Les Bâteaux Mouches'** "Le Pont Battant." *(☎ 03 81 68 05 34. Available Apr.-Oct. 100min.; 4 per day; €8, children €6.50. Days and tours vary; call ahead.)*

■ NIGHTLIFE

Most nights of the week, the students of Besançon pack bars and discos until early morning, especially in the area extending from **rue Claude Pouillet** to **Pont Battant**. Small, friendly bars proliferate throughout the town, particularly on **rue Pasteur.**

Pop Hall, 26 rue Proudhon (☎ 03 81 83 01 90), across from the post office, is the hippest pool hall you'll ever see. Its nondescript facade hides everything from antique chandeliers to gondolas to cars appropriated from amusement parks. The high point is the bathrooms, which feature chipped Victorian mirrors, Roman vases, bronze cowhead sinks, and a toilet bowl lamp. Beer €2; cocktail €2.50-4.50. Happy Hour 6:30-7:30pm: drinks half-off. Open M-Th 6pm-1am, F and Sa 6pm-2am, Su 6pm-1am.

Madigan's, pl. 8 Septembre (☎ 03 81 81 17 44), fills to bursting every night with a young crowd seeking its authentic Irish experience. €2.50 margaritas, beer €2-2.80 on tap. Open Su-Th 7am-1am, F and Sa 7am-2:30am.

The Cactus Café, 79 rue des Granges (☎ 03 81 82 01 18), is the closest thing in France to a frat party with its rowdy student crowd. 7000-song karaoke Th-Sa 10pm-2am. Beer €2-2.60 on tap. Open M-Th 9am-1am, F-Su 9am-2am. MC/V.

Le Bar, 15 rue de Vignier (☎ 03 81 82 01 00), is the only gay bar in town. The basic theme is sex, from the porn playing on a big screen TV to the condoms and gloves available downstairs. Ring bell to enter. Beer on tap €2.50, cocktails €5. Open M-Th 8pm-1am, F and Sa 9pm-2:30am, Su 9pm-2am.

Le Privé, 1 rue Antide Janvier (☎ 03 81 81 48 57), is the only gay and lesbian nightclub in town. Plays a variety of French and American music from the 80s on its two floors. This 22-year old club has never been renovated, as testified by the green fluorescent neon lights, red and black striped couches, and prominent mirrors. Cover F €9, Sa €10, Tu-Th €8; includes one drink. Open Tu-Su 11pm-5am.

ALSACE

Le KGB, 8 av. de Chardonnet (☎03 81 61 17 49), about 1km from the tourist office, is the best of Besançon's dance clubs. A large dance floor with London Underground decor is surrounded by plush couches, two bars, and many drunken students. Av. de Chardonnet is not well lit; be cautious. Cover €7.70, F-Sa €9.10; W and Th students €3.90. Open W-Th 10:30pm-4am and F-Sa 10:30pm-5am. MC/V.

🎭 FESTIVALS

The tourist office publishes several comprehensive lists of events. In July and August, the city sponsors **Festiv'été,** with theater, music, dance, expositions, and a film festival. (Many events are free. Call the tourist office for info.) **Jazz en Franche-Comté** brings a flurry of concerts in June and July, uniting jazz musicians from across France and abroad. (☎03 81 83 39 09 for info. Most tickets €5-16, many free and all with student discounts.)

The **Festival International de Musique** fills the air with nightly classical concerts during the middle two weeks of September. Orchestras from across Europe perform well-worn favorites as well as more recent compositions in 85 concerts, 60 of which are free. (☎03 81 25 05 80; fax 03 81 81 52 15; contact@festival-besan-con.com. Tickets €10-36 depending on locale; student discounts up to 25%.)

For more info on the three festivals, check out Besançon's website at www.besancon.com. The Foyer les Oiseaux hostel (see **Accommodations,** p. 752) sponsors an array of events each month; pick up a schedule at the tourist office.

THE JURA MOUNTAINS

France's forgotten mountain range, the Jura, is often overlooked by travelers who flock to the Alps farther south. Much older than its neighbor, the Jura range has become rounder and smoother with age and is covered with dense pine forests, sunny meadows, and countless trails for hiking, biking, and skiing.

ARBOIS

Though frequented by tourists, this peaceful wine-tasting center has not yet lost its down-to-earth, regional feel. Residents are still firmly tied to the local vineyards; for every air-conditioned tour bus zipping by, there is a tractor rattling through the town. Vine-covered houses and blooming gardens, set beside 16th-century ramparts and a cascading river, make Arbois a picturesque and worthwhile visit.

🔷🔷 **ORIENTATION AND PRACTICAL INFORMATION. Trains** and **SNCF buses** will take you to Besançon (45min., 7 per day, €7.20) and Dole (5 per day, €6.25). The **train station** is a good 15min. hike from the town center; go straight from the station onto av. de la Gare, take your second left onto av. Pasteur, and follow it straight into town as it becomes rue de Courcelles and, a block later, Grande Rue, and finally reaches the central **pl. de la Liberté.**

To get to the **tourist office** from the train station, follow the directions above to pl. de la Liberté. From there, turn right onto rue de l'Hôtel de Ville; the tourist office is on the left side of the Hôtel de Ville, with a SNCF office. Get yourself a free map, a list of hotels and restaurants, a flood of brochures, and a free tour of the town in French. Audio tours available in English for €1.60. (☎03 84 66 55 50; www.arbois.com. Open July-Aug. M-Sa 9am-12:30pm and 2-6:30pm, Su 10am-noon and 3-6pm; low-season hours vary.) The **police** can be reached at ☎03 84 66 14 25. The **hospital** is at 23 rue de l'Hôpital (☎03 84 66 44 00). The **post office** is on av. Général Delort (☎03 84 66 01 21). **Postal code:** 39600.

ACCOMMODATIONS AND FOOD. The ritzy Arbois hotels often reach ungodly prices (up to €215), but there are a surprising number of decent and centrally located budget options. **Hôtel Mephisto ❷**, has seven spacious, slightly dark, occasionally too warm rooms with classy furnishings and recently renovated bathrooms. A bar is downstairs. (☎03 84 66 06 49. Breakfast €4.50. Reception 8am-10pm, later on weekends. June-Aug. reserve in advance. Singles €16, with shower €20.60; doubles €23/€30; triples €27/€30; quads with shower €40.60. MC/V.) **Hôtel de la Poste ❷**, 71 Grande Rue, is cheap but very simple. (☎03 84 66 13 22. Shower on first floor, toilets on every floor. Breakfast €4.60. Reception 7am-11pm; closed Tu. Singles €16.80; doubles €21.35.) A good mini-splurge is **Hôtel les Messageries ❸**, 2 rue de Courcelles, a Victorian-style establishment with stone archways, bright rooms, floral trimmings, and great views. (☎03 84 66 15 45. Reception 7am-10pm. Breakfast €6. Singles €27, with shower and toilet €45; doubles €30/€51; extra bed €8, under 10 free.) The three-star **Municipal des Vignes ❶** campsite, av. du Général Leclerc, offers modern amenities including hot showers, snack bar, nearby pool, laundry, and TV. (☎/fax 03 84 66 14 12. Open Apr.-Sept. July-Aug. 1-2 people €10.40; electricity €11.50. Apr.-June and Sept. 1-2 people €9.40; electricity €10.60. €1.40 per child. Bank cards and traveler's checks accepted.)

The mysteriously compelling *vin jaune*, fermented with sauvignon grapes and walnuts, is the pride of Arbois, as is the even more elaborate *vin de paille*, made from grapes that have been dried on beds of straw. Many *caves* in Arbois offer free *dégustations*, and many upscale restaurants have local wines by the glass. Not nearly as glamorous, but much cheaper, are the exquisite wines of **Supermarché Casino**, 55 Grande Rue, including a selection of *vins jaunes*. (☎03 84 66 05 92. Open M-Sa 8:30am-12:30pm and 3-7:15pm, Su 9am-noon.)

There are only a few good cheap eateries in Arbois. **La Cuisance ❷**, 62 rue de Faramand, fills with locals who delight in the generous *plats* (€6) and *menus* (€10). Kids eat for €5.35. (☎03 84 37 40 74. Open Th-M 9am-3pm and 5pm-midnight, Tu-W 9am-3pm. MC/V.) For a quick bite, head to **Restaurant Agor Kebab ❶**, 73 Grande Rue, a cheerful, crowded Middle Eastern stronghold in a land of expensive *coq-au-vin-jaune* eateries. Falafel and kebab sandwiches run €3.50-5, and platters are €7. (☎03 84 66 33 64. Open M-F noon-2pm and 6-10pm, Sa-Su 6pm-midnight.) Bring a date to **La Finette: Taverne d'Arbois ❸**, 22 ave. Louis Pasteur, a rustic place surrounded by candles, wooden tables, stone, animal heads, shotguns, and 3-course meals for €15. (☎03 84 66 06 78. Open daily 11am-midnight.) The big hit is ▓**Hirsinger's Chocolatier and Salon de thé**, 38 Grande Rue. Acclaimed by glossy gourmet magazines and locals alike, award-winning homemade ice cream goes deliciously with the view of pl. de la Liberté from the terrace. (☎03 84 66 06 97. 1 scoop €2, 2 scoops €3.)

SIGHTS AND FESTIVALS. The **Maison de Pasteur,** 83 rue de Courcelles, showcases the famous scientist's original vineyards and laboratory, where he made several crucial observations on the nature of alcoholic fermentation. The Maison continues to bottle wine under Pasteur's name. (☎03 84 66 11 72. Open June-Sept. daily 9:45-11:45am and 2:15-6:15pm; Apr.-May and Oct. daily 2:15-5:15pm. €5.35, children €2.75.) If you're not sick of viticulture yet, head over to the **Musée de la vigne et du vin,** in Château Pécauld on rue des Fossés. (☎03 84 66 40 45. July-Aug. guided tours available. Open March-Oct. W-M 10am-noon and 2-6pm; Nov.-Feb. W-M 2-6pm; July-Aug daily. €3.30.) The tower of **Eglise St-Just,** as well as the nearby 16th-century ramparts, offer an exquisite view of **La Cuisance** river.

A little French folk music complements a lot of wine-tasting, at the **Festival du Vin,** during the second to last weekend in July. During the **Fête du Biou,** the first Sunday in September, a procession of *vignerons* (wine producers) offers the first grapes of the season to God.

ALSACE

PONTARLIER

The town of Pontarlier, 840m above most of Alsace, is a gateway to some of life's higher pleasures—namely, the oft-overlooked Haut-Jura mountains. Pontarlier's current status as a friendly, slow, not-so-happening town belies its history as the absinthe capital of Europe (until the hallucinogenic liqueur was banned in 1915). In addition to great mountain views and beautiful chalet-style houses, Pontarlier serves as a good base for hiking, riding, and biking in the Jura and a trip to Switzerland, only 12km away.

☑ PRACTICAL INFORMATION. The **train station** is on pl. de Villingen-Schweningen. (☎03 81 46 56 99. Open M-F 5am-9pm, Sa-Su 7am-9pm.) **Trains** go to Dijon (1½hr., 6 per day, €18.10); Dole (1hr., 3 per day, €13.50); and Paris (3½hr., 6 per day, €53.36). Monts Jura **buses** leave from in front of the train station for Besançon (55min., 6 per day, €7.30). The **tourist office** is at 14bis rue de la Gare. From the train station, cross through the rotary and head left one block on rue de la Gare. The office is to the left of the bus station, down rue Michaud. The staff has info on hiking, skiing, and other outdoor sports, and free regional guides *Les Doubs: Massif de Jura* and *Guide Pratique*, which list cheap mountain lodgings. (☎03 81 46 48 33; fax 03 81 46 83 32. Office open M-Sa 9am-12:30pm and 1:30-6pm; July-Aug. also Su 10am-noon.) **Cycles Pernet,** 23 rue de la République, rents **bikes.** (☎03 81 46 48 00. €15 per day, €34 for 3 days. Passport deposit. Open Tu-Sa 9:30am-noon and 2-7pm; May-Aug. also M 3-6pm. MC/V.) The **police** are at 19 Rocade Pompidou (☎03 81 38 51 10); the **hospital** is at 2 fbg. St-Etienne (☎03 81 38 53 60). The **post office** is across the street at 17 rue de la Gare. (☎03 81 38 49 44. Open M-F 8am-6:30pm and Sa 8am-noon). **Postal code:** 25300.

⌂⌂ ACCOMMODATIONS AND FOOD. The cheapest place in town is the quiet, centrally located **Auberge de Pontarlier (FUAJ) ❶,** 2 rue Jouffroy. From the tourist office, go left on rue Marpaud, and the easy-to-miss hostel is the white stucco building on your left. The friendly folk at reception have many suggestions for activities, and organize hiking and skiing trips. (☎03 81 39 06 57; fax 03 81 39 06 57. Common room with big-screen TV. Breakfast €3.20. Kitchen. Sheets €2.70. Reception 8am-noon and 5:30-10pm. Reservations advised. Dorms €8 per bed. **Members only.**) TVs, wood panelling, spacious rooms, and a central location make up for the dim lighting and stale smell in the rooms of **Hôtel de France ❷,** 8 rue de la Gare. (☎03 81 39 05 20; fax 03 81 46 24 43. Reception daily 7am-11pm. Singles €16-26; doubles €26, with shower €27; triples €33; quads with shower €50. MC/V.)

The most scenic option is the **campground** on rue du Tolombief . From the train station, turn right onto Rocade Georges Pompidou, cross the river, and bear left onto rue de l'Industrie. Take the first right onto av. de Neuchâtel and follow the signs. (15min.) Amenities include a TV, ping-pong, a game room, and a bar. (☎03 81 46 23 33; fax 03 81 46 83 34. July-Aug. 1 person and tent/car €10, 2 people and tent/car €12.70; Sept.-June €8.90/€9.80; children €1.20. Electricity €3.10. Châlets €45.80 per day for 2 people, €366 per week, €1250 per month. Extra person €3.10. 6-person max. July-Aug. 1-week min. stay.)

The relaxed and small Pontarlier populace tends to eat at home, a fact reflected in the town's dearth of restaurants. Join the crowd at the **Casino supermarket** on rue de la République. (Open M-F 8am-12:30pm and 2:30-7pm, Sa 8:30am-7pm). The wood oven of **Pizzeria Gambetta ❷,** 15 rue Gambetta (off rue de la Gare), cooks over 20 varieties of pizza, ranging from pepperoni to eggs, tuna, and potatoes. Pizzas, regional meat dishes, and pastas can be made to go, but stay for the incredible chocolate mousse. (☎03 81 46 67 17. Pizzas from €6, design your own for €8.90;

mousse €3.80. Open W-Su noon-1.30pm and 7-9:30pm.) A variety of galettes (€5-8) and sweet crêpes (€2-6) are served at the bright and centrally-located **P'tit Delice** ❷, on 10 rue de la République. (☎03 81 46 57 74. Open Tu-Su noon-10pm. MC/V.)

🖪 **SKIING, HIKING, BIKING, AND RIDING.** The Jura mountains, best known for **cross-country skiing**, are covered with 60km of long-distance trails. Eight trails on two slopes (**Le Larmont** and **Le Malmaison**) cover every difficulty level. (Daily pass for cross-country skiing €5, under age 17 €2; for downhill skiing €10, under age 17 €7.) Le Larmont is the alpine ski area nearest to Pontarlier. (☎03 81 46 55 20.) For ski conditions, call **Info-Neige**, Massif de Jura. (☎03 81 39 91 66.) The Jura are much colder than the Alps, so wear layers. **Sport et Neige**, 4 rue de la République, rents ski equipment. (☎03 81 39 04 69. €7.60 per day, €38.10 per week; children €6.10 per day, €33.55 per week. Open daily 9am-noon and 2-7pm. MC/V.) Prices all around are far cheaper than those in the Alps, but the snow quality is less reliable. **Metabief Mont d'Or**, accessible by shuttle bus from Pontarlier, has day and night skiing. (☎03 81 49 13 81. Shuttle 30min., 4 per day from Mont Jura bus station, €7.10. Lift tickets €18 per day, under age 12 €12.)

In the summer, skiing gives way to fishing, hiking, and mountain biking. There are two mountain bike departure points in Pontarlier, one to the north just off rue Pompée and one to the south, about 2km west of Forges. Hikers can choose between a swath of the **GR5**, an international 262km trail, and the **GR6**, which leads to a narrow valley dominated by the dramatic **Château de Joux.** The thousand-year-old castle's collection of rare arms makes you wonder if the Franco-Swiss border has always been so peaceful. (☎03 81 69 47 95. Open July-Aug. daily 9am-6pm; Apr.-June and Sept. 10-11:30am and 2-4:30pm; Oct.-Mar. 10-11:15am and 2-3:30pm; Nov. 15-Dec. 15 by request only. €5, students €4.25.) The tourist office gives out a map (€2.50) that marks departure points for biking and hiking around town, including one near the train station at pl. St-Claude. More detailed maps can be found at **Librairie Rousseau**, 20 rue de la Republique (☎03 81 39 10 28. Open M-Sa 9am-noon and 2pm-7pm. Closed M afternoon.) **Le Poney Club**, 37 rue du Cret, adjacent to the campground rents well-trained horses for riders of all skill levels. (☎03 81 46 71 67. Take bus #2, dir: Poney Club. €6.50 for 30min., €10 per hr. For rides with a free guide, call a day in advance.)

LONS-LE-SAUNIER

Lons-le-Saunier (pop. 22,000) is an agreeable mountain town, not quite so convenient a base as Pontarlier for exploration of the Jura, but prettier and more pleasant. The town is best known as the birthplace of Rouget de Lisle, composer of *La Marseillaise*. As an ancient spa site, Lons possesses its share of Roman ruins; still, most visitors come here for the nearby mountains and the locals' highly developed *joie de vivre* rather than for any specific attraction.

📧 **TRANSPORTATION. Trains** run frequently to Besançon (12 per day, €11.13) and Dole (8 per day, €10.67). **SNCF** (☎08 36 35 35 35) also runs seven **buses** per day from the train station to Dole. Local buses run from Lons to the outlying villages (usually 6am-6pm; inquire at the tourist office for a schedule). **Taxis** are available outside the station. (☎03 84 24 11 16. €1.70 base fee; €1.30 per km, €1.50 after 7pm. 24hr.) You can rent **bikes** at **Dominique Maillard**, 17 rue Perrin. (☎03 84 24 24 07. Open M-F 9am-1pm and 2-6:30pm. MC/V.)

🖿🔃 **ORIENTATION AND PRACTICAL INFORMATION.** To get to the **tourist office**, pl. du 11 Novembre, cross the street in front of the station and head up rue Aristide Briand until it forks. Take the right fork (av. Thurel) to rue Rouget de Lisle on the left. Continue straight across rue Jean Jaurès. The office is in the old theater to your left. They offer free maps, hotel and restaurant listings, guides to excursions in the Jura, and a mountain of friendly suggestions for what to do in town. The office leads tours of the town and into the Jura on a highly variable schedule. (☎03 84 24 65 01; fax 03 84 43 22 59; www.ville-lons-le-saunier.fr. Tours €3. Open M-F 8am-noon and 2-6pm, Sa 8am-noon and 2-5pm.) For info on countryside tours, particularly with groups of 10 or more, contact **Juragence,** 19 rue Jean Moulin. (☎03 84 47 27 27. Open M-F 9am-12:30pm and 2-7pm, Sa 9am-noon and 2-5:30pm.) There is a **laundromat** at 26 rue des Cordeliers. (☎06 80 92 08 37. Open daily 7am-9pm.) The **Commissariat de Police** is at 6 av. du 44ème R.I. (☎03 84 35 17 10), and the **Centre Hospitalier** is at 55 rue docteur Jean Michel. (☎03 84 35 60 00.) Hook up to the **Internet** at **Car'Com,** next to the tourist office in the old theater. (€6.85 per hr., students €3.80 per hr. Open M-F 8am-noon and 2-6pm, Sa 10am-noon and 2-6pm.) The **post office** is on av. Aristide Briand. (☎03 84 85 83 60. Open M-F 8am-7pm, Sa 8am-noon.) **Poste Restante:** 39021. **Postal code:** 39000.

▮▯ ACCOMMODATIONS AND FOOD. Lons has no hostels, but there are a couple of decent cheap hotels near pl. de la Liberté. Reserve a week in advance during the summer. The **Hôtel les Glaciers ❷,** 1 pl. Philibert de Chalon, is probably your best bet. From the train station, proceed on av. Aristide for four blocks and take an abrupt left. Go one block and turn right onto rue St-Desiré. Walk one block and you'll be at pl. Liberté; diagonally across the *place* will be the arcaded rue du Commerce. Take this for two blocks to a fork, then veer to the left and continue to the end of the block. The hotel will be on your right, across from the museum. Nine bright, simple, and fairly new rooms go for snap-'em-up budget rates. (☎03 84 47 26 89. Breakfast €5. Reception 7am-11pm. Singles €20, with shower €25; doubles €23/€28. MC/V.) If Glaciers is full, try the central **Hôtel des Sports ❷,** at 21 rue St-Desiré. The hallways, which you follow up past two floors of private rooms, are dark and cramped, but the rooms are surprisingly spacious and bright and have TVs. Roll out of bed and get breakfast at the daily market next door. (☎03 84 24 04 42. Breakfast €4.60. Reception M-Sa 6am-10:30pm, Su 8:30am-1:30pm and 5-10:30pm. Singles and doubles with shower €22; triples €33. AmEx/MC/V.)

Charcuteries, pâtisseries, and *boulangeries* live side by side on **rue du Commerce.** A produce **market** appears there each Thursday morning. The rest of the week, you'll discover goodies at the local markets surrounding the **pl. de la Liberté.** The small and cheerful **La Ferme Comtoise,** 23 rue St-Desiré will find the slice of *fromage de Comte* perfect for you. (☎03 84 24 06 16. Open M-Sa 7am-7:30pm, Su 8am-1pm.) Fill up your picnic hamper at the **Casino supermarket,** rue du Commerce. (☎03 84 24 48 84. Open M-F 8:30am-12:30pm and 2:30-7:30pm, Sa 8am-7:30pm.) Locals leisurely sip their *kirs* at the **Grand Café du Théâtre,** 4 rue Jean-Jaurès (☎03 84 24 18 45), next to the tourist office, quite possibly the classiest looking *fin de siècle* cafe in France.

◙ SIGHTS. All roads in Lons lead to **pl. de la Liberté,** site of the old theater. The theater's Rococo facade was reconstructed in 1901 following a devastating fire. One of the additions was a clock that keeps time by chiming out a refrain from *la Marseillaise* on the hour. Fire also played a role in the development of the pretty **rue du Commerce,** off the *place,* whose houses were rebuilt in stone after the great conflagration of 1637. Number 24, the birthplace of Rouget de Lisle, is now the **Musée Rouget de Lisle.** It displays a smattering of personal and *Marseillaise*-related memorabilia, including a re-creation of his birth chamber and various editions of the famous song. (☎03 84 47 29 16. Open mid-June to mid-Sept. M-F 10am-noon and 2-6pm, Sa-Su 2-5pm. Free.) Following the rue du Commerce to its end and bearing left leads to the **Musée des Beaux Arts,** pl. Philibert de Chalon. This provincial museum boasts a splendid collection of Perraud statuary, a couple of nice Courbets, and precious little else. Even if you only have half an hour, stop by to get a glimpse of the incredible garden of human figures. (☎03 84 47 64 30. €2, students €1, under 18 free. Open M and W-F 10am-noon and 2-6pm, Sa-Su 2-5pm.)

To get to the **Musée d'Archéologie,** 25 rue Richebourg, veer right when the rue du Commerce forks and follow it as it becomes rue Trouillot, then turn right onto rue Richebourg. Housed in an old stone *fromagerie*, the museum exhibits artifacts from excavations in or near Lons, including France's oldest dinosaur, the Plateosaurus. (☎03 84 47 12 13. Open W-M 10am-noon and 2-6pm, Sa-Su 2-5pm. €2, students €1, under 18 free; all free W.) Between the museums, on rue Puits Salé and the corner of rue de l'Aubepin, you can see the off-kilter parabolic archway to the **Puits Salé,** the remains of the old saltwater baths that first drew the Romans to Lons. The spring is now connected via an underground canal to the **Thermes Ledonia** on the other side of town. This luxurious salt-water spa in the center of the shady green public **Parc des Bains** allegedly cures ailments like rheumatism and cellulite. Full-scale treatment costs thousands of euros, but €8.80 will get you a dip in the pool and a sauna session. (☎03 84 24 20 34. Open Apr.-Oct. M-Th 1:45-8pm and F-Sa 1:45-7pm.) Following rue Richebourg back toward the center of town, you'll hit **place de la Chevalerie** and an astonished-looking statue of Rouget de Lisle sculpted by Bartholdi. The sculptor recycled Rouget's stirring pose, one arm aloft, a few years later for a little lady now known as the Statue of Liberty.

◙ **EXCURSIONS.** Just 10km from Lons slumbers the little town of **Baume-les-Messieurs.** The magnificent **abbey** there was founded in the 6th century by St. Columban. Originally called *Baume-les-moines* (Baume-the-monks), by the 18th century the abbey had attracted so many *messieurs* (nobles) that its name had to change. (☎03 84 44 99 28. Open June 15-Sept. 15 daily 10am-6pm.) There is no direct bus route between Lons and Baume, but you can take a bus from Lons to the very nearby Crançot and follow the signs to Baume. Ask at the tourist office for a current bus schedule. There is an extensive network of caves near the town, with underground lakes and vaults up to 80m high. (☎03 84 48 23 02. €3.50, under 14 €2.50. Caves open Apr.-Sept. M-Su 10am-6pm.)

If you're seeking nature in all her splendor, the tourist office will happily bombard you with suggestions for exploring the cascading waterfalls, crystal lakes, and green hills and forests of the Jura. Several **hiking trails,** and paths for **biking** and **horseback riding,** run near Lons. Some tour operators guide trips through the Jura; try **Juragence,** 19 rue Jean Moulin. (☎03 84 47 27 27.)

If you really like the outdoors, try spending the night under the stars of Baume at **Campground La Toupe**, a one-star campground, with showers but no laundry service. (☎03 84 44 63 16. €2.50 per person, €2 per car or tent. Electricity €2.50.)

CHAMPAGNE

Brothers, brothers, come quickly! I am drinking stars!
—Dom Pérignon

According to European law, the word "champagne" may only be applied to wines made from grapes from this region and produced according to a rigorous, time-honored method which involves the blending of three varieties of grapes, two stages of fermentation, and frequent realignment of the bottles by *remueurs* (highly trained bottle-turners) to facilitate removal of sediment. So fiercely guarded is their name that when Yves Saint-Laurent brought out a new perfume called "Champagne," the powerful *maisons* sued to force him to change it—and won. You can see (and taste) the *méthode champénoise* in action at the region's numerous wine cellars (*caves*), at their best in the glitzy towns of Reims and Epernay. Even regional gastronomical specialties tend to center around a champagne base; try *volaille au champagne* (poultry) or *civet d'oie* (goose stew).

Champagne

Today, small as it is, Champagne is strikingly diverse. The golden vineyards and *beaux arts* flavor of the north seem a world away from the quiet citadels and forests of the south. The grape-fed high life may buoy the whole region economically, but smaller towns both near and far from the vines have quite distinct characters. Be sure to also drink in the monuments of the region's rich history: the inspiring grandeur of the Reims Cathedral, the Roman ramparts of Langres, the half-timbered houses and crooked streets of Troyes.

1	■ **Reims:** Champagne, coronations, and flagrant public *joie de vivre* **(p. 763)**
2	**Châlons-en-Champagne:** An industrial town known for churches and gardens **(p. 768)**
3	■ **Epernay:** Where the wealthy (and you) go to drink champagne **(p. 768)**
4	**Troyes:** The best-preserved medieval town in its area; renowned Gothic churches **(p. 770)**
5	■ **Langres:** One of France's most beautiful towns; eminently walkable ramparts **(p. 775)**

REIMS

Reims today (pop. 185,000; pronounced "rrrrahnce") is an active, vibrant city, all champagne and nightlife. The city's famous cathedral has witnessed some of France's most pivotal moments, from Clovis's baptism in AD 496 to the 1429 crowning of Charles VII, after being brought to Reims by Joan of Arc. The city also won the dubious honor of witnessing Napoleon's last victory, the so-called "last smile of Fortune." Fortune frowned on another would-be conqueror on May 7, 1945, when the German army surrendered in Reims's little red schoolhouse. Reims has since built over its war scars to return to its 19th-century glory. Bar-packed plazas and tree-lined avenues suit the comfortable lives and *joie de vivre* of the locals.

C H A M P A G N E

▐ TRANSPORTATION

Trains: bd. Joffre (☎03 26 88 11 65). Info office open M-F 8:30am-7pm, Sa 9am-6pm. To: **Epernay** (20min., 11 per day, €5.20); **Laon** (1hr., 7 per day, €7.50); **Paris** (1½hr., 11 per day, €18.75).

Public Transportation: Transport Urbains de Reims (TUR) buses stop in front of the train station. Info office at 6 rue Chanzy (☎03 26 88 25 38). Open M-F 7am-8pm, Sa 7am-7pm. €0.80 per ticket, *carnet* of 10 €5.75, day pass €2; buy from driver. All bus lines run 6:35am-9:45pm; 5 lines run until midnight. Regional **buses** leave from the bus station to Troyes and Chalons-en-Champagne. Schedules at the tourist office.

Taxis: ☎03 26 47 05 05 or 03 26 02 15 02. 24hr.

Car Rental: Avis, cour de la Gare (☎03 26 47 10 08). Open M-F 8am-noon and 2-7pm, Sa 8am-noon and 2-6pm. **Hertz,** cour de la Gare (☎03 26 77 87 77). **Budget,** 47 av. Nationale (☎03 26 77 66 66). **Europcar,** 76 bd. Lundy (☎03 26 88 38 38).

Bike Rental: Centre International de Séjour, chaussée Bocquaine (☎03 26 54 60 00). Half-day €7.60, full day €10.65, weekend €18.30. Deposit €76.25 or passport.

✈ ▐ ORIENTATION AND PRACTICAL INFORMATION

Tourist Office: 2 rue Guillaume de Machault (☎03 26 77 45 25; fax 03 26 77 45 27; tourismReims@netvia.com), in a pint-sized ruin beside the cathedral. Free map with sights and *caves* and free same-night **accommodations service** (with deposit). Ask for the student guide *Le Monocle*. **Tours** of the town and audio guides in 6 languages (€7.65). Office open mid-Apr. to mid-Oct. M-Sa 9am-7pm, Su 10am-6pm; mid-Oct. to mid-Apr. M-Sa 9am-6pm, Su 10am-5pm. Walking tours of Reims in French July-Aug. Tu 2:30pm. Tour of Basilique St-Rémi in French Th 2:30pm. Tour of cathedral daily, except Su morning; 10:30am and 4:30pm in French; 2:30pm in English, Spanish, or German, on a rotating basis. Tours €5.35, students and over 60 €3.05, under 12 free.

Budget Travel: Wasteels, 26 rue Libergier (☎08 03 88 70 55). ISIC cards, cheap flights. Open M-Sa 9am-noon and 2-6pm.

Youth Center: Centre d'Information et de Documentation, 41 rue Talleyrand (☎03 26 79 84 79; fax 03 26 79 84 72). Info on jobs and local events. Message board with job offers for seasonal work, including camp counselor positions and field work during the harvest. Contact ANPE Saisonnière (☎03 26 77 62 98) for more info about harvest work. Open M-Th 10:30am-12:30pm and 2-6pm, F 10:30am-12:30pm and 2-5pm.

Laundry: Laverie de Vesle, 129 rue de Vesle. Open daily 7am-9pm.

Police: 40 bd. Louis Roederer (☎03 26 61 44 00), by the train station.

Hospital: 45 rue Cognac Jay (☎03 26 78 78 78).

Internet Access: Clique & Croque, 27 rue de Vesle (☎03 26 86 93 92). 1st hr. €4.30, hours after €3.80. Open M-Sa 10:30am-12:30am, Su 2-9pm. Free **Internet** at **Centre Régionale d'Information Jeunesses**. Time limit 30min.; no e-mail checking, but this policy is loosely enforced.

Post Office: rue Olivier-Métra (☎03 26 50 58 82), at pl. de Boulingrin, near Porte Mars. Open M-F 8am-7pm, Sa 8am-noon. Central **branch office,** 1 rue Cérès (☎03 26 77 64 80), on pl. Royale. Open M-F 8:30am-6pm, Sa 8:30am-noon. **Poste Restante:** 51084 Reims-Cérès. Another branch on rue de Veste close to hostel. **Postal Code:** 51100.

▶ ACCOMMODATIONS AND CAMPING

Inexpensive hotels cluster west of pl. Drouet d'Erlon, in the region above the cathedral, and near the *mairie*. Reims is a popular destination; call ahead.

▣ **Centre International de Séjour/Auberge de Jeunesse (HI),** chaussée Bocquaine (☎03 26 40 52 60; fax 03 26 47 35 70), next to La Comédie-Espace André Malraux. Cross the park in front of the station, following the right-hand side of the traffic circle. Turn right onto bd. Général Leclerc, follow it to the canal and cross the first bridge (Pont de Vesle) on your left. Bocquaine is the first left. (15min.) Friendly staff houses a mix of backpackers and noisy school groups. Renovated rooms, brightly colored hallways, and new comfortable beds. Breakfast €4. Kitchen. Laundry. Reception 24hr. 4- to 5-bed rooms €9 per person. Singles €14, with shower €24; doubles €20/€30; triples €27/ €36. **Non-members** €2 one-time fee. MC/V. ❶

Au Bon Accueil, 31 rue Thillois (☎03 26 88 55 74; fax 03 26 05 12 38), off pl. Drouet d'Erlon. A sunny, spotless guest house with a slightly scruffy clientele. Reserve ahead and you may get a better, less expensive room than at the hostel. Breakfast €4.50. Hall shower €1.50. Reception 24hr. Singles €18-21, with shower €30; doubles with shower €36-44; extra person €7.50; extra bed €15. MC/V. ❷

Ardenn' Hôtel, 6 rue Caqué (☎03 26 47 42 38; fax 03 26 09 48 56), near pl. Drouet d'Erlon and the station. 14 romantic, chandeliered, velvety rooms, priced accordingly. All rooms with shower. Breakfast €5.58. Reception M-Sa 24hr., Su after 6pm. Singles €31-41; doubles €47-49; triples and quads €59; extra bed €6. MC/V. ❸

Hôtel Thillois, 17 rue Thillois (☎03 26 40 65 65), to the west of pl. Drouet d'Erlon. Rooms vary greatly in quality, from ratty and worn-down to bright and cheery; ask to see yours before you commit. Breakfast €4.30. Singles €19.85, with shower €24.40-27.45; doubles €22.90/€27.45-30.50. MC/V. ❷

▶ FOOD

The heart of Reims's street life, **pl. Drouet d'Erlon** is also its stomach; bakeries and sandwich shops compete for space with cheap cafés and classier restaurants. A **Monoprix** supermarket is in a 19th-century building on the corner of rue de Vesle

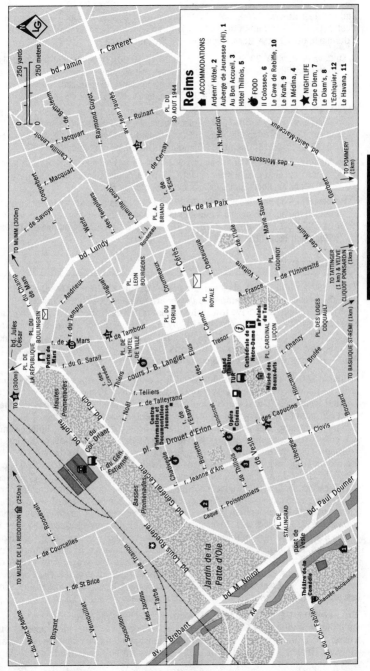

CHAMPAGNE

Reims

▲ ACCOMMODATIONS
Ardenn' Hôtel, 2
Auberge de Jeunesse (HI), 1
Au Bon Accueil, 3
Hôtel Thillois, 5

🍴 FOOD
Il Colosseo, 6
Le Cave de Rebiffe, 10
Le Kraft, 9
La Médina, 4

★ NIGHTLIFE
Carpe Diem, 7
Le Diam's, 8
L'Echiquier, 12
Le Havana, 11

and rue de Talleyrand (open M-Sa 8:30am-9pm); a smaller **Marché Plus** is on rue de Vesle. (Open M-Sa 9am-9pm, Su 9am-1pm.) The main **open-air market** is on pl. du Boulingrin near Porte Mars. (Open W and Sa 6am-1pm.)

■ **La Cave de Rebiffe,** 23 rue de Mars (☎03 26 46 10 00). Oenologists (wine specialists) run this brightly colored establishment, answering all conceivable grape-related questions and serving the greatest variety of wine and champagne around. A few full meals, but mostly appetizers. Open Tu-Sa 9am-8pm. MC/V. ❶

■ **Le Kraft,** 5 rue Salin (☎03 26 05 29 29). Restaurant, bar, gallery, cocktail lounge, and concert hall. The library is a perfect place to smoke, sip a glass of champagne (€5.95), and compose poetry to the beats of Ella Fitzgerald or heavy metal, jazz, and salsa concerts. Entrees €5-15. Open Tu-Sa 6pm-3am, food served until 2am. MC/V. ❷

La Médina, 13 rue de Chativesle (☎03 26 88 43 34). Serves North African food to Moroccan music. Couscous with meat €11-16.70. Open Sept.-June Tu-Sa noon-2pm and 7-10pm, Su noon-2pm; July-Aug. closed for lunch. ❸

Il Colosseo, 9-11 rue Thillois (☎03 26 47 68 50). Makes a valiant attempt to maintain a Roman theme, with plaster busts and fake fluted columns. Serves good Italian food. Pasta €7.90-11.50. Pizza €7.20-10.60. Salads €8-10.50. Open Tu-Sa 11:30am-2:30pm and 6:30-11:30pm. ❷

🔘 SIGHTS

The most popular sights are near the center of town, all easily reached on foot. The cathedral and the champagne *caves* are unquestionably the biggest draws. Many champagne firms give tours; the tourist office has info on hours, prices, and reservations. It may not be cheaper to buy champagne directly from the firms; ask the advice of wine shops near the cathedral, where there are often sales on local brands, and check the prices at Monoprix (see **Food,** above). Good bottles start at €9.15, half the price for champagne outside of France.

■ **CHAMPAGNE CAVES.** Four hundred kilometers of *crayères* (Roman chalk quarries) and two hundred kilometers of more modern French-built *caves* shelter bottled treasures. The most elegant tour is at the massive **Champagne Pommery.** Mme. Pommery took over her husband's business and became one of France's foremost vintners; her wealth allowed her to bring art into the workplace, lining the *cave* with exquisite carvings by Gustave Navlet. The firm boasts the largest *tonneau* (vat) in the world, carved by Emile Galle and sent to the 1904 World's Fair in St. Louis as a 75,000L gesture of goodwill. *(5 pl. du Général Gouraud. ☎03 26 61 62 56. Tours Mar. 18-Nov. 15 daily 11am-5pm; Nov. 18-Mar. 14 by reservation only. €7, students €3.50, children free.)* **Veuve Clicquot Ponsardin** is slightly less elegant, but with a free tour and tasting, who can complain? Tours pass by a small sample vineyard, wind through cellars made from ancient chalk mines, and offer a tasting. *(1 pl. des Droits de L'Homme. ☎03 26 89 53 90. Tours M-Sa 10am-6pm, Nov.-Mar. Sa closed; by reservation only. Free.)* If caves are your thing, you'll love **Taittinger**'s spectacularly spooky tunnels, dug by the Romans. Taittinger boasts an unbelievably informative (if self-aggrandizing) tour. You can see the largest champagne bottle in the world and watch the *dégorgement*, an exciting name for the sediment removal process. *(9 pl. St-Nicaise. ☎03 26 85 45 35. Open Mar.-Nov. M-F 9:30am-noon and 2-4:30pm, Sa-Su 9-11am and 2-5pm; last tours 1hr. before closing; Dec.-Feb. M-F 9:30am-noon and 2-4:30pm. €5.50.)*

CATHÉDRALE DE NOTRE-DAME. The three churches that have stood on this spot held the coronations of Clovis and 25 other French sovereigns. More recently, the current building witnessed the reconciliation between President de Gaulle and German Chancellor Adenauer in 1962. The present edifice is made of blocks of golden limestone quarried from the *caves*. WWI bombing destroyed most of the original stained glass, giving way to the most spectacular element of the modern cathedral, a sea-blue set of replacement windows by Marc Chagall. Outside, statues of local martyrs decorate the left porch, including the famous smiling angel of Reims. (☎03 26 77 45 25. *Open daily 7:30am-7:30pm. Tours in French July-Aug. M-Sa 10:30am and 4:30pm, Su 11am; in English daily 2:30pm; less frequent tours Oct. and late Mar. to mid-June. Tourist office also gives tours. €5.35, ages 12-25 and seniors €3.05.)*

PALAIS DU TAU. This former archbishop's residence got its name from its original floor plan, which resembled a "T." Its dazzling collection includes reliquaries dating back to Charlemagne; the show-stoppers are the magnificent 16th-century tapestries, sumptuous 50 ft. robes of Charles X, and massive statues. (*Pl. du Cardinal Luçon.* ☎03 26 47 81 79. *Open May-Aug. Tu-Su 9:30am-6:30pm; Sept.-Apr. 9:30am-12:30pm and 2-5:30pm. €5.50, ages 18-25 €3.50, under 18 free.)*

BASILIQUE ST-RÉMI. The basilica rises from a bed of lavender at the other end of town from the cathedral, near the Pommery and Taittinger *caves*. This Romanesque church with Gothic tinges was built around the tomb of St-Rémi, the bishop who baptized Clovis. (*Pl. St-Rémi. Open daily 9am-7pm. Light-and-sound shows July-Aug. Sa 9:30pm.)* Next door, the **Abbaye St-Rémi** shelters an extensive collection of religious art, military uniforms, and artifacts from the Merovingian and Carolingian eras. Look for the Enamels of St-Timothy, a fascinating series of engraved tiles depicting life under oppressive Roman rule. (*53 rue Simon.* ☎03 26 85 23 36. *Open M-F 2-6:30pm, Sa-Su 2-7pm. €2.)*

OTHER SIGHTS. Germany signed its surrender to the Allies on May 7, 1945, in a schoolroom across the railroad tracks. That schoolhouse is now the small **Musée de la Reddition.** A short film and several galleries of photos and timelines lead to the preserved, glassed-off room, which contains the thirteen chairs in which the British, French, American, Soviet, and German heads of state sat. (*12 rue Franklin Roosevelt.* ☎03 26 47 84 19. *Open W-M 10am-noon and 2-6pm. €3, children and students free. Ticket valid for one month, gains entry into 5 other sites and museums.)* The largest arch in the Roman empire still rises over the modern pl. de la République. The **Porte Mars** is decorated with reliefs of Romulus and Remus, who gave the city its name.

🔊🎭 ENTERTAINMENT AND FESTIVALS

The best nighttime entertainment is a stroll by the illuminated cathedral. The sidewalk then leads to the **Comédie de Reims,** chaussée Bocquaine, which presents a variety of plays. (☎03 26 48 49 10. *Tickets €15.25, students €4.60. Open Sept.-June.)* **Opéra Cinémas,** 3 rue Théodore Dubois, shows a range of films, some undubbed. (☎03 26 47 29 36. *Tickets €6-8. Ticket office open 1:30-10pm.)* The **Grand Théâtre de Reims,** rue de Vesle, hosts operas and ballets. (☎03 26 47 44 43. Box office at 13 rue Chanzy. *Open Oct.-June Tu-Sa 2:30-6:30pm. Tickets €7-42.)* In July and August, Reims hosts the fantastic **Flâneries Musicales d'Eté,** with more than 100 free concerts in 60 days.

At night, people concentrate in the cafés and bars of **pl. Drouet d'Erlon.** At **Le Kraft** (see **Food,** above), a window on the second floor looks down on a concert room which features jazz, salsa, blues, and world music. (*Concerts free-€9. Ask tourist office for schedule.)* Hidden off rue de Vesle, tropical-style **Le Havana,** 27 rue de Vesle, is the most diverse watering hole in town; live Afro-Cuban music fills the bar every other Friday. (☎03 26 86 85 07. *Happy hour daily 6-7pm with 2 beers for €2.50.)* **Carpe Diem,** 6 rue des Capucins, is a gay-friendly bar with three small rooms. (☎03 26 02 00 41. *Beer €2.50-3.30. Cocktail €3.90-4.60. Open Th 9pm-midnight, F-Sa 9pm-1:30am, Su 4-11pm).* The enormous club **L'Echiquier,** 110 av. Jean

Jaurès, is just outside the pedestrian district—walk in a group. Three tiers of top 40, techno, and rock make for a flashy, pheromone-filled evening. (☎03 26 89 12 38. Cover €6 for men, women €9; includes one drink. Open Th-Sa 10pm-5am. MC/V.) **Le Diam's,** 15 rue Lesange, is a gay dance club. Recently opened, it caters to an attractive bunch. (☎03 26 88 33 83. Cover F-Sa after 1am €12, free with *Let's Go* guide. Open Th-Su 11pm-4am, F-Sa 11pm-5am.)

🔲 DAYTRIP FROM REIMS: CHÂLONS-EN-CHAMPAGNE

Trains run from av. de la Gare to **Reims** *(30min., 8 per day, €5.05) and* **Paris** *(1½hr., 7-10 per day, €19). To reach the* **tourist office,** *3 quai des Arts, go left from the train station, and take another left at the roundabout onto av. Jean Jaurès and follow it across the tracks and the river; the office is several blocks down, on a little side street on the left, facing a canal. (15-20min.) (☎03 26 65 17 89; fax 03 26 65 35 65. Open June-Aug. M-Sa 9am-12:00pm and 1:30-6:30pm, Su 10:30am-12:30pm and 2:30-5:30pm; Sept.-May M-Sa 9am-noon and 1:30-6:30pm.)*

Having hidden out for years under the alias Châlons-sur-Marne, Châlons-en-Champagne (pop. 50,000) recently reverted to its original name. Not much else has changed here for centuries. As administrative center of Champagne, Châlons possesses little glamor or stunning scenery, but the churches of this river-knit city and a fascinating medieval cloister make it a worthwhile daytrip from Reims.

Alongside the Mau canal, in one of the prettier areas of town, sits Châlons's pride, the graceful **Notre-Dame-en-Vaux.** Constructed in a mix of Romanesque and Gothic styles between 1157 and 1217, the church boasts the largest peal of bells—56—in all of Europe. (Open June-Sept. M-Sa 10am-noon, 2-6pm, Su 2:30-6pm, Oct.-Apr. M-Sa 10am-noon and 2-6pm.) Behind the church, the tiny **Cloître de Notre-Dame-en-Vaux,** rue Nicolas-Durand, displays statuary unearthed from the ancient church cloister, much of it dating from the 12th century. The statues are beautifully detailed and virtually unique in the world. (☎03 26 64 03 87. Open W-M Apr. 1-Sept. 30 10am-noon and 2-6pm; Oct. 1-Mar. 31 10am-noon and 2-5pm. €4, students and children €2.50.) On the other side of the Marne river are the crypt and one remaining tower of the Romanesque **Cathédrale St-Étienne.** The remarkable stained glass ranges from the 13th-20th centuries. (Open M-Sa 10am-noon, 2-6pm, Su 2:30-6pm.) Châlons is prettiest in the magnificently sculpted gardens along the Marne River. **Le Petit Jard,** a country garden in the style of Napoleon III, is famous for its fantastical floral clock, while the nearby **Grand Jard** is criss-crossed by vast tree-lined esplanades.

EPERNAY

Wedged between three wealthy grape-growing regions, Epernay (pop. 30,000) is an appropriately ritzy town. The world's most distinguished champagne producers—Moët & Chandon, Perrier-Jouet, and Mercier, among others—inhabit the palatial mansions along av. de Champagne and keep their 700 million bottles of treasure in the 100km of tunnels underneath. If you're burning for bubbly, Epernay is for you; tour a cave, raise a glass, and taste the stars. At the heart of the *Route Touristique du Champagne,* Epernay is also an excellent base for exploring the countryside, including the Champagne route, a set of hikes through vineyards, châteaux, and mountains.

🔲 TRANSPORTATION. Epernay loses no time introducing you to its main attraction; entering by train from the east, you'll encounter the colorful tiled roofs and blue enameled signs of the de Castellane maison de champagne, on av. de Champagne. The train station is two blocks from the central pl. de la République. **Trains**

leave cours de la Gare. (Ticket office open Su-F 6am-8pm, Sa 6am-8pm. Info office open M-Sa 9am-6pm.) To: Paris (1¼hr., 18 per day, €16.60); Reims (25min., 16 per day, €5.20); Strasbourg (4½hr., 3 per day, €34). **STDM buses** (☎03 26 51 92 10) serve Paris, Reims, and small towns in Champagne. **Local buses** are run by **Sparnabus,** 30 pl. des Arcades. (☎03 26 55 55 50. Tickets €1, *carnet* of 10 €6.40. Open M 2-6pm, Tu-F 9am-noon and 2-6pm, Sa 9am-noon.) Rent **bikes** at **Rémi Royer,** 10 pl. Hugues Plomb. (☎03 26 55 29 61. €11 per half-day, €17 per day, €77 per week. Open Tu-Sa 9am-noon and 2-7pm. MC/V.)

■ ▨ **ORIENTATION AND PRACTICAL INFORMATION.** To get to the **tourist office,** 7 av. de Champagne, from the station, walk straight ahead through pl. Mendès France, pass a fountain, walk one block up rue Gambetta or rue J. Moët to **pl. de la République,** and turn left onto av. de Champagne. (5min.) The welcoming staff gives you free maps, a list of hotels, info on Epernay's *caves,* and suggestions for *routes champenoises.* They also publish *On Sort?,* a free monthly list of local events and festivities. (☎03 26 53 33 00; fax 03 26 51 95 22. Open Easter-Oct. 15 M-Sa 9:30am-12:30pm and 1:30-7pm, Su 11am-4pm; mid-Oct. to Easter M-Sa 9:30am-12:30pm and 1:30-5:30pm. Train tours 50min. Tu-Su 7 per day; €4.60, under 16 €2.80.) Other services include: **currency exchange** at **Banque de France,** pl. de la République (M-F 8:45am-noon and 1:45-4pm; no bills larger than US$50); **Laundremat,** 8 Ave Jean Jaurés (☎03 26 54 96 15; open daily 7am-8pm); **police,** 7 rue Jean-Moët (☎03 26 56 96 60); the **hospital,** 137 rue de l'Hôpital (☎03 26 58 70 70). Access the **Internet** at **l'Icone Café,** 25 rue de l'Hôpital Auban Moët. (☎03 26 55 73 93. €4.60 per hr. Open July-Aug M-Th noon-midnight, F-Sa noon-1am, Su 3pm-midnight; Sept-June M noon-11pm, Tu-Th 11am-11pm, F-Sa 11am-1am, Su 3-8pm. MC/V.) Or try **Le Babylone,** 25 rue Gambetta. (☎03 26 55 96 44, €4 per hr. Open Tu-Sa noon-8pm.) The **post office,** pl. Hugues Plomb, has **currency exchange.** (☎03 26 53 31 60. Open M-F 8am-7pm, Sa 8am-noon.) **Postal code:** 51200.

▨ ▢ **ACCOMMODATIONS AND FOOD.** Epernay caters to the champagne set—budget hotels are rare. ▨**Hôtel St-Pierre ❷,** 14 av. Paul-Chandon, near pl. d'Europe, is the best bet for your money. Luxuriously floral halls lead to three floors of spacious, antique-furnished rooms. (☎03 26 54 40 80; fax 03 26 57 88 68. Breakfast €5. Reception 7am-10pm. Singles and doubles €21, with shower €25-32; extra bed €5. MC/V.) For hostel-style accommodations without the ambience, try the **Foyer des Jeunes Travailleurs ❶,** 2 rue Pupin, which maintains large, four-bed rooms with desks and sinks, laundry facilities, and a cafeteria. From the station, cross the grassy square, turn left onto rue de Reims, and make a quick right onto rue Pupin. Only five rooms are available to travelers; reserve ahead. (☎03 26 51 62 51; fax 03 26 54 15 60. Cafeteria open M-F lunch and dinner, Sa lunch only. Breakfast €2.30. Meals €7.95. Laundry. Kitchen. Reception M-F 9am-8pm, Sa 10am-2pm. Bunks €11.) There is a **campground ❶** about 1.5km from the station (dir: Reims) at allée de Cumières. (☎03 26 55 32 14. Open mid-Apr. to mid-Sept. 7am-10pm. €2.50 per person, €1.30 per child, €3 per tent and car. Electricity €2.80.)

The pedestrian district around pl. des Arcades and pl. Hugues Plomb is dotted with delis and bakeries. There are Italian, Moroccan, Asian, and Turkish eateries on rue Gambetta. There's a **Marché Plus** at 13 pl. Hugues Plomb. (☎03 26 51 89 89. Open M-Sa 7am-9pm, Su 9am-1pm.) Halle St-Thibault hosts a **market.** (Open W and Sa 8am-noon.) You might consider the cafeteria at the **Foyer.** (Open daily 11:30am-1:30pm.) **Le Kilimanjara ❶,** 15 pl. de la République, is not a bit African, but has a mountainous selection of salads (€2.90-8.50), pastas (€6.80), and the most garish green-and-yellow decor this side of a pineapple skin. (☎03 26 51 61 60. Open W-Su noon-2pm and 7-10pm, Tu noon-2pm. MC/V.)

CHAMPAGNE

⬛ **SIGHTS.** The name says it all: **av. de Champagne** is a long, broad strip of palatial *maisons de champagne* pouring out bubbly to hordes of visitors. The tours
below are all offered in French or English; no reservations are required. All
include a *petite dégustation* (ages 16+ only). *Caves* are usually around 10°C;
bring a sweater. Each firm's tour may give more or less the same explanation of
the process, but everything from the dress of the guides to the design of the lobby
reflects the status and character of the producer. The grandaddy of them all, the
producer of Dom Perignon, is ⬛**Moët & Chandon,** 20 av. de Champagne, which has
been "turning nature into art" since 1743. The mansion is full of as much old-
money elegance as you'd expect. The 50min. tour details the basic steps in champagne production and gives a detailed history of champagne and M&C in particular. The *caves* feel authentic, though the 7min. film fairly tingles with pompous
melodrama. (☎03 26 51 20 20. Open Apr.-Nov. 11 daily 9:30-11:30am and 2-4:30pm;
Nov. 12-Mar. M-F only. Tour with one glass €7, two glasses €15, three glasses
€19; ages 12-16 €4, under 12 free.). Slightly less famous but equally swanky, **Mercier,** 70 av. de Champagne, 10min. away, is in the middle of a vineyard. The self-proclaimed "most popular champagne in France" certainly knows how to market
itself. The film is a slick advertisement, but their 30min. tour in roller coaster-style
cars is fun. (☎03 26 51 22 22. Open Mar.-Nov. M-F 9:30-11:30am and 2-4:30pm, Sa-
Su until 5pm; Dec. 1-19 and Jan. 13-Feb. Th-M only. €6, ages 12-16 €3, under 12
free.) Across the street is **De Castellane,** 57 rue de Verdun. Their tour is less romantic than at M&C and Mercier, but it gets into the nitty-gritty of champagne production. Visitors during the week can observe factory workers unloading, corking,
and labeling. (☎03 26 51 19 11. Open Apr.-Dec. 24 daily 10am-noon and 2-6pm, last
tours 11:15am and 5:15pm. Full *cave* tour with tasting €6, tower and museum with
tasting €3.) **Demoiselle Vranken,** 42 rue de Champagne, is a relatively new arrival.
The lively, hip staff leads small, casual tours. (☎03 26 59 50 50. Open M-Sa 9:30am-
noon and 2-5pm; Oct.-Apr. Sa closed. Tour with tasting €3.50, under 15 free.)

For a laid-back and cheap but authentic alternative to the big maisons, ask the
tourist office about *l'esprit de champagne*, a free presentation and sampling
given by several smaller companies in the tourist office. (June to late Oct. F-Sa;
July-Aug. Th. Obtain tickets in advance.)

🎭 **ENTERTAINMENT.** The city's limited selection of watering holes tend to fill up
surprisingly at night. **Le Progrès,** 5 pl. de la République, draws a mix of 20-some-
things and their elders for languorous champagne sipping on a packed terrace.
(☎03 26 55 22 72. Glass of champagne €5.70. Food served Tu-Su 6am-midnight.)
From the end of June to the third week in August, free **concerts** are held at 7pm at
the Château Perrier on av. de Champagne. (Tu classical, Th jazz.) There is occasional rock and world music at **pl. Mendès France.**

TROYES

With its principal roads cleverly forming the shape of a champagne cork, Troyes
(pop. 60,000) may cause visitors to wonder whether the city plan is a serendipitous
historical quirk or a tourist gimmick. If the latter were true, the Troyes founders
must have been very far-sighted, for Troyes has been a prominent city since the
Middle Ages. It was here that Chrétien de Troyes wrote *Parsifal*, Jewish scholar
Rashi translated the Bible and the Talmud, and a local shoemaker's son became
Pope Urbain IV. In addition to its relaxed, family-centered culture, Troyes boasts
one of France's best-preserved *vieille villes*, filled with Renaissance half-timbered fountains and narrow alleyways.

CONNING CONNOISSEURSHIP Follow these steps and you'll rival Dom Perignon for bubbly expertise. (1) Choose your champagne wisely. *Brut* is an apéritif, but *vintage brut* goes with meat and mild cheese. *Chardonnay* accompanies fish or shellfish, while *Rose* or *demi-sec* complements dessert. (2) Look at the label. *Tête de Cuvée* is made from the finest juices. *Grand Cru* comes from the higest quality grapes. *Premier Cru* is a step below that, *Cru* is from the bottom of the barrel. *Millésime* is a vintage bottle. (3) When the champagne is served, take it by the stem to avoid warming the liquid with your hand. (4) Inspect before you drink. When freshly poured, there should be a string of bubbles shooting straight up from the bottom of the glass. The more delicate the champagne, the smaller the bubbles. (5) Smell the champagne once, swish it around and smell it again. The odor will change between the two sniffs and should reveal aromas like coffee, brioche, lemon, grapefruit, and spice. For best effect, refrain from smoking, wearing perfume, or eating pungent foods beforehand. Taste the champagne, rolling it around your tongue to reveal different tastes. Rinse and repeat often—you'll pay double for far lowlier champagne back home.

TRANSPORTATION

Trains: av. Maréchal Joffre (☎08 36 35 35 35 for info and reservations). Open M-Sa 9-11:45am and 2:15-6:30pm. To **Mulhouse** (3hr., 9 per day, €31.80) and **Paris** (1½hr., 14 per day, €8.60).

Buses: Go left as you exit the train station and enter the door just around the corner labeled *Gare Routière*. **SDTM TransChampagne** (☎03 26 65 17 07) runs to **Reims** (2hr., 2 per day, €18.50). **Les Rapides de Bourgogne** (☎03 86 94 95 00) runs to **Auxerre** (2½hr., M-Th 1 per day, €13).

Public Transportation: L'Autoville (☎03 25 70 49 00), in front of the market. Open M-Sa 8am-12:45pm and 1:30-7pm. Extensive and frequent (every 12-23min.) service. Tickets €1.10, 3 for €2.90.

Taxis: Taxis Troyens (☎03 25 78 30 30), across the street from the station on the curb in front of the Grand Hôtel. Base charge €2.30; before 7pm €1 per km, after 7pm €1.55 per km. Service Su-Th 4am-midnight, F-Sa 24hr.

Car Rental: Europcar, 6 av. President Coty (☎03 25 78 37 66). Open 7:30am-12:30pm and 1:30-6:30pm. **Budget,** 10 rue Voltaire (☎03 25 73 27 37). Open daily 8am-noon and 2-6:30pm.

ORIENTATION AND PRACTICAL INFORMATION

Troyes's train station is just three blocks from the *vieille ville*. The main tourist office is one block from the train station exit, on your right, at the corner of bd. Carnot; a branch office is near the town center on rue Mignard.

Tourist Office: 16 bd. Carnot (☎03 25 82 62 70; www.tourisme-troyes.fr) and rue Mignard off rue Emile Zola (☎03 25 73 36 88). Free detailed city map. Accommodations service. Both branches open M-Sa 9am-12:30pm and 2-6:30pm, July-mid-Sept. extended to 10am-7pm; rue Mignard branch also open Su 10am-noon and 2-5pm.

Money: Société Générale, 11 pl. Maréchal Foch (☎03 25 43 57 00; fax 03 25 43 57 57), has **currency exchange** for a hefty commission. Open M-F 8:30am-12:20pm and 1:30-6pm, Sa 8:30-12:45pm. When banks are closed, the **tourist office** on rue Mignard (see above) will exchange currency.

FROM THE ROAD

GAY TRIPPER

Whenever I get to a new town, my eyes hunt for signs of a Lesbian, Gay, Bisexual, Transgender community. I'm not looking for romance of any sort. I just want to be with folks who have an identity similar to mine, find a place where I'm not in the minority anymore. Okay, and maybe a few flirtatious glances for fun. But cultural cues can be frustratingly different in France. I'll see a woman with short, spiky hair and my "gay-dar" will start ringing, until I realize that she's looking lovingly at the boy next to her.

I was feeling pretty lonely when I got to Troyes until I saw a timid rainbow flag hanging above an otherwise average-looking hotel. I excitedly asked the owner about it, and he introduced me to his friend, a gay nightclub manager. In response to my onslaught of questions, he brought me to his favorite gay-friendly café, where I met the bartender and a bunch of people. From that point on, I was practically one of the gang.

In retrospect, the situation makes sense. In small towns, LGBT tourists are pretty rare. I found local folks much more friendly than big city folk, where hundreds of temporary travelers like me are trying to discover their subculture every weekend. Of course, having some new friends didn't hurt.

Finding that hotel in Troyes was dumb luck, and I haven't had the same fortune in many other small towns. But finding a town with an LGBT community has reassured me that there are more LGBT French folks are out there, even if I can't always find them. —*Laure de Vulpillières*

Cultural Center: Maison du Boulanger, 16 rue Champeaux (☎03 25 43 55 00; tickets and administration around the corner at 42 Paillot de Montabert). Info on festivals, exhibits, and concerts. Open M-F 9am-noon and 2-6pm, Sa 10am-noon and 2-5pm.

Laundromat: 11 rue Clemenceau. Open daily 7:30am-8pm.

Police: ☎03 25 43 51 00.

Hospital: 101 av. Anatole France (☎03 25 49 49 49). For emergency medical service, call ☎03 25 71 99 00.

Internet Access: Open Games, 24 rue Huez (☎03 25 41 58 71). €2.80 per hr. Open daily M 2pm-10pm, Tu-Th 11am-10pm, F-Sa 11am-midnight, Su 2pm-8pm. **Cyber Wan,** 20 rue Hetz (☎03 25 40 86 95). €3 per hr. Open M-Th noon-8pm, F-Sa 2pm-10pm.

Post Office: 2 pl. Général Patton (☎03 25 45 29 00). From the train station, turn right onto bd. Carnot and walk down one block. Open M-F 9am-noon and 1:30-6:30pm, Sa 9am-noon. **Postal code:** 10000. **Poste Restante:** 10013 Troyes-Voltaire.

🏠 ACCOMMODATIONS AND CAMPING

Les Comtes de Champagne, 56 rue de la Monnaie (☎03 25 73 11 70; fax 03 25 73 06 02). On a quiet street just minutes from the train station and city center. It's hard to imagine a nicer place to stay in Troyes than this 16th-century mansion and its spacious, modern, tastefully decorated rooms with TV. Breakfast €4.90. Reception 7am-10:30pm. Reserve ahead. Singles with shared shower €24.40, with private shower €30.50; doubles from €27.45, €33.55; triples €44.20-54.90; quads €48.90-58; some large rooms fit 5 or 6. Extra bed €4.90. DC/V. ❷

Hôtel le Trianon, 2 rue Pithou (☎03 25 73 18 52). Clean, unspectacular, fairly quiet rooms. Breakfast €4.50. Reception 6:30am-8pm. One person €20; 2 people €25, with shower €34. Extra person €4.60. MC/V. ❷

Hôtel Ambassy Club, 49 rue Raymond Poincaré (☎03 25 73 12 03). With the town hall to your left, proceed down rue de la République as it becomes rue Raymond Poincaré. The hotel is 3 blocks down on the left, above a smoky *brasserie.* Breakfast €4.60. Reception (at bar) 7am-3am. Singles €20.60; one double and one triple €24.40 per person. Closed weekends. AmEx/MC/V. ❷

Camping Municipal (☎03 25 81 02 64), on N60 2km from town. Take bus #1 (dir: Pont St-Marie) to this 3-star site. Includes the creature comforts of showers, toilets, TV, and laundry. Open Apr. 1-Oct. 15. €4 per person, €4.60 per tent or car. ❶

📷 FOOD

The **quartier St-Jean** is the place to be for a meal and local chatter. Cafés, *brasseries*, and inexpensive *crêperies* line the pedestrian **rue Champeaux** on the way to pl. Alexandre Israël. On the other side of the *vieille ville*, reasonably priced kebab places dot the **rue de la Cité** near the cathedral. Government regulations and a relaxed lifestyle result in many restaurants being closed on weekends.

It would be a shame not to take full advantage of Troyes's beautiful parks—the pl. de la Libération is the perfect backdrop for a mid-afternoon snack. **Les Halles,** an English-style market behind the bus station (turn left down rue de la République from the town hall), offers a fresh selection of produce, meats, and baked goods from the Aube region. Try creamy *fromage de Troyes* or the *andouillette de Troyes*, a popular tripe sausage. (Open M-Th 8am-12:45pm and 3:30-7pm, F-Sa 7am-7pm, Su 9am-12:30pm. Many stalls take MC/V.) Grab generic grub at the **Monoprix** supermarket, 71 rue Emile Zola. (☎03 25 73 10 78. Open M-Sa 8:30am-8pm.)

🦪 **Aux Crieurs de Vin,** 4-6 pl. Jean Jaurès (☎03 25 40 01 01). This cool, minimalist eatery is part restaurant, part wine cellar. The knowledgeable staff will help you choose the perfect local wine to complement your charcuterie. A meal and glass of wine run €10.50. Open Tu-Sa 10am-2pm, 7:30-10:30pm; bar 11am-11pm; *cave* M 3-7pm, Tu-Sa 10am-9pm. MC/V. ❷

La Taverne de l'Ours, 2 rue Champaux (☎03 25 73 22 18). Located right off the town's main plaza, pl. Alexandre Israël, this popular restaurant's terrace is a great way to see and be seen. All-you-can-eat mussels or pork for €10.50, generous salads for €15. Open daily noon-2:30pm and 7-11pm. MC/V. ❸

Café-Restaurant l'Union, 34 rue Champeaux (☎03 25 40 35 76). This newly established hotspot serves up traditional favorites to local folk on its private terrace. Open noon-2pm and 7-11pm, bar 11am-3am. ❸

📷📷 SIGHTS AND OUTDOORS

CATHÉDRALE ST-PIERRE ET ST-PAUL. The sheer verticality of this cathedral with fluted pillars is only slightly less stunning than its spectacular stained glass. Ranging in age from a youthful 100 to an ancient 700, the *vitraux* are in many cases as delicate as lace. In the late morning, those on the east rose window scatter a kaleidoscope of light on the floor. Suffering invasions and natural disasters, the cathedral has been frequently rebuilt, making it a living history of Troyen architecture. (☎03 25 76 26 80. Pl. St-Pierre, down rue Clemenceau past the town hall. Enter the courtyard to the right of the cathedral; the entrance to the museum is on the right. No charge. Open daily 10am-noon and 2-5pm, except M morning.)

MUSÉE D'ART MODERNE. This collection of over 2000 works of French art from 1850 to 1950 is Troyes's cultural centerpiece. Sculptures, paintings, and drawings by Degas, Rodin, Picasso, and Seurat are joined by a garden filled with African and Oceanic sculptures that have influenced 20th-century French art. (Pl. St-Pierre; directions as above. €6, under 25 €0.80; free W. Open Tu-Su 11am-6pm.)

BASILIQUE ST-URBAIN. Come at night to see the basilica's spear-like spires illuminated against the dark sky or visit in daylight to whistle appreciatively at its flying buttresses. The archetypally Gothic structure was commissioned when Jacques Pantaléon became Pope Urbain IV; it lies upon the site of the Pope's father's cobbler shop. (☎03 25 73 37 13. Walk down rue Clemenceau from the Hôtel de Ville. Open daily 10am-noon and 2-5 pm; closed Su and M morning.)

MUSÉE DES BEAUX-ARTS. The Abbaye St-Loup has been converted into a museum with an interesting hodge-podge of archaeological finds, medieval sculptures, and 15th- to 19th-century paintings. Contained within is one of France's oldest libraries, with some volumes dating back 1300 years. (☎03 25 76 21 60. *4 rue Chrétien-de-Troyes, near the cathedral. Walking from the canal along rue de la Cité, take a left on rue Mitantier; the entrance is on the left. Open W-M 10am-noon, 2-6pm. €5.60, under 25 €0.80; free W and first Su of month. Ticket accesses Musée de la Pharmacie and Musée de Vauluisant.)*

OTHER SIGHTS. Troyes's museums delve deeply into the rich local social history, particularly the craft traditions that put it on the map in medieval times. The **Maison de l'Outil et de la Pensée Ouvrière** is a beautifully restored 16th-century *hôtel*. Once the central workshop of the town's knitwear industry, it now exhibits over 7000 tools from the 17th- and 18th-century *(7 rue de la Trinité, off rue Emile Zola. ☎03 25 73 28 26. Open M-F 9am-1pm and 2-6:30pm, Sa-Su 10am-1pm and 2-6pm. €6.50, students €5, families €16.)* The **Musée de Vauluisant** displays a collection of medieval Troyen sculpture, and also houses the textile-oriented **Musée de la Bonneterie**, whose cave details the history of tile-making. *(☎03 25 42 33 33. 4 rue de Vauluisant. Open W-Su 10am-noon and 2-6pm.)* The 12th-century **Eglise Ste-Madeleine**, off ruelle des Chats (so named because the houses are close enough for cats to stroll from roof to roof), is proud owner of an impressive stone screen that separates the nave from the chancel. *(☎03 25 73 82 90. Open Tu-Sa 10am-noon and 2-5pm, M and Su 2-5pm.)*

EXCURSIONS. Over 12,500 acres of freshwater lakes dot the region around Troyes. The sunny waters of Lake Orient welcome sunbathers, swimmers, and windsurfers. Wilder Lake Temple is reserved for fishing and bird watching. Lake Amance roars with speedboats and screaming waterskiers. The **Comité Départemental du Tourisme de l'Aube,** 34 quai Dampierre, provides free brochures. *(☎03 25 42 50 00; fax 03 25 42 50 88. Open M-F 8:45am-noon and 1:30-6pm.)* The tourist office has bus schedules for the Troyes-Grands Lacs routes. In July and August, the **Courriers de l'Aube** takes travelers to Lake Orient three times daily (one-way €4.95).

🎵 ENTERTAINMENT

Movie theaters, arcades, and pool halls neighbor chic boutiques on **rue Emile Zola.** On warm evenings, lots of Troyens and even more tourists swarm the cafés and taverns of **rue Champeaux** and **rue Mole** near pl. Alexandre Israël. **Bar Montabert,** 24 rue Paillot de Montabert, has a gregarious owner and loyal pub crowd and is one of the many fine bars on this happening street. *(☎03 25 73 58 04. Open daily noon-3pm and 6pm-3am.)* The friendly but non-descript **Berny's Café,** 43 rule Molé, is the central hang-out spot for Troyes's gay and lesbian population, though the clientele is 40% straight. *(☎06 22 63 06 62. Open daily 10am-midnight.)*

The hottest nightclub in Troyes is the appropriately-named ▓**Privilège**, 5 rue de la Republique, which goes by the motto "que la fête soit avec vous,"—i.e., the DJs tailor the music to suit the changing tastes of the crowd. On F and Sa nights, Privilège is 25+, but it often joins forces with its less agist neighbor **Atlantide** to help out the younger crowd. *(☎03 25 73 85 76. Cover €3.60-5.50, includes 1 drink; no cover Tu for women, Th for everyone. Drinks €5.50. Open daily F-Sa 10pm-4am, Su-Th 11pm-4am.)*

Lest it become known solely for the art of imbibing the bubbly, Troyes hosts a number of festivals and special events. **Le Chemin des Bâtisseurs de Cathédrales,** a free sound-and-light spectacle, is held in the Cathedral of St-Rémy Friday and Saturday nights at 10pm, from the last weekend in June to the end of the summer. Summer in Troyes also sees **Ville en Musique,** a series of concerts held in churches or outside. *(☎03 25 43 55 00 or stop by the Cultural Center for more info.)*

LANGRES

Perched prettily above the fertile Marne valley, tiny Langres (pop. 10,000) deserves its reputation as one of France's 50 most beautiful towns. Because of its elevation and central position between Champagne, Burgundy, and Franche-Comté, the town was founded by the Romans as a stronghold. Years later, it became famous as the birthplace of philosopher Denis Diderot, who ambitiously recorded the known world in his 18th century encyclopedia (see p. 23). To walking on the well-preserved ramparts of this friendly and charmingly proud little town is to feel on top of the world.

⌁ TRANSPORTATION. Langres sits 3km away—and half a kilometer up—from its train station. **Trains** roll north to Paris (3hr., 9 per day, €29.20) and west to Reims (2½hr., 7 per day, €23.60) and Troyes (1¼hr., 7 per day, €15.50). Local **buses** run sporadically between the station and the town center (1 ticket €0.85, 10 tickets €5.55). Schedules of departure times and stops are posted at the train station and the tourist office. The impatient can call a **taxi** (☎ 03 25 87 47 31; €9 from the station to pl. Bel'Air). For the way down, the brave rent **bikes** from **Diderot Cycles et Loisirs,** 67 rue Diderot (☎ 03 25 87 06 98; open Tu-Sa 9am-noon and 2-6pm; €9 per half-day, €13 per day, €22 for the weekend; €200 deposit).

▣ ⁊ ORIENTATION AND PRACTICAL INFORMATION. The **tourist office,** located in sq. Olivier Halle, is just across from the pl. Bel'Air bus stop. The friendly staff provides a free and very useful regional guide and reserves rooms in person for €1. **Value tickets** (€5, students €3.50, under 18 free) provide access to all the major local sights. The office also provides **audio guides** in English (€3). (☎ 03 25 87 67 67. Open July 15-Aug. 15 M-Sa 9am-12:30pm and 1:30-7pm, Su 10:30am-12:30pm and 2-6pm; Apr. and Oct. M-Sa 9am-noon and 1:30-6pm; rest of year M-Sa 9am-noon and 1:30-6:30pm, Su 10:30am-12:30pm and 2-6pm.) You can also rumble along the ramparts for an hour on the shameful *train touristique*. (Leaves from pl. Bel'Air. Tickets €4.80, under 12 €3.20. July-Aug. 7 per day 10am-6pm; May-June and Sept. W and Sa-Su afternoons 3 per day.) The **police** are at the Hôtel de Ville on rue Charles Beligne (☎ 03 25 87 00 40). Medical care is available at the **Centre Hospitalier,** 10 rue de la Charité (☎ 03 25 87 88 88). On Mondays, the only **currency exchange** option is at the **post office,** rue Général Leclerc. (☎ 03 25 84 33 30. Open M-F 8am-noon and 1:30-6pm, Sa 8am-noon.) **Postal code:** 52200.

⌂ ACCOMMODATIONS AND CAMPING. Set right outside the Porte des Moulins by the tourist office. the **Foyer des Jeunes Travailleurs (HI) ❶,** pl. des États-Unis, offers pleasant, modern dorm rooms, kitchen access, and an adjoining cafeteria. Though slightly institutional, it has outstanding views and is the best bargain in town. From the tourist office, walk out through the 17th century gateway and take a left; the hostel will be on your immediate left. (☎ 03 25 87 09 69. Breakfast €2.50. Lunch daily 11:45am-1:30pm, dinner 7-8:15pm. Sheets €2.50. Reception M-F 9am-12:30pm and 2-7pm, Sa 10:30am-noon. Singles €11.20; doubles €16. Discount after 4 nights.) When the Foyer is full, try the smaller and more expensive **Auberge Jeanne d'Arc ❸,** 26 rue Gambetta, on pl. Jenson across from Eglise St-Martin, which has small but elegant rooms. (☎ 03 25 86 87 88. Breakfast €6.10. Reception daily 7am-11pm. Singles and doubles with shower €27.45-38.10. Extra person €4.60. MC/V.) The **Hôtel de la Poste ❷,** 8 & 10 pl. Ziegler, is a comfortable, inexpensive, and centrally located establishment with medium-sized rooms that would seem spacious if their ceiling were not covered by garish wallpaper. (☎ 03 25 87 10 51; fax 03 25 88 46 18. Breakfast €5. Reception open daily 7am-10pm. Singles €22, with shower €35; doubles and triples with shower €44. MC/V.)

CHAMPAGNE

REINVENTING DIDEROT. For more than 40 years, the students of the local Collège Diderot have celebrated on their graduation day at the expense of their celebrated namesake and fellow Langrois. Each year in late May, the students dress poor Diderot in themed costumes to mark the end of their high school careers. "Zon Zon," as the statue is affectionately known, generally remains in costume for more than a week. In past manifestations, the hapless philosopher has become a hippie, a priest, and a member of *Loft Story*—a popular teen reality TV show. Fulfilling every college guy's dream, he has even been endowed with a 1.5m phallus. This year he sacrificed sex for finance. A cardboard euro was hung around his neck, a cardboard euro skirt placed around his waist, and authentic euros scattered all over his pedestal.

Camping Navarre ❶ occupies prime hilltop space right next to the 16th-century Tour de Navarre at the edge of the old town, with fabulous views over the ramparts. (☎/fax 03 25 87 37 92. Reception July-Aug. 6-8am and 4-10:30pm; Sept.-June 6-8am and 4-8pm. Gates closed 10pm-6:30am. €1.70, €1 under 7, €3.50 with tent or car. Electricity €2.75.)

◻ **FOOD.** From fresh *foie gras* to the soft orange-cased *fromage de Langres* to the local sweet currant apéritif *rubis de groseilles*, Langrois's *spécialités de terroir* are still made the old-fashioned way: on the farm. Many of these farms provide *dégustation* tours; the regional guide available at the tourist office provides contact info. Those who wish to remain protected by the city walls can still sample the Langrois cuisine. The **market** at pl. Jenson is open Friday mornings, and cafés on the side streets near pl. Diderot offer plates of *fromage de Langres*. The cafetaria at the Foyer is cheap but surprisingly tasty (closed F and Sa night). You'll find cheap, generic goods at **Aldi** supermarket, rue des Chavannes just before pl. Bel'Air. (Open M-F 9am-12:15pm and 2-7pm, Sa 9am-7pm.) Restaurants, like everything else in town, keep close to **rue Diderot. Café de Foy ❷**, pl. Diderot, serves up fresh local specials. Everybody orders the salad with walnuts and warm *fromage de Langres* (€6.60), although you might not want to pass up the *formule rapide*, the dish of the day with dessert and coffee for €11.50. (☎03 25 87 09 86. Open June-Aug. Su-Th 7am-midnight, F-Sa 7-1:30am. MC/V.)

◪ **SIGHTS.** The ramparts have been the soul of Langres for millennia; fittingly, the best sights can be viewed from their lofty height. A good starting point is the squat **Tour de Navarre,** on the southeast corner. Erected in 1521 by François Ier, this outpost defended the city with 7m-thick walls and spiral ramp for moving artillery. (Tower open July-Aug. daily 10am-12:30pm and 2:30-7pm; May-June and Sept. Sa-Su 2-6pm. €2.50, under 12 €1.50.) The first-century AD **Porte Gallo-Romane,** toward the center of the south wall, is the oldest of the seven gates that allow entrance into the fortifications. Farther clockwise stands the **Tour du Petit Sault,** now closed. On the north wall there remains one lonely and immobile train car to commemorate the **Old Cog Railway,** the first link between the town and the valley below. **Place de la Crémaillère,** just after the railway, overlooks farmland and the glittering **réservoir de la Liez,** which offers swimming, boating, and camping. A few steps ahead lies the **Table d'Orientation,** a fun 19th-century panel noting visible landmarks as well as far-flung destinations like Moscow and Constantinople. Last is the zippy glass-and-steel **Panoramics,** a 20th-century answer to the cog railway, which whisks down the ramparts to the parking lot and road below free of charge.

The best view in town is from the south tower of the 12th-century **Cathédrale St-Mammès,** which dominates the center of town. The cathedral is an impressive combination of Burgundian-Romanesque and Gothic styles. It was given the name and patronage of St-Mammès when his relics were donated to Langres. Two gold reliquaries still house the grisly remains of the saint. (€2.50, under 12 €1.50. Tours in French 2:30pm, 3:30pm, 4:30pm, and 5:30pm. Cathedral open daily 8am-7pm. Treasury open July-Aug. W-M 2:30-6pm.) For the **Ronde des Hallebardiers,** locals in full Renaissance costume recreate the night watchman's patrol of more turbulent times. (Aug. F and Sa 9:15pm.) If your French is up to par, get your cape and galli-vant about the town banishing the bandits and spooks of yore; otherwise chortle over the proceedings along the sidelines. It all ends in music and drink at a Renais-sance tavern. (Info ☎03 25 90 77 40. €12, students €9. Begins at the cathedral cloister.) Every Saturday in June, the **Fête du Petard** celebrates the defense of Lan-gres in 1591 against attackers from Lorraine who unsuccessfully tried to destroy the city gates with a pétard (bomb). Dancers, fire eaters, and jugglers mark the three-century old tradition. (For info, call ☎03 25 90 77 40).

In the center of town sits the **Musée d'Art et d'Histoire,** pl. du Centenaire, which exhibits artifacts from Langrois prehistory, Egypt, and Rome. The panels are in French, but are so impressive that non-French speakers will appreciate them. (☎03 25 87 08 05. €4, students €1.70, under 18 free. Open Apr.-Oct. W-M 10am-noon and 2-6pm, Nov.-Mar. 10am-noon and 2-5pm.)

FLANDERS AND THE PAS DE CALAIS

Even after five decades of peace, the memory of two world wars is never far from the inhabitants of northern France. Nearly every town bears scars from merciless bombing in World War II, and German-built concrete observation towers still peer over the dunes. Regiments of tombstones stand as reminders of the terrible toll exacted at Arras, Cambrai, and the Somme.

Flanders (on the Belgian border), the coastal Pas de Calais, and Picardy (farther inland) remain the final frontiers of tourist-free France. Although thousands traveling to and from Britain pass through the channel ports every day, few take the time to explore the ancient towns between the ports and Paris. This has left the countryside unspoiled by commercial traffic and the natives welcoming to travelers. Chalk cliffs loom over the beaches along the rugged coast, and cultivation gives way to cows and sheep grazing near collapsed bunkers. Once part of an independent state, the wooden windmills and gabled houses still show Flemish influence. In Picardy, seas of wheat extend in all directions, broken in spring and summer by eruptions of red poppies. As you flee the ferry ports, don't overlook the hidden treasures: the cathedrals of Amiens and Laon, the intriguing Flemish culture of Arras, the world-class art collections of Lille, and the rural charm of small towns like Montreuil-sur-Mer, whose imposing ramparts top a green valley.

TRANSPORTATION

A logical base for a visit to the North is **Lille,** capital of the region and a major transportation hub. Getting to smaller towns often involves changing trains in **Amiens.** Ferries usually dock in the **Channel Ports,** where no one wants to linger; **Boulogne** is the most pleasant port of arrival. The **Channel Tunnel** connects France to Britain at Calais and provides a viable alternative to ferries (for more info, see **Getting There: By Channel Tunnel,** p. 66). The countryside is flat enough to allow bicycling, but towns are far apart. Consult local tourist offices for maps and routes.

1	**Lille:** Big city; lots of foreigners; untouristed for its size and appeal; great baroque **(p. 779)**
2	**Douai:** A quintessentially Flemish town, with a belfry and canal **(p. 783)**
3	**Arras:** Known for its gabled houses, chalk tunnels, and nearby WWI memorials **(p. 785)**
4	**Laon:** One of France's finest cathedrals—*really.* Check out the fabulous views **(p. 787)**
5	**Dunkerque:** Minor channel port famous for the Allied scramble there; don't go **(p. 792)**
6	**Calais:** Lively ferry port flooded with British tourists; don't stay **(p. 790)**
7	**Boulogne-sur-Mer:** Most genial of the Channel ports; exceptional fine-arts museum **(p. 789)**
8	**Montreuil:** A surprisingly stylish, art-loving, flower-lined little town **(p. 794)**
9	**Amiens:** More lively than most; known for its cathedral and floating gardens **(p. 795)**

778

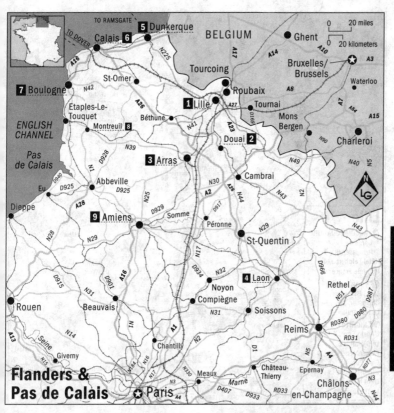

LILLE

Lille (pop. 175,000) has been an international hub since the 11th century, but Charles de Gaulle's hometown retains a Flemish flavor, from the architecture of the beautiful *vielle ville* to its inhabitants's rabid consumption of mussels and beer. France's 4th largest metropolis is much more inviting and exciting than the region's ports. With 100,000 students nearby and 25% of the population under 25, the nightlife in Lille is the best in the North, with tons of great bars and clubs.

⌫ TRANSPORTATION

Flights: Aéroport de Lille-Lesquin (☎03 20 49 68 68). Cariane Nord **shuttles** leave from rue le Corbusier at Gare Lille Europe (☎03 20 90 79 79; M-F, Sa-Su 5-6 per day according to flight times; €4.60).

Trains: Lille has two stations.

  Gare Lille Flandres, pl. de la Gare. To: **Arras** (40min., 18 per day, €8.30); **Brussels**, Belgium (1½hr., 20 per day, €22); **Paris** (1hr., 21 per day, €34-44.10). **Currency exchange.** Info desk open M-Sa 9am-7pm.

FLANDERS & CALAIS

Lille

🏠 **ACCOMMODATIONS**
Auberge de
  Jeunesse (HI), **7**
Hôtel Faidherbe, **4**
Hôtel de France, **6**

🍴 **FOOD**
Les 3 Brasseurs, **1**
Chinostar, **10**
Le Maharajah, **5**

⭐ **NIGHTLIFE**
L'Anglo-Saxo, **3**
Le Djoloff, **12**
Father Moustache, **9**
Gino Pub, **8**
L'Irlandais, **11**
L'Ptit Marais, **2**
Le Tchouka, **13**

Gare Lille Europe, av. le Corbusier (☎08 36 35 35 35). M: Gare Lille Europe. **Eurostar** runs to **London** and **Brussels**. **TGVs** run to the south of France and **Paris** (1hr., 4 per day, €32.60-44). Open M-F 9am-1pm and 2-6pm.

Bus Station: Eurolines, 23 Parvis St Maurice (☎03 20 78 18 88). Open M-F 9:30am-12:30pm and 1:30-6pm, Sa 1-6pm.

Public Transportation: The **Transpole** central **bus terminal** is next to the train station. **Métro (M)** and **trams** serve the town and periphery daily 5:12am-12:12am. Tickets €1.15, *carnet* of 10 €10. Info at the tourist office or the office below Gare Flandres (☎08 20 42 40 40). Kiosks open M-F 7am-7pm, Sa 9am-5pm.

Taxis: Taxi Union (☎03 20 06 06 06).

Bike Rental: Peugeot Cycles, 64 rue Léon Gambetta (☎03 20 54 83 39). €8 per day. €160 deposit. Open Tu-Sa 9am-12:30pm and 2-7pm. MC/V.

✈ 🛈 ORIENTATION AND PRACTICAL INFORMATION

In general, Lille is easy to navigate; it even has a métro. Still, get a map before tackling *vieille Lille*, a maze of narrow streets running from the tourist office north to the cathedral. The newer part of town, with wide boulevards and 19th-century buildings, culminates in the **Marché de Wazemmes.** Lille's largest shopping district is off **pl. du Théâtre.** Lille is a big city, and can be unsafe. Be cautious in the areas near the train station, the Marché de Wazemmes, the sidestreets between the Gare Lille Flandres and bd. Carnot, rue Molinel, and many areas in the east of the city.

Tourist Office: pl. Rihour (☎03 20 21 94 21; fax 03 20 21 94 20). M: Rihour. From Gare Lille Flandres, head straight down rue Faidherbe for 2 blocks and turn left through pl. du Théâtre and pl. de Gaulle. Beyond pl. de Gaulle, there's a huge war monument; the tourist office is behind it. Free maps, an essential mass transit guide, free **accommodations service,** and a detailed city guide (€2). Excellent city tours with minibus and bike, including of *vieux Lille* and a night tour with a beer tasting. Less thrilling **currency exchange** rate. The **Lille Metropole City Pass** (€15) gets you one day of unlimited transportation, entrance into museums and monuments, a panoramic tour, and additional discounts valid for one week. Open M-Sa 9:30am-6:30pm, Su 10am-noon and 2-5pm.

Budget Travel: Wasteels, 25 pl. des Reignaux (☎08 03 88 70 41). Open M-Th 9am-noon and 2-6pm, F 9am-1pm and 2-6pm, Sa 9am-noon.

Youth Information: Centre Regional Information Jeunesse (CRIKJ), 2 rue Nicolas Leblanc, has information about seasonal work and long-term lodging. Open Tu and Th 10am-8pm, W and F 10am-6pm, Sa 10-12:30pm.

Laundromat: 57 rue du Molinel. Open daily 8am-9pm. Also **Lavarama,** 2 rue Ovigneuz. Open daily 7am-8pm.

Police: 10 rue Ovigneur (☎03 20 62 47 47).

Hospital: 2 av. Oscar Lambret (☎03 20 44 59 62). M: CHR-Oscar Lambret.

Internet access: NetPlayer Games, 25 bd. Carnot (☎03 20 31 20 29). €3.05 per hr. Open M-Sa 10am-1am, Su 2pm-midnight. **Agence France Télécom,** pl. Général de Gaulle, facing the Vieille Bourse (☎03 20 57 40 00). €0.15 per min., students half-price. Open M 2-7pm, Tu-Sa 9am-7pm.

Post Office: 8 pl. de la République (☎03 28 36 10 20). M: République. Decent rate of **currency exchange.** Open M-F 8am-7pm, Sa 8am-noon. **Poste Restante:** 59035 Lille Cédèx. **Branch** on bd. Carnot, near pl. du Théâtre. Open M-F 8am-6:30pm and Sa 8am-noon. **Postal code:** 59000.

ACCOMMODATIONS AND CAMPING

Auberge de Jeunesse (HI), 12 rue Malpart (☎03 20 57 08 94; fax 03 20 63 98 93; lille@fuaj.org). M: Mairie de Lille. From Gare Lille Flandres, circle around the station to the left and turn onto rue du Molinel, take the 2nd left onto rue de Paris, and then the 3rd right onto rue Malpart. Friendly reception, international atmosphere, and spacious quarters. Co-ed bathrooms. Bar open 7:30pm-1am. Breakfast included. Sheets €2.70. Kitchen. Laundry. Luggage storage €2 per day. Check-out 10am; curfew 1am. Reception 7-11am and 3pm-1am. Open Jan. 31-Dec. 17. 3- to 6-bed dorms (some with private shower) €12.50 per person; deposit of €10 required for key. ❶

Hôtel Faidherbe, 42 pl. de la Gare (☎03 20 06 27 93; fax 03 20 55 95 38). M: Gare Lille Flandres. A tiny elevator and spackled halls lead to institutional-feeling rooms with a splendid view of...the train station! Breakfast €4.12. Reception 24hr. Singles and doubles €27.50, with shower €36.60-42.70; triples €50.30. Tax €0.30 per person per day. 10% discount with *Let's Go* guide. AmEx/MC/V. ❸

Hôtel de France, 10 rue de Béthune (☎03 20 57 14 78; fax 03 20 57 06 01). TVs in all rooms, great location in the pedestrian district. Price strongly correlates to quality—from newly renovated to small and ratty; ask to see yours ahead of time. Breakfast €4.50. Singles €29.45, with shower €39.45-54.45; doubles €33.90/€38.90-60.90; triples with shower €47.35-65.36. Extra bed €4.60. AmEx/MC/V. ❸

Camping Les Ramiers, 1 chem. des Ramiers (☎03 20 23 13 42), in Bondues. Take bus #35 (dir: Halluin Colbras) or #36 (dir: Comines Mairie) to "Bondues Centre," then follow rue César Loridan for 1km. (25min.) Fences and garden plots divide spacious private spots. Reception July-Aug. 8am-7:30pm; Sept.-May 8am-7:30pm. Open mid-Apr. to Nov. €2.40 per site, €1.60 per person, €0.80 per car. Showers €1. Electricity €2.

■ FOOD

Lille is known for *maroilles* cheese, *genièvre* (juniper berry liqueur), and (this being Flanders) mussels. Decently priced restaurants and cafés fill the fashionable pedestrian area around **rue de Béthune.** The highest value food, catering to students, is south of the Blvd. de la Liberté, near rue Solférino, rue Masséna, and the Halles Centrales. Dusty **rue Léon Gambetta** is a picnicking paradise, culminating in the enormous **Marché de Wazemmes,** pl. de la Nouvelle Aventure. You'll find **markets** both indoors (open M-Th 7am-1pm, F-Sa 7am-8pm, Su 7am-3pm) and out. (Open Su, Tu, Th 7am-3pm.) **EuraLille,** the big shopping center next to the Eurostar station, has an enormous **Carrefour supermarket.** (Open M-Sa 9am-10pm.) **Monoprix** is on rue du Molinel near Gare Lille Flandres. (Open M-Sa 8:30am-8pm.)

Le Maharajah, 4 rue du Sec Arembault (☎03 20 57 67 77), in the pedestrian district. Fabulous Indian food, from drool-worthy lamb to vegetarian plates (€8.50-12). Long dinner lines. Open M-Sa noon-2pm and 7-10:30pm. AmEx/MC/V. ❷

Les 3 Brasseurs, 22 pl. de la Gare (☎03 20 06 46 25). A branch of the micro-brewery micro-chain. As a garnish for your beer, try a *tarte flambée* (from €5). Menus €10.50-11. Open Su-Th 11am-midnight, F-Sa 11am-1am.

Chinostar, 37 rue Léon Gambetta (☎03 20 57 62 44), is a fine Chinese restaurant with rich decorations, quality food, and low prices. €5.34 gets you a starter, main meal, rice, and dessert. Open daily 11am-3pm and 6pm-midnight. ❶

◎ SIGHTS

MUSÉE DES BEAUX-ARTS. Housed in a 19th-century mansion, surrounded by the lovely gardens of the pl. de la République, this well-respected museum holds the second-largest collection in France, including an encyclopedic display of 15th- to 20th-century French and Flemish masters. *(Pl. de la République. M: République. ☎03 20 06 78 00. Open M 2-6pm, W-Th and Sa-Su 10am-6pm, F 10am-7pm. €4.60, students €3.)*

LA PISCINE. This fantastic new museum is in a renovated interior pool. It has a collection of paintings from the 19th and early 20th centuries, as well as vases, needlepoint work, stained glass, and emotive statues. *(23 rue de L'Esperance. Take M: Gare Jean Lebas, follow large boulevard in front of you, then take a right on rue des Champs, and it'll be right ahead. ☎03 20 69 23 60. Open Tu-Th 11am-6pm, F 11am-8pm, Sa-Su 1-8pm. €3.)*

MUSÉE D'ART MODERNE. More impressive from the outside than the inside, this museum houses works by Cubist and Postmodernist masters, including Braque, Picasso, Léger, Miró, and Modigliani. Temporary exhibits can be interesting, but the museum is mostly for hard-core fans of Cubism. *(1 allée du Musée, in the suburb of Villeneuve d'Ascq. Take tram (dir: 4 Cantons) to "Pont du Bois" Then take bus #41 (dir: Villeneuve d'Ascq) to "Parc Urbain-Musée." ☎03 20 19 68 68. Open W-M 10am-6pm. Tours Sa 3pm and Su 11am; €2.29. €6.50, under 25 €1.50, under 12 free; free first Su of every month 10am-2pm.)*

VIEILLE BOURSE. Lille's old stock exchange epitomizes the Flemish Renaissance; the garland-like moldings encircling the building give it the appearance of an elaborate, oversized wedding cake. *(Pl. du Général de Gaulle, between rue des Sept Acaches and rue Manneliers. Markets Tu-Su 9:30am-7:30pm.)*

OTHER SIGHTS. The **Citadel** on the city's north side was redesigned in the 17th century by military genius Vauban. *(In French. May-Aug. Su 3-5pm. Tourist office gives tours of the army base. €7.)* Have some civilian fun across the street at the **Jardin Vauban,** which has fields for Frisbee-playing, a carousel, and carnival games. The **Musée de l'Hospice** has served as a hospital, hospice, and orphanage. Check out the fascinating *enseigne de la fille mal gardée*, a rather primitive sculpture of a suspiciously young woman holding out a baby, designed as a moralistic lesson for children. The downstairs chapel is directly across the hall from the massive sick ward; on Sunday, the doors were opened and patients watched the services from their beds. *(☎ 03 28 36 84 00. Open M 2-6pm, W-F 10am-12:30pm and 2-6pm. €2.50; children, students, and teachers of art history free.)*

ENTERTAINMENT AND FESTIVE MARKETS

Lille is a huge party town, with endless bars and clubs. The atmosphere is calmer in the summer, but still very lively. Partyers head to two separate neighborhoods. Around les Halles Centrales, pubs line **rue Solférino** and **rue Masséna,** popular college-student hangouts. On the other end of town, the winding *vieille ville* is home to a more sophisticated nightlife scene.

■ **L'Irlandais,** 160-162 rue Solférino (☎ 03 20 57 04 74). Fairly typically Irish decorations, but distances itself from the pack with an interactive setting. Don't be shy: grab a young lad or lass by the arm and join in the jig. Beer €2.50. Open daily 4pm-2am.

■ **Le Tchouka,** 80 bis rue B. Delespaul, is a gay bar, but is usually filled with an even number of men and women. After other places have shut down, seemingly half the city heads here to dance under 20 disco balls and sing along to the French music.

Le Djoloff, 37 rue des Postes (☎ 03 20 30 84 23). Bamboo, wall hangings, and colorful painted boats mark this African bar. Try the *ventillateur*, a mixed drink with rum, ginger, curacao, and a secret ingredient (€6). Open daily 6pm-2am.

Father Moustache, 19 rue Masséna (☎ 03 20 30 19 17), is a romantic place to go with that special someone. Dim lights, wood decor, and a dance floor downstairs set the stage for that move you've been planning. Beer €2-4. Cocktail €6. Open Sept.-May.

L'Angle-Saxo, 36 rue d'Angleterre (☎ 03 20 51 88 89), will give you a tamer, relaxed experience with jazz four or five nights a week. Open daily 9pm-2am.

Gino Pub, 21 rue Masséna. (☎ 03 20 54 45 55 is a good place to find the college crowd, pheromone cocktails, billiards, and €1.50 beer (!). Open daily noon-2am.

L'Ptit Marais, 45 rue Lepelletier (☎ 03 20 51 30 09), is a friendly lesbian bar. Almost exclusively women fill the terrace out front, especially on Fridays. Beer €2-3. Cocktail €5.50. Open Tu 3pm-10pm, W 3-midnight, Th 3pm-2am, F 3pm-3am, Sa 3pm-2am.

Opera Night, 84 rue de Trevise (☎ 03 20 88 37 25), blasts "house-happy techno" (in the owner's words) to a 20- and 30-something clientele. A favorite among clubbers.

The **Marché aux Fleurs** carpets the center of town at the end of April, while the flea market **La Braderie** is held in the city's central squares on the first weekend of September. For a dose of culture, contact the **Orchestre Nationale de Lille,** 30 pl. Mendes France. (☎ 03 20 12 82 40; www.onlille.com. Tickets €23, students €8.) The tourist office has information on **film festivals,** held at **Le Métropole,** rue des Ponts de Comines (☎ 08 36 68 00 73), and the **Majestic,** 54 rue de Béthune. (☎ 03 28 52 40 40.)

DOUAI

Staying a night in Douai (pop. 45,000) makes one realize that a Flemish town is a quite different animal from a classically French one. The pace of life here is dawdling, best experienced strolling beside Douai's placid canals. As the seat of the

Flemish parliament from 1713 until the Revolution, Douai acquired elegant mansions and government buildings that bear surprisingly few scars from the world wars; they now redeem the grungy, commercial blocks of the modern city.

█ █ ORIENTATION AND PRACTICAL INFORMATION. Trains run to: Arras (15min., 17 per day, €4.20); Lille (30min., 22 per day, €5.50); Paris (1hr., 16 per day, €28). Douai is divided by the river Scarpe, with the shopping district and the tourist office on one side and the museum on the other. Turn left from the train station exit; at the Porte de Valenciennes roundabout take the third street (rue de Valenciennes) to the right and follow it for two blocks to **pl. d'Armes,** the center of town and home to the **tourist office,** 70 pl. d'Armes. The staff offers a map with major sights, a list of hotels and restaurants, and a tour of the Hôtel de Ville. (☎03 27 88 26 79; fax 03 27 99 38 78. Tour €3.50, under 14 €2. Open May-Oct. M-Sa 10am-1pm and 2-7pm, Su 3-6pm; Nov.-Apr. M-Sa 10am-12:30pm and 2-6:30pm.) **Local transport** is provided by TUB. (☎03 27 95 77 77. Tickets €1. Office at pl. de Gaulle open M-F 8:30am-noon and 2-5:30pm.) For a **taxi,** call ☎03 27 96 96 05. The **police** are at 150 rue St-Sulpice (☎03 27 92 38 38) and the **hospital** is at rte. de Cambrai (☎03 27 99 61 61). **Net Gamer,** 64 rue St-Christophe, has **Internet access,** but little ambience. (☎03 27 88 69 85; €5 per hr.) The **post office** is on pl. Général de Gaulle. (Open M-F 8am-6:30pm, Sa 8am-1pm.) **Postal code:** 59500.

█ █ ACCOMMODATIONS AND FOOD. If you can, stay overnight in Arras or Lille. In a pinch, try **Le Djurdjura ❸,** 370 pl. du Barlet, just down the road from the pl. d'Armes, which has airy, pastel rooms with baths. (☎03 27 88 74 65; fax 03 27 87 05 86. Reception 8am-midnight. Singles and doubles €27-40; triples €45. MC/V.)

The **Monoprix Supermarket** is at 171 rue de Bellain. (Open M-Sa 9:30am-7pm.) Cheap cafés line the **pl. d'Armes** and **pl. Carnot.** Lots of bakeries are on **rue de Bellain.** Get tender pasta or delicious pizzas served hot from the brick oven at █**La Fata Morgana ❶,** 68 rue des Ferronniers, off rue de Bellain. (☎03 27 88 60 95. Pizza €5-12. Open daily noon-2pm and 7:30-10pm; June-Aug. closed Su. MC/V.)

█ █ SIGHTS AND ENTERTAINMENT. The star attraction here is the fantastic **Hôtel de Ville,** just up the road from pl. d'Armes. Popularized by Victor Hugo, its 64m belfry is crowned with a delightfully gaudy assortment of tourelles and spires. It holds 62 bells, the largest collection in Europe. Every 15min. the bells play a short tune; there are concerts every Sa at 10:30am. (Tours July-Aug. daily 10am-5pm; Sept.-June M-Sa 2-5pm, Su 10am-5pm. €2, children €1.) Following rue Gambetta to the right of the Hôtel de Ville, you'll arrive at the **Eglise St-Pierre.** It appears to be two churches welded together, its 16th-century Gothic facade joined with a 1903 red-brick addition. (Open Tu-Sa 10-11:30am and 3-4:30pm, Su 3-5pm.) On the other side of the river, the **Musée de la Chartreuse,** 130 rue de la Chartreuse, inhabits an ancient monastery. The collection of painting and sculpture includes 16th-century Flemish altarpieces, Rodin bronzes, and an exceptional array of 17th-century Northern masters. Look for Jean Bellegambe's gruesome, yet provocative *Martyrdom of Ste-Barbara.* (☎03 27 71 38 80. Open W and F-Su 10am-noon and 2-6pm. €3, students and seniors €1, under 18 free.)

Douai is most festive during the **Fête des Géants,** a tradition that began in 1479 with a procession through the streets to celebrate a Flemish victory over France. The highlight of the parade is the march of family of giants constructed by local basket makers. The *fête* is always held the first weekend after July 5; call tourist office for info. Haggle for antiques at the **Puce du Nord,** a flea market held the 3rd Sunday of each month from September to June, in the Gayant Expo hall.

ARRAS

Rows of gabled townhouses, Flemish arcades, and the lilting melody of the belfry bells are a reminder of this city's vibrant past as capital of the Artois province. Arras (pop. 80,000) merits a short visit for its well-preserved collection of 17th- and 18th-century buildings and the still-intact if pock-marked World War I trenches of the nearby Vimy Memorial. Unfortunately, Arras is now a dull, humdrum city, and unless you have an extended interest in architecture or war memorials, you'll want to move on after a day.

TRANSPORTATION AND PRACTICAL INFORMATION. Trains leave pl. Maréchal Foch. (Info desk open M-F 8am-7pm, Sa 8am-6pm.) To: Amiens (1hr., 12 per day, €10); Dunkerque (1½hr., 11 per day, €14.20); Lille (45min., 20 per day, €8.80); Lyon (3hr., 2 per day, €59.30); Paris (50min., 12 per day, €26-34.20). To get to the **bus station** from the train station, turn left onto rue du Dr. Brassart. At the end of the road, turn right; the bus station will be ahead to your left. (☎03 21 51 34 64. Open July-Aug. M-F 8am-noon and 4-6:30pm, Sa 10am-1pm; Sept.-June M-F 7am-7pm, Sa 7am-1pm.) **Local transportation** is operated by **STCRA** (☎03 21 58 08 58; tickets €1.10). **Arras Taxis** (☎03 21 23 69 69) wait at the train station. (24hr.) **Avis Car Rental** is near the train station on 4 rue Gambetta. (☎03 21 51 69 03. Open M-F 8am-noon and 2-6pm, Sa 9am-noon and 4-6pm.)

To get to the **tourist office**, pl. des Héros, from the station, walk straight across pl. Foch onto rue Gambetta. Continue straight on Gambetta for five blocks, then turn left on rue Desiré Delansorne. Walk for two more blocks; the tourist office is across pl. des Héros in the elaborate Hôtel de Ville. The bilingual staff offers a **reservations service**, a free map, and a booklet of local walking trails. (☎03 21 51 26 95; fax 03 21 71 07 34. Open May-Sept. M-Sa 9am-6:30pm, Su 10am-1pm and 2:30-6:30pm; Oct.-Apr. M-Sa 9am-noon and 2-6pm, Su 10am-12:30pm and 3-6:30pm.) The town's other main square, **Grand'Place,** is on the opposite side of pl. des Héros. **Crédit Agricole,** 9 Grand'Place, has the best rates of **currency exchange** and 24hr. exchange machines. (☎03 21 50 41 80. Open M 2-6pm, Tu-F 8:45pm-12:30pm and 2-6pm, Sa 8:45am-12:45pm.) Do your **laundry** at **Superlav,** 17 pl. d'Ipswich, next to the Eglise St-Jean-Baptiste. (Open daily 7am-8pm.) The **police station** is in the Hôtel de Ville (☎03 21 23 70 70, after 6pm ☎03 21 50 51 60); the **hospital** is at 57 av. Winston Churchill. (☎03 21 24 40 00.) The **post office,** 13 rue Gambetta, **exchanges currency.** (☎03 21 22 94 94. Open M-F 8am-6:30pm, Sa 8am-noon.) **Postal code:** 62000.

ACCOMMODATIONS AND FOOD. Arras has previous few budget hotels. **Auberge de Jeunesse (HI) ❶,** 59 Grand'Place, offers 3- to 7-bed rooms; though spartan and tiny, they are cheerfully maintained and some have pleasant views of the *place* in an unbeatable location. (☎03 21 22 70 02; fax 03 21 07 46 15. Breakfast €3. No door locks; safes €0.15. Sheets €2.80. Reception 8am-noon and 5-11pm. Lockout noon-5pm. Curfew 11pm. June-Aug. reserve ahead. Open Feb.-Nov. Bunks €8. **Members only.**) If it's full, try the **Ostel des Trois Luppars ❹,** 47 Grand'Place, in the oldest house in Arras. A beautiful lobby and dining room lead to large, antiseptically clean rooms. (☎03 21 60 02 03; fax 03 21 24 24 80. Breakfast €7. Reception 7am-11pm. All rooms with shower. Singles €46; doubles €51; triples €64; quads €69. Sauna €5 for 30min. AmEx/MC/V.) Another option is the quiet, aging **OK Pub et Hôtel,** 8 pl. de la Vacquerie, behind the Hôtel de Ville, above a bar. (☎03 21 21 30 60; fax 03 21 21 30 61. Breakfast €5.50. Reception daily 8am-1am. Some larger rooms have kitchens. Singles €23; singles and doubles with shower €33-39; triples with shower €45-55. Extra bed €5. AmEx/MC/V.) The local **campsite ❶,** 138 rue du Temple, is basically a parking lot with a few grassy plots. From the station, turn left onto rue du Dr. Brassart, then left on av. du Maréchal Leclerc. Cross the bridge; after 10 min., rue du Temple will on the left. (☎ 03 21 71 55 06. Reception 7am-10pm. Open Apr.-Sept. €3 per person; €1.80 per car or tent. Electricity €2.30.)

The pedestrian shopping area between the post office and the Hôtel de Ville bustles with bakeries and other specialty shops. There's a huge **Monoprix supermarket** across from the post office on rue Gambetta. (Open M-Sa 8:30am-8pm.) The **pl. des Héros** springs to life for Arras's boisterous open-air **market**. (Open W and Sa 8am-1pm.) Inexpensive cafés skirt **pl. des Héros** and the pedestrian area; more elegant restaurants adorn the **Grand'Place.** You'll smell *Les Best Ribs in Town*—and probably the only ribs in town—all the way across the *place* at **Le Saint-Germain ❷**, 14 Grand'Place, where France and suburban America shake greasy hands. Gorge on a plateful of ribs (€9) or grab 'em to go (€7.80). Try the all-you-can-eat *mousse chocolat* or *crème caramel* for €4.60. (☎ 03 21 51 45 45. Open daily noon-12:30am. AmEx/MC/V.) **La Cave de l'Ecu**, 54 Grand'Place, serves huge salads (€7.30-12.10), and free-range chicken (€9-13) raised on a local farm. (☎ 03 21 50 00 39. Open daily noon-2:30pm and 7-10pm; July-Aug. Su afternoon closed.)

◎ 🎹 SIGHTS AND ENTERTAINMENT. Arras's two great squares are framed by rows of nearly identical houses. **Grand'Place's** Flemish homogeneity is ruffled by a lone Gothic housefront (Ostel des Trois Luppars), which dates from 1430. A block away, shops, bars, and cafés line the smaller, livelier **pl. des Héros.** The current **Hôtel de Ville** is a faithful copy of the 15th-century original, which reigned over pl. des Héros until its destruction in WWI. The best view of Arras is from its 75m **belfry.** (Open M-Sa 10-11:45am and 2-5:45pm, Su 10am-12:15pm and 2-6:15pm. €2.30, students €1.50.) Beneath the town hall are the eerie maze-like underground tunnels of **Les Boves,** bored into the soft chalk in the 10th century. The tourist office leads fascinating tours. (☎ 03 21 51 26 95. €3.80, children and students €2.29.) A few blocks behind the Hôtel de Ville lies the **Abbaye St-Vaast,** built in 667 on the hill where St-Vaast used to pray. Its traditional Gothic floor plan accommodates massive Corinthian columns with striking success. (Open daily 2:15-6:30pm; Dec.-Feb. until 6pm.) Inside the abbey, the sophisticated **Musée des Beaux-Arts** displays medieval architecture and tapestries. Look for the gruesome skeletal sculpture of Guillaume Lefrançois and his worm-infested entrails. (☎ 03 21 71 26 43. Open W and F-Su 9:30am-noon and 2-5:30pm, Th 9:30am-5:30pm. €3.90, students €2.)

Place des Héros, Grand'Place, and the surrounding pedestrian roads are the centers of local nightlife; just follow the young blood coursing into bars and cafés all over town. **Dan Foley's Irish Pub,** 7 pl. des Héros, is filled with well-dressed youngsters who love karaoke Tuesdays. **Le Couleur Café,** 35 pl. des Héros (☎ 03 21 71 08 70), draws the college set with a house and drum'n'bass DJ. Take a break from the bars at cosmopolitan **Noroît,** 6-9 rue des Capucins, which plays foreign artsy films and hosts several concerts and plays each month. (☎ 03 21 71 30 12.)

▶ DAYTRIP FROM ARRAS: VIMY MEMORIAL AND TRENCHES

The Vimy Memorial is a 3km walk from the town of Vimy. You can catch a taxi in Arras (€17-18, after 7pm €21-23) or a bus from Arras to Vimy (20min., M-Sa 8 per day, €2.40); ask the bus driver to point you toward the monument and follow the signs.

The Vimy Memorial, 12km northeast of Arras along N17, honors the more than 66,000 Canadian soldiers killed during WWI. The memorial itself is a vast limestone monument, consisting of two pylons rising from a rectangular base. Sculpted figures surround the edifice, the most poignant being a sorrowful woman carved from a single 30-ton limestone block. The surrounding park, whose soil was shipped from Canada, is dedicated to the crucial victory at Vimy Ridge in April 1917. The land surrounding the Vimy Memorial is morbidly beautiful; tiny hills and large craters, carved out by shells and underground mines, are now covered in grass. You can explore trenches, both Canadian and German, in some areas no more than 25m apart. **Stay on the marked paths,** as there are still undetonated mines in the area. The kiosk near the trenches is the starting point for an underground tour of the crumbling tunnels. Little details evoke the realities of life on the front lines: the registration room, the commander's desk, a maple leaf chiseled in the wall by an anonymous soldier. (☎03 21 58 19 34 or 03 21 48 98 97. Memorial open daily sunrise to sunset. Tours Apr.-Nov. 10am-6pm in English and French; every 30min.; free. Museum open daily 10am-6pm.)

LAON

The cathedral of Laon, one of France's Gothic masterpieces, presides over the surrounding farmland from its hilltop throne. The birthplace of both Charlemagne's mother and the great folk hero Roland, Laon (pop. 28,000; pronounced "Laahn") was the capital of the mighty Carolingian Empire in the 9th and 10th centuries. While residence in the fortified *haute ville* was once limited to kings and nobles, there's no royalty here today, and the *basse ville* seems somewhat depressed. Still, Laon offers some giddy thrills and glorious views for a day or two.

■ ◪ **ORIENTATION AND PRACTICAL INFORMATION.** Laon's *haute ville* is built around one main street, whose name is rue du Cloître by the cathedral and rue de Bourg by the Hôtel de Ville. **Trains** leave pl. de la Gare (☎03 23 79 10 79). (Ticket office open M-F 4:55am-9:15pm, Sa 6am-8:35pm, Su 6:45am-9:20pm.) To: Amiens (1½hr., 7 per day, €13.40); Paris (1¼hr., 12 per day, €16.50); Reims (50min., 9 per day, €7.50). The **POMA car** runs every two minutes from the station to the *haute ville* and tourist office, passing breathtaking views of the *basse ville* from above. (☎03 23 79 07 59. Open July-Aug. M-Sa 7am-8pm, Su 2:30-7pm; Sept.-June Su closed. Round-trip ticket €1.) From the POMA station in the *haute ville*, exit straight, cross the parking lot and turn left across pl. Gén. Leclerc onto rue Sérurier. Turn right when you reach the art center (old hospital) and walk one block to reach the **tourist office**, pl. du Parvis, occupying the Hôtel-Dieu, a squat 12th-century stone structure that was France's first hospital. For the athletic, the path on foot from the base is straightforward, but involves a lot of steps. From the train station, go straight out toward the hill, past the rotary, onto av. Carnot, and up the endless steps. At the top, circumvent the POMA tracks, and take the pedestrian path to your left that head uphill and to the right. Find the cathedral tower and head toward it. The tourist office is right next to it. Tours of the the medieval city and cathedral in French and English. (☎03 23 20 28 62; fax 03 23 20 68 11. Cathedral tours July-Aug. M-F 3pm, Sa-Su 4:30pm; Sept.-June Sa-Su 4:30pm. City tours July-Aug. M-F 10:30am, Su 2:30pm; Sept.-June Sa-Su 2:30pm. Tours €5.50, students €3, under 12 free. Office open July-Aug. M-Sa 9:30am-1pm and 2-6:30pm, Su 10:30am-1pm and 2-6:30pm; Sept. and June-Mar. M-Sa 9am-12:30pm and 2-6:30pm, Su 11am-1pm and 2-6pm; Oct.-Mar. M-Sa 9am-12:30pm and 2-6pm, Su 11am-1pm and 2-5pm.) The **police** are at 2 bd. de Gras Boncourt (☎03 23 20 28 62) and the **hospital** is at rue Marcellin-Berthelot. (☎03 23 24 33 33.) There is a **post office** next to the station on pl. de la Gare, with **currency exchange.** (☎03 23 21 55 74. Open M-F 8am-7pm, Sa 8am-noon.) **Postal code:** 02000.

▛◪ **ACCOMMODATIONS AND FOOD.** Popular with backpackers, the **Hôtel Welcome ❷**, 2 av. Carnot in the *basse ville*, lets simple, worn rooms with thin walls. (☎03 23 23 06 11. Breakfast €3.85. Reception M-Sa 7am-noon and 2-10pm, Su 7am-noon. Singles and doubles €22.10, with shower €24.50; triples and quads

€27.50. MC/V.) Château-like **Les Chevaliers** ❸, 3-5 rue Sérurier, has handsome, dark rooms just a block from the cathedral. (☎03 23 27 17 50; fax 03 23 79 12 07. Breakfast included. Reception 6:30am-8:30pm. Singles €30, with shower €40-48; doubles €40/€50-60; triples with shower €60-80; quads with shower €70. Extra bed €10. MC/V.) Rural **Camping Municipale** ❶, allée de la Chênaie, about 3km from the train station, is mostly full of caravans but has some private areas for tents. (☎03 23 20 25 56. Reception 7am-10pm. Open May-Sept. €3 per person; €2 per site, €1.60 per car. Electricity €2.60.)

The ever-reliable **Monoprix supermarket** lies on rue de Bourg. (Open M-F 8:30am-7pm, Sa 9am-noon and 2-7pm.) **Rue Chatelaine,** which leads left from pl. Général Leclerc toward the cathedral, is full of bakeries and cheap sandwich shops. ▓**La Bonne Heure** ❷, 53 rue Chatelaine, is the best restaurant in Laon, possibly the region. The friendly owner cooks with fresh produce from local farms. An expert on Laon, he has invented a crust for his specialty *tourtinette* (€7.50-8), a pizza-like food topped with ingredients like leeks, ham, smoked trout, lemon, tomatoes, mozzarella, and escargot. Be sure to try the *montagne couronnée* (€3), a chocolate-covered wafer filled with berries and dessert cheese; it honors Laon's nickname, the "crowned mountain." (☎03 23 20 57 09. Open Tu-Su 9am-9pm. MC/V.)

◙▟ **SIGHTS AND FESTIVALS.** A maze of narrow, twisting alleys and medieval walls surrounds Laon's airy **Cathédrale de Notre-Dame,** one of the earliest and finest examples of Gothic architecture in France. The striking white interior contrasts with a simple, sumptuous rose window. Look for the winged hippopotamus and miracle oxen. (☎03 23 25 14 18. Open daily 9am-6:30pm. French tours €5.50, students €3.) The **ramparts** encircling the *haute ville* offer a panoramamic view of the *basse ville* and the surrounding countryside. Nearby is the lovely, cool **Eglise St-Martin,** the neglected sister of the cathedral. Behind a lush courtyard on rue Georges Ermant are the tiny **Musée de Laon** and the crumbling 13th-century **Chapelle des Templiers.** The chapel holds the carved 14th-century cadaver of Laon native Guillaume de Harcigny, the celebrated physician to Charles VI, who cured the king of madness. The museum's collection of paintings and Greek and Egyptian antiquities doesn't merit a detour. (☎03 23 20 19 87. Both open June-Sept. Tu-Su 11am-6pm; Oct.-May Tu-Su 2-6pm. Museum €3.10, students €2.40.)

From October to early November, the **Festival de Laon** presents mainly modern classical music. (☎03 23 20 87 50. Tickets €12-26; students and over 65 €10-21. Tickets at tourist office June-Sept. and over the phone in Sept.) On the last weekend of May, **Les Fêtes de Laon Médiéval** brings jousts, falconry, street performers, and medieval food. (Free.) The last week of March and first week of April sees the **Festival International du Cinéma Jeune Public,** an international film and animation festival aimed at kids. (☎03 23 79 39 37.) **Jazzitudes** hits a number of venues in Laon during June. (www.jazztitudeslaon.free.fr. Tickets €4-18.)

▓ **DAYTRIPS**

South of Laon, basically reached only with a car, the **Chemin des Dames** winds across the Aisne region, a scenic route of great importance since Roman times. The route follows a 200m ridge whose value as a natural barrier was first noticed by Caesar when he conquered Northern Gaul in 57 BC. The Chemin was the scene of Napoleon's last battle before Waterloo and later the site of crucial strategic depot during WWI, which the Germans held from 1914 to 1918. Today the route is peppered with monuments to this turbulent history, including the ▓**Caverne des Dragons,** a former quarry used by the Germans as a barracks, hospital, and chapel during WWI and now a museum of remembrance. At the height of the war, both Germans and the French used the dark, dreary tunnels as sleeping quarters, but refused to fight each other except when they emerged into the light. (☎ 03 23 25 14 18. Open May-June and Sept.-Apr. daily 10am-6pm. €5, students €2.50. 1½hr. tours every 30min.; Sept.-June daily 10am-4:30pm; July-Aug. M-Sa 10am-5:30pm; free.)

THE CHANNEL PORTS (COTE D'OPALE)

They're big, they're bad, they're ugly. Such is the conventional wisdom regarding the sprawling ports that give the first taste of France to travelers from Britain and beyond. Towns fronting the English Channel were fought over for centuries, but today's visitor has to wonder what made them such hot items; with soggy weather, schlocky boutiques, and cafés promising genuine steak and kidney pie, the ports seem to combine the worst of both sides of the water. It's no wonder many get off the ferry only long enough to stock up on cheap wine, beer, and cigarettes before heading back to Blighty. Under the surface, however, these towns reveal a unique charm and character, from Boulogne's ancient walled *haute ville* to Dunkerque's lively beach at Malo-les-Bains. Don't go out of your way to get here, but take some time as you pass through and you may be pleasantly surprised.

BOATS TO BRITAIN. All three towns offer frequent service to the UK; Calais is by far the busiest. **Eurostar** trains zip under the tunnel from London and Ashford, stopping outside Calais on their way to Lille, Brussels, and Paris. **Le Shuttle** carries cars between Ashford and Calais. **Ferries** from Calais cross to Dover, while Boulogne services Dunkerque and Ramsgate. For details on operators, schedules, and fares, see **Getting There: By Boat** (p. 67) and **Getting There: By Channel Tunnel** (p. 66).

BOULOGNE-SUR-MER

With a refeshing sea breeze and bright floral displays, Boulogne (pop. 46,000) is by far the most attractive of the channel ports. The busy harbor is the heart of town, the *vielle ville* is its most charming aspect, and the aquarium its most entertaining.

⊟ TRANSPORTATION. Trains leave **Gare Boulogne-Ville**, bd. Voltaire, for Calais (30min., 13 per day, €6.40); Lille (2½hr., 11 per day, €17.20); Paris-Nord (2-3hr., 11 per day, €25.46-46.30). Info office open M-Sa 8:15am-6:30pm. **BCD** buses leave pl. Dalton for Calais (30min., 4 per day, €6) and Dunkerque (80min., 4 per day, €10). **TCRB** (☎ 03 21 83 51 51) sends **local bus #10** from the train station and pl. de France to the *haute ville* (€1). **Taxis** (☎ 03 21 91 25 00) wait at the station.

⊞ ▨ ORIENTATION AND PRACTICAL INFORMATION. The river Liane splits Boulogne in two: the ferry terminal is on the west bank, everything else on the east bank. The train station posts a large map on its doors. To reach central **pl. de France** from Gare Boulogne-Ville, turn left on Blvd. Voltaire, then right on Blvd Diderot. Follow Diderot till you hit pl. de France. To get to the tourist office, walk along Diderot past pl. de France; after the roundabout, the tourist office is on the right. On the other side of pl. de France, **Pont Marquet** leads to the **ferry port**. The streets between **pl. Frédéric Sauvage** and **pl. Dalton** form the town center.

The **tourist office**, 24 quai Gambetta, has bus info, reservations service, and a free fold-out town map. (☎ 03 21 10 88 10; fax 03 21 10 88 11; www.tourisme-boulognesurmer.com. Port tours F; €5.50, students €4, under 12 free. Open late June to mid-Sept. M-Sa 9am-7pm, Su 10am-1pm and 3-6pm; Sept.-June M-Sa 8:45am-12:30pm and 1:30-6:15pm, Su 10am-1pm and 3-6pm; mid-Sept. to June 8:15am-12:30pm and 1:30-6:30pm.) **Crédit Agricole**, 26 rue Nationale, has a 24hr. **currency exchange** machine. There's a **laundromat** at 62 rue de Lille in the *haute ville*. (Open daily 8am-7pm.) The **police** are at 9 rue Perrochel (☎ 03 21 99 48 48), the **hospital** on allée Jacques Monod. (☎ 03 21 99 33 33.) The **post office** is on pl. Frédéric Sauvage. (☎ 03 21 99 09 03. Open M-F 8am-6:30pm, Sa 8am-12:30pm.) **Postal code:** 62200.

ACCOMMODATIONS. Many hotels in the €17-25 range are near the ferry terminal; the tourist office has a list. The █Auberge de Jeunesse (HI) ❶, 56 pl. Rouget de Lisle, across from the train station, mixes pine cabin and fine hotel in its 2- to 4-bed rooms. Lively, backpacker-packed bar. (☎03 21 99 15 30; fax 03 21 80 45 62. Internet access €2 per 40min. Breakfast included. Late-night snack until 1am. Sheets included. Wheelchair accessible. Reception 8am-1am, Dec.-Feb. till midnight. Check-in 5pm; check-out 11am. Curfew 1am. 2- to 4-bed dorms €15. Nonmembers €2.90 extra per night first six nights. MC/V.) The Hôtel Au Sleeping ❷, 18 bd. Daunou, has spotless, lovingly decorated, newly renovated little rooms minutes from the train station, above a *brasserie*. All rooms have shower. (☎03 21 80 62 79; fax 03 21 80 62 79. Breakfast €5. Reception 7am-10pm. June-Aug. reserve ahead. Singles €23; doubles €27-34; triples €34; €0.45 tax per person per day. Dec.-Feb. prices around €3 lower. MC/V.) The central Hôtel de Londres ❹, 22 pl. de France, behind the post office, is pricey, but slightly luxurious. (☎03 21 31 35 63; fax 03 21 83 50 07. Breakfast €5.40. Reception 7:30am-midnight. Singles and doubles €38.11; quads €59.46. Extra bed €7.60. Tax €0.61 per person per day. MC/V.)

FOOD AND ENTERTAINMENT. There are lots of restaurants, cafés, bakeries, and other food shops in the center of town. An excellent market is held on pl. Dalton. (Open W and Sa 6am-1pm.) A Champion supermarket, rue Daunou near bd. de la Liane, in the Centre Commercial de la Liane mall, is up the road from the hostel. (Open M-Sa 8:30am-8pm.) Rue de Lille is undoubtedly the finest place to dine, though the ambience is costly. In the evening, check out the many neon-lit bars at pl. Dalton or its tiny offshoot rue Doyen. Drink a glass in memory of JFK and son at the Pub "J.F. Kennedy," 20 rue du Doyen. (☎03 21 83 97 05. Mussels €7.30. Beer €2.30. Open daily 9am-1am, food served 11am-3pm and 7-11pm.)

SIGHTS. Boulogne's *vieille ville* was built atop a hill by Roman conquerors. Its ramparts have exhilarating views of the harbor, town, and countryside. The massive Château-Musée, rue de Bernet, dominates the east corner of the battlements. Its collection is more striking for its size and variety than for any individual works, which include a bare-faced Egyptian mummy and Napoleon's second-oldest hat. (☎03 21 10 02 20, tours 03 21 80 56 78. Open M and W-Sa 10am-12:30pm and 2-5pm, Su 10am-12:30pm and 2:30-5:30pm. €3.50, students €2.50, under 12 free, all free Oct.-May 1st Su of the month. Tours €5, students €3.) Just down rue de Lille, the domed 19th-century Basilique de Notre-Dame sits above 12th-century crypts. (Basilica open Apr.-Sept 14 daily 9am-noon and 2-6pm; Sept. 15-Mar. 10am-noon and 2-5pm. Crypt open Tu-Su 2-5pm; €2, children €1.)

Boulogne capitalizes upon its main source of commerce and nutrition at the huge aquarium █Le Grand Nausicaä, bd. Ste-Beuve. Climb a ladder down into the lagoons, admire the shark tank, and pet sting rays. (☎03 21 30 99 99; www.nausicaa.fr. Open July-Aug. daily 9:30am-8pm; Sept.-June 9:30am-6:30pm. €12, students €8.50.) Next to Nausicaä is the beach, where Le Club de Voile rents windsurfers and catamarans. (☎03 21 31 80 67. Windsurfers €9 per hr., €15 for 1hr. lesson. Catamarans €21 per hr., €23 for 1hr. lesson. Open M-F 10am-5pm, Sa-Su 1-5pm.)

CALAIS

Calais (pop. 80,000) is the most lively of the Channel Ports, and the least French; with the Chunnel next door, you'll hear almost as much English as French on the streets. The town lacks charm, due in large part to the trauma it suffered in WWII, but if you're here for the day, check out Rodin's *Burghers of Calais* or gaze at the white ships gliding by the town's wide beaches.

⟐🔢 TRANSPORTATION AND PRACTICAL INFORMATION. Free buses connect the ferry terminal and train station every 30 minutes. Avoid the area around the harbor at night. **Eurostar** stops outside town at the new Gare Calais-Fréthun, but most **SNCF trains** stop in town at the Gare Calais-Ville, bd. Jacquard. They go to Boulogne (45min., 8 per day, €6.30); Dunkerque (1hr., 2 per day, €12.80); Lille (1¼hr., 8 per day, €13.40); Paris-Nord (3¼hr., 6 per day, €40.10). Ticket office open M-Sa 6:30am-8:30pm, Su 8:30-9:30am and 1:30-8:30pm. **BCD buses** (☎03 21 83 51 51) stop in front of the station on the way to Boulogne (30min.; 5 per day, Sa 2 per day; €6.40) and Dunkerque (40min.; M-F 6 per day, Sa 3 per day; €7). **OpaleBus,** 22 rue Caillette (☎03 21 00 75 75), operates **local buses.** Line #3 (dir: Blériot/VVF) runs from the station runs to the beach, hostel, and campground (M-Sa 7:15am-7:20pm, Su 10:30am-7:15pm; €0.90). For a **taxi,** call ☎03 21 97 13 14. (24hr.)

The **tourist office,** 12 bd. Clemenceau, is near the train station; cross the street, turn left, cross the bridge, and it's on the right. Free **reservations service.** (☎03 21 96 62 40; fax 03 21 96 01 92. Open M-Sa 9am-7pm, Su 10am-1pm.) **Exchange currency** at the ferry or Hovercraft terminals (both 24hr.) or more cheaply at the post office or banks. The **police** are on pl. de Lorraine (☎03 21 19 13 17), the **hospital** at 11 quai du Commerce. (☎03 21 46 33 33.) **Internet access** at **Dixie Bar,** 10 pl. d'Armes. (☎03 21 34 71 56. Free with purchase of drink or food. Open daily 7am-2am.) The **post office** is on pl. d'Alsace (☎03 21 85 52 72; open M-F 8:30am-6pm, Sa 8:30-noon); there's a **branch** on pl. du Reims. (Open M-F 8:30am-6pm, Sa 9am-noon.) **Postal code:** 62100.

🔢⟐ ACCOMMODATIONS AND FOOD. The few budget hotels fill up quickly in summer; call 10-14 days in advance. The tourist office provides a list of hotels and their prices. Better than any hotel is the modern, recently renovated **Centre Européen de Séjour/Auberge de Jeunesse (HI) ❶,** av. Maréchal Delattre de Tassigny, one block from the beach. From the station, turn left and follow the main road through various name changes past pl. d'Armes; cross the bridge and take a left at the roundabout onto bd. de Gaulle. Walk past the high-rise and go right on tiny rue Alice Marie; the white hostel is the 3rd building on your left. Or take bus #3 to "Pluviose." From the ferry, take a shuttle bus to pl. d'Armes and then follow the above directions. There are 42 bathrooms for the 84 doubles, some of which have beach views. Pool table, bar, library, and an attentive staff. (☎03 21 34 70 20; fax 03 21 96 87 80. Breakfast and sheets included. Cafeteria open M-F 7-9am, noon-1pm, and 5-7pm; Sa 7-9am and noon-1pm. Wheelchair accessible. Reception 24hr. Check-out 11am. Bunks €14.50 first night, €12.20 every extra night. **Non-members** €1.50 extra.) A down-to-earth 40-something runs two hotels. Homey **Hôtel Bristol ❷,** 13-15 rue du Duc de Guise, off the main road, has newly renovated, quiet rooms and the reception for both establishments. (☎/fax 03 21 34 53 24. Free **Internet.** Breakfast €5. Reception 24hr. Reservations suggested. Singles €25; doubles with shower €36. MC/V.) The more adorable **Hôtel Tudor,** 6 rue Marie Tudor, off rue Duc de Guise, has larger, fancier rooms. (☎03 21 96 08 15. Singles and doubles with shower €31-36; triples, quads, and quints €46-70. Reservations suggested. AmEx/MC/V.) **Camping Municipal de Calais ❶,** av. Raymond Poincoiré, has cramped sites with little privacy. (☎03 21 34 73 25. Reception July-Aug. daily 7:30am-12:30pm and 2:45-7:30pm; Sept.-June M-F 8am-noon and 2-5pm, Sa 9am-noon, Su 10am-noon. 1 person €3.30, children €2.68; €2.20 per site. Electricity €1.80.)

Calais caters to that rare breed of human looking for unexciting food at middling prices. Morning **markets** are held on pl. Crèvecœur and pl. d'Armes. (Both open W and Sa.) Otherwise, look for bakeries on **bd. Gambetta, bd. Jacquard,** and **rue des Thermes** or one of two supermarkets: **Match,** pl. d'Armes (open M-Th 9am-12:30pm and 2:30-7:30pm, F-Sa 9am-7:30pm) and **Prisunic,** 17 bd. Jacquard. (Open M-Sa 8:30am-7:30pm, Su 10am-7pm.) The hostel and campsite cafeterias are inexpensive

LEAVING SANGATTE

On the road to Sangatte, a refugee camp near Calais, a billboard shows a seagull hovering above the English Channel with the promising words *l'Angleterre à deux pas* ("England's two steps away") written below. But for the immigrants and refugees seeking temporary shelter at Sangatte's camp, the sign is only a bitter reminder of the difficulties they must face to gain passage to England.

Sangatte was opened in 1999 by the French Red Cross to provide homeless refugees with food and shelter. The camp was a response to the influx of immigrants escaping the crisis in Kosovo crisis, but today it holds up to 1500 Kurds, Afghans, and Iranians—mostly literate single young men—in a space designed for 600. Sangatte is the last stop in France before emigration to England, where housing and welfare benefits are better. While many refugees seek legal entrance to England, many make the dangerous attempt to emigrate illegally, sneaking across the Chunnel on trains and the undersides of trucks.

Sangatte remains a bitter point of contention between France and England, who complains that millions of pounds have already been spent enforcing border control. The Eurotunnel commission reported in 2002 that in eight months, there were 30,000 attempts to break into the Calais terminal. For their part, the French see Sangatte as a humanitarian duty. With the UN stepping in to moderate in July 2002, hopefully a compromise for England, France, and the refugees will not be far in the future.

options. Restaurants line **rue Royale** and **bd. Jacquard.** Try fresh pies at **Le Napoli Pizzeria,** 2 rue Jean de Vienne. (☎03 21 34 49 39. Open Tu-F until 10:30pm; Sa-Su until 11:30pm; Sa afternoon closed. MC/V.)

⬛ SIGHTS. Rodin's evocative sculpture of **The Burghers of Calais** stands in front of the **Hôtel de Ville** at the juncture of bd. Jacquard and rue Royale. When Calais was captured during the Hundred Years' War, six of the town's leading citizens—the burghers in this statue—surrendered the keys to the city and offered their lives to England's King Edward III in exchange for those of the starving townspeople. Edward's French wife Philippa pleaded for mercy, and they were spared. The best part of Calais is its **beach;** follow rue Royale to rue de Mer until the road ends, then walk west along the shore away from the harbor.

DUNKERQUE

Dunkerque entered the history books in June 1940, when the last defenders of France were evacuated on battleships, yachts, rowboats, and anything else the British could round up. The last French city to be liberated, over 80% of Dunkerque was destroyed before the Allied victory. Drab buildings are complemented by a gloominess among the *dunkerquois*. The only fun to be had here is in the lively beach area of Malo-les-Bains, a short bus ride from the city center.

⬛⬛ TRANSPORTATION AND PRACTICAL INFORMATION. Trains leave pl. de la Gare for Arras (1½hr., 14 per day, €14.50); Calais (1hr., 7 per day, €13); Lille (1¼hr., 14 per day, €11.35); Paris (1½hr., €33.45-45). Ticket windows open M-Sa 6am-7pm, Su 7am-7pm. **BCD buses** (☎03 21 83 51 51) leave the train station for Boulogne (1hr.; M-F 5 per day, Sa 2; €9.15) and Calais (40min.; M-F 8 per day, Sa 3; €6.10). Local transportation is provided by **DK'BUS,** 12 pl. de la Gare (☎03 28 59 00 78). Routes #3 and 3A connect the station and town center with the hostel and Malo-les-Bains (every 10-20min. 6:30am-9pm; tickets €1.25, students and children €0.60, *carnet* of 10 €7.60) and **Taxibus** (every 30min. 10pm-midnight; tickets €1.20). **Taxis** wait at pl. de la République and pl. Jean Bart. (☎03 28 66 73 00; 24hr.)

Bd. Alexandre III connects pl. de la Gare and the town center, whose two main squares are **pl. Jean Bart** and **pl. Général de Gaulle.** Along the beach, **digue de Mer** turns into **digue des Alliés** on the west side, which is closer to the town center. To reach the **tourist office,** rue Amiral Ronarch from the station, cross pl. de la Gare to rue du Chemin de Fer on the left, and follow the main road, bd. Alexandre III, which becomes rue Clemenceau at pl. Jean Bart. Here you'll find free maps and a lousy rate of **currency exchange.** (☎ 03 28 26 27 28; fax 03 28 63 38 34; dunkerque@tourisme.norsys.fr. Open July-Aug. M-Sa 9am-6:30pm, Su 10am-noon and 2-4pm; Sept.-June M-F 9am-12:30 and 1:30-6:30pm, Sa 9am-6:30pm, Su 10am-noon and 2-4pm.) For the **police,** call ☎ 03 28 23 50 50. A **hospital** is at 130 av. Louis Herbeaux. (☎ 03 28 28 59 00.) The **post office,** 20 rue du Président Poincaré, next to pl. de Gaulle, has good rates of **currency exchange.** (☎ 03 28 65 91 65. Open M-F 8:30am-6:30pm, Sa 8:30am-1pm.) **Postal codes:** Dunkerque 59140; Malo-les-Bains 59240.

⊞ ⊡ ACCOMMODATIONS AND FOOD. The busy, uncongenial **Auberge de Jeunesse (HI) ❶,** pl. Paul Asseman in Malo-les-Bains, is right on the beachfront. From the station, take bus #3 or 3A to "Piscine." Turn left and walk past the pool and rink; the hostel will be on your right. Walking, follow bd. Alexandre III across town through its various name changes. At pl. de la Victoire, turn left onto av. des Bains, cross the bridge, and turn left onto allée Fenelon; pl. Asseman is on the right. (30min.) The single-sex barracks are cramped and perpetually sandy. (☎ 03 28 63 36 34; fax 03 28 63 24 54. Breakfast €2.90. Meals €7.20. Sheets €2.70. Reception 9am-noon and 6-11pm. Lockout noon-2pm. Curfew Sept.-June 11pm. June-Aug. 11pm-6am entry but no check-in. Bunks €8. **Non-members** €2.90 extra per night first 6 nights. June-Aug. **members only.**) Also on the beach is **Hôtel le Central ❷,** 2 pl. de Turenne. Take bus #3 or 3A to "pl. Turenne" and walk past the church toward the beach; the hotel is over a bar called Café Leffe. This hotel has comfortable, but unspectacular rooms. (☎ 03 28 69 13 64; fax 03 28 69 52 57. Reception daily 7:30am-11pm. Singles and doubles €25, with shower €35; triples and quads €43. AmEx/MC/V.) **Hôtel le Lion d'Or,** 2 rue de Chemin de Fer, is near the station. Rooms are well-sized, clean, and attractive. (☎/fax 03 28 66 08 24. Reception M-F 8am-midnight. Singles and doubles €30-37. MC/V.) Camp near the sand at **Dunkerque Camping Municipal ❶,** bd. de l'Europe. Take bus #3 or 3A to "Malo CES Camping" or follow av. des Bains east for 4km. (☎ 03 28 69 26 68. Reception 8am-8pm. Open Apr.-Nov. 1 person and tent €7.50, with car €15; extra person €4.80. MC/V.)

Dunkerque's speciality is *potje vlesch,* a gelatinous dish of rabbit, chicken, and lamb served cold in aspic. The cheapest, and most generic, pizzerias and *crêperies* lie between #30 and #60 digue de Mer in Malo. Various indistinguishable cafés offer lunchtime *formules* on bd. Alexandre III around pl. Jean Bart. There's a **Monoprix** supermarket at pl. République. (Open M-Sa 8:30am-8pm.) There is also a **market** at pl. Général de Gaulle (open W and Sa 9am-4:30pm) and a smaller suburban version at pl. Turenne. (Open June-Aug. Tu 7am-2pm; Dec.-Feb. 7am-1pm.) Or try **Primfruit,** 70 ave. A. Geeraert, a fruit-and-wine stand near the beach. (Open M-Sa 6:30am-8pm, Su 6:30am-1pm.)

⊡ ⊡ SIGHTS AND ENTERTAINMENT. Opposite the tourist office on rue Clemenceau, the 15th-century **Eglise St-Eloi** holds Flemish paintings within its spare spidery walls. The church is the final resting place of Jean Bart (1650-1702), the famous swashbuckling local pirate knighted by Louis XIV after saving France from famine. The church's 500-year-old **belfry** is open June to August.

Although the coastline is marred by cranes and industrial buildings, the beach region **Malo-les-Bains** is very active on sunny summer days. The boardwalk overflows with tackiness. Rent **windsurfing** equipment and catamarans at the **Office de Tourisme de la Plage,** 48bis digue de Mer. (☎ 03 28 26 28 88. €12 per hr.) On warm summer weekends, the beachfront is an all-night party along **digue de Mer** and **digue des Alliés.** Twenty-somethings pile into the **Milk Bar,** 46 digue de Mer, for milkshakes (€3.35) and videogames. (☎ 03 28 59 12 52. Open daily 10am-2am.) The nightclub **NASA,** 67 digue de Mer, launches reggae in the jungle-like interior from 10pm until dawn. (☎ 03 28 69 07 75. Beer €3.50-5. Cocktail €6.50.)

MONTREUIL-SUR-MER

Though its name is misleading (not a drop of salt water has been seen here since the 13th century, when the ocean began to recede considerably), Montreuil could hardly be more idyllic if it actually were on the ocean. Its unmanicured *vieille ville* and the rough, peaceful hills outside have a simple, authentic appeal, in part because the tourist hordes have not yet discovered them.

■ ⚡ TRANSPORTATION AND PRACTICAL INFORMATION. The **train station** lies just outside the walls of the citadel (☎03 21 06 05 09. Office open M-Sa 6am-9:30pm, Su 8:30m-9:15pm.) **Trains** go to: Arras (1½hr., 4 per day, €11.50); Boulogne (40min., 6 per day, €6); Calais (1hr., 3-4 per day, €11); Lille (2hr., 4 per day, €13.90); Paris (3hr., 3 per day, €32.10) via Etaples.

To reach the **tourist office,** beside the citadel at 21 rue Carnot, climb the stairs across from the train station and turn right on av. du 11 Novembre. Turn right at the sign for "Auberge de Jeunesse" and follow the quiet rue des Bouchers to its end, then take a left onto the footpath at the shrine of Notre-Dame; the office is straight ahead. It distributes a map and brochures. (☎03 21 06 04 27; fax 03 21 06 57 85. Open Apr.-Oct. M-Sa 9:30am-12:30pm and 2-6pm, Su 10am-12:30pm and 3-5pm; Nov.-Mar. Su 10am-12:30pm only.) **BNP,** pl. Darnétal, **exchanges currency.** (☎03 21 06 03 98. Open Tu-W 8:30am-noon and 1:30-5:30pm, Th 8:30am-noon, F 1:30-5:30pm, Sa 8:45am-12:30pm.) Call the **police** at ☎03 21 81 08 48. The closest **hospital** is in Rang du Fliers. (☎03 21 89 45 45.) The **post office** is on pl. Gambetta. (☎03 21 06 70 00. Open M-F 8am-noon and 2-5:30pm, Sa 8:30-11:30am.) **Postal code:** 62170.

■ ⬛ ACCOMMODATIONS AND FOOD. The ■**Renards,** 4 av. du 11 Novembre, offer huge, old-fashioned **chambres d'hôte** at the top of the stairs from the train station. All rooms have fireplaces, rugs, and heavy old furniture; they may be the nicest accommodations for style and price in northern France. (☎03 21 86 85 72. Breakfast included. All rooms with bath. Singles €31; doubles €34-39. Extra bed €12.50.) The **Auberge de Jeunesse "La Hulotte" (HI)** is inside the citadel on rue Carnot. It offers rustic, summercamp-style accommodations and sweeping hilltop views. (☎03 21 06 10 83. Kitchen. Reception 2-6pm. Open Mar.-Oct. Bunks €7.) The **Hotel le Vauban ❹,** 32 pl. de Gaulle, has sun-drenched yellow-and-blue rooms in a petal-pink building on the central *place*. (☎03 21 06 04 95; fax 03 31 06 04 00. Breakfast €6. Reception 8am-8pm. Singles €39; doubles €46.) The beautiful, forested **campground ❶,** 744 rte. d'Etaples, is by the banks of the river, not far from a pool, restaurant, and tennis courts. (☎03 21 06 07 28. Reception 9am-noon and 2-6pm. 1 or 2 people with car or tent €6; extra person €1.50. Electricity 2.50.)

Restaurants crowd **pl. de Gaulle,** and there are bakeries on the adjacent streets. There is a **Shopi** at pl. de Gaulle. (Open Tu-F 9am-12:15pm and 2:30-7:15pm, Sa 9am-7:15pm, Su 9am-12:15pm.) **La Crêperie Montreuil ❶,** 3 rue du Clape en Bas, serves velvety crepes and offers free, rock, jazz, and blues shows. (Crepes €1.50-6. Shows July-Aug. Th 9:30am, Su 5pm. Open July to mid-Sept. daily 4pm-midnight).

■ ◀ SIGHTS AND ENTERTAINMENT. A walk along the 3km long **ramparts** is like the first glorious minute after take-off. Green rivers cut through fields of wildflowers, grazing cows, and sooty red rooftops. Return to earth to visit the 16th-century **citadel,** on the site of the old royal castle. (Open July-Aug. W-M 10am-noon and 2-6pm; Sept.-June 10am-noon and 2-5pm. €2.50, children €1.25.)

Picture-perfect tumbledown cottages line the **rue du Clape en Bas** and the **Cavée St-Firmin;** the latter has actually been featured in several films, including the first version of *Les Misérables*. The liveliest streets are **rue d'Herambault** and those surrounding **pl. de Gaulle.** The **Chapelle de l'Hôtel Dieu** and the **St-Saulve Abbey** are both heavily carved Gothic churches on pl. Gambetta. **Club Canoë Kayak,** 4 rue Moulin des Orphelins, across the canal from the train station, runs canoe and kayak excursions on the river Canche. (☎03 21 06 20 16. Open daily 9am-noon and 2-5pm. Sessions start at €9, different difficulty levels available.)

In late July and early August, the townsfolk stage a huge *son-et-lumière* behind the citadel, with 250-300 actors. It's based on Victor Hugo's *Les Misérables,* in which the reformed mayor of Montreuil, Jean Valjean, flees from Inspector Javert to claim the child Cosette. (Contact tourist office for info. €14, children €9.50.) August 15 brings the **Day of the Street Painters,** an exuberant and artsy celebration.

AMIENS

Amiens (pop. 135,929), the capital of Picardy, is a friendly, livable place, more agreeable than any other city in the region, and a lively student center. Tourists come for its fine Gothic cathedral, twisting old quarter of streets and canals, and the tranquil *hortillonages,* marshlands cultivated since Roman times.

🖪🖪 TRANSPORTATION AND PRACTICAL INFORMATION. Trains leave Gare du Nord, pl. Alphonse Fiquet. (Ticket office open M-F 5am-9pm, Sa 6am-9pm, Su 6am-10pm. Info open M-Sa 9am-6pm.) To: Boulogne (1¼hr., 13 per day, €15.20); Calais (2hr., 10 per day, €19.10); Lille (1¼hr., 14 per day, €15.60); Paris (1¼hr., 20 per day, €6); Rouen (1½hr., 3 per day, €15). **Buses** leave from under the shopping center to the right of the station for Beauvais (1-1½hr., 5 per day, €6.70). **SEMTA,** left as you exit the station on 10 pl. Alphonse Figuet, provides **local transportation.** All buses stop at the train station; buy tickets on board or at the office. (☎03 22 71 40 00. Office open M-F 7am-7pm, Sa 8am-5:30pm. Buses run 6am-9pm; tickets €1.10.) **Rent bikes** at **Buscylette,** in front of train station. (€0.91 per hr., €3.05 per half-day, €4.57 per day. Open M-Sa 6:30am-9pm, Su 9am-noon and 2-7pm.) For a **taxi,** call ☎03 22 91 30 03. (24hr.)

To reach the **tourist office,** 6bis rue Dusevel, turn right from the station parking lot, pass the mall, and turn left onto rue Gloriette. Continue through several name changes and pl. St-Michel; after the cathedral, turn left onto rue Dusevel. The staff organizes tours, takes care of **hotel reservations** (€3, in-person), and has an excellent map of the town. (☎03 22 71 60 50; fax 03 22 71 60 51. Open Apr.-Sept. M-Sa 9am-7pm, Su 10am-noon and 2-5pm; Oct.-Mar. M-Sa 9am-6pm, Su 10am-noon and 2-5pm. Call for info about cathedral and city tours. €5.50, students €4, under 12 €3.) **Net Express,** 10 rue André, is a **laundromat,** not a cybercafé. (☎03 22 72 33 33. Open daily 7am-9pm.) Surf the **Internet** cheaply at **Score Games,** 5 rue Lamarck (☎03 22 80 06 06. €3.10 per hr. Open M-Sa 10am-7pm, July-Aug. closed noon-2pm.) **Hôpital Nord** is on pl. Victor Pauchet (☎03 22 66 80 00); take bus #10 (dir: Collège César Frank). The **police** are at 1 rue Maré-Lanselles (☎03 22 71 53 00). The **post office** is at 7 rue des Vergeaux, down the block from the Hôtel de Ville (☎03 22 44 60 00. Open M-F 8am-7pm, Sa 8am-12:30pm.) **Poste Restante:** 80050. **Postal code:** 80000.

🖪🖪 ACCOMMODATIONS AND FOOD. Amiens has no youth hostel or nearby campgrounds. There is, however, a cluster of hotels in the €23-27 range near the train station. The tourist office publishes a list of hotels and price ranges. The rooms at the two-star **Hôtel Victor Hugo ❸,** 2 rue l'Oratoire, are large, well-kept, and varied in style. (☎03 22 91 57 91; fax 03 22 92 74 02. Breakfast €5. Reception 24hr. Singles and doubles €35; triples €41; quads €51. MC/V.) The spacious rooms at **Hôtel Puvis de Chavannes ❷,** 6 rue Puvis de Chavannes, were once worn-down, but are now being renovated. They're some of the cheapest around and are right by the Musée des Beaux-Arts. (☎03 22 91 82 96; fax 03 22 72 95 35. Breakfast €4.12. Shower €1.53. Reception M-Sa 7:20am-9:30pm, Su 7:20-11am and 8-9:30pm. Singles and doubles €21-25; triples with shower €41; extra bed €9. MC/V.) Snuggled in a prime location on a small street behind the cathedral, the **Hôtel le Prieuré ❺**, 6 rue Porion, combines grandmotherly luxury and modern amenities. Beautiful four-poster beds and swirly floral wallpaper. (☎03 22 71 16 71. Breakfast €6. Reception M-Sa 7pm-9pm, Su 7am-6pm. Singles and doubles €52; triples €61. MC/V.) The **Spatial Hôtel ❻**, 15 rue Alexandre Fatton, between the train station and the cathedral, has impersonal but spacious rooms, all with TV. (☎03 22 91 53 23; fax 03 22 92 27 87. Breakfast €5. Reception 7:30am-9:30pm. Singles €25.50-41; doubles €28.50-44; triples €48-50. Extra bed €7. AmEx/MC/V.) A **Match supermarket** is in the mall to the right of the station. (Open M-Sa 9am-8pm.) Amiens's main **market** in pl. Pasmentier sells vegetables grown in the *hortillonages* on Sa (see **Sights,** below). Smaller markets are held on pl. Beffroi. (Open W and Sa.) There's plenty of food in the shops around the **Hôtel de Ville.** *Crêperies, brasseries,* and Italian eateries line the **Rue Belu** and the canal in the **Quartier St-Leu.** The **Restaurant Tante Jeanne ❶,** 1 rue de la Dodane, serves a super *ficelles picardie* (thin crepe, €6.50) along the waterfront in St-Leu. (☎03 22 72 30 30. Open daily noon-2pm and 7-10:30pm. V.)

◪ SIGHTS. The soaring **Cathédrale de Notre-Dame,** the largest Gothic cathedral in the world, was built for a less-than-space intensive task—holding John the Baptist's head, brought home from the unsuccessful Fourth Crusade. Look behind the choir for the small Weeping Angel, made famous during WWI when French soldiers mailed home thousands of postcards of it. (Open Apr.-Sept. daily 8:30am-6:30pm; Oct.-Feb. M-Sa 8:30am-noon and 2-5pm. French tours June 15-Sept. daily 11am and 4:30pm; low-season Sa 11am and Su 3pm. Lightings June 10:45pm; July 10:30pm; Aug. 10pm; Sept. 9:30pm.)

Just north of the Somme River, the **Quartier St-Leu** is the oldest, most attractive part of Amiens. Its narrow, cobbled streets and flower-strewn squares are built along a system of waterways and canals; locals even call it "Venice of the North." Nearby are the **hortillonages,** market gardens spread over the inlets that jut past canals into the marshland. There is a daily antique market and countless small art studios on passage Belu. (Open daily Apr.-Oct. €4.80, teens €4, children €2.40.)

The **Picardy Museum,** 48 rue de la République, houses a distinguished collection of French paintings and sculpture. Don't miss Pierre Coisin's sculpture of Daphnis embracing the nymph Naïs. (☎03 22 97 14 00. Open Tu-Su 10am-12:30pm and 2-6pm. €5.50, students and ages 6-17 €3.)

▣ ▣ ENTERTAINMENT. The gas-lit, cobbled **pl. du Don** and **rue Belu,** in the Quartier St-Leu, teem with French students at night. Walking into **Le Living,** 3 rue des Bondes, makes you feel like you're in a cartoon. (☎03 22 92 50 30. Happy hour 6-8pm with beer €2.50. Open daily M-Sa 2pm-3am.) Across the street, **Le Zeppelin II,** 2 rue des Bondes, is a stairway to heaven full of partiers, cheap beer, and trip-hop. (☎03 22 92 38 16. Open M 2pm-3am, Tu-Su 10am-3am.)

On the 3rd weekend in June, the **Fête dans la Ville** fills the streets with concerts, street festivals, jugglers, and circus performers. For one week in mid-November, the **Festival International du Film** presents international films and documentaries.

APPENDIX

CLIMATE

The chart below gives average temperatures and rainfalls for major French cities. For a rough estimate of Fahrenheit, double the Celsius and add 32.

	AVERAGE TEMPERATURE (LO/HI) AND PRECIPITATION											
	January			April			July			October		
	°C	°F	mm	°C	°F	mm	°C	°F	mm	°C	°F	mm
Ajaccio	4/13	39/55	7.5	9/19	48/66	5.5	18/29	64/84	7.0	13/22	55/71	9.5
Bordeaux	1.6/9	35/48	6.8	7/17	45/63	6.5	14/27	57/81	5.0	8/19	46/66	9.5
Brest	4/8	39/46	8.8	7/13	45/55	6.3	13/21	55/70	5.0	9/16	48/61	9.0
Cherbourg	4/8	39/46	8.3	6/12	43/54	5.0	14/19	57/66	4.8	10/15	50/59	11.5
Lille	0.5/6	33/43	5.0	4/14	39/57	7.0	13/24	55/75	7.0	7/15	45/59	7.5
Lyon	-1/5	30/41	5.3	6/16	43/61	7.0	14/27	39/81	7.0	7/16	45/61	7.8
Marseille	3/12	37/54	5.0	5/15	41/59	1.5	14/26	57/79	1.5	13/24	55/75	9.3
Paris	0/6	32/43	4.3	5/16	41/61	5.3	13/24	55/75	5.3	6/15	43/59	5.5
Strasbourg	0/4	32/39	6.5	5/15	41/59	8.5	14/26	39/79	8.5	6/14	43/57	6.8
Toulouse	19/26	66/79	6.3	7/17	45/63	3.8	15/28	59/82	3.8	9/19	48/66	5.5

TIME ZONES

France lies in the Central European time zone, which is one hour ahead of GMT. From Easter to Autumn, French time moves one hour ahead. Both switches occur about a week before such changes in the US.

MEASUREMENTS

France invented, and still uses, the metric system of measurement. The basic unit of length is the **meter (m)**, which is divided into 100 **centimeters (cm)**, or 1000 **millimeters (mm)**. 1000 meters make up one **kilometer (km)**. Fluids are measured in **liters (L)**, each divided into 1000 **milliliters (mL)**. A liter of pure water weighs one **kilogram (kg)**, divided into 1000 **grams (g)**, while 1000kg make up one metric **ton**.

MEASUREMENT CONVERSIONS	
1 inch = 25.4mm	1mm = 0.039 in.
1 foot = 0.30m	1m = 3.28 ft.
1 yard = 0.914m	1m = 1.09 yd.
1 mile = 1.61km	1km = 0.62 mi.
1 ounce = 28.35g	1g = 0.035 oz.
1 pound = 0.454kg	1kg = 2.202 lb.
1 fluid ounce = 29.57ml	1ml = 0.034 fl. oz.
1 gallon = 3.785L	1L = 0.264 gal.

FRENCH PHRASEBOOK AND GLOSSARY

ENGLISH	FRENCH	PRONOUNCED
GENERAL		
Hello./Good day.	Bonjour.	bohn-ZHOOR
Good evening.	Bonsoir.	bohn-SWAH
Hi!	Salut!	sah-LU
Goodbye.	Au revoir.	oh re-VWAHR
Good night.	Bonne nuit.	bonn NWEE
yes/no/maybe	oui/non/peut-être	wee/nohn/p'TET-rh
Please.	S'il vous plaît.	see voo PLAY
Thank you.	Merci.	mehr-SEE
You're welcome.	De rien.	de rhee-AHN
Pardon me!	Excusez-moi!	ex-KU-zay-MWAH
Go away!	Allez-vous en!	ah-lay vooz ON!
Where is...?	Où se trouve...?	oo s'TRHOOV...?
What time do you open/ close?	Vous ouvrez/fermez à quelle heure?	vooz ooVRAY/ ferhMAY ah ke-UHR?
Help!	Au secours!	oh-sekOOR
I'm lost.	Je suis perdu(e).	zh'SWEE pehr-DU
I'm sorry.	Je suis désolé(e).	zh'SWEE day-zoh-LAY

OTHER USEFUL PHRASES AND WORDS

ENGLISH	FRENCH	ENGLISH	FRENCH
PHRASES			
Who?	Qui?	No, thank you.	Non, merci.
What?	Quoi?	What is it?	Qu'est-ce que c'est?
I don't understand.	Je ne comprends pas.	Why?	Pourquoi?
Leave me alone.	Laissez-moi tranquille.	this one/that one	ceci/cela
How much does this cost?	Ça coûte combien?	Stop/Stop that!	Arrête! (familiar) Arrêtez! (pl.)
Please speak slowly.	S'il vous plaît, parlez moins vite.	Please repeat.	Répétez, s'il vous plaît.
I am ill/I am hurt.	J'ai mal./Je suis blessé(e).	Please help me.	Aidez-moi, s'il vous plaît.
I am (20) years old.	J'ai (vingt) ans.	Do you speak English?	Parlez-vous anglais?
I am a student (m/f)	Je suis étudiant/étudi- ante.	What's this called in French?	Comment-on dit...en français?
What is your name?	Comment vous appelez- vous?	The check, please.	L'addition, s'il vous plaît.
Please, where is/ are...?	S'il vous plaît, où se trouve(nt)...?	I would like...	Je voudrais...
a doctor	un médecin	the cash machine	le guichet automatique
the toilet	les toilettes	the restaurant	le restaurant
the hospital	l'hôpital	the police	la police
a bedroom	une chambre	the train station	la gare
with	avec	single room	une chambre simple

a double bed	un grand lit	double room	une chambre pour deux
a shower	une douche	two single beds	deux lits
lunch	le déjeuner	a bath	bain
included	compris	without	sans
hot	chaud	breakfast	le petit déjeuner
cold	froid	dinner	le dîner

DIRECTIONS

(to the) right	à droite	(to the) left	à gauche
straight	tout droit	near to	près de
north	nord	far from	loin de
south	sud	east	est
follow	suivre	west	ouest

NUMBERS

one	un	ten	dix
two	deux	fifteen	quinze
three	trois	twenty	vingt
four	quatre	twenty-five	vingt-cinq
five	cinq	thirty	trente
six	six	forty	quarante
seven	sept	fifty	cinquante
eight	huit	hundred	cent
nine	neuf	thousand	mille

TIMES AND HOURS

open	ouvert	closed	fermé
What time is it?	Quelle heure est-il?	It's 11am	Il est onze heures.
afternoon	l'après-midi	until	jusqu'à
night	la nuit	public holidays	jours fériés (j.f.)
today	aujourd'hui	January	janvier
morning	le matin	February	fevrier
evening	le soir	March	mars
yesterday	hier	April	avril
tomorrow	demain	May	mai
Monday	lundi	June	juin
Tuesday	mardi	July	juillet
Wednesday	mercredi	August	août
Thursday	jeudi	September	septembre
Friday	vendredi	October	octobre
Saturday	samedi	November	novembre
Sunday	dimanche	December	decembre

MENU READER

agneau (m)	lamb	bière (f)	beer
ail (m)	garlic	bifteck (m)	steak
asperges (f pl)	asparagus	blanc de volaille (m)	chicken breast
assiette (f)	plate	boeuf (m)	beef
aubergine (f)	eggplant	boisson (f)	drink
bavette (f)	flank	brochette (f)	kebab
beurre (m)	butter	canard (m)	duck

APPENDIX

bien cuit (adj)	well done	**carafe d'eau (f)**	pitcher of tap water
cervelle (f)	brain	**maison (adj)**	homemade
champignon (m)	mushroom	**marron (m)**	chestnut
chaud (adj)	hot	**fraise (f)**	strawberry
chèvre (m)	goat cheese	**miel (m)**	honey
choix (m)	choice	**moules (f pl)**	mussels
choucroute (f)	sauerkraut	**moutarde (f)**	mustard
chou-fleur (m)	cauliflower	**nature (adj)**	plain
ciboulette (f)	chive	**noix (f pl)**	nuts
citron (m)	lemon	**œuf (m)**	egg
citron vert (m)	lime	**oie (f)**	goose
civet (m)	stew (of rabbit)	**oignon (m)**	onion
compote (f)	stewed fruit	**pain (m)**	bread
confit de canard (m)	duck confit	**pâtes (f pl)**	pasta
coq au vin (m)	rooster stewed in wine	**plat (m)**	course (on menu)
côte (f)	rib or chop	**poêlé (adj)**	pan-fried
courgette f)	zucchini/courgette	**poisson (m)**	fish
crème Chantilly (f)	whipped cream	**poivre (m)**	pepper
crème fraîche (f)	thick cream	**pomme (f)**	apple
crêpe (f)	thin pancake	**pomme de terre (f)**	potato
eau de robinet (f)	tap water	**potage (m)**	soup
échalot (f)	shallot	**poulet (m)**	chicken
entrecôte (f)	chop (cut of meat)	**pruneau (m)**	prune
escalope (f)	thin slice of meat	**rillettes (f pl)**	pork hash
escargot (m)	snail	**riz (m)**	rice
farci(e) (adj)	stuffed	**salade verte (f)**	green salad
faux-filet (m)	sirloin steak	**sanglier (m)**	wild boar
feuilleté (m)	puff pastry	**saucisse (f)**	sausage
figue (f)	fig	**saucisson (m)**	hard salami
foie gras d'oie/de canard	liver of fattened goose/ duck	**saumon (m)**	salmon
frais (fraîche) (adj)	fresh	**sel (m)**	salt
haricot vert (m)	green bean	**steak tartare (m)**	raw steak
huîtres (f pl)	oysters	**sucre (m)**	sugar
jambon (m)	ham	**tête (f)**	head
lait (m)	milk	**thé (m)**	tea
lapin (m)	rabbit	**tournedos (m)**	beef filet
légume (m)	vegetable	**truffe (f)**	truffle
magret de canard (m)	duck breast	**viande (f)**	meat

FRENCH-ENGLISH GLOSSARY

Le is the masculine singular definite article (the); *la* the feminine; both are abbreviated to *l'* before a vowel, while *les* is the plural definite article for both genders. *Un* is the masculine singular indefinite article (a or an), *une* the feminine; while *des* is the plural indefinite article for both genders ("some"). Where a noun or adjective can take masculine and feminine forms, the masculine is listed first and the feminine in parentheses; often the feminine form consists of adding an "e" to the end, which is indicated by an "e" in parentheses: étudiant(e).

abbaye (f): abbey
abbatiale (f): abbey church
accueil (m): reception
addition (f): the check
allée (f): lane, avenue
alimentation (f): food
aller-retour (m): round-trip ticket
an (m)/année (f): year
appareil (m): machine; commonly used for telephone
appareil photo (m): camera
arc (m): arch
arènes (f pl.): arena
arrivée (f): arrival
auberge (f): hostel, inn.
auberge de jeunesse (f): youth hostel
autobus (m): city bus
autocar (m): long-distance bus
autoroute (f): highway
banlieue (f): suburb
basse ville (f): lower town
bastide (f): walled fortified town
bibliothèque (f): library
billet (m): ticket
billetterie (f): ticket office
bois (m): forest, wood
boucherie (f): butcher shop
boulangerie (f): bakery
brasserie (f): beer salon and restaurant
bureau (m): office
cap (m): cape
car (m): long-distance bus
carte (f): card; menu; map
cave (f): cellar, normally for wine
centre ville (m): center of town
chambre (f): room
chambre d'hôte (f): bed and breakfast room
chapelle (f): chapel
charcuterie (f): shop selling cooked meats (gen. pork) and prepared food
château (m): castle or mansion; headquarters of a vineyard
cimetière (m): cemetery
cité (f): walled city
cloître (m): cloister
collégiale (f): collegial church
colline (f): hill
comptoir (m): counter (in a bar or café)
côte (f): coast; side (e.g. of hill)

côté (m): side (e.g. of building)
couvent (m): convent
cour (f): courtyard
cours (m): wide street
cru (m): vintage
dégustation (f): tasting
départ (m): departure
donjon (m): keep (of a castle)
douane (f): customs
école (f): school
église (f): church
entrée (f): appetizer; entrance
épicerie (f): grocery store
étudiant(e): student
faubourg (m; abbr. fbg): quarter (of town; archaic)
fête (f): celebration, festival; party
ferme (f): farm
fleuve (m): river
foire (f): fair
fontaine (f): fountain
forêt (f): forest
fronton (m): *jai alai* arena
galerie (f): gallery
gare or gare SNCF (f): train station
gare routière (f): bus station
gîte d'étape (m): rural hostel-like accommodations, aimed at hikers
grève (f): strike, French national pastime
guichet (m): ticket counter, cash register desk
haute ville (f): upper town
horloge (f): clock
hors-saison (f): off-season
hôpital (m): hospital
hôtel (particulier) (m): town house, mansion
hôtel de ville (m): town hall
hôtel-Dieu (m): hospital (archaic)
île (f): island
jour (m): day
jour férié (m): public holiday
location (f): rental store
lycée (m): high school
madame (f; abbr. Mme): Mrs.
mademoiselle (f; abbr. Mlle): Miss
magasin (m): shop
mairie (f): town hall
maison (f): house
marée (f): tide
marché (m): market
mer (f): sea
mois (m): month
monastère (m): monastery

monsieur (m; abbr. M): Mr.
montagne (f): mountain
mur (m): wall
muraille (f): city wall, rampart
nuit (f): night
palais (m): palace
parc (m): park
pâtisserie (f): pastry shop
place (f): town square
plan (m): plan, map
plat (m): course (on menu)
pont (m): bridge
poste (f; abbr. PTT): post office
pourboire (m): the tip
puy (m): hill, mountain (archaic)
quartier (m): section (of town)
randonnée (f): hike
rempart (m): rampart
rivière (f): river
route (f): road
rue (f): street
salon (m): living room
salle (f): room; in a café it refers to indoor seating as opposed to the bar or patio
semaine (f): week
sentier (m): path, lane
service compris: tip included
soir (m): evening
son-et-lumière (m): sound-and-light show
source (f): spring
supermarché (m): supermarket
syndicat d'initiative (m): tourist office
tabac (m): cigarette and newsstand
table (f): table
télépherique (m): cable car
terrasse (f): terrace, patio
TGV (m): high speed train
thermes (m pl): hot springs
tour (f): tower
tour (m): tour
traiteur (m): delicatessen
université (f): university
val (m)/vallée (f): valley
vélo(m): bicycle
vendange (f): grape harvest
vieille ville (f): old town
ville (f): town, city
visite guidée (f): guided tour
vitraux (m pl): stained glass
voie (f): road
voiture (f): car

PDAs & Travel

LG
LET'S GO

(it's not what you're thinking)

Let's Go City Guides
are now available for
Palm OS™ PDAs.
Download a free trial at
http://**mobile.letsgo.com**

INDEX

MAP INDEX

Hospital	Bus Station	Church	Hotel/Hostel
Police	Airport	Synagogue	Food & Drink
Post Office	Train Station	Museum	Pubs/Nightlife
Tourist Office	MÉTRO STOP	Mountain	Clubs
Bank	RER Station	Winery	
Embassy	Cablecar	TAXI Taxi	The Let's Go thumb always points NORTH.
Site or Point of Interest	Ferry Landing		

-10	0	10	20	30	40	°Celsius

°Fahrenheit 30 40 50 60 70 80 90 100 110 120

100 meters (m) = 328 feet (ft.)   500m = 1640 ft. = 0.31 miles (mi.)
1 kilometer (km) = 0.625 mi.   50km = 31.25 mi.   1 hectare (ha) = 2.47 acres